EDPSYCH

MODULES

Lisa Bohlin

Cheryl Cisero Durwin
Southern Connecticut
State University

Marla Reese-Weber
Illinois State University

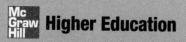 **Higher Education**

Boston   Burr Ridge, IL   Dubuque, IA   New York   San Francisco   St. Louis
Bangkok   Bogotá   Caracas   Kuala Lumpur   Lisbon   London   Madrid   Mexico City
Milan   Montreal   New Delhi   Santiago   Seoul   Singapore   Sydney   Taipei   Toronto

Connect
Learn
Succeed™

Published by McGraw-Hill, an imprint of The McGraw-Hill Companies, Inc., 1221 Avenue of the Americas, New York, NY 10020. Copyright © 2012, 2009. All rights reserved. No part of this publication may be reproduced or distributed in any form or by any means, or stored in a database or retrieval system, without the prior written consent of The McGraw-Hill Companies, Inc., including, but not limited to, in any network or other electronic storage or transmission, or broadcast for distance learning.

This book is printed on acid-free paper.

1 2 3 4 5 6 7 8 9 0 DOW/DOW 1 0 9 8 7 6 5 4 3 2 1

ISBN: 978-0-07-809786-7
MHID: 0-07-809786-X

Sponsoring Editor: *Allison McNamara*
Marketing Manager: *Julia Flohr Larkin*
Developmental Editor: *John Sisson*
Editorial Coordinator: *Sarah Kiefer*
Production Editor: *Ruth Sakata Corley*
Manuscript Editor: *Janet Tilden*
Design Manager: *Allister Fein*
Text Designer: *Lisa Buckley*
Cover Designer: *Nicole Hayward*
Photo Research: *Editorial Image LLC, Emily Tietz*
Buyer: *Louis Swaim*
Media Project Manager: *Jennifer Barrick*
Composition: *10/12 Minion by Thompson Type*
Printing: *45# New Era Matte Plus, R. R. Donnelley & Sons*
Vice President Editorial: *Michael Ryan*
Publisher: *Michael Sugarman*
Director of Development: *Dawn Groundwater*
Cover: © David Ward/Photographer's Choice/Getty Images

Credits: The credits section for this book begins on page 655 and is considered an extension of the copyright page.

Library of Congress Cataloging-in-Publication Data
Bohlin, Lisa.
    Edpsych : modules / Lisa Bohlin, Cheryl Cisero Durwin, Marla Reese-Weber.—2nd ed.
        p. cm.
    Includes bibliographical references and index.
    ISBN-13: 978-0-07-809786-7 (pbk.)
    ISBN-10: 0-07-809786-X ()
    1. Educational psychology.   2. Child development.   3. Learning.   4. Classroom management.   5. Teaching.
6. Education—Evaluation.   I. Durwin, Cheryl Cisero.   II. Reese-Weber, Marla.   III. Title.
    LB1051.B46395 2011
    370.15--dc23
                                                                        2011039772

The Internet addresses listed in the text were accurate at the time of publication. The inclusion of a website does not indicate an endorsement by the authors or McGraw-Hill, and McGraw-Hill does not guarantee the accuracy of the information presented at these sites.

www.mhhe.com

Dedication

We would like to dedicate this book to all the instructors and students who provided valuable feedback on the first edition and gave us the inspiration to complete a second edition.

To our husbands, Mike, Mike, and John, whose continued support, patience, and understanding have made this textbook possible. And, to our children, Ben, Holly, Sammy-Kate, Mark, Andrea, Payton, and Reese, who inspire us every day to be the best mothers and educators that we can be.

Authors' Acknowledgments

We would like to thank Allison McNamara, Dawn Groundwater, Sheryl Adams, David Patterson, and many others at our McGraw-Hill family for their continued enthusiasm and support for our vision. We also would like to thank several students who have helped us on various tasks related to this project: Rebecca Nemecek, Allison Rhoades, Shenira James, and Jessica Pittman. We are especially grateful to have our Developmental Editor, John Sisson, working with us again to guide us through many aspects of this project.

BRIEF CONTENTS

Introduction

Case Study   2

Module 1: Using Science to Inform Classroom Practices   4

Unit 1: Personal Development

Unit 1 Case Studies   22

Module 2: Contexts of Development   30

Module 3: Social Development   45

Module 4: Emotional Development   61

Module 5: Moral Development   76

Unit 2: The Developing Learner

Unit 2 Case Studies   92

Module 6: The Brain and Development   100

Module 7: Cognitive Development   118

Module 8: Language Development   133

Unit 3: Learning Theories

Unit 3 Case Studies   150

Module 9: Behavioral Learning Theories   158

Module 10: Social Cognitive Theory   173

Module 11: Information Processing   183

Unit 4: Cognitive Processes

Unit 4 Case Studies   202

Module 12: Metacognition   210

Module 13: Transfer of Skills and Knowledge   225

Module 14: Critical Thinking and Problem Solving   238

Unit 5: Motivation

Unit 5 Case Studies   256

Module 15: Behavioral Theory   264

Module 16: Cognitive Theories   278

Module 17: Self Theories   298

Unit 6: Classroom Management and Instruction

Unit 6 Case Studies   318

Module 18: Creating a Productive Learning Environment   326

Module 19: Understanding and Managing Student Behavior   346

Module 20: Instruction: Behavioral, Cognitive, and Constructivist Approaches   363

Module 21: Grouping Practices   377

Unit 7: Learner Differences

Unit 7 Case Studies   394

Module 22: Intelligence   402

Module 23: Giftedness and Creativity   418

Module 24: Cognitive Disabilities   432

Module 25: Emotional, Social, and Behavioral Disorders   449

Unit 8: Classroom Assessment

Unit 8 Case Studies   468

Module 26: Assessing Student Learning   476

Module 27: Test Construction and Use   492

Module 28: Performance Assessment   509

Unit 9: Standardized Testing

Unit 9 Case Studies   528

Module 29: Standardized Tests and Scores   536

Module 30: Issues in Standardized Testing   551

How Does *EdPsych* Help You Prepare for the Praxis Exam?   566

Glossary   574

References   589

Credits   655

Subject-Name Index   661

Introduction

Case Study 2

Module 1: Using Science to Inform Classroom Practices

Outline and Learning Goals   4
Teaching as Decision Making   5
   Opportunities and Challenges of Teaching   5
   Educational Psychology: A Resource for Teachers   5
Educational Psychology: The Science   6
   Research Designs   7
   Samples   9
   Measures   10
Educational Psychology: Classroom Practices   10
   Developing Your Philosophy of Teaching   10
   Addressing Diversity Using a Case Study Approach   16
Summary   17
Key Concepts   17
Video Applications   17
Case Study: Reflect and Evaluate (annotated)   18

Unit 1: Personal Development

Unit 1 Case Studies   22

Module 2: Contexts of Development

Outline and Learning Goals   30
Bronfenbrenner's Bioecological Theory   31
Family Context   31
   Parenting Practices   32
   Divorce and Remarriage   34
Peer Context   36
   Friendships and Peer Groups   36
   Peer Statuses   38
Broader Contexts   40
   Parental Employment   40
   Cultural Factors   41
Summary   43
Key Concepts   43
Video Applications   43
Case Studies: Reflect and Evaluate   44

Module 3: Social Development

Outline and Learning Goals   45
Erikson's Psychosocial Theory   46
Aspects of Identity   49
   Identity Statuses   49
   Ethnic Identity   50
   Gender Identity   51

Understanding the Self   52
   Self-Concept   53
   Self-Esteem   53
Social Competence   54
   Social Adjustment   54
   Social Performance   55
   Social Skills   55
Summary   58
Key Concepts   58
Video Applications   59
Case Studies: Reflect and Evaluate   59

Module 4: Emotional Development

Outline and Learning Goals   61
What is Emotion?   62
   Emotions and Temperament   62
   How Parents, Gender and Culture Influence Emotion   62
Emotions and Individual Performance   63
   Dimensions of Emotional Intelligence   63
Applications: Emotionally Intelligent Teaching   68
   What is Social-Emotional Learning (SEL)?   70
   Benefits of SEL Programs   71
Summary   73
Key Concepts   73
Video Applications   73
Case Studies: Reflect and Evaluate   74

Module 5: Moral Development

Outline and Learning Goals   76
Cognitive-Developmental Moral Reasoning   77
   Piaget's Theory   77
   Kohlberg's Theory   77
   Gilligan's Criticism   78
Prosocial Behavior   79
   Eisenberg's Theory   80
   Perspective Taking   81
   Empathy   81
Aggressive Behavior   82
   Social-Cognitive Domains   83
   Social-Information Processing   83
Applications: Advancing Moral Development   84
   Family Context   84
   Peer Context   85
   School Context   86
Summary   88
Key Concepts   88
Video Applications   88
Case Studies: Reflect and Evaluate   89

TABLE OF CONTENTS

Unit 2: The Developing Learner

Unit 2 Case Studies   92

Module 6: The Brain and Development
Outline and Learning Goals   100
The Relevance of Brain Research   101
Brain Structure and Function   102
The Developing Brain   104
  Factors Affecting Brain Development   105
Brain Activity During Learning   108
Applications: How Brain Research Can Inform Learning   110
  Current State of Research in Memory, Reading, Math, and Emotion   110
Summary   115
Key Concepts   115
Video Applications   116
Case Studies: Reflect and Evaluate   116

Module 7: Cognitive Development
Outline and Learning Goals   118
Constructivist Theories of Cognitive Development   119
  Individual and Social Constructivism   119
  Piaget's Theory   119
  Vygotsky's Theory   124
Issues in Cognitive Development: Piaget and Vygotsky   126
  What Comes First: Development or Learning?   126
  Role of Language in Cognitive Development   127
  Role of Play in Cognitive Development   128
Applications: Constructivist Principles for Effective Teaching   128
Summary   130
Key Concepts   130
Video Applications   131
Case Studies: Reflect and Evaluate   131

Module 8: Language Development
Outline and Learning Goals   133
Understanding Language Acquisition   134
  Biological Basis of Language   134
  Imitation and Reinforcement   134
  Social Interactions   135
Development of Language Skills   136
  Language Acquisition Through Early Childhood   136
  Language Acquisition Through Adolescence   138
  Bilingual Language Acquisition   139
  Individual Differences in Language Acquisition   141
Applications: Encouraging Language Development in the Classroom   143
Summary   145
Key Concepts   145
Video Applications   146
Case Studies: Reflect and Evaluate   146

Unit 3: Learning Theories

Unit 3 Case Studies   150

Module 9: Behavioral Learning Theories
Outline and Learning Goals   158
Assumptions of Behavioral Learning Theories   159
Classical Conditioning   159
Operant Conditioning   161
  Basic Tenets of the Theory   161
  Using Consequences Effectively   163
Applications: Applied Behavior Analysis   167
  Strategies for Increasing Appropriate Behavior   167
  Strategies for Decreasing Inappropriate Behavior   168
Summary   170
Key Concepts   170
Video Applications   171
Case Studies: Reflect and Evaluate   171

Module 10: Social Cognitive Theory
Outline and Learning Goals   173
Assumptions of Social Cognitive Theory   174
Observational Learning   174
  Model Characteristics   174
  Imitators Characteristics   176
  Environmental Characteristics   176
Personal Factors in Learning   177
  Self-Efficacy   177
  Self-Regulation   179
Applications: Improving Students' Self-Efficacy and Self-Regulation   180
Summary   181
Key Concepts   181
Video Applications   181
Case Studies: Reflect and Evaluate   181

Module 11: Information Processing
Outline and Learning Goals   183
Assumptions of the Information Processing Approach   184
The Three-Stage Model of Information Processing   184
  Sensory Memory   184
  Working Memory   185
  Long-Term Memory   189
  Individual Differences in Information Processing   192
Applications to Teaching   193
  Helping Students Pay Attention   193
  Helping Students Store and Retrieve Information Effectively   194
Summary   197
Key Concepts   197

Video Applications   198
Case Studies: Reflect and Evaluate   198

Unit 4: Cognitive Processes

Unit 4 Case Studies   202

Module 12: Metacognition

Outline and Learning Goals   210
What Is Metacognition and Why Is It Important?   211
Special Cases of Metacognition   212
   Theory of Mind in Childhood   212
   Egocentrism in Adolescence   214
Factors Affecting the Development and Use of Metacognition   215
Applications: Learning Strategies   215
   Reading Comprehension   215
   Writing Skills   218
   Note Taking   218
   Studying   220
Summary   222
Key Concepts   222
Video Applications   223
Case Studies: Reflect and Evaluate   223

Module 13: Transfer of Skills and Knowledge

Outline and Learning Goals   225
What Is Transfer and Why Is It Important?   226
   Specific Versus General Transfer   226
   Low-Road Versus High-Road Transfer   226
Do We Readily Transfer What We Learn?   227
   The Success of Low-Road Transfer   227
   The Problem of High-Road Transfer   228
Application: How to Facilitate Transfer   230
   Develop Automaticity of Skills   231
   Promote Meaningful Learning   231
   Teach Metacognitive Strategies   234
   Motivate Students to Value Learning   234
Summary   236
Key Concepts   236
Video Applications   236
Case Studies: Reflect and Evaluate   236

Module 14: Critical Thinking and Problem Solving

Outline and Learning Goals   238
Thinking Skills and Dispositions   239
   What Are Higher-Order Thinking Skills?   239
   What Are Thinking Dispositions?   240
Critical Thinking   241
   What Is Critical Thinking?   241
   Application: Fostering Critical Thinking   242
Problem Solving   245
   What Is Problem Solving?   245
Obstacles to Successful Problem Solving   246
Application: Teaching Problem-Solving Strategies   246
Summary   250
Key Concepts   250
Video Applications   251
Case Studies: Reflect and Evaluate   251

Unit 5: Motivation

Unit 5 Case Studies   256

Module 15: Behavioral Theory

Outline and Learning Goals   264
A Behavioral Definition of Motivation   265
   Defining Intrinsic and Extrinsic Motivation   265
   Factors Influencing Intrinsic and Extrinsic Motivation   265
Rewarding Students for Learning   266
   Task-Contingent and Performance-Contingent Rewards   267
   Applications: Using Rewards Effectively   268
Praising Students for Learning   269
   Process, Performance, and Person Praise   269
   Applications: Using Praise Effectively   270
When the Reward Is the Activity Itself   272
   Flow Theory   272
Applications: Creating an Intrinsically Motivating Learning Environment   273
Summary   275
Key Concepts   275
Video Applications   275
Case Studies: Reflect and Evaluate   276

Module 16: Cognitive Theories

Outline and Learning Goals   278
Cognitive Theories of Motivation   279
   Expectancy-Value Theory   279
   Goal Theory   280
   Attribution Theory   282
Developmental and Cultural Differences in Motivation   285
   Developmental Changes in Motivation   285
   Gender Differences in Motivation   287
   Ethnic Differences in Motivation   289
Applications: Enhancing Students' Motivation   289
   Student-Level Techniques   289
   Classroom-Level Techniques   290
Serious Motivational Problems   292
   Learned Helplessness   292
   Anxiety   292
Summary   295
Key Concepts   295

TABLE OF CONTENTS

Video Applications   296
Case Studies: Reflect and Evaluate   296

Module 17: Self Theories
Outline and Learning Goals   298
Self-Efficacy Theory   299
  Self-Efficacy and Motivation   299
  Teacher Efficacy   302
Self-Worth Theory   303
  Self-Worth and Motivation   303
  Types of Students   303
Self-Determination Theory   305
  Self-Determination and Motivation   307
  Becoming Self-Determined   307
Integrating the Self Theories   309
  Self-Theories Compared   309
  Applications: Enhancing Intrinsic Motivation   310
Summary   313
Key Concepts   313
Video Applications   314
Case Studies: Reflect and Evaluate   314

Unit 6: Classroom Management and Instruction

Unit 6 Case Studies   318

Module 18: Creating a Productive Learning Environment
Outline and Learning Goals   326
Planning and Organization   327
  Environmental Competence   327
  Instructional Planning   330
  Time Management   332
Establishing Norms and Expectations for Behavior   333
  The First Days of School   333
  Classroom Rules and Consequences   335
  Procedures and Routines   337
Establishing a Climate for Positive Relationships   338
  Caring, Productive Student-Teacher Relationships   338
  Positive Student-Student Relationships   340
  Building Strong Home-School Connections   341
  Building a Sense of Community within the School   343
Summary   344
Key Concepts   344
Video Applications   344
Case Studies: Reflect and Evaluate   345

Module 19: Understanding and Managing Student Behavior
Outline and Learning Goals   346

Defining Student Misbehavior   347
  Degrees and Types of Misbehavior   347
  Common Causes of Misbehavior   348
  Application: General Ways to Address Behavior Management   350
  Establish Clear, Positive Expectations for Behavior   352
  Model and Reinforce Desired Behaviors   352
  Anticipate and Prevent Potential Behavior Problems   353
  Teach Self-Regulation Skills   353
  Respond Effectively to Behavior Problems as They Occur   354
Application: How to Handle Specific Misbehaviors   355
  Routine Disruptions   355
  Intermediate Concerns   356
  Immoral Behaviors   356
  Dangerous Behaviors   358
Summary   361
Key Concepts   361
Video Applications   361
Case Studies: Reflect and Evaluate   362

Module 20: Instruction: Applying Behavioral, Cognitive, and Constructivist Approaches
Outline and Learning Goals   363
Planning Instruction   364
Teaching Methods Based on Behaviorism   365
  Direct Instruction   365
  Mastery Learning   367
Teaching Methods Based on Cognitive Learning Theory   368
  Discovery Learning and Guided Discovery   368
  Expository Teaching   368
Teaching Methods Based on Constructivism   369
  Inquiry Learning   370
  Cooperative Learning   370
  Methods of Fostering Comprehension   371
Summary   375
Key Concepts   375
Video Applications   375
Case Studies: Reflect and Evaluate   376

Module 21: Grouping Practices
Outline and Learning Goals   377
Grouping by Ability   378
  Within-Class Ability Grouping   379
  Between-Class Ability Grouping   380
  Flexible Grouping Methods   381
Cooperative Learning   382
  Characteristics of Cooperative Learning   382
  Is Cooperative Learning Effective?   383
Applications: Best Practices   385

Elementary School: Using Within-Class Ability Grouping Effectively   385

Middle School and High School: To Track or Not to Track   386

Using Cooperative Learning Effectively   386

Summary   389

Key Concepts   389

Video Applications   389

Case Studies: Reflect and Evaluate   390

Unit 7: Learner Differences

Unit 7 Case Studies   394

Module 22: Intelligence

Outline and Learning Goals   402

What Is Intelligence?   403

Classic Views   403

Contemporary Views   403

Intelligence Measured as IQ   406

Individually Administered and Group Administered Tests   406

Interpreting IQ Scores   407

Caveats for Interpreting IQ   408

Biological, Social, and Cultural Issues   408

Intelligence: Heredity or Environment?   408

Socioeconomic and Cultural Factors   409

Applications: Intelligence Theories in the Classroom   412

Multiple Intelligences in the Classroom   412

Teaching for Successful Intelligence   413

Summary   415

Key Concepts   415

Video Applications   415

Case Studies: Reflect and Evaluate   416

Module 23: Giftedness and Creativity

Outline and Learning Goals   418

Giftedness and Creativity: Are They More Than Just Intelligence?   419

Giftedness   420

Characteristics   420

Identifying Giftedness   421

Applications: Teaching Gifted Students   422

Creativity   424

Characteristics   424

Identifying Creativity   425

Applications: Promoting Creativity in the Classroom   427

Summary   429

Key Concepts   429

Video Applications   430

Case Studies: Reflect and Evaluate   430

Module 24: Cognitive Disabilities

Outline and Learning Goals   432

Cognitive Disabilities in Today's Classrooms   433

Special Education Referral and Eligibility   433

Planning and Placement   434

Intellectual Disabilities   435

Identification of Intellectual Disabilities   435

Applications: Guidelines for Teachers in the General Education Classroom   436

Specific Learning Disabilities   438

Identification of Specific Learning Disabilities   438

Reading Disability   441

Mathematics Disability   443

Summary   446

Key Concepts   446

Video Applications   446

Case Studies: Reflect and Evaluate   447

Module 25: Emotional, Social, and Behavioral Disorders

Outline and Learning Goals   449

Emotional, Social, and Behavioral Disorders in Today's Classrooms   450

Special Education Referral and Eligibility   450

Planning and Placement   452

Characteristics of Disabilities   453

Anxiety and Depression   453

ADHD and Conduct Disorder   455

Autism Spectrum Disorders   459

Applications: Interventions   460

Types of Interventions   460

Effectiveness of Interventions   461

Summary   463

Key Concepts   463

Video Applications   463

Case Studies: Reflect and Evaluate   464

Unit 8: Classroom Assessment

Unit 8 Case Studies   468

Module 26: Assessing Student Learning

Outline and Learning Goals   476

What is Assessment?   477

Purposes of Assessment in Education   477

Standards for Teacher Competence   478

Applications: Assessment Planning   479

Choosing Assessment Methods   480

Using Assessment Data   482

Applications: Communication of Classroom Assessment Information   483

Grading Procedures   483

TABLE OF CONTENTS

Report Cards and Narrative Reports   485
Parent-Teacher Communication   486
Summary   489
Key Concepts   489
Video Applications   489
Case Studies: Reflect and Evaluate   490

Module 27: Test Construction and Use
Outline and Learning Goals   492
Characteristics of High-Quality Classroom Tests   493
Validity   493
Reliability   494
Fairness and Equivalence   495
Practicality   496
Application: Developing a Test Blueprint   496
Application: Developing Test Items   497
Alternate-Choice (True/False Items)   498
Matching Exercises   499
Multiple Choice Items   500
Short-Answer Items/Completion Items   502
Essay Tasks   502
Application: Test Analysis and Revision   504
Summary   506
Key Concepts   506
Case Studies: Reflect and Evaluate   507

Module 28: Performance Assessment
Outline and Learning Goals   509
A Broader View of Assessment   510
Performance Assessment   510
Authentic Assessment   511
Application: Developing Performance Assessments   512
Presentations   512
Projects   514
Portfolios   514
Application: Evaluating Performance Assessments   516
Checklists   516
Rating Scales   516
Rubrics   517
Advantages and Disadvantages of Performance Assessment   520
Summary   522
Key Concepts   522
Video Applications   523
Case Studies: Reflect and Evaluate   523

Unit 9: Standardized Testing

Unit 9 **Case Studies**   528

Module 29: Standardized Tests and Scores
Outline and Learning Goals   536
Types of Standardized Tests   537
Categories of Standardized Tests   538
Criterion-Referenced and Norm-Referenced Tests   539
Basic Concepts of Measurement   541
Central Tendency and Variability   541
Normal Distribution   542
Types of Test Scores   542
Raw Scores   542
Percentile Scores   542
Grade-Equivalent Scores   544
Standard Scores   544
Characteristics of Good Tests   545
Validity   545
Reliability   546
Summary   548
Key Concepts   548
Video Applications   549
Case Studies: Reflect and Evaluate   549

Module 30: Issues in Standardized Testing
Outline and Learning Goals   551
High-Stakes Testing and Accountability   552
What is High-Stakes Testing?   552
No Child Left Behind   553
Negative Outcomes and Test Score Pollution   554
Applications: Accommodating Students at Risk   556
Test Fairness and Test Bias   558
Teacher Certification and Licensure   560
Summary   563
Key Concepts   563
Video Applications   564
Case Studies: Reflect and Evaluate   564

How Does *EdPsych* Help You Prepare for the Praxis Exam?   566
Glossary   574
References   589
Credits   655
Subject-Name Index   661

Preface

Teaching is about making instructional decisions. We wrote this book to help new students of educational psychology learn how to make better instructional decisions. This second edition of *EdPsych: Modules* helps students to:

- Develop a personal teaching philosophy that guides how they will make informed decisions

- Apply educational theory and research findings to diverse instructional situations

- Understand student differences and how instruction must be adapted to their individual needs

Our Approach

Flexible

A book that adapts to your course

Our modular approach and our inclusion of developmental case studies allow you flexibility in designing your course. Our modules are succinct (about half the length of a typical chapter), stand-alone topics that represent every topic found in a traditional chapter textbook. The modules are organized into themed units that correspond to chapter topics found in conventional textbooks. However, we do not expect any two instructors to teach a selection of modules in the same order, nor would we expect an instructor to teach all the modules in a single course! With this modular approach, instructors can easily select only those modules relevant to their courses and can arrange the topics in any order, and even skip entire modules or units if they choose. Our case studies also allow instructors flexibility. Instructors can choose to use one particular educational level (only early childhood), several (elementary and high school), all levels, or may choose to skip the cases altogether. Our stand alone modules and developmental cases allow you to tailor content to your particular course and student audience.

BRIEF CONTENTS

Introduction
Case Study 2
Module 1: Using Science to Inform Classroom Practices 4

Unit 1: Personal Development
Unit 1 Case Studies 22
Module 2: Contexts of Development 30
Module 3: Social Development 45
Module 4: Emotional Development 61
Module 5: Moral Development 76

Unit 2: The Developing Learner
Unit 2 Case Studies 92
Module 6: The Brain and Development 100
Module 7: Cognitive Development 118
Module 8: Language Development 133

Unit 3: Learning Theories
Unit 3 Case Studies 150
Module 9: Behavioral Learning Theories 158
Module 10: Social Cognitive Theory 173
Module 11: Information Processing 183

Unit 4: Cognitive Processes
Unit 4 Case Studies 202
Module 12: Metacognition 210
Module 13: Transfer of Skills and Knowledge 225
Module 14: Critical Thinking and Problem Solving 238

Unit 5: Motivation
Unit 5 Case Studies 256
Module 15: Behavioral Theory 264
Module 16: Cognitive Theories 278
Module 17: Self Theories 298

Unit 6: Classroom Management and Instruction
Unit 6 Case Studies 318
Module 18: Creating a Productive Learning Environment 326
Module 19: Understanding and Managing Student Behavior 346
Module 20: Instruction: Behavioral, Cognitive, and Constructivist Approaches 363
Module 21: Grouping Practices 377

Unit 7: Learner Differences
Unit 7 Case Studies 394
Module 22: Intelligence 402
Module 23: Giftedness and Creativity 418
Module 24: Cognitive Disabilities 432
Module 25: Emotional, Social, and Behavioral Disorders 449

Unit 8: Classroom Assessment
Unit 8 Case Studies 468
Module 26: Assessing Student Learning 476
Module 27: Test Construction and Use 492
Module 28: Performance Assessment 509

Unit 9: Standardized Testing
Unit 9 Case Studies 528
Module 29: Standardized Tests and Scores 536
Module 30: Issues in Standardized Testing 551

How Does EdPsych Help You Prepare for the Praxis Exam? 566
Glossary 574
References 589
Credits 655
Subject-Name Index 661

iv   brief contents

The Power of Customization: Create

Craft your teaching resources to match the way you teach. The flexibility of ***EdPsych: Modules*** provides the perfect opportunity to create the book you've always wanted. With McGraw-Hill Create, **www.mcgrawhillcreate.com,** you can easily rearrange modules, combine material from other content sources, and quickly upload content you have written, such as your course syllabus or teaching notes. McGraw-Hill Create even allows you to personalize your book's appearance by selecting the cover and adding your name, school, and course information. Order a McGraw-Hill Create book and you'll receive a complimentary print review copy in 3–5 business days or a complimentary **electronic review copy** via e-mail in **about an hour.** Go to **www.mcgrawhillcreate.com** today and register. Experience how McGraw-Hill Create empowers you to teach *your* students *your* way.

Applied

Opportunities for practical application of theories and concepts

In each module, our coverage of educational theories and concepts provides examples that illustrate application and reflective prompts that encourage practical application and critical thinking about individual differences and instructional contexts.

- In every module, **Application** sections provide an in-depth look at the theories in action. Coverage is focused on evidence-based teaching methods that are linked to research.

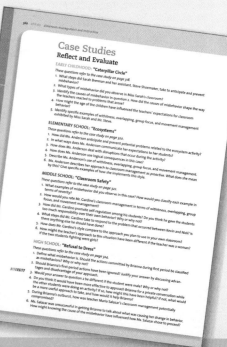

- **Guidelines and Examples** provide instances of classroom practice that reflect the theories and research covered within the module. These sections provide examples of curriculum that demonstrate the direct connection between theory and practice.

- **Case studies**—37 in all— provide opportunities for students to apply theories and concepts. Our case studies are rich, detailed glimpses into classroom and school settings. Each unit begins with four case studies: early childhood, elementary school, middle school, and high school which are relevant to all modules in that unit.

- At the end of each case study ASSESS questions prompt students to assess their existing knowledge and to identify assumptions, preconceptions, and personal beliefs prior to reading a particular module.

- REFLECT AND EVALUATE questions at the end of each module encourage students to check their comprehension of important concepts, to apply what they have learned about the research presented in the modules, and to evaluate the situations and instructional decisions presented in the case.

Our developmental approach of presenting cases at various certification levels enables students to meaningfully apply the concepts they are learning to the grade levels they intend to teach. Whether you use the case studies out of class or for class discussions, students will have the opportunity to practice applying what they've learned.

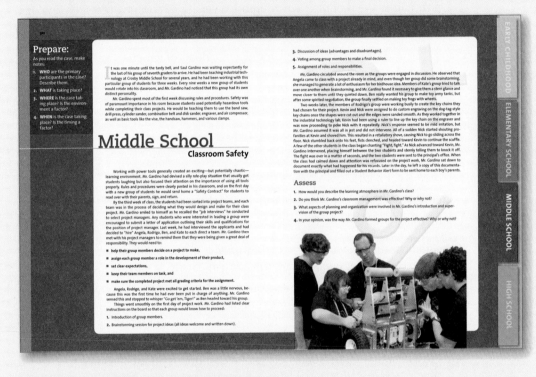

Current, Relevant, and Connected

Balance of classical and contemporary

We present research on traditional topics, such as cognitive development, learning, information-processing, and motivation, as well as more contemporary educational topics such as the brain, emotional development, response to intervention, and underserviced areas.

Focused coverage with depth and connections

The scope of each module provides a deeper examination of core topics. For example, while typical chapter textbooks combine behavioral and social cognitive learning theories into a single chapter, we treat each of these topics as separate modules to allow more meaningful discussion of the theory, research, and practice. We also offer more in-depth coverage of topics that may only be minimally covered in chapter textbooks such as constructivist teaching approaches, intelligence, grouping practices, and metacognition. Concepts in our modules that are discussed in more detail in other modules are cross referenced to provide linkages and to create a larger instructional framework.

Integrated Issues of Diversity

Our book treats diversity—characteristics such as ethnicity, race, socioeconomic status, gender, and disabilities—not as a separate topic but as a facet of most instructional situations.

DIVERSITY A marginal icon indicates where pertinent coverage of diversity appears in the modules. In the modules, we have chosen to emphasize information as a diversity issue only if it is supported by sufficient research or theoretically relevant. Within the modules, we integrate diversity by covering research findings that:

- indicate important differences among individuals of various diversity groups on psychological constructs such as intelligence, motivation, or language;

- reveal differences among individuals of various groups in values, practices, or social interactions;

- suggest differential responses to treatments, interventions, or teaching methods for individuals of varying diversity groups; and

- highlight differential treatment of individuals from various diversity groups within the classroom.

These findings are relevant because they provide essential information to help teachers make informed decisions that affect the success and well-being of their students.

In the case studies, you will find students and teachers of diverse backgrounds and Reflect and Evaluate questions at the end of the modules that probe students to evaluate their personal beliefs or assumptions about diversity.

Unit-by-Unit Changes

EdPsych: Modules, 2e,

- Includes nearly 800 new research citations

- New attention given—in every module—to the application of educational theory to instructional contexts

- Coverage of diversity—including race, gender, ethnicity, and even learning contexts—is strengthened throughout the book, with new and existing coverage better annotated for the reader

- New information on rural and urban teaching contexts

- Additional video applications illustrate application of theories

Unit-by-unit updates include:

Introduction

Module 1 Educational Psychology: Using Science to Inform Classroom Practices

- Revised to provide a more cohesive introduction to this field of study

- Frames teaching as decision-making
- Examines how we use science to improve instructional practices
- Provides a thorough introduction to issues of diversity in the classroom.

Unit 1: Personal Development

- Includes 80 new reference citations

Module 2: Contexts of Development

- New coverage of bullying and intervention relating to types of student and different contexts
- Added coverage of high poverty and highly segregated school systems

Module 3: Social Development

- Completely reorganized to provide a more logical flow from Erikson's theory to aspects of identity (statuses, ethnic, gender) and understanding the self (self-concept and self-esteem)
- New section on social competence broadened to include three components: social adjustment, social performance, and social skills.
- Updated coverage of ethnic identity
- New attention to rural and urban settings

Module 4: Emotional Development

- Updated coverage of milestones in emotional development, bullying
- New coverage of social and emotional learning (SEL) programs
- New coverage of parental beliefs about emotional expression
- New coverage of gender and cultural differences in emotional expression
- New coverage of emotional intelligence in relationships

Module 5: Moral Development

- New coverage of overt and relational aggression
- New coverage of processing deficits and cyber aggression.

Unit 2: The Developing Learner

- Includes 82 new reference citations

Module 6: The Brain and Development

- Significantly expanded to provide the most thorough coverage of any educational psychology textbook

- Examines new concerns with correlating neuroscience data to educational practice
- Expanded coverage of brain structure and function
- Expanded coverage of developmental processes
- Expanded coverage of brain activity during learning
- Provides the most current review of research in memory, reading, and math
- New coverage on emotion as it relates to learning and how brain research may offer insights
- New material on evaluating claims about "brain-based learning"

Module 7: Cognitive Development

- Added coverage of teaching methods based on constructivist principles
- Added perspective on Piaget's contributions—and criticism of his theories.
- More coverage of the differences between Piaget and Vygotsky
- Additional coverage of Vygotsky's view on socio-dramatic play
- More applied examples of concrete operational thinking

Module 8: Language Development

- New coverage of methods used with English language learners, such as instructional conversations
- Additional connections to instructional planning

Unit 3: Learning Theories

- Includes 40 new reference citations

Module 9: Behavioral Learning Theories

- Updated art program and research citations

Module 10: Social Cognitive Theory

- New material on self efficacy and challenging tasks

Module 11: Information Processing

- Added material on phonologically rehearsal as a memory strategy
- New coverage of distinctions between distributed practice and massed practice
- More on Individual differences in working memory capacity
- New coverage of processing time and cognitive load

- Added cultural findings on different patterns of thinking and perception in different societies
- Additional insights on information encoding and retrieval

Unit 4: Cognitive Processes

- Includes 58 new reference citations

Module 12: Metacognition

- New coverage of instructional strategy "Questioning the Author"
- New coverage of the SOAR method

Module 13: Transfer of Skills and Knowledge

- Added coverage of deliberate practice
- New material on using worked-out examples for practice at problem-solving
- New material on the use of question-answering and self-explanation strategies
- New tip on students constructing models for calculation problems

Module 14: Critical Thinking and Problem Solving

- Revised coverage of questioning and critical thinking
- New research on the influence of standardized testing on the teaching of thinking skills
- New research on the effectiveness of higher-order thinking lessons for students with and without special needs
- Added material on different cultural values regarding thinking skills and intellectual dispositions
- Added material on developmental differences in children's problem-solving
- More coverage on the application of general and specific problem-solving strategies
- Expanded coverage of problem-based learning—and its challenges

Unit 5: Motivation

- Includes 146 new reference citations

Module 15: Behavioral Theory

- Updated coverage of task-contingent rewards, competition, performance-contingent rewards
- New material on process praise and other types of praise
- Additional material on flow theory

- New material on authentic learning activities
- New material on the balance of challenge and skill level

Module 16: Cognitive Theories

- New material explaining the difference between a competency belief and self-efficacy
- Added coverage of mastery-approach goals and performance-approach goals
- New material on entity view of ability
- New material on developmental changes in expectancies and values
- New material on gender and ability beliefs
- New material on cultural norms and ethnic differences
- Added coverage of applications for enhancing student motivation

Module 17: Self Theories

- New coverage on the role of cultural expectations on gender differences
- New coverage of gender and ethnicity in relation to self-efficacy
- Added material on mastery learning experiences
- Added material on developmental changes in self-efficacy
- New insights on teachers with higher efficacy
- Expanded coverage of Maslow's hierarchy of needs and common misinterpretations of his theory
- More coverage of self-determination
- Revised coverage on integrating and applying self theories of motivation

Unit 6: Classroom Management and Instruction

- Includes 133 new reference citations

Module 18: Creating a Productive Learning Environment

- New: incorporates coverage of instructional planning
- Reorganized section on planning and organization offers logical overview of environmental competence, planning, and time management
- Added guidelines on developing strong teacher-student relationships

Module 19: Understanding and Managing Student Behavior

- New coverage of teachers' expectation of misbehavior

John Gutowski, Middlesex County College

Michelle Hanson, University of Sioux Falls

Stephanie Lewis Hinson, West Chester University

Emily Hixon, Purdue University—Calumet

Bob Hoffman, University of Central Florida

Steven M. Hoover, St. Cloud State University

Sachi Horback, Bucks County Community College

Christy A. Horn, University of Nebraska, Lincoln

Peggy Hsieh, University of Texas at San Antonio

Judy Hughey, Kansas State University

Richard E. Hult, University of South Carolina

John H. Hummel, Valdosta State University

Mona Ibrahim, Concordia College

Miranda E. Jennings, University of Massachusetts, Amherst

Emilie Johnson, Lindenwood University

Nancy Johnson, Geneva College

Martin H. Jones, University of Memphis

Pamela Kidder-Ashley, Appalachian State University

David A. Kilpatrick, SUNY Cortland

Kristopher J. Kimbler, Troy University

Kimberly Kinsler, Hunter College

> "The treatment of diversity throughout as opposed to its inclusion in one chapter mirrors the educational practice of including students of diverse backgrounds in the mainstream."
>
> [Al Longo, *Ocean County College*]

Kathleen Kleissler, Kutztown University

Catharine C. Knight, University of Akron

Elaine C. Koffman, Northeastern Illinois University

Tina Kruse, Macalester College

William Lan, Texas Tech University

Jennifer Lara, Anne Arundel Community College

Susan Leckart, Middlesex County College

Mary Beth Leibham, University of Wisconsin—Eau Claire

Judith R. Levine, Farmingdale State University of New York

Dennis A. Lichty, Wayne State College

Jeffrey Liew, Texas A&M University

> "I am very impressed with the approach described by the author team. I have to say that this is something I have been waiting years for."
>
> [Renee Mudrey-Camino, *University of Akron*]

Frank R. Lilly, California State University, Sacramento

Reinhard W. Lindner, Western Illinois University

Kimberly S. Loomis, Kennesaw State University

Alfred P. Longo, Ocean County College

Edward Lonky, SUNY Oswego

Cheryl Lovett, University of Central Oklahoma

Cleborne D. Maddux, University of Nevada, Reno

Pamela Manners, Troy University

Smita Mathur, University of South Florida, Lakeland

James Mbuva, National University

Catherine McCartney, Bemidji State University

Michael Meloth, East Carolina University

Lakeisha D. Meyer, Western Kentucky University

Elisa Michals, Sacramento State University

Ted Miller, University of Tennessee—Chattanooga

Michelle Montgomery, Central Washington University

Renee Mudrey-Camino, University of Akron

Ron Mulson, Hudson Valley Community College

Bob Nelson, University of Texas at Dallas

Sharon L. Nichols, University of Texas at San Antonio

Nicole Nickens, University of Central Missouri

Roseann O'Connor, Luzerne County Community College

ACKNOWLEDGMENTS

Sansanee Ohlson, Bowling Green State University

Comfort O. Okpala, Fayetteville State University

Scott Paris, University of Michigan, Ann Arbor

"Case material: This is a real strength. These make sense, they are well written, and they address crucial questions of pedagogy that are happening in schools consistently. They are compelling and ethically charged situations. "

[J'Anne Affeld, *Northern Arizona University*]

Leonard W. Parker, Liberty University

Kathryn Penrod, South Dakota State University

Jim Persinger, Emporia State University

Sarah Anne Polasky, Arizona State University

Carrie Pritchard, Western Kentucky University

Steven Pulos, University of Northern Colorado

Mary Ann Rafoth, Indiana University of Pennsylvania

Israel Ramos, The College of Saint Rose

Shelley C. Randall, Bloomsburg University of PA

Guynel Reid, Minnesota State University–Mankato

Peter Rich, Brigham Young University

Aaron S. Richmond, Metropolitan State College of Denver

Anne N. Rinn, University of Houston, Downtown

Kelly A. Rodgers, University of Texas at San Antonio

Susan Rogers, Columbus State Community College

Lawrence Rogien, Boise State University

Paul Rooney, University of California–Davis

Cary Roseth, Michigan State University

Terri Rothman, Monmouth University

Darrell Rudmann, Shawnee State University

Ruth Sandlin, California State University–San Bernardino

Jeff Sandoz, University of Louisiana of Lafayette

Tom Scheft, North Carolina Central University

Thomas R. Scheira, Buffalo State College

Roberta Scholes, University of Missouri

Dorothy Scotten, Lesley University

Donna Seagle, Chattanooga State Technical Community College

Thomas D. Sepe, Community College of Rhode Island–Knight Campus (Warwick)

Linda Sidoti, The College of Saint Rose

Joy Springer, Pepperdine University

Penee Stewart, Weber State University

Jeremy Sullivan, University of Texas at San Antonio

Sapna V. Taggar, University of Michigan, Flint

"This is the best writing of an ed psych text that I've seen in years. In addition to the writing style, I like the philosophy that aims at promoting knowledge and skills for professional development of the prospective teachers. The closing statement strikes a major point by emphasizing learning and application of the knowledge and skills in the process of becoming a teacher. This is very important to me. The purpose of an ed psych class should not only cover theory and research, but also and more importantly, develop students' competency to apply them in practice. "

[Li Cao, *University of West Georgia*]

Carol Thompson, Rowan University

Jennifer Titus, Tarleton State University

Patti Tolar, University of Houston

Ellen Usher, University of Kentucky, Lexington

Rick Van Sant, Ferris State University

Manuel Vargas, Winston-Salem State University

Craig Vivian, Monmouth College

Paul Wagner, University of Houston–Clear Lake

Rhea Walker, Winona State University

Faith Wallace, Kennesaw State University

Christopher Was, Kent State University

Deborah L. Watkins, York College of Pennsylvania

Carol L. Webb, Bridgewater College

Nicole Webb, Grand Canyon University

Marie C. White, Nyack College–Manhattan Campus

Keith Williams, Richard Stockton College of New Jersey

Barbara Wilson, Towson University

Steven Wininger, Western Kentucky University

Barbara N. Young, Middle Tennessee State University

Supplements Reviewers

Frank D. Adams, Wayne State College

Shane Cavanaugh, Central Michigan University

C. Allen Colebank, Fairmont State University

John V. Connor, Daytona Beach Community College

Jaclyn Finkel, Anne Arundel Community College

Richard A. Giaquinto, St. Francis College

Judith R. Levine, Farmingdale State College

Alfred P. Longo, Ocean County College

Renee Mudrey-Camino, University of Akron

Comfort O. Okpala, Fayetteville State University

Thomas R. Scheira, Buffalo State College

Teleconference Focus Group

Frank D. Adams, Wayne State College

Jerrell C. Cassady, Ball State University

Gregory Cutler, Bay de Noc Community College

Shelley Dubkin-Lee, Oregon State University

Richard A. Giaquinto, St. Francis College

Michelle Hanson, University of Sioux Falls

Karen Huxtable-Jester, University of Texas at Dallas

Nancy Knapp, University of Georgia

Catharine C. Knight, University of Akron

Tina Kruse, Macalester College

"Case studies were realistic, especially the So Yoon. This is a good example to discuss diversity and the implications, if any, to students' success and challenges."

[DeAnna M. Burney, *Florida A&M University*]

Renee Mudrey-Camino, University of Akron

Jim Persinger, Emporia State University

Jeff Sandoz, University of Louisiana at Lafayette

Dorothy Scotten, Lesley University

Craig Vivian, Monmouth College

Sapna Vyas, University of Michigan, Flint

Supplements Teleconference Focus Groups

Frank D. Adams, Wayne State College

C. Allen Colebank, Fairmont State University

John V. Connor, Daytona Beach Community College

Shane Cavanaugh, Central Michigan University

Jaclyn Finkel, Anne Arundel Community College

Richard A. Giaquinto, St. Francis College

Kimberly Kinsler, Hunter College

Judith R. Levine, Farmingdale State University of New York

Alfred P. Longo, Ocean County College

Smita Mathur, University of South Florida, Lakeland

Renee Mudrey-Camino, University of Akron

Comfort O. Okpala, Fayetteville State University

Thomas R. Scheira, Buffalo State College

Rayne A. Sperling, The Pennsylvania State University

Jason Stephens, University of Connecticut

ACKNOWLEDGMENTS

Case Studies Workshop Participants

Li Cao, University of West Georgia

Gypsy Denzine, Northern Arizona University

Kellah M. Edens, University of South Carolina

Bernie Frank, Suffolk County Community College

"I especially appreciate the authors for putting all these terms and theories into practice. Textbooks often neglect to help students make the connection between what they read/learn and how they should perform in classrooms. I must commend the authors' efforts in preparing the high-level thinking questions at the end of each case study. Most case studies I have seen ask low-level thinking questions where answers are most obvious, which makes the activity somewhat futile. These questions that the authors prepared are very meaningful and appropriate. "

[Peggy Hsieh, *University of Texas at San Antonio*]

Marina Gair, Pace University

Richard E. Hult, University of South Carolina

Ruth Sandlin, California State University, San Bernardino

Marie White, Nyack College, Manhattan Campus

Design Reviewers

Kathleen Beauvais, Eastern Michigan University

Dorothy Espelage, University of Illinois at Urbana–Champaign

Alfred P. Longo, Ocean County College

Sarah Anne Polasky, Arizona State University

Dorothy Scotten, Lesley University

Jay Thomas, Aurora University

Educational Psychology Symposium Participants

Every year McGraw-Hill conducts symposia, which are attended by instructors from across the country. These events are an opportunity for editors from McGraw-Hill to gather information about the needs and challenges of instructors teaching the educational psychology course. They also offer a forum for the attendees to exchange ideas and experiences with colleagues they might not have otherwise met. The feedback we received at our educational psychology symposium has been invaluable and has contributed to the development of *EdPsych Modules*.

Lisa Bohlin, Purdue University

Carol Crumbaugh, Western Michigan University

Cheryl Cisero Durwin, Southern Connecticut State University

Fernando A. Hernandez, California State University at Los Angeles

Brent Igo, Clemson University

Jack Judkin, Bemidji State University

Nancy Knapp, University of Georgia

Patricia Lanzon, Henry Ford Community College

Bryan Moseley, Florida International University

Marla Reese-Weber, Illinois State University

James L. Rodriguez, California State University-Fullerton

Jill Stamm, Arizona State University

Jason M. Stephens, University of Connecticut

David J. Tarver, Angelo State University

Class Test Participants

John V. Connor, Daytona Beach Community College

Carol Davis, Spoon River College

Kellah M. Edens, University of South Carolina

Lynne Ekdale, Illinois State University

Emilie Johnson, Lindenwood University

Nancy Johnson, Geneva College

Tina Kruse, Macalester College

Jennifer Lara, Anne Arundel Community College

Sansanee Ohlson, Bowling Green State University

David Sears, Purdue University

Rhea R. Walker, Winona State University

Deborah L. Watkins, York College of Pennsylvania

Marie White, Nyack College–Manhattan Campus

Corinne Zimmerman, Illinois State University

Video Participants

Boswell Elementary School
Pam Brooks
Angie Harmon

Burnett Creek Elementary School
Rebecca Combs
Jeanne Dano
Karen Miller
Mark Pearl
Michelle Webb

Cumberland Elementary School
Kim Bowers
Emily Pool

Harrison High School
Tanya Van Hyfte

Hershey Elementary School/East Tipp Middle School
Dr. Melanie Davis, school psychologist

Key Learning Community (K–12)
Beverly Hoeltke
Dr. Christine Kunkle
Renee Motz

Klondike Elementary School
Rich Brown
Elizabeth Dunlap
Carol Goodrich
Jessica Harris
April Lyons
Scott Peters
Mary Raub
Mary Ruley
Joyce Sheets
Angie Shondell
Kim Steiner
Marie Wellman
Tammy Younts

Klondike Middle School
Shelly Buck
Beth Buss
Christine Cannon
Amy Craig
Karen Hail
Sue Nail
Neil Radtke

West Lafayette Junior/Senior High School
Larry Allen
Dave Collins
Steve Florence
John Levy
Joel Munoz
Jane Schott
Gracie Shukle

EDPSYCH

MODULES

using science to inform classroom practices

Case Study

"Achievement Gap" 2

Module 1:
Using Science to Inform Classroom Practices

Teaching as Decision Making 5

Educational Psychology: The Science 6

Educational Psychology: Classroom Practices 10

Summary 17

Key Concepts 17

Video Applications 17

Case Study: Reflect and Evaluate 18

Prepare:

As you read the case, make notes:

1. **WHO** are the central characters in the case? Describe them.

2. **WHAT** is taking place?

3. **WHERE** is the case taking place? Is the environment a factor?

4. **WHEN** is the case taking place? Is the timing a factor?

Jarrod and Tamara Patterson met during college and are both teachers in the Chicago area. They live in the suburbs, where Jarrod teaches third grade. Tamara completed her student teaching at an inner-city school. She wanted to continue in a similar school district, so she takes the train into the city each day to teach history in a public middle school.

Over the years, Jarrod and Tamara have had a number of arguments about education. Some of their disagreements stem from the developmental differences in their students—as Jarrod works with younger students—but their liveliest disagreements involve the differences between suburban and urban classrooms. Ninety percent of Tamara's students are African American and live in households where the median annual income is around $33,000. In contrast, 79% of Jarrod's students are White, 9% are Latino, 8% are Hispanic,

Middle School
Achievement Gap

and only 3% are African American. The median annual income for households in Jarrod's school district is $83,000.

As they begin their drive into the city to run errands on Saturday morning, Tamara reminds Jarrod that she needs to stop by her classroom to pick up some papers. She forgot them yesterday and needs to finish grading them before Monday morning. Jarrod doesn't respond—he has taken the opportunity to read the newspaper while Tamara drives.

"Listen to this," he begins. "A new study examined the 'achievement gap'—you know, the idea that African Americans perform more poorly compared to Whites. Says here that some researchers found that the differences in achievement levels between African Americans and Caucasians no longer exist."

Tamara responds skeptically, "How did they determine that?"

"Well, it says that the researchers found no differences in the GPAs of students from several ethnic backgrounds, including African-American and Caucasian students," replies Jarrod.

Tamara pushes the issue. "Who were the students? How did they get information about GPA? Did they use the official records?"

★ *Daily News* ★

January 2012

Achievement Gap Vanishes

Jarrod replies, "It doesn't give that many details."

As they pull into the school parking lot, Tamara announces, "The newspaper shouldn't print those statements without supplying more details." She grabs the newspaper out of Jarrod's hands and says, "Come on; while we are inside getting my papers, we can probably find more information about the study on the Web."

"Do we have to do this today?" moans Jarrod, wishing he had kept his mouth shut.

"Yes," replies Tamara.

As they enter Tamara's classroom, Jarrod says, "I still can't get over how old everything seems in the building. When are they going to update the decor, not to mention your textbooks?"

Tamara ignores his comment. She turns on the only computer in the room and retrieves her papers while she waits for the computer to get up and running. Then she launches her Internet browser and begins to alphabetize her papers, because she knows it will take several minutes before the computer is ready.

Jarrod waits impatiently. "How long is this going to take?"

"Well, if we had new computers with wireless Internet connections like at your school, we'd be out of here by now. But I don't have those perks, so just give me a couple of minutes."

Tamara uses the researchers' names from the newspaper article to find the original study online. "Good, it was published early this year," she says, and sends the print job to the printer in the main office. "Come on. I'll grab the printout. I can read while you drive us."

As they walk to the office, Tamara can't help herself. "I suppose you have your own printer in your classroom and don't have to walk to the main office all the time."

"As a matter of fact, I do," replies Jarrod. "You know you could get a job in my school district anytime. Remember, you chose to work here. Don't give me a hard time because I chose not to."

As they drive to their next stop, Tamara begins to read and launches into a tirade: "Well, they used college students, not K–12 students. Oh, can you believe this? They didn't even use official records to find GPA. They simply asked students to provide their GPA on a survey."

"Why do you care so much? It's just one newspaper article in the back of the paper," replies Jarrod.

Tamara continues her tirade. "Because parents and most other teachers won't take the time to read the actual study and see that the newspaper article is misleading. People won't realize that the achievement gap is still present in K–12 classrooms and will expect all teachers to have students with similar achievement levels. That's unrealistic. If journalists were actually trying to inform the public—instead of spewing out stories on movie stars in rehab—they would explain why the achievement gap exists. It's not even about ethnicity; it's about socioeconomic status."

"Maybe you should write a letter to the editor," suggests Jarrod.

"Maybe I will," Tamara says.

Assess

1. How might the different schools in which Tamara and Jarrod work influence the importance each places on understanding achievement differences?

2. Should teachers be concerned with what type of students participate in research studies like the one reported in the newspaper article? Why or why not?

3. How would you respond to a parent whose child is not achieving as well as others but who believes that all students should perform equally well?

MODULE 1

Using Science to Inform Classroom Practices

Outline	Learning Goals
Teaching as Decision Making	
■ Opportunities and Challenges of Teaching ■ Educational Psychology: A Resource for Teachers	1. Explain why educational psychology is an important resource for teachers.
Educational Psychology: The Science	
■ Research Designs ■ Samples ■ Measures	2. Describe three elements of research studies that help determine which studies are worthy of consideration.
Educational Psychology: Classroom Practices	
■ Developing Your Philosophy of Teaching ■ Addressing Diversity ■ Using a Case Study Approach	3. Define *philosophy of teaching* and explain why it is important for teachers to base their philosophy on scientific evidence. 4. Describe four diversity characteristics that can define an individual's group membership, and explain why teachers need to understand differences between groups.
Summary **Key Concepts** **Video Applications** **Case Study: Reflect and Evaluate**	

TEACHING AS DECISION MAKING

Teaching is about making decisions. Within and outside the classroom, teachers face instructional questions every day, whether they are planning a course or creating an assignment, whether they are assessing student performance or addressing student behavior. *Which works of literature should I assign? How could I best measure student understanding of this chapter on molecules? Why is this student no longer engaged in class?*

If you become a teacher, you will face many instructional situations that require you to make a decision and act on it. How will you make sure those decisions are good ones? Think about professionals in many fields, such as health care, who use scientific research as the basis for evaluating situations and responding to them. Like them, teachers use the science of educational psychology to make informed decisions about instruction. But teachers need more than an understanding of scientific facts. Effective teachers are confident in their problem-solving abilities and skilled in meeting the instructional needs of a diverse group of students (Steffy, Wolfe, Pasch, & Enz, 2000). To become an effective teacher, you will need to do the following things:

■ develop a personal teaching philosophy that guides you in making informed decisions,

■ understand student differences and how instruction must be adapted to their individual needs,

■ practice adopting research findings to your teaching philosophy and applying them to diverse instructional situations.

Opportunities and Challenges of Teaching

Some readers of this book have always wanted to be teachers. Others may not be sure, but they are curious and want to find out more. Teaching can be a very rewarding profession. Over the course of a teaching career, a teacher has the opportunity to make a positive difference in the lives of hundreds, if not thousands, of students. The typical elementary teacher receives a new group of 20 to 30 students each fall and spends an average of seven hours per day with them—more than 1,400 hours over the course of the school year. At the secondary level, teachers spend less time with individual students, yet they may touch the lives of as many as 150 students each day.

Students come to school with diverse life experiences and a range of ethnic, socioeconomic, and language backgrounds. These students will have differing levels of ability, prior achievement, and motivation. Some also may have physical disabilities that may or may not affect learning, and others may have intellectual, learning, emotional, social, or behavioral disabilities that affect their achievement. Students who are intellectually gifted or have creative talents also may need special consideration.

Today's diverse classrooms present many unique opportunities for teachers to promote learning and personal growth in the students they encounter. Those who choose to become teachers will have the opportunity to help students negotiate the challenges they face as they experience physical, social, emotional, and cognitive changes. You can help them learn a tremendous amount about themselves by teaching them to evaluate their own thinking processes, identify their strengths and weaknesses, and pay attention to the way they interact and collaborate with peers. You will help students discover new interests, build on their prior knowledge, and even challenge their preconceptions by exposing them to different ideas and perspectives—those in the curriculum as well as those of their peers. You can help students learn to be sensitive to the perspectives of peers with disabilities as well as those with academic and cultural backgrounds different from their own.

Teaching can be very rewarding, but it requires a high degree of commitment. In today's educational climate, teachers are held accountable for the academic success of each student. That can create a lot of pressure. Making wise choices about how to teach effectively is made more complex by the diverse nature of today's classrooms. What types of instructional approaches will you use to meet the individual needs of your students? How will you deal with differing levels of ability and achievement? How will you adapt your teaching for students from different cultural and socioeconomic backgrounds? Moreover, how will you confront your own preconceptions and identify biases you might not even be aware of? Educational psychology helps us answer questions such as these.

Educational Psychology: A Resource for Teachers

When teachers need help dealing with issues of diversity, motivation, achievement differences, behavioral problems, and other concerns, they turn to the field of educational psychology. **Educational**

psychology links the science of psychology to educational practice and provides teachers with evidence-based knowledge to support their day-to-day decision making in the classroom. Teachers who use research and theory to guide their practices are more deliberate and more thoughtful classroom problem solvers (Bigge & Shermis, 1999; Eisner, 1985; Leu & Kinzer, 1995). In short, educational psychology can help teachers to become better teachers.

People who work outside educational settings may assume that good teaching practices are simply common sense. Yet, common-sense approaches to classroom management and instruction often are ineffective or even counterproductive. Assume, for example, that an elementary student continues to get out of his seat during a lesson. A common-sense approach would be to politely ask the student to sit down. However, if the student is misbehaving to attract attention from the teacher and classmates, this approach might simply encourage the behavior.

Scientific Approaches Versus Common Sense. Research informs teachers about how best to approach situations in the classroom, such as children playing with one another rather than completing their work, as shown here. The common-sense approach does not always lead to best practices.

Research suggests that a more effective approach would be to ignore the unwanted behavior, *depending on the individual characteristics of the student.* Hence, scientific evidence helps teachers determine the best practices for effective teaching. As a teacher, you will encounter situations for which, despite all your training, you are unprepared. When that happens, research can help you formulate an informed response.

Although the field of educational psychology has always relied on science, the No Child Left Behind (NCLB) Act of 2001 has lifted the importance of science to a new level. NCLB states that schools and educational programs must use "scientifically based research" in order to receive federal funding. For example, the Reading First program makes federal funds available to help certain reading teachers strengthen existing skills and foster new ones, using instructional techniques shown to be effective by scientifically based research. Following the recommendations of NCLB, we are writing this text to provide theories and empirical evidence you can use to develop a repertoire of skills and knowledge on your path to becoming an effective teacher.

No Child Left Behind: See page 552.

To make the most of educational psychology, teachers need both a basic understanding of scientific principles (the science) and an awareness of how these principles can apply to real situations (classroom practices). In this text, you will be considering the same major challenges that face scholars in this field:

- The science: formulating theories and conducting research studies.
- Classroom practices: developing applications of current theories and research to enhance teaching and learning.

EDUCATIONAL PSYCHOLOGY: THE SCIENCE

The science of educational psychology involves formulating **theories**—sets of ideas that are used to explain a phenomenon and make predictions about behavior—and then conduct research to determine how well those theories explain the phenomenon. The relationship between theory and research is reciprocal. Research findings may support a theory, but researchers also may alter theories or develop new ones based on accumulated evidence. This process is ongoing—scientists today are building upon (or tearing down) the work of twentieth-century scientists.

For today's teachers, the amount and variety of research material available can be intimidating. The first step in evaluating research is to find appropriate resources (see Guidelines 1.1: Finding Reputable Research). After you have located good research articles, you need to determine which studies are worthy of consideration. In order to evaluate the quality of research, you need to understand three elements of research:

1. Design: What was the purpose of the study (to describe, to show cause-and-effect)?
2. Sample: Who was being studied (elementary-aged children, college students)?
3. Measures: How were constructs of interest measured (surveys, observations)?

> ### GUIDELINES 1.1: Finding Reputable Research
>
> Teachers need to become informed consumers of research. News stories and Web sites commonly misinterpret scientific findings. The first step in evaluating research is to find appropriate resources. To obtain reputable research:
>
> - Don't use newspaper and magazine articles, because they are not research articles.
> - Don't do Internet searches using search engines, because they may not yield credible sources.
> - Do find peer-reviewed articles in scholarly journals at a local university library.
> - Do find peer-reviewed articles in databases such as ERIC and PSYCINFO.
> - Do visit Web sites of professional associations to see if they have links to educational research groups such as the American Educational Research Association (AERA) and the American Psychological Association (APA).

Research Designs

Researchers must choose a method for investigating variables of interest. **Variables** are events, characteristics, or behaviors that can be measured, such as age, family divorce, medication, diagnosis of attention–deficit hyperactivity disorder (ADHD), math scores, or aggression. To focus on a specific question about certain variables, researchers choose a particular **research design**—a method for investigating how and whether the variables selected are related. Table 1.1 describes four designs that are commonly used in educational research.

Descriptive designs provide basic information about variables in a population without making connections between behaviors, events, or conditions. For example, a descriptive research study might determine what percentage of school-age children are diagnosed with ADHD.

Two descriptive designs can provide in-depth perspectives:

- *Case study* research examines a single individual and creates a rich picture of that individual's psychological functioning. Researchers might observe a child diagnosed with autism both at home and at school, interview teachers and parents, and examine test scores, school records, and other sources of information.
- *Ethnographic study* research closely examines a particular group through direct participation within the group. For example, a researcher might attend a school of Latino students, taking extensive field notes to capture the unique educational values and social challenges of this ethnic group.

To move beyond simply *describing* behaviors, researchers use **correlational designs,** which answer questions about the connections between two variables. For example, in exploring the connection between study time and grades, the researcher might ask whether students who spend more time studying get better grades. These connections are expressed in a statistical computation called a *correlation coefficient*, a number between –1.0 and +1.0 that indicates the type and strength of the relationship between two variables.

- The sign (positive or negative) indicates the type of relationship between the two variables. A positive correlation (+) between study time and grades means that as study time increases, grades also increase. A negative correlation (–) between school absences and grades means that as absences increase, grades decrease.
- The closer a correlation coefficient is to +1 or –1, the stronger the relationship between the two variables. For example, a correlation coefficient of –.56 indicates a stronger connection than a correlation coefficient of +.43 because the absolute value of the number is larger.

Although correlation studies measure the relationships between different variables, they *cannot* determine cause and effect. Although we may find that study time and grades are positively correlated, increased study time *does not cause* better grades. Instead, this positive correlation may suggest several possibilities: (1) more study time causes better grades, (2) better grades cause a person to enjoy academics and therefore to study more, or (3) some other variable, such as parental involvement, accounts for the high levels of study time and grades.

TABLE 1.1	Summary of Research Designs			
	Descriptive	**Correlational**	**Experimental**	**Quasi-experimental**
Definition	To systematically explain a situation factually and accurately.	To assess how changes in one variable correspond with changes in another variable.	To establish a cause-effect relationship between variables.	To infer a cause-effect relationship between variables when the researchers cannot manipulate the independent variable.
Researcher's questions	What percentage of students passed a state mastery test? Does the percentage differ by grade level or socioeconomic status?	To what extent are reading achievement scores correlated with socioeconomic status? How are science project scores correlated with parents' level of interest in science?	How is third-grade reading achievement affected by classroom reading-training? (Researchers randomly assign students into two groups, one with reading, training and one without, and then compare scores on reading achievement tests).	How is third-grade reading achievement affected by classroom reading-training? (Researchers study two existing classrooms at the same school, one with reading-training and one without, and then compare scores on reading achievement tests).
Limitations	Cannot show connections between different variables.	Can show connections between variables, but cannot prove one variable causes changes in the other.	Requires random assignment into experimental and control groups, which is often not possible.	Can show connections between variables and even infer causation, but cannot confirm that the results were due solely to the independent variable.

When researchers want to establish whether a cause-effect relationship exists, they turn to experimental and quasi-experimental designs. **Experimental designs** are used to establish a cause-effect relationship between an independent variable and a dependent variable. An independent variable is the variable of interest that is presumed to have an effect on the dependent variable, which is the outcome of the study. Researchers conduct experimental studies in two steps:

1. Randomly assign participants to one of two groups: an experimental group and a control group.
2. Manipulate the independent variable (a treatment or intervention) with the experimental group but not the control group.

Suppose researchers want to determine whether using computers in elementary classrooms (independent variable) affects the academic achievement of students (dependent variable). They might give an academic achievement test to students and then randomly assign some to a computer classroom (experimental group) and others to a no-computer classroom (control group). The experimental group would use computers in the classroom over a specified period of time, while the control group would not. At the end of the study, researchers would give the same academic achievement test to each student. If the experimental group showed greater improvement over time than the control group, researchers could make a claim about a cause-effect relationship: that the independent variable (the use of computers in the classroom) affected the dependent variable (academic achievement).

In situations in which researchers cannot randomly assign individuals to groups or manipulate an independent variable, they use **quasi-experimental designs** to *infer* a cause-effect relationship. Obviously, researchers cannot randomly assign children to divorced and nondivorced families, abusive and nonabusive homes, male and female genders, or high and low socioeconomic groups. In other cases, researchers' actions may be limited by school district rules or by time or expense, making the manipulation of experimental and control groups impossible. As a result, quasi-experimental designs cannot establish that an independent variable directly affects a dependent variable, and therefore they leave open the possibility that the outcome of the study may be due to other variables the researcher could not control. Say, for example, that researchers study an existing group of students in a computer classroom and compare their achievement to that of students enrolled in a no-computer classroom. Changes in the academic achievement of students in the computer classroom (dependent variable) may not depend *solely* on the presence of computers (independent variable) but may also be affected by variables beyond the researchers' control: the computer classroom having more high-level readers, fewer behaviorally challenging children, or a teacher with more teaching experience than the teacher in the no-computer classroom. Researchers employ safeguards to account for and control all other possible variables that might affect the experimental and control groups, but their presence and the lack of random group assignment are limiting factors.

Despite these shortcomings, quasi-experimental research does allow researchers to examine questions involving differences between groups or differences over time. Two examples are cross-sectional studies and longitudinal designs, described below.

1. *Cross-sectional studies* examine two or more groups to compare behaviors. Researchers might examine whether middle school students have more or fewer hours of homework than high school students.

2. *Longitudinal designs* examine the same group of people repeatedly over time in order to provide information about how behaviors change over time or how earlier events can be connected to later events. A longitudinal study might follow children over time to determine whether children whose parents divorce in elementary school have more academic difficulties in adolescence than children whose parents did not divorce.

To use science effectively in decision making, teachers need to be informed consumers of research. When you encounter scientific evidence presented in the media, in journals, or at workshops, you should be aware of the various inferences that can be made with each research design, as shown in Figure 1.1. Experimental studies are the only type that can answer questions about cause-effect relationships. However, correlational and quasi-experimental designs are more common in educational research because they are more practical than experimental designs for investigating many hypotheses regarding teaching and learning. They also provide more information than descriptive designs. Nevertheless, you must be cautious when interpreting correlational and quasi-experimental designs. You should always question whether other variables not identified in the studies might account for the findings.

Samples

Once the research design is determined, researchers must identify the population of interest and select a sample. Suppose researchers want to study how students of different ages respond to the stress of transferring to a new school. Because the researchers cannot observe or survey all transferring students—the population of interest—they rely on a **sample,** a smaller set of individuals from the population of interest. The sample needs to be representative, meaning that it has gender, ethnicity, and age characteristics similar to the population of interest. The best method for ensuring a representative sample is to use a **random sample,** meaning every person in the population of interest has an equal chance of being included. Many computer programs can take a large list of individuals (for example, all students registered in a school district) and create a random subset of individuals to be included in a study.

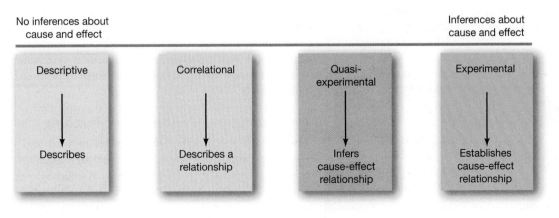

No inferences about cause and effect

Inferences about cause and effect

Descriptive	Correlational	Quasi-experimental	Experimental
Describes	Describes a relationship	Infers cause-effect relationship	Establishes cause-effect relationship

Figure 1.1. A Continuum of Research Designs. Design dictates what inferences we can make from educational research studies.

Even when a random sample of individuals within the population is selected, not all the people selected will agree to participate in the research study. (How many Web site surveys have you declined?) This is called **volunteer bias,** the tendency of those who choose to participate in research studies to differ in some way from those who do not participate. Typically, individuals who have strong feelings or opinions, or who are invested in the outcome of a particular research study, are more likely to participate than are those who do not have a vested interest. For example, a college student might be more willing to participate in surveys and interviews regarding opinions on the effectiveness of the university's financial aid office, and less likely to participate in research on the effectiveness of the university president.

Measures

Once researchers have chosen a research design and representative sample, they must decide on a method for taking measurements, which will provide a framework for gathering information. If researchers are investigating the amount of time students spend during school hours completing assignments, they must decide whether to ask students verbally, have them complete a paper-and-pencil survey, or observe them within the school setting. Some measures commonly used in educational research are these:

- **Observations,** or watching or viewing the behavior of individuals, might be used to examine how many times a teacher calls on a girl versus a boy in relation to the number of students from each gender who raise their hands.

- **Interviews,** or questions presented to participants, can be highly structured lists of simple questions (*How many hours do you spend on homework each night?*) or can include open-ended questions (*How do you study for a test?*). Even though open-ended questions allow more information to be gathered, they often result in less consistency across participants. Participants might talk about the number of hours spent studying, the use of a study guide, or strategies they use for reading, note taking, memorizing, and testing themselves.

- **Tests and surveys** typically are paper-and-pencil measures that include a number of questions. Test-and-survey research can be done very easily with large groups of individuals in a relatively short amount of time. One requirement for participation in survey research is the ability to read and write. This might exclude younger children and individuals with language barriers.

Research Measures. Observations allow researchers to view the behaviors of teachers and students during instruction, such as whether boys or girls are called on more frequently by teachers.

When you examine research findings, consider the measurement strategy that the researchers chose. Each measurement approach has limitations. In interviews, the researcher must speak the same language as the participant. On a test or survey, the participant must be able to read and write in the same language. Observation research is less valid for measurements of internal states of mind such as self-confidence or sadness.

Consider the research scenarios presented in Example 1.1 and see if you can classify them according to research design.

EDUCATIONAL PSYCHOLOGY: CLASSROOM PRACTICES

In addition to understanding educational research, teachers must be able to translate practical findings of specific research studies into school settings—diverse school settings. To do this, every teacher needs a systematic process for developing his or her personal educational philosophies.

Developing Your Philosophy of Teaching

Effective teachers develop **philosophies of teaching**— their views about how they will structure their classrooms, teach students, and respond to problems. A philosophy of teaching provides a lens or filter through which teachers consider the merits of various teaching strategies before

> ### EXAMPLE 1.1   Applications of Research to Educational Settings
>
> How would you classify each of the following research designs?
>
> 1. There are two sections of a class. Both sections are taught by the same instructor, cover the same content, and have the same number of students. In one class the teacher uses a $150 textbook, and in the other class the teacher uses no textbook. The final exam scores are compared to determine which practice is a better option.
> 2. An educational psychologist examines how students' levels of motivation toward studying compare with their IQ scores.
> 3. In an effort to decrease obesity and increase movement among students, a superintendent has all the gym teachers in a district record the average number of hours in a week spent doing cardio work in gym class.
> 4. A researcher goes to an urban school and a rural school to observe differences. After much study, the researcher writes a report comparing and contrasting the two schools.

they select or reject them for use in the classroom (Campoy, 2005). Philosophies of teaching should be based on sound scientific evidence and be continually reevaluated as new information becomes available. Essentially, teachers are lifelong learners. Table 1.2 shows the standards set forth by the *Interstate New Teacher Assessment and Support Consortium (INTASC)*, used by many education programs at colleges and universities across the country to evaluate competencies of graduates of teaching programs. Notice that the criteria for effective teaching do not state *what* subject matter to teach or *what* instructional methods or motivational and management strategies to use. Rather, the criteria address whether the teacher possesses the skills necessary to make informed decisions in these areas.

In other words, the skills necessary for informed decision making are just as important as the content and methods that teacher-preparation students learn in their education programs—perhaps even more so. Teachers must make decisions for themselves rather than merely adopting methods, strategies, and techniques because they have been traditionally used, fit their personal beliefs, or are currently in vogue. If you were a physician, would you consider using the best medical practices and equipment of 50 years ago? Of course not. Teachers cannot assume that the approaches that worked well many years ago are equally effective today. Today, professionals use *evidence-based practice*, or approaches that have scientific support. As knowledgeable users of scientific information, teachers must always be ready to evaluate empirical findings and to decide how they can use those findings in the classroom to enhance students' learning. However, research findings in educational psychology often do not provide

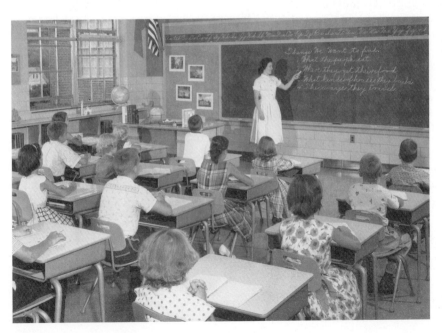

Best Practices. Teachers need to examine current resources and up-to-date scientific evidence in making decisions about instructional methods and techniques, rather than relying on techniques used decades ago.

TABLE 1.2   INTASC Core Teaching Standards 2011

The standards have been grouped into four general categories to help users organize their thinking about the standards:

The Learner and Learning

Standard #1: Learner Development. The teacher understands how learners grow and develop, recognizing that patterns of learning and development vary individually within and across the cognitive, linguistic, social, emotional, and physical areas, and designs and implements developmentally appropriate and challenging learning experiences.

Standard #2: Learning Differences. The teacher uses understanding of individual differences and diverse cultures and communities to ensure inclusive learning environments that enable each learner to meet high standards.

Standard #3: Learning Environments. The teacher works with others to create environments that support individual and collaborative learning, and that encourage positive social interaction, active engagement in learning, and self-motivation.

Content

Standard #4: Content Knowledge. The teacher understands the central concepts, tools of inquiry, and structures of the discipline(s) he or she teaches and creates learning experiences that make the discipline accessible and meaningful for learners to assure mastery of the content.

Standard #5: Application of Content. The teacher understands how to connect concepts and use differing perspectives to engage learners in critical thinking, creativity, and collaborative problem solving related to authentic local and global issues.

Instructional Practice

Standard #6: Assessment. The teacher understands and uses multiple methods of assessment to engage learners in their own growth, to monitor learner progress, and to guide the teacher's and learner's decision making.

Standard #7: Planning for Instruction. The teacher plans instruction that supports every student in meeting rigorous learning goals by drawing upon knowledge of content areas, curriculum, cross-disciplinary skills, and pedagogy, as well as knowledge of learners and the community context.

Standard #8: Instructional Strategies. The teacher understands and uses a variety of instructional strategies to encourage learners to develop deep understanding of content areas and their connections, and to build skills to apply knowledge in meaningful ways.

Professional Responsibility

Standard #9: Professional Learning and Ethical Practice. The teacher engages in ongoing professional learning and uses evidence to continually evaluate his/her practice, particularly the effects of his/her choices and actions on others (learners, families, other professionals, and the community), and adapts practice to meet the needs of each learner.

Standard #10: Leadership and Collaboration. The teacher seeks appropriate leadership roles and opportunities to take responsibility for student learning, to collaborate with learners, families, colleagues, other school professionals, and community members to ensure learner growth, and to advance the profession.

Council of Chief State School Officers. (2011, April). Interstate Teacher Assessment and Support Consortium (InTASC) Model Core Teaching Standards: A Resource for State Dialogue. Washington, DC: Author.
http://www.ccsso.org/Documents/2011/InTASC_Model_Core_Teaching_Standards_2011.pdf

definitive solutions to a particular instructional issue. That's okay. As you consider the available research findings and develop your own philosophy of teaching, you must decide how you will respond to specific instructional issues. As new research findings become available, and as you develop practical experience in the classroom, your teaching philosophy will evolve.

Addressing Diversity

Determining effective classroom practices is made more complex by the increasingly diverse nature of the student body in U.S. schools. Aspects of diversity will shape your teaching and the choices you make about the methods, techniques, and strategies you employ in the classroom. Because diversity can be found in all educational interactions, we discuss issues of diversity within specific educational contexts. An icon (like the one in the margin here) will point to pertinent coverage of diversity within a particular topic. In order to provide a basic understanding of diversity, some of the most important guidelines and concepts related to diversity and effective classroom practices are summarized here.

Effective teachers are aware of the diversity they are likely to encounter in the classroom. Individuals and environments can exhibit a wealth of diverse characteristics. To begin to understand individual and group differences, researchers often ask participants of studies to report their ethnicity or race, sex or gender, socioeconomic status, and disabilities. By grouping people based on these characteristics, researchers can divide any population into subsets for analysis. For example, in the 2010 U.S. Census, respondents were asked to report their race by choosing among the following categories:

- White
- Black, African American, or Negro
- American Indian or Alaska Native
- Asian (with specific check box responses for Asian Indian, Chinese, Filipino, Japanese, Korean, Vietnamese, Other Asian, Native Hawaiian, Guamanian or Chamorro, Samoan, or Other Pacific Islander)
- Some other race (Individuals of "multiracial, mixed, interracial, or a Hispanic, Latino, or Spanish group" could respond in a write-in space under this category. Also, people of two or more races could fill in multiple race response check boxes and provide additional responses.)

The inclusion of multiple-race categories is relatively new but will be required by all K-12 institutions for all reports published for the No Child Left Behind Act of 2001 (Meyer & Setzer, 2009).

A group may be considered a **minority group** if it has less power than the majority group, even if the group is not smaller in number. For example, more women than men live in the United States, but women are considered a minority group due to their relative lack of power in business (lower-paying jobs), politics (fewer political positions), and religion (in some religions, women still are not allowed to hold leadership positions). Let's examine group membership further.

- The terms *ethnicity* and *race* are often used interchangeably to express cultural differences, but they actually have different meanings (Betancourt & López, 1993). Although each term has a definition that is so complex that entire courses are taught to differentiate the two, our purpose here is to provide a basic distinction. **Ethnic group** includes people who share a similar culture—an environment with a unique history, traditions, rules, and attitudes and perhaps a specific language. In contrast, **racial group** categorizes people who share common biological traits (such as hair texture and skin color). The biological traits that distinguish races are socially defined. In other words, there is nothing particularly important about hair texture or skin color. Our society could have chosen, or defined as important, other biological traits (eye color, height, and so on). Certain traits were most likely chosen to establish social standing between groups (Markus, 2008). Most often, a person's ethnicity and racial group overlap. However, because ethnicity is based on environment and race is based on biology, they can diverge. For example, how would researchers categorize the race and ethnicity of an Asian-born child who is adopted and raised by a middle-class, White family living in the rural midwestern United States? Classrooms today are rich with such complexity.

- Like ethnicity and race, the terms *sex* and *gender* are often used interchangeably but differ technically. **Sex** refers to the biological status of male (penis) or female (vagina), whereas **gender** is the social definition including behaviors learned in the environment about being either male (masculine) or female (feminine). Sexual orientation is another concept related to sex and gender that has been used to denote diversity. The term **sexual orientation** denotes homosexuality, heterosexuality, or bisexuality.

DIVERSITY

1 | Using Science to Inform Classroom Practices

■ Many people believe that socioeconomic status (SES) is based solely on income, with families who have higher incomes being considered high-SES and families with low income considered low-SES. A more accurate definition of **socioeconomic status** relies on the educational level and occupation of family members rather than on their level of income. Although in most circumstances educational attainment and occupation are highly related to income (more education and/or more prestigious occupations lead to higher incomes), in many circumstances less-educated individuals have higher incomes than those who are highly educated. The typical example is the college professor who holds a doctoral degree but whose income is modest.

■ **Disability** refers to being unable to perform some behavior, task, or skill. The term can refer to physical disabilities (hearing impairment, cerebral palsy), cognitive disabilities (intellectual disabilities, learning disabilities, language delays), or behavioral or emotional disabilities (attention-deficit hyperactivity disorder, anxiety). We consider disability to be a diversity characteristic because a student's disability will result in different learning needs and perhaps different levels of achievement in comparison with students who have no disabilities.

DIVERSITY

Effective teachers attempt to understand the possible causes of differences among groups. Teachers who understand why differences exist can learn to be sensitive to the individual needs of students from various backgrounds. Typically, environmental differences, not biological or genetic differences, are the root of group differences. Consider SES as an example. Students from high-SES homes tend to score higher on achievement tests, receive higher grades, and stay in school longer than students in lower-SES homes (Gutman, Sameroff, & Cole, 2003; McLoyd, 1998). These outcomes can be traced to several environmental differences (Evans, 2004; National Center for Education Statistics, 2000):

■ poorer nutrition and more exposure to pollution in lower-SES homes;

■ less exposure to school readiness materials such as books and computers in lower-SES homes due to lack of financial resources or lack of knowledge about the importance of reading to children at a young age;

■ less parental involvement in lower-SES homes, which may be due to work schedules or to less education; and

■ less well-qualified teachers and higher turnover rates among teachers in lower-SES schools and preschools.

One might think that these factors are most influential in early childhood, but the SES achievement gap for math actually widens around age 12, typically during the transition to middle school (Caro, McDonald, & Willms, 2009).

Recent social and political events have highlighted the connection between SES and academic achievement in underserved areas such as urban and rural communities. For example, the popular documentary *Waiting for Superman* follows five urban students, identifying the failure of the current public school system. Although the film was met with controversy and viewed by some as blaming teachers' unions, one result was a bright spotlight placed on urban education for the public.

Achievement and SES. Achievement differences stemming from socioeconomic status may be due to differences in access to resources such as books and computers.

Issues surrounding urban education have been highlighted within higher education for several years now. For example, in 2003 the University of Chicago Urban Education Institute began a two-year master's program for Urban Teacher Education. Similarly, the City University of New York (CUNY) Graduate Center has developed a doctoral program in Urban Education. Both programs focus on training individuals to work in urban educational systems and conducting research to determine the best classroom practices in these areas.

In a similar fashion, many universities have centers focused on rural education within their state. Washington State University has a Rural Education Center that focuses on exchanging information between rural schools and providing a voice in policy development. Likewise, Kansas State University established the Center for Rural Education and Small Schools, which focuses on improving education in those areas. Finally, the National Research Center on Rural Education Support (NRCRES) was established in 2004 with funding from the U.S. Department of Education. The research center examines issues related to retaining qualified teachers, increasing opportunities for advanced courses, and decreasing student dropout rates in rural schools. Knowledge of current research can help inform teachers' practices. For example, teachers may take extra time with students who lack readiness skills, allow students to borrow books from the classroom for use at home, or find creative ways to involve parents in their children's education, particularly during the transition to middle school.

Effective teachers address and embrace diversity. Their teaching is not guided by assumptions about individuals from diverse groups. **Prejudice feelings** are rigid and irrational generalizations about a group or category of people. Prejudice feelings appear to emerge very early in life, with more than half of 6-year-old White children and 85% of 5-year-old White children showing signs of pro-White, anti-Black biases (Doyle & Aboud, 1995; Katz, 2003). Almost every individual has some prejudice feelings toward one or more groups, even though they may not be aware of those feelings. Teachers themselves may believe that lower-achieving students need to focus on basic skills. They may assume that students from lower socioeconomic backgrounds are lower achievers, that girls are not as capable in math as boys, that Asian-American students are naturally smarter than members of other ethnic groups, and that gifted students are socially immature. Prejudice feelings tend to become more intense over time due to confirmation bias and belief perseverance. **Confirmation bias** is the tendency for people to seek evidence that confirms what they already believe to be true, rather than searching for facts that might refute their beliefs (Myers, 2005). **Belief perseverance** is the tendency to hold onto our beliefs even in the face of contradictory evidence (Andersen, Klatzky, & Murray, 1990; Savion, 2009). For example, if a woman believes that green-eyed people are exceptionally intelligent, she will notice or pay attention to all instances in which a green-eyed person says something intelligent (confirmation bias). Likewise, she will ignore or assume it was just a fluke when a green-eyed person says something silly or unintelligent (belief perseverance).

Prejudice feelings can affect the way a teacher makes decisions about instruction, grouping, motivation, and assessment. Treating individuals differently based on prejudice feelings or biased beliefs about a particular group is **discrimination.** A recent study found that 6- to 7-year-old White children discriminated against Black children when distributing coins, even in the presence of an adult. Slightly older White children, 9 to 10 years old, also discriminated against Black children in the same task, but only when the adult was out of the room (Monteiro, de Franca, & Rodrigues, 2009). Children are not the only ones who might discriminate.

Teachers and educators must identify their own feelings of prejudice and educate themselves on the scientific evidence regarding diversity issues. However, even scientific evidence that points to group differences should be interpreted with caution due to individual differences within each group. For example, Figure 1.1 shows that average math scores are higher for boys than girls, but the amount of overlap in scores is great.

Consider your own experiences and group membership. Have you ever treated someone differently because of the person's race, socioeconomic status, gender, or disability? If you have experienced prejudice feelings—or been on the receiving end of prejudice feelings—how and why have those beliefs persevered?

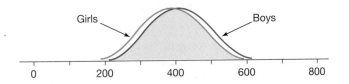

Figure 1.2. Similarities > Differences. Comparing boys' and girls' math performance historically has found mean differences, but the overlap of scores between these two groups is great, emphasizing the enormous variability within groups.

Using a Case Study Approach

Did you read the opening case study on page 2? You may have skipped it, thinking, *Why do I need to read this? How will reading this before I read the content help me?* Case studies allow pre-service teachers to develop decision-making skills by considering how to apply scientific evidence to specific classroom practices. In each unit, there are four cases: (1) early childhood, (2) elementary school, (3) middle school, and (4) high school. Your instructor may ask you to read one or more of the case studies, depending on which certification level you are pursuing. Reading one or more case studies before reading a module will provide you with a realistic classroom situation to consider as you learn about the theories, research, and their application as presented in the module. To get the most out of the case study approach, pay close attention to the different categories of questions we have provided. These prompts will help you uncover important elements, make connections between science and practice, and build problem-solving skills.

PREPARE

The Prepare questions that precede each case study will help you identify the relevant pieces of information within the case study.

- *Who?* Pay attention to characteristics of teachers, students, and parents and the relationships among them. These characteristics may include gender, ethnicity, disabilities, or the SES of students, parents, the teacher, or the school district.

- *What?* Attempt to identify the main problem described in the case study. Is it a behavioral problem, a learning problem, an instructional problem, or a classroom management problem? Each case may address more than one problem.

- *Where?* Consider where the events take place. Is it a traditional classroom, a chemistry lab, an art room, the gym, the hallway, or the principal's office? Try to envision that context and identify any characteristics that might contribute to the problem or to its solution.

- *When?* Identify time-relevant information. Does the story unfold in the morning or the late afternoon; at the beginning, middle, or end of the school year; before or after a holiday? Start thinking about how time might be related to the main problem.

ASSESS

At the end of each case study, you will find three or four Assess questions to help you evaluate your initial understanding and interpretation of the case. Because you will not yet have read the modules in the unit, you will not have the science and application to aid your thinking. Here, we will be asking you to use prior knowledge to make predictions or draw preliminary conclusions. These questions may focus on asking:

- *How* you might respond to the situation;

- *What* characteristics of the individuals involved contributed to the situation; or

- *Why* solutions described did not work well.

REFLECT AND EVALUATE

At the end of each module, a series of Reflect and Evaluate questions will ask you to use the information presented in the module to formulate a more educated, scientific-based response to each case study.

- *How?* Rather than relying on your own opinions and experience, use the science and application discussed in the module to address the situation described in the case.

- *What?* Identify examples of key concepts in the modules.

- *Why?* Move beyond the facts of the case and focus on the characteristics and motivations of individuals. What aspects of the case study were most important, or why did one solution succeed when another failed?

- *What if . . . ?* Consider how the problem and solution presented in the case study would change if some aspect of the case were changed, such as the gender or ethnicity of students or teachers in the case study.

The Reflect and Evaluate questions will help you gauge your level of comprehension of important concepts. They will also encourage you to apply what you have learned in realistic contexts, letting you practice the same type of informed decision making experienced teachers do.

Summary

Explain why educational psychology is an important resource for teachers. Educational psychology links the science of psychology to educational practice and provides teachers with evidence-based knowledge to support their day-to-day decision making in the classroom. Teachers' choices of techniques and strategies should rely not on common-sense approaches but on scientific research. The importance of using evidence-based knowledge is apparent in the No Child Left Behind (NCLB) Act of 2001, which mandates that school systems use scientific-based practices in order to receive federal funding.

Describe three elements of research studies that help determine which studies are worthy of consideration. First, the sample selection process for conducting research studies should attempt to use randomized samples and minimize volunteer bias. Second, measures should be selected based on how well the measure answers the research question. Third, the findings of research studies should be interpreted accurately given the limitations of the research design used, such as whether cause and effect can be established.

Define philosophy of teaching and explain why it is important for teachers to base their philosophy on scientific evidence. Philosophy of teaching is a broad view about how to structure a classroom, teach students, and respond to problems. Because popular views of appropriate teaching methods have changed throughout history and will continue to change in the future, teachers should base their philosophy on current scientific information by acquiring the skills needed to evaluate research and to become lifelong learners.

Describe four diversity characteristics that can define an individual's group membership, and explain why teachers need to understand differences between groups. (1) Ethnic groups share a common culture or environment, while race denotes a group of people who share common biological traits. (2) An individual's sex refers to his or her biology, whereas gender refers to the social definitions of masculine and feminine. (3) Socioeconomic status (SES) is defined by the educational level and occupational status of family members. (4) Disabilities also can be used as a characteristic of diversity, because individuals differ in physical, cognitive, and emotional capabilities. Teachers need to understand that group differences typically result from environmental differences and to be aware of their own prejudice feelings, which may easily be reinforced by attending to information that confirms their beliefs and by ignoring information that contradicts their beliefs or prejudice feelings.

Key Concepts

belief perseverance   15

confirmation bias   15

correlational designs   7

descriptive designs   7

disability   14

discrimination   15

educational psychology   5–6

ethnic group   13

experimental designs   8

gender   13

interviews   10

minority group   13

observations   13

philosophies of teaching   10

prejudice feelings   15

quasi-experimental designs   8

racial group   13

random sample   9

research design   7

sample   9

sex   13

sexual orientation   13

socioeconomic status (SES)   14

tests and surveys   10

theories   6

variables   7

volunteer bias   10

Video Applications

www.mhhe.bohlin2e

Video 1: Celebrating Diversity (5 minutes)
A fifth-grade student explains the accommodations made for his religious beliefs, which forbid making music. A kindergarten teacher uses sign language to include a hearing-impaired student in her class. A teacher describes her use of ethnically diverse Barbies in the classroom. Four teachers discuss how issues of diversity are handled within their classrooms and school.

Video 2: Philosophy of Teaching (*1 minute*)

Two fourth-grade teachers discuss the importance of developing a philosophy of teaching and staying current within their field.

Video 3: Culture in the Classroom (*2 minutes*)

A first-grade teacher describes how students from different cultural backgrounds may vary in aspects of classroom behavior such as eye contact and may use learning strategies that differ from those taught in American classrooms.

Case Study
Reflect and Evaluate

DIVERSITY   **MIDDLE SCHOOL: "Achievement Gap"**

These questions refer to the case study on page 2.

1. Why are the resources available in school districts important for understanding differences among teachers and students?

2. Why is knowledge that the sample was college students important for interpreting the results of the study?

3. Why is the survey measure used in the study problematic? What might be an alternative measure?

4. What type of research design was used in the study? What type of information can be interpreted from this type of research design?

5. Based on the information presented in the module about prejudice feelings, why would some people have a difficult time believing that African-American students and Caucasian students can achieve at equal levels?

6. If the study had been done with K-12 students in various school districts assessing their GPA from official records over several years, how would this alter the way the results might be interpreted?

unit one

Case Studies

Early Childhood: "Cry Baby" 22

Elementary School: "Team" 24

Middle School: "Basketball Star" 26

High School: "Steal, Cheat, and Fight" 28

Module 2:
Contexts of Development
Outline and Learning Goals 30
Bronfenbrenner's Bioecological Theory 31
Family Context 31

Peer Context 36
Broader Contexts 40
Summary 43
Key Concepts 43
Video Applications 43
Case Studies: Reflect and Evaluate 44

Module 3:
Social Development
Outline and Learning Goals 45
Erikson's Psychosocial Theory 46
Aspects of Identity 49
Understanding the Self 52
Social Competence 54
Summary 58

personal development

Key Concepts 58

Video Applications 59

Case Studies: Reflect and Evaluate 59

Module 4:
Emotional Development

Outline and Learning Goals 61

What Is Emotion? 62

Emotions and Individual Performance 63

Applications: Emotionally Intelligent Teaching 68

Summary 73

Key Concepts 73

Video Applications 73

Case Studies: Reflect and Evaluate 74

Module 5:
Moral Development

Outline and Learning Goals 76

Cognitive-Developmental Moral Reasoning 77

Prosocial Behavior 79

Aggressive Behavior 82

Applications: Advancing Moral Development 84

Summary 88

Key Concepts 88

Video Applications 88

Case Studies: Reflect and Evaluate 89

Prepare:

As you read the case, make notes:

1. **WHO** are the central characters in the case? Describe them.

2. **WHAT** is taking place?

3. **WHERE** is the case taking place? Is the environment a factor?

4. **WHEN** is the case taking place? Is the timing a factor?

Edward Abbott and Linda Harsted are teachers at a local child care facility in the 4-year-old preschool room. The 20 students are from diverse backgrounds with a range of socioeconomic status. At this preschool, the children are taught letter recognition, colors, fine and large motor skills, and many other readiness skills. The teachers also spend a large portion of the day encouraging social behaviors such as sharing, helping, expressing assertiveness without aggression, and behaving respectfully toward others. Each year the teachers prepare kindergarten readiness reports to share with parents during a brief individual conference. To prepare for parent-teacher conferences, Ms. Harsted spent last week observing the children during centers to assess their educational skills while Mr. Abbott supervised the children. This week, Mr. Abbott will observe the children to assess their social behaviors while Ms. Harsted supervises. Centers include a

Early Childhood

Cry Baby

number of activities, including playing house, snack, coloring, blocks, and puzzles. Children in groups of four spend 15 minutes on each activity.

Mr. Abbott begins during snack, when the children are having cheese crackers and juice. He quickly notices that Joe is helping Allison clean up her spilled juice that has soaked her crackers. Joe offers to share his crackers with Allison. Mr. Abbott thinks about how typical this behavior is of Joe. He is a very considerate child, always willing to help others. Mr. Abbott then turns his attention to Annie and Zada, who are beginning to argue.

Annie says, "Zada, you aren't my best friend anymore!"

Zada replies, "Well, you didn't share your crayons with me before, so I don't have to share my crackers with you. You got your crackers! I don't have to give you some of mine."

Mr. Abbott has already commented in his notes for Annie and Zada that both girls tend to be natural leaders, which can result in problems from time to time as both want to be "boss." Ms. Harsted intervenes and asks Zada, "How did you feel earlier when Annie wouldn't share her crayons?"

Zada replies, "She was mean, so I was sad."

"Well, I bet that Annie is sad now because you won't share with her," states Ms. Harsted.

"Okay, she can have this one cracker, but only if I get to be the mommy when we play house," replies Zada.

Annie quickly responds, "Okay."

Mr. Abbott and Ms. Harsted exchange looks, because both know that Annie's home life is much different from Zada's. Zada's parents are married and middle-class. Her parents spend much of their extra time with Zada and her brother. Both children were adopted when their parents were in their 40s. Yesterday, Zada told everyone about a recent family trip to a museum. Annie's parents are divorced. Her father lives halfway across the country with his new wife and Annie's new baby sister. Annie's mother works first shift at the local hospital as a nurse's aide and spends several evenings a week socializing with friends.

Mr. Abbott moves over to the block area. He notices that Tyler and Tanner are building a tall tower. Erica begins to place more blocks on the tower, but Tyler shouts, "That one doesn't go there!" The loud shout startles Erica, who bumps the tower, and all the blocks come tumbling down.

Tanner yells, "You did that on purpose. We told you that girls aren't supposed to play with blocks."

"Yeah," adds Tyler, "you ruined everything!"

Erica begins to cry. Tyler adds, "See, you are just a little cry baby. Cry baby. Cry baby. . . ."

"Boys, I want you to stop talking to Erica that way," interjects Mr. Abbott. "I saw the whole thing, and Erica didn't mean to knock down the tower. How do you think she feels when you make fun of her like that?"

Tyler jumps in, "Well, she's probably sad, but that's not our fault. We didn't knock down the tower."

"Maybe she's sad because you were blaming her for an accident and then calling her a cry baby," says Mr. Abbott. "Wouldn't you be sad too if someone blamed you and called you a cry baby?" he asks.

"I wouldn't care," answers Tanner.

Mr. Abbott comments in his observation notes that Tyler is always quick to blame others yet rarely takes responsibility for his own actions. Mr. Abbott thinks about how all the children have difficulty understanding how another child might feel, but some have more trouble than others.

Assess

1. How typical are the behaviors in this classroom?

2. Why do you think some children are so eager to be helpful and to share while other children are so quick to assign blame and respond in a negative manner?

3. How do you think the gender of each child plays a role in his or her behaviors?

Prepare:

As you read the case, make notes:

1. **WHO** are the central characters in the case? Describe them.

2. **WHAT** is taking place?

3. **WHERE** is the case taking place? Is the environment a factor?

4. **WHEN** is the case taking place? Is the timing a factor?

Rocío Barone is one of two first-grade teachers at a small rural elementary school. She was raised in a large metropolitan area and is continually amazed at the connections her students share. For example, three students in the first grade this year—Patricia, Kelly, and Samantha—are all cousins. In addition to familial connections, many of the parents attended high school together and have been friends for years, with their children growing up highly connected to one another outside school. Ms. Barone has always had a soft spot for the children who lack those connections within the community. Kashi is a good example. She moved to the small rural community last year. Kashi is the only student in first grade who is African American. All the other students and almost everyone in the community are Caucasian. She had a rough transition to the school, because her parents were getting a divorce that led to the move. Kashi seemed to have made

Elementary School
Team

friends and to have adjusted to the new curriculum last year. But this year she is struggling academically, and the children appear uninterested in playing with her on the playground or being her partner during classroom activities.

As Kashi enters the classroom, she squabbles with Patricia, one of the oldest but smallest children in the class, who also has experienced challenges adjusting to first grade. After kindergarten, Patricia was placed in a special pre–first grade program for children who need extra time to develop academically or socially. Having her cousins in the same class has helped with the transition, but she continues to struggle with reading and math.

"Well, if you don't want to sit with me at lunch," says Kashi, "then you can't be on my team."

"I don't want to be on your team," Patricia replies. "My mom says I can do whatever I want on the playground. You know, Kashi, you aren't the boss!"

Ms. Barone intervenes and attempts to calm the situation. "Girls, please try to get along and speak nicely to each other. Now, take your seats so we can start our day."

As the day continues, Ms. Barone notes that Patricia and Kashi appear to have resolved their differences for the moment and are working on their science project together without bickering. This is typical for these two girls. One minute they are playing or working nicely together, referring to each other as "best friends," and the next minute one is telling on the other for saying or doing something "mean." Ms. Barone has always had trouble getting either of them to give specifics of the mean behavior.

As Ms. Barone asks the children to form their line and leave for lunch, two boys—Bill and Zach—begin pushing and shoving each other in the back of the line. Bill shouts, "I am tired of you always bumping into me!"

Ms. Barone moves quickly to the back of the line and begins to say, "Boys, please keep your hands to . . ."

Zach interrupts, "Well, I didn't mean to bump you, and besides I am tired of you always cutting in line at lunch. You are such a bully to everyone—my dad says you are just like your dad was in school!"

"At least my dad isn't a sissy," says Bill, who is very tall and athletic. "I didn't hurt you or anyone else. You're just like a little girl."

Ms. Barone states firmly, "Both of you stop right now. You should be ashamed of yourselves for talking to each other that way."

Both boys keep looking at each other with angry faces, but they discontinue their verbal and physical assaults. Ms. Barone sends the other children to lunch and has a short talk with the boys.

"Now, Bill, accidents do happen, and Zach may not have meant to bump into you. And Zach, it is not nice to call others names. You both need to keep your hands to yourself."

The boys give a quick "okay" and walk to lunch.

During the lunch break, Ms. Barone checks her e-mail. Patricia's mom, Mary, has sent an e-mail to tell Ms. Barone that Patricia has been very upset about how Kashi treats her at school. The e-mail reads:

Ms. Barone,

We have been having several conversations in the evening about Patricia and Kashi. Patricia tells me that Kashi has a "team" of girls and if Patricia doesn't do what Kashi asked then she cannot be on the "team." Her dad and I have tried to explain that Patricia should not allow others to boss her around and talk her into doing things she doesn't want to do. I am already somewhat concerned about Patricia's self-esteem and want her to have enough self-confidence to stand up for herself. I typically would have continued to try and work with Patricia at home on this issue, but now something else has happened and I thought you should be aware. Last week I was told by my friend who works in the cafeteria that Patricia doesn't always take all the food options because Kashi is whispering to her to only take the food that Kashi likes. I understand that a teacher cannot know everything that happens during the day, especially on the playground or at lunch, but I wanted you to know about this issue. Any advice you can give us to help Patricia deal with these issues would be helpful.

Mary

Assess

1. How well do you think Ms. Barone handled the girls entering the classroom? How well do you think she handled the boys during lunch line? Do you think gender played a role in her treatment of the incidents?

2. What examples of aggression did you notice?

3. What factors in the children's lives might have contributed to their behavior?

4. How would you respond to Mary's e-mail?

Prepare:

As you read the case, make notes:

1. **WHO** are the central characters in the case? Describe them.

2. **WHAT** is taking place?

3. **WHERE** is the case taking place? Is the environment a factor?

4. **WHEN** is the case taking place? Is the timing a factor?

Tyrone Martin is the middle school girls' basketball coach. The middle school is located in a suburb of a large metropolitan city with students from mostly middle- to upper-middle-class homes. Mr. Martin has been teaching English at the school for three years. He was the coach for boys' basketball at his last job and enjoyed the out-of-class experience with his students. When he was asked by the principal to coach girls' basketball this year while the usual coach takes a leave of absence, he was excited about the opportunity. However, he has experienced some difficulties getting the girls to work as a team.

As Jill and Sierra enter the gym for practice, he overhears them whispering about Darla. Darla is very athletic but doesn't seem to fit in with the "popular" group of girls. Darla is already practicing and too far away to hear their conversation.

Middle School

Basketball Star

Mr. Martin overhears Jill saying, "If she thinks we are going to let her steal the show on the basketball court, she can forget it."

"The only reason she is any good is because her dad makes her play basketball every night for like three hours!" adds Sierra. "He thinks Darla is going to be some big star! Too bad she doesn't have a mother around to show her how to act."

Claudia, who appears to socialize with Darla, walks up behind the girls and overhears their conversation. She states loudly, "Well, Sierra, you have had three mothers now with all your dad's divorces and remarriages, and you're still not a lady. Maybe you should spend a little more time with your father. Oh, that's right, he's too busy to pay attention to anything you're doing."

Mr. Martin defuses the situation by announcing that the girls need to take their positions for a scrimmage. He begins to think about Darla. Mr. Martin has noticed in the past that Darla does not seem to have many friends. Claudia has repeatedly attempted to include Darla in social events, but Darla doesn't seem to respond with excitement, appreciation, or even a simple "Thanks, but no thanks." Rather, she seems to be uninterested in having friends or a social life.

Mr. Martin decides to have a talk with Darla after practice to see if he can help determine what might be the problem. He begins by asking Darla, "How do you like basketball this year?"

Darla replies, "I like it. I just wish the other girls were more dedicated to the game. They seem to think they are going to be movie stars or models."

"Well, what would you like to be when you grow up?" asks Mr. Martin.

"My dad says I should be a basketball player because I have a lot of natural talent. That's why I don't worry too much about those other girls and what they say about me. I know I am a good athlete. And I am going to take business classes in high school so that I can manage my own career and money when I make it big," says Darla with a slight smile.

Mr. Martin pushes her on the issue a bit. "Have you ever considered doing anything else?"

Darla replies quickly, "No way! My dad really wants me to be a basketball player. That's who I am. It's in my blood. Basketball is what makes me Darla. I am not good at many other things, especially school and making friends off the basketball court. So I'm sure I'll be a basketball player."

Mr. Martin ends the conversation, saying, "Well, Darla, I am glad you have such a clear vision of your future, but don't be afraid to change that vision. As people make their way through high school and college, most change their minds about what and who they want to be in the future. Just keep your options open, okay?"

"Okay, but I already know who I am and where I'm going," says Darla.

As Mr. Martin begins to put away the equipment, he thinks about a boy at his last school, Mark. Mark was very similar to Darla in a number of ways. He didn't have many friends or the skills to make friends. Rather, Mark had a short temper and typically was in other students' faces about something they had done to him or, at least, what Mark thought they had done to him. He never thought his remarks or retaliatory behaviors were as bad as those of the other kids. Mark and Darla were also alike in their family backgrounds. Their parents had divorced, and they each had ended up living with their father instead of with their mother. Mr. Martin wonders how two children from such similar yet unusual backgrounds could both end up very different yet both have few friends.

Assess

1. Darla seems to be a loner. Is this a bad thing? Why or why not?

2. What are some examples of appropriate social behavior? What are some examples of aggressive behavior?

3. How likely do you think it is that Darla will become a basketball player? Give the reasons for your answer.

Rebecca Durbin is the principal at one of the three high schools located in a small city with a population of approximately 100,000. The school enrollment is approximately 2,500 students. Recently, there have been a number of incidents related to cheating, stealing, and drinking, as well as a number of verbal and physical fights. Rebecca decides to use next Friday's school improvement day to address these behavioral issues. To prepare for the workshop, Principal Durbin sends an e-mail to all the teachers and staff asking for examples of these behaviors and suggestions for how the school system should handle these issues and situations. She receives a number of responses, including the following:

Mr. Smith (freshman English) wrote: Last week I wasted five minutes of class time breaking up an exchange between Lisa and Kiana. Basically, the girls were engaged in a

High School
Steal, Cheat, and Fight

verbal assault on each other, saying things such as "You're fat and ugly" and "Your mom is a slut." I was very disturbed by their comments, but don't have many suggestions. I am just thankful they didn't start a cat fight during my lecture!

Ms. Baxter (advanced mathematics) wrote: I know we have several groups of students who don't apply themselves. For instance, there is that whole group of kids who stand across the street after school smoking (one of whom spent the night in jail last weekend for driving under the influence) and the group of girls who walk around the school like they are dressed for a night out on the town. However, I don't think it is the school's place to dictate how they dress or to meddle in their behavior outside the school. I am much more concerned about the students who are here to learn and their inability to determine their career paths. Many of them are very academically talented yet have no direction or ideas about where to go to college or what their major will be in college. I think our time is better spent guiding them into good colleges and career paths.

Ms. Presley (office staff manager) wrote: I have been working in high schools for over 20 years now and honestly believe that the school has little control over these teenagers. The problem is the breakdown of the family. So many of our students come from broken homes without a mother or a father, or they have the opposite problem—too many parents and stepparents. Plus, almost all of our mothers are out working full-time jobs, leaving no one at home to take care of these children when they leave school in the afternoon. I suggest we offer parenting classes and family counseling to keep families together.

Mr. Ruestman (biology) wrote: The problem is that we simply don't have the time to deal with all these issues. I have too much course content to cover to continually be dealing with the problems students have with their friends. Very few seem to know how to control their anger or how to think about how others might be feeling, or understand that the world does not revolve around them. They all seem to be overly concerned about their friendships, who is friends with whom, who was and wasn't invited to the party, yet they lack the skills to make and keep friends. Maybe some form of social skills training would help, but not during my class time.

Mr. Cargill (physical education) wrote: Just yesterday, Jimmy was sent to the office for hitting Bob. Apparently, Bob was talking about another Jim, commenting on his sister. The whole thing was taken out of context, and Jimmy hauled off and hit him. If Jimmy would have taken two seconds to look at Bob and pay attention to his tone of voice and nonverbal behaviors, Jimmy would have realized that the comments were not inappropriate or derogatory, and were not even about his sister but another Jim's sister. Bob was actually commenting on how nice this young lady had been helping him with his math homework during study hall. These kids need a lesson in how to read others' intentions and behaviors as well as how to handle their own emotions.

Ms. Kennel (chemistry) wrote: I am mostly concerned about the girls and minority students in our school. The girls seem to be lacking in confidence, particularly in academics and even more so in math and science. I think we need to find a way to boost their egos and give them the confidence they will need out there in the real world. Maybe with a little more confidence they would stop worrying so much about their friends, boyfriends, and other relationships. The minority students may also need a boost, but even more they need to stop grouping together according to their ethnicity. Do you know we now have a whole group of students who are referred to as the "Spans" because they all speak Spanish? We need to incorporate all ethnic groups into our school and educate every student on the issues of diversity in our country.

Ms. May (special education) wrote: The behaviors of stealing, cheating, and aggression in this school are due to a basic lack of respect for authority. We need to have firm policies on these issues and stick to them. Most students simply don't think it is a big deal to cheat, lie, or steal, and in many classes it is because teachers let them get away with these behaviors. We need every teacher on board to enforce the rules of the school.

Assess

1. What are some of the recurring themes within these responses from the teachers and staff?

2. For each person's e-mail, give a score based on how much you agree with the view (1 = completely disagree, 2 = somewhat disagree, 3 = somewhat agree, 4 = completely agree). Briefly explain why you agree or disagree with each e-mail response and whether your rating is based on experience, observation, or opinion.

3. Do you think gender might be important in handling these issues? Why or why not?

4. Do you think it is appropriate for the principal and teachers to use school time to address issues related to students' social and emotional behaviors?

MODULE 2

Contexts of Development

Outline

Bronfenbrenner's Bioecological Theory

Family Context

- Parenting Practices
- Divorce and Remarriage

Peer Context

- Friendships and Peer Groups
- Peer Statuses

Broader Contexts

- Parental Employment
- Cultural Factors

Summary
Key Concepts
Video Applications
Case Studies: Reflect and Evaluate

Learning Goals

1. Describe Bronfenbrenner's bioecological theory.

2. Describe how parenting styles and family transitions interact with the school system.

3. Describe how aspects of the peer context interact with the school system.

4. Explain how broader contexts of development influence microsystems and individual outcomes.

BRONFENBRENNER'S BIOECOLOGICAL THEORY

Who is the most influential person in your life now? Who was it five years ago? You can probably think of several people who have made a difference in your life. As children and adolescents, we grow and develop with the support and influence of people and places: our family members, friends, and teachers, and our neighborhoods and schools. Because of their influence on development, these people and places are considered *contexts of development*. Bronfenbrenner's bioecological theory of human development (1994, 2005), the best-known theory on the contexts of development, emphasizes the combined function of person (or genetics) and the many systems that exist in the environment and interact to influence development, as shown in Figure 2.1. Let's examine this model more closely. It will be the framework for our discussion on the contexts of development throughout this module.

- The **microsystem,** the immediate environment surrounding an individual, includes the people, relationships, and systems that directly interact with the developing individual, such as family, peers, and school.

- The **mesosystem** links two or more microsystems. For example, the communication between parents and teachers links home and school environments or home and child care settings.

- The **exosystem** is the interaction among two or more environments, one of which does not directly include the individual. For developing children and adolescents, the exosystem includes links between home and their parents' places of work. The developing child typically has no direct interaction with a parent's workplace but is influenced by that environment indirectly. For example, parental work stress influences children's adjustment.

- The **macrosystem** includes many of the broader cultural patterns, such as beliefs, customs, knowledge, and morals. Bronfenbrenner suggests that this is not simply the ethnicity or social class of individuals but rather the social features that affect individuals. For example, low-income children may experience more stressors in their macrosystem—substandard housing, crowding, or community violence—than do middle-class children (Evans & English, 2002).

- The **chronosystem** refers to the chronological nature of development within the individual as well as the history of the surrounding environment. The social environment changes over time and affects developing individuals differently at various points in history. For example, the impact of divorce on child development was viewed more negatively during the 1950s than it is today.

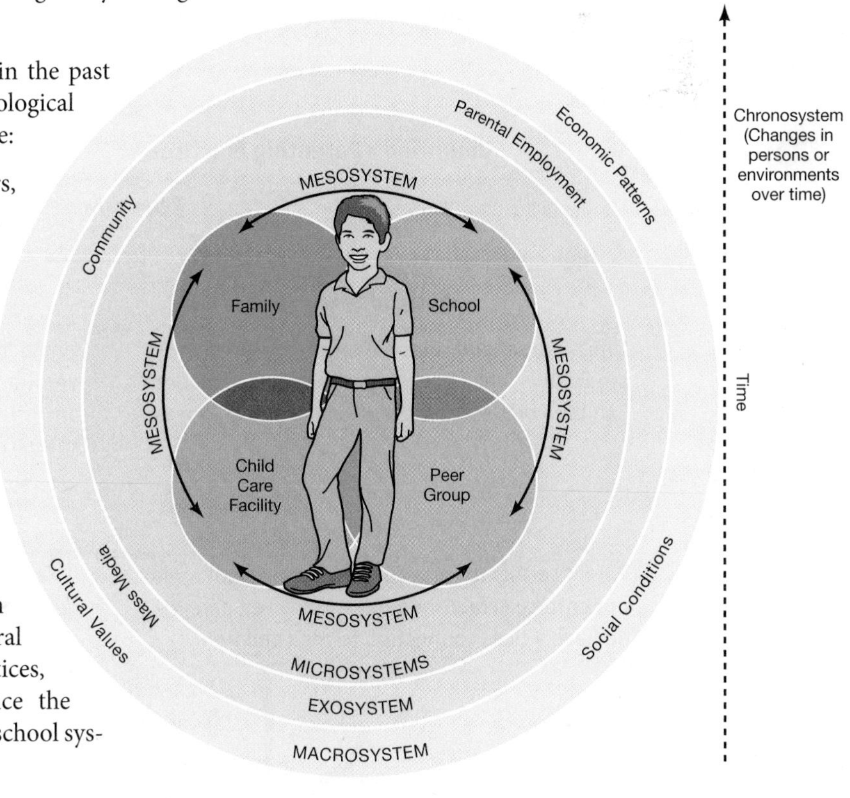

Much of the research on development in the past 30 years has been conducted from a bioecological perspective. In this module, we will examine:

- the microsystems of families and peers, with special emphasis on the interaction of these within the educational system (in other words, mesosystems)

- the influence of parental employment on development (exosystem)

- connections to ethnicity and socioeconomic status (macrosystem) as they relate to the microsystems

FAMILY CONTEXT

Arguably, the most influential microsystem in the lives of individuals is the family. Several basic aspects of families—parenting practices, divorce and remarriage—directly influence the child and how the family interacts with the school system as a component of the mesosystem.

**Figure 2.1.
Bronfenbrenner's
Bioecological Model**

Chronosystem
(Changes in persons or environments over time)

Time

Parenting Practices

Parenting practices, also called parenting styles, are the patterns of discipline and affection parents display with their children. These have an important influence on child and adolescent development. Diana Baumrind (1966) describes parenting practices as typically including two broad dimensions: control and responsiveness. **Control** is the manner and strictness with which parents provide their children with limits and discipline. **Responsiveness** includes the affection, acceptance, and caring involved in parenting. In short, control describes the *behavioral* aspects of parenting, while responsiveness describes the *emotional* aspects. Based on the levels of these two dimensions, Baumrind describes four parenting styles, as shown in Table 2.1.

- **Authoritative parenting** includes setting limits or having rules for children and adolescents, and enforcing those rules. Parents and children also exhibit a high level of emotional connectedness that allows the parents to be flexible when necessary. For example, parents may be less strict than usual because they understand that their child is having difficulty with peers at school or is upset about not making the cheerleading squad.

- **Authoritarian parenting** includes a high level of control in which limits are set and rules are enforced yet emotional connectedness is lacking. Parents may be viewed as "dictators" who are inflexible, unable to bend the rules to accommodate special or unusual circumstances. For example, a parent might make a negative comment regarding the B on the child's report card when all the other grades are As.

- **Permissive parenting** involves less control, with parents either not setting rules for behavior or not enforcing rules. However, parents do have a close connection to their children such that observers might refer to them as "friends" rather than parents. For example, parents may show their affection by giving in to their child's tantrums in the grocery line and buying candy, or they may ground their adolescent but not monitor whether the teenager is home.

- **Uninvolved parenting** lacks both control and responsiveness. Parents typically are unaware of their child's behavior, friends, difficulties, or achievements. For example, a parent may not know when reports come home from school or may be unable to name his child's friends. These parents are at risk of being neglectful or abusive. You can read more about how child abuse and neglect is an example of a poor family context in Example 2.1. Besides the family context, child abuse can occur in various other microsystems for example, neighborhoods, child care settings, schools, and churches). Learn how to identify signs of abuse in Table 2.2.

TABLE 2.1	Baumrind's Parenting Practices

	Responsiveness	
	High ←————————————————→ Low	
High	**Authoritative**	**Authoritarian**
	Limits are set and rules are enforced, but parents are flexible when necessary. Parents and children exhibit a high level of emotional connectedness.	Limits are set and rules are enforced, yet emotional connectedness is lacking. Parents are inflexible—unable to bend the rules in special or unusual circumstances.
Control	**Permissive**	**Uninvolved**
	Parents either do not set rules for behavior or do not enforce established rules. However, parents do have a close connection to their children.	Parenting lacks both control and responsiveness. Parents typically are unaware of their child's behavior, friends, difficulties, or achievements.
Low		

EXAMPLE 2.1   **Example of a Detrimental Family Context—Child Abuse and Neglect**

Child abuse and/or neglect can have a very negative impact on a child's behavior and general well-being, and its consequences reach across physical, psychosocial, and environmental domains. A classroom teacher is one of the people in a child's life with the greatest opportunity to detect signs of abuse or neglect and to intervene on the child's behalf to help stop the cycle of abuse.

Approximately 872,000 children were determined to have been victims of child maltreatment in the United States in 2004 (U.S. Department of Health and Human Services, 2006). Even though over half the nation's abused and neglected children are in school on any given day, only 10% of abuse and neglect reports originate in schools (McIntyre, 1990). One reason for this low rate of reporting from teachers may be that teachers do not recognize the signs of abuse. In one survey, only 4% of the teachers were "very aware" of the signs of sexual abuse, 17% could recognize obvious signs, and 75% were completely unable to recognize the signs of abuse (McIntyre, 1990). Every teacher should know how abuse is defined and be able to recognize potential indicators of abuse.

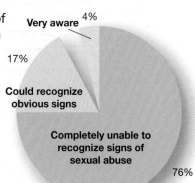

Source: McIntyre, 1990.

Reporting suspected child abuse or neglect is not only a moral obligation, it is the law. The key federal legislation addressing child abuse and neglect is the Child Abuse Prevention and Treatment Act (CAPTA), originally enacted in 1974 (P.L. 93-247). This act has been amended several times and was most recently amended and reauthorized by the Keeping Children and Families Safe Act of 2003 (P.L. 108-36). Reporting requirements vary by state, but most states require any person who has reasonable cause to suspect that abuse has occurred to make a report to their community's local Child Protection Services or law enforcement agency. Teachers may be reluctant to make a report without absolute proof; however, reporting in good faith protects the person making the report from any liability if the report is found to be unsubstantiated (Fischer, Schimmel, & Kelly, 1999). Failure to report suspected abuse or neglect can lead to criminal and/or civil liability. Most states have a hotline for reporting abuse and neglect (open 24 hours a day, 7 days a week). Additional information about how to file a report can be obtained by calling the Child Help National Child Abuse Hotline at 1-800-4-A-CHILD.

Research studies consistently link authoritative parenting with positive outcomes. Children and adolescents with authoritative parents tend to have higher levels of healthy adjustment and fewer mental health issues or problem behaviors (Kaufmann et al., 2000; Shek, 2005). However, the optimal parenting style may depend on the broader cultural context within which the parents and children are living. Specifically, authoritarian parenting may be important for deterring antisocial behavior among young adolescents residing in low-income neighborhoods with high rates of unemployment and an insufficient police presence (Eamon, 2001).

DIVERSITY

How do parenting practices interact with the school system? Remember that an interaction between two microsystems—in this case family and school—is called the mesosystem. The interaction between the family and school microsystems is evident because authoritative parenting is related to academic benefits among a variety of ethnic groups for both elementary-age students and high school students (Gonzalez, Holbein, & Quilter, 2002; Mandara, 2006; Pong, Hao, & Gardner, 2005; Tam & Lam, 2003). For example, students with authoritative parents tend to have higher achievement and better attitudes toward school, spend more time on homework, are more engaged with teachers and learning, and have lower levels of maladaptive behavior in the classroom (Simons-Morton & Chen, 2009; Walker & Hoover-Dempsey, 2006). Teachers are unlikely to be able to change the parenting practices a student experiences at home, but they can gain much insight into the reasons for children's and adolescents' behaviors in the classroom based on knowledge about those parenting practices.

Can you determine which parenting practice was used in your home? If you had two parents, were their parenting practices the same or different? How do you think parenting practices influenced your educational experiences or academic achievement?

TABLE 2.2	Identifying Physical and Behavioral Indicators of Abuse		
Type	**Definition**	**Physical indicators**	**Behavioral indicators**
Physical abuse	Any nonaccidental injury to a child or allowing non-accidental injury to occur. This includes hitting, burning, shaking, and whipping.	Physical signs of this type of abuse may include bruises, lacerations, welts, lumps, unexplained fractures, burns by cigarettes, burns by immersion. Suspicious examples include handprints on skin; repeated injuries in various stages of healing; bath scalding pattern; injuries in fleshy, noncontact areas.	Behavioral indicators of possible abuse may include verbal reports of abuse, depression, behavioral extremes, role reversal, appearing frightened of caretaker, exaggerated startle response, school absenteeism, low self-esteem.
Sexual abuse	Any sexual act between an adult (or child with power) and a child, or permitting another to use a child. This includes fondling, penetration, intercourse, pornography, exhibitionism, child prostitution, oral sex, and forced observation of sexual acts.	Physical signs of sexual abuse may include any venereal disease; bruised or dilated genitals or rectum; difficulty or pain in walking or sitting; foreign matter in bladder, urethra, or rectum; pelvic inflammatory disease; recurrent urinary tract infections; stained or bloody underclothing; pregnancy under 16 years of age.	Behavioral indicators of possible sexual abuse may include premature knowledge of explicit sexual acts; aggressive, overt sexual behavior; sleep disorders; taking frequent baths; starting fires; self-inflicted injuries; cruelty to animals; drawing pictures of people with genitals or vagina; expressing fear of particular person or place; reports of sexual abuse.
Emotional abuse	Any attitude or behavior that interferes with a child's mental health or social development. This includes yelling, shaming, put-downs, failure to provide affection and support, withdrawal of attention, threats, lack of praise, and systematic destruction of child's self-esteem.	N/A	Behavioral indicators of possible emotional abuse may include low self-esteem, difficulty in forming positive relationships, inability to trust, poorly developed ability to empathize with others, defiant behavior, elimination disorders, speech disorders, eating disorders, deriving pleasure from hurting others, suicide attempts, reports of maltreatment.
Neglect	Deprivation of conditions necessary for normal development (food, shelter, supervision, education, medical care).	Physical indicators of possible neglect may include poor hygiene; torn, dirty, or inappropriate clothing for the weather; developmental lags; underweight; sickly appearance.	Behavioral indicators of possible neglect may include dull or listless behavior, begging/stealing food, constant fatigue, alcohol or drug use, reports of being left alone or abandoned.

Divorce and Remarriage

Today, approximately 50% of all first marriages and 60% or more of second marriages end in divorce (Fine & Harvey, 2006). As a result, nearly half of all children in the United States will live in a single-parent family for some length of time (Hetherington, Henderson, & Reiss, 1999). Although not all children and adolescents experience problems following divorce, some do. Children and adolescents may also experience difficulties prior to the divorce. In fact, they tend to have the greatest difficulties a few years before and after the divorce, as indicated by poorer academic performance (Sun & Li, 2002). The difficulties surrounding divorce are thought to be the result of changes in the *functioning* of the family rather than *structural* changes (Demo & Acock, 1996). Changes in the functioning of families include a number of possible issues:

1. *Family conflict* surrounding divorce is an important aspect of family functioning related to children's and adolescents' adjustment (Amato & Cheadle, 2008; Bing, Nelson, & Wesolowski, 2009). Although marital conflict occurs prior to the divorce, the level of conflict often increases around the time of divorce. Children living in high-conflict, intact families experience difficulties similar to those experienced by children in divorced families. In particular, school problems may arise as a result of attention difficulties. Children who are worried or concerned about the stability of their parents' relationship may be less able to focus, leading to poor peer relations and behavioral problems at school (Bascoe, Davies, Cummings, & Sturge-Apple, 2009).

2. *Disorganized parenting practices,* which may occur during divorce as parents are coping with their own distress, play a role in children's social and cognitive functioning as rated by their teachers (Forehand, Thomas, Wierson, Brody, & Fauber, 1990). Parents who once were authoritative may become overwhelmed by their own problems, have few cognitive resources available for their children, and become lax in their monitoring and supervision of children (Hetherington, 1991; Nair & Murray, 2005). Children tend to have fewer difficulties following divorce when parental discipline is consistent across homes.

3. *Decreases in family economics* also can have a negative impact on the functioning of families (Amato & Keith, 1991; Pong, 1997, 1998). Parents who were not employed outside the home may need to obtain employment, or parents who were employed may need to work longer hours or earn a second income in order to sustain the level of economics within the home (exosystem). Post-divorce economics may lead to the family's moving to a smaller home or a lower socioeconomic status neighborhood (macrosystem), which may lead to poorer school achievement.   *DIVERSITY*

Some children—because of their developmental level, gender, personality, or relationships—may have a tougher time dealing with divorce than others do (Davies & Windle, 2001; Hetherington, Bridges, & Insabella, 1998), especially: *DIVERSITY*

- younger children
- boys more than girls
- children placed in custody with the opposite-sex parent (typically boys)
- children who have a difficult temperament or who have always been less able to adjust to change within their environment
- children who do not have a supportive relationship with an adult outside the immediate family (for example, teacher, aunt, uncle, coach)

Although most difficulties occur around the time of divorce, children whose parents have been divorced for years may encounter problems again during adolescence; this is called the **sleeper effect** (Hetherington, 1993). Adolescents experiencing the sleeper effect exhibit difficulties such as drug and alcohol use, behavioral problems, poor school performance, and poor interpersonal relationships—including higher rates of divorce themselves later in life. The awakening of these difficulties is thought to occur because the period of adolescence introduces more opportunity to engage in drugs and alcohol use and to develop intimate relationships with peers and romantic partners, typically not a factor during childhood.

Some of the same family functioning issues surrounding divorce, such as family conflict and disruptions in parenting styles, continue to exist in remarried homes (Hetherington et al., 1998). Children's and adolescents' well-being suffers each time a transition or change occurs within the family. Remarriage adds a second transition to the family dynamics. As a result, adolescents from stepfamilies may have lower academic achievement and more involvement in delinquent acts than adolescents from single-parent homes (Amato & Keith, 1991; Hetherington, 1993; Sun & Li, 2009). Some children are particularly at risk for experiencing difficulties following remarriage, including (Hetherington et al., 1998; Sun & Li, 2009):

- older children,
- girls more than boys, and   *DIVERSITY*
- children with more difficult temperaments.

Family Transitions. Children and adolescents experience fewer difficulties during family transitions when they have a supportive relationship with an adult outside the family, such as a teacher or coach.

Social competence and self-esteem: See page 54.

How do divorce and remarriage within the family interact with the school in the mesosystem? Children from both divorced and remarried families are more likely to have lower academic achievement and more problematic school behavior than children from intact families (Kurdek & Sinclair, 1988; Potter, 2010). Understanding that family functioning may be the reason for such difficulties and that particular children may be more likely to experience these difficulties allows educators the opportunity to provide the support necessary to assist these children during family transitions. Children and adolescents who have a supportive adult relationship outside the family—such as a strong relationship with a particular teacher—are less likely to experience difficulties (Dornbusch et al., 1985; Hetherington, 1993). On the other hand, teachers also may unwittingly form negative expectations about students based on their individual characteristics and family circumstances. This could lead to a **self-fulfilling prophecy**—an unfounded expectation that becomes true simply because it was expected. For example, a teacher who is aware of the relationship between divorce and achievement may expect less of children of divorce, which can lead to behaviors that cause the student to achieve less in school.

Teachers in today's classrooms encounter children from various family structures. Knowledge about family functioning and structure provides teachers with a context for understanding why some children may experience difficulties in the school setting. However, family background should not be used as a rationale to lower expectations for some students. Instead, it can provide information about who is most likely to need additional support and assistance within the microsystem of the school.

PEER CONTEXT

After families, peers are considered the second most important microsystem influencing development. Let's examine the development of friendships and peer groups among children and adolescents, as well as how peer status can interact with the educational experience (mesosystem).

Friendships and Peer Groups

Friendships are important because having friends during childhood and adolescence is related to several positive outcomes. For example, children with close friendships tend to have more social competence, greater self-confidence, and higher self-esteem, as well as fewer difficulties with school transitions and better academic performance (Hartup, 1996). Parents and teachers therefore should attempt to promote friendships among children and adolescents while understanding that friendships undergo changes throughout development.

Friendships among preschool-age children are qualitatively different from friendships among adolescents. In early and middle childhood, children base their friendships on moment-to-moment interactions. For example, two preschool-age children might be playing well together and consider themselves best friends, but a moment of not sharing or an unwillingness to submit to the other's request can lead to anger resulting in the children announcing that they are no longer friends. Within a few minutes, the children may resume interactions and once again announce that they are friends. Friendships among children in later childhood and early adolescence are based on more stable and similar qualities, such as typical play interests (we both like Barbies or video games) or typical qualities of sharing and kindness. In adolescence, friendships become based on common values and more complex interests, such as attitudes toward school, career aspirations, and achievement (Hartup, 1996). As a result, distinct peer groups begin to emerge during adolescence.

Over the past 20 years, much of the research on peer group formation during adolescence has been conducted and written by B. Bradford Brown and his colleagues (Brown, 1990, 2004; Brown & Klute, 2006; Brown, Mory, & Kinney, 1994). During middle school, groups of peers begin to form cliques and crowds. **Cliques** are small groups of two to eight people who know each other very well. Cliques provide opportunities to learn social skills, to discover how to communicate in interpersonal relationships, and, for some, to practice leadership roles within small groups. Many times these small groups have a social structure or place in which time is spent together. For example, one clique may hang out at the local restaurant, another may congregate at the school, and another may gather at one adolescent's home.

Social skills: See page 55.

Clique members typically are very similar on a number of demographic characteristics, such as age, socioeconomic status, and race, as well as on shared activities (for example, dress and music) and values (Hamm, 2000; Hartup, 1996). For example, members of a clique typically have similar beliefs about the importance of school and similar levels of involvement in delinquent behavior and substance use (Crosnoe, 2002; Hussong, 2002). In addition, cliques typically include same-sex friends during middle school but develop into mixed-sex groups during high school (Xie & Shi, 2009). The similarities among clique members may be due to the following processes:

- *peer selection process*—adolescents seeking out others similar to themselves
- *peer socialization process*—dissimilar adolescents becoming more similar over time

In contrast to the small, interaction-based peer cliques, **crowds** are larger, reputation-based peer groups that typically have common labels across school districts and vary across gender (Youniss, McLellan, & Strouse, 1994). They include:

Identity development: See page 48.

- populars/preps—having many friends, being well known, being cool, being highly social (more likely to be girls than boys)
- jocks—participating in sports and physical activities (more likely to be boys than girls)
- brains/nerds—being smart and showing high academic performance (equally likely to be girls or boys)
- normals—being average or normal, being cool, being highly social (more likely to be girls than boys)
- loners—belonging to a small group, having few friendships, being nonconforming (more likely to be girls than boys)
- druggies/partiers/burnouts—using drugs, alcohol, and physical aggression (more likely to be boys than girls)

By ninth grade, most adolescents agree on who belongs to which crowd within the school system, and these labels provide adolescents with a basis for identity development—that is, understanding who they are and how they fit into society (Newman & Newman, 2001). Crowds tend to be hierarchical during middle school and hence are related to self-esteem, or how positively individuals feel about themselves. Adolescents in higher-status crowds such as preps and jocks typically have higher self-esteem than individuals in lower-status crowds such as druggies (Prinstein & La Greca, 2002). The hierarchy of crowds changes over time, and membership within these crowds is more easily changed during the later years of high school, such that individuals may be members of more than one crowd (Youniss et al., 1994).

Friendship Development. Preschool-age friendships are based on moment-to-moment interactions.

Self-esteem: See page 54.

The interaction between the peer and school microsystems is another example of the mesosystem in Bronfenbrenner's bioecological model. As discussed earlier, children with friends tend to have better school performance and to handle school transitions, such as the move from elementary to middle school, better than children who lack friendships. Similarly, affiliation with cliques and crowds during adolescence promotes social skills and identity formation, both of which are related to higher levels of academic achievement (Denham et al., 2003; Streitmatter, 1989). As a result, teachers should attempt to foster friendships among peers early in students' development and should continue to support peer group formation throughout adolescence.

Can you list the friends who were in your clique during high school? Which crowd label best represents you during high school? How did those peer groups help or hinder your academic progress?

Peer Statuses

In addition to friendships and peer groups, the social status of individuals among their peers is an important factor in the microsystem of peers. Peer social status typically is determined by both socially appropriate behaviors (for example, caring, leadership skills) and aggressive behaviors. Positive social behaviors and aggression are important determinants of peer status across developmental levels—with preschool-age children as well as elementary, middle, and high school students—and among rural African-American adolescents (Burr, Ostrov, Jansen, Cullerton-Sen, & Crick, 2005; Farmer, Estell, Bishop, O'Neal, & Cairns, 2003; Rose, Swenson, & Carlson, 2004).

DIVERSITY

In discussing the peer context, aggression typically sparks ideas of physical or **overt aggression,** such as fighting, with the intent to harm another physically. Recent research has defined a second type of aggression: relational aggression (Crick & Grotpeter, 1995). **Relational aggression** refers to behaviors specifically intended to damage another child's friendships, social status, or feelings of inclusion in a peer group. Such behaviors include gossiping, rumor spreading, and excluding someone as a way to control them. In childhood and adolescence, boys are more likely to use overt aggression, whereas girls are more likely to display relational aggression, especially during middle school (Crick & Grotpeter, 1995; Mathieson & Crick, 2010; Ostrov & Crick, 2007).

DIVERSITY

Children and adolescents have been categorized into several peer statuses based on socially appropriate and aggressive behaviors with peers: popular, rejected, or neglected.

POPULAR

Gender and Aggression. During middle school, boys are more likely to use overt aggression, and girls are more likely to use relational aggression.

Using different approaches, researchers have determined that there are actually two separate forms of popularity (Cillessen & Rose, 2005). In the first type, **sociometric popularity,** students nominate peers whom they most like and most dislike within their classroom or grade. In **perceived popularity,** students nominate peers who are the most popular or "cool" and those who are the least popular or "cool." Both sociometric and perceived popularity include characteristics of positive behavior, such as being cooperative and/or displaying socially appropriate behaviors. Unlike individuals with sociometric popularity, those with perceived popularity sometimes receive high numbers of nominations both for

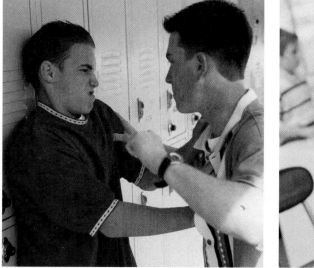

being liked and for being disliked—meaning that their popularity is controversial. The main difference between the two types of popularity, however, appears to be whether these peer status positions include displays of aggression. Sociometric popularity is not related to aggressive behaviors, whereas individuals with high levels of perceived popularity are likely to show higher levels of overt or relational aggression (LaFontana & Cillessen, 2002; Puckett, Aikins, & Cillessen, 2008). However, relational aggression appears to play a more important role in peer status than does overt aggression, and more so with girls' perceived popularity than with that of boys. Using relational aggression to obtain or maintain high peer status is more likely to occur following the transition from elementary school to middle school (LaFontana & Cillessen, 2002). Middle school students with advanced social skills may be more effective in delivering threats of friendship withdrawal, excluding others from the peer group, or orchestrating rumor spreading (Adler & Adler, 1998; Xie, Cairns, & Cairns, 2005).

DIVERSITY

REJECTED

Not all individuals who display relational or overt aggression are perceived as popular (Rose et al., 2004; Vaillancourt & Hymel, 2006). Individuals who display aggressive behaviors but do not display the positive behaviors of cooperation and social skills typically are considered **rejected youth.** Rejected youth tend to be less well liked by peers, including those within their own peer clique, and are members of smaller peer cliques (Bagwell et al., 2000). In addition, violence may beget violence in rejected students. For example, rejection status and the use of relational aggression are related to increases in relational aggression for girls. Similarly, rejection and overt aggression are related to increases in overt aggression for both boys and girls (Werner & Crick, 2004). Many consider a pattern of aggressive and coercive behavior over time to be *bullying.* Yet, being the victim of aggression also may lead to higher levels of aggression, meaning victims of aggression may themselves become aggressive. For example, one study of African-American eighth graders found that students who were the victims of overt or relational aggression by their peers also were more likely to be aggressive themselves (Sullivan, Farrell, & Kliewer, 2006). Unfortunately, students with mild disabilities may be more likely to be perceived as bullies and victims as compared with general education students who are more likely than gifted students to be perceived as bullies or victims (Estell et al., 2009).

DIVERSITY

Bullying: See page 67.

DIVERSITY
DIVERSITY

NEGLECTED

The final category of peer status includes those individuals who are neither popular nor aggressive but rather are considered **neglected youth.** Individuals who are considered neglected typically are not nominated as liked or disliked and do not show high rates of overt or relational aggression (Brown, 2004). Because little research evidence is available concerning this category of peer status, less is known about related characteristics among these individuals.

Think about people at your high school who would have been considered popular because they were well liked and those who were popular but not well liked. Did aggressive behaviors contribute to these popular students being disliked by their peers?

How does peer status interact with the school in the mesosystem? Students perceived as popular but not necessarily well liked tend to be less academically engaged, whereas students who are well liked by peers are considered to be more academically engaged (de Bruyn & Cillessen, 2006). Because popularity and aggression are related to academic engagement and later disruptive behaviors, teachers need to identify and eliminate aggressive behaviors. A study by Frank Barone (1997) reported that counselors, teachers, and administrators tend to underestimate the amount of bullying that occurs within a school. When eighth-graders were surveyed, 60% reported having been bothered by a bully in middle school; however, school personnel reported that they thought only 16% of the students had ever been bullied. When teachers recognize and react to overt aggression displayed by elementary-age boys, they typically assign more blame for the aggression to more popular boys than to less popular boys (Nesdale & Pickering, 2006). Teachers may attribute more blame to popular boys because of concerns that popular children will have more influence on the behaviors of other children. Even though popularity may influence teachers' views of who is to *blame,* the popularity of the aggressive boys does not affect the teachers' *punishment* of their behavior.

Research has not examined how teachers react to episodes of girls' overt aggression or relational aggression toward boys or girls. We might assume that teachers have more difficulty identifying acts of relational aggression and determining who is to blame because the behaviors are less obvious and more indirect. For example, teachers might clearly see overt aggression when one child hits, kicks, or slaps another child, but they might not "see" the rumor spreading or gossiping behaviors characteristic of relational aggression. Given the link between relational aggression and negative outcomes, teachers

DIVERSITY

should be on the lookout for instances of relational aggression and react as swiftly to these aggressive behaviors as they do to instances of overt aggression. A recent intervention program for rural schools has been successful in improving teachers' abilities to identify students involved in bullying (Farmer, Hall, Petrin, Hamm, & Dadisman, 2010). Education and training of school personnel on the significance of relational aggression may also see benefits.

DIVERSITY

BROADER CONTEXTS

Although the microsystems of families, peers, and schools most directly influence children, Bronfenbrenner's model also includes systems that have less direct influence on the developing individual—the exosystem and the macrosystem.

Parental Employment

In today's economy, both parents typically are employed outside the household, making parental workplaces a common element of a student's exosystem—that is, an indirect influence on development. Thirty years ago, as more mothers began rejoining the workforce, researchers examined the effects on child and adolescent outcomes and did not find negative results. Instead, a number of positive outcomes were found, particularly for girls (Hoffman, 1974):

DIVERSITY
- Girls with working mothers tended to have higher achievement aspirations or greater desire to excel academically, as well as higher achievement in school, compared to girls with nonworking mothers.

DIVERSITY
- Girls with working mothers tended to have higher intelligence scores (IQ scores) compared to girls with nonworking mothers.

- Children of working mothers were not more likely to be involved in delinquent acts than were children of nonworking mothers.

- Children of working mothers had more household responsibilities than did children of nonworking mothers, a situation related to positive, rather than negative, outcomes, such as advanced social development.

More recent research on parental employment as an exosystem suggests that having both parents employed outside the home does not generally affect children in either a negative or a positive manner (Crouter & McHale, 2005). For example, working mothers spend slightly less time with their children than do nonworking mothers; however, fathers whose wives are employed become more involved in child rearing than do fathers whose wives are not employed outside the home. In short, parental

Parental Employment. Fathers with working wives become more involved in child rearing than do fathers whose wives do not work outside the home.

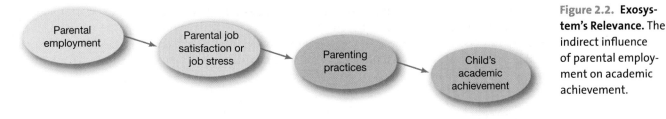

Figure 2.2. Exosystem's Relevance. The indirect influence of parental employment on academic achievement.

employment appears to have little impact on children and may even be related to positive academic achievement, aspirations, and intelligence among girls.

Parental satisfaction or job stress may have an indirect influence in the lives of children and adolescents. Data from the 1970s suggested that children of working mothers who were satisfied with their jobs had more positive outcomes than did children of unemployed mothers who preferred to work or working mothers who did not want to work (Hoffman, 1974). Similarly, more recent research suggests that job stress may be related to parenting practices. Higher levels of job stress may lead to a mother's withdrawal from her preschool-age child or to conflict with her adolescent (Crouter, Bumpus, Maguire, & McHale, 1999; Crouter & McHale, 2005).

Because parental satisfaction and job stress are components of the exosystem, the interaction with the school system is less direct, but it is not completely absent. Parents who are employed and experience high levels of job stress and dissatisfaction may exhibit less effective parenting practices, which can influence the academic achievement of their children (see Figure 2.2). Teachers might not be able to change the employment, job satisfaction, or parenting styles of parents, but they need to understand that this aspect of the exosystem indirectly affects the students in their classrooms.

A more direct influence of parental employment on the school system is the need of many families to use child care facilities. Child care facilities are considered a microsystem within a child's life, but they exist within the broader context of parental employment. Approximately 50% of mothers with children under one year of age and 75% of mothers with school-age children use child care facilities (Scarr, 1998). A variety of options for child care are available, including home or center care, licensed or unlicensed care, and for-profit or not-for-profit organizations. The amount of time spent in child care is not as important as the quality of care (McCartney et al., 2010). Quality of care from birth through age four can have positive effects on academic achievement through adolescence (Vandell et al., 2010).

Quality care typically means a safe environment with warm, supportive interactions that enhance children's development. Specific characteristics of quality care include:

- small group sizes within homes or classrooms
- low teacher-to-child ratios within classrooms
- qualified teachers or child care providers with early childhood education or child development training
- high stability or low turnover rates among teachers

Although quality of care is an important microsystem to consider, other factors appear to have an even greater influence on later development. A government-funded study has examined child care since 1991, following children from birth through sixth grade. The most recent findings indicate that parenting practices as well as a child's temperament are better predictors of later cognitive and social development outcomes than are experiences in child care facilities (Belsky et al., 2007; Pluess & Belsky, 2010). Broader contextual factors may also have a stronger impact on the cognitive and academic performance of children than quality of child care. For example, although quality of child care is related to language and cognitive development in children, this connection can be explained by family income and socioeconomic status, because families living in higher socioeconomic status neighborhoods have better access to quality child care (Brooks-Gunn, Han, & Waldfogel, 2002; Scarr, 1998). Figure 2.3 depicts the complex nature of how microsystems, mesosystems, exosystems, and macrosystems together influence an individual.

DIVERSITY

Cultural Factors

Like parenting practices (microsystem) and parental employment (exosystem), even broader contextual factors—socioeconomic status (macrosystem)—can shape child and adolescent development. More specifically, high-poverty school systems and highly segregated African-American school systems can

Figure 2.3. Interre-lationships. Systems are interdependent and exert direct and indirect influences on the individual.

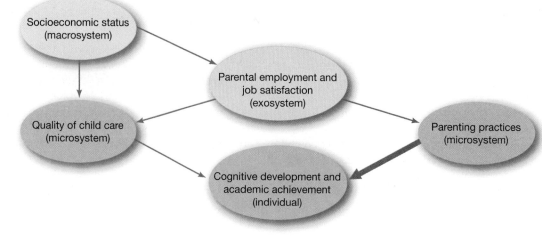

DIVERSITY have a negative impact on educational outcomes beyond individual differences (Borman & Dowling, 2010). Similarly, cultural values regarding education can play a major role in children's and adolescents' academic performance. Almost all parents want their children to excel academically and become successful, yet parental expectations may vary based on ethnicity and socioeconomic status. For example:

- Asian-American students report that their parents have higher expectations and standards for school success than parents of Caucasian-American students (Chen & Stevenson, 1995).

- African-American students also report that their parents have high expectations for them, but the expectations are not as high as the parents of Caucasian-American students (Ogbu, 2003).

These different expectations among parents may reflect their beliefs about the benefits of education. For example, African Americans are more skeptical of how helpful education will be, because many believe that even with an education their children will be discriminated against and their opportunities for suc-
DIVERSITY cess will be limited (Ogbu, 1994, 2003). Hence, African-American students have fewer negative views of the future when they think about not being educated, whereas Asian-American students have a greater fear of negative outcomes or failure when they think about not being well educated (Steinberg, 1996).

Broader cultural beliefs about the benefits of education may lead to parents' being either more or less involved in their child's education. The connection between parental involvement and broader cultural beliefs is important because higher parental involvement is consistently linked to higher academic achievement (Jeynes, 2008). African-American parents have been found to participate less in school functions, such as parent-teacher organizations, workshops, and open houses, than Caucasian-American parents and to be less likely to help their children with homework or check that homework has been completed (Ogbu, 2003). Lower parental involvement among African-American parents most
DIVERSITY likely results from a misconception that the school does not need their help to educate their children, with the result that these parents may not understand the importance of their role at school or as homework facilitators (Ogbu, 2003; Steinberg, 1996). In contrast, Asian Americans are highly invested in the school system, and Asian-American students spend substantially more time on homework than do Caucasian Americans (Steinberg, 1996). In short, families (microsystem) are influenced by cultural beliefs (macrosystem), particularly with regard to parental involvement in education, and to interactions with the school setting (mesosystem).

Teachers and educators need to be reminded that differences among beliefs in and support for education exist not only between ethnic groups but also within ethnic groups. The value each student's family places on education should be considered outside of his or her ethnicity. As with many of the contexts of development we have discussed, teachers may have little ability to change the cultural values or beliefs held by their students' parents. Teachers should, however, continue to provide encouragement and support for the importance of education among all students, regardless of race, ethnicity, or socioeconomic status.

Summary

Describe Bronfenbrenner's bioecological theory. Bronfenbrenner's bioecological theory emphasizes the interaction between the biological person and the environmental systems, including microsystems, mesosystems, exosystems, macrosystems, and the chronosystem. Research examining families and peers has relied on this theory to help explain developmental outcomes.

Describe how parenting practices and family transitions interact with the school system. The four parenting practices vary by level of control and responsiveness. Authoritative parenting appears to be most beneficial to children's and adolescents' academic achievement and school performance. Although children from both divorced and remarried families are more likely to have lower academic achievement and to exhibit more problem behaviors in school than children from intact families, not all such children experience difficulties. Difficulties do tend to increase with each family transition, meaning that academic achievement may be lower in remarried families than in single-parent families. Teachers should use information about the family context to help them understand children's difficulties and provide additional support to children and families.

Describe how aspects of the peer context interact with the school system. Children with friends or peer group affiliation tend to have better school performance than do children without friends or peer ties. In addition, children or adolescents who are well liked by their peers are more likely to be engaged in school than are those who are disliked or neglected by peers. Because of the link between overt aggression and negative outcomes as well as between relational aggression and negative outcomes, teachers need to identify both overt and relational aggression.

Explain how broader contexts of development influence microsystems and individual outcomes. The presence of an exosystem such as parental employment is not as important to a child's development as the indirect influence on the child via job satisfaction and stress. In addition, the presence of parental work outside the home may lead to an additional microsystem in the child's life—child care—but the child's development may be influenced more by the macrosystem of socioeconomic status and neighborhood. The macrosystem also varies by ethnicity and cultural values such that parental expectations and support for educational achievement may vary across and within ethnic groups to help explain differences in academic performance among students.

Key Concepts

authoritarian parenting   32

authoritative parenting   32

chronosystem   31

cliques   37

control   32

crowds   37

exosystem   31

macrosystem   31

mesosystem   31

microsystem   31

neglected youth   39

overt aggression   38

parenting practices   32

perceived popularity   38

permissive parenting   32

rejected youth   39

relational aggression   38

responsiveness   32

self-fulfilling prophecy   36

sleeper effect   35

sociometric popularity   38

uninvolved parenting   32

Video Applications

www.mhhe.com/bohlin2e

Video 1: Family to School Connections (*3 minutes*)
An elementary principal and a middle school principal discuss various ways to involve parents in their children's education.

Video 2: Peer Groups (*2 minutes*)
A group of eighth-grade students talk about peer groups and popularity in middle school.

Video 3: Bullying with Relational Aggression (*2 minutes*)
An elementary teacher explains how bullying includes more than physical aggression.

Case Studies
Reflect and Evaluate

DIVERSITY **EARLY CHILDHOOD: "Cry Baby"**

These questions refer to the case study on page 22.

1. Based on the information provided in the case study, speculate on the parenting strategies most likely used by Annie's mom and Zada's parents.
2. How might the family structures of Annie and Zada influence their behavior?
3. How developmentally appropriate is Annie's comment about not being best friends with Zada?
4. How might Tyler's aggressive behavior become a problem with peers as he continues into elementary school?
5. How does the employment of Annie's and Zada's parents play a role in their development?
6. How does the value placed on education differ in Annie's and Zada's homes? What factors might account for these differences?

DIVERSITY **ELEMENTARY SCHOOL: "Team"**

These questions refer to the case study on page 24.

1. How might Bronfenbrenner's bioecological theory be important in understanding Kashi's experiences?
2. Based on the information provided in the case study, speculate on the type of parenting strategy most likely used by Patricia's mom Mary.
3. In what specific ways might the divorce of Kashi's parents have influenced her behavior?
4. What does Kashi's "team" most likely refer to regarding peer groups?
5. Based on the information provided in the case study, is Zach correct in labeling Bill a bully? Why or why not?
6. Does Ms. Barone handle the girls and boys differently? Based on the research presented in the module, how are teachers' reactions typically different based on types of aggression and children's gender?

MIDDLE SCHOOL: "Basketball Star"

These questions refer to the case study on page 26.

1. What parenting strategy is most likely used by Sierra's dad? Darla's dad?
2. How might the family structures of Sierra, Darla, and Mark influence their behavior?
3. Identify an example of a clique and a crowd in the case study. Would these be expected to be formed during middle school? How might they change over the next several years?
4. What are the peer statuses of Jill, Sierra, Darla, and Mark? Give specific examples of their behavior that indicate these statuses. How might their peer status affect their school performance?
5. What type of aggression is used by Jill and Sierra? By Claudia? By Mark? Why might teachers react differently to aggressive behaviors displayed by these students?

DIVERSITY **HIGH SCHOOL: "Steal, Cheat, and Fight"**

These questions refer to the case study on page 28.

1. How could the content of these e-mails be combined to better reflect the bioecological model?
2. Ms. Presley believes that the family is responsible for these behaviors. To which aspects of family life might she attribute these behaviors?
3. How might Ms. Presley be accurate and inaccurate in her descriptions of divorce, remarriage, and parental employment?
4. What examples of cliques and crowds are given by the teachers and staff? Are these typical groupings in a high school? Why or why not?
5. What examples of relational and physical aggression are given by the teachers and staff? Based on the research presented in the module, is the gender of the adolescent who is displaying a particular type of aggression in the case study typical or atypical?

MODULE 3

Social Development

Outline	Learning Goals
Erikson's Psychosocial Theory	1. Describe the environmental influences in the development of the eight psychosocial crises.
Aspects of Identity	
■ Identity Statuses ■ Ethnic Identity ■ Gender Identity	2. Describe the four types of identity statuses. 3. Explain the development of ethnic identity and gender identity.
Understanding the Self	
■ Self-Concept ■ Self-Esteem	4. Compare and contrast self-concept and self-esteem.
Social Competence	
■ Social Adjustment ■ Social Performance ■ Social Skills	5. Explain the three components of social competence.
Summary **Key Concepts** **Video Applications** **Case Studies: Reflect and Evaluate**	

ERIKSON'S PSYCHOSOCIAL THEORY

Cognitive development: See Module 7.

Family and peer contexts: See page 36.

Erik Erikson (1959/1980) proposed one of the only theories of development that extends over the entire lifespan. Other theories typically begin in infancy and end during adolescence, including Piaget's cognitive development theory. Erikson's theory focuses on the social elements that influence individual development throughout a person's life, such as the importance of family and peer contexts, and identifies eight stages of development, as illustrated in Table 3.1. During each developmental stage, an individual faces and (ideally) masters a new psychological and social challenge, called a **psychosocial crisis.** Each psychosocial crisis has two developmental outcomes—one positive and one negative. The first five of Erikson's eight developmental stages apply directly to children in educational settings, whereas the latter three stages apply to adults, including teachers and administrators in educational settings. Let's examine each of these stages:

1. *Trust versus mistrust:* The first stage includes the period of infancy. Parents and primary caregivers are dominant environmental or social influences. Caregivers who dependably respond to the infant's needs provide a world in which the infant believes that his or her needs will be taken care of and learns to trust the world. Infants who experience lapses in having their needs met learn that the world may or may not meet their needs and develop a sense of mistrust. Similarly, attachment theory describes the importance of the mother-infant bond in providing infants with a warm, safe environment (Bowlby, 1969, 1973). Empirical data support the connection between responsive parenting and a perception of the self as lovable and a view of others as dependable or trustworthy, while parenting that is harsh and rejecting is related to seeing the self as unlovable and others as untrustworthy (Cassidy, 1999).

2. *Autonomy versus shame/doubt:* The second stage focuses on the period of toddlerhood, during which children continue to be most influenced by parents' and primary caregivers' responses. Toddlers are becoming more mobile and are attempting to do things on their own, such as toilet training, walking, and playing alone. Parents who provide opportunities for their children to explore their surroundings without guilt for accidents or mistakes are likely to instill a sense of autonomy in their children. In contrast, parents who are either punitive—disciplining children for mistakes and accidents—or overly protective—not allowing their children to move forward on their own—will instill in their children a sense of shame or doubt about their own capabilities.

TABLE 3.1   Erikson's Psychosocial Theory

Stage	Developmental period	Psychosocial crisis	Significant relations	Significant event
1	Infancy	Trust versus mistrust	Parents or primary caregivers	Feedings, diaper changing
2	Toddlerhood	Autonomy versus shame/doubt	Parents or primary caregivers	Toilet training, walking
3	Preschool	Initiative versus guilt	Family and early childhood educators	Learning to color, write; using pretend play
4	School-age	Industry versus inferiority	Parents, teachers, and peers	Learning to read and complete tasks
5	Adolescence	Identity versus identity diffusion	Peer groups and role models	More time with friends and romantic partners
6	Young adulthood	Intimacy versus isolation	Friends and romantic partners	Opportunities to try many new things
7	Middle adulthood	Generativity versus stagnation	Co-workers	Career choices and volunteer experiences
8	Late adulthood	Integrity versus despair	Mankind, society	Reflecting on one's life

Source: A. Lefton Lester, *Psychology* (5th ed.). Boston, MA: Allyn and Bacon. Copyright 1994 by Pearson Education. Adapted from Erikson (1959), *Identity and the Life Cycle (Psychological Issues,* Vol. 1, no. 1).

As children's motor skills develop and language capacity increases, how and whether they comply with the wishes of parents and caregivers also becomes an important facet of their developing autonomy. Children can choose to follow adult directives, such as cleaning up toys when asked to do so, or they can choose to defy authority, typically by saying no. At this stage, toddlers begin to test parental limits, requiring parents and caregivers to establish rules and address the issue of discipline. The child's temperament and the parents' style of parenting affect how the child resolves the autonomy crisis. Basically, warm and responsive parenting—setting reasonable expectations and choices and providing suitable guidance (neither overcontrolling nor undercontrolling)—will allow the child to positively develop autonomy.

Parenting styles: See page 32.

Application: Although parents primarily facilitate autonomy, the following guidelines can help teachers continue autonomy development during the preschool years:

- Provide reasonable choices (for example, giving the child a choice between two activities, such as "Would you like a story or time to color?").

- Allow children to do things for themselves, and do not punish mistakes (for example, accidents in toilet training).

- Be accepting of attempts to master skills even if the results are not perfect (for example, a shirt that's on backward).

- Provide reasonable expectations for the child's age (for example, don't expect a 2-year-old to sit quietly listening to stories for two hours).

- Provide opportunities for developing independence (for example, toddler eating utensils and cups, safety scissors, large crayons).

- Expect occasional noncompliance—the child is testing independence.

3. *Initiative versus guilt:* Stage three focuses on preschool-age children. Early childhood education contexts include increasing interaction with peers. Peers, along with parents and primary caregivers, influence the resolution of this stage's crisis. Preschoolers who are rewarded for trying new things—such as coloring, writing, and using their imagination in pretend play—are likely to develop a sense of initiative. Initiative gives children a sense of purpose and offers opportunities to master the environment, which may involve taking risks but not behaving impulsively. Therefore, parents, child care providers, and teachers must find a delicate balance between allowing children to try new things and potentially fail and doing things for children (that is, being overprotective). Adults who respond to failures by being overly critical or who ridicule children's creative and innovative behaviors are likely to instill guilt in children.

Application: The following guidelines can help teachers boost children's sense of initiative and decrease their feelings of guilt:

- Provide tasks and activities that are age-appropriate and in which children can experience success (for example, helping pass out supplies or materials prior to doing a project, picking up toys, watering plants using a small cup, etc.).

- Refrain from providing unsolicited help, because this suggests that you believe they cannot do the task alone.

- Avoid being overly critical of failures or setbacks, because this will lead to guilt. In response to failure, provide alternative strategies for tackling the task (for example, "Maybe next time you can try . . .").

- Provide toys for pretend play.

4. *Industry versus inferiority:* The fourth stage of Erikson's theory focuses on children in elementary and middle school contexts who are learning to master many skills, such as reading, school subjects, physical skills (for example, bike riding), and sports. Although parents continue to be an important context for development, teachers and peers within the school

Initiative Versus Guilt. Teachers can boost children's sense of initiative by allowing them to help with tasks and activities in the classroom.

system become increasingly influential. Children will develop a sense of industry when they have parents, teachers, and peers who provide opportunities for them to successfully complete tasks, learn information, and become competent or skilled in particular areas. Children develop inferiority when they believe that they are not competent in areas of school-related functioning ("I can't read") or home functioning ("I can't make breakfast"). Unfortunately, children with learning disabilities are less likely to develop a sense of industry (Pickar & Tori, 1986), so teachers should be sensitive to these individuals' attempts to increase their feelings of success and competence.

DIVERSITY

Application: Many aspects of the school environment can affect a sense of industry. The following guidelines may help teachers control some of these influences:

Ability grouping: See page 378.

- Be aware that activities or teaching approaches that emphasize competition among students— such as spelling bees, competitive sports, and team captains picking players in physical education class— draw attention to skill-level differences among children, which could lead to feelings of inferiority.

- Minimize comparisons of ability among students, particularly ability grouping in elementary school. Most students are aware of their position in the hierarchy, and for students in lower ability groups, grouping can reinforce feelings of inferiority.

- Emphasize mastery of skills (academic, physical, and so on) over competition with other students (for example, "You are in the reading level that *you* need to be in—the one that is right for *you*.").

- Have high expectations for all students. When teachers have different expectations for students, they convey these expectations in subtle ways, such as giving unsolicited help and praising for effort or a "good try." Such practices can lead students to believe that they lack competence.

5. *Identity versus identity diffusion:* Erikson's fifth stage focuses on adolescence. Beginning with this stage, the individual's own internal states play an important role along with environmental contexts of development such as family, peers, and school. Identity is a sense of self or understanding about "Who am I?" In contrast, identity diffusion involves a lack of clear goals and aspirations about the self. During this period of development, adolescents need a **psychosocial moratorium,** a time with few responsibilities and many opportunities for exploring different roles. Many adolescents will be in a state of moratorium for many years as they contemplate familial and educational aspirations and career or occupational goals, as well as determine their own set of morals and values.

   Application: Although peers become increasingly important during adolescence, teachers can also support adolescents in their formation of identity development. Strategies include the following:

   - Allow students to enroll in a variety of courses and to engage in numerous extracurricular activities.

   - Welcome individual or peer group preferences for music, clothing, and other minor issues.

   - Prompt students to consider alternatives and consequences for multiple options (for example, pros and cons of attending college versus gaining employment following graduation, or choosing one career path over another).

   - Debate moral issues to provide students with multiple perspectives as they explore their own views and value systems.

6. *Intimacy versus isolation:* The period of young adulthood was considered by Erikson to be focused on developing close, personal relationships with others. Erikson did not limit this stage to the development of romantic relationships, but included intimacy in close friendships and family relationships. In this sense, isolation is not necessarily about being a "loner" but is a characteristic demonstrated by individuals who move from one relationship to another and typically have an elevated fear of rejection, never becoming completely intimate with others.

7. *Generativity versus stagnation:* The seventh stage of development occurs primarily in middle adulthood and focuses on giving back to the next generation. Individuals who believe they have given to society in meaningful ways are likely

Identity Development. Teachers and parents can support adolescents' identity development by accepting individual preferences in the areas of clothing, body piercing, and hair style.

to have a sense of generativity. In contrast, individuals who fail to contribute to society in meaningful ways may feel bored with life and develop a sense of stagnation. Most teachers and administrators will be in this stage of development during most of their careers. Providing educational opportunities to the next generation may be one way teachers and administrators can successfully resolve this psychosocial crisis.

8. *Integrity versus despair:* The final stage is focused on the elderly or the period of old age. Integrity is a feeling that life was worth living and that death is not a threat. Despair involves dissatisfaction with one's life, a strong desire for more time, and a fear of dying.

At first glance, you might think that the eight psychosocial crises imply an either-or situation, but these labels were intended to illustrate a continuum (Marcia, 1994), a spectrum of possibilities rather than a list of either-or choices. The way individuals resolve each crisis affects their view of themselves as well as their view of society.

Erikson clearly stated that a positive resolution of one crisis does not imply a positive resolution of the next crisis. Nor does a negative resolution of one crisis suggest that all the other crises will be negatively resolved. One exception, however, was the resolution of the intimacy versus isolation crisis. Erikson's early work suggested that an individual must have achieved a sense of self or identity in order to successfully resolve the crisis of intimacy. In other words, in order to achieve true intimacy, an individual must have developed a coherent identity. This aspect of Erikson's theory has been criticized for focusing on the development of men rather than women. In fact, early studies conducted with college men indicated that individuals with identity achievement had the highest levels of intimate relationships, whereas identity diffusion was characterized by the lowest levels of intimacy (Orlofsky, Marcia, & Lesser, 1973). More recent research suggests that in women intimacy may develop prior to identity formation, or identity and intimacy may codevelop (Josselson, 1988).

DIVERSITY

Which stage of Erikson's theory best represents your current stage of development? How will your own personal strengths and weaknesses, as well as your relationships with your family and peers, help support your resolution of this psychosocial crisis?

ASPECTS OF IDENTITY

Identity Statuses

Developmental psychologist James Marcia (1966, 1987) conducted studies with adolescents and young adults to better understand the period of identity development described by Erikson. His research led him to discuss identity in terms of two variables: exploration and commitment. **Exploration** is a period of role experimentation and trying new behaviors, including contemplation of morals and values. **Commitment** is making decisions about areas of one's life such as educational and career goals, family obligations or goals, and political and religious beliefs. Marcia used the presence and absence of these two qualities to derive four identity statuses during adolescence, as shown in Table 3.2. Identity statuses have been linked to parenting practices (Harter, 1990) as well as to school attendance and math performance (Streitmatter, 1989).

Parenting practices: See page 32.

- **Identity achieved:** These adolescents are provided with opportunities to explore many options involving occupations, academic skills, friendships, and values and to commit themselves to certain goals and values. They typically have parents who use an authoritative parenting style. Identity achievement is related to better performance on math achievement tests.

- **Identity foreclosure:** These adolescents are not given time to explore but have accepted the commitments laid out by their parents. They have parents who typically use an authoritarian style of parenting—telling them who they are, what they will become, or where they will attend college. These students are less likely to be absent from school but also are less likely to perform well academically.

- **Moratorium:** These adolescents are actively involved in the exploration process but have not yet made decisions or commitments. Moratorium would be considered developmentally appropriate for most high school students and early college students. Their parents may use an authoritative style of parenting, allowing them to try new things while deferring decisions. These students are more likely to be absent from school than are other students, but surprisingly they score well on math achievement tests.

- **Identity diffusion:** These adolescents either have not yet begun the process of exploration (as you might expect of younger children) or have been through the exploration process but were unable to

TABLE 3.2 Marcia's Categories of Identity Achievement Commitment

		Commitment	
		Yes	**No**
Exploration	**Yes**	**Identity achieved** Adolescents are provided with opportunities to explore many options involving occupations, academic skills, friendships, and values and to commit to certain goals and values. *Parenting practice:* Individuals who have achieved identity typically have parents who use an authoritative parenting style. *Achievement:* Identity achievement is related to better performance on math achievement tests.	**Moratorium** Adolescents are actively involved in the exploration process but have not yet made decisions or commitments. Moratorium would be considered developmentally appropriate for most high school and early college students. *Parenting practice:* Parents who use an authoritative style of parenting provide a moratorium for their children by allowing them to try new things while deferring decisions until they have had ample time to explore their options. *Achievement:* Students who are in a state of moratorium are likely to be absent from school but, surprisingly, score well on math achievement tests.
	No	**Identity foreclosure** Adolescents have parents who typically use an authoritarian style of parenting, such as telling their adolescents who they are, what they will become, or where they will attend college. *Parenting practice:* Adolescents are not given time to explore but rather have accepted the commitments laid out by their parents. *Achievement:* Adolescents are less likely to be absent from school but also less likely to perform well academically.	**Identity diffusion** Adolescents either have not yet begun the process of exploration (as you might expect for younger children) or have gone through the exploration process but are unable to make commitments to their goals and values. *Parenting practice:* Parents are permissive and have allowed their adolescents to explore in the past but have never asked them to make commitments. *Achievement:* Individuals are more likely to be absent from school and to perform poorly on math achievement tests.

make commitments to their goals and values. Their parents may be permissive, allowing them to explore but not asking them to make commitments. These individuals are more likely to be absent from school and to perform poorly on math achievement tests.

DIVERSITY Ethnic Identity

Self-concept, self-esteem, and identity development all include a number of domain-specific areas. For many individuals, **ethnic identity,** or psychological attitudes toward and behaviors related to membership in an ethnic and racial group, is an important aspect of social development in these areas (Phinney, 1990). Developmental psychologist Jean S. Phinney (1990) defines ethnic identity as having several components:

- *self-identification,* or the ethnic label an individual uses regarding his or her group membership;
- a *sense of belongingness,* which includes the level of importance or concern given to one's ethnic group;
- *positive or negative attitudes* toward one's ethnic group (essential to ethnic identity), typically in the form of acceptance (positive) or denial (negative) of one's ethnic group;
- *ethnic involvement,* or the participation in social and cultural aspects of the ethnic group. Women of minority groups are more likely to achieve ethnic identity and to become active in cultural organizations and practices than are men of minority groups (Dion & Dion, 2004).

⑤ **Is this person Spanish/Hispanic/Latino?**	⑥ **What is this person's race?** *Mark (X) one or more races* *to indicate what this person considers himself/herself to be.*	
Mark (X) the "No" box if not Spanish/Hispanic/Latino. ☐ **No**, not Spanish/Hispanic/Latino ☐ Yes, Mexican, Mexican Am., Chicano ☐ Yes, Puerto Rican ☐ Yes, Cuban ☐ Yes, other Spanish/Hispanic/Latino — *Print group.* ⤵ ▭	☐ White ☐ Black or African American ☐ American Indian or Alaska Native – *Print name of enrolled or principal tribe.* ⤵ ▭	☐ Asian Indian ☐ Chinese ☐ Filipino ☐ Japanese ☐ Korean ☐ Vietnamese ☐ Other Asian – *Print race.* ⟶ ▭	☐ Native Hawaiian ☐ Guamanian or Chamorro ☐ Samoan ☐ Other Pacific Islander – *Print race below.* ☐ Some other race – *Print race below.* ▭ ↵

Ethnic Identity. On questionnaire forms, individuals must self-identify an ethnic label regarding their group membership.

DIVERSITY

Research with Latino adolescents indicates that each of these components may develop at different rates but development typically occurs during the high school years (Umana-Taylor, Gonzales-Backen, & Guimond, 2009). The combination of these components determines the ethnic identity stage of an individual. Ethnic identity stages mirror those proposed by Marcia for general identity development. Phinney (1989) found that Asian-American, Hispanic, and African-American high school students tend to fall into one of three ethnic identity stages, which are highly related to global identity development:

1. *Diffusion/foreclosure* includes individuals who have not yet examined their ethnicity.

2. *Moratorium* refers to those who currently are exploring the components described above.

3. *Achieved* describes those who are committed to their ethnic group membership.

Gender Identity

DIVERSITY

Any discussion of gender must begin by defining a number of concepts used in developmental psychology. **Sex** typically is used to refer to the biological identity of male or female, whereas **gender** is a social definition that includes behaviors learned from the environment about being either male or female. The latter term has several facets:

1. **Gender identity,** typically developed by age 4, refers to knowledge that one is biologically male or female.

2. In adolescence, gender identity often is referred to as **gender-role identity,** or the knowledge that one behaves appropriately according to societal expectations for one's gender. Gender-role identity may be defined as follows (Bem, 1974, 1975):

   ■ **masculine:** stereotypical male behaviors such as being athletic, aggressive, dominant, self-reliant, and independent;

   ■ **feminine:** stereotypical female behaviors such as being affectionate, warm, gentle, cheerful, and loyal; or

   ■ **androgynous:** having both masculine and feminine characteristics.

3. **Gender-role attitude** refers to approval or disapproval toward societal expectations for one's gender.

Would you consider yourself masculine, feminine, or androgynous? What characteristics in your past, such as family or peer and media influences, may have contributed to your gender-role identity?

Let's examine the three main theories used to explain issues surrounding gender (for reviews, see Eisenberg, Martin, & Fabes, 1996; Galambos, Berenbaum, & McHale, 2009):

1. *Biological theories* suggest that males and females behave differently and have different expectations due to the biological differences between the sexes—for example, boys are more likely to engage in rough-and-tumble play based on hormonal differences. In actuality, most gender differences do not originate solely from biological differences but rather interact with cultural and environmental influences—such as parents using rough-and-tumble play with boys more than with girls.

2. *Social learning theory* suggests that children develop a sense of gender identity by observing the behaviors and attitudes displayed by their parents, teachers, peers, and people depicted in the mass

Social cognitive learning: See page 174.

media (television, movie, and book characters). Children imitate the behaviors and attitudes of others and find that they typically are rewarded for behaving in gender-appropriate ways; hence, they continue to display those behaviors, taking on that gender identity.

3. *Gender schemas,* as the theory with the most empirical support, focus on the thought processes included in gender identity. Gender schemas develop in three distinct steps:

- In **gender labeling** (between ages 2 and 3) children can label themselves and others as male or female. First, children are able to correctly label *themselves* as either male or female. By age 2, children can correctly identify adults as either male or female. Finally, by age 3, they can also label other children correctly.

- In **gender stability** (between ages 3 and 4), children form the knowledge that gender will not change over time. For example, they understand that a girl will grow up to be a woman, not a man.

- In **gender constancy** (age 4 or 5), children understand that gender will remain the same regardless of behaviors, clothing, hairstyle, or other qualities. For example, a man holding a purse is still a man, not a woman.

Once children develop gender identity, they will begin to prefer the gender-role behaviors expected by society (Maccoby, 1990). Several factors influence the adoption of these behaviors, chief among them being the family and peer group. Typically, parents and siblings model and encourage gender-appropriate behaviors in their toy selection during childhood and assigned chores during adolescence. For example, boys are more likely to receive trucks and sports equipment for gifts and to be asked to *DIVERSITY* mow the grass and take out the garbage. Girls are more likely to receive dolls and kitchen sets for gifts and to be asked to help with dishes and laundry. Peers also provide models of gender-appropriate behaviors and will reward or punish (in the form of teasing) children for their displays of normal or contrary gender-role behaviors. For instance, if a kindergarten girl takes a Spiderman lunch box to school, her peers may tease her by saying that Spiderman is for boys. The girl would quickly learn to leave other Spiderman objects at home and to refrain from talking about "boy" things with her peers.

By adolescence, most individuals have a clear sense of the expected behaviors for males and females but develop **gender-role flexibility,** or the ability to alter expectations of their own and others' behaviors (Bem, 1974, 1975). Gender-role identity during adolescence includes incorporating that flexibility and choosing how closely to follow societal expectations. For girls and women, androgynous *DIVERSITY* gender-role identity has the best outcomes for psychological well-being, as compared with masculinity or femininity (Galambos et al., 2009). The need for girls to have some masculine qualities is related to the higher value placed on those characteristics in our society. For example, strong leadership skills and a competitive nature are highly valued qualities for upper-level administration and for skilled professions such as law and medicine. In contrast, professions characterized by feminine qualities of nurturing and caring, such as teaching and providing child care, receive less attention and fewer financial rewards in our society. Not surprisingly, given these societal expectations, adolescent boys and men who are considered predominantly masculine tend to have better psychological well-being than feminine or androgynous males.

UNDERSTANDING THE SELF

Although the terms *self-concept* and *self-esteem* frequently are used interchangeably, they have quite different meanings. **Self-concept** refers to a cognitive aspect in which individuals have a perception about themselves, such as "I am a student." **Self-esteem** refers to an affective aspect in which an individual evaluates components of him- or herself, such as "I am a good student." Self-concept can influence self-esteem depending on

Gender Constancy. Around age 4 or 5, children understand that gender will stay the same. A man holding a purse is still a man.

how much the individual values the component being considered (Harter, 1990). For example, a secondary education student may perceive that she has weak creative writing skills. Because she plans to attend college to major in accounting and places little value on creative writing skills, her self-esteem may not be influenced. In contrast, a student who has career aspirations to become a journalist may devalue himself because he highly values creative writing skills. Let's take a closer look at how self-concept and self-esteem function in educational settings.

Think about an aspect of yourself that is not particularly positive yet doesn't play an important role in your level of self-esteem.

Self-Concept

The structure of self-concept is related to educational settings because it includes the perceptions of one's knowledge and abilities in a number of activities, such as math, science, reading, athletics, and friendships (Bornholt, 2005; Byrne & Shavelson, 1986). Self-concepts or perceptions of oneself within particular domains are related to achievement in those domains. Contemporary educational psychologist Herbert W. Marsh and his colleagues (Guay, Marsh, & Boivin, 2003; Marsh, Trautwein, Ludtke, Koller, & Baumert, 2005) have repeatedly found that the relationship between academic self-concept and achievement is reciprocal: positive self-concept may lead to higher achievement, and higher achievement in turn will lead to an even more positive self-concept. The connection between academic self-concept and achievement has been found with children in elementary, middle, and high schools, as well as in a number of domain-specific areas such as math, science, and English. For example, Wilkins (2004) found, in an international sample of over 40 countries, children with positive self-concepts for math and science were more likely to have high achievement in those areas as compared with children who had more negative self-concepts in math and science. More recently, research with students in both rural and urban settings suggests that positive self-concepts in specific domains may lead to more interest and value for those domains, which in turn leads to greater participation and academic achievement (Bornholt & Wilson, 2007).

DIVERSITY

Because self-concept is related to academic achievement through various means, educators should understand who is most likely to have a positive self-concept.

- Self-concepts tend to be more positive for young girls than young boys in elementary education, but the reverse is found in middle school, where boys have more positive self-concepts than girls (Bornholt, 2005). In particular, boys are found to have higher self-concepts for math and science than girls (Steffens, Jelenec, & Noack, 2010; Wilkins, 2004).

DIVERSITY

- Differences are also found for middle school children with speech and language impairments, who report less positive self-concepts for academic competence than do typically developing children (Lindsay, Dockrell, Letchford, & Mackie, 2002).

DIVERSITY

While some influences on self-concept, such as gender and learning difficulties, are beyond the control of educators, teacher-student interaction is important for the development of positive self-concepts. For example, teachers tend to ask ever more difficult questions of students for whom they have high expectations. They also tend to wait longer for a response, provide cues and prompts, and interrupt these students less often than they do students for whom they have lower expectations of success (Allington, 1980; Rosenthal, 1995). Positive teacher-student relationships have been linked to academic self-concept as well as academic motivation (Martin, Marsh, McInerney, Green, & Dowson, 2007). Hence, educators should focus on quality interactions in order to facilitate positive self-concepts among students, which in turn will facilitate students' academic motivation and achievement.

Motivation: See Unit 5, starting on page 254.

Researchers who have examined the effectiveness of interventions designed to increase self-concept have made the following recommendations (O'Mara, Marsh, Craven, & Debus, 2006):

1. *Focus on domain-specific self-concept:* Help students focus on domain-specific aspects of self-concept such as math or science but not both.

2. *Focus on praising students and providing feedback on their performance:* Praising students when they have succeeded on academic tasks conveys important information about their level of mastery and helps foster an intrinsic motivation to learn—that is, it motivates students to learn for the sake of curiosity, interest, and mastery (Deci, Koestner, & Ryan, 1999a, 199b).

Intrinsic motivation and praise: See page 265 and page 269.

3. *Focus on at-risk populations:* Interventions have the best results for students with existing problems, such as behavioral disorders or learning disabilities.

Self-Esteem

We can look at self-esteem in two ways:

- as global self-esteem, a singular and relatively stable characteristic of the self, or
- as domain-specific self-esteem, separate components related to particular domains such as self-esteem in academics or self-esteem in relationships (Harter, Waters, & Whitesell, 1998).

Global self-esteem is related to overall psychological well-being, whereas domain-specific self-esteem is related to specific behavioral outcomes. The latter may be more important for teachers, because academic self-esteem has a greater effect on academic performance than does global self-esteem (Rosenberg, Schooler, Schoenbach, & Rosenberg, 1995).

DIVERSITY   Like self-concept, self-esteem is influenced by a number of factors, including socioeconomic status (SES), gender, ethnicity, and generational factors:

- Students from higher-SES families are more likely to have higher self-esteem (Twenge & Campbell, 2002).

- Girls tend to score higher than or equal to boys on levels of global self-esteem until adolescence, when girls score lower than boys (Simmon, 1987). Although boys have higher self-esteem than girls following adolescence, the difference in levels of self-esteem is small, indicating that boys and girls actually are very similar (Kling, Hyde, Showers, & Buswell, 1999). This small difference may result from the importance of physical appearance for global self-esteem during adolescence, particularly for girls who report being less satisfied with their appearance (Harter, 1990; Gentile et al., 2009).

- While both boys and girls may be affected by the transition from elementary school to middle school, this has a more detrimental influence on self-esteem for girls (Dusek & McIntyre, 2006). Often, girls are experiencing biological changes (puberty) in conjunction with the social transitions of school, whereas boys typically begin puberty later and are not faced with two simultaneous changes (Galambos et al., 2009).

- African Americans tend to have higher levels of self-esteem than Whites (Gray-Little & Hafdahl, 2000), including academic self-esteem, although their academic achievement is lower than that of Whites. African Americans tend to attribute their poorer academic achievement to causes outside their control, such as poor school systems and discrimination, an association that has less influence on their feelings about themselves (van Laar, 2000). Ethnic identity also plays a larger role in self-esteem for individuals from minority groups than it does for Whites (Gray-Little & Hafdahl, 2000).

- Overall levels of self-esteem have increased from previous generations. High school students in 2006 reported higher global self-esteem than high school students in 1975; however, few explanations have been tested to explain this difference (Twenge & Campbell, 2008).

SOCIAL COMPETENCE

Psychologists offer different definitions of the concept of social competence. **Social competence** comprises social adjustment, social performance, and social skills that lead to positive social outcomes such as having friends and social status (Cavell, 1990; Hubbard & Coie, 1994). Let's look at these three components in more detail:

1. *Social adjustment* includes how individuals behave in particular social situations, for example, whether individuals express or hide their emotions.
2. *Social performance* focuses on interpersonal processes such as actively participating in social situations and focusing on other people's needs in social situations.
3. *Social skills* are specific behaviors in interpersonal contexts including greeting ability and conflict resolution skills.

See Module 4 regarding emotions and emotional development.

Social Adjustment

One specific aspect of social adjustment is the ability to express, understand, and regulate emotions within the self and others, called **emotional competence.** There are three major elements of emotional competence (Denham et al., 2003; Hubbard & Coie, 1994):

- *Emotional expressiveness* is the ability to express positive and negative emotions appropriately. Teachers are more likely to rate children who express more positive and less negative emotions as

| EXAMPLE 3.1 | Characteristics of Social Competence during Childhood and Adolescence |

Developmental period	Characteristics
Early childhood	■ Beginning of strong reciprocity in social exchanges (matching, fitting, and coordinating social acts) ■ Rapid development in synchronizing interactions with peers ■ Movement from nonverbal signals to strong verbal communication patterns ■ Onset of self-classification of gender, age, and race
Early elementary	■ High levels of mutuality in social responding ■ Can respond simultaneously to more than one peer ■ Self-system concept becoming reasonably stable and independent of contradictory evaluations ■ Learning how to recruit others into ongoing activity ■ Increased reliance on verbal, rather than physical, strategies in interpersonal control
Late elementary	■ Peer group formation and identification of role in the group ■ Continued reliance on authority figures to guide behavior, but with increasing reliance on peers as a mechanism of norm establishment ■ Continued reciprocity and increased integration of patterns of social exchange
Early adolescence	■ Employment of peer group affiliation to achieve particular ends ■ Peers now taking primary role as a mechanism of norm establishment
Middle adolescence	■ Sharp delineation between strategies for same-sex and opposite-sex relations, along with norms, behaviors, goals, and outcomes ■ Development of more rigid social structures and evolution of subgroup norms for behavior ■ Formation of transient cross-sex liaisons for mutual support or gratification
Late adolescence	■ Divergence of interaction styles as a function of the social groups in which individuals engage (code switching) ■ Sharpening of sexual stereotypes ■ Employment of cognitive capabilities to enhance social relations (better social cognition) ■ More sophisticated use of skills to inhibit, remove, or control the behavior of others

Source: Adapted from Cairnes, 1986.

Summary

Describe the environmental influences in the development of the eight psychosocial crises. Erikson suggested that parents or caregivers are the most important influences for the first two stages (trust and autonomy) and continue to play an important role in the development of industry and identity. However, teachers and peers begin to become important during the third stage (initiative) and play an increasing role in the fourth stage (industry). Although environmental influences such as parents and peers continue to support the fifth and sixth stages (identity and intimacy), adolescents and young adults take a more active role in the resolution of these stages. The final two stages (generativity and integrity) are based almost exclusively on the individual's own processes.

Describe the four types of identity statuses. Identity statuses are determined by the presence or absence of commitment and exploration. Identity-achieved adolescents have explored options and made commitments to personal values and future goals. Identity-foreclosure status lacks exploration but involves a strong commitment to goals and values, typically based on parental aspirations. The status of moratorium includes actively exploring goals and values without yet having made commitments. Identity-diffused adolescents either have not begun exploration or following exploration have been unable to make commitments.

Explain the development of ethnic identity and gender identity. Ethnic identity develops from self-identification with an individual's ethnic group, a sense of belongingness to the group, attitudes toward the ethnic group, and participation within the group. The stages of ethnic identity development mirror those of identity in other areas, as described by Marcia. Gender identity implies different meanings at different levels of development. For young children, gender identity is the knowledge of being biologically male or female. By adolescence, gender-role identity includes behaving appropriately according to the social expectations for one's biological status as male or female. Boys and men who consider themselves masculine tend to have the best psychological outcomes, whereas androgyny, not femininity, is related to better psychological well-being for girls and women.

Compare and contrast self-concept and self-esteem. Although self-concept refers to the cognitive perceptions of the self and self-esteem to the affective evaluation of the self, both are influenced by the environment and are related to school achievement. Educators should be aware of the demographic variables related to these concepts and of strategies for improving self-concept and self-esteem among students.

Explain the three components of social competence. First, social adjustment includes how individuals behave in specific situations, such as their level of emotional competence. Second, social performance includes interpersonal processes such as sociability and prosociality. Third, social skills include thinking about social situations and making decisions about how best to respond.

Key Concepts

androgynous   51

commitment   49

emotional competence   54

ethnic identity   50

exploration   49

feminine   51

gender   51

gender constancy   52

gender identity   51

gender labeling   52

gender-role attitude   51

gender-role flexibility   52

gender-role identity   51

gender stability   52

identity achieved   49

identity diffusion   49

identity foreclosure   49

masculine   51

moratorium   49

prosociality   55

psychosocial crisis   46

psychosocial moratorium   48

self-concept   52

self-esteem   52

sex   51

sociability   55

social competence   54

social skills   55

Video Applications

www.mhhe.com/bohlin2e

Video 1: Gender Role Behavior (2 minutes)
A middle/high school science teacher discusses how difficult it is to recruit girls into his technology and engineering class and the steps he takes to encourage girls to participate.

Video 2: Identity Development (2 minutes)
A middle/high school science teacher discusses an afterschool robotics team and how the program can aid students in learning leadership skills and developing their identities.

Case Studies
Reflect and Evaluate

EARLY CHILDHOOD: "Cry Baby"   *DIVERSITY*

These questions refer to the case study on page 22.

1. Based on Erikson's psychosocial theory, what crisis are most of these children experiencing?

2. What examples in the curriculum may help children with the psychosocial crisis for this stage?

3. Why would a preschool program spend so much time and effort on facilitating and observing social behaviors?

4. What types of developmentally appropriate social skills are evident in the classroom? Which social skills should be emphasized more?

5. Tanner seems to have clear ideas about gender appropriateness. Is this typical of children his age? How might these ideas change over time?

ELEMENTARY SCHOOL: "Team"   *DIVERSITY*

These questions refer to the case study on page 24.

1. Based on Erikson's psychosocial theory, what crisis are most of these children experiencing? What factors in Patricia's and Kashi's experiences can you identify that are important to their resolution of this crisis?

2. Can you think of ways Ms. Barone can help her students develop a sense of industry and avoid feelings of inferiority?

3. Why would Mary be concerned about her daughter's self-esteem? Is this a legitimate concern?

4. How might Kashi's ethnic identity be compromised in this particular school system?

5. Why would the comments made by Bill about Zach's father be hurtful given the boys' stage of gender identity?

6. How might comments such as Bill's about Zach's being "like a little girl" influence the gender identity of the girls and boys in his class?

MIDDLE SCHOOL: "Basketball Star"   *DIVERSITY*

These questions refer to the case study on page 26.

1. Based on Erikson's psychosocial theory, what crisis are most of these adolescents experiencing? What evidence is given that these adolescents are in that stage of development?

2. How might Mr. Martin attempt to foster Darla's social competence? Give specific suggestions.

3. Describe Darla's self-concept and self-esteem based on the information provided in the case.

4. What identity status does Darla appear to be in currently? To what factors is her status most likely attributed?

5. How does Mr. Martin attempt to foster identity development in Darla?

6. What is the gender-role behavior of Darla? How does Darla view the gender-role behavior of the other girls on the basketball team?

DIVERSITY HIGH SCHOOL: **"Steal, Cheat, and Fight"**

These questions refer to the case study on page 28.

1. Based on Erikson's psychosocial theory, what crisis are most of these adolescents experiencing? What evidence is given that these adolescents are in that stage of development? What evidence is given that they might also be entering the next stage?

2. Based on theory and research, is Principal Durbin correct in taking school time to consider social behavior? Is Mr. Ruestman correct in not wanting his class time to be used to address these behaviors by including social skills training?

3. How likely is it that Ms. Kennel's concern about the girls' self-concepts and self-esteem is accurate? What can be done?

4. Ms. Baxter is concerned that students should be making decisions about college and career paths. Is this a legitimate concern at this developmental level? Why or why not?

5. How might the ethnic identity of the Spanish-speaking students be enhanced or compromised by the creation of a peer group based on their ethnicity?

MODULE 4

Emotional Development

Outline	Learning Goals
What Is Emotion?	
■ Emotions and Temperament ■ How Parents, Gender, and Culture Influence Emotion	1. Describe the general influences of temperament, parenting practices, gender, and culture on children's emotional expressiveness.
Emotions and Individual Performance	
■ Dimensions of Emotional Intelligence ■ Emotions in the Classroom	2. Identify the five dimensions of emotional intelligence outlined in Goleman's model, and discuss at least one way that teachers can facilitate the development of each dimension. 3. Describe two primary ways that emotions can influence learning.
Applications: Emotionally Intelligent Teaching	
■ What Is Social-Emotional Learning (SEL)? ■ Benefits of SEL Programs	4. Define social-emotional learning and discuss the three essential principles that underlie SEL interventions.
Summary **Key Concepts** **Video Applications** **Case Studies: Reflect and Evaluate**	

WHAT IS EMOTION?

Every day of every school year, teachers witness a broad spectrum of emotional displays by students. They may notice physiological signs such as sweaty palms or flushed cheeks, behavioral signs such as worried facial expressions or fists clenched in anger, or conscious expressions of feelings such as entries in students' reflective journals or persuasive arguments made during a class discussion. As you will see throughout this module, **emotions** are complex constellations of physiology, behavior, and feeling that can have a direct impact on students' performance in school.

Emotions and Temperament

Temperament refers to genetically based individual differences in emotions, activity, and self-control that determine our patterns of response to environmental stimuli and events. It encompasses our capacity for adaptability, persistence, adventurousness, shyness, inhibitedness, irritability, and distractibility (Keogh, 2003; Pfeifer, Goldsmith, Davidson, & Rickman, 2002; Thomas & Chess, 1977). Although temperament includes more than emotions, variations in emotionality are central to modern conceptions of temperament (Lemerise & Arsenio, 2000). Researchers have identified different temperament styles that emerge early in life and seem to be relatively enduring. From the first days of life, some babies are easygoing, cheerful, and relaxed, while others are difficult, reactive, and fidgety. Inhibited and fearful 2-year-olds often are still relatively shy as 8-year-olds, and about half will continue to be introverted as adolescents (Kagan et al., 1994; Kagan, Snidman, & Arcus, 1998). Young children who are observed to be highly irritable, impulsive, and hard to control at age 3 are more likely to have drug problems, difficulties at work, and relationship conflicts by the time they are 21 (Caspi, 2000; Williams et al., 2010). Teachers who recognize some of these persistent patterns can help provide students with tools to understand and manage their emotions in a way that will optimize their chances for life success (Rudasill, Gallagher, & White, 2010).

Temperament affects how students engage in and respond to classroom activities and also affects students' academic achievement (Keogh, 2003). For example, high levels of persistence and low levels of distractibility can facilitate school success. The genetic underpinnings of temperament establish a predisposition for certain kinds of emotional behavior. However, culture plays an important role in shaping how and whether those behaviors ultimately will unfold (Keogh, 2003; Thompson, 1998). For example, European-American families tend to encourage children to be assertive and independent, while families in Mexico, Japan, or India are more likely to encourage children to be reserved and obedient (Joshi & Maclean, 1994; Rothbaum, Weisz, Pott, Miyake, & Morelli, 2000). While no one best temperament guarantees success, teachers may need to consider students' temperamental characteristics in trying to create an optimal learning environment that meets the needs of every student. For example, students who are highly anxious may be overwhelmed in a noisy, chaotic classroom and may need a calmer space in which to work productively. Students who are shy and sensitive may need help finding supportive peer connections.

How would you describe your own temperament? What examples can you think of that indicate whether your own temperament has been relatively stable over the years? How does your temperament affect the way you approach school activities?

How Parents, Gender, and Culture Influence Emotion

Children first learn to express emotion within a family context, so the degree to which family members express their emotions, and the form those emotions take, shape the emotional patterns that children adopt (Dunsmore et al., 2009; Warren & Stifler, 2008). Parents' beliefs about emotion seem to have two important dimensions: beliefs about the acceptability of emotions and beliefs about active socialization/coaching with respect to children's emotional expression (Hakim-Larson et al., 2006). Research with preschool-age children has demonstrated that parents who value teaching children about emotions have children with greater emotion knowledge (Denham & Kochanoff, 2002). More specifically, parents' belief about guiding their children's emotions have been linked to preschool children's emotion talk, emotion understanding, and peer relations (Cervantes & Seo, 2005; Dunsmore & Karn, 2001, 2004), suggesting a link to children's emotional recognition skill. The influence of family **emotional expressiveness** declines over the first six years of life, which suggests that schools may be an appropriate transition point for assisting children with managing their emotions (Halberstadt & Eaton, 2002).

Emotions in the Classroom. Every day, teachers see a broad spectrum of emotional displays by students.

Differences in emotional expressiveness by gender may also, in part, be traced back to socialization within the family. Parents typically attempt to encourage emotional expression in girls, with the exception of anger. They are more likely to attempt to regulate boys' emotional expressiveness, particularly sadness and pain. Hence, boys may be less emotionally expressive when it comes to emotions such as sadness or fear but may be more likely than girls to express feelings of anger or dominance (Brody & Hall, 2008; Eisenberg, Martin, & Fabes, 1996; Fuchs & Thelen, 1988). Achievement situations are more likely to produce anxiety responses in boys, whereas girls are more likely to become anxious in interpersonal situations (Steinberg & Morris, 2001). Gender differences in emotional expression have been found across multiple cultures, and they are most pronounced in cultures where there is greater differentiation in gender roles (Brody, 1999; Hofstede, 2001; Safdar et al., 2009).

Each culture has its own **display rules** governing the degree of emotional expression considered appropriate in different situations, along with the coping strategies considered acceptable (Elfenbein, 2006; Mesquita & Frijda, 1992). For example, Asians rarely display negative or self-aggrandizing emotions that might disrupt the communal feeling within close-knit groups, but they are more likely than Americans to display emotions of sympathy, respect, and shame that reflect their social connection and interdependence. A recent cross-cultural study comparing the emotional expressiveness of Japanese, Canadian, and American students also found that Japanese students varied their display rules for different interaction partners more than the two North American groups did (Safdar et al., 2009). A teacher's ability to recognize and respond to students' emotional states requires awareness of the ways emotions may be expressed by different individuals, as well as awareness of how parenting practices, gender, and culture influence emotional expression.

EMOTIONS AND INDIVIDUAL PERFORMANCE

Research on the connection between emotion and learning suggests that thinking, learning, and emotions are interconnected processes and that teachers need to address multiple goals of cognition and emotions in every facet of classroom learning (Coles, 1998). Let's examine how emotional competence contributes to personal success in both academic and broader life arenas and how emotions influence learning.

Dimensions of Emotional Intelligence

Psychologists have begun to explore whether students who have a better command of their own emotions and are more attuned to the emotions of others have a social or an academic edge of some kind. Psychologists Peter Salovey and John Mayer first introduced the term **emotional intelligence (EI)** and defined it as the ability to perceive, express, understand, and manage emotions (Mayer, DiPaolo, & Salovey, 1990; Salovey & Mayer, 1990). With the 1995 publication of psychologist Daniel Goleman's best-selling trade book *Emotional Intelligence: Why It Can Matter More Than IQ*, public attention became focused on the construct of emotional intelligence.

The concept of emotional intelligence has shifted the academic emphasis from isolated cognitive abilities as a predictor of school and life success to the contributions of emotional and social factors. IQ accounts for only about 20% of a person's career success, leaving a large portion of success determined by other factors (Goleman, 2006). Studies have shown that:

See Module 3 for more about emotions and social competence.

- overall emotional intelligence uniquely explains individual cognitive performance beyond the level attributable to general intelligence (Lam & Kirby, 2002);
- emotional intelligence during preschool is related to social competence in elementary school students (Denham et al., 2003; Hubbard & Coie, 1994);
- children's high emotional intelligence is associated with bonding to teachers and peers in school, whereas low emotional intelligence is associated with academic outcomes such as dropping out of school (Hawkins, Catalano, Kosterman, Abbott, & Hill, 1999).

Daniel Goleman (1995, 2006) broadened Salovey and Mayer's definition of emotional intelligence (EI) to include five main dimensions:

1. Emotional understanding
2. Responding to others' emotions
3. Emotional regulation
4. Self-motivation
5. Emotions in relationships

Whereas the original definition focused exclusively on understanding and managing emotions, Goleman's version blends those emotional components with motivation and social skills. Let's consider each dimension of emotional intelligence and explore how a teacher might facilitate the development of students' skills.

DEFINING EMOTIONAL UNDERSTANDING

How well can students of various ages understand their own emotional reactions and those of others? **Emotional understanding,** the ability to differentiate and interpret one's own emotions and to perceive and understand the emotions of others, becomes possible only when certain cognitive milestones have been reached. Between 18 and 24 months of age, the cognitive capacity for **self-awareness** emerges. This is the ability to recognize our own thoughts and feelings and to observe them in a way that allows us to understand them and make decisions about how to act on them (Goleman, 1995). Children who lack such self-awareness may find it difficult to control impulsive actions, make appropriate decisions, and communicate what they mean (Elias, Tobias, & Friedlander, 1999). Children's understanding of other people's emotions is closely tied to their ability to understand their own emotions (Bretherton, Fritz, Zahn-Waxler, & Ridgeway, 1986; Shatz, 1994).

Researchers have noted several developmental trends in the various aspects of emotional understanding, summarized in Table 4.1. As language development occurs, toddlers begin to acquire emotion words like *happy* and *sad* to express how they feel (Bretherton & Beeghly, 1982; Bretherton et al., 1986). By their fourth year, they can engage in simple dialogues about the causes and consequences of emotions (Dunn, Brown, & Beardsall, 1991). A child's ability to evaluate behavior based on external standards emerges between 2 and 3 years of age, making emotions such as pride, shame, and guilt possible (Kochanska, Gross, Lin, & Nichols, 2002; Lindner, 2006). By the middle elementary grades, most children are also capable of feeling shame when they fail to meet standards for moral behavior set for them by adults (Damon, 1988). Guilt comes from within the child, while shame comes from knowing that someone else might see and criticize what the child has done (Tangney, 2001). Although guilt and shame are experienced as unpleasant emotions, they are a good sign that children are developing a sense of right and wrong. Between ages 3 and 6, children's understanding of causes, consequences, and the behavioral signs of emotion improves in accuracy and complexity. By age 5, children are nearly adult-like in their ability to recognize happy facial expressions; however, their sensitivity to subtle expressions of surprise, disgust, fear, anger, or sadness develops more slowly and may not reach its full potential until age 10 or later (Gao & Maurer, 2010). Between ages 7 and 11, individuals demonstrate the ability to consider multiple sources of information (for example, situational and personality factors) in explaining the emotions of others (Gnepp & Gould, 1985). Teachers' expectations of students in regard to emotional maturity in different situations should reflect an awareness of developmental norms and changes.

Students' ability to understand their emotions is linked to greater self-confidence, because understanding emotions allows them to feel greater control over their inner self (Goleman, 1995; Hamacheck, 2000). In a longitudinal study that controlled for verbal aptitude and temperament, 5-year-olds

TABLE 4.1	Milestones in Emotional Development	
Age	**Emotional Regulation**	**Emotional Understanding**
Birth–6 months	Signs of almost all basic emotions are present. Social smile emerges. Laughter appears. Expressions of happiness are greater when interacting with familiar people.	Resonance to the emotional cues of others is present.
7–12 months	Anger and fear increase. Use of caregiver as a secure base emerges. Emotional self-regulation improves as crawling and walking permit approach and retreat from stimulation.	Ability to detect the meaning of others' emotional signals emerges. Social referencing develops.
1–2 years	Self-conscious emotions appear but depend on the presence of others.	Vocabulary of words for talking about feelings expands. Empathic responding appears.
3–6 years	As representation and language improve, active behavioral and cognitive strategies for engaging in emotional self-regulation develop.	Understanding of causes, consequences, and behavioral signs of emotion improves in accuracy and complexity. As language develops, empathic responding becomes more reflective.
7–11 years	Self-conscious emotions become integrated with inner standards for right action. Strategies for engaging in emotional and self-regulation increase in variety, become more cognitive, and are adjusted to situational demands. Conformity to and conscious awareness of emotional display rules improve.	Ability to consider multiple sources of information when explaining others' emotions appears. Awareness that people can experience more than one emotion at a time emerges. Empathic responding increases as emotional understanding improves.
12 years and above	At this point, adolescents are developing the ability to: ■ Regulate intense emotions ■ Modulate rapidly vacillating emotions ■ Achieve awareness of and successfully attend to their own emotions without becoming overwhelmed by them	Adolescents begin to demonstrate the following capabilities: ■ Understand the consequences to self and others of genuine emotional expression versus dissemblance ■ Separate momentary emotional experience from identity and recognize that the self can remain intact and continuous despite emotional fluctuation ■ Use cognitive skills to gather information about the nature and sources of emotion ■ Negotiate and maintain interpersonal relationships in the presence of strong emotion

Note: These milestones represent overall age trends, but individual differences may exist.

who could most accurately discern others' emotions became 9-year-olds who easily made friends, co-operated with their teacher, and effectively managed their own emotions (Izard, 2001).

Children's understanding of right and wrong: See page 77.

RESPONDING TO OTHERS' EMOTIONS

As human beings, we communicate our emotions verbally through emotional language, tone or attitude, and pitch (high or low volume), as well as nonverbally through our facial expressions, posture, and hand gestures. **Paralinguistic cues** such as changes in speaking rate, pitch level, or vocal quality

Figure 4.1. Facial Expressions. Facial expressions of basic emotions are culturally universal. See if you can identify the individuals displaying the following emotions: happiness, sadness, disgust, anger, surprise, and fear.

typically are used to reinforce language content. From the first months of life, babies can pick up on emotional cues in spoken conversation (Cooper & Aslin, 1990; Morton & Trehub, 2001).

Facial expressions, a nonverbal indicator of emotion, seem to be culturally universal (Ekman, 1994; Matsumoto & Ekman, 1989). For example:

- Studies of adults across a wide range of cultures show high levels of agreement on the meaning of facial displays of basic emotions such as happiness, sadness, disgust, anger, surprise, and fear (Ekman, 1994). Try it yourself. Figure 4.1 presents six photographs of facial expressions (Matsumoto & Ekman, 1989). See if you can match the six basic emotions with the faces pictured.

- The facial expressions children use to express various emotions, even among blind children who have never seen another face to imitate, are universal (Eibl-Eibesfeldt, 1971; Galati, Scherer, & Ricci-Bitti, 1997).

Empathy: See page 81.

As children and adolescents improve at reading and interpreting emotions, empathetic responding tends to increase. **Empathy** is the ability to experience and understand the feelings, situation, or motives of someone else. Children as young as age 2 to 3 are able to understand another's emotional expressions of distress and to respond with appropriate behaviors (Denham, 1986, 1998). At the early elementary level, children show empathy more frequently toward people they know personally. As they reach the upper elementary grades, their feelings of empathy begin to extend to people they may not know, such as homeless people or children orphaned by war (Eisenberg, 1982; Hoffman, 1991).

EMOTIONAL REGULATION

Children and adolescents vary in the intensity with which they experience and express emotions and in their skills for regulating emotions. **Emotional regulation,** the ability to tolerate and manage emotions, enables students to prevent stress from overwhelming them and to stay on task and think and work productively (Elias et al., 1997). Students who are poor regulators have a higher risk of maladjustment and demonstrate limited social competence (Eisenberg et al., 1996; Hughes, Dunn, & White, 1998; Silk, Steinberg, & Morris, 2003). Emotional regulation involves, among other things, following certain rules about when and how to display emotions. Children become more proficient at this as they get older and gain a better understanding of what emotions are considered appropriate in different contexts (Barnes, 1995). Children and adolescents often use **social referencing,** a strategy of observing other people's reactions to help them interpret a situation and decide how to respond (Campos & Sternberg, 1981). Teachers can guide students' emotional reactions by being in tune with their own emotions and by modeling the types of emotional expression that are appropriate in various circumstances.

Some situations involve stimuli that trigger an almost uncontrollable emotional response. The amygdala, a limbic structure within the brain that controls emotions such as fear, anger, and aggression, reacts instantly to stimuli that individuals perceive as threatening and triggers a series of behavioral, physiological, and endocrine responses (LeDoux, 2000; Winston, Strange, O'Doherty, & Dolan, 2002). This quick response pattern has an adaptive function, as in cases where students react to a fire alarm with an increased heart rate, a fight-or-flight reaction, and a search for an exit from the building. The state of arousal created in such situations makes self-regulation, planning, and thoughtful reflection more difficult (Metcalfe & Mischel, 1999). However, by participating in a fire drill (discussing and role playing), students can learn what behavior is expected and practice it without the increased emotional arousal and potential cognitive interference that may accompany an actual emergency.

Emotional regulation allows the individual to move from an automatic, hot emotional response to a cooler, well-reasoned, reflective response that gives access to a wider range of cognitive resources (Mischel, Shoda, & Rodriguez, 1989). Early in their development, children have difficulty regulating and inhibiting hot responses (which often involve some form of impulsiveness or aggression). A preschooler might hit another child when provoked by teasing (hot response) rather than considering other possible options such as using words to ask the child to stop or to ask the teacher to intervene (cool responses). Cool responses may include dialogue and negotiation, conflict resolution skills, or self-calming actions such as deep breathing. Cool system processes begin to emerge around age four and become increasingly dominant over the lifespan (Rothbart, Ellis, & Posner, 2004).

SELF-MOTIVATION

Self-motivation refers to the ability to generate feelings of enthusiasm, zeal, confidence, and persistence, especially during challenges and setbacks (Goleman, 1995). Students who have an optimistic attitude toward learning motivate themselves to expect success. To be motivated, students need to set goals that they value and to feel that, with effort, their goals are attainable. According to Nicki Crick and Kenneth Dodge (1994), emotions can serve to facilitate the achievement of particular goals, and goal selection or attainment can modify an individual's emotional state. Children who have deficits in reading the emotions of others or in expressing empathy may pursue more destructive goals because they are unable to "feel other children's pain" (Cohen & Strayer, 1996). When children are involved in a conflict with a peer, friendship ties can motivate them to work hard to pursue social-relational goals that maintain the bonds of friendship. If the children are not friends, they may focus on very different goals, such as revenge or avoidance.

Goal theory: See page 280.

EMOTIONS IN RELATIONSHIPS

In day-to-day classroom interactions, peers provide one another with various forms of emotional support necessary to accomplish social and academic tasks (Schunk, 1987). Positive, supportive peer relationships translate into greater social adjustment and academic success (Zins, Bloodworth, Weissberg, & Walberg, 2004). Children who do not express positive feelings, who have difficulty regulating their emotions, or who are unable to understand others' emotional states are likely to experience peer difficulties (Denham et al., 2003; Wilson, Fernandes-Richards, Aarskog, Osborn, & Capetillo, 2007). The process of initiating, building, and maintaining social relationships involves a merging of social and emotional competencies. Consider the following skills:

- *Greeting ability:* Greeting a friend involves more than just saying hello. Our facial expressions, body language, and tone of voice all communicate a certain attitude toward the person we are greeting and send a message about whether we are happy to see that person.

- *Timing and staging:* When a friend tells you that her beloved pet has just died, it probably is not an appropriate time to tell a joke or ask for fashion advice. Friends need to be able to read emotional contexts and make good judgments about how to respond.

Emotional intelligence in relationships is also related to bullying (Mayer et al., 2004). Research gathered via observations, peer reports, and child self-reports suggests that bullying may be the result of

Making Connections. Building teacher-student relationships can begin with something as simple as greeting students each day as they arrive for class.

young children learning to regulate their emotions and behavior in response to peer conflict (Snyder et al., 2003). It is not just the potential bully who may need support in emotional regulation. While victimization does appear to be largely situational for young children—dependent on what the child is doing, and where and with whom the child is playing—evidence suggests that children who respond to aggression by peers in ways that diminish the effects of that aggression ultimately discourage harassment, which becomes increasingly intermittent (Snyder et al., 2003). That is, children who display "victim tendencies"—identified by researchers as the manifestation of social disengagement and recognizable anxiety—tend to experience more harassment for longer periods than children who do not (Snyder et al., 2003). Over time, some children learn how to manage their emotional response to harassment, and consequently manipulate the emotional responses of others. The concept of emotional intelligence provides one way to understand bullying behavior.

If you were asked in a job interview to describe five ways you would promote emotional intelligence within your classroom, how would you respond? (Hint: Guideline 4.1 provides numerous examples of how to foster emotional intelligence. Which ones seem most relevant to you?)

Emotions in the Classroom

Emotions can affect *how* students learn as well as *what* students learn. The emotions students bring to a classroom can potentially help or hinder their performance. Students learn and perform more successfully when they feel secure, happy, and excited about the subject matter (Boekaerts, 1995). Negative emotions, in contrast, can hamper performance on cognitive tasks (Izard, 2001). Students whose minds are cluttered with distracting thoughts and emotions may find it more difficult to focus their limited attentional resources on learning tasks within the classroom (Ellis, 2001; Hertel, 1994). Some distractions, such as a fight with a friend on the school bus, may be temporary. Others, such as dealing with their parents' divorce, may require more intensive intervention to provide students with the necessary coping skills and enable them to keep their intellectual resources focused on learning. In these situations, students may need extra prompts to help them stay on-task, or one-on-one time with a teacher or counselor to help them talk through their feelings or resolve a problem.

Classroom factors also affect students' emotional well-being. Students can become upset by an event such as a failed test or a negative comment from a peer and may react in a way that impedes further learning. Their reactions can unfold in different ways depending on how the student perceives the problem (Weiner, 1994) or whether the situation triggers emotional memories (LeDoux, 2000). If two students watch the same movie in class about a skyscraper collapsing, one might say that the film is entertaining, while the other finds it quite disturbing. Knowing that the latter student lost a close family member in the 2001 terrorist attacks on the World Trade Center may help the teacher understand the differences in how the students process and react to the same movie.

Can you recall a classroom experience from your student days that triggered an emotional response? How did that response influence your attentiveness to the lesson?

APPLICATIONS: EMOTIONALLY INTELLIGENT TEACHING

Psychologist Robert Sternberg (1996b) argues that traditional schooling neglects practical skills that prepare individuals to deal with real-life problems and challenges. Ideally, the skill sets students learn should prepare them to face social and emotional challenges that arise over the course of their lives. Several studies conducted by Rutgers psychologist Maurice Elias and his colleagues have emphasized the need for social and emotional learning in public education across the grade levels (Elias et al., 1997; Elias & Weissberg, 2000). The best approach may be to focus on a broad array of skills acquired through personal experience, modeling, and observation (Lopes & Salovey, 2004). Some skills cannot be learned

GUIDELINES 4.1   Ways Teachers Can Help Foster Emotional Intelligence

Dimensions	Ways teachers can help foster emotional intelligence in students
Emotional Understanding	■ Model the use of self-reflective language in the classroom (for example, "I felt embarrassed when . . .") ■ Create opportunities to talk about positive and negative feelings (for example, classroom meetings, journal exercises, creative writing) ■ Guide students in learning to identify complex emotions (for example, through role playing, storytelling, case studies, discussing emotional themes in novels, and so on) ■ Give students the language to express how they are feeling (for example, the use of "I" statements such as "I feel frustrated when . . ." rather than blaming statements)
Responding to the Emotions of Others	■ Help students recognize the emotions that others are feeling ■ Develop perspective-taking skills so that students can better understand what kind of support the other person may need ■ Acknowledge and positively encourage instances of empathetic responding ■ Model ways to be caring and considerate of others' feelings
Emotional Regulation	■ Show students how to maintain a sense of emotional balance so that destructive emotions do not flare out of control in the first place. This approach involves teaching students to monitor and identify their own positive and negative feelings, accepting emotions as a normal part of human experience, practicing perspective-taking skills, and developing patience. Managing emotions requires learning to redirect disruptive impulses and to "shake off" negative moods ■ Use modeling, direct instruction, or coaching to help students acknowledge and fully experience emotions when they arise, while encouraging students to refrain from acting out in a way that adversely affects others. This step requires teaching students strategies to stop, collect their thoughts, and consider multiple alternative responses to the emotional situation ■ Help students to view an emotional disruption as a learning experience and help them identify ways to handle the situation more effectively in the future ■ Provide training in conflict resolution skills
Self-Motivation	■ Provide students with specific, concrete feedback so that they can learn from their mistakes ■ Identify strengths on which students can build ■ Encourage students to keep trying their best ■ Share your own enthusiasm for a topic with students ■ Model perseverance in the face of challenges ■ Develop meaningful lessons that connect with students' lives ■ Provide opportunities for students to be successful
Emotions in Relationships	■ Foster a set of attitudes and skills that strengthen student-student relationships, including (1) effective communication skills, (2) emotional self-control and appropriate expression, (3) empathy and perspective taking, (4) optimism and sense of humor, and (5) nonviolent conflict-resolution and problem-solving skills ■ Provide students with opportunities to get to know one another better and to practice many of the skills through well-chosen classroom experiences ■ Select activities that involve cooperation and collaboration rather than competition ■ Create rituals that involve all members of the class, such as class meetings

through direct instruction alone. Children need opportunities to practice and refine these social and emotional skills in the classroom.

What Is Social-Emotional Learning (SEL)?

The concept of **social-emotional learning (SEL)** emerged in a systematic way with the publication of *Promoting Social and Emotional Learning: Guidelines for Educators* (Elias et al., 1997). The term reflects a strong recognition of the role of both social and emotional factors in successful academic learning (Elias, 2004). SEL refers to the competencies students need to acquire in order to manage their emotions, develop caring for others, make responsible decisions, establish positive relationships, and handle challenging situations effectively (Ji & Weissberg, 2010). Three essential SEL principles have been articulated to guide classroom interventions (National Center for Innovation and Education, 1999):

1. Caring relationships are the foundation of all lasting learning.

2. Emotions affect how and what we learn.

3. Goal setting and problem solving provide focus, direction, and energy for learning.

Teacher-student and student-student relationships: See page 338.

These principles emphasize the importance of the learning environment and the teacher's role in establishing caring relationships with students and helping students develop the skills needed to develop positive relationships with others.

The social-emotional challenges facing students vary, depending on developmental level and environmental context (Payton et al., 2008). Teachers may not be able to eliminate all sources of frustration, anxiety, or conflict in the classroom, but they can take steps to minimize these negative emotions and provide students with the skills necessary to manage difficult emotions when they arise. Important attitudes and skills to foster include the following (Payton et al., 2008):

- effective communication skills (listening and communicating accurately and clearly)
- emotional self-control and appropriate expression
- empathy and perspective taking
- optimism and a sense of humor
- nonviolent conflict resolution and problem-solving skills
- respect for others and oneself and an appreciation of differences

In the United States, many districts and even entire states currently make SEL a curriculum requirement. In Illinois, for instance, specific learning standards in SEL abilities have been established for every grade from kindergarten through the last year of high school (Goleman, 2006). SEL skills may be taught, modeled, and practiced so that children and adolescents use them as part of their behavior set in dealing with daily life challenges. Some programs teach pupils to apply SEL skills to prevent risky behaviors (for example, substance abuse, violence, and bullying) or to contribute positively to their class, school, or community (for example, service learning) (Durlak & Weissberg, 2010; Katulak, Brackett, & Weissberg, 2009). SEL initiatives in classrooms vary widely, but the best-designed programs share two important features:

Emotional Triggers. Incidents in the classroom can trigger emotional memories that influence how students process information. Viewing a film clip in history class about the collapse of the World Trade Center twin towers on 9-11 might be especially disturbing for a student who lost a family member in the terrorist attacks.

1. They match social-emotional learning (SEL) skills to particular intervention goals. For example, if violence prevention is a top priority, a teacher might prioritize conflict resolution skills.

2. They focus attention on teaching skills that can be generalized across multiple settings—for example, the ability to delay gratification and persist in the face of difficulties.

TABLE 4.2	Planning Lessons that Integrate Emotional Intelligence	
Subject	**Lesson objective**	**Emotional intelligence benefits**
Reading	Cause and effect	The teacher reads various passages from well-known stories. Students determine the cause and effect. The class discusses how the characters could have solved their problems in more appropriate ways.
Writing	Personal narrative	During an essay writing exercise, students have the opportunity to share a time in their lives when they reacted appropriately in a bad situation.
Social studies	Understanding the Confederate point of view in the Civil War	In cooperative groups, students discuss the feelings and emotions of the Confederate soldiers.
Health	Smoking cessation	Students engage in a class discussion in which they are given the chance to discuss the loss of a loved one because of conditions resulting from tobacco use.

Reprinted from Doty, G. (2001). *Fostering emotional intelligence in K-8 students* (p. 14). Thousand Oaks, CA: Corwin Press, Inc.

As teachers, we may be skeptical about our ability to help students develop emotional competencies. With all of the academic content we are expected to teach, how can we take on the extra tasks required by an SEL curriculum? To be most productive, an effective SEL program must make sense to teachers, be acceptable to pupils, and fit the existing curriculum. Effective social and emotional regulation programs generally require about one lesson length of teaching time a week (Little & Hopkins, 2010). The integration of SEL content into the curriculum need not be burdensome. Table 4.2 shows how social-emotional skills can be integrated into academic content without compromising academic instruction. SEL skills can be taught by taking advantage of impromptu teachable moments (reflecting and coaching), modeling, and building opportunities for skill development into the curriculum.

Benefits of SEL Programs

The implementation of classroom, school-level, or district-level programs targeted at developing social and emotional competence is a relatively new undertaking. The effectiveness of SEL programs has not been conclusively determined, because rigorous evaluations of their results over time are relatively limited (Lopes & Salovey, 2004). The development of an evidence-based program must be guided by good science and then evaluated to establish whether the predicted effects on children's health and development actually occur. Among the dozens of SEL programs in use today, around 20 have passed this first test (Little & Hopkins, 2010; Durlak & Dupre, 2010). Based on evidence from some of the best-designed programs, the outcomes are very encouraging (Durlak & Weissberg, 2010; Hawkins et al., 1999; Kusche & Greenberg, 2001; Weissberg & Greenberg, 1998). The PATHS curriculum, one of the oldest and most widely adopted SEL programs, was developed in the United States and is a school-based, universal prevention program. It has been evaluated in mainstream education, as well as with pupils who have specific needs (including hearing impaired, special educational needs, and gifted). Successful implementations of the original PATHS program have been carried out in 22 countries. The rigorous evaluations demonstrate significant improvements in self-control, understanding and recognition of emotions, coping skills, and conflict resolution strategies (Eacott & Frydenberg, 2009; Magee & Perkins, 2010; Payton et al., 2008). Other benefits of SEL programs include the following:

- up to 50% of children showing improved achievement scores
- up to 38% of students improving their grade-point average
- a drop in incidents of misbehavior by an average of 28%, in suspensions by 44%, and in other disciplinary actions by 27%, with 63% of students demonstrating significantly more positive behavior
- a rise in attendance rates

(Conduct Problems Prevention Research Group, 2010; Durlak & Weissberg, 2005; Goleman, 2006)

One-on-One Time. Sometimes students need to meet with a teacher or counselor to talk through their feelings or resolve a problem.

Schools that effectively implement evidence-based SEL programs do achieve successful outcomes. However, implementing SEL programs is challenging for many teachers. Reasons for this include lack of support from school leadership, limited professional development for staff, failure to adopt evidence-based programming, and an inability to integrate SEL into existing school operations (Payton et al., 2008). Furthermore, in today's educational climate, there is a tendency to marginalize the teaching of non-tested subjects and increase the time required for exam preparation. Funds, staff time, teaching time, and professional development activity are channeled towards teaching the specific content and skills that are *tested*. "Educating the whole child"— that is, attending to children's social, emotional, ethical, aesthetic, and physical development as well as their academic development—has become a secondary if not tertiary consideration (Schaps, 2007, 2010). For SEL programs to affect school culture and be internalized by pupils, it is essential that they become part of the fabric of school life rather than an isolated lesson implemented a couple of times a week by a few teachers (Osher et al., 2008).

Understandably, educators need models and strategies to guide their efforts to implement SEL in an efficient, effective way. The Collaborative for Academic, Social, and Emotional Learning (CASEL) has been a leader in the field for the past 20 years and maintains a Web site (www.casel.org) to support SEL initiatives. The site provides empirical research (via searchable database), program descriptions, implementation guides, assessment tools, and a variety of other ongoing professional development resources.

A final consideration with respect to SEL is that teaching SEL involves a process of behavior change in the teacher as well as the student (Hamre & Pianta, 2007; Zins et al., 2007). Teachers must cultivate their own levels of emotional intelligence in order to model adaptive social-emotional skills and to create an emotionally supportive learning environment (Jennings & Greenberg, 2009). Teachers' emotional support directly provides students with experiences that foster motivational and learning-related processes important to academic functioning (Crosnoe, Johnson, & Elder, 2004; Greenberg et al., 2003; Gregory & Weinstein, 2004; Zins, Bloodworth, Weissberg, & Walberg, 2004). Theories of motivation suggest that students who experience sensitive, responsive, and positive interactions with teachers perceive them as more supportive and are more motivated within the academic contexts of schooling (Fredriksen & Rhodes, 2004; Wentzel, 2002). For children at risk of problems in school, a supportive relationship with a school-based mentor functions as an important resilience mechanism (Noam & Herman, 2002; Noam, Warner, & Van Dyken, 2001).

How would you respond to a parent who claimed that teachers who promote social-emotional skills are wasting valuable learning time? Do you think that SEL interventions are a worthwhile undertaking? Why or why not?

Summary

Describe the general influences of temperament, parenting practices, gender, and culture on children's emotional development. Temperament refers to genetically based individual differences in emotions, activity, and self-control that determine our patterns of response to environmental stimuli and events. Socialization practices within the family shape the way patterns of emotional expressiveness develop in children. Parents are more likely to attempt to regulate boys' emotions, particularly sadness and pain, whereas girls are encouraged to express emotions, with the exception of anger. Cultural differences are also seen in emotional expressiveness. Some cultures rarely display negative emotions but more often display emotions of sympathy, respect, and shame that reflect their social connection and interdependence.

Identify the five dimensions of emotional intelligence outlined in Goleman's model, and discuss at least one way teachers can facilitate the development of each dimension. Emotional intelligence can be described in terms of five major dimensions: (1) emotional understanding, (2) responding to others' emotions, (3) emotional regulation, (4) self-motivation, and (5) emotions in relationships. Approaches for developing these dimensions include, but are not limited to, (1) giving students the language to express how they are feeling, (2) guiding students in learning to identify complex emotions, (3) teaching students how to calm themselves down and think through nonviolent solutions to problems, (4) providing conflict resolution training, (5) selecting activities that involve cooperation and collaboration rather than competition, and (6) creating rituals that involve all members of the class, such as class meetings.

Describe two primary ways in which emotions can influence learning. Emotions can affect *how* students learn as well as *what* students learn. Students perform more successfully when they feel secure, happy, and excited about the subject matter, and they perform more poorly when they are experiencing negative emotions such as anger or depression. Students' perceptions of classroom events (for example, receiving a low grade on a test) can cause them to react in a way that impedes further learning or one that motivates them to try harder. Aspects of classrooms situations can trigger strong emotional memories that influence the ways students attend to, process, and react to information.

Define social-emotional learning and discuss the three essential principles that underlie SEL interventions. The term "social-emotional learning" (SEL) was developed to recognize the role of both social and emotional factors in successful academic learning. Three essential SEL principles guide interventions: (1) caring relationships are the foundation of all lasting learning; (2) emotions affect how and what we learn; and (3) goal setting and problem solving provide focus, direction, and energy for learning. Well-designed SEL programs match social-emotional learning (SEL) skills to particular intervention goals and focus attention on teaching skills that can be generalized across multiple settings.

Key Concepts

display rules   63

emotional expressiveness   62

emotional intelligence (EI)   63

emotional regulation   66

emotional understanding   64

emotions   62

empathy   66

paralinguistic cues   65

self-awareness   64

self-motivation   67

social-emotional learning (SEL)   70

social referencing   67

temperament   62

Video Applications

www.mhhe.com/bohlin2e

Video 1: Promoting Emotional Intelligence through Community (2½ *minutes*)
In this video clip, a 4/5multiage teacher uses a community circle (class meeting) to foster communication skills, social-emotional skills, and problem solving.

Video 2: Promoting Emotional Intelligence Through Life Skills Training (2½ *minutes*)
In this video clip, a first-grade teacher discusses the value of teaching life skills in her classroom and a group of fifth-grade students produce an elementary school news segment (BobCat TV) in which life skills are taught.

Case Studies
Reflect and Evaluate

DIVERSITY   EARLY CHILDHOOD: **"Cry Baby"**

These questions refer to the case study on page 22.

1. Erica begins to cry when Tyler yells at her. What if Erica had been a boy? Would you expect a boy in this situation to react by crying? Why or why not?

2. Tyler and Tanner are both very quick to express their anger when the block tower gets knocked over. Based on what you read about cultural differences in emotional expressiveness, how might their reactions have been different if they had been raised in an Asian culture rather than an American culture?

3. When Mr. Abbott talks with the boys about the falling tower incident, he asks, "How do you think she [Erica] feels when you make fun of her like that?" At what age are children developmentally capable of understanding and interpreting the feelings of others? What cues do they use to identify how others are feeling?

4. At the beginning of the case study, Joe is described as a very considerate child, always willing to help others. Is empathy a trait a person is born with, or is it learned? Support your answer with evidence from the module.

5. Annie and Zada are both extroverted girls whom Eddy describes as "natural leaders." According to temperament research, do these characteristics have a genetic basis? What kind of temperaments might you expect Annie and Zada to have 10 years from now?

6. Based on what you read about emotional intelligence, how might these teachers include social-emotional learning in their classroom?

DIVERSITY   ELEMENTARY SCHOOL: **"Team"**

These questions refer to the case study on page 24.

1. Patricia's parents have encouraged her to stand up for herself in interactions with Kashi. Is it typical for parents to encourage their daughters to express their feelings openly?

2. Ms. Barone tells the boys they should be ashamed of themselves for the way they are speaking to each other. When do complex emotions such as shame first develop? How do complex emotions such as shame, guilt, and pride differ from basic emotions such as anger and fear?

3. If Ms. Barone wants Bill and Zach to use conflict resolution skills to resolve their problem, what steps should she suggest they take? How might Patricia and Kashi use conflict resolution skills to resolve the tension between them?

4. In terms of emotional regulation, Bill and Zach are engaging in hot responses. How would their actions be different if they were resorting to cool responses instead?

5. How might Ms. Barone use the incidents in her classroom as teachable moments to strengthen her students' SEL (social-emotional learning) skills?

DIVERSITY   MIDDLE SCHOOL: **"Basketball Star"**

These questions refer to the case study on page 26.

1. Mark is emotionally reactive and has difficulty with self-regulation. According to the research on emotional self-regulation, what negative outcomes are students such as Mark likely to face?

2. Darla doesn't seem to get angry when others say bad things about her, yet Mark gets angry quite easily. What might account for the difference in their levels of anger management?

3. Darla and Mark are being raised by their fathers. How might being raised by a male parent affect a child's emotional development differently from being raised by a female parent?

4. Darla seems to take pride in her talent as a basketball player. What are the developmental precursors to feelings of pride?

5. What actions has Coach Martin taken to provide an emotionally supportive coaching environment? What additional steps could he take?

HIGH SCHOOL: "Steal, Cheat, and Fight"

These questions refer to the case study on page 28.

1. Is Mr. Ruestman's refusal to include social skills training during class justified? What arguments could be used to overcome Mr. Ruestman's reluctance to provide SEL skills training during his class time?

2. The e-mail comments submitted by Ms. Baxter and Mr. Ruestman imply an either-or situation: the idea that teachers must address social-emotional issues *or* academics but not both. What is the relationship between socioemotional development and academic achievement?

3. The high school's parent-teacher association has asked the school board to implement a school uniform policy to resolve behavioral problems such as fighting and cheating. They argue that a strict dress code will reduce fighting by minimizing competition among students regarding clothes and other status symbols and will help students focus on academic success (minimizing cheating). Based on the research evidence in the module regarding social-emotional learning (SEL), provide a rationale for implementing an SEL program instead of requiring uniforms.

4. Mr. Smith complains that he wasted class time to break up a verbal argument between two girls. How could the situation have been different if he had modeled conflict resolution skills rather than just breaking up the fight?

5. Ms. Baxter complains that her students don't apply themselves. How does her comment relate to self-motivation as a form of emotional intelligence? What could she do to try to increase her students' self-motivation in the classroom?

6. Mr. Cargill describes a situation in which Jimmy lost his temper and hit Bob. Based on what you read about managing destructive emotions, how could Mr. Cargill have used this conflict as a teachable moment?

MODULE 5

Moral Development

Outline	Learning Goals

Cognitive-Developmental Moral Reasoning

- Piaget's Theory
- Kohlberg's Theory
- Gilligan's Criticism

1. Explain how thinking or reasoning about moral issues becomes more sophisticated over time, and identify any gender differences in moral reasoning.

Prosocial Behavior

- Eisenberg's Theory
- Perspective Taking
- Empathy

2. Describe the importance of perspective taking and empathy to prosocial behavior, and identify any gender differences that exist in prosocial behaviors.

Aggressive Behavior

- Social-Cognitive Domains
- Social-Information Processing

3. Describe the cognitive deficits that may explain why some individuals are more likely than other individuals to use aggression.

Applications: Advancing Moral Development

- Family Context
- Peer Context
- School Context

4. Explain how families, peers, and schools contribute to the moral development of children and adolescents.

Summary
Key Concepts
Video Applications
Case Studies: Reflect and Evaluate

COGNITIVE-DEVELOPMENTAL MORAL REASONING

Do you think lying is wrong? We have all told "white lies," perhaps to spare people's feelings or shelter them from bad news. But how do we distinguish between a harmless fib and a more serious deception? When we think about such moral issues, a process called **moral reasoning,** we are seeking rationales for determining right and wrong.

As you already know, people might *think* about what is right and wrong, but they don't always *behave* consistently with those thoughts. However, individuals must be able to distinguish right from wrong before they can behave in appropriate ways. Hence, theories on moral reasoning focus on the thought processes individuals use to determine what is right or wrong, not on the moral (or immoral) behaviors individuals may exhibit. Before we can discuss how an understanding of moral development can serve teachers in the classroom, we need to summarize the prominent moral development theories.

Piaget's Theory

Developmental psychologist Jean Piaget is best known in the fields of education and psychology for his theory of cognitive development. In one of his early writings, *The Moral Judgment of the Child* (1932), he proposed a two-step process of cognitive moral development. According to Piaget, in the first stage of cognitive moral development, labeled **moral realism,** children believe that right and wrong are determined by the consequences of behavior as given by adult authority figures. Rules are absolute and are not meant to be broken or bent under any circumstances. At this stage, intentions are not important. As they develop more advanced thinking skills, children move into the stage of **morality of cooperation,** or autonomy, and understand that in certain situations or under particular circumstances rules can be bent. In other words, children begin to see the complexities of right and wrong, for example, understanding that lying may be necessary to spare someone's feelings or that killing someone may be acceptable in war or self-defense.

Piaget's theory of cognitive development: See page 119.

Kohlberg's Theory

Lawerence Kohlberg, one of Piaget's students, believed that moral reasoning was much more complex than the two-stage process proposed by Piaget. Kohlberg (1963, 1981) developed his own theory of moral reasoning, framing it in three levels, each of which encompasses two stages, as summarized in Table 5.1.

The **preconventional level** is defined by an egocentric, self-interested view of right and wrong, and disregards the conventions or standards of society. **Egocentrism** is a focus on the self with little consideration for other people or their perspectives. Children in the first stage of this level, *punishment/obedience*, focus on the consequences of their behavior, similar to Piaget's moral realism. For example, "Cheating is wrong because I might get caught and fail the course." In the second stage, *naive hedonistic* or *personal reward*, children focus on whether there will be a reward for their behavior: "What's in it for me?" Here individuals are concerned with the quid pro quo of behavior, a more or less equal exchange also called manipulative

TABLE 5.1   Kohlberg's Theory of Moral Reasoning

Level	Stage	Description
Preconventional	Punishment/obedience	■ Focus on the consequences of behavior
	Naive hedonistic	■ Focus on equal exchange, manipulative reciprocity
Conventional	Interpersonal authority	■ Focus on conforming to rules of parents and other family members
	Social authority	■ Focus on conforming to laws and norms of society
Postconventional	Morality of social contract	■ Focus on personal decisions to determine when and how rules should be bent
	Morality of individual principles	■ Focus on what will most benefit society as a whole or the greater good

reciprocity. For example, "If you are nice to me, then I will be nice to you." An individual also may justify misbehavior by invoking manipulative reciprocity. For example, "Cheating is okay because the teacher's tests are unfair." Children need to be exposed to people and situations that introduce new ideas, outside their own perspectives, in order to advance beyond the preconventional level (Shaffer, 2000).

At the **conventional level,** the individual focuses on external authorities, such as the conventions and standards of society, in determining right and wrong. Because of their less egocentric focus and more advanced thinking skills, children at the conventional level are capable of judging the intentions of actions—for example, "He didn't mean to trip me." In the third stage, *interpersonal authority* has the highest priority, meaning that children want to hold the same beliefs as their parents and other family members. Therefore, they will conform to rules to gain the approval of authority figures and avoid disapproval—for example, "Cheating is wrong because my mother says you are only cheating yourself and should do your own work." The next stage of conventional reasoning, *social authority,* focuses on social systems in determining laws and norms of behavior. Here an individual may claim that cheating is wrong because it is against school policy.

The **postconventional level** moves beyond simple consequences and away from external authorities to an internal authority, as the individual establishes personal convictions about what is right and wrong. Again, advances in cognitive development allow individuals to move into the postconventional level of reasoning such that individuals who attend college or have more years of formal education show more complex reasoning than individuals who lack those educational experiences (Speicher, 1994). *Morality of social contract,* the fifth stage, includes personal decisions about when, why, and how rules should be bent or under which circumstances actions that typically are considered misbehaviors may actually be appropriate. For example, cheating is okay only if the task is unimportant (for example, playing a card game with friends) or when it benefits someone else (for example, cheating to let a younger child win in order to boost his or her confidence). In the sixth stage of moral reasoning, *morality of individual principles,* individuals focus on the system of morality that will most benefit society, or the greater good. For example, stealing should never be tolerated because societal chaos and disruption will follow.

Kohlberg measured an individual's level of moral reasoning by presenting moral dilemmas and rating responses according to the stages. Moral dilemmas have no right or wrong answer, so Kohlberg was interested not in the individual's choice to do or not do something but rather in a person's stage of moral development as determined by his or her rationale or reasoning for the choice.

The classic dilemma used by Kohlberg to measure moral reasoning follows. Read the dilemma and think about whether you would make the same choice as Heinz, the character in the story. More important, explain why you would or would not make that choice.

> *In Europe, a woman was near death from a rare form of cancer. There was one drug that the doctors thought might save her, a form of radium that a druggist in the same town had recently discovered. The druggist was charging $2,000, ten times what the drug cost him to make. The sick woman's husband, Heinz, went to everyone he knew to borrow the money, but he could only get together about half of what the drug cost. He told the druggist that his wife was dying and asked him to sell it cheaper or let him pay later. But the druggist said no. So Heinz got desperate and broke into the man's store to steal the drug for his wife. (Kohlberg, 1984, p. 186)*

Kohlberg believed that his theory of moral reasoning was universal across all cultures, but he was convinced that not all adults function at the highest levels of reasoning (Carpendale, 2000). While adults have been found to use a mix of moral reasoning strategies, children appear to progress developmentally from preconventional to postconventional thinking, as Kohlberg hypothesized (Colby, Kohlberg, Gibbs, & Lieberman, 1983; Rest, Thomas, & Edwards, 1997; Walker, de Vries, & Trevethan, 1987). For example, high school students are likely to provide responses to moral dilemmas consistent with the interpersonal authority stage (conventional level), whereas college students provide responses consistent with the postconventional social contract stage (Boom, Brugman, & van der Heijden, 2001). Support for Kohlberg's hypothesized order of cognitive-developmental moral reasoning has been found in Israel and Turkey, suggesting that, as he proposed, the theory applies universally across cultures (Colby & Kohlberg, 1987).

DIVERSITY

Gilligan's Criticism

DIVERSITY Carol Gilligan has criticized several developmental theories for their lack of attention to women and exclusion of a feminine perspective. Most notably, Gilligan has criticized Kohlberg's theory of moral

HAZING

Soliciting, encouraging, aiding, or engaging in hazing is prohibited. Hazing means any intentional, knowing, or reckless act directed against a student for the purpose of being initiated into, affiliated with, holding office in, or maintaining membership in any organization, club, or athletic team whose members are or include other students. Students engaging in hazing will be subject to one or more of the following disciplinary actions:

1. Detention assignment.
2. Removal from the extra-curricular activities.
3. Conference with students and parents.
4. In-school suspension.
5. Referral to appropriate law enforcement agency.
6. If serious enough, possible recommendation for expulsion.

BULLYING/HARASSMENT

Bullying is defined, but not limited to: taunting, insults, teasing, aggression, exclusion, humiliation, alienation, harassment, intimidation, or any behavior repeated with the intent of hurting someone physically or emotionally.

CHEATING

Cheating is the most serious of academic crimes and an inarguable deceitful act which a school cannot afford to foster. Cheating will be defined as a student's intentional presentation of academic work which is not his/her own. Cheating will be constituted any time a student submits work which (1) has been fraudulently borrowed from another individual, including but not limited to current students and graduates; or (2) has been fraudulently borrowed from a published author. Furthermore, any student who knowingly lends his/her work to another in a circumstance where cheating exists will be considered an aide to cheating.

The consequences for those who cheat or are aides to cheating are as follows:

1. Resubmission of work in question.
2. No credit received for the work submitted, regardless of length and magnitude.
3. A semester's failing grade for the course.

Conventional Reasoning. Students at this stage may consider some behaviors wrong or immoral because the behaviors are against school policy as outlined in the student handbook.

reasoning for focusing on justice as the overarching theme in determining the level of moral reasoning. Gilligan (1977) suggests that men, who typically are more focused on independence and individuality, will have a **justice orientation** that focuses on the rights of individuals. Women, however, who typically are more focused on interpersonal relationships, will have a **caring orientation** that focuses on responding to others' needs in intimate relationships. Gilligan suggested that the moral dilemmas presented to measure an individual's level of moral reasoning needed to be real-life situations rather than the hypothetical situations presented by Kohlberg (Walker, 2006).

Early research using Kohlberg's methodology was conducted only with men, leading Gilligan to criticize the sample on which the theory was based. In addition, early studies using samples of women suggested that women's responses to the moral dilemmas were more likely to be scored in the third stage, interpersonal authority, while men's responses were scored more often in the fourth or fifth stage of moral reasoning (Walker, 2006). However, Kohlberg's scoring system for the moral dilemmas was revised following the first few empirical studies due to a number of problems. Lawrence Walker (2006) reviewed the literature on gender differences in moral reasoning and found that, overall, men and women do not differ in their moral reasoning. Moreover, no evidence suggests that two separate orientations—justice versus caring—exist. Rather, most people use a combination of justice and caring to determine what is right and wrong in a given situation (Jorgensen, 2006). Although Gilligan's basic premise that men and women have different moral orientations has not been supported, her criticism did spark interest in moral development, issues of measurement in moral development, and the roles of caring and empathy in moral reasoning.

PROSOCIAL BEHAVIOR

Separate from the cognitive-developmental perspectives of Piaget and Kohlberg, other researchers have studied the foundations of individual compassion and self-sacrifice. Why do people voluntarily care for and comfort one another? Why do they cooperate and share with one another? Psychologists call this human tendency **prosocial behavior,** and it encompasses those voluntary actions that are intended to benefit others through helping or sharing (Eisenberg, Spinrad, & Sadovsky, 2006).

Eisenberg's Theory

Nancy Eisenberg's theory of prosocial moral reasoning is different from the cognitive-developmental perspectives of Piaget and Kohlberg due to its focus on *positive justice* (Lapsley, 2006). In essence, positive justice focuses on why we do the right thing, such as helping others or sharing. Eisenberg (1986) developed levels of prosocial reasoning based on her longitudinal research. Although Eisenberg's levels refer to prosocial reasoning (thinking), many of the outcomes also include actions (behavior). She identified five levels of prosocial thinking:

- *Level 1—hedonistic or self-focused orientation:* Individuals focus on the consequence to the self or self-interest as a motive for prosocial behavior. "I will share my crayons because the teacher will be happy and say something nice to me."

- *Level 2—needs orientation:* Individuals focus on the needs of others even when those needs conflict with one's self-interest. "I will share my crayons with Jenny because she can't find hers today."

- *Level 3—approval/interpersonal orientation:* Individuals engage in prosocial behavior based on the stereotypical beliefs about a person, helping a person considered to be "a good person" and not helping a person considered to be "a bad person," in order to gain approval from or acceptance by others. "I will share my crayons with Billy because he is a nice person, but I won't share with Tommy because he is always mean to people."

- *Level 4—self-reflective empathetic orientation:* To determine whether their actions will result in positive feelings or feelings of guilt, individuals use empathy and **perspective taking,** the ability to understand another person's situation or psychological state, such as their thoughts or feelings (Damon, 1988). "I will share my lecture notes with Lisa, who missed class due to her grandfather's funeral, because I feel bad for her and I would want someone to help me."

- *Level 5—internalized orientation:* Individuals behave in prosocial ways due to their personal values rather than external authority or expectations. "Because I believe more fortunate people should help others, I will give some of my holiday bonus to the local charity that provides gifts for underprivileged children."

DIVERSITY   Prosocial reasoning and behavior increase throughout childhood and adolescence, with girls being more likely than boys to use prosocial behaviors, particularly in relationships (Eisenberg & Fabes, 1998; Eisenberg et al., 2009). Perspective taking and empathy are two components that help explain why older children and girls are more likely to exhibit higher levels of prosocial reasoning and behavior.

Prosocial Behaviors. Even preschool-age children can focus on others' needs by sharing.

Perspective Taking

Perspective taking is vital to the development of prosocial moral reasoning, which Kohlberg also considered important for cognitive-developmental moral reasoning. Individuals capable of perspective taking can appreciate that different people facing the same event may think or feel differently due to their unique backgrounds and qualities. For example, when two middle school students lose a homework assignment, their teacher understands that the incident will affect each child differently based on their commitment to education and the consequences they face at home for failure. Preschool children, however, are not yet able to grasp the perspectives of others, because children develop that ability gradually during their school years. Robert Selman (1971a) proposed five stages of perspective-taking development from early childhood through adolescence and beyond:

- *Stage 0—egocentric viewpoint:* Preschool-age children (ages 3 to 6) understand that other individuals have thoughts and feelings but confuse their own emotions with those of others or have difficulty understanding the causes of others' feelings.

- *Stage 1—social-informational role taking:* Early elementary children (ages 6 to 8) understand that others have thoughts and feelings that may be different from their own but do not yet understand how different perspectives are related; hence, children are likely to focus on one perspective only. "I know she is sad, but I am happy I got the bigger piece of cake."

- *Stage 2—self-reflective role taking:* Older elementary children (ages 8 to 10) can understand the relationship between self and others' perspectives, enabling them to speculate on how another will feel or what another will think prior to the circumstances. "Johnny will be mad if I cut in line."

- *Stage 3—mutual role taking:* Early adolescents (ages 10 to 12) are also able to take the perspective of a third party in order to understand how two individuals influence each other in a mutual, simultaneous manner. "I can understand why both Jenny and Jill want first prize at the science fair and why each thinks the other's project is not as good as her own."

- *Stage 4—social and conventional system role taking:* By middle adolescence (ages 12 to 15) and beyond, individuals are capable of understanding social conventions that are relevant to everyone rather than to only one individual: "I can understand that you shouldn't cheat even if the teacher's tests are too hard."

Selman (1971b) found that role-taking ability was related to Kohlberg's moral reasoning stages, with low role-taking ability related to preconventional reasoning and higher role-taking ability related to conventional reasoning. While perspective-taking abilities help individuals develop prosocial reasoning, those abilities do not necessarily lead to prosocial behavior. Some individuals may have the ability to take perspective but may not be motivated to consider the other person's perspective (Gehlbach, 2004). Others may use their perspective-taking abilities to their own advantage, understanding exactly what will anger or sadden another person and using that understanding to manipulate or con others (Damon, 1988).

Empathy

The development of prosocial behavior also relies on **empathy,** the ability to experience the emotions or feelings of another person, as when an individual feels sad because someone else feels sad (Eisenberg et al., 1987; Eisenberg et al., 2006). In order to experience empathy, an individual must have perspective-taking abilities (Hoffman, 2000), so both of these skills appear to be essential for prosocial moral development. Note that empathy differs from sympathy. *Sympathy* is the emotional response of concern for another person's emotional state. For example, we may express sympathy toward others when their loved one dies, yet we do not experience their grief. Psychologist Martin Hoffman (2000) has suggested that empathy development occurs in three stages early in life:

- *Stage 1—global empathy:* Infants may cry when other infants cry, but they are unable to differentiate between self and other. They will seek comfort for their own distress when they are exposed to another's cry or emotional distress.

- *Stage 2—egocentric empathy:* Toddlers begin to differentiate between self and others and may attempt to comfort others' emotional distress, but they do so from their own egocentric perspective. For example, a child may provide another person, including adults, with their comfort toy or blanket when, in actuality, it provides comfort only to himself or herself.

■ *Stage 3—empathy for another's feelings*: Children as young as age 2 or 3 have an increasing awareness of others' emotions and different perspectives of needs. Hence, children begin to understand that what comforts them may not be what comforts others. With language and cognitive development, older children and adolescents can understand another person's emotions without having any direct experiences with that person (for example, reading about someone).

Research supports Hoffman's stages of empathy development as well as empathy's relationship to prosocial behavior. For example, toddlers respond to both researchers' and mothers' injuries with empathy, and slightly older children will attempt to comfort siblings who are distressed (Eisenberg et al., 2006). Toddlers are even capable of responding with concern when someone is harmed but does not overtly express negative emotions (Vaish, Carpenter, & Tomasello, 2009). Empathy continues to develop throughout adolescence and has been linked to prosocial behavior, with more advanced empathy related to a higher degree of prosocial behavior.

DIVERSITY

Women and girls tend to be more empathetic than men and boys (Eisenberg & Fabes, 1998; Maite, 2009), yet research findings are not conclusive. The methods used to measure empathy may explain the gender differences found in some studies (Eisenberg et al., 2006). Studies that ask individuals to report their own levels of empathy or rely on reports from teachers or parents favor girls slightly. The expectation that girls will be more emotional and caring may bias these reports. Researchers who use behavioral observations to determine empathy have not found gender differences. Hence, girls may be expected to have higher levels of empathy, but in actuality they may have levels similar to those of boys.

Think of some examples that illustrate how a person could have perspective-taking skills but not be empathetic. Is it possible for a person to be empathetic, but not have perspective-taking skills? Why or why not?

AGGRESSIVE BEHAVIOR

Types of aggression:
See page 38.

Although some theories of moral development have focused on the positive, or prosocial, behaviors of individuals, aggression has also been a point of interest among scholars investigating moral development. Aggression typically refers to physical or *overt aggression* in which a person intends to harm another person physically. Yet, *relational aggression* in which a person attempts to harm another person's relationships or social standing can also be examined from a moral perspective. Regardless of the type of aggression used, the question becomes: Why are some individuals more likely to use aggression than others? Possible answers to that question include the following:

■ biological predispositions, such as genetics or hormones that may increase aggression;

■ family influences, such as direct experiences with violence and abuse from parents and siblings;

■ peer influences, such as having friends who are aggressive;

■ cultural differences; and

■ other variables, such as exposure to violent television or video games.

Most often, the factors listed interact to increase the chance that a particular individual will become aggressive. The interaction among these factors can lead to differences in the ways individuals think about aggression. Much of the research on moral development has examined the cognitive deficits that accompany the use of aggression. Psychologist John C. Gibbs (1991) suggests that some individuals have a **sociomoral developmental delay,** or a self-centered, egocentric orientation that is not replaced by the more typical advanced moral development. This sociomoral developmental delay is maintained by two cognitive distortions:

1. *Externalizing blame:* Individuals see themselves as the victim, rather than those whom they have victimized. For example, students may explain their aggressive behavior toward a peer by declaring that the peer has always mistreated them.

2. *Mislabeling or minimizing:* Individuals will escape responsibility for their actions by viewing their behavior as less serious than social conventions might judge. For example, they might declare that an aggressive act was not that bad or that it did not really hurt the other person.

Gibbs suggests that these cognitive distortions are used by individuals to decrease their feelings of **empathy-based guilt,** or the pain and regret felt for causing distress or pain in another person (Hoff-

Aggressive Behaviors. A number of factors can contribute to the development of aggressive behavior, such as exposure to violence in the home, on television, or in video games.

man, 2000). To decrease their feelings of guilt and pain, individuals may rationalize their aggressive behaviors or may believe that others do not experience negative emotions following victimization (Malti, Gasser, & Buchmann, 2009).

Social-Cognitive Domains

A common approach to evaluating aggressive behaviors is based on the social domain model, which examines how cognitions play a role in aggression (Turiel, 1983). Through their interactions with the environment, children and adolescents may consider social situations within three domains:

1. The *moral domain* includes situations and circumstances related to the rights of others as well as the welfare of others.

2. The *conventional domain* focuses on the rules of conduct necessary for social organization.

3. The *personal domain* focuses on situations that affect the individual.

The moral domain is the area of the most serious infractions, and the personal domain encompasses the least. Conventional domain issues fall in the middle. When surveyed, elementary students typically view aggressive behavior as being in the moral domain because it affects human welfare and issues of fairness (Murray-Close, Crick, & Calotti, 2006). Children and adolescents who view aggressive behavior as being in the conventional domain may have a cognitive deficit similar to minimizing (Tisak, Tisak, & Goldstein, 2006).

Social-Information Processing

Another theory used to explain aggressive behaviors in children and adolescents comes from the social-information processing model developed by Kenneth Dodge (Crick & Dodge, 1994). The model suggests that individuals process social information in six steps. Let's walk through those steps in the context of the commonplace event of an individual being bumped into by the school bully.

1. *Encoding cues:* Individuals pay attention to some information in their social environment and dismiss other information. (I noticed a shocked looked on his face when he bumped into me.)

2. *Interpretation of cues:* Individuals determine meaning for those cues and the causes of the behavior of others in the social environment. (His shocked look must mean that he was surprised to see me standing there.)

Social-Information Processing. Aggressive behaviors may occur because an individual interprets social information as intentional rather than accidental, such as bumping into someone.

3. *Clarification of goals:* Individuals determine goals or outcomes for the situation. (I don't want to make him mad.)

4. *Response access:* Individuals attempt to remember past responses to similar situations. (Last time he bumped into me, I just said, "Excuse me.")

5. *Response decision:* Individuals evaluate the past responses and select the most appropriate response based on the expected outcome. (If I don't want trouble, I should just walk away.)

6. *Behavioral enactment:* Individuals behave according to their decision to respond. (I'll walk away.)

Although this model focuses on the cognitive or thought processes of individuals, emotions are considered to be important as well (Palmer, 2005). For example, emotional arousal may be an internal cue encoded in the first step. Similarly, empathy-based guilt may be considered in the response-decision step. However, aggressive children tend to process information differently from nonaggressive children (Tisak, Tisak, & Goldstein, 2006) and may be less attentive to cues—such as not noticing that the person who bumped into them was surprised. A specific difference is found between aggressive and nonaggressive children in the interpretation of cues. Aggressive individuals may have what is called a **hostile attributional bias,** or a tendency to interpret another person's intentions as hostile. For example, an aggressive student might interpret someone's bumping into them in the hallway as *intentional* when in fact the collision was *accidental*. Aggressive children are likely to have this bias (Bradshaw et al., 2009; Crick & Dodge, 1996), leading them to externalize blame for their own aggressive behavior. The cognitive deficits of externalized blame, minimizing or mislabeling the situation, and hostile attributional bias contribute to aggressive children's inability to process social information correctly (Palmer, 2005). A recent study found that these same types of processing deficits are associated with cyber aggression as well (Pornari & Wood, 2010).

Would you expect all individuals who have used aggression in the past to have cognitive deficits? Under what circumstances might someone without a cognitive deficit resort to aggression?

APPLICATIONS: ADVANCING MORAL DEVELOPMENT

We've made a fast and furious survey of the theories of moral development. You may have noticed that some of these theories overlap, despite using different terminology (see Table 5.2 for a developmental comparison of theories). Many aspects of these theories have been studied in the contexts of family, peers, and schools to provide suggestions on how to advance moral development among children and adolescents (Eisenberg et al., 2009).

Family Context

Although parents begin as external authority figures who provide consequences, the norms for behavior become the child's own moral code as they outgrow the need for external consequences (Dunn, 2006; Hoffman, 2000). More specifically, maternal support and responsiveness are related to empathy and prosocial behavior in children. The children of parents who use consistent discipline that includes providing reasons for misbehavior and suggesting appropriate alternatives are more likely to exhibit higher levels of empathy and social responsibility (Bronstein et al., 2007; Eisenberg et al., 2006). In addition, siblings may play an important role in moral development by engaging in imaginative play that includes moral issues (for example, your Barbie stole something from my Barbie, so she has to go to jail) and by modeling empathy for younger siblings (Dunn, 2006; Eisenberg et al., 2006).

TABLE 5.2	Comparison of Moral Development Theories			
Theorist	**Emphasis**	**Infancy to childhood**	**Childhood to adolescence**	**Late adolescence to adulthood**
Piaget	Cognitive	Moral realism	Morality of cooperation	
Kohlberg	Cognitive	Preconventional level	Conventional level	Postconventional level
Eisenberg	Prosocial reasoning	Hedonistic or self-focused orientation Needs orientation	Approval/interpersonal orientation Self-reflective empathetic orientation	Internalized orientation
Selman	Perspective taking	Egocentric viewpoint Social-informational role taking	Self-reflective role taking Mutual role taking	Social and conventional system role taking
Hoffman	Empathy	Global empathy Egocentric empathy	Empathy for another's feelings	
Developmental trends across theories		Focus on the self, with little consideration for others (egocentrism)	Beginning to consider others through perspective of external sources such as parents, society, and stereotypical views of others	Development of personal convictions and concern for society as a whole

In examining the importance of family, psychologists have identified several parenting strategies that may help advance moral development (Berkowitz & Grych, 1998; Berkowitz, Sherblom, Bier, & Battistich, 2006):

Parenting: See page 32.

- *induction,* in which parents explain discipline by verbally providing the consequences of choices as well as asking children to think about others' emotions (empathy);

- *nurturance,* in which parents express warmth and affection toward their child as an indication of their concern for the child's emotional state (perspective taking);

- *demandingness,* in which parents set high standards of behavior for their children and support children in their attempts to meet these standards;

- *modeling,* in which parents "practice what they preach" such that they become examples of moral conduct; and

- *democratic processes,* in which parents include children in decisions, particularly those that require them to hear and appreciate another's perspective.

These parenting strategies can provide a model for teachers to follow in developing instructional strategies that promote moral development. For example, teachers should also ask children to consider others' feelings in order to promote empathy and perspective taking, two qualities essential to prosocial behavior. Also, teachers, like parents, are authority figures who model appropriate behavior and need to practice what they preach regarding moral conduct.

How can parents and teachers balance the need to be demanding and set high standards for behavior with the need to follow a democratic process and allow children to participate in making decisions?

Peer Context

Peer relationships must include reciprocity—aspects of sharing, fairness, and equality—because most children will discontinue relationships with other children who refuse to share or play fair. According to psychologist William Damon (1988), sharing in young children is an early sign of empathy and is considered an important aspect of prosocial behavior. He further suggests that the specific skill of perspective taking in prosocial behavior develops within peer interactions. Piaget and Kohlberg also both suggested that peer interaction is an essential component of moving into higher levels of cognitive moral reasoning and learning to cooperate with others to determine fairness and justice.

Hence, parents and teachers should encourage peer interaction among children. Teachers can ensure that children have adequate peer interaction by using cooperative learning strategies. Cooperative learning requires students to work collaboratively on projects and has been found to enhance both empathy and perspective-taking skills (Solomon, Watson, & Battistich, 2001). Therefore, requiring peer interaction among children and adolescents provides an opportunity for teachers to monitor and model the skills necessary for higher levels of moral reasoning.

School Context

Although teachers can benefit from the research in the family and peer contexts, several specific approaches to enhancing moral development in educational settings have also been proposed (Berkowitz & Hoppe, 2009; Jackson, Boostrom, & Hansen, 1993; Nucci, 2006; Watson & Ecken, 2003):

Cooperative learning: See page 378.

Immoral behavior in the classroom: See page 356.

1. *Climate of trust:* The classroom and school system should have a climate of trust and an ethic of caring. Children should feel safe to express emotions, knowing that they are supported and cared for by teachers and staff. Specific strategies have been suggested based on observational research:
   - Teachers can interact with students outside of instructional time, such as having lunch with students, engaging students in ordinary conversations about events, joking with students, and allowing students time to be "goofy."
   - Teachers can share minor personal information such as family, pets, and hobbies with students as well as spend time getting to know about students' hobbies, interests, and family life.
   - Teachers can use a physical posture that relays a trusting, caring attitude, such as leaning down to a young child's level, standing close to a student, or putting a hand on a student's shoulder.
   - Teachers should be consistent and predictable in their responses and routine behaviors in order to impart a sense of trustworthiness.

2. *Developmental discipline:* Just as parents can use induction and a democratic process to establish standards and consequences as well as encourage empathy, teachers should employ those same strategies within the classroom:
   - Teachers should help students understand the reasons behind rules.
   - Rules should include prosocial behaviors such as sharing, taking turns, and respecting others.
   - Teachers can hold regular class meetings and include collaborative problem solving to stop misbehavior in the classroom.
   - Because adolescents will begin to view more and more issues as personal rather than conventional, desiring more power and control, teachers should give adolescents more opportunities to contribute to the development of rules and to make choices within the classroom (democratic governance).

3. *Service learning:* Service learning is a method of instruction that combines learning with service to the community. It can involve community service (typical volunteer activities such as tutoring, helping at a nursing home, or volunteering with an organization such as Race for the Cure), community exploration (experiential education, such as internships within the community or outdoor/ environmental education), or community action (civic reform, community enhancement). Engaging in service learning has been linked to increases in prosocial behavior, decreases in aggressive behaviors, and increases in levels of civic skills, attitudes, and knowledge. In order for service learning to be effective, students should have choices in selecting activities and opportunities to reflect on their experiences in ways that help them prepare for, be successful in, and learn from those experiences (for example, through journals or papers). Schools can reinforce the beneficial effects of service learning by offering some sort of acknowledgment and honoring of students' contributions or of the student-community partnership (holding a party to celebrate a job well done, awarding certificates of appreciation, providing community-sponsored scholarships).

4. *Curriculum:* The moral curriculum should not be separated from academic content, but rather the two should be connected and intertwined within the classroom and school (Berkowitz & Bier, 2007):
   - History lessons and classic literature typically include moral dilemmas, as do current events in social studies classes.

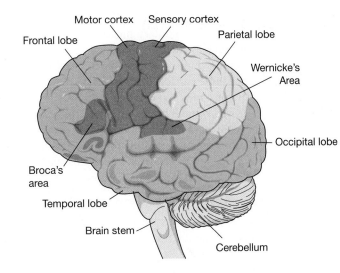

Figure 6.1. Review of Brain Structures and Functions

Brain stem:	connects the cerebrum to the spinal cord; controls many important vital functions such as motor and sensory pathways, cardiac and respiratory functions, and reflexes.
Broca's area:	located in the left hemisphere and processes the understanding of language, speech, and the control of facial neurons.
Cerebellum:	controls complex motor functions such as walking, balance, posture, and general motor coordination.
Cerebrum (or cerebral cortex):	associated with conscious thought, movement and sensation; it consists of two hemispheres (symmetrical halves), each controlling the opposite side of the body. Hemispheres contain four lobes: frontal, temporal, parietal, and occipital. The hemispheres are connected by the corpus callosum, which delivers messages between them.
Frontal lobe:	one of four sections of the cerebral cortex; controls attention, behavior, abstract thinking, problem solving, creative thought, emotion, intellect, initiative, judgment, coordinated movements, muscle movements, smell, physical reactions, and personality.
Hypothalamus:	(not visible in this diagram) a region of the brain that acts in partnership with the pituitary gland that controls the hormonal processes of the body as well as temperature, mood, hunger, and thirst.
Motor cortex:	an area located in the middle, top part of the brain that helps control movement in various parts of the body.
Occipital lobe:	one of the four lobes of the cerebral cortex; controls vision.
Parietal lobe:	one of four lobes of the cerebral hemisphere; controls tactile sensation, response to internal stimuli, sensory comprehension, some language, reading, and some visual functions.
Pituitary gland	(not visible in this diagram) a small, bean-sized organ located at the base of the brain; controls the secretion of many essential hormones for growth and sexual maturation.
Sensory cortex:	located in the front part of the parietal lobe, it receives information from the spinal cord about the sense of touch, pressure, pain, and the perception of the position of body parts and their movements.
Temporal lobe:	one of four lobes of the cerebral hemisphere of the cerebral cortex; controls auditory and visual memories, language, some hearing and speech, language, plus some behavior.
Wernicke's area:	part of the left temporal lobe that surrounds the auditory cortex and is thought to be essential for understanding and formulating speech. Damage in Wernicke's area causes deficits in understanding spoken language.

(Adapted from http://massoudbina.com/neurodisorders/BrainAnatomy.php)

Executive control functions: See page 212.

parietal lobe, occipital lobe, and temporal lobe. The cerebral cortex is largely responsible for higher brain functions including sensation, voluntary muscle movement, thought, reasoning, and memory, as well as executive functions such as attention, planning, organizing, and monitoring. Although many learning tasks involve processing that is distributed across multiple areas of the brain, certain brain structures are specialized to handle particular functions, such as vision (occipital lobe) and control of physical movements (the motor cortex). The cortex is the last area of the brain to develop, and it accounts for 85% of the weight of an adult's brain (Schacter, Gilbert, & Wenger, 2009).

The various parts of the brain work together through connections among brain cells called **neurons.** As shown in Figure 6.2, neurons send information to other cells through a **synapse,** a gap between two neurons that allows the transmission of chemical messages, called **neurotransmitters.** Although neurons can vary in shape and size, they have certain features in common (see Figure 6.3):

- a *cell body* that contains a nucleus;
- *dendrites,* branchlike structures that receive messages from other neurons;
- an *axon,* a long armlike structure that transmits information to other neurons by releasing neurotransmitters;
- *myelin,* an insulating fatty substance around the axon of a neuron that speeds the transmission of information from one neuron to another.

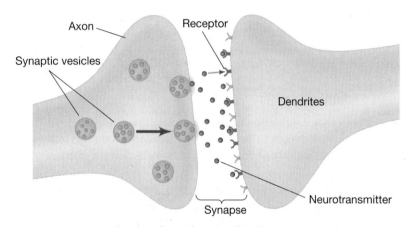

Figure 6.2. Communication Through Brain Chemistry. Scientists have learned a great deal about neurons by studying the synapse—the gap where a signal passes from a neuron to another cell. Synaptic vesicles release neurotransmitters to cross the synapse and attach to receptor sites on the dendrite of another neuron. This is how information is transmitted within the brain.

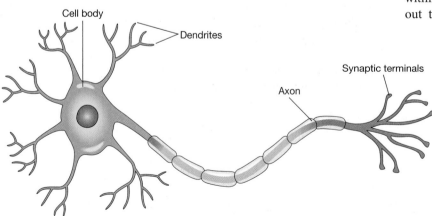

Figure 6.3. The Neuron. A neuron is comprised of a cell body, an axon, and dendrites. The axon of most neurons is covered in a sheath of myelin, which speeds the transmission of impulses down the axon.

THE DEVELOPING BRAIN

Developmental Processes

The brain of a human fetus, by the twentieth week of fetal life, has developed more than 200 billion neurons. Over time, however, half of these original cells will be eliminated. This early overproduction of neurons and neural networks guarantees that the young brain will be capable of adapting to virtually any environment into which the child is born, whether San Francisco, São Paulo, or Shanghai. Consider the case of language development. At birth, every child has the innate capacity to master any of the 3,000 languages spoken on Earth. Instead of being preprogrammed to speak any one particular language, the cerebral cortex will focus its developmental activities around just those sounds that have regularity and meaning within its environment and will start to weed out those neurons that seem unnecessary, a process called **neural pruning** (cell death and/or differentiation).

A toddler's brain has twice as many synaptic connections among its neurons as does the brain of a college student, as shown in Figure 6.4. The toddler brain also appears to expend more energy than does an adult brain, as toddlers encounter more sensory data that is completely new to them (requiring more attention and energy to process) and are trying to master skills that will become automatic and effortless by adulthood (Shore, 1997). Between ages 3 and 6, extensive production and pruning of synapses takes place within the frontal lobe, which is responsible for executive control functions such as organizing actions, planning activities, and focusing attention (Thompson et al., 2000). This process primes the child to meet the demands of formal schooling encountered in kindergarten or first grade.

Although the *overall size* of the brain does not change much after age 6, neurons continue to grow in number and size at least through adolescence. Part of the size increase can be attributed to the process of myelination, the creation of myelin sheaths around axons. Performance and speed of processing on many tasks depends on the development of **myelin**. Rates of myelination (and subsequent processing speed) have been linked to stages of development:

■ Myelination of brain cells related to hand-eye coordination is not complete until about 4 years of age.

■ Myelination in areas of the frontal lobe responsible for focusing attention is not complete until around age 10 (Posner & Rothbart, 2007).

■ The most extensive myelination in the areas of the brain that are responsible for thinking, reasoning, and executive functions does not take place until adolescence (Nelson, Thomas, & de-Haan, 2006).

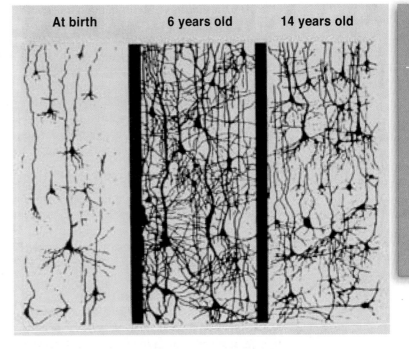

At birth   **6 years old**   **14 years old**

Figure 6.4. Synaptic Density in the Human Brain. The number of synaptic connections between neurons peaks during early childhood. Over time, these connections are "pruned" to allow for more directed and efficient functioning of the brain.

Image reprinted from R. Shore (1997). *Rethinking the brain: New insights into early development* (p. 20). New York: Families and Work Institute.

Understanding these myelination patterns can give teachers additional insight about how long it takes for children and adolescents to become efficient at various learning tasks.

From ages 6 to 13, individuals may experience striking growth spurts in the temporal and parietal lobes, the areas connecting brain regions specialized for language and understanding spatial relations. Just prior to puberty, a second wave of neuron overproduction and pruning occurs, predominantly in the frontal lobe. During the teen years, many parts of the brain undergo additional refinement. Areas associated with more basic functions, including the motor and sensory areas, mature early, while areas involved in planning and decision making do not appear to reach adult dimensions until the early twenties. This includes the prefrontal cortex, the cognitive or reasoning area of the brain important for controlling impulses and emotions (Perrin et al., 2008). The brain's reward center, the ventral striatum, is more active during adolescence than in adulthood, and the adolescent brain still is strengthening connections between its reasoning- and emotion-related regions (Choudbury, Charman, & Blakemore, 2008; Gogtay et al., 2004; Sowell et al., 2010). These findings may indicate that cognitive control over high-risk behaviors is still maturing during adolescence, making teens more likely than adults to engage in risky behaviors (Giedd et al., 1999; Sowell et al., 1999).

Today, functional magnetic resonance imaging (fMRI) allows scientists to measure, at essentially all ages, how different brain regions engage in cognitive tasks. From infancy to adulthood, psychological functioning becomes less reflexive, less stimulus bound, more goal directed, more self-organized, and more flexible (Johnson & Munakata, 2005; Brown, 2007). In short, the brain is a work in progress, and it's important for educators to be aware that brain areas controlling different skill sets and functions are developing at different rates.

Factors Affecting Brain Development

Are some people good at certain cognitive functions, such as learning languages, math, or reading, simply because they were "born that way," or do developmental experiences shape each individual's cognitive abilities? When we examine brain development, how do we assess the roles of nature and nurture? For example, let's say one group of individuals excels at a certain cognitive function. If research also shows that this group exhibits patterns of brain functioning that differ from those of other groups, we must ask:

- Did the different patterns of brain functioning give rise to these cognitive abilities?
- Or did different experiences (for example, poor readers receiving less reading practice) lead to altered brain functioning?

It's a chicken-and-egg question: Which came first, the developmental experience or the cognitive ability? The brain is dynamic, remodeling itself in response to environment and experience (Begley, 2007; Tashiro et al., 2007). Still, neuroscience cannot yet tease apart the direction of this relationship. Research indicates that the relationship is bidirectional, meaning that certain patterns of brain functioning have a genetic basis, but patterns of brain functioning can change as a result of experience. Let's explore some of the factors that affect brain development.

GENETICS

Some characteristics of brain development seem to have a hereditary component, but research suggests that genes alone do not determine brain structure. For example, identical twins, who have exactly the same genetic instructions, sometimes develop brains that are structurally different, indicating that other factors besides genetics are at work (Edelman, 1992; Steinmetz, Herzog, Schlaug, Huang, & Lanke, 1995; Yoon, Fahim, Perusse, & Evans, 2010).

ENVIRONMENTAL STIMULATION

In a classic study conducted by Mark Rosenweig (1969), rats and other animals were randomly assigned different environmental conditions in which to live. Some animals were placed in an enriched environment that had stimulating features such as wheels to rotate, steps to climb, levers to press, and toys to manipulate, while other animals were placed in standard cages or in deprived and isolated conditions. Compared to the brains of animals raised in the standard or deprived conditions, the brains of the animals living in enriched conditions were heavier and had thicker layers, more neuronal connections, and higher levels of neurochemical activity. Similarly, studies have shown that humans need a stimulating environment in order to achieve optimal learning and development (Farah et al., 2008; Molfese, Molfese, Key, & Kelly, 2003; Yang et al., 2007). Features of a stimulating, enriched environment include social interaction, sensory stimulation, positive emotional support, novel changes, and challenging but achievable tasks (Diamond & Hopson, 1998).

CRITICAL AND SENSITIVE PERIODS

Environmental stimulation can have different effects on brain structure depending on when it occurs in development. For example, in a famous study of visual deprivation in kittens, researchers found that kittens reared in total darkness (with their eyelids surgically sewn shut) for two weeks right after birth would be permanently blind; however, if the visual deprivation occurred somewhat later in the postnatal period, the kittens were able to develop normal visual skills (Hubel & Weisel, 1962). Findings such as this led to the notion of a **critical period** in human brain development, a window of opportunity during which certain experiences are necessary if the brain and corresponding cognitive skills are to develop normally. The assumption underlying critical periods is that the window of opportunity will close after a certain period of time, making it nearly impossible to develop normal levels of skill. However, there is limited neuroscientific evidence in studies with human beings to support this assumption (Blakemore & Firth, 2005; Bruer, 1999).

Most neuroscientists now believe that development is characterized by **sensitive periods.** During a sensitive period, the brain is particularly receptive to environmental influences (Knudsen, 1999, 2004). Although it is possible to develop certain capacities after the sensitive period has passed, skills acquired after that time are subtly different and may rely on different strategies and brain pathways (Hensch, 2004). For example, individuals who learn a second language after puberty do not acquire the same level of grammatical skill that is attained by younger children who learn a second language (White & Genesee, 1996; Wartenburger et al., 2003).

PLASTICITY

Studies of patients with brain damage indicate that the brain can rewire itself in an attempt to compensate for loss of function (Johnston, 2009; Meehan, Randhawa, Wessel, & Boyd, 2010; Ward & Frackowiak, 2006). The brain's ability to reorganize itself by forming new neural connections throughout life is called **plasticity.** Some brain systems are more plastic than others, some are highly plastic during limited periods, and some change more quickly in response to targeted interventions (Begley, 2007). Plasticity may be considered as *experience-expectant* or *experience-dependent* plasticity (Greenough,

Black, and Wallace, 1987). **Experience-expectant plasticity** is available from conception and describes the brain's ability to fine-tune its powers to adapt to environmental conditions. For example, although the brain is equipped to interpret visual signals from both eyes, it will restructure itself to compensate for a nonseeing eye. Experience-expectant plasticity involves windows of opportunity that may gradually close (or at least narrow) if the brain identifies the skills involved as unnecessary for the individual. **Experience-dependent**

Stimulating experiences such as playing basketball or painting enhance brain development.

plasticity refers to the emergence of skills that are unique to particular cultures and social groups. For example, a student who moves from rural Indiana to New York City will have to activate or develop new neural connections that help her negotiate her new and different living conditions (for example, going to sleep to the sounds of cars, horns, and sirens). This form of plasticity involves strengthening weak synapses and forming new ones and seems to be viable throughout the lifespan (Bruer & Greenough, 2001; Merzenich, 2001).

NUTRITION

Experimental studies with animals and correlational studies with humans have shown that malnutrition can have different effects on brain development, depending on the timing of the malnutrition and how long it lasts (Beard, 2003; Schlotz, Jones, Phillips, Gale, Robinson, & Godfrey, 2010). The brain of a human fetus grows very rapidly from the tenth to the eighteenth week of pregnancy, and good nutrition during this formative period is believed to be particularly critical to healthy development (Chafetz, 1990; Dhopeshwarkar, 1983). Malnutrition during periods of rapid brain growth can have devastating effects on the nervous system and on myelin development (Byrnes, 2001). Malnutrition can impair the flow of neurotransmitters, thereby placing an individual at higher risk for neurological and mental disorders (Coleman & Gillberg, 1996; Edelson, 1988).

Types of research designs: See page 7.

TERATOGENS

Teratogens are any foreign substances that can cause abnormalities in a developing fetus. For example, maternal consumption of alcohol has consistently been linked to a range of cognitive, motor, and interpersonal deficits (McGee et al., 2009; Victor, Wozniak, & Chang, 2008; Weiss, St. John Seed, & Harris-Muchell, 2007). Infants born to mothers who were heavy drinkers during pregnancy may have some form of mental retardation or behavioral problems (Henry, Sloane, & Black-Pond, 2007). Prenatal exposure to alcohol can occasionally lead to a disorder called **fetal alcohol syndrome (FAS),** which has an incidence of 3 per 1,000 births. FAS is a permanent condition characterized by abnormal facial features, growth deficiencies, and central nervous system problems. Children with FAS might have problems with learning, memory, attention span, communication, vision, hearing, or a combination of these. These problems often lead to academic difficulties as well as social difficulties (Centers for Disease Control and Prevention, 2007). Figure 6.5 shows the dramatic differences between the brain of a healthy 6-week-old infant and the brain of an infant with fetal alcohol syndrome.

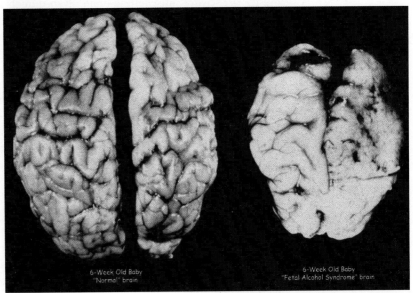

Figure 6.5. The Effects of Fetal Alcohol Syndrome on the Brain. The image on the left shows the brain of a healthy 6-week-old infant. The image on the right shows the brain of a 6-week-old infant with fetal alcohol syndrome. (Image retrieved from http://www.acbr.com/fas/fasbrail.jpg)

DIVERSITY **GENDER DIFFERENCES**

Do you think there might be differences in brain structures and processes based on gender? Consider these examples:

- Gender differences in prenatal brain development may result in males having brains that are more specialized for right-hemisphere functions, such as visual-spatial, music, and nonverbal tasks, and females having brains that are more bilaterally organized (Bitan et al., 2010; Halpern, 1997).

- Significant gender differences also exist in the metabolism of neurotransmitters known to play an important role in cognition (Becker and Hu, 2008; Laakso et al., 2002; Staley et al., 2001).

- Differences in circulating sex hormone levels, in addition to their role in regulating reproductive behavior, have also been shown to modulate working memory, verbal memory, and organization of the developing brain (Bramen et al., 2010; Grigorova et al., 2006; Neufang et al., 2009; Sherwin & Tulandi, 1996).

Although many neuroanatomic differences have been noted, the connection between these gender differences in the brain and differences in cognitive performance is still unclear. Correlational studies have indicated a link between brain volume, IQ scores, and cognitive performance but have not proved causality (McDaniel, 2005). Likewise, researchers have discovered a correlation between social behaviors such as higher cooperativeness in females and larger gray matter volume in "social" brain regions within the prefrontal cortex (Yamasue et al., 2008) but this doesn't provide definitive evidence about the direction of the relationship. Are females more cooperative because they have more gray matter in social brain areas, or do they have more development in these areas of the brain because they tend to act cooperatively?

> Types of research designs: See page 7.

Think about other areas of physical development, such as your height. How have those aspects of physical development been affected by genetics, environmental stimulation, plasticity, nutrition, and teratogens?

BRAIN ACTIVITY DURING LEARNING

What happens in the brain when a child is learning to read, play the piano, or ride a bike? During these learning activities, neurons reach out to one another to form new connections or strengthen old ones. The adult brain contains about 100 billion neurons, and many cognitive tasks require millions of interconnected neurons (Blakemore & Firth, 2005).

But when we speak of "reading words," "adding numbers," "playing music," or "forming a hypothesis," we are not referring to the work of individual brain cells. There are no specific "reading," "math," "music," or "science" areas of the brain. Even though specific brain areas do carry out characteristic kinds of processing, such as the left hemisphere's specialization for language, all types of cognitive tasks involve the development of connections between neural networks spread across many regions of the brain (Immordino-Yang & Fischer, 2009). For example, the process of reading activates various areas of the left hemisphere, as shown in Figure 6.6.

Learning changes the very architecture of the human brain, as the learner acquires new skills and competencies. **Synaptogenesis,** the growth of new connections in the brain, continues throughout life as individuals adapt to changing life conditions and experiences (Kelsch et al., 2010). Certain skills and behaviors have a greater likelihood of developing elaborate neural connections that become almost impervious to destruction. These are skills and behaviors that:

- receive significant amounts of time, attention, and practice; and

- are vital for survival and/or emotional or personal well-being.

> Constructivism: See Module 7 and Module 20.

The constructivist theory of learning suggests that knowledge is *constructed*—that each individual builds knowledge through interaction and experience. This implies that each learner's neural networks may differ depending on biological factors and the cultural, physical, and social context in which the skills are built (Immordino-Yang, 2008). In other words, individual learners can take various routes to effectively develop the same skills, as researchers in reading (Fischer, Bernstein, & Immordino-Yang, 2007) and math (Singer, 2007) have demonstrated. Children use whatever capacities they have to learn the most important skills in their lives. Although there may be a more common or typical way to learn a specific skill (for example, learning to do arithmetic), individuals can adapt and learn that same skill in diverse ways (Immordino-Yang & Fischer, 2009).

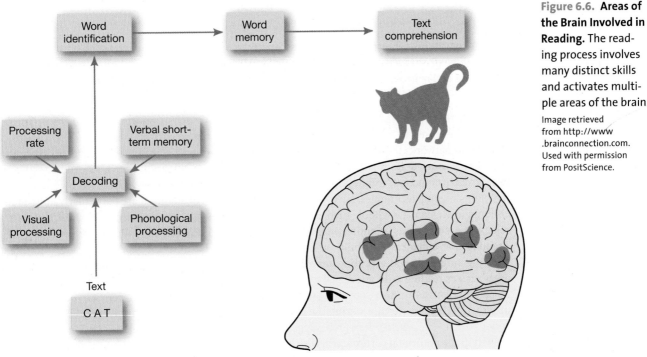

Figure 6.6. Areas of the Brain Involved in Reading. The reading process involves many distinct skills and activates multiple areas of the brain.

Image retrieved from http://www .brainconnection.com. Used with permission from PositScience.

As an individual uses certain combinations of skills repeatedly, the brain begins to recognize the pattern and becomes faster and more efficient at performing the task (Begley, 2007; Hebb, 1949). Certain brain cells actually learn to fire in unison. Neuroscientists describe this pattern of increasing efficiency as **"Cells that fire together, wire together."** Research suggests that when memory-related neurons in the brain fire in sync, the resulting image recognition and memories are stronger than if this synchronization does not occur (Cedars-Sinai Medical Center, 2010). Well-entrenched behaviors that are practiced to automaticity (becoming fast and error-free and needing few cognitive resources) become centered in the regions of the brain responsible for automatic, unconscious processing. This frees up the conscious cerebral cortex for new learning, because deep-rooted skills no longer demand a learner's full attention for their execution. For example, as you read this sentence, you have already developed automaticity of word identification (identifying words and their meanings) allowing you to focus more cognitive resources on comprehending what you are reading.

Automaticity: See pages 193 and 230.

Just as practice strengthens neural connections, infrequent use of certain skills may cause synaptic connections to weaken or degenerate in a process called **synaptic pruning.** The brain is the quintessential example of the **"use-it-or-lose-it" principle.** Synaptic pruning also eliminates redundant connections and makes it possible for the remaining connections to operate more efficiently. Some loss of synapses is both inevitable and desirable.

How do synaptogenesis and pruning apply to classroom experiences? Teachers should clearly identify important skills and concepts and make sure they are reviewed on a regular basis to ensure they are retained or learned.

What skills have you practiced to a level of automaticity? What skills have you lost or become less efficient in performing because you haven't used them often enough? For example, what problem would you solve with Pythagoras' Theorem ($a^2 + b^2 = c^2$)? Hint: It's a skill you may have acquired in a high school geometry class.

APPLICATIONS: HOW BRAIN RESEARCH CAN INFORM TEACHING

Recent advances in neuroscience, combined with studies in educational psychology, have validated some of the educational practices that teachers have intuitively considered educationally sound. Let's review some of these findings and discuss their implications for teachers and students.

Current State of Research in Memory, Reading, Math, and Emotion

MEMORY

The psychological model of memory suggests that instruction is most likely to succeed if it involves practice and helps students create detailed representations. This model is highly consistent with both psychological and neuroscientific evidence (Byrnes, 2001). Specific findings regarding human memory include these:

Three-Stage Model of Information Processing: See Module 11.

1. *Attention.* The problem of forgetting is not always a memory problem. Several attention-related problems can be traced to neural factors. In the past decade, researchers have identified three distinct attentional networks important in the learning process: those for alerting, orienting, and executing attention (Posner & Rothbart, 2007). Individual differences in attention networks can be related to genetic, environmental, and developmental factors. Psychological studies, supported by findings using brain-imaging techniques, have shown that some aspects of attention are particularly difficult for children in elementary school (such as filtering out unimportant information) and other aspects are relatively easy (such as orienting attention where directed) (Posner, 1995; Posner & Raichle, 1994). Training that enhances the ability to regulate one's focus on different aspects of the environment (alerting, orienting, and executing attention) can improve preschoolers' academic abilities in various areas such as reading skills and social interaction at school (Berger, Kofman, Livneh, & Flenik, 2007).

ADHD: See Module 25.

Neuroscientists are also examining the possible neural basis of attention-deficit hyperactivity disorder (ADHD) and are considering the effects of drugs such as Ritalin on the brain (Durston et al., 2004; Sowell et al., 2010). Research suggests ADHD may be due to underactivation and delayed growth in the prefrontal cortex areas, which are responsible for attention, planning, impulse control, and movement (Ellison-Wright, Ellison-Wright, & Bullmore, 2008; Emond, Joyal, & Poissant, 2009).

2. *Building patterns and connections.* Learning involves the establishment of relatively permanent synaptic connections among neurons. The *hippocampus,* a brain structure that plays an important role in memory formation, may temporarily bind separate sites in the cerebral cortex associated with a memory (for example, what an object looks like, what it is called, and so on) until connections that constitute a more permanent record are established in the brain (Squire & Alvarez, 1998). Neuroscientists recently discovered the existence of a miniature "mental map" of all the things one can pay attention to. Interestingly, this map is reproduced in at least 13 different places in the brain, and these duplicate maps are connected to each other. Yet, each copy appears to do something different with the information: one map processes eye movements while another processes analytical information, and so on (Anderson et al., 2010). An individual's ability to pay attention emerges from complex interactions among these connected regions of the brain.

Practice Makes Perfect. Students can develop expertise by practicing essential skills such as basic math exercises.

While articles and popular books may emphasize that certain teaching approaches build synaptic connections and that the brain encodes information in multiple ways, neuroscientific research has not been able to demonstrate that one particular instructional technique is better than any other for actually generating synapses in the brain (Begley, 2007; Byrnes, 2001).

3. *Novices versus experts.* When we compare brain images of "novices" and "experts" performing the same task or playing the same game, the differences are vividly apparent. Experts organize and interpret information in their brains differently from nonexperts (National Research Council, 2000a). In one study, researchers made fMRI scans of a skilled portrait artist and a nonartist as each drew a series of faces. During the task, both exhibited a discernible increase in blood flow in the right-posterior parietal region of the brain, a site normally associated with facial perception and processing. However, the level of activation appeared lower in the expert than in the novice, suggesting that a skilled artist may process facial information more efficiently. In addition, the skilled artist showed greater activation in the right frontal area of the brain than did

the novice, which may indicate that such an artist uses "higher-order" cognitive functions, such as the formation of associations and planning motor movements, when viewing and drawing a face (Solso, 2001).

In a similar study, expert golfers demonstrated patterns of brain activation during their pre-shot routine that radically differed from patterns seen in novices. These differences are apparent even before the golfer swings the club, suggesting that differences in the performance of novice and expert golfers lie at the level of the organization of neural networks during motor *planning*—not just during execution of a swing. Novice golfers have difficulty filtering out irrelevant information, whereas experts, through extensive practice, develop a focused and efficient organization of the relevant task-related neural networks (Milton, Solodkin, Hlustik, & Small, 2007). Teachers can support the development of expertise by giving students plenty of opportunities to practice essential skills. Many psychological studies have confirmed the importance of practice and repetition, as well as the value of a variety of metacognitive strategies to aid learning, memory, and transfer (Anderson, 1995; Flavell, Green, & Flavell, 2000; Weinstein & Mayer, 1986).

Memory, metacognition, and transfer: See pages 184, 211, and 226.

READING

Reading is probably the area with the highest degree of research convergence between educational psychology and neuroscience. Educational researchers have developed sophisticated theories of reading and reading disability based on behavior, and these theories have guided the interpretation of neuroscientific data (Willingham & Lloyd, 2007). Here are some classroom implications suggested by research in these two fields:

Reading disability: See page 441.

1. Based on studies of neural development and psychological studies of cognitive development, reading instruction is likely to be relatively ineffective before age 3 or 4 (Goswami, 2008; Katzir & Pare-Blagoev, 2006).

2. Sophisticated brain-imaging technology reveals that individuals with a reading disability show decreased functioning in the temporal-parietal region of the brain while performing reading tasks that require phonological processing—a skill needed for mapping sounds onto printed words, called *decoding* (Begley, 2007; Perfetti & Bolger, 2004; Shaywitz et al., 2002). However, it is not yet clear to what extent differences in brain functioning are a *cause* of phonological processing deficits or a *product* of the phonological deficits that individuals with a reading disability experience when learning to read (the chicken-and-egg phenomenon). The relationship seems to be bidirectional. Neurological research of phonological processes in reading has led to a reevaluation of how reading disabilities are defined and understood (Perfetti & Bolger, 2004).

Decoding and reading: See page 441.

3. Brain scans reveal that intervention makes a difference in the reading performance of students with a reading disability. Individuals with reading disabilities who participated in systematic phonics instruction—intensive practice applying sounds to printed letters—improved their reading performance, and their brain activation patterns began to more closely resemble those of typical readers (Shaywitz et al., 2004; Simos et al., 2007, 2009). One reading software program that is receiving a great deal of attention is Fast ForWord®, which provides intensive training to help children discriminate rapid auditory signals, and develop phonological skills, auditory attention and memory, and listening comprehension. Cognitive-behavioral research and neurological findings indicate that specific remediation programs such as this, which provide intensive training to improve auditory and phonological processing deficits, can alter the functioning of the brain (Katzir & Pare-Blagoev, 2006; Temple et al., 2003).

4. Cultural differences in reading disability: MRI research indicates cross-cultural differences in the brain areas underlying reading disability. A study comparing brain images demonstrated that individuals with reading disability showed similar patterns of underactivation in the temporal-parietal area of the left hemisphere whether they were speakers of Italian, French, or English (Paulesu et al., 2001). This pattern of brain activation among alphabetic languages differs from brain patterns found in logographic languages such as Chinese, in which meaning is conveyed through hieroglyphs, icons, or pictographs. Research comparing disabled and nondisabled readers of Chinese found that individuals with a reading disability showed reduced activation in visual attention areas but not in the areas implicated in reading disability for alphabetic languages (Siok et al., 2004). The hypothesis—so far untested—is that logographic and alphabetic languages will require different remediation programs. This finding also leads to the intriguing question of whether individuals with reading disabilities in one language would be normal readers in another (Varma, McCandliss, & Schwartz, 2008).

DIVERSITY

MATH

Research evidence in this area presents tentative conclusions about where math is processed in the brain (Duffau et al., 2002; Varma & Schwartz, 2008):

■ Individual math facts and procedures seem to be stored in their own separate areas of the cortex (one area for multiplication facts, another for subtraction procedures, and so on).

■ Calculation skills seem to be largely confined to the left hemisphere (though not always).

■ Skills of comparing and ordering information seem to be localized in the posterior regions of the right hemisphere (though not always).

Remediating math:
See page 444.

Yet, these findings contribute little to our understanding *how to teach* math. Some of the most useful findings about math instruction come from studies in educational psychology that examine children's conceptual understanding, factual knowledge, and calculation processes (Peterson, Fennema, Carpenter, & Loef, 1989; Resnick & Omanson, 1987).

Although fewer educational implications exist for math skills because the number of neuroscientific studies is presently limited, some existing studies have provided valuable insights for educators. Let's consider a few examples.

1. *Different learning contexts require different strategy use.* Delazer et al. (2005) compared two ways of learning novel arithmetic operations. One group of participants used a memorization technique; the other used a more strategic approach to solving the problems. A subsequent fMRI scan revealed that memorization led to greater activation in brain areas specialized in the retrieval of verbally-coded information, whereas strategy use resulted in greater activation in brain areas responsible for visuo-spatial processing. This study suggests that different strategies used to solve the same problem lead to different patterns of brain activation.

2. *Domain-general versus domain-specific learning.* As students acquire experience and practice within various domains (for example, math, reading, science, playing chess, and so on), they appear to shift from **domain-general strategie**s (general reasoning and memory strategies) to **domain-specific strategies** (useful strategies within a given subject area). Rivera et al. (2005) took brain images of children between the ages of 8 and 19 as they solved simple arithmetic problems. Although children of all ages solved problems equally well, speed increased with age. Neuroimaging data revealed that the age-related improvement in speed was *not* the result of a change in the efficiency of a particular brain area involved in arithmetic, but a shift involving the use of different brain areas for solving arithmetic problems. Younger children used areas of the brain that control general memory and reasoning skills, while older children used brain areas controlling visual and verbal processes, suggesting that older children encoded the problems in a different way.

DIVERSITY

3. *Cultural differences in math processing.* Tang et al. (2006) imaged native English- and Chinese-speaking participants as they added and compared Arabic numbers. English-speaking participants showed greater activation in language areas (including **Broca's** and **Wernicke's areas**), presumably because in our culture children use verbal encoding when learning basic arithmetic calculations (saying "two plus two equals four"). In contrast, Chinese participants showed greater activation in motor areas (including premotor and supplementary areas). This may be the result of Chinese children learning arithmetic using the abacus, which enables a visuomotor understanding of numbers that they retain even as adults. This study raises a number of interesting educational questions. For example, children are often introduced to place-value through physical manipulation of blocks (called base-10 blocks). When they later reason without manipulatives, do they visualize those blocks while problem solving? If so, does this have implications for the sequencing of hands-on and paper-and-pencil lessons?

EMOTION

Emotions and learning: See page 63.

There is still much to learn about the ways emotion relates to learning and how brain research on emotions might apply to classroom practice. However, let's consider two contemporary avenues of research:

Cooperative learning: See Module 21.

1. Psychologists have hypothesized that human brains may reflect an inherent sociability and need for affiliation (Lefebvre, 2006; Pinker, 1997). This "social brain" hypothesis could explain why children perform better in school when they view their teachers as caring and also could have implications for the use of independent versus collaborative approaches in the classroom (Wentzel, 1997). Additional research with human subjects needs to investigate further the connection between social and emotional centers in the human brain and related learning outcomes.

The "Social Brain." Children perform better in school when they believe their teachers care about them.

2. Stress and fear affect social judgments, responses to reward and risk, and the ways in which the brain assesses the value of information being received (Goswami, 2004). Chronic stress and fear can lead to the physical destruction of neurons in the *hippocampus,* an area buried deep in the forebrain that helps regulate emotion and memory (McEwen, 1995). The *amygdala,* a structure in the forebrain responsible for emotions, fears, and memory, is activated in response to stress. When the amygdala is activated, it interrupts action and thought, and triggers rapid body responses essential for survival. One implication of this response is that classroom fear or stress may reduce students' ability to pay attention to the learning task (LeDoux, 2000). This finding is consistent with educational psychology research indicating that high anxiety can interfere with learning by distracting a student's attention from the material to be learned (Cassady & Johnson, 2002). Teachers should be aware of classroom conditions that elevate student anxiety, such as severe consequences for failure and competitive comparisons among students (Wigfield & Eccles, 1989).

EVALUATING CLAIMS ABOUT BRAIN-BASED LEARNING

The No Child Left Behind Act of 2001 and the Individuals with Disabilities Education Improvement Act of 2004 have required schools to provide students with academic instruction that uses scientific, research-based methods. Unfortunately, many claims about brain-based education are an oversimplification or inappropriate interpretation of complex neuroscience research (Alferink & Farmer-Dougan, 2010). Also, "brain-based learning" recommendations often are based on findings from educational psychology studies rather than on neuroscientific evidence (Bruer, 1999; Coles, 2004; Hyatt, 2007). Other studies have been conducted with animals and the results generalized to humans, with no real understanding of the differences across species.

The rapid explosion of brain research has sparked the interest of educators who have drawn premature conclusions about educational implications. Consider, for example, these claims:

■ *Suggestions by Geoffrey and Renata Caine (1997) and Howard Gardner (2000) that brain research justifies a shift toward more thematic, integrated activities.* Currently, no neuroscientific evidence supports such a sweeping conclusion.

■ *The assertion by Gardner (2000) that brain research supports active learning.* This assertion is based on behavioral studies, not neuroscientific findings.

■ *Brain Gym, a popular commercial program marketed in more than 80 countries, is claimed to lead to neurological repatterning and greater whole-brain learning (see the Official Brain Gym Web site at*

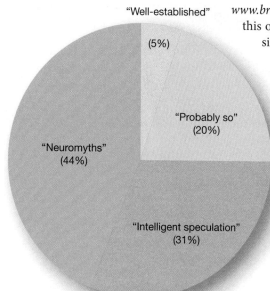

"Well-established" (5%)

"Probably so" (20%)

"Neuromyths" (44%)

"Intelligent speculation" (31%)

Figure 6.7. Survey of Mind, Brain, and Education Concepts. In a comprehensive survey of the concepts in the emerging area of mind, brain, and education, Tracey Tokuhama-Espinosa (2008) found:

■ only five beliefs experts considered "well-established" concepts,

■ 19 they considered "probably so,"

■ 29 that were "intelligent speculation," and

■ 42 that were "neuromyths."

In short, three-quarters of the concepts were considered speculative or worse.

www.braingym.org). The brain is dynamic and is constantly repatterning itself, so this outcome is not unique to Brain Gym. Such commercial programs describe simple physical exercises for "switching on the brain before a lesson," "increasing information flow between the left and right hemispheres," and so on. Regardless of the efficacy of these programs, their claims are not founded on what is actually known about brain function (Varma, McCandliss, & Schwartz, 2008).

Although some prescriptions for brain-based learning may eventually turn out to be valid, data to support these claims remain insufficient, as indicated in Figure 6.7. When sorting through claims made about brain-based learning, we must proceed with caution and analyze the data with a critical eye. To do so, we must develop scientific literacy skills, learn relevant terminology, and read research analytically in order to successfully navigate the field of brain-based education (Ansari & Coch, 2006; Wolfe, 2001).

Evaluating brain-based products and programs objectively can be especially challenging because of the appeal that neuroscience holds. For example, the mere presence of brain images in an article is more successful than other data representations in leading readers to boost their ratings of scientific reasoning in arguments (McCabe & Castel, 2008). Even including irrelevant neuroscience information in articles, without brain images, can sway readers' judgment of scientific reasoning (Weisberg, Keil, Goodstein, Rawson, & Gray, 2008). It is important for teachers to find and evaluate empirical, peer-reviewed papers written by scientists or practitioners regarding specific brain-based interventions. Sylvan and Christodoulou (2010) have presented a five-step approach to help educators evaluate brain-based educational products, as outlined in Guidelines 6.1.

You hear from a friend that listening to classical music boosts infants' brain power. How can you judge whether this claim is valid?

GUIDELINES 6.1   **Evaluating Brain-Based Educational Products**

1. Identify educational goals and target student populations.

2. Determine a match between educational goals and the purpose of the brain-based product.

3. Evaluate the brain-based rationale and the empirical research supporting the product.

4. Identify benefits and limitations of the product and consider alternatives.

5. Evaluate how the product will affect behavioral performance.

Summary

Describe the major arguments for and against the relevance of brain research for educators. Critics have argued that neuroscience data are still too new, too inconclusive, and too different from educational frameworks to be of any real value to educators. Advocates, on the other hand, emphasize that new research methods in neuroscience can provide tangible evidence to support what has been found in traditional educational and psychological research. They suggest that educational decision making can be best informed by combining scientific data from psychology, education, and neuroscience, using multiple research methods in different settings.

Name the four lobes of the cerebral cortex and identify their primary functions. Lobes of the cerebral cortex include the *frontal lobe* (attention, behavior, abstract thinking, problem solving, creative thought, emotion, intellect, initiative, judgment, coordinated movements, muscle movements, smell, physical reactions, and personality), *temporal lobe* (auditory and visual memories, language, some hearing and speech, plus some behavior), *parietal lobe* (tactile sensation, response to internal stimuli, sensory comprehension, some language, reading, and some visual functions), and the *occipital lobe* (vision, spatial working memory).

Identify the major factors that can lead to individual differences in brain development. Several factors produce individual differences in brain structure and development: (1) genetics; (2) environmental stimulation; (3) plasticity, which allows the neurons (nerve cells) in the brain to compensate for injury and disease and to adjust their activities in response to new situations or changes in their environment; (4) nutrition; (5) teratogens, or foreign substances that can cause abnormalities in a developing fetus, and (6) gender.

Identify the contributions from neuroscience to our understanding of what it means to *learn*. During learning, neurons respond by reaching out to one another in an elaborate branching process that connects previously unaligned brain cells, creating complex neural circuits. Neurons are constantly rearranging their connections in response to new information and experiences. Learning can involve strengthening existing synapses or forming new ones. In some cases,

cognitive development can require the elimination of synapses through synaptic pruning. Teachers should clearly identify important skills and concepts and make sure they are used and reviewed on a regular basis—otherwise students' ability to remember and use these skills is likely to weaken or disappear altogether. Practice strengthens neural connections and allows more efficient retrieval of information.

Discuss those areas in which neuroscience findings have led to implications for classroom practice. Research now suggests that brain development is not determined solely by genetics. How a brain develops hinges on a complex interplay between the genes people are born with and the experiences they have. Studies of memory and attention have shown that experts organize and interpret information in their brains differently from nonexperts. Teachers can support the development of expertise by giving students plenty of time to practice essential skills. Classroom interventions, such as the Fast ForWord Program used with students who experience reading difficulties, can help students make cognitive adaptations that cause the brain to rewire itself in more efficient and interconnected ways. Unfortunately, the rapid explosion of brain research has sparked the interest of educators who have drawn some premature conclusions about the educational implications. Neuroscientific research does not support the specific claims of many "brain-based learning" programs that promise to boost brain power.

Describe how teachers can best evaluate claims about brain-based learning. Teachers need to develop scientific literacy skills, learn relevant terminology, and read research analytically in order to successfully navigate the field of brain-based education. Guidelines for evaluating brain-based educational products include: 1. Identify educational goals and target student populations, 2. Determine a match between educational goals and the purpose of the brain-based product, 3. Evaluate the brain-based rationale and the empirical research supporting the product, 4. Identify benefits and limitations of the product and consider alternatives, and 5. Evaluate how the product will affect behavioral performance.

Key Concepts

brain hemispheres   101

Broca's area   112

"cells that fire together, wire together" principle   109

cerebral cortex   102

critical period   106

domain-general strategies   112

domain-specific strategies   112

experience-dependent plasticity   107

experience-expectant plasticity   107

fetal alcohol syndrome (FAS) 107

myelin 105

neural pruning 104

neuron 104

neurotransmitters 104

plasticity 107

sensitive period 106

synapse 104

synaptic pruning 109

synaptogenesis 108

teratogens 107

"use-it-or-lose-it" principle 109

Wernicke's area, p. 112

Video Applications

www.mhhe.com/bohlin2e

Video: How the Brain Learns (2 minutes)
In this video clip, a kindergarten teacher and a first-grade teacher use strategies that are consistent with current research on how the brain learns (for example, making meaningful connections and providing opportunities for practice).

Case Studies
Reflect and Evaluate

EARLY CHILDHOOD: "Fire Safety"

These questions refer to the case study on page 92.

1. Define *sensitive period* and explain why the preschool years may be a sensitive period for language development.

2. Explain the relationship between a stimulating environment and a child's brain development. What types of activities, toys, and interactions would characterize a stimulating preschool environment? Based on this, evaluate whether Rolling Hills Preschool is a stimulating preschool environment.

3. Suppose there was a child at Rolling Hills Preschool with fetal alcohol syndrome. How might this child's learning, memory, and communication skills compare with those of the other children in the case?

4. Miss Angela encouraged the children to practice their safety information so they would know it by heart. Explain what happens in the brain as individuals practice skills until they become automatic.

5. Preschoolers often are said to have limited attention spans. Evaluate the validity of this claim with respect to the evidence on age-related patterns in the brain.

6. Miss Angela introduced several different ways to practice and remember phone numbers. How would you describe what happens in the brain as each new method is introduced and used?

ELEMENTARY SCHOOL: "Project Night"

These questions refer to the case study on page 94.

1. Evaluate Mr. Morales's assumptions about right-brained and left-brained students. Based on your reading of the research in the module, what would you say to him?

2. Explain why practicing research techniques such as using the Internet and an encyclopedia is so important in developing automaticity, and explain what happens in the brain as this occurs.

3. According to brain research on attention, why would you expect the fifth-graders to have difficulty distinguishing important information from less important information in their project resources?

4. Based on the discussion of age-related patterns of brain development, why might the exchange and evaluation of information in the "research teams" be challenging for fifth-grade students?

5. Mr. Morales's project unit helps students build elaborate and meaningful representations of their social studies knowledge. Explain what happens in the brain as this occurs.

MIDDLE SCHOOL: "Frogs"

These questions refer to the case study on page 96.

1. Tyler has fetal alcohol syndrome (FAS). Describe the problems associated with FAS, and provide suggestions for modifications Ms. Thesdale might need to make in biology lab for Tyler.

2. Ms. Thesdale assumes that because Tyler is 13, there is not much she can do to help him improve his language skills because the critical period for language development has passed. Explain why Ms. Thesdale's reasoning is flawed.

3. A student in Ms. Thesdale's class who has struggled academically throughout upper elementary school has just been diagnosed as having a specific reading disability. He asks Ms. Thesdale to help him understand why he processes written text differently from his peers. Based on brain research presented in this module, what might Ms. Thesdale say to this student?

4. If Ms. Thesdale's students never have an opportunity to do another dissection, what is most likely to happen to their dissection skills? Give your answer in terms of what is known about the way the brain functions.

5. How might the saying "Cells that fire together, wire together" explain why students would be expected to become more efficient at doing the steps involved in dissection if they repeated them multiple times?

HIGH SCHOOL: "The Substitute"

These questions refer to the case study on page 98.

1. Dylan appears to have begun engaging in some risk-taking behavior. Explain the brain changes taking place during adolescence that might contribute to decisions about risk-taking.

2. The students Mr. Matthews encounters on his first day are not accustomed to being actively engaged in class. Explain how the teaching methods Mr. Matthews introduces might shape the way knowledge of British literature is processed in the brain.

3. A teacher meets Mr. Matthews in the hall and says, "You've had quite an impact on your British literature students. So, I hear you're using brain-based teaching." Explain why the teacher's comment about brain-based teaching is inaccurate. How should teachers use brain research to support and inform their teaching?

4. If a student in Mr. Matthews's class had a reading disability, would it be possible to change the way that student's brain processes information during reading? Explain based on evidence from neuroscience research.

MODULE 7

Cognitive Development

Outline

Constructivist Theories of Cognitive Development

- Individual and Social Constructivism
- Piaget's Theory
- Vygotsky's Theory

Issues in Cognitive Development: Piaget and Vygotsky

- What Comes First: Development or Learning?
- Role of Language in Cognitive Development
- Role of Play in Cognitive Development

Applications: Constructivist Principles for Effective Teaching

Summary
Key Concepts
Video Applications
Case Studies: Reflect and Evaluate

Learning Goals

1. Contrast individual and social constructivism.
2. Describe cognitive development through Piaget's stages, and identify what causes changes in thinking.
3. Describe intersubjectivity, internalization, and scaffolding within the Zone of Proximal Development.

4. Compare and contrast the views of Piaget and Vygotsky on issues in cognitive development.

5. Discuss how teachers can use constructivist theories to develop effective instruction.

CONSTRUCTIVIST THEORIES OF COGNITIVE DEVELOPMENT

Constructivism is a paradigm in psychology that characterizes learning as a process of actively constructing knowledge. Individuals create meaning for themselves or make sense of new information by selecting, organizing, and integrating information with other knowledge, often in the context of social interactions (Bruning, Schraw, Norby, & Ronning, 2004; Mayer, 2003). Constructivist ideas about intellectual development can be traced back to the early 1900s and two notable theorists: Jean Piaget, a Swiss scientist and philosopher, and Lev Semenovich Vygotsky, a Russian educational psychologist. Their work has significantly influenced U.S. educational practices. Many constructivist approaches continue to be studied by psychologists and used by teachers in today's classrooms.

During the 1940s and 1950s, schools typically used teacher-centered instructional approaches based on behavioral learning theories. Teachers were dispensers of information, and learning involved breaking down complex skills into subskills, learning those subskills in isolation, memorizing, and practicing. In the 1970s and 1980s, educational thinking began to shift toward teaching approaches that emphasized the teacher as facilitator and involved knowledge construction (rather than memorization) and peer interaction.

Constructivist teaching approaches: See page 369.

Behavioral learning theories: See Module 9.

Individual and Social Constructivism

Constructivism is often defined as individual or social. In **individual constructivism,** a person constructs knowledge by using cognitive processes to gain knowledge from experience rather than by memorizing facts provided by others. In **social constructivism,** individuals construct knowledge through an interaction between the knowledge they bring to a situation and social/cultural exchanges within that context. For example, a child who is interested in how wheels and axles work may engage in individual construction of knowledge by tinkering with a bicycle, or she may socially construct knowledge by working alongside an adult who is fixing a bike.

While Piaget often is considered an individual constructivist and Vygotsky a social constructivist, the line between individual and social constructivism can easily become blurred:

■ Even though Piaget was interested primarily in how meaning is *individually* constructed, he acknowledged *social experiences* as an important factor in cognitive development (Lourenço & Machado, 1996; Paris, Byrnes, & Paris, 2001).

■ While Vygotsky was interested primarily in social and cultural interactions as triggers of cognitive change, his theory actually emphasizes knowledge construction as both *socially* mediated and *individually* constructed (Moshman, 1997; Palincsar, 1998; Windschitl, 2002).

Let's further explore Piaget's and Vygotsky's views on knowledge construction.

Piaget's Theory

BASIC TENETS

Piaget's first intellectual interests were the study of nature and *epistemology,* a branch of philosophy that is concerned with the origins of knowledge. These interests shaped his views of cognitive development, leading him to propose a theory of *genetic epistemology*—the idea that knowledge develops from an interaction between nature and nurture. He proposed that all children's thinking evolves as a result of four factors (Piaget, 1970):

1. Biological maturation (nature)

2. Active exploration of the physical environment (nurture)

3. Social experiences (nurture)

4. Equilibration (or self-regulation)

Biological maturation. Maturation implies a biological "readiness" to learn, opening the door for a person to profit intellectually from social experiences and active exploration. Our current level of cognitive functioning determines what knowledge we are able to construct from our experiences. On a trip to an aquarium, knowledge construction for a toddler or preschooler might be limited to acquisition of concepts (for example, dolphin, whale, turtle), whereas an older child might be able to classify aquatic life and an adolescent could engage in discussions about how aquatic life evolved.

Active exploration of the physical environment. Individuals construct new knowledge when they engage in active self-discovery, as they interact with objects in their environment. In infancy, the acquisition of **schemes**—organized patterns of physical action—is the basis of all further development. Infants' schemes, such as grasping and sucking or filling and emptying containers, allow them to learn about the world. Schemes in preschoolers, older children, and adolescents are performed mentally and are called **operations** (Zigler & Gilman, 1998). For example, figuring out 2 + 2 = 4 is an operation that involves mentally combining two objects and two more objects to get four.

Social experiences. Social interaction is necessary for the development of logic in older children and adolescents. Here the process (interactions) as well as the product (solution) are stored mentally (Piaget, 1976a). To be effective, the exchange of ideas and cooperation with others should occur between peers instead of between adults and children, because peers are more likely to cooperate as equals, can more easily see each other's point of view, and can more easily challenge each other (Karpov, 2006; Piaget, 1976b). In discussing opposing points of view, students are able to see multiple perspectives and may change their existing way of thinking (Brown & Palincsar, 1989). However, social interactions alone are not sufficient for intellectual development (Lourenço & Machado, 1996; Piaget, 1950).

Equilibration. Because Piaget (1950, 1985) believed that nature and nurture were insufficient in themselves to explain changes in thinking, he proposed equilibration to regulate—or control—all the individual influences on development. Intellectual development involves continual adaptation whereby individuals construct new and more sophisticated cognitive structures (schemes or operations). **Equilibration** is a process of maintaining a cognitive balance between our existing knowledge and new experiences. When individuals are confronted with new experiences, they have a sense of **disequilibrium,** a discrepancy between their existing way of knowing and the new experiences. This motivates them to explore and to reach a conclusion that restores balance in their cognitive system (Piaget, 1985). For example, a student learning the commutative property of addition—that changing the order of addends does not change the sum—may be confused by the assertion that 4 + 3 = 3 + 4, having learned these as separate and unrelated facts. This student's disbelief may lead him to test the commutative property with several addends (such as 5 + 7 and 7 + 5, or 8 + 9 and 9 + 8) in order to achieve a cognitive balance—knowledge that the commutative property "works."

Cognitive adaptation can be achieved through assimilation and accommodation, which work together to help the individual maintain equilibration (Piaget, 1970; Sternberg, 2003):

- **Assimilation** involves integrating new information or a new experience into an existing cognitive structure. For example, on a trip to the grocery store, a young girl might see a Granny Smith apple and call it "apple" because it looks like the Macintosh apple that she eats. Sometimes new experiences can be incorrectly assimilated, as when a preschooler learning the alphabet mistakes the letter R for the letter P, which he already knows and easily recognizes.

- **Accommodation** involves any modification of an existing scheme or formation of a new cognitive structure when it is not possible to fit information into an existing structure. For example, after many repeated experiences, the preschooler will develop the correct concept for the letter R.

Think of some ways you could promote disequilibrium in your future students.

STAGE MODEL

In his book *The Psychology of Intelligence* (1950), Piaget explained how knowledge evolves through four stages, shown in Example 7.1. Stage theories often suggest distinct and abrupt changes from one stage to the next, with children shifting to a qualitatively different way of thinking than before. In contrast to this stage view, Piaget considered children's progression from stage to stage as a continuous adaptation of cognitive structures, with each new capability growing out of the achievements of the previous stage. Each stage is defined by new cognitive abilities not evident in previous stages as well as cognitive limitations compared to later stages. While Piaget was not interested in the ages at which children acquire different levels of thinking, numerous studies indicate ages at which these cognitive abilities typically emerge. Let's take a closer look at Piaget's four stages:

- Sensorimotor
- Pre-operational
- Concrete operational
- Formal operational

| EXAMPLE 7.1 | Piaget's Stages of Cognitive Development |

Sensorimotor (birth to 2 years)

Infants explore their world using sensory and motor actions. Object permanence is a major attainment necessary for the next stage. If you distract an infant and remove a toy from his view as shown here, he will not look for it—"out of sight, out of mind"—but an older infant will search for the toy.

Pre-operational (2–7 years)

One-way thinking is characteristic of this stage. Children at this stage typically show centration. This girl is selecting blocks by shape and ignoring color.

Concrete operational (7–11 years)

This student learning about weights and measures illustrates the ability of children in this stage to think logically using concrete materials.

Formal operational (11 years to adult)

This student, who is testing a hypothesis about evaluating which combination of solutions causes a chemical reaction, illustrates the abstract, logico-mathematical thinking of this stage.

Sensorimotor stage. Acquiring a capacity for internalized thinking is the central goal of the sensorimotor stage. During much of infancy, intelligence is external and behavioral, with infants constructing knowledge from sensory perceptions and motor actions (Brainerd, 2003). Infants initially do not realize that they exist as separate entities apart from objects and people in their environment or that objects and people exist independent of their perceptions (Zigler & Gilman, 1998). Throughout the first year

EXAMPLE 7.2   Concept Formation

A large part of lesson planning in K–12 classrooms involves figuring out how to teach **concepts,** abstract ideas generalized from specific examples (Klausmeir, 1992, 2004). Concept formation helps us organize large amounts of information into more manageable units. Promoting concept formation in the classroom can be challenging, because we tend to resist changing our existing understanding of concepts even though they sometimes are inaccurate (Chinn & Brewer, 1998). Teachers can use the following guidelines to help them introduce concepts in ways students will understand and accept:

■ *Assess prior knowledge.* Identifying inaccurate or incomplete conceptual understanding is the first step in promoting conceptual change. Based on this knowledge, a teacher can show students how new information contradicts what they currently believe and can motivate them to change their thinking.

■ *Initiate learning using a best exemplar or prototype of the concept.* Using prototypes or best exemplars—common examples of a concept—capitalizes on students' prior knowledge. When introducing a concept such as *quadrilateral* (a shape with four sides) to second-graders, teachers might begin with examples such as *square* and *rectangle.* As students' understanding of quadrilaterals becomes more sophisticated, teachers can add more unfamiliar examples, such as *parallelogram* and *trapezoid.*

■ *Use visual aids.* Teachers can improve students' understanding of complex concepts by using visual aids such as maps, diagrams, charts, graphs, or illustrations (Anderson & Smith, 1987; Mayer, 2001).

of life, infants gradually develop knowledge of themselves as separate entities, and by 8 to 12 months, they begin to acquire **object permanence**—an awareness that objects and people continue to exist even when they are not visible. Acquiring object permanence gives infants the capacity to represent objects, people, and events as entities that exist mentally, an important ability for the next stage. Children's acquisition and use of language allows them to progress cognitively from sensorimotor capabilities in infancy to mental representations in the pre-operational stage (Piaget, 1970).

Pre-operational stage. In the pre-operational stage, children develop **semiotic functions.** Semiotic (or symbolic) function is an ability to represent an object or action with signs and symbols, such as language, imagery, drawing, symbolic games, and deferred imitation (mentally storing an action and reproducing it later). The development of concepts is a major task at this stage, and teachers can facilitate it using guidelines discussed in Example 7.2.

The term *pre-operational* indicates that children are unable to engage in operations that involve two-way thinking, a characteristic of the next stage. Instead, their operations are limited to one-way thinking (Piaget, 1970):

■ Pre-operational children are **egocentric.** They think about the world primarily from their own physical and cognitive perspective and are unable to think of future actions or events that they have not seen or engaged in (Zigler & Gilman, 1998). They may hold up a drawing so that they can see it rather than turning the picture around to show the viewer, or they may nod while talking on the phone to grandma, not realizing that she cannot see them. Pre-operational children typically engage in **egocentric speech,** talking aloud about things that interest them without regard for the interests and conversational contributions of the listener.

■ Pre-operational children exhibit **centration,** an inability to focus on two dimensions simultaneously. For example, the child in Example 7.1 sorting blocks may start sorting them by shape, failing to see that they can also be sorted by color.

■ Pre-operational children cannot engage in **reversibility** of operations. For example, they have not yet acquired **conservation,** the realization that quantity or amount remains the same (is conserved) despite changes in appearance. Consider Piaget's classic conservation tasks in Figure 7.1. A child who sees two rows of objects lined up as shown will acknowledge that each row has the same number of objects. When an adult spreads out one row of objects as the child observes and asks if the rows have the same number of objects, a pre-operational child will say that the longer row has more, while a more cognitively advanced child will say that the rows have the same number because "you can put them back the way they were" (mentally reversing the operation).

In the classroom we see many signs of one-way thinking, as when children identify with a character in a story based on their own experiences or when they need to use manipulatives to solve an arithmetic problem.

Along with semiotic functions, **identity constancy** is an important milestone of the pre-operational stage (Zigler & Gilman, 1998). Toward the end of this stage, children realize that an object remains qualitatively the same even if its appearance may have changed in some way (DeVries, 1969). For example, putting a ferocious dog mask on a cat does not change the cat into a dog. Identity constancy may be necessary for children to acquire conservation.

Concrete operational stage. In the concrete operational stage, children form mental representations that accurately reflect possible actions and events in the physical world (Zigler & Gilman, 1998). Unlike pre-operational children, they are able to manipulate their operations—that is, to engage in two-way thinking. This in turn allows them to acquire reasoning skills (Brainerd, 2003). Concrete operational children who have acquired conservation will conclude that the two rows of objects, two pieces of clay, or two different-sized jars of liquid shown in Figure 7.1 have the same amount because they are able to mentally reverse the operation without having to test that hypothesis physically. While children's thinking becomes more logical and systematic, they are not yet able to manipulate abstract operations. In the classroom, we see signs of concrete operational thinking when students write a persuasive essay, solve a complex math problem, or test hypotheses in science using hands-on experiments. We also see difficulties related to concrete thinking, as when students have trouble making predictions in narratives or seeing the relevance of historical events to the present time.

Formal operational stage. While concrete operational thinkers are limited to concrete problems and tools, formal operational thinkers have achieved a characteristic way of thinking that allows them to solve many physical, logical, and mathematical problems. They:

- exhibit abstract reasoning that is reflective and analytical (Brainerd, 2003),

- can solve a problem without needing concrete representation, and

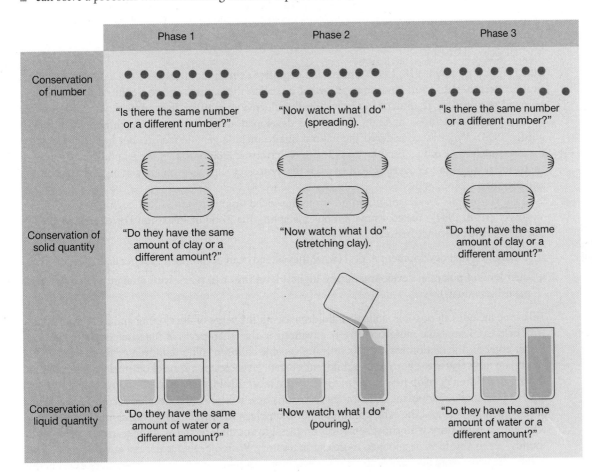

Figure 7.1. Piaget's Conservation Tasks. These tasks distinguish the pre-operational stage from the concrete operational stage.

Source: R. S. Siegler & M. W. Alibali (2005). *Children's thinking* (4th ed.). Upper Saddle River, NJ: Prentice-Hall.

■ can consider implications and incompatibilities, think hypothetically, search for alternatives, and reject inappropriate solutions without physically needing to test them (Piaget, 1970; Zigler & Gilman, 1998).

At this stage, we see students who are able to debate and to think about future plans.

Piaget believed that cognitive development culminated in formal operational reasoning, the point at which we have developed all the cognitive processes necessary for thinking—from schemes and symbolic thinking to concrete and abstract operations (Inhelder & Piaget, 1955). However, does everyone reach formal operational thinking, and do individuals develop cognitively after this stage? Based on research indicating that in many cultures the development of formal operational reasoning depends on extensive schooling, Piaget acknowledged that differences in the acquisition of formal operational thinking can occur among individuals (Ashton, 1975; Goodnow, 1962; Laurendeau-Bendavid, 1977). An individual may acquire formal operational thinking in one domain but not another (Piaget, 1972a). Also, the rate at which individuals reach the formal operational stage, like any of the other stages, depends partly on cultural and educational factors (Piaget, 1970; Zigler & Gilman, 1998). While we may reach a final way of thinking about the world with formal operations, Piaget believed that we continue throughout adulthood to acquire new knowledge and accumulate more content in our cognitive systems (Piaget, 1972a; Zigler & Gilman, 1998). Research suggests that the formal operational stage provides a solid foundation for understanding the development of wisdom, moral reasoning, and expertise in adulthood (Baltes, 1987; Kohlberg, 1984; Sternberg, 1990).

Piaget made scientific contributions to fields such as biology, philosophy, and sociology, as well as psychology, and his writings gave rise to a proliferation of developmental research for several decades. The vast amount of research based on Piaget's theory has led to several criticisms, outlined in Table 7.1. It is important for teachers to be aware of *all* of the evidence—support for the criticisms and counter-support—in order to fully understand students' cognitive development. Also keep in mind that all theories are flawed. No single theory can perfectly explain or predict a psychological construct—in this case, intellectual development. Despite any criticisms, Piaget undoubtedly changed our understanding of the cognitive potential of children (Lourenço & Machado, 1996).

Vygotsky's Theory

Like Piaget, Vygotsky (1978, 1993) argued that cognitive development results from a complex interaction between heredity and environment—what he called the natural and the cultural lines of development, respectively. To understand how culture influences cognitive development, we need to know what cognitive structures the child already has developed and brings to the learning situation (Vygotsky, 1994). Vygotsky considered the natural line to include genetic factors, but he did not discuss these as much as he did cultural factors (Tudge & Scrimsher, 2003). Rather, he emphasized the role of social interactions in the development of cognitive processes such as problem solving, self-regulation, and memory.

Zone of Proximal Development. To illustrate the social origins of individual cognitive functioning, Vygotsky (1978, 1994) created a now-famous metaphor, the **Zone of Proximal Development (ZPD).** The ZPD is the difference between

■ children's actual developmental level (what they already can accomplish independently), and

■ their level of potential development (the highest level they can reach with guidance from more capable individuals).

This zone includes all possible skills that children are on the verge of developing and can perform only with help from someone more cognitively advanced (rather than peers at the same cognitive level, as Piaget argued). Interaction with adults or more capable children (older children or those with higher ability) on tasks that are slightly above children's current level creates a zone of optimal learning. Within this zone, children develop new skills and internalize more advanced ways of thinking, reaching a new level of potential development. When they reach this new level of thinking, this becomes their actual developmental level, and the cycle continues. For example, a first-grader working alone may be able to write only a brief story with short sentences and simple vocabulary, but with help from a third-grade "buddy" she is able to write a longer, more elaborate story. With repeated experiences working with her buddy, she will eventually be able to write longer, more complex stories on her own. Let's examine the factors involved in cognitive growth within the ZPD.

Mechanisms of cognitive change. Within the ZPD, adults and learners engage in **intersubjectivity,** or co-construction of knowledge. Intersubjectivity is a process in which two individuals who begin a task

TABLE 7.1	Criticism of Piaget's Theory: Support and Counterarguments	
Criticism of Piaget's theory	**Support for the criticism**	**Counterarguments**
1. Underestimates children's cognitive abilities.	■ Infants achieve object permanence earlier than Piaget proposed. ■ Pre-operational children can pass concrete-operational tasks when tasks are modified to simplify instructions or to reduce memory and language demands.	■ Research findings with younger infants may indicate only an awareness that the perceptual array has changed, rather than clear acquisition of object permanence. ■ Children's success on simplified concrete operational tasks may be due to lower-level cognitive competencies (for example, using a counting strategy on number conservation) rather than logico-mathematical reasoning (reversibility).
2. Proposes that cognitive development cannot be meaningfully accelerated.	Pre-operational children can learn conservation (not just memorize answers) through various methods, such as providing corrective feedback (right or wrong), directing their attention to the appropriate visual cues, adult modeling, and working with peers who have mastered conservation.	Piaget was not interested in the rate of development, accelerations, and delays, but in describing processes that account for developmental changes. The rate of progression through the stages will vary, depending on individuals' previous experiences.
3. Wrongly proposes that self-discovery is necessary for cognitive development.	There is little available evidence to support unguided, self-discovery as necessary for cognitive development.	Discovery can enhance thinking when students are given appropriate structure and guidance.
4. May not be stagelike.	Children master different conservation tasks at different ages—number conservation around age 7, mass somewhat later, and liquid conservation toward the end of concrete operations—even though conservation is a concrete operational acquisition.	Piaget's theory allowed for asynchrony in development, proposing continual transformations and integration of less advanced thinking into more complex forms of thinking. The stages give us a "big picture" of these transformations.
5. Is limited to Western cultures.	Critics argue that Piaget's theory is not universal as he originally proposed.	■ The sequence of development through the four stages has been found in cultures around the world, from Mexico and Australia to Thailand, Rwanda, Papua, Iraq, and Ghana. *DIVERSITY* ■ Research showing that the rate of development through stages varies across cultures supports Piaget's assertion that intellectual development depends on specific cultural and educational environments.

Sources: Au, Sidle, & Rollins, 1993; Baillargeon, 1991; Brainerd, 2003; Chandler & Chapman, 1991; Dasen, 1977; Greenfield, 1976; Lourenço & Machado, 1996; Miller & Baillargeon, 1990; Piaget, 1924, 1932, 1972b; Rogoff & Chavajay, 1995; Smith, 1993; Sternberg, 2003; Zigler & Gilman, 1998.

with different knowledge and perspectives come to a shared understanding as each person adjusts to the perspective of the other (Newson & Newson, 1975; Vygotsky, 1978). Both the learner and the more skilled individual are active partners in co-construction. In the first-grade example, even though the first-grader and the third-grader have different levels of writing skill and perhaps different ideas about what to include in the story, they must bridge the gap between them and *together* create the story.

How do the more experienced and less experienced partners bridge the gap? During a joint activity, adults, older children, and more capable peers use **psychological and cultural tools** (what Piaget called semiotic functions) to mediate the child's thinking and shape the development of more complex thought (Rowe & Wertsch, 2002; Vygotsky, 1978). Broadly speaking, tools can be signs and symbols (primarily language), mnemonics, concepts, or any activities, interactions, or symbolic systems the culture provides (Das, 1995). To illustrate the adult's role, David Wood, Jerome Bruner, and Gail Ross (1976) used the metaphor **scaffolding,** based on Vygotsky's writings. Like the temporary platforms used in the construction of a building, scaffolding is a temporary social support to help children accomplish a task. It supports preschoolers as well as older students when they are learning new tasks (Barron et al., 1998; Brown & Kane, 1988).

As children master the use of psychological and cultural tools, a gradual **internalization** occurs, in which they slowly acquire more cognitive responsibility for the task, and scaffolding gradually is withdrawn (called *fading*) (Vygotsky, 1962; Wood, 1989). Children shift from performing cognitive processes *socially* with an adult to performing them *mentally* by themselves (Leontiev, 1961; Webb & Palinscar, 1996). The tools become part of children's repertoires, the children's new cognitive processes become part of their actual developmental level, and a new zone is created, with a new level of potential development (Karpov & Bransford, 1995; Vygotsky, 1978).

Teachers should keep in mind two points when applying the Zone of Proximal Development to their classroom:

1. The zone of optimal learning will differ among students. Two same-age students can have the same actual developmental level but differ considerably in their learning potential in particular subjects or in their ability to benefit from external assistance (Sternberg, 2002; Vygotsky, 1978). Some students may have a narrower ZPD and may need more frequent and explicit assistance (Day & Cordon, 1993).

2. Scaffolding actually is driven by the learner rather than controlled by the more experienced person (Tudge & Scrimsher, 2003). To be effective, adults must match their communication and support to the learner's needs and current cognitive level (Dennen, 2004; Jacobs & Eccles, 2000). Vygotsky saw adults as both pushing and pulling development, yielding a co-constructive, bidirectional process within the ZPD rather than a one-way transmission from the adult to the learner (Tudge & Scrimsher, 2003).

Constructivist teaching methods: See page 369.

It is difficult to critically evaluate Vygotsky's theory due to its smaller research base in comparison with Piaget's theory. Even though Vygotsky wrote extensively on the science of child development from 1928 until 1934, his career was cut short when he died at age 37 from tuberculosis. Also, in the Soviet Union, the study of child development and all references to it (including Vygotsky's theory) were denounced and banned from 1936 to the 1950s, and researchers and educators in the United States have only recently had access to translations of his writings (Tudge & Scrimsher, 2003). Researchers have begun to evaluate Vygotsky's theory and its impact on education by investigating the efficacy of various constructivist teaching methods based on his ideas about the co-construction of knowledge and intersubjectivity within the ZPD.

Can you think of ways in which Piaget's and Vygotsky's theories are similar, different, and complementary?

ISSUES IN COGNITIVE DEVELOPMENT: PIAGET AND VYGOTSKY

Piaget and Vygotsky simultaneously developed theories of cognitive development during the early twentieth century. Vygotsky wrote critiques of Piaget's work, but Piaget did not read any of Vygotsky's writings until years after Vygotsky's death (Piaget, 1962). Even though they never met in person, their views provide us with a dialogue on important issues in cognitive development. Let's examine these issues next.

What Comes First: Development or Learning?

Development involves acquiring concepts spontaneously through natural experiences, and learning involves applying the newly developed cognitive structures to new situations (Lawton & Hooper, 1978; Piaget, 1970). According to Piaget, development precedes learning because an individual must be developmentally ready to learn (Wink & Putney, 2002). A child's stage of development places constraints on what and how much he or she can learn from instruction (Brainerd, 1978; Inhelder, Sinclair, & Bovet, 1974). We must know a child's current stage before we can know what it is possible to teach the child (Piaget, 1970).

Vygotsky used the ZPD to explain how *theoretical learning,* a form of learning that occurs in school, pulls development to higher levels (Karpov & Bransford, 1995). Before children enter school, they engage in *empirical learning,* a simple form of learning that results in *spontaneous concepts.* Spontaneous concepts are unsystematic, unconscious, and sometimes incorrect ideas generalized from children's everyday concrete experiences (Davydov, 1972, 1988). Spontaneous concepts provide the conceptual framework—prior knowledge—for acquiring *scientific concepts,* or concepts acquired during theoretical learning (Karpov, 2006; Vygotsky, 1962).

During instruction, teachers should provide problem-solving activities that enable students to use scientific concepts in practical ways. This allows scientific concepts to meet students' personal, concrete experiences so their spontaneous concepts become structured and conscious (Karpov, 2006; Vygotsky, 1987). For example, elementary school students may begin school with knowledge of how a flower grows from a seed (an everyday experience). In school, they will learn the definitions of concepts related to plants and engage in scientific observation and recording of factors that affect plant growth (amount of water, sunlight, etc.). Their spontaneous concept or everyday knowledge about plant growth is transformed and restructured into scientific concepts.

Vygotsky cautioned that learning leads to development only if instruction has been organized properly to focus on cognitive functions not yet completely mastered (Karpov & Bransford, 1995). Teachers should create a ZPD in which social interaction and collaboration lead the student to use and develop new cognitive processes and skills (Vygotsky, 1978).

Role of Language in Cognitive Development

Piaget and Vygotsky shared similar views on the role of language in thinking. They agreed that internalized (not spoken) language:

- is needed for conscious thoughts—that we think in words (Das, 1995; Moll, 2001; Vygotsky, 1987);
- serves a reflective function, allowing individuals to refer to the past, present, and future (Das, 1995); and
- serves a planning function, whereby individuals practice a dialogue with a hypothetical other person before actually engaging in it (Piaget, 1926).

They also agreed on the role of language in logical thinking, but they differed in the importance they placed on language. For Vygotsky, language and thought are intertwined: Thinking is a mental process that needs language as its base (Leontiev & Luria, 1972). For Piaget, language plays a necessary but not primary role in logical thinking. During the concrete and formal operational stages, children use language as a tool for developing logical thinking, to think through problems and express what they know and do not know (Das, 1995; Inhelder & Piaget, 1955). However, because logical thinking involves a continual coordination of actions—from organizing sensorimotor schemes to coordinating logical operations—thinking comes *before* language (Piaget, 1970).

Piaget and Vygotsky also disagreed on the role of externalized speech in cognitive development. In Vygotsky's theory, social situations provide the initial context in which children develop planning and self-regulation strategies (Rowe & Wertsch, 2002). Adults and children use **socialized speech** (speech used to communicate with others) as a tool for coordinating their actions with those of others. Children gradually learn to regulate their thoughts and actions using **inner speech,** a self-regulatory, internalized speech.

In Piaget's theory, externalized speech takes the form of egocentric speech and is a cognitive limitation of pre-operational thinking. Egocentric speech gradually diminishes as children progress through the pre-operational stage and develop the two-way thinking characteristic of the concrete operational stage. Vygotsky, however, saw Piaget's egocentric speech as a necessary transition between socialized speech and

Pretend Play and Symbolic Thinking. Both Piaget and Vygotsky considered pretend play to be important to the development of symbolic thinking.

inner speech (Rowe & Wertsch, 2002). Vygotsky conducted research on Piaget's egocentric speech that showed substantial increases in egocentric speech during cognitively challenging activities (Kohlberg, Yaeger, & Hjertholm, 1968; Rowe & Wertsch, 2002). Therefore, externalized speech is a useful tool for independently planning and regulating actions, for example, when students solve a difficult word problem in math or organize an essay on their own.

Can you think of other examples when children and adolescents may need to talk themselves through a problem out loud?

Role of Play in Cognitive Development

The importance of play in the intellectual development of preschool-age children is evident in both Piaget's and Vygotsky's theories. Piaget (1945/1962) regarded pretend play as evidence of the child's ability to use and understand symbols, emerging at the end of the sensorimotor stage and developing throughout the pre-operational stage (Smith, 2002). He also emphasized pretend play as an individual process, suggesting that the child alone invented and used symbols (Smolucha & Smolucha, 1998).

Vygotsky (1978) considered pretend play to be a more social phenomenon than did Piaget. Imaginative play creates a ZPD in which children behave beyond their current developmental level and advance to higher levels of cognitive functioning (Moll, 2001; Whitington & Floyd, 2009). In pretend play, children advance their thinking by:

- creating actions that originate from ideas ("Let's pretend we're dinosaurs"),
- detaching the meaning of objects from their typical appearance (a stick for a gun), and
- creating imaginary contexts for practicing roles, rules, and expectations they have experienced in their everyday life (playing a parent role and punishing a doll).

Sociodramatic play is a particular form of pretend play in which children jointly create and act out an imaginary context. In sociodramatic play, children learn to guide their behavior because they must think before acting (Vygotsky, 1978). They also use intersubjectivity by sharing a joint focus on the task, exchanging knowledge, and moving between pretend and reality to negotiate the play experience (for example, stepping out of play to decide on roles) (Goncu, 1993; Whitington & Floyd, 2009). This type of play advances cognitive development and prepares children for later symbol-based learning such as reading and writing (Berk, 2006; Bodrova & Leong, 1997).

Current research suggests that play experiences may continue to support children's cognitive development through the later elementary school years. Peer play in elementary school is related to academic success and the development of social skills (Bjorklund & Pellegrini, 2000; Coie & Dodge, 1998; Waters & Sroufe, 1983). Allowing time for recess, which may involve peer play as well as physical activities, reduces students' attention and memory demands and allows them to more efficiently process information when they return from the break (Pellegrini & Bohn, 2005; Toppino, Kasserman, & Mracek, 1991). In a series of studies, elementary school students were more attentive after recess than before, even when recess was held indoors, with less opportunity for physical activity (Pellegrini, Huberty, & Jones, 1995; Pellegrini & Smith, 1993).

Attention and memory: See page 184.

APPLICATIONS: CONSTRUCTIVIST PRINCIPLES FOR EFFECTIVE TEACHING

The constructivist theories we've discussed in this module can provide teachers with several guidelines for effective teaching.

Consider students' developmental level when designing curricula and activities. Both theorists recognized the importance of knowing a child's current level of thinking before planning instruction. Based on Piaget's theory, teachers can use a student's stage of cognitive development to determine appropriate instructional materials and activities (Brainerd, 1978; Piaget, 1970). Likewise, Vygotsky recommended that teachers identify what the child brings to the situation and then arrange activities to foster the development of cognitive processes on the verge of emerging (Tudge & Scrimsher, 2003; Vygotsky, 1998). Teachers can use dynamic testing to determine what students are able to learn with assistance (their ZPD) rather than relying on assessments that show only what a student already knows (Campione & Brown, 1990; Vygotsky, 1998). *Dynamic testing* is an interactive assessment in which teachers probe students' thinking and provide guidance and feedback during the testing. This points to students' learning

[handwritten margin note:] Constructivist = Student Centered

potential by identifying how much they can achieve *above* their current level with appropriate support (Brown & Ferrara, 1985; Grigorenko & Sternberg, 1998).

Whether we consider stages or ZPD, students profit from experiences that are within their reach cognitively. When teachers design tasks that are moderately challenging, students will be operating in their ZPD—or, in Piagetian terms, they will experience disequilibrium.

Encourage students to be active learners. Encouraging students to be active learners does not mean that we must always use social interactions and group work (a common misapplication of Vygotsky's theory) or that all learning must be discovery-based (an assumption based on Piaget's theory). Social interactions are beneficial only if they occur appropriately within students' ZPDs and if students are given the proper scaffolding. Also, unguided self-discovery is less effective than other teaching methods for learning and transfer of knowledge to new situations, because learning may not occur if students are given too much freedom in the discovery process (Mayer, 2004; Mayer & Wittrock, 1996). Rather, **active learning** can be defined more broadly as any type of meaningful learning in which students construct a rich knowledge base (rather than memorizing facts) of interconnected concepts, prior knowledge, and real-life experiences (Bransford & Schwartz, 1999; Murphy & Woods, 1996; Renkl, Mandl, & Gruber, 1996).

Discovery learning: See page 368.

Promoting meaningful learning: See page 231.

Link new concepts to students' prior knowledge. Teachers can encourage meaningful learning (as well as transfer of learning to new settings) by capitalizing on what students already know. According to Piaget, individuals first assimilate a new experience into their existing cognitive framework (thinking a whale is a fish) and later may reorganize their cognitive structure to accommodate the new experience (modifying the fish concept) (Piaget, 1970; Zigler & Gilman, 1998). Vygotsky likewise believed that children's spontaneous concepts from their everyday experiences form the basis for the development of more sophisticated concepts in school (Karpov & Bransford, 1995).

Prior knowledge: See page 226.

Use teaching methods based on constructivist principles. To encourage active, meaningful learning, teachers can use a variety of strategies that are based on constructivist principles:

Constructivist teaching methods: See page 369.

- Cognitive apprenticeships involve opportunities to develop cognitive skills within the context of authentic activities. Students participate at a level commensurate with their abilities and move gradually toward full participation. Within cognitive apprenticeships, teachers use techniques such as modeling, scaffolding, and fading.

- To teach reading comprehension, teachers can use methods such as reciprocal teaching and instructional conversations—methods based on Vygotsky's Zone of Proximal Development. Both methods contain elements of cognitive apprenticeships such as modeling and scaffolding. Reciprocal questioning, another method that relies on co-construction of knowledge, can be used from elementary through high school to help students understand new concepts or skills through structured conversations.

- Methods such as inquiry learning, in which students solve problems by following research steps, and cooperative learning, in which students work together to achieve a shared goal, can be used for any subject and with students from elementary through high school.

Provide multiple exposures to content. Returning to content at different times, in different contexts, for different purposes, and from different perspectives will enhance students' knowledge acquisition (Haskell, 2001; Spiro, Feltovich, Jacobsen, & Coulson, 1991). Examining content from differing perspectives, such as in class debates and discussions, may lead students to restructure or modify their existing knowledge. Revisiting content over time and in different contexts also encourages transfer of knowledge by preventing learned information from being tied to specific situations or contexts (Salomon & Perkins, 1989).

Recognize cultural context in learning situations. Consistent with Vygotsky's theory, teachers need to consider how the setting of particular instructional activities and the larger cultural context may affect learning (Griffin & Cole, 1999; Tharp & Gallimore, 1988). In arranging instructional activities that involve social interaction, such as collaborative projects or class discussions, teachers need to consider how styles of interaction may differ among students from different cultural backgrounds. For example, Native Hawaiian children, who tend to engage in negative wait time (children talking at the same time), and Navajo children, who wait a long time to be sure a speaker has finished talking, may have different needs during social interactions in the classroom (Tharp, 1989).

Transfer: See page 226.

DIVERSITY

Think about the grade level of students you expect to teach. How can you use the guidelines presented here in your classroom?

Summary

Contrast individual and social constructivism. In individual constructivism, a person constructs knowledge independently by using cognitive processes to abstract information from experiences. In social constructivism, individuals construct knowledge within a social/cultural context—the social interactions and what they bring to the learning situation are interconnected.

Describe cognitive development through Piaget's stages, and identify what causes changes in thinking. In the sensorimotor stage, infants construct knowledge from sensory and motor experiences, preparing them for later symbolic thinking. While pre-operational children are able to form mental representations, their thinking is one-way. Operations develop further in the concrete operational stage, in which children can think logically and mentally reverse their thinking, albeit concretely. Formal operational thinkers can mentally manipulate abstract concepts. Maturational changes, active exploration, social interactions, and equilibration together cause thinking to evolve through the four stages.

Describe intersubjectivity, internalization, and scaffolding within the Zone of Proximal Development. In the ZPD, a child and an older individual engage in intersubjectivity, an active co-construction of knowledge. As the adult provides scaffolding, the child gradually gains more skill and takes over more responsibility for the task. Cognitive processes that initially were shared between the adult and the child and were scaffolded by the adult gradually become internalized by the child, and the adult slowly removes the scaffolding.

Compare and contrast the views of Piaget and Vygotsky on issues in cognitive development. Piaget argued that development precedes learning, while Vygotsky proposed that formal learning in school pulls development to a new level. Both theorists emphasized the importance of play in young children's cognitive development. However, Piaget considered pretend play to be an individual process, while Vygotsky considered it to be social as well as individual. The theorists also agreed on the role of language in logical thinking and shared similar ideas about the role of internalized language in thinking. They differed in their view of the role of externalized speech in planning actions and regulating thoughts—Piaget considered it a cognitive weakness of pre-operational children, while Vygotsky viewed it as a tool for planning and regulating actions.

Discuss how teachers can use constructivist theories to develop effective instruction. Teachers can begin by considering students' level of thinking when designing curricula and activities because students will benefit from experiences that are within their reach cognitively. During instruction, teachers should encourage students to be active learners and to link new concepts to their prior knowledge. Both Piaget and Vygotsky believed that children continually modify their existing thinking through active construction of knowledge. To encourage meaningful learning, teachers can choose among a variety of constructivist methods based on Piaget's and Vygotsky's theories. Examining content from different perspectives can also help students restructure or modify their existing knowledge, and revisiting content in different contexts will promote transfer. Finally, teachers should consider how the social settings within the classroom, as well as the larger cultural context, may affect students' learning.

Key Concepts

accommodation 120
active learning 129
assimilation 120
centration 122
concepts 122
conservation 122
constructivism 119
disequilibrium 120
egocentric 122

egocentric speech 122
equilibration 120
identity constancy 123
individual constructivism 119
inner speech 127
internalization 126
intersubjectivity 124
object permanence 122
operations 120

psychological and cultural tools 126
reversibility 122
scaffolding 126
schemes 120
semiotic functions 122
social constructivism 119
socialized speech 127
Zone of Proximal Development (ZPD) 124

Video Applications
www.mhhe.com/bohlin2e

Video 1: Piaget's Stages (*5 minutes*)
This clip shows segments of instructional activities from classrooms at different grade levels to illustrate stages of Piaget's theory.

Video 2: Piaget and Vygotsky in the Classroom (*4 minutes*)
Carol Goodrich, a teacher in a fourth/fifth-grade self-contained gifted classroom, challenges students to discover whether Madison, Wisconsin, is closer to the North Pole or the Equator.

Video 3: Vygotsky in the Classroom (*3 minutes*)
This clip shows segments of instructional activities from classrooms at different grade levels to illustrate aspects of Vygotsky's theory.

Video 4: Using Play to Promote Cognitive Development (*7 minutes*)
This clip shows how preschool and kindergarten teachers encourage cognitive development through the use of centers.

Case Studies
Reflect and Evaluate

EARLY CHILDHOOD: "Fire Safety"

These questions refer to the case study on page 92.

1. Using the concept of egocentrism, explain why Michala wanted to sit on the letter M on the carpet.

2. Use the case situation in which Brianna and Michala are coloring their flashcards to contrast Piaget's and Vygotsky's views on externalized speech.

3. According to Piaget's theory, why would demonstrations be an effective way to teach preschoolers about fire safety? Would demonstrations be effective for elementary school students, according to his theory?

4. Identify Miss Angela's use of scaffolding in the case, and explain how scaffolding helps children in the Zone of Proximal Development.

5. Think of one original fire safety activity (not already mentioned in the case) that would be consistent with Piaget's theory of cognitive development. Think of another original fire safety activity that would be consistent with Vygotsky's theory of cognitive development. Describe how each activity is supported by the theory. What factors, consistent with these theories, do teachers need to consider when planning instruction at the early childhood level?

ELEMENTARY SCHOOL: "Project Night"

These questions refer to the case study on page 94.

1. Explain in your own words why the project-based unit would be considered a constructivist approach to learning.

2. Based on the students' current stage of cognitive development, why was it necessary for Mr. Morales to break down the project into smaller, more manageable steps?

3. Based on Piaget's stage theory of cognitive development, would you have expected students' self-evaluations to be so superficial? Why or why not?

4. How does the "research team" format exemplify Vygotsky's social construction of knowledge within the Zone of Proximal Development?

5. Explain how the "research team" activity might stimulate disequilibrium in students. Explain how assimilation and accommodation would be involved in this activity.

MIDDLE SCHOOL: "Frogs"

These questions refer to the case study on page 96.

1. According to Piaget's theory of cognitive development, what factors should Ms. Thesdale consider in planning biology lessons?

2. Explain how Ms. Thesdale could stimulate disequilibrium in her students before the frog dissection and why disequilibrium is important for cognitive change.

3. Ms. Thesdale assumed that the social interaction of working together in groups on dissection would foster cognitive growth. Based on the processes that stimulate cognitive change within the Zone of Proximal Development, evaluate the effectiveness of the group dissection activity.

4. Based on Vygotsky's Zone of Proximal Development, was it appropriate for Ms. Thesdale to place Tyler with Jay and Vincent? Why or why not? What types of support would Tyler need from other students and from Ms. Thesdale in order to benefit from instruction involving social interaction?

5. How can Ms. Thesdale encourage active learning in her students? Provide specific suggestions, and explain whether each is supported by Piaget's or Vygotsky's theory.

HIGH SCHOOL: "The Substitute"

These questions refer to the case study on page 98.

1. Is it valid for a teacher to assume that high school students should be at the formal operational stage of development? Use Piaget's theory to support your answer.

2. Based on Piaget's theory of cognitive development, is a skit an effective method for helping Mr. Matthews's high school students understand *A Tale of Two Cities*? Why or why not?

3. From your reading of the case, what mistakes did Mr. Reddy make in teaching his British literature class, based on the four factors necessary for developmental change in Piaget's theory?

4. Explain how the group discussions at the end of the case exemplify intersubjectivity and internalization.

5. Assume that you are teaching a junior-level British literature course in high school. What would be your expectations of the students, and how would you approach teaching this subject? Explain how your response fits with either Piaget's or Vygotsky's theories, or both.

MODULE 8

Language Development

Outline	Learning Goals
Understanding Language Acquisition	
■ Biological Basis of Language ■ Imitation and Reinforcement ■ Social Interactions	1. Explain the factors that contribute to language development.
Development of Language Skills	
■ Language Acquisition Through Early Childhood ■ Language Acquisition Through Adolescence ■ Bilingual Language Acquisition ■ Individual Differences in Language Acquisition	2. Describe changes in semantics, syntax, pragmatics, and metalinguistic awareness from birth through adolescence. 3. Explain the advantages and disadvantages of the methods of teaching English-language learners. 4. Describe the language differences that emerge from early childhood through the early school-age years.
Applications: Encouraging Language Development in the Classroom	
	5. Describe ways teachers can support language development in the classroom.
Summary **Key Concepts** **Video Applications** **Case Studies: Reflect and Evaluate**	

UNDERSTANDING LANGUAGE ACQUISITION

Language development forms the basis of much school learning from early childhood through secondary education. Language skills allow children to form concepts, engage in pretend play, and interact socially—all of which advance children's cognitive development. In elementary through secondary school, oral language skills enable students to learn from lessons and lectures, to demonstrate knowledge by answering questions, and to participate in discussions and group activities. Oral language also provides a foundation for reading and writing skills, as well as for acquisition of a second language in English-language learners. Before we discuss the progression of language development and its impact on school-age learners, let's explore the factors responsible for language acquisition.

Biological Basis of Language

The brain and its development: See Module 6.

Our brains are well designed for the production and acquisition of language. The cerebrum, the largest portion of our brain, consists of two halves called hemispheres. Although both hemispheres are involved in language, in most individuals the left hemisphere has more responsibility for many language functions and becomes specialized for language functions early in infancy (Holowka & Petitto, 2002; Obler & Gjerlow, 1999). When the left hemisphere is damaged, the brain's *plasticity*—its ability to adapt to environmental experiences—allows the right hemisphere to take over many of the functions of the left hemisphere, leading to relatively normal language development (Stiles & Thal, 1993). Because plasticity decreases with age, however, it is more difficult for the right hemisphere to take on language functions after infancy (Stiles, Bates, Thal, Trauner, & Reilly, 2002).

Humans may acquire language so readily and easily because we are genetically predisposed—that is, biologically ready—to acquire language (Ritchie & Bhatia, 1999; Spelke & Newport, 1998). From birth, infants prefer sounds that have characteristics of human speech: sounds in the frequency range of 1,000–3,000 Hz and sounds with a variation in frequencies rather than monotones (Schneider, Trehub, & Bull, 1979).

DIVERSITY The similarities among cultures in many features of language also suggest an innate capacity for language:

1. Children around the world acquire language within a short period of time and at roughly the same rate despite differences in cultures (Kuhl, 2004). This is true both in cultures where children initiate and participate in conversations with adults and in cultures that discourage adults from conversing with children (Snow, 1986).

2. The sequence of language skills is similar across cultures for signed and spoken languages (Kent & Miulo, 1995; Petitto, Holowka, Sergio, & Ostry, 2001).

3. The sounds *b, p, m, d,* and *n* appear across many languages in infants' **babbling,** or repetitive consonant-vowel combinations (for example, dadadadada) (Gopnik, Meltzoff, & Kuhl, 1999; Locke, 1983).

4. All signed and spoken languages share:

   ▪ first words such as *juice, milk,* and *dog* (Caselli et al., 1995; Marschark, West, Nall, & Everhart, 1986); and

   ▪ rules to indicate changes in tense and plurality and to organize words into grammatical sentences (Goldin-Meadow & Morford, 1985; Goldin-Meadow & Mylander, 1983).

Imitation and Reinforcement

Positive reinforcement: See page 162.

Language learning partly involves imitation and reinforcement (Skinner, 1957). In response to adult modeling of language, children will attempt to produce language by spontaneously imitating sounds, words, and phrases. Parents also may encourage *elicited imitation* when they ask the child to produce a word spoken by the adult (say "bottle" instead of "ba-ba"). In many instances, children receive *positive reinforcement* (a positive consequence for behavior) for their efforts, as when a caregiver responds to infants' babbling with more dialogue or responds to a toddler's request ("want milk").

DIVERSITY Modeling and imitation vary by culture. In cultures that do not encourage children to initiate conversations or to talk before a certain age, children are expected to learn by listening and by observing adult language (Schieffelin & Ochs, 1986). In the United States, elicited imitation is not considered a crucial teaching method. Children implicitly discover the usefulness of imitation as a way to expand their communication skills. In recurrent, predictable events in their lives, children often repeat an utterance previously spoken by an adult during the same events (Snow & Goldfield, 1983). However, imitation and parental reinforcement cannot entirely explain children's development of grammatically appropriate language (James, 1990). Consider these findings:

■ Children produce sentences they have never heard adults say ("I falled on the playground"). Also, children use imitation much less after age 2, even though they still have much more language to acquire (Otto, 2006).

■ Reinforcement of children's grammar is not necessary for language development. Rather than correcting a child's grammar, parents tend to reinforce and correct children's utterances based on meaning or truth value (Brown & Hanlon, 1970). When a school-age child announces "I don't got no more money," a parent might respond, "Really, you *don't have* any more money? Where did you spend it?"

■ We are motivated to learn to speak grammatically even though ungrammatical statements can convey our message just as well (Siegler & Alibali, 2005).

Social Interactions

Language acquisition is also a product of children's early social interactions with adults. Infants communicate and interact socially even before they are able to produce language. They make different babbling sounds in response to adults' pitch and intonation, move in rhythm to adults' intonations, and vocalize more when adults stop talking—a pattern similar to typical conversation (Ginsburg & Kilbourne, 1988; Locke, 1995; Masataka, 1992).

Communication During the First Year. The mother shown here might be describing the flower and asking her daughter questions about the flower. Providing experiences such as these encourages expressive language in young children.

Adults also behave in certain ways that elicit communication and foster language development. They initiate communication in response to infants' eye contact, burping, or gurgling and respond to infants' babbling or first attempts at saying words. Toward the end of infants' first year, adults in many cultures encourage the development of language skills with additional techniques, described in Table 8.1. Caregiver techniques may not be universal, though (Harkness, 1977; Ochs

TABLE 8.1	Social Interaction Techniques of Caregivers		
Caregiver technique	**Description**	**Outcome**	**Example**
Child-directed speech	Language directed to infants and children characterized by high pitch, exaggerated intonations, elongated vowels, short and simple sentences, and repetition	Increases infants' attention to language, facilitating their comprehension and acquisition of language	(playing peek-a-boo) *Where—is—Tommy?* (exaggerated intonation) *Peek—a—boo—I—see—you!*
Joint attention	Adults labeling and talking about objects on which the child's attention is focused	Encourages vocabulary acquisition	An adult noticing an infant looking at a bird and saying: *That's a bird. Do you hear it chirping?*
Expansion	Adults adding to—or expanding—the child's incomplete statement as a way to model more complex language	Encourages the development of more complex grammar	When a child says: *doggie sleep*, an adult saying: *Yes, the doggie is sleeping. She's tired.*
Recasting	Adults reproducing the child's utterance as a semantically similar expression that adds new information to model more complex language	Encourages the development of more complex grammar	A child saying: *We go home?* and the adult replying: *No, we're going to the store.*

Sources: Adamson, 1996; Brown & Bellugi, 1964; Butterworth, 2001; Campbell & Namy, 2003; Fernald, 1985; Karrass, Braungart-Rieker, Mullins, & Lefever, 2002; Kasari, Sigman, Mundy, & Yirmiya, 1990; Rollins, 2003; Sachs, 1989; Scherer & Olswang, 1984.

& Schieffelin, 1984). Therefore, while adult behaviors may not be *necessary* for language acquisition, they can *enhance* language development. Recent research suggests that several forms of caregiver responsiveness contribute to infants' development of expressive language: using expansions, describing objects, asking questions about objects ("What is that?"), using verbal prompts ("Let's feed the doll"), providing a rich vocabulary, and producing more complex sentences (Hoff, 2003a, 2003b; Tamis-LeMonda, Bornstein, & Baumwell, 2001).

DIVERSITY   Adults' behaviors may have long-term benefits as well. Regardless of the family's socioeconomic status or ethnic group identity, parents who vary their speech, label objects, ask questions, respond to children's questions, and provide positive feedback for children's participation in conversations are more likely to have children with advanced language development (Hart & Risley, 1995; Snow, Tabors, & Dickinson, 2001). The amount of verbal interaction between caregivers and children is a significant predictor of a child's vocabulary, language skills, and reading comprehension at age 9 (Hart & Risley, 1999, 2003). Talking with children during activities and about activities should be a regular part of the day both at home and in early-childhood classrooms.

Imagine a child growing up in another part of the world. How might his language development be similar to that of a child in the United States? How might it be different?

DEVELOPMENT OF LANGUAGE SKILLS

Language Acquisition Through Early Childhood

Babbling is the first sign of an infant's ability to produce language, beginning at about 6 months. Around age 8 to 12 months, infants can more easily communicate with adults through gestures and joint attention (adult labeling and talking about objects the child is gazing at). They also become increasingly skilled at comprehending the meaning of words and can respond appropriately to commands (Benedict, 1979; Morrisette, Ricard, & Gouin-Decarie, 1995). With the acquisition of their first words at about 1 year of age, children gradually acquire the ability to use semantics, syntax, the pragmatics of language, and metalinguistic awareness.

Holophrastic Speech. "Juice" may mean "Mommy, I want some more juice."

SEMANTICS

Semantics (how words convey meaning) is evident in infants' first words. Their language is often referred to as **holophrastic speech,** because they use single words to express a larger meaning. For example, "juice" may mean "The juice is all gone" or "I spilled the juice." Children in the holophrastic stage will commit errors known as:

- **overextensions,** or using a word to cover a range of concepts, such as saying "kitty" to refer to all four-legged animals; and
- **underextensions,** or limiting the use of a word to a subset of objects it refers to, such as using "kitty" only for the family cat.

SYNTAX

The development of **syntax** (the logical combination of words into meaningful sentences) begins with **telegraphic speech,** a way of ordering two or three words according to the grammatical rules of the child's language (Brown & Fraser, 1963; Tager-Flusberg, 1997). Such speech is called telegraphic because it resembles a telegram, consisting mostly of content words (nouns and verbs) and omitting function words (articles, conjunctions, etc.). For example, "sit floor mommy" conveys the request "Sit on the floor with me, mommy." Children also develop several other forms of syntax throughout early childhood, including:

- **morphemic inflections,** or word endings (dog*s*, dog*'s*, runn*ing*, bak*ed*),

- negations (I can't do it!),
- questions (What is Mommy doing?), and
- conjoining clauses (I went to a party *and* I ate cake).

Caregivers and early-childhood educators should not be concerned about children's **overregularizations** of past tense endings (for example, saying "winned" for "won"), because these are typical in this stage of development and continue through school age (Brown, 1973; Otto, 2006).

PRAGMATICS

Pragmatics (knowledge about how to use language in communicative contexts) emerges in toddlerhood as children learn to use language for many purposes (Otto, 2006):

- regulating others' behaviors ("No!" or "Daddy, look!"),
- imagining (as in pretend play),
- learning about their environment by asking questions ("Why?" "What's this?"), and
- informing others ("I have a new baby sister").

Preschool children begin to use language for a wider range of purposes, such as asking permission, invoking social rules, expressing emotions, making judgments, joking and teasing, and making requests (Owens, 1988).

METALINGUISTIC AWARENESS

Metalinguistic awareness, our knowledge about language and how it works, is an important skill that emerges in early childhood and develops throughout the early elementary grades. Some early signs of metalinguistic awareness are:

- adjusting speech to different listeners, as when children as young as 2 years of age talk to a younger sibling differently from the way they talk to a parent (Warren-Leubecker & Bohannon, 1983);
- pretend reading of books, as when preschoolers turn pages and recite a story they have heard many times;
- asking "Are you making words?" to a parent typing on a computer; and
- "writing," in which preschoolers make marks on paper and ask an adult to read them (Schickedanz, York, Stewart, & White, 1990).

Phonological awareness, the knowledge that spoken words contain smaller units of sound, is a form of metalinguistic awareness that is important for later reading acquisition. Words can be divided into:

- *syllables,* the largest units of sound (but-ter);
- *onsets* and *rimes;* for example, in a word such as "bat," the onset is the sound corresponding to the initial consonant ("b"), and the rime is the vowel and the remaining consonant sound ("at"); and
- *phonemes,* the smallest units of sound ("b," "a," "t" sounds in the word "bat").

During kindergarten and first grade, children continue to develop awareness of phonemes as they acquire experience with printed words during reading instruction.

Phonological awareness and knowledge of letter names enable children to make progress in beginning reading instruction (Adams, 1990; Wagner, Torgesen, & Rashotte, 1994). Phonological awareness helps children acquire the skill of **decoding,** or sounding out (Liberman, Shankweiler, & Liberman, 1989). Children with awareness of phonemes

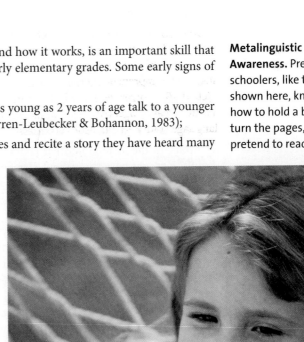

Metalinguistic Awareness. Preschoolers, like the girl shown here, know how to hold a book, turn the pages, and pretend to read.

TABLE 8.2	Benchmarks of Normal Development in Phonological Awareness
Grade level	**Average child's ability**
Beginning kindergarten	Can tell whether two words rhyme, can generate a rhyme for a simple word (e.g., *cat* or *dot*), or can easily be taught to do these tasks.
End of kindergarten	Can isolate and pronounce the beginning sound in a word (e.g., /n/ in *nose* or /f/ in *fudge*). Can blend the sounds in two-phoneme words [e.g., *boy* (/b/-/oi/) or *me* (/m/-/e/)].
Midway through first grade	Can isolate and pronounce all the sounds in two- and three-phoneme words. Can blend the sounds in four-phoneme words containing initial consonant blends.
End of first grade	Can isolate and pronounce the sounds in four-phoneme words containing initial blends. Can blend the sounds in four- and five-phoneme words containing initial and final blends.

Reprinted with permission from J. K. Torgesen & P. G. Mathes (2000). *A basic guide to understanding and teaching phonological awareness*. Austin, TX: Pro-Ed.

are able to apply sounds to letters in printed words to help them identify new words while reading. Direct instruction in awareness of phonemes can help children learn to read and spell (National Reading Panel, 2000). Preschool and kindergarten teachers also can teach phonological awareness skills through fun activities such as songs, nursery rhymes, and games. The guidelines in Table 8.2 can help early-childhood educators determine whether a child is progressing adequately in phonological awareness development.

Language Acquisition Through Adolescence

Contrary to the assumption that children have mastered language by their fifth birthday, language acquisition continues throughout elementary school, with some language forms not mastered until adolescence.

SEMANTICS

As elementary school students learn many concepts in and outside of school, their vocabularies grow at a rate of several new words per day—ranging from about 6,000 words in first grade to as many as 40,000 words in fifth grade (Anglin, 1993; Johnson & Anglin, 1995). The understanding and use of figurative language, an aspect of semantics, also evolves from elementary through high school (Owens, 2005). By third grade, students appreciate puns and riddles because they realize that words can have two meanings (McGhee, 1979; Pepicello & Weisberg, 1983). Elementary school students also begin to understand similes (He eats like a pig), metaphors (She's an angel), proverbs (Haste makes waste), and idioms (Did the cat get your tongue?), and they begin to realize that figures of speech are not to be taken literally ("stealing" home base). However, children do not master the more complex figurative language found in proverbs and sophisticated forms of humor until late adolescence (Lund & Duchan, 1988; Nippold & Duthie, 2003). Middle school and high school teachers should be aware that poetry and literature containing figurative language will be challenging for many students.

SYNTAX

Children's sentences become more elaborate and consist of more complex grammatical structures in both oral and written language:

- By age 10 or 11, students begin to produce subordinate clauses with complex conjunctions such as "because," "if," and "then" (Hulit & Howard, 2006; Wing & Scholnick, 1981).

- They begin to understand and use embedded sentences around age 7 (I saw a movie *that you would really like*). By age 12, they begin to understand embedding that occurs in the middle of sentences (The dog *that chased the cat* ran away) (Abrahamsen & Rigrodsky, 1984).

- Between ages 8 and 11, they also become better at understanding and producing passive sentences (Baldie, 1976; Horgan, 1978). For example, in the sentence "The boy was loved by the girl," younger children have difficulty determining who is the subject and who is the object of the loving.

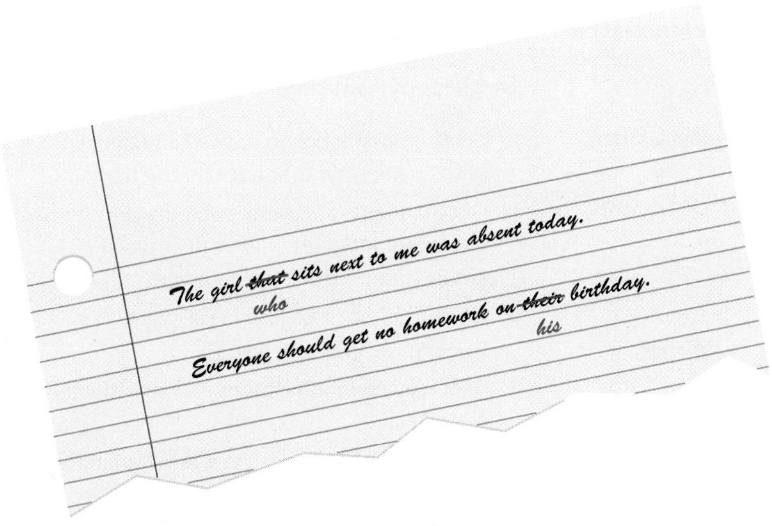

Figure 8.1. Syntax.
Even though adolescents' syntax continues to expand, they still may have difficulty with complex forms in their writing, as shown here.

> The girl ~~that~~ sits next to me was absent today.
> who
>
> Everyone should get no homework on ~~their~~ birthday.
> his

Secondary education teachers should expect adolescents to continue to have difficulty with some aspects of syntax, particularly when writing. Even adults have difficulty producing the syntactic forms who/whom/that and I/me in oral language (Otto, 2006). Adolescent writers also have problems using pronouns to refer to nouns in their writing. Teachers commonly see errors in adolescents' writing such as those shown in Figure 8.1.

PRAGMATICS

Elementary school students become more aware of the intent of indirect requests and the appropriate responses to such requests (Menyuk, 1988; Owens, 2005). Indirect requests are a more polite way of requesting an action from another person, such as "Can you turn off the TV?" rather than "Please turn off the TV." While preschoolers tend to respond literally by simply saying yes, 6-year-olds begin to respond appropriately to many types of indirect requests, with complete mastery occurring by adolescence (Cherry-Wilkinson & Dollaghan, 1979). By adolescence, most pragmatic skills related to common social experiences are well developed (Berko Gleason, Hay, & Cain, 1988).

METALINGUISTIC AWARENESS

While knowledge about language and how it works dramatically increases between ages 5 and 8, development continues throughout adulthood (Bernstein, 1989). Students in upper elementary through secondary grades are better able to understand words with multiple meanings, to know when words are used incorrectly in sentences, and to understand how to construct sentences of varying types (active, passive, etc.). They also become better able to use reading and writing strategies, such as consulting a dictionary or thesaurus, monitoring their comprehension, and planning and revising their writing.

Reading and writing strategies: See page 215.

How would you promote students' development of semantics, syntax, pragmatics, and metalinguistic awareness in the grade you intend to teach?

Bilingual Language Acquisition

Even though native English-speaking children and bilingual children (children speaking two languages) may have very different cultural and social experiences, they learn language in a very similar way (Bialystok, 2001):

- Children who acquire two languages from birth follow the same overall pattern and reach the same developmental milestones at the same rate as monolingual children (Genesee, Paradis, & Crago, 2004; Nicoladis & Genesee, 1997).

- Bilingual children say their first words and acquire a 50-word vocabulary at approximately the same age as monolingual children (Nicoladis & Genesee, 1997).

- Bilingual children have at least as large a vocabulary as monolingual children when vocabularies from both languages are combined (Nicoladis & Genesee, 1996; Pearson, 1998).

Becoming bilingual involves developing two separate language systems that interact with and complement each other. Even before children produce their first words, they have the capacity to differentiate

TABLE 8.3	Bilingual Instructional Approaches	
Instructional method	**Aim**	**Language of instruction**
Transitional bilingual education	To ensure that English-language learners do not fall behind academically by initially teaching school subjects in their native language .	■ Content instruction in native language; English as a Second Language instruction. ■ Once students are proficient, they transition to content instruction in English, usually around grades three through five.
English immersion	To make English-language learners fluent in English as soon as possible.	■ All instruction in English in classes with native English-speaking peers. ■ Generally no modifications in instruction or materials.
Structured English immersion	To facilitate a rapid transition to English-language instruction.	■ All instruction in English in classes separate from native-English speakers typically for one year. ■ Curricula and teaching methods designed to accommodate students who are learning the language. ■ Minimal use of native language. ■ Once students are "reasonably proficient" in English, they are transitioned into classes conducted in English with native English-speaking peers.
Two-way bilingual immersion	To facilitate acquisition of two languages in English-language learners and native English-speaking students.	■ Instruction in English and a non-English language for native English speakers and students who speak a non-English language (e.g., Spanish). ■ Instruction and classwork in both languages, with the non-English language used at least 50% of the time. ■ Only one language is used, without translation, during periods of instruction.

Sources: Crawford, 1997; Kogan, 2001; Lessow-Hurley, 2000; Lindholm-Leary, 2004–2005.

between two languages, including sign languages (Petitto, Katerelos, et al., 2001). **Code mixing,** using words or phrases from one language as a substitute in the other language, is normal for bilingual children and adults and does not suggest confusion between the two languages (Genesee et al., 2004; Nicoladis & Genesee, 1997). It allows individuals to use competencies in each language to communicate in a way that is more complete than if either language were used alone (Genesee et al., 2004). Elementary school children also are able to transfer their native-language competence in phonological awareness, vocabulary, and word recognition skills to their second language (Carlo & Royer, 1999; Cisero & Royer, 1995; Proctor, August, Carlo, & Snow, 2006). Experts disagree, however, about which instructional method is most effective for facilitating English language proficiency in English-language learners. Table 8.3 describes the aim of each instructional method.

Transitional bilingual education, which emphasizes the development of native language skills, was popular for almost 30 years. Because native language skills transfer to the second language, students experience greater academic success when they are given instruction in their native language in the early elementary grades (García, 1992; Marsh, Hau, & Kong, 2002). In contrast, students struggle academically in English immersion classrooms *without any instructional modifications* because they find it difficult to understand the teacher and to demonstrate their knowledge (DaSilva Iddlings, 2005; Gutiérrez, Baquedano-López, & Asato, 2001).

Two-Way Bilingual Immersion. This bilingual instructional method leads to beneficial academic and nonacademic outcomes for native English speakers and English-language learners.

Recent passage of the English Acquisition Act has shifted the bilingual education debate toward favoring immersion approaches, especially structured English immersion and two-way bilingual immersion, described in Table 8.3. Some recent research on two-way bilingual immersion (TWBI) offers intriguing results:

- In 3- and 4-year-olds, TWBI improved the Spanish language skills of both the English-language learners and monolingual children without any loss in English-language skills (Barnett, Yarosz, Thomas, Jung, & Blanco, 2007).

- English-language learners and native English-speaking students who attended TWBI programs since the early elementary grades have shown oral language, reading, and writing proficiency in both languages in the upper elementary grades (Howard, Sugarman, & Christian, 2003; Perez, 2004; Serrano & Howard, 2003). They have also scored at or above grade level in reading and math in both languages in middle school (Collier & Thomas, 2004; Lindholm-Leary, 2001).

- High school students who were enrolled in TWBI programs since elementary school, especially those from Hispanic backgrounds, have reported very positive attitudes about school (Lindholm-Leary, 2001).

Individual Differences in Language Acquisition

Typical language development varies considerably among young children in terms of the rate of acquisition and the style of acquiring words. Infants begin producing their first words at about 8 to 18 months, and telegraphic speech at about 18 months to 3 years. Children between ages 1 and 2 years typically have a vocabulary of 20 to 170 words (de Boysson-Bardies, 1999; Morrow, 1989). However, even these are rough estimates—some 2-year-olds may have fewer than 10 words, while others have as many as 668 words in their oral vocabulary (Fenson et al., 1994).

Children's distinct approaches to acquiring words may indicate that they have different ideas about pragmatics (Flavell, Miller, & Miller, 2002). Some children who acquire many words for the names of people and objects (milk, dog, cup) have a *referential style* that focuses on the informational aspect of language. Others who build a vocabulary of words used in social relationships (no, yes, want, please, love you) have an *expressive style* that focuses on the interpersonal aspect of language. Differences, however, are a matter of degree rather than kind, as all children learn both types of words (Goldfield & Snow, 2005).

EXAMPLE 8.1   **Common Articulation Problems in Early Childhood**

Articulation problem	Example
Substituting one sound for another that is similar in manner of articulation	Saying _free_ for _three_ Other, similar substitutions are _s_ for _sh_ sound, _w_ for _l_ sound, and _th_ for _s_ sound (a lisp).
Substituting across manners of articulation, using a sound produced with the teeth for a sound produced at the back of the mouth	Saying _tookie_ for _cookie_
Omitting sounds, sometimes whole syllables	Saying _mote_ for _remote_ or _puter_ for _computer_
Producing sound distortions	Saying _run_ as _wun_
Mispronouncing consonant blends	Saying _pasketti_ for _spaghetti_

DIVERSITY   Girls typically are faster than boys at acquiring first words, tend to have larger vocabularies, and are more likely to have a referential style of acquisition (Bauer, Goldfield, & Reznick, 2002; Flavell et al., 2002). Differences are small, however, and there are many exceptions. As with other cognitive abilities, males and females appear to be more alike than different.

As children continue to develop through the preschool years and into the early elementary grades, many experience language problems involving articulation of sounds or lack of fluent speech that they eventually overcome. Others, however, experience more pervasive language difficulties. Children from toddlerhood through the preschool years produce many common articulation errors, as shown in Example 8.1 (Kostelnik, Soderman, & Whiren, 2004; McLean & Snyder-McLean, 1999). An **articulation disorder** is diagnosed when a familiar adult cannot understand children's speech at age 3 or when articulation errors are still evident at age 8 (Patterson & Wright, 1990). Like articulation errors, **dysfluency** (a lack of fluency in speech production) typically is outgrown by the first year of elementary school (Weir & Bianchet, 2004). Dysfluency involves several types of errors, including the following (Gottwald, Goldbach, & Isack, 1985; Swan, 1993):

- repetition of syllables, words, or phrases (that . . . that doll);
- interjections (I saw . . . uh . . . a school bus);
- pauses (Mommy, I want . . . some juice);
- revisions (I went . . . we went to the doctor); and
- sound prolongation (r----abbit).

Children may experience dysfluency due to a heightened emotional state or hurried speech or, more likely, from experimentation with their rapidly expanding phonetic, syntactic, semantic, morphemic, and pragmatic knowledge (Otto, 2006).

Stuttering is the most common speech dysfluency. Approximately 80% of children who develop stuttering overcome it within 18 to 24 months after its onset (Ratner, 2004). Stuttering involves an involuntary repetition of isolated sounds or syllables, prolonged speech sounds, or a complete halt in the flow of speech (Cook, Tessier, & Armbruster, 1987). Speech problems that may indicate the onset of stuttering are (Otto, 2006; Yairi & Ambrose, 2005):

- sound and syllable repetitions that persist over time,
- repetition of part of a word more than twice or repetition of two sounds or syllables in 100 words, and
- frequent sound prolongations or sound prolongations of more than one second.

Unlike students with articulation problems or dysfluency, students with specific language impairment experience considerable delays in overall language development. Children with **specific language impairment (SLI)** have difficulties in receptive and expressive language, resulting in language development that is significantly below age level despite normal hearing, average nonverbal intelligence, and an absence of developmental disabilities (Bishop, 1997; Montgomery, 2002). Compared with normally developing children, children with SLI have smaller vocabularies, produce simpler sentences with more grammatical errors, and have difficulty with the pragmatic aspect of language (problems understanding others or being understood in conversations) (Fey, Long, & Finestack, 2003; Fraser, Goswami, & Conti-Ramsden, 2010). SLI usually is first identified in the preschool years when a child shows difficulty in conversational settings. In elementary school, language impairment may be observed when children experience difficulty in comprehending and composing both oral and written language, reading, or interacting with peers (Fey et al., 2003; Fraser et al., 2010).

How would you respond to a parent who is concerned because her 2-year-old produces only a few words? A parent concerned about her 8-year-old's stuttering?

APPLICATIONS: ENCOURAGING LANGUAGE DEVELOPMENT IN THE CLASSROOM

A responsive curriculum that recognizes language experiences as the foundation for academic learning will lead to beneficial student outcomes (García, 1992). Let's consider some general guidelines.

Talk, sing, and read to young children. Caregivers and early childhood educators can support language development by talking with children, singing songs with them, and reading to them.

- Stimulating verbal interactions promote expressive language skills and vocabulary development (Hart & Risley, 2003; Tamis-LeMonda et al., 2001).

- Singing songs encourages attention to rhythm, repetition, and expressive intonation (Squibb & Deitz, 2000). The rhymes in songs also promote the development of phonological awareness by calling attention to the component sounds in words (Maclean, Bryant, & Bradley, 1987).

- Native English-speaking and bilingual children who are read to three or more times per week, have books in the home, and make frequent trips to the library have more advanced vocabulary and emergent literacy skills than children without these experiences (DeTemple, 2001; Payne, Whitehurst, & Angell, 1994; Santiago, 1994). *DIVERSITY*

- Preschoolers and kindergartners with specific language impairment can learn to communicate their thoughts, questions, and ideas with storybook sharing (McNeill & Fowler, 1996). During storybook sharing, a teacher elicits responses from children about what is being read, uses expansion to elaborate on their comments, and praises them for appropriate comments about the content or about their interest in what was read or illustrated. *DIVERSITY*

Encourage the development of listening skills. During class discussions and conversations, teachers can model effective listening strategies such as **active listening,** which involves listening in a nondefensive way and responding by clarifying the message rather than criticizing (Farris, Fuhler, & Walther, 2004; Wolvin & Coakley, 1985). Students need listening skills to help them understand oral directions and explanations of concepts, listen during class discussions, and listen to peers during collaborative group work.

Provide vocabulary instruction. Not only does reading practice influence vocabulary acquisition, but increased vocabulary knowledge contributes to students' reading comprehension (Aarnoutse & van Leeuwe, 1998; Verhoeven, van Leeuwe, & Vermeer, 2011). Teachers can foster vocabulary development through direct instruction with repeated exposure to words in varying contexts, as well as through indirect methods such as reading and class discussions (National Reading Panel, 2000).

Provide opportunities for oral and written language use. Explicit grammar instruction and practice (e.g., writing stories, essays, and journals) help students develop oral language skills such as vocabulary, knowledge of morphology, syntax, and semantics. Also, collaborative group activities, social interaction, and discussions can provide better opportunities for students to develop language and literacy skills than large group lessons, lectures, and independent activities or seatwork (Raphael &

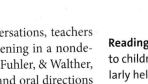

Reading. Reading to children regularly helps promote language and literacy skills.

Instructional
conversations:
See page 372.

Hiebert, 1996). For example, open-ended discussions of culturally relevant books can facilitate meaning-ful dialogue and reading comprehension in English-language learners as early as first grade (Martinez-Roldan & Lopez-Robertson, 2000). A teaching method known as *instructional conversations* can also be effective with English-language learners. Here, teachers scaffold students in the interpretation of texts through conversations that resemble spontaneous discussions, rather than evaluating students' responses in traditional question-and-answer sessions (Bauer & Manyak, 2008; Saunders & Goldenberg, 1999).

   Be sensitive to individual differences among students. Rather than explicitly correcting language, teachers should focus on supporting language acquisition in *all* students by asking questions, clarify-ing, and expanding on students' utterances. Open-ended questioning helps elicit language participation from students with specific language impairment and builds their self-confidence and their competen-cies in responding to questions (McNeill & Fowler, 1996). Teachers also can encourage positive class-room experiences and promote language development in students who stutter or exhibit dysfluency by using the guidelines summarized in Table 8.4.

DIVERSITY   In addition, showing sensitivity to the needs of English-language learners will promote their English-language acquisition and improve their academic achievement. Teachers can encourage language de-velopment by offering English-language learners opportunities to read at their appropriate levels and to listen to rich, stimulating stories, in contrast with providing these experiences only when students show oral language proficiency (Bauer & Manyak, 2008). Teachers also need to recognize that the interaction styles of English-language learners may be different from the type of communication they are expected to use in the classroom (Crago, 1992; Genesee & Nicoladis, 1995). For example, while native English-speaking children know that it is appropriate to initiate conversations with adults, compete verbally with other children, make eye contact during conversations, and demonstrate their knowledge, some Native American children are expected to remain silent in the presence of adults and to not make eye contact. Their behavior could be misinterpreted as a language delay or a lack of knowledge (Nicoladis & Genesee, 1997). Also, when teachers accept students' use of their native language for understanding content and answering questions, bilingual learners show positive attitudes toward both languages, leading to better linguistic, academic, and social achievement (Bhatnagar, 1980; Brisk, 1991; Jalava, 1988).

Think about the grade level of students you expect to teach. How can you use the guidelines in Table 8.4 to promote language development in your students?

TABLE 8.4	Guidelines for Promoting Language Development in Students with Dysfluency
Early childhood teachers should:	**Elementary school teachers should:**
Reduce conversational demands on children by modeling slow, smooth speech.	Speak with students in an unhurried way.
Maintain eye contact and be patient so children do not feel that the teacher is uncomfortable talking with them.	Convey that they are listening to the content of students' utterances (rather than their grammar) by using appropriate eye contact, body language, and feedback.
Avoid telling children to slow down, start over, think, or take a deep breath, because these indicate that their speech is unacceptable, potentially increasing their anxiety and dysfluency.	Inform all students to take their time and think about their answers rather than answering questions in a hurry.
Discourage other children from interrupting or trying to finish an utterance for a child who is having difficulty talking.	Monitor social interactions so that peers do not tease or embarrass a student who stutters, and encourage all students to take turns when speaking.
Include group singing, choral responses, or choral reading in curricula, because these provide opportunities for children who stutter to participate in fluent speech. Recent neurological research has shown that choral speech is activated in the brain differently from speech that occurs in conversations.	Encourage all students to practice reading in pairs (taking turns or in unison) and to practice reading their stories at home before reading them orally to the class.

Sources: Büchel & Sommer, 2004; Scott, 2007; Weir & Bianchet, 2004.

Summary

Explain the factors that contribute to language development. Humans are biologically ready to learn language, and our brains are well equipped to produce and acquire language. Language acquisition also requires experiences that facilitate language learning. Caregivers model language for children, and children receive reinforcement for their language attempts. Caregivers also engage in verbal and nonverbal interactions that teach children about language. While cultures vary in their emphasis on techniques used to support language development, children in all cultures develop language at about the same rate.

Describe changes in semantics, syntax, pragmatics, and metalinguistic awareness from birth through adolescence. Children rapidly acquire language skills during early childhood. They begin to babble at 6 months and acquire first words at about 1 year of age. From ages 2 to 5, children's syntax expands. Toddlers and preschoolers also acquire pragmatics by using their emerging language skills to achieve different goals. Preschoolers develop metalinguistic awareness as they begin to understand how reading, writing, and the sounds of their language work. From elementary through high school, students' semantic knowledge continues to expand as their vocabularies rapidly increase and they begin to understand figurative language. Students' sentences also become more elaborate and consist of more complex grammatical structures. Pragmatics and metalinguistic awareness improve through adolescence as students become better able to understand and use their language skills in reading, writing, and social interactions.

Explain the advantages and disadvantages of the methods of teaching English-language learners. Transitional bilingual programs encourage academic success because native-language skills facilitate acquisition of English-language skills and students do not fall behind academically. English-language learners struggle in English-immersion methods that have no curricular modifications to help them learn content in English. Structured English immersion improves on traditional immersion by providing appropriate support to accommodate the needs of students learning the language. Two-way bilingual immersion results in academic success in both languages and in positive attitudes toward school for students of all language backgrounds.

Describe the language differences that emerge from early childhood through the early school-age years. Children exhibit differences in their rate of language development and in how they acquire words. Girls typically are faster than boys to acquire first words and tend to have larger vocabularies. Young children commonly exhibit articulation errors and fluency problems. A specific language impairment is identified in the preschool and early elementary grades when a child's receptive or expressive language development is significantly below age level despite normal hearing, average nonverbal intelligence, and lack of developmental disabilities.

Describe ways teachers can support language development in the classroom. Teachers can promote language development by showing sensitivity to differences in children's language patterns, both with students who have language disorders and with students from different language backgrounds. They can support all students' language capabilities by asking questions, clarifying, and expanding on students' utterances rather than explicitly correcting language usage. Teachers also can model active listening strategies, incorporate vocabulary instruction into their curricula, and provide opportunities for oral and written language practice to encourage language acquisition in all students.

Key Concepts

active listening   143

articulation disorder   142

babbling   134

child-directed speech   135

code mixing   140

decoding   137

dysfluency   142

English immersion   140

expansion   135

holophrastic speech   136

joint attention   135

metalinguistic awareness   137

morphemic inflections   136

overextensions   136

overregularizations   137

phonological awareness   137

pragmatics   137

recasting   135

semantics   136

specific language impairment (SLI)   142

structured English immersion   140

syntax   136

telegraphic speech   136

transitional bilingual education   140

two-way bilingual immersion   140

underextensions   136

Video Applications

www.mhhe.com/bohlin2e

Video 1: Promoting Language Development in Young Children (*3 minutes*)
This clip highlights some methods of promoting native language and second language acquisition in young children.

Video 2: Promoting Language Development in Elementary School Students (*2 minutes*)
This clip shows one teacher's approach to encouraging the language development of elementary school students.

Case Studies
Reflect and Evaluate

DIVERSITY **EARLY CHILDHOOD: "Fire Safety"**

These questions refer to the case study on page 92.

1. Identify examples of *expansion* and *recasting* in the case study.

2. Identify the *overregularizations* of past-tense verbs in the case study. Is this typical of preschool children's language development? Based on research on language development, explain why correcting children's overregularizations and other grammatical errors may not be necessary.

3. Miss Angela read a rhyming book about fire safety. Explain how calling attention to rhymes can help promote phonological awareness and later reading development. In what other ways can preschool teachers promote the development of phonological awareness?

4. Story reading is a common practice in preschools. Explain how it helps foster language development.

5. Imagine that Miyu, a 4-year-old girl who recently immigrated to the United States from Japan and speaks little English, enrolled at Rolling Hills Preschool. Based on the research on bilingual two-way immersion programs, explain why it would be beneficial for the English-speaking preschoolers to learn Japanese while Miyu is learning English at preschool (assuming there is a Japanese-speaking bilingual teacher).

6. Suppose a parent approaches Miss Angela with a concern that her child has a language disorder. Many of the child's utterances are not understandable because he substitutes the "s" sound for the "sh" sound (saying *see* for *she*). What would you say to the parent about these articulation errors? How could you enhance the child's language development in the preschool classroom?

DIVERSITY **ELEMENTARY SCHOOL: "Project Night"**

These questions refer to the case study on page 94.

1. Mr. Morales included writing a poem as a project option. Based on school-age children's language development, explain why poetry might be challenging for fifth-grade students.

2. How does Mr. Morales attempt to promote language development in his students? What changes could he make to the project unit to further support language development?

3. How well does Mr. Morales support the language development of his bilingual students?

4. How do the "research teams" help students develop more sophisticated language skills?

5. Based on your reading of the module, would you make any modifications to the research teams activity for students with a specific language impairment or for English-language learners?

DIVERSITY **MIDDLE SCHOOL: "Frogs"**

These questions refer to the case study on page 96.

1. Describe the language achievements of children in the school-age years. Based on the information in the case, identify weaknesses in the eighth-grade students' language skills.

2. What changes can Ms. Thesdale make to the dissection lab to foster language development in her eighth-grade students?

3. What specific changes to her teaching can Ms. Thesdale make to support the language development of bilingual students in her class?

4. How can Ms. Thesdale support the language development of students, like Tyler, who have language impairments? Try to think of modifications you would make as a teacher to the biology lab activity and to your teaching in general.

5. Ms. Thesdale is attending a required workshop on children's language development but is frustrated at having to learn about the acquisition of language skills in young children. "What does this have to do with my adolescent students?" she thinks. Based on your reading of the module, explain to Ms. Thesdale how learning about language development from infancy onward can improve her understanding of adolescent language development.

HIGH SCHOOL: "The Substitute"   *DIVERSITY*

These questions refer to the case study on page 98.

1. Describe the language achievements of students from elementary through high school. Why might reading material such as *A Tale of Two Cities* be challenging for adolescents?

2. What techniques did Mr. Matthews use to foster language development in his students? What other recommendations would you suggest to Mr. Matthews?

3. What recommendations would you suggest to Mr. Matthews for supporting the language skills of bilingual students like Demeri?

4. What if some of the students in this case had language impairments? What recommendations would you suggest to Mr. Matthews for supporting the language skills of students with language impairments in his British literature class?

5. Imagine that you are at a school board meeting regarding bilingual education. Make a persuasive argument for K–12 two-way bilingual immersion (TWBI) based on the particular benefits to adolescents who have participated in TWBI programs.

unit three

Case Studies

Early Childhood: "Pinch" 150

Elementary School: "Silly Students" 152

Middle School: "Study Hall" 154

High School: "Bending the Rules" 156

Module 9:
Behavioral Learning Theories

Outline and Learning Goals 158

Assumptions of Behavioral Learning
Theories 159

Classical Conditioning 159

Operant Conditioning 161

Applications: Applied Behavior
Analysis 166

Summary 170

Key Concepts 170

Video Applications 171

Case Studies: Reflect and Evaluate 171

learning theories

Module 10:
Social Cognitive Theory

Outline and Learning Goals 173

Assumptions of Social Cognitive
Theory 174

Observational Learning 174

Personal Factors in Learning 177

Summary 181

Key Concepts 181

Video Applications 181

Case Studies: Reflect and Evaluate 181

Module 11:
Information Processing

Outline and Learning Goals 183

Assumptions of the Information Processing
Approach 184

The Three-Stage Model of Information
Processing 184

Applications to Teaching 193

Summary 197

Key Concepts 197

Video Applications 198

Case Studies: Reflect and Evaluate 198

Prepare:

As you read the case, make notes:

1. **WHO** are the primary participants in the case? Describe them.

2. **WHAT** is taking place?

3. **WHERE** is the case taking place? Is the environment a factor?

4. **WHEN** is the case taking place? Is the timing a factor?

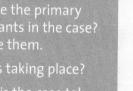

Miss Rana (*RAH-nah*) is the head teacher at the local preschool for at-risk children. The preschool is state-funded and typically includes children ages 3 to 5 from lower-SES homes, from single-parent families, and/or with developmental delays. Arriving early one morning to prepare the art area for a sponge painting activity, Miss Rana begins setting up space for pairs of children to share art materials. Miss Amber, the assistant teacher, arrives and provides the list of paired children that she has prepared for the art project.

Miss Rana reads the list and says, "I'm glad to see you paired Reagan and Emily for art. Emily has been so reluctant to participate in art ever since that day when she spilled the paint all over Billy's shoes."

"Yes," Miss Amber replies. "I thought it would be a good idea. Reagan loves art. I just hope she can keep her hands to herself today."

Early Childhood

Pinch

Reagan, a 3-year-old, is one of the youngest children in the preschool. Unlike the parents of many of the students, Reagan's parents are married and highly educated. Reagan qualified for the preschool due to a severe speech impairment. She was very hard to understand at the beginning of the school year, but her daily sessions with the school speech pathologist have resulted in markedly improved speech over the first three months of the school year. Although Reagan generally is a well-behaved child, during circle time she has a habit of pinching the children sitting next to her on the rug. Reagan does not attempt to conceal her misbehavior and readily admits to it if confronted by her teachers. Miss Rana and Miss Amber first tried ignoring the behavior, but that only resulted in a number of other children pinching their classmates. They have also tried telling her to stop pinching the other children and have even removed her from the rug area a few times, with no

result. Recently, they decided to give Reagan a sticker at the end of the day contingent on no instances of pinching anyone. Stickers typically are used as special rewards when a child does something that deserves recognition. Only once during the past three weeks has Reagan earned the sticker—every other day she has pinched at least one child. Yesterday afternoon, Miss Rana and Miss Amber discussed the issue again and decided to try yet another strategy. They hope to "catch" Reagan early in circle time, before she has a chance to pinch, praise her for keeping her hands to herself, and then every couple of minutes praise Reagan and the other children for keeping their hands to themselves.

As the children begin to enter the classroom, Miss Rana gives her usual morning greeting: "Good morning, boys and girls!"

Emily enters the room and quietly walks to her space along the wall, where she hangs her coat on the hook and places her book bag below her name. As Emily sits down at her special spot on the rug, Miss Amber greets her. "Hello, Emily. I sure like the way you put your things away and sat down. You look ready to begin this morning."

As usual, Emily does not respond to this praise. However, a number of other children who were wandering off to inspect the art supplies quickly scramble to their own special spots on the rug. Reagan has just sat down, and Miss Rana quickly says, "Reagan, I like the way you have your hands in your lap—look everyone—Reagan is giving a wonderful example of how to sit with our hands to ourselves during circle time." Reagan's face clearly displays her pride at being the good example.

Circle time includes doing the calendar and weather, followed by Miss Amber reading the morning book. Miss Amber holds the children's attention during the story by asking them to clap each time they hear the word *leaf*. The teachers praise Reagan a number of times—along with many of the other children—for sitting with her hands to herself and for clapping along with the story. After she finishes reading, Miss Amber says, "Yesterday we read a different story about leaves. How is today's story like that one? How is it different from the one we read yesterday?" Several children raise their hands to share their ideas. Following circle time, the children are told who will be their partner for art that day and are sent to the space designated for them.

Miss Amber stands in front of four pairs of children, while Miss Rana stands in front of the other four pairs of children. "Eyes up here," Miss Rana says, as she notices some of the children whispering to each other. Each teacher holds up the art supplies and demonstrates how to gently put the leaf-shaped sponge into the paint tray and then gently place the sponge on their large piece of paper. Miss Rana tells the children to begin painting and quietly observes the interactions between Reagan and Emily.

Reagan asks Emily, "Do you want the red paint first?"

"Um, you pick," Emily quietly replies.

"Red is my favorite color," says Reagan. When Emily does not respond, Reagan asks, "What is your favorite color?"

Emily answers, "I don't know. I guess pink."

Emily has too much paint on her sponge and gets too much paint on her paper. Under her breath, she says: "I can't do it."

Miss Rana approaches and offers a few words of encouragement.

Reagan, mimicking the teacher, offers similar comments, such as "I like it too."

The two children continue to talk and share the art supplies. As Miss Rana walks around the room to provide assistance, she notices that Reagan and Emily are talking and giggling. She thinks about how she has never heard Emily giggle during class.

Miss Rana quickly takes the opportunity to encourage Emily: "You are doing a wonderful job! You are quite a little artist!"

Assess

1. Why do you think the initial attempts to stop Reagan from pinching were unsuccessful?

2. Do you think the teachers would have reacted the same way if a boy were pinching other children? Why or why not?

3. Why do you think Miss Amber makes a point of getting the children's attention when a new activity begins? What might happen if she failed to do this?

Prepare:

As you read the case, make notes:

1. **WHO** are the primary participants in the case? Describe them.

2. **WHAT** is taking place?

3. **WHERE** is the case taking place? Is the environment a factor?

4. **WHEN** is the case taking place? Is the timing a factor?

Aidan Lindsay is in his first year of teaching at a small rural school where most students are from lower- to middle-SES homes. His fourth-grade class has 25 students, with about equal numbers of boys and girls. Mr. Lindsay designed his room so that desks are arranged in clusters of three or four, which allows students to work together on some projects. The students seem to like this arrangement. However, some disruptive behaviors have occurred during the first few weeks of the school year.

Mr. Lindsay is seeking the assistance of the other fourth-grade teachers, Anna Vargas and Elsa Klendworth. During their lunch break in the teachers' lounge, he asks, "What do the two of you do with a group of three children who do not seem interested in anything but talking with one another and giving silly answers to questions?"

Ms. Klendworth presses him for more information. "What exactly do you ask of your students, and how do they respond?"

Elementary School
Silly Students

"Many times I will show the students how to do something, such as multiplication, on the white board and then ask them to complete worksheets," Mr. Lindsay says. "I inform them that they should not copy the work of others in their group, but I encourage them to ask others for help. This typically works well. I have seen students showing other students how to complete the problems. However, these three children, Billy, Jason, and Megan, all pretend to help each other by talking and pointing to the worksheets, but as I walk past they obviously are talking about other things and typically end up getting little work done. In addition, their laughing and giggling disrupt the other students, particularly the fourth child in their group, Sara. Of course, given this silly behavior, it is not surprising that Billy, Jason, Megan, and Sara all received low scores on the math quiz I gave last week."

Ms. Vargas asks, "What have you tried in order to get them back on track?"

"Well, of course, I have repeatedly told them to calm down and get back to work. I have also tried ignoring their laughing and giggling, but they are just too disruptive to the other children around them. So yesterday I started taking away their recess time when their work is not completed, but I don't know yet how well that is going to work," says Mr. Lindsay.

"I would suggest that you give them extra time to talk with one another *only* if their project is completed," Ms. Vargas suggests.

Ms. Klendworth adds, "Yes, you might even begin by telling them that if they can just be quiet and not disrupt the other children you will give them a few minutes at the end of the period to talk with one another quietly."

Mr. Lindsay leaves the teachers' lounge somewhat skeptical about rewarding students for doing what all the other students already are doing, but he decides to try these suggestions because Ms. Klendworth and Ms. Vargas have been teaching much longer than he has and have been very supportive and helpful over the past several weeks.

As the children enter the classroom after their lunch and recess time, Mr. Lindsay asks them to sit in their seats. On the white board he demonstrates the day's lesson on multiplication. As the children begin working in their groups, he walks over to the table where Billy, Jason, Megan, and Sara are working.

"I have a new idea," Mr. Lindsay says. "If the three of you can work quietly for the next ten minutes while others are also trying to complete their math worksheets, I will give you three minutes to talk with one another. You can use quiet voices to help one another, but you need to stay focused on the math work. Sound good?"

The following week at lunch in the teachers' lounge, Ms. Klendworth asks, "So, how is that problem with your group of silly students going?"

"Oh, your suggestions worked like a charm. The three misbehaving students are paying more attention and actually helping one another finish their work so they have time to talk together. However, now the problem is the fourth student in that group, Sara. She has become increasingly frustrated that the other students finish before her. Many times I hear her say 'I can't do it' or 'This is too hard.' She even went so far as to throw her pencil down on the table and start crying.

"I have tried to explain to her that she does good work and should ask for help if she needs it, but Sara insists that she is not good at math. Do you have any suggestions?" asks Mr. Lindsay.

"What if you make the three minutes contingent on all *four* students completing the assignment?" Ms. Klendworth suggests. "Then the students will be more interested in helping Sara, and Sara will not need to ask for their help."

"Yes," Ms. Vargas agrees. "I would also suggest that you take as many opportunities as possible to prove to Sara that she is doing well. You can continue to tell her that she is doing well, but you should also remind her of previous work she has completed well—maybe even start a bulletin board where you can spotlight the students' work."

Assess

1. Do you think having fourth-grade students "help" each other is a good idea? Why or why not?

2. Do you think Mr. Lindsay's reliance on the other teachers is a sign of incompetence? Why or why not?

3. If you were the teacher in this classroom, what strategies would you use to help the three disruptive students focus on their schoolwork?

154

Prepare:

As you read the case, make notes:

1. **WHO** are the primary participants in the case? Describe them.

2. **WHAT** is taking place?

3. **WHERE** is the case taking place? Is the environment a factor?

4. **WHEN** is the case taking place? Is the timing a factor?

Milos Havel is one of three seventh-grade teachers at a middle school in a small but ethnically diverse city. The three seventh-grade teachers cover reading and social studies in their own "homeroom" classes, but each one instructs all the seventh-graders in one subject area (math, English, or science). Mr. Havel's specialty is English.

Mr. Havel is worried about Jamie, a student in his homeroom class. Jamie appears to be a very bright child when he applies himself. He readily participates in class by explaining difficult concepts and providing good examples of the material, particularly during his favorite subject, social studies. His difficulties appear to be in the sixth-period mathematics class. Although Gladys DeBrick does not complain about Jamie's compliance in her class, his academic performance is weak. He rarely finishes his homework on time and ap-

Middle School

Study Hall

pears to have fallen behind in the subject. For example, he lacks an understanding of basic mathematical principles taught the previous year in sixth grade.

During their weekly Thursday morning meeting, the three seventh-grade teachers discuss their students' performance. It turns out that Ms. DeBrick's student Jasamine is having problems completing her English assignments for Mr. Havel's sixth period. Much like Jamie, Jasamine does not have many behavioral problems within the classroom. Nor does she appear to struggle with the content of Mr. Havel's English class. Nevertheless, Jasamine typically doesn't have the homework completed.

Mr. Havel and Ms. DeBrick develop a plan. Mr. Havel will help Jamie with his math homework during the study hall period immediately following Jamie's sixth-period math class. In turn, Ms. DeBrick will help Jasamine with her English homework during the study hall period immediately following Jasamine's sixth-period English class. Although both need to attend to other students during the study hall period, Mr. Havel and Ms. DeBrick will try to give Jamie and Jasamine as much extra help with homework as possible.

Several issues arise while trying to implement this plan with Jamie. On the first day, Mr. Havel walks by Jamie's desk and states, "I will be around to help you with your mathematics homework, so take out the assignment and get started."

Jamie replies, "I thought we could talk about the social studies lesson you gave today, like we usually do."

"No, I think your time is much better spent completing your math homework while you are here and have my help available to you," says Mr. Havel.

"I don't think I have the worksheets Ms. DeBrick gave us to complete. I guess I will have to do them tomorrow. So we can discuss social studies, right?" asks Jamie.

This pattern of forgetting the homework assignment and diverting the conversation to social studies continues for several days. Finally, Mr. Havel tells Jamie that he will not discuss social studies with him during study hall until his math homework is complete. After only one day of Mr. Havel's refusing to talk with him about social studies, Jamie begins to bring his math homework. Although he struggles with completing the problems, he puts forth effort to complete the assignments so he will have a few extra minutes at the end of the class study hall period to discuss social studies with Mr. Havel.

In Ms. DeBrick's homeroom, the plan works wonderfully from the start. Jasmine seems to enjoy the extra attention she receives in completing her English assignments. Ms. DeBrick notices that Jasmine does not seem to have difficulty completing the work once she has given Jasmine an example or two to get her started. Ms. DeBrick decides to pair Jasmine with a student who excels in English, so that Ms. DeBrick is able to spend her time helping the other children and preparing her lessons for the next day.

Assess

1. Why do you think the initial plan to get Jamie to complete his math homework during study hall was unsuccessful? Why did the same plan work so well for Jasmine's English homework?

2. Do you think that Ms. DeBrick's plan to have another student help Jasmine will be as effective? Why or why not? Would this strategy work for Jamie?

3. How might memory play an important role in completing math problems for Ms. DeBrick's class? How might memory be important for completing assignments for Mr. Havel's English class?

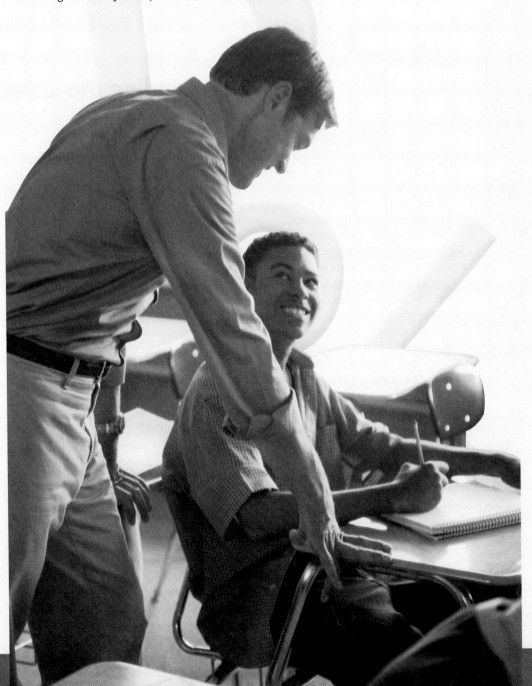

Prepare:

As you read the case, make notes:

1. **WHO** are the primary participants in the case? Describe them.

2. **WHAT** is taking place?

3. **WHERE** is the case taking place? Is the environment a factor?

4. **WHEN** is the case taking place? Is the timing a factor?

Dan Hardy is a teacher of U.S. history, the only subject he has taught during his five years at a high school in an upper-socioeconomic community. The students are highly motivated to do well and to continue their education at the top universities in the state. Mr. Hardy is well liked by most of his students. He spends a lot of class time providing examples of how to relate concepts in history to current events. He also uses group work during class, such as debating a controversial historical issue and predicting what would have happened if a particular event had not occurred. Mr. Hardy assigns homework that typically involves thinking and writing about issues discussed during class. Because his assignments are thought-provoking and because most of his students are eager to learn, Mr. Hardy rarely has problems with students completing the assignments.

High School

Bending the Rules

At the beginning of Mr. Hardy's third class period, he asks students to pass their homework forward to the front person in each row. As he reaches the third row, he notices that Jason's assignment is missing from the stack. This is the fourth day in the past two weeks that his assignment has not been completed. Jason was told after missing his last assignment that one more incomplete grade would earn him a trip to detention.

After class Mr. Hardy asks Jason to stay for a minute. Mr. Hardy asks, "Why didn't you turn in your homework assignment today?"

"I don't know," Jason answers. "I guess I forgot about it, Mr. Hardy."

Mr. Hardy wonders whether he really forgot about it or instead was having difficulty understanding the material or organizing his thoughts. "Well, you will need to spend one hour in detention after school today to complete the missed work. Please be sure to stop by the office and notify your parents that you will be home late today," Mr. Hardy requests.

"I can't stay today—I have basketball practice," Jason replies. "If I miss practice, I will have to miss the game Friday night."

"Well, I warned you after your last missed homework assignment that you would be sent to detention if you missed another assignment," Mr. Hardy states. "You were aware of this classroom rule. I suggest you spend your hour today completing your missing assignments for the class."

When the last bell rings at the end of the day, Jason walks to Coach Gil Hanson's office and tells him why he will not be at basketball practice. Coach Hanson, upset that Jason's detention would mean facing the school's archrival without a star player, offers to discuss the issue with Jason's teacher and with the principal, Ms. Alice Krug.

In the principal's office, the coach makes his case to Mr. Hardy and Principal Krug. "I understand that Jason has missed some assignments in history class and is now in detention," he says. "As a result, he is missing basketball practice today and, by the rules, cannot play in Friday night's game. Is there something we can work out as a compromise?"

Principal Krug turns to Mr. Hardy and says formally, "What is your class rule about completing assignments and detention?"

"The rule is four incompletes result in detention until the student no longer has four incompletes. I rarely need to enforce this rule, but Jason is missing four assignments," Mr.

Hardy explains. "I gave him a warning when he had missed three assignments, but he came to class again today without his homework."

"Can't you make an exception in this case?" Coach Hanson suggests. "Jason is overall a good student and an excellent athlete."

Principal Krug interjects, "I believe that a rule is a rule. If this is the system that Mr. Hardy has set up for his class, then we must all support his efforts. Jason will not be at practice and hence cannot play in the game Friday night."

"Well, the no practice–no game rule is my own team rule, not a school rule. I am willing to bend the rule in this case. The rule has been bent before for cases of illness and family vacations," Coach Hanson replies.

"I was not aware of that," the principal says. "I suggest that you change the rule to better reflect the practice. However, you and I can discuss this issue at a later date, in private."

Back in detention, Jason begins to gather his notes for the assignments he did not complete during the past few weeks. He quickly realizes that he has not taken good notes and cannot remember clearly Mr. Hardy's demonstration of how to complete the assignment. Nor has he really participated with his classmates during the group work. Jason remembers that he did not do well in history during middle school because he wasn't good at keeping dates and facts straight.

Assess

1. Was the strategy of placing Jason in detention helpful to Jason? Why or why not?

2. Do you think the teachers would have reacted the same way if a girl had been experiencing the same problems with homework and missing an extracurricular event? Why or why not?

3. What strategies would you use to help you remember dates and facts in history, and what types of skills or strategies would you need to complete Mr. Hardy's homework assignments?

MODULE 9

Behavioral Learning Theories

Outline	Learning Goals
Assumptions of Behavioral Learning Theories	
	1. Describe the basic assumptions of traditional behavioral learning theories.
Classical Conditioning	
	2. Explain classical conditioning and its relevance to educational settings.
Operant Conditioning	
■ Basic Tenets of the Theory ■ Using Consequences Effectively	3. Explain how reinforcement and punishment influence future behavior and how often each should be used to be effective. 4. Explain how teachers can use consequences effectively.
Applications: Applied Behavior Analysis	
■ Strategies for Increasing Appropriate Behaviors ■ Strategies for Decreasing Inappropriate Behaviors	5. Describe strategies teachers can use to increase appropriate behaviors and decrease inappropriate behaviors.
Summary **Key Concepts** **Video Applications** **Case Studies: Reflect and Evaluate**	

ASSUMPTIONS OF BEHAVIORAL LEARNING THEORIES

How did you *learn* to write your name? How did you *learn* to raise your hand during class? Although most psychologists and educators might define **learning** as a change in either behavior or knowledge, traditional behavioral theories have focused on learning *behaviors,* with little focus on knowledge, mental processes, or memories.

As behavioral psychologists have studied how learning occurs, their theories traditionally have fallen into one of two categories: classical conditioning or operant conditioning. We'll examine each of these theories separately, but first let's consider their shared assumptions about how learning occurs:

Contiguity Learning. Young children learn to associate golden arches with fast food.

- *Learning must include a change in behavior.* To show that learning has occurred, traditional behaviorists assert that new information must cause behavior to change (Watson, 1913). If one cannot determine that behavior has changed, learning has not occurred.

- *Behavior occurs due to experiences in the environment.* British philosopher John Locke (1632–1704) stated that children are born as blank slates who can be taught to do, or not do, any behavior based on experiences in their environment (Locke, 1892).

- *Learning must include an association between a stimulus and a response* (Kimble, 2000). Stimuli are events that individuals link or associate with certain responses. Learning by associations, called **contiguity learning,** is important for learning the vast amount of information children and adolescents are presented with. For example, letter and word recognition in early childhood is based on repeated exposure.

- *The stimulus and the response must occur close together in time.* Remember that time is relative. Immediate consequences are needed for young children, who view 30 minutes as an eternity. In contrast, cross-cultural studies have found that older children and adults are more likely to delay small rewards and wait much longer in exchange for larger rewards (Green, Fry, & Myerson, 1994; Rotenberg & Mayer, 1990). Although this developmental trend implies that older children and adolescents can wait longer, immediate feedback in educational settings is optimal. For example, studies repeatedly find that immediate feedback is more effective than delayed feedback with respect to performance on classroom quizzes and success with learning materials (Kulik & Kulik, 1988).

- *Learning processes are very similar across different species.* Rats, pigeons, and humans learn in similar ways. Because traditional behaviorists believe most learning processes are the same across species, few behavioral studies have focused on differences across ethnicity, gender, socioeconomic status or other issues of diversity within the human species. According to traditional behaviorists, it does not matter whether you are Black, White, female, or male—all humans (and all animals) learn behaviors through similar mechanisms.

DIVERSITY

Can you think of examples of contiguity learning from your own experiences, both in and outside school?

CLASSICAL CONDITIONING

We are all aware of involuntary behaviors, such as the body's many reflexes. For example, people automatically blink when an object quickly moves toward their eyes (the "you flinched" game played by children). These involuntary behaviors include two elements:

- an **unconditioned stimulus,** the behavior or event that evokes an automatic response (for example, moving your hand quickly toward someone's face); and

- an **unconditioned response,** the automatic behavior caused by the stimulus, which can be physiological (e.g., someone flinching when your hand approaches) or emotional (e.g., fear).

Behavioral Perspective. Behaviorists assume that learning processes are very similar between animals and humans.

In short, we don't learn to connect an unconditioned stimulus with an unconditioned response; rather, we inherit these involuntary behaviors.

Classical conditioning, or classical learning, is based on the pairing of these involuntary behaviors with events that do not evoke an automatic response. These **neutral stimuli** include shapes, behaviors, sounds, and smells. In classical conditioning, learning will occur when a neutral stimulus is paired repeatedly with an unconditioned stimulus, as in the famous study by Ivan Petrovich Pavlov (1849–1936), a physiologist who was studying the digestive systems of dogs. (Note that he was not a psychologist.) In Pavlov's study (Pavlov 1927/1960), his researchers would release the alarm on the doors to the dogs' cages, sounding a bell, and then bring food to the dogs. After they had done this repeatedly, Pavlov noticed that the dogs started to produce saliva when the bell sounded rather than when the food was presented.

Classical conditioning states that an unconditioned stimulus (in this case, the presentation of food) and its unconditioned response (the dogs salivating automatically) can be paired with a previously neutral stimulus (a bell sounding). As a result, the previously neutral stimulus becomes a **conditioned stimulus,** or a learned stimulus that evokes a **conditioned response,** or a learned response. The dogs produced saliva (conditioned response) when they heard the bell (conditioned stimulus), not when presented with food. According to the first assumption we discussed, the change in behavior showed that learning had occurred.

While Pavlov's study illustrates a physical response, classical conditioning also demonstrates how emotions, particularly fear, can be learned (Watson & Rayner, 1920). In one study, researchers began by placing an infant, Little Albert, in the middle of a table and then made a loud noise behind him (unconditioned stimulus, UCS), automatically producing a startled fear response (unconditioned response, UCR). A neutral stimulus—a white rat—was paired repeatedly with the loud noise. After several pairings, Little Albert learned to be afraid of the white rat and would cry and attempt to crawl away when the white rat appeared, even in the absence of the loud noise. The once neutral stimulus, the white rat, became a conditioned stimulus (CS), and the fear of the white rat became a conditioned response (CR), as depicted in Figure 9.1. Again, the change in behavior confirmed that learning had occurred. (It is important to note that current ethical guidelines would not allow similar studies to be conducted.)

Once learning—or a change in behavior—has occurred, the behavior can be expanded on, altered, or eliminated. These additional learning opportunities are referred to by traditional behavioral theorists as generalization, discrimination, and extinction, respectively.

- **Generalization:** Conditioned learning can be expanded beyond a specific stimulus to other, similar stimuli. After conditioning with the white rat, Little Albert was presented with a white rabbit and more quickly learned to fear the rabbit as well—he generalized the meaning of "white rat" to the white rabbit.

- **Discrimination:** Species can learn to differentiate between similar but different stimuli. For example, Little Albert could have been taught to discriminate between white rabbits and white rats by being presented with white rabbits *without* the loud noise. Little Albert would have learned to distinguish, or discriminate, between the animals.

- **Extinction:** If the conditioned stimulus is presented repeatedly without the unconditioned stimulus, the previously learned behavior will disappear or become extinct. Consider the example of Pavlov's dogs. Researchers could have presented the bell repeatedly without food. Eventually, the dogs would no longer respond to the bell by producing saliva. The conditioned response would have become extinct.

Although classical conditioning is widely used in modern psychology in the areas of cognitive science and neuroscience, there are fewer examples of how it may be applied in classroom settings (Rescorla, 1988). However, classical conditioning can affect students' emotional states regarding teachers, schools, and academic subjects. (Remember that emotions are automatic responses.) For example, a child who has been harassed and victimized on the playground by other children may begin to associ-

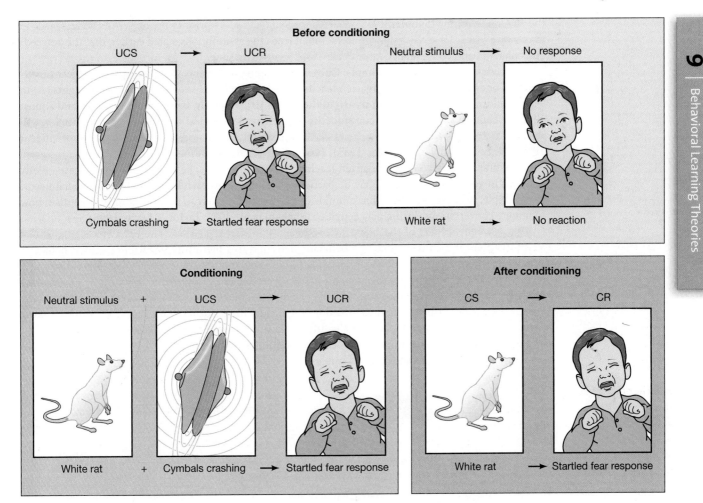

Figure 9.1. Watson's Classical Conditioning of Little Albert. A once neutral stimulus, the white rat, became a conditioned stimulus (CS). Fear of the white rat became a conditioned response (CR).

ate recess with fear. High school students may associate a teacher who is critical and harsh with feelings of humiliation or may associate the subject matter with fear and inferiority (e.g., math anxiety). In contrast, students may associate a teacher who is positive and supportive with feelings of pride and may learn to associate the subject matter with pleasure and happiness. Many other examples, including test anxiety and school phobia, illustrate how specific situations, people, and events often come to be associated with certain emotions.

Can you think of examples from your educational experiences that might have led to feelings of anxiety or fear about a particular subject? What might have been the unconditioned stimulus, the conditioned stimulus, and the conditioned response in those experiences?

OPERANT CONDITIONING

Operant conditioning, like classical conditioning, includes a pairing of events. However, operant conditioning does not depend on involuntary behaviors such as physiological responses or emotional states. Rather, it includes new, voluntary behaviors such as raising your hand in class.

Basic Tenets of the Theory

Operant conditioning originated with Edward Thorndike (1874–1949), who, like many behaviorists, was conducting experiments with animals. The results of his experiments led to the **law of effect,** which states that behaviors associated with good consequences (satisfiers) are more likely to occur again in the future, whereas behaviors associated with bad consequences (annoyers) are less likely to occur again (Thorndike, 1898). For example, when a child is praised for class participation (good consequence), he or she is *more* likely to participate in the future. In contrast, when a child is laughed at or humiliated by the teacher or by other students when he or she attempts to participate in class (bad consequence), that child is *less* likely to participate in the future. B. F. Skinner (1904–1990) expanded on these ideas to form the ABCs of learning (Skinner, 1953). The antecedent (A) occurs prior to the behavior (B) and leads to the consequence (C) of the behavior. Remember, from the assumptions stated earlier, that the antecedent, behavior, and consequence must occur close together in time.

Antecedents can be cues or prompts. **Cues** refer to nonverbal events that signal that a behavior is expected. For example, many kindergarten teachers use the nonverbal cue of shutting off the lights (A) to signal children to quiet down and return to their seats (B). Similarly, many middle schools and almost all high schools use a bell (A) to cue students that a new class period has begun. Teachers' nonverbal cues are very important for maintaining classroom management and increasing the level of student performance (Woolfolk & Brooks, 1985). **Prompts** typically are verbal reminders that accompany a cue. The first few times the kindergarten teacher turns off the lights, he or she also says "Please quietly sit down in your seats." Prompts may be particularly effective in teaching students with special needs. For example, studies have found that prompts can be used effectively to teach children with autism how to initiate conversations during play activities (Shabani et al., 2002; Taylor & Levin, 1998).

DIVERSITY

The consequence (C) of the behavior can either increase or decrease the behavior in the future. **Reinforcement** is a consequence of a behavior that increases the future occurrence of that behavior. When a teacher praises a student for participating in class and the student considers the praise good, he or she is likely to participate again—in order to receive more praise. **Punishment** is a consequence of a behavior that decreases the future occurrence of that behavior. Most children, after participating in class, would consider being laughed at and humiliated by their teacher and peers a bad thing, making them less interested in participating in the future—in order to avoid such consequences.

Reinforcement and punishment can occur by adding (+) something desirable or by taking away (–) something undesirable, as shown in Example 9.1.

EXAMPLE 9.1   Examples of Reinforcement and Punishment

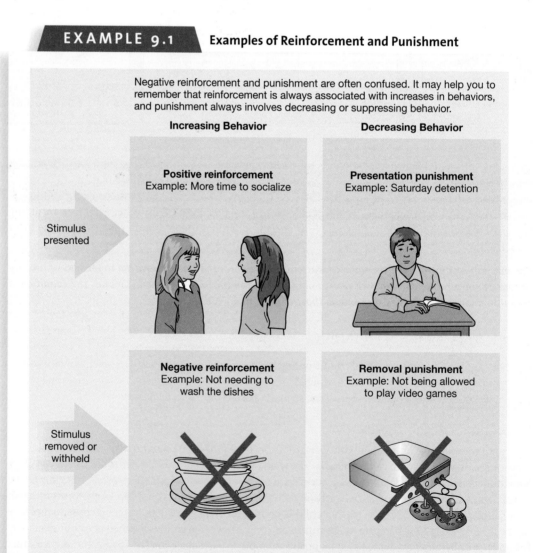

Negative reinforcement and punishment are often confused. It may help you to remember that reinforcement is always associated with increases in behaviors, and punishment always involves decreasing or suppressing behavior.

	Increasing Behavior	**Decreasing Behavior**
Stimulus presented	**Positive reinforcement** Example: More time to socialize	**Presentation punishment** Example: Saturday detention
Stimulus removed or withheld	**Negative reinforcement** Example: Not needing to wash the dishes	**Removal punishment** Example: Not being allowed to play video games

- *Positive reinforcement* is adding (+) something that is desired by the individual, such as praise, candy, or wanted attention.
- *Negative reinforcement* is taking away (–) something undesired by the individual, such as an annoying noise, an unpleasant chore, or unwanted attention.
- *Positive punishment,* also called presentation punishment, is adding (+) or presenting something undesired by the individual, such as physical pain, unpleasant chores, or unwanted attention.
- *Negative punishment,* also called removal punishment, is taking away (–) something desired by an individual, such as toys, free time, or wanted attention.

Regardless of whether the reinforcement is positive or negative, reinforcement *increases* the behavior, whereas both positive and negative punishments *decrease* the behavior.

When a behavior is first being developed, consequences are needed every time the behavior occurs in order for individuals to make the association and perform the behavior consistently—a **continuous schedule.** After the behavior has been well established, reinforcement is needed only periodically to continue supporting the behavior (Skinner, 1954). Reinforcement can occur on an **intermittent schedule.** Intermittent reinforcement schedules, shown in Example 9.2, may be:

- *ratio* schedules, based on the number of times a behavior occurs, such as every third time the child raises his or her hand;
- *interval* schedules, based on the time elapsed after the behavior has occurred, such as providing praise for every five minutes a student is quietly working on an assignment;
- *fixed* schedules, occurring exactly every third time the behavior occurs (fixed ratio) or exactly every five minutes (fixed interval), such that individuals know when to expect the reinforcement; or
- *variable* schedules, providing reinforcement every third time (variable ratio) or every five minutes (variable interval) on average but varying across time. Variable schedules typically are more effective and efficient because students are unaware of exactly when the reinforcement will be provided.

Although intermittent schedules work well for reinforcement, punishment needs to occur after every single infraction in order to work effectively. In other words, punishment requires a continuous schedule. Let's examine more closely the effective use of consequences.

Using Consequences Effectively

Here we present several tips for using consequences effectively, summarized in Guidelines 9.1. Many apply similarly to both reinforcement and punishment, but we'll also address some important differences in the use of reinforcement and punishment.

Know the developmental level of the individual. To use consequences effectively, teachers should understand what typically is considered good and bad by students in a particular developmental period. Stickers and smiley faces may be desired consequences for early childhood and elementary students, but they will not be as effective for influencing the behavior of middle school and high school students, who may instead desire free time to talk with friends.

Know the individual's likes and dislikes. In order to provide reinforcement and punishment, teachers must know what individual students consider to be positive and negative. One student may love chocolate and another may not, so chocolate might work great as positive reinforcement for one student's behavior but not another's. Individuals choose different reinforcements due to preference and are more

EXAMPLE 9.2	Examples of Intermittent Schedules	
	Fixed	**Variable**
Ratio	Feedback on book reports is given for every third book report completed.	Slot machines pay out based on the number of pulls, but you don't know which pull will be the big winner.
Interval	Every Friday, popcorn is given to all students who meet their weekly reading goal.	Extra credit for class participation is given on random days throughout the semester.

likely to increase their behavior for a highly preferred reinforcement than for other reinforcements (Damon, Riley-Tillman, & Fiorello, 2008; Fischer & Mazur, 1997). Teachers must find out what is preferred by the students in their classrooms. Some examples of specific classroom strategies based on student preferences are described in Table 9.1.

Understand the function of attention. Just as students have individual preferences for tangible rewards, attention given to students can be a powerful consequence, as either reinforcement or punishment (Maag, 2001). For example, a teacher who repeatedly asks a student to sit down and be quiet may actually be increasing the behavior by providing the student with attention for the misbehavior—positive reinforcement. Peers can also reinforce inappropriate behaviors by providing attention, such as looking and laughing at disruptive behaviors (Flood, Wilder, Flood, & Masuda, 2002). In contrast, a teacher who repeatedly praises a student publicly for appropriate behavior may be decreasing the likelihood of that behavior because the student does not want the attention—positive punishment. By increasing or decreasing the amount of attention given, the teacher can alter problem behavior in the classroom (McComas, Thompson, & Johnson, 2003). Teachers must assess whether the attention they give to problem behavior is increasing or decreasing that behavior for each individual student and alter the amount of teacher and peer attention accordingly.

Know when and how often to provide consequences. As we discussed earlier, behavior and consequence must occur close together in time. The sticker given to a preschooler one day after the child has sat quietly for a story is no longer associated with the child's behavior the day before due to the elapsed time. Also, remember that scheduling how often to provide a consequence differs for reinforcement and punishment. Intermittent reinforcement can be as effective as continuous reinforcement in children and adolescents (Bowman et al., 1997; Freeland & Noell, 1999). Although teachers can use either schedule with similar results, an intermittent schedule of reinforcement is more efficient because it does not require teachers to "catch" every instance of positive behavior. In contrast, teachers *do* need to catch every instance of misbehavior if punishment is to be effective. Students who "get away" with a negative behavior learn that punishment can be avoided.

Use reinforcement more than punishment. Because it is difficult to use punishment on a continuous schedule, punishment is considered less effective than reinforcement. Also, punishment alone tends

GUIDELINES 9.1	Guiding Principles for Using Consequences Effectively
Guiding Principles	**Tips**
Know the developmental level of the individual.	Younger children may like pencils, candy, and stickers. Older children and adolescents may prefer time to socialize with friends or listen to music.
Know the individual's likes and dislikes.	Although we assume most young children will like candy and stickers, some won't. Know what is considered desirable by particular students.
Understand the function of attention.	Some students will want the teacher's attention (praise and criticism alike), whereas other children may not want attention or may want only positive attention, such as praise.
Know when and how often to provide consequences.	Reinforcement can be given on an intermittent schedule without needing to catch every appropriate behavior. Punishment must be given on a continuous schedule by catching every infraction.
Use reinforcement more than punishment.	Because reinforcement is more efficient on an intermittent schedule, reinforcement should be used often and punishment sparingly.
Some punishments should not be used.	Physical or psychological punishment, extra homework, withdrawal of recess, and out-of-school suspensions all are ineffective punishments.

TABLE 9.1	Classroom Strategies Based on Students' Likes and Dislikes	
Strategy	**Description**	**Note of caution**
Token economy	Students are given a token for appropriate classroom behavior or good academic work. The tokens are exchanged periodically for toys or prizes that children can choose based on their own preferences.	Managing this complex system of tokens and exchanges is very time consuming.
Contingency contract	Teachers write a contract for each student specifying goals for behaviors that will be reinforced and what reinforcement will be given based on student preferences. Students can be involved in setting the goals and determining the rewards.	Teachers must be able to remember the goals and rewards specified for numerous students.
Group consequences	Reinforcement is based on the behavior or academic achievement of the class as a whole. The students may help choose the class reward.	Individual students who struggle in the subject area or who have behavioral difficulties can be singled out as holding back the whole class.

to teach a student only what *not* to do rather than encouraging a more appropriate behavior (Alberto & Troutman, 1999). Given these limitations of punishment, psychologists tend to agree that teachers should focus on using reinforcement to increase wanted behaviors and focus less on punishing unwanted behaviors (Cheyne & Walters, 1970; Maag, 2001).

Historically, teachers were more likely to use disapproval (punishment) than approval (reinforcement) in the classroom. Many teachers may learn to use punishment. For example, the first time a teacher yells, students typically react with immediate silence and obedience; hence, the teacher experiences positive reinforcement for her yelling. Yet the students eventually adjust to the yelling, and the punishment becomes less effective. More recent studies have found that teachers use approval more often than disapproval. Although this signals an important shift in the behaviors of teachers, research also indicates that approval is used primarily for academic learning and rarely to increase appropriate social behavior. Teachers would also benefit from using reinforcement for appropriate classroom behavior in order to increase on-task time for academic learning (see Beaman & Wheldall, 2000, for a review of approval and disapproval).

Some punishments should not be used. Several types of punishment are considered ineffective. First we need to define what we mean by effective and ineffective punishment. If effective punishment means simply getting the individual to stop engaging in some behavior, then most punishments work extremely well when given on a continuous schedule. However, most scholars think that effective punishment should not only stop the unwanted behavior but also lead to an understanding of why a behavior should not be used, enabling individuals to generalize to other, similar behaviors (Pfiffner & Barkely, 1998). In addition, effectiveness usually implies that the reasons for using the punishment outweigh its negative effects (Alberto & Troutman, 1999). The following five types of punishment do not meet this requirement of effectiveness:

1. *Physical punishment.* Physical punishment typically is viewed as spanking, but it also includes washing someone's mouth out with soap or making someone remain in a physically uncomfortable environment (e.g., extremely cold, extremely hot). One negative effect of physical punishment is that it teaches individuals that it is acceptable for older or more powerful individuals to hit, push, or slap others. Although empirical data do not support the use of physical punishment, many educators still believe that it is a necessary evil, and changing their belief has proved difficult (Robinson, Funk,

DIVERSITY

Beth, & Bush, 2005). Specifically, teachers in Botswana, Africa, have been found to strongly believe that physical punishment (e.g., caning) is inherent in their culture (Tafa, 2002).

2. *Psychological punishment:* Psychological punishment can include public humiliation, such as a teacher ridiculing a student in front of the class, and may lead to loss of self-esteem (Davis & Thomas, 1989). The negative impact of this type of punishment on an individual's long-term well-being far outweighs the potential effect of decreasing an unwanted behavior. Hence, scholars agree that psychological punishment should not be used (Walker, Shea, & Bauer, 2004).

3. *Extra homework.* By giving additional homework as a punishment, teachers send the message that homework is undesirable. Teachers should be sending the message that learning is important, essential, and positive—not negative, bad, or unwanted (Corno, 1996).

4. *Withdrawal of recess.* Recess may be necessary in order for children to focus attention and behave appropriately, in addition to the usefulness of physical activity for health purposes (DeAngelis, 2004; Rich, 2004). Attention appears to decrease after long periods of confinement in classrooms and to improve following recess (Holmes, Pellegrini, & Schmidt, 2006). In addition, classroom behavior, as rated by teachers, is better among children who have at least some recess during the day (Barros, Silver, & Stein, 2009). One study examining the importance of recess for children with ADHD found inappropriate behaviors more likely to occur on days when the children did not have recess (Ridgway, Northup, Pellegrin, LaRue, & Hightshoe, 2003). In addition to increasing attention and decreasing inappropriate behaviors, activities typically engaged in by students during recess help foster cognitive development and social skills (Pellegrini & Bohn, 2005). The positive effects of recess far outweigh any benefit of using the elimination of recess as a form of punishment.

5. *Out-of-school suspensions.* In most cases, students who are given out-of-school suspensions do not view missing school as a punishment. Most of those students will see the suspension as negative reinforcement—taking away something undesired (attending school). In addition, empirical data suggest that out-of-school suspensions are given disproportionately to children from lower-socioeconomic homes and minority ethnic groups, and to boys more than girls (Gregory & Weinstein, 2008; Krezmien, Leone, & Achilles, 2006; Mendez & Knoff, 2003). An alternative approach is in-school suspensions that can be used to more closely supervise students and to provide assistance for their academic struggles (Gootman, 1998; Huff, 1988). However, in-school suspensions also may serve as a negative reinforcement—as some students may misbehave because they do not want to be in class. In addition, teachers and administrators must be careful not to give in-school suspensions disproportionately to lower-SES students, ethnic minority students, or boys.

DIVERSITY

DIVERSITY

Think of some ways you might use positive and negative reinforcement in a classroom. What are some things that students would consider desirable or undesirable to have taken away? (Remember, don't assign additional academic work—you don't want to imply that you consider it bad.)

APPLICATIONS: APPLIED BEHAVIOR ANALYSIS

We've discussed many examples regarding the use of operant conditioning in classroom settings. However, teachers can use specific strategies based on operant conditioning to influence behaviors in their classrooms. These specific strategies typically are referred to as applied behavior analysis or behavior modification. Many of these strategies focus on increasing appropriate behaviors, while others focus on decreasing inappropriate behaviors. Let's examine some of these strategies more closely.

A Necessary Break. Recess provides positive outcomes, such as increased attention. The withdrawal of recess should not be used as a punishment.

Strategies for Increasing Appropriate Behaviors

Premack principle: Using the Premack principle (Premack, 1959, 1965), a teacher may increase one behavior of students by providing

Premack Principle.
Reinforcement can include preferred activities such as listening to music or talking with friends.

9 | Behavioral Learning Theories

an activity as reinforcement (e.g., playing a game, socializing with friends, drawing) rather than giving tangible rewards (e.g., stickers, smiley faces). Early studies found the Premack principle extremely effective for teaching young children (3-year-olds) to sit quietly and look at the teacher by using free time as reinforcement (Homme, DeBaga, Devine, Steinhorst, & Rickert, 1963). The principle applies to older students as well. Middle school or high school students who complete an assignment early could use the rest of the class period to listen to music on an iPod or talk quietly with their friends.

Operant conditioning in classroom settings: See page 161.

Shaping: Shaping is used when a behavior is not currently being displayed and therefore cannot be reinforced, such as when a student *never* brings a pencil and paper to class. The teacher does not have the opportunity to reinforce the behavior because it doesn't occur. Shaping involves reinforcing small steps that move toward the behavior until the entire behavior is displayed (Skinner, 1953, 1954).

Teachers can use shaping for both academic learning and classroom behavior. For a child who struggles with learning to read, teachers can shape behavior by first praising the student for attempts to sound out a difficult or an unfamiliar word, then for each time the child correctly sounds out words, then for increased reading fluency, and finally for answering comprehension questions. In middle school or high school classrooms, class participation can be shaped by reinforcing any effort at participation by students, such as making eye contact, raising their hand, or providing an answer, even if it is incorrect (Hodge & Nelson, 1991).

Reinforcing incompatible behaviors: In this strategy, teachers use reinforcement to increase the appropriate behavior (e.g., working on the assignment) while decreasing the behavior it is incompatible with (e.g., passing notes). While this strategy is effective for a number of behaviors, it must be used correctly, with consistent and frequent reinforcement of the appropriate behavior, so students do not return to the original, inappropriate behavior (Alberto & Troutman, 1999).

Praise-and-ignore: Like the strategy of reinforcing incompatible behaviors, the praise-and-ignore strategy suggests that teachers ignore inappropriate behaviors displayed by an individual while praising the appropriate behaviors of others. For example, the teacher may ignore a student who blurts out the answer to a question while praising the other students for raising their hands and being patient. Several early studies found this technique to be very effective for increasing appropriate behaviors (Becker, Madsen, Arnold, & Thomas, 1967; Madsen, Becker, & Thomas, 1968). Remember, however, that certain students may consider public praise a positive reinforcement, while others may consider it a positive punishment. In addition, some behaviors cannot be ignored, such as physically harming others or destroying property. Ignoring such behaviors would be unsafe and unethical.

Positive practice: In using positive practice, the teacher has a student perform the right or appropriate behavior (Kazdin, 2001). Students may write words they misspelled to practice the correct way to spell them. Teachers also can have students who run down the hallway return to the end of the hall and practice walking, decreasing the likelihood that the student will run in the hallway again and increasing the likelihood that the student will walk.

Strategies for Decreasing Inappropriate Behaviors

Satiation: In this strategy, the teacher asks the student to perform the negative or inappropriate behavior repeatedly, until it is no longer rewarding. Satiation diminishes the desirability of an inappropriate behavior by requiring the student to perform it over and over (Krumboltz & Krumboltz, 1972). For example, a student caught throwing spitballs is required to spend the entire class period creating those balls and spitting them at a specified target. At first, the other students may reinforce the behavior with their laughing and attention to the student (as they probably have done in the past), but eventually the spitball making and spitball watching behaviors will become satiated and no longer fun, entertaining, or desirable. The trick is to make sure that everyone has had enough. Don't give up too quickly. When the student appears bored with the behavior, let it go on a bit longer. Satiation should be used only when the behavior is not seriously harmful to the individual (Krumboltz & Krumboltz, 1972). In other words, do not use satiation with behaviors that may result in harm, such as smoking or lighting matches.

Satiation also can occur unintentionally, making a particular reinforcement no longer effective. Suppose, for example, a high school teacher reinforces students' completion of their homework with class time for talking and socializing. If other teachers begin to use the same reinforcement strategy in their classrooms, the importance and desirability of social time may be reduced. So teachers should continually reevaluate the effectiveness of the reinforcement strategies they use and alter them when the original reinforcement is satiated or no longer desirable enough to effect a change in behavior.

Extinction: Similar to its use in classical conditioning, extinction means that the behavior ceases or is eliminated. However, according to operant conditioning, extinction occurs because reinforcement no longer is given for that behavior (Skinner, 1953). Extinction can be useful for addressing a number of inappropriate behaviors (for a review, see Alberto & Troutman, 1999). For example, suppose a teacher stops giving a disapproving look to a student who continually speaks out of turn. The teacher is eliminating the positive reinforcement (attention), and the inappropriate behavior (speaking out of turn) should decrease or cease altogether. Like satiation, however, extinction should be used only when the undesired behavior can easily be ignored and is not harmful or dangerous, such as aggression (Krumboltz & Krumboltz, 1972).

A word of caution on using extinction: When a teacher withdraws reinforcement that has been given on an intermittent schedule, the student is likely to display an *extinction burst*—an initial increase in behavior due to the withdrawal of reinforcement. Consider the student who continually speaks out of turn. The teacher has been providing the positive reinforcement of attention (a disapproving look) to the student's unwanted behavior (talking out of turn). When the teacher eliminates the reinforcement, the student likely will increase the unwanted behavior in hopes that the teacher will "give in" and again provide the previous reinforcement. Over time, the student will learn that talking out of turn will no longer gain the teacher's attention, and the behavior will decrease. Individuals are less likely to display an extinction burst when extinction is used in conjunction with other behavioral methods, such as reinforcing the appropriate behavior (Lerman & Iwata, 1995).

Overcorrection: Overcorrection includes making restitution for inappropriate behavior (Alberto & Troutman, 1999). A student who writes on a desk in the classroom may be asked to remove the markings not only from that desk but from all the other desks in the classroom—overcorrecting for his or her own behavior.

Reprimand: Reprimands are verbal criticisms of behavior intended to be positive punishment. When teachers confront a student in class for an inappropriate behavior, they are providing attention. Some students will find this attention desirable, because they enjoy being in the spotlight, while other students will find it undesirable. Teachers must assess whether their reprimands (attention) are increasing or decreasing the behavior. When giving a verbal reprimand, teachers should make eye contact with the student and should stand close to the student rather than several feet away. The quiet, private approach allows the teacher to point out the behavior without providing the spotlight effect (O'Leary, Kaufman, Kass, & Drabman, 1970; Van Houten, Nau, MacKenzie-Keating, Sameoto, & Colavecchia, 1982).

Response cost: The concept of response cost is illustrated by the substance abuse policies of many athletic programs. Student athletes who use drugs or alcohol face the response cost of being suspended for a certain number of games or banned from the team. Response cost, a type of negative punishment, always involves taking away something the individual desires. For adolescents, the cost may be social time with peers, such as not being allowed to eat lunch in the cafeteria with friends or not being able to attend the class field trip. Response cost interventions effectively decrease disruptive behavior and tend to have lasting effects (Sullivan & O'Leary, 1990). One study of children with ADHD found that losing free time as a response cost was more effective in increasing on-task behavior and academic learning than was the use of the prescription medicine Ritalin (Rapport, Murphy, & Bailey, 1982). The effectiveness of this strategy may be one reason why teachers prefer this type of punishment to others (McGoey & DuPaul, 2000). The key in using response cost is to determine—both at the developmental level and at the individual level—what is desired and to consistently take that away following inappropriate behavior.

Social isolation (time-out): The time-out strategy includes removing an individual from one setting, where reinforcement is given, to another setting, where reinforcement is denied (Walker et al., 2004). In the best-known form of time-out, the student either is moved to an empty, uninteresting room or is removed from an activity to sit alone. When implementing time-out, teachers should consider these guidelines for using it effectively:

DIVERSITY

- Time-out should be used only when other strategies have failed and after careful consideration of time and age guidelines (Lentz, 1988). The duration of the time-out should not exceed one minute per year of age and should not be used with children younger than age 2. Hence, 5-year-olds should not be in time-out longer than five minutes. The use of a timer will increase the consistency and fairness of the strategy and serve to alert both teacher and student to the duration (Walker et al., 2004).

- Time-out is effective only if reinforcement is not present and the student desires to be with others in the classroom. Children who prefer to be alone and do not want attention from others may view removal from the classroom as desirable, making it a negative reinforcement (Walker et al., 2004). Also, in child-care centers and preschools, time-out may be ineffective because the teacher is not able to place the child in a separate room away from other children. So the child may draw attention from other children or from the teacher if he or she is being supervised by the teacher. In such cases, the attention associated with the time-out actually may be a positive reinforcement rather than a punishment.

Think about the grade level you want to teach. How could you use the Premack principle and response cost with this group of students? Think of specific examples.

Summary

Describe the basic assumptions of traditional behavioral learning theories. Learning processes are very similar across species and include an association between a stimulus and a response that occur close together in time. The association between stimulus and response results in a behavioral change, which indicates that learning has occurred.

Explain classical conditioning and its relevance to educational settings. Classical conditioning is the pairing of an unconditioned stimulus with a neutral stimulus, resulting in learning by association. Classical conditioning provides an explanation for why some children may experience anxiety or fears related to school. Emotions—which are unconscious, involuntary responses—can be linked to important aspects of educational settings, such as particular teachers, a certain subject, or school more generally.

Explain how reinforcement and punishment influence future behavior and how often each should be used to be effective. Reinforcement following a behavior will increase the likelihood that the behavior will occur again. When a behavior is first being developed, reinforcement must be given continuously. Once the behavior is established, only intermittent reinforcement is needed to maintain the behavior. Punishment following a behavior will decrease the likelihood that the behavior will occur again. For punishment to eliminate a behavior and keep the behavior from occurring in the future, every instance of the behavior must be followed by the punishment.

Explain how teachers can use consequences effectively. Teachers must understand how developmental level and individual preference influence the use of reinforcement and punishment—in particular, the preference for attention from the teacher. Reinforcement should be given more often than punishment yet can be used on an intermittent schedule. Some punishments should not be used, and all others should be used consistently and continuously to be effective.

Describe strategies teachers can use to increase appropriate behaviors and decrease inappropriate behaviors. A number of strategies can be used to increase appropriate behaviors. The Premack principle focuses on using activities for reinforcement, and shaping uses reinforcement of small steps toward a goal behavior. Reinforcing incompatible behaviors and praise-and-ignore strategies focus on reinforcing appropriate behaviors and ignoring other behaviors. Positive practice increases appropriate behaviors by having students practice the appropriate behaviors and providing reinforcement. Strategies to decrease inappropriate behaviors are also available. Satiation, extinction, overcorrection, and social isolation eliminate previous reinforcement of inappropriate behaviors in various ways. Reprimands, or verbal criticism, are a specific case of positive punishment. Response cost, a specific case of negative punishment, involves taking away something desired by the student following an inappropriate behavior.

Key Concepts

conditioned response 160

conditioned stimulus 160

contiguity learning 159

continuous schedule 163

cues 162

discrimination 160

extinction 160

generalization 160

intermittent schedule 163

law of effect 161

learning 159

neutral stimuli 160

overcorrection 168

positive practice 167

praise-and-ignore 167

Premack principle 166

prompts 162

punishment 162

reinforcement 162

reinforcing incompatible behaviors 167

reprimand 168

response cost 168

satiation 168

shaping 167

social isolation (time-out) 169

unconditioned response 159

unconditioned stimulus 159

Video Applications

www.mhhe.com/bohlin2e

Video 1: Reinforcement in the Classroom (*3 minutes*)
Several teachers describe how they implement behavioral strategies such as positive reinforcement, praise-and-ignore, the Premack principle, and reinforcing incompatible behaviors.

Video 2: Marble Jar (*4 minutes*)
A first-grade classroom is shown during a lesson. The behavioral management strategies of using a marble jar and stickers are shown throughout the lesson, followed by the teacher's rationale for using this system.

Case Studies
Reflect and Evaluate

EARLY CHILDHOOD: "Pinch"

These questions refer to the case study on page 150.

1. Why didn't the verbal reprimands of Miss Rana and Miss Amber deter Reagan from pinching others? Why was Reagan so eager to admit to her behavior?

2. Why was providing the sticker for reinforcement at the end of the day ineffective in decreasing Reagan's inappropriate pinching behavior? What could have been done differently to increase the effectiveness of the sticker strategy?

3. It may be difficult for Miss Rana and Miss Amber to continue to provide Reagan with so much praise for keeping her hands to herself. How might they change this strategy over time?

4. Could shaping be used to increase Emily's behavior during art or Reagan's behavior during circle time? If so, explain how.

5. What techniques for increasing appropriate behavior and for decreasing inappropriate behavior were used in the preschool classroom?

ELEMENTARY SCHOOL: "Silly Students"

These questions refer to the case study on page 152.

1. What strategies were originally used by Mr. Lindsay with the three students who were being disruptive? According to operant conditioning, why didn't those strategies work well for decreasing their disruptive behavior?

2. Mr. Lindsay focused on punishment as a behavioral strategy, whereas the other fourth-grade teachers suggested a focus on reinforcement. Explain why this shift in focus toward reinforcement most likely increased appropriate behavior.

3. Although taking away recess time may have decreased the students' disruptive behaviors, why is this a poor option?

4. Providing students with three minutes of "free time" to talk after each subject will decrease the time available for Mr. Lindsay to present lessons and/or decrease the time available for students to complete work. How might Mr. Lindsay change the three-minute reward over time?

5. Do you think the same reinforcement would have been equally effective with younger and older children? Why or why not?

MIDDLE SCHOOL: "Study Hall"

These questions refer to the case study on page 154.

1. What types of reinforcement could be included in the English, mathematics, and study hall periods to increase homework completion?

2. How might the same reinforcements have different outcomes for different students? How might these reinforcements be different than rewards used with elementary students?

3. How was the Premack principle used with Jamie?

4. How is the importance of receiving attention from the teacher illustrated in this case? How might attention be used as a reinforcer within the English and mathematics class periods to enhance performance?

5. What other strategies could be used to increase homework productivity for Jamie? For Jasamine? How might the strategies be different for these two students, and why?

HIGH SCHOOL: "Bending the Rules"

These questions refer to the case study on page 156.

1. Does this school appear to focus on reinforcement or punishment? What are some specific examples of reinforcement and punishment within the school?

2. Do some teachers use behavioral strategies better than others? Which strategies are used, and why are they effective or ineffective?

3. How and why might bending the rules influence Jason's future completion of homework? What about other students' completion of homework?

4. What other specific strategies could the teacher, the coach, and the principal implement to increase appropriate behavior and decrease inappropriate behavior?

5. Are the behavioral strategies used in the classrooms and the school appropriate, given the developmental level of the students? Why or why not?

MODULE 10

Social Cognitive Theory

Outline	Learning Goals
Assumptions of Social Cognitive Theory	
	1. Describe the basic assumptions of social cognitive theory.
Observational Learning	
■ Model Characteristics ■ Imitator Characteristics ■ Environmental Characteristics	2. Describe those characteristics of models, imitators, and the environment needed for observational learning.
Personal Factors in Learning	
■ Self-efficacy ■ Self-regulation ■ Applications: Improving Students' Self-efficacy and Self-regulation	3. Explain how self-efficacy and self-regulation are related to positive outcomes for students. 4. Explain how teachers can promote self-efficacy and self-regulation among their students.
Summary **Key Concepts** **Video Applications** **Case Studies: Reflect and Evaluate**	

ASSUMPTIONS OF SOCIAL COGNITIVE THEORY

Maybe you've heard a young child say a swear word and thought to yourself, *Well, she heard that somewhere*. Would you ever consider teaching children how to shoot a basketball or write their name without showing them how? Many times children imitate our behaviors when we don't necessarily want them to, such as when they repeat swear words, but often we want them to imitate our behaviors as a way for them to learn. In the 1960s, Albert Bandura began to study how individuals could learn by observing others' experiences in the environment. His ideas about observational learning were first termed *social learning theory*. As the theory evolved and included more personal characteristics such as cognition, the theory was relabeled *social cognitive theory*. Let's examine several assumptions of Bandura's (1986) social cognitive theory before we address the specifics of the theory:

Learning: See Module 9.

- *Learning can occur by observing others.* An individual does not need to directly experience environmental stimuli, such as through reinforcement and punishment of behavior. Instead, an individual can observe others' environmental experiences in order to learn new behaviors or to learn which behaviors will receive rewards or punishments. Learning by observing others' behaviors is called vicarious learning, or **observational learning.**

Stimuli: See page 159.

- *Learning may or may not include a behavior change.* Learning can include observing others' behaviors and gaining knowledge but not performing those behaviors. For example, an individual may learn how to put a pencil in the sharpener and sharpen it through observation but might not sharpen the pencil if it is already sharp.

- *Personal characteristics are important in learning.* Behavior is not simply a direct effect of the environment but also includes personal characteristics, such as beliefs in one's ability. For example, a student who believes she can succeed on a history test is more likely to learn the material. Personal characteristics can be enhanced by the environment to promote learning, as when the student's high score on the history test further solidifies her belief in her success.

The best-known example of observational learning is the classic experimental study examining aggressive behaviors (Bandura, Ross, & Ross, 1961). Preschool-age children in the experimental group were taken individually to a toy room and exposed to an adult model exhibiting aggression toward a Bobo doll. Preschool-age children in the control group were taken individually to the same toy room and exposed to an adult model playing quietly and ignoring the Bobo doll. Then the adult model exited the room, and the children's behavior in the toy room was observed for aggression. As expected, the children exposed to the aggressive model exhibited more aggressive behaviors—both physical and verbal—than did children in the control group.

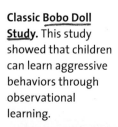

Classic Bobo Doll Study. This study showed that children can learn aggressive behaviors through observational learning.

Think of some instances when you have learned through observation. Did your learning include a change in behavior? What factors were important in your observational learning?

OBSERVATIONAL LEARNING

Observational learning includes several components that influence what information will be learned. Both specific characteristics of the model performing the behavior and specific characteristics of the imitator influence whether learning will occur. Even with the most effective models and imitators, environmental conditions also influence whether behaviors will be performed.

Model Characteristics

For observational learning to occur, someone must perform a behavior while being observed by another individual. The **model,** the individual whose behavior is being observed, performs (or models) a behavior that can be imitated by others. Models can be either live or symbolic (Bandura, 1986, 2002). **Live models**—individuals who are observed directly—can be the observer's friends, parents, siblings, fellow students, or teachers. **Symbolic models**—individuals who do not live within the same environment as the observer—can be observed through various media such as movies, books, and television

Symbolic Models.
Models can be found
in the media, such as
singer Taylor Swift
and athlete Peyton
Manning.

programs. Both live and symbolic models provide individuals with many opportunities to observe the behaviors of others.

Certain characteristics of models, whether live or symbolic, increase the likelihood that their behaviors will be observed:

1. *Relevance:* The behavior of models must be relevant for the individual observing the behavior—the individual must be interested in the behavior being performed, and the model must be similar to the individual (Schunk & Hanson, 1989). For example, some children may not be interested in chess and will not pay attention to the behavior of the stellar chess player in school. Also, individuals are more likely to imitate the behaviors of models who appear similar to them based on age, gender, race, socioeconomic status, and so on. Students who observe a peer of the same age will increase their level of mathematical performance more than students who observe a teacher (Schunk & Hanson, 1989).

2. *Competence:* The model must be viewed as competent in the behavior being observed. Students learning math will pay more attention to the behavior of other students who have strong academic performance in math than to that of students who are failing or struggling in math.

3. *High status:* The model is more likely to be imitated if he or she is someone with high status. High status can include power:

   ■ within the family (parents and older siblings),

   ■ within the peer group (the popular students at school),

   ■ of authority (teachers and principals),

   ■ within the popular media (celebrities), or

   ■ within a particular culture (political or religious figures).

4. *Gender-appropriateness:* An effective model is more likely to be someone of the same sex who is performing gender-appropriate behaviors. Gender-appropriate behaviors are those viewed by mainstream society as specific to either males or females (Bussey & Bandura, 1999). In the classic Bobo doll study described earlier, boys and girls were more likely to imitate a male model being aggressive than they were a female model. The strongest relationship was between a male model and male child, most likely because physical aggression is deemed more appropriate for males than for females by society (Bandura et al., 1961).

Gender: See page 51.

Teachers provide an excellent example of models in the classroom. Teachers may not have all the characteristics described, such as being of the same gender or race, but they can facilitate observational learning by making sure they are competent in the subject matter and maintaining their high status as authority figures. Teachers must be careful not to model inappropriate behaviors, which also can be imitated by students.

Imitator Characteristics

Many times, teachers with several of the characteristics described model academic skills or appropriate social behaviors, yet those behaviors are not imitated by students. In addition to requiring certain characteristics of models, observational learning requires the imitator to meet several conditions (Bandura, 1986; Schunk, 2004):

Attention: See page 185.

1. *Attention:* The imitator must be paying attention to the model. Teachers can perform behaviors that are intended to be imitated by students, such as completing mathematical equations on the white board, but students must pay attention to the behavior in order to perform the behavior themselves later. Teachers can enhance student attention by keeping the content relevant and interesting.

2. *Retention:* Students not only must pay attention to the teacher who is completing the mathematical equation on the white board, but also must be able to remember the behavior later that evening while they are completing the homework assignment. Providing students with memory strategies such as numbering the steps in a math equation or creating a mnemonic for a list of items can increase the likelihood that the information will be retained for later imitation.

3. *Production:* The imitator must be able to produce the behavior. For example, many individuals paid attention to Michael Jordan's legendary basketball skills in the 1990s and even memorized his physical moves; however, few people could produce those same behaviors.

Motivation: See page 265.

4. *Motivation:* An imitator who pays attention, retains the information, and can produce the behavior also must have the motivation to perform that behavior in the future. A math student may have attended to and retained the model's behavior and may be able to produce the behavior but may not be motivated to complete the math homework. Recent research suggests that a program using students' personal information (name, friends' names, favorite store) can create math word problems that are more interesting to students. Nigerian students provided with this personalized program had much higher achievement scores than those using the traditional math word problems (Akinsola & Awofala, 2009). By keeping the information personally interesting, teachers can increase a student's motivation to imitate the behavior or performance.

DIVERSITY

Students may be more or less likely to meet these conditions. For example, young children do not have the same attention span or memory strategies as older individuals. As cognitive development becomes more advanced, individuals are able to imitate more complex behaviors. Similarly, physical strength and ability grow throughout childhood and adolescence, allowing some behaviors to be more easily produced at a later time. In addition, some cultures, such as the country of Samoa, use observational learning as a primary mode of teaching social behavior, a strategy that may give students practice in using the skills involved in learning by observation (Odden & Rochat, 2004).

Environmental Characteristics

Assume that we have a model who has all the necessary characteristics to be effective and an imitator who also has all the necessary characteristics to be effective. Will all the modeled behaviors be imitated? No. Environmental conditions increase or decrease the likelihood that a modeled behavior actually will be imitated by an individual (Bandura, 1986; Schunk, 2004). Let's look at some of these environmental conditions:

Live Models. Teachers can model learning tasks and behaviors for students, such as completing mathematical equations on a white board, but students must be paying attention in order to perform the behavior themselves later.

- *Response facilitation effect:* A behavior is imitated more frequently if a model has been reinforced for that behavior—called **vicarious reinforcement.** An adolescent who views another student receiving free time to talk with friends because she has completed her homework during class time is more likely to complete the homework (increase behavior) to receive that same reinforcement.

Reinforcement: See page 162.

- *Response inhibition effect:* A behavior is imitated less frequently if a model has been punished for that behavior—called **vicarious punishment.** An elementary student is less likely to swear in class if a classmate has been sent to the principal's office for swearing in class.

Punishment: See page 162.

- *Response disinhibition effect:* A behavior is imitated more frequently if a model's behavior is not punished when the behavior typically is punished. For example, cheating on an exam typically results in punishment. If some students are successful in cheating on an exam without receiving punishment, other students are more likely to perform that same cheating behavior.

Researchers continue to find support for learning by observation. For example, a recent study of aggression, based on natural observations of preschoolers in a low-income, urban day care center, found that aggression occurred more frequently after an aggressive act resulted in a positive outcome—vicarious reinforcement—than after aggression was followed by a negative outcome—vicarious punishment (Goldstein, Arnold, Rosenberg, Stowe, & Ortiz, 2001). Support has also been found for using observational learning in academic domains, such as preschool-age reading and middle school writing (Braaksma, Rijlaarsdam, van den Bergh, & van Hout-Wolters, 2004; Horner, 2004). Teachers should not only model academic skills and appropriate behaviors themselves, but also reinforce students' appropriate behaviors, as other students may imitate their peers.

DIVERSITY

Celebrities and athletes are symbolic models with extremely high status who may not model appropriate behaviors and may not be punished for inappropriate behaviors. How can teachers compete with such models?

PERSONAL FACTORS IN LEARNING

Bandura (1986) has expanded his theory of observational learning to move beyond the historical link between environment and behavior and include variables unique to individuals. The advances in his theory led to the *triadic reciprocal determinism model of causality* to explain the interaction among three aspects (see Figure 10.1):

1. *Behavior,* including choices in actions and performance.
2. *Environment,* consisting of the various contexts (family, school, mass media) and the socialization factors within those contexts (parents, teachers, symbolic models).
3. *Person,* including personality, temperament, emotions, and physical characteristics (gender and race) as well as internal cognitive processes (goals, beliefs, and attitudes).

Note two features of this model. First, the influence of these three aspects on one another is bidirectional, or reciprocal. A teacher's instructional style (environment) may influence a student's performance (behavior), and the student's performance may influence the teacher's instruction. Second, personal characteristics are important and interact with environment to influence behavior. A student with high levels of anxiety (personal characteristic) who is attending a school in a low-socioeconomic district with few resources (environment) may score lower on a standardized test than a student with high levels of confidence (personal characteristic) who is attending a school in a high-socioeconomic district with the best teachers and resources (environmental characteristic). Although many personal characteristics contribute to learning, two that have received much attention in the educational field are self-efficacy and self-regulation.

Self-efficacy: See page 299.

Self-efficacy

Self-efficacy, an individual's belief about his or her capabilities for success, has been studied extensively (Bandura, 1977, 1997). Individuals with high self-efficacy believe that they are capable of success, whereas individuals with low self-efficacy believe

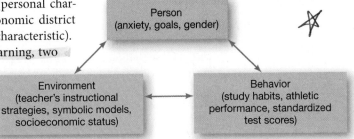

Figure 10.1. Bandura's Triadic Reciprocal Determinism Model of Causality. In this model, behavior, environment, and person have bidirectional influences on each other.

that they are likely to fail or that they are not capable of success. Self-efficacy develops from four influences:

1. *Past performance:* Individuals who have been successful in a given domain in the past are likely to have high self-efficacy for it. For example, a student who has performed well in math is likely to expect to achieve success in math in the future. In contrast, the student who has struggled with math or has had many instances of failure likely expects to fail again in the future. Teachers who provide students with ample opportunities to be successful may enhance a student's self-efficacy for more challenging tasks.

2. *Modeling:* When individuals see others similar to themselves experience success, they are likely to have high self-efficacy and to believe that they too can be successful.

3. *Verbal persuasion:* Individuals who are told that they can be successful are more likely to believe in their own success and to develop high self-efficacy. Students who are told that they are unlikely to succeed may develop low self-efficacy and a belief that they will fail. Here, simple words of encouragement may increase a student's self-efficacy.

4. *Physiological states:* Physical strength or fatigue can influence levels of self-efficacy. A student who is physically weak may have lower self-efficacy in areas of athletic performance than a student who is physically strong; or students who are tired may be less likely to view their capabilities as leading to success.

High Self-efficacy. Individuals with high self-efficacy believe that they are very capable of success and would be more likely to participate in class by raising their hand.

DIVERSITY

Cultural differences also may influence the development of self-efficacy (Bandura, 2002; Schunk & Pajares, 2002). Teachers and media figures often are less likely to represent a minority group. Because students from minority groups may have fewer similar models available, they may have lower self-efficacy. For example, one study found that minority students predicted their own performance on standardized tests—as well as that of others in their minority group—to be below average. Similarly, women had lower self-efficacy than men for performance on a standardized test (Mayo & Christenfeld, 1999). Historically in American culture, girls had few female role models in successful careers, and verbal persuasion toward participation in certain academic areas, particularly math and science, was not encouraging but rather discouraging (Bussey & Bandura, 1999). Recent research suggests that this pattern may be disappearing in some cultures. A cross-national study found that middle school-age girls had *higher* self-efficacy for academic activities than boys in Eastern and Western European countries (Pastorelli et al., 2001). Teachers can counter the limited models available for minority students and girls by using verbal persuasion and providing examples of successful similar models whenever possible.

Self-efficacy is considered an important cognitive process in learning because it influences choice of behavior, effort and persistence, and achievement (Bandura, 1982, 1989, 1997). Let's examine each of these more closely.

- Choice of behavior: Individuals will choose more difficult behaviors for which they have high self-efficacy, whereas individuals with low self-efficacy will avoid those behaviors. For example, the student with high self-efficacy for reading will choose more difficult books to read, while the student with low self-efficacy for reading will avoid it (Mucherah & Yoder, 2008). Similarly, one study found that middle school students who had high self-efficacy for math and science were more likely to continue taking classes in those areas (Fouad & Smith, 1996).

- *Effort and persistence:* Students with high self-efficacy will increase their effort and persistence for success even when they are struggling. For example, students with high self-efficacy for mathematics who do not perform well on the first homework assignment will put more time and energy into the next assignment. These students will continue to strive for success because they believe that they can be successful. In contrast, students with low self-efficacy for mathematics will view their first failure or struggle in math as verification that indeed they cannot be successful, and they will give up more easily (Bandura, 1982).

■ *Achievement:* Individuals with high self-efficacy tend to have higher levels of academic achievement than individuals with low self-efficacy (Tella, Tella, & Adeniyi, 2009; Weiser & Riggio, 2010; Valentine, DuBois, & Cooper, 2004). Specifically, self-efficacy for learning is related to mathematical performance, reading, and writing skills (see Schunk, 2003, for a review).

Think about your own self-efficacy. Do you have high self-efficacy in some academic areas and low self-efficacy in others? What factors most influenced your self-efficacy in those areas?

Self-regulation

Another personal characteristic in the triadic reciprocal model that has received much attention in educational settings is **self-regulation**—the ability to control one's emotions, cognitions, and behaviors by providing consequences for oneself. Bandura (1989) proposed that individuals need to learn self-regulation because the external environment cannot always provide reinforcement and punishment. Because learning processes can be very different in different domains and contexts, self-regulation is not a general trait but rather is highly situational and context-specific (Schunk, 2001). For example, a student may have the ability to master his learning rather than relying on others in the subject of math but not in American literature.

Minority Status. The election of President Barack Obama was significant for many people, as he provided the first presidential model of diversity in our nation's history.

Self-regulation: See page 301.

Self-regulation for learning includes a cyclical process with three major components, as shown in Figure 10.2 (Bandura, 1986; Zimmerman, 2001).

1. **Self-observation,** or self-monitoring: viewing one's own behavior and possibly recording one's own behavior.

2. **Self-judgment:** comparing one's performance to a predetermined goal or standard.

3. **Self-evaluation:** determining the quality of the judgment (good or bad) and possibly providing self-imposed consequences (reinforcement or punishment).

Let's examine these three components using the example of a student studying for an exam. The student would self-observe her study strategies, including recording the number of hours spent reading the text or taking notes. Then, assuming the student set a goal of an 80% score and achieved a 90% score on the exam, the student would self-judge that she had met the goal. Finally, she would evaluate her performance positively and possibly self-impose a reward, such as going to a movie with a friend. The cyclical process suggests that the student would use the self-judgment and self-evaluation processes to conclude that her study strategies are effective and should be used in the future. When the judgment and evaluation processes are less favorable, the student may choose to change study strategies and start the process of self-observation again.

The development of self-regulation begins in social interactions with parents, teachers, and peers who model learning strategies and provide verbal persuasion. The learning processes demonstrated in these social experiences become more self-directed through internal standards, beliefs, and self-reinforcement. Achieving self-regulation is more difficult for younger children than for older children, because younger children:

■ have a shorter attention span,

■ possess fewer memory strategies,

■ tend to overestimate or underestimate their progress (exhibit poor self-judgment and self-evaluation), and

■ need more immediate consequences.

Given these limitations, self-regulation does not begin to develop until the elementary school years (Schunk & Zimmerman, 1997; Zimmerman & Schunk, 2001). Self-regulation skills continue to grow

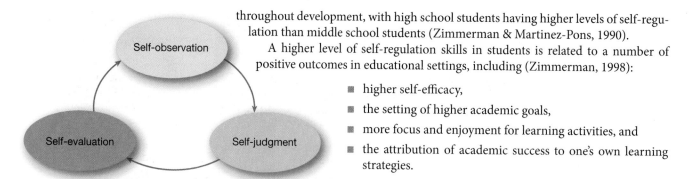

throughout development, with high school students having higher levels of self-regu-lation than middle school students (Zimmerman & Martinez-Pons, 1990).

A higher level of self-regulation skills in students is related to a number of positive outcomes in educational settings, including (Zimmerman, 1998):

- higher self-efficacy,
- the setting of higher academic goals,
- more focus and enjoyment for learning activities, and
- the attribution of academic success to one's own learning strategies.

Figure 10.2. Self-regulation. Cyclical process between major components of self-regulation.

Applications: Improving Students' Self-efficacy and Self-regulation

Given the link between self-efficacy and academic achieve-ment, educators need to promote self-efficacy. To do this, teachers can provide students with accurate, specific feedback rather than undeserved positive feedback (Linnenbrink & Pintrich, 2003). Self-efficacy that is based on accurate appraisals of an individual's ca-pabilities is more beneficial for positive outcomes than are inaccurate appraisals. This is especially true for younger children, who are less likely to assess their capabilities accurately due to their limited cogni-tive abilities and limited past performances (Schunk & Pajares, 2002). Teachers also can provide verbal persuasion for their students, particularly young children, in order to enhance accurate appraisals and increase self-efficacy.

Teachers should also model self-efficacy (Bandura, 1989). **Teacher efficacy** is a teacher's belief in his or her capability to transmit knowledge as well as manage the classroom well. Teacher efficacy is im-portant because it influences student self-efficacy and can affect student achievement (Woolfolk & Hoy, 1990). Teachers with high efficacy develop more challenging lessons, spend more time on academic ac-tivities, and are more persistent in working with students who are struggling. Conversely, teachers with low efficacy tend to have a pessimistic view of student motivation, are more easily stressed by students' misbehaviors, and have lower job satisfaction (Bandura, 1997; Schunk, 2004; Viel-Ruma, Houchins, Jolivette, & Benson, 2010). Teacher efficacy can be increased by observing other teachers, practicing performance (e.g., student teaching), and gaining more knowledge in one's subject areas.

Student self-efficacy and teacher self-efficacy can be increased through collective efficacy within school systems (Viel-Ruma et al., 2010). **Collective efficacy** is the belief in success with respect to a group or social system, such as beliefs about teachers and administrators in a school system as a whole (Schunk, 2004). Bandura (1997) suggests a number of characteristics needed for collective efficacy in a school system:

- administrations seek to improve instruction;
- administrators and teachers have high expectations and standards;
- teachers provide activities that promote self-efficacy in students;
- classroom behavior is well managed, resulting in more time spent on instruction and less on disci-pline issues; and
- the school encourages a collaborative effort with parents, including open communication.

Teacher efficacy: See page 302.

Self-regulation also can be enhanced by modeling learning strategies and guiding the practice of learning strategies (Schunk & Zimmerman, 2007). Teachers first need to act as models and to pro-vide feedback. Teachers then can provide students with opportunities for independent practice that require more self-evaluation, such as homework. Training in self-regulation processes (goal setting, self-reflection) has been found to lead to remarkable improvements in learning skills and self-efficacy (Schunk, 2001), including increases in performance and learning processes in individuals with learning disabilities (Butler, 1998).

DIVERSITY

Summary

Describe the basic assumptions of social cognitive theory. Learning can occur through observation as well as through direct experiences with the environment but may not always lead to a change in behavior. Learning is not simply a product of the environment but includes individual, personal characteristics such as cognitive beliefs.

Describe those characteristics of models, imitators, and the environment needed for observational learning. Models are more likely to be imitated if they are similar to the imitator, have a high status, and competently display gender-appropriate behaviors that are of interest to the imitator. Observational learning can take place only when the imitator is paying attention, can remember the behaviors observed, can actually produce the behaviors, and is motivated to imitate the behaviors. Behaviors are more likely to be imitated if the model was reinforced for the behavior, and less likely to be imitated if the model was punished for the behavior. When the model is not punished for behaviors that typically are punished, the behavior is likely to be imitated.

Explain how self-efficacy and self-regulation are related to positive outcomes for students. Self-efficacy, or beliefs about one's ability to be successful, are related to choice of behavior, effort and persistence, and achievement. Self-regulation involves a cyclical process among self-observation, self-judgment, and self-evaluation that enhances self-efficacy and promotes the setting of higher goals, the attribution of academic success to the self, and enjoyment of learning activities.

Explain how teachers can promote self-efficacy and self-regulation among their students. Teachers can provide students with successful models and accurate, positive feedback on their performance to increase self-efficacy. In addition, teachers who have high self-efficacy for instruction and are involved in school systems with collective efficacy are more capable of increasing student self-efficacy. Teachers can increase self-regulation among students by first providing a model and feedback and then giving students opportunities for independent learning.

Key Concepts

collective efficacy   180

live models   174

model   174

observational learning   174

self-efficacy   177

self-evaluation   179

self-judgment   179

self-observation   179

self-regulation   179

symbolic models   174

teacher efficacy   180

vicarious reinforcement   177

vicarious punishment   177

Video Applications

www.mhhe.com/bohlin2e

Video 1: Modeling and Self-Efficacy (*3 minutes*)
An eighth-grade math teacher models how to change fractions into decimals. He begins by reminding the students of their past performance (self-efficacy) and letting them know that he will do the first problems (model behavior) and they will do the following problems (imitate the behavior).

Case Studies
Reflect and Evaluate

EARLY CHILDHOOD: "Pinch"

These questions refer to the case study on page 150.

1. Identify an example of vicarious reinforcement being used in the preschool classroom.

2. Although ignoring misbehaviors can be effective at times, why did that strategy lead to increased pinching by other students?

3. Why did Miss Rana and Miss Amber both demonstrate how to use the sponge for painting?

4. What are some reasons why Emily was unable to use the sponge and paint in the way it was demonstrated by her teachers?

5. How did self-efficacy influence Emily's art project? How did pairing Emily with Reagan help improve Emily's self-efficacy? What else can Miss Rana and Miss Amber do to increase Emily's self-efficacy?

ELEMENTARY SCHOOL: "Silly Students"

These questions refer to the case study on page 152.

1. What are some examples of how modeling is used within Mr. Lindsay's classroom? How might these be improved upon?

2. What characteristics of imitators needed to be improved upon for the students to increase their ability to complete the work?

3. What methods of increasing Sara's self-efficacy were suggested by Ms. Vargas? What else can Mr. Lindsay do to increase her self-efficacy?

4. Mr. Lindsay asks the other two fourth-grade teachers for help quite often during their lunchtime. Why is this type of interaction among teachers important for Mr. Lindsay and for the school system?

5. In what specific ways did Mr. Lindsay attempt to increase self-regulation among his students?

6. How might the knowledge that Mr. Lindsay is African American and his students are predominantly White change your expectations for modeling and increasing self-efficacy? Why?

MIDDLE SCHOOL: "Study Hall"

These questions refer to the case study on page 154.

1. What modeling characteristics were important in order for Jamie to complete his math homework and for Jasamine to complete her English homework?

2. Do you think this plan would work as well if Jamie were a girl and Jasamine were a boy? Do you think this plan would work as well if Mr. Havel were a woman and Ms. DeBrick were a man? Explain your answers.

3. Is Ms. DeBrick's idea of having Jasamine work with another student a good idea? Why or why not, based on effective modeling?

4. How might Jamie's past performance in mathematics influence his ability to complete the homework? How might Jasamine's past performance in English influence her ability to complete the homework? What other factors might influence their performance?

5. How might "helping" Jamie and Jasamine with their homework increase or decrease self-regulation? What strategies could be used to increase self-regulation?

HIGH SCHOOL: "Bending the Rules"

These questions refer to the case study on page 156.

1. What specific aspects of observational learning does Mr. Hardy include in his classroom?

2. According to social cognitive theory, what specific characteristics of imitators make completing the homework assignments easy for most of the students? What characteristics of imitators give Jason difficulty? How could these characteristics be changed?

3. How and why might bending the rules influence the other basketball players' future completion of homework?

4. What factors might be influencing Jason's self-efficacy? How might his self-efficacy be changed?

5. How would you describe the collective self-efficacy within this school system? How might it be changed?

Information Processing

Outline	Learning Goals
Assumptions of the Information Processing Approach	
	1. Describe the assumptions that underlie information processing theory.
The Three-Stage Model of Information Processing	
■ Sensory Memory ■ Working Memory ■ Long-term Memory ■ Individual Differences in Information Processing	2. Describe the steps in the three-stage model of information processing, and discuss memory capacity and duration at each stage in the model. 3. Contrast the effectiveness of rehearsal and encoding strategies for storing information in long-term memory.
Applications to Teaching	
■ Helping Students Pay Attention ■ Helping Students Store and Retrieve Information Effectively	4. Discuss the methods for getting and maintaining students' attention. 5. Summarize the instructional strategies for helping students store and retrieve information effectively.
Summary **Key Concepts** **Video Applications** **Case Studies: Reflect and Evaluate**	

ASSUMPTIONS OF THE INFORMATION PROCESSING APPROACH

Human beings are constantly attempting to make sense of their environment and experiences. When we see, hear, smell, touch, or taste something, our mind immediately tries to figure out what it is, how it relates to previous experiences, and whether it is something worth remembering. In this module, we will consider how we process information, how we remember and forget, and how teachers can help students better understand and remember critical information, skills, and concepts. Before we examine how information processing works, let's first consider some basic assumptions about how learning occurs:

- *Cognitive processes influence learning.* Cognitive psychologists have offered many explanations of how people mentally process information. When students have difficulty learning, it may indicate ineffective or inappropriate cognitive processes. Teachers must consider not only *what* students need to learn but also *how* students can most effectively process the information they are learning.

- *People are selective about what they pay attention to and learn.* Students are constantly bombarded with sensory stimuli and information, so they need to be selective and focus only on what they think is important. Teachers must help students make wise choices about what concepts or information to pay attention to, process, and save in memory.

- *Meaning is personally constructed by the learner and is* influenced *by prior knowledge, experiences, and beliefs.* Individuals take many separate bits of information and piece them together to make sense of the world around them. Students bring different sets of prior knowledge, experiences, and beliefs with them to the classroom, and these influence the way they interpret new ideas and events. Although a teacher may present similar information to all students during a lesson, individual students may understand and remember that information differently.

Have you ever compared notes with someone and realized that you each focused on different things? Have you ever reminisced with a family member or friend about a past event and found that you remember different details?

THE THREE-STAGE MODEL OF INFORMATION PROCESSING

Behavioral learning theories: See Module 9

Information processing theory encompasses a variety of specific theories about the process of human cognition (Bereiter, 1997; Schunk, 2004). These theories challenge the behaviorist perspective that all learning involves associations between stimuli and responses. Cognitive theorists are concerned less with external behaviors than with the internal mental processes that occur as learners select and attend to features of the environment, transform and rehearse information, relate new information to prior knowledge, and organize knowledge to make it meaningful (Mayer, 1996).

Of the many different theories that attempt to explain human memory and learning, the most common are information processing approaches (Ashcraft, 2006). Early information processing theories compared human learning to the way computers process information (Atkinson & Schiffrin, 1968; Broadbent, 1958; Newell & Simon, 1972). Like a computer, the mind takes in information, performs operations on it to change its form (**encoding**), stores it, and retrieves it when needed. Figure 11.1 illustrates the three-stage information processing model, which suggests that our memories undergo three stages of processing: sensory memory, working memory, and long-term memory.

Sensory Memory

As you sit in a classroom, your **sensory memory** registers countless bits of data, including the firmness of the chair you're sitting in (touch), the perfume someone nearby is wearing (smell), the sound of chalk against the blackboard (hearing), the outfit your instructor is wearing (sight), and so on. If you were interviewed later in the day, would you remember all these details? Of course not. Not all of this information is perceived at a conscious level. You ignore some stimuli, give others cursory attention, and examine relatively few in depth.

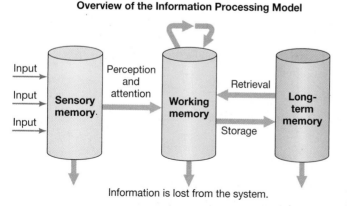

Overview of the Information Processing Model

Figure 11.1. **Three-Stage Model of Information Processing.**

Classroom Stimuli. During a typical lecture, sensory memory is bombarded with huge amounts of data.

As the first stop in the information processing system, sensory memory holds an unlimited amount of sensory data in a raw form, exactly as we sensed it (visual, auditory, olfactory, etc.), but the information has not yet been processed or interpreted (Neisser, 1967). However, the duration of sensory memory is extremely limited. Visual information lasts for only one second, auditory information only two or three seconds. One classic study by George Sperling (1960) showed that human beings have a very fleeting photographic memory (*iconic memory*). While our eyes can register an incredibly detailed amount of visual information, that mental picture decays very quickly. Auditory stimuli, held in *echoic memory*, appear to be similarly short-lived (Cowan, 1995, 2007; Lu, Williamson, & Kaufman, 1992). The onslaught of incoming information interferes with and quickly replaces the existing sensory data. If the mind does not perceive the sensory information as noteworthy, it is immediately discarded, never reaching the next stage in the memory system. Our fleeting sensory memory is actually advantageous. If every sensory stimulus in the environment commanded our full **attention,** our mental processes would become so bogged down that we couldn't function effectively (Mangels, Piction, & Craik, 2001).

To manage the constant barrage of data, we pay attention to some things and ignore others (Anderson, 2005; Mather & Sutherland, 2011). We might intentionally turn our attention to searching for a friend we have lost in a crowded cafeteria or to scanning our cluttered desk for a pencil. But sometimes stimuli seem to seek us out—something about a particular stimulus draws our attention to it. Advertisers clearly recognize what qualities of stimuli attract attention and capitalize on that information in selling their products. Humans use at least six criteria to determine the amount of attention particular stimuli deserve (Franconeri & Simons, 2003; Hommel & Akyurek, 2009):

1. *Size:* large things
2. *Intensity:* bright and loud stimuli
3. *Novelty:* new and unusual things
4. *Incongruity:* things that don't make sense within a given context
5. *Emotion:* stimuli with strong emotional attachments
6. *Personal significance:* stimuli personally important to us

Attention determines which stimuli will receive further processing.

What kinds of things attract and hold your attention in the classroom? Can you think of certain classes during which your mind has wandered easily?

Working Memory

Once we pay attention to a stimulus, we transfer its information to our **working memory,** where the information is put to use. Our working memory processes information from sensory memory, maintains new information in a heightened state of activity, and retrieves task-relevant information from long-term

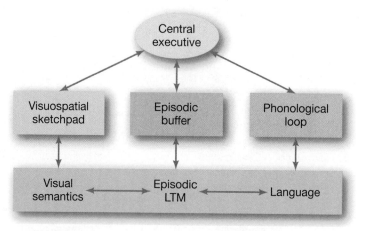

Figure 11.2. Baddeley's Model of Working Memory.

Source: Redrawn from figure retrieved from http://www.smithsrisca.demon.co.uk/ PSYbaddeley2000.html, copyright © 2004, Derek J. Smith. Based on a black-and-white original in Baddeley (2000, p. 421; Figure 1). Reprinted by permission of Derek Smith.

memory so that we can work with it, as when we recall a formula to use during an exam (Unsworth & Engle, 2007). Working memory can be understood as an active system that involves a central executive and three assistants: the phonological loop, the visuospatial sketchpad, and the episodic buffer, as shown in Figure 11.2 (Baddeley, 2001; Baddeley & Hitch, 1974). The **central executive** acts as the information supervisor within working memory, focusing attention on what is deemed important, integrating information from both sensory and long-term memory, selecting what strategies to apply when processing information, and planning and organizing complex behavior (Carlson & Moses, 2001; Willingham, 2004).

Executive control strategies: See Module 12.

The **phonological loop** allows us to store auditory information for a few seconds and to repeat phonological information over and over to extend its availability within working memory and increase the chances of remembering it. The **visuospatial sketchpad** temporarily stores and allows rehearsal of visual and spatial information. The **episodic buffer** is a temporary storage system that integrates information from the visuospatial sketchpad, the phonological loop, and long-term memory (LTM) into a single representation (Baddeley, 2000). These components of working memory explain why we are generally unable to process two verbal tasks or two auditory tasks at the same time, but we are sometimes able to perform tasks that require different modalities, such as listening to music while reading a book.

CAPACITY AND DURATION

In contrast with the unlimited capacity of sensory memory, working memory is finite. For the past 50 years, researchers thought the average adult could hold only five to nine chunks of data at a time (Miller, 1956). However, more recent research suggests that it is not the exact number of items that influences recall but how many items we have *time* to rehearse before the information fades. For example, if a list of words flashes on a computer screen, we are able to remember more one-syllable words, like *hat,* than polysyllabic words, like *opportunity,* because we can process shorter words faster (Baddeley, 1999; Byrnes, 2001). Longer processing time has been found to result in poorer recall in both children and adults (Portrat, Camos, & Barrouillet, 2009). Some tasks have a higher **cognitive load,** making more demands on working memory than others (Nesbit & Adesope, 2006). The extent of cognitive load depends on many things, such as the complexity of the task, the student's prior knowledge and skills, and the types of supports provided (van Merrienboer & Sweller, 2005).

Although the concept of *working memory* has proved useful, it cannot account for complex cognitive activities such as language comprehension, for which greater amounts of data must be available than what can be processed within a few seconds. In recent years, researchers have introduced *active long-term memory (ALTM)* models to address this issue (Oberauer, 2002, 2005; Woltz & Was, 2007). These models have several ideas in common:

1. Working memory can include memory processes that are outside of our conscious awareness.

2. Some information in working memory is more readily available than other information.

3. Our capacity for processing information in working memory changes based on the degree of memory activation (how recently the information has been in use).

Information in working memory typically is lost within 5 to 20 seconds; however, we can extend the duration of information in working memory indefinitely if we actively use it (Anderson, 1995; Baddeley, 2001). When we stop thinking about something, that information leaves working memory and may be either discarded or stored in long-term memory. Items can be displaced from working memory when incoming information interferes with it or when our attention to it wavers, as when a secondary task distracts us (Davelaar, Goshen-Gottstein, Ashkenazi, Haarmann, & Usher, 2005).

ENCODING PROCESSES

Encoding is a process in which we modify or reformat information to prepare it for long-term storage. Some encoding occurs automatically, freeing the mind to process other information that requires conscious effort. For example, brushing your teeth is handled by **automatic processing.** Once tooth brushing has become a daily habit, you no longer need to consciously think about it, enabling you at the same time to plan what to pack for lunch or mentally review for an upcoming quiz. Other information or skills require **effortful processing,** which involves conscious effort and attention. For example, learning to read is an effortful process whereby beginning readers focus attention on basic reading skills such as "sounding out" words, often at the expense of comprehending what they've read. More complex tasks may have a higher cognitive load, requiring more effortful processing and more working memory capacity. Fortunately, over time, effortful processing becomes automatic processing—otherwise our ability to learn

Automatic Processing. With practice, skills like brushing teeth become automatic, freeing up working memory to concentrate on other things.

new information and skills might be considerably limited. How can individuals prepare information for long-term storage? There are a number of ways, as described below.

Automaticity: See page 231.

Individuals can retain new information through **rehearsal,** *or repeating the information over and over to themselves.* You may do this when you've just been introduced to someone and are trying to commit that person's name to memory. Unless it is rehearsed, verbal information may be forgotten quickly (Peterson & Peterson, 1959). Children begin to phonologically rehearse at around 7 years of age, and their use of such memory strategies becomes more sophisticated over time (Lehmann & Hasselhorn, 2010; Tam et al., 2010).

Rehearsal can take two different forms:

Effortful Processing. Some tasks such as reading, especially when they initially are learned, require intense concentration.

- **Maintenance rehearsal** involves repeating information over and over so it can be maintained indefinitely in working memory. If you are assigned a new locker with a combination number, you might repeat that number over and over as you try to memorize it.

- **Elaborative rehearsal** involves connecting new information you are trying to remember to prior knowledge. When we create passwords for our computers and Internet access, we often create strings of digits related to important dates in our lives (birthdays and anniversaries of relatives) that are part of our long-term memory. This strategy transforms the stimuli from a meaningless string of digits into something that has contextual meaning.

Individuals can retain new information by using **mnemonics,** *aids designed to help us remember information by making it more meaningful.* Mnemonics include strategies such as acronyms, chain

EXAMPLE 11.1 Mnemonic Devices

Mnemonic	Description
Acronym	A form of abbreviation, such as "ROY G BIV" for the colors of the rainbow.
Chain mnemonic	Connecting items to be memorized in a jingle, such as "i before e, except after c" for a common spelling rule.
Keyword method	Associating sounds or images with concepts. An English-speaking student learning Spanish might imagine a cow on vacation to remember *vaca*, the Spanish word for cow.
Loci method	Associating items that need to be memorized with locations in a familiar setting. For example, to memorize a grocery list, you might picture items on the list sitting around your house: milk in the refrigerator, cereal on the table, pretzels on a TV tray, and so on.
Verbal mediation	Using a word or phrase to connect two pieces of information, such as "the principal is my pal" to remember that the word for the school official ends in "pal," not "ple."

mnemonics, the keyword method, the loci method, and verbal mediation, as described in Example 11.1. Mnemonics are most useful for students when they have trouble finding relationships between new material and their prior knowledge or when information to be learned does not seem to have a logical, organized structure.

*Individuals can also retain information by using various **organizational strategies**.* For example:

- **Chunking** involves grouping individual bits of information in a meaningful way. Consider the following two sets of numbers:

6 1 3 9 7 5 2 4 8   and   1 2 3 4 5 6 7 8 9

Which set seems easier to remember? You probably chose the second set. The first set challenges us to remember the individual numbers, but we immediately recognize the second set as the digits 1 through 9, a chunk we can easily remember. The mind actively searches for meaningful patterns (Lichtenstein & Brewer, 1980). For example, confronted with the list of words *couch, orange, banana, dog, pear, rug, pineapple, lamp, horse, rat, table,* and *sheep,* an individual might attempt to remember the words by organizing them into the categories of furniture, fruit, and animals. Chunking can enhance meaning and increase efficiency. When a child is first learning the alphabet, each letter represents a discrete piece of data to remember. Once the child has memorized the alphabet, the ABCs are only one chunk of information, freeing up processing space within working memory.

- The use of **hierarchies** means dividing broad concepts into narrower concepts and facts. When information is organized into hierarchical groups, as shown in Figure 11.3, it is remembered two to three times better (Bower, 1969).

- **Visual imagery** involves constructing mental pictures (drawing, modeling, or graphing). Research has demonstrated that people are better able to remember visual images than words. For example, think of what you know about Abraham Lincoln. Is it easier for you to retrieve a visual image of Lincoln or verbal facts about the president, such as the years of his term in office or his place of birth? When words and pictures

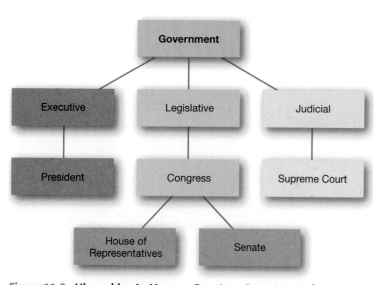

Figure 11.3. Hierarchies As Memory Boosters. Organizing information into a hierarchy such as this one makes it two to three times more likely that the information will be remembered.

EXAMPLE 11.2   Characteristics of Each Component of the Information Processing System

	Sensory Memory	Working Memory	Long-term Memory
Capacity	Unlimited	Five to nine bits of data	Unlimited
Form of Storage	Raw form in which the information was sensed (visual, auditory, olfactory, etc.).	Actively processed data from sensory memory and long-term memory	Declarative, procedural, episodic, or conceptual knowledge of various forms (visual, auditory)
Duration	One second for visual information Two to four seconds for auditory information	Five to twenty seconds, unless it's actively used; then it can be held indefinitely	Relatively permanent
Implications for Teachers	If students are to retain information, they must pay attention to information, and teachers must direct their attention to the most important ideas or concepts.	Students need opportunities for repetition and review as they process new information, and they must be able to connect new information with prior knowledge.	Effective use of long-term term memory requires students to encode the information in a meaningful way for long-term storage and then to use retrieval strategies to recall the information when needed.

are combined during learning, the pictures are easier to remember than the words (Duthie et al., 2008; Roediger, 1997).

Think about the memory strategies we've just discussed. Which ones have you used? How effective have they been as you've tried to commit information to memory?

Long-term Memory

Long-term memory, the third memory stage in the information processing system, enables us to store huge amounts of information and retain it for days, weeks, or years (see Example 11.2).

TYPES OF KNOWLEDGE

Our minds store both explicit and implicit knowledge. **Explicit knowledge** refers to all the information we are consciously aware of and use, including academic information like multiplication facts or grammar rules. We are not as aware of **implicit knowledge,** which may involve conditioned responses (habits), memories of common routines and procedures, or the triggering of related concepts stored in long-term memory. Implicit information can influence our behavior or thoughts even if we are not conscious of it. Say, for example, that a snake crosses your path. You may not consciously remember any previous incidents with snakes, yet an implicit memory of such an event may cause you to respond with fear.

Conditioned responses: See page 160.

Within the explicit/implicit dichotomy, people have four types of knowledge (Byrnes, 2001; Sadoski & Paivio, 2001):

1. **Episodic knowledge** is the memory of a certain episode or event that you have experienced, sometimes referred to as autobiographical memory (Shimamura, 1995).

2. **Declarative knowledge,** also called *semantic knowledge,* is a compilation of verbal information or facts.

3. **Procedural knowledge,** or knowing how to do something, is a compilation of all the skills and habits you have formed (Byrnes, 2001).

4. **Conceptual knowledge** indicates *why* something is the case. It reflects an *understanding* of declarative and procedural information (Byrnes, 2001). It is one thing to know a declarative fact ("The sky is blue") and another to understand why the fact is true.

HOW MEMORIES ARE STORED

We know that explicit and implicit knowledge are associated with different areas of the brain (Ashcraft, 2006), but we know relatively little about the brain's filing system. We do know that mental records stored in long-term memory can be encoded in more than one format (Anderson, 1995; Paivio, 1971). For example, suppose you are told "If you add two things to two others, you have four things in all." You can represent this statement mentally as

$$2 + 2 = 4$$

or

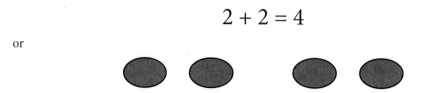

Dual coding theory suggests that information is remembered best when it is encoded in both visual and verbal forms (Kulhavy, Lee, & Caterino, 1985; Winn, 1991). Theorists have offered several explanations of how the various pieces of information in long-term memory may be connected. Let's look at two of them:

- **Network theory** suggests that information can be stored as a *proposition,* the smallest unit of knowledge that can be judged true or false. Propositions that share information can be linked in what is called a *propositional network.* Consider the sentence "Sarah is wearing my new raincoat." This communicates two linked propositions: (1) Sarah is wearing my raincoat, and (2) the raincoat is new. Cognitive psychologists have suggested that most information is stored and represented in these propositional networks, although the networks are not part of our conscious awareness. One task, such as facial recognition, may involve several levels of association and processing within a network. Recollection of one piece of information can activate recall of related or linked information in the network in a process known as **spreading activation** (Anderson, 2005).

- **Schema theory** suggests that information is easier to understand and remember if it fits easily into an existing schema, or conceptual framework (Anderson & Bower, 1973). For example, Figure 11.4 illustrates a schema for the concept "wave." A *script,* or event schema, is a pattern of representing the typical sequence of events in aneveryday situation (for example, the steps involved in getting ready for school each morning). Another type of schema, *story grammar,* helps students understand and remember stories by presenting a familiar structure to guide them through the stories (for example, the pattern in a typical detective mystery).

Figure 11.4. Concept Map for "Wave." A schema for "wave" might include many of the elements shown on this concept map.

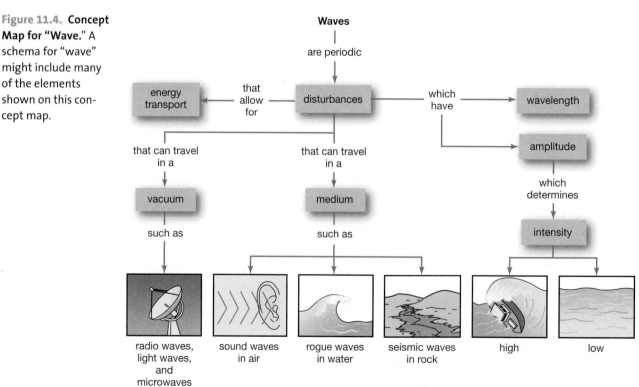

We've considered how information is put into long-term memory, but information is useful only if we can access it when we need it.

HOW MEMORIES ARE RETRIEVED

How do we get information out of long-term memory? And why do we easily remember certain (sometimes trivial) information and struggle to remember other (more important) things?

Facts or procedures that are practiced on a regular basis and learned well come to mind easily when we try to remember them; information not practiced or used often is harder to retrieve (Byrnes, 2001; Karpicke & Roediger, 2008). Educational psychologists distinguish between *distributed practice* (learning spaced out over several sessions) and *massed practice* (learning crammed into one big study session). Distributed practice has been found to be more effective than massed practice in terms of long-term retention and retrieval of information (Bird, 2010; McCabe, 2008).

Importance of practice: See pages 109 and 227.

Information in our long-term memory has an **activation level** that indicates its current degree of availability at a conscious level. Information in a high state of activation is available for immediate use. Other information, which is in a low state of activation, idles in long-term memory while awaiting future retrieval (Anderson, 1995). **Retrieval cues,** or hints about where to look for a particular piece of information, can be used to move information from a low to a high state of activation (Watkins, 1979). Retrieval cues that jog our memories can be in any sensory format (such as a familiar scent, a visual image, a sound). For example, if asked to recall details about the elementary school you attended as a child, you might find that you remember few details. However, if you visit the school in person, you might be flooded with sights, sounds, and smells that trigger memories from your elementary years. Retrieval cues also are related to **context,** the setting or circumstances around a particular place, feeling, or event (Godden & Baddeley, 1975). For example, the hallways and classrooms of your elementary school provide a *physical context* for your memories. *Emotional contexts* also may facilitate long-term memory storage and retrieval. When we have a strong emotional reaction to something, the event is processed at a deeper level, and our memory of that information or event is longer lasting (Ainley, Hidi, & Berndorf, 2002; Pintrich, 2003). Can you recall exactly where you were and what you were doing on September 11, 2001?

We use retrieval cues when we're trying to match previously encoded information with the needs of our current situation (Brown, Preece, & Hulme, 2000; Rugg et al., 2008), a process that requires us to discriminate between relevant and irrelevant information stored in long-term memory (Unsworth & Engle, 2007). Some tasks require that we remember the gist or general meaning of something previously learned, while others demand recall of very specific information (Koustaal & Cavendish, 2006). **Recall** is the ability to retrieve information not in conscious awareness, as when a student is asked to write an essay during an exam. **Recognition tasks,** such as identifying items on a multiple-choice test, contain retrieval cues and require individuals only to identify items previously learned. Recall and recognition tasks place different demands on the memory system. The greater the similarity between how information was first encoded and the cues being used to retrieve it (called *study-test overlap*), the greater the likelihood of successful retrieval (Roediger & Guynn, 1996; Rugg et al., 2008; see Nairne, 2002, for caveats). For example, if a student studies new vocabulary words by simply matching words to their definitions, the student may find it more challenging to complete a quiz that requires him to use each word correctly in a sentence.

Recognition Versus Recall. One study showed that people who had graduated 25 years earlier could not recall the names of many of their old classmates, but they could recognize 90% of their pictures and names from a high school yearbook (Bahrick, Bahrick, & Wittlinger, 1975).

FORGETTING

Suppose you studied for a test last night and did well on the test this morning, but next week, in a surprise quiz, you can't recall the same information. What happened to the information? Cognitive psychologists offer three main reasons for why we forget things:

1. *Encoding failure.* Failure to encode the information successfully means that it may never have reached long-term memory storage.

2. *Storage decay.* Memory for new information fades quickly and then levels off in a process often referred to as **decay** (Bahrick, 1984; Wixted & Ebbesen, 1991). Psychologist Hermann Ebbinghaus (1885) called this the "forgetting curve."

3. *Retrieval failure.* Stored information may be unavailable due to **retrieval failure,** which occurs when we are certain we have learned a piece of information but cannot pull up the mental record of it (Cohn, Emrich, & Moscovitch, 2008).

Retrieval failure has many potential causes. A common cause is **interference,** which occurs when the learning of some items interferes with the retrieval of others (MacLeod & Saunders, 2008). Interference can happen proactively or retroactively (Dallett & Wilcox, 1968; Jang & Huber, 2008; Osgood, 1949). **Proactive interference** occurs when French words you learned in high school (prior knowledge) get mixed up with Spanish words you are learning in college. **Retroactive interference** occurs in the opposite direction. If you have just learned some new steps in a dance class and then try to rehearse steps you learned last month, the new routine may interfere with your memory of the steps you learned previously. In a form of retrieval failure called **reconstruction error,** we may recall only limited pieces of information about a topic or event and then, without realizing it, fill in the information gaps with assumptions or guesses based on other things we know (Hemmer & Steyvers, 2008). The information we've retrieved in this way is incomplete and potentially inaccurate.

Have you ever had the experience of knowing that you learned something but not being able to dig it out of your memory when you needed it? What might have caused the memory failure?

Individual Differences in Information Processing

Two individuals witnessing the same event might pay attention to different aspects, encode the information in different ways, and recount the event very differently when asked later what they remember. The way they process information reflects their own interests, skills, and experiences. In a classroom context, teachers must understand that students respond to a lesson or an activity in different ways. Their responses are influenced by factors such as gender, age, and cultural background. Let's consider some of these influences at various stages of information processing.

SENSORY MEMORY

Developmental differences affect the speed with which sensory information is transmitted, as well as the speed with which visual information is extracted for interpretation (LeBlanc, Muise, & Blanchard, 1992). This means that younger children process information more slowly than older children and therefore lose more information before it can be encoded and retained in memory (Demetriou, Mouyi, & Spanoudis, 2008). Our ability to filter stimuli, called *selective attention,* increases with age, and as a result older children also are better at focusing on what's important (Bjorklund, 1995). Girls may have *DIVERSITY* a slight advantage over boys in keeping their attention focused (Das, Naglieri, & Kirby, 1994; Halpern & LaMay, 2000).

WORKING MEMORY

Individual differences in working memory capacity arise from differences in both the ability to actively maintain information and the ability to retrieve task-relevant information in the presence of irrelevant information (Unsworth & Engle, 2007). Young children seem to have less working memory capacity than older children and adults. Two factors may explain this developmental difference. First, older individuals simply may process information faster and thus can retrieve more of it before it decays. *DIVERSITY* Second, as novices, young children may be encountering information for the first time, so they initially process things in an effortful way that consumes more space (Schneider & Shiffrin, 1985). Over time, children develop the ability to resist interference from extraneous information and to inhibit the intrusion of task-inappropriate thoughts that might interfere with working memory (Dempster, 1993; Engle & Kane, 2004; Harnishfeger, 1995). They also gain more experience with many types of knowledge, and their greater knowledge base allows them to process information more efficiently in working memory. The more a person already knows about something, the better he or she is able to understand, organize, and retain new information on that topic (Engle, Nations, & Cantor, 1990; Kuhura-Kojima & Hatano, 1989). Girls may have a slight advantage over boys in performing specific kinds of memory tasks, such as remembering items in a list or recalling details of life events (Das, Naglieri, & Kirby, 1994; Halpern & LaMay, 2000).

DIFFERENCES IN STRATEGY USE

Children as young as 18 to 24 months show some rehearsal-like behaviors when processing information during play (DeLoache, Cassidy, & Brown, 1985). During middle childhood, rehearsal strategies become more effective. Older children use a wide variety of strategies, whereas young children typically use maintenance rehearsal (Ornstein, Naus, & Liberty, 1975). Training children and adolescents to develop and use strategies does not guarantee that they will spontaneously use these skills when learning or that they will transfer them to new situations.

Several developmental limitations can affect strategy use. Attention resources are more limited in younger children. A limited and less organized knowledge base reduces a child's ability to chunk information in working memory (Chi, 1978). Furthermore, subroutines (simpler procedures necessary to perform more complex tasks) are not yet automatic. For example, in math, it is important for students to memorize basic addition and subtraction facts until knowledge of them is retrieved quickly and easily. When the addition-facts subroutine reaches a level of **automaticity,** students can complete complex math problems more efficiently. Until then, completing each problem will require more sustained attention and effort (Anderson, 2005).

Automaticity: See page 231.

Cultural differences also may affect the degree of experience students have with different types of learning tasks and strategies. For example, students from North America and Asia are likely to have had experience learning lists, whereas students from certain cultures in Africa, Australia, and Central America may have had more experience recalling oral histories or spatial locations (Purdie & Hattie, 1996; Rogoff, 2001, 2003). Cultural psychologists have consistently found different patterns of thinking and perception in different societies, with some cultures demonstrating a more analytic pattern and others a more holistic pattern (Kitayama et al., 2009; Varnum et al., 2010).

DIVERSITY

APPLICATIONS TO TEACHING

Helping Students Pay Attention

Effective teachers use many strategies to arouse student interest in a topic and maintain student attention throughout a lesson. Some of these strategies are described below.

Plan for attention. Plan lessons with students' developmental level in mind. Students' ability to attend to incoming information and to identify what is most important changes over time. Plan to engage students' curiosity by bringing variety and novelty to the lesson (keep in mind the features that attract attention, discussed earlier in this module). Construct seating arrangements in a way that focuses students' attention on the teacher or on one another (depending on what an activity requires). Seat easily distracted students near you. Proximity to the teacher will help these students pay closer attention (Murray, 2006). Plan to minimize distractions in the room so they do not interfere with learning.

Planning: See page 364.

Use attention signals. Develop a signal that reminds students to stop what they are doing and focus their attention on you (e.g., the sound of chimes, a clapping pattern, a familiar tagline to begin a lesson). During a lesson, direct students' attention to the most important ideas or concepts and to the reasons *why* they are important (Jensen, 1998). Students' sensory memories are bombarded with huge amounts of information, and they may have difficulty separating essential from nonessential data. Use repetition to focus students' attention on key ideas.

Engaging student interest: See pages 273, 279, and 312.

Keep students' attention engaged. Incorporate a variety of instructional methods into your lessons to engage students in different ways. When possible, get students physically involved with the lesson through role playing, demonstrating, experimenting, or researching. Encourage students to interact with the content by having them take notes, create concept maps, or draw diagrams. Ask students questions about the material to direct their attention. Posing questions to the class, and to specific students, can help students attend to pertinent information and begin to process it (Bybee, 2002). In addition to asking students to give verbal responses, have them write their responses before sharing their thoughts with a small group or with the entire class. This ensures that all students, not just a few, are attending to the question. As a transition from one activity or subject to another, have students write in a journal a question or summary about what was just learned or discussed. This practice encourages students to

Note-taking strategies: See page 218.

Respect Attentional Limits. If students seem restless or bored during a lesson, a useful strategy is to pick up the pace, add some variety, or get students physically engaged.

attend to activities, discussions, and lectures while they are occurring and to do additional information processing after they are finished (National Research Council, 2000a).

Respect attentional limits. Read students' body language and facial expressions to discern when they need a change of pace. Provide frequent breaks from sedentary activities, especially when working with younger children. If a lesson starts with several minutes of lecture or teacher demonstration, consider pausing to give students the opportunity to discuss or practice new concepts or to work in collaborative groups to complete a task.

If you were to create a Top Ten List of "Effective Ways to Get and Keep Students' Attention," what strategies would you include in your list?

Helping Students Store and Retrieve Information Effectively

Skilled teachers know their content areas, but—perhaps even more important—they also know the kinds of teaching activities that will help students understand the content for themselves. These teachers know what kinds of difficulties students are likely to encounter, how to tap into students' existing knowledge in order to make new information meaningful, and how to assess their students' progress (National Research Council, 2000a). Example 11.3 reviews the encoding strategies discussed earlier in this module. Let's consider the teacher's role in helping students effectively encode information in various areas.

Meaningful learning: See pages 231, 232, and 233.

Organization. Individuals differ in their ability to organize information, and they can be taught strategies that will assist them (Pressley & Woloshyn, 1995). Instructional strategies that facilitate organization include the following (Mestre & Cocking, 2000; Murray, 2006):

- Present information in a clear, logical way. Give students an outline to follow, and provide a summary at the end of a lesson.

- To help students see how information is related, provide visual organizers such as concept maps, diagrams, and graphs.

- Allow students time to organize their thoughts and responses by using appropriate **wait time.** When teachers ask students a question in class, they typically wait one second or less to get a response. When teachers extend their wait time to three seconds or longer, they find an increase in student participation and a better quality of responses (Rowe, 1987).

Conceptual understanding. Experts in various disciplines organize their problem solving around big ideas and are attentive to key concepts (Bransford et al., 1988; Sabers, Cushing, & Berliner, 1991). Teachers can strengthen students' conceptual understanding and help students develop expertise in several ways:

- Help students identify key concepts and recognize meaningful patterns. Connect new information to students' prior knowledge by presenting analogies that relate topics to situations and concepts that are familiar to the students and by activating prior knowledge through questions, discussions, and review before introducing new material.

- Focus on meaning rather than memorization.

- After you make an important point, pause, repeat, and ask students to paraphrase.

- Provide time for students to practice and review important information through homework assignments, quizzes, and in-class activities. Correct misconceptions and clarify understanding by providing students with frequent feedback on their work.

- Distribute practice opportunities over time within a single unit, and strive to cover the same material several times in different contexts over the course of the semester or year. This additional pro-

11 | Information Processing

EXAMPLE 11.3   Encoding Strategies to Promote Storage in Long-term Memory

Strategy	How to Use It	Effectiveness
Rehearsal	Drill and practice over and over.	Least effective. This method is a good first choice when first encountering sensory data, but the information then needs to be processed in a deeper way.
Meaningful Learning	Have students put information in their own words. Provide examples to enhance comprehension.	Effective. Information is interpreted and understood in terms of existing knowledge.
Organization	Provide organized structures, such as hierarchies, outlines, and timelines, to help students chunk information.	Effective if it results in a schema that ties the information together well.
Elaboration	Add to new information by helping to fill in gaps in students' knowledge.	Effective if meaningful inferences are drawn.
Visual Imagery	Provide visual aids such as photos, graphs, concept maps, and charts.	Using visuals to illustrate certain points can be very effective.

cessing leads to elaboration, building stronger connections to other information and increasing the likelihood that students will be able to transfer their knowledge effectively to new situations (Murray, 2006).

Transfer: See page 227.

Task analysis. Students can actively process only a limited amount of information at a time, so teachers must consider ways to maximize the effectiveness of information processing within working memory. Overloading of information impedes learning. If tasks are complex, limit the number assigned and consider breaking them down into smaller parts. **Task analysis** is a common method for breaking down a large instructional task into manageable parts. From a cognitive perspective, task analysis involves identifying the specific knowledge, behaviors, or cognitive processes necessary to master a particular skill. For example, the task of working on a set of math problems may involve *first* understanding how to classify the problems (Do they require addition or subtraction? Do they require using a formula?) and *second,* retrieving math facts or formulas that apply to each problem.

Relevance. Sometimes students complete an assignment but fail to fully understand the specific context in which that knowledge is useful. For example, a student might successfully complete a math worksheet related to a unit on multiplying fractions but be overwhelmed when a test presents problems randomly from the entire unit. Unfortunately, some teachers present facts and formulas without giving sufficient attention to teaching students when the use of that information will be relevant. Well-designed activities can help students better understand when, where, and why to use particular strategies and pieces of information (Lesgold, 1988).

Automaticity versus external memory aids. Students can benefit from opportunities to practice basic skills until they become automatic. Information learned to a level of automaticity takes up less processing space. In some cases, it is possible to free up space in working memory by using external aids to working memory (such as calculators or dictionaries). The use of such external memory aids should match the objective of the lesson. For example, if the objective of a trigonometry assignment is to select the correct formulas to use, a teacher might allow the use of a calculator. Performing calculations with this tool would not interfere with the ultimate goal of the assignment. However, if the objective of the assignment is to practice computing formulas by hand, the use of a calculator would be inappropriate. The use of external memory aids should not take the place of automaticity in learning basic skills, as automatic basic skills form the basis for higher-level thinking and problem solving.

Transfer of automatic skills: See page 331.

Organization Gone Awry.
With permission from
Harley Schwadron.

"REFRESH MY MEMORY, MS. HAMISH. WHICH LITTLE SQUARE AM I--ON THE ORGANIZATIONAL CHART?"

Acquisition of procedural knowledge. Procedural knowledge may range from simple to very complex sets of activities and may include a combination of motor and cognitive skills. Learning complex procedures involves a combination of the following activities and skills:

Observational learning: See page 174.

- watching someone else successfully perform the task (observational learning),
- receiving guidance and/or feedback from a mentor,
- applying encoding strategies (e.g., breaking down the information into a series of smaller, manageable tasks), and
- learning by doing (practice, practice, practice).

Which of these strategies might you select to help a student write a term paper? Solve a word problem in math? Learn to shoot a free throw?

Summary

Describe the assumptions that underlie information processing theory. (1) Because cognitive processes influence learning, teachers must consider not only *what* students need to learn but also *how* they can most effectively process the information they are learning. (2) Individuals are selective about what they pay attention to and learn. Teachers must help students make wise choices about what concepts to pay attention to, process, and save in memory. (3) Students bring different sets of prior knowledge, experiences, and beliefs with them to the classroom, which influences the way they interpret new ideas and events. Although a teacher may present similar information to all students during a lesson, individual students may understand and remember that information differently.

Describe the steps in the three-stage model of information processing, and discuss memory capacity and duration at each stage in the model. The three-stage model states that memory involves a sequence of three stages: sensory memory, working memory, and long-term memory. Raw sensory data from the environment first enters sensory memory, where it is captured initially as fleeting sense memory. The capacity of sensory memory is unlimited, but data are held only briefly. From there data can be processed into working memory, which can hold selected chunks of information for 5 to 20 seconds—or indefinitely if the information is actively being used. Long-term memory seems to have an unlimited capacity and is relatively permanent, although difficulties can impede the retrieval of information stored in long-term memory.

Contrast the effectiveness of rehearsal and encoding strategies for storing information in long-term memory. Maintenance rehearsal is a good choice when first encountering sensory data, but the information then needs to be processed in a deeper way. Elaborative rehearsal, in which information is interpreted based on prior knowledge, helps make the information meaningful and thus more memorable. The use of mnemonics lends a meaningful structure to information that does not have its own easily remembered structure or connection to prior knowledge. Organizational strategies, such as the use of chunking or hierarchies, can connect new information to prior knowledge. Research suggests that visual imagery is remembered more easily than words alone and that dual encoding in both visual and auditory formats is most effective for long-term storage and retrieval.

Discuss the methods for getting and maintaining students' attention. It is vital that teachers draw students' attention to important concepts, facts, or procedures to be learned and help students discriminate between relevant and irrelevant information. Teachers need to consider ways to plan for attention, use signals to direct students' attention at the beginning of and throughout the lesson, apply a variety of instructional methods to engage students, and respect students' attentional limits.

Summarize the instructional strategies for helping students store and retrieve information effectively. Teachers must emphasize the importance of *understanding* classroom material and must encourage students to make connections to prior knowledge, synthesize information, organize ideas, actively apply new information in a meaningful context, and practice basic skills to a level of automaticity in order to free up processing space for more complex thinking.

Key Concepts

acronym 188

activation level 190

attention 185

automatic processing 187

automaticity 193

central executive 186

chain mnemonic 188

chunking 188

cognitive load 186

conceptual knowledge 189

context 191

decay 192

declarative knowledge 189

effortful processing 187

elaborative rehearsal 187

encoding 184

episodic buffer 186

episodic knowledge 189

explicit knowledge 189

hierarchies 188

implicit knowledge 189

information processing theory 184

interference 192

keyword method 188

loci method 188

long-term memory 189

maintenance rehearsal 187

mnemonics 187

network theory 190

organizational strategies 188

phonological loop 186

proactive interference 192

procedural knowledge 189

recall   191

recognition tasks   191

reconstruction error   192

rehearsal   187

retrieval cues   190

retrieval failure   192

retroactive interference   192

schema theory   190

sensory memory   184

spreading activation   190

task analysis   195

verbal mediation   188

visual imagery   188

visuospatial sketchpad   186

wait time   194

working memory   185

Video Applications

www.mhhe.com/bohlin2e

Video 1: Information Processing Strategies in Action (*3 minutes*)
Clip 1 (kindergarten classroom): *Practice and repetition*
Clip 2 (kindergarten classroom): *Music and memory*
Clip 3 (kindergarten classroom): *Graphing the temperature*
Clip 4 (kindergarten classroom): *Zoo phonics*
Clip 5 (kindergarten classroom): *Using context clues*

Video 2: The Importance of Paying Attention (*3 minutes*)
In this video clip, teachers use a variety of strategies to get and maintain students' attention. As you view this video, identify the strategies the teachers use to focus students' attention on the lesson.

Case Studies
Reflect and Evaluate

EARLY CHILDHOOD: "Pinch"

These questions refer to the case study on page 150.

1. Why does Miss Amber have the children clap at certain points during her story?

2. When the children are asked to compare today's story with the one from yesterday, what memory system(s) is (are) being activated? Explain.

3. What does Miss Rana do to focus the children's attention on her instructions for the art project? Why is this important?

4. How do the teachers help the children acquire *procedural knowledge* for the painting activity?

5. Emily has been reluctant to paint since she accidentally spilled paint on Billy's shoes. From an information processing perspective, why might this incident be very memorable for Emily?

ELEMENTARY SCHOOL: "Silly Students"

These questions refer to the case study on page 152.

1. How did the cluster seating arrangement affect the attention level of Billy, Jason, Megan, and Sara?

2. Billy, Jason, Megan, and Sara receive low scores on the math quiz. What might explain their inability to successfully retrieve the information they needed in order to answer the questions on the quiz?

3. What strategies could Mr. Lindsay use to help his students organize their ideas in a meaningful way during his math lesson?

4. Sara began to feel frustrated in trying to complete her math problems. What strategies could Mr. Lindsay have used to help her acquire the *procedural knowledge* necessary to successfully complete the problems?

5. Under what conditions would it have been appropriate for Mr. Lindsay's students to use a calculator? How would the use of a calculator affect the way they process information in working memory?

MIDDLE SCHOOL: "Study Hall"

These questions refer to the case study on page 154.

1. Jamie does not seem to remember basic mathematical principles taught the previous year in sixth grade. According to information processing theory, what are three possible explanations for his forgetting?

2. What strategies could Mr. Havel use to help increase Jamie's *conceptual understanding* of the basic math concepts?

3. What strategies could Mr. Havel use to help Jamie develop the *procedural knowledge* necessary to complete the math problems?

4. When Ms. DeBrick works with Jasamine, she discovers that Jasamine has not been writing down the homework assignments for English class. How can writing down these assignments in a daily planner help Jasamine?

5. What strategies could Jasamine's classmates share to help Jasamine complete her English homework successfully?

6. How might the examples Ms. DeBrick gives Jasamine serve as retrieval cues for her?

HIGH SCHOOL: "Bending the Rules"

These questions refer to the case study on page 156.

1. Jason has forgotten Mr. Hardy's demonstration of how to complete the assignment. Explain the role of attention in his forgetting.

2. What strategies could Mr. Hardy implement to help focus students' attention during his lessons?

3. Jason recalls not doing well in history during middle school. Assume he used maintenance rehearsal as his primary memory strategy. Explain the limitations of this approach to Jason and offer better ways to remember information over the long term.

4. What types of strategies, consistent with information processing, would you use to study for a history test? Give specific examples.

5. How does Mr. Hardy incorporate conceptual knowledge and episodic knowledge into his history class? In what other ways can teachers emphasize conceptual understanding in their classes?

unit four

Case Studies

Early Childhood: "Air" 202

Elementary School: "Reading About Pirates" 204

Middle School: "King Washington" 206

High School: "I Don't Understand" 208

Module 12:
Metacognition

Outline and Learning Goals 210

What Is Metacognition and Why Is It Important? 211

Special Cases of Metacognition 212

Factors Affecting the Development and Use of Metacognition 215

Applications: Learning Strategies 215

Summary 222

Key Concepts 222

Video Applications 223

Case Studies: Reflect and Evaluate 223

cognitive processes

Module 13:
Transfer of Skills and Knowledge

Outline and Learning Goals 225

What Is Transfer and Why Is It
Important? 226

Do We Readily Transfer What We
Learn? 227

Application: How to Facilitate
Transfer 230

Summary 236

Key Concepts 236

Video Applications 236

Case Studies: Reflect and Evaluate 236

Module 14:
Critical Thinking and Problem Solving

Outline and Learning Goals 238

Thinking Skills and Dispositions 239

Critical Thinking 241

Problem Solving 245

Summary 250

Key Concepts 250

Video Applications 251

Case Studies: Reflect and Evaluate 251

B arb Carson, a veteran elementary school teacher of 15 years, is in her sixth year of teaching full-day kindergarten at Roosevelt Elementary. She loves working with the kindergarteners and was surprised to see how much this age group could achieve when given the right amount of support and encouragement.

This morning the children are seated on the floor around Ms. Carson's rocking chair, listening attentively as she reads a story about the wind from an oversize book with colorful pictures. She begins by showing the children the cover of the book and asking them what they think the story is about. She enthusiastically discusses their suggestions and then ends the suspense by turning to the first page and beginning the story. As she nears the end of the story, she asks Dominique to summarize what has happened in the book. Then Ms. Carson spreads out a set of simple sentence cards on the floor, each with a pic-

Early Childhood

Air

ture depicting a main event from the story. She tells the students that they are going to play a game in which they mix up the story and try to put it back in order. She calls on Jose to pick the card that describes the first event in the story. Jose struggles to figure out the words on each card, and Ms. Carson reminds him that he can also use the pictures as a clue. Jose successfully picks the first card, and Ms. Carson then invites Maria to find the next event in the story. One by one, Ms. Carson calls on students to help put the story back in order, reminding the whole group that they need to watch carefully and help if someone has trouble figuring out what comes next.

When the class has finished this activity, Ms. Carson sends the students back to their seats, clustered around four tables. During the story session, a parent volunteer had placed materials for an experiment on a large table at the front of the classroom and put a prediction sheet at each child's seat.

"We just read a story about the wind," Ms. Carson says. "What is the wind made out of?"

"Air!" several children shout at once.

"Okay," Ms. Carson replies. "We are going to do an experiment to see what happens with air, some water, a cork, and a plastic cup."

The children squirm with delight. They know these classroom experiments are usually fun.

"Let's put on our scientist hats today," says Ms. Carson as she walks over to the front table, drops a cork in a clear bowl of water, and holds up a plastic cup. "See if we can figure out what will happen to this cork if we trap it under this plastic cup while it is still in the water. Take a minute and draw a picture on your prediction sheet to show me what you think will happen to the cork." Ms. Carson walks around the room, looking on as the children draw pictures on their sheets. When it seems that most children have finished, she calls on Tony.

"Tony, tell us about your prediction," she says.

Tony holds up his drawing and explains, "I drew the cork way down near the bottom of the bowl, under the plastic cup."

"Did anybody else draw the cork down on the bottom of the bowl?" Several children raise their hands. "Does anyone have a different prediction about what will happen to the cork?"

Shelby raises her hand.

"Yes, Shelby. Tell us about your prediction."

"I drew the cork floating near the top, right under the cup." Several other students nod that they made the same prediction.

"How do we find out what will really happen to the cork?"

"We test it!" reply several students.

"Yes, we test our predictions. Scientists, look up here and pay close attention." Ms. Carson places the cup over the cork, and it sinks down closer to the bottom of the bowl.

"What happened?" she asks.

"The cork got pushed way down," Tony replies.

"Why do you think that happened, Maria?" asks Ms. Carson.

Maria pauses to think for a few seconds and then replies, "Well, the cup was pushing down and that pushed the water down more."

"It was the air," interjects Jose. "There was air in the cup and the air pushed the water down more."

Ms. Carson continues to ask questions to clarify what the students are thinking and to help them make connections between the experiment and things they learned earlier in the week about properties of air. When she feels that they all have a clear understanding of the outcome of the experiment, she has the students record the result by drawing a picture in the "Now I Know" column on their prediction sheet.

After lunch, Ms. Carson challenges the children to create kites that will fly really high during "Kindergarten Kite Day," a special event later in the week when parents and siblings are invited to fly kites with the students in the field behind the school. "How can you make your kite aerodynamic?" Ms. Carson asks. Kiontee smiles because he remembers that *aerodynamic* is Ms. Carson's "million-dollar word of the week." She likes to use accurate terms when possible during her lessons and has found that the students feel very important when she sprinkles a few challenging words into her lessons for them to remember. For the next few minutes the children brainstorm ideas about how to design kites that will really catch the wind. After they have come up with a long list of possibilities, Ms. Carson teaches them how to evaluate critically the set of ideas and narrow down their choices. As the children settle down to work on their own designs, they seem to lose all track of time, becoming completely absorbed in their plans for making the greatest kite ever.

Assess

1. What kinds of learning behaviors and attitudes does Ms. Carson model for her students?

2. How would you describe the level of challenge that Ms. Carson includes in her curriculum? Does the level of challenge fit with your image of a kindergarten classroom?

3. How do you think Ms. Carson's students would describe their experiences in her classroom?

Prepare:

As you read the case, make notes:

1. **WHO** are the primary participants in the case? Describe them.

2. **WHAT** is taking place?

3. **WHERE** is the case taking place? Is the environment a factor?

4. **WHEN** is the case taking place? Is the timing a factor?

Ian McPherson is a second-grade teacher at an elementary school that has entered into a PDS (Professional Development School) partnership with a local university. The PDS Alliance provides collaborative research, training, and professional development opportunities for public school teachers, university faculty, and teacher education students, with the ultimate goal of improving public school education for all children. Recently, Mr. McPherson participated in a focus group exploring evidence-based practice in teaching. As a follow-up activity, teachers were encouraged to keep a journal of classroom activities and then go back and assess areas they wanted to improve through the use of evidence-based practices. Here is an excerpt from Mr. McPherson's journal:

Yesterday I began the morning reading session by assigning my students three short story booklets to read followed by questions to complete. I instructed the students to

Elementary School
Reading About Pirates

color the pictures in the stories when they were finished so they would be able to remain busy. Once the students understood what they were supposed to be doing and began working industriously, I called my first reading group back to our designated reading table. As the students collected themselves at the reading table, I made certain that everyone else was working constructively at their desks, and then I took my seat at the reading table as well. As I began my reading lesson with the group of students at the table, I was interrupted by Kiana, who said she was tired and couldn't work. I had seen this behavior before. Kiana's reading skills were on par with her classmates, but she often lacked the motivation to stay on task at her desk during our morning reading group rotations. After making sure she wasn't ill, I told her to continue working and that we'd all take a break together in a little while to have morning snack. I tried to sound caring but firm, and Kiana returned to her seat to begin work on her storybooks.

As I continued my session with the reading group, I involved each of the students in the group by asking direct questions, giving students turns to read short passages out loud, and making sure everyone understood what we were reading. As we worked with our reading selection about pirates and buried treasure, we analyzed it to look for vowel-pairs that we had talked about in class last week. At the end of the reading group lesson, I reviewed basic skills in using a dictionary. We discussed alphabetical order and letter position, and we practiced strategies like looking at the bolded word at the top of the page to quickly orient yourself to where you are in the dictionary. I then had students complete a worksheet in which they searched for certain words and wrote down the dictionary page number where each word could be found. One of the students commented that finding the words was kind of like a treasure hunt—and indeed it was. The word list included words like gold, silver, jewel, chest, and map. This activity enabled the students to move from talking and working in a group to working alone. This prepared the students to work on their own again when they returned to their seats after the reading group was concluded.

As I neared the end of our reading group session, I was disappointed to see that several of the students who were supposed to be doing independent seat work were off task. They weren't being noisy or disruptive, but it was clear that they were not doing their work either. Kiana was doodling, Randy was slouched in his seat ready to take a nap, and Kelsey was fidgeting with the key chain collection attached to her bookbag.

Later in the day, Mr. McPherson looked back over what he had written about the morning work. He saw things that he thought were successful, as well as areas that could be improved. As he reviewed his notes, he identified the reading tasks assigned for independent seat work as an area for improvement. He tried to better define his own expectations about how the reading session should run, and then he began to make a list of the ways he could have been more effective in working with his reading group as well as ways he could have improved the learning experience for the children working independently at their desks. He wasn't sure he had really hit on a plan that would work any better than what he was already doing, so he stopped in to speak with Linda Ariano, a second-grade teacher in the classroom next door. Mr. McPherson and Ms. Ariano brainstormed possibilities together. When he left to head home, Mr. McPherson felt optimistic about his plans for the next morning. He wouldn't really be sure he was on the right track until he had an opportunity to test his ideas with the class, but he felt he had two or three options for adjusting the morning routine that were worth a try.

Assess

1. In what areas do you think Mr. McPherson did an effective job with his morning session?

2. What areas would you suggest he try to improve?

3. Mr. McPherson kept a classroom journal. Do you think keeping a journal about your teaching would be useful? Why or why not?

Prepare:

As you read the case, make notes:

1. **WHO** are the primary participants in the case? Describe them.

2. **WHAT** is taking place?

3. **WHERE** is the case taking place? Is the environment a factor?

4. **WHEN** is the case taking place? Is the timing a factor?

Tom Radcliffe looked out into the sea of faces in his second-period eighth-grade social studies class. He knew his students were paying attention to his lecture on the Revolutionary War period because of the way he started the class. He began by asking Carrie Johnson, "Who was the first president of the United States?"

"George Washington," replied Carrie, amazed that he had asked her something so easy yet worried that she wasn't off the hook yet.

"Why do we care?" asked Mr. Radcliffe.

Carrie hesitated and then said, "I don't know."

"Clayton, is knowing that George Washington was the first president going to make you rich?" Mr. Radcliffe asked.

Middle School

King Washington

Clayton, a slightly disheveled student in the third row, sat up. "No, not unless I get to be on *Who Wants to Be a Millionaire?* and that is the final question to win the million," Clayton responded, to mild laughter from his classmates.

"Not likely," chimed in Clayton's friend Brad.

"Is knowing that George Washington was the first president going to make you a better friend, Cathy?" Mr. Radcliffe asked a girl in the front row.

"No," Cathy replied.

"Is knowing that George Washington was the first president going to make you more popular with the ladies?" Mr. Radcliffe asked, pointing to Chuck, an outgoing basketball player.

"No, but I don't think I need any help in that category," Chuck joked. Cathy rolled her eyes.

"Okay, so why do we care?"

When the class sat there stumped, Mr. Radcliffe said, "Knowing that fact all by itself may not really mean very much. But what if you knew the characteristics that made Washington a great man and a great leader? What if you understood how he handled power? How many of you knew that George Washington had the opportunity to be king and turned it down?" A couple of hands went up; most students looked surprised.

"How many of you would have given up a chance to be king?" He had them hooked, and he knew it. The questions Mr. Radcliffe asked in order to launch this topic stirred up a little controversy and got everyone interested. He proceeded with his lecture, confident that the students now really wanted to know more about George Washington.

A week later, Mr. Radcliffe gave a test on the social studies unit. His students did well on the questions about big ideas related to George Washington, but they missed much more than he had expected when it came to details. The next day he did a "notes check," asking students to pull out their notebooks and flip to their notes from the previous week. Their notes were very sparse—and in some cases nonexistent.

"Come on, guys. How come no one took good notes?" He heard a variety of responses.

"I was too busy listening."

"I already knew about George Washington so I didn't think I needed to write anything down."

"You didn't tell us what we should be writing down."

"I didn't realize that stuff was going to be on the test."

Mr. Radcliffe paused dramatically and said, "I am getting ready to give you some absolutely free advice that countless hordes of people would spend at least five bucks to hear me share." The students smiled. He turned and wrote in great big letters on the board, TAKE GOOD NOTES! "The process of taking notes helps most people retain information better—even if they never go back and look at those notes. If they actually do look over the notes the next day, they get another little boost in memory. And if they go back to review those notes again five days later, they get an additional memory boost."

Over the next few days, Mr. Radcliffe made a point of teaching his students different note-taking strategies. He encouraged them to take thorough notes by giving an unannounced "notes quiz" in which the correct answer was something they could easily copy down directly from their class notes—*if* they had taken the time during his lecture to write down the information. As a culminating activity for the unit on events surrounding the Revolutionary War, Mr. Radcliffe presented his students with the following scenario:

You are to be a colonial delegate to the Second Continental Congress in May 1775, just a few weeks after the battles at Lexington and Concord. In preparation for the Congress session, develop a list of talking points to express your opinion about how the colonists should respond in light of recent events, giving particular attention to the Intolerable Acts. On Wednesday we will convene our own Continental Congress, and you will have the opportunity to come together to decide the course of history.

Assess

1. What did Mr. Radcliffe do well as a teacher in the opening scenario about George Washington?

2. What mistakes did Mr. Radcliffe make?

3. What changes did Mr. Radcliffe institute after seeing how his students performed on the exam? How might these changes make a difference for his students?

Prepare:

As you read the case, make notes:

1. **WHO** are the primary participants in the case? Describe them.

2. **WHAT** is taking place?

3. **WHERE** is the case taking place? Is the environment a factor?

4. **WHEN** is the case taking place? Is the timing a factor?

Ms. So Yoon Park is a first-year teacher in her second month at Sunnyside High School. She recently completed a lesson with her tenth-grade algebra class that left her feeling very frustrated. That evening, she e-mailed the following message to a mentor teacher to get some advice:

Mr. Kim,

Today did NOT go as well as I had hoped. My assignment was to teach the class to change repeating decimals into fractions. I began by instructing the students to open their books to the section and take out some paper for notes. I went through a review of terminating decimals and fractions on the board. The students did not have any questions about the review. I continued with the problems on the board by writing a

High School

I Don't Understand

repeating decimal and asking the class how to change the decimal to a fraction. A few students had some suggestions, but they realized that a correct fraction could not be found with previous methods they had learned in converting fractions and decimals. I taught them a step-by-step process that would change the repeating decimal into a fraction. I had the attention of the class, and I was confident in my abilities.

I went through the example and then asked if there were any questions. The entire class looked at me with confusion. I did not know what was confusing them, so I asked questions about each step in the example. This helped me target the problems, and I changed the approach I used to explain the process. I used different vocabulary, related steps to previous lessons, and asked students more detailed questions for each step. I believe a few students caught on to the idea, but the majority of the class was still saying "I don't understand."

I answered individual questions from students raising their hands, and I also had students answer some questions in hopes they had an explanation their peers would understand. As I continued to show examples, many students still did not comprehend the lesson, and I was running out of ideas to help them. I felt like the students were losing all interest in learning the strategy I was trying to teach. I was afraid that their minds were shutting down because they began to show very little skill even in the individual steps which involved previously learned material, such as subtracting equal amounts from each side of an equation. My students were becoming frustrated, and the classroom became unsettled with chatter and distractions. I was frustrated, too, but I tried not to let it show because I did not want to add my own aggravation to the already tense feeling in the room.

I realized that I was failing as a teacher, and I did not know what to do. There were still many questions from the students and I wasn't sure what to do next. I noticed that the students were more focused on finding shortcuts or quick ways to solve the problem to lessen the amount of work they had to put into the solution. My students had missed out on the strategy being taught because they were so focused on finding a way to skip steps. I had not anticipated that they would dislike putting in the effort to complete the few lines of actual work for each problem.

I did not expect the students to be so confused with new material. New ideas and processes are taught in school all the time, and I really expected that the students could transfer some of what we had done previously to help them approach these math problems. I am sure no other teacher has ever felt so out of control, unprepared, and unorganized as I did while teaching this class. I was not prepared for students to give up, and I was not ready to manage an entire class confused by the lesson topic. I thought I had prepared a successful lesson, but I failed to really teach my students today. You seem to handle your own lessons so well. Do you have any suggestions about what I could have done differently? I need help!

Ms. Park

Mr. Kim replied:

Ms. Park,

Don't be so hard on yourself. Based on what you described to me, it sounds like you really made an effort to get through to the class. Although you didn't think the lesson would be a particularly difficult one, many students shut down their minds when they see something totally new. . . .

Assess

1. Ms. Park is worried that her entire lesson was a failure. Is there anything that she did well during the lesson?

2. What should the teacher do when the majority of the class does not understand the material presented in the lesson?

3. Are you surprised that the class was not able to apply previously taught material to the decimal lesson? Why or why not?

Metacognition

Outline	**Learning Goals**
What Is Metacognition and Why Is It Important?	
	1. Describe the two main components of metacognition.
Special Cases of Metacognition	
■ Theory of Mind in Childhood	2. Explain four characteristics of children's theory of mind.
■ Egocentrism in Adolescence	3. Explain two consequences related to adolescent egocentrism.
Factors Affecting the Development and Use of Metacognition	
	4. Explain the factors that influence the development and use of metacognitive skills.
Applications: Learning Strategies	
■ Reading Comprehension	5. Describe how teachers can assist students with reading comprehension and writing skills.
■ Writing Skills	
■ Note Taking	6. Explain the importance of note taking and study time and describe how teachers can help students improve these learning strategies.
■ Studying	
Summary	
Key Concepts	
Video Applications	
Case Studies: Reflect and Evaluate	

WHAT IS METACOGNITION AND WHY IS IT IMPORTANT?

As you begin to read this module, you might have a pencil, pen, or highlighter in hand, ready to begin identifying important concepts and examples. Did you look over the outline on the preceding page? How many of the six learning goals can you recall? Do you plan to memorize the key concepts? These questions are prompting you to engage in **metacognition**—thinking about your own thinking processes, including study skills, memory capabilities, and the ability to monitor your learning (Hertzog & Robinson, 2005; Metcalfe, 2000).

Metacognition is important for both teaching and learning. The more students know about *what* learning strategies are and *how, when,* and *where* to apply different learning strategies effectively, the more likely they are to use such strategies and thereby increase their academic achievement (Perkins, 1995; Peterson, 1988). Rather than expect students to spontaneously acquire metacognition on their own, teachers need to explicitly teach students metacognitive skills along with content instruction (Kistner et al., 2010). Teaching students about their metacognition and how to use it requires an understanding of its two main components: metacognitive knowledge and metacognitive regulation (see Figure 12.1).

Metacognitive knowledge is knowledge about our own cognitive processes and an understanding of how to regulate those processes to maximize learning. Metacognitive knowledge falls into three categories (Flavell, Miller, & Miller, 2002; Manning, 1991):

1. **Person knowledge,** also called *declarative knowledge,* refers to understanding our own capabilities: "I am good at memorizing lists" or "I am poor at comprehending what I read in textbooks." This type of knowledge changes considerably from kindergarten through high school. Older school-age children become much more accurate in determining how much information they can learn within a specific time frame (Flavell et al., 2002).

2. **Task knowledge,** or *procedural knowledge,* relates to how we perceive the difficulty (or ease) of a task. In school, students may make this judgment based on the following aspects of the task:

   - content ("This is a review of irregular verbs in Spanish"),

   - length ("This chapter is very long"), and/or

   - type of assignment ("Essay exams require recall of information rather than recognition, as in multiple-choice exams").

   Very young children understand that fewer items will be easier to learn than more items and that learning a list of similar concepts (three colors) is easier than learning concepts with little connection to one another (Flavell et al., 2002). Older children also understand that the difficulty level of a task will influence the study strategies they use (e.g., studying to summarize information versus studying to repeat the information verbatim) (Schunk, 2004).

3. **Strategy knowledge,** or *conditional knowledge,* describes our capability for using strategies to learn information. In general, young children are not good at using strategy knowledge (Flavell et al., 2002). Three-year-olds can be taught a learning strategy for a specific task but will not spontaneously apply that strategy in a similar learning task (Hertzog & Robinson, 2005; Palincsar, 2003). By age 8, children will use strategies on their own without prompting (Beal & Fleisig, 1987; Ritter, 1978). In the upper elementary grades, students start to develop a better understanding of which cognitive

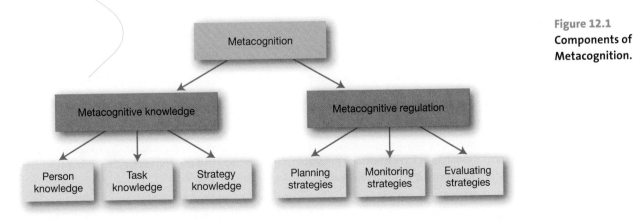

Figure 12.1
Components of Metacognition.

strategies are effective in which situations, and they begin to apply them with increasing consistency (Flavell et al., 2002).

In general, young children, especially those in early childhood education programs, are less likely to accurately estimate memory abilities (person knowledge), judge task difficulty (task knowledge), or apply appropriate strategies in new contexts (strategy knowledge).

Metacognitive regulation is the purposeful act of attempting to control our own cognitions, beliefs, emotions, and values. It allows us to use our metacognitive knowledge to function efficiently in learning situations. Metacognitive regulation requires using *executive control functions,* a collection of mental processes that include planning, monitoring, and evaluating strategies (Brown, 1987; Flavell et al., 2002; Tajika, Nakatsu, Nozaki, & Maruno, 2007).

1. **Planning** involves scheduling learning strategies and selecting which strategies to use in different contexts.

2. **Monitoring** involves periodically checking on how well the planned strategy is working. For example, we can monitor our performance through self-testing and self-explanation.

3. **Evaluating** involves appraising the outcomes of the cognitive strategies used. More than just "getting a good grade," this process measures to what degree our performance is affected by our planning and monitoring of selected learning strategies.

Children in early childhood are less likely to plan the use of memory strategies. They also are less accurate at monitoring their learning progress, being more likely to insist that they understand or have learned material that in fact is not yet well learned (Chi, 1987). Monitoring skills increase with age, with 11- to 12-year-olds becoming much more accurate in their monitoring than younger children (Krebs & Roebers, 2010). Young children also are not good at evaluating the effectiveness of learning strategies and memory skills (Hertzog & Robinson, 2005). Children need explicit feedback about the outcomes of strategy use in order to increase experience and hence metacognitive regulation. Even adults, however, are poor judges of their comprehension in some tasks, such as reading comprehension (Schunk, 2004).

Where did you learn metacognitive knowledge and regulation? Did your teachers provide information to help you develop metacognitive skills?

SPECIAL CASES OF METACOGNITION

Theory of Mind in Childhood

As early as age 2, children begin to recognize that others have their own minds. This recognition helps them understand why others' perceptions and feelings differ from their own. This early understanding of the mind and the "mental world" is called **theory of mind** (Flavell et al., 2002). Just as other theories have linked cognition and language, theory of mind also develops in relation to language skills (Lockl & Schneider, 2007). Studies on theory of mind have defined four characteristics:

1. **False-beliefs:** the understanding that a belief is only one of many mental representations, which can be false or accurate. Three-year-olds are not capable of understanding that someone could have a false-belief. Rather, they perceive only one belief—the correct one. However, by age 4 or 5, most children understand that people can believe one thing but be wrong (Flavell et al., 2002). The candy box experiment described in Example 12.1 provides an example of false-beliefs.

2. **Appearance-reality distinctions:** a person's ability to understand that something may look one way (appearance) but actually be something else (reality), such as a well-designed plastic spider (reality) that appears to be alive (appearance). One experiment presented preschool-age children with a fake egg (appearance). Once the children learned that the "egg" was actually a painted rock (reality), they insisted that it looked like a rock, not an egg (Flavell, Flavell, & Green, 1983). Similar experiments have been conducted with numerous stimuli, such as sponges (reality) that look like rocks (appearance). The findings suggest that children are not capable of understanding that appearances can be deceiving or false until they reach age 4 or 5.

3. **Visual perspective-taking:** understanding that views of physical objects differ based on one's perspective. Researchers have been able to establish the development of perspective-taking in preschool as occurring on two levels (Flavell et al., 2002):

| EXAMPLE 12.1 | **Candy Box Experiment** |

Trial one, with 5-year-old:

A developmental psychologist shows a 5-year-old a candy box and asks her, "What is in it?"

"Candy," she says. She then looks inside the box and to her surprise discovers that it actually contains pencils, not candy.

"What would another child who had not yet opened the box think was in it?" the experimenter asks.

"Candy!" says the child, amused at the trick.

Trial two, with 3-year-old:

The experimenter then tries the same procedure with a 3-year-old. "What is in the box?"

"Candy," she says. She then looks inside and is also surprised to discover the pencils.

When asked "What would another child who had not yet opened the box think was in it?" the child responds, "Pencils." The child also insists that she had originally thought the box held pencils.

Conclusion:

The 3-year-old does not understand that other people or they themselves can have a false belief.

Source: Flavell et al., 2002.

- Level one (2 to 3 years of age): Children understand that another person can see something if the person's eyes are open and looking in the appropriate direction without any visual obstructions. At this level, perspective-taking involves determining *whether* something is seen (e.g., "Mom can see the game board").

- Level two (4 to 5 years of age): Children understand that another person can see something in a different way or from a view that differs from how they see it. Here perspective-taking involves determining *how* something is seen (e.g., "Mom's view of the game board is upside down because she is sitting across from me at the table").

4. **Introspection:** children's awareness and understanding of their own thoughts (Flavell, Green, & Flavell, 1995, 2000; Flavell, 2000, 2004). By age 5, children are likely to both overestimate and underestimate the amount of thinking they and others are capable of. For example, 5-year-olds believe that people know when they are sleeping (overestimate) yet believe that a person can go days without thinking (underestimate). Even when they do understand that thoughts are occurring within the mind, 5-year-olds are not clear about what is being thought about within their own mind or that of another person. For example, children who are asked to think about where in their house their

Visual Perspective-taking. Children understand that another person may see the same object from a different view, such as a game board that faces the child and not his or her opponent.

toothbrush is kept will deny having been thinking about their bathroom (Flavell et al., 1995). By age 8, children are better able to describe their own stream of thoughts and understand that it is very hard, if not impossible, to stop thinking for any length of time (Flavell et al., 2000).

Hence, the theory of mind becomes increasingly sophisticated over the preschool and school-age years.

Egocentrism in Adolescence

As the awareness of thoughts within one's own and others' minds develops, early adolescents become increasingly *self-conscious,* having a heightened sense of the self and a concern for how and what others think of them. Egocentrism in young children involves difficulty differentiating between their view of an object and another's view of an object, while **adolescent egocentrism** is difficulty differentiating between one's own thoughts and the thoughts of others. Elkind (1967) proposed two specific consequences of adolescent egocentrism:

1. **Imaginary audience:** The adolescent imagines or believes that he or she is the focus of attention in social settings due to a lack of differentiation between self and others' thoughts. For example, an adolescent boy may believe that others' thoughts are focused on him, just as his own thoughts are (e.g., "I can't stop thinking about the zit on my chin, and everyone else is looking at it too!"). Imaginary audience can manifest itself in two ways:

   - An adolescent girl might be highly critical of herself and expect others to judge her negatively as well. Let's say she tries a new hairstyle and is very concerned that it does not look well on her. When no one in her group of friends comments on the hairstyle, she might ask, "What do you think of my new haircut?" and be unconvinced by the answer "We didn't even notice."

   - An adolescent boy might be self-admiring and assume that others also will find his qualities endearing and positive. Perhaps he believes that his joking, sarcastic style of classroom behavior is a flattering and attractive quality. He will have difficulty understanding why his parents and teachers do not approve of this behavior.

2. **Personal fable:** Adolescents mistakenly believe that they are unique, such that no one else can understand their situation. For example, most adolescents do not believe that their teachers can understand the difficulty they might have in studying or receiving good grades. They might believe that their friends do not experience the same pressure to do well or have the same feelings of disappointment (e.g., "None of my friends have this much trouble in math class").

Piaget's theory of cognitive development, see page 119.

Imaginary Audience. Adolescents may believe or imagine that other people are watching or thinking about them, especially about their appearance.

Two separate explanations for the rise of the imaginary audience and the personal fable during adolescence have been offered. The first, based on Piaget's theory of cognitive development, suggests that imaginary audience and personal fable are negative consequences that arise as the individual moves into formal operational thinking (Alberts, Elkind, & Ginsberg, 2007; Elkind, 1967). The development of formal operational thinking not only enables adolescents to use metacognition, but also leads them to think too much about themselves and about what others think of them. The second explanation proposes that imaginary audience and personal fable are not negative side effects but rather adaptive coping processes that arise because of the changing relationship between adolescents and their parents (Lapsley, 1993). In the course of adolescence, as the child becomes an adult, the relationship between child and parent must be renegotiated to balance separateness and connectedness (Gavazzi & Sabatelli, 1990; Sabatelli & Mazor, 1985). Imaginary audience helps adolescents maintain their connectedness with others, whereas personal fable helps them maintain their separateness and uniqueness. Imaginary audience and personal fable may continue to be used as coping mechanisms throughout adulthood, although less often and intensely than during adolescence (Frankenberger, 2000; Lapsley, 1993; Quadrel, Fischhoff, & Davis, 1993).

Think of a time when you thought no one could possibly understand your situation or emotions.

FACTORS AFFECTING THE DEVELOPMENT AND USE OF METACOGNITION

A number of factors influence the development of metacognition, including biological differences and environmental differences (Flavell et al., 2002). Neurological impairments can impede the development of metacognition. For example, children with autism are considered to have neurological deficits in their ability to understand the mind and thoughts of people (Flavell et al., 2002; Hamilton, Brindley, & Frith, 2009), and children with intellectual disabilities have difficulty with processes such as planning, monitoring, and evaluating strategies for task performance (Campione, Brown, & Ferrara, 1982). In addition, frontal brain damage can impair metacognitive abilities (Shimamura, 1994).

Our environment—in particular, our family experiences—also plays a role in the development of metacognition. Children learn about metacognition by listening to parents' and siblings' conversations about beliefs, emotions, knowledge, how to learn, and how to study. Family conversations may be more influential for girls than for boys because parents tend to express their thoughts and emotions more with daughters than with sons (Flavell et al., 2002).

Students also possess individual characteristics that determine whether they choose to use the metacognitive skills they have developed:

- *Belief about the nature of the task (task knowledge):* Students who believe that the information to be learned is easy will not use more advanced skills and strategies such as planning, monitoring, and evaluating (Schunk, 2004). Also, when the task involves memorization rather than connections between important ideas or elaboration of ideas, students are more likely to use lower-level strategies (e.g., rote memorization) or to alter their strategies to reflect the type of exam or task identified by the teacher (Van Meter, Yokoi, & Pressley, 1994).

- *Motivation:* Students who are highly motivated to learn are more likely to invest time and energy in metacognitive strategies than are students who are less interested in learning (Schunk, 2004).

- *Prior knowledge about the topic:* The more students know about a topic, the better they are able to understand, organize, and retain new information (Engle, Nations, & Cantor, 1990; Kuhura-Kojima & Hatano, 1991). Students who are aware of what they know and do not know are better able to use planning strategies to increase their study time for information not well understood (Brown, Bransford, Ferrara, & Campione, 1983).

- *Prior success using metacognitive skills:* Successful use of metacognitive skills will lead to increased use of those skills. Students who do not understand how metacognitive strategies improve their learning are less likely to use those strategies in the future (Schunk, 2004).

Think of some specific ways teachers can help students understand the importance of metacognitive skills and encourage them to use these skills.

APPLICATIONS: LEARNING STRATEGIES

Students typically equate learning or study strategies with basic memory skills that help them remember information (see Example 12.2). Several other learning strategies are related to metacognition, notably reading comprehension, writing skills, note taking, and study time. Reading and writing are introduced early in educational settings, whereas note taking and studying typically are not required until later elementary school or middle school. Let's examine each of these learning strategies more closely.

Reading Comprehension

Learning strategies include extracting information from reading materials, or reading comprehension. Reading comprehension increases with age, partly due to increases in metacognitive skills (Palincsar, 2003; Peverly, Brobst, & Morris, 2002) and to repeated exposure across multiple tasks and domains (Schunk, 2004). Two popular instructional techniques are used to increase reading comprehension: reciprocal teaching, commonly used with younger children, and the PQ4R strategy, typically used with older students.

Reciprocal teaching is a structured conversation in which teachers and students discuss sections of a text (Palincsar & Brown, 1984), as depicted in Example 12.3. Reciprocal teaching involves four steps:

1. *Summarizing:* Students must verbally summarize the text, which requires them to attend to the main points and check or monitor their understanding.

Intellectual disabilities: See page 435.

DIVERSITY

The brain and its development: See Module 6.

DIVERSITY

Motivation and cognitive factors: See page 279.

Prior knowledge: See page 184 and page 226.

Memory: See page 184.

12 | Metacognition

EXAMPLE 12.2   Memorization Strategies

Memory strategy	Description
Rehearsal strategies	
Maintenance rehearsal	Simply repeating the information over and over.
Elaborative rehearsal	Connecting new information to prior knowledge.
Chunking	Grouping individual pieces of information in a meaningful way.
Mnemonic devices	
Acronym	Forming a word from the first letter of each word to be remembered or forming a phrase or sentence from the first letter of each item in a list to be remembered.
Chain mnemonic	Connecting the first item to be memorized to the second, the second to the third, and so on, or incorporating items to be remembered into a catchy jingle.
Keyword method	Associating new words and concepts with similar-sounding cue words and images.
Method of loci	Imagining a familiar place, picking out particular locations, and using those locations as pegs on which to hang items to be remembered from a list.

2. *Questioning:* Students must create questions based on the text, a form of monitoring their understanding.

3. *Clarifying:* Students are asked to clarify difficult points in order to critically evaluate their understanding of the material.

4. *Predicting:* Students are asked to make predictions about future content in order to test their inferences between main points.

As with many learning strategies, teachers first need to model good reading comprehension skills using this strategy. Then students begin to use the strategy with the support of teachers, who provide cues, prompts, and feedback (Palincsar, 2003). Teachers' prompts can be derived from a related instructional strategy, "Questioning the Author" (Beck & McKeown, 2001). Examples of teacher prompts include questions such as the following:

■ What is the author trying to say?

■ What does the author want us to know?

Teachers can provide follow-up to student responses by asking questions such as these:

■ That is what the author said, but what did he or she mean?

■ Why does he or she want us to know that?

DIVERSITY

Teacher training on reciprocal teaching and Questioning the Author approaches suggests that teachers first use the strategies with a focus on the procedures, but later learn to use these instructional strategies as a springboard for more analytical discussions that foster reading comprehension (Kucan, Palincsar, Khasnabis, & Chang, 2009). Results of using these instructional strategies to improve reading comprehension are substantial across various age groups, from elementary students to adults, as well as among elementary and middle school students with learning disabilities (Gajria, Jitendra, Sood, & Sacks, 2007; Lederer, 2000; Rosenshine & Meister, 1994). The strategy is also effective when used in peer interaction or cooperative learning instruction (Palincsar, Brown, & Martin, 1987).

A traditional system for teaching older students reading comprehension skills involves a series of steps known as **PQ4R** (Robinson, 1961; Thomas & Robinson, 1972). These steps are described below:

EXAMPLE 12.3	Reciprocal Dialogue Example
Text:	In the United States salt is produced by three basic methods: solar (sun) evaporation, mining, and artificial heat evaporation. For salt to be extracted by solar evaporation, the weather must be hot and dry. Thus, solar salt is harvested in the tropic-like areas along our southern ocean coasts and at Great Salt Lake.
Chris:	Name three different basic methods how salt is produced.
Angela:	Evaporation, mining, evaporation . . . artificial heat evaporation.
Chris:	Correct, very good. My summary on this paragraph is about ways that salt is being produced.
Teacher:	Very good. Could you select the next teacher?
	(Chris selects another student to read)
Text:	The second oldest form of salt production is mining. Unlike early methods that made the work extremely dangerous and difficult, today's methods use special machinery, and salt mining is easier and safer. The old expression "back to the salt mine" no longer applies.
Logan:	Name two words that often describe mining salt in the old days.
Ken:	Back to the salt mines?
Logan:	No, Ken. Angela?
Angela:	Dangerous and difficult.
Logan:	Correct. This paragraph is all about comparing the old mining of salt and today's mining of salt.
Teacher:	Beautiful!
Logan:	I have a prediction to make.
Teacher:	Good.
Logan:	I think it might tell when salt was first discovered, well, it might tell what salt is made of and how it's made.
Teacher:	O.K. Can we have another teacher?
Text:	Table salt is made by the third method—artificial evaporation. Pumping water into an underground salt bed dissolves the salt to make a brine that is brought to the surface. After purification at high temperatures, the salt is ready for our tables.
Ken:	After purification at high temperatures the salt is ready for what?
Chris:	Our tables.
Ken:	That is correct. To summarize: After its purification, the salt is put on our tables.
Teacher:	That was a fine job, Ken, and I appreciate all that work, but I think there might be something else to add to our summary. There is more important information that I think we need to include. This paragraph is mostly about what?
Angela:	The third method of artificial evaporation.
Brian:	It mainly tells about pumping water from an underground salt bed that dissolves the salt to make a brine that is brought to the surface.
Teacher:	Angela hit it right on the money. This paragraph is mostly about the method of artificial evaporation and then everything else in the paragraph is telling us about that process. O.K. Next teacher.

Source: Palincsar & Brown, 1984.

1. *Preview:* Consistent with the executive control process of planning, the first step in reading comprehension is to survey or preview the material to be read. Students read chapter outlines, scan the chapter for general topics, and identify major sections within the reading assignment.

2. *Question:* Developing questions based on the outline or section headings allows students the opportunity to plan or identify the important information that will be obtained from the reading assignment. For example, the heading "Theory of Mind" might be rephrased as the question "What is theory of mind?"

3. *Read:* While reading the assigned chapter, article, or book, students attempt to answer the questions developed from the outline or the section headings.

4. *Reflect:* The process of monitoring one's reading comprehension includes taking breaks from the reading material to relate information to prior knowledge and create examples beyond those

provided in the text. Reflection includes asking questions such as these: "Did I grasp the main points?" "Do I understand the content?" "How does this relate to other information in the text?" "Can I think of an example?"

5. *Recite:* Reciting or rehearsing the information in the text is an attempt to store the information in long-term memory. One strategy is to answer the questions developed from the outline or section headings (step 2) without looking back at the text material.

6. *Review:* Although it might be thought that review implies rereading, it actually requires the student to mentally, rather than physically, think through the chapter contents in order to monitor how much of the material has been learned.

DIVERSITY

Empirical studies have consistently found that the use of reading comprehension strategies such as reciprocal teaching and PQ4R improves students' recall and understanding of important ideas presented in the text (Anderson, 1990; Palincsar, 2003). This also applies to children with learning disabilities (Schewel & Waddell, 1986).

Writing Skills

Writing skills increasingly require metacognitive skills such as planning, monitoring, and evaluation (Bereiter & Scardamalia, 1987). However, even kindergarten children are capable of answering questions about their planning strategies or their ability to put thoughts onto paper. When interviewed about their writing skills, kindergarten children typically use words such as "thought," "remembered," and "idea." They also are increasingly able to answer questions about where or how they formulated ideas for their writing assignments (Jacobs, 2004). Revision becomes an important part of the writing process in middle school and high school as students become better able to engage in monitoring and evaluation of their writing and develop an increasing ability to think abstractly (Berninger, Mizokawa, & Bragg, 1991).

Intervention strategies suggest that direct instruction and modeling of metacognitive skills can improve writing skills (Conner, 2007; Hooper, Wakely, de Kruif, & Swartz, 2006). Teachers can:

■ provide instruction in and modeling of planning strategies such as (1) determining the audience, (2) identifying the main ideas, (3) outlining the organization, and (4) making rough drafts and revising. *Procedural facilitations,* shown in Example 12.4, are a set of prompts used during planning and revision (Bereiter & Scardamalia, 1987; Scardamalia & Bereiter, 1985). Elementary students using procedural facilitations spend more time planning and improve the quality of their writing (Scardamalia, Bereiter, & Steinbach, 1984). Similarly, middle school students who plan their writing by developing rough drafts perform at levels comparable to those of some college students (Brown, Day, & Jones, 1983).

■ provide assistance in monitoring and evaluating progress. With younger children, this might include asking them to think aloud or answer questions about their ideas as they engage in writing assignments (Jacobs, 2004). For older children and adolescents, teachers might ask students to reread (aloud or silently) and substantially revise, not simply edit, their papers.

Note Taking

As students continue to develop metacognitive skills, note taking becomes necessary in many middle school and high school classes. Learning the best practices of note taking is important because the amount of information and the techniques used during note taking are related to academic achievement.

Functions of note taking: Before we examine best practices for note taking, we need to understand the three functions of taking notes (Kiewra, 1985; Kiewra et al., 1991).

Encoding and storage of information: See page 184.

1. Encoding: The process provides assistance in the encoding of material because writing down ideas from lecture material is a second form of encoding that goes beyond simply listening to the lecture. Some research supports the encoding function, suggesting that taking notes, even without time for review, leads to superior academic performance over not taking notes (Kiewra, 1985; Peverly, Brobst, Graham, & Shaw, 2003).

2. Encoding plus storage: While taking notes may serve an encoding function, reviewing notes provides the additional benefit of returning to the lecture material for review and storage of the information in memory. Empirical studies consistently find that students who take notes and review their

EXAMPLE 12.4   **Sample Procedural Facilitations: Planning Cues for Opinion Essays**

New Idea
An even better idea is . . .
An important point I haven't considered yet is . . .
A better argument would be . . .
A different aspect would be . . .
A whole new way to think of this topic is . . .
No one will have thought of . . .

Improve
I'm not being very clear about what I just said, so . . .
I could make my main point clearer . . .
A criticism I should deal with in my paper is . . .
I really think this isn't necessary because . . .
I'm getting off the topic, so . . .
This isn't very convincing because . . .
But many readers won't agree that . . .
To liven this up I'll . . .

Elaborate
An example of this . . .
This is true, but it's not sufficient, so . . .
My own feelings about this are . . .
I'll change this a little by . . .
The reason I think so . . .
Another reason that's good . . .
I could develop this idea by adding . . .
Another way to put it would be . . .
A good point on the other side of the argument is . . .

Goals
A goal I think I could write to . . .
My purpose . . .

Putting It Together
If I want to start off with my strongest idea I'll . . .
I can tie this together by . . .
My main point is . . .

Source: Adapted from Scardamalia, Bereiter, & Steinbach, 1984.

notes have higher achievement levels than students who do not review notes (Kiewra, 1985; Kiewra et al., 1991).

3. External storage: External storage—or the review of notes borrowed from another student—can still benefit the storage of information. While less beneficial than encoding or encoding plus storage for tasks of recall, external storage may actually have more benefit than merely encoding (listening to lectures) for tasks that ask students to integrate or synthesize ideas (Kiewra et al., 1991).

Amount of information recorded: One important aspect of note taking is the amount of information included in students' notes. Increased amounts of noted lecture material are related to higher achievement. For example, information that is recorded in notes has about a 50% chance of being recalled on an examination, whereas nonnoted information has only a 15% chance of being recalled (Aiken, Thomas, & Shennum, 1975). However, most students record only about 30% of the important information (Kiewra, 2002). Students may not record important information because they lack the metacognitive knowledge to understand the usefulness of note taking as well as to determine what is and is not relevant information (Garcia-Mila & Anderson, 2007).

Teachers can increase the amount of important information that is identified and recorded by students in a number of ways (see Kiewra, 2002, for a complete review):

■ Provide lecture notes, which offer a model for identifying important concepts. However, many teachers, particularly those in secondary education and beyond, believe that students should be responsible for their own note taking. Providing detailed notes to students does not encourage them to develop and improve their note-taking skills.

■ Provide skeletal notes that contain the main points plus space for students to add detail. Skeletal notes provided by teachers and completed by students include over 50% of the important information, compared to only 30% of important information contained in notes taken without assistance.

■ Provide lecture cues to signal important ideas, such as writing concepts on the board, verbally repeating information, pausing after stating the information, or explicitly identifying the organization (e.g., "There are three categories"). Organization cues increase the percentage of important information recorded to close to 65%, while approximately 80% of the information presented on the board is recorded in students' notes.

DIVERSITY

- Allow—and even encourage—students to audiotape or videotape lectures as an opportunity to hear the lecture a second time and add to their existing notes. Audio- or videotapes should not be used as a substitute for note taking during the lecture, except when students are unable to take notes—such as in cases of physical or learning disabilities. Students who hear or view a lecture can recall 30% of the important information, while students who hear or view it twice recall more than 50%.

- Allow students the opportunity to compare notes with other students in order to make corrections or add details they missed. Reconstructing notes with a partner increases the amount of important information recorded to 50%.

Note-taking techniques: Several studies have compared the use of conventional outline notes to use of matrix notes (Figure 12.2 gives a sample of each technique). Matrix notes consistently have resulted in greater learning (Kiewra, 2002; Risch & Kiewra, 1990). The advantage of matrix notes may be due to their completeness: Students' matrix notes typically include 47% of the lecture ideas, compared with only 32% of lecture ideas contained in conventional outline notes. In addition, matrix notes allow connections and comparisons to be made between key concepts and ideas, possibly resulting in improved integration and synthesis of the information presented in lectures (Kiewra et al., 1991). Teachers can assist students in creating matrix notes in a number of ways:

- Completed matrix notes can be prepared by the teacher and provided to students.

- The matrix framework can be prepared by the teacher and provided to students for them to complete.

- Teachers can train students to construct matrix notes through direct instruction, modeling, feedback, and practice.

Studying

Figure 12.2. Note-taking Techniques. Outline notes and matrix notes provide the same information but organize that information very differently.

Source: K. A. Kiewra (2002). How classroom teachers can help students learn and teach them how to learn. *Theory into Practice*, 41, 71–80.

Students can read the class material, complete writing assignments, and take notes, but quizzes and tests also require *studying*. The developmental level at which studying begins varies considerably. Early elementary students typically are quizzed in spelling and math. In later elementary grades, social studies tests may be added and spelling tests may become vocabulary tests, with students needing to study definitions as well as spelling. At the middle school level, science tests are included and social studies tests are common. However, great variability exists among schools, classrooms, and teachers regarding the introduction and difficulty level of study skills required.

More advanced metacognitive abilities include **study-time allocation,** or the amount of time devoted to studying as well as whether studying will take place over a long period of time or be crammed into a few hours. Specifically, study-time allocation has been closely linked to procedural knowledge or judgments about the difficulty of learning. For example, one student might believe that the list of vocabulary words for this week's English quiz is easy, whereas another student judges the list to be very

Wildcats: Outline Notes

I. Tiger
  A. Call
    1. Roar
  B. Weight
    1. 450 pounds
  C. Life span
    1. 25 years
  D. Habitat
    1. Jungle
  E. Social behavior
    1. Solitary

II. Lion
  A. Call
    1. Roar
  B. Weight
    1. 400 pounds
  C. Life span
    1. 25 years
  D. Habitat
    1. Plains
  E. Social behavior
    1. Groups

III. Cheetah
  A. Call
    1. Purr
  B. Weight
    1. 125 pounds
  C. Life span
    1. 8 years
  D. Habitat
    1. Plains
  E. Social behavior
    1. Groups

IV. Bobcat
  A. Call
    1. Purr
  B. Weight
    1. 30 pounds
  C. Life span
    1. 6 years
  D. Habitat
    1. Forest
  E. Social behavior
    1. Solitary

Wildcats: Matrix Notes

	Tiger	Lion	Cheetah	Bobcat
Call	Roar	Roar	Purr	Purr
Weight	450	400	125	30
Life span	25	25	8	6
Habitat	Jungle	Plains	Plains	Forest
Social behavior	Solitary	Groups	Groups	Solitary

difficult to learn. According to the *discrepancy reduction model,* individuals with advanced metacognitive skills will determine the difficulty level of items to be studied and allocate more study time to more difficult items (Dunlosky & Hertzog, 1998). However, the extra time spent on difficult items is not consistently related to better performance on tests or evaluations (Metcalfe, 2002).

In an alternative view of study-time allocation, a student should focus on material that is not easy or extremely difficult but just out of grasp, an area Vygotsky termed the *Zone of Proximal Development.* A model based on Vygotskian theory, the **region of proximal learning,** suggests that individuals will study items close to being learned but not yet mastered (Metcalfe, 2002). Study-time allocation gradually shifts toward more difficult items, as reflected in changes in the individual's region of proximal learning. Experimental studies have confirmed that allocating study time based on one's own region of proximal learning, rather than on the most difficult items (as the discrepancy reduction model proposes), results in better performance (Kornell & Metcalfe, 2006; Metcalfe & Kornell, 2005).

Zone of Proximal Development: See page 124.

In order for the region of proximal learning to be effective, students must engage in metacognitive regulation, particularly in planning and monitoring skills.

- *Planning:* Students must be able to make accurate judgments about what they know and do not know and must plan or prioritize the information to be learned (Metcalfe & Finn, 2008). Teachers can assist students in planning study time by asking them to make a list of items to be learned, arranging the items from easiest to most difficult.

- *Monitoring:* Students must be able to monitor their learning by continually making judgments about what has and has not been learned during their study time. However, even college students are not good at monitoring their level of preparedness for exams (Peverly et al., 2003).

One study strategy that combines many of the ideas presented here is the **SOAR method.** Although this strategy was designed to be used with college students, it can be taught to high school students as well. The SOAR method includes four components that directly address common study errors (Jairam & Kiewra, 2009, 2010):

- **S** – *Selection.* The teacher provides complete notes, skeletal notes, or cues to combat the common student tendency not to record all of the important information. Many times students highlight text material as a form of selection, but they often select too much or too little material. Teachers' assistance in identifying important material within the text, such as providing an outline of the text material, can be particularly beneficial.

- **O** – *Organization.* Students receive or create graphic organizers such as matrix notes or hierarchies rather than lists or linear notes. Teachers can present visual material in the form of matrices and hierarchies to model this strategy.

- **A** – *Association.* Students identify similarities between items to be learned (comparisons) and differences between items to be learned (contrasts) rather than studying each item separately, one at a time. Again, teachers can model this skill by presenting concepts or material in comparison with other concepts or materials.

- **R** – *Regulation.* Students move beyond simple rehearsal of the material and use self-testing, which involves asking themselves questions to help them gauge whether newly learned material has been mastered. Students can learn to turn headings in their textbook chapters into questions for self-testing. Teachers also can provide sample questions, give quizzes, or ask students to write practice exam questions themselves.

Instruction for the specific learning and study strategies just discussed should follow these general guidelines (Bruning, Schraw, & Ronning, 1995):

- Explain the value of the learning strategy. Many students do not use strategies because they do not understand how strategy use improves learning and performance.

- Introduce only a few learning strategies at one time to decrease the probability of cognitive overload.

- Model strategy use for students.

- Provide ample opportunity for students to practice learning strategies.

- Provide feedback to students about their use of learning strategies and improvement in their use.

- Encourage reflection on strategy effectiveness.

- Note opportunities for the transfer of learning strategies to other classes or domains.

Transfer: See page 226.

How will you promote the use of learning strategies in the grade level you expect to teach?

Summary

Describe the two main components of metacognition. Metacognitive knowledge, the first component of metacognition, refers to knowledge about our own cognitive processes. It is divided into person (declarative), task (procedural), and strategy (conditional) knowledge. Metacognitive regulation is the purposeful act of controlling our own thinking, emotions, and values and includes the functions of planning, monitoring, and evaluation. Both metacognitive knowledge and metacognitive regulation develop over time and are related to higher academic achievement.

Explain four characteristics of children's theory of mind. Theory of mind, which describes a child's early understanding of the mental world, involves four characteristics that begin in preschool and become increasingly sophisticated throughout the school-age years: (1) false-beliefs, an understanding that beliefs can be accurate or inaccurate; (2) appearance-reality distinctions, the understanding that objects may look one way but actually be something different; (3) visual perspective-taking, an ability to understand that another person may visually see something differently from the way you do; and (4) introspection, an awareness of thoughts within one's own and others' minds.

Explain two consequences related to adolescent egocentrism. Egocentrism in adolescence includes (1) imaginary audience, the belief that others' thoughts are focused on the individual, and (2) personal fable, or the belief that the individual is so unique that no one else can understand his or her emotions or thoughts. Egocentrism in adolescence begins in an attempt to renegotiate parent-child relationships so they become more adult-adult by balancing separateness and connectedness. The balance of separateness and connectedness continues into adulthood, as does the use of imaginary audience and personal fable, albeit less intensely.

Explain the factors that influence the development and use of metacognitive skills. Metacognitive development is influenced by several factors. Biological factors such as neurological deficits and brain damage and familial factors such as conversations between children and their parents and siblings about thinking, learning, and knowledge influence the development of metacognition. Once metacognitive skills begin to develop, individual factors will determine whether those skills are used in learning situations. These factors include the nature of the task and the individual's level of motivation, prior knowledge, and prior success with metacognitive skills.

Describe how teachers can assist students with reading comprehension and writing skills. Teachers can improve students' reading comprehension by using reciprocal teaching with younger students and the PQ4R strategy with older students. Both of these strategies require the use of metacognitive skills such as planning, monitoring, and evaluation and improve students' recall and understanding of important ideas. Teachers can improve students' writing skills by encouraging the use of planning techniques such as making rough drafts. They can also assist students in increasing their monitoring skills by asking younger children to think aloud or answer questions about their ideas and by asking older students to reread their initial drafts and make revisions.

Explain the importance of note taking and study time and describe how teachers can help students improve these learning strategies. Note taking and study time are both related to higher achievement. Although greater amounts of note taking are related to higher achievement, most students do not record the bulk of important information. Teachers can improve the amount of information students record by teaching them specific note-taking strategies such as using matrix notes. Study time should be based on an individual's region of proximal learning, which requires being able to make accurate judgments about prior knowledge and to-be-learned knowledge. Teachers can assist students in planning and monitoring their study time by asking them to list items to be learned from easiest to most difficult, teaching them self-testing skills, and providing them with sample questions.

Key Concepts

adolescent egocentrism   214

appearance-reality distinctions   212

evaluating   212

false-beliefs   212

imaginary audience   214

introspection   214

metacognition   211

metacognitive knowledge   211

metacognitive regulation   212

monitoring   212

personal fable   214

person knowledge   211

planning   212

PQ4R   217

reciprocal teaching   216

region of proximal learning   221

SOAR method   221

strategy knowledge   211

study-time allocation   220

task knowledge   211

theory of mind   212

visual perspective-taking   212

Video Applications

www.mhhe.com/bohlin2e

Video 1: Reading Strategies (*4 minutes*)

The teacher asks her fourth-grade students to summarize the reading strategies they have been learning during the year, such as inference, predictions, and so on.

Video 2: Reading in Class (*7 minutes*)

As this fourth-grade teacher reads a book, the students use reading strategies to help comprehend the story.

Video 3: Note-Taking (*2 minutes*)

A middle school social studies teacher gives a lesson on the Civil War. His notes appear on the overhead projector, and students are seen taking notes.

Case Studies
Reflect and Evaluate

EARLY CHILDHOOD: "Air"

These questions refer to the case study on page 202.

1. What strategies did Ms. Carson use to aid students' reading comprehension?

2. What characteristic of theory of mind is illustrated by Maria and Jose? What does this tell you about Jose's theory of mind?

3. The nature of the task can influence the way students use metacognitive strategies. How do you think students viewed the nature of the science experiment task Ms. Carson presented them with? How did this view affect their use of metacognitive strategies?

4. How did Ms. Carson incorporate planning and monitoring into her students' kite project? Why are those skills important?

5. How could Ms. Carson's students use the strategy of evaluation on Kindergarten Kite Day to assess how well their aerodynamic ideas work?

ELEMENTARY SCHOOL: "Reading About Pirates"

These questions refer to the case study on page 204.

1. Assume that some students who were completing seat work protested that the reading group had an easier assignment. Explain what type(s) of metacognitive knowledge might lead some students to this conclusion.

2. What metacognitive strategies did Mr. McPherson use with his reading group? Be specific.

3. What specific metacognitive strategies could Mr. McPherson have taught his students to use in order to improve their reading comprehension?

4. How could Mr. McPherson have used reciprocal teaching with the students who were not in his reading group?

5. How might Mr. McPherson have helped the students working at their desks to monitor their progress?

6. How could writing skills have been incorporated into the lesson for the students working at their desks? For the students in the reading group?

MIDDLE SCHOOL: "King Washington"

These questions refer to the case study on page 206.

1. What metacognitive factors may have contributed to the students' failure to remember details from the lessons when it came time to take their exam?

2. What is adolescent egocentrism, and how might it have contributed to the students' failure to take notes?

3. How might prior knowledge about George Washington have been a factor in students' use of metacognitive skills during this unit?

4. Why was it important for Mr. Radcliffe to take time to teach different note-taking strategies rather than just telling his students to be sure to take notes?

5. What advice could Mr. Radcliffe have given his students to help them make the best use of their study time before the exam?

6. How could students have used planning and monitoring strategies as they wrote down their talking points for the Continental Congress?

HIGH SCHOOL: "I Don't Understand"

These questions refer to the case study on page 208.

1. What types of metacognitive knowledge are evident in Ms. Park's reflection on her teaching? What types of metacognitive knowledge are evident in the students' responses and actions during the lesson?

2. How might students' understanding of the repeating decimals task have influenced their use of metacognitive strategies during the math lesson?

3. In what way does Ms. Park display characteristics of having a personal fable? Is it realistic to think that a teacher would have a personal fable?

4. Could students have used their notes from previous class sessions to help them better understand the materials? Explain.

5. How could students have used self-monitoring and evaluation during the lesson? How could Ms. Park have helped students use monitoring and evaluation during the lesson?

6. How did Ms. Park use self-monitoring as a metacognitive strategy during her delivery of the lesson?

MODULE 13

Transfer of Skills and Knowledge

Outline	Learning Goals
What Is Transfer and Why Is It Important?	
■ Specific Versus General Transfer ■ Low-road Versus High-road Transfer	1. Contrast the specific versus general view of transfer with the high-road versus low-road view.
Do We Readily Transfer What We Learn?	
■ The Success of Low-road Transfer ■ The Problem of High-road Transfer	2. Explain why high-road transfer is more difficult to achieve than low-road transfer.
Application: How to Facilitate Transfer	
■ Develop Automaticity of Skills ■ Promote Meaningful Learning ■ Teach Metacognitive Strategies ■ Motivate Students to Value Learning	3. Identify four teaching principles that support transfer, and explain how each facilitates transfer.
Summary **Key Concepts** **Video Applications** **Case Studies: Reflect and Evaluate**	

WHAT IS TRANSFER AND WHY IS IT IMPORTANT?

As teachers, we would all like our students to take what they have learned in our classrooms and find ways to apply that knowledge in other courses and in other contexts of their lives—that is, to transfer their learning. But the transfer of skills and knowledge is easier said than done. Researchers have found it difficult to demonstrate that we spontaneously and successfully transfer our learning from instructional situations to other contexts (Haskell, 2001; Marini & Genereux, 1995). The research findings tell us that we cannot teach students and *expect* them to find a way to use the information outside school. Rather, we must teach *for* transfer. To do this, teachers must clearly understand the nature of transfer and carefully design instruction with transfer in mind (Marini & Genereux, 1995).

Transfer can be defined broadly as the influence of prior knowledge, skills, strategies, or principles on new learning. We should be careful not to assume that all transfer is **positive transfer,** in which previous learning facilitates learning on new tasks. Learners can also experience **negative transfer,** in which previous learning hinders learning on new tasks. For example, an elementary school student's misconception that a whale is a fish may lead to making incorrect animal classifications in science class. Learners also may experience **zero transfer,** in which previous learning has no effect on the performance of a new task. For example, a high school student might not apply knowledge learned from a business course to managing money earned from a part-time job.

How, exactly, does prior knowledge influence our behavior in new situations? Psychologists have long debated whether transfer involves specific responses or more general principles and strategies. This debate has led to different definitions of transfer.

Specific Versus General Transfer

An idea popular at the turn of the twentieth century, the **doctrine of formal discipline,** advocated a *general* view of transfer in which the study of subjects such as Latin and geometry could improve individuals' logical thinking, and their improved mental functioning then would transfer to other disciplines. In the early 1900s, Edward Thorndike (1923, 1924) provided evidence against the doctrine of formal discipline, showing that students who studied Latin or geometry did not perform better on tests of intellectual reasoning than students who studied other subjects.

Thorndike's alternative to the doctrine of formal discipline, called the **theory of identical elements,** is a *specific* view of transfer. According to this theory, transfer will occur between two learning tasks if the new skill or behavior contains elements that are identical to a skill or behavior from the original task. For example, mastering single-digit addition helps the learning of two-column addition because single-digit addition is a component skill required for two-column addition (Mayer & Wittrock, 1996). The more a new learning situation resembles the context in which a skill was learned, the more likely it is that transfer will occur.

Automaticity:
See page 193 and
page 441.

Low-road Transfer.
Acquiring automaticity at ice skating enables low-road transfer to the sport of in-line skating, allowing these teammates to practice playing hockey during warm weather.

Low-road Versus High-road Transfer

Gavriel Salomon and David Perkins (1989) provide a more detailed account of transfer than did earlier theories of specific and general transfer. Unlike these earlier theories, their model of transfer specifies *what* exactly transfers and *how* it transfers. Let's explore the types of transfer in their model.

Low-road transfer involves the "spontaneous, automatic transfer of highly practiced skills, with little need for reflective thinking" (Salomon & Perkins, 1989, p. 118). Low-road transfer results from extensive practice of a skill in a variety of contexts until it becomes flexible and developed to automaticity (Salomon & Perkins, 1989). **Automaticity** occurs when a person performs a skill very quickly, very accurately, and with little attention or other cognitive load. Developing automaticity of a skill allows a person not only to perform the skill without much thought but also to transfer the skill to other, similar situations. Reading and arithmetic are examples of automatic skills that transfer to many situations in and outside school because they have been extensively practiced in varied contexts.

In **high-road transfer,** an individual purposely and consciously applies general knowledge, a strategy, or a principle learned in one situation to a different situation (Salomon & Perkins, 1989). For example, a child who has mastered a puzzle may approach a new and more challenging puzzle by first thinking of the strategies used with the original puzzle. Just as automaticity is the key characteristic of low-road transfer, **mindful abstraction** is the defining feature of high-road transfer. Abstraction is the process of retrieving meaningful information (that has been consciously and actively learned rather than memorized) and applying it to a new learning context. Abstraction is *mindful* when it is guided by metacognition (our awareness, monitoring, and regulation of our thinking), allowing the learner to recognize transfer situations and apply abstract knowledge across contexts (Fuchs et al., 2003). In the puzzle example described, the child reflects on what she knows about puzzle solving and applies this knowledge to the new puzzle.

Problem-solving Transfer. Strategies the child is learning about solving puzzles, such as starting with the edge pieces first, can be consciously retrieved and applied to solving new and more challenging puzzles.

The puzzle example illustrates a type of high-road transfer called **problem-solving transfer,** in which we recall a general strategy or principle that we have learned from solving one type of problem and apply it to solve another type of problem. **Analogical transfer,** another example of high-road transfer, involves creating or using an existing analogy to aid in understanding a new concept, as when science teachers compare the orbit of an electron in an atom (new knowledge) to the orbit of a planet in the solar system (existing knowledge).

Metacognition: See Module 12.

High-road transfer can also be described in simple chronological terms. **Forward-reaching transfer** involves learning a principle or strategy so well that an individual selects it quickly and easily when it is needed in future situations. For example, a high school student who has developed a deep, conceptual understanding of geometry might easily think of ways he could use geometric principles in other classes, real-life situations, or future careers. **Backward-reaching transfer,** in contrast, occurs when an individual deliberately looks for strategies or principles learned in the past to solve a current problem or task. A high school student building a birdhouse in a woodworking class might think *back* to last year's geometry class for knowledge that could help her calculate the dimensions for the birdhouse.

Problem solving: See page 245.

Think of your own learning experiences. When have you used forward-reaching or backward-reaching transfer?

DO WE READILY TRANSFER WHAT WE LEARN?

The Success of Low-road Transfer

Consider all the skills you are able to perform automatically. As elementary school students you learned how to read, and as college students you apply those reading skills broadly, to magazines, mass transit maps, Facebook pages, and so on. These examples illustrate the success of low-road transfer: Once students develop a skill to automaticity, they can transfer it readily to novel situations. Just as experts such as chess players, musicians, and athletes must engage in thousands of hours of practice at their craft, students must devote an extensive amount of time to honing their skills in areas such as reading, mathematics, computer use, speaking a foreign language, athletics, and playing a musical instrument (Anderson, 1982; Hayes, 1985). At least 100 hours of practice are needed for an individual to develop modest levels of skill proficiency (Anderson, 1982).

Practicing skills to automaticity: See page 441.

Keep in mind that extensive practice alone is not sufficient for effective transfer to occur. Extensive practice using **rote memorization** (memorizing without understanding) leads to discrete bits of information or skills in long-term memory that are not meaningfully connected and that fade over time, making transfer less likely. To ensure that low-road transfer occurs, students should engage in reflective and deliberate practice rather than rote memorization (Haskell, 2001). **Reflective practice** involves developing a conceptual understanding. For example, students must practice $2 \times 3 = 6$ to automaticity, but

Deliberate practice. Musicians engage in many hours of deliberate practice to acquire skill proficiency.

they also need to understand the concept behind this fact. **Deliberate practice** involves an intrinsic motivation to engage in extensive and long-term repetition with the goal of learning the skill and improving performance, not just "going through the motions" of practicing (Ericsson, 2006).

The Problem of High-road Transfer

In order to understand the problem of high-road transfer, first read the following story and problem, used in research by Mary Gick and Keith Holyoak (1980, 1983):

Military story

A small country was ruled from a strong fortress by a dictator. The fortress was situated in the middle of the country, surrounded by farms and villages. Many roads led to the fortress through the countryside. A rebel general vowed to capture the fortress. The general knew that an attack by his entire army would capture the fortress. He gathered his army at the head of one of the roads, ready to launch a full-scale direct attack. However, the general then learned that the dictator had planted mines on each of the roads. The mines were set so that small bodies of men could pass over them safely, since the dictator needed to move his troops and workers to and from the fortress. However, any large force would detonate the mines. Not only would this blow up the road, but it would also destroy many neighboring villages. It therefore seemed impossible to capture the fortress. However, the general devised a simple plan. He divided his army into small groups and dispatched each group to the head of a different road. When all was ready he gave the signal and each group marched down a different road. Each group continued down its road to the fortress so that the entire army arrived together at the fortress at the same time. In this way, the general captured the fortress and overthrew the dictator. (Gick & Holyoak, 1980, p. 351)

Medical problem

Suppose you are a doctor faced with a patient who has a malignant tumor in his stomach. It is impossible to operate on the patient, but unless the tumor is destroyed the patient will die. There is a kind of ray that can be used to destroy the tumor. If the rays reach the tumor all at once at a sufficiently high intensity, the tumor will be destroyed. Unfortunately, at this intensity the healthy tissue that the rays pass through on the way to the tumor will also be destroyed. At lower intensities the rays are harmless to healthy tissue, but they will not affect the tumor either. What type of procedure might be used to destroy the tumor with the rays, and at the same time avoid destroying the healthy tissue? (Duncker, 1945, pp. 307–308)

Did you solve the medical problem? If not, reread the military story for a hint. In the study, college students read the medical problem after reading the military story, which provides an analogous solution to the medical problem. When prompted to use the military story to help solve the medical problem, the majority of students arrived at the correct solution: Use the convergence of several rays at lower intensities from different angles. However, significantly fewer students were able to generate the solution without the hint given by the military story. This example, like several other classic experimental studies, illustrates a well-known finding—students often fail to *spontaneously* transfer what they have learned from a previous problem to a structurally similar problem, even when the new problem is presented immediately after the original problem (Gick & Holyoak, 1983; Hayes & Simon, 1977; Reed, Ernst, & Banerji, 1974).

Experimental studies indicate that high-road transfer involving problem solving and analogies is rare because students lack one or more of three skills needed for successful transfer (Mayer & Wittrock, 1996):

1. *Recognition.* Students often fail to recognize that they have an analogous solution in their memory that they can apply to solving a new problem. In the study described above, for example, most stu-

| EXAMPLE 13.1 | The Difficulty of Mapping Solutions Between Problems |

Training problem:
A nurse mixes a 6% boric acid solution with a 12% boric acid solution. How many pints of each are needed to make 4.5 pints of an 8% boric acid solution?

Transfer problem:
A grocer mixes peanuts worth $1.65 a pound and almonds worth $2.10 a pound. How many pounds of each are needed to make 30 pounds of a mixture worth $1.83 a pound?

Adapted from Reed, 1987.

dents did not think of the convergence solution to the tumor problem unless the researcher explicitly directed them to search previously read stories for a hint about the solution.

2. *Abstraction.* Students often fail to abstract the general principle or strategy. In the study described, reading two stories with the same solution enhanced students' ability to abstract the analogy for the tumor solution, compared to reading one story with the solution and one irrelevant story. This suggests that students may need a lot of varied exposure to problems in order for them to become successful at recognizing and abstracting analogous strategies.

3. *Mapping.* Students may fail to transfer because of difficulty mapping—making appropriate connections between the original and the new problem—especially when the problems appear very dissimilar on the surface (Holyoak & Koh, 1987; Reed, 1987). The two mathematical problems in Example 13.1 involve an identical solution but look very different—one is about mixtures of boric acid, and the other is about mixing peanuts and almonds. Learning how to solve one problem often does not help students solve a new problem that looks different but has the same solution (Gick & Holyoak, 1983; Hayes & Simon, 1977; Reed, 1987).

Research on the transfer of school learning to other contexts is equally discouraging. Although some research demonstrates successful transfer of strategies from one subject to a different learning context in school (Adey & Shayer, 1993; Chen & Klahr, 1999), other research shows a general failure of students to apply what they have learned in school to novel tasks (Brown, Campione, Webber, & McGilly, 1992; Nickerson, Perkins, & Smith, 1985). For example, students typically do not exhibit transfer of mathematical problem solving (Bransford & Schwartz, 1999; Mayer, Quilici, & Moreno, 1999). This is especially true for elementary school students who have difficulty applying computational skills when problems change in minor ways, as in the training and transfer problems in Example 13.1 (Durnin, Perrone, & MacKay, 1997; Larkin, 1989). Likewise, children and adults rarely apply school-taught procedures to problems they encounter in real life, such as determining a better buy in a supermarket (Lave, 1988; Saxe, 2002; Schliemann & Acioly, 1989).

Why do individuals seldom transfer school-learned knowledge to real-life contexts? One line of research suggests that they may not have learned the knowledge in a meaningful way in the first place (Bereiter, 1995). Instruction that relies primarily on rote memorization or *convergent thinking* (obtaining the one right answer to a question) produces a narrow ability to answer only certain kinds of questions rather than encouraging students to acquire flexible knowledge that can be abstracted to new situations. Experimental studies have shown that learners who understand concepts and procedures are more likely to transfer their learning to novel contexts than students who learn by rote memorization (Adams et al., 1988; Bransford et al., 2000). For example, fourth- and fifth-grade students were more likely to engage in transfer of mathematical problems if they learned conceptual principles rather than simply memorizing procedures (Perry, 1991).

Convergent thinking: See page 424.

Another line of research suggests that high-road transfer of school-learned knowledge may be limited by the extent to which the learning and transfer contexts are similar (Barnett & Ceci, 2002). As Table 13.1 illustrates, learning and transfer contexts may differ on several dimensions, including subject matter, physical features, and purpose. We may readily engage in **near transfer,** which involves applying prior knowledge to new situations that are very similar, but not identical, to the learning context. However, we may be less likely to engage in **far transfer,** or applying prior knowledge to a context that is very different from the learning context. We may not realize that our knowledge is relevant in a context that is very different from the learning context (Driscoll, 2005; Singley & Anderson, 1989). We

TABLE 13.1 Distinguishing Between Near and Far Transfer

Domain	Description	Near example	Far example
Subject matter	Knowledge may transfer to a similar or very different subject matter.	Using knowledge from a calculus class to solve equations in a physics class	Using knowledge of the scientific method (science class) as part of a persuasive writing assignment (English class)
Physical context	Knowledge may transfer from one context to a similar physical context or to a different environment.	Applying knowledge about liquid measures to solving word problems at school	Applying knowledge about liquid measures to bake a cake at home
Functional context	Knowledge learned for one purpose may transfer to a similar purpose or to a very different purpose.*	Using knowledge of calculating percentages in math class to solve word problems (both academic purposes)	Using knowledge of calculating percentages (academic) to figure out batting averages of favorite baseball players (recreational)
Temporal context	Near and far transfer can be distinguished by the length of time between learning and transfer.	Transferring knowledge over a short period of time (same or next day)	Transferring knowledge over a longer time lapse (weeks, months, or years later)
Social context	Knowledge in the learning and transfer situations may involve a similar social context or different social contexts.	Working alone in both learning and transfer situations	Using what has been learned from a group activity to do independent research
Modality	Knowledge in learning and transfer situations may involve the same or a different modality.	Listening to a lecture on fetal pig dissection and being able to describe the process to a friend (oral modality for both)	Listening to a lecture on fetal pig dissection and being able to perform the dissection (oral versus hands-on)

Source: Adapted from Barnett & Ceci, 2002.

[a] Physical and functional contexts sometimes overlap. For example, baking a cake at home can be far transfer in terms of physical context (outside school) and functional context (real-life purpose). However, physical and functional context can also be distinct. A student may use percentages to calculate his or her favorite players' batting averages at an after-school program at school (similar physical context, different purpose).

also may find it difficult to recognize uses for our school-learned knowledge when faced with real-life tasks if the content taught in school is disconnected from a clear goal or purpose for learning it (Barnett & Ceci, 2002; Gick & Holyoak, 1987). Transfer across very different contexts may occur rarely simply because it requires so much effort (Gage & Berliner, 1992).

Think about your school experiences. Were you encouraged to memorize, or to think, problem-solve, and practice using your knowledge? How might teaching methods have affected transfer opportunities?

APPLICATION: HOW TO FACILITATE TRANSFER

Teachers can use several research-based principles to help them design instruction that will foster transfer. Similarly, the guidelines can help students adopt learning strategies that lead to more efficient transfer. These principles include:

- develop automaticity of skills,
- promote meaningful learning,
- teach metacognitive strategies, and
- motivate students to value learning.

Develop Automaticity of Skills

To facilitate low-road transfer of academic skills, teachers should provide students with many opportunities to practice and achieve automaticity of academic skills. To be effective, practice needs to (Haskell, 2001):

- be reflective rather than rote,
- occur in a variety of contexts, and
- involve **overlearning,** in which students engage in continued practice after they have demonstrated mastery. Skills continue to improve long after individuals achieve complete accuracy (Schneider, 1985).

Developing automaticity does not necessarily mean that teachers need to use drill and practice, a method that relies on flashcards and rote memorization. The use of drill and practice has declined since the 1970s, after it acquired a reputation as "drill and kill," meaning that its lack of meaningful context or purpose for learning *killed* students' motivation. However, extensive practice leading to automaticity can occur within the context of meaningful and fun academic tasks such as problem solving, collaborative activities, computer games, and classroom games.

Developing automaticity can also facilitate high-road transfer. Students who attain automaticity of lower-level skills, such as word decoding and arithmetic computation, are able to focus more cognitive resources on higher-level cognitive skills, such as comprehension, planning, monitoring, and problem solving (Case, 1985; Geary, 1994; Perfetti, 1992). Greater attention to higher-level skills during learning will increase the likelihood of high-road transfer in elementary as well as middle and high school students. For example, a high school student who can automatically perform the arithmetic operations of algebra is more likely to understand and transfer algebraic problem solving than is a student who struggles with arithmetic operations.

Even though automaticity enables the development of higher-level cognitive skills such as reading comprehension, problem solving, and reasoning, a lack of automaticity should not be used as an excuse for delaying students' exposure to complex cognitive skills. Often, lower-achieving students will continue to receive basic skills instruction and drill and practice as a prerequisite for progressing to instruction in higher-level skills. As a result, lower-achieving students receive less instruction in these skills and fall farther behind their peers as they move through higher grades, when complex cognitive skills become increasingly important (Means & Knapp, 1994). In working with lower-achieving students, teachers are encouraged to do the following things:

- Create problem-solving tasks that remove the constraint of automaticity. Students can use calculators for mathematical problem solving, dictate essays to remove grammatical constraints, and draft essays or journals without worrying about handwriting, spelling, or punctuation (Glynn, Britton, Muth, & Dogan, 1982; Scardamalia, Bereiter, & Goelman, 1982).

- Balance basic skills instruction with teaching methods that focus on complex cognitive skills. Teachers can focus on mathematical problem solving with lower-achieving students who have not yet achieved automaticity of math facts, as Example 13.2 shows. They also can use *reciprocal teaching*, a method of teaching metacognitive strategies important for reading comprehension, with students who have poor reading skills. In this method, the teacher models strategies of summarizing, questioning, clarifying, and predicting and provides *scaffolding* (support, hints, and prompts) to help students acquire and later demonstrate these strategies on their own, without the teacher's assistance. Reciprocal teaching has improved the reading comprehension of students with poor reading comprehension from elementary through secondary education (Palincsar & Brown, 1984; Rosenshine & Meister, 1994). It is also effective when used with students with learning disabilities from elementary through middle school (Gajria, Jitendra, Sood, & Sacks, 2007; Lederer, 2000).

Reciprocal teaching: See page 215.

Scaffolding: See page 126.

DIVERSITY

Promote Meaningful Learning

High-road transfer relies on active, meaningful learning in which students possess deep-level knowledge structures (not discrete facts acquired by rote memorization) that are connected to similar concepts, prior knowledge, and real-life experiences (Bransford & Schwartz, 1999; Renkl, Mandl, & Gruber, 1996; Salomon & Perkins, 1989). Teachers can use a variety of techniques for encouraging meaningful learning.

Take inventory of students' prior knowledge before beginning a new lesson or topic. Teachers can prevent negative transfer by determining what students already know about a topic, identifying inaccurate prior knowledge, and correcting it before teaching new information. Tapping into students' prior knowledge will also help students see the relevance of new material and enable them to integrate it with their existing knowledge, facilitating forward-reaching transfer. Teachers can do this by asking students

Meaningful learning: See page 368.

EXAMPLE 13.2   Mathematical Problem Solving with Lower Achievers

While most of the children in this first-grade class are solving word problems independently or in small groups, Ms. J. is sitting at a table with three students—Raja, Erik, and Ernestine. Each child has plastic cubes that can be connected, a pencil, and a big sheet of paper on which are written the same word problems. They read the first problem together: "Raja made 18 clay dinosaurs. Ernestine has nine clay dinosaurs. How many more clay dinosaurs does Raja have than Ernestine?"

The students work on the problem in different ways. Raja puts together 18 cubes. She removes nine of them and counts the rest. She gets 11. She writes down the answer and looks up at the teacher for confirmation. Ms. J. looks at the answer, looks back at the problem, and then says, "You're real close." As Raja recounts the cubes, Ms. J. watches her closely. This time Raja counts nine.

Ernestine also connects 18 cubes. Then she counts nine and breaks them off. She counts what she has left. Ernestine exclaims, "I've got it!" Ms. J. looks at Ernestine's answer and says, "No, you're real close." Ernestine does the same procedure over again.

Erik connects nine cubes, and in a separate group he connects 18 cubes. He places them next to each other and matches them up, counting across each row to make sure there are nine matches. Then Erik breaks off the unmatched cubes and counts them. "I've got it!" he announces.

Turning to the group, Ms. J. queries, "Okay now, how did you get your answers? Remember, that's what's always the important thing: How did you get it? Let's see if we can come up with different ways this time. [*Erik has his hand raised.*] Erik, what did you do?"

Erik: I had nine cubes, and then I put 18 cubes and then I put them together. And the 18 cubes . . . I took away some of the 18 cubes.

Ms. J.:   Okay, let's see if we can understand what Erik did. Okay, you got—show me 18 cubes.

Erik: Okay. [*He puts together two of the three sets of nine he has lined up in front of him.*]

Ms. J.:   Okay, so you have 18 cubes. Then you had nine.

Erik takes nine cubes in his other hand and puts them side by side.

Ms. J.:   Then you compared.

Erik: [*simultaneously with Ms. J.*] Then I put them together.

Ms. J.:   Then you put them together.

Erik: Then I took . . .

Ms. J.:   Nine away.

Erik: Nine away, and I counted them [*the ones left*], and there were nine.

Ms. J.:   Okay. So that's one way to do it. Nice job, Erik. Which way did you do it, Raja?

Ms. J. discusses their solution methods with Raja and Ernestine.

Ms. J.:   So we had—how many different ways did we do that problem? [*The group discusses the different ways.*] So we did the problem in three different ways. Let's read the next problem.

Adapted from Means & Knapp, 1994.

to brainstorm what they know about a topic, and students can adopt a strategy of asking themselves "What do I know about this topic already?" when they read a textbook or research a topic. **KWL,** a popular method used in schools (Figure 13.1), taps into prior knowledge by requiring students to list their *Knowledge* about a topic and *What questions* they have before instruction begins (Ogle, 1986). To complete the process, students list what they *Learned* from instruction.

Require students to construct relationships between new information and their prior knowledge. Teachers can ask students to think of their own example of a concept rather than memorizing the example given in a textbook. Such methods have been used successfully in subjects that include reading, mathematics, science, economics, and geography (Mackenzie & White, 1982; Osborne & Wittrock, 1983; Peled & Wittrock, 1990) and with students from lower-socioeconomic backgrounds (Kourilsky & Wittrock, 1992). In subjects that involve calculating a solution to a problem, such as math or science, teachers can encourage students to construct their own representations or models of the problems to aid their understanding. Elementary school students might draw five groups of six circles to help calculate

DIVERSITY

K What I *know*	W What I *want* to learn	L What I have *learned*
Magnets stick to metal. Magnets are black.	How do they attract things? Why don't they attract some objects?	Opposite poles attract; same repel. Magnets work in water. Magnets don't attract plastic or aluminum.

Figure 13.1. Tapping Into Prior Knowledge. KWL, shown here, can help prevent negative transfer by assessing students' prior knowledge before a lesson.

a story problem involving the operation 5 × 6, or high school students might draw an incline and other attributes of a physics problem. Constructing one's own problem representation improves students' learning and transfer of their knowledge to new, complex problems, benefiting both low and high achievers (Terwel, van Oers, van Dijk, & van den Eeden, 2009).

Encourage the use of question-answering and self-explanation strategies. Teachers can provide questions for students to answer while reading their textbooks. Questions that focus on applying knowledge to situations outside of the learning context, rather than finding answers to factual questions, are best because they facilitate students' transfer of knowledge to new examples or new problems (Shavelson, Berliner, Ravitch, & Loeding, 1974; Watts & Anderson, 1971). Teachers can also encourage self-explanation, as when students explain expository texts, solve math or science problems, or use steps in their problem solving. Students show deeper learning and greater transfer when using self-explanation because it promotes the integration of new content with existing knowledge (Chi, 2000; Tajika & Nakatsu, 2005; Tajika et al., 2007).

Use manipulatives. These are materials that encourage active learning and help students make a connection between a concrete situation and a more abstract principle (Mayer & Wittrock, 1996). Hands-on activities involving experiments can be used in science, and beads, Dienes blocks, or any other concrete objects can help elementary school students learn computational principles in math (Champagne, Gunstone, & Klopfer, 1985; Montessori, 1964).

Teach by analogy. Science educators are increasingly using analogies as a way to tap students' prior knowledge about topics (Haskell, 2001). For example, teachers can use the flow of water through pipes to introduce the concepts of current and voltage in electrical circuits (Brooks & Dansereau, 1987; Gentner & Gentner, 1983). Because students have difficulty mapping—making appropriate connections between the analogy and a new problem—teachers should check students' understanding to prevent incorrect application of the analogy (negative transfer).

Use worked-out examples for practice in problem solving. In a worked-out example, students can see the solution and the steps involved in reaching the solution. Worked-out examples are most effective for learning and transfer when:

- they are structurally similar to the current problem, which is especially important for younger learners (Gentner, Loewenstein, & Thompson, 2003; Reed, 1987);
- students actively attempt to understand the example problem rather than merely re-reading it (Chi, Bassock, Lewis, Reimann, & Glaser, 1989; Zhu & Simon, 1987); and
- students compare two examples rather than examining a single example or studying two examples independently (Gentner & Namy, 2004; Silver, Ghousseini, Gosen, Charalambous, & Strawhun, 2005).

Use multiple examples or similar concepts in multiple contexts. Optimally, instruction should continually return to topics or concepts, but on different levels and in different contexts (Haskell, 2001). Teachers also should encourage students to learn general strategies or principles in many contexts so they can flexibly apply what they have learned to a variety of situations (Perkins, Jay, & Tishman, 1993; Prawat, 1989). This will encourage mindful abstraction and prevent students from tying knowledge only to specific situations or contexts (Salomon & Perkins, 1989).

Metacognition: See Module 12.

Teach Metacognitive Strategies

Because successful transfer requires the ability to identify appropriate transfer situations, it is important to teach students metacognitive strategies for recognizing situations in which they can use their knowledge. A recent study on teaching mathematical problem solving in third-grade classrooms indicates that (Fuchs et al., 2003):

- explicitly teaching students what transfer is leads to greater transfer on novel problems in comparison with students not instructed about transfer. Teachers in this study taught students the concept of transfer (meaning to move), gave examples of how students transfer skills (moving from two-digit horizontal problems to two-digit vertical problems), and reviewed the meaning of transfer in every unit. Both lower and higher achievers benefited from this instruction, in contrast to earlier research suggesting that transfer is difficult for low-achieving students (Fuchs, Fuchs, Kams, Hamlett, & Karzaroff, 1999; Mayer, 1998; Woodward & Baxter, 1997).

- instruction and practice in metacognitive strategies can facilitate transfer. In this study, students practiced classifying different types of problems, solved partially worked-out examples, and were reminded to think of previous solutions when solving new problems. Practice with multiple types of problems can help students overcome their difficulties both in *abstracting* principles or solutions and in *mapping* solutions from previously learned problems to new ones.

Teachers can incorporate metacognitive strategies in their lessons in many ways, from simple cuing to more explicit instruction. They can begin by having students cue themselves: "Do I know anything from [other subjects or problems] that might help here?" (Salomon & Perkins, 1989). Cuing the relevance of recently learned information or the similarities across tasks facilitates backward-reaching transfer (Catrambone & Holyoak, 1989; Ross, 1987, 1989). To get students to independently recognize transfer situations without the aid of external cues, teachers can explicitly teach metacognitive strategies—such as the scientific method, Internet research, reading comprehension strategies, and problem-solving strategies—in many different subjects. Both in-class activities and out-of-class assignments can provide students with opportunities for practicing strategies in the context of subject-matter instruction. Explicit instruction in reading and mathematics strategies can encourage high-road transfer, especially among lower achievers (Fuchs et al., 2003; Gajria et al., 2007).

DIVERSITY

Motivate Students to Value Learning

Motivation to learn: See page 254.

Mastery goals: See page 280.

Students' motivation to learn and to take advantage of transfer opportunities can lead to higher levels of transfer (Colquitt, LePine, & Noe, 2000; Pea, 1987). Teachers can facilitate transfer by using several techniques to encourage students to take an interest in and value learning.

Encourage students to set mastery goals. Students with **mastery goals** focus on mastering a task, growing intellectually, and acquiring new skills and knowledge (in contrast with learning for the sake of passing a test or getting a good grade). As a result, they are more likely to (Grant & Dweck, 2003; Wolters, 2004):

- engage in meaningful learning (or deep-level processing),
- use metacognitive strategies, and
- show high levels of effort.

All of these behaviors have been linked to greater likelihood of transfer (Pugh & Bergin, 2006). Students with mastery goals are more likely to engage in backward-reaching transfer—looking for learned information that may be helpful to their current understanding, and forward-reaching transfer—looking for ways to apply their newly learned knowledge. Part of being a good student is acquiring a tendency to independently look for transfer opportunities (Salomon & Perkins, 1989).

Capitalize on students' natural interests when teaching new topics. Students who come to school with **individual interest**—an intrinsic interest in a particular subject or activity—are more likely to use deep-level processing in learning content (Ainley, Hidi, & Berndorff, 2002; Schiefele, 1991). A student who is interested in a particular topic may consciously look for ways the material can be applied in other contexts, facilitating forward-reaching transfer (Salomon & Perkins, 1989). For example, a high school student who wants to become a doctor might be interested in ways science topics can be applied to medicine and therefore be more likely to engage in forward-reaching transfer in science classes.

Use techniques to create situational interest. Introducing new material using enthusiasm, novelty, and surprise can spark **situational interest**—an immediate interest in a particular lesson (Covington, 2000;

Stipek, 1996). While some studies suggest that situational interest fosters deep-level processing, and therefore transfer (Hidi, 2001; Hidi & Harackiewicz, 2000; Krapp, 1999), other research has found that situational interest might *not* lead to transfer because it can be superficial and unrelated to learning goals (Bergin, 1999; Lepper & Malone, 1987). Consider these examples:

- Elementary school teachers who believed in using manipulatives to teach mathematics often used them to make math fun rather than to foster thinking about mathematical principles (Moyer, 2002).

- Students who read a science text that included **seductive details**—highly interesting segments of a text conveying nonessential information—recalled fewer main ideas and solved fewer transfer problems than did students who read the same text without seductive details (Harp & Mayer, 1997, 1998; Lehman, Schraw, McCrudden, & Hartley, 2007; McCrudden & Corkill, 2010). These details activate prior knowledge that is not directly related to the material to be learned, making it less likely that students will deeply process the important points (Harp & Mayer, 1998; Pugh & Bergin, 2006). Using seductive details in lessons and lectures can attract students' interest, but it may undermine effective learning that would lead to transfer.

Encourage students to acquire critical dispositions (attitudes and values) about thinking and learning. High-road, far transfer requires students to develop a conscious and purposeful approach to acquiring knowledge (Langer, 1993; Salomon & Globerson, 1987). If students are taught to think scientifically and to think critically about concepts in particular subjects such as science, math, or literature, they will learn to value this type of thinking and will be more likely to transfer this disposition to other subjects and to real-life experiences (Bereiter, 1995).

Think of some specific ways you can implement these guidelines in the grade you intend to teach.

Summary

Contrast the specific versus general view of transfer with the high-road versus low-road view. The general view of transfer proposes that certain school experiences allow transfer of general mental functions to new situations, while the specific view claims that specific behaviors transfer, but only to the extent that the original and new situations share common elements. The low-road versus high-road distinction provides a more detailed account of transfer than earlier theories of specific and general transfer. This distinction specifies *what* exactly transfers and *how* it transfers. In low-road transfer, highly practiced skills are automatically applied from one situation to the next, whereas high-road transfer involves the conscious and reflective application of abstract knowledge from one context to a very different context.

Explain why high-road transfer is more difficult to achieve than low-road transfer. Low-road transfer—the spontaneous transfer of automatic skills—is relatively easy to achieve because students have extensively practiced skills in a variety of contexts and have developed them to automaticity. High-road transfer—a conscious retrieval of abstract knowledge, principles, or strategies from one situation to a very different situation—is more difficult to achieve because knowledge sometimes is not learned in a meaningful way. Also, applying knowledge from one context to very dissimilar physical, functional, or social contexts requires a lot of cognitive effort.

Identify four teaching principles that support transfer, and explain how each facilitates transfer. (1) Require students to develop automaticity of skills. This leads to low-road transfer and frees up cognitive resources for use on higher-level tasks. (2) Promote meaningful learning, in which students form a rich, interconnected knowledge base of concepts, principles, and strategies. Deep-level knowledge is more likely to transfer to a variety of situations. (3) Teach metacognitive strategies so students recognize high-road transfer situations. (4) Motivate students to value learning, which may enhance the likelihood of transfer. Students with individual interest in a topic and with mastery goals are more likely to process information deeply and to look for ways to apply their knowledge.

Key Concepts

analogical transfer   227

automaticity   226

backward-reaching transfer   227

deliberate practice   228

doctrine of formal discipline   226

far transfer   229

forward-reaching transfer   227

high-road transfer   227

individual interest   234

KWL   232

low-road transfer   226

mastery goals   234

mindful abstraction   227

near transfer   229

negative transfer   226

overlearning   231

positive transfer   226

problem-solving transfer   227

reflective practice   227

rote memorization   227

seductive details   235

situational interest   234

theory of identical elements   226

transfer   226

zero transfer   226

Video Applications

www.mhhe.com/bohlin2e

Video 1: Promoting Transfer in the Classroom (*6 minutes*)
This clip illustrates transfer in various subjects and across several grade levels.

Case Studies
Reflect and Evaluate

EARLY CHILDHOOD: **"Air"**

These questions refer to the case study on page 202.

1. Explain how Shelby's prediction about the cork represents negative transfer.

2. How did Ms. Carson give her students opportunities to construct knowledge in a meaningful way, and how does that affect transfer?

3. Ms. Carson's lesson on air began with a story, was followed up by an experiment, and ended with kite designing. Using Table 13.1, discuss whether the kite-designing activity would be considered near or far transfer.

4. Would you expect students in Ms. Carson's classroom to transfer their knowledge of aerodynamics to new learning situations? Why or why not?

5. Summarize the teaching principles Ms. Carson used to encourage transfer.

6. Several parents approach Ms. Carson with a concern that she is not focusing enough on teaching basic reading and mathematics skills. While they appreciate her commitment to teaching complex problem-solving and thinking skills, they believe that automaticity of lower-level skills should come first. Imagine that you are Ms. Carson. How would you respond to the parents?

ELEMENTARY SCHOOL: "Reading About Pirates"

These questions refer to the case study on page 204.

1. Using Table 13.1, discuss whether the dictionary worksheet activity completed by the reading group would be considered near or far transfer.

2. What strategy did Mr. McPherson use to try to make the dictionary assignment more interesting for his students? Was he successful at stimulating students' interest? Consider the students' point of view, as well as how Mr. McPherson might have evaluated this portion of his teaching.

3. Based on your reading in the module, how might stimulating interest facilitate transfer?

4. What skills that were used in Mr. McPherson's reading group should be developed to a level of automaticity? Why would automaticity of these skills be important for transfer?

5. Use the teaching principles discussed in the module to evaluate how well Mr. McPherson's approach promotes high-road transfer. Offer Mr. McPherson specific strategies for improving his teaching.

MIDDLE SCHOOL: "King Washington"

These questions refer to the case study on page 206.

1. How did Mr. Radcliffe try to motivate his students to value what they were learning? Why is this important for transfer?

2. Mr. Radcliffe sparked students' interest with his questions about George Washington, and once they were hooked he proceeded to lecture. Explain why a lecture might not be conducive to meaningful learning, and provide an alternative that would better facilitate transfer.

3. What metacognitive strategies did Mr. Radcliffe teach his students? Could these strategies help facilitate transfer of learning? Explain.

4. Summarize those teaching principles used by Mr. Radcliffe that are most likely to support transfer.

5. Provide an example of one way a skill or piece of information learned in Mr. Radcliffe 's class might transfer to a new learning situation. Does your example illustrate high-road or low-road transfer?

HIGH SCHOOL: "I Don't Understand"

These questions refer to the case study on page 208.

1. How did students' prior math knowledge play a role in their understanding of the lesson on changing repeating decimals to fractions? Think of some techniques Ms. Park could have used to ensure that students had appropriate prior knowledge before starting the lesson.

2. The class was learning how to change repeating decimals into fractions. Would transfer of this skill to a new context be considered high-road or low-road transfer? Support your answer.

3. Students in Ms. Park's algebra class learned how to convert fractions into decimals in elementary school. Using Table 13.1, discuss whether learning to change repeating decimals into fractions can be considered near or far transfer.

4. How could Ms. Park have made the assignment more meaningful for her students? What is the likelihood of transfer outside algebra class in this case?

5. How did Ms. Park try to encourage backward-reaching transfer of students' previous math knowledge? Think of some other ways she could have encouraged backward-reaching transfer.

6. Use the teaching principles discussed in the module to evaluate how well Ms. Park's teaching approach promotes high-road transfer. Offer Ms. Park specific strategies for improving her teaching.

MODULE 14

Critical Thinking and Problem Solving

Outline	Learning Goals
Thinking Skills and Dispositions	
■ What Are Higher-Order Thinking Skills? ■ What Are Thinking Dispositions?	1. Explain the difference between a higher-order thinking skill and a thinking disposition, and discuss why both skills and dispositions are important.
Critical Thinking	
■ What Is Critical Thinking? ■ Application: Fostering Critical Thinking	2. Explain what critical thinking means. 3. Identify five instructional strategies that can be used to foster critical thinking.
Problem Solving	
■ What Is Problem Solving? ■ Obstacles to Successful Problem Solving ■ Application: Teaching Problem-Solving Strategies	4. Define problem solving and explain the difference between a well-defined and an ill-defined problem. 5. Discuss the roles of algorithms, heuristics, the IDEAL approach, and problem-based learning in teaching problem solving.
Summary **Key Concepts** **Video Applications** **Case Studies: Reflect and Evaluate**	

THINKING SKILLS AND DISPOSITIONS

Socrates challenged the loose thinking of the youth of his day by asking questions such as "What is the evidence?" and "If this is true, does it not follow that other things must also be true?" He promoted an approach that disciplined his students' thinking and guarded against the human tendency to accept fallacious arguments and draw unwarranted conclusions (Resnick, 1987). Today, teachers in every grade level and every discipline often ask themselves the same question: "How can I get my students to think?" Educational and professional success requires the development of thinking skills and a consistent internal motivation to use those skills in appropriate situations (Facione, Facione, & Giancarlo, 2000).

What Are Higher-Order Thinking Skills?

Higher-order thinking involves complex cognitive processes that transform and apply our knowledge, skills, and ideas. Norman R. F. Maier (1933, 1937) used the term *reasoning* or *productive behavior* to describe higher-order thinking and described lower-order thinking as *learned behavior* or *reproductive thinking.* He demonstrated experimentally that the two are qualitatively different types of behavior patterns. Learning the multiplication tables through repeated practice is an example of lower-order thinking—reproducing a behavior previously observed or practiced. Higher-order thinking moves beyond reproducing previous learning and draws on analysis, synthesis, and evaluation skills (Lewis & Smith, 1993). For example, a student may know how to compute the area of a rectangle but may be faced instead with a problem that asks for the area of a parallelogram. If the student is able to see how to convert the parallelogram to a rectangle of the same size and proportion, he has produced new knowledge from the integration of previous learning experiences. Simple repetition of a previous behavior is insufficient. The student has to transform and apply previous learning in a new way.

Thinking Skills. Effective teachers encourage their students to be critical thinkers and problem solvers.

Bloom's taxonomy: See page 365.

The idea that thinking can be divided into higher and lower levels was elaborated on by Benjamin Bloom and colleagues in their *Taxonomy of Educational Objectives,* usually called Bloom's taxonomy (Anderson & Krathwohl, 2001; Bloom, Englehart, Frost, Hill, & Krathwohl, 1956). Table 14.1 provides additional distinctions between lower-order and higher-order thinking. Higher-order thinking skills frequently are interwoven with basic skills during the teaching and learning process (Resnick, 1987; Shaw, 1983). For example, in order for children to understand what they read, they have to be able to make inferences and to use knowledge or information that goes beyond the written text; thus, teaching reading involves interweaving both basic reading skills and higher-order thinking processes.

Many have argued that in order to compete in the twenty-first century, students need to be taught a curriculum that balances core knowledge—such as math, science, and reading—with instruction in how to think—such as critical thinking, problem solving, and making connections between ideas (Songer, Kelcey, & Gotwals, 2009; Wallis & Steptoe, 2006). Research in the field of cognitive psychology has shown that these thinking characteristics can be measured and that they relate to important real-world decisions in domains such as personal finance, employment, health, and public policy (Baron, Bazerman, & Shonk, 2006; Hilton, 2003; Lichtenstein & Slovic, 2006; Myers, 2002; Reyna & Farley,

TABLE 14.1	A Comparison of Lower-Order and Higher-Order Thinking
Lower-Order Thinking	**Higher-Order Thinking**
Reproductive behavior	Productive behavior
Repeating past experiences	Integrating past experiences
Routine or mechanical application of previously acquired information	Challenges student to interpret, analyze, or otherwise manipulate information
Recalling information	Manipulating information
Knowledge, comprehension, and application	Analysis, synthesis, and evaluation

Sources: Bloom et al., 1956; Maier, 1933; Marzano, 1993; Newman, 1990.

2006; Reyna & Lloyd, 2006; Sunstein, 2005). Unfortunately, the domination of standardized testing in schools has undercut the teaching of thinking skills (Hanneke, 2009; Jones, 2010).

DIVERSITY

Enhancing the quality of thinking of all children is important, but it may have particular significance for those minority students who historically have not performed as well as their more economically advantaged peers (Armour-Thomas, Bruno, & Allen, 2006). A curriculum that emphasizes higher-order thinking skills has been found to substantially increase the math and reading comprehension scores of economically disadvantaged students (Pogrow, 2005). Although learning theorists see the development of higher-order thinking as an important goal for all students, teachers often believe that stimulating higher-order thinking is appropriate only for high-achieving students (Torff, 2005). According to this view, low-achieving students are, by and large, unable to deal with tasks that require higher-order thinking skills and thus should be spared the frustration generated by engaging in such tasks. This rationale for reserving higher-level thinking for high achievers is not supported in the research literature, however. Rather, research strongly suggests that teachers should encourage students of all academic levels to engage in tasks that involve higher-order thinking skills (Miri, David, & Uri, 2007; Zohar & Dori, 2003). Research also suggests that sound teaching practices, such as cognitively engaging students in higher-order thinking, are effective for students with and without special needs (Jordan, Schwartz, & McGhie-Richmond, 2009).

DIVERSITY

What Are Thinking Dispositions?

What sets good thinkers apart from others? The most important factor is not simply superior cognitive ability or particular skills; rather, it is their "tendencies to explore, to inquire, to seek clarity, to take intellectual risks, to think critically and imaginatively" (Tishman, Jay, & Perkins, 1992, p. 2). These tendencies can be called **thinking dispositions.** Teaching for thinking involves nurturing dispositions such as the following (Facione, 2011; Tishman, Jay, & Perkins, 1992):

- *truth-seeking*—a desire to understand clearly, to seek connections and explanations;
- *open-mindedness*—the tendency to explore alternative views, to generate multiple options;
- *analytical thinking*—the urge for precision, organization, thoroughness, and accuracy;
- *systematic planning*—the drive to set goals, to make and execute plans, and to envision outcomes;
- *intellectual curiosity*—the tendency to wonder, probe, and identify problems; a zest for inquiry;
- *confidence in the use of reasons and evidence*—the tendency to question assumptions, to demand justification, and to weigh and assess reasons; and

Metacognition: See Module 12.

- *metacognition*—the tendency to be aware of and to monitor the flow of one's own thinking and the ability to exercise mature judgment.

Empirical research has shown that thinking skills and thinking dispositions are two distinct entities (Ennis, 1996; Perkins, Jay, & Tishman, 1993; West, Toplak, & Stanovich, 2008). A thinking skill is a cognitive strategy, whereas a thinking disposition is a personal attribute (Dewey, 1933). There is a difference be-

Dispositions such as open-mindedness, intellectual curiosity, and analytical thinking played a key role in the achievements of inventor Thomas Edison and entrepreneur Bill Gates.

tween teaching a thinking skill and motivating students to cultivate a curious, inquisitive nature in which thinking skills are used consistently (Fisher & Scriven, 1997). Skills and dispositions are mutually reinforcing and thus should be explicitly taught and modeled together (King & Kitchener, 2002; Yang & Chou, 2008). Teachers have a responsibility not only to promote thinking skills, but also to motivate students to make higher-order thinking a habit. It should be noted that although this view is prevalent in Western societies, Eastern students may not place the same value on thinking skills and dispositions. In countries such as China, Japan, and Taiwan, educators have typically focused on providing students with knowledge through rote memorization rather than with activities designed to promote critical thinking (McBride, Xiang,Wittenburg, & Shen, 2002; Yu & Suen, 2005; Zhang, 2006). This may stem from the tendency of Western cultures to place more value than Eastern cultures on individuality of thought and action.

Motivation: See page 254.

DIVERSITY

What intellectual dispositions have become consistent features of the way you think? In what areas do you have thinking skills but lack the motivation to use them?

CRITICAL THINKING

What are we talking about when we say *critical thinking*? The term is often cited and possibly overused, so it's important to know exactly what it means. The American Philosophical Association defines it as follows:

> *The ideal critical thinker is habitually inquisitive, well-informed, trustful of reason, open-minded, flexible, fair-minded in evaluation, honest in facing personal biases, prudent in making judgments, willing to reconsider, clear about issues, orderly in complex matters, diligent in seeking relevant information, reasonable in the selection of criteria, focused in inquiry, and persistent in seeking results which are as precise as the subject and circumstances of inquiry permit. (American Philosophical Association, 1990, p. 3)*

What Is Critical Thinking?

Critical thinking is the process of evaluating the accuracy and worth of information and lines of reasoning. A disposition toward critical thinking could be characterized as the consistent internal motivation to use critical thinking skills to decide what to believe and do (Facione et al., 2000; Facione, 2011). A critical thinker not only *is capable of* reflecting, exploring, and analyzing, but *chooses to* think in advanced, sophisticated ways (Esterlee & Clurman, 1993). We use aspects of critical thinking all the time in tasks such as comparing food labels to see which foods are most nutritious, deciding which candidate to vote for in an election, and evaluating advertising claims. In any instance of critical thinking or reasoning, at least one question is at issue. For example, in an elementary classroom, students might be given a set of objects and asked to form and test a hypothesis about whether each object will sink or float. During the critical thinking process, students deconstruct a problem, issue, or argument using guidelines such as those listed here (Marzano et al., 1988; Paul & Elder, 2006).

- *Frame of reference or points of view involved:* Clearly identify the point of view from which a problem is expressed.
- *Assumptions made:* Identify what is assumed or taken for granted in thinking about the issue.
- *Central concepts and ideas involved:* Identify the most important ideas that are relevant to the issue.
- *Principles or theories used:* Identify the principles or theories used to support an argument. Clarify them, question them, consider alternatives, and apply theories precisely and appropriately.
- *Evidence, data, or reasons given:* Identify lines of reasoning and the evidence on which the reasoning is based. Use logic in trying to determine whether a statement or an argument has a solid basis in fact. Identify contradictions.
- *Interpretations or claims made:* Examine whether the interpretations or claims made are valid and grounded in evidence.
- *Inferences made:* Rationally argue in favor of the inferences being made. Formulate and consider possible objections to inferences.
- *Potential implications and consequences:* Figure out the implications and consequences of a line of reasoning or course of action.

Let's think about these skills within the context of reading a piece of literature. As a critical thinker, the reader might consider the points of view of different characters, identify central themes in the book, look for evidence to support assertions being made, and consider alternative endings, noting the possible implications these would have for the various characters.

The critical thinking process is similar to Piaget's concept of cognitive equilibrium: See page 120.

Automaticity: See page 226.

Critical thinking abilities emerge gradually (King & Kitchener, 1995; Pillow, 2002). The development of critical thinking proceeds in stages that reflect an increasing ability to analyze one's own thinking with a view toward improving it (Paul & Elder, 2006). In the initial stage, individuals may be completely unaware of any significant problems in their thinking. Once they are faced with problems in their thinking (through self-discovery or through direct challenge of their ideas and beliefs by someone else), they may try to improve. At the next stage, they recognize the need for regular practice and take advantage of ways to practice good thinking habits. In the final stage, critical thinking habits become second nature (automatic) as the individual becomes a "master thinker" (Paul & Elder, 2006). Qualitative dimensions that reflect an individual's skill in critical thinking include clarity, accuracy, precision, relevance, depth, breadth, and use of logical reasoning (Paul & Elder, 2006), as shown in Table 14.2.

Application: Fostering Critical Thinking

Improvement in students' critical thinking cannot just be an implicit expectation; research indicates that critical thinking skills must be explicitly taught (Abrami et al., 2008). The first step in fostering critical thinking in the classroom is to make students aware of what it means to think critically. Teachers can have students examine the lives and works of individuals who were critical thinkers or have them examine and discuss their own thinking processes. After students have been given the opportunity to identify the characteristics of critical thinking, they can be encouraged to monitor their own thinking for evidence of these characteristics. When a basic foundation for critical thinking has been established, teachers can use specific instructional strategies to help students think critically. These include questioning during class discussion, applying writing techniques, hypothesis testing, inductive and deductive reasoning, and argument analysis. Let's examine each of these.

QUESTIONING IN CLASS DISCUSSION

Questioning is one of the most frequently used methods for sparking critical thinking and analysis (Marzano, 1993; Murphy et al., 2009). Class discussion, which provides a logical venue for intro-

TABLE 14.2		Qualitative Dimensions of Critical Thought
	Dimension	**Description**
1	Clarity	If a student's statement is unclear we cannot really tell much else about the level of thinking reflected, because we don't know what the student is trying to say.
2	Accuracy	A statement can be clear but not accurate, as in " Most dogs weigh more than 300 pounds."
3	Precision	A statement can be clear and accurate, but not precise. For example, "Jack is overweight." We don't know if Jack is 2 pounds overweight or 200 pounds overweight.
4	Relevance	A statement can be clear, accurate, and precise, but irrelevant to the issue at hand. "Jack is overweight. *FOOD, Inc.* is a good movie."
5	Depth	A statement can be clear, precise, accurate, and relevant, but still be very superficial. For example, the statement "Just Say No," often used to discourage kids from using drugs, lacks depth in response to the very complex issues of drug use and peer pressure.
6	Breadth	A line of reasoning can display all of the dimensions listed above, but lack breadth. For example, a political argument may only look at a question from the liberal standpoint and ignore the conservative view.
7	Logic	Students may pull together a combination of thoughts that are contradictory or do not make any sense. Their thinking in this case is illogical.

Source: Paul & Elder, 2006.

EXAMPLE 14.1   Question Sets That Can Be Used Effectively in Class Discussions

Question Type	Examples
Questions of *Clarification*	What do you mean by _____ ? How does _____ relate to _____ ? Could you give me an example? Why do you say that?
Questions that probe *Assumptions*	All of your reasoning seems to be based on the idea that _____. Why have you based your reasoning on _____ rather than _____ ? Is that always the case? Why do you think that assumption holds here? What could we assume instead? How would that change our conclusions?
Questions that probe for *Reasons and Evidence*	What is your reason for saying that? What other information do we need to know? Is there reason to doubt the evidence or sources of our information? What led you to that conclusion? What would convince you otherwise?
Questions about *Viewpoints or Perspectives*	You seem to be approaching the issue from _____ perspective. Why have you chosen this rather than that perspective? How might other groups/people respond to this issue? What would someone who disagrees say? How are Ken and Roxanne's ideas alike? How are they different?
Questions that probe *Implications and Consequences*	What are you implying by your statement? But if that happened, what else would happen as a result? What effect would that have?

Adapted from Paul, R., Binker, A. J. A., Martin, D., & Adamson, K. (1989). *Critical Thinking Handbook: High School.* Rohnert Park, CA: Center for Critical Thinking and Moral Critique.

ducing different types of questioning, can take three main forms (Paul, Binker, Martin, & Adamson, 1989):

- **Spontaneous discussion** can provide a model of listening critically and exploring personal beliefs. It is especially useful when students become interested in a topic, when they raise an important issue during class, or when they are on the brink of grasping an idea.

- In an **exploratory discussion,** the teacher raises questions in order to assess students' prior knowledge and values and to uncover their beliefs or biases. Exploratory discussion also can be used to identify areas where students' thinking is fuzzy or unclear.

- **Issue-specific discussion** is used to "explore an issue or concept in depth, evaluate thoughts and perspectives, distinguish the known from the unknown, and synthesize relevant factors and knowledge" (Paul et al., 1989, p. 28).

Example 14.1 provides general questions that can be used effectively in any of these discussion formats. In order to maximize critical thinking during class discussion, teachers need to provide sufficient **wait time** by pausing for several seconds after posing a question to give students time to think before they are called on to respond (Tobin, 1987). When teachers wait an average of at least 3 seconds after posing a question, the result is greater student-to-student interaction during learning and increased student participation in class discussions (Honea, 1982; Swift & Gooding, 1983).

In recent years, researchers have explored the use of online discussion formats as a vehicle for higher-order thinking (Dutton, Dutton, & Perry, 2002; Garrison, Anderson, & Archer, 2001). Content analyses of online discussions have shown that students' messages are lengthy and cognitively deep, incorporating critical thinking skills such as inference and judgment as well as metacognitive strategies related to reflecting on experience and self-awareness (Hara, Bonk, & Angeli, 2000). While there are advantages to holding discussions in either setting (face-to-face or online), well-structured online discussions can expand the time spent focusing on course objectives and allow more time for reflection (Meyer, 2003; Yang & Ahn, 2007). In order to extend the uses of discussion, teachers can do the following things (Pierce, Lemke, & Smith, 1988):

Metacognition: See Module 12.

- break down an initial exploratory discussion about a complex issue into simpler parts and have students choose aspects they want to research or explore, or

- have students write summaries immediately after a discussion, allowing them to work together to fill in gaps, provide clarification, or add new thoughts or questions.

WRITING TECHNIQUES

Writing and cognition: See page 218.

Although the importance of writing as a basic skill has always been recognized, it was Raymond Nickerson (1984) who first noted the value of writing as a tool for enhancing higher-order thinking. Composing a piece of writing is a complex task that involves planning, reviewing, weighing alternatives, and making critical decisions (Marzano, 1995; Scardamalia & Bereiter, 1986). A great advantage of writing is its versatility—teachers can utilize writing in virtually every content area (Martin, 1987). Journal writing is a format commonly used in classrooms to enhance students' understanding of content, elucidate students' thinking processes in a way that teachers can react to, and provide opportunities for self-reflection (Marzano, 1993). Teachers need to be aware that many students experience a delay in being able to transfer the skills of problem-solving, reasoning, and justifying from oral discourse to written text, and so teachers must provide the necessary instruction and reflective guidance for these skills to emerge (Gillies & Khan, 2009).

HYPOTHESIS TESTING

Hypothesis testing involves examining research data and results to determine what conclusions reasonably can be drawn to support or refute a stated hypothesis. In an elementary classroom, a teacher might organize students into groups and present each group with a tray of materials to use in making a small lightbulb work. The students would begin by forming hypotheses about how the materials could be used in combination to make their lightbulb turn on and would follow up by actually testing their hypotheses. Hypothesis testing is germane not only to science activities but to other disciplines as well. For example, students in a literature class might be asked to form hypotheses about how they think a story will end based on what they have read so far and then be asked to compare their hypotheses with the actual ending.

INDUCTIVE REASONING AND DEDUCTIVE REASONING

Teachers can provide opportunities for students to practice **inductive reasoning,** logical thinking that moves from specific examples to formulation of a general principle. For example, a teacher might present a set of souvenirs from different countries and have students work together to discover a general principle that describes what all the items have in common. Students also can benefit from activities that require them to use **deductive reasoning,** a form of logical thinking that moves from the general to the specific. For example, if a student is presented with several characteristics of Native Americans and asked to identify which tribe the characteristics best describe, the student must use deductive reasoning. When Sherlock Holmes takes a general set of clues and pieces them together to find the solution to a crime, he is using deductive reasoning—moving from the general to the specific.

ARGUMENT ANALYSIS

Argument analysis involves challenging students to evaluate reasons critically in order to discriminate between those that support a particular conclusion and those that do not. For example, a teacher might organize a class debate on the merits of wearing school uniforms, with one side presenting arguments for the wearing of uniforms and the other side presenting arguments against. Each side not only would present its own arguments, but also would analyze the arguments presented by its opponents in order to decide which were valid in support of the conclusion being drawn.

Deductive Reasoning. Detective Sherlock Holmes said, "If you eliminate the impossible, whatever remains—however improbable—must be the truth." Like Holmes, students reason deductively, narrowing the possibilities and drawing conclusions based on the available evidence.

EXAMPLE 14.2   **Tips for Creating a Classroom Environment Conducive to Critical Thinking**

Model critical thinking skills and dispositions.

Explain different thinking strategies and focus students' attention on important aspects of critical thought (e.g., examining evidence).

Reward good critical thinking.

Challenge poor critical thinking.

Actively engage students in critical thinking by providing diverse contexts for practicing reasoning skills.

Create a climate of reasoned inquiry through assignments, class discussions, and collaborative learning.

Encourage metacognition by teaching students how to examine their own thinking processes.

Sources: Facione, Facione, & Giancarlo, 2000; Tishman, Perkins, & Jay, 1995.

While specific teaching strategies are useful, the intellectual climate of the classroom is equally important in fostering critical thinking. Students need an open, stimulating, supportive climate in which they are encouraged to explore and express opinions, examine alternative positions on controversial topics, and justify their beliefs (Glassner & Schwarz, 2007; Gough, 1991). See Example 14.2 for a summary of tips for creating a classroom environment conducive to critical thinking.

Think about the classrooms you have spent time in over the years, and identify specific classroom events or assignments that fostered critical thinking. How does the promotion of critical thinking vary by grade level or by discipline?

PROBLEM SOLVING

Critical thinking is an important part of defining and solving problems. In everyday situations, we are called on to solve problems of various levels of complexity. Let's consider what the problem-solving process involves.

What Is Problem Solving?

A **problem,** quite simply, is any situation in which you are trying to reach some goal and you need to find a means to do so. It has a starting point, a goal (desired outcome), and one or more paths for achieving that goal. **Problem solving** is the means we use to reach a goal in spite of an obstacle or obstacles. Some problems have clear goals and solutions; others don't. Problems can range from well defined to ill defined, depending on a variety of problem characteristics (Hamilton & Ghatala, 1994). In **well-defined problems,** a goal is clearly stated, all the information needed to solve the problem is available, and only one correct solution exists. For example, a kindergartener who needs to match the word *two* to its numeral faces a well-defined problem with a clear goal and a single answer. An **ill-defined problem** is one in which the desired goal may be unclear, information needed to solve the problem is missing, and/or several possible solutions exist. High school juniors who are participating in a discussion of First Amendment rights in a U.S. history course face an ill-defined problem because the specific goals are unclear, many important facts may not be in evidence, and there probably is more than one "right" answer.

Problem solving requires a complex range of skills that develop at different rates. There are developmental differences in the degree of flexibility in children's problem solving, as well as variability in their strategy choices across different educational contexts (Farrington-Flint, Vanuxem-Cotterill, & Stiller, 2009). Children are naturally curious and often will try to figure out solutions to problems on their own; however, their strategies may not be the most effective or efficient ways to approach the problem. Preschoolers are able to use available information appropriately in problem solving, but they often fail to identify or retrieve useful information from memory. Upper elementary students not only can use current information effectively but also can draw on prior knowledge to aid in understanding and solving a problem (Kemler, 1978). Older children remember what did or did not work on previous occasions and permanently reject hypotheses that failed, whereas young children are less likely to reflect on how well their previous strategies worked and may continue to use an ineffective strategy (Carr & Biddlecomb, 1998; Davidson & Sternberg, 1998).

Research on novice and expert problem solvers provides further information about how students' approaches to problem solving may differ based on their level of experience. Novice or inexperienced problem solvers tend to apply problem-solving strategies mindlessly or inflexibly, without any real understanding of what they are doing or why they are doing it (Carr & Biddlecomb, 1998; Davidson & Sternberg, 1998; Star & Rittle-Johnson, 2007). Expert problem solvers are more likely to do the following things (Bruning, Schraw, Norby, & Ronning, 2004; Chi, Glaser, & Farr, 1988; Star & Seifert, 2006):

- recognize potential problems,
- perceive meaningful patterns in the information they are given,
- perform tasks quickly and with few errors,
- hold a larger quantity of information in working and long-term memory,
- take time to carefully analyze a problem before implementing a solution,
- consider a broader range of strategies to solve the problem, and
- monitor their own performance and make adjustments.

Obstacles to Successful Problem Solving

Problem solving may break down due to the inexperience of the problem-solver or as a result of several cognitive obstacles. Let's examine each of these obstacles in turn.

- **Functional fixedness** is the inability to use objects or tools in a new way (Duncker, 1945). For example, you need to draw a straight line and have a ruler nearby; however, you are thinking of the ruler only as an instrument for measuring length, so you don't use it as a straightedge.

- **Response set** is our tendency to respond to events or situations in the way that is most familiar to us. Consider this problem: You are presented with Figure 14.1 and are asked to connect all the dots by drawing four lines or fewer without lifting your pen. The solution to this problem (found in Figure 14.2) requires breaking your response set and drawing lines that extend beyond the mental border you instinctively visualize around these dots.

- **Belief perseverance** is the tendency to hold onto one's beliefs even in the face of contradictory evidence. For example, students tend to be overconfident about how quickly they can complete a writing assignment. Even when the writing process takes twice as long as they expect, students tend to remain overly confident and fail to adjust their estimates for future writing assignments (Buehler, Griffith, & Ross, 1994).

The common theme in all these obstacles is lack of flexibility. A rigid mindset narrows possibilities, while an open mind increases the chance that you will be able to reframe a problem in a way that suggests a workable solution. Though our mindsets can be very resistant to change, teaching approaches that help students identify obstacles, destabilize them through critical analysis, and reconstruct new understandings can be effective (Peterfalvi, 2001; Skoumios & Hatzinikita, 2008).

Application: Teaching Problem-Solving Strategies

Teachers can enhance students' problem-solving skills by teaching and modeling strategies that students will use frequently within a particular area, by providing students with general rules of thumb that may work in a variety of contexts, and by presenting varied contexts and opportunities for students to practice their problem-solving skills.

GENERAL AND SPECIFIC STRATEGIES

Problem-solving strategies often are specific to a particular content area (e.g., formulas for calculating area or perimeter; strategies for identifying common grammar or punctuation errors when editing a paper). Although content area often is very important, certain problem-solving strategies tend to be helpful across a variety of contexts (Davidson & Sternberg, 1998; Dominowski, 1998). John Bransford and Barry Stein (1993) use the acronym IDEAL to identify five important steps found in many different problem-solving approaches: (1) identify the problem, (2) define goals, (3) explore possible strategies, (4) anticipate outcomes, and (5) look back and learn. Table 14.3 describes each of these steps.

Figure 14.1. Mental Set Problem. Assume that you are given a sheet of paper showing these nine dots. Connect the nine dots with four straight lines. You must draw all four lines without lifting your pencil from the paper. You may not fold, cut, or tear the paper in any way.

TABLE 14.3 IDEAL Problem-Solving Steps	
Step	**Description**
Identify problems and opportunities	Identifying that a problem exists is a critical first step in the problem-solving process.
Define goals and represent the problem	Success in problem solving often depends on how one represents the problem. This step involves focusing on relevant information, understanding what the problem is asking, and activating prior knowledge schemas that might relate to the problem.
Explore possible strategies	Identify possible options and strategies that might be used to solve the problem.
Anticipate outcomes and *act*	Consider possible consequences of different strategies proposed in the previous step, and implement the chosen strategy.
Look back and *learn*	After implementing a strategy, evaluate whether the problem is solved effectively.

Source: Bransford & Stein, 1993.

People seem to move back and forth from general strategies, such as those described in the IDEAL method, to content-specific approaches, depending on the needs of the situation and their own level of expertise. When we have little experience in an area, we are more likely to rely on general knowledge and problem-solving strategies. However, as we develop expertise within a content area, we are more likely to apply specific strategies that we know are effective (Alexander, 1996).

ALGORITHMS AND HEURISTICS

Solutions to some problems can be found by using an **algorithm,** a prescribed sequence of steps for achieving a goal. For example, if you want to calculate the area of a cylinder and know its dimensions, you can apply a specific formula that will give you the correct answer. The problem-solving process may take a little time, but the solution is clearly achievable if the appropriate algorithm is chosen and its steps are followed accurately.

Not all problems come with directions to follow. In the absence of specific directions, you might need to use a heuristic to solve the problem at hand. A **heuristic** is a general problem-solving strategy that might lead to a right answer or to a solution that usually is reasonably close to the best possible answer. It's a rule of thumb, an educated guess, or common sense. Basically, algorithms use formal steps, while heuristics use informal rules of thumb. Algorithms seek accurate answers, while heuristics provide approximations. Students are using heuristics when they guess a close answer to a multiplication problem, rounding to the nearest large unit (for example, 19 times 18 is about 400); shoppers are using heuristics when they examine the price tag as an indicator of which electronic device probably has the most features. Heuristics help us narrow down possible solutions to find one that works (Stanovich & West, 2000).

Let's consider three common heuristics:

- **Means-end analysis** is a heuristic in which the main problem-solving goal is divided into subgoals. For example, the main goal of developing a classroom management plan for your first year of teaching could be broken down into subgoals of defining your rules, outlining your classroom procedures, arranging your classroom in an orderly way, and developing a schedule to help your students understand the classroom routine.

- The **working-backward strategy** is a systematic approach in which you start with the final goal and think backward to identify the steps necessary to reach that goal. For instance, students who have a major term paper due in three weeks can work backward to figure out how much time they will need to allow for each step in the research and writing process and set intermediate deadlines for themselves.

- **Analogical thinking** limits the search for solutions to situations that are most similar to the one at hand. A class that is analyzing sources of pollution in a local river might consider the sources of pollution in other waterways in the region for comparison.

GUIDELINES 14.1   Using Algorithms and Heuristics in Instruction

Use of algorithms

- Describe and demonstrate specific algorithms.

- Work on a particular problem together and talk students through each step of the algorithm.

- Help students learn to check their work and catch errors in their applications of an algorithm.

- Ask students to explain what they are doing as they work through a problem, or ask them to show their written work. This makes it easier for the teacher to pinpoint specific misunderstandings or errors and provide corrective feedback to the students.

- Define the situations in which the algorithms should be used. This step is essential. In math, for example, students may memorize formulas for calculating the area of different shapes; however, if they do not understand when to apply a particular formula, they will not be able to solve their math problems correctly.

Use of heuristics

- Teach students how to better define ill-defined problems. This may involve taking a large, vague problem and breaking it into several smaller problems or steps to be tackled.

- Teach students how to distinguish essential from nonessential information as they gather data to solve a problem.

- Show students where and how to find missing information that is needed for solving a problem.

- Give students the opportunity to problem-solve in groups. Group work can be fertile ground for problem solving if students have the opportunity to share ideas, model different approaches for one another, and discuss the merits of different approaches to solving a problem

Sources: Atkinson, Derry, Renkl, & Wortham, 2000; Renkl & Atkinson, 2003; Rogoff, 2003.

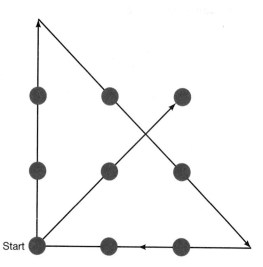

Figure 14.2. Solution to Mental Set Problem.
If you had never seen this problem before, you probably approached it with a specific set of expectations—you assumed the four lines had to remain within the perimeter of the nine dots. To solve the problem, you must go beyond the perimeter of the dots.

Explicit instruction in the use of algorithms and heuristics is very useful in helping students become better problem solvers (Dominowski, 1998; Kramarski & Mevarech, 2003). Guidelines 14.1 provides tips for instruction in the use of each of these problem-solving methods. In the real world, students are faced with many problems that are ill-defined and are not solvable by a clear algorithm. Teachers therefore need to pay particular attention to providing students with authentic learning experiences that give practice in solving complex problems (Resnick, 1988; Sternberg et al., 2000).

You may not have heard the terms algorithm *and* heuristic *prior to reading this module, but you undoubtedly have used these problem-solving strategies many times. In what situations have you used an algorithm to solve a problem? When have you used a heuristic?*

PROBLEM-BASED LEARNING

Problem-based learning (PBL) is experiential, hands-on learning organized around the investigation and resolution of ill-defined, real-world problems (Loyens, Kirschner, & Paas, 2009; Torp & Sage, 2002). PBL was designed to foster several learning outcomes (Hmelo-Silver, 2004; Loyens, Magda, & Rikers, 2008; Otting & Zwaal, 2006), namely to help students:

1. construct an extensive and flexible knowledge base,
2. become effective collaborators,
3. develop effective problem-solving skills,
4. become intrinsically motivated to learn, and
5. develop self-directed learning skills.

Imagine that you want to teach your students how to identify minerals. A traditional lesson might involve providing students with several tools (for example, mineral key, pictures of crystal shapes, streak plate, glass plate, nail, penny, weak acid, hand lens), a step-by-step demonstration of how to use the tools, and an activity in which students are asked to identify minerals based on the demonstrated procedure. In a PBL unit designed to cover the same curriculum, you might tell your students that they are playing the roles of geologists. Their task is to identify the minerals at a couple of local sites in order to facilitate the modification of local zoning ordinances. Tools and various minerals are made available, and the students work in small groups to identify the minerals. The lesson content in each case is similar; however, the PBL lesson is designed to engage students' curiosity and tie their learning to a real-life context.

PBL has its challenges. The emphasis on personal responsibility and self-directedness can result in student confusion, lack of shared vision, insufficient teacher feedback, and poor communication of expectations (Maudsley, Williams, & Taylor, 2008; Nel et al., 2008; Park & Ertmer, 2008; Spronken-Smith & Harland, 2009). Students experience PBL differently—many find it stimulating and challenging—but the added personal responsibility leaves others feeling anxious and seriously hindered in their learning process (Duke, Forbes, Hunter, & Prosser, 1998). Studies reporting challenges with the implementation of PBL have led to investigation of how these concerns can be addressed (Ertmer et al., 2009). Suggestions for more effective implementation include provision of online resources to better prepare students, evaluation of group discussion and functioning, and efficient time use (for example, asking students to identify central issues of the problem before class and then share and discuss them in class) (Vardi & Ciccarelli, 2008).

Problem-Based Learning. Experiential, hands-on learning is centered around real-world problems.

What elements of problem-based learning have you been exposed to as a student? Do you think PBL is a valuable approach? Why or why not?

Summary

Explain the difference between a higher-order thinking skill and a thinking disposition, and discuss why both skills and dispositions are important. Empirical research has shown that thinking skills and thinking dispositions are two distinct entities. Higher-order thinking skills reflect an individual's ability to manipulate and transform information to solve problems or make decisions. Thinking dispositions reflect an individual's consistent internal motivation to use thinking skills. Having the ability to engage in higher-order thinking does not guarantee the disposition to do so; therefore, teachers must understand how to build intellectual skills in students as well as how to foster the dispositions to use those skills on a regular basis.

Explain what critical thinking means. Critical thinking is the process of evaluating the accuracy and worth of information and lines of reasoning. During the critical thinking process, students deconstruct a problem or an issue to identify and carefully consider characteristics such as (1) the frames of reference or points of view involved, (2) the assumptions being made, (3) the evidence or reasons being advanced, (4) the validity of the interpretations and claims being made, and (5) the implications and consequences that follow from a particular decision.

Identify five instructional strategies that can be used to foster critical thinking. Teachers can use one of five popular and effective strategies for promoting critical thinking: (1) Questioning techniques to help identify students' prior knowledge, clarify values, and uncover students' beliefs or biases. (2) Writing techniques (in virtually every content area) to challenge students to plan, review, weigh alternatives, and make critical decisions. (3) Hypothesis testing to foster examination of research data and results, and to determine what conclusions reasonably can be drawn. (4) Inductive and deductive reasoning to spur students to formulate a general principle from specific examples (inductive), or to discern a solution from a general set of clues (deductive). (5) Argument analysis to challenge students to evaluate reasons critically and discriminate between those that support a particular conclusion and those that do not.

Define problem solving and explain the difference between a well-defined problem and an ill-defined problem. A problem is any situation in which you are trying to reach some goal and need to find a means to do so. Problem solving has a starting point, a goal (desired outcome), and one or more paths for achieving that goal. A well-defined problem is one in which a goal is clearly stated, all the information needed to solve the problem is available, and only one correct solution exists. An ill-defined problem is one in which the desired goal is unclear, information needed to solve the problem is missing, and/or several possible solutions to the problem exist.

Discuss the roles of algorithms, heuristics, the IDEAL approach, and problem-based learning in teaching problem solving. An algorithm is a prescribed sequence of steps for achieving a goal. A heuristic is a general problem-solving strategy that might lead to a right answer or to a solution that usually is reasonably close to the best possible answer. The difference between *algorithms* and *heuristics* basically comes down to formal steps leading to an accurate answer versus informal rules of thumb that provide an approximation. The acronym IDEAL identifies five important steps found in many different problem-solving approaches: (1) identify the problem, (2) define the goals, (3) explore possible strategies, (4) anticipate outcomes, and (5) look back and learn. Problem-based learning (PBL) is experiential, hands-on learning organized around the investigation and resolution of messy, real-world problems.

Key Concepts

algorithm 247

analogical thinking 247

argument analysis 244

belief perseverance 246

critical thinking 241

deductive reasoning 244

exploratory discussion 243

functional fixedness 246

heuristic 247

higher-order thinking 239

hypothesis testing 244

ill-defined problem 245

inductive reasoning 244

issue-specific discussion 243

means-ends analysis 247

problem 245

problem-based learning (PBL) 248

problem solving 245

response set 246

spontaneous discussion 243

thinking dispositions 240

wait time 243

well-defined problems 245

working-backward strategy 247

Video Applications

www.mhhe.com/bohlin2e

Video 1: Reasoning and hypothesis testing in elementary school (*5 minutes*)
In this series of short clips, teachers demonstrate different ways to foster critical thinking among elementary students.

Clip 1 (first-grade classroom): *Inductive reasoning*

Clip 2 (first-grade classroom): *Working backward strategy*

Clip 3 (kindergarten classroom): *Deductive reasoning*

Clip 4 (fourth-grade classroom): *Hypothesis testing*

Video 2: Critical Thinking and Problem Solving (*4½ minutes*)
In this video, third-grade teacher Michelle Webb uses a crime lab simulation to enhance her students' critical thinking and problem-solving skills.

Clip 1: *Introducing the forensic lab*

Clip 2: *Recap of prior findings*

Clip 3: *Doing a thorough job before drawing conclusions*

Clip 4: *Use of questioning*

Clip 5: *Red herrings*

Clip 6: *Who looked guilty?*

Case Studies
Reflect and Evaluate

EARLY CHILDHOOD: "Air"

These questions refer to the case study on page 202.

1. What thinking dispositions did Ms. Carson foster in her classroom? How would you describe the motivation and engagement level of her students?

2. Describe how Ms. Carson used questioning techniques to promote critical thinking during the experiment with the cork and the cup.

3. How did Ms. Carson challenge her students to think critically during the discussion of kite aerodynamics?

4. Was the kite project an example of a well-defined or an ill-defined problem? Explain.

5. Which steps of the IDEAL problem-solving sequence did you notice during the kite project?

ELEMENTARY SCHOOL: "Reading About Pirates"

These questions refer to the case study on page 204.

1. How would you describe Kiana's thinking dispositions during the reading rotations?

2. Which features of higher-order thinking, if any, did you see represented in the learning events that transpired in Mr. McPherson's classroom?

3. Was Mr. McPherson's assignment for the students completing the short story booklets at their seats beneficial, or could he have given them a more thought-provoking assignment? Explain.

4. How could Mr. McPherson incorporate aspects of critical thinking into his reading-group activities?

5. What steps of the IDEAL problem-solving model did you see used in this case?

MIDDLE SCHOOL: "King Washington"

These questions refer to the case study on page 206.

1. Which thinking dispositions did you see represented in the learning events that transpired in Mr. Radcliffe's classroom?

2. How could Mr. Radcliffe's discussion of George Washington promote students' critical thinking about the concept of leadership?

3. What dimensions of critical thought should Mr. Radcliffe consider when evaluating his students' thinking during the Continental Congress activity?

4. Does the Continental Congress activity present students with a well-defined or an ill-defined problem to solve? Explain.

5. Is the Continental Congress activity an example of problem-based learning as defined in your reading? Explain.

HIGH SCHOOL: "I Don't Understand"

These questions refer to the case study on page 208.

1. What thinking dispositions could Ms. Park have tried to enhance in order to facilitate students' learning of the new math concept?

2. How might *belief perseverance* have interfered with students' decision making about how to approach the math problems?

3. Did the type of problems Ms. Park assigned require the use of algorithms or the use of heuristics? Explain.

4. What steps from the IDEAL model could have been utilized by Ms. Park's students?

unit five

Case Studies

Early Childhood: "The Worksheets"

Elementary School: "Writer's Block"

Middle School: "The Math Review"

High School: "Exam Grades"

Module 15:
Behavioral Theory

Outline and Learning Goals ooo

A Behavioral Definition of Motivation ooo

Rewarding Students for Learning ooo

Praising Students for Learning ooo

When the Reward Is the Activity Itself ooo

Summary ooo

Key Concepts ooo

Video Applications ooo

Case Studies: Reflect and Evaluate ooo

motivation

Module 16:
Cognitive Theories

Outline and Learning Goals ooo

Cognitive Theories of Motivation ooo

Developmental and Cultural Differences in Motivation ooo

Applications: Enhancing Students' Motivation ooo

Serious Motivational Problems ooo

Summary ooo

Key Concepts ooo

Video Applications ooo

Case Studies: Reflect and Evaluate ooo

Module 17:
Self Theories

Outline and Learning Goals ooo

Self-Efficacy Theory ooo

Self-Worth Theory ooo

Self-Determination Theory ooo

Integrating the Self Theories ooo

Summary ooo

Key Concepts ooo

Video Applications ooo

Case Studies: Reflect and Evaluate ooo

Prepare:

As you read the case, make notes:

1. **WHO** are the central characters in the case? Describe them.

2. **WHAT** is taking place?

3. **WHERE** is the case taking place? Is the environment a factor?

4. **WHEN** is the case taking place? Is the timing a factor?

Elizabeth Garvey, a second-year teacher at Fitzgerald Elementary School, enjoys teaching kindergarten because the children are eager to learn new things and approach each new experience with excitement. As with any kindergarten class, it is typical for some students to have trouble adjusting to the structured, academic environment of elementary school. Elizabeth tries to balance formal instruction with opportunities for social interaction and play. This year seems especially challenging, as she has a large class of 21 students with diverse backgrounds. Three students are English-language learners, many students have had no preschool experience, and there are large disparities in readiness skills among the children.

After morning meeting, during which Mrs. Garvey and the children go over the date, the day's weather, the lunch count, and any special news or events, Mrs. Garvey begins a

Early Childhood

The Worksheets

lesson on math concepts that includes a game of "Numbers I Spy." After the group lesson, the children return to their seats to complete some worksheets. Mrs. Garvey gives them instructions to match digits on the left side of the page to sets of objects on the right side of the page. She shows them how to complete the first one, drawing a line from the number 5 to the five hats. "When you're finished, use the color key at the bottom of the page to color the sets of objects," Mrs. Garvey says, pointing to the bottom of the page.

As the children begin working, Mrs. Garvey walks around the room to check on their progress. She notices Melissa coloring instead of doing the worksheet. "Melissa, why haven't you started your math sheet?" whispers Mrs. Garvey.

"I can't do it," replies Melissa, slouching in her chair.

"I know you can do it if you just try," says Mrs. Garvey with a reassuring smile. Melissa tends to need a little extra coaxing and then ends up doing fine work. "I'll come back and check on you."

Melissa has been raised by her grandmother since she was a year old. From the age of 3, she has attended Head Start, a preschool program for economically disadvantaged children. Her academic skills are steadily improving, but she still lacks confidence in her abilities.

As Mrs. Garvey continues moving around the room, she notices Emanuel, Kristina, and Martin at the building center playing with Legos. She approaches the children and says, "Now is not the time for building."

"But we're already done with our math sheets!" exclaims Martin. "I already know numbers and adding so I don't need to do baby worksheets. My mom says I'm smart at math."

"Yes, I know you three are good at doing math," Mrs. Garvey says. "Show me your worksheets so I can check to see if they are correct and neatly colored, and then you can play with the blocks while the others finish."

Because Mrs. Garvey needs to follow the district's curriculum, she often lets advanced students play while others finish their work. She's not sure whether their playing affects other students' motivation, though. She always has a few students who want to rush through their work so they can play as well.

Mrs. Garvey walks past the next table and says, "Nice work, Alannah and Mahiro!" She then stops at Kayvon, and leans over his shoulder saying, "The seven fish don't go with that number, Kayvon. It's this one. Count them with me."

Tugging at her shirt is Claire. Claire is anxiously waiting for Mrs. Garvey to check her answers, as she does with all her work, even art projects. Claire never wants to get anything wrong.

"Mrs. Garvey, I'm done with the numbers. Are they all right? I want to color the pictures now," says Claire. Mrs. Garvey glances at the sheet and gives her a nod. *Everyone looks like they're doing fine,* she thinks as she goes back to check on Melissa and Kayvon.

Assess

1. How motivated do you think Melissa, Martin, Kayvon, and Claire are to learn in this case study? What evidence supports your point of view?

2. In your opinion, should Mrs. Garvey allow Martin and the others to play while they wait for other students to finish their work? Why or why not?

3. Which student's motivation would you be concerned with most? Why?

Prepare:

As you read the case, make notes:

1. **WHO** are the central characters in the case? Describe them.

2. **WHAT** is taking place?

3. **WHERE** is the case taking place? Is the environment a factor?

4. **WHEN** is the case taking place? Is the timing a factor?

Yuiko Okuda is a third-grade teacher at White Eagle Elementary School who believes that hands-on experiences are essential to students' understanding and skill development. Mrs. Okuda uses many different activities to help her students improve their writing skills. Every week, she has her students write a letter home to their parents about what they have learned in school that week, any upcoming events they are looking forward to, and any exciting activities they will be participating in. Most of the students enjoy writing letters home to their parents. Every Thursday morning Mrs. Okuda uses another activity, called "free writing," in which students are given 30 minutes to write about a given subject, such as a favorite season or family traditions. Mrs. Okuda gives the essays a grade based on whether or not they are completed. She displays them all on the bulletin board outside the classroom.

Elementary School
Writer's Block

This Thursday morning Mrs. Okuda announces, "The topic of the day today will be your favorite pastime during summer vacation. After you've completed your assignment, you may read, use the computer, or play a board game quietly at the back of the class." James, Zara, Ronnie, and Shanti begin chatting as they quickly take out a piece of paper to start writing.

"I love writing!" says Shanti, eagerly beginning her assignment.

"I like that we get to show the other kids in the school our writing work," whispers Zara.

"I just like to write about things I like. It's more fun than other subjects like reading," adds James. "Plus we don't get graded on it." James dislikes reading and would much rather be doing math, playing sports, or using the classroom computer. But he generally likes school and is a good student because his parents have tried to instill in him the value of hard work and a good education.

Carter takes out a piece of paper and a pencil, writes his name at the top of the page, and then turns pale, quietly staring at the blank paper. Carter is a high-achieving and popular student who turns in letters to parents, journals, and other writing assignments that have all been above average. But he seems to have difficulty when it comes to the free writing activity. Lately he has asked to go to the nurse after Mrs. Okuda announces the topic, but Mrs. Okuda has caught on to his attempt to avoid the assignment.

Mrs. Okuda notices Carter's demeanor and asks, "What's wrong, Carter?"

"I don't know what to write about," Carter replies, as he typically says at every free-writing activity. "I want this to be the *best* story, but I don't know where to start."

Mrs. Okuda sits down with Carter and begins to help him brainstorm. "What was the most fun for you during your last summer vacation?"

"I went on a sailboat for the first time!" Carter replies. A smile spreads across his face and he begins to write.

Before Mrs. Okuda returns to her desk, she walks by Mason to see how he is doing. Mason has a learning disability in reading and spelling and usually needs some help with writing, although he never asks for it. She is happy to see Mason working hard. "Here's a suggestion. Try to use more adjectives so that the story is more descriptive," Mrs. Okuda says as she glances over his shoulder.

After about 15 minutes, Shanti and James place their essays on Mrs. Okuda's desk. Shanti heads to the reading corner with a book from the shelf, and James hurriedly walks over to the computer before anyone else gets there. Mrs. Okuda glances over their essays and gets up.

At the reading corner, she whispers, "Great use of vocabulary in your story, Shanti." She then goes over to the computer, kneels by James, and sternly says, "James, your thoughts are very incomplete and you've forgotten about the rules of punctuation. Go back to your seat and finish your work. I know you can do better than that."

Assess

1. Which student do you identify with and why? In your own words, describe this student's motivation.

2. Do you think it is okay for Mrs. Okuda to allow the students to read, use the computer, or play a board game quietly at the back of the class after completing their assignments? What might be some problems with this? What might be some alternatives?

3. In your opinion, is Mrs. Okuda's practice of hanging all the papers on the bulletin board outside the classroom a good idea? Why or why not?

Prepare:

As you read the case, make notes:

1. **WHO** are the central characters in the case? Describe them.

2. **WHAT** is taking place?

3. **WHERE** is the case taking place? Is the environment a factor?

4. **WHEN** is the case taking place? Is the timing a factor?

A s the bell rings for the start of third period at Washington Middle School, Jack Pantera announces to his eighth-grade class, "Today we'll be doing a math review for the state mastery test next week." The room fills with groans and sighs. Mr. Pantera understands the students' reaction, but he also realizes the importance of this test. Last year Washington Middle School did not meet its annual goals for math, with only 27% of the eighth graders in the district performing at the proficiency level.

"Come on, everyone, we're going to make this fun," he explains. "I've assigned all of you to four-member teams. Each of you will be given a set of problems and will first work on the problems by yourselves. When everyone on the team is done, you will compare answers and work together to make sure everyone understands how to solve the problems. The first team to finish all the problems correctly gets a prize, and . . ."

Middle School

The Math Review

"What is it?!" Jeremy interrupts.

"That's a surprise," Mr. Pantera replies. "Let me finish. If *all* teams complete the problem set correctly by the end of the period, the entire class will get a surprise."

Mr. Pantera hopes the prize will encourage students to work together and help each other. Some students in the class are very skilled in math, and others either struggle with math concepts or have anxiety about math.

While students are working in their teams, Mr. Pantera moves around the room to monitor their progress. As Mr. Pantera approaches the first team, he notices Aaron missing. Aaron had gone to sharpen pencils and stopped to talk to Ben. "Aaron, this isn't time for socializing. You should be helping your team. I see you haven't even started the problems yet," says Mr. Pantera, a bit exasperated. Aaron appears to lack a strong work ethic, although he gets good grades.

"Team Two looks like a contender for the first prize. Everyone's working hard!" Mr. Pantera announces. He stops at the next team because he notices Sam erasing all her answers. "Sam, what are you doing?" he asks.

"I'm no good at math. All my answers are wrong," she replies, holding back tears.

"How do you know they're wrong? Sam, you just need a little confidence in yourself," says Mr. Pantera, a bit perplexed. "You get As on all your homework assignments and got a B– on the midterm exam. I'd say you're doing fine," Mr. Pantera says, trying to be reassuring.

"That's just it. I think I know the stuff. But when it comes time for an exam or a competition like this, I go blank! I must not be smart at math," Sam sighs.

"Math is about working hard and practicing. Just try a little harder and I'm sure it will pay off," says Mr. Pantera.

"But Aaron doesn't try at all and he gets As," Sam retorts.

Knowing that he has to check on the other groups, Mr. Pantera discourages Sam from comparing herself to other students, asks her to finish the problems, and suggests that they talk further after class.

Mr. Pantera overhears some arguing and heads over to Team Five to check out the disturbance. "Hurry up, you guys! I want to win this prize," Jeremy shouts to Gabriel and Rachel.

"I want to be sure I understand how to do the problems myself before we all go over them. It's not all about the stupid prize, you know!" Rachel replies.

"Rachel's right," says Mr. Pantera, looking over Jeremy's shoulder. "Jeremy, you used all the correct procedures. But you should double-check your work. You made simple computation errors on three of the problems. Slow down and concentrate on what you're doing."

Mr. Pantera looks around at all the students and musters a serious tone. "I want to see everyone working together."

"We're all done," announces Renee from Team Four, with her hand raised. Mr. Pantera goes over to check the team's answers.

"We have a winner!" Mr. Pantera announces. "The remaining teams should keep working. We have 15 minutes left, and we can still get the class prize."

Assess

1. In your opinion, was it a good idea for Mr. Pantera to encourage his students to do math problems by making it into a friendly competition? Why or why not?

2. In your opinion, how effective was Mr. Pantera in motivating Sam? What would you have done differently?

3. What experiences have you had with state-wide or district-wide testing? How did these experiences affect your own motivation?

Prepare:

As you read the case, make notes:

1. **WHO** are the central characters in the case? Describe them.

2. **WHAT** is taking place?

3. **WHERE** is the case taking place? Is the environment a factor?

4. **WHEN** is the case taking place? Is the timing a factor?

It's Monday morning at Davis High School, which is located in a large metropolitan city and boasts a variety of programs such as Advanced Placement (AP) classes, vocational/technical, and the arts. Today, Curtis Womack, a first-year teacher, is handing back exams in his classes. As the bell rings for his second-period sophomore general science class, Mr. Womack begins distributing the exams and says, "Class, I'm very disappointed that the highest grade was a C+. But I must say that I'm not very surprised. Many of you turned in exams after only 20 minutes. With 25 multiple-choice questions and one essay, that meant you weren't putting a lot of effort into answering the questions. I don't know what's going on. Can you help me with this?"

"A C+ sounds pretty good," Reggie says with a sly smile.

High School

Exam Grades

"Yeah, pretty good for not studying," Tamika adds. "I mean we can drop the lowest grade we get, and we can even do an extra-credit project at the end of the marking period."

"But those options are supposed to help you get the *best* grade you can," replies Mr. Womack, "not make it easy for you to get out of work."

"Mr. Womack, I'm not trying to get out of work," Carla explains. "I just want to focus on my other classes, ones that are more important to my arts program, no offense!"

"Yeah, why do we need to know this stuff anyway?" adds Reggie. "It's not like we're going to be engineers or scientists, or something."

Mr. Womack's concern over his students' motivation is apparent. He spends almost half the period discussing their aspirations, motivation, and work habits. He is eager to understand their perspectives on school and ways to motivate them. But the day's schedule leaves him little time to think about it further. The bell rings, signaling the end of the period, and he begins gathering another set of exams to hand back to his next class, AP physics.

"Good morning, everyone. I have exams ready to hand back," Mr. Womack announces. The classroom fills with groans and sighs.

"Not to worry," says Mr. Womack, "the scores were actually quite good. The highest grade was an A–,—congratulations to Madelyn—and the lowest grade was a C–. There's definitely room for improvement, but you all are doing fine."

As Mr. Womack continues distributing the exams, Nicholas leans over to his longtime friend Chelsea and whispers, "What'd you get?"

Chelsea hesitates. "C+. I can't believe it. I've never gotten a C in my life," she admits. "What'd you get?"

"I got a C+ too," he says. "I guess we'll have to study harder next time if we want to get a good grade."

"That's just it. We've always gotten As and hardly ever studied," says Chelsea. She doesn't tell her best friend that she *did* study and wondered whether he did too.

After class, Chelsea approaches Mr. Womack about her grade. "Mr. Womack, I'm not sure what to do. I studied for the exam and am not happy with my grade. I think I want to drop AP physics and take another science class," Chelsea says.

"I wouldn't make such a drastic decision based on one test score, Chelsea. I'm sure you'll improve next time. Maybe you just need to study more," replies Mr. Womack. "Tell me, why did you choose AP physics in the first place?"

"Because I like math and science, and my dad's an engineer, and ever since I can remember I've wanted to be an engineer too. I figured AP physics might be a good preparation for an engineering major in college."

"So you want to give up your dream?" Mr. Womack persists.

"No, uh, I don't know. I know I don't want to fail or hurt my GPA. That will hurt my chances of getting into a good college. That is, if I even want to choose engineering. I must not be as good at science as I thought. I was always the 'smart' kid in the class. Getting a C+ must mean I'm stupid compared to the other kids."

"No, I wouldn't say that at all," says Mr. Womack in a reassuring tone. "I say sleep on this and let's talk more tomorrow."

Assess

1. Which student do you identify with in terms of motivation? Why?

2. What recommendations would you give to Mr. Womack for dealing with Chelsea? For dealing with students in general science?

3. Do you think it was a good idea for Mr. Womack to announce who received the highest grade in the AP physics class? Why or why not?

MODULE 15

Behavioral Theory

Outline	Learning Goals
A Behavioral Definition of Motivation	
■ Defining Intrinsic and Extrinsic Motivation ■ Factors Influencing Intrinsic and Extrinsic Motivation	1. Explain how motivation changes from elementary through middle school, and discuss what factors might account for this trend.
Rewarding Students for Learning	
■ Task-Contingent and Performance-Contingent Rewards ■ Applications: Using Rewards Effectively	2. Explain why task-contingent rewards tend to diminish intrinsic motivation and performance-contingent rewards tend to enhance intrinsic motivation.
Praising Students for Learning	
■ Process, Performance, and Person Praise ■ Applications: Using Praise Effectively	3. Discuss the conditions under which praise can enhance or diminish intrinsic motivation, and explain individual and developmental differences in the effectiveness of praise.
When the Reward Is the Activity Itself	
■ Flow Theory ■ Applications: Creating an Intrinsically Motivating Learning Environment	4. Discuss methods teachers can use to create an intrinsically motivating learning environment.
Summary **Key Concepts** **Video Applications** **Case Studies: Reflect and Evaluate**	

A BEHAVIORAL DEFINITION OF MOTIVATION

Many students pursue careers in teaching because they were once inspired by a teacher. For teachers, can anything be more gratifying than sparking students' interest in school subjects and fostering a love of learning in young minds? The importance of motivation to student success begins early and remains significant through adolescence (Gottfried, Fleming, & Gottfried, 2001; Vansteenkiste, Simons, Lens, Sheldon, & Deci, 2004).

Defining Intrinsic and Extrinsic Motivation

Most early research on motivation was rooted in the study of behavioral learning theory, specifically the theory of operant conditioning. It suggests that an individual who receives **reinforcement,** a positive consequence for a behavior, would be likely to perform the behavior again under similar circumstances (Skinner, 1953). Reinforcement, in other words, can motivate behavior. Early researchers called this **extrinsic motivation,** meaning it is "external" to the behavior—in other words, participants engage in an activity to obtain an outcome that is distinct from the activity itself (deCharms, 1968; Lepper & Greene, 1978). Extrinsic motivators can be tangible—such as trophies, awards, stickers, prizes, and grades on report cards—or they can be intangible, such as praise, attention, or recognition.

Operant conditioning: See page 161.

Of course, individuals do not need external incentives for some activities, such as reading or playing video games. When the reward is an intrinsic part of the activity itself, it is called **intrinsic motivation.** Humans and many animals engage in many exploratory and curiosity-driven behaviors in the absence of reinforcement (White, 1959). For example, young children build towers of blocks, color, and play dress-up with no need for extrinsic rewards. Elementary-school children enjoy recreational reading, adolescents blog or listen to music, and adults engage in hobbies. In school, teachers strive to encourage **academic intrinsic motivation,** which is an orientation toward learning characterized by curiosity; persistence; attraction to challenging, novel tasks; and a focus on mastery of knowledge and skills (Gottfried, Fleming, & Gottfried, 1994; Gottfried & Gottfried, 1996).

Think of some ways in which you are intrinsically and extrinsically motivated. For example, list three activities you do now that you wouldn't do without some external reward.

Factors Influencing Intrinsic and Extrinsic Motivation

Researchers now believe that discussing motivation as intrinsic or extrinsic may oversimplify what's really happening. Many learning activities are both intrinsically and extrinsically motivating. Students reading this textbook might work hard in their course because they enjoy learning about educational psychology *and* because they want to get a good grade. The issue may not be whether a student is extrinsically *or* intrinsically motivated, but *when* and *how much*—under what conditions and to what degree the student is extrinsically *and/or* intrinsically motivated.

Students' upbringing and cultural background can significantly influence their motivation:

DIVERSITY

- Children's early experiences at home may affect their motivation. Regardless of the family's socioeconomic level, cognitively stimulating home environments encourage academic intrinsic motivation through early adolescence. Conversely, parental reliance on extrinsic motivational practices to promote achievement may lower academic intrinsic motivation (Gottfried et al., 1994; Gottfried, Fleming, & Gottfried, 1998).

- Extrinsic and intrinsic motivation may be more interrelated in cultures that emphasize interdependence. Asian-American children view the desire to please adults (extrinsic) and intrinsic motivation as interrelated, whereas Caucasian children tend to view external pressures from adults and intrinsic motivation as distinct forces (Lepper, Corpus, & Iyengar, 2005).

Extrinsic rewards may not be necessary in early childhood because children at this developmental level generally are curious, inquisitive, and motivated to learn new things (Harter, 1978). Students tend to become less intrinsically motivated as they move from upper elementary grades through middle and high school (Lepper et al., 2005; Spinath & Spinath, 2005). They prefer less challenging tasks and show less interest in and curiosity about learning (Dotterer, McHale, & Crouter, 2009; Harter & Jackson, 1992). Students also tend to like reading, math, and science less as they advance in grade level (Gottfried et al., 2001; Jacobs, Lanza, Osgood, Eccles, & Wigfield, 2002).

The structure and climate of classrooms and schools in middle and high school may help explain the developmental trend toward extrinsically motivated learning. In middle and high schools, students

Competition and Extrinsic Motivation. This boy looking to see if he made the honor roll illustrates the increased academic competition in middle school and high school that can lead to greater extrinsic motivation.

have multiple teachers, switch classes, and often have schedules with academic subjects organized into short periods. Teachers in middle and high schools have many students to teach and tend to use more lecture and fewer hands-on activities. This may lead to *decontextualized learning*, where students do not see the relevance of academic material (Lepper et al., 2005). Middle and high schools also have stricter academic and behavioral policies than elementary schools, leading to a more extrinsic and controlling atmosphere (Eccles, Wigfield, & Schiefele, 1998; Lepper & Henderlong, 2000). As a result, students may have few opportunities to make decisions, encounter more rules and discipline, and experience poorer teacher-student relationships (Anderman & Maehr, 1994). As students progress beyond elementary school, they also experience a greater emphasis on performance goals such as looking smart and getting the highest grades rather than mastery and learning for the sake of learning (Lepper & Henderlong, 2000; Wigfield & Wagner, 2005). This increasing emphasis on competition among students can be seen in honor rolls, class rankings, and standardized testing. As children develop, they also spend more time comparing their own skills and performance in academic subjects with those of their classmates, which could lead to the increased competition and focus on performance goals that we see during adolescence (Wigfield & Wagner, 2005; Wigfield, Eccles, Schiefele, Roeser, & Davis-Kean, 2006).

All of these experiences lead students to become more extrinsically motivated and perhaps shift from an internal to an external locus of control. **Locus of control** is a belief that the result of one's behavior is due to either external factors outside one's control, such as luck or other people's behaviors (i.e., external locus), or internal factors under one's control, such as ability or effort (i.e., internal locus) (Rotter, 1966, 1990). Keep in mind that not all extrinsic motivators lead to an external locus of control or are detrimental to motivation. Extrinsic motivators can be an important part of teachers' motivational techniques when used appropriately. Let's look at two extrinsic approaches teachers use to encourage motivation for learning: rewards and praise.

REWARDING STUDENTS FOR LEARNING

Educators often attempt to stimulate students' intrinsic motivation for academic tasks by using extrinsic motivators. Teachers give tangible rewards such as stickers or smiley faces on classwork or homework that is well done, no-homework passes, or opportunities to pick a prize from a treasure box. They also use intangible rewards, such as extra time for recess or to chat with classmates, as rewards for completing required assignments or tasks (Premack, 1959, 1963). How do extrinsic motivators such as these affect students' intrinsic motivation?

Consider the Pizza Hut Book It!® national incentive program used by teachers to encourage interest in reading with about 10 million children each year. When students reach reading goals set by their teachers, they receive a voucher for a free personal pan pizza. According to the operant conditioning model, rewarding reading in this way will increase the likelihood that the behavior (reading) will be performed again, enhancing motivation to produce the behavior in that environment (Skinner, 1953).

The question, however, is whether students continue to read after they no longer receive rewards. Operant conditioning predicts that when the reward is withdrawn, individuals will perform the behavior just as frequently as they did before (Skinner, 1953). However, in classic experimental research, Edward L. Deci and colleagues provided the first evidence that individuals performed a task *less frequently* after withdrawal of extrinsic rewards than they did before rewards were introduced (Deci, 1971). Therefore, rewards actually *undermined* intrinsic motivation.

Rewards. Rewards can take many forms such as extra recess, stickers, no-homework passes, or choosing a toy from a treasure box, as shown here.

To use rewards effectively for enhancing intrinsic motivation, teachers should consider not only *what* rewards to offer and *why*, but also *how* and *when*. Rewards can have different effects on intrinsic motivation depending on several factors:

- the purpose of the reward,
- how students perceive the reward, and
- the context in which the reward is given.

Task-Contingent and Performance-Contingent Rewards

Task-contingent rewards are given for *participating in* an activity (a certificate or extra free time for working on a science project) or for *completing* an activity (a sticker for completing a set of math problems). Students tend to perceive task-contingent rewards as controlling—the student must only do what the teacher wants to get the reward. Such rewards undermine intrinsic motivation. When given task-contingent rewards, students show less interest in the activity and choose to engage in the activity less often than before the reward (Deci, Koestner, & Ryan, 1999a, 2001).

Like task-contingent rewards, educational practices that students perceive as controlling may also lead to diminished intrinsic motivation. These practices include:

- close monitoring by the teacher (Plant & Ryan, 1985),
- deadlines and imposed goals (Amabile, DeJong, & Lepper, 1976; Manderlink & Harackiewicz, 1984),
- threats and directives (e.g., "get started," or "no, do it this way") (Assor et al., 2005; Koestner, Ryan, Bernieri, & Holt, 1984),
- external evaluation (Harackiewicz, Manderlink, & Sansone, 1984; Hughes, Sullivan, & Mosley, 1985), and
- competition (Reeve & Deci, 1996; Vansteenkiste & Deci, 2003).

The effect of any of these educational practices, though, depends on the context and emphasis (Stipek, 2002). For example, goals may enhance intrinsic motivation if students are encouraged to participate in establishing the goals and if the emphasis is on mastery or personal growth (Deci, Koestner, & Ryan, 1999b; Stipek, 2002). In a competition, how students feel about the outcome is of primary importance. When students feel pressure to win above all else, even the winners experience diminished intrinsic motivation (Vansteenkiste & Deci, 2003). When students lose competitions, such as spelling bees, science fairs, or even receive a lower grade than other students, they still can feel enhanced intrinsic motivation if they receive positive feedback about their performance. Positive performance feedback, which provides students with information about mastery, can facilitate intrinsic motivation more than winning a competition (Vansteenkiste & Deci, 2003).

In contrast with task-contingent rewards, **performance-contingent rewards** are those given for doing well or achieving a certain level of performance (receiving a sticker for *correctly* completing all math problems). Students perceive such rewards to be informational—conveying meaningful feedback about one's achievement on a given task. Compared with task-contingent rewards, performance-contingent rewards are less likely to undermine intrinsic motivation. Students who receive performance-contingent rewards for successful performance on an activity continue to express interest and enjoyment in that activity, although they may choose to engage in the activity less frequently (Deci et al., 1999a). Performance-contingent rewards may enhance intrinsic motivation by providing positive feedback about students' competence (Cameron, 2001; Deci et al., 1999b).

Even performance-contingent rewards can undermine intrinsic motivation in certain situations. When students expect a performance-contingent reward for achieving a certain level of mastery, the anticipation of being evaluated may interfere with their intrinsic interest in the subject (Harackiewicz, Manderlink, & Sansone, 1984). For example, elementary school students may be told in advance that if they earn an A on their math test, they will receive a no-homework pass, or high school students may know that if they pass a standardized test at the end of their AP History course, they can receive college credit. These students may be more focused on the anticipated evaluation and outcome than the subject matter itself.

Also, feedback that is negative may not enhance intrinsic motivation because the feedback suggests a lack of ability (Stipek, 2002). For example, in research that closely reflected what happens in classrooms, where only the top-performing participants received a reward and lower-performing participants received a smaller reward or no reward at all, performance-contingent rewards clearly undermined intrinsic motivation for individuals receiving lesser rewards (Deci et al., 2001).

Think of some instances when you have received rewards for learning in or out of school. Were these rewards task-contingent or performance-contingent, and did they increase or decrease your intrinsic motivation?

Applications: Using Rewards Effectively

Educators can adopt the following research-based guidelines for using rewards in ways that are minimally detrimental to intrinsic motivation (Deci et al., 2001):

Occasionally use unexpected rewards. Unexpected rewards, such as surprising students with a movie after a job well done on a group activity, do not significantly affect intrinsic motivation. Students are not specifically working for the opportunity to receive a reward and are more likely to be intrinsically motivated by the task (Cameron, 2001; Deci, Ryan, & Koestner, 2001).

Use expected tangible rewards sparingly. Expected tangible rewards (e.g., prizes or certificates) generally undermine intrinsic motivation, especially for children in elementary school (Deci et al., 1999a, 2001). Rewarding students in this way can cause them to shift from an internal to an external locus of control (Deci & Ryan, 1985). For example, if students who initially were interested in recreational reading receive rewards for reading, they may at first believe that they received rewards for their ability to read well (internal locus of control) but eventually may consider rewards as externally imposed constraints by the teacher (external locus of control). Over time, students may believe that their successful performance is due more to the reward than to internal causes such as ability, effort, or interest (Brockner & Vasta, 1981; Pittman, Cooper, & Smith, 1977). One exception may be tangible rewards that are related to the activity being rewarded, such as receiving a book as a reward for reading (Marinak & Gambrell, 2008).

Withdraw rewards as soon as possible. Rewards may be useful in situations where school tasks are necessary but seem to have little intrinsic value or interest to students. Elementary students may groan at practicing spelling words, middle school students may not particularly enjoy working through sets of math problems, and high school students may not initially appreciate reading the Greek tragedies. In these instances, educators can use rewards to draw students into an activity because students who develop an initial interest in a topic or activity are more likely to develop intrinsic motivation (Hidi, 2000). However, when teachers use rewards to encourage engagement in a task for which students have little initial interest, they should withdraw rewards as soon as possible to prevent students from engaging in the activity solely to get the reward (Stipek, 2002).

Use the most modest reward possible. Individuals will attribute their involvement in an activity to the most obvious explanation. Receiving a reward leads individuals to attribute their successful performance more to the reward itself—a very obvious reason for engaging in an activity—and less to internal causes such as intrinsic interest, enjoyment, or ability (Deci & Ryan, 1985; Deci et al., 1999a). As a result, individuals may shift from an internal to an external locus of control. The use of smaller rewards, however, will not become the primary reason for students' participation in a learning activity because they are not very prominent as explanations for student behavior (Stipek, 2002).

Make rewards contingent on quality of work (Ames & Ames, 1990; Deci, Eghrari, Patrick, & Leone, 1994). Remember that performance-contingent rewards are informational—conveying feedback about one's achievement on a given task. Teachers can give performance-contingent rewards to reinforce effort as well as achievement. Rewarding students' efforts toward mastering a particular task fosters intrinsic motivation (Harter, 1978). Performance-contingent rewards for increased effort and improvement over past performance may be especially beneficial to students who do not recognize that effort has an effect on task success (Seligman, 1994; Urdan, Midgley, & Anderman, 1998). Teaching them that effort leads to greater achievement will increase their achievement level (Craske, 1985; Van Overwalle & De Metsenaere, 1990).

Minimize the use of an authoritarian style. Authoritarian teaching styles that involve controlling language, directives, threats, and close monitoring have been shown to decrease students' intrinsic motivation (Deci et al., 1994; Koestner et al., 1984). Teachers should avoid using disapproval as a way to motivate students when they fail to achieve mastery on tasks. Punishment for failing to master a task inhibits intrinsic interest (Harter, 1978). Disapproval or punishment for failures also leads students to prefer easy tasks and thus to avoid risking the failure that sometimes occurs when initially attempting a challenging task (Stipek, 2002).

PRAISING STUDENTS FOR LEARNING

In some situations, the performance of a skill or behavior itself provides an individual with direct reinforcement (Stipek, 2002). A 5-year-old who successfully ties her shoes and an adolescent who beats his highest score on a video game have immediate feedback about mastery of their skills. In other situations, reinforcement of an individual's performance requires social input. Knowing that your batting swing has improved, your term paper is persuasive, or your homework assignment is correct requires feedback from an adult. In these cases, **praise,** or positive feedback in the form of written or spoken comments, is useful for providing individuals with feedback.

In developmental terms, praise has a limited window of effectiveness. Children younger than age 7 interpret praise as affirmation that they are pleasing authority figures, rather than as feedback about their performance (Brophy, 1981). Elementary school students tend to benefit from praise because they come to realize that praise should occur only after certain types of behavior, such as compliance and academic success. By the time students reach high school, however, they interpret praise from the teacher as an indication of low ability (Henderlong & Lepper, 2002). For praise to be effective with older students, it has to be sincere, provide positive information about one's competence, and not be given for tasks that are too easy (Henderlong & Lepper, 2002).

Praise may also benefit some students more than others because of the way they perceive the praise.

- Students with an external locus of control—a belief that teacher praise is caused by external factors (teacher's attitude or liking of them) rather than internal factors (their own success)—are more receptive to praise (Brophy, 1981).
- Lower-achieving students and students from lower socioeconomic backgrounds tend to benefit academically from praise. Students who are more likely to be discouraged academically may interpret teacher praise as more meaningful (Brophy, 1981).

DIVERSITY

Praise is widely recommended as a reinforcement method because it is free and has the potential to provide encouragement and enhance self-esteem (Brophy, 1981). Praise also may have positive effects partly because it is unexpected, leading students to believe that they genuinely have done something praiseworthy (Brophy, 1981; Deci et al., 1999a). However, like the rewards discussed earlier, praise can enhance or undermine intrinsic motivation depending on the type of praise, how it is given, and how it is perceived.

Process, Performance, and Person Praise

Teachers can give students process praise or performance praise as feedback to encourage improvement. **Process praise** is an evaluation of the process taken to complete a task—"What a careful job you did coloring inside the lines!" **Performance praise** (or outcome praise) is an evaluation of the end-product—"The argument in your term paper is clear and compelling" (Corpus & Lepper, 2007).

Researchers refer to process or performance praise as *informational praise* because it provides students with information about what they have done well and what to do the next time.

Informational praise enhances students' intrinsic motivation. Specific praise that provides detailed information about one's competence promotes a sense of mastery, leading to the following outcomes (Cameron, 2001; Corpus & Lepper, 2007; Zentall & Morris, 2010):

- increased interest;
- more positive self-evaluations;
- more positive attitudes about the activity;
- persistence after experiencing failure; and
- a greater likelihood of choosing the activity during free time.

Person praise involves a favorable judgment about a person's attributes or behaviors, such as "You're so good at math" (Corpus & Lepper, 2007). In contrast with process and performance praise, this form of praise does not indicate specifically what the student does well. It is also considered by researchers to be *controlling praise*. The teacher's favorable evaluation, rather than students' intrinsic interest or self-evaluation, provides the motivation. Students work to receive another favorable evaluation.

Entity view of ability: See page 282.

Learned helplessness: See page 292.

Self-worth: See page 303.

Person praise may be detrimental to intrinsic motivation. This form of praise may result in a belief that ability is fixed and uncontrollable—called an entity view of ability (Corpus & Lepper, 2007; Mueller & Dweck, 1998). This may lead students to acquire learned helplessness when faced with repeated failures (Kamins & Dweck, 1999). They attribute their failures to causes beyond their control and give up trying (Seligman & Maier, 1967). Person praise may also foster a poor sense of self-worth because it may teach students to make inferences about a global sense of worth based on their performance (Kamins & Dweck, 1999).

Like person praise, positive feedback given using controlling language, such as *should* and *ought*, tends to undermine intrinsic motivation even when teachers are attempting to give students encouragement (Kast & Connor, 1988; Ryan, Mims, & Koestner, 1983). An example is "Thank you for turning in neat homework. You should keep up the good effort." Instead, a teacher could say, "I've noticed your homework is neater; I appreciate your efforts."

DIVERSITY

Girls and boys react differently to person, process, and performance praise. In comparison with girls, elementary school boys are more intrinsically motivated by person praise, particularly praise of their ability when they succeed (Corpus & Lepper, 2007; Koestner, Zuckerman, & Koestner, 1989). Elementary school girls are more intrinsically motivated by performance and process praise, particularly praise for effort on their successes (Corpus & Lepper, 2007; Koestner et al., 1989). Girls also tend to perceive praise as controlling even when the praise is relatively ambiguous with respect to its informational or controlling qualities (Kast & Connor, 1988; Koestner, Zuckerman, & Koestner, 1987).

Applications: Using Praise Effectively

Teachers' appropriate use of praise can encourage students to focus on the intrinsic value of learning. Jere Brophy (1981) provides many suggestions, shown in Table 15.1, for using praise in ways that do not hinder intrinsic motivation. To use praise effectively, keep in mind these guidelines.

Make praise specific to the particular behavior being reinforced. Teachers should refrain from using vague phrases such as "Nice work," "Good job," or "You're so smart!" Instead, they should use process or performance praise to identify exactly what is *good* about the behavior. Specific praise is more credible and is informational, providing feedback about students' performance. Also, praising children and adolescents for being smart leads them to believe that learning is about looking smart and not making mistakes (Dweck, 1999). These children believe intelligence to be innate and fixed, and they experience lowered motivation when they are confronted with failure. When using specific praise, teachers also should not include social comparisons—comparing a student's performance to that of other classmates— because it may undermine students' later perseverance (Henderlong & Lepper, 2002). If students learn to judge their personal success by comparing themselves with others rather than focusing on individual mastery, they may not learn to cope with situations in which others show superior performance.

Be sure praise is sincere. Teacher praise must be credible in order for students to believe that their performance is praiseworthy. Praise can undermine intrinsic motivation, so teachers need to be careful to:

- not praise everyone, because students will be less likely to attribute praise to anything special (Brophy, 1981);

TABLE 15.1   Guidelines for Effective Praise

Effective Praise . . .	Ineffective Praise . . .
is delivered contingently	is delivered randomly or unsystematically
specifies the particulars of the accomplishment	is restricted to global positive reactions
shows spontaneity, variety, and other signs of credibility; suggests clear attention to the student's accomplishment	shows a bland uniformity that suggests a conditioned response made with minimal attention
rewards attainment of specified performance criteria (which can include effort criteria, however)	rewards mere participation, without consideration of performance processes or outcomes
provides information to students about their competence or the value of their accomplishments	provides no information at all or gives students information about their status
orients students toward better appreciation of their own task-related behavior and thinking about problem solving	orients students toward comparing themselves with others and thinking about competing
uses students' own prior accomplishments as the context for describing present accomplishments	uses the accomplishments of peers as the context for describing students' present accomplishments
is given in recognition of noteworthy effort or success at difficult (for this student) tasks.	is given without regard to the effort expended or the meaning of the accomplishment
attributes success to effort and ability, implying that similar successes can be expected in the future	attributes success to ability alone or to external factors such as luck or low task difficulty
fosters endogenous attributions (students believe that they expend effort on the task because they enjoy the task and/or want to develop task-relevant skills)	fosters exogenous attributions (students believe that they expend effort on the task for external reasons—to please the teacher, win a competition or reward, and so on)
focuses students' attention on their own task-relevant behavior	focuses students' attention on the teacher as an external authority figure who is manipulating them
fosters appreciation of, and desirable attributions about, task-relevant behavior after the process is completed	intrudes into the ongoing process, distracting attention from task-relevant behavior

Source: J. Brophy (1981), "Teacher praise: A functional analysis." *Review of Educational Research, 51*(1), 5–32. Copyright © 1981 American Educational Research Association. Reprinted by permission of Sage Publications.

- not praise students for easy tasks, because students see the praise as undeserved (Marzano, Pickering, & Pollack, 2005). They perceive praise for performing an easy task as an indication of low ability (Miller & Hom, 1997; Weiner, 1990).

- not praise students for completing a task quickly and easily because it conveys that "being smart" does not involve effort (Dweck & Master, 2008). This promotes a perception that ability is fixed and uncontrollable. Instead, teachers should say that the task is too easy and offer a more challenging task, which conveys that teachers value challenging tasks that require effort (Dweck & Master, 2008).

Entity view of ability: See page 282.

Give praise that is contingent on the behavior to be reinforced. When teachers give praise that is contingent on success, students interpret it as feedback that success has been achieved (Brophy, 1981; O'Leary & O'Leary, 1977). However, praise is often noncontingent because of the unsystematic way that teachers apply praise during lessons (Beaman & Wheldall, 2000). Teachers have been found to:

- give praise for success relatively infrequently—only about 10% of the time—suggesting that they do not consistently offer praise despite observing many examples of successful performance in their students (Brophy, 1981);

- shift their criteria for "success," leading them to praise a student for a certain achievement on one occasion and not on another (Mehan, 1974); and

- praise incorrect responses in addition to correct responses (Anderson, Evertson, & Brophy, 1979). For example, teachers gave similar praise to students whose oral reading was errorless and to students whose reading contained mistakes.

Think of some instances when you have been praised. Did the praise increase your intrinsic motivation or decrease it? Why do you think this happened?

WHEN THE REWARD IS THE ACTIVITY ITSELF

Flow Theory

Some students are intrinsically motivated by the nature of the task in which they are involved and do not need any external reward. Have you ever been surprised by how much time has passed when you've been engaged in an interesting experiment or activity in one of your college classes? If so, you were in a state of flow, also called optimal experience or, using a sports metaphor, being "in the zone." **Flow** is a feeling of intrinsic enjoyment and absorption in a task that is challenging and rewarding, making a person feel at one with the task. Mihalyi Csikzentmihalyi (1990, 2000) created flow theory to describe the subjective experiences of individuals who are motivated to engage in an activity for its own sake.

Some activities are more likely than others to create the level of engagement and absorption characterized by flow. Playing chess, rock climbing, sailing, and playing a musical instrument are activities conducive to flow. In general, experiences that promote flow tend to:

- have rules that require the learning of new skills,
- establish goals,
- provide feedback,
- allow the participants to have a sense of control, and
- facilitate a high level of concentration and involvement.

State of Flow. Experiences such as playing chess can promote flow. When have you been in a flow state?

Based on these characteristics, what classroom experiences do you suspect might be flow-inducing? At the upper elementary level, vocabulary relay races in which teams of students compete against one another to define a set of vocabulary terms could have flow-inducing components: rules of the relay, immediate feedback (as each vocabulary word's definition is checked), heightened concentration, and active participation. At the middle school or high school level, flow might be induced by a living history assignment in which students learn about the Civil War and then spend time planning and implementing a live reenactment of a certain battle.

Flow state is difficult to achieve and maintain (Schweinle, Turner, & Meyer, 2008). To achieve a state of flow, an individual must have the right balance between the degree of challenge in the activity and the degree of mastery of the necessary skills for engaging in the activity (Brophy, 2008; Csikszentmihalyi, 1997). A student whose skills exceed the requirements of the activity likely will find the task boring and not conducive to flow. Likewise, a student who lacks skills for a particular activity may find it frustrating and will not experience a state of flow. If individuals are willing to devote an extensive amount of time and practice to mastering new skills, an activity that at first requires conscious focus and effort can become conducive to flow (Csikszentmihalyi, 1990). For that reason, flow experiences may be easier to attain in older students. Older students might better understand that time and sustained effort devoted to a challenging task are needed for improving skills. They also may have a more sophisticated view of challenge as a vehicle for helping them improve their skills, which can lead to enhancing an area of talent (Schweinle et al., 2008).

Applications: Creating an Intrinsically Motivating Learning Environment

Teachers can create an intrinsically motivating learning environment through the way they introduce material, design learning tasks, group students for activities, and display students' work. Let's explore each of these components.

Introduce a lesson by conveying its importance or relevance. Students often ask teachers, "Why do I have to know this?" When students know why it is important to learn something and when and where to use this new knowledge, they will be more likely to value what they are learning, which can lead to increased intrinsic motivation (Brophy, 2008; Turner & Paris, 1995). Relating information to students' interests is particularly effective in conveying the value of to-be-learned material (Brophy, 2008; Covington, 2000). For example, if a high school physics teacher begins a lesson on mass and velocity by telling students how it relates to driving a car or another use relevant to their lives, this should pique their interest and intrinsically motivate them to learn. When students have a personal interest in material, they are more likely to process information meaningfully and to learn more (Ainley, Hidi, & Berndorff, 2002; Cordova & Lepper, 1996).

Another way to emphasize the importance of lessons is to ground them in authentic learning activities that are real-life tasks, such as designing experiments in science, writing letters to members of Congress in an English class, or conducting an interview for a social studies class. Authentic activities encourage the acquisition of skills for solving problems and completing tasks that are important in the real world (Brown, Collins, & Duguid, 1989; Collins, Hawkins, & Carver, 1991). Students may be motivated in these instances because learning has real-world significance.

Use enthusiasm, novelty, and surprise. Introducing new material through the use of enthusiasm, novelty, and surprise can spark *situational interest* in learning—an immediate interest in a particular lesson (Hidi, 2000; Silvia, 2005, 2006). Using novelty and surprise is consistent with Piaget's (1954, 1963) notion of *disequilibrium*, a state of cognitive imbalance in which new information does not fit with an individual's existing way of thinking. In Piaget's theory of cognitive development, individuals are motivated to learn in order to resolve their disequilibrium.

Design tasks of optimal difficulty (Covington, 2000; Stipek, 1996). Providing tasks that are just slightly beyond the skill level of students is an effective way to challenge them (Piaget, 1985; Vygotsky, 1978). Optimal challenge fosters feelings of competence and self-esteem. Teachers must be careful to tailor tasks to the ability levels of their students (Stipek, 2002). Work that is too difficult increases anxiety, but tasks that are too easy can lead to boredom. The right balance between challenge and skill level can also foster flow experiences. When middle school or high school students are allowed to choose their classes, such as electives or foreign languages, this presents them with an opportunity to choose courses at an appropriate difficulty level for their skills, and may facilitate flow experiences in these classes (Schweinle et al., 2008).

Provide students with choices for learning activities (Deci & Ryan, 1992; Ryan & Stiller, 1991). Even though students might develop feelings of competence in response to praise and extrinsic rewards, they might not become intrinsically motivated unless they have a sense of autonomy, or self-determination (Ryan & Deci, 2000a). In other words, students should feel that they have control over their learning. Teachers who promote autonomy by offering students opportunities to make choices that affect their learning create more responsible, independent, self-regulated learners. If students are provided with too many choices, however, they can become overwhelmed. An effective teacher must be selective about how and under what circumstances to involve students in the decision-making process. For example, a teacher might *require* groups of students to develop social studies projects about a particular country but *allow* each group to choose which country to research based on their personal interests.

Create tasks that involve collaborative grouping. Collaborative group activities can focus students' attention on the intrinsic value of learning (Turner & Paris, 1995). Learning in a social context not only challenges students to think in more advanced ways but also can satisfy students' need for affiliation (Deci & Ryan, 2000; Vygotsky, 1978). Collaboration works best when:

- students depend on one another to reach a desired goal,
- they are shown how to work together effectively, and
- group performance is valued or rewarded in some way (Driscoll, 2005).

Display student work to emphasize effort, creativity, and pride in accomplishments. Displaying students' work on an art wall, bulletin board, or Web site or at events like a science fair can lead to an increase in intrinsic motivation depending on what teachers choose to display (Malone & Lepper, 1983).

Authentic tasks: See situated learning on page 369 and authentic assessment on page 481.

Disequilibrium: See page 120.

Self-determination: See page 305.

Collaborative grouping activities: See page 383.

Using Surprise When Teaching. Novelty or surprise, as shown here by the teacher demonstrating a chemical reaction, can spark intrinsic motivation.

Putting only A papers on a bulletin board can undermine feelings of competence in students who did well but did not earn an A. This competitive focus can foster feelings of incompetence in students who have performed well but did not outperform classmates (Stipek, 2002). In contrast, displaying students' work is effective if it is intended to show improvement over past performance or conveys the message that there is more than one way to complete a project (Fryer & Elliot, 2008). This recognition process creates positive feelings about effort, ownership, achievement, and responsibility (Turner & Paris, 1995).

Imagine a grade level you intend to teach. How would you use these guidelines to create an intrinsically motivating classroom environment?

Summary

Explain how motivation changes from elementary through middle school, and discuss what factors might account for this trend. Students' motivation shifts as they grow, from an intrinsic focus to an extrinsic focus. With extrinsic motivation, students may engage in an activity to obtain an external reward, while intrinsic motivation means the activity is itself rewarding. Students' intrinsic motivation for academic tasks declines from elementary through middle school. This may be due to changes in the structure of the classroom environment, a greater focus on grades and evaluations of performance, decontextualized learning, and the overuse of extrinsic rewards for learning.

Explain why task-contingent rewards tend to diminish intrinsic motivation and performance-contingent rewards tend to enhance intrinsic motivation. Task-contingent rewards, given for merely completing a task or an activity, diminish intrinsic motivation. Students perceive task-contingent rewards as controlling and work only to get the reward. Performance-contingent rewards are less likely to undermine intrinsic motivation and may even enhance it, because they provide information about a student's level of mastery. However, even performance-contingent rewards can undermine intrinsic motivation if the feedback is negative.

Discuss the conditions under which praise can enhance or diminish intrinsic motivation, and explain individual and developmental differences in the effectiveness of praise. Praise generally enhances intrinsic motivation because it is unexpected and provides feedback about a student's competence. However, praise may diminish intrinsic motivation if teachers use it as feedback for easy tasks or convey it in a controlling or insincere manner. Praise is more likely to benefit students in the middle elementary grades, lower-achieving students, students from lower socioeconomic backgrounds, males, and students with an external locus of control.

Discuss methods teachers can use to create an intrinsically motivating learning environment. Teachers have several options for creating intrinsically motivating environments. In general, they can convey the importance of a new lesson or concept and spark interest in academic subjects by using enthusiasm, novelty, and surprise. Teachers can create tasks that involve collaborative learning, provide students with a choice in learning tasks, and be sure that tasks are optimally challenging for all students. Teachers can appropriately display students' work, making sure that these create positive feelings about effort, achievement, and responsibility.

Key Concepts

academic intrinsic motivation 265

extrinsic motivation 265

flow 272

intrinsic motivation 265

locus of control 266

performance-contingent rewards 268

performance praise 269

person praise 270

praise 269

process praise 269

reinforcement 265

task-contingent rewards 267

Video Applications

www.mhhe.com/bohlin2e

Video 1: Intrinsic and Extrinsic Motivation (*2 minutes*)
Joel Muñoz, a second-year Spanish teacher, is shown teaching Spanish to first-graders and high school students, and he discusses the motivational differences between younger and older students when learning Spanish.

Video 2: Using Positive Reinforcement to Motivate Students (*1 minute*)
First-grade teacher Jessica Harris discusses methods of motivating her students.

Video 3: Fostering Intrinsic Motivation (*2 minutes*)
Christine Kunkel, principal of the Indianapolis Key Learning Community, discusses ways that teachers can promote intrinsic motivation in the elementary school classroom. This clip is also applicable to middle school and high school students.

Case Studies
Reflect and Evaluate

EARLY CHILDHOOD: "The Worksheets"

These questions refer to the case study on page 256.

1. Is the kindergarten class as a whole extrinsically motivated or intrinsically motivated? Are there any students for whom your answer would be different? Based on the research presented in the module, would you expect the same type of motivation in a sixth-grade class? Explain.

2. Mrs. Garvey is rewarding Emanuel, Kristina, and Martin by allowing them to play after satisfactorily completing their seat-work. What type of reward is this called? Is this reward effective in promoting students' intrinsic motivation, according to the research evidence?

3. Does Claire have an external locus of control or an internal locus of control? How do you know? How might that influence the effect that praise has on her motivation?

4. What guideline did Mrs. Garvey violate when praising Alannah and Mahiro? What alternative praise would you suggest Mrs. Garvey use? Give an example.

5. Some of the children want to rush through their work so they can play like Martin and his friends. How can you use rewards to motivate these children to focus on their schoolwork?

6. How can Mrs. Garvey encourage Martin to have an intrinsic motivation to learn math?

ELEMENTARY SCHOOL: "Writer's Block"

These questions refer to the case study on page 258.

1. Identify the instances of extrinsic and intrinsic motivation in this case.

2. Mrs. Okuda announces that students may select an activity of their choice after they've completed their writing. What type of reward is this called? Is this effective in promoting intrinsic motivation, according to the research evidence?

3. Based on the research evidence, explain why Mrs. Okuda's free-writing activity might discourage intrinsic motivation. What could she do differently to enhance students' intrinsic motivation for writing?

4. What type of praise did Mrs. Okuda use with Shanti—controlling or informational? According to the guidelines for praise discussed in the module, is the praise given to Shanti effective? Why or why not?

5. Based on your reading of the module and the information presented in the case, does the practice of displaying students' writing on the bulletin board motivate students? If so, which students and in which way, intrinsically or extrinsically? How would you display students' work in your own classroom?

6. Outside of writing activities, identify strategies Mrs. Okuda can implement to foster intrinsic motivation in her third-graders.

MIDDLE SCHOOL: "The Math Review"

These questions refer to the case study on page 260.

1. Do the eighth-graders appear to be intrinsically or extrinsically motivated in math class? According to the research evidence presented in the module, is their motivation typical of middle school students?

2. Based on the research evidence discussed in the module, are the first prize and class prize likely to enhance students' intrinsic motivation for math? Why or why not?

3. Is the feedback Mr. Pantera gives to Jeremy likely to be perceived as informational or controlling? How might that affect Jeremy's motivation?

4. Based on the guidelines for effective praise, evaluate Mr. Pantera's interaction with Sam. Imagine that Mr. Pantera and Sam talk further after class. What can Mr. Pantera say to increase Sam's intrinsic motivation for math?

5. What should the first prize and class prize be? How would that enhance students' intrinsic motivation?

6. Instead of creating a competition, what other things could Mr. Pantera do to foster intrinsic motivation for math?

HIGH SCHOOL: **"Exam Grades"**

These questions refer to the case study on page 262.

1. Contrast the motivational orientation—intrinsic or extrinsic—of students in general science and students in AP physics.

2. Is the motivational orientation of students in Mr. Womack's classes typical of high school students? What factors might contribute to their motivational orientation?

3. According to the research presented in the module, is praising Madelyn for the highest grade on the physics exam an effective motivator? Why or why not?

4. How can Mr. Womack encourage students like Chelsea to focus more on learning and less on grades?

5. If Mr. Womack wants to use rewards to stimulate students' intrinsic motivation and interest in science in his general science class, what types of rewards would you recommend? Be sure your answer is supported by the research evidence discussed in the module.

6. Aside from offering rewards, how can Mr. Womack create an intrinsically motivating environment in his general science class?

Cognitive Theories

Outline

Cognitive Theories of Motivation

- Expectancy-Value Theory
- Goal Theory
- Attribution Theory

Developmental and Cultural Differences in Motivation

- Developmental Changes in Motivation
- Gender Differences in Motivation
- Ethnic Differences in Motivation

Applications: Enhancing Students' Motivation

- Student-Level Techniques
- Classroom-Level Techniques

Serious Motivational Problems

- Learned Helplessness
- Anxiety

Summary
Key Concepts
Video Applications
Case Studies: Reflect and Evaluate

Learning Goals

1. Define expectancies and values, and explain how they influence students' motivation.
2. Compare and contrast the two types of mastery and performance goals.
3. Identify attributions that enhance motivation and those that lower motivation.

4. Explain the major developmental changes in motivation.
5. Identify gender and ethnic differences in motivation.

6. Identify student-level and classroom-level strategies for enhancing motivation.

7. Explain how learned helplessness and anxiety affect students' motivation to learn.

COGNITIVE THEORIES OF MOTIVATION

What does *thinking* have to do with motivation? According to cognitive theories of motivation, changing students' motivation to learn requires changing the way they think. To do this, we need to understand students' expectations for success and valuing of learning tasks, their goals for learning activities, and their attributions (or explanations) for their successes and failures. In this module, we will discuss:

- expectancy-value theory;
- goal theory; and
- attribution theory.

But before we discuss *how* to motivate student learning, let's review *what* motivation is. When students study for a test to get a good grade, they are exhibiting **extrinsic motivation,** which focuses on external rewards for their behavior. When students study out of interest or enjoyment, they show **intrinsic motivation,** in which learning is the reward itself. And some learning may be prompted by both, as when a student wants a good grade (extrinsic motivation) *and* enjoys the subject matter (intrinsic motivation).

Our goal as teachers is to foster **academic intrinsic motivation,** in which students exhibit curiosity and persistence and focus on mastery of knowledge and skills (Gottfried, Fleming, & Gottfried, 1994; Gottfried & Gottfried, 1996). From elementary school through high school, students with high academic intrinsic motivation have positive views of their ability, display lower anxiety and greater persistence, and show deeper learning and higher achievement than students with lower academic intrinsic motivation (Gottfried, Fleming, & Gottfried, 2001; Vansteenkiste, Simons, Lens, Sheldon, & Deci, 2004). To encourage academic intrinsic motivation in all students, we first need to understand the thinking that underlies students' motivation. Let's begin with expectancy-value theory.

Expectancy-Value Theory

What motivates students to participate in class, study, or complete homework assignments and projects? According to the expectancy-value model, the answer involves two components (Eccles, 2005; Wigfield & Eccles, 2000, 2002):

1. **Expectancy:** Students' expectation for success (Can I do this task?)
2. **Value:** Reasons for undertaking a task (Why should I want to do this task?)

Expectancies and values are related to each other. Individuals tend to value what they are good at (Jacobs et al., 2002; Wigfield et al., 1997). Expectancies and values also predict motivational behaviors such as choice of activities as well as performance, effort, and persistence on activities (Denissen, Zarrett, & Eccles, 2007; Wigfield, Tonks, & Klauda, 2009).

EXPECTANCIES

Students have different expectancies for success. Some children and adolescents with positive expectancies believe that they can succeed on a task when they are presented with a new challenge, while others with negative expectancies believe that they are likely to fail. Expectancy depends on the student's **competency belief,** a judgment about one's relative ability in one domain compared to the ability of other individuals and compared to one's ability in other domains (Eccles et al., 1983). For example, a student may say "Math is my strongest subject and I am better at it than my friends." Competency beliefs are determined by past experiences, our interpretations of those experiences (why we think we've succeeded or failed), and social and cultural factors such as parental beliefs and gender-role stereotypes (for example, the idea that males are better at math and females are better at reading) (Eccles, 2005; Wigfield & Cambria, 2010a). Note that competency belief differs from an individual's sense of self-efficacy. Self-efficacy is a belief about a particular task and does not involve a comparison of one's ability to others' ability or to one's ability in other skill areas (Wigfield & Cambria, 2010a).

Self-efficacy: See page 299.

VALUES

Why do students choose to complete academic tasks? Individuals may choose to engage in tasks because of:

- **intrinsic value**—satisfying interest, curiosity, or enjoyment (completing a science project because the topic is interesting);

- **attainment value**—the *intrinsic* importance of being good at a task (studying spelling words to be a good speller); and

- **utility value**—*extrinsic* usefulness for meeting short-term and long-term goals (choosing to take calculus to prepare for college).

Students also might choose to engage in tasks or to avoid tasks because of their **cost,** or the expense of engaging in the activity. A cost may be the amount of effort needed to complete a task, time away from other activities (e.g., going to the mall), or psychological risks such as anxiety, fear of failure, or social consequences of success (e.g., being labeled a nerd).

Many factors influence how we value a task (Wigfield, Eccles, Schiefele, Roeser, & Davis-Kean, 2006). For example, a high school girl may decide to take calculus because she likes math (intrinsic value), is good at it (attainment value), and needs it for college (utility value). She has developed these values based on her view of herself (self-schema), long- and short-term goals, competency beliefs about math, and past experiences. Her parents' beliefs about math and their expectations for her success, as well as gender roles and cultural stereotypes, are environmental factors that also affect task values (Meece, Glienke, & Askew, 2009).

The values students ascribe to academic tasks or subjects influence their achievement-related choices. For example, the value elementary school students place on reading, math, and science is predictive of the number of courses they will choose in high school in English, math, and science, respectively (Durik, Vida, & Eccles, 2006; Simpkins, Davis-Kean, & Eccles, 2006). Values are also related to adolescents' achievement-related choices, such as course selection decisions, involvement in sports, occupational choices, and anticipated college major (Eccles, Wigfield, & Schiefele, 1998).

Think about your past experiences in school. Describe your expectancies and values. Do they differ for different subjects?

Goal Theory

Individuals form goals for a variety of academic and nonacademic pursuits. An **achievement goal** includes both (1) the reason for choosing to do a task and (2) the standard that individuals construct to evaluate their performance (Ames, 1992; Pintrich, 2000). For example, an adolescent may want to earn better grades to gain admission into college and may decide that successful performance means earning a B in history. Our *goal orientation,* or what drives our behaviors and choices, can be described by two types of mastery goals and two types of performance goals, as shown in Table 16.1.

Mastery-approach goals and performance-approach goals are grounded in a need for achievement. Students with these goals are motivated to approach situations in which they have an opportunity to achieve. Students with **mastery-approach goals** focus on improving intellectually, acquiring new skills and knowledge, and developing competence (Hulleman & Senko, 2010). Students who hold **performance-approach goals** are motivated simultaneously by a need to achieve and a fear of failure (Elliot & Church, 1997). Because these students fear failure and have perceptions of low ability, their goal is to demonstrate their ability to others and outperform others (Hulleman et al., 2010; Urdan & Mestas, 2006).

Mastery-approach and performance-approach goal orientations result in positive outcomes such as persistence and effort (Hulleman & Senko, 2010; McGregor & Elliot, 2002). Performance-approach goals are often linked to students' use of superficial learning strategies, such as memorizing, although this behavior nonetheless results in achievement most of the time. However, mastery-approach goals are not always linked to high achievement despite students' tendency to use deep-level learning strategies, such as planning and organizing material, relating information to prior knowledge, and monitoring comprehension while learning (Hulleman, Schrager, Bodmann, & Harackiewicz, 2010).

While some individuals may be motivated to *approach* achievement situations, others may be motivated to *avoid* situations that may lead to failure. Students with **mastery-avoidance goals** want to avoid situations in which they might fail to achieve mastery. They judge their competence by personally created, absolute standards, such as avoiding a strikeout when coming up to bat or avoiding the possibility of answering a question incorrectly. Perfectionists are considered mastery-avoidant because they never want to be wrong or incorrect

Performance-Approach Goals. Some students are motivated to show others their ability, like the boy showing off his spelling trophy.

TABLE 16.1	**Comparing Mastery and Performance Orientations**

	Mastery	**Performance**
Approach State	**Focus:** mastering task, learning, understanding **Standards:** self-improvement, progress, deep understanding of task **Outcomes:** ■ intrinsic motivation, interest, enjoyment ■ deep-level learning strategies to enhance understanding and recall ■ preference for challenging tasks and moderate risk taking ■ adaptive help seeking ■ effort and persistence ■ positive self-efficacy and self-regulation	**Focus:** being superior, being the smartest, besting others **Standards:** getting best or highest grades, being best performer in class (comparing to the norm) **Outcomes:** ■ intrinsic motivation ■ effective, but often superficial, learning strategies (e.g., rote memorization) ■ effort and persistence ■ low anxiety and positive self-efficacy ■ acceptance of cheating
Avoidance State	**Focus:** avoiding misunderstanding, avoiding not learning or not mastering task **Standards:** not being wrong, not performing incorrectly relative to task **Outcomes:** ■ disorganized studying ■ increased test anxiety ■ negative feelings about failure ■ avoidance of help-seeking ■ less intrinsic motivation	**Focus:** avoiding inferiority, not looking stupid or dumb in comparison to others **Standards:** not getting the worst grades, not being lowest performer in class (comparing to the norm) **Outcomes:** ■ surface-level learning strategies (e.g., memorizing, studying only what is likely to be on the test) ■ disorganized study habits ■ self-handicapping strategies (e.g., not trying, procrastination, minimizing participation, making excuses for incomplete work, possibly cheating) ■ anxiety and negative feelings about failure ■ avoidance of help-seeking ■ disengagement ■ lower performance

SOURCES: Cury et al., 2006; Daniels et al., 2008; Elliot & Church, 1997; Elliot & McGregor, 2001; Elliot, McGregor, & Gable, 1999; Elliot & Moller, 2003; Elliot, Shell, Bouas Henry, & Maier, 2005; Harackiewicz, Barron, Pintrich, Elliot, & Thrash, 2002; Harackiewicz, Barron, Tauer, Carter, & Elliot, 2000; Hulleman & Senko, 2010; Hulleman, Schrager, Bodmann, & Harackiewicz, 2010; Karabenick, 2003; Leondari & Gonida, 2007; Maatta & Nurmi, 2007; Middleton & Midgley, 1997; Moller & Elliot, 2006; Murayama & Elliot, 2009; Payne, Youngcourt, & Beaubien, 2007; Pintrich, 2000; Turner, Meyer, Midgley, & Patrick, 2003; Urdan, 2004; Wolters, 2004.

(Elliot & McGregor, 2001; Pintrich, 2000). In contrast, students with **performance-avoidance goals** are concerned with judging their competence relative to others, such as failing a test they believe others will succeed on (Elliot & Church, 1997; Elliot & McGregor, 2001). To avoid failure, these students use several self-handicapping strategies listed in Table 16.1, which are a useful way to attribute failure to causes other than low ability, leading to less shame (Stipek, 2002).

Mastery and performance goals can work together to enhance students' motivation. Mastery goals are important during the process of skill acquisition, while performance goals tend to promote interest once skills have been developed (Zimmerman & Kitsantas, 1997). For example, mastery-approach goals may be necessary for learning to calculate fractions in fourth grade and learning to write term papers in high school, but once students have acquired proficiency at these skills, they may need to adopt performance goals in order to maintain their interest (e.g., writing a paper to impress the teacher and get an A). Students also may be influenced by both types of goals in any given learning situation (Fryer & Elliot, 2008; Linnenbrink, 2005). For example, the classroom atmosphere may emphasize competition and outperforming others (a performance-approach orientation), while a student's own personal

Self-handicapping strategies: See page 304.

goal may be mastery. Conversely, students who initially approach learning with performance goals may develop interests as a result of their engagement in the activity, which may lead to a mastery orientation (Hidi, Weiss, Berndorff, & Nolan, 1998). For example, high school students consider both grades and interest to be their major motivators (Hynd, Holschuh, & Nist, 2000). Students who pursue both mastery and performance goals have greater interest and intrinsic motivation, higher self-regulation and self-efficacy, and better grades than students who adopt only one or neither type of goal (Barron & Harackiewicz, 2000; Midgley, Anderman, & Hicks, 1995).

Describe your own goal orientation in school. Does your goal orientation differ depending on the subject?

Self-efficacy: See page 178 and self-regulation: See page 179.

Attribution Theory

Think about a time when you studied for a test and were surprised to find out that you received a lower grade than expected. What caused this outcome? According to attribution theory, humans naturally seek to understand why events have occurred, especially when the outcome is important or unexpected (Moeller & Koeller, 1999; Weiner, 1992). We all try to explain our performance through **causal attributions,** interpretations of events based on past performance and social norms (Weiner, 2010).

To better understand how attributions influence students' motivation, consider the three dimensions of attributions.

For a similar concept, see *locus of control* on page 283.

1. **Locus:** where we place the cause of the outcome. Do we believe our success or failure results from *internal* causes such as ability and effort? Or do we believe our success or failure is due to *external* causes such as asking the teacher for help? Compared to external attributions, ability and effort attributions for success lead to higher levels of pride, confidence, satisfaction, and self-esteem (Graham & Weiner, 1996).

2. **Stability:** whether we perceive the cause as being stable or unstable over time. We expect future success when we attribute success to a *stable* cause (the typical effort you make every time you study). However, our expectation decreases when we attribute failure to a stable cause, such as our belief that the teacher makes her tests too difficult (Weiner, 1982). Our expectations for future success are not hampered when we attribute failure to an *unstable* cause—say, missing several classes because of illness.

3. **Controllability:** our personal responsibility for the cause of the success or failure. Was success or failure *controllable* (the amount you studied) or *uncontrollable* (unfairness of the test)? Attributing success or failure to amount of effort generally leads to positive expectations for future performance, because we believe that effort is under our control (Weiner, 1994). Our future motivation is not likely to be affected by attributing success to uncontrollable causes such as luck. However, when we attribute failure to uncontrollable causes, such as believing we have low ability that cannot improve, we might experience shame and avoid situations that may lead to failure (Covington & Omelich, 1984a; Graham & Weiner, 1996).

Figure 16.1 shows common attributions students make and characterizes them according to locus, stability, and controllability. Two students who get the same grade on the same test might make completely different attributions for their performance. The attributions we make are affected not only by our own beliefs about our ability, but also by the evaluations others make about our academic performance. Let's examine these two factors next.

BELIEFS ABOUT ABILITY

Attributing success and failure to ability has different effects on motivation, depending on our belief about ability.

Individuals with an **incremental view of ability** perceive ability as unstable and controllable; they consider it to be ever-changing (Dweck & Leggett, 1988). When students with an incremental view attribute success to their ability, they will be motivated to continue to improve their knowledge and skills. When they attribute failure to low ability, they will become motivated to find alternative strategies for succeeding next time.

Students with an **entity view of ability** believe that ability is stable and uncontrollable; they see it as fixed and unchangeable (Dweck, 2000; Molden & Dweck, 2000). When such students experience success, they want to continue to demonstrate their competence if they believe that competence is valued by others, such as teachers and peers (Stipek, 2002). When they attribute failure to lack of ability, their expectations for future success diminish, negatively affecting their motivation to learn (Dweck & Sorich, 1999; Hong, Chiu, Dweck, Lin, & Wan, 1999).

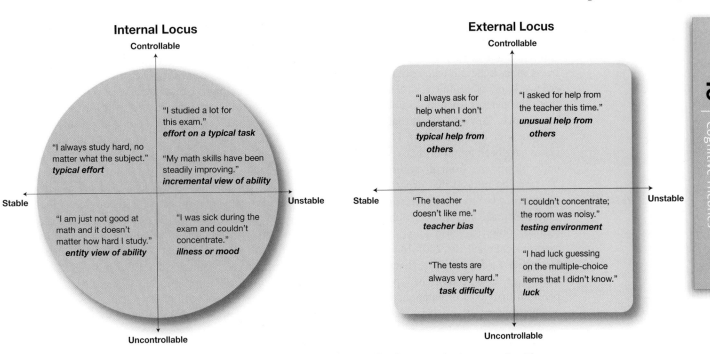

Figure 16.1. Locus, Stability, and Controlabilty Dimensions of Attributions. Students can make different attributions for past successes and failures, each of which has a different effect on their future motivation.

For students with an entity view, preventing a negative impression of their ability is more important than actually succeeding (Dweck & Master, 2008). When they experience failure, they often engage in self-handicapping behaviors, such as not trying, procrastination, and making excuses, which further undermine their performance (Cury, Elliot, Da Fonseca, & Moller, 2006). Because students with an entity view believe that exerting effort indicates a lack of ability, they tend to use lack of effort as an excuse for failure ("I failed because I didn't study"), which suggests to others that lack of effort is the reason for failure, not low ability (Blackwell et al., 2007; Hong, Chiu, Dweck, Lin, & Wan, 1999). Making low effort excuses can result in more peer approval, especially during adolescence when popularity and minimizing the importance of effort go hand in hand (Juvonen, 2000).

Self-handicapping:
See page 304.

Think of a recent academic success and a recent failure. What attributions did you make for each?

TEACHER REACTIONS AND EVALUATIONS

When evaluating student performance, teachers' beliefs and reactions affect the attributions students make (Reyna & Weiner, 2001; Weiner, 2000). Many teachers tend to have an entity view of ability, believing it to be fixed and unchangeable (Oakes & Guiton, 1995; Reyna, 2000). Teachers with this belief tend to pass judgment more quickly on the basis of initial performance and resist changing their judgments when students' performance contradicts their initial assumptions (Butler, 2000; Plaks, Stroessner, Dweck, & Sherman, 2001). If teachers with an entity view of ability hold low expectations for students, their initial perceptions may lead students to attribute failure to low ability or teacher bias (stable and uncontrollable attributions), with serious motivational consequences. Students from lower socioeconomic backgrounds and minority students are especially susceptible to low-ability messages from teacher expectations and behaviors (Banks & Banks, 1995; Graham, 1990; McLoyd, 1998).

Teachers may not be consciously aware of their own beliefs, but they can be mindful of the types of reactions to student performance that can lead to diminished motivation. Students tend to adopt an entity view of ability when teachers praise or reward them for easy tasks, offer unsolicited help, express pity for failures, or fail to blame students for poor performance (Dweck, 2000; Graham & Barker, 1990; Graham & Weiner, 1993). Also, when teachers tell students to work harder after poor performance, students may adopt entity beliefs about ability if they believe they are already trying as hard as they can (Ames, 1990). In contrast, high school students—but not elementary school students—tend to make high-ability attributions when teachers react to successes with neutral feedback ("Yes, that's correct.") or more demanding criteria ("I know you can do better!") (Brophy, 1981; Meyer et al., 1979).

Praising students for being *smart* or telling them they have natural ability also fosters an entity view of ability and can lower students' intrinsic motivation because it implies that learning is about looking smart and not making mistakes (Dweck, 2000; Dweck & Master, 2008). Children who are praised for being smart believe intelligence to be innate and dislike when tasks become more challenging (Mueller & Dweck, 1998). Middle school students of *all* ability levels who believe that intelligence is fixed think that poor performance in school implies low intelligence and that making an effort means they lack intelligence. They also report that they would consider cheating if they did poorly on a test (Blackwell, Trzesniewski, & Dweck, 2007; Henderson & Dweck, 1990). The negative effects of praising for intelligence have been found in children from preschool age through adolescence in urban and rural settings and with students from all ethnic backgrounds (Dweck, 2007).

DIVERSITY

Have you noticed that expectancy-value, goal, and attribution theories overlap? Students develop competency beliefs and expectations for success (expectancy-value theory) based partly on the attributions they make for past accomplishments and failures (Wigfield & Cambria, 2010a; Wigfield, Tonks, & Klauda, 2009). They also adopt mastery or performance goals based on their beliefs about ability (Linnenbrink & Fredericks, 2007; Maehr & Zusho, 2009). For example, students with an entity view of ability tend to have a fear of failure that becomes the basis for mastery-avoidance and performance-avoidance goals (Cury et al., 2006). The types of strategies that students use—adaptive or non-adaptive—also depend on their goal orientations and beliefs about ability. As Table 16.2 illustrates, these theories are complementary—they work together to give us a more complete understanding of students' motivation.

TABLE 16.2 — Integrating Cognitive Theories of Motivation

		Students with an Incremental View of Ability	Students with an Entity View of Ability
Attribution theory	**Success** Attributions due to:	Effort (unstable, uncontrollable)	Unstable factors (luck) External factors (help from others)
	Feelings:	Pride and satisfaction	Lack of pride, lack of personal responsibility
	Failure Attributions due to:	Lack of effort (unstable, controllable) or low incremental ability (unstable, uncontrollable)	Stable causes (low entity ability)
	Feelings:	Guilt	Shame
Expectancy-value theory	Competency beliefs:	Perceive ability to be high	Perceive ability to be low
Goal theory	Goal orientation:	Mastery-approach goals (try to improve skills)	■ Performance-approach goals (try to look smart); or ■ Performance-avoidance goals (try to avoid looking inferior)
	Types of strategies:	■ Increasing effort ■ Trying new learning strategies ■ Help seeking	■ Avoidance of help seeking ■ Selecting very easy tasks (to ensure success); or ■ Selecting very difficult tasks (failure would be due to task difficulty, not low ability) ■ Using self-handicapping strategies

SOURCES: Ames, 1992; Covington & Omelich, 1979; Cury et al., 2006; Dweck & Master, 2008; Linnenbrink & Fredericks, 2007; Maatta & Nurmi, 2007; Maehr & Zusho, 2009; Stipek, 2002; Tollefson, 2000; Turner, Meyer, Midgley, & Patrick, 2003; Urdan, 2004; Weiner, 1982.

DEVELOPMENTAL AND CULTURAL DIFFERENCES IN MOTIVATION

To influence students' motivation, teachers need to understand the developmental changes in motivation and individual differences among students based on their cultural backgrounds. Let's consider these factors next.

Developmental Changes in Motivation

Most children are intrinsically motivated when they begin school. They tend to value learning, have positive competency beliefs, and endorse mastery-approach goals and attribute successes to effort and ability and failures to low effort or unstable causes. As students progress from elementary through secondary education, their competency beliefs and their values, goals, and attributions gradually change.

CHANGES IN EXPECTANCIES AND VALUES

Children as early as first grade have competency beliefs—beliefs about what they are good at—and are able to make judgments about their competencies in school subjects, music, and sports (Wigfield & Eccles, 2000; Wigfield et al., 1997). Prior to about second grade, young children's perceptions of their abilities are overly optimistic (Stipek, 1984; Wigfield & Cambria, 2010a). Of course, there are always exceptions. Some preschoolers show negative attitudes about their ability after failure, and may be more at-risk for motivational problems as they progress through school (Dweck, 2002).

Children in the early elementary grades value a task primarily according to how much it interests them (Wigfield & Cambria, 2010b). Elementary school boys in the United States, Taiwan, and Japan more highly value sports, while girls in these countries more highly value reading and music (Debacker & Nelson, 2000; Jacobs, Lanza, Osgood, Eccles, & Wigfield, 2002). As students move from elementary through middle school, they begin to value tasks based on interest, attainment value, and utility value (Wigfield & Cambria, 2010b). Other components of a task's value—such as the skill at performing a task (attainment value), the difficulty level of the task (cost), and the relevance of the task to future goals (utility)—become important in students' achievement-related choices (Wigfield & Eccles, 2000). For example, a boy might decide to play baseball out of enjoyment, but as he grows older and the game becomes more competitive, requiring greater skill, he might choose not to play.

DIVERSITY

Both competency beliefs and academic values decline from elementary school through high school, with the greatest changes occurring after the transition to middle school (Wigfield & Eccles, 1994; Watt, 2004). Students' beliefs about their abilities in math, language arts, and sports decline from elementary school through high school (Fredericks & Eccles, 2002; Jacobs et al., 2002; Watt, 2004). The values students place on these domains as well as the value they place on achievement and effort also decline (Jacobs et al., 2002; Watt, 2004). Research on gender differences in the decline of competency beliefs and task values is mixed, with some studies showing declines consistent with gender stereotypes (girls experiencing more rapid declines in math, boys in language arts), and others showing different patterns (Fredericks & Eccles, 2002; Jacobs et al., 2002; Watt, 2004).

DIVERSITY

CHANGES IN GOAL ORIENTATIONS

Many children come to school with mastery goals. As early as third grade, approach and avoidant forms of mastery and performance goals become evident, but performance-approach and performance-avoidant goals are not as distinct as in older students (Bong, 2009).

Students may become socialized to adopt performance goals in response to the goal orientations underlying classroom practices (Linnenbrink & Fredericks, 2007; Maehr & Zusho, 2009). Students tend to adopt performance-approach goals in classrooms in which their achievement is compared to others through grades and test scores, and in which teachers recognize student achievements by displaying only the best projects (Ames & Archer, 1988; Elliot, Shell, Bouas Henry, & Maier, 2005). When students with performance goal orientations are placed in performance-oriented classrooms, they are more likely to use self-handicapping strategies, especially if they have lower achievement (Leondari & Gonida, 2007; Urdan, 2004). For example, a student motivated to look smart may "forget" his math homework in a classroom where the teacher emphasizes getting the right answer. In contrast, when teachers emphasize mastery over performance, students attribute success to effort and effective learning strategies, and they deal with failures positively by finding new strategies (Ames & Archer, 1988; Kaplan & Midgley, 2000). For example, a mastery-oriented teacher may allow a student to re-do a difficult homework assignment that was incorrectly done, leading the student to adopt positive strategies for dealing with challenges the next time.

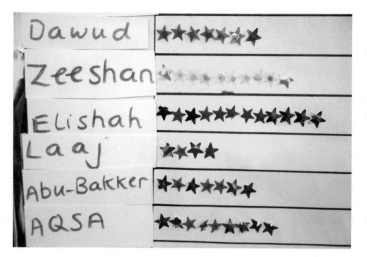

Competitive Classroom Practices.
Competitive classroom practices, such as earning a star for each new book read, can lead students to adopt performance goals.

As students move from elementary to middle school, and later to high school, many adopt a **work-avoidance goal** orientation—a motivation to avoid academic work (Nicholls, Cobb, Wood, Yackel, & Patashnick, 1990). Students motivated by work avoidance often use surface-level learning strategies and engage in behaviors such as the following (Dowson & McInerney, 2001; Meece & Miller, 2001):

- pretending they don't understand something,
- complaining about assignments,
- engaging in off-task behavior,
- taking the easiest path when given choices, and
- not contributing their fair share in group activities.

Students do these things because they believe that putting forth effort indicates low ability, a trait they consider to be stable and unchanging. Therefore, they value performance goals and try to avoid exerting effort on academic tasks (Dweck & Leggett, 1988; Dweck & Sorich, 1999).

CHANGES IN ATTRIBUTIONS

Children in preschool and early elementary school think of *ability* broadly, as comprising social behavior, conduct, work habits, and effort (Stipek & Daniels, 1990; Stipek & Tannatt, 1984). They have an optimistic view of ability, believing that individuals who try hard are smart (Folmer et al., 2008; Schunk, 2008). As a result, they have high expectations for success and are resilient after failure (Stipek, 1984).

As children progress through elementary school, their beliefs about effort and ability change, as Table 16.3 shows. At age 7 or 8, children begin to compare themselves to others more, to understand normative comparisons, and to pay increasing attention to grades and teachers' evaluations (Blumenfeld, Pintrich, & Hamilton, 1986; Dweck, 2002). As a result, their perceptions of ability become more consistent with teachers' evaluations of their ability (Eccles et al., 1999; Harter, 1999). They also consider effort and mastery to be less important than grades (Blumenfeld et al., 1986; Nicholls, 1979).

In middle school, students begin to use normative criteria to judge their ability and tend to view ability more as a stable trait and less a result of effort than they did earlier (Dweck, 2002; Feldlaufer, Midgley, & Eccles, 1988). They also believe that differences in ability will lead to different amounts of effort and different outcomes (Tollefson, 2000). In general, middle school students think that putting in a lot of effort compared to others who complete a task with less effort implies lower ability (Anderman & Maehr, 1994; Folmer et al., 2008).

Think about how your own competency beliefs, values, goals, and attributions have changed throughout your schooling.

TABLE 16.3	Developmental Changes in Effort and Ability Attributions	
Age	**View of Ability**	**View of Effort**
Preschool and early elementary	Optimistic Incremental belief	Equated with ability ("smart = tries hard")
Elementary school (age 7 or 8)	Less optimistic More accurately reflects teachers' evaluations	Less important for success than ability
Middle school through high school	More pessimistic entity belief	Implies lack of ability

DEVELOPMENTAL FACTORS AFFECTING MOTIVATIONAL CHANGE

What are the reasons for students' gradual shift toward more negative attributions, their declining competency beliefs and academic values, and their shift toward performance goals? A student's cognitive development and changes in the learning environment may account for this evolution.

Young children's incremental view of ability and their optimistic expectancies for success may be the result of two factors:

1. *An emphasis in early childhood education on positive feedback and improving skills.* Parental modeling of mastery behaviors may promote a mastery-orientation in preschool-age children (Turner & Johnson, 2003). Preschool and early elementary teachers also focus on mastery (Anderman & Anderman, 1999; Midgley, 2002). They provide positive feedback through praise, happy faces, and stickers and rarely criticize children's achievement efforts (Blumenfeld, Pintrich, Meece, & Wessels, 1982). Teachers in the early elementary grades also emphasize effort and work habits (Blumenfeld, Hamilton, Bossert, Wessels, & Meece, 1983; Brophy & Evertson, 1978). These practices boost children's confidence in their abilities.

2. *Children's level of cognitive development.* Young children have a limited ability to compare their performance to that of their peers and to reflect on and evaluate behaviors of others. Therefore, they tend to interpret praise as an indicator that they are pleasing authority figures rather than as an indicator of ability (Stipek, 1984). Also, young children don't understand the compensatory relationship between effort and ability—that those with lower ability must put forth greater effort to succeed and those with higher ability can succeed with less effort (Graham & Williams, 2009).

As students progress from elementary to high school, their competency beliefs and achievement values decline, and students shift toward an entity view of ability. These changes may be the result of the following two factors (Wigfield & Eccles, 2002):

1. *Improved ability to interpret evaluative feedback and to compare their performance to that of their peers.* Older children's self-assessments become more realistic, leading to more negative beliefs relative to those of younger children (Wigfield & Cambria, 2010a).

2. *Changes in the school environment that may make evaluation more salient and increase competition among peers.* As students move to the middle elementary grades (grades 3 to 5), their abilities are more systematically evaluated through grades, reading groups, standardized test scores, and so on (Wigfield, Tonks, & Klauda, 2009). Also, children begin to make more social comparisons based on their accomplishments due to advances in their cognitive development (Wigfield & Cambria, 2010a). Pressures placed on students to perform on high-stakes tests also can weaken the competence beliefs of students who do poorly in areas being tested (Deci & Ryan, 2002).

High-stakes testing:
See page 552.

Once students transition to middle school, they often encounter an environment characterized by a performance-oriented approach in which students experience ability grouping, harsher grading practices, and competitive recognition practices such as honor rolls and class rankings (Anderman & Maehr, 1994; Wolters & Daugherty, 2007). Adolescents tend to endorse performance goals more than mastery goals because many middle school teachers use approaches that are consistent with a performance goal orientation (Anderman & Anderman, 1999; Midgley, 2002). High school teachers also tend to be performance-oriented, particularly those who teach in lower-level tracks (Retelsdorf, Butler, Streblow, & Schiefele, 2010).

Grouping practices:
See Module 21.

Gender Differences in Motivation

DIVERSITY

Boys and girls in both Eastern and Western cultures generally have similar beliefs about their overall academic competence (Stetsenko, Little, Gordeeva, Granshof, & Oettingen, 2000). However, students' attributions, beliefs about ability, expectancies, and values differ by gender.

On different school subjects, elementary school boys and girls differ in their competency beliefs and values. Elementary school boys have more positive competency beliefs about math, science, and sports while girls have more positive beliefs about music, reading, and language arts (Baker & Wigfield, 1999; Eccles, Barber, Jozefowicz, Malenchuk, & Vida, 2000; Freedman-Doan et al., 2000). As students transition to middle school, girls more highly value English, and boys more highly value sports (Jacobs, Lanza, Osgood, Eccles, & Wigfield, 2002; Stephanou, 2008).

In elementary school, girls also begin to develop an entity belief about their ability in general (Dweck, 2000, 2002).

Giftedness: See page 420.

■ Girls are less likely to attribute success to ability and tend to rate their ability lower than boys even when they outperform boys (Freedman-Doan et al., 2000; Stetsenko, Little, Gordeeva, Grasshof, & Oettingen, 2000).

■ Even girls who are gifted and high-achieving hold an entity view of ability more often than do boys (Eccles, Barbar, Jozefowica, Malenchuk, & Vida, 2000; Freedman-Doan et al., 2000).

■ While results are not consistent across studies, this effect tends to be true for gender-stereotyped domains such as math and science (Eccles et al., 2000; Meece & Painter, 2008).

Girls' negative perceptions may be due to lower confidence levels or a greater sensitivity to adult evaluations of ability (Meece, Glienke, & Burg, 2006; Oakes, 1990b). By adolescence, boys more often make internal attributions for success, leading to higher self-esteem and more subsequent effort, while girls tend to be more discouraged after failure, which reduces their confidence (Dweck, Goetz, & Strauss, 1980; Oakes, 1990a).

Cultural norms, such as the expectation that math and science are male achievement domains, may lead to sex-role stereotypes—the idea that boys are better at math and girls are better at language arts. These societal values may in turn contribute to gender differences in competency beliefs and values. Boys may value math and sports because they have been socialized to believe these are male achievement domains (Eccles, 2005; Wigfield & Cambria, 2010a). Some parents may unknowingly convey their belief that boys are more competent than girls in math and science (Meece et al., 2009). For example, they may offer different types of encouragement to boys and girls in math. Parental involvement in children's activities may also affect boys' and girls' choices of activities differently (Meece et al., 2009). For example, in one study mothers were more likely to buy math and science items for boys than girls, which affected subsequent math and science interests (Bleeker & Jacobs, 2004). Parents and teachers also provide information about the usefulness of different school activities, through their enthusiasm for and support of activities, which can affect whether or not children value certain activities (Wigfield et al., 2006). Teacher-student interactions also convey different expectations for boys and girls (Brophy & Good, 1974). Teachers tend to praise boys only for successful performance while praising girls for success as well as easy or unimportant achievements, such as neatness or following instructions, leading to a perception of low ability among girls (Dweck, Davidson, Nelson, & Enna, 1978).

Nevertheless, we should interpret these gender differences in motivation with caution. No clear gender differences in students' achievement goal orientations have been found, and gender differences in causal attributions are small (Meece et al., 2006). Gender differences in *actual* achievement domains such as math also are very small (Lindberg, Hyde, Peterson, & Linn, 2010).

Gender Differences in Motivation. Gender differences in competence beliefs are more pronounced in gender-stereotyped domains for boys and girls (e.g., sports for boys and reading for girls).

Ethnic Differences in Motivation

Ethnic differences in motivation have been found across cultures as well as within our own culture. Let's explore some findings.

Students from Asian cultures tend to have a motivational outlook different from that of most students in Western cultures. Students in Western cultures such as the United States, Canada, and England typically have higher competence beliefs in various subjects than do students in East Asian cultures (Zusho & Pintrich, 2003; Wigfield & Cambria, 2010a). This is possibly due to the emphasis that East Asian cultures place on self-criticism versus the emphasis Western cultures place on self-enhancement (Heine & Hamamura, 2007). For example, Chinese parents tend to de-emphasize their children's successes and provide more negative emotional responses to their failures (Ng, Pomerantz, & Lam, 2007). Japanese and Chinese students attribute outcomes more to effort and less to ability than do American students (Heine et al., 2001). Asian parents' negative reactions to failures may lead their children to focus on self-improvement (Ng et al., 2007). This attitude is consistent with the Asian philosophy emphasizing the importance of striving for improvement and the belief that ability is malleable (Stipek, 2002).

Within American culture, African-American and Hispanic adolescent boys may be most at risk motivationally. African-American elementary school students believe in personal responsibility for their achievements and failures and have high expectations for success (Graham, 1984, 1994). During adolescence, however, African-American and Hispanic boys are more likely than other groups to reject achievement-related values and become disengaged in education (Mau & Bikos, 2000; Taylor & Graham, 2007). The tendency of minority students to devalue academic achievement may result from several factors:

- an increasing tendency to make external attributions for academic success—believing that school success is determined by external forces beyond their control (van Laar, 2000)
- their belief that education has limited usefulness for long-term social and economic success because discrimination will narrow their opportunities (Mickelson, 1990; Ogbu, 1994, 2003)
- low teacher expectations and negative classroom climates (Meece et al., 2009; Wood, Kaplan, & McLloyd, 2007)

Researchers are unsure why this shift in motivational orientation on the part of minority students occurs at adolescence. The changes students experience in their transition from elementary school to more advanced grades may affect students' values about education, regardless of their ethnicity. Some Caucasian adolescents from middle- and upper-socioeconomic backgrounds also have expressed doubt in the utility of school despite their average school performance. These anti-academic values appear to be rooted in a sense that teachers were not supportive, curricula were not meaningful, and the school environment was competitive and stifled autonomy (Roeser, Eccles, & Sameroff, 1998, 2000).

As with gender differences, we should interpret ethnic differences in motivation with caution. Even though research cites *average* differences in motivational orientations among ethnic groups, we should be careful not to make stereotypical assumptions about a student's motivation based on ethnicity. Students' motivation is more likely due to their achievement experiences, the beliefs and values of their family, and the classroom climate than to their ethnic or racial identification. Much more research needs to be conducted in order for us to understand ethnic differences in motivation.

APPLICATIONS: ENHANCING STUDENTS' MOTIVATION

The cognitive theories we've examined provide many useful strategies for improving students' motivation. Teachers can use certain techniques to stimulate the motivation of individual students and can structure their classroom and tasks to encourage motivation in all students.

Student-Level Techniques

Change students' attributions for success and failure. We should not assume that individuals with an entity view are doomed to have low overall motivation and performance. Entity and incremental views of ability are domain-specific (Dweck, Chiu, & Hong, 1995), meaning students may believe that they have fixed ability in math but malleable ability in other subjects or in sports.

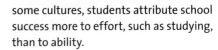

Ethnic Differences in Motivation. In some cultures, students attribute school success more to effort, such as studying, than to ability.

| EXAMPLE 16.1 | **Sample Questions to Assess Student Attributions** |

Using student responses to questions such as these can help teachers determine student attributions.

1. Are you better now than you were when you started doing this kind of work? (Circle one response.)

| not much better | a little bit better | quite a bit better | a lot better |

2. Do you feel confident that you could do harder problems, or do you need practice and help on these kinds of problems? (Circle one response.)

| I'll never be able to do this | I still need help on these | I need a little more practice on these | I can do harder problems now |

3. Do you think you will be able to do this assignment well? (Circle one number.)

| 1 | 2 | 3 | 4 | 5 | 6 | 7 |

I definitely won't do it well   I'll do OK   I definitely will do it well

4. Look at your math work for today. How hard do you think this work will be for you? (Circle one number.)

| 1 | 2 | 3 | 4 | 5 | 6 | 7 |

really easy   medium hard   really hard

SOURCE: D. Stipek (2002). *Motivation to Learn: Integrating Theory and Practice.* Boston: Allyn & Bacon. Reprinted with permission from the publisher.

Training students to attribute failure to lack of effort rather than to low ability can be done in classrooms using simple techniques such as having students read persuasive articles or participate in discussions that focus on strategies for dealing with challenges and that emphasize ability as improvable (Blackwell, Trzesniewski, & Dweck, 2007; Niiya, Crocker, & Bartmess, 2004). Re-attribution training in academic settings has led to improvement in grades, decreases in attributions to uncontrollable factors, and increased motivation (Blackwell et al., 2007; Horner & Gaither, 2006; Good, Aronson, & Inzlicht, 2003). The first step is to identify whether students have low perceptions of ability by asking questions such as "How good are you at math?" (Stipek, 2002). Teachers can also ask students about their expectancies and their views about skill improvement and difficulty level of tasks, as shown in Example 16.1.

Teach students to value challenge, improvement, and effort. Encourage students to view challenge as necessary for learning instead of something low-achieving students experience (Dweck & Master, 2008). Also, help students realize that success should be defined as improvement in knowledge or skills rather than looking smart or outperforming others. This conveys the message that effort is important for everyone, not just for students with low ability (Covington & Omelich, 1984b; Dweck & Master, 2008). Some students are not aware that effort can affect task success (Urdan, Midgley, & Anderman, 1998). Teaching them that increased effort leads to greater achievement increases their actual achievement (Craske, 1985; Van Overwalle & De Metsenaere, 1990).

Provide short-term goals and strategies for making progress toward goals (Ames, 1990). When teachers help students set short-term, mastery goals, students are more willing to put forth effort because they learn that both effort and ability contribute to success (Schunk, 1989; Tollefson, 2000). This technique will prepare elementary school students to accept that students with different levels of ability need different amounts of effort to obtain the same level of achievement. In middle school and high school, encouraging mastery may prevent adolescents from viewing academic tasks as a measure of their ability (Tollefson, 2000).

Classroom-Level Techniques

Reduce the competitive atmosphere of the classroom. Students at all levels of K–12 education, regardless of their motivational orientation, consider school to be competitive (Maehr & Midgley, 1991; Thorkildsen & Nicholls, 1998). When students are focused on extrinsic goals such as outperforming others, they are more likely to compare themselves with other students and seek contingent approval from the teacher (Kernis, 2003; Patrick, Neighbours, & Knee, 2004). This is likely to draw their attention away from the learning activity and therefore reduce their intrinsic motivation (Vansteenkiste, Matos, Lens, & Soenens, 2007). Teachers can reduce competition and enhance students' motivation by using:

- mastery learning, a method in which students work at their own pace on curricular units once teachers present material, and repeat the units until they have achieved a certain level of mastery;

- cooperative learning, an approach in which students of varying ability levels work together to achieve a single goal on a task or project;

- a variety of academic tasks, which tend to foster a mastery orientation because students have less opportunity or need to engage in social comparisons of performance (Marshall & Weinstein, 1984; Rosenholtz & Simpson, 1984).

Mastery learning: See page 367.

Cooperative learning: See page 382.

Use appropriate methods of evaluation and recognition. Consider these methods when evaluating students' learning:

- Praise students only when they learn or do something well, not for being smart, perfect at a task, or completing a task quickly or easily (Dweck, 2000; Dweck & Master, 2008). Saying something positive just to praise a student backfires because usually it is about something that is unimportant or irrelevant to the task requirements, implying that the student has low ability (Ames, 1990). Such praise will undermine intrinsic motivation.

Praise: See page 269.

- Take developmental level into account when using praise. In young children, praise for effort enhances self-confidence and is considered an indicator of high ability because young children do not differentiate between ability and effort (Schunk, 2008). However, in middle and high school students, who have differentiated concepts of ability and effort, praising effort and praising for success on easy tasks can be interpreted as signs of low ability (Barker & Graham, 1987; Henderlong & Lepper, 2002).

- Offer opportunities for improvement so students know that effort is important and that performance is not due solely to fixed ability (Covington & Omelich, 1984b).

- Be aware that motivational strategies such as announcing highest and lowest scores, posting grades, displaying students' work, and charting progress emphasize social comparisons. When ability comparisons are heightened, this can decrease intrinsic motivation and lead high achievers to experience anxiety about keeping up their success and low achievers to give up when they fail (Rose, 1989; Weinstein, 1993). Such practices need not undermine intrinsic motivation, though. For example, if the reason for displaying student work is to show improvement over past performance or reaching a standard of performance, the display would promote feelings of mastery (Fryer & Elliot, 2008).

Emphasize the value of learning. When teachers emphasize the relevance of to-be-learned knowledge, students will appreciate its utility value—its usefulness to students' goals in or out of school (Brophy, 2008). Students who see utility value in what they are learning are more likely to engage in meaningful learning—learning that results in rich, interconnected knowledge structures rather than discrete facts—which can lead to increased effort, interest, and achievement (Brophy, 1999; Wagner et al., 2006). Teachers can foster an appreciation for learning by doing the following things (Brophy, 2008):

Meaningful learning: See page 368.

- making abstract content more concrete and personally relevant to students,

- connecting content to students' interests and backgrounds,

- modeling interest and enthusiasm, and

- emphasizing applications outside of school.

A utility value approach may not work for all students. When students believe they have low ability, simply informing them about the usefulness of content to their future goals may not be beneficial (Durik & Harackiewicz, 2007; Godes et al., 2007). For example, if students struggle with math, why would they view it as helpful to their future? Instead, having students generate ways the content is relevant to them may be more effective (Hulleman & Harackiewicz, 2009). For example, students may find calculating percentages important for understanding batting averages or for figuring out sale prices at the mall. Because much of the research on utility value has been conducted with adolescents in high school and college, we do not yet know about the efficacy of this approach with students in lower grades.

Think of some specific ways you can implement these guidelines in the grade you intend to teach.

SERIOUS MOTIVATIONAL PROBLEMS

Learned Helplessness

Learned helplessness occurs when students who have experienced repeated failures attribute their failures to causes beyond their control (Seligman & Maier, 1967). They might attribute failure to *external,* stable, and uncontrollable causes such as teacher bias ("the teacher doesn't like me") or task difficulty ("math is too hard for me"). Or they might attribute failure to *internal,* stable, and uncontrollable causes such as lack of ability (entity) (Dweck, 2000; Dweck & Goetz, 1978).

Example 16.2 lists characteristics teachers can use to identify learned helplessness in students. Learned helplessness can be domain-specific, occurring in one subject but not another (Sedek & McIntosh, 1998). Even high-achieving students can experience learned helplessness (Dweck, 2000). Because learned helplessness results from experiences of failure, it is less common in preschool children, who typically receive reinforcement and encouragement of their efforts and products (Rholes, Blackwell, Jordan, & Walters, 1980).

Teachers should be aware that simply providing opportunities for success will not alleviate learned helplessness (Dweck, 1985). For several reasons, it is difficult to convince students with learned helplessness that they can succeed in the future, because they (Ames, 1990; Diener & Dweck, 1978):

- believe others performed better than they did,
- do not take responsibility for their successes (i.e., believe successes are uncontrollable),
- underestimate their performance when they do succeed, and
- interpret a new failure as further evidence of their lack of ability.

To reduce learned helplessness, teachers can use a combination of the motivational techniques discussed earlier. In general, learned helplessness is less common in classrooms where teachers emphasize understanding (rather than memorizing), stimulate creative thinking, and value students' opinions (Sedek & McIntosh, 1998).

Anxiety

All students occasionally experience anxiety in achievement situations in which their abilities are being evaluated. For most students, a small amount of anxiety does not impair performance and may even facilitate it, especially if the task is not too difficult (Ball, 1995; Sieber, O'Neil, & Tobias, 1977). However, for other students anxiety can significantly impair motivation and academic performance.

EXAMPLE 16.2   **Behaviors Indicating Learned Helplessness**

The following behaviors may indicate the presence of learned helplessness.

The student:

- says "I can't,"
- doesn't pay attention to the teacher's instructions,
- doesn't ask for help, even when it is needed,
- does nothing (e.g., stares out the window),
- guesses or answers randomly without really trying,
- doesn't show pride in successes,
- appears bored, uninterested,
- is unresponsive to the teacher's exhortations to try,
- is easily discouraged,
- doesn't volunteer answers to the teacher's questions, or
- maneuvers to get out of or to avoid work (e.g., has to go to the nurse's office).

SOURCE: D. Stipek (2002). *Motivation to Learn: Integrating Theory and Practice.* Boston: Allyn & Bacon. Reprinted with permission from the publisher.

Anxiety has both a cognitive and an emotional component (Sapp, 1999; Zeidner, 1998). Students with anxiety experience mental worry, which most directly interferes with learning and task performance (Tobias, 1992; Zeidner & Nevo, 1992). They also experience negative emotions such as nervousness or tension, which are indicated physically by increased heart rate, sweaty palms, and so on.

Anxiety: See page 292.

Anxiety is more common in school-age children and adolescents than in preschool children (Stipek, 1984), because parents and early childhood educators frequently reinforce young children's efforts and rarely criticize failures. Young children also do not reflect on their performance due to their level of cognitive development. Therefore, their anxiety may at first result from emotional responses to failure (e.g., becoming upset at repeated failures) and later may involve cognitive responses (Harter, 1983; Wigfield & Eccles, 1989).

Anxiety can interfere with the performance of school-age children at three points during the instructional process (Tobias, 1992):

1. *Preprocessing stage:* Anxiety can cause interference when students are forming representations of material initially being presented to them. This anxiety may impair students' ability to pay attention or take notes. A student with anxiety about math may not listen carefully to the teacher's explanation for solving an algebraic equation.

2. *Processing stage:* Anxiety can impair students' ability to learn material after it is presented to them. These students possess less effective study skills than lower-anxiety students and perform more poorly even when they study more (Naveh-Benjamin, McKeachie, & Lin, 1987; Topman, Kleijn, van der Ploeg, & Masset, 1992). A student with math anxiety may use ineffective algorithms when studying and therefore perform more poorly on a test than other students.

3. *Output stage:* Anxiety can impair students' ability to retrieve information in evaluative situations. Students with *text anxiety* at this stage have good study habits and learning strategies but perform poorly because they divide their attention between the task and thoughts about their performance (Naveh-Benjamin et al., 1987). They don't attend to important information during testing, show more off-task behavior than low-anxiety students, and have poorer test-taking strategies such as not accurately interpreting instructions, pacing themselves, nor completing easy questions first (Bruch, Juster, & Kaflowitz, 1983; Nottlemann & Hill, 1977). A student with anxiety about math may "go blank" when completing the test.

DIVERSITY

Girls typically show higher anxiety levels than boys do (Eccles et al., 2000; Randhawa, 1994). However, boys may be more reluctant to admit anxiety. Also, girls and boys may become anxious for different reasons. Girls may be more sensitive to social approval from adults (worrying about making parents or teachers proud of them), while boys may be more concerned with peer evaluation (Dweck & Bush, 1976; Maehr & Nicholls, 1980). During adolescence, girls may become more anxious about certain school subjects, such as math and English, because of the stereotypes these subjects elicit (Meece, 1981).

Anxiety has several possible sources. Parents may promote anxiety when they blame and punish children for failures or setbacks rather than reinforce their successes and also when they control and restrict children's behaviors (Krohne, 1992; Stipek, 2002). Students with an entity view of ability (the view that ability is stable and uncontrollable) may develop anxiety about evaluation of their ability if they have experienced repeated failures (Covington, 1986). Even high-achieving students may become anxious because of unrealistic parental, peer, or self-imposed expectations (Wigfield & Eccles, 1989). Also, factors in the school environment can affect anxiety, including:

- harsh criticism of students' efforts or extremely high standards (Zatz & Chassin, 1985),

- introduction of timed tests (Plass & Hill, 1986),

- changes in grade reporting from nonletter grades in early elementary school to letter grades in upper elementary through high school (Wigfield & Eccles, 1989), and

- school transitions (elementary to middle school or middle to high school) (Eccles, Midgley, & Adler, 1984).

How can teachers reduce students' anxiety? As Guidelines 16.1 shows, students with anxiety at different points in the learning process require different approaches to reducing their anxiety (Naveh-Benjamin, 1991). Developmental level is also an important consideration in choosing methods to reduce anxiety in students. Because younger children are more responsive to praise and feedback from adults than are older children, teachers can alleviate anxiety by providing additional support and

GUIDELINES 16.1   Approaches for Reducing Student Anxiety

Approach	Outcome
Improve students' perceptions of their ability (e.g., re-attribution training).	Reduces anxiety about performance situations.
Modify the presentation of material by: ■ providing clear, unambiguous instructions, ■ presenting well-organized lessons, and ■ allowing students to reinspect material (e.g., provide access to a film that was shown in class).	Reduces anxiety that can interfere with the learning and organizing of new information.
Teach effective study skills.	Reduces anxiety and improves performance in students who do not store or organize information well due to anxiety at initial stages of learning.
Teach test-taking strategies and coping skills.	Reduces anxiety, especially in students who have no difficulty learning the material but experience anxiety when attempting to retrieve information.
Use relaxation techniques prior to testing situations.	Reduces anxiety and improves performance in students who have no difficulty learning the material but experience anxiety when attempting to retrieve information.
Relax time limits, describe tests in a way that deemphasizes their focus on ability, and provide instructions that reduce students' worries about being evaluated.	Reduces test anxiety.

SOURCES: Algaze, 1995; Dendato & Diener, 1986; Dweck, 1975; Fletcher & Spielberger, 1995; Hill & Wigfield, 1984; Linn & Gronlund, 2000; Naveh-Benjamin, 1991; Plass & Hill, 1986; Sapp, 1999; Stipek, 2002; Vagg & Spielberger, 1995; Wigfield & Eccles, 1989.

encouragement and by ensuring that academic tasks are at an appropriate level of difficulty so students do not experience multiple failures (Wigfield & Eccles, 1989). Older students may benefit more from techniques that focus on changing their negative views of ability, attributions for failure, and worries, in addition to study skills training (Wigfield & Eccles, 1989).

Can you remember a time when you have felt anxiety or helplessness? Think about what may have caused these feelings and what you did to overcome them.

Summary

Define expectancies and values, and explain how they influence students' motivation. Expectancies are an individual's expectations for success on a task, which are based partly on one's competency beliefs. Values are the reasons for choosing to do a task (attainment value, intrinsic value, utility value, and cost). Expectancies and values, in combination, determine an individual's motivation to engage in a particular task.

Compare and contrast the two types of mastery and performance goals. Mastery-approach goals (improving knowledge) and performance-approach goals (besting others) both lead students to be intrinsically motivated and are associated with many beneficial outcomes. Mastery-avoidance and performance-avoidance goals both involve avoiding situations that show one's incompetence, but the standard for incompetence is absolute (e.g., the best, the worst) for mastery avoidance and normative (in comparison with others) for performance avoidance. Performance-avoidance goals are related to poor intrinsic motivation.

Identify attributions that enhance motivation and those that lower motivation. Attributing success and failure to amount of effort leads to subsequent motivation to learn. Attributing success to controllable causes leads to further motivation, while attributing failure to stable and uncontrollable causes, as with an entity view of ability, hinders motivation. Teachers who give praise for easy tasks, express sympathy or pity for failures, or offer unsolicited help may inadvertently convey a sense of low ability in students. Praising intelligence also leads to an entity view of ability, which could lower motivation when students encounter failure or difficult tasks.

Explain the major developmental changes in motivation. Young children begin school with a mastery orientation. They have an incremental belief about ability, have high expectancies, and choose tasks based primarily on intrinsic value. As children progress from elementary through high school, they shift toward a performance orientation. Adolescents place less emphasis on mastery and effort and believe that ability is fixed. As a result, they have lower competency beliefs, expectancies, and intrinsic values for academic tasks.

Identify gender and ethnic differences in motivation. Girls tend to hold an entity view of ability and to rate their ability lower than that of boys, especially in math and science. While research suggests that African-American and Hispanic adolescents may be most at risk motivationally compared to other ethnic groups, motivation is the result of many cultural and environmental factors rather than simply the product of a person's ethnicity.

Identify student-level and classroom-level strategies for enhancing motivation. Teachers can improve the motivation of students by:

- changing students' attributions for success and failure,
- emphasizing values that promote intrinsic motivation,
- providing short-term goals and strategies for making progress toward goals,
- reducing the competitive atmosphere of the classroom, and
- using appropriate methods of evaluation and recognition.

Explain how learned helplessness and anxiety affect students' motivation to learn. Students with learned helplessness believe that they have no control over learning outcomes and therefore expect to do poorly, lowering motivation. Anxiety may affect an individual's performance while learning, studying, or retrieving material. The expectation of performing poorly as a result of anxiety lowers motivation to learn.

Key Concepts

academic intrinsic motivation   279

achievement goal   280

anxiety   293

attainment value   280

causal attributions   282

competency belief   279

controllability   282

cost   280

entity view of ability   282

expectancy   279

extrinsic motivation   279

incremental view of ability   282

intrinsic motivation   279

intrinsic value   279

learned helplessness   292

locus   282

mastery-approach goals   280

mastery-avoidance goals   280

performance-approach goals   280

performance-avoidance goals   281

stability   282

utility value   280

value   279

work-avoidance goal   286

Video Applications

www.mhhe.com/bohlin2e

Video 1: Teacher Feedback and Motivation (5 minutes)
This clip shows elementary school students participating in a guitar lesson. It provides an up-close example of the forms of encouragement and feedback that teachers provide to students in the classroom.

Case Studies
Reflect and Evaluate

EARLY CHILDHOOD: "The Worksheets"

These questions refer to the case study on page 256.

1. According to expectancy-value theory, what is Melissa's expectancy for completing her schoolwork? Based on evidence from the case study and the module, what attribution do you think Melissa might make for her math ability?

2. Kristina, like Emanuel and Martin, appears to like math and to be good at math. Based on the research evidence in the module, predict how her competency beliefs in math and the value she places on math might change as she progresses through the upper elementary grades and middle school. How might her attributions change?

3. Imagine that you are having a parent-teacher conference with Martin's mother. Explain to her why she should not praise him for being smart. What effect might this have on Martin's subsequent motivation?

4. Which student(s) might be most difficult to motivate based on goal theory? Based on attribution theory? Cite evidence from the case study to support your position.

5. Based on research evidence regarding the effects of praise, explain why Mrs. Garvey's encouraging Melissa to try harder would be appropriate for a kindergartner but not for a student in middle school or high school.

6. Mrs. Garvey realizes that Martin, Melissa, and Claire have different motivational needs. Help Mrs. Garvey create a motivational plan for each student. Think about modifications to the following: her expectations for each student, goals, feedback about successes and failures, offering help on tasks, and types of tasks and assignments. Create a plan for each student and explain how the modifications would affect each student's expectancies, values, goals, and attributions.

ELEMENTARY SCHOOL: "Writer's Block"

These questions refer to the case study on page 258.

1. According to expectancy-value theory, what is Carter's expectancy for completing his writing assignment? Which type of value—intrinsic value, attainment value, or utility value—does Carter have for writing?

2. Based on the information in the case study regarding goal orientations, which student—Shanti, Zara, or Carter—would be most difficult to motivate? Why? Which student would be easiest to motivate? Why?

3. Reread Mrs. Okuda's interactions with James and Mason. Based on these interactions, what attribution might James and Mason make for their writing performance? Are they likely to have motivation for free writing in the future?

4. What information do students at this developmental level use in making attributions for their performance?

5. Based on the research evidence regarding teacher-student interactions, evaluate Mrs. Okuda's use of feedback.

6. Carter appears to have anxiety about writing when he starts his assignments. What can Mrs. Okuda do to help reduce his anxiety about writing?

MIDDLE SCHOOL: "The Math Review"

These questions refer to the case study on page 260.

1. In your own words, define *expectancy* and *value.* What is Aaron's expectancy for and value of the math game activity? Which type of value—intrinsic value, attainment value, or utility value—do Jeremy and Rachel have for the math activity?

2. According to goal theory, which student—Sam, Jeremy, or Rachel—would be most difficult to motivate? Why? Which student would be easiest to motivate? Why?

3. What attribution does Mr. Pantera likely make for Aaron's performance in his class? Does Mr. Pantera view math performance to be the result of an entity view of ability or an incremental view of ability?

4. What attribution does Sam make for her math performance? Cite research evidence related to gender differences in attributions that might help explain Sam's attributional pattern.

5. What error did Mr. Pantera make in his feedback to Sam?

6. At what point in the instructional process does Sam's anxiety affect her performance? What specific strategies can Mr. Pantera use to help reduce Sam's anxiety?

7. Identify specific techniques Mr. Pantera might use to intrinsically motivate Aaron, Sam, and Jeremy. Explain how each suggestion would improve intrinsic motivation using expectancy-value, goal, or attribution theory.

HIGH SCHOOL: "Exam Grades"

These questions refer to the case study on page 262.

1. What is Chelsea's expectancy for success in physics? Speculate on the social, cultural, and individual factors that might contribute to this expectancy.

2. Explain how physics holds *intrinsic value, attainment value,* and *utility value* for Chelsea. If Chelsea decides not to drop AP physics, what are the *costs* resulting from this decision?

3. Explain why students in AP physics are likely to adopt performance goals. What factors in their environment might contribute to this orientation?

4. What type of goal orientation do students in general science have? Be sure to support your answer with details from the case. Explain how this goal orientation is typical of adolescents.

5. Assume that Reggie is an African-American student. Based on details in the case and on research on ethnic differences in motivation, why would you be concerned about Reggie's motivation? What could you do to intrinsically motivate him?

6. What attribution do Nicholas and Chelsea make for their C+ grades in physics? Based on the research on gender differences in attributions, why is Chelsea's attribution not surprising?

7. What specific suggestions would you give Mr. Womack for intrinsically motivating students in general science? Would your suggestions differ for students in AP physics? If so, why and how? If not, why not?

MODULE 17

Self Theories

Outline	Learning Goals
Self-Efficacy Theory	
▪ Self-Efficacy and Motivation ▪ Teacher Efficacy	1. Describe outcome expectations and efficacy expectations with respect to student and teacher efficacy.
Self-Worth Theory	
▪ Self-Worth and Motivation ▪ Types of Students	2. Explain how self-worth affects the motivation of success-oriented students, overstrivers, and failure-avoiding and failure-accepting students.
Self-Determination Theory	
▪ Self-Determination and Motivation ▪ Becoming Self-Determined	3. Explain how autonomy, competence, and relatedness can facilitate intrinsic motivation. 4. Define internalization and explain how educational contexts can facilitate internalization of behaviors.
Integrating the Self Theories	
▪ Self Theories Compared ▪ Applications: Fostering Self-Efficacy, Self-Worth, and Self-Determination	5. Describe techniques teachers can use to enhance students' intrinsic motivation, and identify which self theory supports each technique.
Summary **Key Concepts** **Video Applications** **Case Studies: Reflect and Evaluate**	

The *self* in self theories of motivation refers to characteristics within individuals that cause them to be motivated: self-efficacy, self-worth, and self-determination. We'll examine each of these characteristics as theories of motivation and consider how they apply to students' intrinsic motivation for learning. All three theories have two things in common. They all focus on:

- a *competence* that underlies the self and an individual's motivation, and
- **intrinsic motivation,** a tendency to engage in an activity for its own sake or out of interest, which can be achieved through feelings of competence. This contrasts with **extrinsic motivation**, engaging in a behavior (in this case learning) for external reasons such as rewards, praise, grades, or recognition.

However, the theories differ in several respects, as we will discuss in the following pages.

SELF-EFFICACY THEORY

Albert Bandura's (1986, 2001) social cognitive theory provides us with three concepts necessary for understanding student motivation and achievement: self-efficacy, self-regulation, and teacher efficacy. Let's explore each of these and how they affect students' intrinsic motivation.

Self-Efficacy and Motivation

Self-efficacy, an expectation that we are capable of performing a task or succeeding in an activity, influences our motivation for the task or activity. To be motivated, we must have high outcome and efficacy expectations. **Outcome expectations** are beliefs that particular actions lead to particular outcomes—in this case, success. **Efficacy expectations** are beliefs that we have the requisite knowledge or skills to achieve the outcome. An elementary school student might believe that learning spelling words makes students better spellers (outcome expectation), but to be motivated to achieve she also needs to believe that *she* has the ability to memorize the assigned spelling words (efficacy expectation). Likewise, a middle school or high school student might believe that studying leads to performing well in school, but he also must believe that *he* has the appropriate study skills to achieve success in school subjects. Students with high efficacy and outcome expectations approach difficult school tasks as challenges to be mastered, set moderately challenging goals, and persist when tasks are difficult—that is, they are motivated. Students with low efficacy and outcome expectations are easily discouraged by failure and therefore are not motivated to learn (Bandura & Schunk, 1981; Schunk & Pajares, 2009).

Self-efficacy is a critical determinant of behavior in school, sports, and social relationships (Bandura, 1977, 1997). It is domain-specific, meaning that a student may have high self-efficacy in math but not

Intrinsic motivation: See pages 265 and 279.

Extrinsic motivation: See pages 265 and 279.

Social cognitive theory: See Module 10.

17 | Self Theories

Self-efficacy. The Little Engine That Could is a good example of self-efficacy, with the engine saying, "I think I can, I think I can. . . ." as she climbs the hill.

in other subjects, or in athletics but not in academics. Boys tend to have higher self-efficacy in math and science, while girls tend to have higher self-efficacy in writing (Anderman & Young, 1994; Pajares & Valiante, 2001; Pintrich & DeGroot, 1990). Gender differences may be due partly to cultural expectations that influence parents' perceptions that boys are better at math and science (Meece, Glienke, & Askew, 2009). Because cultural expectations also affect parental behaviors, they may indirectly influence children's self-efficacy and motivation. In one study, for example, mothers were more likely to buy math and science items for boys than for girls, regardless of the child's age (Bleeker & Jacobs, 2004).

DIVERSITY

Students from various ethnic backgrounds also show differences in self-efficacy depending on subject matter. Students from minority groups tend to have self-efficacy for reading that is comparable to that of their Caucasian peers (Mucherah & Yoder, 2008). However, self-efficacy for math appears to be lower for African-American and Hispanic students (Pajares & Kranzler, 1995; Stevens, Olivárez, Lan, & Tallent-Runnels, 2004). Also, Hispanic students tend to have lower writing self-efficacy than Caucasian students (Pajares & Johnson, 1996). Because self-efficacy is domain-specific, the challenges of second language acquisition may partly explain the lower self-efficacy of Hispanic students in writing. Despite any group differences in self-efficacy for certain subjects, we should remember that students from diverse ethnic and cultural backgrounds tend to have positive overall academic self-efficacy (Graham, 1994; Lay & Wakstein, 1985; Stevenson, Chen, & Uttal, 1990). Also, group differences in self-efficacy may be less important for teachers' understanding of self-efficacy than knowing about the experiences that shape self-efficacy and the relative importance of these experiences for different cultural groups.

How do individuals develop beliefs about their own self-efficacy? For example, why does a high school student think she's good at physics? Research shows that, over time, individuals develop self-efficacy beliefs as they interpret information from four influences (Bandura, 1982; Usher & Pajares, 2008):

Four influences on self-efficacy: See page 177.

1. *Past performance.* Students' self-efficacy improves when they achieve mastery and attribute their success to ability or effort (Scholz, Dona, Sud, & Schwarzer, 2002; Zimmerman, 2000). Mastery experiences are the most influential of all four sources of information for developing self-efficacy (Pajares, Johnson, & Usher, 2007; Usher & Pajares, 2006a, 2006b). Parents' use of authoritative parenting—allowing children to try new things, setting reasonable limits, and responding in a firm, but warm manner—increases children's sense of mastery and self-efficacy (Boon, 2007).

Authoritative parenting: See page 32.

Modeling: See page 174.

2. *Vicarious experiences.* Vicarious experience, or observing the performance of someone else, can help an individual develop self-efficacy. Parents who model effort, persistence, and coping with difficulties have children with greater self-efficacy (Bandura, 1997). When students lack personal experience with a task, it is especially important that the model be similar to them (Schunk & Miller, 2002). For example, observing peers complete a task leads students to greater self-efficacy than does observing a teacher (Schunk & Hanson, 1985). However, if the model is considered to be abler or more talented, observers will not have high efficacy expectations after viewing the model's performance (Zimmerman, 2000).

3. *Verbal persuasion.* Reassuring individuals that they will succeed or encouraging their efforts can foster positive self-efficacy. Parents who encourage their children to try different activities and provide them with support for doing so encourage their children's self-efficacy (Bandura, 1997). Verbal persuasion is less effective than both past mastery performance and vicarious experiences because success outcomes are merely described, not witnessed or experienced, and depend on the credibility of the persuader (Zimmerman, 2000).

4. *States of emotional arousal.* Fatigue, stress, and anxiety often are interpreted as indicators of lack of competence (Scholz et al., 2002; Tollefson, 2000). Confidence and eagerness, in contrast, are emotional signs of competence. Individuals with higher self-efficacy show decreased stress, anxiety, and depression when they are confronted with demanding school tasks, while those with lower self-efficacy tend to exhibit depression, anxiety, and helplessness (Bandura, 1997; Scholz et al., 2002).

Vicarious Experiences. The most effective model for this young boy learning to tie his sneaker is a child of a similar age, like his sister shown here.

Students of varying backgrounds are influenced differently by the sources of information described above, and these varied experiences may be the cause of gender and ethnic differences in self-efficacy.

DIVERSITY

Praise: See page 269.

- For example, boys report stronger mastery experiences and lower anxiety in math and science while girls have stronger mastery experiences and lower anxiety in writing (Britner & Pajares, 2006; Lent et al., 1996; Pajares et al., 2007). General academic efficacy is influenced more by vicarious experiences for boys and by verbal persuasion for girls (Usher & Pajares, 2006a, 2006b). This suggests that the right type of praise and encouragement could be effective in motivating girls.

- The self-efficacy of Caucasian students seems to be influenced by all four sources of information, while African-American students' self-efficacy is influenced mainly by mastery experiences and verbal persuasion (Usher & Pajares, 2006a, 2006b). In contrast, Mexican-American students may be more influenced by vicarious experience than their Caucasian peers (Stevens, Olivárez, & Hamman, 2006).

- Students with learning disabilities and students in lower ability groups have lower self-efficacy than their peers, and report fewer mastery experiences, vicarious experiences, and verbal persuasions. They also have higher anxiety than students with average or above-average achievement (Hampton & Mason, 2003; Usher & Pajares, 2006b).

To better understand how to increase students' self-efficacy, we need to discuss how school experiences help shape self-efficacy. Young children's beliefs about their ability are overly optimistic (Wigfield & Cambria, 2010a). They interpret praise as an indication of exceptional performance and pay little attention to social comparisons of performance (Usher & Pajares, 2008). Self-efficacy declines developmentally (Anderman & Midgley, 1997; Eccles & Midgley, 1989). As children progress through school, their cognitive development and school practices that involve evaluation (grades, displaying best work, etc.) lead them to make comparisons of their performance with others. These comparisons may lead to more realistic perceptions of ability, and consequently decreased self-efficacy.

School transitions from elementary to middle school and from middle school to high school can cause further declines in self-efficacy (Friedel, Cortina, Turner, & Midgley, 2010; Schunk & Meece, 2006). Middle school students perceive school as more focused on performance-approach goals (competing for grades, showing off ability) than mastery-approach goals (focusing on learning and improving (Midgley, 2002). In response to the increasing emphasis on grading and evaluation that they experience as they transition to middle school, adolescents continually reassess their self-efficacy in various subjects (Schunk & Miller, 2002).

Performance-approach goals and mastery-approach goals: See page 280.

Regardless of grade level, classroom practices can influence self-efficacy. In classrooms where teachers make explicit comparisons of ability, lower-achieving students have lower self-efficacy. For example, ability grouping, which involves placing students into homogeneous groups based on their achievement level (e.g., for reading or math in elementary classrooms), can undermine the self-efficacy of students in the lower groups (Schunk & Miller, 2002). Explicit comparisons are less likely in middle school and high school, because in many schools students are assigned to curriculum tracks in which all students within a class are of the same ability level.

Ability grouping: See page 378.

During any particular grade, outcome and efficacy expectations may also change over the school year. Students may have high outcome and efficacy expectations on the first day of school. But as the school year progresses and they receive feedback about their performance, they may come to believe that while it is possible for students to be successful (outcome expectation), they personally do not have the requisite skills, abilities, or work ethic to achieve success in that particular environment (efficacy expectation) (Tollefson, 2000).

The second of the three motivation-related concepts from Bandura's social-cognitive theory is **self-regulation**, the ability to control one's emotions, cognitions, and behaviors by providing consequences to oneself. Self-efficacy influences self-regulation in learners (Bong & Skaalvik, 2003; Pintrich & Schunk, 2002). Students with high self-efficacy are more likely to engage in self-regulatory processes such as goal setting, self-monitoring, self-evaluation, and effective strategy use (Zimmerman, 2000). Many of these processes are linked to intrinsic motivation. For example, students with high self-efficacy tend to:

Self-regulation: See page 301.

- choose more difficult tasks and set mastery goals (Seijts & Latham, 2001; Zimmerman, Bandura, & Martinez-Pons, 1992). Intrinsically motivated students set moderately challenging goals that allow them to achieve mastery of knowledge or skills.

Goal theory: See page 280.

- respond more positively to negative feedback and persist when faced with failure (Pugh & Bergin, 2006; Seijts & Latham, 2001). Intrinsically motivated students do not fear failure; rather, they consider feedback to be useful information for improving themselves.

- choose more effective strategies such as organizing information, making connections, rereading material, making outlines, and monitoring performance (Bouffard-Bouchard, Parent, & Larivee, 1991; Pintrich & DeGroot, 1990). This is true of students at all levels of K–12 education (Zimmerman &

Martinez-Pons, 1990). Students who are intrinsically motivated to achieve mastery are more likely to use effective learning strategies (Pintrich & DeGroot, 1990; Pintrich & Garcia, 1991). As a result, students with high self-efficacy attain higher achievement through their efficient use of self-regulatory skills (Bandura & Locke, 2003; Valentine, DuBois, & Cooper, 2004).

Think of a subject that you find enjoyable and one that you find challenging. Describe your self-efficacy in each. How do your outcome and efficacy expectations differ in each subject?

Teacher Efficacy

The third and final motivation-related concept we'll examine from Bandura's social-cognitive theory is **teacher efficacy,** a belief by teachers that they have the skills necessary to teach all students effectively. Teacher efficacy positively influences student achievement (Goddard, Hoy, & Woolfolk-Hoy, 2004; Hines & Kritsonis, 2010). Over time, teachers develop outcome expectations (a belief that all students can learn the material) and efficacy expectations (beliefs about their own ability to help all children learn) (Ashton & Webb, 1986; Gibson & Dembo, 1984).

Like students, teachers possess different levels of efficacy. Teachers may have low teaching efficacy for a variety of reasons. New teachers, who tend to feel overwhelmed and sometimes unprepared, might believe that all teachers can have a positive effect on the education of students (outcome expectation) but that *they* lack the skills required to teach students effectively (efficacy expectation) (Stipek, 2002). Teachers also may have low efficacy because they believe that:

- a lack of school resources hinders their ability to teach effectively, or that the district or state requires them to teach in ways that are not effective (Stipek, 2002);
- a lack of parental support for academics contributes to students' low achievement (Guskey & Passaro, 1994; Weinstein, Madison, & Kuklinski, 1995); or
- students' low ability contributes to their poor achievement.

Entity view of ability and incremental view of ability: See page 282.

Many teachers tend to have an **entity view of ability**—the belief that ability is stable and uncontrollable (Oakes & Guiton, 1995; Reyna, 2000). Teachers with an entity view tend to pass judgment more quickly on the basis of initial performance and to resist changing their judgments when they are confronted with evidence that contradicts their initial assumptions (Butler, 2000; Plaks, Stroessner, Dweck, & Sherman, 2001). In contrast, other teachers have an **incremental view of ability,** in which ability is seen as improvable (unstable and controllable).

DIVERSITY

Teachers who believe that low student ability, low levels of effort, and lack of parental involvement are stable factors leading to poor academic achievement may develop low outcome expectations for both their students and themselves (Tollefson, 2000). This, in turn, may affect their expectations for and interactions with students. Teachers with low teacher efficacy tend to call on low achievers less often, give them less praise and more busy work, and interact more with high achievers (Ashton & Webb, 1986). Also, teachers are more likely to give students from lower socioeconomic backgrounds and minority students low-ability messages, such as expressing pity for students' failures, praising students for easy tasks, or offering unsolicited help (Graham, 1990; McLoyd, 1998). As a result, students may develop an entity belief about their ability—believing that they have low ability and cannot change it—and may experience lower intrinsic motivation (Dweck, 1999; Graham & Weiner, 1993).

To understand how teacher efficacy can enhance students' intrinsic motivation, consider these characteristics of highly efficacious teachers. Teachers with higher efficacy:

- spend more time on planning and organizing (Gibson & Dembo, 1984; Tschannen-Moran & Woolfolk-Hoy, 2001).
- are more willing to try new instructional methods (Ross, 1998; Supovitz & Turner, 2000). They tend to use more self-directed activities and small group discussions (Tschannen-Moran, Woolfolk-Hoy, & Hoy, 1998). They also are more open to using interactive approaches such as cooperative learning, peer tutoring, and problem-based learning because they believe that these types of activities enhance learning (outcome expectation) (Tollefson, 2000).

Cooperative learning: See page 378.

- modify curricula so that students with different levels of ability can achieve success with moderate effort (Tollefson, 2000).
- use classroom management strategies that keep students on task and promote achievement (Ross & Bruce, 2007; Woolfolk, Rosoff, & Hoy, 1990).
- show persistence when helping students who are having difficulty and foster positive self-esteem in students (Ross & Bruce, 2007; Tschannen-Moran et al., 1998).

In sum, teachers with high efficacy tend to have a mastery-oriented focus to teaching practices, meaning that they emphasize the importance of learning, improvement, and overcoming challenges over performance goals such as outperforming other students (Wolters & Daugherty, 2007).

Goal theory: See page 280.

SELF-WORTH THEORY

According to self-worth theory, as proposed by Martin Covington (1998, 2009), humans naturally strive to maintain a sense of **self-worth,** or an appraisal of one's own value as a person. Humans are motivated to protect their self-worth by maintaining a belief that they are competent (Ames & Ames, 1984; Covington, 2009).

Self-Worth and Motivation

Because schools value and reward competencies (being able, smart, successful), students' perceptions of ability contribute to their self-worth (Covington, 1998). Proving their ability, therefore, becomes a primary focus of students' learning. This leads students to be motivated to avoid a negative consequence—such as looking less competent than their peers (Covington & Müeller, 2001). Consequently, students become *extrinsically motivated*—that is, motivated by external factors—and their intrinsic motivation to learn becomes compromised.

Students may be both intrinsically and extrinsically motivated but appear extrinsically motivated because of external pressures to prove their self-worth. When college students (like you) were asked why they would do extra, unassigned work for a course, they most often reported that it would satisfy their curiosity and interest (intrinsic motivation). In practice, however, college students didn't take time to pursue topics that interested them because it would take time away from studying for exams (extrinsic motivation) (Covington & Müeller, 2001).

As students progress from elementary school through middle school and high school, they experience greater emphases on competition and performance evaluation, and their self-worth increasingly depends on their ability to achieve competitively (Gottfried, Fleming, & Gottfried, 2001; Harari & Covington, 1981). Extrinsic rewards for learning, such as good grades and high performance on standardized tests, are symbols of success that maintain self-worth. However, because success is defined by comparing one's performance with that of others, the self-worth of low-achieving students may be threatened when they face standards that are too high for them to have success (Stipek, 2002). For example, the No Child Left Behind (NCLB) Act of 2001, which mandates states to set proficiency goals in reading and mathematics and to report assessment of progress toward meeting those goals, requires documentation of proficiency levels from students in various groups: socioeconomic status, ethnicity, disability, and limited English proficiency. The academic challenges faced by students with disabilities and students with limited English proficiency put them at risk for low self-worth. Students from lower socioeconomic backgrounds and minority students, who traditionally have performed poorly on standardized tests, also may experience low self-worth (Kim & Sunderman, 2005). A focus on extrinsic factors such as grades and test scores therefore may decrease students' intrinsic motivation (Lepper, Corpus, & Iyengar, 2005; Lepper, Sethi, Dialdin, & Drake, 1997).

No Child Left Behind: See page 552.
DIVERSITY

Types of Students

According to self-worth theory, the distinction between "approaching success" and "avoiding failure" is central to understanding students' motivation (Covington, 2009; Covington & Beery, 1976). This distinction allows us to understand the motivation of four different types of students, as shown in Figure 17.1, based on how much each student is driven to approach success and to avoid failure.

Success-oriented students are intrinsically motivated. Because they value ability as a tool to achieve mastery on personally meaningful goals, they define success in terms of becoming the best they can be, regardless of the achievements of others. Students in the other three categories define success (and their resulting self-worth) as doing better than others, so they are motivated to avoid failure or to avoid looking as if they have low ability (Covington & Müeller, 2001).

Success-oriented students: See mastery-approach goals on page 280.

Like success-oriented students, **overstrivers** are driven by high hopes for success, but unlike success-oriented students they have an excessive fear of failure (Beery, 1975). Therefore, they are motivated to prove their ability by performing better than others. To do this, they use several strategies to ensure their success (Covington, 1984; Stipek, 2002):

Overstrivers: See performance-approach goals on page 280.

1. *Attempting only very easy tasks.* This guarantees success with little learning.

Self-worth. Schools often reward students for their competencies, leading students to develop a sense of self-worth based on beliefs about their own abilities.

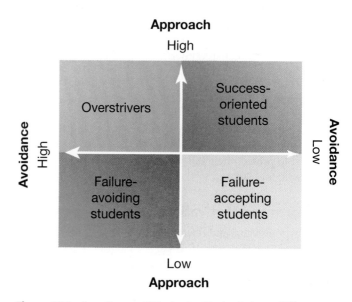

Figure 17.1. Four Types of Students. Students have different types of motivation, according to self-worth theory.

SOURCE: From M. V. Covington and K. J. Mueller (2001), "Intrinsic versus extrinsic motivation: An approach/avoidance reformulation," *Education Psychology Review, 13,* (2), 157–176. Copyright © 2001. Reprinted by permission of Springer.

2. *Having low aspirations.* A student might announce that he is not prepared for a test and hopes simply to pass. Doing better than passing (success) with minimal effort implies that the student has high ability.

3. *Rehearsing responses.* An elementary school student might rehearse a section of text that she expects to read aloud to minimize any reading errors. Likewise, a student in a high school foreign language or math class might practice the answer to a question before being called upon.

4. *Excessive attention to detail.* Overstrivers doubt their actual abilities and attribute success to extreme effort, such as being overprepared or showing excessive attention to detail (Covington, 1984; Covington & Beery, 1976). An elementary school student might ask the teacher if he is on the right track with a math worksheet after every few problems, or a middle or high school student might ask the teacher for clarification or feedback several times while working on an individual project.

5. *Cheating.* Students might cheat as an extreme measure to ensure success because they believe that asking for help indicates low ability (Butler, 1998).

Overstrivers are motivated by a sense of pride stemming from their success and by the temporary relief of not failing (of avoiding negative consequences), creating a continual cycle of having to prove themselves (Covington & Müeller, 2001).

Failure-avoiding students also are highly motivated to avoid failure, but unlike overstrivers they do not have high expectations for success. Failure-avoiding students are motivated to temporarily avoid a negative outcome—the anxiety of being identified as incompetent—and learn to internalize feelings of relief rather than pride (Covington & Müeller, 2001). To avoid looking incompetent, they use several self-handicapping strategies that prevent any real learning (Covington, 1984; Covington & Beery, 1976):

1. Minimizing or withdrawing participation (not raising one's hand, sitting at the back of the room out of the teacher's view, note taking with head down, pretending to pay attention with a pensive look, or being absent on the day of a test)

2. Making excuses (for missing or incomplete homework; "forgetting" a presentation at home)

3. Procrastination (studying or starting a term paper the night before an exam or due date)

4. Setting unattainable goals or selecting very difficult tasks

5. Not trying or making others think one didn't try

Students with lower achievement from elementary school through high school tend to use more self-handicapping strategies than students who are doing well in school (Leondari & Gonida, 2007). Research on gender differences in self-handicapping is inconclusive, with some studies showing

Failure-avoiding students: See performance-avoidance goals on page 281.

DIVERSITY

boys using these strategies more often than girls do, while other studies find no gender difference (Leondari & Gonida, 2007; Urdan, Midgley, & Anderman, 1998).

To failure-avoiding students, self-handicapping strategies are a useful way to attribute failure to causes other than low ability, enabling them to feel less shame (Stipek, 2002). If a student puts in a lot of effort to succeed on a task—one that others master with less effort—the student would feel this implies low ability. Worse, to fail after putting in effort would, to the student, be a public admission of low ability (Covington & Omelich, 1979). Failure without effort, though, does not reflect negatively on the student's ability (Covington & Beery, 1976).

Learned Helplessness. This student may believe that she cannot possibly succeed in reading all of these sources for a term paper. Students like this one may develop learned helplessness, accepting failure and not trying at all.

However, lack of effort can become a "double-edged sword" (Covington & Omelich, 1979). Because teachers value effort, students who purposely do not try risk teacher disapproval and punishment (Urdan et al., 1998; Weiner, 1994). Teachers may require elementary school students to complete work during recess or as a homework assignment, and in the upper grades they may give detentions or failing grades. Therefore, the student is stuck between two competing alternatives: being punished for not trying, or trying and risking a demonstration of low ability.

Unlike the other three types of students, **failure-accepting students** neither approach success nor avoid failure. Rather, in response to repeated failures to perform up to their expectations, they accept failure and give up the struggle to demonstrate their ability and maintain their self-worth (Covington & Omelich, 1985). Failure-accepting students (Covington, 1984):

- take little credit for success and believe that success is determined by external, uncontrollable factors;
- blame themselves (i.e., their low ability) for failure; and
- view a new failure as confirmation of their belief that they lack ability.

Failure-accepting students are similar to students with *learned helplessness*, those who are not motivated to learn because they believe that past failures are due to causes they do not control. Therefore, these students are the most difficult to motivate because positive reinforcement for successes does not work, and convincing them that they could succeed in the future is difficult (Ames, 1990; Covington & Omelich, 1985).

Learned helplessness: See page 292.

Failure-avoiding and failure-accepting students, whose sense of ability is threatened, may attempt to maintain positive self-worth by discounting the importance of school success (Harter, Whitesell, & Junkin, 1998). Some adolescents use this strategy as a last resort. They shift their attention to developing competencies in nonacademic areas such as sports, music, art, or delinquent behavior (Stipek, 2002). It is important for teachers to identify students with failure-avoiding or failure-accepting orientations so they may help them develop more positive mastery behaviors.

Which type of student do you consider yourself? Has your motivational orientation changed during your schooling? If so, how has it changed?

SELF-DETERMINATION THEORY

According to self-determination theory, humans possess *universal*, innate needs for autonomy, competence, and relatedness (deCharms, 1976; Ryan & Deci, 2000b). We need to feel **autonomy**—that our behavior is internally controlled or self-regulated and that we have choices in our actions rather than being controlled or pressured (Deci & Ryan, 1985; Vansteenkiste, Niemiec, & Soenens, 2010). We also have a **need for competence,** that is, an innate desire to explore and attempt mastery of skills (White, 1959). To feel safe enough to explore our environment, though, we also need to feel **relatedness,** or a sense of being securely connected to others (Ryan, Deci, & Grolnick, 1995). When these needs are supported in our environment, we feel a sense of **self-determination**, or a freedom to pursue goals and activities that are personally relevant and interesting to us. These needs are important for psychological well-being of individuals in Western cultures and Eastern collectivistic cultures, including Bulgaria, South Korea, Russia, and China (Vansteenkiste et al., 2010).

Self-determination theory shares some characteristics with **Maslow's hierarchy of needs,** a once-popular humanistic theory. **Humanistic theories** emphasize factors intrinsic to the individual, such as needs, as sources of motivation. In Maslow's (1943, 1987) theory, individuals are motivated by basic human needs:

1. physiological needs (food, water, shelter, and clothing),
2. safety needs (feeling nonthreatened and having a sense of order and stability),
3. love and belongingness (a need to give and receive love, and to experience friendship, appreciation, and belonging),
4. esteem needs (desire for achievement and for respect from others), and
5. **self-actualization**, a need to satisfy their full potential.

Maslow proposed that the needs are organized according to their biological urgency, with the most urgent ones needing to be satisfied first. Lower-level needs, such as physiological and safety needs, need to be at least partially satisfied in order for an individual to focus on higher-level needs. The four basic needs (physiological comfort, safety, love, and self-esteem) are all **deficiency needs** (Maslow, 1954), meaning we are motivated to obtain them when they are lacking in our environment. The fifth, self-actualization, is a **growth need** because individuals are continually motivated from within by a need for growth, maturation, and fulfillment (Maslow, 1954). Even though Maslow never used a pyramid or triangle to depict the hierarchy, these needs are often shown in this way, as in Figure 17.2 (Wininger & Norman, 2010).

A common misconception of Maslow's theory is that individuals need to fully satisfy one need before addressing the next need in the hierarchy (Wininger & Norman, 2010). However, the hierarchy is not rigid; the order in which needs are met may vary (Maslow, 1954, 1987). For example, a student who desires to do well in school and attend a prestigious college may spend countless hours studying (motivated by esteem needs) and neglect spending time with family and friends (love and belongingness needs). Also, the satisfaction of needs is not "all-or-none." Most individuals in our society have all of their basic needs partially satisfied to different degrees (Maslow, 1987; Wininger & Norman, 2010).

Maslow's theory has been influential in research on motivation because it gave us the idea of innate needs as important sources of information. The theory remains popular in practice because it gives teachers a way to understand the possible obstacles to learning and motivation. Maslow's theory proposes that if lower needs are *mostly* unmet, this would interfere with students' interest in learning. Similarly, self-determination theory suggests that if needs for autonomy, competence, and relatedness are not supported, students will not be intrinsically motivated. Let's explore this idea further.

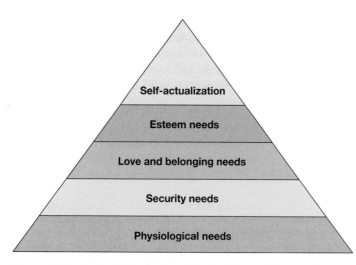

Figure 17.2. Maslow's Hierarchy of Needs. Maslow's hierarchy provides teachers with an understanding that when certain needs are extremely deficient in a student, such as when children from poor environments do not have food to eat every day, these can become obstacles to learning and self-fulfillment.

Self-Determination and Motivation

As we discussed with regard to self-efficacy and self-worth theory, feelings of competence can facilitate intrinsic motivation. Engaging in optimally challenging tasks fulfills the need to feel competent, encouraging intrinsic motivation (Deci & Ryan, 1992; Grolnick, Gurland, Jacob, & DeCourcey, 2002). When cognitive tasks are slightly above children's skill levels, they spend more time on them, show more intrinsic motivation, and exhibit intense joy and pride when they master the tasks (Harter, 1978b; McMullin & Steffen, 1982). Increases in feelings of academic competence from elementary school to middle school result in increased intrinsic motivation for schoolwork, while lowered feelings of competence over the years decrease intrinsic motivation (Harter, 1992; Harter, Whitesell, & Kowalski, 1992). High school students whose perceptions of competence increased over the semester found the subject they were learning more interesting at the end of the semester than at the beginning (MacIver, Stipek, & Daniels, 1991).

Feelings of competence enhance intrinsic motivation only when they are supported by autonomy (Ryan & Deci, 2000a), meaning that behaviors are internally regulated. Earning an A on an exam (feeling competent) will lead you to be intrinsically motivated if you believe that your actions—studying—were autonomous. Highly autonomous students are more engaged in school, achieve higher academic performance, and stay in school until graduation (Grolnick et al., 2002; Soenens & Vansteenkiste, 2005. However, if you study hard because your parents expect you to do well in school or because you want to impress the teacher, your studying behavior is not internally regulated, leading you to be more extrinsically motivated.

Intrinsic motivation also is more likely to flourish when students feel relatedness (Ryan & Deci, 2000a). Students who feel secure in their environment and connected to others are more likely to seek out mastery experiences, promoting a sense of competence. They may develop intrinsic motivation for academic tasks and activities if these are modeled or valued by others with whom they feel (or want to feel) attached (Ryan & Deci, 2000a). For example, students may become intrinsically motivated to learn if they have "bonded" with a teacher who shows them the value of learning. Students who believed their teachers to be cold and uncaring had lower intrinsic motivation (Ryan & Grolnick, 1986). Relatedness may positively affect the motivation of girls more than that of boys. Girls report closer relationships with teachers, and teachers consider their relationships with girls to be closer than their relationships with boys (Howes, Phillipsen, & Peisner-Feinberg, 2000; Valeski & Stipek, 2001).

DIVERSITY

Teacher-student relationships: See page 338.

Becoming Self-Determined

Like self-efficacy, self-determination is specific to a particular activity or subject (Grolnick et al., 2002). Individuals can develop self-determination for behaviors such as schoolwork, chores, or attending religious functions (Grolnick, Deci, & Ryan, 1997). Individuals develop self-determination through a developmental process called **internalization**, where they acquire beliefs, attitudes, and behaviors from external sources and progressively transform them into personal attributes, values, and self-regulatory behaviors (Grolnick, Deci, & Ryan, 1997). Figure 17.3 shows the developmental continuum from non-self-determined behavior (no self-regulatory behavior) to self-determined behavior (fully autonomous and intrinsically regulated behavior). Let's remember that self-determination theory does not imply

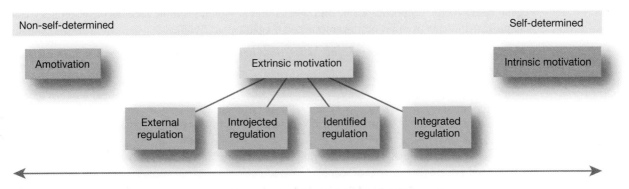

Figure 17.3. A Taxonomy of Human Motivation. The degree of autonomy we have affects our level of motivation from non-self-determined to self-determined.

SOURCE: Adapted from R. M. Ryan, & E. L. Deci (2000). "Self-determination theory and the facilitation of intrinsic motivation, social development, and well-being." *American Psychologist, 55*(1), 72, January 2000. Copyright © 2000 American Psychological Association. Used with permission.

movement through each form of motivation (Vansteenkiste, Lens, & Deci, 2006). Rather, individuals may show different types of motivation that vary in their degree of autonomy depending on how successful they are at internalization (Deci & Ryan, 1985; Ryan & Deci, 2000a). To intrinsically motivate students, it is important for teachers to know what type of motivation along the continuum students currently exhibit.

Amotivation is a lack of motivation. Individuals with this orientation do not show any self-regulation. Instead, they simply "go through the motions" or are unwilling to act at all. Students may be amotivated because the academic task is unappealing to them or they do not value the learning activity (Legault, Green-Demers, & Pelletier, 2006; Ryan, 1995). Students may also be amotivated because they do not feel competent to do the activity or they do not feel they can put forth the effort needed to succeed (Bandura, 1986; Legault et al., 2006). Amotivation may be more likely to occur in boys than girls (Alvernini, Lucidi, & Manganelli, 2008).

DIVERSITY

External regulation is the least autonomous form of extrinsic motivation. Externally regulated individuals perform behaviors in response to external contingencies such as rewards, praise, punishments, and deadlines. An elementary school student who studies to get money for As and Bs on her report card exhibits external regulation of behavior, as does a high school student who completes homework assignments to avoid detentions.

Introjected regulation is a form of extrinsic motivation in which individuals engage in an activity in order to comply with external pressure. Because individuals have partially internalized the behavior and have not taken ownership of it, they perform the behavior to avoid guilt or anxiety or to achieve a sense of pride (Ryan & Deci, 2000a; Vansteenkiste et al., 2010). A middle school student who studies before going to baseball practice (because he would feel guilty if he put sports ahead of schoolwork) is showing introjected regulation, as is a high school student who feels intense pressure to ace an exam in order to prove her self-worth (because she has not yet accepted studying as part of her internal values).

Identified regulation is a slightly internalized form of regulation that approximates intrinsic motivation. Individuals identify with the value of an activity, have accepted regulation of the activity as their own, and more willingly engage in the activity because they see its personal relevance. An elementary school student who says "I do my schoolwork because learning new things makes you smarter" exhibits identified regulation, as does a high school student who chooses to learn a foreign language because of its importance for career goals.

Integrated regulation occurs when individuals have fully accepted extrinsic regulations by integrating them with other aspects of their values and identity (Ryan, 1995). A high school student might study regularly because it has become a part of his identity as a student.

Finally, the most self-determined and autonomous form of motivation is **intrinsic motivation.** A high school study might study regularly because it satisfies her curiosity, interests, or need for competence.

Amotivation and external and introjected regulation are considered controlled (pressured or coerced), while intrinsic motivation and well-internalized forms of extrinsic motivation (identified and integrated regulation) are considered autonomous, or self-determined (Vansteenkiste et al., 2010). Girls tend to be more self-determined in school than boys, showing higher levels of identified and introjected regulation (Vallerand, Pelletier, Blais, Briére, Senécal, & Vallières, 1993). Consistent with research showing a general decline in intrinsic motivation from elementary through high school, amotivation and external regulation are typically found more often in high school students (Alvernini et al., 2008; Legault et al., 2006). Supportive home and peer contexts, which promote feelings of relatedness, can help prevent students from becoming amotivated (Legault et al., 2006).

DIVERSITY

What level of self-determination do you have? How have your parents or teachers influenced your self-determination?

Home or school contexts that fulfill individuals' needs for competence, autonomy, and relatedness—called autonomy-supportive contexts—can facilitate internalization and encourage intrinsic motivation (Grolnick et al., 1997; Ryan & Deci, 2000a). Autonomy-supportive parents spend time with their children, know about their daily life, and provide them with opportunities to explore and master their environment (Grolnick et al., 1997). As a result, their children tend to be mastery-oriented and to have increased self-esteem, connection to school, and academic achievement (Eccles, Early, Frasier, Belansky, & McCarthy, 1996; Grolnick et al., 1997). Teachers with a strong sense of autonomy in their teaching tend to be more autonomy-supportive (Roth, Assor, Kanat-Maymon, & Kaplan, 2007; Reeve, 2009). Their behaviors lead to numerous positive outcomes for students, as outlined in Table 17.1. The advantages of autonomy-supportive environments have been found in Western and non-Western cultures (Chirkov, Ryan, & Willness, 2005; Jang, Reeve, Ryan, & Kim, 2009; Vansteenkiste, Zhou, Lens, & Soenens, 2005).

DIVERSITY

TABLE 17.1	Autonomy-Supportive Teaching Practices and Beneficial Student Outcomes

What Autonomy-Supportive Teachers Do	Beneficial Outcomes of Autonomy-Supportive Teaching
■ empathize with the students' perspectives, showing an understanding of their complaints and negative emotions ■ encourage students to express opinions and preferences ■ allow students to work at their own pace ■ solicit students' opinions ■ provide classroom structure, conveying their expectations for students in a non-controlling way and providing sufficient information and support for meeting those expectations ■ give feedback about students' competence and express confidence in students' abilities ■ avoid the use of controlling educational practices such as controlling language, directives, threats, imposed deadlines, and close monitoring	■ better time management and concentration ■ deep, meaningful learning ■ greater creativity ■ better academic performance ■ greater identified regulation for schoolwork ■ higher intrinsic motivation ■ enhanced well-being

SOURCES: Assor et al., 2005; Deci, Eghrari, Patrick, & Leone, 1994; Jang, Reeve, & Deci, 2010; Koestner, Ryan, Bernieri, & Holt, 1984; Levesque, Zuehike, Stanek, & Ryan, 2004; Patall, Cooper, & Wynn, 2010; Reeve, 2009; Reeve, Jang, Carrell, Barch, & Jeon, 2004; Sierens, Vansteenkiste, Goossens, Soenens, & Dochy, 2009; Soenens & Vansteenkiste, 2005; Vansteenkiste, Lens, De Witte, De Witte, & Deci, 2004; Vansteenkiste et al., 2010; Vansteenkiste, Simons, Lens, Sheldon, & Deci, 2004; Vansteenkiste, Zhou, Lens, & Soenens, 2005.

Autonomy-supportive learning contexts are beneficial for students from preschool through high school, including students with special needs (Deci, Hodges, Pierson, & Tomassone, 1992; Reeve, 2009). This type of context may be especially important during adolescence, when students are experiencing important changes such as going through puberty, establishing their independence and identity, and transitioning to middle and high school. Self-determination is critical during times of change. It facilitates problem solving and flexible strategies in new situations and helps promote healthy sociocognitive development in early adolescence (Eccles, Midgley, et al., 1993; Grolnick et al., 2002). Ironically, schools seem to become more controlling just as students' autonomy needs begin to increase (Eccles, Midgley, et al., 1993; Midgley & Feldlaufer, 1987). In middle school, students face more rules and discipline, have fewer opportunities to make decisions, and experience harsher grading practices (Anderman & Maehr, 1994). In high school, teachers tend to rely on extrinsic motivators to engage students in learning, to use controlling language without explanations for their requests, and to reject students' complaints and negative emotions (Reeve, Jang, Carrell, Barch, & Jeon, 2004; Jang, Reeve, & Deci, 2010). The structure of middle schools and high schools—in which students have multiple teachers, switch classes, and often are grouped by ability—also may discourage connectedness (Juvonen, 2007).

DIVERSITY

INTEGRATING THE SELF THEORIES

Have you noticed similarities among the theories? You may have asked yourself why we need three separate theories related to the self. While the theories do overlap, they each bring a unique perspective to understanding intrinsic motivation. As a teacher, it is important to become familiar with these differing perspectives and to understand how each can inform best practices for enhancing motivation.

Self Theories Compared

Table 17.2 presents the self theories side-by-side to illustrate where they overlap and where they diverge. As our examination of self-efficacy, self-worth, and self-determination has shown, all three theories place importance on competence and intrinsic motivation. Self-efficacy depends on whether

TABLE 17.2 Self Theories Compared

	Self-efficacy	Self-worth	Self-determination
Description	Expectations for success on a particular task	Overall evaluation of our worth as individuals	Feeling that we have choice in our actions
Core needs	To believe we have the knowledge or skills to succeed on a task	To protect our perception of competence	To feel autonomous, competent, and related
Domain specific	Yes	No	Yes
Focus	Perceived competence		A need to develop competence

individuals believe they have the knowledge or skills to succeed on a task. Self-worth relies on a basic need to protect our perception of competence. Self-determination has at its core the individual's need to feel competent.

However, while self-efficacy and self-worth theories both focus on *perceived* competence—on whether individuals *think* they have ability—self-determination theory emphasizes the *need* for competence, the individual's need to develop mastery of knowledge and skills.

Both self-efficacy and self-determination are domain-specific, meaning they refer to specific learning situations (e.g., biology lab) or fields of study (e.g., calculus). For self-efficacy, that means our expectations about accomplishing a specific goal. Likewise, for self-determination it means our *feelings* of autonomy, competence, and relatedness can vary depending on the situation. However, remember that our *strivings* for autonomy, competence, and relatedness represent universal human needs. Like our needs for autonomy, competence, and relatedness, our need to protect self-worth is a general human characteristic.

Despite differences among the theories, they provide similar suggestions for enhancing students' intrinsic motivation. We'll explore these next.

Applications: Fostering Self-Efficacy, Self-Worth, and Self-Determination

Students with high self-efficacy, positive self-worth, and self-determination are more likely to be intrinsically motivated than are students with lower levels of these traits. According to the self theories, teachers can enhance students' intrinsic motivation by following the guidelines described below.

Capitalize on interest and relevance. When teachers point out the relevance of new material, students are more likely to become self-determined in their learning (Assor, Kaplan, & Roth, 2002; Deci et al., 1994). This is especially true when students have low initial interest. Students also are more likely to value what they are learning and to enjoy it more when they are studying something of personal interest. In one study, students valued learning more when it involved a topic of interest to them, even when they experienced failure (Covington & Müeller, 2001). Students are more likely to become engaged with assignments that yield tangible but intrinsically oriented rewards, such as sharing the results of their work with others or explaining to someone why what they learned is important (Covington & Müeller, 2001).

Another way to make content relevant to students is to ground it in authentic learning activities that are real-life tasks, such as designing experiments in a science class, writing a persuasive letter to a local politician for English class, or creating a plan to reduce pollution in a civics class. Authentic activities encourage the acquisition of skills for solving problems and completing tasks that are important in the real world (Brown, Collins, & Duguid, 1989; Collins, Hawkins, & Carver, 1991). Students may be intrinsically motivated because learning has real-world significance.

Provide realistic choices among tasks. Teachers can enhance students' autonomy by giving all students realistic choices, as when elementary school students choose which book they want to read or when middle and high school students select their own topics for research projects. When students have choices such as these, they tend to enjoy tasks more, feel more competent, and have higher achievement (Patall, Cooper, & Wynn, 2010). Giving students control over the process or the product of a task also fosters autonomy, promotes self-determination, and enhances intrinsic motivation (Deci, Vallerand,

Situated cognition: See page 369.

Pelletier, & Ryan, 1991; Reeve & Jang, 2006). To be effective, choices should be relevant to students' interests and goals and consistent with their cultural values (Katz & Assor, 2007; Vansteenkiste et al., 2010). Also, teachers should offer a moderate number of choices at an optimally challenging level (Katz & Assor, 2007).

Teach and model skills necessary for success. Rather than expect that students will acquire learning strategies on their own, teachers need to explicitly teach strategies such as study skills, mnemonic techniques, and math algorithms. Students who learn strategies improve their self-efficacy as well as their academic skills (Pintrich & De Groot, 1990; Zimmerman & Martinez-Pons, 1990). Teacher modeling of cognitive strategies can also promote higher self-efficacy and achievement than independent learning where students read and answer questions without guidance (Schunk, 1981).

Focus on mastery. When students complete tasks that are moderately difficult—just slightly beyond their capabilities—they are more likely to prefer the tasks and be motivated to master them (Harter, 1974). Emphasizing mastery encourages students to be success-oriented rather than failure-avoiding. Covington (1992) describes a mastery approach called the "grade-choice arrangement," in which students can earn any grade they choose by accruing credits (a specific number for an A, fewer for a B, etc.), but the higher the grade they choose to aim for, the more they must accomplish and the better they must perform. Students compete not against one another but for a standard of performance. Students working under this approach learned more and were more motivated than students in a typical competitive environment (Covington, 1998; Covington & Omelich, 1984b). Teachers should not allow students to select a grade option that allows them to minimize effort, protect self-worth, or avoid failure (Ryan et al., 1985). For example, allowing students to choose a C grade option when you know they are capable of B or A work reinforces their attempt to minimize effort and avoid failure rather than encouraging them to strive for mastery.

Help students set appropriate goals. Teachers can break down tasks and assignments into smaller components; provide short-term, moderately difficult goals; and offer strategies for making progress toward goals. Mastering small components of tasks teaches students to accept credit for their successes (Covington, 1984). Also, when students learn to set short-term, realistic goals and learn ways to make progress toward goals, they (Schunk & Miller, 2002; Tollefson, 2000):

- learn that effort as well as ability contributes to success,
- are more willing to put forth effort,
- improve their academic skills, and
- develop positive self-efficacy and self-worth.

However, assigning easy tasks or helping students complete an assignment they could not have done independently will not necessarily enhance efficacy expectations, because students will not attribute their success to their own ability or effort.

Provide appropriate feedback. When teachers give students feedback indicating that their success was due to increased effort, students feel greater self-efficacy and higher motivation (Schunk, 1987; Schunk & Miller, 2002). Be aware, however, that telling students to work harder following poor performance may lower their self-efficacy, especially if they believe they already are trying as hard as they can (Ames, 1990; Tollefson, 2000). Whenever possible, teachers should use informational feedback rather than controlling feedback. Informational feedback provides information about students' competence and enhances their intrinsic motivation (Deci, Koestner, & Ryan, 1999a; Grolnick et al., 1997). For example, stating "The argument in your paper is clear and compelling" conveys what the student has done well. In contrast, giving positive feedback in a controlling manner undermines intrinsic motivation (Kast & Connor, 1988; Ryan, Mims, & Koestner, 1983). Students perceive words like *should* and *ought* as controlling even when teachers intend the feedback to be positive and motivating, as in "Excellent, you *should* study that hard all the time."

Limit the use of external constraints in teaching. Some educational practices—such as close monitoring, the use of threats and directives, and the imposition of goals and deadlines—can be perceived as controlling and lead to diminished intrinsic motivation (Ryan & Deci, 2000b; Sierens, Vansteenkiste, Goossens, Soenens, & Dochy, 2009). However, the way such tools are introduced, expressed, or administered makes a difference. For example, goals and deadlines are a necessary part of instruction, but the more students see them as a valued component of the learning process and the more autonomy they have in learning, the more likely goals and deadlines will support intrinsic motivation.

Mastery goals: See page 280.

Grading practices: See page 483.

Controlling educational practices: See page 267.

Establishing positive relationships in the classroom: See page 333.

Foster relatedness in the classroom. Show students that you care about them as individuals. Feelings of relatedness promote internalization, the integration of extrinsic values, and intrinsic motivation (Deci et al., 1994). Also, show students that you trust them. For example, an elementary school student might be trusted to bring the lunch count to the main office, and high school students might be asked to abide by an "honor system" when the teacher leaves the classroom during an exam. Lastly, use strategies to build a sense of community in the classroom. Adolescents who believe they are valued and respected members of the classroom tend to have higher self-efficacy and mastery goals, to show greater responsibility, and to attain higher levels of achievement (Anderman & Anderman, 1999; DeBacker & Nelson, 1999). Ideas for creating a classroom community include: highlighting group achievements, increasing opportunities for students to interact with one another during the school day, and engaging students in relationship-building activities (Burden, 2003).

Summary

Describe outcome expectations and efficacy expectations with respect to student and teacher efficacy. A student may believe that studying leads to good grades (outcome expectation) and that *he* has adequate study skills to obtain good grades (efficacy expectation). Teachers also have outcome expectations about the ability of all students to learn, as well as efficacy expectations, which are beliefs about their own teaching effectiveness.

Explain how self-worth affects the motivation of success-oriented students, overstrivers, and failure-avoiding and failure-accepting students. Because our sense of competence contributes to our overall feeling of self-worth, we are motivated to protect our self-worth by maintaining a positive feeling of competence. Success-oriented students, who are intrinsically motivated, value learning as an opportunity to improve their ability and are not discouraged by failure. Overstrivers have high hopes for success but fear failure, so they use strategies to ensure that they will perform better than other students. Failure-avoiding students use many self-handicapping strategies to avoid situations that lead to failure or to avoid looking incompetent. Failure-accepting students neither approach success nor avoid failure because they have learned to accept failure.

Explain how autonomy, competence, and relatedness can facilitate intrinsic motivation. Individuals are more likely to be intrinsically motivated to perform activities over which they feel they have autonomy. Autonomy-supportive contexts lead to many benefits, including increased autonomy, perceived competence, and intrinsic motivation. Feelings of competence are associated with increased intrinsic motivation for schoolwork. Optimally challenging tasks enable students to feel competent, increase students' sense of pride, and stimulate intrinsic motivation. Students also are more likely to be intrinsically motivated to engage in school activities if teachers have a connectedness with their students.

Define internalization and explain how educational contexts can facilitate internalization of behaviors. Within the context of motivation, internalization is a developmental process in which individuals move from less self-determined (more extrinsically motivated) to more self-determined behavior. Educational contexts can facilitate internalization and encourage students' intrinsic motivation if they allow for the satisfaction of autonomy, competence, and relatedness needs.

Describe techniques teachers can use to enhance students' intrinsic motivation, and identify which self theory supports each technique. Teachers can encourage intrinsic motivation with these techniques: (1) capitalizing on interest and relevance, (2) providing realistic choices of tasks, (3) teaching skills necessary for success, (4) focusing on mastery, (5) helping students set appropriate goals, (6) providing appropriate feedback, (7) limiting external constraints in teaching, and (8) fostering relatedness. Pointing out the relevance of new material and providing students with choices among tasks may make students more self-determined. Teaching students the skills needed to achieve success will increase their self-efficacy. When teachers focus on mastery and help students set moderately challenging, short-term goals, students become success-oriented and develop positive self-efficacy and self-worth, increasing their intrinsic motivation. Feedback that is informational and focuses on effort also increases self-efficacy and intrinsic motivation. Limiting external constraints and fostering relatedness in the classroom also will enhance self-determination.

Key Concepts

amotivation   308

autonomy   305

deficiency needs   306

efficacy expectations   299

entity view of ability   302

external regulation   308

extrinsic motivation   299

failure-accepting students   305

failure-avoiding students   304

growth needs   306

humanistic theories   305

identified regulation   308

incremental view of ability   302

integrated regulation   308

internalization   307

intrinsic motivation   299

introjected regulation   308

Maslow's hierarchy of needs   305

need for competence   305

outcome expectations   299

overstrivers   304

relatedness   305

self-actualization   306

self-determination   305

self-efficacy   299

self-regulation   301

self-worth   303

success-oriented students   303

teacher efficacy   302

Video Applications

www.mhhe.com/bohlin2e

Video 1: Student Choice and Motivation ($2\frac{1}{2}$ minutes)
This clip shows fourth- and fifth-grade gifted and talented students in their reading groups, some students picking out a new novel to read and others in their group discussing a novel, as teacher Carol Goodrich discusses novel reading groups and the use of student choice.

Video 2: Teacher Feedback and Motivation (5 minutes)
This clip shows elementary school students in a guitar lesson. It provides an up-close example of the forms of encouragement and feedback that teachers provide to students in the classroom.

Case Studies
Reflect and Evaluate

EARLY CHILDHOOD: "The Worksheets"

These questions refer to the case study on page 256.

1. According to self-efficacy theory, what is Melissa's efficacy expectation for completing her schoolwork? How would you characterize Claire's self-efficacy? Martin's?

2. Explain why asking a peer to show Melissa how to complete the math sheet might improve her self-efficacy.

3. How can Mrs. Garvey improve the self-efficacy of students in her class?

4. Based on self-worth theory, which student—Melissa, Martin, or Claire—would be most difficult to motivate? Why? Which student would be easiest to motivate? Why?

5. Based on the case study, speculate on the degree of Mrs. Garvey's teaching efficacy.

6. Assume that Mrs. Garvey seeks advice from a more experienced teacher about how to enhance her students' feelings of autonomy and competence. Think of specific suggestions that her colleague would provide, and explain how each would enhance students' motivation.

ELEMENTARY SCHOOL: "Writer's Block"

These questions refer to the case study on page 258.

1. Contrast Carter's and Shanti's self-efficacy for writing. What failure-avoiding tactics does Carter use during free writing?

2. Using your response to the previous question, explain why you would expect to see a failure-avoiding motivational pattern in Carter and not in Shanti, according to the research on gender differences discussed in the module.

3. What specific things can Mrs. Okuda do to increase Carter's self-efficacy for free writing? Would your suggestions for increasing self-efficacy change if the student you were considering were Mason? Why or why not?

4. According to self-worth theory, how can Mrs. Okuda encourage James and Carter to be more intrinsically motivated for writing activities?

5. How are *self-regulation* and *internalization* similar? Which students in Mrs. Okuda's class are most self-regulated? How can Mrs. Okuda encourage all her students to be self-regulated in writing? How will this affect their self-determination?

6. What changes can Mrs. Okuda make to increase her students' autonomy? How will this affect their motivation?

7. Based on the information in the case, speculate on the degree of relatedness in Mrs. Okuda's classroom. Now think outside the writing activity. How can Mrs. Okuda foster relatedness in her classroom, and how will this affect students' self-determination and motivation?

MIDDLE SCHOOL: "The Math Review"

These questions refer to the case study on page 260.

1. How would you describe Sam's self-efficacy for completing the math problems?
2. Speculate on whether Mr. Pantera has high teaching efficacy. Use details in the case to support your answer.
3. What can Mr. Pantera do to promote positive self-efficacy in his students?
4. Discuss the effects a state mastery test might have on students' perception of competence, self-worth, and intrinsic motivation.
5. According to self-worth theory, which student—Aaron, Sam, or Rachel—would be most difficult to motivate? Why? Which student would be easiest to motivate? Why?
6. The eighth-graders feel external pressures due to the need to perform on the state test. Provide Mr. Pantera with suggestions for creating a classroom that promotes student autonomy to improve their motivation. How can Mr. Pantera promote feelings of competence and relatedness in his classroom in general?

HIGH SCHOOL: "Exam Grades"

These questions refer to the case study on page 262.

1. How would you describe Chelsea's self-efficacy? Compare this with Nicholas's self-efficacy. Based on research evidence regarding gender differences, how typical is this motivational pattern?
2. Based on the comments of Reggie, Tamika, and Carla, describe the self-efficacy of students in the general science class. Assuming that general science is a class for students with lower achievement than students in AP physics, explain how this practice of ability grouping (assigning students to different levels of classes) might affect students' self-efficacy. What are the outcome expectations in science for students in the general science class?
3. Is Mr. Womack's reassuring of Chelsea that she will do better next time likely to improve her self-efficacy? Why or why not?
4. According to self-worth theory, which student—Nicholas, Chelsea, or Reggie—would be most difficult to motivate? Why? Which student would be easiest to motivate? Why?
5. Mr. Womack realizes that the general science class and the AP physics class have different motivational needs. Help Mr. Womack create a motivational plan for each class for increasing students' self-efficacy, enhancing their self-worth, and facilitating their self-determination. Provide specific examples that are consistent with each theory. How do the motivational plans differ for the general science class and the AP physics class?

unit six

Case Studies

Early Childhood: "Caterpillar Circle" 318

Elementary School: "Ecosystems" 320

Middle School: "Classroom Safety" 322

High School: "Refusal to Dress" 324

Module 18:
Creating a Productive Learning Environment

Outline and Learning Goals 326

Planning and Organization 327

Establishing Norms and Expectations for Behavior 333

Establishing a Climate for Positive Relationships 338

Summary 344

Key Concepts 344

Video Applications 344

Case Studies: Reflect and Evaluate 345

Module 19:
Understanding and Managing Student Behavior

Outline and Learning Goals 346

Defining Student Misbehavior 347

Application: General Ways to Address Behavior Management 350

Application: How to Handle Specific Misbehaviors 355

Summary 361

Key Concepts 361

classroom manage- ment and instruction

Video Applications 361

Case Studies: Reflect and Evaluate 362

Module 20:
Instruction: Applying Behavioral,
Cognitive, and Constructivist
Approaches

Outline and Learning Goals 363

Planning Instruction 364

Teaching Methods Based on
Behaviorism 365

Teaching Methods Based on Cognitive
Learning Theory 368

Teaching Methods Based on
Constructivism 369

Summary 375

Key Concepts 375

Video Applications 375

Case Studies: Reflect and Evaluate 376

Module 21:
Grouping Practices

Outline and Learning Goals 377

Grouping by Ability 378

Cooperative Learning 382

Applications: Best Practices 385

Summary 389

Key Concepts 389

Video Applications 389

Case Studies: Reflect and Evaluate 390

Prepare:

As you read the case, make notes:

1. **WHO** are the primary participants in the case? Describe them.

2. **WHAT** is taking place?

3. **WHERE** is the case taking place? Is the environment a factor?

4. **WHEN** is the case taking place? Is the timing a factor?

Sarah Brennan is the lead teacher in a university-based, half-day preschool program where she teaches a morning class from 8:30 to 11:30 and an afternoon class from 1:00 to 4:00. She gets some help from Steve Shoemaker, a graduate student who works part-time while completing his degree in Early Childhood Education. The children call them "Miss Sarah" and "Mr. Steve." Sarah really enjoys working in this environment because of its diversity. In her morning class, 5 of the 18 children were born outside the United States. Mudiwa's family is from Nigeria; Jun-ho and his twin brother, Soon-Kim, are from Korea; and Ellia and Constantine are both from Greece. Some of her students also have special needs. Holly sees a speech therapist once a week for her articulation difficulties, and Brady has a degenerative condition called Newman-Picks disease, which affects his muscular control.

Early Childhood

Caterpillar Circle

This morning, the children have just taken their seats for snack time. There are four snack tables, each equipped with a plastic pitcher of milk, paper cups, napkins, and a box of granola bars. Constantine uses the pitcher on his table to carefully fill the cups of other children at his table. Ben passes out the napkins and Mudiwa hands everyone at the table a granola bar. Soon the room is filled with giggling and chatter. Miss Sarah and Mr. Steve each pick a group to sit with today, and they join in the conversation. The teachers make a point of alternating the groups they sit with so they have an opportunity to visit with all the children over the course of the week. As they finish their last sips of milk and bites of granola bar, the children begin to get up, push in their chairs, and throw away their paper cups and napkins. Brady helps Mr. Steve wash off the tables as Miss Sarah calls her class of 3- and 4-year-olds over to the carpet for circle time.

"Today we'll be reading one of our favorite stories, *The Very Hungry Caterpillar,* by Eric Carle," she tells them. "I've brought something special today to go along with our story."

Miss Sarah has brought some flannel pieces for the children to stick on the flannel board as she reads the story. Eleven children sit quietly in various spots on the floor in the story area, while four others are struggling to sit closest to the teacher and two remain over by the sink, where they have just finished washing their hands after snack. Brady heads toward the circle, having finished his job as table cleaner.

Miss Sarah rings a set of chimes to indicate that it is time to begin the story and opens an oversize book to the first page. Holly and Mudiwa ignore the chimes and begin splashing in the water at the sink. Mr. Steve, who has been doing a final survey of the snack area, quickly intervenes to redirect the girls to join the group. Ben, Jacob, Austin, and Tyler are still shoving one another as they try to get a favored spot next to Miss Sarah.

"On your carpet squares, boys," Miss Sarah says as she points to the four empty carpet remnants, each labeled with a child's name. As Miss Sarah reminds the boys where to sit, they grin sheepishly and crawl over to their designated spots. Once everyone is settled and quiet, Miss Sarah begins reading.

Mr. Steve takes a seat near the reading circle. Miss Sarah keeps the children engaged by inviting them up one at a time to place items from the story on the flannel board. "I'm looking for someone who is sitting quietly to help me put Mr. Caterpillar on our flannel board. Then I'll need some helpers to feed him."

To Ellia, who is wiggling and shouting "Pick me, pick me," Miss Sarah simply says, "Show me that you're ready."

"Tyler, you are waiting patiently," says Miss Sarah. "How about coming up to help with Mr. Caterpillar?"

Tyler eagerly hops up to add the first piece to the flannel board. When she sees that Ellia is sitting quietly, Miss Sarah invites her to come up and take a turn. As she nears the end of the story, she notices that Jun-ho has started to fiddle with the magnet blocks in a basket on the shelf behind him.

"Jun-ho, how do you think this story is going to end?" she asks. Jun-ho stops playing with the blocks and tells her about the butterfly that will appear on the next page. It has taken much practice, but the children seem to be getting used to the morning routine.

Assess

1. Based on this short scenario, how would you rate the teachers' classroom management skills?

2. What examples of misbehavior did you notice?

3. Which elements in this scenario might have required advance planning and preparation on the part of Miss Sarah and Mr. Steve?

4. How might interacting with children of various backgrounds and abilities influence a child's learning?

Prepare:

As you read the case, make notes:

1. **WHO** are the primary participants in the case? Describe them.

2. **WHAT** is taking place?

3. **WHERE** is the case taking place? Is the environment a factor?

4. **WHEN** is the case taking place? Is the timing a factor?

Leilani Anderson teaches third grade at Lincoln Elementary School. This year her class includes 23 students with a wide range of learning characteristics. A few of her students, Missy, Tamika, and Steven, still struggle with basic reading skills, while Jackson and Alissa already can read at a fifth-grade level. Some students, like Kelly, Jason, and Megan, have great verbal skills but really struggle in math. Jorge, who recently moved here from Mexico with his family, speaks very little English.

The wide range of skills and ability levels makes lesson planning, as well as general classroom management, a real challenge. Ms. Anderson has found that things run much more smoothly when she plans ahead and tries to anticipate potential behavior problems, rather than waiting until problems occur. This bit of teaching wisdom was passed along to

Elementary School
Ecosystems

her when she was a first-year teacher, and she has found that a proactive approach works well for her—in both traditional and mixed-age settings.

Today Ms. Anderson's class is making ecosystems out of 2-liter soft drink bottles. On the tables at the front of the classroom, Ms. Anderson has amassed large amounts of dirt, rocks, grass seed, and water. These materials alone could quickly have set the stage for a messy free-for-all, but Ms. Anderson has a plan—and she also has a parent volunteer who should be arriving any minute to lend a hand. Before distributing any materials, Ms. Anderson has the students gather around her dry erase board.

"Class, before you get started with the exciting project we have planned, we need to make sure everyone knows exactly what to do," she explains. "When the project is finished, this room should look just as clean and organized as it does right now. I need each of you to listen very carefully to the instructions and help one another remember them."

They go over the supplies and instructions needed for their groups to make the ecosystem. Ms. Anderson holds up an example of what a finished ecosystem might look like. "Cool!" several of the children murmur. She has the group repeat the instructions to her and then sends them back to their seats, with four or five students seated at each table in the room.

Students are called up one table at a time to get their supplies. Robyn Walsh, the parent volunteer, helps the students measure out the amount of each item they need. When a group is finished getting their supplies, those students return to their seats and are told to sit quietly and patiently until everyone is ready to begin. Ms. Anderson has put an ecosystem handout with a set of instructions and questions at each student's seat. As they continue to wait for their turn, students are encouraged to read through the questions they will need to answer.

Things seem to be getting a bit backlogged so Ms. Anderson joins Mrs. Walsh in passing out the materials. With two adults helping, the process moves quickly, and soon every group is ready to get started on building the ecosystem. As the groups are working, Ms. Anderson notices the students at two tables getting too loud. She does a hand clap beat, signaling the class to stop what they are doing and repeat the clapping pattern. Once she has their full attention, she says, "I see everyone working busily, but I need to remind you to keep your voices low so we don't disturb other classes."

Then she and Mrs. Walsh circulate around the room, reminding students of what they are supposed to be doing and providing assistance when necessary. Ms. Anderson notices that Austin has spilled the water at his table. Having expected an occasional spill, Ms. Anderson takes it in stride.

"Austin, grab a couple of paper towels from that dispenser by the sink and let's get this cleaned up," she says. Austin grabs a wad of paper towels and hurries back to the table. After Austin has wiped up the spilled water, she tells him to refill the cup and continue working.

At one table an argument ensues, and Ms. Anderson walks over to see what is going on.

"I worked the hardest on this project, so I get to take it home," says Hannah.

"No way!" shouts Kelsey. "I worked just as hard as you did."

Cole interjects, "Hey, we all worked on it, so it's not fair for one person to keep it."

Brandon groans and says in a mocking voice, "What should we do, Stupid? Rip it into four pieces so we can all take it? Impossible!"

Ms. Anderson interrupts the work session to tell the whole class that they have done a great job today. "Let's take out our reflection sheets. Start by listing three things you learned. Then write down what worked well in your groups today, what problems you encountered, how you solved them, and any ideas you have for improving collaboration next time." The students quickly settle down, take out their reflection sheets, and begin writing.

Assess

1. How well did Ms. Anderson manage the ecosystem activity? Would you have done anything differently if it were your class?

2. What strategies did Ms. Anderson use to get the students' attention quickly? Do you know of any other strategies that might work to signal students to be quiet and give the teacher their full attention?

3. Describe what might have happened if Ms. Anderson had simply set materials out on each table in advance, along with an instruction sheet. What other issues do you think she had to consider when planning her ecosystem lesson?

4. In your opinion, was it a good idea for Ms. Anderson to arrange the project groups according to the tables at which the students sat? Are there any other ways to form groups for this type of project?

Prepare:

As you read the case, make notes:

1. **WHO** are the primary participants in the case? Describe them.

2. **WHAT** is taking place?

3. **WHERE** is the case taking place? Is the environment a factor?

4. **WHEN** is the case taking place? Is the timing a factor?

It was one minute until the tardy bell, and Saul Gardino was waiting expectantly for the last of his group of seventh graders to arrive. He had been teaching industrial technology at Crosby Middle School for several years, and he had been working with this particular group of students for three weeks. Every nine weeks a new group of students would rotate into his classroom, and Mr. Gardino had noticed that this group had its own distinct personality.

Mr. Gardino spent most of the first week discussing rules and procedures. Safety was of paramount importance in his room because students used potentially hazardous tools while completing their class projects. He would be teaching them to use the band saw, drill press, cylinder sander, combination belt and disk sander, engraver, and air compressor, as well as basic tools like the vise, the handsaw, hammers, and various clamps.

Middle School
Classroom Safety

Working with power tools generally created an exciting—but potentially chaotic—learning environment. Mr. Gardino had devised a silly role-play situation that usually got students laughing but also focused their attention on the importance of using all tools properly. Rules and procedures were clearly posted in his classroom, and on the first day with a new group of students he would send home a "Safety Contract" for students to read over with their parents, sign, and return.

By the third week of class, the students had been sorted into project teams, and each team was in the process of deciding what they would design and make for their class project. Mr. Gardino smiled to himself as he recalled the "job interviews" he conducted to select project managers. Any students who were interested in leading a group were encouraged to submit a letter of application outlining their skills and qualifications for the position of project manager. Last week, he had interviewed the applicants and had decided to "hire" Angela, Rodrigo, Ben, and Kate to each direct a team. Mr. Gardino then met with his project managers to remind them that they were being given a great deal of responsibility. They would need to:

- help their group members decide on a project to make,

- assign each group member a role in the development of their product,

- set clear expectations,

- keep their team members on task, and

- make sure the completed project met all grading criteria for the assignment.

Angela, Rodrigo, and Kate were excited to get started. Ben was a little nervous, because this was the first time he had ever been put in charge of anything. Mr. Gardino sensed this and stopped to whisper "Go get 'em, Tiger!" as Ben headed toward his group.

Things went smoothly on the first day of project work. Mr. Gardino had listed clear instructions on the board so that each group would know how to proceed:

1. Introduction of group members.

2. Brainstorming session for project ideas (all ideas welcome and written down).

3. Discussion of ideas (advantages and disadvantages).

4. Voting among group members to make a final decision.

5. Assignment of roles and responsibilities.

Mr. Gardino circulated around the room as the groups were engaged in discussion. He observed that Angela came to class with a project already in mind, and even though her group did some brainstorming, she managed to generate a lot of enthusiasm for her birdhouse idea. Members of Kate's group tried to talk over one another when brainstorming, and Mr. Gardino found it necessary to give them a stern glance and move closer to them until they quieted down. Ben really wanted his group to make toy army tanks, but after some spirited negotiation, the group finally settled on making toy frogs with wheels.

Two weeks later, the members of Rodrigo's group were working busily to create the key chains they had chosen for their project. Kevin and Nick were assigned to do custom engraving on the dog-tag-style key chains once the shapes were cut out and the edges were sanded smooth. As they worked together in the industrial technology lab, Kevin had been using a ruler to line up the key chain on the engraver and was now proceeding to poke Nick with it repeatedly. Nick's response seemed to be mild irritation, but Mr. Gardino assumed it was all in jest and did not intervene. All of a sudden Nick started shouting profanities at Kevin and shoved him. This resulted in a retaliatory shove, causing Nick to go sliding across the floor. Nick stumbled back onto his feet, fists clenched, and headed toward Kevin to continue the scuffle. A few of the other students in the class began chanting "Fight, fight." As Nick advanced toward Kevin, Mr. Gardino intervened, placing himself between the two students and sternly telling them to knock it off. The fight was over in a matter of seconds, and the two students were sent to the principal's office. When the class had calmed down and attention was refocused on the project work, Mr. Gardino sat down to document exactly what had happened for his records. Later in the day, he left a copy of this documentation with the principal and filled out a Student Behavior Alert form to be sent home to each boy's parents.

Assess

1. How would you describe the learning atmosphere in Mr. Gardino's class?

2. Do you think Mr. Gardino's classroom management was effective? Why or why not?

3. What aspects of planning and organization were involved in Mr. Gardino's introduction and supervision of the group project?

4. In your opinion, was the way Mr. Gardino formed groups for the project effective? Why or why not?

Prepare:

As you read the case, make notes:

1. **WHO** are the primary participants in the case? Describe them.

2. **WHAT** is taking place?

3. **WHERE** is the case taking place? Is the environment a factor?

4. **WHEN** is the case taking place? Is the timing a factor?

The time is 7:15 A.M., 15 minutes before the bell rings for the start of first period at Valley High School. Maria Salazar makes her way to the main office, greets the secretary and principal, and picks up her mail. She is in her second year of teaching and notes with relief that fewer students and faculty are mistaking her for a high school student this semester. When she first arrived at Valley High, Ms. Salazar felt conspicuous as the new kid on the block, and at 22 years of age she was very aware of being only a few years older than her students.

Ms. Salazar is the physical education teacher, and she works with a wide spectrum of students, from freshmen to those seniors trying to get required credits for P.E. at the last minute so they can graduate. Some of the kids in her class tower over her, but she has

High School

Refusal to Dress

gained a reputation as a "petite powerhouse." She is energetic and enthusiastic and really cares about her students.

It is the middle of the semester. As Ms. Salazar gets set up for her first-period class, she wonders how the day will unfold. At 7:26 A.M., with a whistle around her neck, a pen behind her ear, and a grade book in hand, she is waiting patiently for her freshmen to arrive in the West Gym. The students are in the locker room changing into their required gym uniforms, but one by one they begin to enter the gymnasium. The late bell rings, class has begun, and Ms. Salazar blows her whistle, signaling the students to be in their assigned squad positions. She opens the grade book and gives the students their first assessment of the day: dressed or not dressed?

". . . Jacobson, okay; Jennings, all right; Jones, good but keep jewelry in your locker next time; . . . Johnson . . ?" Ms. Salazar thinks her eyes must be deceiving her. Brianna Johnson dresses in uniform for gym every day. Ms. Salazar walks in her direction, asking, "Not dressing today, Brianna? Is everything going okay?" She is genuinely concerned.

"I'm not dressing, and you can't tell me what to do. Only my momma can do that, and the last time I checked, your name wasn't Cynthia Johnson," roars Brianna as she storms over to the bleachers.

This certainly is not the reaction Ms. Salazar expected. She is uncertain about how to handle Brianna's tantrum, but she decides not to dwell on it too much because there are many other students in the class. Brianna is usually a very good student, so for the moment, Ms. Salazar decides to completely ignore Brianna's outburst and move on.

Participation is a major component of assessment in this class. Even students who are not dressed for gym can still receive points for the class—minus points for not dressing in the required uniform. Brianna opts to fall asleep after she has huffed and puffed while sitting awhile on the bleachers. Ms. Salazar continues to ignore Brianna's actions and to focus on the rest of the class. The students are rotating through four series of basketball drills, and fortunately none of the other students have chosen to act up this morning.

At 8:19 A.M., the second-period bell rings. Ms. Salazar finally decides to say something to Brianna, but Brianna storms out of the room after the bell has rung.

Brianna walks into her second-period class, English composition, where David Williams has written sentences on the board for students to find and correct grammatical errors. The students who are taking this class have very low language and reading skills. There are some students with learning disabilities, and several students are English language learners with limited English proficiency.

Brianna stomps to the back of the class, slouches in her desk, and closes her eyes. As a second-year teacher, Mr. Williams is used to motivational and behavioral problems in this second-period class, although he's not always sure how to handle them. He knows, however, that confronting a student in front of the class backfires, especially with someone who already appears very agitated. So today he chooses to ignore Brianna and continue with the lesson.

Assess

1. In your opinion, does Ms. Salazar's gender make a difference in this situation? Why or why not?

2. Do you think Ms. Salazar handled the situation with Brianna appropriately during her first-period class? Would you have responded the same way?

3. Are you surprised that the focus of a high school English class is on a basic skill like teaching grammar? Why or why not? Is your response based on prior personal experience, observation, or knowledge gained from other classes?

4. Why do you think students in Mr. Williams's second-period class have motivational and behavioral problems?

MODULE 18

Creating a Productive Learning Environment

Outline	Learning Goals
Planning and Organization	
■ Environmental Competence ■ Instructional Planning ■ Time Management	1. Describe the ways in which the organization of classroom space, instructional planning, and time management influence students' behavior.
Establishing Norms and Expectations for Behavior	
■ The First Days of School ■ Classroom Rules and Consequences ■ Procedures and Routines	2. Discuss the various ways norms and expectations for behavior are established in the classroom.
Establishing a Climate for Positive Relationships	
■ Caring, Productive Teacher-Student Relationships ■ Positive Student-Student Relationships ■ Building Strong Home-School Connections ■ Sense of Community Within the School	3. Explain the teacher's role in establishing a climate for positive relationships at different levels of interaction: teacher-student, student-student, home-school, and school-wide.
Summary **Key Concepts** **Video Applications** **Case Studies: Reflect and Evaluate**	

PLANNING AND ORGANIZATION

Effective teachers make classroom management and academic instruction look relatively effortless. Yet in truth, a well-organized, productive learning environment is the result of intentional decisions and choices, most of which are made before the teacher steps into the classroom (Borko & Shavelson, 1990; Clark & Yinger, 1979; Osher et al., 2010). Let's consider three critical skills that each teacher must master in order to establish the best possible context for learning: environmental competence, instructional planning, and time management.

Environmental Competence

More than 30 years of research indicates that the way teachers organize the physical environment of the classroom influences student mood and behavior (Burke, 2003; Dunn & Griggs, 2003). For example, attractive environments make individuals feel more comfortable, happier, more productive, more persistent on learning tasks, and more willing to help others (Bell, Fisher, Baum, & Greene, 1990; Weinstein & Mignano, 2007). Teachers need to develop **environmental competence,** an awareness of how the physical environment affects learning and an understanding of how to manipulate the environment to reach behavioral goals (Steele, 1973; Doyle, 2006). Classroom management involves organizing space, time, materials, and processes so that instruction flows smoothly and misbehavior is minimized.

ROOM ARRANGEMENT

A well-planned room arrangement helps the teacher cope with the complex demands of teaching by minimizing interruptions and delays while offering a comfortable, safe learning environment (see Example 18.1). There are several important factors to consider (Burden, 2003; Weinstein & Mignano, 2007):

- *Fixed features.* Doors, windows, closets, electrical outlets, and lab stations are examples of room elements that are fixed and immovable. The location of these features will influence teacher planning and organization.

- *Instructional materials and supplies.* Accessibility of materials and efficient storage make it possible to begin and end instructional activities promptly and to minimize time wasted on transitions.

- *Traffic areas.* High-traffic areas should be kept free of clutter. If possible, students should be seated away from congested areas (such as the space around doorways, cubbies, or the pencil sharpener) so that they are not easily distracted.

- *Visibility.* The room arrangement should allow a clear line of sight between teacher and students. This allows the teacher to easily see when a student needs assistance, as well as to provide supervision and minimize behavior problems or time off-task.

- *Flexibility.* Instructional needs change, so the classroom design should be flexible enough to be easily modified for different activities and grouping patterns.

- *Ambience.* Good classroom managers create a warm, inviting atmosphere. This includes attention to physical comfort, safety, a sense of order, and personal touches that give students a sense of ownership and connection (e.g., displays of student work or photographs).

- *Accommodation of students with disabilities.* Students with disabilities need to be considered when decisions are made about classroom design. For example, a student in a wheelchair needs space to move around the room without obstruction. A student with a hearing impairment may need to be seated close to the teacher in order to read the teacher's lips.

DIVERSITY

SEATING PATTERNS

Seating arrangements elicit distinct patterns of behavior from students (Adams & Biddle, 1970; Rosenfield, Lambert, & Black, 1985). Teachers should choose the seating that best matches the learning goals and types of instruction that will take place within the classroom space. Three options are illustrated in Example 18.2.

Teachers often begin the year with students seated in rows because this arrangement makes it easier to maintain control of the classroom. Once behavioral norms and expectations have been established, students can be arranged into clusters, circles, or other arrangements that facilitate different types of learning experiences (Burden, 2003). No matter which arrangement is chosen, the teacher should be able to see all students at all times (Emmer & Worsham, 2006).

EXAMPLE 18.1 **Classroom Floor Plan**

An effective classroom floor plan makes use of fixed features (doors and windows), ambience (light and noise), storage, traffic areas, and action zones. The plan also provides teacher-student visibility and flexible space for different activities. To accommodate students with disabilities, the floor plan may address issues of access and seating, including seating for in-class aides, and the best location for adaptive equipment such as a raised desk and special lighting.

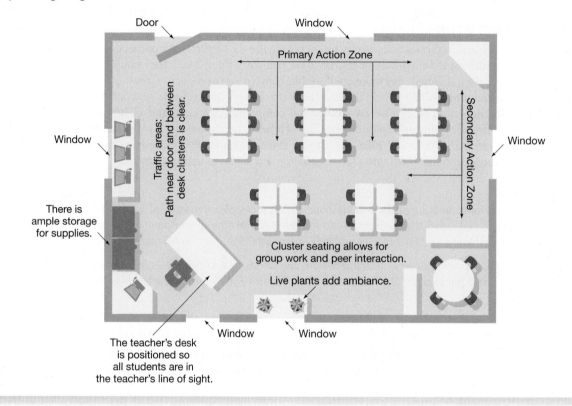

When creating seating arrangements, teachers also should be aware of the effect that an action zone has on teacher-student interactions. An **action zone** is an area in which the teacher is most likely to interact with students. With forward-facing rows, the teacher is most likely to interact with students in the front and center rows of the classroom. Students seated in this area also are more likely to ask questions and initiate discussion than students seated in more peripheral locations (Adams & Biddle, 1970). It is a good idea to place any misbehaving or unengaged students closer to the teacher in order to help them pay attention and participate more actively (Doyle, 1986). Because action zones vary depending on seating arrangement, the teacher must be sensitive to levels of interaction and make an effort to give attention to *all* students. Teachers can do this by moving around the room when possible, making eye contact with and calling on students seated farther away, and occasionally shuffling the seating arrangement (Weinstein & Mignano, 2007).

ENVIRONMENTAL CUES

Environmental cues are stimuli that suggest appropriate behavior. In the classroom, student decisions about what to do next are influenced by environmental conditions that signal the desirability of certain actions (March & Olson, 1989; Doyle, 2006). For example, in a classroom where the teacher has placed an activity sheet on each desk and has written instructions on the board directing students to begin the activity as soon as they arrive, the range of choices has been narrowed. The teacher has provided two environmental cues (activity sheet and instructions on the board) that focus students' behavior and make getting to work the most salient option. Additional examples of environmental cues include:

■ color-coded materials for different subject areas,

■ posted instructions to indicate how a particular area of the room is to be used,

EXAMPLE 18.2   **Seating Arrangements and Their Purposes**

Teachers should choose the seating that best matches the type of instruction they intend to use.

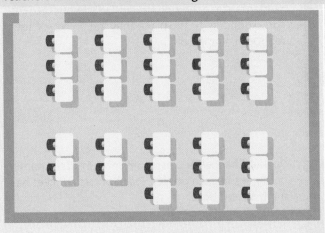

The traditional *auditorium arrangement,* with all desks in rows facing the teacher, is most effective when the teacher wants students' attention to be focused on direct instruction and wants to minimize interaction between students (Renne, 1997).

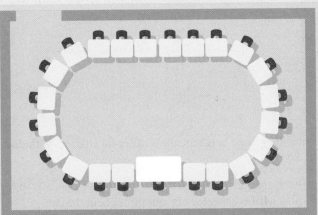

Students seated in a *large circle* participate more during a whole-class brainstorming activity than do students seated in clusters or rows (Rosenfield et al., 1985).

In general, face-to-face seating (such as *clusters*) leads to higher student distraction; however, this seating arrangement is ideal to facilitate collaboration during small-group activities.

- a checklist of assignments due, and
- a green/yellow/red traffic light system to indicate acceptable levels of noise during an activity.

Example 18.3 presents two additional tools that help direct student behavior. Such environmental cues provide important reminders of classroom procedures, routines, and expectations.

In inclusive classrooms, careful organization of the physical environment can be particularly help-ful in structuring and supporting the learning of students with disabilities (Villa & Thousand, 2000).   *DIVERSITY* Students with learning and behavior problems may be easily distracted by what is happening in their

EXAMPLE 18.3 Organizational Tools

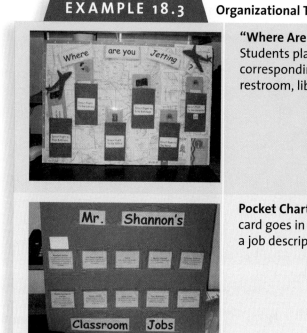

"Where Are You Jetting?" Hall Pass Pocket Chart: Students place their photo card in the pocket corresponding to the place they are going (office, restroom, library, etc.).

Pocket Chart with Classroom Jobs: Student name card goes in each pocket. Front of each pocket has a job description.

environment. Teachers can follow the guidelines listed here to make it easier for students with disabilities to focus on learning tasks (Swanson, 2005):

■ Minimize auditory and visual distractions.

■ Provide a daily schedule so students know what is expected of them throughout the day.

■ Provide transitioning cues at the beginning and end of activities.

■ Designate a specific place for turning in completed assignments.

■ Establish clear physical and visual boundaries that indicate how different areas of the room are to be used.

■ Keep clutter to a minimum and establish a definite place for materials.

What environmental cues have you seen teachers use to shape student behaviors and attitudes? How do you think the cues might differ depending on the age of the students in a classroom?

Instructional Planning

Effective classroom management involves gaining and maintaining students' cooperation in the activities that organize and shape classroom life (Osher et al., 2010). Teachers must plan effectively and students must be encouraged to come to class ready to attend and be engaged (Osher et al., 2008). Let's consider some of the decisions effective teachers make prior to teaching a lesson (Evertson & Emmer, 1982, 2008; Thompson, 2002):

Set Instructional Goals

■ Align curriculum with state standards.

■ State learning objectives and how students will demonstrate knowledge or skills.

Consider Student Preparedness

■ Identify necessary prior knowledge and determine whether a review of certain knowledge is needed.

DIVERSITY Consider Student Differences

■ Differentiate instruction to meet the needs of students at varying ability levels.

■ Accommodate students with special needs.

EXAMPLE 18.4   **Basic Components of a Lesson Plan**

Component	Criterion for evaluation
Statement of topic	Lesson/topic is tied to state standards.
Objectives	Objectives are clearly stated in behavioral terms.
Materials needed	Learning materials are appropriate for students' age, interests, developmental level.
Prerequisites/prior knowledge needed	Students have mastered the necessary prerequisites for this lesson.
Attention getter	Lesson includes an appropriate opening that engages students' attention.
Teacher input (e.g., explanation or demonstration)	Lesson is presented in a logical sequence and designed in a way that helps students master the material.
Opportunities for student engagement/active learning	Lesson includes a variety of activities or presentation formats that will appeal to different students.
Practice (guided and/or independent)	Students are given sufficient opportunity to practice new skills.
In-class assessments (formal or informal)	Assessments fairly and accurately evaluate students' learning.
Potential accommodations (remediation, enrichment, or adjustments)	Lesson includes activities for enrichment and remediation that can be used to meet individual needs.
Closure	Lesson includes appropriate closing.

SOURCE: Adapted from Thompson, 2002.

Select Appropriate Resources and Assessments

- Select relevant instructional materials and resources.
- Select assessment techniques to indicate whether objectives have been met (which should happen in advance, not as an afterthought).

Comprehensive instructional planning unfolds in three stages (Schell & Burden, 1992):

1. *Long-range plans* determine how much time is to be spent on each unit of the curriculum and what state standards will be met by the end of the school year.

2. Teachers construct *unit plans* to decide how much to accomplish in a given time period (usually two to four weeks). Because unit plans often involve a particular theme or set of concepts to be learned, they are more specific than long-range plans.

3. *Daily lesson plans* are completed last. Although the lesson plan format may vary depending on grade level and subject area, typical lesson plans include many of the components listed in Example 18.4.

As effective teachers plan daily lessons, they pay attention to how those lessons address multiple facets of instruction such as learning objectives, student needs, preparation of materials, and time constraints. Novice teachers commonly focus too much on the teaching of content and not enough on student learning, leading them to create plans that rush through coverage of a large amount of material (Thompson, 2002). This content-driven approach often overemphasizes what the teacher will do and say and fails to specify what students need to do to master the material. At any grade level, teachers should allow students sufficient time to process new information and ample opportunities to apply what they have learned (Jensen, 2000). Practice opportunities can be provided during designated work periods in the school day and/or through the assignment of homework. When students are given a choice of homework options, they report higher intrinsic motivation to do homework, feel more competent regarding the homework, and perform better on the unit test than they perform when they are not given any choice (Patall, Cooper, & Wynn, 2010).

An effective lesson should include both focused attention and movement or hands-on activities. For example, a high school chemistry teacher might facilitate learning by breaking up the lecture with a demonstration and an opportunity for hands-on experimentation. Elementary school students need time for recess and other unstructured activities to get a mental break from focused academic work, which reduces demands on their attention and memory, and leads to more efficient processing of information during learning tasks (Bjorklund & Harnishfeger, 1987; Toppino, Kasserman, & Mracek, 1991).

Because students in every classroom have varying abilities, teachers need to carefully target an appropriate difficulty level for instruction. When necessary, teachers differentiate instruction in a way that considers individual differences among students. For example, they plan how to accommodate students who finish a task earlier than expected as well as students who require extra time to complete a task (Richards, 2006). Teachers may need to create different lessons, activities, or assignments or use a different teaching method for students with disabilities and students who are gifted. Proactive teachers anticipate potential challenges that could arise at any point in the lesson and are prepared to address them, making on-the-spot adjustments as needed to achieve the learning goals they've defined. After the lesson, they reflect on what did and did not work so that they can improve their instruction the next time.

DIVERSITY

Teaching gifted students: See page 422.

Time Management

An effective teacher understands that **academic learning time**—the time students spend engaged in meaningful, appropriate tasks—helps predict academic achievement (Berliner, 1988; Evans, Evans, Gable, & Schmid, 1991; Jones & Jones, 2007). Even though most states mandate more than 1,000 hours per year of instruction, two-thirds of those hours are not directly educational. The actual time spent in academic learning drops to an average of only 333 hours when we consider absences, recess, lunch, time spent in lulls and transitions, and time spent off-task (Weinstein & Mignano, 2003). Lack of planning or poor time management by instructors often leads to time-wasting practices such as the following (Karweit, 1989; Thompson, 2002):

- using the first few minutes or last few minutes of class ineffectively,
- failing to establish efficient daily routines and procedures,
- using poor transitions between activities, and
- straying off topic.

USING TEACHING TIME EFFICIENTLY

Effective teachers use even small blocks of time wisely to maximize academic learning time. They approach teaching purposefully by developing clear learning objectives, choosing among a variety of effective, engaging instructional methods, and using assessments to determine whether learning goals have been met. In a series of studies on the characteristics of effective teachers, Carolyn Evertson and Edmund Emmer (Evertson & Emmer, 1982; Evertson, 1989) found that effective teachers also use time wisely by

1. having materials ready in advance,
2. selecting materials that are directly useful in instruction,
3. using consistent routines for delivering information about assignments (e.g., having students copy assignments from the board into an assignment notebook), and
4. reminding students that class time is for work-relevant activities, that they are aware of what students are doing, and that students will be held accountable for their work.

Teachers' effective classroom management is reflected in students' greater behavioral and cognitive self-control, higher behavioral engagement, and less time spent off-task in the classroom (Rimm-Kaufman et al., 2009).

MAINTAINING STUDENT ENGAGEMENT

Academic learning time is not simply the number of hours a teacher is engaged in instruction; it is also critical that the students be engaged in learning during that time. If classroom activities lack the power to hold students' attention, it is unlikely that school discipline will make up for this deficiency. Students are more likely to pay attention and stay on task when lessons are designed to be meaningful and relevant to their interests (Weinstein & Mignano, 2003). The teacher's own level of interest and engagement can be contagious, crossing over to influence student attitudes (Bakker, 2005; Basom & Frase, 2004). Instruction should be targeted to a difficulty level that is challenging but not overwhelming, with varied modes of presentation and frequent opportunities for students to participate actively (Acee et al., 2010; Finn & Cox, 1992; Schussler, 2009). Numerous research studies conclude that meaningful engagement is composed of two independent conditions—academic intensity and a positive emotional response—and that optimal learning environments combine both in order to make learning both playful and challenging, both spontaneous and important (see, for example, Andersen, 2005; Rathunde & Csikszentmihalyi, 2005; Shernoff & Csikszentmihalyi, 2009; Turner & Meyer, 2004).

Have you ever been in a class where a teacher rushed through content or did not adjust instruction to meet the needs of different students? How did this influence your level of learning and engagement?

> For more information on creating an engaging learning environment, see page 338.

ESTABLISHING NORMS AND EXPECTATIONS FOR BEHAVIOR

Psychologists Roger Barker and Herbert Wright pursued an intriguing line of research by examining the ways in which the norms and expectations within particular settings affect individual behavior (Barker & Wright, 1949; Barker, 1968, 1971). They examined stable situations in the environment known to be correlated with specific patterns of behavior (a basketball game, choir practice at a Methodist church, a meeting of a Boy Scout troop, etc.). They formulated the concept of a **behavior setting** to describe situations that coerce children who enter them to behave in relatively homogeneous ways, regardless of the individual characteristics of the children. Behavior settings can be identified by examining physical and social features of a particular environment and asking, "What is it appropriate to do here?" (Barker & Wright, 1949). Understanding that behavior settings are coercive, a teacher can structure the learning environment in ways that elicit desired behavioral outcomes.

Students may enter the classroom at the beginning of a new school year with preconceived ideas about how to act in that classroom setting. Teachers can redefine the **standing pattern of behavior,** or the norms and expectations associated with the classroom setting, through clear communication of rules and expectations in the first days of school. "Effective classroom management, especially in the early grades, is more an instructional than a disciplinary enterprise" (Brophy & Evertson, 1976, p. 185). In other words, skilled teachers socialize their students to the student role through instruction and modeling of desired behaviors rather than through disciplinary actions.

Behavior Setting. What behaviors are expected in a library setting? How do you know?

What behaviors do you assume will be expected of you when you attend a college class? How do these differ from the behaviors expected in a dining hall?

The First Days of School

Learning environments begin to take shape on the first day of school and, once established, tend to remain fairly stable (Patrick, Anderman, Ryan, Edelin, & Midgley, 2001; Wilson & Wilson, 2007). The norms and expectations established by the teacher in the first days of school determine which behavior patterns are most likely to persist throughout the year. Guidelines 18.1 presents a list of suggestions for setting the stage for good behavior and high academic achievement.

Various studies of effective versus ineffective teachers have shown that the first few days of school are critical to the establishment of a productive, smoothly managed learning environment (Israel, 2001; Patrick, Turner, Meyer, & Midgley, 2003; Wong & Wong, 1998). In

GUIDELINES 18.1   Establishing Norms and Expectations

Time/Instructional Management

- Establish and follow a classroom schedule.
- Develop guidelines for daily routines.
- Manage nonacademic time efficiently.
- Identify goals and responsibilities.
- Emphasize individual achievement.
- Use purposeful and relevant teaching methods and activities.
- Monitor progress and provide corrective feedback.

Behavior Management

- Post, teach, and enforce rules that are positive, concise, and fair.
- Administer clear and appropriate consequences.
- Provide specific feedback for behavior.
- Maintain a 3 to 1 ratio of positive to negative events.
- Use a variety of interventions and reinforcers.
- Individualize interventions.
- Use punishment sparingly.
- Encourage self-management and monitoring techniques.

Teacher Effectiveness

- Maintain high expectations.
- Know students as individuals and accommodate diversity.
- Model good behavior and values.
- Communicate the belief that every student can learn.
- Show a sense of humor, confidence, and enthusiasm.

SOURCE: Adapted from Stewart, Evans, & Kaczynski, 1997.

a series of classic studies conducted at the University of Texas, researchers analyzed the behavior of teachers in 27 third-grade classrooms and 26 junior high classrooms during the first weeks of school and found striking differences between the behaviors of effective and ineffective teachers (Emmer, Evertson, & Anderson, 1980; Evertson & Emmer, 1982). When teachers established excellent classroom management at the very beginning of the school year, the classroom was more orderly and student achievement was higher at midyear.

Rather than simply reacting to disruptive behaviors when they occur, effective teachers anticipate and prevent potential behavior problems and use the first days of school to teach students appropriate behavior (Koegel, Koegel, & Dunlap, 1996; Nilson, 2003). Several principles should guide teacher planning and decision making at the start of the school year (Burden, 2003; Good & Brophy, 2000):

- Be sensitive to student uncertainty in the first days of school and plan ways to help students become oriented to the teacher, their classmates, and the demands of the classroom.
- Plan activities and assignments for the first few days of class that ensure maximum student success so students can begin the year on a positive footing.
- Be available, visible, and in charge.
- Begin to assess the range of student abilities and tailor instruction to meet individual needs.

GUIDELINES 18.2	Establishing Classroom Rules

General Guidelines

1. Establish rules early, at the beginning of the school year.
2. Involve students in establishing the rules and identifying why they are important.
3. Limit the number of rules.
4. State rules positively in short, clear terms. Rules should communicate what behavior is expected rather than all the types of behavior that are inappropriate.
5. Identify rewards and consequences.
6. Post rules in the classroom or give each student a copy to keep.
7. Practice and review rules frequently, particularly at the beginning of the school year.
8. Inform parents of rules and expectations at the beginning of the school year. This can be done in a letter, by e-mail, at a parent orientation, or via a class Web site.
9. Remember that rules necessarily will vary with the age and maturity of the students.

Grade-based Examples

Kindergarten:

- Walk inside.
- Use an inside voice.
- Follow directions.
- Use words to let others know what you need.
- Be kind to others.

Upper elementary school:

- Be polite. Raise your hand to speak.
- Be kind. Keep your hands to yourself except when helping someone.
- Be responsible. Always do your personal best on classwork and homework.
- Be considerate. Remember that we all are here to learn.

Middle school:

- Be on time—that means being in your seat and ready to go when the bell rings.
- Be respectful—we are all equally important in this class and deserve respect.
- Be ready to learn. Have your homework and other materials out and ready to go. Be a follower of classroom procedures.
- Be safe. Don't create a hazard for yourself or your classmates.
- Be thoughtful. Treat others as you would want to be treated.

18 | Creating a Productive Learning Environment

- Clearly communicate rules, procedures, and expectations on the first day of school.
- Closely monitor student compliance with rules and procedures and intervene quickly to correct problem behaviors.

Classroom Rules and Consequences

Effective classroom managers have clear rules for general conduct, as well as procedures or routines for carrying out specific tasks (Emmer et al., 1980; Evertson, Emmer, & Worsham, 2006). The **rules** describe those behaviors necessary to ensure a safe and productive learning environment, such as "Respect other people's property" or "Always do your best work." Rules should reflect one of these purposes:

- to enhance work engagement,
- to promote safety and security,
- to prevent disturbance to others or to ongoing classroom activities, or
- to promote acceptable standards of courtesy and interpersonal relations.

Each classroom rule should be reasonable, necessary, and consistent with school-wide policies (Weinstein & Mignano, 2007). Guidelines 18.2 provides tips for developing rules.

The "Judicious Discipline" program, developed by Forrest Gathercoal, suggests a unique approach to the development of rules. In this program, rules emerge from the principle that "you may do what you want in this classroom, unless what you do interferes with the rights of others" (Gathercoal, 1993,

Discipline models, see Module 19.

p. 20). The program is framed around the rights and responsibilities of a citizen under the Constitution. Students develop the classroom rules based on these principles and formally agree to adhere to those rules (Gathercoal & Crowell, 2000). In her book *Cooperative Discipline,* educator Linda Albert (1996) takes a slightly different approach, giving attention to what she calls the three Cs: helping students to feel *capable,* to *connect* with others, and to make positive *contributions* to the class. She suggests that teachers and students work cooperatively to develop a code of conduct and to decide on a set of consequences to be enforced on transgression of the classroom code of conduct (Albert, 1996).

In addition to developing the rules (alone or with the class), teachers must invest time in teaching and reinforcing those rules. In fact, research findings indicate that effective teachers spend more time covering rules, procedures, and routines than they do on academic content in the first four days of school (Leinhardt, Weidman, & Hammond, 1987). When introducing the rules to the class, the teacher might discuss the reasons for the rules, provide examples of appropriate behaviors, and inform students of the consequences when rules are followed and when they are broken. To ensure that the rules are understood and remembered, the elementary school teacher should send a copy of the discipline plan home to parents, post the rules in a prominent location within the classroom, and review the rules regularly, especially in the first weeks of school (Burden, 2003). In secondary classrooms, rules and expectations often are communicated as part of a course syllabus distributed on the first day of class.

Consequences are steps taken by the teacher when a rule is violated.

- **Conventional consequences** are those commonly practiced in today's classrooms, such as time out, loss of privileges, removal from the room, and suspension from school. These tend to be applied in a generic fashion and are intended to serve as a form of punishment that deters future misbehavior. A **discipline hierarchy** lists generic consequences in increasing order of severity (Canter & Canter, 1992).

- **Logical consequences** allow students to make right what they have done wrong. If they make a mess, they clean it up. If they break something belonging to another student, they replace the broken item. Logical consequences are specific to the misbehavior itself and serve a corrective rather than punitive function (Charney, 2002).

- **Instructional consequences** teach students how to correct the behavior and provide examples of how to behave properly. For example, kindergarteners who push, shove, and talk loudly while lining up to go to the library may be asked to go back to their seats. The teacher then reminds them how to line up properly, has one student demonstrate the correct procedure for lining up quietly, and invites the rest of the class to follow (Curwin & Mendler, 1999).

Educators and authors Jane Nelsen, Lynn Lott, and Stephen Glenn urge teachers to move beyond consequences as a form of punishment and focus instead on involving students in generating real solutions for problem behaviors (Nelsen, Lott, & Glenn, 2000). Consider the following example (Nelsen, 1997).

During a class meeting, students in a fifth-grade class were asked to brainstorm consequences for two students who didn't hear the recess bell and were late for class.

Their list included the following consequences:

1. Make them write their names on the board.
2. Make them stay after school that many minutes.
3. Take away that many minutes from tomorrow's recess.
4. No recess tomorrow.
5. The teacher could yell at them.

The students then were asked to forget about consequences and brainstorm solutions that would help the students come to class on time. Following is their list of solutions:

1. Someone could tap them on the shoulder when the bell rings.
2. Everyone could yell together, "Bell!"
3. They could play closer to the bell.
4. They could watch others to see when they are going in.
5. Adjust the bell so it is louder.
6. They could choose a buddy to remind them that it is time to come in.

The first list focuses on the past and makes the students pay for their mistake. The second list focuses on helping the students do better in the future and frames the situation as a learning opportunity.

Class meetings have become a widely used format for participatory classroom management in which teachers and students make joint decisions about class rules and consequences, room arrangement, and preferred activities (Gordon, 1999; Kohn, 1996; Nelsen et al., 2000). They provide a vehicle for establishing a caring, supportive, cooperative climate in which students are taught skills such as listening, taking turns, considering different points of view, negotiating, thinking critically, and problem solving. In a typical class meeting, students form a circle and the teacher identifies a problem or an issue on that day's agenda. Students take turns expressing their opinions and concerns, brainstorming possible solutions, and/or making decisions.

Procedures and Routines

The class meeting establishes a routine for joint decision making in the classroom. At all grade levels, teachers use routines and procedures to manage the daily events of classroom life (Ball, 2002).

A **routine** is a predictable schedule or course of action. Students move through many activities during the course of a typical day, from whole-group lessons to small-group work, from reading time to science lab, from in-class work to lunch. Predictable routines allow students to move smoothly from one activity to the next without losing learning time.

Procedures describe how to accomplish activities in the classroom. Before the school year begins, a teacher must identify those actions or tasks that will require specific procedures for completion in order to keep the classroom running smoothly.

Here are three main categories of classroom procedures (Leinhardt et al., 1987; Weinstein & Mignano, 2003):

1. **Class-running procedures** are the nonacademic routines that help the classroom run smoothly. These include taking attendance, sharpening pencils at the beginning of class, using a hall pass when going to the restroom, and recording upcoming assignments in a student planner. Example 18.3 presents organizational tools commonly used by elementary school teachers to accomplish routine tasks. What organizational tools have you seen in middle school or high school classrooms?

2. **Lesson-running procedures** support instruction by identifying the specific behaviors required in order for teaching and learning to happen. These include collecting homework, completing makeup work, transitioning between learning centers, and distributing materials.

3. **Interaction procedures** refer specifically to rules for talking. They specify when talking is permitted in the classroom and how it should occur. Some contexts that might need their own set of talking procedures are whole-class lessons, independent seat work, small-group work, free time, transitions, and cooperative learning activities. Interaction procedures also include those procedures teachers and students use to gain one another's attention at various times of the day, such as when students raise their hands to be called on or when a teacher uses a certain phrase or hand signal to indicate that a lesson is about to begin.

How might rules and procedures differ across developmental levels?

Class Meetings. Class meetings are a useful format for making joint decisions about class rules, consequences, room arrangement, and preferred activities.

ESTABLISHING A CLIMATE FOR POSITIVE RELATIONSHIPS

Effective teachers take a proactive approach to classroom management by creating an environment in which positive relationships can flourish and optimal behavior and learning can occur (Freiburg & Lamb, 2009). Numerous research studies attest to the crucial role of the teacher in creating and maintaining a positive classroom atmosphere conducive to academic learning (Elias & Weissberg, 2000; Patrick et al., 2003; Weinstein & Mignano, 2007). Important aspects of this atmosphere include social-emotional emphasis, a feeling of school connectedness, and student self-discipline (Waters, Cross, & Shaw, 2010).

Thoughtful planning with students' best interests in mind can result in the creation of a caring, supportive classroom community. Students who feel supported and cared about are more persistent, set higher goals for themselves, achieve more academically, are less likely to report experiencing depressive or anxious symptoms, and are less likely to misbehave (Carter, McGee, Taylor, & Williams, 2007; Jones & Jones, 2001; Niebuhr & Niebuhr, 1999; Shochet, Dadds, Ham, & Montague, 2006; Wilson, 2006). Classroom life is a web of interconnected relationships.

Positive student-teacher relationships. The relationships change according to developmental level.

Caring, Productive Teacher-Student Relationships

I have come to a frightening conclusion. I am the decisive element in the classroom. It is my personal approach that creates the climate. It is my daily mood that makes the weather. I possess tremendous power to make a child's life miserable or joyful. I can humiliate or humor, hurt or heal. My response decides whether a crisis will be escalated or de-escalated, and a child humanized or dehumanized.

Haim Ginott in *Teacher and Child*

Empirical research indicates that quality academic instruction and positive student-teacher relationships can lessen the impact of factors commonly associated with poor achievement (Greenwood, 2001; Osher et al., 2004; Gable, Hester, Hester, Hendrickson, & Sze, 2005). Students who perceive that their teachers care about them are more likely to adhere to classroom rules and expectations (Wentzel, 1997), to expend effort on their schoolwork (Kaufman & Dodge, 2009), and to use self-regulated learning strategies (Rimm-Kaufman et al., 2009; Ryan & Patrick, 2001). Students reported liking school more and experiencing less loneliness if they had a close relationship with their teachers (Birch & Ladd, 1997).

Positive student-teacher relationships are important at all grade levels, although *what* students need from the relationship may vary according to their developmental level. The relationships students in the early elementary grades develop with their teachers have been shown to greatly influence academic achievement throughout the students' school careers (Berry & O'Connor, 2009; Esposito, 1999). The middle school context reflects a significant change in relationship dynamics, including a larger, more bureaucratic system with many more teachers, peers, and curricular choices (Hill & Chao, 2009).

Self-regulation: See page 353.

In a recent study, middle school students were asked to describe caring teachers. The students tended to define caring teachers as individuals who:

- demonstrate democratic communication styles designed to elicit student participation and input,
- develop expectations for student behavior and performance in light of individual students' differences and abilities,
- model a "caring" attitude and interest in their instruction and their interpersonal dealings with students, and
- provide constructive rather than harsh and critical feedback.

In contrast, middle-schoolers described teachers who do *not* care as teachers who yell, interrupt them, communicate low expectations of students, and show no willingness to provide individual help or ex-

GUIDELINES 18.3   Dos and Don'ts in Developing Strong Teacher-Student Relationships

Do	Don't
■ Make an effort to get to know each student in your classroom. Always call them by name and strive to understand what they need to succeed in school (Croninger & Lee, 2001).	■ Don't assume that being kind and respectful to students is enough to bolster their achievement. Ideal classrooms have more than a single goal. In ideal classrooms, teachers hold their students to appropriately high standards of academic performance and offer students an opportunity to form emotional connections with their teachers, their fellow students, and the school (e.g., Gregory & Ripski, 2008; McCombs, 2001).
■ Make an effort to spend time individually with each student, especially those who are difficult or shy. This will help you create a more positive relationship with them (Rudasill, Rimm-Kaufman, Justice, & Pence, 2006).	■ Don't give up too quickly on your efforts to develop positive relationships with difficult students. These students will benefit from a good teacher-student relationship as much as or more than their easier-to-get-along-with peers (Baker, 2006; Birch & Ladd, 1998).
■ Be aware of the explicit and implicit messages you are giving to your students (Rimm-Kaufman et al., 2002). Be careful to show your students that you want them to do well in school through both actions and words.	■ Don't assume that respectful and sensitive interactions are only important to elementary school students. Middle and high school students benefit from such relationships as well (Croninger & Lee, 2001; Meece, Herman, & McCombs, 2003; Wentzel, 2002).
■ Create a positive climate in your classroom by focusing not only on improving your relationships with your students, but also on enhancing the relationships among your students (Donohue, Perry, & Weinstein, 2003).	■ Don't assume that relationships are inconsequential. Some research suggests that preschool children who have a lot of conflict with their teachers show increases in stress hormones when they interact with these teachers (Lisonbee, Mize, Payne, & Granger, 2008).

Source: American Psychological Association, http://www.apa.org/education/k12/relationships.aspx

planations (Wentzel, 2003a). These negative interaction patterns contribute to student disengagement, misbehavior, poor achievement, and dropping out, especially in high-poverty schools (Balfanz, Herzog, & MacIver, 2007; Sutton, Mudrey-Camino, & Knight, 2009). Recent educational reform efforts have focused on making the middle grades more developmentally appropriate for young adolescents and providing more caring, personalized, and supportive learning environments (Dickinson, 2001; National Association of Secondary School Principals, 2006). Guidelines 18.3 describes actions teachers can take to establish strong relationships with students, as well as pitfalls to avoid.

In addition to understanding students' developmental needs, teachers also need to consider several factors that specifically affect their ability to make meaningful connections with ethnically and culturally diverse students (Brown, 2002; Delpit, 1995; Gay, 2000; Howard, 1999). Effective urban teaching requires implementing culturally responsive instructional strategies and communication styles, linking content with student experience, and recognizing, honoring, and responding to the many cultural and language differences among students (Abbate-Vaughn, Frechon, & Wright, 2010). An approach known as Culturally Responsive Classroom Management (CRCM) includes five essential components: (a) recognition of one's own ethnocentrism; (b) knowledge of students' cultural backgrounds; (c) understanding of the broader social, economic, and political context; (d) ability and willingness to use culturally appropriate management strategies; and (e) commitment to building caring classrooms (Weinstein, Tomlinson-Clarke, & Curran, 2004). Consider the following examples of cultural differences that affect classroom interactions:

DIVERSITY

■ Students who are African American, Native American, Mexican American, Puerto Rican, Southeast Asian, or Pacific Islander tend to benefit from instructional methods that rely on interaction and collaboration, because these styles more closely match the students' family values and practices (García, 1992, 1995; Lomawaima, 2003).

Addressing Diversity: See page 13.

■ Teachers need to recognize that interaction patterns that don't match typical White, middle-class expectations may reflect students' culturally specific, valued actions. Students from diverse ethnic backgrounds who shout out answers and fail to adhere to turn-taking rules in class discussions often are seen as disruptive, and other students' lack of verbal assertiveness may be interpreted incorrectly as a lack of motivation or resistance to instruction (Cartledge, Kea, & Simmons-Reed, 2002; Irvine, 1990).

DIVERSITY

Regardless of the age or ethnic background of students, three teacher actions are essential for the development of positive teacher-student relationships (Parsley & Corcoran, 2003):

1. *Show a high level of trust in students.* A teacher might do this by giving students positions of responsibility in the classroom. For example, an elementary school student might be asked to care for a class pet, or a high school student might be asked to design the program for a school play.

2. *Show students that they care about them as individuals.* Teachers can show they care by giving students individual attention, expressing appreciation and encouragement for students' efforts, acknowledging their positive personality traits, and showing an interest in activities important to them.

3. *Create a supportive learning environment in which students feel comfortable taking risks.* In his **congruent communication approach,** Haim Ginott (1972) outlines several positive communication strategies that create a supportive environment. He suggests that teachers acknowledge students' feelings, avoid using sarcasm, focus on misbehavior without damaging self-esteem, and express anger appropriately. Ginott explains that in every classroom encounter a teacher should ask "How can I be helpful right now?" This approach avoids finding fault, establishing guilt, and meting out punishment as responses to students' mistakes.

Students tend to be more accepting of peers who show engagement in the tasks of school (e.g., show attention, participate in classroom activities), and positive teacher-student relationships enhance students' engagement. Positive teacher-student relationships improve student-to-student acceptance in both current and future years (Hughes & Kwok, 2007).

Positive Student-Student Relationships

Peer relations:
See page 67.

Positive, supportive peer relationships offer students many advantages that translate into greater social adjustment as well as greater academic success (Dubois, Felner, Brand, Adan, & Evans, 1992; Zins et al., 2004). In the course of day-to-day classroom interactions, students provide one another with various forms of support necessary to accomplish both social and academic tasks (Schunk, 1987; Sieber, 1979). For example, students clarify and interpret the teacher's instructions about what they should be doing, answer one another's questions, and model social competencies (Wentzel, Battle, Russell, & Looney, 2010).

A good teacher can foster a set of attitudes and skills that strengthen student-student relationships. Skills that enhance a student's ability to build and sustain relationships include the following (Elias & Weissberg, 2000):

Emotional regulations and emotional expressiveness: See pages 62 and 67.

- effective communication skills,
- emotional self-control and appropriate expression,
- empathy and perspective taking,
- optimism and a sense of humor, and
- nonviolent conflict-resolution and problem-solving skills.

Empathy and perspective taking: See page 79.

Beginning in the first days of school, effective teachers stress community values, students' encouragement of one another, and adherence to good manners as a sign of respect (Bohn, Roehrig, & Pressley, 2004).

Listed below are life skills commonly taught on a school-wide basis at the elementary, middle, and high school levels (Stipek, de la Sota, & Weishaupt, 1999):

INTEGRITY: acting in accordance with what is right and wrong

INITIATIVE: doing something because it needs to be done

FLEXIBILITY: being able to alter plans when necessary

PERSEVERANCE: keeping at a task and not giving up

ORGANIZATION: working in an orderly way

SENSE OF HUMOR: laughing and being playful without hurting others

EFFORT: doing your very best

COMMON SENSE: thinking everything through

PROBLEM SOLVING: seeking solutions

RESPONSIBILITY: doing what is right

PATIENCE: waiting calmly

FRIENDSHIP: making and keeping a friend through mutual trust and caring

CURIOSITY: investigating and seeking understanding

COOPERATION: working together toward a common goal

CARING: feeling and showing concern for others

School-wide prevention programs focusing on these life skills have resulted in a decrease in verbal aggression, fighting, delinquency, and substance abuse (Botvin, Griffin, & Nichols, 2006; Spoth, Clair, Shin, & Redmond, 2006). In addition to providing life skills training, teachers can take specific actions to build a sense of community and supportiveness in the classroom, including the following (Burden, 2003; Nelsen et al., 2000; Osterman, 2010; Soodak, 2003):

- establish norms for cooperation, altruism, and social responsibility;

- provide increased opportunities for students to interact with and work with one another during the school day;

- highlight group achievements; and

- foster the development of friendships through activities that involve cooperation and collaboration or through rituals that involve all members of the class.

Teachers need to be responsive to students whose behavior impedes their own or others' sense of community (Stainback & Stainback, 1996). Rather than resorting to punishments and suspensions for students who exhibit disruptive behavior, many teachers are turning to positive interventions that focus on supporting students by making changes in the school environment (such as changing seating arrangements, schedules, or patterns of supervision) or teaching students new or alternative behaviors (Soodak, 2003).

Understanding and managing student behavior: See Module 19.

Building Strong Home-School Connections

Students benefit in many ways from good communication between home and school and a shared commitment to support students' education. Parental involvement in children's education is associated with the following outcomes (Henderson & Berla, 1995; Hill & Chao, 2009; Seginer, 2006):

- better attendance,

- more positive student attitudes and behavior,

- a greater willingness to complete homework, and higher levels of academic achievement.

Family–school relations and parental involvement in education have been identified as a way to close demographic gaps in achievement and maximize students' potential (Dearing, Kreider, Simpkins, & Weiss, 2006). Continuous efforts to involve parents by informing them about school discipline policies, routinely updating them on their children's behavior, and involving them in the school-wide discipline procedures are common practice for safe and effective schools (Dwyer, Osher, & Warger, 1998). **Home-based reinforcements,** in which students are given rewards (e.g., verbal or tangible rewards or privileges) and sanctions (e.g., loss of privileges such as television time, snacks, or later bedtime) at home, based on their behavior at school, have been shown to improve student behavior, classroom attentiveness, and academic productivity (Atkeson and Forehand, 1979; Jurbergs, Palcic, & Kelley, 2007; Leach and Byrne, 1986).

DIVERSITY

Whereas some aspects of parental involvement in education may decline in amount or in effectiveness during middle school, such as involvement at school (Singh et al., 1995; Stevenson & Baker, 1987), other aspects of involvement may increase in significance (Chao, Kanatsu, Stanoff, Padmawidjaja, & Aque, 2009). Of the many forms of parental involvement in education, *academic socialization* has the strongest positive relationship with achievement during middle school (Hill & Tyson, 2009). Parents provided academic socialization when they communicate their expectations for achievement and value for education, foster educational and occupational aspirations in their adolescents, discuss learning strategies with children, and make preparations and plans for the future, such as linking material discussed in school with students' interests and goals. School-based involvement was also

Parent-teacher conferences: See page 486.

positively related to achievement, but less strongly so. Finally, the results for home-based involvement were mixed. Involvement that entailed assisting with homework was not consistently associated with achievement. Parental participation in general education traditionally has focused on sharing information about student achievement and ensuring that parents provide the context and supervision needed for students to complete assignments (Chao et al., 2009; Hoover-Dempsey, Bassler, & Brissie, 1992). Today, information about students' progress is commonly communicated through work sent home in a weekly folder, updates posted on school Web sites, report cards, and parent-teacher conferences. Frequent communication is important for building alliances between home and school that support the child's education and development.

Certain parents may be reluctant to get involved with their children's education for many reasons. Some parents recall unhappy experiences they had as students and have a negative attitude or are uncomfortable about working with school personnel. Parents of children who have a history of misbehavior may disengage from school participation as a way to cope with self-doubt, denial, hostility, or frustration (Walker & Shea, 1995). Other parents may view teachers as experts and feel that as parents they have little to contribute (Turnbull & Turnbull, 2001). These issues are often magnified for parents of English language learner (ELL) students as the parents themselves may have minimal proficiency in **DIVERSITY** English and vastly different formal schooling histories (Panferov, 2010). Teachers can overcome some of this resistance by creating an inviting atmosphere that welcomes parents into the school and/or classroom and values parents' knowledge of their children.

Sometimes practical concerns interfere with a parent's school involvement. Inadequate transportation, a lack of child care, or inflexible work schedules may make it difficult for parents to attend school functions. Also, cultural, ethnic, or socioeconomic differences in the parent population may make parents feel uncomfortable about interacting with school personnel whom they perceive to be very different from them. Teachers need to be aware of these barriers to parent involvement and find ways to dismantle them. For example, a teacher can schedule time outside regular school hours in which to meet with parents who work during the day. If lack of child care is a barrier to parent involvement, the teacher might occasionally host events that the entire family can attend. If the teacher and the parent do not speak the same language, the teacher might ask a staff member, a parent, or another student who can translate to sit in on a parent-teacher conference.

The home-school partnership is especially important when working with students from diverse cul-**DIVERSITY** tural backgrounds. Students raised in nonmajority cultures or communities are likely to experience more diverse goals and expectations than those espoused by the school. They may struggle with competing goals across family, peer, and classroom contexts (Hidalgo, Siu, Bright, Swap, & Epstein, 1995; Wentzel, 2003a). For example, some Asian-American students may not feel comfortable correcting other students' verbal mistakes or responding competitively during class discussions. The conflict arises because at home they have been socialized to value collectivism, saving face, interdependence, and harmony (Gay, 2000).

Effective teachers communicate with parents in order to better understand conditions in a student's home life that may affect classroom behavior and learning. Guidelines 18.4 presents several culturally responsive strategies for forging strong home-school connections (adapted from Panferov, 2010).

What do teachers need to do to connect with parents and maximize student success? Effective teachers make an effort to communicate early and often with parents. Parents need to be kept informed about school events, academic expectations, their child's progress, and disciplinary expectations and actions taken.

Multiple forms of communication can be initiated to strengthen school-home connections. Before the school year begins, a teacher can forge connections with parents by sending home an introductory letter. This can be followed by an event such as a Back to School Night or Open House in which parents are invited into the school to meet the teacher and become familiar with the school, the classroom, and the curriculum. Other common forms of communication include the following:

- weekly or monthly newsletters,
- assignment sheets that parents review and sign,
- individual notes and letters sent home,
- phone calls,
- e-mails or text messages, and
- postings on a class Web site.

GUIDELINES 18.4   **Developing Culturally Responsive Home–School Connections**

- Use regular multi-modal (written and spoken) forms of communication, ideally in the parents' native language.
- Conduct home visits to establish mutual respect for both home and school cultures.
- Pair ELL parent with another parent in the school who can answer questions and provide support.
- Offer bilingual parent workshops that help parents understand how to best support their children's education and successfully navigate school issues.
- Create opportunities for parents to share aspects of their culture.

Building a Sense of Community Within the School

A sense of community within the school can add to the sense of connectedness in the classroom (Battistich, Solomon, Kim, Watson, & Schaps, 1995; Battistich, Solomon, Watson, & Schaps, 1997; Waters, Cross, & Shaw, 2010). Ideally, in a spirit of cooperation, all faculty and students work to help one another. When teachers and students share a strong sense of community, the students have a more positive attitude toward school and show higher motivation, and teachers experience a greater sense of self-efficacy about their teaching effectiveness (Langer, 2000). Research demonstrates that when teachers have high **collective self-efficacy**—the belief that they can have a positive impact on student learning by working together—students make greater academic progress (Bandura, 2000; Goddard, Hoy, & Woolfolk Hoy, 2000). Support from colleagues can enhance the professional environment of the school and provide insights about how to address problems within the classroom (Sykes, 1996). A strong support network is particularly helpful to novice teachers and has been shown to increase both job satisfaction and teacher retention (Betoret, 2006; Klassen & Chiu, 2010).

Think about the many interconnected relationships that have influenced your own school experiences. What teacher, student, or home-school interactions stand out most in your mind? How did relationships at these levels shape your attitudes toward school?

Good News!

Dear _Mrs. Jackson_

Brandon did a great job listening and following directions this morning. He set a great example for his classmates.

Teacher _Mrs. Newton_

Date _10/1/11_

Great Work!

Communication. Frequent communication with parents is an important factor in students' educational progress and overall development.

Summary

Describe the ways in which the organization of classroom space, instructional planning, and time management influence students' behavior.

Several organizational issues influence students' mood and behavior in the classroom. Good classroom managers create a warm, inviting atmosphere and make intentional choices about environmental factors such as traffic patterns, seating arrangements, and use of environmental cues to direct student behavior. As they plan daily lessons, they pay attention to how those lessons address multiple facets of instruction such as learning objectives, student needs, preparation of materials, and time constraints. They maximize academic learning time by planning efficiently and implementing strategies that maintain student attention and interest.

Discuss the various ways norms and expectations for behavior are established in the classroom. Norms and expectations are established through the constraints of the behavior setting of the classroom, the tone the teacher sets during the first days of school, and the rules, consequences, routines, and procedures students are taught. Many educators advocate involving students in the process of developing rules and consequences, as well as giving them shared responsibility for making decisions and solving problems involving the classroom learning environment.

Explain the teacher's role in establishing a climate for positive relationships at different levels of interaction: teacher-student, student-student, home-school, and school-wide. To build a positive relationship with students, the teacher needs to show a high level of trust in students, care about the students as individuals, create a supportive learning environment in which students feel comfortable taking risks, and help students feel that they belong and are accepted. Teachers can help students form good relationships with one another by giving them opportunities to work together and to get to know one another better. Teachers can build strong home-school connections by communicating early and often with parents, welcoming parents into the classroom as volunteers, and supporting parents' efforts to create good conditions for learning in the home. Finally, teachers can contribute to a school-wide sense of community by collaborating with other teachers and with school personnel to meet students' needs.

Key Concepts

academic learning time   332

action zone   328

behavior setting   333

class meetings   337

class-running procedures   337

collective self-efficacy   343

congruent communication approach   340

conventional consequences   336

discipline hierarchy   336

environmental competence   327

environmental cues   328

home-based reinforcements   341

instructional consequences   336

interaction procedures   337

lesson-running procedures   337

logical consequences   336

procedures   337

routine   337

rules   335

standing pattern of behavior   333

Video Applications

www.mhhe.com/bohlin2e

Video 1: Ways to Facilitate a Productive Learning Environment (*3 minutes*)

Clip 1 (Kindergarten teacher interview): *Establishing norms and expectations for behavior*

Clip 2 (Kindergarten classroom): *Warmth*

Clip 3 (Middle school teacher interview): *Seating arrangements*

Video 2: Creating a Productive Learning Environment (*2½ minutes*)

Eighth-grade social studies teacher Neil Radtke talks about how to build rapport with middle school students and how to create a positive, open learning environment.

Case Studies
Reflect and Evaluate

EARLY CHILDHOOD: "Caterpillar Circle"

These questions refer to the case study on page 318.

1. What environmental cues were used in Miss Sarah's classroom to guide the children's behavior?
2. How does Miss Sarah respond to Jun-ho's inattentive behavior during story time? Is this response effective?
3. Miss Sarah's classroom has a fairly predictable morning routine. How might such a routine affect student behavior in the classroom?
4. Describe the seating arrangement during story time. How might this arrangement influence the way the children interact?
5. Brady has a noticeable physical disability that may become more pronounced over the course of the school year. How is he made to feel valued? What additional steps could the teachers take to help Brady feel accepted and valued within the classroom?

DIVERSITY

ELEMENTARY SCHOOL: "Ecosystems"

These questions refer to the case study on page 320.

1. What are the seating arrangements in Ms. Anderson's classroom? What are the advantages and disadvantages of this particular arrangement?
2. How effectively are classroom procedures implemented during the ecosystem activity? Explain.
3. Would the ecosystem activity be a good choice during the first few days of a new school year? Why or why not?
4. How might the completion of this group project in Ms. Anderson's class promote student-student relationships?
5. How does parent involvement play a role in this case? Do you think it makes a difference in the success of the project?

MIDDLE SCHOOL: "Classroom Safety"

These questions refer to the case study on page 322.

1. Why are classroom rules and procedures particularly important in an industrial technology classroom?
2. How were Mr. Gardino's rules and procedures communicated to students?
3. How did Mr. Gardino allow students to share in some aspects of classroom decision making?
4. Mr. Gardino did several things to build relationships in his classroom. Comment on the ways he established connections with his students.
5. In what ways can parents be involved in issues of classroom management? How did Mr. Gardino make parents a part of the process?

HIGH SCHOOL: "Refusal to Dress"

These questions refer to the case study on page 324.

1. What is meant by the term *behavior setting*? How might the behavior setting of the gym differ from the behavior setting of a traditional classroom?
2. Do you think Ms. Salazar has established a clear routine for the opening minutes of gym class? Why or why not?
3. What evidence did you see in this case to indicate Ms. Salazar's attitude about teacher-student relations?
4. This case does not reveal whether Ms. Salazar has had any prior contact with Brianna's parents. Do you think Brianna's parents should be informed about her behavior at school on this occasion? Why or why not?
5. How would your response to question 4 differ if Ms. Salazar were teaching fourth-graders rather than high school students?

MODULE 19

Understanding and Managing Student Behavior

Outline	Learning Goals
Defining Student Misbehavior	
■ Degrees and Types of Misbehavior ■ Common Causes of Misbehavior	1. Define *misbehavior* and identify the various causes of misbehavior.
Application: General Ways to Address Behavior Management	
■ Establish Clear, Positive Expectations for Behavior ■ Model and Reinforce Desired Behaviors ■ Anticipate and Prevent Potential Behavior Problems ■ Teach Self-regulation Skills ■ Respond Effectively to Behavior Problems As They Occur	2. Discuss five proactive ways to address behavior management issues in the classroom.
Application: How to Handle Specific Misbehaviors	
■ Routine Disruptions ■ Intermediate Concerns ■ Immoral Behaviors ■ Dangerous Behaviors	3. Summarize important considerations in responding to mild, moderate, and severe misbehaviors.
Summary **Key Concepts** **Video Applications** **Case Studies: Reflect and Evaluate**	

Numerous studies identify discipline problems as one of the biggest concerns in education. Over the years, this concern has been reflected in polls of public opinion (Phi Delta Kappa/Gallup, 2010; Rose & Gallup, 1999), as well as in reports from teachers (Curwin, 1992; Greenlee & Ogletree, 1993; Marshall, 2002; Micklo, 1993). Teachers report that misbehavior is their primary source of career-based stress, often leading to symptoms such as lethargy, exhaustion, tension, depression, and high blood pressure (Charles, 1999; Kendziora & Osher, 2000). Teacher stress may influence how effective teachers are in the classroom, with potential consequences for their students' behavior and learning (McIntyre, 2011). Former teachers cite student misbehavior as the number one reason they left the field (Luekens, Lyter, & Fox, 2004; Osborn, 2006). Urban, rural, and minority communities are hardest hit by the high rate of teacher attrition (National Commission on Teaching and America's Future, 2003). Also, experienced teachers often try to transfer away from schools with high levels of misbehavior, leaving those schools in the hands of less experienced teachers who have not yet developed strong discipline skills (Charles, 1999).

DIVERSITY

DEFINING STUDENT MISBEHAVIOR

Misbehavior can be any student behavior that disrupts the learning environment in the classroom, including behavior that (Levin & Nolan, 2000):

- interferes with teaching,
- interferes with the rights of others to learn,
- is psychologically or physically unsafe, or
- destroys property.

Degrees and Types of Misbehavior

A teacher notices that one of her students is staring off into space during individual seat work. Is this misbehavior? While it is not disrupting the work of others or harming other students, it may indicate that the student is off-task. This student could be daydreaming or simply pausing to think about how to answer the next question on the assignment. Even if the student clearly is off-task, the teacher probably will address this behavior differently from an incident in which a student is distracting others or engaging in violent behavior. Teachers must be able to distinguish the type and severity of different behaviors in order to know whether, and how, to intervene. Behaviors that may seem quite similar will elicit different reactions from teachers depending on the particular student involved, the time, or the context in which the behavior occurs (Burden, 2003; Doyle, 1986). For example, talking with peers may be unacceptable when students are taking an exam, but it may be perfectly acceptable when they are working in cooperative learning groups. Expectations also change with age. A recent study that followed students from the last year of elementary school through the first year of middle school demonstrated that teachers were more likely to discipline students in middle school, especially for subjectively defined infractions like class disturbance or failure to follow rules (Theriot & Dupper, 2010).

Misbehavior can range from mildly to severely disruptive (Burden, 2003). Teachers frequently classify misbehaviors into three main categories:

1. *Mild misbehaviors* generally are related to a student's being off-task.
2. *Moderate misbehaviors,* such as arguing or clowning around, are slightly more serious and are likely to disrupt the learning of others.
3. *Intolerable behaviors* involve dangerous or immoral actions that absolutely will not be tolerated under any circumstance.

Examples of student misbehavior in each of these three categories can be found in Example 19.1.

While teachers may express their greatest anxiety about having to deal with more serious misbehaviors such as aggression, immorality, or defiance, the less serious misbehaviors occur more frequently and waste valuable instruction

Mild, Moderate, or Intolerable? Student misbehavior disrupts the learning environment.

EXAMPLE 19.1	Various Degrees of Misbehavior in the Classroom

Mild misbehaviors	Moderate misbehaviors	Intolerable misbehaviors
<ul><li>Getting out of seat without permission</li><li>Not doing assigned tasks</li><li>Dawdling</li><li>Daydreaming</li><li>Sleeping in class</li><li>Occasional tardiness</li></ul>	<ul><li>Failing to do what the teacher asks; not listening</li><li>Talking loudly</li><li>Calling out</li><li>Tossing objects</li><li>Clowning around</li><li>Making rude sounds</li><li>Arguing</li><li>Teasing</li></ul>	<ul><li>Immoral behaviors: cheating, lying, stealing, vandalism</li><li>Aggressive or violent behaviors (verbal or physical attacks)</li><li>Bullying</li><li>Substance abuse</li><li>Harassment of teacher or students</li><li>Openly defiant behaviors</li><li>Leaving school grounds without permission</li></ul>

time (Osher et al., 2010; Shen et al., 2009). Some isolated off-task behaviors may seem harmless but, if left unchecked, can lead to a chaotic and unproductive classroom environment that interferes with learning (Canter & Canter, 1998; Conoley & Goldstein, 2004).

Common Causes of Misbehavior

Students may misbehave at school for hundreds of potential reasons, including (Curwin & Mendler, 1999; Fish, Fish, & Scott, 2008):

- boredom,
- feelings of powerlessness,
- unclear limits,
- a lack of appropriate outlets for their feelings, and
- attacks on their sense of dignity.

Behavior is not caused entirely by internal or external factors; rather, it results from the interaction between the person and the environment (Burden, 2003), including developmental, physical, psychosocial, and other environmental factors.

DEVELOPMENTAL FACTORS

One source of potential behavior problems at school involves developmental factors. At the early childhood level, young children are just learning about appropriate classroom behavior and expectations (Rimm-Kaufman et al., 2009; Webster-Stratton, Reid, & Stoolmiller, 2008). They may show higher anxiety levels about being in school, especially if being away from home for several hours a day is a new experience for them. Teachers can respond to these developmental characteristics by explicitly teaching students what behaviors are acceptable and unacceptable and by providing a nurturing environment that eases the transition from home to school and builds connections with peers.

Students in elementary school still have a high desire for teacher approval, but the attention and approval of their peers become important too. At the upper elementary level, students who consistently have experienced academic and/or social failure may become increasingly disengaged. Teachers can help reduce anxiety during this period by communicating regularly with students about both social and academic issues and by helping students gain the skills necessary to form and sustain close, supportive relationships (Catalano et al., 2003).

As students transition to middle school, they are entering an unfamiliar school structure and might again feel anxious. Heightened concerns about "fitting in" and social demands may take precedence over academics (Murdock, 1999). Not surprisingly, bullying behaviors reach their highest levels during the middle school years (Pellegrini, 2002). Teachers can support students during this period by reaching out to students who seem socially unconnected and making it clear that bullying will not be tolerated.

Emotional understanding and dimensions of emotional intelligence: See page 64.

Developmental, Physical, Psychosocial, or Environmental? Recognizing and meeting students' needs is an important part of classroom management.

At the high school level, teachers see a higher incidence of cheating and a disdain for classmates who work too hard to get teacher approval (Cizek, 2003). Violence and substance abuse issues also become more common among adolescents (Fingerhut & Christoffel, 2002).

At every grade level, teachers are more likely to be successful in creating optimal learning environments when they take developmental needs and challenges into consideration.

PHYSICAL FACTORS

General physical health can influence student misbehavior. Lack of sleep, poor nutrition, inadequate exercise, allergy, or illnesses can make it difficult for a student to pay attention, focus, and think clearly. Conditions with a neurological component, such as attention-deficit hyperactivity disorder (ADHD) or fetal alcohol syndrome, can, among other things, lead to impulsive or hyperactive behavior. Physical factors also may include serious impairments such as vision or hearing loss, paralysis, or a severe physiological disorder. Students with such impairments may become frustrated or overwhelmed if they are unable to complete classroom tasks successfully.

ADHD and conduct disorder: See page 455.

DIVERSITY
Fetal alcohol syndrome: See page 107.

PSYCHOSOCIAL FACTORS

Psychosocial factors include any of the social networks in which the student is embedded. In Urie Bronfenbrenner's bioecological model of human development (Bronfenbrenner, 2005), children affect and are affected by multiple social systems—family, peers, schools, media—that are interconnected and change over time. For example, students, particularly those who feel unsuccessful or unsupported in other ways, may find a niche in peer groups whose members devalue school achievement and prosocial behavior (Wentzel, 2003b). Delinquent acts among middle school and high school students usually are done in groups, in which these delinquent behaviors are fueled by antisocial peer norms (Perkins & Borden, 2003).

Bronfenbrenner's bioecological model: See page 31.

ENVIRONMENTAL FACTORS

Another broad source of influence on student behavior includes numerous environmental factors. Aspects of the classroom's physical environment can be both direct and indirect influences, including:

See Module 18: Creating Productive Learning Environments

- seating arrangement,
- traffic flow,
- overcrowding,
- scarcity of resources,
- quality of lighting, and
- room temperature (Proshansky & Wolfe, 1974).

Consider the direct and indirect influences of seating arrangement. If students are seated in straight rows, they may be less likely to carry on discussions among themselves because they cannot hear each other as well (*direct impact*). Also, face-forward seating can send the message that the teacher expects attention to be focused on the front of the classroom and not on other students (*indirect impact*).

Seating arrangements: See page 327.

Sometimes it is not the physical environment itself but the teacher's actions within that environment that cause behavior problems. When teachers fail to maintain a high level of self-awareness, they may

More Disadvantages than Advantages. Harsh reprimands and threats are often counterproductive.

engage in counterproductive actions that actually increase the likelihood of students' misbehaving (Kellough, 2005; Thompson, 2002). For example, harsh reprimands, threats, and physical punishment consistently produce more disadvantages than advantages (Gottfredson, Gottfredson, Payne, & Gottfredson, 2005; Weber & Roff, 1983). Failure to plan meaningful activities that hold students' attention and keep them engaged is another teacher action that invites misbehavior (Doyle, 2006).

In some cases, the reasons for misbehavior may be complex and unpredictable; in others, misbehavior may arise from common, predictable causes that can be anticipated and prevented. As effective classroom managers, teachers must be very aware of their own behavior (Leflot et al., 2010). When students misbehave, novice teachers often focus on what the students are doing wrong. Experienced teachers are more likely to consider what they themselves can do differently to better understand and meet the students' needs (Emmer & Stough, 2001). Many classroom management/discipline programs are based on the belief that when students' basic needs are met, misbehavior can be avoided (Albert, 1996; Dreikurs, 1968; Fay & Funk, 1995; Glasser, 1998; Nelsen, 1997; Nelsen, Lott, & Glenn, 2000).

How prepared do you feel to deal with behavior problems of various types? Which types of misbehavior concern you most? Which causes of misbehavior do you as a teacher have the power to change?

APPLICATION: GENERAL WAYS TO ADDRESS BEHAVIOR MANAGEMENT

Ultimately, each teacher develops a personal discipline model or approach, whether explicit or implicit, that guides classroom management decisions. A discipline model is a set of cohesive practices for establishing, maintaining, and restoring order in the classroom (Burden, 2003). Example 19.2 lists the main features of several well-known models of classroom management and discipline. Each model emphasizes different aspects of classroom management, and no single model has been shown to be the most successful. Together these models present a wide range of perspectives to consider when developing your own behavior management philosophy. Each teacher must incorporate a management style that fits his or her belief system while staying within research-based guidelines (Cotton, 1990; Little & Akin-Little, 2008).

If you were asked in a job interview to summarize your own approach to classroom management and discipline in just three sentences, how would you respond? Which of the models in Example 19.2 best fits your own classroom management style?

We've all heard the adage, "An ounce of prevention is worth a pound of cure," and research underscores its relevance to teaching. Academic climate and effective teaching practices promote high task engagement and positive attitudes that prevent misbehavior (Winzer and Grigg, 1992). Effective teachers understand that discipline problems disrupt learning, and they take a proactive approach to classroom management (Kame'enui and Darch, 1995; Kerr and Nelson, 1998; Marzano & Marzano, 2009). **Proactive classroom management** has three distinctive characteristics (Gettinger, 1988):

1. It is preventive, rather than reactive, in nature.
2. It integrates behavioral management methods with effective instruction to facilitate achievement.
3. It focuses on the group dimensions of classroom management rather than the behavior of individual students.

Let's consider some successful elements commonly found in proactively managed classrooms.

EXAMPLE 19.2   **Models of Classroom Management and Discipline**

Proponents	Main focus	Practical tips for the classroom
Fritz Redl and William Wattenberg	Group dynamics	■ Establish control by applying principles of group dynamics. ■ Use diagnostic thinking to assess causes of misbehavior and apply appropriate consequences. ■ Use peer influence to curb misbehavior.
Jacon Kounin	Effective lesson management and supervision	■ Prevent misbehavior by keeping students actively engaged. ■ Rely on good teaching techniques to keep students on track. ■ Use withitness, personal accountability, challenge, enthusiasm, and variety to prevent student boredom and restlessness.
Haim Ginott	Communication skills	■ Speak to a misbehaving student as you would like to be spoken to yourself in the same situation. ■ Invite student cooperation by focusing on what needs to be done rather than on what was done wrong. ■ Show self-discipline and model desirable behaviors.
Rudolf Dreikurs	Collaborative decision making and sense of belonging	■ Give every student a sense of belonging. ■ When misbehavior occurs, identify what is driving the behavior. ■ Help students redirect their behavior in positive ways.
B. F. Skinner	Behavior modification through reinforcement	■ Strengthen desired behavior by providing immediate reinforcement. ■ Extinguish undesired behaviors by providing *no* reinforcement. ■ Shape complex behaviors gradually through successive approximations.
Lee and Marlene Canter	Teacher assertiveness/ clear rules and consequences	■ Establish a climate of mutual trust and respect. ■ Remain in charge in the classroom, but not in a hostile or authoritarian manner. ■ Teach each student how to behave responsibly. ■ Develop clear rules and consequences.
Thomas Gordon	Discipline as self-control	■ Involve the students in problem solving and decision making about class rules and procedures. ■ Identify problem ownership—who is bothered by the problem situation?
William Glasser	Student satisfaction with school	■ Help meet students' needs for belonging, freedom, power, and fun. ■ Assign work that is meaningful and relevant to students, and expect students to do their very best. ■ Hold classroom meetings to discuss curriculum, procedures, behavior, and other educational topics.
Richard Curwin and Allen Mendler	Discipline with dignity	■ Always interact with students in a way that preserves their dignity. ■ Provide interesting activities, opportunities for academic success, and encouraging feedback to students who are behaviorally at-risk (those who have a chronic history of misbehavior).
Barbara Coloroso	Developing inner discipline	■ Help students develop inner discipline by giving them opportunities to solve their own problems. ■ Give students the power and responsibility to make decisions and accept the consequences. ■ Use natural and logical consequences instead of bribes, rewards, or threats.

Adapted from Charles, 1999, pp. 8–9.

Establish Clear, Positive Expectations for Behavior

It is crucial that the teacher, rather than the students, have ultimate control over the classroom. If this sense of control is not established early, then a constant struggle for power will disrupt the learning environment for the entire school year. Educators Ann Harrison and Frances Spuler (1983) make these suggestions:

- Set limits at the very beginning of the school year and be prepared to enforce them all year, because students will test them from time to time.

- Only introduce rules that you can enforce consistently.

DIVERSITY

If the list of rules is too cumbersome, the teacher will become exhausted trying to enforce each one and will begin to ease up or ignore the misbehavior when students break one of the rules. This results in the teacher losing credibility with the class. Students are more likely to work harder and to be more persistent when they perceived that their teachers provide clear, consistent expectations (Bear, 2009; Skinner & Belmont, 1993). Also, students with special needs adapt to a general education setting more easily when the procedures for performing certain tasks are outlined clearly, expectations for student behavior are clear, and misbehaviors are treated consistently (Pfiffner & Barkley, 1998; Scruggs & Mastropieri, 1994).

Model and Reinforce Desired Behaviors

Observational learning: See page 174.

Interpreting the teacher's own words, thoughts, and actions, students create a set of expectations for what is appropriate and valued within the classroom. **Observational learning,** watching and imitating the behavior of a model, is an efficient and effective way to develop skills and behaviors (Bandura, 1986; Schunk, 2000). In order to build and maintain credibility with students, a teacher should model the behaviors expected of the students (Kellough, 2005). Research indicates that the degree of respect teachers show students significantly predicts students' behavior toward one another (Matsumura, Slater, & Crosson, 2008).

Reinforcement: See page 161.

When students do perform desired behaviors, many different methods can be used to reinforce those behaviors. The use of praise and positive attention can be one of the most powerful tools for motivation and classroom management (Alber & Heward, 2000). Effective praise should be contingent on the behavior being reinforced, clearly state the behavior that is valued, and be genuine (Landrum & Kaufman, 2006). While praise is a good starting point for reinforcing desired behaviors, in some cases teachers may need to use other reinforcers, such as awarding special privileges or tangible rewards, to maintain or increase a desired behavior (Menendez, Payne, & Mayton, 2008; Schloss & Smith, 1994). The key for teachers is to find a reinforcer that is personally meaningful or valuable to the student, understanding that perceptions of what is a valuable reinforcer will vary from one student to the next. Some teachers use interest surveys to get to know students better and to identify activities or rewards that appeal to individual students. Also, teachers may ask students to brainstorm ideas together and vote on a group reward.

Praise as motivation: See page 269.

Reinforcing Behaviors. The use of praise and positive attention can be a powerful motivational tool.

To chart group progress toward a desired goal, teachers can choose among many tangible reward systems. In elementary school classrooms, this approach may include:

- filling a marble jar (the class earns one or two marbles each time a desirable behavior is displayed by all),

- earning letters to spell out PIZZA PARTY, and

- filling in sticker charts.

At the secondary level, genuine praise and positive attention continue to be effective reinforcers. Other options teachers can use include awards or certificates of recognition, free time, access to special equipment or resources, food, and passes or tickets to special events.

Earning a Pizza Party. Behavioral incentives can be individual or group-oriented.

Anticipate and Prevent Potential Behavior Problems

An effective classroom manager must cultivate supervision skills. Jacob Kounin (1970), in his classic study of classroom management, compared the behaviors of effective teachers whose classes were relatively orderly and productive with those of ineffective teachers whose classrooms were centers of chaos and confusion. What he discovered was that effective and ineffective teachers responded in similar ways when misbehavior occurred. The main difference between them lay in the fact that effective teachers were much better at taking steps to anticipate misbehavior and prevent it from occurring in the first place. Kounin identified four main areas in which effective classroom managers were highly skilled: withitness, overlapping, group focus, and movement management.

1. **Withitness** refers to the ability to remain aware of and responsive to students' behaviors at all times. Teachers who possess this skill scan the classroom frequently, read students' facial expressions and body language, and interpret the mood of the class as a whole. In particular, teachers notice when students are getting restless and losing interest and react by making adjustments to the lesson to raise the level of student engagement (Carter, Cushing, Sabers, Stein, & Berliner, 1988).

2. **Overlapping** refers to the ability to deal with misbehaviors without interrupting the flow of an ongoing lesson or activity. For example, while explaining an assignment, the teacher might walk over to a student who is passing notes, quietly collect the notes, and redirect the student's attention by pointing to the assignment being discussed. The ability to keep the main activity going in the classroom while simultaneously dealing with problem behaviors contributes to better classroom order (Copeland, 1983).

3. **Group focus** refers to the ability to keep as many students as possible actively engaged in appropriate activities. A teacher who excels at this skill will not spend too much time focusing on one particular student at the risk of diminishing the level of attention and on-task behavior of the group as a whole.

4. **Movement management** refers to the ability to keep a lesson moving at an appropriate pace, to maintain smoothness (logical organization and sequencing) of instruction, and to successfully manage transitions from one activity to the next.

Teach Self-regulation Skills

At times, even the most effective teacher has difficulty monitoring the behavior of all students. Teaching students to use *self-regulation,* or to monitor and manage their own behavior, gives them a greater sense of autonomy and helps them develop personal responsibility (Bear, 2005). Researchers have observed behavioral improvements in settings in which students are taught to attribute their success or failure to their personal effort and in which they (1) learn to check their own behavior and judge its appropriateness; (2) talk themselves through a task using detailed, step-by-step instructions; and (3) learn problem-solving steps to take when they confront classroom issues (Anderson & Prawat, 1983; Cotton, 1990).

In studying the classroom management approaches of elementary and secondary teachers, researchers found that effective teachers at both levels had well-planned systems for encouraging students to

Self-regulation: See page 179.

Attribution theory: See page 282.

manage their own behavior (Emmer, Evertson, & Worsham, 2006; Evertson, Emmer, & Worsham, 2006). Teachers have implemented self-monitoring techniques to increase desired behaviors, such as improved academic skills and on-task behaviors, and to decrease inappropriate behaviors (Rhode, Jensen, & Reavis, 1992). Toward this end, students should be encouraged to take responsibility for keeping track of their belongings, for completing assignments, and for managing their time well. Additional examples of self-management techniques include personal goal setting, charting personal progress, and reinforcing oneself (Briesch & Chafouleas, 2009). The ultimate goal of an effective classroom manager is to help students develop responsibility and self-control. If the teacher is absent or is called away from the room for a moment, the class should be able to function smoothly in the teacher's absence.

Respond Effectively to Behavior Problems As They Occur

The **principle of least intervention** states that a teacher should react in the least intrusive way possible when dealing with misbehavior in the classroom to minimize disruption to the instructional process. If the least intrusive strategy does not work, the teacher then moves up a level to a more intrusive approach until an effective strategy is found. Guidelines 19.1 summarizes intervention options that move

GUIDELINES 19.1   Using the Principle of Least Intervention

STEP 1: *Move closer to the student.*

STEP 2: *Make eye contact.*

STEP 3: *Gesture.* Walk over to the troublesome student while you are teaching and use a gesture like shaking your head or putting a finger to your lips to let it be known that the behavior is inappropriate.

STEP 4: *Use a one-liner,* stated with authority, that requires no answer. "Cool it!" or "Knock it off!" usually works well. You usually can catch three other students you didn't yet know were misbehaving.

STEP 5: *State the problem behavior* ("Your talking is distracting the class") and *redirect the student.*

STEP 6: *Time-out.* Move the student quietly and quickly to a predesignated spot.

STEP 7: *Talk with the student privately.* Speak to the student outside the classroom. You might ask the student to wait for you outside the classroom, but because you are legally responsible for the student, you should join the student outside as soon as possible. Use your best judgment in each situation to decide how long a student can safely wait for you. When you speak to the student, try not to become angry. You want the student to stop the inappropriate behavior. Documenting begins here. Write on an index card "Pat distracting class with talking; spoken to outside of class, March 24, 2006, 10:45 A.M."

STEP 8: *Contact parents.* Write a brief note to the student's parent(s) describing the child's misbehavior and the methods you have taken to try to eliminate it. Include the effects the behavior is having on the student. Document the fact that you sent the note, or keep a copy of it. If you know the parent is easier to contact via e-mail, the note could be sent electronically.

　　Alternatively, you might want to call the parent directly so you can gain the parent's cooperation in eliminating the unacceptable behavior that the child is exhibiting. Realize that while the parent probably is angry at the child, the parent may displace that anger toward you. Listen quietly and then ask the parent to work with you to help the child. The message you want to convey is that you care about the student. Document this contact with the parent. Ask for suggestions to eliminate the problem behavior, and arrange to get together again to discuss improvements. Keep in mind that no matter what the reason for the behavior, you want it stopped. For instance, sad as it may be that the child's home life is unhappy, the student's incessant talking in class is distracting you and other students. Your goal is to help children handle crises, not to allow them to make excuses for unacceptable behavior. Document the conference.

STEP 9: *Send the student to the principal's office.* Inform the principal of the unacceptable behavior, share the intervention steps you have taken up to this point, and ask for suggestions.

STEP 10: *Get outside help for the student.* Some persistent behavioral problems may require additional interventions by other professionals. The school counselor, school psychologist, child's physician, etc. may be able to offer helpful suggestions or services to address the problem.

gradually from low to high levels of intrusiveness (Harrison & Spuler, 1983). This approach is designed to guide students toward the goal of self-control and to minimize disruption of the flow of classroom instruction.

If the behavior in question is mildly annoying to the teacher but does not disrupt other students or interfere with the learning of the student in question, it may be best for the teacher to simply *ignore it.* This may be an appropriate strategy for student behaviors such as momentary daydreaming, getting off to a slow start with seat work, tapping a pencil, or squirming. A teacher also might decide that it is appropriate to be more lenient when temporary, contextual factors cause a rise in off-task behaviors. For example, students may be more easily distracted if it is unusually warm in the classroom or if they are excited about an upcoming holiday or special event.

Sometimes the best response is not to completely ignore a misbehavior but to delay taking action in order to avoid further disruption. For example, if a student is using a pencil during a timed quiz when the correct procedure is to use a pen, it might be best to wait until the quiz is over and then remind the student of the correct procedure for future reference. Correcting the student during the quiz and asking him to track down a pen might break his concentration and/or distract other students.

When the teacher chooses to respond to misbehavior, *logical consequences* specific to the misbehavior should be implemented (Curwin & Mendler, 1999; Dreikurs, Grunwald, & Pepper, 1982; Elias & Schwab, 2006). For example, a student who is talkative and disruptive when she is seated next to a close friend should be assigned a different seat where she will be less tempted to get off-task.

Teachers learn to apply the principle of least intervention over time, as they become informed by both past classroom experience and knowledge of current individual students. This system works best with mild to moderately serious misbehaviors. Severe student misbehavior may require the teacher to skip several of the less intrusive steps and move immediately to a more direct response.

Trick or Treat. Students may be easily distracted at school when they are anticipating a special holiday or event.

Logical consequences: See page 336.

What might be some advantages and disadvantages of the principle of least Intervention?

APPLICATION: HOW TO HANDLE SPECIFIC MISBEHAVIORS

In addition to using research to inform their practice, teachers can benefit from the advice and experience of other teachers. Suggestions for how to handle various behavior problems that reflect strategies frequently used by K–12 teachers follow.

Routine Disruptions

Passing notes: While still continuing to deliver instruction, the teacher can walk toward students who have just passed a note, extend a hand for the students to hand it over, pocket it, and continue with instruction. The teacher should not interrupt valuable instruction time to read a passed note out loud to the whole class or make comments that embarrass the students involved.

Excessive talking: A teacher must communicate the importance of being a courteous, active listener and model that behavior by listening attentively to students at the appropriate times. When the teacher is giving instructions, students should stop what they are doing and give the teacher their full attention. The teacher can elicit students' attention through the use of a prearranged signal such as a responsive hand clap, raising one hand in the air, or ringing chimes. If the teacher has taken these preventive measures and certain students still are talking excessively, the teacher can follow the steps of the principle of least intervention to bring the students' behavior back into line.

Complaining or malingering: Often, at the heart of student complaints or malingering is an unmet need. Students need attention and need to feel successful. By allowing opportunities for both of these needs to be met on a daily basis, teachers can prevent cases of chronic complaining. Student complaints do need to be taken seriously. The teacher should listen to what the student has to say and, if the complaint is legitimate, show appreciation for the fact that the student has brought the problem to attention. If the complaint is not legitimate, the teacher can briefly explain why and then refocus the student's attention on the task at hand.

Intermediate Concerns

Teasing: Teasing can leave lasting emotional scars, so it's important for teachers to educate students about being sensitive to the feelings of others. It may be helpful to discuss the following guidelines with respect to teasing (Weinstein, 2003):

- know the difference between friendly joking around and hurtful ridicule;

- pay attention to others' body language and facial expressions to read whether their feelings are hurt—even if they don't tell you;

- never tease about sensitive issues such as someone's body, family, or personal weaknesses;

- accept teasing from others if you tease, and avoid being overly sensitive about teasing that is meant in a friendly way; and

- speak up if being teased about a certain topic bothers you.

Talking back: It is natural for a teacher to feel a sudden rush of anger when a student talks back in a belligerent or hostile way. However, it is very important that the teacher remain calm and not react defensively. Teachers should make it clear that they are willing to listen to what students have to say, but only if students are willing to speak respectfully and show the same courtesy. Issues like talking back are likely to be minimal if the teacher models respect for students, establishes clear expectations for acceptable behavior, and provides students with the tools to resolve their conflicts peacefully. This is also true of related behaviors such as the use of profanity and arguing among students.

See Module 26 for more information about homework policies.

Failure to do homework: Homework should be meaningful (have a clear purpose), reasonable in length and difficulty level, and clearly explained. Given many students' busy schedules and responsibilities outside school, the teacher should provide in-class opportunities to complete assignments when possible. Students can be given some autonomy in the homework process by having the option of skipping an assignment if they have passed a pretest or otherwise demonstrated mastery over the material. If, despite a teacher's best efforts, a student still will not turn in homework, the teacher can respond by meeting with the student individually to discuss the problem and to generate solutions together with the student. Some possible solutions include:

- creating a **contingency contract** (see Example 19.3), or an agreement, preferably written, between the teacher and student that provides the following information: (a) specification of appropriate student behavior, (b) specification of inappropriate student behaviors, (c) description of consequences for both appropriate and inappropriate behaviors (Henson & Eller, 1999), in this case behaviors specific to completing homework;

- encouraging a student to use a homework hotline or study buddy to get support when needed; and

- getting the student's parents involved in setting up a homework schedule and/or designating a space in the home that is conducive to doing homework (quiet, relatively free of distractions, with good lighting).

Chronic tardiness: The teacher can model promptness by being prepared for class and starting class on time. Students might not recognize tardiness as a real problem. Through class discussion early in the school year or one-on-one discussion with tardy students, the teacher can raise students' awareness of how tardiness disrupts the learning environment. Let students know that arriving late can:

- distract the teacher and the student's classmates,

- send the message that the student doesn't care about the class, and

- leave the student unprepared due to missing valuable instruction or discussion.

If a student has a legitimate reason for consistently getting to class late, consider seating that student close to the door in order to minimize disruption for the rest of the class.

Immoral Behaviors

For detailed coverage of moral development, see Module 5.

Cheating: Some behaviors clearly are considered cheating: copying someone else's homework, looking at someone else's answer sheet on an exam, plagiarizing someone else's work for a report. Other behaviors, such as working with a classmate to complete an assignment, can be ambiguous. An effective teacher will make it clear when students are allowed to work together or exchange ideas and when they are expected to complete their work independently. In an age of increased Internet use, students need to have a clear understanding of the rules with respect to plagiarism or cheating with Internet sources as well (Ma, Wan, & Lu, 2008). Some effective strategies for reducing the incidence of cheating include:

EXAMPLE 19.3 **Sample Contingency Contract**

Note how this contract ties appropriate and inappropriate student behavior to specific goals.

My Contract:

Name: Bobby Klosterman

Date: 10/1/12

These are my goals:

1. Write all homework assignments down in my notebook.

2. Complete all work and check it off as I get it finished.

3. Put completed homework in the "In" box as soon as I get to class.

These are my consequences if I don't meet my goals:

I will stay inside during recess to get my work finished.

I will lose 10% of the points possible on late assignments.

Three Strikes rule: After 3 late assignments, I will get an automatic zero on any late work.

These are my rewards/reinforcers if I meet my goals:

① I will get a sticker on my homework chart each day that my work is completed and turned in on time.

② For 5 stickers in a row, I'll earn a prize from the class Treasure Chest.

My contract will be reviewed on 10/14/12

Signatures: *Bobby Klosterman*

Marie Klosterman — Mom

Mrs. Newton (Teacher)

- discussing cheating policies openly with the class,
- emphasizing mastery over performance goals,
- communicating the value of understanding the material well,
- varying projects and assignments from year to year,
- separating desks so students cannot easily see one another's papers,
- using multiple forms of a test,
- asking students to put all materials in or under their desks before a test begins,
- reminding students not to talk to one another during a test session, and
- circulating around the room to monitor students' behavior.

If, despite taking preventive measures, cheating does occur, the teacher should talk privately with the student involved and present logical consequences (e.g., the student will receive no points and has to redo the assignment or retake the test).

Stealing: Most stealing incidents occur in the early grades, when students have less control over their impulses (Weinstein & Mignano, 2003). As with cheating, one of the best approaches is to reduce the

Logical Consequences. If a student writes all over a desk, having that student clean the desk would be a logical consequence that fits the misbehavior.

See Module 4: Bullying and emotional intelligence.

opportunity to steal things in the first place. The teacher can make sure all students have the supplies they need by:

- sending home a school supply list before the school year begins, and
- setting up a system in which students can borrow supplies from the teacher on the rare occasion that they forget or misplace their own.

The teacher can prevent theft of other personal property by never leaving a purse, field trip money, or other valuables unattended and by discouraging students from bringing valuables to school. If a theft does occur and the teacher knows who is responsible, the teacher can talk privately with the student in a nonconfrontational way. Sometimes a low-key statement is best: "I noticed you put Kevin's book in your bag as you left yesterday. Please make sure it is returned to him. I wouldn't want anyone to think you stole it." If the teacher does not know who took the stolen item, accusing particular students is inappropriate. The teacher can make an appeal to the entire class, letting students know that the item has been "misplaced" and encouraging anyone who knows where it might be to return it as soon as possible. If a particular student persists in stealing things even after a private talk with the teacher, the student's parents and the principal should be contacted.

Vandalism: As with many other types of misbehavior, prevention is the key to discouraging vandalism. Students are less likely to be destructive if they have been taught the importance of respecting other people and their belongings and if they feel a sense of ownership in the classroom. If vandalism does occur, it is best handled through the use of logical consequences. For example, if a student scribbles all over a desk, the student should be asked to stay after school to clean the desk.

Dangerous Behaviors

Bullying: Approximately 160,000 children avoid going to school every day and thousands more drop out of school completely because they feel victimized or afraid at school (Garbarino & deLara, 2002). Bullying is one of the most inadequately addressed problems in schools. A study by Frank Barone (1997) reported that when eighth-graders were surveyed, 60% reported having been bothered by a bully in middle school; however, school personnel thought that only 16% of the students had ever been bullied. The problem is compounded because peer harassment and teasing are seen as somewhat acceptable (Hoover & Oliver, 1996).

A report by the Pew Internet and American Life Project (2007) concluded that about 32% of teens have been the target of cyberbullying, and the percentage is even higher (41%) among high school girls. **Cyberbullying** can take a number of forms, including misrepresenting one's identity online in order to trick someone, spreading lies or rumors, and posting embarrassing pictures. Early intervention is one of the best approaches to preventing problems with bullying and aggression later in life (Aber, Brown, & Jones, 2003). Teachers can decrease the amount of verbal bullying by:

- encouraging students to be respectful of one another both in person and online,
- teaching students to show empathy for one another and to try to see things from someone else's perspective, and
- making it clear that threats and intimidation are totally unacceptable and that any students engaging in these behaviors will face serious consequences.

Fighting or other forms of violence: Violence in the classroom is every teacher's worst nightmare. Fortunately, it is relatively infrequent and has decreased in the past decade (Lynch, 2002). A study conducted by researchers at the Centers for Disease Control found that from 1993 to 1997 the percentage of students who said they had carried a weapon "such as a gun, knife or club" to school decreased from 11.8% to 8.5%. The percentage of students engaging in a physical fight on school property dropped from 16.2% to 14.8% (Brener, Simon, Krug, & Lowry, 1999). The most common types of school-based conflicts are verbal harassment, verbal arguments, and physical fights that involve hitting, kicking, scratching, and/or pushing. Fortunately, most of these fights do not involve serious injury or violations of the law (DeVoe et al., 2003).

Teachers can use a wide array of preventive methods to minimize the likelihood of violence in the classroom. Here are a few suggestions:

- Model respectful, courteous, caring behaviors at every opportunity.
- Allow opportunities for students to work together and to get to know one another better, but be sure to structure the interactions to ensure a positive outcome.
- Set up activities and experiences that help students practice patience, generosity, honesty, and thoughtful speech (no lying, gossiping, insulting, teasing).
- Help students understand cause and effect so they can better understand how their words and deeds affect others.
- Teach students to *own* their reactions. They do not get to choose how someone treats them, but they do get to choose how they react (or choose not to react) to what others say or do.
- Vigilantly monitor what is going on at all times in the classroom (withitness).
- Teach step-down skills that can help students deescalate a potentially violent situation (e.g., breathe, count to 10, go to a separate space to cool off).
- Make it clear that there are serious penalties for fighting.
- Praise and encourage students who attempt to resolve conflicts peacefully.
- Know the warning signs of impending violence.
- If you hear a rumor that a student has brought a weapon to school, report it to the principal at once.

In 1998, the U.S. Department of Justice and the U.S. Department of Education published a guide to assist schools with violence prevention (Dwyer, Osher, & Warger, 1998). The guide includes a list of early warning signs that indicate a potential for violence, as shown in Example 19.4. Students typically exhibit multiple warning signs, so a teacher should be careful not to overreact to single words, signs, or actions. If a physical fight does break out, follow the procedures in Guidelines 19.2. Some actions, like assault and battery or possession of a weapon on school property, are crimes and must also be reported to the police. Follow your school's policy with regard to the consequences of fighting.

EXAMPLE 19.4   **Early Warning Signs of Potential Violence**

- Social withdrawal
- Excessive feelings of isolation and being alone
- Excessive feelings of rejection
- Being a victim of violence
- Feelings of being picked on and persecuted
- Low school interest and poor academic performance
- Expression of violence in writings or drawings
- Uncontrolled anger
- Patterns of impulsive and chronic hitting, intimidating, and bullying behaviors
- History of discipline problems
- History of aggressive or violent behavior
- Intolerance of differences; prejudice
- Drug and alcohol use
- Affiliation with gangs
- Inappropriate access to, possession of, or use of firearms
- Serious threats of violence

Source: Dwyer, Osher, & Warger, 1998.

GUIDELINES 19.2   Procedures for Managing Physical Fights

1. Do not leave the area.

2. Immediately send a student to get help from other adults in the building.

3. Issue a short, firm command telling students to stop.

4. Do not try to restrain or physically intercede between fighting students without another adult present.

5. Make sure the rest of the class is a safe distance from the students who are fighting, and ask the class to sit quietly.

6. Do not, under any circumstances, permit other students to incite further violence by cheering for either participant in the fight or chanting "Fight, fight!"

7. If a student is injured in the fight, get help from the school nurse or call EMTs if necessary to get additional, skilled help in treating the injuries.

8. Document all the details of the fight as soon afterward as possible and provide a copy of the documentation to the parents of the students involved and to the principal. Be sure to specify when and where the fight happened, who was involved, and what action was taken.

A cautionary note about zero tolerance and exclusionary policies. Zero Tolerance is the most popular and widespread discipline reform effort in American schools today (Gregory & Cornell, 2009). Virtually every public school in the United States is mandated by federal law to use a zero tolerance approach for firearms violations (Gun Free Schools Act of 1994), and many apply a similar approach to other weapons, illegal drugs, over-the-counter medications, and other prohibited behaviors (APA Zero Tolerance Task Force, 2006). Zero tolerance is a highly structured disciplinary policy that permits little flexibility in outcome by imposing severe sanctions (often long-term suspension or expulsion) for violations of a school rule. Zero tolerance policies permit little or no consideration of the student's intentions or the circumstances of his or her misbehavior (Skiba & Peterson, 1999; Tebo, 2000).

Advocates of zero tolerance claim that it prevents school violence by removing dangerous students immediately after an infraction and, simultaneously, sending a strong deterrent message to other students. These claims have not been empirically tested; to the contrary, available research suggests that expulsion policies have a negative impact on students and no preventive effect (APA Zero Tolerance Task Force, 2006; Osher et al., 2010). Suspension and expulsion disproportionately affect students with emotional and behavioral disorders and students of color, contributing to school disengagement, lost opportunities to learn and dropout (Gregory, Skiba, & Noguera, 2010; Osher, Morrison, & Bailey, 2003). Because of their high potential for negative effects, exclusionary policies such as these should be used as a last resort.

DIVERSITY

Think about the types of misbehavior you are likely to see at the grade level you plan to teach. How might a proactive approach, as shown in many of the examples in this module, help to minimize incidents of misbehavior?

Summary

Define *misbehavior* and identify the various causes of misbehavior. Misbehavior can be any student behavior that disrupts the learning environment in the classroom. It includes behavior that interferes with teaching or with the rights of others to learn, is psychologically or physically unsafe, or destroys property. Students may misbehave at school for hundreds of potential reasons. The common causes of misbehavior vary according to the age and developmental level of the student. Physical, psychosocial, and environmental factors all contribute to student behavior patterns in the classroom.

Discuss five proactive ways to address behavior management issues in the classroom. Proactive behavior management involves planning ahead in order to prevent or minimize behavior problems rather than simply reacting to misbehavior after it occurs. First, effective teachers provide expectations of behavior early in the school year and are consistent in enforcing consequences for breaking the rules. Second, effective teachers model appropriate behaviors, such as behaving respectfully toward others, and follow up by rewarding students who behave in desired ways. Third, effective teachers anticipate problems and prevent them from occurring by using skills such as withitness, overlapping, group focus, and movement management. Fourth, effective teachers have systems in place for encouraging students to manage their own behavior—self-regulation. Finally, when addressing misbehavior in the classroom, effective teachers use the principle of least intervention to minimize disruption to the instructional process.

Summarize important considerations in responding to mild, moderate, and severe misbehaviors. Mild misbehavior may include disruptive actions such as note passing, excessive talking, or complaining. The teacher should follow the principle of least intervention by responding to these behaviors in a way that is least disruptive to the instructional environment (e.g., gesturing to students to remind them to get back on track, redirecting students to the task at hand). Moderate misbehaviors include slightly more serious actions such as teasing, talking back, failure to do homework, or chronic tardiness. When these behaviors occur, the teacher must help the student better understand the negative impact the behaviors have on their own learning and on the learning of others. The most serious misbehaviors include actions such as cheating, vandalism, bullying, and violence. It is critical that the teacher be aware of conditions that may precipitate such behaviors and of signs that these behaviors are occurring or are imminent. Responses to serious misbehavior vary depending on the situation. In general, teacher responses should be consistent with school-wide policies, should involve communication with a broader network (parents, administrator, school counselor, etc.), and should prioritize student safety and well-being.

Key Concepts

contingency contract   356
cyberbullying   358
group focus   353
misbehavior   347

movement management   353
observational learning   352
overlapping   353
principle of least intervention   354

proactive classroom management   350
withitness   353

Video Applications

www.mhhe.com/bohlin2e

Video 1: Addressing Behavior Management (*4 minutes*)

Clip 1 (First-grade classroom): Praise and positive attention

Clip 2 (First-grade classroom): Praise

Clip 3 (First-grade classroom): Rules and expectations

Clip 4 (Interview with middle school teachers): Rules and expectations

Clip 5 (Interview with middle school principal and guidance counselor): Handling behavioral issues in middle school.

Case Studies
Reflect and Evaluate

EARLY CHILDHOOD: "Caterpillar Circle"

These questions refer to the case study on page 318.

1. What steps did Sarah Brennan and her assistant, Steve Shoemaker, take to anticipate and prevent misbehavior?
2. What types of misbehavior did you observe in Miss Sarah's classroom?
3. Identify the causes of misbehavior in question 2. How did the *causes* of misbehavior shape the way the teachers reacted to problems that arose?
4. How might the age of the children have influenced the teachers' expectations for classroom behavior?
5. Identify specific examples of withitness, overlapping, group focus, and movement management exhibited by Miss Sarah and Mr. Steve.

ELEMENTARY SCHOOL: "Ecosystems"

These questions refer to the case study on page 320.

1. How did Ms. Anderson anticipate and prevent potential problems related to the ecosystem activity?
2. In what ways does Ms. Anderson communicate her expectations to her students?
3. How does Ms. Anderson deal with disruptions that occur during the activity?
4. How does Ms. Anderson use logical consequences in this case?
5. Describe Ms. Anderson's use of withitness, overlapping, group focus, and movement management.
6. Ms. Anderson describes her approach to classroom management as *proactive*. What does she mean by this? Give specific examples of how she implements this style.

MIDDLE SCHOOL: "Classroom Safety"

These questions refer to the case study on page 322.

1. What examples of misbehavior did you observe in this case? How would you classify each example in terms of severity?
2. How would you rate Mr. Gardino's classroom management in terms of withitness, overlapping, group focus, and movement management?
3. How did Mr. Gardino promote self-regulation among his students? Do you think he gave the students too much responsibility over their own behavior? Why or why not?
4. What steps did Mr. Gardino take to respond to the problem that occurred between Kevin and Nick? Is there anything else he should have done?
5. How does Mr. Gardino's style compare to the approach you plan to use in your own classroom?
6. How might the teacher's approach to this situation have been different if the teacher was a woman? If the two students fighting were girls?

HIGH SCHOOL: "Refusal to Dress"

These questions refer to the case study on page 324.

1. Define what misbehavior is. Should the actions committed by Brianna during first period be classified as misbehaviors? Why or why not?
2. Should Brianna's first-period actions have been ignored? Justify your answer by discussing advantages and disadvantage of your approach.

DIVERSITY 3. Would your answer to question 2 be different if the student were male? Why or why not?

4. Do you think it would have been more effective to approach Brianna for a private conversation while the other students were doing an activity? If so, how might this have been helpful? If not, what would be a more useful approach to take, and how would it help Brianna?
5. During Brianna's outburst, how was teacher Maria Salazar's classroom management potentially compromised?
6. Ms. Salazar was unsuccessful in getting Brianna to talk about what was causing her change in behavior. How might knowing the cause of the misbehavior have influenced how Ms. Salazar chose to proceed?

Instruction: Applying Behavioral, Cognitive, and Constructivist Approaches

<table>
<tr><th>Outline</th><th>Learning Goals</th></tr>
</table>

Planning Instruction

1. Define *learning objective* and explain why it is important for a lesson to have clear learning objectives.

Teaching Methods Based on Behaviorism

- Direct Instruction
- Mastery Learning

2. Describe the goals of mastery learning and direct instruction, and discuss the advantages and disadvantages of each approach.

Teaching Methods Based on Cognitive Learning Theory

- Discovery Learning and Guided Discovery
- Expository Teaching

3. Explain how discovery learning and expository teaching foster meaningful learning.

Teaching Methods Based on Constructivism

- Inquiry Learning
- Cooperative Learning
- Methods of Fostering Comprehension

4. Describe the techniques based on cognitive apprenticeships that are used in constructivist teaching.

Summary
Key Concepts
Video Applications
Case Studies: Reflect and Evaluate

In many of your classes for teacher preparation, you often learn about the *"what"* and *"how"* of teaching—that is, you learn about the content that you will be teaching (the what) and how to develop lesson plans and implement various teaching methods. Effective teachers are not just skilled at developing and delivering instruction. They are also skilled at planning instruction before they step into the classroom, considering what they want students to know and choosing teaching methods that are appropriate to the learning goals they set. In this module, you will learn the *"why"* and *"when"* of teaching. For example:

- Why is it important to develop learning objectives?
- When should teachers choose lower-level or higher-level objectives?
- For what purposes and in what contexts should teachers use different teaching methods?
- Why and when are some teaching methods more effective than others?

Before we explore the answers to these questions, it is important to point out that the teaching methods you will encounter can be considered teacher-centered or student-centered in their approach to instruction. In *teacher-centered approaches,* teachers control the amount and pace of information and the structure of the learning environment. In *student-centered approaches,* the learning environment is structured to optimize students' construction of meaning from their interactions with content material and peers. In this approach, teachers often are mediators or facilitators of student learning rather than dispensers of information. As you read about the variety of instructional methods, think about their teacher-centered or student-centered orientation and whether this focus is best suited for the particular students you are working with and your learning objectives. Let's start where all good teaching begins—with learning objectives.

PLANNING INSTRUCTION

Learning objectives are the foundation for a good lesson and the standard by which teachers evaluate student learning. Teachers develop **learning objectives** to describe and specify what students will know or be able to do after they have completed a lesson (Mager, 1975; Thompson, 2002). Three features are common to all learning objectives:

1. Performance: *what* the learner is expected to do. What knowledge do students need to demonstrate? What task will they need to accomplish?

2. Conditions: *how* the learner is expected to do it. Describe the conditions under which students will perform. What methods and materials will they need to use?

3. Criteria: *how well* the student needs to perform. What constitutes acceptable performance? When possible, specify how the learner's performance of an objective will be measured (Mager, 1975).

Example 20.1 provides two illustrations of performance, condition, and criteria elements of a learning objective. The conditions and criteria aspects of learning objectives refer to assessment and evaluation of student learning once instruction is completed—a topic that is discussed in Module 26, "Assessing Student Learning," and Module 27, "Performance Assessment." When you are planning instruction, it is most helpful to think through the performance component of learning objectives.

Declarative knowledge: See page 189.

Begin by asking yourself what types of knowledge students will be required to show. Will students be required to learn *declarative knowledge,* information that can be communicated verbally, as when they

EXAMPLE 20.1	Defining Features of Learning Objectives		
	Performance	**Conditions**	**Criteria**
Geography example	Correctly identify continents and oceans.	When given an unlabeled map of the world, . . .	The student will correctly label all seven continents and all five oceans.
English example	Correctly use grammar, spelling, and punctuation rules.	When given five sentences to correct, . . .	The student will identify 90% of the grammar, spelling, and punctuation errors in the sentences and make the appropriate corrections.

TABLE 20.1	Levels of Bloom's Taxonomy	
Category	**Description**	**Instructional Activities**
Remember	Recall or recognize information, ideas, or principles without necessarily understanding or using the information	List, label, name, state, or define
Understand	Make sense of information based on prior learning, without necessarily making new connections	Explain, summarize, paraphrase, or describe
Apply	Select and use data and principles to solve a problem or complete a task with minimal direction	Use, compute, solve, demonstrate, or apply knowledge
Analyze	Break something down into its parts	Analyze, categorize, compare, or contrast information
Evaluate	Judge the value of materials, methods, or ideas in a particular situation	Critique information, make judgments or recommendations, provide justifications
Create	Combine ideas into an original product, plan, or proposal to create something new	Create, design, invent, develop, hypothesize

memorize the capitals of all 50 states? Will students acquire *procedural knowledge* —how to perform a task or skill—as when they learn to operate a microscope? Will they learn *conceptual knowledge,* reflecting an understanding of the relationship or connections between ideas, as when they explain the events leading up to World War I?

Procedural knowledge: See page 189.

Conceptual knowledge: See page 189.

Next, ask yourself what students should be able to do with this knowledge. How will they demonstrate what they have learned? **Bloom's taxonomy** for cognitive tasks, revised and updated in 2001, specifies six ways students can demonstrate their knowledge (Anderson & Krathwohl, 2001; Bloom, Englehart, Frost, Hill, & Krathwohl, 1956), as shown in Table 20.1. Educators often view these levels in Bloom's taxonomy as a hierarchy, with each skill building on those that precede it. When deciding on learning objectives, ask yourself whether the content to be learned involves lower-level objectives (remember, understand, apply) or higher-level objectives (analyze, evaluate, create). Mastering the multiplication of fractions is a lower-level objective, while comparing and contrasting two literary pieces is a higher-level one.

Thinking about the type of knowledge you want students to acquire and the level at which you expect them to demonstrate their knowledge will help you choose a teaching method that is most appropriate for these outcomes. Keep this in mind as we explore various teacher-centered and student-centered teaching methods. Let's begin with teacher-centered approaches based on behaviorism.

TEACHING METHODS BASED ON BEHAVIORISM

Behavioral learning theory proposes, simply, that learning leads to a change in an individual's behavior. This school of thought has its roots in *operant conditioning*, which proposes that an individual's behavior is the result of two environmental stimuli: antecedents and consequences. Antecedents are stimuli or situations that signal that a behavior is expected, while consequences are stimuli that either strengthen the likelihood that the behavior will occur again or reduce the future occurrence of the behavior. For example, a typical classroom interaction would involve a teacher asking a question (antecedent), a student providing a response (behavior), and the teacher offering feedback (consequence). Behavioral learning theory is equated with teacher-centered instructional approaches in which teachers serve as dispensers of information and structure the learning environment to help students progress from simple to more complex skills. Two examples of this approach are direct instruction and mastery learning, in which teachers create an antecedent for learning and consequences that strengthen students' knowledge and skills.

Operant conditioning: See page 161.

Direct Instruction

The goal of **direct instruction** is to maximize academic learning time—the time that students spend in meaningful, appropriate tasks—by emphasizing completion of learning tasks and by minimizing off-task behavior such as puzzles, games, and teacher-student interactions not directly related to academic tasks (Joyce, Weil, & Calhoun, 2004; Rosenshine, 1979). With this approach, teachers use a high degree of control to create a structured learning environment and monitor student progress. Direct instruction assumes students learn best when teachers structure the learning environment to present accurate information in small chunks and offer many opportunities for practice and feedback (Kirschner, Sweller, & Clark, 2006; Mayer, 2004; Rosenshine, 1985). This approach also requires all students to move through the content at the same pace. Let's examine the typical components of direct instruction by discussing what occurs before, during, and after a lesson.

Teachers using direct instruction would begin a lesson by reviewing the previous day's lecture and checking student work. This allows teachers to identify concepts or skills where students committed errors so that they can re-teach the material to the entire class. Next, teachers would introduce new content by activating prior knowledge through discussion of the learning objective or an overview of the lesson (Joyce et al., 2004; Rosenshine, 1985). Identifying the learning objective or lesson overview provides students with a purpose for learning the material and an overall procedure for how material is to be learned. Preparing students for the lesson using these steps improves student achievement (Fisher et al., 1980; Medley, Soar, & Coker, 1984).

During a lesson, teachers control the pace and presentation of new material. They present information in small steps to be mastered one step at a time, provide varied examples, use modeling, and re-explain challenging concepts. They also check for understanding by asking convergent questions that call for a right answer or questions that require students to explain their answers (Rosenshine, 1985).

Once students have learned material, they have an opportunity to progress through four structured types of practice.

1. In *controlled practice,* the teacher leads students through examples, providing immediate corrective feedback. This stage requires careful monitoring to prevent students from learning incorrect procedures or concepts. Rather than simply giving the right answers, effective teachers provide feedback, telling students what they have done correctly, prompting them for clarification or improved answers, and reteaching when necessary (Fisher et al., 1980; Rosenshine, 1971).

2. In *guided practice,* students practice on their own while the teacher provides reinforcement and corrective feedback. For example, high school students might complete a worksheet conjugating Spanish verbs as teachers move through the classroom to check on their progress.

3. Students move to *independent practice* when they are able to practice knowledge or skills with about 85% to 90% accuracy. Traditional homework is an example of independent practice.

4. Students also need to engage in *distributed practice,* a process of spreading out practice over a period of time. These short and frequent practice periods are more effective than fewer but longer practice opportunities, especially for children in early elementary grades. To foster long-term learning, teachers also provide weekly and monthly reviews and re-teach as necessary.

Direct instruction is a popular method in elementary grades 1–3, where much of instruction is focused on basic skills such as reading, mathematics, spelling, handwriting, and early science and social studies knowledge. Direct instruction is effective:

■ for lower-level objectives in Bloom's taxonomy and for improving students' basic skills in reading and mathematics (Brophy & Evertson, 1976; Denham & Lieberman, 1980; Joyce et al., 2004);

■ as an initial instructional strategy for lower-achieving students (Good, Biddle, & Brophy, 1975); and

■ for teaching basic skills to students with disabilities (Reddy, Ramar, & Kusama, 2000; Turnbull, Turnbull, Shank, Smith, & Leal, 2002).

Direct instruction can also be used for teaching more complex skills and subjects. Elementary school students have learned how to design controlled experiments in science through direct instruction and were able to transfer their newly learned strategies to new contexts (Chen & Klahr, 1999; Klahr & Nigam, 2004). Direct instruction has proven effective for teaching multi-step procedures typically found in high school subjects such as algebra, geometry, and computer programming (Anderson, Corbett, Koedinger, & Pelletier, 1995; Klahr & Carver, 1988).

Yet, direct instruction is not effective for all students and all situations (Joyce et al., 2004). This method may not benefit high-achieving students or task-oriented students who are intrinsically driven to perform and succeed on tasks (Ebmeier & Good, 1979; Solomon & Kendall, 1976). Also, direct instruction should not become the sole instructional method for lower-achieving students. Rather, as

Transfer: See page 226.

these students achieve more success, teachers should transition to less structured learning experiences and emphasize more complex knowledge and skills (McFaul, 1983; Means & Knapp, 1991). Furthermore, direct instruction may not be sufficient alone for encouraging long-term retention and transfer of complex skills (Dean & Kuhn, 2006). Teachers should follow direct instruction with opportunities for extended practice with problem solving and application of strategies. For a more balanced emphasis on basic and complex learning skills, direct instruction can effectively be used together with more student-centered approaches (Dean & Kuhn, 2006; Kierstad, 1985).

Mastery Learning

Mastery learning is based on the idea that *all* students can learn curricular material if given sufficient time (Carroll, 1971). Teachers set a pre-specified mastery level, such as 80% on a unit test. Students who do not master a certain unit are allowed to repeat it or an equivalent version at their own pace and to take another unit test until they have mastered the material (Joyce et al., 2004). The approach consists of (Bloom, 1971):

- the development of major learning objectives representing a course or unit;
- dividing major learning objectives into smaller units from simple to complex, with each unit having its own learning objectives;
- conducting a *formative assessment*—a brief diagnostic test to assess students' current level of performance before instruction and to determine areas needing improvement;
- presenting material to students, who typically work individually and independently;
- providing students with feedback about their progress (reinforcement of learning); and
- conducting a *summative assessment*—a test to determine what the student has learned.

Formative and summative assessment: See page 480.

This sequence of instruction has been used with students at all grade levels and for curricula ranging from basic skills to complex material (Joyce et al., 2004). Mastery learning is also appropriate for students of varying achievement and ability levels. By adjusting the amount of time and the amount of feedback given to students with different needs, mastery learning increases the likelihood that most students will achieve a pre-specified mastery level set by the teacher.

Teachers also should be aware of potential disadvantages of mastery learning. In research comparing students taught with mastery learning and those taught the same material using a different method, mastery-learning students have shown modest learning gains on teacher-made tests but no gains when

Mastery learning. In mastery learning, shown here, students work independently at their own pace.

standardized tests are used to measure achievement (Kulik, Kulik, & Bangert-Drowns, 1990; Slavin, 1990; Wambugu & Changeiywo, 2008). Also, this method may widen the *achievement gap* between students rather than narrowing it. While lower-achieving students are given extra time to repeat content in order to achieve mastery, we must assume that higher-achieving students are progressing to more advanced units.

Think about the grade level you intend to teach. Would you consider using mastery learning or direct instruction? Why or why not?

TEACHING METHODS BASED ON COGNITIVE LEARNING THEORY

Meaningful learning: See page 231.

Cognitive learning theory proposes that learning involves actively constructing knowledge. Teaching methods based on this perspective are considered student-centered because they focus on the *mental processes* students use in knowledge construction rather than the external stimuli teachers use in behaviorist approaches. An important concept in cognitive learning theory is **meaningful learning**—actively forming new knowledge structures by (Mayer, 2003):

- selecting relevant information,
- organizing the information into a coherent structure, and
- integrating the information with relevant prior knowledge.

Teachers can foster meaningful learning using one of two distinct teaching methods—discovery learning and expository teaching—or both of them. Today's elementary and secondary school teachers consider these two methods to be complementary, as each has features that encourage meaningful learning when used appropriately.

Discovery Learning and Guided Discovery

Discovery learning, proposed by Jerome Bruner (1961), encourages students to discover and internalize a concept, rule, or principle through unstructured exploration of to-be-learned information (Bruner, 1961). For example, high school students might be given various inclines and objects and be expected to experiment with the materials—without explicit guidance from the teacher—to "discover" certain physics principles.

However, discovery learning without any guidance from the teacher generally does not benefit learning (Alfieri, Brooks, Aldrich, & Tennenbaum, 2011). Students may not be able to integrate the to-be-learned principle into their memory because they may lack prior knowledge or may activate inappropriate knowledge (Klahr & Nigam, 2004). Students also may fail to stumble across the principle at all because of too much freedom in the discovery process (Mayer, 2004). As a result, the discovery process often leads to gaps in understanding and results in *negative transfer* (incorrectly applying prior knowledge to the problem) or *zero transfer* (failing to recognize when they can apply their knowledge).

Transfer: See Module 13.

A form of discovery learning called **guided discovery** is considered more effective than pure discovery in facilitating the learning and transfer of knowledge (Alfieri et al., 2011; Mayer, 2004). In this approach, the teacher provides enough guidance to ensure that students discover the rule or principle to be learned. For the high school students discovering physics principles, the teacher would provide general guidelines for experimentation and monitor their progress, steering their activities in the right direction when needed. The structure and guidance allow the student to focus cognitive resources on integrating and reorganizing knowledge and making inferences rather than on figuring out how to carry out the discovery process itself (Alfieri et al., 2011; Chi, 2009; Fletcher, 2009). To be successful using guided discovery, teachers must consider the individual abilities and needs of students in determining how much and what type of guidance to provide (Mayer, 2004). Recent research suggests that a guided discovery approach can be effective for learning and transfer of new scientific knowledge for students from elementary through high school (Akinbobola & Afolabi, 2009; Balim, 2009; Dean & Kuhn, 2007).

Expository Teaching

In David Ausubel's (1963, 2000) **expository teaching** (also called *meaningful verbal learning*), the goal is not to have students independently discover to-be-learned content but to ensure that new information will be integrated into the learner's memory in a meaningful way.

Teachers begin by emphasizing the relevance of the new content to what students already know and to real-life examples and situations. To do this, they use an **advance organizer,** a tool that presents general information and that provides a structure into which new information can be integrated. Take a moment to flip back to the beginning of this module and examine the outline on page 363. It is one example of an advance organizer. Advance organizers are not just outlines. They can be visual presentations, such as a flow chart that introduces a process, or an *analogy* that compares a new concept (a molecule) to a familiar one (a solar system). Advance organizers that consist of concrete models or analogies presented either verbally or graphically, rather than abstract examples or principles, are most effective (Mayer, 1992; Robinson, 1998). Advance organizers also enhance learning and promote transfer (application of knowledge to new situations), especially when new material is unfamiliar or difficult (Corkill, 1992; Luiten, Ames, & Ackerson, 1980; Morin & Miller, 1998). For example, a camera might be used as an analogy to teach elementary school students about the workings of the human eye.

After activating students' relevant knowledge, teachers present topics in a highly organized process that moves from general, or prerequisite, knowledge to more specific topics. This structuring provides a relevant foundation on which students can build. Teachers also offer students opportunities to practice their knowledge in many different contexts to be certain they develop a thorough understanding of the new content. Implemented in this way, expository teaching is an efficient method for teaching subject-matter content, such as science, math, social studies, or health, especially with students from the upper elementary grades through high school (Ausubel, 2000; Luiten et al., 1980).

Have you ever experienced discovery learning, guided discovery, or expository teaching? Reflect on how effective these methods were for your learning.

TEACHING METHODS BASED ON CONSTRUCTIVISM

Teaching methods based on constructivism are considered student-centered because constructivism emphasizes the individual's active role in exploring and socially interacting within his or her environment. Many constructivist theories of learning are based on *situated cognition,* a conceptual framework with roots in the writings of Russian educational psychologist Lev Semenovich Vygotsky, Swiss psychologist Jean Piaget, and philosopher/educator John Dewey (Cobb & Bowers, 1999; Rogoff, 1990). Situated cognition is about learning in authentic contexts, such as apprenticeships, in which individuals work alongside experts and acquire necessary skills for solving problems and completing tasks that are important in the real world (Brown, Collins, & Duguid, 1989; Collins, Hawkins, & Carver, 1991).

Piaget's and Vygotsky's theories: See pages 119 and 124.

Educators can bring situated cognition into schools by creating what are called **cognitive apprenticeships,** in which students develop cognitive skills through guided participation in authentic activities (Brown et al., 1989; Collins, Brown, & Newman, 1989; Lave & Wenger, 1991). Students participate in activities at a level commensurate with their ability and move gradually toward full participation. For example, young children at first may only be able to participate in conversation around the dinner table by talking about their day at school, but they will gradually move on to discussing current events and social issues with increasing cognitive and language development and with support from family members. Cognitive apprenticeships involve many techniques (Dennen, 2004; Enkenberg, 2001):

Modeling: See page 174.

- *modeling* (performing a behavior for others to imitate) by the adult or the more experienced individual,

- *explaining* (discussing one's reasoning or the need for certain strategies),

- *coaching* (monitoring students' activities and assisting and supporting them when necessary),

Cognitive Apprenticeships. Cognitive apprenticeships, like actual apprenticeships (shown here), involve guided participation in authentic activities.

Scaffolding and fading: See page 126.

- *practicing,*
- *scaffolding* (providing support to students so they can accomplish a task) and *fading* (gradually withdrawing scaffolding),
- *exploration* (forming and testing hypotheses; finding new ideas and viewpoints),
- *reflection* (assessing and analyzing one's learning performance), and *articulation* (verbally expressing the results of one's reflection).

These techniques are found in many of the constructivist teaching methods described next. As you read, try to identify the techniques in each teaching method.

Inquiry Learning

In **inquiry learning,** students construct knowledge and develop problem-solving skills in the context of an inquiry activity (Lave & Wenger, 1991). This process typically involves several phases:

1. formulating appropriate research questions,
2. collecting and organizing data,
3. analyzing and evaluating data, and
4. communicating the research results in a presentation.

More than a finite list of steps, however, the process of inquiry usually is practiced as a continuous cycle (Bruner, 1965), as Figure 20.1 illustrates. While this approach appears similar to the *scientific method,* inquiry learning assignments can be designed for any discipline and any developmental level.

   In inquiry learning, teachers serve as facilitators, using their expertise to guide the inquiry lesson and to evaluate students' progress and the direction of the inquiry process. This approach requires the teacher to design and monitor inquiry groups to ensure that students are working collaboratively. If some students are allowed to take over the inquiry process of the group, the opportunity for all students *DIVERSITY* to "construct" knowledge for themselves may be reduced. Students with intellectual disabilities, who typically show a weakness in independent insight and inductive thinking relative to normally achieving students, may require additional coaching and scaffolding in order to benefit from the inquiry process (Mastropieri et al., 1996; Mastropieri, Scruggs, & Butcher, 1997).

Cooperative Learning

Cooperative learning: See page 378.

Cooperative learning involves students working together to achieve a shared goal. In a high school U.S. history course, for example, a cooperative learning group might create a presentation on the Bill of Rights in which group members work together to develop the content of the presentation, each member presents a portion, and the group is graded on the final product. Cooperative learning can be used for any subject and with students from elementary through high school (Johnson & Johnson, 1986), but a cooperative group activity must contain these five elements (Johnson & Johnson, 1999, 2009):

1. *Positive interdependence:* Members of the group work together and depend on one another so that all group members succeed.
2. *Individual and group accountability:* Each member must contribute to the group in order for the group to succeed and be rewarded.

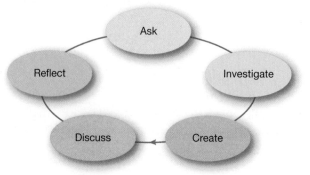

Figure 20.1. The Cycle of Inquiry Learning. Students begin by asking research questions and end by reflecting on the research process and its outcomes.

| GUIDELINES 20.1 | Tips for Effective Use of Cooperative Learning |

Characteristic	Teaching tips
Positive interdependence	■ Establish a group goal stating that all group members must reach their learning goals.
	■ Provide rewards based on the success of the group (e.g., a group grade, bonus points, or tangible rewards).
	■ Distribute limited resources.
	■ Assign each member a specific role.
	■ Divide the work so that one member's assignment is necessary for the next member to complete his or her assignment.
Individual and group accountability	■ Randomly select one student's product to represent the group.
	■ Test all group members and average the scores.
Interpersonal skills	■ Teach communication skills, especially in the elementary grades.
	■ Include interpersonal objectives for a cooperative lesson.
	■ Inform students of the collaborative skills needed to work successfully in their groups.
Face-to-face interaction	■ Monitor group members' use of resources and level of challenge and feedback.
	■ Monitor and scaffold interactions and collaboration, especially for students in elementary grades.
Group processing	■ Allow time for groups to reflect on their functioning so students do not assume that speed and finishing early are more important than meaningful learning.
	■ Have students identify what was helpful and unhelpful in their interactions.
	■ Use information about group processing to make decisions about what to change for the next task or what changes to make in group placements.

Sources: Johnson & Johnson, 1986, 1990; McCaslin & Good, 1996.

3. *Interpersonal skills:* Trust, communication, decision making, leadership, and conflict resolution are all important to the success of cooperative learning.

4. *Face-to-face interaction:* Offering effective help and feedback, exchanging resources effectively, challenging one another's reasoning, and motivating one another to achieve goals are all necessary for effective learning.

5. *Group processing:* Reflecting on how well the group is functioning and how to improve is important for successful cooperative learning.

Teachers can use Guidelines 20.1 to create activities that incorporate these five essential elements.

Decades of research show that cooperative learning yields many beneficial academic and social outcomes, including the following:

■ higher-level reasoning, creative thinking, and long-term retention and transfer of learned information (Johnson & Johnson, 1998);

■ higher achievement in reading and mathematics (Slavin, Lake, Chambers, Cheung, & Davis, 2009; Rohrbeck, Ginsburg-Block, Fantuzzo, & Miller, 2003);

■ increased self-esteem, especially in students with disabilities (Johnson & Johnson, 1998);

■ greater intrinsic motivation for learning (Johnson & Johnson, 1985); and

■ improved peer relationships in general, among students with disabilities and nondisabled students, and between students of different ethnicities (Johnson & Johnson, 2000, 2002; McMaster & Fuchs, 2002).

Methods of Fostering Comprehension

Teachers can use several methods to promote students' comprehension, all of which foster the construction of knowledge through social interactions and embody several characteristics of cognitive apprenticeships.

DIVERSITY

Students with disabilities: See Modules 24 and 25.

Intrinsic motivation: See page 265 and page 279.

RECIPROCAL TEACHING

Reciprocal teaching: See page 215.

Zone of Proximal Development: See page 124.

Based on Vygotsky's Zone of Proximal Development, **reciprocal teaching** teaches metacognitive strategies necessary for skilled reading comprehension. Using this method, a group of students would be jointly responsible for understanding and evaluating an assigned text (which is why it is called *reciprocal*). The teacher would first model four comprehension strategies (questioning about the main idea, clarifying, summarizing, and predicting) and then provide scaffolding to students, who take turns leading discussions (Brown & Palincsar, 1987; Palincsar, 2003). Scaffolding by the teacher (and later by the students) may involve asking questions and rephrasing or elaborating on statements (Brown & Palincsar, 1989; Rosenshine & Meister, 1994). Students are given as much support as they need to complete the activity (Collins et al., 1989). Students with lower reading ability can participate and contribute to the level of their ability, while learning from those with more ability or experience (Brown & Palincsar, 1989). As students acquire skill, they take greater responsibility over the reciprocal teaching process, and scaffolding gradually fades.

Reciprocal teaching is most appropriate at the elementary school level, when instruction in reading focuses on the acquisition of comprehension skill. The method results in substantially improved reading comprehension in students of all ages (Rosenshine & Meister, 1994; Slavin et al., 2009). It also improves the comprehension skills of elementary and middle school students with intellectual disabilities and learning disabilities (Alfassi, Weiss, & Lifshitz, 2009; Gajria, Jitendra, Sood, & Sacks, 2007). Because students are required to articulate what makes a good question, prediction, and summary, their strategies become decontextualized, meaning students are able to use them in many domains, which improves transfer (Collins et al., 1989).

Transfer: See page 226.

INSTRUCTIONAL CONVERSATIONS

In many elementary school classrooms, students' verbal contributions during reading lessons are limited to known answers (Gallimore & Goldenberg, 1992), as when a teacher asks "Who is the main character in this story?" Teachers can move away from the traditional role of evaluating students' responses toward *assisting* students in interpreting texts by using **instructional conversations,** a method that assumes that (1) students have something important to say and (2) their input is valued (Gallimore & Goldenberg, 1992). This method consists of ten elements (see Table 20.2) that reflect Vygotsky's notion of assisted learning in the Zone of Proximal Development.

Teachers and students engage in a joint conversation about a text that looks like a spontaneous discussion where each person contributes to the dialogue by building upon, extending, or challenging a previous comment. However, the discussion is a planned interaction with instructional and conversational purposes (Gallimore & Goldenberg, 1992; Gallimore & Tharp, 1990). The instructional purpose focuses on learning objectives—what the teacher wants students to acquire from reading the text (e.g., vocabulary, comprehension, themes). The conversational purpose involves creating a joint understanding and interpretation of the text through genuine communication.

Teachers have used instructional conversations to promote elementary school students' interaction with and comprehension of stories during reading lessons (Gallimore & Goldenberg, 1992; Saunders & Goldenberg, 1999). Students participating in instructional conversations have achieved grade-level or higher reading skills and mastery of more complex, differentiated concepts than children receiving traditional reading comprehension instruction (Saunders & Goldenberg, 1992; Tharp & Gallimore, 1988). These findings have primarily come from research with culturally diverse populations, as the instructional conversations method was initially developed and used with native Hawaiian children in grades **DIVERSITY** K–3 in urban Honolulu and was later adapted for use with Latino students in Los Angeles, California (Au, 1979; Goldenberg, 1987). Although research results are promising, more empirical support for this approach is needed (Gallimore & Goldenberg, 1992). The effectiveness of instructional conversations with other grade levels and other student populations has yet to be tested. Another potential obstacle to the widespread adoption of this method is that effective implementation requires one year of teacher training (Moll, 2001).

RECIPROCAL QUESTIONING

Reciprocal questioning, which is a method of reinforcing new concepts, information, or procedures that students have learned in class, encourages structured conversations among students. Because each student's understanding of new material may differ from that of others, the social negotiation of conflicting perspectives can lead to a restructuring of knowledge (Bearison, 1982; Glachan & Light, 1982).

TABLE 20.2	Components of Instructional Conversations
Instructional elements	**How to implement**
1. Thematic focus	■ Select a theme or idea as a starting point for focusing the discussion. ■ Make a general plan for how the theme will unfold.
2. Activation and use of background knowledge	■ Provide students with necessary background knowledge for understanding the text by weaving the knowledge into the discussions.
3. Direct teaching	■ When necessary, teach a skill or concept directly.
4. Promotion of more complex language and expression	■ Elicit more complex language by asking students to expand on their thoughts, questioning them, and restating their contributions using more complex grammar and vocabulary.
5. Promotion of bases for statements or positions	■ Encourage students to use text, pictures, and reasoning to support an argument or a position. ■ Probe for the bases of students' statements (e.g., ask "How do you know?").
6. Fewer "known-answer" questions	■ Focus on questions for which there might be more than one correct answer.
7. Responsiveness to student contributions	■ Be responsive to students' statements and the opportunities they provide for further discussion, while maintaining the focus and coherence of the discussion and the initial plan for the discussion.
8. Connected discourse	■ Be sure the discussion involves interaction and turn-taking so that succeeding contributions build on and extend previous ones.
9. A challenging but nonthreatening atmosphere	■ Create an open, supportive environment that challenges students to negotiate and construct the meaning of the text.
10. General participation	■ Encourage students to volunteer to speak or to influence the selection of speaking turns rather than directly determining who speaks.

Source: Adapted from Goldenberg, 1992/1993.

For example, after high school students participate in a history lesson on the consequences of the Missouri Compromise of 1820, they would independently generate two or three questions using question stems, shown in Example 20.2, and then take turns in cooperative groups asking and answering each other's questions. This approach is called *reciprocal* because students help each other achieve an understanding of material.

The question stems are the most important aspect of this approach, because they guide discussions by encouraging students to do the following things (King, 1990, 2002):

■ provide explanations to others,

■ think about the material in new ways by confronting different perspectives, and

■ monitor their own thinking through metacognitive questions.

Providing students with more instruction on how to generate the questions is better than offering less instruction. In research by King (1990, 2002), students trained in the use of "why" and "how" questions

Metacognition: See Module 12.

EXAMPLE 20.2 Question Stems for Reciprocal Questioning

Type of prompt	Purpose	Examples
Comprehension-checking	Self-testing	▪ What does . . . mean? ▪ Describe in your own words . . . . ▪ What is a new example of . . . ?
Knowledge-constructing	To construct new knowledge and integrate it with prior knowledge by: ▪ explaining ▪ making evaluative, comparative, or evidential connections within the material	▪ Explain why . . . . ▪ Explain how . . . . ▪ How do you account for . . . ? ▪ How does . . . tie in with what we learned before? ▪ What conclusions can you draw about . . . ? ▪ What would happen if . . . ? ▪ How would . . . affect . . . ? ▪ What do you think causes . . . ? ▪ What are the strengths and weaknesses of . . . ?
Thought-provoking	To create cognitive conflict through expression of different points of view	▪ What do you think would happen if . . . ? ▪ Do you agree or disagree with this statement? Why or why not? ▪ What is the best . . . and why?
Metacognitive	To monitor thinking and learning	▪ What made you think of that? ▪ What is your reasoning?

Source: Adapted from King, 2002.

asked more critical thinking questions and gave and received more elaborated explanations than untrained students.

Reciprocal questioning results in several positive academic outcomes. Students using this technique generate more high-level (critical thinking) questions than those involved in group discussion (King, 1990, 2002). Students who give explanations of lesson content in peer groups also improve their own comprehension of the material (Dansereau, 1988; Webb, 1989). Research with students in elementary school through college shows that reciprocal questioning improves comprehension more effectively than group discussion, unguided peer questioning (i.e., no question stems provided), and a general review of material (Fantuzzo, Riggio, Connelly, & Dimeff, 1989; King, 1991). Reciprocal questioning may also be appropriate for students with disabilities. A recent study with children with Autism Spectrum Disorder indicates that these students were able to increase the frequency of questioning and responding while reading in peer groups after being taught reciprocal questioning (Whalon & Hanline, 2008).

DIVERSITY

Autism Spectrum Disorder: See page 459.

Summary

Define *learning objective* and explain why it is important for a lesson to have clear learning objectives. A learning objective describes what students will know or be able to do after they have completed the lesson. Objectives form the foundation for a good lesson and provide the standard by which student learning is evaluated. Bloom's taxonomy of cognitive objectives is a useful tool for planning learning goals at six different levels of thinking: remember, understand, apply, analyze, evaluate, and create.

Describe the goals of mastery learning and direct instruction, and discuss the advantages and disadvantages of each approach. Mastery learning encourages *all* students to achieve mastery of course content by adjusting the amount of time and feedback provided to meet students' needs as they progress through individual curricular units. Mastery approaches are applicable to all grade levels and to material of varying complexity, but they may widen the achievement gap between lower- and higher-achieving students. Direct instruction maximizes academic learning time through use of teacher control, structured lessons, practice, and feedback. The approach is effective for teaching basic skills, especially with lower-achieving students and students with disabilities, but it may not be beneficial when used with high-achieving or task-oriented students or as a teacher's only instructional method.

Explain how discovery learning and expository teaching foster meaningful learning. Both approaches promote *meaningful learning,* in which students form new knowledge by selecting and organizing information and relating it to prior knowledge. In discovery learning, students actively discover and internalize a concept, rule, or principle through unstructured exploration of lesson content. Expository teaching promotes meaningful learning by: (1) activating students' prior knowledge through advance organizers, (2) emphasizing how new material relates to what students already know and to real-life examples and situations, and (3) providing opportunities for students to practice their knowledge in many different contexts.

Describe the techniques based on cognitive apprenticeships that are used in constructivist teaching. Inquiry learning, cooperative learning, instructional conversations, reciprocal teaching, and reciprocal questioning are all constructivist teaching methods that use a variety of techniques based on cognitive apprenticeships. Students engage in exploration, practice of skills, explanations of their reasoning, reflection, and articulation. Teachers use explanation whenever necessary, as well as modeling, coaching, scaffolding, and fading. More experienced students also use scaffolding and fading of cognitive strategies to assist their less experienced peers.

Key Concepts

advance organizers   369

Bloom's taxonomy   365

cognitive apprenticeships   369

cooperative learning   370

direct instruction   365

discovery learning   368

expository teaching   368

guided discovery   368

inquiry learning   370

instructional conversations   372

learning objectives   364

mastery learning   367

meaningful learning   368

reciprocal questioning   372

reciprocal teaching   372

Video Applications

www.mhhe.com/bohlin2e

Video 1: Direct Instruction in Spanish (*2 minutes*)
This clip illustrates direct instruction in Spanish in a first grade and high school class.

Video 2: Promoting Meaningful Learning (*1 minute*)
This clip shows Mr. Radtke introducing a lecture on the Civil War in his middle school class. The segment illustrates expository teaching (explicit instruction) using an advance organizer.

Video 3: Direct Instruction in High School (*5 minutes*)
Mr. Florence illustrates the direct instruction approach in a high school technology course.

Video 4: Teacher-centered and Student-centered Approaches (*1 minute*)
This high school Spanish class taught by Mr. Muñoz illustrates both teacher-centered and student-centered approaches.

Case Studies
Reflect and Evaluate

EARLY CHILDHOOD: "Caterpillar Circle"

These questions refer to the case study on page 318.

1. How might you describe the behavioral objectives of Miss Sarah's reading circle? State possible objectives in terms of performance, conditions, and criteria.
2. Explain how Miss Sarah can use guided discovery with her preschool class. Choose a specific topic or lesson and describe how she would need to structure the lesson for optimal learning.
3. Explain how Miss Sarah can use inquiry learning with her preschoolers.
4. Explain how Miss Sarah can use cooperative learning with her preschoolers.
5. Describe any benefits and caveats for using inquiry learning and cooperative learning with students who have disabilities.

ELEMENTARY SCHOOL: "Ecosystems"

These questions refer to the case study on page 320.

1. Does Ms. Anderson tell students the purpose of the activity? Does she identify behavioral learning objectives? How does a statement of behavioral objectives relate to assessment?
2. Explain how Ms. Anderson could use inquiry learning for the ecosystem project. With such a diverse class of students, what potential problems must Ms. Anderson anticipate when forming inquiry groups?
3. If you were the teacher, would you approach a lesson on ecosystems using an expository teaching method or a guided discovery method? Why? What aspects of the approach you've chosen fit with your philosophy of teaching?
4. Imagine that Ms. Anderson does a follow-up activity in which she has students in each group engage in reciprocal questioning about ecosystems. Explain the benefits of this method and the reasons why it is more effective than having students summarize what they have learned.
5. Assume that Ms. Anderson uses direct instruction to teach reading. What factors does she need to consider to meet the needs of diverse learners such as Missy, Tamika, Steven, Jackson, Alissa, and Jorge? What other specific teaching methods discussed in the module could she use to complement direct instruction?

MIDDLE SCHOOL: "Classroom Safety"

These questions refer to the case study on page 322.

1. What do you think the objectives were for Mr. Gardino's group project?
2. Explain how the learning objectives could have been communicated to Mr. Gardino's students in terms of performance, conditions, and criteria.
3. Identify techniques used in cognitive apprenticeships, and describe how Mr. Gardino could use these in his industrial technology class.
4. You are Mr. Gardino's colleague. Explain to him how he could use cooperative learning to improve the effectiveness of the assigned project.

HIGH SCHOOL: "Refusal to Dress"

These questions refer to the case study on page 324.

1. Identify two learning objectives that would be appropriate for Ms. Salazar's first-period class.
2. Which instructional methods discussed in the module seem most applicable to Ms. Salazar's class? Explain.
3. Assume from the details in the case that Mr. Williams uses direct instruction in his second-period English composition class. Pretend that you're his colleague, and explain to Mr. Williams the disadvantages of this method.
4. If you were teaching second-period English composition, describe the teaching method(s) you would use with the students in the case. Provide a rationale for your choice of teaching method(s).
5. Imagine that Brianna was walking into an AP English class during second period. Describe the teaching method you might expect to see. Does your answer differ from the answer you gave for question 4? Why or why not?

Grouping Practices

Outline	Learning Goals

Grouping by Ability

- Within-class Ability Grouping
- Between-class Ability Grouping
- Flexible Grouping Methods

1. Discuss the pros and cons of within-class and between-class ability grouping.
2. Discuss the advantages of flexible grouping methods.

Cooperative Learning

- Characteristics of Cooperative Learning
- Is Cooperative Learning Effective?

3. Identify the characteristics of cooperative learning and discuss the effectiveness of this approach.

Applications: Best Practices

- Elementary School: Using Within-class Ability Grouping Effectively
- Middle School and High School: To Track or Not to Track
- Using Cooperative Learning Effectively

4. Describe effective practices for addressing student differences in elementary and secondary education and for implementing cooperative learning.

Summary
Key Concepts
Video Applications
Case Studies: Reflect and Evaluate

A primary challenge for teachers is resolving how to deal with differences in their students' prior knowledge and achievement levels. When students in a group show variation on an attribute, such as achievement or ability, it is called **heterogeneity.** When little variability occurs among students on an attribute, it is referred to as **homogeneity.** Historically, the first attempt at reducing heterogeneity among children was the transition from the one-room schoolhouse to grouping by age, now called grades. Grouping by age, an innovation of the nineteenth century, still left a great deal of variability in student ability within each grade (Goodlad & Anderson, 1987).

Starting around 1900 and through most of the twentieth century, ability grouping was a common practice for reducing heterogeneity (Barr, 1995; Mills & Durden, 1992). **Ability grouping** is a method of creating groups of students who are homogeneous in achievement or ability. **Cooperative learning,** a more recent approach, is a method of grouping students to work collaboratively, usually with students of different achievement levels within each group. Although students within ability groups also may work collaboratively, ability grouping creates a more competitive atmosphere than does cooperative learning. The segregation of students into distinct groups of higher- and lower-achievers often results in higher- and lower-achievers experiencing different teacher expectations and working toward different learning goals, usually with different curricula (Weinstein, 1993).

The distinction between ability grouping and cooperative learning does not necessarily mean that one grouping structure is better than the other. In choosing a grouping structure to address heterogeneity in student ability, teachers need to consider many factors, both academic and socioemotional. Let's examine the different approaches and discuss some best practices for grouping students.

GROUPING BY ABILITY

The aim of ability grouping is to enhance learning for students of all ability levels by allowing teachers to adapt learning goals, activities and materials, and the pace of instruction to meet the specific needs of students within each particular group or class. When ability grouping is implemented correctly, students of *all* ability levels show achievement gains (Fielder, Lange, & Winebrenner, 1993; Shields, 1995; Slavin & Madden, 1989). Students from minority groups and economically disadvantaged backgrounds also benefit from well-implemented ability grouping (Lynch & Mills, 1990).

DIVERSITY

Teachers may decide whether to use ability grouping based partly on their beliefs about the approach (Chorzempa & Graham, 2006). Beliefs aside, in order to objectively evaluate the benefits of ability grouping, we should consider two key questions:

1. How effective is ability grouping?
2. Are the advantages (and disadvantages) of ability grouping the same for all students?

Within-Class Ability Grouping. This method is commonly used in elementary schools for teaching reading and math.

Within-class Ability Grouping

Within-class ability grouping is the practice of dividing students within a self-contained classroom into groups that are homogeneous in ability. This type of grouping is common practice for reading instruction—and sometimes math instruction—in the elementary grades. For example, a teacher might divide the class into high-, average-, and low-achieving groups for reading, devoting time to each group for read-aloud and comprehension activities while students from other reading groups complete independent seat work. While within-class ability grouping still is commonly used for reading instruction in the early grades, current trends show a movement toward whole-class reading instruction (Baumann, Hoffman, Duffy-Hester, & Moon Ro, 2000; Chorzempa & Graham, 2006).

Research has shown that within-class ability grouping has positive effects on student learning compared to other methods.

- Within-class ability grouping generally is more effective than traditional teacher-led whole-class instruction, heterogeneous grouping, or individual seat work (Kulik & Kulik, 1992; Lou et al., 1996).

- It is also more effective than individualized mastery learning (Lou et al., 1996). *Mastery learning* is a practice in which teachers present a lesson and test students. Students who fail to meet a preset mastery criterion (e.g., 80% on the test) receive additional instruction, while students who exceed the criterion do enrichment activities.

Mastery learning: See page 367.

- Ability grouping for math and science, in particular, is more effective than heterogeneous instruction (Lou et al., 1996). Math and science instruction, more than other disciplines, is hierarchical, meaning that new concepts and skills often build on earlier content. Within-class ability grouping allows teachers to specifically tailor instruction to the current achievement level of students in each group. In mixed-ability classes, in contrast, math instruction may cover some material that lower-ability students have not yet learned and higher-ability students have already mastered.

While ability grouping does not appear to have detrimental effects on students' self-esteem, it does promote the achievement of some students over that of others (Kulik & Kulik, 2004). Students from higher ability groups and gifted students benefit most from within-class ability grouping (Kulik & Kulik, 1990, 1992). Average students tend to benefit somewhat from ability grouping, while lower-achieving students benefit more from heterogeneous grouping (Lou et al., 1996; Saleh, Lazonder, & Jong, 2005). Thus, a major criticism of ability grouping is that it widens the gap between high and low achievers (Calfee & Brown, 1979; Hiebert, 1983; Moody, Vaughn, & Schumm, 1997).

The gap between ability groups may widen partly because students in lower and higher groups receive different levels and paces of instruction. Compared with students in higher reading groups, students in lower reading groups spend more time reading orally and being read to by the teacher, spend less time reading silently, and spend more time on rote learning of skills than on comprehension, discussion, and interpretation (Allington, 1983; Chorzempa & Graham, 2006). Teachers also tend to interrupt oral reading to correct errors more often with students in lower reading groups, slowing the pace of instruction (Allington, 1980, 1983). As a consequence, students in different ability groups get different amounts

DIVERSITY

of practice (Biemiller, 1977/1978; Juel, 1988; Nagy & Anderson, 1984). Students in higher groups read about three to four times as many words per day as those in lower groups (Allington, 1984; Biemiller, 1977/1978). Grouping students for reading, coupled with more out-of-school reading practice by good readers than by below-average readers, creates a so-called **Matthew effect**—above-average readers increase their reading achievement at a faster rate than below-average readers (Stanovich, 1986).

In addition, within-class ability grouping seriously disadvantages minority students and students from lower socioeconomic backgrounds. Students from higher socioeconomic backgrounds usually make up the highest ability groups, while students from lower-income families or from minority groups typically are placed in lower ability groups (Saleh et al., 2005; Tach & Farkas, 2006). Many factors may influence these placement decisions, including teacher expectations, past performance, and standardized test scores.

Matthew Effect. Good readers, like the boy shown here, read more often outside of school and increase their reading skills at a faster rate than below-average readers.

Schedule for a high track:

Name: Darcy Lindquist	Level: Freshman	
Homeroom Teacher: Ms. Benoit	Homeroom Number: 214	
Schedule for School Year 2012–2013		
English: Honors English Composition		
Math: Algebra II		
Science: Biology		
Foreign Language: Honors Spanish I		
Elective: American Government		

Schedule for a low track:

Name: David Holmes	Level: Freshman	
Homeroom Teacher: Mrs. Klein	Homeroom Number: 211	
Schedule for School Year 2012–2013		
English: Freshman Composition		
Math: Introduction to Algebra		
Science: Physical Sciences		
Foreign Language: Spanish I		
Elective: American Government		

Figure 21.1. Class Schedules for a High-track Student and a Low-track Student. Students in higher and lower tracks experience different curricula and teacher expectations.

DIVERSITY

Giftedness: See page 420.

Between-class Ability Grouping

Between-class ability grouping (also called *tracking*) is a common practice in high school and sometimes middle school, in which students are placed into homogeneous classes based on their level of achievement. Depending on the district or school, a student's past grades or test scores in a single subject (e.g., math or language arts) may be used to determine placement in a track, or a combination of scores or grades from several subjects may be used. Students' ability group placement in elementary school is often another criterion for determining placement in middle school or high school (Moore & Davenport, 1988; Rist, 1970; Rosenbaum, 1980). A student who was in the low reading group in elementary school is likely to be placed in a lower track in middle school or high school. Based on the selected criteria, students are assigned to curriculum tracks (e.g., honors, college prep, remedial/vocational) in which all their classes—English, math, science, history, and so on—are with students of similar ability. Figure 21.1 shows a sample schedule for a student in a high track and a student in a low track.

One criticism of tracking is that it reinforces racial and socioeconomic segregation. As discussed earlier, students from minority groups and impoverished backgrounds frequently are placed into lower ability groups in elementary school. Because tracking decisions in middle school and high school are based partly on past group placement in elementary school, students who are African American, Latino, or Native American and students from low-income environments are disproportionately assigned to lower tracks (Darling-Hammond, 1995; Loveless, 1999; Oakes, 1992).

Before discussing the effects of tracking on students, we should remember that the effects are caused not by tracking itself but by the different experiences students have in their respective tracks. Tracking affects higher- and lower-achieving students differently partly because of the different approaches teachers use (Gamoran, 1992; Wheelcock, 1992). Students in gifted programs, honors classes, and advanced placement courses clearly benefit from tracking (Kulik & Kulik, 2004; Robinson & Clinkenbeard, 1998). Teachers use instructional approaches with gifted students that are different from the ones they use with students who are not gifted, providing enrichment and accelerated instruction that have been shown to be effective in teaching gifted students (Brown, 1993; Rogers, 2002). Teachers of higher-track students (Finley, 1984; Oakes, 1985, 1990b):

- spend more time preparing lessons,
- use more interesting instructional materials,
- give more demanding and longer reading assignments,
- present more complex material, and
- convey more enthusiasm in their teaching.

In contrast, students in lower tracks often are offered fewer courses in English, math, and science (Darling-Hammond, 1995; Loveless, 1999). Their classes also are characterized by low-level instruction, rote drills, and a lack of higher-level content (Banks, 2006; Gamoran, 1990; Oakes, 1992). As a result, tracking leads to a clear academic advantage for students in high tracks.

Research indicates that students in middle and lower tracks experience a small disadvantage due to tracking (Kulik & Kulik, 2004). However, looking at the overall effects of tracking—by comparing higher-track and lower-track students—does not give the entire picture. The effects of tracking vary depending on factors such as subject matter and gender.

In some subjects that are hierarchical, such as math, tracking may benefit even students in the lower tracks. Research on approximately 1,052 schools and 24,000 students in middle school indicates that tracking has a positive effect on math achievement for students of *all* ability levels (Mulkey, Catsambis, Steelman, & Crain, 2005). This finding supports previous research indicating that middle school students in mixed-ability (nontracked) algebra classes did not learn as much as students in tracked algebra classes (Epstein & MacIver, 1992).

Tracking also may affect males and females differently. In middle school, high-achieving males tend to have lower aspirations than high-achieving females when tracked for English and math (Catsambis, Mulkey, & Crain, 1999, 2001). In math—a subject considered to be a "male domain"—high-achieving females spend more time on homework, perhaps because they work harder to compete with their male peers. In contrast, males—who place a greater emphasis on social comparisons in male achievement domains—may no longer feel superior to other students when they are placed in higher tracks because they now are grouped with peers of comparable ability (Catsambis et al., 2001; Schwalbe & Staples, 1991). Low-achieving male students placed in low tracks have more positive feelings than do low-achieving females (Butler, 2008; Catsambis et al., 2001).

DIVERSITY

Before drawing your own conclusions about tracking, let's consider some effects on nonacademic outcomes. Students in higher tracks and gifted students placed in separate classes for the gifted may experience slight decreases in self-concept—an evaluation of one's competence (Butler, 2008; Preckel, Götz, & Frenzel, 2010). This may be due to greater competition for grades and comparing their performance with that of other same-achieving students (Mulkey et al., 2005). These students are motivated by performance-approach goals—wanting to demonstrate superior ability to others—and are less likely to seek help from the teacher when experiencing difficulty (Butler, 2008). Students in lower tracks, particularly boys, may experience a small boost in academic self-concept (Butler, 2008; Mulkey et al., 2005). They are motivated to avoid performing worse than others (performance-avoidance goals) and are more likely to seek help when struggling (Butler, 2008).

Self-concept: See page 52.

Performance-approach goals: See page 280.

DIVERSITY

Performance-avoidance goals: See page 281.

Imagine that you teach at a school that uses ability grouping. What are the disadvantages of ability grouping at the grade level you teach? How might you reduce these negative effects when teaching your students?

Flexible Grouping Methods

Flexible grouping methods can be used as alternatives to ability grouping. Like ability grouping, flexible grouping methods reduce the heterogeneity in skill level among students, allowing teachers to tailor instruction to the needs and ability levels of students. Unlike within-class grouping and tracking, however, flexible approaches allow for greater movement of students between ability groups as their achievement changes and thereby avoid the stigmatization of becoming stuck in a low group.

Regrouping is a method in which students receive reading or math instruction in homogeneous groups based on their current skill level but remain in heterogeneous classrooms for all other subjects (Slavin, 1987b). For example, if two second-grade classes have reading at the same time each day, students would go to separate classes, each designed for a specific reading level. Students may be grouped and regrouped continuously as their achievement changes. Regrouping reduces the number of reading or math groups to one whole-class group, alleviating common problems of within-class ability grouping such as the need to manage various groups and assign independent seat work and the stigmatization of students in rigid ability groups (Gutiérrez & Slavin, 1992; Slavin, 1987b). Regrouping has positive effects on achievement when it is implemented for only one or two subjects and when the curriculum and the pace of instruction are modified to meet students' ability levels (Gutiérrez & Slavin, 1992; Mason & Good, 1993; Slavin, 1987a).

Several **nongraded plans** organize students flexibly into homogeneous groups across grade or age levels (Gutiérrez & Slavin, 1992). **Cross-grade grouping** is the simplest nongraded plan. Students from different grades are assigned to homogeneous groups based on their reading or math achievement level, and each group works with different curricular materials and different methods (Kulik & Kulik, 1992). Because cross-grade grouping involves many more groups than within-class ability grouping, it allows for group placement and instruction that closely match students' skill levels (Kulik & Kulik, 2004). For example, in the first and best-known cross-grade grouping plan—the **Joplin plan** (Floyd, 1954)—students in grades four through six were assigned to homogeneous groups that ranged from second- to ninth-grade reading levels (Kulik & Kulik, 2004). Students in cross-grade grouping, particularly lower-achieving students, show small achievement gains over students in mixed-ability instruction (Kulik & Kulik, 2004). Gifted students benefit from cross-grade grouping because it enables them to interact with peers of the same ability level (Kulik, 1992; Rogers, 1993).

On a wider scale, students may be grouped flexibly for multiple subjects, or entire schools may be structured as nongraded, multiage classrooms (Gutiérrez & Slavin, 1992; Slavin 1987a). In **multiage classrooms,** students of varying ages (e.g., 8, 9, and 10) are grouped within a classroom based on their current achievement, motivation, and interests. This structure reduces heterogeneity among students and fosters a developmentally appropriate curriculum (Gutiérrez & Slavin, 1992; Lloyd, 1999). Consistent with the aims of nongraded plans, this grouping approach benefits student achievement and does not negatively affect socialization or psychosocial adjustment (Gutiérrez & Slavin, 1992; Rogers, 1991). Students in nongraded, multiage classes like school better and have a more developed interpersonal intelligence than do students in graded classes (Anderson & Pavan, 1993; Goodlad & Anderson, 1987; Veenman, 1995).

Note that *multiage* classes are distinct from *multigrade* classes. **Multigrade classes,** also called combination classes or split-grade classes, are an administrative tool for combining grades to address declining enrollments or uneven class sizes (Lloyd, 1999; Veenman, 1997). Students in these classes are exposed to different curricula and therefore maintain separate grade levels. No achievement benefits are to be gained from multigrade classrooms in which students from different grades are taught by the same teacher but separate curricula and grade levels are maintained (Veenman, 1997).

As a student, would you prefer flexible grouping methods over ability grouping? What about as a teacher? Why or why not?

Interpersonal intelligence: See page 405.

COOPERATIVE LEARNING

Cooperative learning as a constructive teaching method: See page 370.

Cooperative learning, a method of grouping students to work collaboratively, has become an increasingly popular approach in education, used for learners from preschool age through college (Johnson, Johnson, & Smith, 2007; Tarim, 2009; Tsay & Brady, 2010). It is used in some form by 79% of elementary school teachers and 62% of middle school teachers (Puma, Jones, Rock, & Fernandez, 1993). This approach differs from **group work,** in which students work in groups but do not necessarily need to work cooperatively. Also, in cooperative learning, as opposed to group work, groups typically are heterogeneous, consisting of low-, average-, and high-achieving students (Johnson & Johnson, 1986; Slavin, 1980).

Characteristics of Cooperative Learning

For group work to be considered cooperative learning, it must contain these five elements (Johnson & Johnson, 1999):

1. Positive interdependence
2. Individual and group accountability
3. Face-to-face interaction
4. Interpersonal skills
5. Group processing

Positive interdependence is the most important factor to consider when structuring a cooperative learning task (Johnson & Johnson, 1998; Slavin, 1991). **Positive interdependence,** a sense of "sink or swim together," can be implemented by doing the following things (Johnson & Johnson, 2009):

- establishing a group goal specifying that all group members must achieve their learning goals,
- providing rewards based on the success of the group (e.g., giving a group grade, bonus points, or tangible rewards when all group members achieve their goals),
- distributing limited resources so that cooperation is required,
- assigning each member a specific role in the group project, or
- dividing the work so that completion of one member's assignment is necessary for the next member to complete his or her assignment.

Structuring tasks so that students work toward a single goal or reward increases student productivity and achievement (Johnson & Johnson, 2009). However, having students rely on each other for resources, roles, or tasks—without establishing a group goal or reward—may undermine achievement and productivity because students focus on obtaining resources from each other without sharing their own (Johnson & Johnson, 2009).

Individual and group accountability, the second most important element in cooperative learning, refers to a sense of personal responsibility to the group (Johnson & Johnson, 1990). Because students are graded or rewarded as a group (group accountability), individual students are held accountable for completing their share of the work and for helping others work toward achieving the group goals (individual accountability). Accountability can be achieved in a variety of ways, such as randomly selecting one student's product to represent the group or testing all members on the material they were learning in the group and then averaging the scores (Johnson & Johnson, 1986).

Cooperative learning also requires face-to-face interaction and interpersonal skills. Beyond simply working together, **face-to-face interaction** requires students to provide each other with *effective* help and feedback to improve performance, exchange resources effectively, challenge each other's reasoning, and motivate each other to achieve goals (Johnson & Johnson, 1990). To that end, students need to have **interpersonal skills** such as trust, communication, decision making, leadership, and conflict resolution. Rather than assume that students possess these skills, teachers should teach and monitor these skills, especially in the elementary grades (Boekaerts, 2009; Johnson & Johnson, 2009). They also should include interpersonal skills as objectives of a cooperative learning activity and discuss the collaborative skills needed for students to work successfully in their groups.

Cooperative learning ends not with the completion of the activity but with group processing. In **group processing,** students identify what was helpful and not helpful and make decisions about what to change before moving on to the next task. Allowing time for group processing is necessary if cooperative learning is to be effective (Johnson & Johnson, 2009).

Teachers can structure cooperative group activities differently for different purposes (Slavin, 1987b):

1. *Johnson methods* (named after creators David and Roger Johnson): Students work together on a joint activity in groups having the characteristics just discussed (Johnson & Johnson, 1975, 1978). For example, a middle school English teacher who has just finished a lecture on poetic devices and figurative language may arrange students in cooperative groups and assign each group a set of poems to compare and contrast, ending with a group presentation to the class. To be effective, groups should be heterogeneous and consist of three or four students (Lou et al., 1996; Marzano, Pickering, & Pollack, 2005). Teachers can create mixed groups based on criteria such as ability, interests, gender, or ethnicity.

2. *Jigsaw method:* Jigsaw was designed to provide an opportunity for interdependence and cooperation among students from culturally diverse backgrounds (Aronson, Blaney, Stephan, Sikes, & Snapp, 1978). Each group member becomes an "expert" on one piece of an assignment and teaches the other members so the assignment can be completed collaboratively. Everyone's contribution is important, and each member contributes to the attainment of a common goal (Aronson, 2000; Aronson et al., 1978). For example, fourth-grade students studying the underground railroad might be assigned different topics for a cooperative project, such as the lives of slaves, routes that slaves took to freedom, roles of the abolitionists, and the role of Harriet Tubman.

3. *Skills-focused methods:* Students in mixed-ability groups study reading, mathematics, or other academic material and are rewarded based on the achievement of all group members. Examples of several of these methods are shown in Table 21.1.

Have you participated in group work or cooperative learning? Did you find either of these beneficial? Why or why not?

Is Cooperative Learning Effective?

Cooperative learning benefits student achievement more than competitive teaching methods, which have students compete for high grades or best scores, and more than individualistic methods, which have students work alone on tasks (Johnson & Johnson, 1998; Johnson, Maruyama, Johnson, Nelson, & Skon, 1981). Also, students in cooperative learning situations (Gillies, 2008; Johnson & Johnson, 1990, 1998):

- spend more time on tasks,
- are willing to take on more difficult tasks,
- show persistence on tasks despite difficulties,

DIVERSITY

Jigsaw Method. Each group member is responsible for a piece of the assignment.

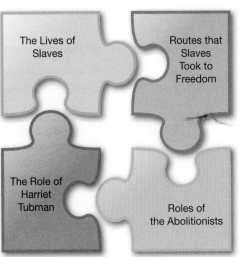

TABLE 21.1	Skills-based Cooperative Methods	
Cooperative method	**Subject**	**Characteristics**
Student Teams–Achievement Division (STAD)	Various	■ Four-member teams heterogeneous in ability, gender, SES, and ethnicity. ■ Group members study together until all members master the material. ■ Based on improvement over past quiz scores, each student contributes points to an overall team score. ■ Individual high scores and team rankings are recognized in a classroom newsletter.
Teams-Games-Tournament (TGT)	Various	■ Students earn points for their team by playing in weekly tournaments against members of other teams with similar ability. ■ Individual winners and highest-scoring teams are recognized in a newsletter.
Team-Assisted Individualization (TAI)	Grades 3-6 mathematics	■ Four- to five-member teams heterogeneous in ability. ■ Team members complete a series of math units at their own pace, with teammates working in pairs to check each other's worksheets. ■ Test scores and number of tests completed in a week contribute to a team score. ■ Certificates are given for improvement over preset team standards of performance.
Peer-Assisted Learning Strategies (PALS)	Beginning reading (K-3)	■ Students who need help with specific skills are paired with another student to assist them with those skills. ■ Students are paired as "coaches" (tutors) and "players" but alternate the role of tutor while reading aloud, listening, and providing feedback in structured activities.
Cooperative Integrated Reading and Composition model (CIRC)	Upper elementary reading and writing/language arts	■ Heterogeneous groups formed by matching pairs of students from one reading level (e.g., above-average) with pairs of students from another reading level (e.g., average). ■ Students in cooperative groups complete independent reading requirements and work on reading assignments and integrated language arts/writing assignments.

Sources: DeVries & Edwards, 1974; Slavin, 1978, 1986; Slavin, Leavey, & Madden, 1984; Slavin, Madden, & Stevens, 1990; Slavin, Lake, Chambers, Cheung, & Davis, 2009; Stevens, Madden, Slavin, & Farnish, 1987; Webb, 2008.

■ exhibit positive attitudes,

■ demonstrate higher-level reasoning, creative thinking, and critical thinking, and

■ achieve better long-term retention and transfer of what was learned.

But is cooperative learning beneficial for everyone?

DIVERSITY   Cooperative learning tends to benefit low-achieving students most and gifted students least. Low-achieving students from elementary through high school benefit from cooperative learning both academically and socially in subjects such as English, math, science, and social studies (Schachar, 2003). Gifted students, however, do not benefit from cooperative learning activities involving groups of mixed abilities (Feldhusen & Moon, 1992; Fielder et al., 1993). Rather, gifted students who spend at least part of the school day in homogeneous groups show greater achievement than gifted students who are grouped heterogeneously (Kulik & Kulik, 1987).

Socioeconomic status and ethnicity also are factors to consider when evaluating the effectiveness of cooperative learning. Students living in urban settings, students from low-income families, and minority students show higher achievement as a result of participating in cooperative learning approaches listed in Table 21.1 such as peer-assisted learning (Rohrbeck, Ginsburg-Block, Fantuzzo, & Miller, 2003). Students who are African American, Native American, Mexican American, Puerto Rican, Southeast Asian, or Pacific Islander tend to benefit from cooperative learning activities because these classroom structures more closely match the family values and practices of these groups, emphasizing cooperative rewards and group achievements (Allen & Boykin, 1992; García, 1992; Lomawaima, 2003). Cooperative activities also may be helpful for second-language learners, because these learners have more opportunity to practice language in this context (Smith, 2006).

DIVERSITY

Cooperative learning has many nonacademic benefits as well (Solomon, Watson, & Battistich, 2001):

- More than 80 studies have shown that cooperative learning enhances self-esteem, especially in students with disabilities (Johnson & Johnson, 2009; Smith, Johnson, & Johnson, 1982).

- Cooperative learning encourages greater academic intrinsic motivation (learning driven by curiosity, interest, and a focus on mastery) than competitive or individualistic approaches (Johnson & Johnson, 1985a).

- Because students in cooperative groups must give and receive personal and academic support, cooperative learning promotes peer relationships, enhancing students' empathy, tolerance for differences, feelings of acceptance, and friendships (Johnson & Johnson, 2009; Solomon et al., 2001). It fosters relationships between students with disabilities and nondisabled students and between students from different ethnic groups (Aronson, 2000; Johnson & Johnson, 2009).

DIVERSITY

Academic intrinsic motivation: See page 265 and page 279.

DIVERSITY

APPLICATIONS: BEST PRACTICES

Elementary School: Using Within-class Ability Grouping Effectively

Although flexible grouping methods may be more effective than within-class ability grouping for reducing heterogeneity among students and increasing student achievement, within-class grouping remains the norm in many elementary schools. The formation of within-class ability groups requires careful consideration—and frequent reassessment—of each student's current achievement level. The following guidelines can help ensure that within-class ability grouping is used appropriately and effectively.

Adapt instructional methods and materials to meet the needs of students within each group. Ability grouping fails when students, regardless of ability group, receive the same instruction (Lou et al., 1996). For example, elementary school teachers tend to spend equal amounts of time with all reading groups even though the pace of instruction often differs among the low, middle, and high groups, with higher-achieving readers moving faster through curricula (Allington, 1983; Barr & Dreeben, 1983). This implies that additional instructional time for students in the lower groups is necessary in order to close the achievement gap (Allington, 1984).

Keep group size small. Teachers historically have formed three homogeneous groups when implementing within-class grouping: below average, average, and above average. However, today's larger class sizes pose a problem for within-class ability grouping because they lead to larger groups. Larger group size has been found to negatively affect achievement, with students in larger groups learning less than students in smaller groups (Hallinan & Sorensen, 1985). The optimal size for within-class ability groups is three or four members (Lou et al., 1996). And recent trends show teachers moving in this direction by forming more groups with fewer members—an average of four groups per classroom (Chorzempa & Graham, 2006).

Change group placement frequently (Smith & Robinson, 1980). In within-class ability grouping, students know that a hierarchy of groups exists, and most students are aware of their position in the hierarchy even when steps are taken to disguise the hierarchy (e.g., calling groups "dolphins" and "sharks") (Eder, 1983; Filby & Barnett, 1982). In the early elementary grades, students also are beginning to compare their abilities to those of others. A fixed hierarchy serves to reinforce feelings of inferiority for students in the lower groups. By changing group placement frequently, teachers can counter the negative effects of students' comparing their group placement to that of other students. This may also prevent the **sustaining expectation effect,** which refers to teachers inadvertently sustaining low-achieving students' achievement at the current level by keeping them in their current group placement. Once groups have been formed, teachers tend to generalize expectations to all members of a group (Amspaugh,

1975). As a result, they sometimes fail to notice a student's improvement in a skill and thus fail to change their expectations for the student. However, recent data suggest that teachers tend to change students' reading groups more frequently than in the past, when students remained stuck in the group in which they originally were placed (Chorzempa & Graham, 2006; Rowan & Miracle, 1983).

Middle School and High School: To Track or Not to Track

Tracking in middle school and high school appears to have mixed effects, with students in higher tracks, advanced placement courses, and gifted programs experiencing greater academic benefits than students in lower tracks. To address the variability of student abilities in middle schools and high schools, educators have at least two options:

- detracking, or
- improving the quality of instruction for students in lower tracks.

While research evidence suggests that eliminating tracking would decrease the achievement level of higher-ability students (Argys, Rees, & Brewer, 1996; Kulik & Kulik, 2004), educator and researcher Jeannie Oakes and her colleagues propose an approach to teaching effectively in secondary education without tracking. This approach would:

- require all students to take a common core of classes,
- eliminate remedial courses, and
- provide advanced courses as options beyond the common core for *all* students, especially minority students.

In place of remedial courses, Oakes suggests incorporating additional instructional time, before- and after-school tutoring, and homework help centers to assist students who are struggling. To accommodate the variability in student abilities and interests, teachers also would need to focus on teaching learning and study strategies, as well as provide honors assignments as options within courses (Oakes, 1990a; Oakes & Wells, 2002).

DIVERSITY As one example of this approach, Robert Cooper (1999) reports research on detracking in a racially mixed high school. In place of tracking for ninth-grade English and history, educators created a common core of English and history classes in which students were heterogeneously grouped based on ability and race. The intent was to provide a challenging curriculum for all students. Students who traditionally were placed in lower tracks were required to take a "back-up" English class in place of one elective as an academic support for learning in the core English class. This allowed them more time to learn the material and work on assignments. Consistent with the proposal of Oakes and Wells (2002), this system offered all students a common core while at the same time providing instructional support to ensure success for all. The majority of students reported that their detracked courses were intellectually stimulating and said they felt that the courses provided a positive learning environment.

Other experts argue that tracking can be modified to enhance the experiences of students in lower tracks. Research by Adam Gamoran (1993) has identified several criteria for improving the achievement level of students in lower tracks:

- high expectations for students,
- a rigorous curriculum,
- encouragement of class discussions, and
- assignment of innovative and experienced teachers to lower-track courses.

Gamoran and his colleagues found that, of tracked middle schools and high schools, those that were effective in providing high-quality instruction for *all* students emphasized intellectually stimulating content, higher-order thinking, and in-depth discussions of material, even in the lower tracks. These successes were due partly to teachers' passion for their subject and a commitment to ensure equity across classes (Gamoran & Weinstein, 1998).

Using Cooperative Learning Effectively

In general, cooperative learning is misused when tasks given to groups are not well structured or when teachers group students out of convenience without ensuring that all elements of cooperative learning have been met (Gillies, 2003; Marzano et al., 2005). Students will not benefit from a cooperative activity

For this activity, all group members will need to:

Listen attentively

State ideas clearly

Take turns

Give constructive criticism

Clarify what others are saying

Clarify your own understanding

Interpersonal Objectives. Teachers need to state interpersonal objectives to foster cooperative learning, as shown here in this PowerPoint slide.

if they are not given specific guidance about the objectives of the lesson and about the expectations for individual contributions and the end-product. Also, cooperative learning can be overused when students spend most of their instructional time in groups, with little time to independently work on and demonstrate their new knowledge and skills (Marzano et al., 2005). Research on cooperative learning has yielded several guidelines that teachers can use to help them effectively implement this approach (Johnson & Johnson, 1986).

Preparing students for a cooperative activity. When preparing students for a cooperative task, specify the academic and interpersonal objectives for the lesson so students are aware of the goals of the task. Teachers often fail to inform students of the collaborative skills needed to work successfully in their groups. Teachers also need to clearly explain positive interdependence to students so they understand that they must work together to achieve success. Teachers can also help groups function effectively during a cooperative activity by:

- teaching collaborative skills,
- monitoring student behavior, and
- providing assistance to groups (e.g., answering questions and clarifying instructions).

Forming cooperative groups. Forming groups of mixed abilities is not a critical element of cooperative learning (Mills & Durden, 1992). However, cooperative groups should be heterogeneous in general. Heterogeneous grouping can be based on a variety of criteria, such as ability, interests, motivation, or even random assignment (Johnson & Johnson, 1986; Marzano et al., 2005). Also, groups of three or four tend to work best—such groups are small enough to ensure that each student actively participates (Lou et al., 1996). However, when students have little experience with cooperative learning or when the teacher has limited time or materials, groups of two or three should be formed (Johnson & Johnson, 1986).

Teachers need to pay careful attention to the gender composition of groups. Balancing the number of girls and boys in a group provides the best opportunity for equal participation (Webb, 1985). When girls outnumber boys, they tend to defer to the boys for input; when boys outnumber girls, they tend to ignore the girls (Webb, 1984, 1985, 1991).

Integration of students with disabilities into cooperative groups also requires careful consideration. Cooperative learning may not be useful for students with disabilities when they are learning new or challenging concepts (Kirk, Gallagher, Anastasiow, & Coleman, 2006), so it should be used only when it is appropriate for the instructional objectives. When implementing cooperative learning to include students with disabilities, the most common concerns teachers encounter are (Johnson & Johnson, 1986):

DIVERSITY

DIVERSITY

- feelings of fear or anxiety on the part of students with disabilities,
- nondisabled students' concerns over their grades, and
- finding ways to encourage active participation by the students with disabilities.

You can address these concerns by adapting lessons so that students of all ability levels can participate successfully in the cooperative group. To adapt a lesson, use different criteria for success for each group member, or vary the amount of material each member is expected to master. This approach should

Figure 21.2. Surveying Group Processing. Teachers can give students surveys like this one to help cooperative group members reflect on the functioning of their groups.

Each of the statements below will ask you how the group worked. Next to each statement is a number. Circle your answer.

Circle number 1 if this almost never happened.
Circle number 2 if this seldom happened.
Circle number 3 if this sometimes happened.
Circle number 4 if this often happened.
Circle number 5 if this almost always happened.

1. All group members felt free to talk.	1	2	3	4	5
2. People listened to one another.	1	2	3	4	5
3. Group members were asked to explain their ideas.	1	2	3	4	5
4. Some members tried to boss others.	1	2	3	4	5
5. Group members tried to help others.	1	2	3	4	5
6. Everyone had a say in the decisions that were made.	1	2	3	4	5
7. The members worked well as a group.	1	2	3	4	5
8. Each member had a job to do.	1	2	3	4	5
9. I felt good about being in this group.	1	2	3	4	5

alleviate the concerns of the nondisabled students as well as the anxieties of the students with disabilities. Also, to lessen the anxiety of students with disabilities, explain the procedures that the group will follow and give these students specific roles or sources of expertise that the group will need, thereby encouraging their active participation (Johnson & Johnson, 1986).

Providing time for group processing. When students evaluate the functioning of their group and plan for improvements, they are less likely to believe that speed and finishing early are more important than meaningful learning (McCaslin & Good, 1996). At the end of an activity, teachers can give students a survey, such as the one in Figure 21.2, to help students identify what was helpful and not helpful. Teachers then can use this information to make decisions about what to change for the next task or what changes to make in group placements.

In sum, remember that both ability grouping and cooperative learning are vulnerable to inappropriate use (Clark, 1990; Robinson, 1990; Slavin, 1990). Whether a grouping strategy is effective depends on the appropriateness of the content and the instruction (Mills & Durden, 1992).

Imagine that you are being interviewed by a school principal for a teaching position. Based on the grade level you intend to teach, provide a statement of your philosophy about ability grouping and cooperative learning.

Summary

Discuss the pros and cons of within-class and between-class ability grouping. In both within- and between-class ability grouping, high achievers and gifted students benefit academically more than students in lower groups, and students from impoverished backgrounds and minority students are disproportionately placed into lower groups. Tracking leads to beneficial nonacademic outcomes such as greater engagement in school, better grades, and positive attitudes toward academic subjects. Within-class ability grouping tends not to affect self-esteem, but tracking yields a small self-esteem benefit for lower-achieving students.

Discuss the advantages of flexible grouping methods. Cross-grade grouping and nongraded plans tend to have positive effects on achievement, especially for lower-achieving students. Flexible methods are effective because they reduce the heterogeneity of skills among students and allow teachers to tailor instructional materials and paces to meet the needs of students. Flexible plans also result in many positive nonacademic outcomes.

Identify the characteristics of cooperative learning and discuss the effectiveness of this approach. To be truly cooperative, tasks must contain five elements: (1) positive interdependence, (2) individual and group accountability, (3) interpersonal skills, (4) face-to-face interaction, and (5) group processing. Cooperative learning benefits students academically more than competitive and individualistic approaches. Girls and minorities tend to benefit more from cooperative learning, while gifted students do not benefit. Cooperative learning also enhances self-esteem, motivation, and peer relationships among students from diverse backgrounds and students with and without disabilities.

Describe effective practices for addressing student differences in elementary and secondary education and for implementing cooperative learning. For within-class ability grouping to be effective, teachers should adapt instruction to meet the needs of students in each group, use many small groups, and change group placement frequently. To meet the needs of middle school and high school students of all ability levels, schools need to eliminate the remedial focus in the lower tracks and emphasize high expectations and higher-level thinking skills for all students. For effective cooperative learning at any grade level, teachers should specify objectives for interpersonal skills, emphasize positive interdependence, form heterogeneous groups, use small groups, and facilitate group functioning. Teachers also must carefully consider several factors when integrating students with disabilities into cooperative groups.

Key Concepts

ability grouping   378

between-class ability grouping   380

cooperative learning   378

cross-grade grouping   381

face-to-face interaction   383

group processing   383

group work   382

heterogeneity   378

homogeneity   378

individual and group accountability   383

interpersonal skills   381

Joplin plan   381

Matthew effect   379

multiage classrooms   382

multigrade classes   382

nongraded plans   381

positive interdependence   382

regrouping   381

sustaining expectation effect   385

within-class ability grouping   379

Video Applications

www.mhhe.com/bohlin2e

Video 1: Cooperative Learning—Algebra Puzzle Activity (*2 minutes*)
This clip shows middle school students working together on algebra problems as team teachers Shelley Buck and Beth Buss monitor their performance. The groups solve problems to earn puzzle pieces, and they need to complete their puzzles by the end of the activity. Although the clip shows middle school students, it is also applicable to cooperative learning at the elementary and high school levels.

Video 2: Cooperative Learning: Building Robots (*2 minutes*)
This clip shows high school students in a technology course working in groups to create arms for robots that they have been building and that they will use to compete in a class-wide game. Although the clip shows high school students, it is also applicable for discussing features of cooperative learning at the elementary and middle school levels.

Case Studies
Reflect and Evaluate

EARLY CHILDHOOD: "Caterpillar Circle"

These questions refer to the case study on page 318.

1. Within-class ability grouping typically is used in elementary school for reading and math. Is there any reason to form homogeneous groups in preschool? Why or why not?

2. Assume that you are in favor of ability grouping. On what criteria would you group preschool students (ability, prior knowledge, age, etc.), and for what types of lessons?

3. Review the guidelines for effective use of within-class ability grouping in the section "Elementary School: Using Within-class Ability Grouping Effectively." Explain why these guidelines would be easier to implement in a preschool classroom than in an elementary school classroom.

4. What are the benefits of using cooperative learning, especially in a class as diverse as Miss Sarah's?

5. Keeping in mind the developmental level of the children, what specific things would you need to do to implement the five elements of cooperative learning discussed in the module? Be sure to give specific examples of how you would implement each of the five elements, and address any challenges you would expect with this age group.

ELEMENTARY SCHOOL: "Ecosystems"

These questions refer to the case study on page 320.

1. If you were teaching this third-grade class, would you use within-class ability grouping for teaching reading or math? Why or why not? What factors and/or research evidence influenced your decision?

2. You want to eliminate within-class ability grouping at the elementary school where you teach, and you arrange a meeting with the principal to discuss a new alternative. Provide a convincing argument against within-class ability grouping, and explain the practice of regrouping and its advantages.

3. Ms. Anderson wants to arrange students in cooperative learning groups for the ecosystem project rather than keep their current group formation, in which they work together at the tables where they sit. What criteria would you use to form cooperative groups (ability, interests, etc.) and why?

4. Based on the argument that broke out at the end of the ecosystem activity, which element of cooperative learning did Ms. Anderson ignore? Give her specific suggestions for improving this component of cooperative learning.

5. Explain why the reflection process at the end of the ecosystem project is an important component of cooperative learning. Speculate on what improvements Ms. Anderson might make for future group projects.

MIDDLE SCHOOL: "Classroom Safety"

These questions refer to the case study on page 322.

DIVERSITY

1. Imagine that Crosby Middle School uses tracking and that the seventh-graders in the case study are in a lower track. Discuss the advantages and disadvantages of tracking for these students. Why might students' gender, socioeconomic status, and ethnicity be important factors to consider when evaluating the effectiveness of tracking?

2. The school board is discussing whether to detrack Crosby Middle School. Provide a convincing argument for detracking. Create an original plan for meeting the needs of both higher achievers and lower achievers within a detracked curriculum.

3. In what ways did Mr. Gardino implement *positive interdependence* successfully? How could he improve on this?

4. How can Mr. Gardino improve the *face-to-face interaction* and *interpersonal skills* of the groups? Provide specific examples or suggestions.

5. Explain why balancing the number of girls and boys is important for Mr. Gardino to consider when forming groups for the project.

6. What modifications might Mr. Gardino need to make to the group project for a student with a disability?

DIVERSITY

HIGH SCHOOL: "Refusal to Dress"

These questions refer to the case study on page 324.

1. Assume that student Brianna is African American. Based on the research on tracking, explain why it would not be surprising to find students from minority groups in a lower-level English class.

DIVERSITY

2. Based on the research on tracking, describe the possible effects of tracking on Brianna's academic achievement and self-esteem. Would your response be different if Brianna were male?

DIVERSITY

3. Imagine that you are giving Mr. Williams teaching advice. Describe how you would use cooperative learning to review grammar in his second-period class. Be sure to give specific examples of how you would implement (a) positive interdependence, (b) individual and group accountability, (c) face-to-face interaction, (d) interpersonal skills, and (e) group processing.

4. Mr. Williams is a bit uneasy about using cooperative learning with his second-period English composition class. He's not sure the students are ready for such an approach and feels more comfortable sticking to his tried-and-true method. Explain to Mr. Williams the benefits of cooperative learning, particularly for students like those in his second-period class.

5. Mr. Williams wants to introduce literature in his second-period English composition class. Explain how he could use the Jigsaw approach.

6. You are at a faculty meeting at Valley High School to discuss detracking. State a convincing case for detracking, and describe a new curriculum that would address the needs of students in higher tracks as well as students in the lower tracks, like Brianna.

unit seven

Case Studies

Early Childhood: "Letter *P* Day" 394

Elementary School: "Cheetahs, Lions, and Leopards" 396

Middle School: "Math Troubles" 398

High School: "Noon Supervised Study" 400

Module 22:
Intelligence

Outline and Learning Goals 402

What Is Intelligence? 403

Intelligence Measured As IQ 406

Biological, Social, and Cultural Issues 408

Application: Intelligence Theories in the Classroom 412

Summary 415

Key Concepts 415

Video Applications 415

Case Studies: Reflect and Evaluate 416

Module 23:
Giftedness and Creativity

Outline and Learning Goals 418

Giftedness and Creativity: Are They More Than Just Intelligence? 419

Giftedness 420

learner differences

Creativity 424

Summary 429

Key Concepts 429

Video Applications 430

Case Studies: Reflect and Evaluate 430

Module 24:
Cognitive Disabilities

Outline and Learning Goals 432

Cognitive Disabilities in Today's
Classrooms 433

Intellectual Disabilities 435

Specific Learning Disabilities 438

Summary 446

Key Concepts 446

Video Applications 446

Case Studies: Reflect and Evaluate 447

Module 25:
Emotional, Social, and Behavioral
Disorders

Outline and Learning Goals 449

Emotional, Social, and Behavioral Disorders
in Today's Classrooms 450

Characteristics of Disorders 453

Applications: Interventions 460

Summary 463

Key Concepts 463

Video Applications 463

Case Studies: Reflect and Evaluate 464

Prepare:

As you read the case, make notes:

1. **WHO** are the primary participants in the case? Describe them.

2. **WHAT** is taking place?

3. **WHERE** is the case taking place? Is the environment a factor?

4. **WHEN** is the case taking place? Is the timing a factor?

It is Monday morning, and the children in Mrs. Anita Cahill's kindergarten class are eagerly waiting to hear what centers they will be assigned for today's language arts lesson. Mrs. Cahill, who also has taught preschool and first grade, is a veteran kindergarten teacher who was chosen to be the school's first teacher for full-day kindergarten this year.

Mrs. Cahill has an interesting way of teaching literacy skills. Each Monday, children are introduced to a new letter of the alphabet. Language arts begins with children sitting on a carpet in the reading corner, listening attentively to Mrs. Cahill reading a nursery rhyme or tongue twister featuring the letter of the week. Today she is reading "Peter Piper" to introduce the letter *P* and its sound.

When she has finished reading, Mrs. Cahill announces: "Boys and girls, I have put name cards at each center. Find your name. That is the center you will be working at this

Early Childhood

Letter *P* Day

morning. Craig, Adriana, and Marcie, you look like you're ready to begin. You may get up and look for your names." Mrs. Cahill continues calling children. Joanna Gallagher, a parent volunteer, is helping the children find their center and get started.

Mrs. Cahill has set up four learning centers—publishing, art, building, and science—each with different activities. The children are able to choose which activity they want to do.

- At the "publishing" center, Miguel, Darnell, and Pat are drawing pictures of words that begin with *P* and writing the words, and Craig is looking through the book *Hop on Pop*, by Dr. Seuss, to find words that contain the letter *P*. Jillian has started writing a "story" in her daily journal, using her favorite words that begin with *P*.

- At the "art" center, children can make the shape of the letter *P* using art supplies. Sam, Tonya, and Marcie are gluing cotton balls onto paper to form a puffy *P*, and Teran and Nicholas are gluing pieces of pink tissue paper to form a pink *P*.

- At the "building" center, Tomás, Adriana, Peter, and Emily are constructing letter *P* shapes with blocks.

- At the "science" center, Daniel, Ryan, Cassie, and Marcus are busy cutting out pictures of objects and classifying them into foods that begin with *P* and animals that begin with *P*.

Mrs. Cahill rotates the children through the centers so that each week they have a different experience rather than picking their favorites each time. She overhears some interesting conversations as she makes her way around the tables.

"I'm glad it was my turn at publishing," Pat says excitedly. "Drawing is my favorite." Pat would rather color, cut and paste, and build than do many other activities and is able to draw very realistic and colorful figures.

"Well, I love to write stories," replies Jillian. She typically spends more time than any other student creating detailed responses to journal prompts in her daily journal. Jillian can already write in complete, but short, sentences.

"How's my puffy *P*?" Marcie asks at the art center.

"My favorite color is purple," Nicholas adds, as he presses sticky pink tissue to his paper.

Teran, who is very quiet, almost seems to ignore Marcie and Nicholas as she glues pink tissues with the help of Mrs. Cahill. Her language and fine motor skills are delayed, and she needs extra time to understand and complete most academic tasks.

Children at the building center are working diligently on their projects, except for Peter. Mrs. Cahill has noticed, as is typical of Peter, that he has gotten up from the center twice during the activity and now is making towers of blocks and loudly knocking them down. She redirects him and heads over to the reading corner, where Nolan is looking at books. Mrs. Cahill gently taps his shoulder, whispering, "Shouldn't you be making the letter *P*?"

"Mrs. C," replies Nolan, "I already know *P* and all my letters. This is boring. I want to learn to read."

"You'll get to reading soon enough," says Mrs. Cahill, smiling reassuringly.

Mrs. Cahill makes her way around to the centers, recalling a parent-teacher conference she recently had with Nolan's mother. His mother reports that when Nolan discovers a new topic of interest, he will spend weeks learning all he can about it by having his parents read books to him, watching educational programs, and going on "field trips" with his parents. He also likes to spend hours on puzzles and on classifying and counting his dinosaur collection. He is an only child, and his mom, who does not work outside the home, spends a great deal of one-on-one time with him. Although she is an experienced teacher, Mrs. Cahill is unsure how to accommodate the varied skill levels of the children, especially the many students who are still adjusting to the routine of full-day kindergarten.

Assess

1. What are the benefits of Mrs. Cahill's approach to language arts? What are the disadvantages? Would you do anything differently?

2. What should Mrs. Cahill do regarding Nolan's academic needs?

3. What experiences in this classroom allow the students to express their creativity?

4. How typical is Teran of most young children you may know? Should Mrs. Cahill give Teran any special assistance or make special accommodations? Why or why not?

5. Did Mrs. Cahill handle Peter's behavior appropriately? Why or why not?

Prepare:

As you read the case, make notes:

1. **WHO** are the primary participants in the case? Describe them.

2. **WHAT** is taking place?

3. **WHERE** is the case taking place? Is the environment a factor?

4. **WHEN** is the case taking place? Is the timing a factor?

I t is 9:00 A.M. on a cold Tuesday morning in February at Glendale Elementary School. Mrs. Fratelli calls a group of her third graders to a corner of the classroom to do oral reading. "Cheetahs, get your books and come to the reading circle," calls Mrs. Fratelli. "The rest of you can work quietly at your tables on the phonics worksheets in your folders until it's time for your group."

Mrs. Fratelli has been teaching at Glendale Elementary for the past 18 years. Glendale is one of nine elementary schools in a large metropolitan city and serves a diverse population of students. Mrs. Fratelli has a class of 24 students this year, a bit larger than usual. She uses whole-class instruction for most subjects. However, in order to manage the diverse levels of reading skill among the students, she has assigned students to one of four reading groups:

Elementary School
Cheetahs, Lions, and Leopards

- Cheetahs, reading books at the fourth-grade level;

- Lions, reading books at the end-of-third-grade level;

- Tigers, reading books at the mid-third-grade level; and

- Leopards, reading at the beginning-third-grade level or below.

As Mrs. Fratelli is reading with the Cheetah group, most of the other children are busy completing their seat work.

Travis is in a dimly lit corner of the classroom working with the help of his aide, Mrs. Cormier. Travis has autism and is very sensitive to the bright lights of the classroom and the noise of the traffic on the busy street below. Most of his classmates have gotten so used to Travis's rocking back and forth in his chair and muttering certain expressions that it hardly distracts them at all.

By now, Denise has finished her worksheets and leans over to whisper to Marcela. "I wish I could be in the Cheetah group and read chapter books like they are. Their stories are so interesting," Denise whispers. "Not like our books. I could do it if Mrs. Fratelli would give me a chance. I just don't read as good when I have to do it in front of the other kids. I get all nervous and make lots of mistakes. Sometimes I feel like my heart is going to jump out of my chest!"

"At least you're not in the 'dummy' reading group," replies Marcela.

Marcela is in the Leopard group, which is slightly behind grade level in reading skill. She struggles with reading fluency. She has difficulty sounding out words and needs some extra help with phonics. Marcela's family immigrated to the United States from Peru when she was three years old because her father had landed a prestigious engineering position. Marcela's parents speak only Spanish at home, but she quickly picked up English at her new preschool. Despite her struggle with reading, Marcela is a bright student with a natural curiosity about the world, especially science.

Carl, who is sitting between Denise and Marcela, whispers, "Shhhhh! You two are gonna get our table in trouble!"

Carl is not at all concerned that he is in the Lions reading group because he likes that the work is easy for him. He finishes his work quickly so he can spend time doodling detailed futuristic sketches of robots, spaceships, and spacemen. Mrs. Fratelli considers him to be very careless in his schoolwork. To encourage his creativity, though, she often sends home pencils and paper for Carl's artwork. Carl's family is struggling financially because his father lost his job when a large factory in town closed. Carl receives free lunch and has few school supplies.

After all reading groups have had a turn in the reading circle, Mrs. Fratelli collects the worksheets and announces that it's time for science.

"Boys and girls, we are starting a new science unit today on solids, liquids, and gases," says Mrs. Fratelli. "Our first experiment is to test which materials dissolve in water and which don't. Each of you has a cup with water and a plastic spoon. On each table there are several materials for you to share."

Mrs. Fratelli passes out small plastic containers of sand, flour, lemon juice, vegetable oil, and sugar. She explains what to do and tells the students to record their results on their worksheets so they can discuss their findings when everyone is done. As students begin the activity, chatter spreads through the classroom. "I want to try the lemon juice," exclaims Marcela.

"I want the sand," Denise states.

"I like it when we do experiments," Carl adds. "It's more fun than worksheets!"

Assess

1. Based on this case, what are areas of strength for Denise, Marcela, and Carl? How do you think Mrs. Fratelli would rate their capabilities?

2. Which students, if any, do you think could be considered gifted? Why?

3. In your opinion, does Mrs. Fratelli provide her class with many opportunities to be creative? Explain.

4. What characteristics would you look for in third-grade students when trying to identify students with a specific reading disability or math disability?

5. Should Mrs. Fratelli include Travis in the science experiment with the other children? Why or why not?

Prepare:

As you read the case, make notes:

1. **WHO** are the primary participants in the case? Describe them.

2. **WHAT** is taking place?

3. **WHERE** is the case taking place? Is the environment a factor?

4. **WHEN** is the case taking place? Is the timing a factor?

It's first period at Chesterfield Middle School, and Miss Elizabeth Barton is teaching the order of operations in seventh-grade pre-algebra. Miss Barton has a diverse class in many respects, especially with regard to ability.

Lindsey struggles with math. She repeated first grade because of difficulties in both reading and math. Even though Lindsey was able to improve her skills with extensive private tutoring and does well in most subjects, she still is easily frustrated and often will not participate in math class. In other situations, Lindsey is very outgoing. She takes on leadership roles in group projects, designs sets for school plays, and is the seventh-grade vice president.

Sam, on the other hand, loves math and is very good at it. In math class, Sam is easily distracted, likes to finish work quickly to talk with friends, and seems to be a step ahead of

Middle School

Math Troubles

the other students. When Miss Barton is reviewing problems with the class, Sam will ask about problem 6 while Miss Barton and the class are on problem 3. This behavior often annoys Miss Barton and breaks the other students' concentration.

Today Miss Barton has assigned students to work on practice problems in groups of four and has begun moving around the room to monitor their progress.

"Did everyone try the first problem on the page?" Miss Barton asks as she approaches the first group.

Derek and Emma already have the question correctly done, while Lindsey and Jessie are still working. Miss Barton notices that the students seem to be working independently and are not helping each other. She had hoped that group work would help Lindsey with her math skills.

"Do you two have the answer yet?" Miss Barton asks.

Lindsey doesn't reply.

"Let me see what you've got there, Lindsey. That's actually incorrect; you needed to multiply before you added those two numbers. Do you understand?"

"Yes," Lindsey nods.

"Let's all try the next problem," says Miss Barton. "It follows exactly like the first."

Emma and Derek finish it quickly. Jessie takes a bit longer. She has always struggled academically in most subjects and is a bit slower at mastery of concepts than her peers. And, again, Lindsey is the last one done. Everyone got the correct answer except Lindsey. While Miss Barton tries to explain the problem to Lindsey, she notices Sam fooling around.

Miss Barton approaches Sam. "Has your group finished *all* the problems already, Sam?" she asks incredulously.

"No, but I'm already finished," Sam quickly responds.

"But you know you should be working with your group members," says Miss Barton.

"Yeah, but working with them is boring," Sam responds.

A bit exasperated, Miss Barton keeps Sam busy by assigning some extra math problems and begins circulating around to the groups again. She returns to Lindsey's group and notices that Lindsey and Jessie are talking and not concentrating on the problems. Miss Barton gently redirects them. "Lindsey and Emma," she asks. "Are you talking about math? Please get back to the problems."

"Why should I?" Lindsey mutters to herself as she begins doodling. "I'm sure I'll get the answers wrong anyway," she sighs.

Later in the teacher's lounge, Miss Barton shares her experience with Dexter Sharp, who teaches the eighth-grade algebra classes. "I feel like I'm losing some of these kids," she says. "I have a few students who struggle with the concepts and others who don't. And I have one student who is completely bored because he is not challenged by the work we are doing. I need to find a way to keep everyone engaged."

Mr. Sharp pauses to think for a minute before he replies. "Last semester I created a Most Creative Word Problem contest," he explains. "If students finished their work and had a little time to spare, they could develop a word problem, and the answer, using our math concepts from that week and submit it in the problem box on my desk. They could also create problems at home to submit. The rules of the contest required that students write out the problem and the correct solution. Every other Friday I created a review sheet with the problems they had submitted, excluding the answers, and let the students vote on the most creative problem."

Assess

1. In your opinion, is finishing one's work quickly a sign of being "smart"?

2. Should Miss Barton give Sam more challenging work or treat him differently from the rest of the class? Why or why not?

3. How successful do you think the Most Creative Word Problem contest would be in Miss Barton's class?

4. In your opinion, what are Miss Barton's expectations of Lindsey?

5. Should Miss Barton give Jessie any special attention academically?

Prepare:

As you read the case, make notes:

1. **WHO** are the primary participants in the case? Describe them.

2. **WHAT** is taking place?

3. **WHERE** is the case taking place? Is the environment a factor?

4. **WHEN** is the case taking place? Is the timing a factor?

Mr. Beau Hardy is starting his second year at Shreveport High School, where he teaches ninth-grade U.S. history. Students typically enjoy Mr. Hardy's classes because he is an enthusiastic and charismatic lecturer. From time to time, he has been known to begin class by reenacting a famous event dressed as an important historical figure. Students in his classes take notes on the lectures and have an exam on each unit.

The bell rings for fourth period. Mr. Hardy begins by collecting homework. Noticing that Jason has not turned in his homework, he asks, "Jason, why didn't you turn in homework today?"

"I don't know, Mr. Hardy. Guess I forgot about it."

"You know that you'll need to attend Noon Supervised Study today," says Mr. Hardy.

High School
Noon Supervised Study

Jason replies, "But I'm already in there for two other classes from yesterday!"

"Jason," Mr. Hardy explains. "You're just going to have to start doing your work at home then. It's critical for you to have your assignments done in time before each class period. How can I be sure that everyone is reading and understanding the material if I don't check homework?"

"But Mr. Hardy, you know I understand it!" Jason argues.

Mr. Hardy gives Jason a slip for Noon Supervised Study, called NSS for short. As Jason leaves the room, Mr. Hardy is disturbed at the many times he has sent Jason to NSS. Jason is an active and energetic participant in class. Although he takes few notes, he enjoys analyzing historical events and discussing alternative routes that history could have taken.

Later at NSS, Jason sits for 40 minutes attempting to finish his homework assignments. He has one from Mr. Hardy, two from his English teacher, and one more from his health teacher. All of them are past due, and he's not sure where to start or even what the instructions were. He realizes he cannot possibly get all the assignments done in 40 minutes, so he starts his health assignment that was due three days ago. He looks around and notices that Tommy, Gabe, Anthony, and Sarah are all back in NSS with him. After NSS is over, the students head to lunch.

Throughout the day, Mr. Hardy can't stop thinking about Jason, Anthony, and Sarah—all U.S. history students from fourth period whom he has sent to NSS several times for not completing their work. At the end of the day, perplexed by this situation, he decides to look through their academic records for answers.

According to Jason's records, he excelled all through elementary school, but his school performance began to decline in fifth and sixth grades. Mr. Hardy wonders why. Anthony, an African American student, was identified as eligible for special education in third grade for a reading disability. Mr. Hardy is aware that Anthony received extended time for tests but had no idea about the extent of his disability. Anthony's disability has not hampered his social prowess. He has many friends and is captain of the freshman football team and vice president of the freshman class.

Mr. Hardy is not surprised to find that Sarah, who gets As on quizzes and tests despite not doing her homework, skipped first grade and was in a gifted and talented program for mathematics in grades three through six. Her record states that, on transferring to

Shreveport High, Sarah chose a lower-level track for math and science, which meant that all other subjects also needed to be basic level to fit into her schedule. Mr. Hardy wonders why she would choose this track.

Assess

1. Which students in your own high school did you consider to be "smart"? What characteristics made them smart?

2. Why do you think Jason and Sarah don't do homework?

3. Recall your own high school experiences. What types of assignments did you have, and what were the expectations of the teachers? How did this affect your motivation and behavior in school?

4. What types of learning accommodations do you think high school teachers need to make for students with disabilities?

5. What types of emotional, social, and behavioral problems do you think high school teachers face with their students?

Intelligence

Outline

What Is Intelligence?

- Classic Views
- Contemporary Views

Intelligence Measured As IQ

- Individually Administered and Group Administered Tests
- Interpreting IQ Scores
- Caveats for Interpreting IQ

Biological, Social, and Cultural Issues

- Intelligence: Heredity or Environment?
- Socioeconomic and Cultural Factors

Applications: Intelligence Theories in the Classroom

- Multiple Intelligences in the Classroom
- Teaching for Successful Intelligence

Summary
Key Concepts
Video Applications
Case Studies: Reflect and Evaluate

Learning Goals

1. Describe Spearman's two-factor theory of intelligence and contrast it with contemporary theories of intelligence.

2. Describe what IQ tests measure and contrast individually administered and group administered tests.

3. Describe how environment, socioeconomic status, and gender influence IQ.

4. Explain the similarities between the theory of multiple intelligences and the theory of successful intelligence in their applications to the classroom.

WHAT IS INTELLIGENCE?

What do you think of when you hear the term *intelligence*? Almost all psychologists agree that intelligence involves adaptation to the environment (Sternberg, 1996a, 2005). Psychologists throughout the past century have emphasized the importance of cognitive skills in adaptation: abstract reasoning, representation, problem solving, decision making, and speed of processing (Hogan, 2007; Sternberg, Conway, Ketron, & Bernstein, 1981). However, the views of these experts contrast markedly with the layperson's views of intelligence in various cultures. Let's examine the meaning of intelligence in different cultural contexts:

DIVERSITY

- In African cultures, such as Kenya and Zimbabwe, an intelligent person possesses skills for facilitating and maintaining intergroup and intragroup relations (Greenfield, 1997; Sternberg & Kaufman, 1998).

- Individuals in Asian cultures, such as Cambodia, Vietnam, and the Philippines, believe that motivation, social skills, and practical skills are just as important as cognitive skills in defining intelligence (Okagaki & Sternberg, 1993; Sternberg, 2004).

- Cultural groups within the United States have different views of intelligence (Sternberg, 2007). In one study, Latino immigrants emphasized social-competence skills as important for intelligence, in contrast to the emphasis of Asian and Anglo parents on the importance of cognitive skills (Okagaki & Sternberg, 1993).

Classic Views

Modern theorists have debated about the definition of intelligence for more than a hundred years—and the debate continues. The debate over whether intelligence is a single trait or many abilities originated with a theory of intelligence advanced by Charles Spearman. Spearman (1904, 1927), after examining the relationship among many cognitive tests, proposed the **two-factor theory of intelligence** shown in Figure 22.1. The two factors are:

- g, which is our overall ability to perform on a variety of cognitive tasks, and
- s, which refers to specific skills such as vocabulary and mathematical skills.

Other twentieth-century theorists proposed that intelligence consists of multiple factors. One theorist identified seven factors in intelligence, called primary mental abilities (Thurstone, 1938, 1947). Another proposed 120 distinct abilities but later revised that number to 180 (Guilford, 1956, 1988). Several other theorists have proposed hierarchical theories of intelligence—a compromise between one intelligence, g, and many intelligences. In one of the most influential hierarchical theories, g is the overall ability and encompasses two secondary abilities (Cattell, 1963; Horn, 1994):

- *general crystallized intelligence* (Gc), our overall knowledge base resulting from formal and informal education (think of it as an individual's pool of knowledge or facts), and
- *general fluid intelligence* (Gf), or abilities that allow us to reason, think, and learn new things (think of it as an individual's potential for learning).

The hierarchical view of intelligence has remained influential for both theoretical and practical reasons. Crystallized and fluid intelligence appear in modern hierarchical theories of intelligence and serve as the basis for some contemporary IQ tests.

How do you define intelligence? As you read the next section, compare your views with contemporary theories of intelligence.

Contemporary Views

While some contemporary theories still focus on g (e.g., Carroll, 1993; Gustafsson, 1994; Horn, 1994), psychologists Howard Gardner and Robert Sternberg argue that g becomes less important if we define intelligence using a broad range of abilities rather than a limited set of academic-related tasks (Sternberg, 2003a). They have proposed multidimensional theories of intelligence that are distinct yet complementary.

Figure 22.1. Spearman's Two-factor Theory of Intelligence. Intelligence comprises general ability as well as specific skills.

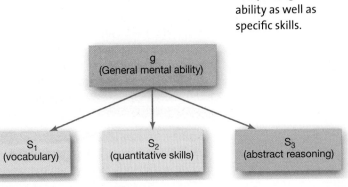

GARDNER'S THEORY OF MULTIPLE INTELLIGENCES

In his **theory of multiple intelligences** (MI theory), Gardner (1983, 1999) proposes that we have eight intelligences:

1. *Linguistic* (using words to describe or communicate ideas).
2. *Logical-mathematical* (reasoning, perceiving patterns in numbers, using numbers effectively).
3. *Spatial* (accurately perceiving and transforming the visual-spatial world).
4. *Bodily-kinesthetic* (having expertise in using one's body).
5. *Musical* (recognizing components of music, expressing musical forms, using music to express ideas).
6. *Interpersonal* (accurately perceiving and appropriately responding to the emotions of other people).
7. *Intrapersonal* (introspection, discriminating one's emotions and perceptions, knowing one's strengths and limitations).
8. *Naturalistic* (recognizing and classifying living things, sensitivity to features of the natural world).

The intelligences are independent of one another, but they interact—or work together—in activities (Gardner & Moran, 2006). For example, playing basketball involves bodily-kinesthetic and spatial intelligences, while ballet dancing incorporates bodily-kinesthetic, spatial, and musical intelligences. Linguistic and logical-mathematical intelligences typically are assessed on IQ tests, but the other six intelligences are not.

Think about your own abilities. How would you describe yourself in terms of multiple intelligences? Your answer—whether it be musical, bodily-kinesthetic, or some combination of intelligences—likely comes from a variety of sources:

- activities in which you excel,
- past experiences and successes, and
- interests or preferences.

Just as you determined your intelligences based on these external sources, Gardner (1993) believes that multiple intelligences exist in the context of a person's interaction with objects and people in the environment, not as abstract entities in the person's mind. For example, we observe intelligence as it is applied every day in *authentic tasks*—that is, tasks that reflect real-life problems, roles, or situations, such as when an elementary school student solving word problems and a high school student designing and conducting a physics experiment show logical-mathematical intelligence.

Gardner's theory has achieved much attention in K-12 education. Many schools have translated MI theory into practice (see Table 22.1), and some, such as the Key Community School in Indianapolis, have developed an entire curriculum using Gardner's ideas. Keep in mind, though, that while Gardner's theory is very appealing to educators, it lacks empirical support. To date, there are no published studies reporting evidence for the validity of MI theory (Gardner & Connell, 2000; Sternberg & Grigorenko, 2004; Waterhouse, 2006). Educators should be cautious about implementing any theory that has not been thoroughly tested and is not supported by research evidence.

Authentic tasks: See page 479.

STERNBERG'S THEORY OF SUCCESSFUL INTELLIGENCE

Like Gardner, Sternberg (1999b; 2010a) does not limit intelligence to capabilities that allow individuals to succeed in school. Rather, he considers intelligence to be a person's ability to succeed in life. According to his **theory of successful intelligence,** an individual defines success according to personal goals, which may be focused on career, extracurricular activities, personal interests, or community service. Our sociocultural context also contributes to defining success, because the types of knowledge needed for success—and what is valued as success—differ across cultural contexts. In Usenge, Kenya, for example, children develop expertise in identifying natural herbal medicines in order to survive in an environment where they are exposed to many parasitic illnesses, just as children in Western cultures engage in formal education because it allows them to be successful within their own cultural context (Sternberg, 1999b, 2004).

DIVERSITY

Sternberg proposes that we all possess analytical, creative, and practical abilities to differing degrees and that individuals who are successfully intelligent find ways to balance the strengths and weaknesses in their abilities (Sternberg, Grigorenko, & Zhang, 2008).

- **Analytical abilities** involve identifying and defining a problem, choosing a strategy for solving the problem, and monitoring the outcome. Analytical skills, typically measured on IQ tests, involve analyzing, evaluating, judging, or comparing and contrasting.

TABLE 22.1	Gardner's Multiple Intelligences

Intelligence	Examples	Instructional activities
1. Linguistic intelligence	writer, comedian, journalist, editor, professor	Write a poem, short story, play about . . . Create an interview of . . .
2. Logical-mathematical intelligence	mathematician, scientist, computer programmer	Design and conduct an experiment on . . . Describe the patterns in . . .
3. Spatial intelligence	interior decorator, architect, artist	Illustrate, draw, or sketch . . . Create a slide show or piece of art about . . .
4. Bodily-kinesthetic intelligence	actor, athlete, mime, dancer	Build or construct a . . . Use hands-on materials to demonstrate . . .
5. Musical intelligence	composer, director, performer, musical technician	Sing a song to explain . . . Indicate rhythmical patterns in . . .
6. Interpersonal intelligence	pastor, counselor, teacher, manager, coach	Participate in a service project . . . Teach someone about . . .
7. Intrapersonal intelligence	religious leader, counselor, writer, philosopher	Write a journal entry on . . . Assess your own work in . . .
8. Naturalistic intelligence	hunter, farmer, environmentalist	Create observation notebooks of . . . Use observational tools (microscope, binoculars) to explore . . .

Sources: Campbell, 1997; Johnson, 2000.

Creativity: See page 424.

- **Creative abilities** involve generating novel ideas for solving problems. Individuals with creative abilities are risk takers because they often generate ideas that initially are unpopular and must convince others of the value of their ideas. Assessing creative intelligence involves evaluating how well people deal with novelty.

- **Practical abilities** involve applying knowledge to real-life contexts, implementing options and solutions, and making them work. Students who are practical learners are better able to learn information if they can see its relevance to their own lives (Sternberg, 1997).

Successful individuals are able to balance their abilities by effectively adapting to, shaping, and selecting their environment (Sternberg, 2002; Sternberg et al., 2008). An elementary student may decide to read more at home to better his oral reading skills in class (adapting to the environment). A middle school student who is excelling academically may ask the teacher for more challenging work (shaping the environment). An adolescent may decide to attend a high school arts academy because it matches her interests and abilities in music and art (selecting the environment). External factors, such as socioeconomic status, education, and cultural background, affect individual students' opportunities to adapt, shape, and select their environments. For example, students from lower socioeconomic backgrounds may not have access to the same resources (books, newspapers, and magazine subscriptions in the home; rigorous curricula; money for private schools) as students from higher socioeconomic backgrounds, limiting their options. Educators need to remember to evaluate students' success within the context of the opportunities afforded them (Sternberg, 1999b).

Teachers can help students identify their strengths and weaknesses in analytical, creative, and practical abilities, but it is especially important for them to recognize students with creative and practical abilities. Traditional methods of instruction and assessment in schools have enabled students with strengths in analytical or memory abilities to be successful, conveying the skewed message that only these abilities are valued in society (Sternberg, 1999b; Sternberg et al., 2008). In reality, many people who have been successful in creative or practical domains were in fact mediocre students (Sternberg, 1997). Designer Tommy Hilfiger, actor/producer Henry Winkler, and Charles Schwab, CEO of the largest brokerage firm in the United States, all have achieved great success in life based on their creative or practical abilities, despite struggling in school academically. A narrow focus on analytical skills also tends to overlook students from culturally diverse backgrounds. By including creative and practical abilities in our conception of intelligence, educators can identify more culturally and socioeconomically diverse students as "smart" on tests of achievement and ability (Stemler, Grigorenko, Jarvin, & Sternberg, 2006; Stemler, Sternberg, Grigorenko, Jarvin, & Sharpes, 2009; Sternberg, 2010a).

DIVERSITY

Unlike MI theory, the theory of successful intelligence is supported by a body of research evidence. Sternberg and colleagues have developed tests based on successful intelligence to identify gifted students, assess achievement, and help determine college admissions (Chart, Grigorenko, & Sternberg, 2008; Sternberg, 2006b, 2010b; Sternberg & Coffin, 2010). Findings generally indicate that performance on these assessments is consistent with the theory of successful intelligence and that the tests better predict success than traditional tests alone. Researchers also have studied whether instruction that balances analytical, creative, and practical abilities is more effective than traditional instruction. Students from elementary school through high school who were taught using a balanced approach typically outperformed those taught by conventional methods on tests of factual memory and on performance assessments where students demonstrate their knowledge in authentic formats (Grigorenko, Jarvin, & Sternberg, 2002; Sternberg, Grigorenko, Ferarri, & Clinkenbeard, 1999; Sternberg, Grigorenko, & Zhang, 2008; Sternberg, Torff, & Grigorenko, 1998a, 1998b).

Performance assessment: See page 510.

INTELLIGENCE MEASURED AS IQ

IQ tests are a set of cognitive tasks used to measure intellectual functioning in children and adults. When used with children, their primary purpose is to predict school achievement.

Individually Administered and Group Administered Tests

The Stanford-Binet Intelligence Scales-V (Roid, 2003) and Wechsler Intelligence Scale for Children, Fourth Edition (WISC-IV) (Wechsler, 2003) are the most common individually administered IQ tests used in school settings. **Individually administered IQ tests** measure individuals' cognitive abilities with a battery of subtests that require no reading and are administered one-on-one by a trained examiner. As an example, the WISC-IV includes ten subtests to measure four general cognitive abilities: verbal comprehension, working memory, perceptual (i.e., nonverbal) reasoning, and processing speed. Table 22.2 provides a description of one subtest from each of these areas. School psychologists use individually administered tests to predict school achievement for very specific purposes, such as:

Giftedness: See page 420.

Intellectual and learning disabilities: See page 435.

- determining eligibility of students for gifted programs, and
- identifying intellectual disabilities and learning disabilities.

Group administered IQ tests contain objective items, such as multiple choice, and are administered in a group setting using a paper-and-pencil format. At one time, schools used group IQ tests as screening tools to help teachers make decisions about instruction and place students into groups based on their ability (Cohen & Swerdlik, 2005; Sternberg, 2003a). Today, schools use group IQ tests less frequently than they did about 20 years ago (Cohen & Swerdlik, 2005). Experts recognize that placement decisions should not be based on a single test score.

When IQ is being used to predict students' academic achievement, individually administered tests are preferred. Because group administered tests are given to large groups of students at once, they have several features that may affect students' scores and

Individually Administered IQ Tests. These IQ tests are given one-on-one by a trained examiner.

TABLE 22.2	Description of Selected WISC-IV Subtests
Cognitive area	**Description of a WISC-IV task**
Verbal Comprehension	*Vocabulary:* Student gives definitions of words presented by the examiner as a question ("What is a . . . ?").
Perceptual Reasoning	*Block Design:* Student views a picture of a design and must re-create it within a specified time period using red-and-white blocks. 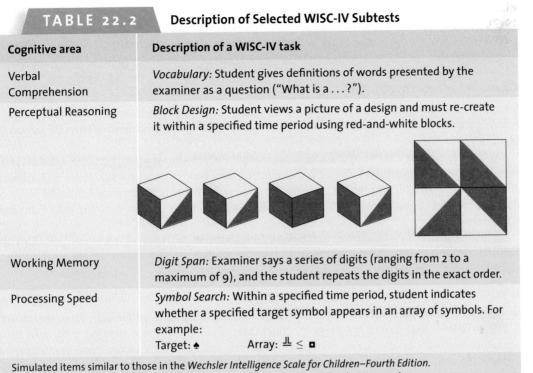
Working Memory	*Digit Span:* Examiner says a series of digits (ranging from 2 to a maximum of 9), and the student repeats the digits in the exact order.
Processing Speed	*Symbol Search:* Within a specified time period, student indicates whether a specified target symbol appears in an array of symbols. For example: Target: ♠ Array: ⊥ ≤ ◻

lead to a narrow interpretation of students' intellectual functioning. These tests rely on a test taker's understanding of the directions, on reading skills, and on test-taking strategies. Group test taking may cause distractions and also may increase a student's anxiety. Individually administered IQ tests provide a more accurate picture of a student's cognitive ability because they require no reading and are given one-on-one with a psychologist, who can establish rapport and determine a student's level of anxiety, motivation, and distractibility.

Interpreting IQ Scores

IQ scores reveal a test taker's relative standing on an IQ test as compared with the scores of other, similar individuals on the same test. This is called a **norm-referenced** interpretation—judging how the student performs compared to others in the **norm group** (all other test takers with similar characteristics). Psychologists make a norm-referenced interpretation by converting a test taker's *raw score,* the number of items correctly answered, to a **deviation IQ,** a score that indicates how far above or below the average a student scored on the IQ test compared to same-age individuals. To interpret a student's deviation IQ, we must compare it to the normal (or bell-shaped) curve shown in Figure 22.2. For any group of same-age individuals, most IQ tests set the average score at 100, with a standard deviation of 15. **Standard deviation (SD)** measures how much a score strays from the average.

Norm-referenced testing: See page 539.

Standard deviation: See page 407.

By using the SD, we can partition the bell curve to allow norm-referenced interpretations. As Figure 22.2 shows:

- Approximately 68% of test takers have IQ scores within 1 SD of the average—that is, between 85 and 115. Performance in this range is considered average.

- Approximately 13.5% of individuals have scores between 115 and 130 (i.e., between 1 and 2 SDs above the average). Similarly, about 13.5% of individuals have scores between 70 and 85 (i.e., between 1 and 2 SDs below the average).

- Almost 2.5% of the population has scores more than 2 SDs away from the mean in either direction. Individuals with IQ scores below 70 may be diagnosed with

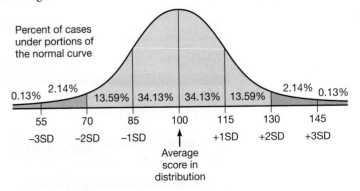

Figure 22.2. Normal Distribution of IQ Scores. The IQ distribution has an average score of 100 and a standard deviation of 15.

intellectual disability (formerly called mental retardation) if they also meet other criteria, such as deficits in adaptive behavior. Students with IQ scores above 132 (top 2% of the population) or above 135 (top 1% of the population) may be eligible for gifted programs (Sternberg, 2002), depending on guidelines that vary from state to state.

Caveats for Interpreting IQ

High-stakes testing: See page 552.

Because IQ tests are used in high-stakes situations in which important educational decisions are made based in part on test scores, educators must be cautious in interpreting students' IQ scores, for several reasons.

IQ tests represent a finite sample of a person's cognitive skills. They capture certain, but not all, abilities that are part of intelligence. Theories of intelligence do not agree on what intelligence is (Sternberg, 2005). Also, different IQ tests do not measure the same skills. Because IQ tests are developed based on different theories of intelligence, each test uses a slightly different set of subtests rather than a standard set of tasks.

IQ is a snapshot of a person's ability *at a given point in time.* Children's IQ scores indicate only their performance at the time of the test administration (Jarvin & Sternberg, 2003). Educators should use caution when they make predictions about future academic performance based on IQ scores.

- Scores on early childhood IQ tests are not very stable in infancy and early childhood (Sternberg, 2002).

- A person's performance on IQ tests can change over time as a result of formal or informal education (Garlick, 2003; Jarvin & Sternberg, 2003). Even fluid abilities that once were thought to be culture-fair, such as abstract or nonverbal reasoning, are affected by cultural and environmental input (Sternberg, 2005). Remember that even though individuals can improve their performance as a result of instruction and environmental input, their performance *relative to the norm group* generally does not change drastically over time. Therefore, IQ scores generally are stable from elementary school through adulthood (Garlick, 2003; Moffitt, Caspi, Harkness, & Silva, 1993).

Validity in testing: See page 545.

- To ensure *validity*—fairness of the test and accuracy of the results—several precautions should be taken with culturally and linguistically diverse students. Students must be tested in their native language on an IQ test that has been developed for use with individuals in their culture. If a test is given in English to a student who does not speak the language, the test score will not be a valid assessment of the student's ability. Use of translated tests also may compromise the validity of the test score (Kaplan & Saccuzzo, 2009). For example, if a student from a Hispanic background obtains a low score on an IQ test translated into Spanish, we can't be sure whether the low score was due to his ability or to the comparability of the translated test to the original English-language IQ test. Similarly, experts caution against the use of interpreters because an interpreter can inadvertently introduce bias into the testing situation, which also will reduce the test score's validity (American Educational Research Association, American Psychological Association, & National Council on Measurement in Education, 1999). When interpreting test results, educators need to take into account the student's sociocultural and linguistic background (Donovan & Cross, 2002; Harry & Klingner, 2006). For example, it is important to consider whether a student has had an opportunity to learn the content being tested.

Test bias: See page 558.

Your friend has received a very high score on a group administered IQ test and believes he is intelligent. Explain to your friend the flaws in his reasoning.

BIOLOGICAL, SOCIAL, AND CULTURAL ISSUES

Intelligence: Heredity or Environment?

Heredity and environment interact to produce all types of behaviors, including intelligence (Carroll, 1992; Sternberg, 1996a). We must be careful not to conclude that genetics predetermines that an individual will have a certain level of intelligence. The environment has been shown to have a dramatic effect on the development of intelligence.

Children's IQ scores may be affected by several factors related to their home environment prior to entering school (Bradley & Caldwell, 1984; Korenman, Miller, & Sjaastad, 1995):

- emotional and verbal responsiveness of parents (responding to children's requests, answering questions),

- parents' involvement with their children (playing with them, reading to them), and
- availability of appropriate play materials, activities, and resources in the home.

Consider the following research on the influence of parent-child interactions. Home observations of 1- and 2-year-old children learning to talk indicated that parents from lower-socioeconomic families spoke about 616 words per hour to their children, middle-socioeconomic parents about 1,251 words per hour, and higher-socioeconomic parents about 2,153 words per hour. Early language experience influenced rate of vocabulary growth, which in turn predicted vocabulary, language skills, and reading comprehension at age 9 (Hart & Risley, 2003). *DIVERSITY*

Most experts also believe that intelligence can be shaped and even improved through various interventions (Grotzer & Perkins, 2000; Mayer, 2000). The Abecedarian project, in which children from impoverished families were provided with an enriching educational environment from age 6 weeks to kindergarten, showed IQ and achievement advantages through age 12 (Ramey, 1994). Head Start, a program that provides at-risk preschoolers with experiences to promote intellectual development, has helped children become cognitively ready for school and has improved their school achievement through middle adolescence (Barnett, 2004; Lazar & Darlington, 1982; Zigler & Berman, 1983). *DIVERSITY*

The **Flynn effect** (Flynn, 1984, 2007), a phenomenon in which IQ scores have increased over successive generations throughout the world (about 3 IQ points per decade since the 1930s), is another example of the effect of environment on cognitive abilities. Possible explanations for the increase in IQ include the following (Lynn, 1998; Kaufman, 2010; Resing & Tunteler, 2007; Sternberg & Kaufman, 1998):

- better nutrition,
- increased schooling,
- greater educational level of parents,
- fewer childhood diseases,
- improved parent-child interactions,
- greater familiarity with taking tests, and
- minor changes in content, instructions, and administration of IQ tests from one version to another.

Socioeconomic and Cultural Factors

DIVERSITY

SOCIOECONOMIC STATUS (SES)

The connection between IQ and socioeconomic status (SES) is well documented (White, 1982). When SES is defined by parents' income, occupation, and educational level, children from higher-SES families tend to have higher IQs than children from lower-SES families. The lower performance of children from poor families may be due to the following influences (Duncan & Brooks-Gunn, 2000; McLoyd, 1998; Sternberg, 2002):

SES as a context of children's development: See page 14.

- fewer resources (books, computers, access to high-quality preschool),
- poorer nutrition,
- poorer health care, and
- strained parent-child relationships due to high levels of parental stress.

However, this correlation does not show the entire picture. When we define a child's home environment based on factors such as parental attitudes about education and parent-child interaction patterns, home environment is a stronger predictor of performance on IQ tests than is a student's socioeconomic status (Bradley & Caldwell, 1984; Suzuki & Valencia, 1997). Children from families in which parents value education, talk with their children, read to their children, and make time for learning—regardless of the financial and occupational status of the family—tend to have higher IQ scores.

What does this research mean for teachers? Teachers form expectations for students based on many sources of information, of which SES is one. Teachers might assume from a student's appearance that he or she is from a lower-SES background and unconsciously form lower expectations for the student, leading to a **self-fulfilling prophecy**—a groundless expectation that leads the teacher to act in ways that make the expectation come true (Merton, 1948). Teachers should regularly monitor their own expectations of student performance to avoid making assumptions or behaving in ways that negatively affect students.

DIVERSITY   ETHNICITY

Like the connection between SES and IQ, the correlation between ethnicity and average IQ scores is well documented. Compared with Caucasian students:

- African-American students score approximately 15 points below average (about 1 SD below the norm) (Nisbett, 1995; Reynolds, Chastain, Kaufman, & McLean, 1987), but the gap between African-American and Caucasian students appears to be narrowing (Hogan, 2007; Nisbett, 1995);

- Hispanic students score approximately average on nonverbal portions of IQ tests but about 7 to 15 points lower ($\frac{1}{2}$ to 1 SD below average) on verbal subtests (Hogan, 2007); and

- students from Chinese and Japanese cultures score about average on verbal subtests and about 1 SD above the average on nonverbal portions (Hogan, 2007).

Remember that these scores represent group averages, which can fluctuate over time (Sternberg, 2002).

What accounts for these differences among ethnic or racial groups? The differences may be due to a **stereotype threat**—an unconscious, automatic activation of prior knowledge about a stereotype that hinders performance on cognitive tasks. For example, African Americans have performed significantly worse on a test when they were told that it was an intelligence test compared to when they were given different instructions about the test (Brown & Day, 2006; Steele & Aronson, 1995). The stereotype they invoked about their ethnic group and intelligence while taking the test may have hindered their performance. Similar stereotype threat effects have been found for individuals from lower-SES groups and Hispanic students (Croizet, Desert, Dutrevis, & Leyens, 2001; Schmader & Johns, 2003).

Also, the labels *Asian, Hispanic,* and *Native American* are so heterogeneous that they are not meaningful indicators of race or ethnicity (Hogan, 2007). *Hispanic* and *Latino* refer to individuals from cultures including, but not limited to, Puerto Rico, Mexico, and Cuba (Neisser et al., 1996). *Asian* includes subgroups from many cultures, such as China, Japan, Vietnam, Cambodia, Korea, Laos, India, Pakistan, and the Philippines (Hogan, 2007; Neisser et al., 1996). And *Native American* includes many different tribes with about 200 different languages (Leap, 1981).

Finally, the differences among ethnic or racial groups are more the result of socioeconomic and environmental influences than of race itself. When we compare the IQ scores of racial or ethnic groups within the same SES level—for example, African-American, Hispanic, and Caucasian students all from higher-SES families—group differences are minimized (Suzuki & Valencia, 1997). Children of the same SES but different racial groups are more similar in IQ than are children from the same racial group but different socioeconomic statuses. It is important to remember that the differences between ethnic groups in IQ scores can occur for many reasons. Therefore, teachers should be careful not to make assumptions about a student's ability based on ethnicity or any other visible characteristic.

DIVERSITY   GENDER

In general, no gender differences are found in overall performance on IQ tests because test makers are careful to remove any items leading to gender bias and to maintain a balance of items that more males answer correctly and more females answer correctly (Halpern & LaMay, 2000; Mackintosh, 1996). Even though males and females do not differ on average, males show more variability in performance on cognitive tests, especially at the extremes of the distribution, leading to more males than females at the highest and lowest levels of measured intelligence (Hyde et al., 2008; Lindberg et al., 2010). Also, males have typically shown advantages on some tasks measuring quantitative and spatial abilities. However, recent research suggests that there are few gender differences in math and spatial skills. Let's consider some of the relevant findings.

Males show an advantage on some but not all tests of spatial ability. Males perform better than females on tasks that require individuals to maintain and transform a visual-spatial image, such as the mental rotations task in Figure 22.3 (Burton, Henninger, & Hafetz, 2005; Masters & Sanders, 1993; Voyer, Voyer, & Bryden, 1995). The gender difference is large (about 1 standard deviation) and is consistently found in adults and children (Geiser, Lehmann, & Eid, 2008; Titze, Jansen, & Heil, 2010). Males also perform better than females on spatial navigation tasks where individuals are required to reconstruct a path through a map, virtual space, or real-world environment (Iaria et al., 2003; Postma et al., 2004; Saucier et al., 2002). However, on tasks that assess memory for the spatial location of objects, research indicates better performance of females or performance that is comparable among males and females (Levy et al., 2005; Postma et al., 2004; Silverman et al., 2007).

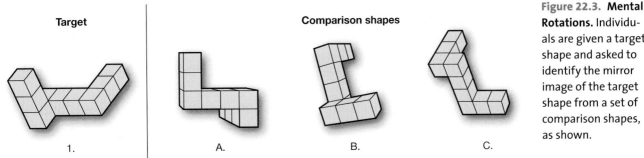

Target   **Comparison shapes**

1.   A.   B.   C.

22 | Intelligence

Figure 22.3. Mental Rotations. Individuals are given a target shape and asked to identify the mirror image of the target shape from a set of comparison shapes, as shown.

The gender stereotyped notion that "males are better at math" also does not always hold true and may have been exaggerated by the popular media (Hyde, 2005). Recent research suggests that there are small to nonexistent gender differences in conceptual understanding and calculation skills in elementary school (Hyde, Fennema, & Lamon, 1990; Lindberg, Hyde, Petersen, & Linn, 2010).

While boys and girls may not differ in their overall math achievement, research is now exploring possible differences in the cognitive processes underlying their math performance. For example, researchers have found either no gender differences or a female advantage in *quickly* recalling arithmetic facts during the early elementary school years (Royer, Tronsky, Chan, Jackson, & Marchant, 1999; Willingham & Cole, 1997). The possibility that girls may be faster at fact retrieval is consistent with findings of a general female advantage on tasks that require rapid retrieval of information from long-term memory (Halpern, 2000; Halpern et al., 2005). Keep in mind, though, that research evidence is inconclusive regarding whether elementary school boys or girls are *more accurate* at fact retrieval (Carr & Davis, 2001; Royer et al., 1999).

Boys and girls may also differ in math performance due to their strategy preference when solving math problems. In a recent study with kindergarteners, no overall gender differences were found on a standardized math test assessing mathematical concepts, calculation, and problem solving. However, the boys' total scores were related to their spatial reasoning skills, whereas the girls' total scores were related to their verbal skills (Klein, Adi-Japha, & Hakak-Benizri, 2010).

At the high school level, there continues to be a small male advantage for complex problem solving (Hyde et al., 1990; Lindberg et al., 2010). Cognitive factors may account for this difference.

■ Differences in strategy use might lead to performance differences. Males tend to favor a spatial imagery strategy when solving mathematical word problems, whereas females are more likely to use a verbal computation strategy (Geary, Saults, Liu, & Hoard, 2000). Girls may have fewer opportunities to learn problem-solving strategies within the context of complex math and science courses such as calculus, physics, and chemistry. However, to date, the gender gap in course taking is nonexistent except for small differences in physics class enrollments (Lindberg et al., 2010; National Science Foundation, 2008).

■ The stereotype threat that "girls are bad at math" may also hinder females' performance on tasks that assess complex mathematical abilities (Halpern, 1997). For example, females who were told that a math test produced gender differences favoring males performed worse than when they were told the test was insensitive to gender differences (Steele, 1997). This effect has consistently been found in research with college students, and more recent research has identified the effect as early as middle school (Muzzatti & Agnoli, 2007; Schmader, 2002; Spencer, Steele, & Quinn, 1999).

The belief of parents and teachers that math is a male domain may also lead them to behave in ways that provide different experiences in and out of school for boys and girls as they develop from early childhood through adolescence, leading to different levels of mathematical ability at the high school level.

■ Parents provide children with different activities and offer different feedback about their performance on those activities (Wigfield & Cambria, 2010a; Wigfield et al., 2006). For example, one study reported that mothers were more likely to buy math and science items for boys than girls, which affected subsequent math and science interests (Bleeker & Jacobs, 2004).

■ Parents and teachers also tend to rate boys as having higher math ability (Lindberg, Hyde, & Hirsch, 2008). These experiences lead children to develop expectancies about what they are good at and what they value as important to them (Jacobs, Davis-Kean, Bleeker, Eccles, & Malanchuk, 2005; Lindberg et al., 2008). In elementary school, when boys and girls generally do not differ in math achievement, boys develop more positive beliefs about their competence in math and science (Eccles, Barber, Jozefowicz, Malenchuk, & Vida, 2000; Else-Quest, Hyde, & Linn, 2010). Girls—even those who are high-achieving and gifted—rate their ability lower than boys even when they outperform boys (Eccles et al., 2000; Freedman-Doan et al., 2000).

- Teachers also can subtly and inadvertently convey the message that girls are not as good as boys at math. A recent study of first- and second-grade female teachers with math anxiety showed that by the end of the school year girls, but not boys, were more likely to believe that boys are better at math. Girls who endorsed this stereotype had lower math achievement in comparison with girls who did not endorse the stereotype and with boys overall (Beilock, Gunderson, Ramirez, & Levine, 2010).

- As students transition to high school, they may acquire additional gender-stereotyped experiences. Teachers tend to assign high-ability boys to top math groups more frequently than high-ability girls (Hallinan & Sorensøn, 1987). High school math teachers also tend to interact less with girls and provide them with less feedback (Oakes, 1990b; Sadker, Sadker, & Klein, 1991).

Let's remember, as we did for ethnic and SES differences, that on average the difference between groups is rather small. Teachers should be careful not to make assumptions about any student's abilities based on membership in a particular gender, ethnic, or socioeconomic group. It is important to understand differences among students and the factors that may cause these differences so that teachers can develop curriculum, methods, and interactions that provide an equitable educational experience for all students.

Why might research on socioeconomic, ethnic, and gender differences in intelligence be important for teachers? How will knowledge of this research influence your teaching philosophy?

APPLICATIONS: INTELLIGENCE THEORIES IN THE CLASSROOM

Multiple Intelligences in the Classroom

Teachers can reach all types of learners using MI theory if they follow general guidelines and avoid common misapplications, shown in Table 22.3. MI theory can be implemented either on a school-wide basis or in individual classrooms.

TABLE 22.3 **Multiple Intelligences Theory: Guidelines and Misapplications**

General guidelines	Common misapplications
Differences among students are taken seriously so that curricula and assessments are constructed to be sensitive to those differences.	Attempting to teach *every* lesson in eight ways
Knowledge about differences is shared with students and parents.	Using MI theory as a mnemonic aid (e.g., using dance or mime to help students remember material from a lesson)
Lessons are presented in a way that allows all students the opportunity to master the material and demonstrate what they have learned.	Promoting musical intelligence by playing background music during learning activities
Students gradually take on responsibility for their own learning.	▪ Using intrapersonal intelligence as a rationale for self-esteem programs ▪ Using interpersonal intelligence as a rationale for cooperative learning

Source: Gardner, 1995.

School-wide approach. Educators can use MI theory to identify the skills and abilities that are valued in society and cultivate those abilities (Gardner, 1995). At the Key Community School in Indianapolis, a group of teachers worked with Gardner and his colleagues to develop a curriculum based on MI theory. The Key School emphasizes the use of all kinds of abilities by students. The curriculum is integrated through the use of school-wide themes that span all grades and all subjects and are studied in depth for nine weeks.

Schools at all levels can create a curriculum that reflects MI theory. In early childhood and elementary classrooms, the curricula should provide students with a variety of experiences to help them discover their interests and talents (Johnson, 2000). Some elementary schools have adopted a themed curriculum, like that of the Key School, integrating language arts, science, mathematics, and social studies. This allows children to experience topics in greater depth and to recognize how they can apply knowledge and skills to multiple subjects. Middle schools and high schools can adapt their existing curricula to reflect an emphasis on MI by adding a stronger arts program, implementing learning stations in classes, using community experts to mentor students in their areas of expertise, or constructing school-wide interdisciplinary units (Campbell, 1997).

Individual classrooms. Teachers should recognize and identify students' different strengths and weaknesses in their intelligence by directly observing students in authentic tasks—real-life activities that are themselves valued (Gardner, 1991, 1999). For example, a teacher might identify spatial intelligence by observing students as they design a new gymnasium, or identify linguistic intelligence by evaluating the process and product of students' writing given a writing prompt.

Authentic assessment: See page 481.

To meet the needs of learners with diverse strengths and weaknesses, teachers should introduce subject matter in more than one way (Gardner, 1991, 1999). For example, as teachers we can learn about intelligence through:

- a narrative (the history of the development of intelligence theories and tests),

- hands-on experiences (looking at IQ tests, learning how to administer them),

- logical-quantitative techniques (practicing the interpretation of IQ scores), or

- an existential inquiry (discussing whether intelligence is due to nature or nurture).

Teaching the same topic using different approaches will provide students with opportunities to learn a topic using their strengths and to develop skills in their weaker areas of intelligence (Kornhaber, Fierros, & Veenema, 2004).

As a result of teaching material through multiple methods, teachers will cover fewer topics, but the topics will be covered in greater depth and more students will be successful (Gardner, 1995). This is not a new concept. International comparisons of mathematics performance have indicated that mathematics instruction in top-performing countries focuses on fewer concepts in greater depth (Schmidt, McKnight, & Raizen, 1996). Schools that have used MI-inspired practices for several years have documented both qualitative and quantitative evidence of the benefits to students' learning (Gardner & Moran, 2006). Of 41 schools implementing MI-inspired curricula, 49% have shown improvement in achievement test scores, 54% have reported fewer discipline problems, and 60% have documented increased parental involvement (Kornhaber et al., 2004).

Teaching for Successful Intelligence

Consistent with an MI approach to teaching, the goal of teaching for successful intelligence is to ensure that *all* students can achieve higher levels of learning. Teachers must use instructional approaches that focus on (Sternberg, 1997, 2010a):

- analytical learning (analyze, compare and contrast; evaluate, judge, assess),

- creative learning (create, invent, imagine, suppose, discover), and

- practical learning (use, apply, employ, put into practice, implement, demonstrate).

Memory-based instruction (factual knowledge or recall) is still an important component of school learning, because students cannot think analytically, creatively, or in a practical manner if they have no knowledge base (Sternberg, 2002). Teachers can use instructional approaches for analytical, creative, or practical thinking in any subject and at any grade level, as illustrated in Table 22.4.

TABLE 22.4	Teaching to Analytical, Creative, and Practical Abilities		
Subject area	**Analytical**	**Creative**	**Practical**
Language Arts	Compare the personality of Tom Sawyer with that of Huckleberry Finn.	Write a very short story with Tom Sawyer as a character.	Describe the general lesson about persuasion that can be learned from Tom Sawyer's way of persuading his friends to whitewash Aunt Polly's fence.
Mathematics	Solve a mathematical word problem (using the D = RT formula).	Create your own mathematical word problem using the D = RT formula.	Show how to use the D = RT formula to estimate driving time from one city to another near you.
Social Studies	Compare, contrast, and evaluate the arguments of those who supported slavery versus those who opposed it.	Write a page of a journal from the viewpoint of a soldier fighting for one or the other side during the Civil War.	Discuss the applicability of lessons of the Civil War for countries today that have strong internal divisions.
Science	Analyze how the immune system fights bacterial infections.	Suggest ways to cope with the increasing immunity bacteria are showing to antibiotic drugs.	Suggest three steps that individuals might take to reduce the likelihood of bacterial infection.

Reprinted with permission from Sternberg, 1997.

Teaching for successful intelligence should empower students to cultivate an ability to adapt to, select, and shape their environments. Guidelines to help students develop successful intelligence include the following:

1. Balance instruction so that over the course of a unit students are exposed to lessons that emphasize analytical, creative, and practical abilities. This enables them to learn how to capitalize on their strengths and correct or compensate for their weaknesses (Sternberg, 2002). Remember, though, that it is not necessary to teach each lesson in three different ways.

2. Be sensitive to individual differences in the way students represent information. Individuals differ in their preferred way of representing content (verbally, quantitatively, spatially) and have preferred modalities for storing information (visual versus auditory) and producing information (written versus oral) (Sternberg, 1998). Teachers should vary the methods they use to assess student learning rather than relying on a single mode of evaluation, such as written tests.

3. Provide students with opportunities to *shape* their environment by choosing activities, paper topics, projects, or portfolio items (Sternberg, 1998). This is consistent with the emphasis on student choice in MI theory.

4. Teach in a "zone of relative novelty" where material is challenging but not too much so (Sternberg, 1998). This approach not only encourages students to develop their creative abilities (responding to novelty) but also is consistent with Piaget's (1972) and Vygotsky's (1978) theories of cognitive development.

5. Encourage *automaticity* of information-processing skills such as reading and mathematics (Sternberg, 1998). Individuals with successful intelligence have information-processing skills that are automatic, allowing them to engage more efficiently in analytical, creative, and practical thinking.

Piaget's and Vygotsky's theories of cognitive development: See page 77 and page 124.

Automaticity: See page 193, page 226, and page 439.

When teachers apply successful intelligence in the classroom, students learn more. In studies of elementary through high school classrooms, students performed better when teachers provided instruction that matched students' strengths *at least some of the time,* compared with students in classes that involved traditional memory-based instruction or instruction that did not match student abilities (Grigorenko et al., 2002; Sternberg et al., 1999). This finding holds true for different subjects and types of assessment (factual knowledge or higher-order thinking).

Think of the grade level you intend to teach. Which theory would you apply to your classroom? What aspects of the theory influenced your decision?

Summary

Describe Spearman's two-factor theory of intelligence and contrast it with contemporary theories of intelligence. Spearman proposed the first hierarchical theory of intelligence, arguing that humans have a general cognitive ability, g, comprised of specific abilities, s. Gardner and Sternberg believe that if we define intelligence more broadly to include other capabilities, g will be less important. Gardner proposed eight intelligences, only two of which are measured by IQ tests, while Sternberg's theory involves a balance between three intellectual abilities—analytical, creative, and practical—of which only analytical skills are measured on IQ tests.

Describe what IQ tests measure and contrast individually administered and group administered tests. IQ tests measure a specific set of skills, which vary from test to test, and they assess an individual's cognitive ability at a specific point in time. Individually administered tests use cognitive tasks that require no reading, and they are administered one-on-one with an examiner. Group administered tests contain objective items that require reading. Psychologists use individually administered IQ tests to diagnose students with intellectual disabilities and learning disabilities and to make eligibility decisions for gifted programs. Group administered IQ tests can be used to help inform placement decisions.

Describe how environment, socioeconomic status, and gender influence IQ. Many factors in children's home environments prior to school entry are related to their IQ. Children tend to have higher IQ scores if their parents are responsive to their needs and provide opportunities that stimulate their cognitive development. Children from higher-SES families also have higher IQs. Although ethnic groups differ in their average IQ scores, we must be cautious in interpreting these differences. The terms *Hispanic* and *Asian*, for example, are imprecise, and the IQ scores of ethnic groups fluctuate over time. SES also may account for a large proportion of the ethnic differences in IQ. Few gender differences in intelligence exist. Researchers are now examining the cognitive and social processes that might account for any gender differences in cognitive skills such as math.

Explain the similarities between the theory of multiple intelligences and the theory of successful intelligence in their applications to the classroom. The goal of both MI theory and the theory of successful intelligence is to reach more learners than traditional education does. Both theories emphasize that teachers should be sensitive to individual differences among students. They also advocate approaching a subject in a variety of ways to capitalize on students' strengths and help them develop in their weak areas. Both theories also stress the importance of allowing students to choose assignments and tasks in a way that helps them demonstrate their strengths and work on their weaknesses.

Key Concepts

analytical abilities   404

creative abilities   405

deviation IQ   407

Flynn effect   409

group administered IQ tests   406

individually administered IQ tests   406

norm group   407

norm-referenced   407

practical abilities   405

self-fulfilling prophecy   409

standard deviation (SD)   407

stereotype threat   410

theory of multiple intelligences   404

theory of successful intelligence   404

two-factor theory of intelligence   403

Video Applications

www.mhhe.com/bohlin2e

Video 1: IQ Testing (*2 minutes*)

This clip shows school psychologist Melanie Davis administering the Block Design subtest of the WISC-IV to an elementary school student. This clip can be used with Module 22 (Intelligence) or with Module 24 video 1 (Title: Categories of Disabilities in Special Education).

Case Studies
Reflect and Evaluate

These questions refer to the case study on page 394.

1. How does Mrs. Cahill's language arts activity reflect Sternberg's theory of successful intelligence?

2. How does Mrs. Cahill's language arts activity reflect Gardner's theory of multiple intelligences?

3. Contrast the capabilities of Jillian and Pat using the theory of multiple intelligences and the theory of successful intelligence.

4. After another parent-teacher conference with Nolan's mother, Mrs. Cahill decides to refer Nolan for a giftedness evaluation. Why would an individually administered IQ test be a more appropriate means to assess Nolan's cognitive ability than a group administered IQ test?

5. Nolan's IQ score is 143. Use the normal curve in Figure 22.2 to interpret what this score means. Based on Nolan's IQ score, would you expect him to have a high IQ in later grades? Why or why not?

ELEMENTARY SCHOOL: **"Cheetahs, Lions, and Leopards"**

These questions refer to the case study on page 396.

1. How would you describe Marcela and Carl according to Gardner's theory of multiple intelligences? How would you describe each student using Sternberg's theory of successful intelligence?

2. The district in which Glendale Elementary School is located uses a group administered IQ test to help teachers place students in the appropriate group level for reading and math instruction. Carl's IQ score is 117. Use the normal curve in Figure 22.2 to interpret what this score means.

DIVERSITY 3. Assume that Carl is African American. Why might his IQ score underestimate his actual cognitive ability?

4. You are addressing the school board. Explain why a group administered IQ test might not be appropriate for determining the placement of students into ability groups. Give specific examples to support your position.

DIVERSITY 5. According to the research on sociocultural issues in intelligence, how do you think Marcela's family background has influenced her interest in science?

6. How can Mrs. Fratelli use the theory of multiple intelligences to teach science? How can she use the theory of successful intelligence to teach science?

MIDDLE SCHOOL: **"Math Troubles"**

These questions refer to the case study on page 398.

1. At the beginning of middle school, Lindsey and her classmates took a paper-and-pencil group administered IQ test. Her IQ score was 113. Use the normal curve in Figure 22.2 to interpret what this score means. How certain are you that this IQ score accurately reflects her cognitive ability?

2. How would you characterize Sam according to Gardner's theory of multiple intelligences?

3. According to Sternberg's theory of successful intelligence, would you say that Lindsey has strengths in analytical, creative, or practical abilities, or in some combination of these?

4. How can Miss Barton incorporate Gardner's theory of multiple intelligences into her pre-algebra class?

5. Which type of ability in Sternberg's theory of successful intelligence does Miss Barton's teaching method emphasize? How can Miss Barton adapt her teaching to include all the abilities in Sternberg's theory?

DIVERSITY 6. Explain how factors such as *gender stereotyping* and *stereotype threat* may be affecting Lindsey's motivation and performance in pre-algebra.

HIGH SCHOOL: "Noon Supervised Study"

These questions refer to the case study on page 400.

1. Sarah was administered the WISC-IV as part of the process of selecting students for the gifted-and-talented program in elementary school. The IQ score in her academic record is 132. Use the normal curve in Figure 22.2 to interpret what this score means.

2. In third grade, Anthony was suspected of having a learning disability and was referred to a school psychologist for testing. He was given the WISC-IV and obtained a score of 125. Use the normal curve in Figure 22.2 to interpret what this score means. (Note that IQ score alone does not determine whether a student has a learning disability.)

3. What expectation do you think Jason has for success in school? How might this create a *self-fulfilling prophecy*?

4. Imagine that you are one of Mr. Hardy's colleagues. Describe the theory of multiple intelligences and the theory of successful intelligence. Give Mr. Hardy some suggestions based on these theories to help him change his all-lecture format.

5. Evaluate Mr. Hardy's use of exams and homework assignments. Which intelligence in MI theory would Gardner say Mr. Hardy is emphasizing? Which ability or abilities in the theory of successful intelligences would Sternberg say Mr. Hardy is emphasizing?

6. Imagine that you are one of Mr. Hardy's colleagues. Based on MI theory and the theory of successful intelligence, give him some suggestions for additional methods of assessing students' learning rather than relying solely on exams and homework assignments.

23

Giftedness and Creativity

Outline	Learning Goals
Giftedness and Creativity: Are They More Than Just Intelligence?	
	1. Describe how intelligence might be related to giftedness and creativity.
Giftedness	
■ Characteristics	2. Discuss the characteristics you would look for in identifying students as gifted.
■ Identifying Giftedness	3. Explain how factors such as race, socioeconomic status, and gender affect the identification of giftedness.
■ Applications: Teaching Gifted Students	4. Discuss the approaches that can be used effectively to meet the needs of gifted students.
Creativity	
■ Characteristics	5. Discuss the characteristics you would look for in identifying creative students.
■ Identifying Creativity	6. Discuss the practices you would use to encourage creative expression in the classroom.
■ Applications: Promoting Creativity in the Classroom	
Summary	
Key Concepts	
Video Applications	
Case Studies: Reflect and Evaluate	

GIFTEDNESS AND CREATIVITY:
ARE THEY MORE THAN JUST INTELLIGENCE?

Students with giftedness or creativity present teachers with unique challenges. They learn in a qualitatively different way from other students their age, often viewing the world and processing information differently and solving problems in unique ways. Teachers need to understand the nature of giftedness and creativity in order to best meet the needs of these students and provide experiences suited to optimal learning. Before we discuss the characteristics of giftedness and creativity and how teachers can identify and teach students with these talents, we need to describe how giftedness and creativity are related to intelligence.

When we think of giftedness, we typically think of someone who is extremely smart and who performs at an exceptional level in school and on standardized tests. A person may be "smart" in this way but not gifted, because giftedness involves much more than just high cognitive ability. Howard Gardner's theory of multiple intelligences (MI theory) and Robert Sternberg's theory of successful intelligence—two contemporary theories of intelligence—consider giftedness to be an extension of intelligence. However, intelligence in these theories is multidimensional, comprising several independent but interacting abilities.

According to MI theory, all individuals have strengths and weaknesses in eight separate intelligences (Gardner, 2006):

1. *Linguistic* (using words to describe or communicate ideas).

2. *Logical-mathematical* (reasoning, perceiving patterns in numbers, using numbers effectively).

3. *Spatial* (accurately perceiving and transforming the visual-spatial world).

4. *Bodily-kinesthetic* (expertise in using one's body).

5. *Musical* (recognizing components of music, expressing musical forms, using music to express ideas).

6. *Interpersonal* (accurately perceiving and appropriately responding to the emotions of other people).

7. *Intrapersonal* (introspection, discriminating one's emotions and perceptions, knowing one's strengths and limitations).

8. *Naturalistic* (recognizing and classifying living things, sensitivity to features of the natural world).

Individuals who are gifted rapidly move through a domain (math, writing, etc.) because they have certain strengths among their intelligences and have had environmental opportunities to nurture those strengths (Gardner, 1993).

According to the theory of successful intelligence, all individuals possess differing degrees of three abilities (Sternberg, 1996b):

1. *Analytical* (analyzing, choosing strategies, evaluating, monitoring outcomes).

2. *Creative* (generating novel ideas for solving problems).

3. *Practical* (applying knowledge to problems, implementing options and solutions, and making them work).

Individuals are intelligent if they find ways to balance the strengths and weaknesses in their abilities in order to adapt to, shape, and select environments in which to succeed (Sternberg & Grigorenko, 2003). In the theory of successful intelligence, giftedness is defined in relation to intelligence. Individuals are gifted if they are able to successfully transform their life experiences into successful outcomes using the abilities they have been given (Sternberg, 2003b). A person can be gifted analytically, creatively, or practically.

The relationship between intelligence and creativity remains controversial (Lubart & Zenasni, 2010). Consider five hypotheses that attempt to explain this relationship (Sternberg & O'Hara, 1999):

1. Creativity is a subset of intelligence.

2. Intelligence is a subset of creativity.

3. Creativity and intelligence are overlapping traits.

The theory of multiple intelligences: See page 404.

Successful intelligence: See page 404.

Bodily-kinesthetic Ability. The ability to use one's body, such as in dance and athletics, is one of eight intelligences that people can possess, according to MI theory.

4. Creativity and intelligence are essentially the same thing.

5. Creativity and intelligence are completely unrelated.

Whether creativity is seen as a part of intelligence or separate from it depends on how we define both *intelligence* and *creativity*.

In MI theory and the theory of successful intelligence, creativity is a part of intelligence. For example, a person may be creative linguistically or musically in MI theory. In the theory of successful intelligence, a person may have a particular strength in creative abilities. However, a person may be intelligent according to these theories and not be particularly creative. For example, an individual may be successfully intelligent because he capitalizes on strengths in analytical skills and compensates for weaknesses in other areas, such as creative ability.

Also, intelligence may be required in varying degrees depending on the domain in which creativity is expressed (Getzels & Csikszentmihalyi, 1976; Sternberg & Lubart, 1995; Sternberg, 2008). The level of intelligence needed to be a creative painter or actress may differ from the level of intelligence required to be a Nobel Prize–winning physicist (Sternberg & O'Hara, 1999). Despite a growing body of research in the field of creativity, there still is no clear consensus about the relationship between creativity and intelligence.

What do you think of when you hear the words gifted **and** creative? **Think of as many characteristics of each as you can. Keep these in mind as you read about giftedness and creativity.**

GIFTEDNESS

Characteristics

What characteristics of **giftedness** did you think of? Let's examine some common traits of students who are gifted:

- Students who are gifted master knowledge or skills in a particular domain earlier than their peers (Steiner & Carr, 2003; Winner, 1996). They tend to have above-average ability in a particular subject, such as reading, mathematics, science, art, or music, or they have above-average ability overall (Renzulli, 2002).

Information processing: See page 184.

- These students process information more efficiently, learn at a faster pace, use more effective strategies, and monitor their understanding better than their non-gifted peers (Davidson & Davidson, 2004; Housand & Reis, 2008; Steiner & Carr, 2003).

- These students are independent learners. They require less direct instruction and support from teachers than their non-gifted peers (Winner, 1996; Hammond, McBee, & Hebert, 2007). They also make discoveries on their own and solve problems in unique ways, showing flexibility and creativity in the way they apply their knowledge to novel situations (Ferrando et al., 2008).

Motivation: See page 265.

- Students who are gifted possess a high level of interest and intrinsic motivation, an internal drive to learn and master topics within their area of giftedness (Winner, 2000). As preschoolers, children who are gifted display unusual curiosity, a high level of questioning, and an intense desire to learn (Creel & Karnes, 1988; Gross, 1993). School-age students who are gifted seek out challenging tasks, exhibit boredom at tasks they consider too easy, and have high personal standards for their performance, sometimes to the point of perfectionism (LoCicero & Ashbly, 2000; Parker, 1997).

According to Joseph Renzulli (1978b, 2002, 2011), an expert on giftedness, giftedness is not a set of distinct traits but an intermingling among three general characteristics that capture many of the traits just discussed.

1. Above-average ability, defined as:

   - general ability, the capacity to process information, synthesize information, or think abstractly; or

   - specific ability, the capacity to acquire knowledge or skill in a specialized domain such as mathematics, poetry, or science.

2. High level of task commitment, or an individual's energy or passion for a particular task, problem, or domain. Higher levels result in behaviors such as perseverance, endurance, hard work, practice, and self-confidence in one's ability to engage in a productive endeavor (Renzulli, 1990).

3. High levels of creativity, the ability to generate many interesting and feasible ideas with respect to a particular problem or domain.

In Figure 23.1, which shows Renzulli's **three-ring conception of giftedness** (1978b, 2002), giftedness is represented as the shaded area—the interaction among the three traits.

Renzulli also describes two forms of giftedness. The first form, **schoolhouse giftedness,** reflects skill in the performance of academic tasks. These are students who have high overall cognitive ability and school achievement, who excel in a particular domain such as reading or science, or who are very efficient at processing information and learning new things. The second form, **creative-productive giftedness,** reflects an individual's ability to generate creative ideas. These are students who enjoy engaging in exploration, creating, and problem solving. As we discuss next, typical methods for identifying giftedness tend to focus on schoolhouse giftedness.

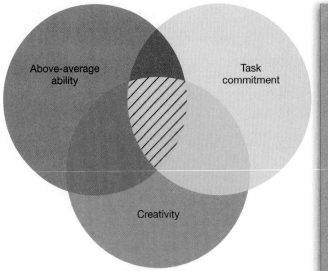

Figure 23.1. Renzulli's Three-ring Conception of Giftedness. Giftedness is the interaction among the three traits, shown as the shaded area in the figure.

IQ tests: See page 406.

Identifying Giftedness

STANDARDIZED IQ SCORES

In 1926, Lewis Terman, creator of the Stanford-Binet IQ test, narrowly defined giftedness as an IQ score in the top 1% of the population, and for most of the twentieth century many experts equated giftedness with a score on an IQ test. IQ tests remain the primary tool for identifying students as eligible for gifted programs (Brown et al., 2005). As shown in Figure 23.2, students with IQ scores above 132 (top 2% of the population) or above 135 (top 1% of the population) may be eligible for gifted programs, although guidelines vary from state to state (Sternberg, 2002). Teacher nominations also are frequently used, but often these nominations serve only to qualify the student to take an IQ test, leaving test scores as the deciding factor (Renzulli, 1990). Identifying giftedness solely on the basis of test scores leads to biases in the selection of students for gifted programs. Students with creative or practical talents in areas such as the arts or leadership are overlooked when educators focus on the identification of schoolhouse giftedness (Renzulli, 1999).

When this single-test score criterion approach is used, females, students with learning disabilities, students from impoverished backgrounds, and minority students typically are underidentified as eligible for gifted programs (Freeman, 1995; Gallagher, 1992; McKenzie, 1986; Stormont, Stebbins, & Holliday, 2001), for several reasons:

■ IQ scores have the potential to discriminate against students from minority groups—who typically do not score well on standardized tests—by restricting their access to gifted programs (Banks, 2006; Kaufman et al., 2009; Maker, 1996). Similarly, students from low-income families are at risk for being overlooked for gifted programs because they lack family and community resources to help them develop their talents (Borland & Wright, 1994; VanTassel-Baska, 1998). The development of gifted talents requires a stimulating learning environment that provides students with opportunities, resources, and encouragement (Renzulli, 2002).

■ Teachers often overlook students from different ethnic backgrounds in favor of White, middle-class students because the characteristics of the latter more closely match teachers' expectations of what giftedness looks like—high academic achievement and good behavior (Bonner, 2000; Bryn, 2008; Miller-Washington, 2010).

■ Students with learning disabilities who also are gifted typically are overlooked for gifted programs because their giftedness may be "masked" by their disability, making them appear to have average abilities (McCoach, Kehle, Bray, & Siegle, 2001; VanTassel-Baska et al., 2009).

■ Girls are underrepresented in gifted programs—particularly in high school, when the percentage of female

DIVERSITY

Cultural issues in intelligence: See page 408.

Figure 23.2. Normal Distribution of IQ Scores. Giftedness typically is identified by IQ scores in the top 1% or 2% of the IQ distribution (shaded purple).

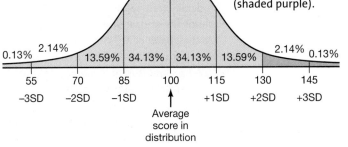

| 0.13% | 2.14% | 13.59% | 34.13% | 34.13% | 13.59% | 2.14% | 0.13% |

55	70	85	100	115	130	145
−3SD	−2SD	−1SD		+1SD	+2SD	+3SD

Average score in distribution

DIVERSITY

participants declines (Read, 1991). Pressure to achieve peer acceptance may lead adolescent girls to hide their cognitive abilities in favor of social acceptance (Basow & Rubin, 1999; Genshaft, Bireley, & Hollinger, 1995; Stormont et al., 2001). For example, adolescent girls score lower than boys on measures of self-concept, interest, and motivation in math—considered a "male" achievement domain—and this difference is even more pronounced among gifted students (Preckel et al., 2008).

MULTIDIMENSIONAL ASSESSMENT

Despite the popularity of IQ tests for identifying students eligible for gifted programs, current theory and research support a multifaceted approach, as illustrated in the definition of giftedness found in the No Child Left Behind (NCLB) Act of 2001 (PL 107–110):

> *The term "gifted and talented," when used with respect to students, children, or youth, means students, children, or youth who give evidence of high achievement capability in areas such as intellectual, creative, artistic, or leadership capacity, or in specific academic fields, and who need services or activities not ordinarily provided by the school in order to fully develop those capabilities. (Title IX, Part A, Section 9101(22))*

To identify students who are gifted—especially those from diverse backgrounds—educators need to move away from using standardized tests and include information from nontest sources (Renzulli, 2002). Experts recommend using a variety of criteria, as outlined here (Pfeiffer & Blei, 2008; Renzulli, 1990; Renzulli & Reis, 1991):

1. Educators first identify the traditional schoolhouse giftedness using intelligence or achievement test scores. According to the three-ring conception of giftedness, students would be considered to have above-average ability if they perform in the top 15% to 20% in a certain subject or skill domain (Renzulli, 1978b, 2002). This differs markedly from requiring an IQ score in the top 1% or 2% of the population, as discussed previously. Demonstration of above-average performance in this case, however, should not be measured solely by tests.

2. Teachers may nominate students who display behaviors not measured by tests, such as creativity, task commitment, interest, or special talents. Students who are creative can come up with many different solutions to problems, as assessed on tests of creativity. Students who have high levels of task commitment are highly fascinated by a certain topic or subject matter and have a strong drive to achieve in that domain (Renzulli, 1978b, 2002). They may show characteristics such as enthusiasm, self-confidence, goal-oriented behavior, persistence, and freedom from feelings of inferiority (MacKinnon, 1965; Ogden, 1968; Roe, 1952; Terman, 1959).

Inferiority is discussed in Erikson's theory of psychosocial development: See page 46.

3. A selection committee then considers students who do not qualify based on test scores or teacher nominations by evaluating alternative criteria, such as parent or peer nominations, self-nominations, tests of creativity, or evaluations of products (e.g., special projects, grades, or portfolios).

4. The selection committee also may consider nominations from previous-year teachers to prevent overlooking students who may not have been identified by present teachers.

Implementation of such a multidimensional identification model would solve the limitations of the single-test score criterion approach and would be consistent with the multi-method approach proposed by federal guidelines for identifying giftedness. Parents, teachers, administrators, and students have reported satisfaction with this type of approach (Renzulli, 1988).

Applications: Teaching Gifted Students

The current definition of giftedness in the NCLB Act states that, to fully develop their potential, students who are gifted need special activities or services not typically provided by schools. However, such students often receive no differentiated instruction for most of the educational activities during the school day, and, at best, teachers make only minor modifications to the curriculum to meet their needs (Archambault et al., 1993; Westberg, Archambault, Dobyns, & Salvin, 1993). Teachers have several approaches available to them in deciding how to meet the needs of students who are gifted.

Advanced instruction in topics or subjects. Teachers can choose to provide students who are gifted with more advanced instruction commensurate with their level of ability. Because a large proportion of the curriculum content in a given school year includes information and skills that gifted students already have mastered, gifted students benefit academically from accelerated instruction (Kulik & Kulik, 2004; Reis & Purcell, 1993; Rogers, 1993). **Acceleration** refers to either moving students quickly through grades (i.e., skipping grades) or providing instruction above grade level in one or two subjects and allowing students to remain with same-age peers for other subjects. Contrary to common beliefs, skipping grades does not appear to be as harmful to social and emotional well-being as once thought (Colangelo & Assouline, 2009; Jones & Southern, 1991; Richardson & Benbow, 1990).

For students who have exceptional achievement in reading or math, teachers can use **cross-grade grouping** to provide accelerated instruction. In this method, gifted students are assigned to classes for reading or math with other students at different grade levels who have similar achievement levels. For example, a gifted second-grade student might go to a fourth-grade class for reading and math and spend the rest of the day with peers, or a gifted ninth-grader might be allowed to take AP calculus with seniors and spend the rest of the day with peers.

Acceleration. Acceleration can be achieved by skipping a grade, which is not as harmful to a student's social and emotional well-being as once thought.

Cross-grade grouping: See page 381.

Enrichment. Because students who are gifted need opportunities for developing critical thinking and problem-solving skills, they benefit greatly from enrichment activities (Johnson, 2000; Miller & Gentry, 2010; Reis & Boeve, 2009). **Enrichment** activities allow them to broaden and deepen their knowledge beyond the regular curriculum. For optimal learning, teachers should create enrichment activities that satisfy the criteria listed in Example 23.1.

Implementing advanced instruction or enrichment. The decision to use acceleration or enrichment activities must take into account the student's interests and learning preferences (independent work, hands-on activities, collaboration, etc.). When teachers uniformly give students more advanced and challenging work without regard for their needs and interests, students quickly learn that if they do their "best work" they are rewarded with more and harder work, perhaps dampening their motivation (Renzulli & Reis, 2004).

When choosing accelerated content or enrichment activities, teachers can use **curriculum compacting,** a useful tool for streamlining the material that needs to be covered with students who are gifted. This method involves evaluating students' existing knowledge of the content in an instructional unit through a pretest and then teaching only material aimed at those instructional objectives not met by the student (Gilman, 2008; Reis & Renzulli, 2004; Renzulli, 1978a). For example, in a high school history class, the student might read the assigned material for a particular unit, demonstrate mastery by taking a test, and then contract with the teacher to do an independent project related to the student's particular interests within the course.

EXAMPLE 23.1   **Criteria for Successful Enrichment Activities**

Enrichment activities should (Renzulli, 1999):	Examples:
Take into account the interests of the student	Allowing a third-grade student who is gifted to pursue an interest in astronomy by researching galaxies and creating a PowerPoint presentation
Be situated within the context of a real problem in order for meaningful learning to occur	Doing a project on alternative fuel sources to help solve global warming
Encourage the use of authentic methods and resources, those used in real life to investigate problems	Using computers, microscopes, library resources, interviewing, experiments
Lead to tangible solutions or products as a result of the activity	Creating models, posters, presentations, plays

Curriculum compacting has several advantages for students who are gifted. It challenges these students by reducing redundancy in the curriculum (Renzulli & Reis, 2004). It also reduces the boredom and lack of motivation that sometimes lead to underachievement in students who are gifted (Baum, Renzulli, & Hebert, 1995). As a result, it leads to greater achievement for such students (Reis & Purcell, 1993; Renzulli, Smith, & Reis, 1982). Curriculum compacting has also been used successfully in many academic subjects with students of above-average ability who show proficiency in certain subjects but have not been identified as gifted (Reis & Purcell, 1993; Renzulli & Reis, 2004).

Can you recall a time when you were bored and thought that certain material was not challenging? Would you have preferred moving on to more challenging material or broadening your knowledge of the current material? Why?

CREATIVITY

Is **creativity** a gift possessed only by certain individuals, or do we all have the potential to be creative? One perspective is that true creativity is indisputable and is limited to geniuses and eminent figures in history such as Newton, Gandhi, and Edison (Big C creativity). An alternate position is that everyone has the potential for creativity, and it is expressed at different levels in everyday life (little c creativity). Different in degree of expression, little c and Big C creativity are at opposite ends of the creativity spectrum (Isbell & Raines, 2007; Lassig, 2009; Root-Bernstein, 2009). To understand the nature of creativity, let's explore the creative process and the characteristics of individuals who are creative.

Creativity appears to happen suddenly and unpredictably in a burst of inspiration, as when we experience a "Eureka" moment (Davis, 2003). However, creativity actually occurs as part of a gradual process interspersed with many smaller insights (Gruber, 1981). Any creative endeavor often first requires irrational and unrestrained fantasy, followed in a second stage by cold logic, analysis, and evaluation (Davis, 2003). The complete fruition of most creative projects or ideas requires four stages (Osburn & Mumford, 2006; Wallas, 1926):

1. *Preparation:* gathering all the facts and existing ideas related to a problem and churning ideas around in one's mind.

2. *Incubation:* the relaxation period in which the problem does not go away but the person can play, sleep, and do things to relax. For example, Archimedes made his "Eureka" discovery while taking a bath, mathematician Henry Poincaré had an insight while boarding a bus, and chemist Frederick von Kekule discovered the molecular structure of benzene while dreaming in bed.

3. *Illumination:* the "ah-ha" moment that hits a person when he or she least expects it.

4. *Verification:* the process whereby the person manifests, evaluates, and verifies his or her new discovery.

Characteristics

Creativity remains difficult to define because the concept is complex and multifaceted, consisting of a variety of traits, skills, and capacities (Runco, 1996).

■ Individuals who are creative display **divergent thinking,** an ability to "think outside the box" by generating multiple ideas or solutions to a problem. They express unusual thoughts, experience the world in novel and original ways, and effect significant changes in culture (Csikszentmihalyi, 1996). Divergent thinking contrasts with the type of thinking typically emphasized in schools—**convergent thinking,** or reaching one conclusion or right answer (Kousoulas, 2010).

■ Creative individuals prefer challenge and complexity, tolerate ambiguity, and take risks (Colangelo & Davis, 2003; Sternberg, 2000). They are not afraid to question assumptions and to redefine problems in new and unconventional

© Randy Glasbergen.
www.glasbergen.com

GLASBERGEN

"Thinking outside of the box is difficult for some people. Keep trying."

Divergent Thinking. Individuals who are creative are able to "think outside the box." Copyright © 2005 Randy Glasbergen. Used with permission.

ways. They also allow themselves to make mistakes and to take risks in creating ideas and products that initially may not be popular. Many major discoveries and inventions, such as the home computer, were considered risky ideas (Sternberg & Lubart, 1995).

■ Creativity also requires domain-relevant knowledge (Amabile, 1983; Sternberg, 2006a). Creative individuals need to have knowledge about the domain in order to create advances in it (Sternberg & Lubart, 1999). For example, a scientist who discovers a gene for obesity needs to have knowledge of genetics.

■ Individuals who are creative exhibit curiosity and intrinsic motivation (Colangelo & Davis, 2003; Sternberg, 2006a). They pursue creative activity out of intense interest and enjoyment. They persist in the face of obstacles, have high *self-efficacy* (a belief that they can perform a task), and are *self-regulated* learners (controlling their own learning) (Colangelo & Davis, 2003; Sternberg & Lubart, 1999).

Self-efficacy and self-regulation: See page 299.

Think of specific situations or classes in which you have used convergent thinking. Now think of specific situations or classes in which you have used divergent thinking.

Identifying Creativity

How can we measure an individual's creativity level? The variety of methods used to measure creativity has increased greatly in the past 25 years. Hundreds of tests, instruments, and rating scales have been developed in recent years (for reviews, see Houtz & Krug, 1995; Hunsaker & Callahan, 1995).

METHODS OF ASSESSING CREATIVITY

When identifying students who might be creative, educators often look for characteristics of creativity using checklists like the one shown in Example 23.2. Creativity researchers often use standardized measures of divergent thinking, such as the Torrance Tests of Creative Thinking (TTCT) (Torrance, 1974). The TTCT consists of relatively simple verbal and figural tasks that involve skills such as divergent thinking and problem solving:

■ asking questions (writing out all questions one can think of based on a drawing of a scene),

■ product improvement (listing all possible ways to change a toy so children would have more fun playing with it),

■ unusual uses (listing interesting and unusual uses for an object), and

■ circles (expanding empty circles into different drawings and giving each drawing a title).

The TTCT can be scored using several criteria. Performance can be scored according to originality, or whether the idea is truly unique. Or it can be evaluated based on the number of ideas produced, called fluency. Individuals also can be evaluated based on their ability to change direction or to think in another way (flexibility) or on their ability to expand an idea to make it more intriguing and complex (elaboration). Paper-and-pencil tests like the TTCT provide a brief, easy-to-administer, objective assessment device. However, these forms of assessment may be undemanding and provide inadequate measures of creativity (Sternberg, 1999a).

Some researchers have focused on the analysis of the products of creativity, rather than the process of creativity itself (Amabile & Hennessey, 1988; Kaufman, Niu, Sexton, & Cole, 2010). Using the **consensual assessment technique,** teachers collect samples of students' creative work and then rate its creativeness (Hennessey, 1994). For example, in a study of elementary school children, teachers evaluated students' creative writing using dimensions such as general creativity, how well they liked the story, novelty, imagination, logic, emotion, grammar, detail, vocabulary, and straightforwardness. Their ratings were very similar, and this method provided an alternative to paper-and-pencil tests of creativity (Amabile & Hennessey, 1988). Application of the consensual technique in the United States, Saudi Arabia, China, and South Korea indicates that this method of rating product creativity is reliable across cultural contexts (Hennessey, Kim, Guomin, & Weiwei, 2008).

Unusual Uses. How many uses can you think of for a paper clip?

Measuring creativity from end results requires that the individuals who are assessing the product be familiar with the domain being assessed (Gardner, 2000). For example, a person who is not considered an expert in art could hardly judge the creativity of a given painting.

EXAMPLE 23.2   **Creativity Checklist**

Schools often use creativity checklists like this one to help identify students who may be eligible for gifted programs.

Checklist for Creativity Characteristics

Student _____   School _____

Teacher _____   Grade _____   Date _____

1 = Never   2 = Very rarely   3 = Rarely   4 = Occasionally   5 = Frequently   6 = Always

This student demonstrates:

Imaginative thinking ability	1	2	3	4	5	6
Sense of humor	1	2	3	4	5	6
Ability to come up with unusual, unique, or clever responses	1	2	3	4	5	6
Adventurous spirit or a willingness to take risks	1	2	3	4	5	6
Ability to generate a large number of ideas or solutions to problems or questions	1	2	3	4	5	6
Tendency to see humor in situations that may not appear to be humorous to others	1	2	3	4	5	6
Ability to adapt, improve, or modify objects or ideas	1	2	3	4	5	6
Intellectual playfulness, a willingness to fantasize and manipulate ideas	1	2	3	4	5	6
Noncomforming attitude, does not fear being different	1	2	3	4	5	6

Subtotals from each column ⬜ ⬜ ⬜ ⬜ ⬜ ⬜

Total the columns together for the grand total.
Place the grand total in this box: ⟶ ☐

DIVERSITY   ETHNICITY, GENDER, AND CREATIVITY

If creativity is highly correlated with traditional measures of intellectual abilities, then we would expect to find the same ethnicity differences on tests of creativity as on the IQ test. However, research conducted over the past 25 years has found few significant differences in creative abilities across ethnicities (Kaufman, 2006). Most studies have relied on the Torrance Tests of Creative Thinking (TTCT) (Torrance, 1966, 1974) or other divergent thinking measures, but findings have been fairly consistent regardless of the type of measurement.

Most studies have found no gender differences in measures of creativity, and those that have found differences have not found any consistent pattern of differences (Baer & Kaufman, 2006; Kogan, 1974). For example, one repeated finding has been that females score higher on verbal creativity and males score higher on figural creativity (DeMoss, Milich, & DeMers, 1993; Fichnova, 2002). Yet the exact opposite results have been found in other studies (e.g., Chan et al., 2001; Dudek, Strobel, & Runco, 1993). When creativity is measured using teacher ratings, the differences in teachers' ratings of creativity are not related to students' gender but to teachers' gender (Kousalas & Mega, 2009).

Creative children seem to diverge from typical gender norms because both sensitivity, which is traditionally a feminine virtue, and independence, which is considered to be a masculine virtue, are essential for creativity (Harrington & Anderson, 1981; Hittner & Daniels, 2002; Norlander, Erixon, & Archer, 2000). However, some children may sacrifice their creativity in order to maintain their masculinity or their femininity (Torrance, 1960, 1962). Teachers who are sensitive to gender issues among their students are in a position to soften the negative impact of sex-role stereotyping (Kim, 2008).

Domain-general and domain-specific creative thinking ability have been found to be distinguishable yet related. Age/grade level, gender, ethnicity, and learning disability status discriminated the two constructs—general and specific creative thinking ability. Different life experiences (schooling and culture) may have stronger impacts on domain-specific creative thinking than on general creative thinking (Hong & Milgram, 2010).

Applications: Promoting Creativity in the Classroom

It was once assumed that creativity was an innate, unteachable characteristic; however, it is now widely accepted that creativity can be learned and enhanced (Do & Gross, 2007; Sternberg, 2006c). The school environment, which often mirrors the expectations of society, plays a crucial role in the development of creativity—or its lack of development (Esquivel, 1995; Simonton, 2000). Too often the creative student's performance in the classroom is based entirely on conformity and convergent thinking, because students typically are asked to find correct answers to problems posed by the teacher (Fleith, 2000; Schirrmacher, 2006). When teachers fail to understand and value creativity, students who are creative may withdraw or refuse to learn (Kim, 2008). Conversely, when creative students are taught and assessed in a way that values their creative abilities, their academic performance improves (Sternberg, Ferrari, Clinkenbeard, & Grigorenko, 1996).

Teacher attitudes. Creativity can be blocked or enhanced by certain emotional or affective conditions (Adams, 2001; Piirto, 2007). Students develop a sense of whether the teacher values or devalues the expression of creative ideas in the classroom by interpreting the teacher's attitudes and behaviors. Teachers who enhance student creativity have an accepting, open interaction style and see students as producers of knowledge rather than simply consumers of knowledge (Lassig, 2009; McWilliam, 2005). To develop creativity, students need to feel safe to share ideas, engage in divergent thinking, take risks, and make mistakes (Fleith, 2000; Sternberg & Williams, 1996). Teachers also can encourage creative expression

Problem solving: See page 245.

by modeling creativity themselves through the types of questions they ask, by implementing problem-solving strategies, and by using innovative practices (Amabile, 1996; Rejskind, 2000).

Teaching strategies. Teachers can promote creativity by helping students discover their interests so they become intrinsically motivated to learn and explore in their area of interest (Sternberg, 2000). Teachers also can help students learn to discriminate between tasks for which convergent thinking is appropriate and sufficient and those that require a more creative engagement (Goswami & Goswami, 1999). Creative thinking can be stimulated in several ways.

- Teachers can ask questions that are divergent, puzzling, or open-ended (requiring explanations or defense of positions) (Gallagher & Gallagher, 1994; Hershkovitz, Peled, & Littler, 2009; Marshall, 1994);

Developing Creativity. Educators can hold science fairs to promote creativity in students.

■ Students can be encouraged to question assumptions and redefine problems, because creative thinking involves knowing what questions to ask and how to ask them rather than learning answers to questions (Csikszentmihalyi, 1990; Sternberg & Williams, 1996);

■ Teachers can also encourage students to generate and evaluate their own ideas, because deciding which projects are worth pursuing is part of being creative (Sternberg, 2000); and

■ Teachers should also give students choices in their learning, such as having them choose their own topics for papers or choose how to solve a problem (Sternberg & Williams, 1996).

Cooperative learning: See page 378.

Teaching activities. Because creative insight does not happen instantaneously, teachers need to allow time for students to practice creative thinking (Sternberg & Williams, 1996). This means not rushing through material but rather designing activities and assignments that encourage students to exercise their creative abilities (Fleith, 2000; Longo, 2010). Cooperative learning, a practice in which students work together in heterogeneous groups and collaborate on a project or an assignment, can stimulate creativity (Sternberg & Williams, 1996). Students learn to see different points of view and to think about the world from more than one perspective. Many widely used curricular programs give students a context for developing creativity (Morrison & Dungan, 1992; Piirto, 2007):

■ Young Authors fairs, where children write their own books;

■ Odyssey of the Mind events, where teams of children compete in categories of problems to make new products;

■ Invention Conventions, where children invent new items;

■ History Day competitions, where children research and role-play historical characters; and

■ Science Fair competitions, where students develop and conduct experiments.

Evaluating learning. Teachers can show that they value creativity by rewarding students for their creativity (Runco & Nemiro, 1994). Teachers cannot show students that they value creativity if they use tests that include only convergent questions (Kousoulas, 2010; Sternberg & Williams, 1996). Rather, they should allow students to take risks and make mistakes without fear of negative evaluation, because recognizing when we have made a mistake and analyzing how to improve is part of creative thinking (Sternberg & Williams, 1996). Teachers should offer opportunities for unevaluated practice, provide constructive criticism, and de-emphasize the evaluation of performance (Rejskind, 2000). They also should praise students who have found ways to overcome obstacles, perhaps in an independent project, even if the final product has flaws (Sternberg & Williams, 1996).

Think of the grade level you intend to teach. Create a philosophy of teaching that specifies particular ways you will use some of the guidelines presented for promoting creativity in your classroom.

Summary

Describe how intelligence might be related to giftedness and creativity. Current theories of intelligence, such as the theory of multiple intelligences and the theory of successful intelligence, propose that giftedness is much more than performing at an exceptionally high level on IQ tests. Because individuals have strengths and weaknesses in different abilities or domains, they can be gifted in a certain ability or domain. Whether creativity is a part of intelligence or separate from it depends on how we define intelligence and creativity. In current theories of intelligence, creativity is a part of intelligence, with a person having a particular strength in creative abilities or perhaps being creative in a certain domain. However, a person may be intelligent and not be particularly creative.

Discuss the characteristics you would look for in identifying students as gifted. Students who are gifted have above-average—and often exceptional—cognitive ability. They learn at a faster pace, master knowledge or skills in a particular domain earlier than their peers, and often are independent learners. They have high levels of task commitment and intrinsic motivation. They are curious, inquisitive, industrious, and self-confident. They seek out challenges, exhibit boredom with easy tasks, and set high personal standards, sometimes to the point of perfectionism. Students who are gifted also may have creative talents.

Explain how factors such as race, socioeconomic status, and gender affect the identification of giftedness. Historically, minorities (particularly African Americans and Native Americans) and students from impoverished backgrounds have performed at a disadvantage on standardized IQ and achievement tests. As a result, these students have been underrepresented in gifted programs. Students with learning disabilities often are overlooked for participation in gifted programs because their giftedness is "masked" by their disabilities. Females also are less likely to be identified for gifted programs, especially in high school.

Discuss the approaches that can be used effectively to meet the needs of gifted students. Students who are gifted benefit from acceleration of content and enrichment activities. Acceleration can be accomplished by more advanced work in the same grade, cross-grade grouping, or skipping a grade. Teachers should identify curriculum content that already has been mastered and teach only material aimed at those objectives not met by the student. Because gifted students need opportunities for challenges, critical thinking, and independent work, enrichment experiences that meet their individual interests should be provided.

Discuss the characteristics you would look for in identifying creative students. Individuals who are creative often tolerate ambiguities, engage in divergent thinking, prefer challenge and complexity, take risks, and are curious and intrinsically motivated. They persist in the face of obstacles, are self-confident, and are self-regulated learners. Students who are creative may generate many ideas for answering a question or solving a problem, may produce work that is unique and original, or may expand on an idea to make it more intriguing and complex.

Discuss the practices you would use to encourage creative expression in the classroom. Teachers can encourage creative expression by establishing a classroom environment in which students feel comfortable taking intellectual risks, sharing ideas, coping with complexities, and making mistakes. Teachers should show that they value creativity, should model creative practices, and should reward students' persistence at tackling challenging tasks. Teachers can promote creativity by asking open-ended questions, encouraging students to ask questions and to generate and evaluate their ideas, giving students choice in learning, and providing opportunities to practice divergent thinking. Teachers should remember to evaluate student learning in a way that does not rely solely on tests and assessment of convergent thinking.

Key Concepts

acceleration   422

consensual assessment technique   425

convergent thinking   424

creative-productive giftedness   421

creativity   424

cross-grade grouping   423

curriculum compacting   423

divergent thinking   424

enrichment   423

giftedness   420

schoolhouse giftedness   421

three-ring conception of giftedness   421

Video Applications

www.mhhe.com/bohlin2e

Video 1: Indication of Gifted Students (1½ minutes)
Carol Goodrich, a teacher for a fourth/fifth grade self-contained gifted class, discusses identification of gifted students.

Case Studies
Reflect and Evaluate

EARLY CHILDHOOD: "Letter *P* Day"

These questions refer to the case study on page 394.

1. Evaluate whether Nolan, Jillian, and Pat could be considered gifted. Use the characteristics of giftedness and the federal definition of giftedness discussed in the module to support your answer.
2. Based on the information given in the case, would you consider Nolan to be gifted according to Renzulli's three-ring conception of giftedness? Why or why not? Would you need additional information about him?
3. If Nolan were assessed and found to be gifted, discuss whether you would choose acceleration or enrichment activities for him. Give specific developmentally appropriate examples of how you would implement your chosen approach.
4. Using the characteristics discussed in the module, explain which student or students you would consider to be creative.
5. Explain how Mrs. Cahill encourages creativity in her classroom.
6. What activities could Mrs. Cahill introduce to encourage divergent thinking?

ELEMENTARY SCHOOL: "Cheetahs, Lions, and Leopards"

These questions refer to the case study on page 396.

1. Using the characteristics of giftedness and the federal definition of giftedness discussed in the module, do you think Marcela or Carl could be considered gifted? Why or why not?
2. Based on the information given in the case, would you consider Marcela or Carl to be gifted according to Renzulli's three-ring conception of giftedness? Why or why not? Would you need additional information?

DIVERSITY
3. Carl appears to come from a lower-socioeconomic family. How might this affect his chances of being identified as gifted, according to the research evidence presented in the module?
4. What strategies could Mrs. Fratelli use to meet the needs of a gifted student in reading and science? How might these strategies be different or similar?
5. Does the science experiment in Mrs. Fratelli's class involve convergent thinking or divergent thinking? Explain.
6. How could Mrs. Fratelli adjust her teaching strategies in reading or science in order to give students greater opportunity to express their creativity in class? Give specific examples.

MIDDLE SCHOOL: "Math Troubles"

These questions refer to the case study on page 398.

1. Do you think Sam may be gifted? Using the characteristics discussed in the module, identify details from the case to support your answer.
2. How should Miss Barton address Sam's academic needs? Give specific examples, and support your answer with research presented in the module.
3. Explain how Miss Barton can use *curriculum compacting* to address the wide diversity of skill levels in her class.

4. Explain how Mr. Sharp's word problem contest represents the four stages of creativity discussed in the module.

5. Based on the information given in the module, what criteria could be used to identify the most creative word problem?

6. In what additional ways can Miss Barton stimulate creativity in her students? Give specific examples.

HIGH SCHOOL: "Noon Supervised Study"

These questions refer to the case study on page 400.

1. Could Jason be gifted? Evaluate this possibility using Renzulli's three-ring conception of giftedness. What additional information would you need to have to help you decide?

2. Evaluate whether Anthony could be gifted according to the federal definition of giftedness. Discuss what factors might cause educators to overlook students like Anthony for eligibility in gifted programs.   *DIVERSITY*

3. According to the research on identification of students for gifted programs, would it surprise you that Sarah chose to be in lower-level math and science classes? Why or why not?   *DIVERSITY*

4. Mr. Hardy suspects that Sarah might be more willing to complete her homework if she found it more challenging and meaningful. If he wants to develop some enrichment activities for Sarah in order to deepen her knowledge of history, what must he take into consideration to ensure that the activities provide the optimal benefit for Sarah?

5. Do you consider Mr. Hardy's reenactment of historical events to be creative? Justify your answer using information discussed in the module.

6. Mr. Hardy notices that his students usually enjoy his lectures; however, they don't seem very enthusiastic about the forms of assessment he uses (tests, papers, and homework). Describe an assessment Mr. Hardy could use in his U.S. history class that would allow students to express their creativity.

Cognitive Disabilities

Outline

Learning Goals

Cognitive Disabilities in Today's Classrooms

- Special Education Referral and Eligibility
- Planning and Placement

1. Describe how cognitive disabilities are identified and served under the Individuals with Disabilities Education Improvement Act.

Intellectual Disabilities

- Identification of Intellectual Disabilities
- Applications: Guidelines for Teachers in the General Education Classroom

2. Discuss the impairments you would expect to see in students with intellectual disabilities and the curricular approaches useful in addressing these deficits.

Specific Learning Disabilities

- Identification of Specific Learning Disabilities
- Reading Disability
- Mathematics Disability

3. Explain how learning disabilities are identified using the IQ-achievement discrepancy and the response-to-intervention approach.
4. Explain the characteristic deficits you would look for in identifying students with reading and mathematics disabilities and how you would approach remediating these deficits.

Summary
Key Concepts
Video Applications
Case Studies: Reflect and Evaluate

COGNITIVE DISABILITIES IN TODAY'S CLASSROOMS

Teachers play a central role in the education of students with disabilities. They not only refer students for special education evaluations but also serve on committees to determine the eligibility of students for special education and implement curricular modifications to address the unique problems of these students in the classroom. Who are the students with disabilities? Let's look to federal special education law for an answer.

The **Individuals with Disabilities Education Improvement Act (IDEIA 2004),** the most recent revision of the first special education law, adopted in 1975, defines a student with a disability as a child:

> *(i) with mental retardation, hearing impairments (including deafness), speech or language impairments, visual impairments (including blindness), serious emotional disturbance (referred to in this title as "emotional disturbance"), orthopedic impairments, autism, traumatic brain injury, other health impairments, or specific learning disabilities; and (ii) who, by reason thereof, needs special education and related services. [PL 108-446, Section 602.3 (A) (i-ii)]*

Students with cognitive disabilities—specific learning disabilities and intellectual disabilities (formerly called mental retardation)—together represent the largest segment of the K–12 special-education population, as the pie chart in Figure 24.1 illustrates (U.S. Department of Education, 2009). In this module, we discuss the learner characteristics and educational needs of students with cognitive disabilities. Other categories of disability shown in the pie chart are topics of other modules.

Speech and language impairments: See page 142.

Emotional, social, and behavioral disabilities: See page 450.

Special Education Referral and Eligibility

IDEIA requires states to provide "a free and appropriate public education" for children between the ages of 3 and 21 with disabilities. An appropriate public education involves curricular methods and modifications designed to provide educational benefit to the student. Specifically, this means special education and related services such as speech and language therapy, counseling, physical therapy, social services, and transportation.

Determining a student's eligibility for special education and related services begins with a referral (see Example 24.1 for a sample referral form), typically by the student's teacher and sometimes by the parent. Parents must consent for a school psychologist to conduct an educational evaluation of the student. Once the evaluation is completed, the next step is to determine whether the student meets eligibility criteria as specified by IDEIA and, if so, to specify a special education plan. Under IDEIA, schools must develop an **Individualized Education Plan (IEP),** a plan outlining curricula, educational modifications, and provision of services intended to enhance or improve the student's academic, social, or behavioral skills. IEPs contain several important features, shown in Example 24.2. A multidisciplinary team called the **IEP team**—consisting of the student's parents (and sometimes the student), teachers, the school psychologist, and other relevant members (e.g., speech-language pathologist, occupational therapist, reading specialist)—determines eligibility and develops and annually revises the IEP.

All those involved in writing the IEP must be informed about the rights of students and their parents:

- Students' records must be kept confidential. According to the **Family Educational Rights and Privacy Act,** only school personnel with a legitimate educational interest may obtain a student's records without written consent from a parent.

- Parents, or an assigned surrogate when parents are unavailable, have a right to examine all relevant records of their child and to participate in every decision related to the identification, evaluation, and placement of their child.

- Parents must be included in the meetings to develop IEPs and may bring an advocate to the meetings.

Figure 24.1. An Overview of Disabilities. This graph shows the percentage of elementary through high school students with various disabilities receiving special education and related services under IDEIA.

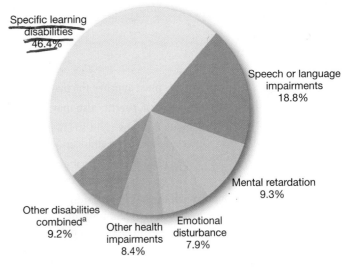

Specific learning disabilities 46.4%

Speech or language impairments 18.8%

Mental retardation 9.3%

Emotional disturbance 7.9%

Other health impairments 8.4%

Other disabilities combined[a] 9.2%

[a]"Other disabilities combined" includes multiple disabilities (2.2 percent), hearing impairments (1.2 percent), orthopedic impairments (1.1 percent), visual impairments (0.4 percent), autism (2.7 percent), deaf-blindness (0.03 percent), traumatic brain injury (0.4 percent), and developmental delay (1.2 percent).

EXAMPLE 24.1 **Sample Referral Form**

Forms such as this one are used to refer students to be evaluated for disabilities under IDEIA.

Referral To Determine Eligibility For Special Education And Related Services

Student: _____ DOB: _____ Age: ____ Grade: _____

Parent/Guardian: _____ Primary Lang: ☐ English ☐ Other: _____

Address: _____ Referred by: _____

_____ Referral date: _____

Telephone: _____ Relationship to child: _____

1. AREA(S) OF CONCERN:

☐ Academic   ☐ Social/emotional   ☐ Gross/fine motor   ☐ Activities of daily living

☐ Health related   ☐ Behavior   ☐ Communication   ☐ Other: (specify) _____

A. Describe specific concerns:

B. Describe alternative strategies attempted and outcomes: (Use additional pages if necessary.)

2. SPECIAL SERVICES HISTORY:

Are you aware of any special services provided for this child now or in the past?   ☐ Yes ☐ No
If Yes, describe the type, location, and provider of the service.

3. OTHER RELEVANT INFORMATION:

4. PARENT NOTIFICATION:

Has the parent/guardian been notified about your concerns regarding this student?   ☐ Yes ☐ No

If Yes, method of notification: _____

Date(s) parent/guardian was notified: _____

- Parents must approve the plans before they go into effect for the first time.
- If they wish, parents also may obtain an independent educational evaluation.
- Parents have the right to challenge or appeal any decision related to identification, evaluation, and placement of their child, and they are protected by due process.
- Parents must receive written notices in their native language before evaluations or changes to their child's placement occur.
- When the IEP meeting involves decisions related to transition (i.e., secondary and post-secondary goals), the student must be invited to attend the meetings, because planning for the student's future must take into account his or her preferences and interests.
- School districts are not required to assess students for determining eligibility for services in post-school environments, but they are required to facilitate students' transition from school to postsecondary education or employment (Madaus & Shaw, 2006).

Planning and Placement

IDEIA ensures a free and appropriate education by requiring students with disabilities to be placed in the general education classroom "to the maximum extent appropriate," known as the **least restrictive**

EXAMPLE 24.2   Information Contained in an IEP

1. The student's present levels of academic achievement and functional performance.

2. Measurable annual goals and short-term instructional objectives.

3. An explanation of how the student's progress toward annual goals will be measured and when progress will be reported to parents.

4. Any appropriate accommodations for test taking on statewide and district-wide assessments, especially those required by the No Child Left Behind Act. In cases where educators determine that the student will take an alternative assessment, the IEP needs to specify why this assessment was selected and why it is appropriate for the student.

5. The types of special education and related services provided to the student and how long the services will be needed. The IEP also needs to specify how much of the student's education will not be in the general education classroom.

6. Measurable postsecondary goals related to education, training, or employment for students age 14 and older.

7. A statement of transition services needed to reach goals involving independent living, continuing education, or employment after high school for students age 16 (or younger, if appropriate).

environment (LRE). Special classes, separate schools, or other pull-out programs should be used only when the nature or severity of the disability prevents the student from functioning in the general education classroom with supplementary aids or services. LRE should not be confused with *mainstreaming* and *inclusion*, LRE approaches that have evolved out of different interpretations of the law over the past three decades.

- In **mainstreaming,** students with special needs are placed with nondisabled peers when appropriate. For example, students may spend most of their day in a special education classroom and be integrated with their peers for subjects such as music, art, and social studies and for activities such as lunch, recess, library, and field trips.

- **Inclusion,** a more recent and popular approach, refers to integrating all students within the general education classroom, even those with severe disabilities (with the assistance of paraprofessionals), for most or all of the school day. Experts continue to debate whether inclusion is the best environment for every student (Benner, 1998; Zigler, Hodapp, & Edison, 1990).

Only about 14% of students with intellectual disabilities spend most of the day in general education classes, while more than half of students with specific learning disabilities in elementary through high school spend most of the school day in the general education classroom (U.S. Department of Education, 2009). In any case, the decision to place students with disabilities in their LRE must be made on a case-by-case basis and in accordance with the intent of the law.

Did you ever have an IEP during your years of education? Did you know someone, such as a friend or relative, who had an IEP? Can you remember what services or accommodations were offered to you or to this individual?

INTELLECTUAL DISABILITIES

Identification of Intellectual Disabilities

IDEIA serves approximately 9% of students ages 6 to 21 for intellectual disabilities (U.S. Department of Education, 2009), a relatively new term that replaced the term *mental retardation*. The American Association on Intellectual and Developmental Disabilities (AAIDD) defines **intellectual disability** as "a disability characterized by significant limitations both in intellectual functioning and in adaptive behavior as expressed in conceptual, social, and practical adaptive skills. This disability originates before age 18" (Luckasson et al., 2002, p. 1; Schalock et al., 2009). Determining whether a student has an intellectual disability involves evaluating whether the student exhibits significant impairment on measures of cognitive ability and adaptive behavior.

IQ tests: See page 406.

Standard deviation: See page 407.

Psychologists assess impairments in cognitive ability using individually administered IQ tests such as the Wechsler Intelligence Scale for Children-IV (Wechsler, 2003) or the Stanford-Binet Intelligence Scales-V (Roid, 2003), which measure a range of cognitive skills: vocabulary, general knowledge, quantitative skills, short-term memory, sequencing ability, and nonverbal reasoning. On such tests, the typical criterion for identifying an intellectual disability is an IQ score of 70 or lower, which is 2 standard deviations below the average IQ score. This means that a student is performing significantly below his or her age group (only 2% to 3% of individuals in the population obtain scores of 70 or below).

It is important not only to assess students' cognitive functioning with IQ tests, but also to assess their everyday functioning, or adaptive behavior. *Adaptive behavior*—acting independently and in a socially responsible manner—includes conceptual, social, and practical skills (Luckasson et al., 2002):

- *Conceptual skills* refer to cognitive skills that are necessary to function in society, such as reading, writing, understanding currency, and communication skills. Communication skills include following instructions, listening skills, asking questions, and providing information about oneself.

- *Social skills* include using good manners, showing responsibility, following rules and societal laws, demonstrating interpersonal skills, and being neither naive nor gullible.

- *Practical skills* comprise daily living skills and work skills, such as dressing, bathing, grooming, cooking, cleaning, shopping, managing money, occupational skills, and using public transportation.

To evaluate adaptive behavior, psychologists use standardized instruments that assess the three dimensions of adaptive behavior outlined above. The Vineland Adaptive Behavior Scales (Sparrow, Balla, & Cicchetti, 1984), a popular instrument for this purpose, uses parent and teacher interviews to gather information about the individual's typical behaviors in areas such as communication, daily living skills, socialization, and motor skills. For example, the interviewer might ask whether a kindergartner brushes his teeth every day (daily living) and whether he can hold a pencil (motor skills).

A deficit in adaptive behavior may be identified by a significant impairment in one of the three dimensions or by a low overall score. The specific criterion for deficiency is:

- a score that is 2 standard deviations below average on a standardized instrument of adaptive behavior in one of the three dimensions (conceptual, social, or practical), or

- an overall score on the instrument that is 2 standard deviations below the average, which indicates that the individual is functioning substantially below the norm.

DIVERSITY

Diagnosis of a disability should involve multiple modes of assessment and should include standardized instruments that are culturally fair to students from ethnically diverse or lower socioeconomic backgrounds. Since the 1960s, ethnic minorities—in particular African-American and Native-American students—have been disproportionately identified as having disabilities and placed in special education classes in elementary through high school (Artiles, Trent, & Palmer, 2004; Blanchett, 2006; Reid & Knight, 2006).

- African-American students are more likely to receive services for an intellectual disability than are students from all other ethnic groups combined (Hosp & Reschly, 2004; U.S. Department of Education, 2009).

- Students from impoverished backgrounds also are more likely to receive special education services for cognitive or behavioral disabilities (Caspi, Taylor, Moffitt, & Plomin, 2000; Evans & English, 2002; U.S. Department of Education, 2009).

The effects of environment on intelligence: See page 408.

We should be cautious *not* to interpret these data to mean that race, ethnicity, or SES is associated with a greater risk for cognitive disabilities. Many environmental factors contribute to a child's intellectual development. For example, children from lower-SES families may have lower IQs because they lack the resources that middle- and upper-SES families provide to promote cognitive development, such as books, computers, and high-quality preschool. Also, students from lower-SES and culturally diverse backgrounds historically have not performed as well as White, middle-class students on IQ and other tests of cognitive ability due to discrimination and bias.

Applications: Guidelines for Teachers in the General Education Classroom

When deciding how to teach students with intellectual disabilities in the general education classroom, educators must first remember that students with and without disabilities are more alike than they are different (Westwood, 2003). For example, two 10-year-old boys, one with an intellectual disability and one without, may both like sports, enjoy gym and art, and prefer to work in groups rather than independently. With this in mind, teachers should start by asking the following questions (Ashman, 1998):

- In which setting will the student learn most successfully?
- What skills need to be taught?
- What are the most effective approaches to teaching those skills?

Teachers can use several guiding principles to maximize learning opportunities for students with intellectual disabilities.

Teach using direct instruction. Direct instruction is a structured instructional method proposed by Barak Rosenshine that involves teaching in small steps, providing ample opportunities for guided and independent practice, giving explicit feedback, and reteaching when necessary (Rosenshine, 1979, 1988; Rosenshine & Stevens, 1986). This method is effective when used with students with disabilities, especially for teaching basic skills (Kroesbergen & Van Luit, 2005; Turnbull, Turnbull, Shank, Smith, & Leal, 2002).

Direct instruction: See page 365.

Focus on overlearning, or practicing a skill past the point of mastery. Many students with intellectual disabilities have difficulty storing information in long-term memory, possibly due to attentional problems or lack of effective memorization strategies (Hallahan & Kauffman, 2000; Westwood, 2003). These students need extensive repetition and practice of skills, which can help them easily and automatically retrieve information from long-term memory (Westwood, 2003).

Overlearning: See page 231.

Encourage hands-on learning. This method is effective for teaching all types of skills and subjects because students with intellectual disabilities typically have difficulty with abstract thinking and need concrete examples (Reddy, Ramar, & Kusama, 2000). Learning math should include not only traditional methods such as textbooks and worksheets, but also real-life situations such as shopping, measuring, cooking, and so on. Similarly, reading skills should be practiced in a variety of realistic contexts, such as reading instructions for a game, recipes, brochures, street signs, and newspapers.

Use cooperative learning when applicable. Cooperative learning requires heterogeneous (mixed) groups of students to work together to achieve a common goal. Cooperative learning can be used when small-group instruction is appropriate (Farlow, 1995). Teachers should adjust the curriculum content, however, to reflect the different cognitive needs and educational objectives of students with disabilities and nondisabled students. For instance, in a middle school social studies activity, nondisabled students might be learning content related to geography and history while students with disabilities are learning vocabulary or social skills. Cooperative learning can raise the self-esteem of students with disabilities and promote positive peer relationships between students with disabilities and nondisabled students (Acton & Zabartany, 1988; Johnson & Johnson, 2009; Salend & Sonnenschein, 1989).

Cooperative learning: See page 378.

Transfer: See page 226.

Foster generalization. Students with intellectual disabilities have difficulty generalizing what they have learned, that is, transferring newly acquired information to new contexts (Meese, 2001; Taylor, Sternberg, & Richards, 1995). Therefore, teachers need to develop ways to encourage and facilitate generalization of knowledge and skills. Often, the teacher needs only to remind the student that he or she has successfully performed the skill in the past. For example, when a student is figuring out how much money to give the clerk at the school store, the teacher may need to remind her that she has practiced counting money in the classroom. Other examples of fostering generalization include (Mastropieri & Scruggs, 1984; Westwood, 2003):

- providing immediate feedback following performance of the skill;
- practicing the skill several times (which also would encourage overlearning);
- providing reinforcement for demonstrating the skill (e.g., privileges, free time, tokens);

Hands-on Learning. Hands-on learning is effective for teaching students with intellectual disabilities.

reteaching the same skill in different contexts, gradually increasing the range of contexts in which to practice the newly acquired information; and

requiring students to decide whether a particular skill or strategy could be used to solve a new problem.

Keep in mind that transfer is difficult for *all* learners when they are acquiring new information and that the above approaches are useful for encouraging generalization in *all* students.

Think about whether you will be teaching in early childhood or elementary school, or whether you plan to teach a certain subject in middle school or high school. How would you use these guidelines in your classroom?

SPECIFIC LEARNING DISABILITIES

Identification of Specific Learning Disabilities

Specific learning disabilities (LD) represent the largest special-educational category under IDEIA (Reid & Knight, 2006; U.S. Department of Education, 2009). When first introduced in 1963, LD referred to students who had learning difficulties but were not eligible for special services under already existing categories such as mental retardation (MacMillan & Siperstein, 2002). Today, excluding mental retardation remains a component of the definition of LD in IDEIA:

> *The term "specific learning disability" means a disorder in one or more of the basic psychological processes involved in understanding or in using language, spoken or written, which may manifest itself in imperfect ability to listen, think, speak, read, write, spell or do mathematical calculations. Such term includes such conditions as perceptual disabilities, brain injury, minimal brain dysfunction, dyslexia, and developmental aphasia. Such term does not include a learning problem that is primarily the result of visual, hearing, or motor disabilities, of mental retardation, of emotional disturbance, or of environmental, cultural, or economic disadvantage. [PL 108-446, Section 602.30 (A-C)]*

For the past several decades, the primary method for determining special education eligibility for a learning disability has been the **IQ-achievement discrepancy.** This method is based on the notion that students with LD have a learning problem that is *not* due to low intelligence (the exclusion of mental retardation as a causal factor in LD in the definition). Students would be identified as learning disabled if their achievement in one or more academic areas was significantly below what would be expected from their IQ. Individually administered achievement tests, typically given by a psychologist, are used for this purpose.

Let's consider an example of the IQ-achievement discrepancy. A 9-year-old boy has a Full-Scale IQ of 105 on the WISC-IV, which is an average score on the IQ test overall. However, the Kaufman Test of Educational Achievement II (KTEA-II) shows that he has standard scores of 70 on the spelling subtest and 68 on the total reading composite. Standard scores below 70 are 2 standard deviations below average, meaning that the boy is far below average for his age group on these skills. In contrast, on the calculations and applied problems subtests of the KTEA-II, the boy exhibits average performance, as shown by standard scores of 92 and 93 (85 to 115 being the average range). Therefore, the 9-year-old boy's reading and spelling performance are significantly below what we would expect from his average IQ, while his mathematics scores are average, in line with his IQ score. The boy probably would be considered eligible for special education services in reading and spelling.

Since the adoption of the IQ-achievement discrepancy, researchers have accumulated evidence challenging the adequacy of this method on theoretical, statistical, and practical grounds (Fletcher, Lyon, Fuchs, & Barnes, 2007; Stanovich, 1991a, 1991b). Several practical problems are important to keep in mind.

- There is wide variation among states and even among districts within a state in how the IQ-achievement discrepancy is implemented (Mercer, Jordan, Allsopp, & Mercer, 1996; Vaughn, Linan-Thompson, & Hickman, 2003). For example, states differ as to the amount of discrepancy between a student's IQ and achievement performance required for a diagnosis of LD (Reschly & Hosp, 2004).

- Finding a discrepancy between IQ and achievement scores does not provide instructionally useful information to help educators develop remedial plans (Aaron, Joshi, Gooden, & Bentum, 2008;

Standard deviation: See page 407.

Semrud-Clikeman, 2005). Collection of additional data (e.g., other tests, student work samples, etc.) is needed to determine students' strengths and weaknesses.

■ Using this approach, minority students tend to be placed in special education for LD at a higher rate than Caucasian students (Blanchett, 2006; U.S. Department of Education, 2009). The disproportionate representation may be due to a variety of factors, including standardized test bias and discrimination.

DIVERSITY

■ IQ-achievement discrepancy is considered by many to be a "wait to fail approach" in which students continue to struggle academically until the discrepancy becomes significant enough to result in eligibility (Bradley, Danielson, & Doolittle, 2005; Fuchs & Fuchs, 2006; Hale, Wycoff, & Fiorello, 2011).

The limitations of the IQ-achievement discrepancy method have led to recent and important revisions. Under IDEIA 2004, LD identification does *not* require use of an IQ-achievement discrepancy and now includes an additional method called **response-to-intervention (RTI).** In most states, educators can choose the identification method used for determining special education eligibility using a multidisciplinary report shown in Example 24.3.

Using RTI, educators determine whether a student responds to "scientific, research-based intervention." A major goal of RTI is to reduce the number of referrals for special education in pre-K through grade 12 by identifying and correcting academic problems at an early stage (Carreker & Joshi, 2010; Fuchs, Mock, Morgan, & Young, 2003). RTI also attempts to reduce the number of students who are

EXAMPLE 24.3   **Form for Determining Special Education Eligibility**

Multidisciplinary Evaluation Report
For Students Suspected Of Having A Learning Disability

Student: _____ Date of birth: _____ Grade: _____

School: _____ Date of report: _____

CRITERIA	CRITERIA MET	
Check the criteria used to determine eligibility for students suspected of having a specific learning disability.	YES	NO
☐ To determine eligibility for students suspected of having a specific learning disability, the District is utilizing an identification process that determines if the child responds to scientific, research based intervention as a part of the evaluation procedures. (H.R. 1350 Section 614(b)(6)(B)) Documentation is attached to the Multidisciplinary Evaluation Report.		
☐ To determine eligibility for students suspected of having a specific learning disability, the District is utilizing a severe discrepancy model and applying the criteria listed below.		
1. Does a severe discrepancy exist between ability and achievement? If yes, indicate which area(s) below: *[Note: at least one area must be identified]* ☐ listening comprehension ☐ reading comprehension ☐ basic reading skills ☐ oral expression ☐ written expression ☐ mathematics calculation ☐ mathematics reasoning		
2. Has a disorder in one of the basic psychological processes in understanding or in using spoken or written language been identified?		

3. (a) Severe discrepancy is *primarily* due to:	YES	NO	
a. Lack of instruction in reading and math ▲ *(Based on Math and Reading Worksheets)*			
b. Visual, hearing or motor impairments			
c. Mental retardation			*Note: If all of the (✔)s are in the NO column, then the student meets the criteria for #3.*
d. Emotional disturbance			
e. Environmental, cultural or economic disadvantage			
f. Limited English proficiency			
g. Motivation			
h. Situational trauma			
3. (b) Has **NO** been (✔)'d for **all** items in #3 above (a-h)?			
4. Are special education and related services required to correct the severe discrepancy identified in #1?			

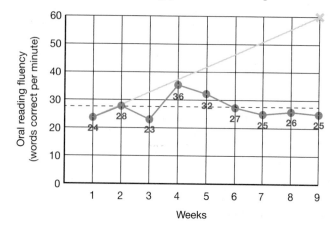

Figure 24.2. A Three-Tiered Model of RTI

High-stakes testing: See page 552.

incorrectly identified as having an LD. For example, students may have reading difficulties that are not due to an actual reading disability involving specific cognitive deficits (as we'll discuss next) but instead are the result of:

- socioeconomic disadvantage (i.e., they have poor readiness skills due to lack of resources, non-English-speaking parents, and so on), or
- lack of appropriate instruction (i.e., they were not taught necessary reading or math skills).

RTI involves screening and monitoring of progress on academic skills for *all* students within a district, and providing increasingly intensive interventions to students who perform below grade-level expectations, as measured by benchmarks (predetermined cut-scores on standardized tests) or adequate yearly progress on high-stakes testing (Bradley et al., 2005; National Research Center on Learning Disabilities, 2007). As of 2007, 37 states have adopted or are developing an RTI model, with some states such as Connecticut mandating the use of *only* RTI for determining special education eligibility (Berkeley, Bender, Peaster, & Saunders, 2009). While there is no single RTI model mandated by IDEIA, the typical model has three tiers, as shown in Figure 24.2:

Tier 1. The preventive tier, which involves whole-class, general education instruction and screening of all students, should be effective for about 80% of students (Bender & Shores, 2007; Cates, Blum, & Swerdlik, 2011).

Tier 2. The secondary intervention tier involves small group, short-term, and intensive interventions, and targets about 15% of students who were not making adequate progress in Tier 1 (Fuchs & Fuchs, 2007).

Tier 3. The tertiary intervention tier is the most intensive intervention (typically one-on-one), which is needed by about 5% of students.

The type of intervention (oral reading fluency, comprehension, math computations) and how often each week students receive the intervention will vary depending on students' needs. An intervention should last about 10 to 15 weeks, during which progress is monitored frequently (Cates et al., 2011).

To accurately identify a student as needing more intensive and more frequent instruction (movement to Tier 2 or Tier 3), a **dual discrepancy method** should be used (Cates et al., 2011). The student's academic performance should be (1) below average (i.e., discrepant) compared with grade-level expectations *and* (2) the student should show a slow rate of improvement toward benchmarks such that the gap widens over time between the student's performance and the benchmark (Cates et al., 2011). Consider Figure 24.3, showing a student's oral reading fluency (number of words correctly read per minute). On the screening measure, the student correctly identified 24 words per minute compared with the benchmark of 60 correctly identified words per minute (shown by the X in the figure), indicating that the student is below grade-level expectations. The student's performance throughout the intervention shows very little progress toward the benchmark, indicating a slow rate of learning that is not sufficient to close the gap between current performance and grade-level expectations. A student can be referred for special education evaluation at any point in the RTI process (VanDer-Heyden & Burns, 2010). However, in most states the process begins after Tier 3 (Berkeley et al., 2009).

Like the IQ-achievement discrepancy, RTI is not without its problems. A major practical problem is the wide variation among states in aspects of implementation such as the following (Berkeley et al., 2009):

- frequency of the Tier 2 and Tier 3 interventions and the size of the instructional groups in each tier;
- requirements for monitoring treatment fidelity (keeping track of how well the teachers or teacher aides are carrying out particular lessons according to the guidelines provided in curriculum manuals, software, or research literature);

Figure 24.3. Oral Reading Fluency Performance of a Student Who Is Not Responding to Intervention

- frequency of progress monitoring; and
- timetable for when the process of determining special education eligibility begins.

RTI may result in as much or greater variation in the number of children identified as having LD than the variation produced by the IQ-achievement discrepancy (Fuchs & Deshler, 2007).

Another practical problem concerns the reliability and validity of the RTI approach. Classifying students as responding or not responding to an intervention based on progress monitoring, without the use of any additional information, may not be a reliable indicator of the presence of LD (Fletcher, Barth, & Stuebing, 2011). Schools measure "failure to respond" using different assessments for screening and progress monitoring and different criteria (cut-points for determining benchmarks and ways to measure progress), leading to inconsistent results (Barth et al., 2008). A student may be considered non-responsive to intervention using one set of tests and criteria and responsive using a different set.

Also, RTI alone also may not be a valid method for determining LD. This method only tells us that a student did not respond to educators' best attempts at intervention, but we do not know why the student failed to respond (Hale, Wycoff, & Fiorello, 2011). This approach would identify both students who are slow learners and students with cognitive deficits indicative of LD (Kavale, 2005). This method also, by itself, cannot differentiate specific learning disabilities from intellectual disabilities and emotional/behavioral disorders (Mastropieri & Scruggs, 2005).

IDEIA mandates that no single test or procedure be used as the sole criterion for determining whether a student has a disability, and that all areas of suspected disability be assessed. Best practices should include assessment of the cognitive processes underlying academic skills (Hale et al., 2011). Most experts agree that a combination of RTI and IQ-achievement discrepancy approaches provides the most well-rounded and accurate evaluation for special education eligibility (Carreker & Joshi, 2010; Feifer, 2008; Kavale et al., 2008).

As you read further about reading and mathematics disabilities, in particular the remediation of these disabilities, keep in mind that remediation is a primary focus of IEPs at the elementary school level and less so at the middle and high school levels. Interventions for RTI are also less common in secondary education (Berkeley et al., 2009). Secondary students with LDs typically do not receive remedial services but instead are offered accommodations to the curriculum in the general education classroom (U.S. Department of Education, 2009). Common examples of accommodations are note takers, books on tape, extended time to complete assignments, extended time on tests, and assistive technology.

Reading Disability

Reading problems often are categorized in research as either developmental delays or cognitive deficits. A **developmental delay** is evident when a student's performance is poorer than that of same-age peers but similar to younger students, indicating that the student acquires cognitive skills in the same way as other students but at a slower rate. This suggests that the student will catch up given proper intervention. A **deficit,** in contrast, indicates a "breakdown" in a specific domain that does not affect a student's general cognitive functioning. Performance in the domain is poorer than the performance of both same-age peers and younger students, indicating that the student acquires skills in a *qualitatively different* way from other students. This suggests that the deficit may not be easily remediated with conventional methods of instruction (Stanovich, 1993).

CHARACTERISTICS

Individuals with a reading disability (RD) have a deficit in phonological processing that inhibits their ability to learn to recognize and decode words (Fletcher et al., 1994; Lyon, 1995; Stanovich & Siegel, 1994). **Decoding** is a strategy of applying sounds to printed letters, or sounding out words. This is necessary for beginning readers to acquire skill in **word recognition,** or identifying individual words in text. Skilled readers have developed word recognition and decoding skills to the point of *automaticity,* which means they can perform the skill very quickly and with few cognitive resources such as attention and strategies (Perfetti, 1992; Stanovich, 1990). Automaticity allows a reader to use cognitive resources for understanding what is being read, as you are doing while you read this paragraph. Conversely, difficulties in word recognition and decoding lead to difficulties in reading comprehension (Perfetti, 1985; Perfetti & Lesgold, 1977).

Automaticity: See page 193.

Compared to normally achieving students, students with RD from elementary through college level lack automaticity of word recognition and decoding (Cisero, Royer, Marchant, & Jackson, 1997; Compton & Carlisle, 1994). They have difficulty holding a phonological representation of a word (e.g., the sounds of letters in a printed word and the name of the word) in working memory in order to decode it during reading. As a result, many words do not become stored in long-term memory as representations that then can be automatically retrieved—even words that students with RD have encountered frequently. Consequently, individuals with RD experience a lack of automatic word recognition and decoding that results in a breakdown in reading comprehension.

Students with RD face difficulties that are distinctly different from those faced by *poor readers.* Students with RD perform more poorly than same-age peers *and* younger children on word recognition and decoding, indicating a *deficit* in reading. In contrast, the performance of poor readers on reading tasks is worse than that of same-age peers but similar to that of younger children, indicating a *developmental delay* (Stanovich, 1988, 1993; Stanovich & Siegel, 1994). While the reading problems of students with an RD are due primarily to phonological processing deficits, the reading problems of poor readers may be due to many factors: difficulty with phonological processing (like students with RD) as well as below-average oral language comprehension, poor strategy use, and lower overall IQ (Stanovich, 1988, 1993).

Teachers and school psychologists can use information about the characteristic deficits of students with RD to choose appropriate assessments for determining whether a student is eligible to receive special education services for a reading disability.

- For children in kindergarten and first grade, an evaluation should include measures of phonological awareness, letter and word recognition, and rapid naming (quickly retrieving labels for objects, letters, colors, and numbers from long-term memory).

- For children in elementary and secondary education, an evaluation should consist of measures of word recognition, decoding, vocabulary, and reading comprehension. Timed measures of word recognition and decoding are particularly important because they provide an indication of automaticity. Timed measures are included in some standardized tests, such as the KTEA-II, the Wechsler Individual Achievement Test-II (The Psychological Corporation, 2001), and the Test of Word Reading Efficiency (Torgesen, Wagner, & Rashotte, 1999).

APPLICATIONS: REMEDIATING READING DISABILITY

Research indicates that extensive and systematic instruction in phonics can help elementary school students with RD acquire word identification and decoding skills (Foorman, Francis, Winikates, Schatschneider, & Fletcher, 1997; Torgesen et al., 1997, 1999, 2001, 2010). **Systematic phonics instruction** focuses on teaching children to recognize and manipulate phonemes—representations of sounds such as /b/ for the initial sound in the word *bat*—and to apply that knowledge to letter-sound correspondences and decoding. As a natural result of many literacy experiences, such as singing songs, reciting nursery rhymes, and reading, nondisabled children develop the **alphabetic principle,** an awareness that letters are represented by sounds. Children with RD fail to acquire the alphabetic principle and have difficulty learning to identify and decode words. Thus, for students with RD, instruction in word recognition and decoding must begin by making them explicitly aware of the phonological structure of their language and of how it maps onto printed letters.

Phonemes: See page 137.

Several caveats must be considered before research findings on RD can be translated into educational practice:

1. Even though research suggests that systematic instruction in phonics may be beneficial for students with RD, this does not mean that the same approach leads to similar levels of improvement for each student. In one study, 24% of children remained below average in their skills after instruction ended (Torgesen et al., 1997). In another study, about one-third to one-half of students continued to perform below average on word recognition and decoding after extensive training (Torgesen et al., 2001).

2. In research studies, children receive an extensive amount of instruction. For example, research interventions ranged from 67 hours of individual instruction to over 80 hours of small-group or individual instruction (e.g., Torgesen et al., 1999, 2001, 2010). Outside of research studies, students are unlikely to receive such a considerable amount of remedial instruction. Many schools do not have the financial and personnel resources to provide sufficient time and intensity of interventions during the school day to accelerate the reading development of students with RD so that they achieve average-level skills (Torgesen et al., 2001, 2010).

3. Teachers should not expect mastery of letter-sound correspondences and phonemic skills to transfer automatically to improved word recognition and decoding. A few research studies suggest that explicit training of phonemic awareness, along with instruction in identifying and decoding words,

did not result in long-term word recognition benefits (Olson, Wise, Ring, & Johnson, 1997; Torgesen et al., 1997). Word recognition and decoding skills must be practiced to the point of overlearning so that automaticity of word identification can support higher-level reading processes such as comprehension (Cisero et al., 1997; Royer, 1997; Royer & Sinatra, 1994). Some research suggests the possibility that **automaticity training** of word recognition can improve the reading skills of students with RD (Royer, 1997).

4. Teachers must remember to offer opportunities for students to read rich, connected text in addition to practicing phonics (Stahl, 1998; Torgesen, 2000). Research indicates that providing simple reading material to students with RD may send the wrong message—that teachers think they are incapable of reading more challenging material and that reading is merely decoding. Also, students may expect to fail when they are given material that they have already encountered without success (Stahl, 1998). Using novel instructional materials helps circumvent this problem and motivates students by providing them with fun and interesting activities.

Additional strategies can be used to help older students who continue to struggle with basic reading skills or comprehension. Interventions that focus on word analysis, such as breaking down multisyllabic words, can be effective for improving reading achievement (Curtis, 2004; Wexler, Edmonds, & Vaughn, 2007). Vocabulary instruction can be used in content courses such as science or social studies. The most effective ways to teach content area vocabulary are to give simple definitions, provide examples and nonexamples, and use semantic maps (Kim, Vaughn, Wanzek, & Wei, 2004). Teachers can improve students' reading comprehension by having them preview headings or key concepts and make predictions to activate their prior knowledge before reading, and by having them revisit their predictions to affirm or refute them after reading (Roberts, Torgesen, Boardman, & Scammacca, 2007; Klingner, Vaughn, & Boardman, 2007). Encouraging students to summarize and to make connections to prior knowledge, other subjects, or to real-life applications also enhances reading comprehension. Reciprocal teaching, a method for teaching metacognitive strategies necessary for skilled reading comprehension (questioning about the main idea, clarifying, summarizing, and predicting), can be used for this purpose.

Reciprocal teaching: See page 216.

Mathematics Disability

Our understanding of mathematics disability (MD) currently is limited to arithmetic skills in elementary school (Geary, 2004). However, when working with students in middle school and high school, a teacher should know the cognitive origin of the disability in order to better plan appropriate curricula and accommodations for students.

CHARACTERISTICS

To understand the nature of MD, let's examine the taxonomy of MD subtypes proposed by researcher David Geary (1993; Geary & Hoard, 2005):

1. Semantic memory,

2. Procedural, and

3. Visuospatial.

The **semantic memory subtype** of MD is characterized by a persistent and stable deficit in the automatic retrieval of math facts from long-term memory (Chong & Siegel, 2008; Jordan, Hanich, & Kaplan, 2003). In the arithmetic problem $3 + 2 = 5$, individuals with MD have difficulty holding number-words (e.g., the words *three* and *two*) in working memory long enough for a memory representation of the problem ($3 + 2$) and the answer ($= 5$) to be associated in long-term memory. Hence, many arithmetic facts do not become stored in long-term memory for automatic retrieval, even after extensive drilling (Geary, 1993, 2004). Compared to students without disabilities, students with the semantic memory subtype of MD (Chan & Dally, 2001; Geary, 2004):

■ retrieve fewer arithmetic facts from long-term memory,

■ commit many more errors when using fact-retrieval as a strategy,

■ overuse counting strategies (e.g., finger counting and verbal counting) rather than using retrieval, and

■ exhibit variability in rates of retrieval of math facts (some slower, some faster), especially compared with younger, normally achieving students.

As with poor readers, the **procedural subtype** of MD is characterized as a developmental delay because students' performance often is similar to that of younger, normally achieving children. Students with a procedural subtype often use developmentally immature procedures for solving arithmetic problems. For example, they tend to use the *counting all* strategy when solving a problem, which means that they begin counting from 1. For example, to solve 3 + 4, they would say "1, 2, 3, 4, 5, 6, 7" to get the answer 7. In contrast, normally achieving children will shift to the *counting on* strategy sometime between first and second grade (Jordan & Montani, 1997; Ostad, 1998). In this strategy, the student identifies the larger addend (4) and counts on from there, "5, 6, 7," to get the answer. Students with the procedural subtype also make frequent errors when doing the following tasks (Geary, 1990; Hanich, Jordan, Kaplan, & Dick, 2001; Russell & Ginsburg, 1984):

- counting,

- executing mathematical procedures, and

- calculating multistep problems that would be common in the middle elementary grades, such as

$$\begin{array}{r} 38 \\ \times\ 13 \\ \hline 494 \end{array}$$

The **visuospatial subtype**—the most recently identified of the three types and not widely investigated—involves difficulties with the spatial representation of numerical information, such as omitting numbers, rotating numbers, misreading operation signs (+, –, ×, and so on), misaligning digits in multicolumn problems, and having difficulty using place value and decimals. Visuospatial difficulties would also affect skills in mathematical areas common to middle school and high school, such as geometry and complex word problems (Dehaene, Spelke, Pinel, Stanescu, & Tsivkin, 1999; Geary, 1996).

Diagnostic evaluations by school psychologists typically include individually administered standardized achievement tests that measure a range of skills, from factual knowledge about math to mathematical calculation (from elementary through secondary level) and problem solving. School psychologists should choose standardized tests that assess mathematical computations in a timed format to assess automaticity of fact retrieval.

In addition, school psychologists or classroom teachers can conduct informal assessments of mathematical competence. An informal assessment requires working one-on-one with students and interviewing them about their knowledge and how they arrived at answers to problems.

- For students from kindergarten through second grade, teachers can give students a variety of arithmetic problems in order to determine what types of counting strategies children are using (Jordan, 1995).

- For students in the upper elementary grades, teachers can conduct an error analysis (Fleischner, 1994). For example, mathematical errors sometimes involve simple misalignment of numbers while writing down partial answers. Students also may make errors due to carrying or borrowing—often called procedural bugs (Brown & Burton, 1978). Consider the following problems, indicating that the student lacks knowledge of carrying and does not understand place value.

$$\begin{array}{r} 93 \\ +\ 57 \\ \hline 1410 \end{array} \qquad \begin{array}{r} 46 \\ +\ 39 \\ \hline 715 \end{array}$$

APPLICATIONS: REMEDIATING MATH DISABILITY

Depending on the nature of the disability, interventions may focus on counting principles, counting strategies, or encouraging automatic fact retrieval. Teachers can use a variety of games to teach counting principles, such as order irrelevance (objects can be counted in any order), abstraction (items of any kind can be counted together), and stable order (counting occurs in a fixed order, always "1, 2, 3 . . .") (Garnett, 1992; Geary, 1994).

For students who use immature counting strategies, teachers need to focus on ways to help them shift to more mature strategies. Students who rely on the *counting all* strategy might practice the *counting on* strategy with their fingers or with objects used for counting, called manipulatives (Garnett, 1992). Using manipulatives facilitates students' understanding of mathematical principles (Gersten et al., 2009). Students also may practice identifying the larger addend and using the commutative property (e.g., 5 + 4 = 4 + 5).

To encourage automatic fact retrieval, teachers should remind their students to ask themselves, "Do I know this one?" For example, when faced with the problem 6 + 8, students should first ask whether this is a known problem that they can directly retrieve from memory, rather than relying on a counting strategy. Overreliance on counting strategies impedes the development of direct fact retrieval.

Teachers also can introduce shortcut strategies to help students develop fact retrieval skill (Jordan, Hanich, & Kaplan, 2003; National Research Council, 2001; Robinson, Menchetti, & Torgesen, 2002). For example, if students know 3 + 3 = 6, they can derive the answer to 3 + 4. Another shortcut is the commutative property (3 + 4 = 4 + 3). Shortcut strategies link similar problems in order to facilitate storage of facts in long-term memory—and thus direct retrieval. Guidelines 24.1 provides two different ways to organize instruction for students with MD. Even though the approaches differ, the intent is the same—reducing the load on working memory in solving arithmetic problems and allowing sufficient practice with calculations so that facts are committed to memory.

Some experts argue against rote memorization of arithmetic facts because it places a heavy load on working memory—a weakness in many children with MD (Geary, 1994). However, other researchers have found success in remediating the fact retrieval deficit by using rote drill, or more specifically automaticity training. In one study involving an at-home intervention for students with math disabilities, six weeks of nightly practice involving speeded retrieval of addition, subtraction, and multiplication facts improved the speed and accuracy of fact retrieval (Royer & Tronsky, 1998). The speeded practice forces students to abandon their less efficient counting strategies and use fact retrieval instead. In the classroom, teachers can use an automaticity training method called Detect-Practice-Repair (DPR) (Poncy, Skinner, & O'Mara, 2006). This approach has several stages (Axtell, McCallum, & Bell, 2009; Poncy et al., 2006):

- a timed assessment to identify the math facts that are not yet automatic;
- multiple repetitions of these facts in sets of five;
- a timed assessment and graphing of scores to show progress.

DPR is likely to be more effective than traditional methods because most classroom approaches use a combination of known and unknown facts, which wastes instructional time because most of the practice is on material the student already knows (Axtell et al., 2009). Research indicates that this method is effective for elementary and middle school students with very low performance in math, and that it may be appropriate as an intervention in RTI models (Axtell et al., 2009; Poncy et al., 2006).

The research and practical applications regarding reading and mathematics disabilities focus on elementary school students. How might middle school and high school teachers assist their students who have been diagnosed with reading or mathematics disabilities?

GUIDELINES 24.1   Organizing Number Facts Instruction for Students with Learning Disabilities

Approach	Instructional sequence	Example
Garnett (1992)	+1 principle and	2 + 1, 3 + 1, etc.
	+0 principle	2 + 0, 3 + 0, etc.
	ties	5 + 5, 6 + 6, etc.
	ties + 1	5 + 6, 6 + 7, etc.
	ties + 2	5 + 7, 6 + 8, etc.
	+10 number facts	1 + 10, 2 + 10, 3 + 10, etc.
	+9 number facts	6 + 9 is one less than 6 + 10
	remaining facts	2 + 5, 2 + 6, 2 + 7, 2 + 8
		3 + 6, 3 + 7, 3 + 8
		4 + 7, 4 + 8
		5 + 8
Thornton and Toohey (1985)	count-ons	+1, +2, +3 facts
	+0 principle	2 + 0, 3 + 0, 4 + 0, etc.
	doubles (i.e., ties)	5 + 5, 6 + 6, etc.
	10 sums	6 + 4, 7 + 3, etc.
	+9s	4 + 9, 9 + 3, etc.
	near doubles	4 + 5, 3 + 4, etc.
	remaining facts	7 + 5, 8 + 4, 8 + 5, 8 + 6

Summary

Describe how cognitive disabilities are identified and served under the Individuals with Disabilities Education Improvement Act. Students with intellectual disabilities and specific learning disabilities are eligible for special education and related services under IDEIA as specified by the law. Students undergo a diagnostic evaluation by a school psychologist after parents give consent. Based on the evaluation results, a multidisciplinary team determines whether the student is eligible for special education. IDEIA requires the development of an educational plan to meet the individual needs of the student and the placement of the student in the least restrictive environment.

Discuss the impairments you would expect to see in students with intellectual disabilities and the curricular approaches useful in addressing these deficits. Individuals with intellectual disabilities have a significant deficiency in both intelligence and one or more areas of adaptive behavior (conceptual, social, and practical behavior). Diagnosis is made based on a score that is 2 standard deviations or more below the average on a standardized IQ test and on a standardized measure of adaptive behavior. Direct instruction and cooperative learning are effective instructional methods for students with intellectual disabilities. Teachers also should encourage hands-on learning, focus on repetition of knowledge and skills, and foster generalization of skills to a variety of contexts.

Explain how learning disabilities are diagnosed using the IQ-achievement discrepancy and the response-to-intervention approach. LD may be diagnosed using a discrepancy between IQ and achievement, where a student's achievement on one or more achievement tests is significantly below what would be expected from his IQ. LD also may be diagnosed using a response-to-intervention approach, in which students are referred for LD diagnosis if they were identified as at-risk in kindergarten or first grade and failed to respond to research-based interventions.

Explain the characteristic deficits you would look for in identifying students with reading and mathematics disabilities and how you would approach remediating these deficits. Students with RD experience a lack of automaticity of word recognition and decoding, which in turn impairs reading comprehension. Similarly, students with a semantic subtype of MD have a fact retrieval deficit, experiencing great difficulty storing and retrieving math facts from long-term memory even after extensive drilling. Both of these are considered deficits, in contrast with the case of poor readers and students with a procedural subtype of MD, who are considered to have a developmental delay. Systematic phonics may be used successfully with some students who have RD, while interventions that encourage the development and automaticity of fact retrieval may be effective for students with MD.

Key Concepts

alphabetic principle   442

automaticity training   443

decoding   441

deficit   441

developmental delay   441

dual discrepancy method   440

family educational rights and privacy act   433

IEP team   433

inclusion   435

Individualized Education Plan (IEP)   433

Individuals with Disabilities Education Improvement Act (IDEIA 2004)   433

intellectual disability   435

IQ-achievement discrepancy   438

least restrictive environment (LRE)   434

mainstreaming   435

procedural subtype   444

response-to-intervention (RTI)   439

semantic memory subtype   443

specific learning disabilities   438

systematic phonics instruction   442

visuospatial subtype   444

word recognition   441

Video Applications

www.mhhe.com/bohlin2e

Video 1: Categories of Disabilities in Special Education (*2 minutes*)
Melanie Davis, a school psychologist who works at the elementary school level, describes categories of disabilities covered by the Individuals with Disabilities Education Improvement Act of 2004.

EXAMPLE 25.1   Disability Referral Form

Forms such as this one are used to refer students to be evaluated for disabilities or disorders under IDEIA.

Referral To Determine Eligibility For Special Education And Related Services

Student: _____ DOB: _____ Age: _____ Grade: _____

Parent/Guardian: _____ Primary Lang: ☐ English ☐ Other: _____

Address: _____ Referred by: _____

_____ Referral date: _____

Telephone: _____ Relationship to child: _____

1. AREA(S) OF CONCERN:

☐ Academic ☐ Social/emotional ☐ Gross/fine motor ☐ Activities of daily living

☐ Health related ☐ Behavior ☐ Communication ☐ Other: (specify) _____

A. Describe specific concerns:

B. Describe alternative strategies attempted and outcomes: (Use additional pages if necessary.)

2. SPECIAL SERVICES HISTORY:

Are you aware of any special services provided for this child now or in the past?   ☐ Yes ☐ No
If Yes, describe the type, location, and provider of the service.

3. OTHER RELEVANT INFORMATION:

4. PARENT NOTIFICATION:

Has the parent/guardian been notified about your concerns regarding this student?   ☐ Yes ☐ No

If Yes, method of notification: _____

Date(s) parent/guardian was notified: _____

---

psychologist, and other relevant members—evaluates whether the student meets the eligibility criteria specified by federal law.

According to IDEIA, a prior diagnosis of a particular disorder such as anxiety, depression, ADHD, or conduct disorder in itself does not warrant eligibility. The student's disability or disorder must:

- persist over a long period of time,
- exist to a marked degree, and
- adversely affect academic performance.

If the disability or disorder fails to meet these requirements, the student is not eligible for special education services under IDEIA.

Teachers should be aware of the limitations of IDEIA that may affect eligibility decisions. The ambiguous language in the definition may lead to inconsistent diagnoses. For example, the definition says that the disability or disorder must persist over a long period of time and exist to a marked degree. How long is long enough? And how do we measure a "marked degree"? The requirement that the disorder "adversely affect academic performance" can also be interpreted in many ways (Jensen, 2005). As a result, the determination of eligibility can vary across states and from one school district to another (Osher et al., 2004; Parrish, 2002).

In addition, students from various ethnic groups are identified for special education disproportionately under the IDEIA category of emotional disturbance. In comparison with Caucasian students,

DIVERSITY   African-American males and Native-American students are overrepresented, while Asian and Latino students tend to be underrepresented (Fierros & Conroy, 2002; Parrish, 2002; U.S. Department of Education, 2009). We should be cautious *not* to interpret these findings to mean that race or ethnicity is associated with a greater risk for emotional and behavioral disorders. The following are likely to be better explanations of the disparity between ethnic groups.

DIVERSITY   ■ Socioeconomic status may be a mediating factor in the relationship between ethnicity and level of risk for emotional and behavioral disorders (Fujiura & Yamaki, 2000; U.S. Department of Education, 2009).

DIVERSITY   ■ Disproportionate identification may be the result of educators' failure to consider cultural context when making special education referrals based on interpretations of students' classroom behaviors. A pattern in which students shout out answers and do not respect turn-taking rules in class discussions may reflect culturally specific, valued actions rather than disruptive behaviors, while the verbally unassertive behaviors of other students may be interpreted incorrectly as a lack of motivation or a resistance to instruction (Cartledge, Kea, & Simmons-Reed, 2002; Irvine, 1990).

Students with special needs who do not meet the IDEIA eligibility requirements may be eligible under **Section 504 of the Rehabilitation Act of 1973,** a federal antidiscrimination law protecting the rights of individuals with disabilities or disorders who participate in any program or activity that receives federal funds from the U.S. Department of Education, including public schools. Students with a physical or mental disability are not automatically eligible for special services under Section 504—their disability or disorder must interfere with learning. Nevertheless, the eligibility requirements under Section 504 are more flexible than those specified by IDEIA.

Planning and Placement

While both IDEIA and Section 504 protect the right to "free and appropriate education," the term *appropriate* implies different accommodations under each law:

■ Under Section 504, *appropriate* means an education that is comparable to that of students who are not disabled. For example, providing books on tape would allow a student who is blind equal access to the same information that is available to his or her sighted peers. Schools develop a **Section 504 plan,** which outlines the type of education (general classroom or special education) and services for allowing the student to function as adequately as nondisabled students.

■ Under IDEIA, *appropriate* refers to a curricular program designed to provide educational benefit to the student. Schools develop an **Individualized Education Plan (IEP),** which outlines curricula, educational modifications, and provision of services intended to enhance or improve the student's academic, social, or behavioral skills. IEPs contain several important features, shown in Example 25.2.

Both IDEIA and Section 504 require educators to place students with disabilities or disorders in the general education classroom "to the maximum extent appropriate," known as the **least restrictive environment (LRE).** Two LRE approaches have evolved from different interpretations of the law over the past three decades.

■ In **mainstreaming,** students with special needs are placed with nondisabled peers when appropriate. For example, they may spend most of their day in a special education classroom and be integrated with their peers for subjects such as music, art, and social studies and for activities such as lunch, recess, library, and field trips.

■ **Inclusion,** a more recent and popular approach, refers to integrating all students within the general education classroom, even those with severe disabilities (with the assistance of paraprofessionals) for most or all of the school day. Experts continue to debate whether inclusion is the best environment for every student (Benner, 1998).

About 30% of elementary through high school students served under IDEIA for emotional disturbance spend most of the school day in the general education classroom. Special education classrooms or *pull-out programs,* in which students are pulled out of the general education classroom for remediation or therapy, are more common at the middle school and high school level (U.S. Department of Education, 2009). Students with disabilities or disorders who are eligible for services under Section 504 may be placed in special education classes or remain in general education classrooms with accommodations and supports, or both, depending on their individual needs.

> **EXAMPLE 25.2**   **Information Contained in an IEP**
>
> 1. The student's present levels of academic achievement and functional performance.
> 2. Measurable annual goals and short-term instructional objectives.
> 3. An explanation of how the student's progress toward annual goals will be measured and when progress will be reported to parents.
> 4. Any appropriate accommodations for test taking on statewide and district-wide assessments, especially those required by the No Child Left Behind Act. In cases where educators determine that the student will take an alternative assessment, the IEP needs to specify why this assessment was selected and why it is appropriate for the student.
> 5. The types of special education and related services provided to the student and how long the services will be needed. The IEP also needs to specify how much of the student's education will not be in the general education classroom.
> 6. Measurable postsecondary goals related to education, training, or employment for students age 14 and older.
> 7. A statement of transition services needed to reach goals involving independent living, continuing education, or employment after high school for students age 16 (or younger, if appropriate).

Did you or someone you know receive special education services for an emotional, social, or behavioral disorder? Do you recall the type of disorder and what services or accommodations were offered to you or this individual?

CHARACTERISTICS OF DISORDERS

We will examine several specific disorders and the collection of behaviors or symptoms that are used to make a diagnosis for these disorders. Before we summarize these specific disorders, it is helpful to examine how they fit within the broad categories of disorders. Two common categories used to describe disorders include (1) *internalizing disorders* and (2) *externalizing disorders* (Achenbach, 1992). Internalizing disorders are those that include emotional states and cognitive distress such as fear, anxiety, and depression. Externalizing disorders are those that include more behavioral characteristics such as impulsivity and aggression. Teachers must be alert to both, especially internalizing symptoms that may not be as readily identified in a busy classroom. Although these two broad categories can be very distinct from one another, some children and adolescents exhibit co-occurring emotional (internalizing) and behavioral (externalizing) problems (Fanti & Henrich, 2010). A third category comprises *developmental disorders* that include symptoms in which a child does not meet expected levels of basic skills, most often related to communication and socialization skills.

In the following sections, we will examine the specific internalizing disorders of anxiety and depression, the specific externalizing disorders of attention-deficit hyperactivity disorder (ADHD) and conduct disorder, and a group of developmental disorders—autism spectrum disorders—that have received increased public attention over the last five to ten years.

Anxiety and Depression

In IDEIA's emotional disturbance definition, anxiety is suggested by the criterion "physical symptoms or fears associated with personal or school problems," and depression is suggested by the criterion "a general pervasive mood of unhappiness or depression." What are the academic and personal characteristics of students with anxiety and depression, and how do these affect their academic and peer relationships? Let's explore these questions further.

ANXIETY

Approximately 20% of children and adolescents suffer from **anxiety disorder,** which includes a variety of disorders: generalized anxiety disorder, obsessive-compulsive disorder, panic disorder, specific phobia, social phobia, and separation anxiety disorder (Albano, Chorpita, & Barlow, 2003; Merikangas,

Anxiety: See page 293.

| EXAMPLE 25.3 | Identifying Behaviors of Individuals with Anxiety |

The following behaviors are typically displayed by individuals with anxiety.

Thoughts about:

- being threatened
- being criticized
- appearing incompetent
- losing control of their thoughts and actions
- hypothetical death of a loved one

Physical symptoms of anxiety:

- increased heart rate
- excessive sweating
- fast breathing
- headache, stomach aches, nausea, bowel problems
- muscle tension
- shaking or chills

Also:

- vivid images of danger and humiliation
- avoidance of or escape from anxiety-provoking situations
- overt signs of negative emotion (e.g., crying, sighing)

Sources: Albano et al., 2003; Cullinan, 2007; Egger, Costello, Erkanli, & Angold, 1999; Freeman, Garcia, & Leonard, 2002; Nishina, Juvonen, & Witkow, 2005.

2005). The description of each of these disorders is beyond the scope of this text, but we can discuss some general features of anxiety disorders.

Anxiety disorders are much more than the occasional anxiety we all feel from time to time. They involve distressingly unpleasant and maladaptive feelings, thoughts, behaviors, and physical reactions (Albano et al., 2003; Albano & Krain, 2005; Ollendick, King, & Muris, 2002). Students with anxiety often worry about their competence, even when they are not being evaluated. Because they tend to be overly conforming, perfectionist, or unsure of themselves, they may redo tasks due to excessive dissatisfaction with what they have produced. Students with anxiety also may worry about catastrophes, violence, and bullying by peers and may engage in avoidance behaviors such as absence from school (American Psychiatric Association, 2000; DeVoe et al., 2003). Teachers can use the behaviors in Example 25.3 to help identify cases of anxiety that may require referral to a psychologist for further evaluation.

Developmental differences. Anxiety is more common in adolescents, particularly females (Cullinan, 2007). However, the type of problem varies by age. Separation anxiety—an anxiety related to separating from parents and caregivers—is typical in infants and younger children, while social phobia—anxiety that is evoked in certain social or performance situations—occurs more frequently in adolescents (Albano et al., 2003; APA, 2000; Verhulst, 2001). Some research has suggested that anxiety at very young ages, such as separation anxiety, is related to later anxiety problems in the form of social anxiety and is likely to persist throughout the adolescent years (Hayward et al., 2008).

Effect on school performance and relationships. Students with anxiety experience impairments in academic and social functioning. They tend to perform below their ability level, to receive lower grades, and score lower on IQ tests (Davis, Ollendick, & Nebel-Schwalm, 2008; Langley, Bergman, McCracken, & Piacentini, 2004; Wood, 2006). Students' heightened state of arousal impairs concentration on academic tasks and interferes with learning and/or recall of subject matter (Ma, 1999; Wood, 2006). Stu-

| EXAMPLE 25.4 | Identifying Symptoms of Depression |

The following thoughts, feelings, and behaviors are typically displayed by individuals with depression.

Symptoms include:

- pervasively sad mood
- general irritability
- inability to sustain attention, think, or concentrate
- decline in school participation and performance
- loss of interest in activities
- drastic change in weight (or failure to gain weight in children), appetite, sleeping, or energy level
- prolonged, unpredictable crying
- hopelessness
- strong feelings of worthlessness or guilt
- social withdrawal
- thoughts about death or self-destruction

Sources: APA, 2000; Garber & Horowitz, 2002; Gresham & Kern, 2004; Harrington, 2002; Lewinsohn & Essau, 2002; Weller, Weller, Rowan, & Svadjian, 2002.

dents who are highly anxious also may avoid peer interactions or may appear less competent in social interactions because of their preoccupation with how they appear to others, preventing them from focusing on social cues (Barrett & Heubeck, 2000; Langley et al., 2004). The long-term effect of anxiety was found in a longitudinal study following African-American children over seven years: Anxiety symptoms in the first grade were related to academic and social difficulties in the eighth grade (Grover, Ginsburg, & Ialongo, 2007).

DIVERSITY

Examine the characteristics of anxiety listed in Example 25.3. What changes can you make to your teaching and to the general classroom environment to help students with anxiety in the grade you intend to teach?

DEPRESSION

We all occasionally feel blue or sad, but this is not depression. **Major depressive disorders** involve at least two weeks of depressed mood or loss of interest, along with at least four additional depressive symptoms, and can last about two months (APA, 2000; Hammen & Rudolph, 2003). To be considered a major depressive episode, symptoms also must cause significant distress or impairment in social, occupational, or other types of functioning and cannot be the result of medication, a medical condition, bereavement, or drug abuse (APA, 2000). Examine the list of depressive symptoms in Example 25.4. Teachers can use tools like this list to help them accurately identify possible cases of depression in students who may require referral to a psychologist for further evaluation.

Developmental differences. Depressive disorders are very rare in young children. While only about 2% of students have experienced some type of depressive disorder by early adolescence, rates of depression rise to about 20% during adolescence (Hammen & Rudolph, 2003; Lewinsohn & Essau, 2002). In late adolescence, females are twice as likely as males to experience some form of depression, in contrast with equal incidence rates for the genders before adolescence (Cullinan, 2007).

Effect on school performance and relationships. Depressive symptoms are linked to lower academic performance as well as a higher dropout rate (Chen, Rubin, & Bo-shu, 1995; Cheung, 1995; Franklin & Streeter, 1995). Depression also may lead to peer isolation and suicidal behaviors in adolescence (Marcotte, Lévesque, & Fortin, 2006).

ADHD and Conduct Disorder

Rather than identifying specific types of behavioral disorders, the IDEIA definition of emotional disturbance broadly lists "inappropriate types of behavior or feelings under normal circumstances." Educators often interpret this criterion as aggression and/or impulsivity. We'll discuss two types of behavioral disorders that fit this criterion: Attention-Deficit/Hyperactivity Disorder (ADHD) and Conduct Disorder.

ADHD

Individuals with **ADHD** have a neurological condition that impairs self-regulation as compared with same-age peers (Barkley, 1997, 2007). A recent examination of several studies found that gray matter in the brains of individuals with ADHD is reduced in areas essential to cognitive control or self-regulation (Ellison-Wright, Ellison-Wright, & Bullmore, 2008). Self-regulation involves maintaining attention, inhibiting impulsive or inappropriate responses, maintaining executive control over planning, monitoring progress, and selecting appropriate strategies in working memory (Douglas, 2005; Martinussen, Hayden, Hogg-Johnson, & Tannock, 2005). Approximately 5% of U.S. children and adolescents have a diagnosis of ADHD, with boys diagnosed more than twice as often as girls (Cullinan, 2007; Pastor & Reuben, 2008; Waschbusch, 2002). ADHD is found in all cultures, although prevalence figures differ (Ross & Ross, 1982). Media coverage as well as information provided by some experts suggests that ADHD is overdiagnosed, yet little empirical data substantiates or disproves this claim (LeFever, Arcona, & Antonuccio, 2003; Sciutto & Eisenberg, 2007).

DIVERSITY

Individuals can have one of three subtypes of ADHD:

1. The *predominantly inattentive* subtype is characterized by symptoms of inattention, such as difficulty sustaining attention, forgetfulness, or difficulty organizing tasks.

2. The *predominantly hyperactive-impulsive* subtype is represented by symptoms of hyperactivity or impulsivity, such as fidgeting, constant physical activity, excessive talking, and difficulty playing quietly.

3. The *combined* subtype consists of both inattentive symptoms and hyperactivity-impulsivity.

For a diagnosis of ADHD, symptoms must persist for at least six months. Additional criteria for an ADHD diagnosis are these:

- Individuals must show some symptoms before age 7. However, this does not mean that the child must be diagnosed prior to age 7. ADHD typically is first diagnosed in elementary school when school adjustment is impaired. Many ADHD-like behaviors of toddlers and preschoolers are normal for their age or developmental stage, making it difficult to distinguish ADHD symptoms from age-appropriate behaviors in young, active children (APA, 2000).

- Symptoms are not due to other disorders. Several other disorders may cause an individual to exhibit difficulties in inattention, impulsivity, or hyperactivity. In those cases, ADHD is not the diagnosis.

- Some symptoms must be present in two or more settings. If a teacher (school setting) believes the child exhibits inattentive or impulsive/hyperactive behaviors but the parents (home setting) do not see those same behaviors, the problem most likely is differences in the environment and not a function of the individual.

- The inattentive or impulsive/hyperactive behaviors must cause *clinically significant impairment* in academic or social functioning. Students who exhibit behavioral symptoms of ADHD but receive good grades and form solid relationships with peers would not qualify for the diagnosis of ADHD.

Comorbidity. Approximately 40% to 60% of children with ADHD have at least one coexisting disorder (Jensen et al., 2001). Although any disability or disorder can coexist with ADHD, common ones include conduct disorder, mood disorder, anxiety, tics, Tourette's syndrome, and specific learning disabilities (Jensen et al., 2001; Mayes, Calhoun, & Crowell, 2000).

Specific learning disabilities: See page 438.

Developmental differences. ADHD affects individuals differently at different ages. Children may be initially identified as having hyperactive-impulsive subtype and later identified as having the combined subtype as their attention problems surface. Impulsiveness also manifests differently in younger and older children. A preschooler may appear fidgety, have a high energy level, have difficulty playing quietly, and have difficulty taking turns, behaviors that tend to continue into elementary school in the form of problems with impulsivity, aggression, and social adjustment (Campbell, Endman, & Bernfield, 1977; Campbell, Ewing, Breaux, & Szumowski, 1986). By the upper elementary grades, students with impulsivity may show disorganized thinking and planning, noncompliance, and academic failure and may become increasingly aggressive and be rejected by their peers (Cullinan, 2007). Adolescents with impulsivity may make hasty, unreflective decisions, such a performing an academic task in a disorganized manner or making disrespectful comments without consideration of ramifications (Schachar

| **EXAMPLE 25.5** | **Identifying Behaviors of ADHD in School Settings** |

The following are examples of behaviors that may be displayed by individuals with ADHD.

Inattentive behaviors in school settings:

- difficulty attending to instructions, explanations, or demonstrations
- missing important details in assignments
- daydreaming, difficulty sustaining attention
- avoidance or dislike of tasks requiring sustained mental effort
- procrastination about assignments
- misplacing needed items, difficulty organizing assignments
- lack of close attention to details, careless mistakes
- ignoring or disobeying teacher directions and school rules

Impulsivity/hyperactivity behaviors in school settings:

- attending only to activities that are entertaining or novel
- responding to questions without fully formulating the best answers
- moving from one task to another without finishing
- careless errors
- appearing fidgety, having difficulty staying seated or playing quietly
- verbal or physical disruptions in class, blurting out answers
- difficulty participating in tasks that require taking turns
- a high energy level often misperceived as purposeful noncompliance

Sources: Barkley, 2003; Cullinan, 2007; Schachar & Tannock, 2002; Weiss & Weiss, 2002; Zentall, 1993.

& Tannock, 2002). They also tend to make friends with other unpopular adolescents, leading to detrimental choices with respect to peer groups, such as defiant and aggressive behaviors, delinquency, reckless behaviors, substance abuse, and illegal acts (Anastopoulos & Shelton, 2001; Barkley, 2003; Hinshaw & Blackman, 2005; Pelham & Molina, 2003; Weiss & Weiss, 2002).

Effect on school performance and relationships. Example 25.5 illustrates typical problems that students with inattentiveness or impulsivity may experience during school. Students with ADHD tend to have difficulties in reading, math, and writing and have lower overall achievement than their peers (Frazier, Youngstrom, Glutting, & Watkins, 2007; Zentall, 1993). Working memory deficits may be partly responsible for poor academic achievement (Gathercole, Pinkering, Knight, & Stegman, 2004; Jarvis & Gathercole, 2003). Teachers can improve students' classroom performance by providing frequent breaks between periods of concentration and structured work (Ridgway, Northup, Pellegrini, LaRue, & Hightshoe, 2003).

ADHD also affects students' social lives. Students with ADHD exhibit several socially incompetent behaviors, including the following (Cullinan, 2007; King et al., 2009; Wehmeier, Schacht, & Barkley, 2010):

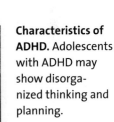

Characteristics of ADHD. Adolescents with ADHD may show disorganized thinking and planning.

Working memory:
See page 185.

- lack of cooperation,
- unwillingness to wait their turn or play by the rules,
- defiance or opposition, and
- aggression.

The inability of children with ADHD to control their behavior may lead to social rejection by peers and to relationships with parents and teachers characterized by conflict (Barkley, 1990; Erhardt & Hinshaw, 1994). As a result, students with ADHD are more likely to be suspended or expelled and to develop peer relationship problems in adolescence (Barkley, 1990; Melnick & Hinshaw, 1996; Stein, Szumowski, Blondis, & Roizen, 1995).

Examine the characteristics of ADHD in school settings listed in Example 25.5. Think of some ways you would handle these behaviors in the grade you intend to teach.

CONDUCT DISORDER

Approximately 3% to 5% of U.S. children and adolescents exhibit aggressive patterns typical of a conduct disorder (Connor, 2002; Hinshaw & Lee, 2003). An individual with a **conduct disorder** shows persistent behaviors such as the following (APA, 2000):

- aggression toward people and animals (e.g., bullying, fights, physical cruelty),
- destruction of property (e.g., setting fires),
- deceitfulness or theft (e.g., home burglary, conning others), and
- serious violation of rules (e.g., truancy, running away).

Individuals must show three or more symptoms over a 12-month period. The characteristic behaviors typically are evident at home, at school, and in the community (APA, 2000; Jensen, 2005). Also, these behaviors must be due to an underlying psychological disorder rather than to behavior patterns that children and adolescents acquire as protective strategies in threatening environments, such as neighborhoods with high poverty levels or high crime rates (APA, 2000).

Developmental differences. Conduct disorder may emerge as early as preschool (APA, 2000). Caregivers and early childhood educators often mistakenly assume that young children who show aggression will outgrow it (Jensen, 2005). Childhood onset of conduct disorder is identified when children demonstrate at least one characteristic behavior before age 10 (typically fighting and hostility). Boys are more likely to develop the childhood-onset type of the disorder and to display aggression through fighting, stealing, vandalism, and discipline problems in school (APA, 2000; Foster, 2005; Hinshaw & Lee, 2003). This type of conduct disorder generally is stable and resistant to change and predicts more severe antisocial, aggressive behaviors through adulthood (Tackett, 2010; Walker, Colvin, & Ramsey, 1995). Without early intervention, antisocial behaviors may escalate from childhood through adolescence to more deviant forms of behavior, such as stealing, property destruction, and victimizing others (Jensen, 2005; Walker et al., 1995).

DIVERSITY   Individuals with conduct disorder who do not show any characteristic behaviors before age 10 develop the adolescent-onset subtype, more commonly found in females. Girls with this disorder typically engage in behaviors such as lying, running away, truancy, substance abuse, and sexual promiscuity (APA, 2000). Those with the adolescent-onset subtype are less likely to have persistent conduct disorders or to develop more serious antisocial disorders in adulthood than those with the childhood-onset type (APA, 2000).

Effect on school performance and relationships. Elementary and middle school students with conduct disorder tend to have lower verbal skills and lower academic achievement overall (APA, 2000; Gresham, Lane, & Beebe-Frankenberger, 2005). However, experts are not certain whether poorer academic achievement is one of several causal factors leading to conduct problems or an outcome of the conduct problems themselves.

Like students with ADHD, students who show highly aggressive and antisocial behaviors gradually become isolated from their peers. By fourth and fifth grades, children who are excluded by their peers may gravitate toward a negative peer group, leading to more serious behaviors in adolescence, such as delinquency, substance abuse, involvement with gangs, and other criminal activities (Jensen, 2005). Delinquent patterns of behavior that continue through adolescence are predictive of adult criminality and substantially limit future opportunities in education, employment, and social relationships (Jensen, 2005; Walker et al., 1995).

Autism Spectrum Disorders

Autism is a developmental disorder that has received considerable attention in the last several years. The classic diagnosis of autism is gradually being replaced with the label **autism spectrum disorders**, which encompasses both severe and milder forms of the symptoms. As a group of developmental disorders, autism spectrum disorders affect social interaction, communication, and behavior in the following ways (Matson & Nebel-Schwalm, 2007; Swinkels et al., 2006):

Appropriate social and emotional development: See Module 3 and Module 4

- Impaired social interaction may be due to difficulties with nonverbal behaviors (eye contact, facial expression, gestures), lack of social or emotional reciprocity, difficulty with sharing interests, or failure to establish developmentally appropriate peer relationships.

- Impairment in communication skills may range from a delay or lack of development of spoken language to lack of spontaneous pretend play, the repetitive use of language (e.g., repeating jingles or commercials), or an inability to engage in or sustain conversations.

- Individuals may also exhibit repetitive patterns of behavior, such as hand flapping or rocking, lining up of toys, self-injurious behavior, or preoccupation with parts of objects (e.g., opening and closing the lid on a jack-in-the-box) (Turner, 1999).

Delays in social interaction, communication, or imaginative play must occur prior to age 3 to be considered an autism spectrum disorder (APA, 2000). Many individuals with autism spectrum disorders also exhibit extreme sensitivity to hearing and touch (Klein, Cook, & Richardson-Gibbs, 2001). For example, a student might find traffic noise outside a classroom window or being touched by others irritating or even painful (Wilson, 2003).

The prevalence rates of autism are difficult to specify because some studies include only the classic disorder of autism which has very low rates, whereas most refer to the prevalence of the broader category of autism spectrum disorders. In addition, the rates have increased over the last 15 years, which may be

Intellectual disabilities: See page 435.

due to (a) other disorders now being labeled as autism, (b) better detection of the spectrum of disorders, or (c) an actual increase in rates of autism (Coo et al., 2008). The most recent data suggest that the rates for autism spectrum disorders are on average 1 in 110 children in the United States, or about 1% (Centers for Disease Control and Prevention, 2009). Similar rates are found in many cultures (Mansell & Morris, 2004; Naoi, Yokoyama, & Yamamoto, 2007).

Comorbidity. Comorbidity refers to the coexistence of two or more disorders. About 75% of individuals with autism also have an intellectual disability (formerly called mental retardation), with about 40% of individuals with autism having a severe intellectual disability (Fombonne, 1999; Howard, Williams, Port, & Lepper, 2001). One criterion for a diagnosis of intellectual disability is significantly lower performance on IQ tests than that of same-age peers (another criterion is deficits in adaptive behavior). Individuals with autism tend to have weaker verbal than nonverbal performance on IQ tests because of their deficits in communication (APA, 2000).

Developmental differences. The degree of social and communicative impairment may change over time (APA, 2000). Infants with autism may appear unresponsive emotionally and socially—not making eye contact, cuddling, showing physical affection, or responding to parents' voices. As children develop, though, they may become more interested in and willing to passively engage in social interaction. However, even in these cases, children with autism tend to interact with others in unusual ways, such as being inappropriately intrusive in interactions or having little understanding of others' boundaries. At adolescence, some individuals experience deterioration in behaviors, while others experience improvements. About two-thirds of individuals with autism do not develop independent living skills by adulthood and continue to struggle with the social aspects of jobs and daily functioning (APA, 2000; Howlin, Mawhood, & Rutter, 2000).

Communication Skills. Individuals with autism, like the character Raymond in the hit 1988 movie *Rain Man*, often exhibit repetitive language and are unable to sustain conversations.

DIVERSITY

While autism is three to seven times more likely to occur in males than in females, the gender difference in rates of occurrence depends on IQ (CDC, 2009; Towle, Visintainer, O'Sullivan, Bryan, & Busby, 2009). Individuals who have more severe cognitive impairments in IQ, especially girls, are more likely to be identified with autism (Bryson, 1997; Ehlers & Gillberg, 1993). Girls who have mild cognitive impairments may be diagnosed less frequently than boys because their communicative abilities might make them appear more socially adept than boys with the same level of cognitive ability, masking some symptoms of autism (McLennan, Lord, & Schopler, 1993; Volkmar, Szatmari, & Sparrow, 1993).

Normal development of empathy: See page 66.

Effect on school performance and relationships. Because of their intellectual disabilities, students with autism face major academic challenges in the general education classroom. Their problems in communication and social interaction present added challenges to learning and impair their ability to develop age-appropriate peer relationships. They often appear aloof, avoid eye contact and physical displays of affection, and sometimes do not develop expressions of empathy (Rutter, 1978). Contrary to common belief, individuals with autism do not prefer to be alone, even though they lack social and communication skills that would allow them to develop friendships. Development of a few close friendships can be very beneficial, as the quality of friendships—not the number—affects whether individuals with autism feel lonely (Burgess & Gutstein, 2007).

APPLICATIONS: INTERVENTIONS

Students with all types of disorders need to learn how to function in the general education classroom. Often, students are prescribed medications by their physicians to reduce anxiety or depressive symptoms and to increase attention and reduce impulsivity, which can improve students' academic and social functioning at school. Pharmacological interventions are outside the teacher's control and therefore are beyond the scope of this text. However, teachers can play a central role in shaping positive student behaviors in the classroom through several behavior modification approaches.

Types of Interventions

Classroom discipline: See page 87.

As part of their general classroom discipline, teachers can use contingency management techniques with students who have disorders. **Contingency management** involves the use of consequences that are tied to specific behaviors exhibited by students. When shaping appropriate classroom behaviors, teachers are encouraged to use *positive reinforcement*—applying a positive consequence (praise, stickers, and so on)—for appropriate behaviors. They also should avoid positively reinforcing misbehaviors by paying attention to them. Calling on, or even reprimanding, a student who is blurting out an answer positively reinforces the inappropriate behavior. Teachers can implement positive reinforcement in a concrete way by using a *token economy* in which students earn tokens for good behavior and cash them in for a small toy or favored activity when they have accumulated a certain number. A student can lose tokens for inappropriate behaviors, a consequence known as *response cost.*

See Applied Behavior Analysis on page 163 for using consequences to shape behaviors.

Negative consequences, or punishments, also can be used to maintain improvements in behavior in students with behavioral disorders such as ADHD (Sullivan & O'Leary, 1990). *Verbal reprimands,* when given consistently and followed with *time out* and loss of privileges, are effective components of classroom discipline for students with behavioral disorders (Abramowitz, O'Leary, & Futtersak, 1988; Acker & O'Leary, 1987; Pfiffner & O'Leary, 1987).

Psychologists also can train teachers to use **cognitive-behavioral treatment (CBT),** a technique that teaches students to regulate their own behavior using a series of instructions that they memorize, internalize, and apply to different school tasks (Barkley et al., 2000; Miranda & Presentación, 2000; Miranda, Presentación, & Soriano, 2002). The goal of CBT is self-management through the development of new thinking patterns and good decision-making skills. CBT techniques include self-monitoring, self-assessment, self-evaluation, and self-reinforcement (Lee, Simpson, & Shogren, 2007). For example, if the goal is for the student to work independently and quietly at his desk on a worksheet, the student can periodically check on his behaviors, assess whether he is achieving the goal, and, if so, put a token in a jar. If not, he can evaluate what he needs to do to get back on track. As a result, students gain an ability to control their own behavior rather than having the behavior be controlled by an adult through consequences. CBT also helps students generalize their behaviors to other classroom settings (Koegel, Koegel, Harrower, & Carter, 1999).

School psychologists also may use systematic desensitization to reduce fears and anxieties in students with anxiety. **Systematic desensitization**—a technique based on the assumption that anxieties and fears are a conditioned (or learned) response to certain stimuli—combines relaxation training with gradual exposure to the anxiety-provoking stimulus. For example, a student who has anxiety about participating in class would engage in relaxation techniques as she moves from answering a question with a class partner to speaking in small groups to giving a response amid all her classmates.

Conditioning: See page 159.

Research has also focused on **multimodal interventions,** interventions that combine more than one approach. For example, students may receive both medication and CBT or both medication and contingency management. Schools increasingly have implemented CBT to augment pharmacological treatment of anxiety and depression. Because medication is a common form of treatment for ADHD, students with ADHD often are exposed to multimodal interventions consisting of medication, behavior modification, and sometimes academic interventions as well.

Effectiveness of Interventions

Because the nature and severity of students' disorders vary, no single intervention is universally effective for every student. Educators need to be aware of the efficacy of interventions for different types of disorders so they can make informed decisions regarding which practices to implement in school settings.

Internalizing disorders. Systematic desensitization is effective in reducing a variety of fears in children and adolescents, including test anxiety, public speaking, and school phobia (Lane, Gresham, & O'Shaughnessy, 2002; Morris & Kratochwill, 1998). Contingency management techniques also can be used effectively to reduce students' fears and anxieties (Lane et al., 2002; Morris & Kratochwill, 1983). Cognitive behavioral treatments (CBT) have been found not only to alleviate the immediate symptoms of anxiety but to continue deterring anxiety symptoms well into adulthood (Saavedra, Silverman, Morgan-Lopez, & Kurtines, 2010). CBT can also be adapted to meet the needs of ethnic minority students whose values may vary as a function of culture (Wood, Chiu, Hwang, Jacobs, & Ifekwunigwe, 2008)

DIVERSITY

Regarding depressive symptoms, studies have found that adolescents who use poor coping strategies, such as consistently talking about negative feelings with peers without the purpose of seeking their support or trying to avoid the problem by never talking with peers or others about their feelings and thoughts, have an increased risk of depressive symptoms (Eacott & Frydenberg, 2009b; Stone, Uhrlass, & Gibb, 2010). Intervention programs aimed at increasing productive coping strategies—such as teaching adolescents to share their problems or feelings with others as a means of gaining support or using problem-solving or planning strategies to eliminate the problem—have been found to decrease depressive symptoms, specifically among rural adolescents who typically have fewer options in obtaining services for mental health disorders (Eacott & Frydenberg, 2009b).

DIVERSITY

Multimodal interventions consisting of CBT and pharmacological intervention are particularly beneficial in treating anxiety and depression because they help change the student's thoughts, feelings, and behaviors (Harrington, 2002; Warner, Fisher, Shrout, Rathor, & Klein, 2007; Weller, Weller, Rowan, & Svadjian, 2002). Research on adolescents with depression indicated that a combination of antidepressant medication and CBT was more effective than either treatment alone (Treatment for Adolescents with Depression Study Team, 2004).

Externalizing disorders. Preschool prevention programs have significantly improved behaviors and delayed the development of more serious behavior problems of children at risk for behavioral disorders (Serna, Lambros, Nielsen, & Forness, 2002; Serna, Nielsen, Mattern, & Forness, 2003). Token economies and response cost have reduced the number of aggressive and disruptive behaviors in school-aged children (McGoey, Schneider, Rezzetano, Prodan, & Tankersley, 2010). Multimodal approaches that include parent training have also been found to decrease disruptive behaviors and increase social skills of children with externalizing problems. The changing of disruptive behavior has been found effective in diverse, urban school settings as well as cross-cultural settings. However, most interventions tend to be less effective in improving academic performance (Walker et al., 2009; Broadhead, Hockaday, Zahra, Francis, & Crichton, 2009). Some interventions that are more effective for academic improvement include working one-on-one with a peer, computer-assisted instruction, and interventions that specifically focus on basic skills such as reading and math (Jitendra, DuPaul, Someki, & Tresco, 2008).

DIVERSITY

Contingency management techniques and parent training of contingency management have been found to reduce the incidence of disruptive behaviors among school-age children and adolescents with ADHD and other behavioral disorders. For example, daily report cards that list children's target behaviors and whether goals were met on that day are found to be effective in reducing disruptive behavior (Fabiano et al., 2010). Students with ADHD respond positively to a combination of academic interventions, behavior management, and modifications of the classroom environment (Fabiano et al., 2009). Research findings include these:

- In one study, a combination of contingency management and academic intervention was more effective than only CBT in reducing disruptive behaviors of students with ADHD (Antshel & Barkley, 2008).
- In the Multimodal Treatment Study of Children with ADHD—the longest and most thorough study of the effects of ADHD multimodal interventions—a combination of medication and behavioral interventions (e.g., parent training, school-based interventions, and summer treatment) improved academic performance, school behaviors, and parent-child interactions and reduced oppositional behavior (MTA Cooperative Group, 1999a, 1999b). The combined medication/behavior treatment and the medication-alone treatment were significantly more effective in reducing the symptoms of ADHD than behavior modification alone (Conners et al., 2001; Swanson et al., 2001). The combined treatment also was effective in improving students' social skills and academic outcomes (Chacko et al., 2005; MTA Cooperative Group, 1999a, 1999b).

Developmental disorders. Because individuals with autism spectrum disorders experience multiple deficits, they often need a variety of interventions, such as speech and language therapy, social-skills training, occupational therapy, and behavior modification techniques. Intensive contingency management techniques have led to improved overall functioning of children with autism spectrum disorders (Eikeseth, 2009). Cognitive behavioral treatments (CBT) that focus not only on the symptoms of autism spectrum disorders but also address issues related to social anxiety appear to be effective as well (Sze & Wood, 2008; Wood et al., 2009). Teachers can improve the social skills of students with autism by including such students in activities with nondisabled peers, providing multiple opportunities to practice social skills in varied settings, and positively reinforcing attempts at appropriate social skills (Kohler, Anthony, Steighner, & Hoyson, 2001; Strain & Danko, 1995). Preschool children, older children, and adolescents with autism have also improved their social skills through cognitive-behavior management (Lee et al., 2007). In short, there is no single effective intervention for individuals with autism. What may be more important than the type of intervention is the timing and length of the intervention. Children with autism benefit from early and intensive interventions—those begun between ages 2 and 4 and involving 15 or more hours per week of treatment over a one- to two-year period with low adult-to-child ratios (Filipek et al., 1999; Rogers, 1996).

Imagine the grade level you intend to teach. Think of some ways you could use contingency management to reduce anxieties and disruptive behaviors and to increase appropriate classroom behaviors in students with internalizing or externalizing disorders.

See Cooperative learning in Modules 20 and 21 for specific suggestions.

Summary

Describe how students with emotional, social, and behavioral disorders are identified and served under IDEIA and Section 504. Students with emotional, social, or behavioral problems may be eligible for special education or related services under IDEIA. They must present symptoms to a marked degree that exist over a long period of time and significantly impair educational performance. Section 504 provides more flexible criteria for eligibility, but eligibility is not guaranteed. Both laws require placement in the least restrictive environment.

Explain how anxiety and depression affect students' academic and social functioning. Students with anxiety perform below their ability, earn lower grades, avoid peer interactions, and may appear less competent in social interactions because of a heightened state of arousal in academic and social situations. Students with depression tend to have lower academic performance and are more likely to be isolated from peers, to have suicidal behaviors, and to drop out of school during adolescence.

Explain how ADHD and conduct disorder affect students' academic and social functioning. Students with ADHD display many behaviors that impair school performance, such as fidgeting and excessive activity in younger children and problems with organization, planning, and decision making in older children. These problems lead to difficulties in reading, math, and writing and to lower overall achievement. Impulsive and hyperactive behaviors may lead to conflict with adults and social rejection by peers, especially in adolescence. Children with conduct disorder tend to have lower levels of verbal skill and academic achievement, gradually become excluded by their peers, and develop delinquent patterns of behavior in adolescence.

Describe the characteristics of autism spectrum disorders, and explain how these affect academic and social functioning. Autism includes deficits in social interaction, communication, and behavior. Because many individuals with autism spectrum disorders have some degree of intellectual disability, they face major academic challenges in the general education classroom. Their problems in communication and social interaction pose added challenges to learning and to the development of peer relationships. Few individuals with severe autism are able to function independently in society.

Describe interventions that are effective in treating emotional, social, and behavioral disorders. Systematic desensitization and contingency management techniques are effective strategies for reducing students' fears and anxieties. Children with autism spectrum disorders need a variety of interventions and benefit most from early and intensive therapies. They respond positively to intensive contingency management and cognitive-behavioral management. Cognitive-behavioral and contingency management techniques also work well for reducing disruptive behaviors. Students with ADHD respond most positively to a combination of interventions.

Key Concepts

ADHD   456

anxiety disorder   453

autism spectrum disorders   459

cognitive-behavioral treatment (CBT)   460

conduct disorder   458

contingency management   460

emotional disturbance   450

inclusion   452

Individualized Education Plan (IEP)   452

Individuals with Disabilities Education Improvement Act of 2004 (IDEIA)   450

least restrictive environment (LRE)   452

mainstreaming   452

major depressive disorders   455

multimodal interventions   461

Section 504 of the Rehabilitation Act of 1973   452

Section 504 plan   452

systematic desensitization   460

Video Applications

www.mhhe.com/bohlin2e

Video 1: Attentional Disabilities (*2 minutes*)
This video clip shows an interview with Melanie Davis, a school psychologist who works at the elementary school level. The clip describes types of emotional, social, and behavioral disabilities.

Case Studies
Reflect and Evaluate

EARLY CHILDHOOD: "Letter *P* Day"

These questions refer to the case study on page 394.

DIVERSITY

1. Based on the information given in the case, is it likely that Peter has ADHD? Why or why not? If Peter were a girl, would that change your decision?

2. What behaviors should Mrs. Cahill look for to determine whether Peter may have ADHD? How might these symptoms differ from symptoms that students might show in higher grades?

3. What specific strategies based on contingency management can Mrs. Cahill use to keep Peter on task?

4. Imagine that Devin is a student with conduct disorder in Mrs. Cahill's class. Using the information presented in the module, describe how Devin might behave during the language arts activity.

5. Does Nolan exhibit symptoms of depression? Why or why not? Use Example 25.4 (on page 455) and the research discussed in the module to support your answer.

6. Why wouldn't you expect to see many anxiety problems in kindergarten? Compare this situation to middle school or high school. What factors might contribute to the development of anxiety in middle school or high school?

ELEMENTARY SCHOOL: "Cheetahs, Lions, and Leopards"

These questions refer to the case study on page 396.

1. Assume that Travis has autism. What challenges might Mrs. Fratelli face in addressing Travis's learning and social needs?

2. Based on Example 25.3 (on page 454) and the information presented in the module, evaluate whether Denise might have an anxiety disorder.

3. Several days this week, one of the students in Mrs. Fratelli's class has come into school very sullen. She's not eating very much or paying attention the way she normally does. What factors does Mrs. Fratelli need to consider to help her determine whether this student has symptoms of a major depressive disorder? What additional information would she need to gather?

4. Based on information in the module, give Mrs. Fratelli specific suggestions for adapting the science experiment so that it helps Travis improve his social functioning.

5. Based on information in the module, give Mrs. Fratelli specific suggestions for easing Denise's anxiety about reading aloud.

6. This case does not include any students with ADHD. Using information in the module, create and describe an elementary school student with ADHD for this case.

MIDDLE SCHOOL: "Math Troubles"

These questions refer to the case study on page 398.

DIVERSITY

1. Use the characteristics in Example 25.3 (on page 454) to evaluate whether Lindsey could have an anxiety disorder. What additional information would you need in order to help you decide? If Lindsey were a boy, would that make a difference?

2. Use the characteristics in Example 25.5 (on page 457) to evaluate whether Sam could have ADHD. What additional information would you need in order to help you decide?

DIVERSITY 3. Did you assume Sam was a boy? How did that affect your evaluation in question 2?

DIVERSITY 4. Assume that Sam is African American. How might that affect your evaluation in question 2? What does the research say about identification of emotional and behavioral disorders in students from minority and lower-socioeconomic backgrounds?

5. How can Miss Barton address Sam's disruptive behaviors? Give specific strategies based on contingency management.

6. How can Miss Barton prevent students like Jessie and Lindsey from developing anxiety about math? Give specific suggestions based on information discussed in the module.

HIGH SCHOOL: "Noon Supervised Study"

These questions refer to the case study on page 400.

1. How might anxiety affect a student's performance in Mr. Hardy's class? Think of specific examples related to in-class performance, performance on assignments, and peer interactions.

2. Mr. Hardy regularly uses student presentations in his class but finds that several students have severe anxiety about public speaking. What specific methods discussed in the module are used to reduce anxiety? Brainstorm additional strategies for reducing student anxiety that Mr. Hardy can use with his students.

3. Why would you expect to find few students with autism in a ninth-grade history class?

4. Use Example 25.5 (on page 457) to evaluate whether Jason could have ADHD. What additional information would you need in order to help you decide?

5. This case does not include any students with conduct disorder. Using information discussed in the module, create and describe a high school student with conduct disorder for this case. Specifically, provide behaviors that Mr. Hardy would see in class or information he would be given by school administrators.

6. Give Mr. Hardy specific suggestions based on contingency management for how to increase homework completion in students like Jason, Anthony, and Sarah.

unit eight

Case Studies

Early Childhood: "The Zoo" 468

Elementary School: "Writing Wizards" 470

Middle School: "Assessment: Cafeteria Style" 472

High School: "Innovative Assessment Strategies" 474

Module 26:
Assessing Student Learning

Outline and Learning Goals 476

What Is Assessment? 477

Application: Assessment Planning 479

Application: Communication of Classroom Assessment Information 483

Summary 489

Key Concepts 489

Video Applications 489

Case Studies: Reflect and Evaluate 490

classroom assessment

Module 27:
Test Construction and Use

Outline and Learning Goals 492

Characteristics of High-Quality Classroom Tests 493

Application: Developing a Test Blueprint 496

Application: Developing Test Items 497

Application: Test Analysis and Revision 504

Summary 506

Key Concepts 506

Case Studies: Reflect and Evaluate 507

Module 28:
Performance Assessment

Outline and Learning Goals 509

A Broader View of Assessment 510

Application: Developing Performance Assessments 512

Application: Evaluating Performance Assessments 516

Advantages and Disadvantages of Performance Assessment 520

Summary 522

Key Concepts 522

Video Applications 523

Case Studies: Reflect and Evaluate 523

Prepare:

As you read the case, make notes:

1. **WHO** are the primary participants in the case? Describe them.

2. **WHAT** is taking place?

3. **WHERE** is the case taking place? Is the environment a factor?

4. **WHEN** is the case taking place? Is the timing a factor?

Sanjay Baterdene is a preschool teacher at a lab school in a large midwestern city. The laboratory preschool is affiliated with a local university and serves as an observation, research, and training facility for students who are pursuing a degree in early childhood education. Mr. Sanjay is currently completing his master's degree. He works four afternoons each week in the preschool classroom alongside a much more experienced lead teacher, Vivian Stanich, who has been at the school for almost 25 years. In addition to working with young children in the classroom, Miss Vivian often teaches a course in the developmental assessment of young children at the university the lab school is affiliated with. Mr. Sanjay is a little in awe of his more experienced counterpart and wants to make sure he is doing his best at all times. Miss Vivian has stressed the importance of develop-

Early Childhood

The Zoo

mentally appropriate assessment practices, and she has set up the classroom to facilitate many opportunities for assessing the students through informal observation.

This afternoon the children (a mix of 4- and 5-year-olds) are engaged in activities in various learning centers around the room. In the tiled area near the sinks, Miriam and Greg are painting on opposite sides of a large free-standing easel. Mr. Sanjay walks over to watch the children as they paint.

"What are you making, Miriam?" he asks. He sees a slightly disapproving look from Miss Vivian and restates his question as "Tell me about that painting, Miriam." Miriam is happily painting thick swirls of color on the paper in front of her. She doesn't answer right away, and Greg shouts, "Hey, Mr. Sanjay, come look at my picture!" Mr. Sanjay crosses over to Greg and admires the scene before him. Greg has painted what appears to be a family, but Mr. Sanjay notices that all the family members have large heads with arms and legs sticking out (no actual torsos). Mr. Sanjay knows that this is a very typical way for young children to represent people in their early drawings. He smiles and tells Greg that he notices the entire page is full all the way to the edges.

"I have a very big family," says Greg.

"Wow! Tell me about all these people who have shown up in your painting," Mr. Sanjay replies. Greg launches into an animated discussion of the various family members he has represented.

Mr. Sanjay then wanders over to the block area but finds that wooden blocks are only one of the many items being utilized by the children. With the blocks, they are building a gigantic zoo housing an assortment of plastic animal figures. Their play has spread well outside the block area and is beginning to encroach on the snack table area. Cindy and Arelio are engaged in a disagreement over whether the cages at the zoo should be locked up or the animals should be allowed to roam free. Ellen pipes up to say that maybe the bad animals can be locked up but the good ones can be let out. Arelio asks how they will know if the animal is bad or good. Mr. Sanjay listens in as the children discuss badly behaved animals. Marcus, another zoo builder, suggests that they reorganize the zoo so that the good animals are in one area and the bad animals are in another. The other children seem to like this idea, and they begin picking up the plastic animal figures and putting them in new locations. Arelio gets a doll figure from the classroom's dollhouse and places it in the "bad zone." He laughs uproariously as he points at the doll and says "My sister." As the zoo grows, the group of zoo builders also grows, and soon more than half the class is engaged in adding features to the zoo. Half an hour later, Mr. Sanjay realizes he needs to have the children clean up and go to the tables for snack.

When he announces clean-up time, he hears a loud groan from several of the children. Marcus asks if they can keep the zoo where it is for the rest of the week. Mr. Sanjay checks with Miss Vivian to make sure she has no objections. He is surprised that she quickly agrees to let the sprawling zoo stay. The children cheer and head over to wash their hands for snack. Cindy and Arelio approach Mr. Sanjay with a piece of paper and a large crayon, asking if he will write "Zany Zoo" on their paper. "How about if I tell you the letters and you write it?" he asks. They agree, and they slowly and carefully make their sign, which they later tape on the floor by the zoo entrance.

As the children are getting settled for snack, Mr. Sanjay takes a minute to jot down a few anecdotal notes to refer to later when he writes up narrative progress reports to share at parent-teacher conferences. He notes some of the skills he has observed various children using this afternoon as well as personal interests he has seen them display. Then he joins the group in the snack area.

When Mr. Sanjay first started working at the lab school, he volunteered to tell the children stories during snack time. "We make our own stories," they said. As Mr. Sanjay learned what they meant, he began to look forward eagerly to the snack time story session. Miss Vivian would begin the session with an outlandish statement, such as "I love to wear pink bubblegum in my hair." The child who happened to be sitting closest to her would respond with a line of his or her own, such as "That's because my name is Hubba Bubba." Each child then would get a turn to add his or her own piece to the emerging story. If the story of the day was really a hit with the children, Miss Vivian would have the students repeat it back to her and she would write it down. On that Friday, the students would stage a production and act out the story. Mr. Sanjay suspected that today's story would somehow involve crazy animals at a zoo.

Assess

1. The children in this preschool classroom are 4 and 5 years old. If you were the teacher, how would you assess their knowledge and skills?

2. In your opinion, what kinds of skills might be important to assess in working with this age group?

3. Why do you suspect there were no traditional tests given in this classroom?

Prepare:

As you read the case, make notes:

1. **WHO** are the primary participants in the case? Describe them.

2. **WHAT** is taking place?

3. **WHERE** is the case taking place? Is the environment a factor?

4. **WHEN** is the case taking place? Is the timing a factor?

Brigita Blaydes beams with pride as she peeks into the school cafeteria to see the Young Authors Fair in full swing. Just a few short months ago, Ms. Blaydes welcomed 27 reluctant writers into her fourth-grade class, and today those same students are displaying their work for parents, classmates, and members of the community. The students, arranged in centers around the cafeteria, are taking turns sharing their writing, illustrating, reading, and storytelling skills with their invited guests.

Ms. Blaydes is passionate about reading and writing and has worked hard to share that passion with her students. Her room is filled with picture books, chapter books, children's magazines, collections of poems, and posters of famous actors, politicians, and sports figures reading a favorite book. In the first days of the school year, Ms. Blaydes welcomed her new students into the classroom by giving each of them a letter written by one

Elementary School
Writing Wizards

of her former students. The letters gave her new crop of students a sense of what they could expect in the year ahead and imparted words of wisdom from the previous year's "writing wizards," as the class had come to call themselves. One letter read:

> *Welcome young wizard! You are about to begin a great adventure, but you'd better come prepared. Ms. Blaydes will cast her reading and writing spell on you just like she did with us—and there will be no turning back. Before you know it you will be carrying a little notebook with you everywhere to jot down "story snippets," searching for "power words," and getting excited about "onomatopoeia." You say you don't know what onomatopoeia is? Don't worry. . . . You soon will. . . .*

These letters helped spark a curiosity about writing that Ms. Blaydes found many ways to sustain throughout the year. As she watches her young authors in action presenting their work in the cafeteria, she reflects on the process that pushed reading and writing into the spotlight in her classroom. Two years ago, Prairie View Elementary School implemented a new writing program after several teachers (including Ms. Blaydes) enrolled in a course on teaching writing as a process and integrating writing across content areas. Ms. Blaydes learned to use many different strategies to help her students grasp the concepts and principles of good writing, and she has given students plenty of time to practice their skills. Every Monday morning, her students have come to expect a "Grammar Slammers" event. This is a quiz—although Ms. Blaydes never actually calls it that. Students are given a practice sheet with ten sentences to correct. They must identify and correct any grammar, punctuation, or spelling mistakes they can find. When they are finished, Ms. Blaydes puts up an answer key on the overhead showing the mistakes and their corrections. Students use this key to correct their responses, and the class discusses which errors were the easiest and the most difficult to catch. Students also take a Friday vocabulary quiz in which they match vocabulary words with their definitions.

Ms. Blaydes believes that students learn to write by writing, so she combines objective tests of basic writing skills with plenty of opportunities to write for different audiences and purposes. Her students have written letters to themselves (and mailed them!) as well as weekly newsletters for parents. To vary the routine a bit, she has introduced writing events like the month-long "Greatest Fan" project for which students were assigned to be the secret fan of a football player on the local high school team. Students wrote weekly letters to their assigned team member, and the football coach taped the letters to the players' lockers. Each week Ms. Blaydes had the students incorporate new writing conventions they had learned into their letters. At the end of the month, the football players were invited to visit her class to meet and take photos with their fans.

This semester the writing wizards in Ms. Blaydes's room have been creating their own memoirs, persuasive pieces, poems, and illustrated picture books as part of the Young Authors project. Students use feedback from classmates and teachers to assess and improve their writing performance. Conferences with peer writing partners and teachers, before and during writing, help students select topics and polish skills. Today's Young Authors Fair is an additional way for the students to get feedback about their writing. The invited guests have been given evaluation forms for providing written comments on several aspects of the students' work. Each guest has been encouraged to provide commentary for at least five students.

Ms. Blaydes's reminiscences about the students' writing journey this year are interrupted as she feels a tug on her arm. Jenny, a quiet fourth-grader who has produced some lovely poems this semester, has come to tell her that she has seen the guest of honor arrive. Ms. Blaydes invited a well-known children's book author to join today's event to read a selection of his stories and discuss his own writing process with the group.

Assess

1. What message do you think Brigita Blaydes is sending her students by spending so much class time on writing?

2. Do you think Ms. Blaydes's approach to writing instruction (and assessment) is likely to be effective in promoting good writing skills? Explain.

3. If you were a student in Ms. Blaydes's class, how would you react to the range of assignments described in this case?

Prepare:

As you read the case, make notes:

1. **WHO** are the primary participants in the case? Describe them.

2. **WHAT** is taking place?

3. **WHERE** is the case taking place? Is the environment a factor?

4. **WHEN** is the case taking place? Is the timing a factor?

Ida Reffert, a social studies teacher at Tecumseh Middle School, couldn't wait for her eighth-grade students to arrive this morning to hear her plans for their final project. With three weeks of the semester to go, Ms. Reffert has been brainstorming to come up with a more interesting and creative way to assess students' understanding of the ideas they have been studying. When the students in her first-period class have settled into their seats, Ms. Reffert points to the board, where she has written "Assessment: Cafeteria Style" in big letters.

She tells them, "I have noticed that you each have your own strengths and talents, and I want to give you a chance to really showcase this as we wrap up our last unit of the school year. Instead of taking our traditional end-of-the-unit exam, you will be designing a project that draws on your strengths and allows you to demonstrate how well you understand the information we've been studying since we returned from spring break."

Middle School
Assessment: Cafeteria Style

The students look puzzled.

"Let me give you an example. Karlee, you've mentioned how much you love to take pictures, right? You might decide to create a photo essay that includes photographs of different objects or events that tie in with our unit and provides a description along with each photo."

"Awesome! You mean I could really do that instead of taking the test?" replies Karlee.

"Sure," answers Ms. Reffert. "And Jarred, I know you've been the announcer this season at the basketball games. Perhaps you could put those vocal talents to use here by creating some kind of radio show that takes us back in history."

Big grins start to emerge on the faces of the students as they realize the wide range of possibilities being made available to them.

"Let's take a few minutes to brainstorm some other ideas just to get everyone thinking about some options. Does anyone have an idea of something that might be interesting for a project?"

Several hands go up, and Ms. Reffert spends the next few minutes jotting down suggestions on the board: building a model, designing a Web-based history activity, creating a historical cartoon strip, designing a poster with a detailed illustrated time line, filming a short talk show episode with historical guests. The class is buzzing with excitement. As the class files out at the end of the period, three students stay behind to talk with Ms. Reffert.

Nettie, the captain of the girls' track team, says, "Ms. Reffert, this is a cool idea and all, and I know you're trying to make this more fun for us, but I am freaking out here. I have track practice every day after school, meets every weekend for the next few weeks, and I also have a regular babysitting job. I'm afraid I won't have time to come up with something great for this project. If it wasn't right during track season I would probably love the idea, but right now I'd much rather just take the test and get it over with." Carla, another student on the track team, voices the same concerns.

Ms. Reffert responds, "Let me think that over, girls, and consider what would be a fair option."

As the girls head to their next class, Angelo, another student, approaches Ms. Reffert and says, "Students are talking about doing cool stuff with digital cameras, video, art supplies, costumes. I don't have those kinds of things. My mom works two jobs and is always reminding me about how hard it is to make ends meet. I'll be lucky if she has time to take me out to buy a piece of posterboard right now. I would rather just take the test. I feel like I will be at a real disadvantage compared to some of the other kids."

"Don't worry, Angelo. We'll work something out. Let me think about it and I'll touch base with you in class tomorrow," Ms. Reffert replies.

She expected all the students to welcome the project idea because it puts them in control and lets them express themselves. Most students seem very excited about the project, but similar concerns were raised by a few students in her other eighth-grade social studies classes. One of her top students raised a good question about how Ms. Reffert was going to be able to grade the projects because they each might be so different. She realizes that she hasn't given that enough thought. She decides to look online to see if she can find some tips to help her create a grading rubric of some kind.

The next day Ms. Reffert distributes the following handout in class:

To wrap up our last unit of the semester, you have two assessment options. Each option is worth 100 points.

Option 1: Take an in-class 50-question multiple-choice **exam** on the material we've been covering since your return from spring break. The exam questions will be drawn from information covered in our class readings, lectures, handouts, and power point slides.

Option 2: Complete an **applied project** that draws on knowledge you've gained during this last unit. You need to get your project idea approved by me before beginning, and you will be graded using the following rubric.

Project Options
Radio show
Photo essay
Poster
Cartoon strip
Model

Project Rubric

	Exemplary	Proficient	Basic
Content (50 pts)	Demonstrates accurate understanding of course theories and concepts.	Demonstrates some understanding of course theories and concepts.	Does not use course theories and concepts in this project.
Organization (10 pts)	Ideas and information are well organized.	Some flaws in organization interfere with understanding of the project.	Project is haphazard. No apparent organization.
Appearance (10 pts)	Appearance of project is neat, with attention paid to every detail.	Appearance of project is good but not excellent.	Project is sloppy, seems hastily thrown together.
Grammar and Syntax (10 pts)	Flawless grammar and syntax are used.	A few grammar and syntax flaws interfere with understanding the author's message.	Several errors. No evidence of proofreading.
Creativity (10 pts)	Format and execution of project are very creative.	Project has some creative elements.	Little or no creativity is involved in this project.
Real-World Relevance (10 pts)	Project includes excellent examples or demonstrates how to apply Unit 3 content.	Project includes some examples of how to apply concepts and principles from Unit 3.	Does not give examples or demonstrate how to implement concepts and principles from Unit 3.

Assess

1. What is your initial reaction to Ida Reffert's plan for assessing her students' learning in the final unit of the semester?

2. Is it appropriate to let students choose how they will be assessed? Why or why not?

3. What challenges do you foresee with this assessment approach?

4. How do you think this plan might affect students' attitudes toward learning the material?

Prepare:

As you read the case, make notes:

1. **WHO** are the primary participants in the case? Describe them.

2. **WHAT** is taking place?

3. **WHERE** is the case taking place? Is the environment a factor?

4. **WHEN** is the case taking place? Is the timing a factor?

For the past 12 years, Joe Medino has been the principal at Jefferson High School, a large public high school within the city limits of a small town in the southeastern United States. He recently attended a conference on Assessment Issues in Education that presented many alternatives to traditional assessment. Intrigued by many of the suggestions he heard, Mr. Medino has decided to share the information with his teachers on his return to school. The school has a Professional Development Day scheduled for the following week, so Mr. Medino has prepared a brief description of some of the assessment options he encountered at the conference. He has asked the teachers to review the material before the workshop and come prepared to discuss it. His memo to the teachers follows.

High School
Innovative Assessment Strategies

MEMO

From: Principal Medino

RE: Interesting alternatives for classroom assessment

At the conference I attended last week, I learned that many schools are designing and using innovative assessment strategies, including authentic assessment, portfolios, process assessment, exhibits, and demonstrations. I'd like to share a few examples with you so we can discuss them as a group during our upcoming professional development workshop. Here are some of the ideas presented by teachers from around the country:

English   At a high school in Oregon, seniors complete a three-part Senior Project to graduate.

1. Students first choose a topic of interest to them, conduct research, and write a paper.

2. Next, they use the information in the papers to create real-life projects. While these projects are to satisfy requirements for senior English, the rich variety of topics chosen makes these efforts interdisciplinary. One aspiring singer wrote and performed a song she had learned to orchestrate. Another student wrote about Big Brothers and Big Sisters programs and recruited students to work with children from broken homes.

3. The third phase of the project is a formal presentation before a panel of teachers and community members, some of whom are experts in the topic. Following the formal presentation, judges ask each senior several questions to evaluate impromptu speaking skills, knowledge level, and poise.

Social Studies   At a high school in Rhode Island, ninth-grade students are asked to complete an oral history project based on interviews and written sources and to present their findings in class. Students are expected to identify central issues they want to explore, identify appropriate sources, develop a set of interview questions, and develop a presentation of their results. Students are evaluated on criteria such as whether they investigated three central issues, described at least one change over time, selected four appropriate sources for the interviews, asked valid questions, noted important differences between "fact" and "opinion" in answers, and effectively organized their writing and their presentation to the class.

In New Hampshire, as a four-part assessment for a twelfth-grade humanities course, students are asked to:

1. Construct their own final test on the semester content, subject to approval by the teacher.

2. Submit a written report on a central topic studied during the semester, conforming to stated grammar requirements.

3. Make a multimedia, 30-minute oral presentation on their chosen topic.

4. Serve on four evaluation teams to evaluate other students' presentations, playing a different role on each team—either a journalist who summarizes important details or a coach who suggests improvements for the presentation.

Math In a California junior high, a math teacher presents a unit or concept and then assigns projects that demonstrate how well students understand the concept. For example, to assess area and perimeter relationships in math, he asked the class to use a particular constant, say "1250 square feet," and design a scale model of a dream home, using graph paper for the floors. These strategies help him judge how much learning the student has retained. He found that "while I thought my students fully understood area relationships before we started on the project, in fact they really learned much more as they went along, when trying to find answers to specific questions such as how many square feet a bathroom should be."

Many of you are currently using traditional test formats to assess your students. When we meet at the workshop next week, I'd like to discuss the advantages and disadvantages of your current assessment plan, and I'd like to discuss ways we might incorporate a broader variety of options into our assessment approach as a school.

Assess

1. What is your initial reaction to the range of assessment options discussed in Joe Medino's memo as a student? As a future teacher?

2. How do these assessment options compare to the way you were assessed in your high school classes?

3. In your opinion, will teachers at Jefferson High School embrace the assessment ideas presented by Mr. Medino? Why or why not?

Assessing Student Learning

Outline	Learning Goals
What Is Assessment?	
■ Purposes of Assessment in Education ■ Standards for Teacher Competence	1. Describe the ways assessment is used in educational decision making.
Application: Assessment Planning	
■ Choosing Assessment Methods ■ Using Assessment Data	2. Explain why developing an assessment plan is an important part of being an effective teacher.
Application: Communication of Classroom Assessment Information	
■ Grading Procedures ■ Report Cards and Narrative Reports ■ Parent-Teacher Communication	3. Discuss the important considerations in determining grading procedures in the classroom. 4. Discuss different methods for communicating assessment information to parents and students.
Summary **Key Concepts** **Video Applications** **Case Studies: Reflect and Evaluate**	

WHAT IS ASSESSMENT?

If you are like many people, when you hear the word *assessment* the first ideas that pop into your head are tests and grades. While these are part of the picture, classroom assessment actually is a much broader term that includes measurement and evaluation. You might hear the terms *assessment, measurement,* and *evaluation* used interchangeably. However, our use of these terms in educational contexts should be more precise. Let's begin by clarifying what each of these terms means:

- **Assessment** is the process of obtaining information to be used for making decisions about curricula, students, programs, and educational policy (Nitko & Brookhart, 2007). This term also describes the actual tools (tests, papers, projects, etc.) used to gather information.

- **Measurement** refers to a quantitative or descriptive number assigned during the process of assessment to describe the extent to which someone possesses a certain attribute or skill (Haladyna, 2002).

- **Evaluation** is the process of making value judgments about the worth of a student's product or performance. Evaluation in classroom assessment often takes the form of assigning letter grades (Haladyna, 2002).

Simply put, measurement and evaluation are parts of the process of assessment.

Purposes of Assessment in Education

Assessment occurs in different forms and for different purposes throughout the learning process. It can take place anywhere students can be found: in the classroom, in the gym, in a lab, or on a field trip. The ultimate purpose of assessment is to support students' learning and development (Earl, 2003; Wiggins, 1998). Assessment involves a variety of data-gathering tools that allow teachers to do the following things (Popham, 2009):

1. provide feedback on students' progress and level of achievement,
2. guide and motivate students in their own learning,
3. improve the general effectiveness of instruction, and
4. identify modifications that will better meet the needs of individual students.

The assessment process provides a sense of *accountability.* Reporting results is one way to hold students, teachers, and school districts responsible for learning.

Student assessment provides valuable information for educational decision making. Consider these uses of assessment data (Kulieke et al., 1990):

Accountability: See page 552.

- *diagnosis:* monitoring students' strengths, weaknesses, and progress in specific areas;

- *placement:* matching students to appropriate levels of instruction, as in determining whether to place an elementary school student in a beginning or advanced reading group or deciding whether to place a secondary school student in a basic or honors-level English course;

- *guidance and counseling:* helping students make appropriate educational and vocational decisions that match their skills and interests;

- *admissions:* choosing students to be admitted into various programs—for example, determining eligibility for a gifted and talented program, making referrals for special education evaluation and services, or identifying candidates for admission to specific organizations such as the National Honor Society; and

- *certification:* determining mastery of specified criteria, such as satisfying the requirements to advance from one grade level to the next or to graduate from a program.

Assessment for Admissions. Assessment data are used to make decisions, including admission into the National Honor Society.

Used with permission of the National Association of Secondary School Principals, parent organization of the National Honor Society.

Think of examples from your own life. How have assessment data on your abilities been used to determine placement in educational programs or admission into organizations? How might your assessment data be used in the future for certification?

A Wider Range of Student Outcomes. Assessment today is not tied only to testing but includes a broad range of student outcomes, such as the dispositions indicators listed here.

Disposition Concerns

Disposition concerns are very important for teacher candidates as disposition becomes increasingly important to the development of collaboration skills and other professional behaviors. Concerns need to be identified early and problems need to be resolved as soon as possible. All teacher candidates will be evaluated on the following disposition indicators*, but only those candidates who have engaged in behaviors that suggest a negative disposition should be reported.

Disposition Indicators

Collaboration Issues: The ability to work together, especially in a joint intellectual effort.

Honesty/Integrity: The ability to demonstrate truthfulness to oneself and to others; demonstration of moral excellence and trustworthiness.

Respect: The ability to honor, value, and demonstrate consideration and regard for oneself and others.

Reverence for Learning: Respect and seriousness of intent to acquire knowledge.

Emotional Maturity: The ability to adjust one's emotional state to a suitable level of intensity in order to remain engaged with one's surroundings.

Reflection: The ability to review, analyze, and evaluate the success of past decisions in an effort to make better decisions in the future.

Flexibility: The willingness to accept and adapt to change.

Responsibility: The ability to act independently, demonstrating accountability, reliability, and sound judgment.

_____   _____   _____
Student's Name (please print)   UID #   Major

Explanation of Concern(s):

This concern has been discussed with the teacher candidate. My signature verifies that I am aware of the document's contents and existence.

_____   _____
Faculty/Staff Signature   Student Signature

_____   _____   _____
Faculty/Staff Name (please print)   Department   Date

Standards for Teacher Competence

Up until the 1980s, very little information was available to teachers about how to design tests or develop other types of assessments for use in the classroom (Popham, 2009). Experts argued that, whenever possible, teachers should use tests developed by experts outside the classroom, and they made little distinction between the kind of assessment data gathered for large-scale policy decisions and that needed by teachers for everyday decision making in the classroom (Pellegrino, Chudowsky, & Glaser, 2001; Shepard, 2006). Today our concept of assessment has expanded beyond the exclusive use of tests. Educators have begun to extend their assessment practices to evaluate a wider range of student outcomes, including knowledge, reasoning skills, performance skills, and dispositions (Costa & Kallick, 2000; Western and Northern Canadian Protocol for Collaboration in Education, 2006).

In 1987, three professional education associations began working to develop standards to address a broader view of teacher competence with regard to student assessment. Representatives from the American Federation of Teachers, the National Council on Measurement in Education, and the National Education Association came together to develop standards that call on teachers to demonstrate skill at selecting, developing, applying, communicating, and evaluating student assessment information and student assessment practices. The standards developed by these associations outline seven skills teachers need in order to fulfill their assessment responsibilities (Sanders et al., 1990). Teachers must be able to:

1. Choose assessment methods appropriate for instructional decisions.

2. Develop assessment methods appropriate for instructional decisions.

3. Administer, score, and interpret the results of both externally produced and teacher-produced assessment methods.

4. Use assessment results when making decisions about individual students, planning instruction, developing curriculum, and recommending school improvements.

5. Develop valid grading procedures.

6. Communicate assessment results to students, parents, and other educators.

7. Recognize unethical, illegal, and otherwise inappropriate assessment methods and uses of assessment information.

The scope of a teacher's professional responsibilities for student assessment at the classroom level can be described in terms of what happens before, during, and after instruction, as detailed in Guidelines 26.1.

APPLICATION: ASSESSMENT PLANNING

What teachers assess and how they assess it reveal what they value in students' learning and help clarify learning objectives for their students, for themselves, and for school administrators. Teachers should not develop assessments after a lesson or unit has been taught; rather, they should choose or design them carefully in advance (Wiggins & McTighe, 1998). The first step in assessment planning is to identify the period the assessments will cover. Teachers may plan for a year, a grading period (often organized in nine-week segments), a unit, or a single lesson. A comprehensive **assessment plan** includes the following elements:

Choosing learning objectives for effective instruction: See page 364.

- learning objectives,
- a time frame,

GUIDELINES 26.1	Assessment Responsibilities Before, During, and After Instruction
Stage	**Teacher responsibilities**
Prior to instruction	■ Understand students' cultural backgrounds, interests, skills, and abilities as they apply across a range of learning domains and/or subject areas. ■ Understand students' motivations and their interests in specific class content. ■ Plan instruction for individuals or groups of students. ■ Match assessments to instructional objectives. ■ Develop a comprehensive assessment plan.
During instruction	■ Monitor student progress toward instructional goals. ■ Identify gains and difficulties students are experiencing in learning and performing. ■ Adjust instruction. ■ Give contingent, specific, and credible praise and feedback. ■ Motivate students to learn. ■ Judge the extent of student attainment of instructional goals.
After instruction (e.g., at the end of a lesson, class, grading period)	■ Determine the extent to which each student has attained both short- and long-term instructional goals. ■ Communicate strengths and weaknesses based on assessment results to students and to parents or guardians. ■ Record and report assessment results for school-level analysis, evaluation, and decision making. ■ Analyze assessment information gathered before and during instruction to understand each student's progress to date and to inform future instructional planning. ■ Evaluate the effectiveness of instruction. ■ Evaluate the effectiveness of the curriculum and the materials in use.

Source: Adapted from http://www.unl.edu/buros/bimm/html/article3.html.

- types of assessment (e.g., in-class assignments, homework, tests, quizzes, self-assessments), and
- types of evaluation (e.g., scoring rubric, weight given to each assessment).

Example 26.1 presents an assessment plan for a science unit at the elementary school level.

Choosing Assessment Methods

Teachers have many different assessment options at their disposal. Research suggests that teachers' preferences for different assessment methods are related to the amount of hands-on experience they have had with those methods (Struyven, Dochy, & Janssens, 2008). Teachers need practice to development assessment expertise (Gearhart & Osmundson, 2009). When thinking about how to assess student learning, teachers must make several decisions about the types of assessment that will best serve their purposes.

Should the assessment be formal or informal? **Formal assessment** is typically a preplanned, systematic attempt to discover what students have learned. Formal assessments, which may include tests, quizzes, homework assignments, and projects, are announced ahead of time to give students time to prepare or study. **Informal assessment** is the spontaneous, day-to-day observation of how students behave and perform in class. It may involve techniques such as listening, observing students' interactions, and asking questions.

Is the purpose of the assessment formative or summative? *Formative* and *summative* refer to how certain assessments are used (Chappuis & Chappuis, 2007–2008; McMillan, 2007b). **Formative assessment** helps both the teacher and the students to determine progress, check for understanding, and make adjustments to improve students' learning while it is still in progress (Popham, 2008). However, simply using formative methods is not enough; the information must be used by the teacher early enough in the decision-making process to influence student learning (Stiggins & Chappuis, 2008). This process of using assessment data to adapt to the immediate needs of students can have profoundly positive effects on student achievement, particularly for low-achieving students and those with special needs (Black & Wiliam, 1998; Cizek, 2009). Both formal and informal methods can be used to gather formative data, but informal assessments tend to be used more often for this purpose. **Summative assessment** helps the teacher evaluate students' progress as well as the effectiveness of instructional methods at the end of a unit or grading period. Summative information often includes written documentation such as tests, quizzes, papers, scores on rating scales, or a student portfolio to determine a student's progress toward achieving specific goals in a class. Summative information may be used to assign grades for report cards, to inform remedial or advanced placement decisions, or to provide accountability and feedback

DIVERSITY

EXAMPLE 26.1	Sample Assessment Plan for a Science Unit at the Elementary Level
UNIT 1: The Water Cycle	
General learning goals	Understanding what the water cycle is, how it works, and how it helps living things. Ability to explain the water cycle and apply this understanding in a real-life context.
Time frame	Unit will take two weeks to complete.
Formative assessment	a. Three homework assignments (taken from Chapter 8 in the science textbook) b. Condensation demonstrations (group activity). Teacher will ask students to explain what they are doing, how it relates to the water cycle, and how it relates to real life. c. Short quiz on basic concepts at the end of week one.
Summative assessment	A written test at the end of the unit (several short-answer questions and one essay task).
Weights	a. Homework: 30% b. Quiz: 10% c. End-of-unit test: 60%

about the teacher's own effectiveness. Formative assessment guides student learning and informs instructional efforts, while summative assessment documents achievement (Shepard, 2006). Ideally, formative and summative assessment work in concert to track progress toward important learning goals and provide information about student understanding and mastery of instructional material.

Is it better to use a paper-and-pencil test or a performance-based assessment task? Teachers often rely on traditional test formats, in which students write their responses on paper. In some cases it may be more appropriate to use performance assessment, in which students demonstrate skills they have learned.

Is it important that the assessment be authentic? **Authentic assessments** measure important abilities using methods that simulate the application of those abilities to real-world intellectual problems, roles, or situations. Rather than relying exclusively on a paper-and-pencil test format, authentic assessments may require students to carry out an activity or develop a product in order to demonstrate skill or knowledge. For example, instead of completing a test matching vocabulary terms with their definitions, students might be asked to define their stand on a particular issue and write a letter to their representative in Congress using rich vocabulary taken from a list of words the class has been studying.

Will assessment involve the use of technology? Traditionally, computers were used primarily to score tests. Today the role of computers in assessment has expanded to include numerous uses (Bitter & Legacy, 2006; Britten & Cassidy, 2006; Gronlund, 2006). For example, software is available that administers quizzes and tests as well as records scores (e.g., WebCT, Blackboard). Some interactive testing software allows the incorporation of multimedia images, audio, and animation in test items (Koong & Wu, 2011; Lai, Chen, & Chen, 2008). Other software programs allow electronic portfolios to be created, and hypermedia programs (e.g., HyperCard) can help students develop their own multimedia presentations. In science classrooms, computers can be used to simulate hands-on investigations (Jarmon et al., 2009; Shavelson & Baxter, 1991). The benefits of providing computers as a part of the learning process vary depending on the age of the students, the kind of computer experiences offered, and the frequency of student access to computers. The potential gains, even for kindergarten and primary children, include improved motor skills, enhanced mathematical thinking, increased creativity, higher scores on tests of critical thinking and problem solving, and higher scores on standardized language assessments (Cardelle-Elawar & Wetzel, 1995; Clements & Sarama, 2003; Denning & Smith, 1997; Haugland & Wright, 1997). Computer-based writing programs can be successfully integrated into process-oriented writing programs in order to:

- provide critical support—or scaffolding—for young writers, enabling them to perform tasks they could not perform by themselves (Clements & Nastasi, 1993);

- allow students to compose longer and more complex stories and worry less about making mistakes (Davis & Shade, 1994); and

- help students gain confidence in their writing and increase their motivation to write more (Apple Classrooms of Tomorrow, 1995).

Computers also provide lower-achieving students with a supportive tool for practice while learning, without exposure to public failure (Bredekamp & Rosegrant, 1994).

Creating an assessment plan can be a challenging task, but it has several benefits for the classroom teacher (Nitko & Brookhart, 2007). Knowing how to choose and/or design assessment components increases the quality of teaching decisions and offers the teacher more flexibility (Stiggins, Rubel, & Quellmalz, 1986). As teachers gain experience in

Use of computer-based assessments, as well as electronic reporting of student grades, are increasingly common in schools today.

Test item formats: See page 497.

Performance assessment design: See page 510.

developing classroom assessments, they develop an appreciation of the strengths and limitations of each type of assessment procedure and improve the accuracy of their interpretations and uses of assessment data (Boothroyd, McMorris, & Pruzek, 1992; Plake, Impara, & Fager, 1993). Table 26.1 describes a variety of common assessment methods used in the classroom.

Using Assessment Data

In today's educational climate, assessment should be a *dynamic* process rather than an "event" signaling completion of instruction (Elliot, 2003; Nirmalakhandan, 2007). Assessment data help teachers evaluate the effectiveness of instruction and curricula. Frequent and varied classroom assessment also gives teachers an opportunity to learn a great deal about their students. During instruction, the effective teacher continually monitors students' progress toward instructional goals. If students seem to be struggling to understand a concept or perform a skill, the teacher can adjust instruction to better meet the students' needs. Assessment facilitates student learning when teachers (Falk, Ort, & Moirs, 2007; Ljungdahl & Prescott, 2009; Shepard, 2000):

- use classroom assessments as a tool to help them become more aware of the knowledge and skills students bring to a task, as well as skills students fail to use or skills they use inaccurately,
- use this knowledge as a starting point for new instruction, and
- monitor students' changing perceptions and understanding as instruction proceeds.

Students also can learn about themselves through assessment. When assessment is used to provide students with feedback about their own learning, students are given the tools to monitor their learning, make corrections, and develop the habit of continually reviewing and challenging what they know (Costa, 1989, 1996; Stiggins & Chappuis, 2008). Effective assessment can help students set personal academic expectations and improve their performance.

TABLE 26.1 — Assessment Tool Kit

Method	Description
Observation	Systematic observation of how students behave or perform, documented through sources such as anecdotal records or observational checklists
Questioning	Asking focused questions in class to elicit understanding
Learning conversations or interviews	Investigative discussions with students about their understanding and sources of confusion
Homework	Assignments to elicit understanding
Demonstrations, presentations	Opportunities for students to show their learning in oral and media performances, exhibitions
Projects and investigations	Opportunities for students to show connections in their learning through investigation and the production of reports or artifacts
Portfolios	Systematic collection of students' work that demonstrates accomplishments, growth, and reflection on their learning
Simulations	Simulated or role-playing tasks that encourage students to show connections among concepts and apply their learning in contexts that emulate real life
Learning logs/ reflective journals	Descriptions students maintain of the process they are achieving in their learning
Quizzes and tests	Opportunities for students to demonstrate their learning through written response
Self-assessments	Process in which students reflect on their own performance and use defined criteria for determining the status of their learning
Peer assessments	Process in which students evaluate the performance of their peers based on preset criteria

Source: Adapted from Western and Northern Canadian Protocol for Collaboration in Education (WNCP), 2006, p. 17.

Think about the developmental level or the subject you intend to teach, and take a look at Table 26.1. What types of assessments will you use for that specific developmental level or specific subject area? How will you evaluate those types of assessments?

APPLICATION: COMMUNICATION OF CLASSROOM ASSESSMENT INFORMATION

At the end of an assessment cycle, the teacher is expected to determine whether each student has met learning goals and to communicate students' strengths and weaknesses to the students and their parents or guardians. The teacher also may report assessment data for school-level analysis and decision-making purposes, such as deciding whether a student has met the criteria for advancement to the next grade level. In order to effectively communicate assessment information, a teacher needs a clear set of grading procedures, a reporting system, and an understanding of what constitutes appropriate, confidential use of assessment information.

Grading Procedures

Grading students' work can be a challenging and controversial task (Marzano, 2000; Trumbull & Farr, 2000). Many systems of assigning grades exist, and it is important that a teacher select grading procedures that are both credible and defensible (Guskey & Bailey, 2001; Linn & Gronlund, 2000). Assessment experts generally recommend that teachers keep the meaning of grades clear by basing them on a student's achievement in meeting specified learning goals (Lalley & Gentile, 2009); however, many teachers confound the grading process by assigning grades that reflect a mixture of attitude, effort, and achievement (O'Connor, 2007; Tomlinson & McTighe, 2006; Waltman & Frisbie, 1994). For example, in some classrooms, if a student meets the mastery criteria on a reading assignment but misbehaves during class, the teacher may dock the reading grade by 10% or more. In others, the teacher may award an A to a student who actually earned a B but seemed to put in a lot of effort. What do those grades mean? They are no longer a pure reflection of academic achievement or progress toward a specific learning goal. For a list of ways to increase the credibility and effectiveness of a grading system, see Guidelines 26.2.

Grading model. Teachers have three different models to choose among as they assign grades based on purpose and context: criterion-referenced, norm-referenced, and growth-based grading.

■ **Criterion-referenced letter grades:** In criterion-referenced grading, the grade represents the degree to which learning objectives have been met (Glaser & Nitko, 1971; Popham, 1978). Criteria for each

---

GUIDELINES 26.2   **Grading Tips**

1. Explain your grading policies to students early in the year.
2. Set reasonable standards and prepare students to be successful.
3. Base grades on as much objective evidence as possible. Guard against bias.
4. Eliminate the mixing of nongrading variables (e.g., deductions for misbehavior) into an academic grade.
5. Grade consistently.
6. Keep students informed of their standing in class.
7. Give students the benefit of the doubt when determining a borderline grade. All measurement techniques involve error.
8. Weight the assessment categories in a rational way. When deciding how many points a task is worth, consider relevance, relationship to what was taught in class, thinking processes and skills required, fairness to all students, objectivity, and reliability of the assessment results.
9. Consider the impact of failure on students. Use an F to represent low achievement rather than "failing to try" or "failing to turn in assignments."
10. Be aware of how much a zero can affect a student's composite score, and consider alternatives to giving a zero.

Sources: Drayer, 1979; Nitko & Brookhart, 2007.

grade level usually are specified in advance (e.g., 60% to 69% = D, 70% to 79% = C, 80% to 89% = B, 90% and above = A). In this system, all students could theoretically earn an A if they meet the preset criteria. Criterion-referenced grading is appropriate for giving students feedback about how close they are to meeting learning goals (a formative use) and can also be appropriate for documenting students' accomplishment of a particular learning goal or standard at the end of a marking period (a summative use).

■ **Norm-referenced letter grades:** In norm-referenced grading, the main influence on a student's grade is comparison with other students in the class. One common type of norm-referenced grading is *grading on the curve.* In this system, a student could study very hard and answer 92% of the questions on a test correctly yet still get a C if the class average was around 92%. Teachers typically have used this model when the class average is very low in an attempt to increase the number of students receiving high grades. Still, this type of grading is often viewed by students as unfair, it generally damages relationships among students and between teachers and students, and it also diminishes motivation for most students (Dalbert, Schneidewind, & Saalbach, 2007; Krumboltz & Yeh, 1996). Norm-referenced grading is not appropriate when assessment is viewed an as integral part of a standards-based program, because it does not accurately reflect mastery of knowledge. For example, the mean score of students could be 50%, indicating that few students had mastery of knowledge, yet many students would receive passing or even relatively high grades.

■ **Growth-based grading** involves assigning grades by comparing students' performance with the teacher's perceptions of their capability. Students performing at or above the level at which they are perceived to be capable would receive better grades, regardless of their absolute level of attainment or their standing in comparison with their classmates. Because the perceptions of teachers often are subjective and can be tinged with personal bias, objective measures of capability should be included. For example, a student who began a unit with very little prior knowledge (based on a pretest score) but made great strides in learning new material might be given the same grade as a student who actually knows more (based on a posttest score) but began with more prior knowledge. Growth-based grading can be an effective tool in formative assessment when the purpose is to provide feedback about how much progress a student has made, but it can be criticized as being an unfair way to determine final grades in a class.

Calculating grades. To calculate grades during a semester or marking period, a teacher must decide whether to use a point-based or percentage-based system. The **point grading system** is a popular approach in which each test, quiz, assignment, or project is given a certain number of points, depending on its overall importance. For example, a test might be worth 100 points, a writing assignment 50 points, and a quiz 10 points. Points are then awarded based on specific criteria, for example, 2 points per correct answer. The **percentage grading system** is another option, in which teachers assign grades based on what percentage of information a student has answered or completed correctly. To determine a final grade at the end of a marking period, the teacher averages all percentage grades the student has accumulated.

In both the point system and the percentage system, a student's score can be converted to a letter grade based on a predetermined cutoff. For example, a student who earned 450 out of 500 possible points or an average of 90% might be given an A. School systems often establish equivalent percentage categories for earning an A, B, C, and so forth; however, the percentages may vary from one school district to the next. In one district, 90% to 100% might be considered A work, while in a neighboring district 94% to 100% might be the range for receiving an A.

Grades and motivation. In the 1960s and 1970s, views of motivation were heavily influenced by behaviorist psychology, in which a schedule of rewards and punishments led to either increasing or decreasing the likelihood of a particular behavior. In that educational climate, teachers and administrators generally believed that assessment and grading motivated students to work hard (Brophy, 2006; WNCP, 2006). In recent years, however, research has shown that the relationship between grades and motivation is more complex and less predictable. Students who receive low grades may withdraw, blame others, decide that the work is "dumb," or feel helpless (Tomlinson, 2005). Low grades may encourage some students to simply give up on themselves or on school. This does not mean that students should never be given low grades or that they should expect only success in the classroom (Clifford, 1990, 1991). Students should be allowed to make mistakes—and even fail sometimes—as part of the learning process. However, the assessments given in class should support students' motivation to learn and improve. For example, teachers need to provide a number of assessment tasks so students have the opportunity to learn from their mistakes and show improvement on subsequent tasks. Students are more likely to show

Behavioral theories of motivation: See page 265.

improvement if a low grade is accompanied by specific, constructive feedback designed to prevent them from repeating the same mistakes.

Grading considerations for students with special needs. The number of students with disabilities included in general classes has increased dramatically in recent years (Handler, 2003). Although the inclusion of students with disabilities yields many positive outcomes (Baker, Wang, & Walberg, 1995; Calculator, 2009; Hunt, Farron-Davis, Beckstead, Curtis, & Goetz, 1994; Rafferty, 2005; Waldron, 1998), the process poses unique challenges for grading and reporting. Should the grades for these students be based on grade-level standards, or should grades somehow be adapted? Should the grades be based on achievement only, or should teachers also consider effort, progress made, or some other combination of factors? Teachers struggle in their efforts to assign fair, accurate, and meaningful grades to students with special needs (Guskey & Jung, 2009).

For students whose education occurs primarily in special education classrooms, the special education teacher typically assigns most grades. General education teachers determine grades only for the few subject areas in which students are included. For students with disabilities who are fully included in general classrooms, however, the division of grading responsibilities is less clear (Bursuck et al., 1996; Polloway et al., 1994). Often, the general education teacher takes responsibility for assigning all grades on the report card, and the special education teacher takes responsibility for a separate report on progress toward IEP goals.

When a student's performance in a general education content area is affected by the student's disability, the grading issues become more confusing (Guskey & Jung, 2009). Consider a sixth-grade student who is unable to demonstrate proficiency on sixth-grade standards because of multiple, severe disabilities but has worked hard and progressed well toward IEP goals. To fail this student, who has shown tremendous effort and progress, seems unfair. Nevertheless, giving passing marks to a student who has not yet met performance standards for that grade level also seems inappropriate.

From a legal standpoint, IEPs must "enable the child to achieve passing marks and advance from grade to grade" (*Board of Education v. Rowley, 1982*). Therefore, a failing grade for a student receiving special education services is considered an indication that appropriate educational services were not provided. To guide educators in developing appropriate policies for grading students with disabilities, Jung and Guskey developed the Five-Step, Inclusive Grading Model (Jung, 2009; Jung & Guskey, 2007). This model, shown in Figure 26.1, is designed to fit standards-based learning environments and meet the legal requirements for reporting on the progress of students who have IEPs.

Think about what you will do if a student in your class receives 89.3% on an assignment and 90% is needed for an A. Will you round up, or will you have a firm and consistent policy that the exact grade earned is the exact grade received? How will you justify your decision?

Report Cards and Narrative Reports

Teachers have many methods at their disposal for recording students' achievement and reporting student progress. Letter grades frequently are used at the upper elementary, middle school, and high school levels, while checklists of skills mastered, abbreviated letter grades (E for excellent,

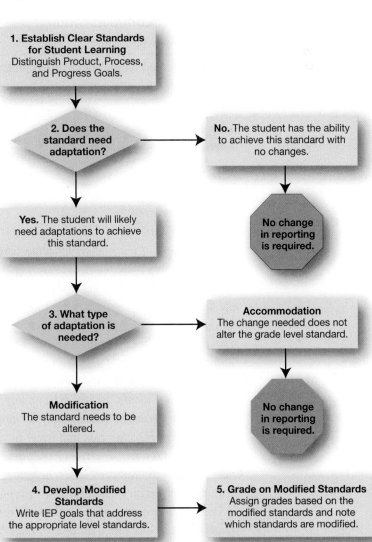

FIGURE 26.1 Five-Step, Inclusive Grading Model.

Reprinted with permission from Guskey, T. R., & Jung, L. A. (2009). Grading and Reporting in a Standards-Based Environment: Implications for Students With Special Needs. *Theory Into Practice, 48,* 53–62.

S for satisfactory, or N for needs improvement), or narrative progress reports are used more often at the early childhood level. **Narrative progress reports** provide detailed, written accounts of each student's learning and performance in class. Example 26.2 provides an example of a narrative report.

Schools may use a combination of methods on a single report card. For example, letter grades may be used to indicate subject-matter achievement, but a checklist or rating scale may be used to convey additional information about student behavior or work habits, with space provided for narrative comments. School administrators and outside evaluators might need a concise, somewhat quantifiable summary of each student's progress for accountability and record-keeping purposes, but parents might want more detailed information about the standards mastered, areas of strength and weakness, or their child's level of attainment compared with that of peers. While a rich description of a student's learning and development may be much appreciated by parents, such reports can be very time-consuming for teachers to prepare, and skill in writing narrative reports requires practice guided by expert teachers (Nitko & Brookhart, 2007). Modified narrative reports that combine a checklist or rating scale with short written comments are a viable compromise.

Any teacher with access to a personal computer can use a simple spreadsheet program to record and calculate student grades. Gradebook software programs allow teachers to choose among a variety of options for recording and reporting grades. School districts sometimes provide and require the use of a particular gradebook program. Some of these programs are linked to confidential Web sites where parents can log in (with a username and unique password) to check their children's grades at any time during the grading period.

Parent-Teacher Communication

Research on home-school communication indicates that parents want to be (Cuttance & Stokes, 2001):

- kept well informed about their children's progress in both academic and nonacademic areas,
- informed about the perceived strengths and weaknesses of their children, and

---

EXAMPLE 26.2 **Narrative Report**

Date: November 2012
Child: Xavier Roberts
Class: Kindergarten

Xavier is one of the younger kindergarteners in the class this year. At the beginning of the year, he was very tentative about entering the classroom. Over the course of the first month as Xavier took the time to get to know his new classmates, he became more comfortable and he is now very willing to jump right into one of the morning learning centers when he arrives. Xavier plays well with a variety of children in the class, but he has developed the strongest bond with Nick and Everett. They like to build structures in the block area, play with the Brio trains, and gather on the beanbags in the reading area to look at picture books.

Xavier has shown an interest in reading in the past month, and he often asks for help in sounding out words. He recognizes many sight words and can easily identify the printed names of his classmates when we do our name card activity in morning circle. We've been working on letter recognition and letter formation this semester. Xavier recognizes all uppercase and lowercase letters of the alphabet, but he is still learning how to write them independently. He can copy letters accurately but sometimes writes them backward when recalling them on his own. That is very typical for this age.

We've been encouraging the children to take responsibility for cleaning up their own materials, and this has been a bit of a struggle with Xavier. He gets wrapped up in the activity he is doing, and it often takes two or three reminders to get him to put away the things he got out and get ready for the next class activity. This will get better with practice. Overall, Xavier is a joy to have in class. He is friendly and curious and has a great imagination.

■ provided with pertinent and constructive advice about how they can support their children's learning.

Parent-teacher conferences are an effective way to build strong home-school connections. They provide parents with a better understanding of children's learning and give teachers the opportunity to gain valuable insights from parents about their children. Parents and teachers may have very different ideas about the meaning of grades, so clear communication with parents about what grades represent within your classroom is very important (Waltman & Frisbie, 1994). Guidelines 26.3 provides a set of organizational tips to follow before, during, and after parent-teacher conferences to make the most of the conference opportunity.

GUIDELINES 26.3   Organizational Tips for Parent-Teacher Conferences

Before the conference	■ Have a clear purpose and a clear understanding of the outcome you would like.
	■ Plan the points you want to discuss.
	■ Plan to have a translator available if necessary.
	■ Gather samples of student work, including progress reports and other information related to grades.
	■ Identify the student's strengths and weaknesses.
	■ Anticipate parents' reactions and questions and jot down notes to address any questions you think may be raised.
	■ Create a seating arrangement that will be comfortable for adults.
	■ Make sure you have pen and paper for yourself and the parents.
	■ Make a conference schedule and a "Do Not Disturb" sign to post on your door so you can meet with parents without distraction.
	■ Meet parents and escort them to your room.
During the conference	Opening:
	■ Be prompt and ready to begin.
	■ Begin by expressing your appreciation that the parents have come to the conference. Try to establish a tone of goodwill and friendly cooperation as quickly as you can.
	■ Begin with positive remarks about the student. Talk about the student's aptitude, special talents, improvements, and potential. Focus on strengths even if the problem you are meeting to discuss is a serious one. Never lose sight of the fact that the child or adolescent is very important to the parents.
	During:
	■ Give parents your full attention.
	■ Use language that will make parents comfortable. Avoid educational jargon.
	■ Convey the attitude that the student's welfare is your primary concern.
	■ Discuss specific examples of the student's work and/or behavior.
	■ If you have a problem to discuss, state the problem in simple, factual terms and express your desire to work together for a successful resolution.
	■ If discussing a recurring problem, let parents know of any improvement you have seen. State what steps you have taken to correct the situation.
	■ Always allow upset or angry parents to speak first.
	Concluding:
	■ End the conference by recapping important points.
	■ Determine what you will do to follow up after the conference.
	■ Express appreciation again for the parents' concern and the time they have spent with you.
After the conference	■ Take the time to jot down detailed notes about what was discussed.
	■ Write down any steps you agreed to take to follow up.
	■ Keep in contact with the parents.

Source: Adapted from Thompson, 2002.

Parent-teacher conferences. Teachers' responsibilities for assessment include communicating students' strengths and weaknesses to parents.

Teachers at all grade levels should make an effort to maintain open lines of communication with parents throughout the school year, not just during the week report cards are distributed. In addition to parent-teacher conferences, home-school communication may include:

- weekly newsletters,
- information and assignments sent home in "Friday folders,"
- information posted on a class or school Web site,
- phone calls, or
- e-mails and notes sent to parents.

Although home-school communication is important, beyond this teachers need to keep students' educational records confidential. For specific uses of educational records, teachers should be familiar with the **Family Educational Rights and Privacy Act (FERPA)** of 1974. FERPA, also called the Buckley Amendment, specifies that parents of children under 18 years of age may review the student's school records; however, the school must have parents' written permission in order to release information about a student's educational record to other sources.

Summary

Describe the ways assessment is used in educational decision making. Assessment data provide information about individual students, quality of teaching, and effectiveness of educational programs. Assessment can be used to diagnose student strengths and weaknesses, match students to appropriate levels of instruction, and help students make appropriate educational and vocational choices that match their skills and interests. It also is used to determine eligibility for admission to various programs and to provide certification of skills. Assessment helps determine the value and effectiveness of instructional programs and provides direction for modifications that will better meet students' needs.

Explain why developing an assessment plan is an important part of being an effective teacher. A comprehensive assessment plan describes the learning objectives, time frame, and types of assessment and evaluation for each lesson or set of lessons. Specifically, it indicates how often assessments will be used, what types of assessments will be used (formal, informal, formative, summative, authentic, technology-based, tests, performance-based), how they will be graded, and how the assessment data will be used to provide helpful feedback to students and to help teachers improve their instructional practices.

Discuss the important considerations in determining grading procedures in the classroom. Teachers have three different models to choose from as they assign grades: criterion-referenced, norm-referenced, and growth-based grading. Teachers also must decide whether to calculate grades using a point system or a percentage system. Finally, grading procedures should be designed to support students' motivation to learn and improve, with measures such as providing frequent assessments with specific feedback.

Discuss different methods for communicating assessment information to parents and students. Assessment information can be communicated to parents and students through report cards that include specific letter grades, a rating scale for student behaviors, or a narrative description of student progress. Parent-teacher conferences allow teachers to communicate exactly what grades indicate in their classroom. In addition to report cards and parent-teacher conferences, home-school communication may include weekly newsletters, information posted on a class or school Web site, phone calls, or notes sent to parents or guardians. All methods of communication should be in accordance with the Family Educational Rights and Privacy Act (FERPA) of 1974.

Key Concepts

assessment   477

assessment plan   479

authentic assessments   481

criterion-referenced letter grades   483

evaluation   477

Family Educational Rights and Privacy Act (FERPA)   488

formal assessment   480

formative assessment   480

growth-based grading   484

informal assessment   480

measurement   477

narrative progress reports   486

norm-referenced letter grades   484

percentage grading system   484

point grading system   484

summative assessment   481

Video Applications

www.mhhe.com/bohlin2e

Video 1: Various Demonstrations of Learning Assessment (*5 minutes*)

Clip 1 (elementary reading session): Informal assessment

Clip 2 (middle school science quiz): Formal assessment

Clip 3 (middle school classroom): Formative assessment

Clip 4 (high school International Relations teacher interview): Authentic assessment

Clip 5 (high school Spanish class): Formative assessment

Case Studies
Reflect and Evaluate

EARLY CHILDHOOD: "The Zoo"

These questions refer to the case study on page 468.

1. Initially, this case might seem to have nothing to do with assessment. As you take a closer look, what types of skills do you see an opportunity to assess?

2. What steps did teacher Sanjay Baterdene take to collect and record assessment information?

3. How can observation be used as a type of formative assessment?

4. What kinds of documentation might be appropriate to use when assessing young children?

5. Would it be meaningful and/or appropriate to issue a report card with letter grades to communicate assessment information about these preschool children? Why or why not?

6. What are the advantages of providing a narrative report to parents, especially when working with 4- and 5-year-olds?

7. What evidence did you see that the teachers modified their plans based on information gathered from informal observation of the students? Why is this process important?

8. If Vivian Stanich, the more experienced teacher, wants Mr. Sanjay to develop an assessment plan for the coming week, what advice should she offer to guide him through the process of developing an effective plan?

ELEMENTARY SCHOOL: "Writing Wizards"

These questions refer to the case study on page 470.

1. Does Ms. Blaydes appear to have a well-designed assessment plan in place with respect to writing skills? Explain your answer.

2. Which assignments or activities in this fourth-grade classroom might serve as sources of formative assessment?

3. Which activities serve as sources of summative assessment?

4. Describe the ways in which students are involved in the assessment process in Ms. Blaydes's classroom.

5. Students in this classroom correct their Grammar Slammer sentences together as a class. Do you think it is necessary for Ms. Blaydes then to collect these assignments and record a grade for them? Why or why not?

6. Referring to the standards for teacher competence in assessment, which areas do you see as a clear strength for Ms. Blaydes? Explain your answer.

MIDDLE SCHOOL: "Assessment: Cafeteria Style"

These questions refer to the case study on page 472.

1. How would you describe the purpose behind Ms. Reffert's assessment approach?

2. Are the test option and the project option likely to be equivalent in assessing how well students understand the content presented in the final unit of the semester? Explain your answer.

3. What conclusions about student learning will Ms. Reffert be able to draw from the test results?

4. What conclusions about student learning will Ms. Reffert be able to draw from the projects she receives?

5. How could Ms. Reffert use the assessment data she gathers on the project/test option to make decisions about the way she teaches? To make decisions about the effectiveness of her assessment plan?

6. What options are available to Ms. Reffert for determining grades to be given on the project?

7. What are some ways information about the students' performance could be communicated to parents?

HIGH SCHOOL: "Innovative Assessment Strategies"

These questions refer to the case study on page 474.

1. Referring to the descriptions of assessment practices in Mr. Medino's memo, identify the practices that are examples of *formative assessment*.

2. Referring to the descriptions of assessment practices in Mr. Medino's memo, identify the practices that are examples of *summative assessment*.

3. Which standard(s) for teacher competence in educational assessment is Mr. Medino addressing in the memo?

4. How would you describe the purpose of the Senior Project used in Oregon?

5. In the New Hampshire humanities course, what advice would you give the teacher about grading the students' work?

6. Give examples of ways teachers can communicate to parents the assessment information described in the memo.

Test Construction and Use

Outline	Learning Goals
Characteristics of High-Quality Classroom Tests	
■ Validity ■ Reliability ■ Fairness and Equivalence ■ Practicality	1. Discuss the importance of validity, reliability, fairness/equivalence, and practicality in test construction.
Application: Developing a Test Blueprint	2. Explain how a test blueprint is used to develop a good test.
Application: Developing Test Items	
■ Alternate-Choice (True/False) Items ■ Matching Exercises ■ Multiple-choice Items ■ Short-answer/Completion Items ■ Essay Tasks	3. Discuss the usefulness of each test item format. 4. Compare and contrast the scoring considerations for the five test item formats.
Application: Test Analysis and Revision	5. Describe the benefits of item analysis and revision.
Summary **Key Concepts** **Case Studies: Reflect and Evaluate**	

CHARACTERISTICS OF HIGH-QUALITY CLASSROOM TESTS

Tests are only one form of assessment that you may find useful in your classroom. Because teachers use tests quite frequently, you will need to become comfortable designing and evaluating classroom tests. Writing good test items takes considerable time and practice. Researchers have identified principles of high-quality test construction (Gronlund, 2006; McMillan, 2007a; National Research Council, 2001). Despite this, countless teachers violate these principles when they develop classroom tests. Poorly constructed tests compromise the teacher's ability to obtain an accurate assessment of students' knowledge and skills, while high-quality assessments yield reliable and valid information about a student's performance (McMillan, 2007a). Let's examine four facets by which to judge the quality of tests:

- validity,
- reliability,
- fairness and equivalence, and
- practicality.

Validity

Validity typically is defined as the degree to which a test measures what it is intended to measure. Validity is judged in relation to the purpose for which the test is used. For example, if a test is given to assess a social studies unit on American government, then the test questions should focus on information covered in that unit. Teachers can optimize the validity of a test by evaluating the test's content validity and creating an effective layout for the test items.

Content validity. **Content validity** refers to evidence that a test accurately represents a content domain—or reflects what teachers have actually taught (McMillan, 2007a). A test cannot cover everything a student has learned, but it should provide a representative sample of learning (Weller, 2001). A test would have low content validity if it covered only a few ideas from lessons and focused on extraneous information or if it covered one portion of assigned readings but completely neglected other material that was heavily emphasized in class. When developing a test, teachers can consider several content validity questions (Nitko & Brookhart, 2007):

Validity as it applies to standardized tests: See page 545.

- Do the test questions emphasize the same things that were emphasized in day-to-day instruction?
- Do the test questions cover all levels of instructional objectives included in the lesson(s)?
- Does the weight assigned to each type of question reflect its relative value among all other types?

Test layout. The layout, or physical appearance, of a test also can affect the validity of the test results. For example, imagine taking a test by reading test items written on the board by the teacher or listening to questions dictated by the teacher. The teacher's handwriting or students' ability to see the board may hinder test performance, lowering the validity of the test score. Writing test items on the board or dictating problems also may put students with auditory or vision problems at a particular disadvantage. The dictation process can slow down test taking, making it very difficult for students to go back to check their answers a final time before submitting them. Have you ever taken a test for which the instructions were unclear? A test-taker's inability to understand the instructions could lower the level of performance, reducing the validity of the test results.

Teachers can follow these guidelines when deciding how to design a test's layout:

- In general, tests should be typed so that each student has a printed copy. Exceptions would be dictated spelling tests or testing of listening and comprehension skills.
- The test should begin with clear directions at the top of the first page or on a cover page. Typical directions include the number and format of items (e.g., multiple-choice, essay), any penalty for guessing, the amount of time allowed for completion of the test, and perhaps mention of test-taking strategies the teacher has emphasized (e.g., "Read each question completely before answering" or "Try to answer every question").
- Test items should be grouped by format (e.g., all multiple-choice items in one section, all true/false items in another section), and testing experts usually recommend arranging like items in order of increasing difficulty. Arranging items from easiest to hardest decreases student anxiety and increases performance (Tippets & Benson, 1989).

Reliability. Consistency among scores on a test given twice indicates reliability.

	Monday	Wednesday	
Claire	87	88	
Jee	83	80	
Kristy	74	73	
Doug	77	78	
Nick	93	92	
Taylor	88	88	
Abby	68	69	
Marcus	70	72	

Reliability

Reliability of test results: See page 546.

Reliability refers to the consistency of test results. If a teacher were to give a test to students on Monday and then repeat that same test on Wednesday (without additional instruction or practice in the interim), students should perform consistently from one day to the next. Let's consider several factors that affect test reliability.

Test length and time provided for test taking. Would you rather take a test that has 5 items or one that has 25 items? Tests with more items generally are more reliable than tests with fewer items. However, longer assessments may not always be a practical choice given other constraints, such as the amount of time available for assessment. When you design tests, make sure that every student who has learned the material well has sufficient time to complete the assessment. Consider the average amount of time it will take students to complete each question, and then adjust the number of test questions accordingly. Example 27.1 provides some target time requirements for different types of test items based on typical test taking at the middle school or high school level. Keep in mind that elementary school students require shorter tests than older students. The time allotted during the school day for each subject might be less than the average class period in middle or high school. So elementary school students might have only 30 minutes to take a test (requiring fewer items), while students in middle school or high school might have a 50-minute period. Students in the elementary grades also need shorter tests because they have shorter attention spans and tire more quickly than older students.

Frequency of testing. The frequency of testing—or how often students are tested—also affects reliability. The number and type of items included on tests may be influenced by the amount of material that has been covered since the last assessment was given. A review of research on frequency of testing yields several conclusions (Dempster, 1991):

- Frequent testing encourages better retention of information and appears to be more effective than a comparable amount of time spent studying and reviewing material.

- Tests are more effective in promoting learning if students are tested soon after they have learned material and then retested on the same material later.

- The use of cumulative questions on tests is key to effective learning. Cumulative questions give students an opportunity to recall and apply information learned in previous units.

Objectivity of scoring. **Objectivity** refers to the degree to which two or more qualified evaluators agree on what rating or score to assign to a student's performance. Some types of test items, such as multiple choice, true/false, and matching, tend to be easier to score objectively than short-answer items and essays. Objective scoring increases the reliability of the test score. This does not mean that the more subjective item formats should be eliminated, because they have their own advantages, as we will see later in the module.

EXAMPLE 27.1   Time Requirements for Certain Assessment Tasks

Type of task	Approximate time per item
True/false	20–30 seconds
Multiple choice (factual)	40–60 seconds
One-word fill-in	40–60 seconds
Multiple choice (complex)	70–90 seconds
Matching (5 stems/6 choices)	2–4 minutes
Short answer	2–4 minutes
Multiple choice (with calculations)	2–5 minutes
Word problems (simple arithmetic)	5–10 minutes
Short essays	15–20 minutes
Data analysis/graphing	15–25 minutes
Drawing models/labeling	20–30 minutes
Extended essays	35–50 minutes

Source: Reprinted from Nitko & Brookhart, 2007, p. 119.

Fairness and Equivalence

Fairness is the degree to which all students have an equal opportunity to learn material and demonstrate their knowledge and skill (Yung, 2001). Consider this multiple-choice question:

Which ball has the smallest diameter?

a. basketball
b. soccer ball
c. lacrosse ball
d. football

If students from a lower-income background answer this geometry question incorrectly, is it because they haven't mastered the concept of diameter or because they lack prior experience with some of the items? Do you think girls also might lack experience with some of these items? Females, as a group, do not score as high as males on tests that reward mechanical or physical skills (Patterson, 1989) or mathematical, scientific, or technical skills (Moore, 1989). African-American, Latino, and Native-American students, as well as students for whom English is a second language, do not as a group perform as well as Anglos on formal tests (Garcia & Pearson, 1994). Asian Americans, who have a reputation as high achievers in American society and who tend to score higher than Anglo students in math, score lower on verbal measures (Tsang, 1989).

A high-quality assessment should be free of *bias,* or a systematic error in test items that leads students from certain subgroups (ethnic, socio-economic, gender, religious, disability) to perform at a disadvantage (Hargis, 2006). Tests that include items containing bias reduce the validity of the test score (Cizek, 2009). Additional factors that tend to disadvantage students from diverse cultural and linguistic backgrounds during testing include:

- speededness, or the inability to complete all items on a test as a result of prescribed time limitations (Mestre, 1984);

DIVERSITY

Test fairness and test bias: See page 558.

Fairness. Tests should be free of bias that would lead certain subgroups to perform at a disadvantage.

- test anxiety and testwiseness (Garcia, 1991; Rincon, 1980);
- differential interpretation of questions and foils (Garcia, 1991); and
- unfamiliar test conditions (Taylor, 1977).

To ensure that all students have an equal opportunity to demonstrate their knowledge and skills, teachers may need to make individual assessment accommodations with regard to format, response, setting, timing, or scheduling (Elliott, McKevitt, & Kettler, 2002).

In addition to assuring fairness among individuals within a particular classroom, assessments must demonstrate fairness from one school year to the next or even one class period to the next. If you decide to use different questions on a test on a particular unit, you should try to ensure equivalence from one exam to the next. **Equivalence** means that students past and present, or students in the same course but different class periods, are required to know and perform tasks of similar (but not identical) complexity and difficulty in order to earn the same grade (Nitko & Brookhart, 2007). This assumes that the content or learning goals have not changed and that the analysis of results from past assessments was satisfactory.

Practicality

Performance
assessment:
See Module 28.

Assessing students is very important, but the time devoted to assessment should not interfere with providing high-quality instruction. When creating assessments, teachers need to consider issues of **practicality**—the extent to which a particular form of assessment is economical and efficient to create, administer, and score. For example, essay questions tend to be less time-consuming to construct than good multiple-choice questions. However, multiple-choice questions can be scored much more quickly and are easier to score objectively. Performance tasks such as group projects or class presentations can be very difficult to construct properly, but there are times when these formats allow the teacher to better assess what students have learned. When deciding what format to choose, consider whether:

- the format is relatively easy to construct and not too time-consuming to grade,
- the time spent using the testing format could be better spent on teaching, and
- another format could meet assessment goals but be more efficient.

Think about a particular test you might give in the grade level you intend to teach. How will you ensure its validity, reliability, and fairness? Evaluate your test's practicality.

APPLICATION: DEVELOPING A TEST BLUEPRINT

Bloom's taxonomy
and its application
to instructional plan-
ning: See page 365.

To increase reliability, validity, fairness, and equivalence, try making a blueprint prior to developing a test. A **test blueprint** is an assessment planning tool that describes the content the test will cover and the way students are expected to demonstrate their understanding of that content. When it is presented in a table format, as shown in Example 27.2, it is called a **table of specifications.** On the table, the row headings (down the left margin) indicate major topics that the assessment will cover. The column headings (across the top) list the six classification levels of Bloom's taxonomy of cognitive objectives (Bloom et al., 1956), which provide a framework for composing tests. The first three categories (knowledge, comprehension, and application) are often called lower-level objectives, and the last three categories (analysis, synthesis, and evaluation) are called higher-level objectives. Think of these six categories as a comprehensive framework for considering different cognitive goals that need to be met when planning for instruction. Each cell within the table of specifications itemizes a specific learning goal. These learning goals get more complex as you move from left to right. In the far left column, the student might be asked to define terms, while in the far right column the student is asked to synthesize or evaluate information in a meaningful way. For each cell, the teacher also needs to decide how many questions of each type to ask, as well as how each item will be weighted (how many points each item will be worth). The weight of each item should reflect its value or importance (Gronlund, 2006; Nitko & Brookhart, 2007).

When planning a test, it is not necessary to cover all six levels of Bloom's taxonomy. It is more important that the test's coverage matches the learning goals and emphasizes the same concepts or skills the teacher focused on in day-to-day instruction. Teaching is most effective when lesson plans, teaching activities, and learning goals are aligned and when all three are aligned with state standards. Assessment is most effective when it matches learning goals and teaching activities. Assuming that learning goals do not change, the same blueprint can be used to create multiple tests for use across class periods or school years.

EXAMPLE 27.2   **Test Blueprint for a High School Science Unit**

Content outline	Major Categories of Cognitive Taxonomy					
	Knowledge	**Comprehension**	**Application**	**Analysis**	**Synthesis**	**Evaluation**
1. Historical concepts of force	*Identify the concepts of force and list the empirical support for each concept. (2 test items)*					
2. Types of force	*Define each type of force and the term velocity. (2 test items)*	*Classify each force as a vector or scalar quantity, given its description. (2 test items)*				
3. Two-dimensional forces	*Define the resultant two-dimensional force in terms of one-dimensional factors. (2 test items)*		*Find the x and y components of resultant forces on an object. (6 test items)*			
4. Three-dimensional forces	*Define the resultant three-dimensional force in terms of one-dimensional factors. (1 test item)*					
5. Interaction of masses	*Define the terms inertial mass, weight, active gravitational mass, and passive gravitational mass. (6 or 7 test items)*		*Calculate the gravitational forces acting between two bodies. (8 test items)*		*Develop a definition of mass that explains the difference between inertial mass and weight. (1 test item)*	

Source: Adapted from Kryspin & Feldhusen, 1974, p. 42.

Use the sample table of specifications in Example 27.2 to create your own test blueprint for a particular unit at the grade level you intend to teach. What topics will your test cover, and how will you require students to demonstrate their knowledge?

APPLICATION: DEVELOPING TEST ITEMS

After you have selected the content to be covered on the test, it is time to consider the format of test items to use. Teachers have several test formats available: alternate response, matching items, multiple choice, short answer, and essay. Alternate response (e.g., true/false), matching items, and multiple choice are called **recognition tasks** because they ask students to recognize correct information among irrelevant or incorrect statements. These types of items are also referred to as **objective testing** formats because they have one correct answer. Short answer/completion (fill in the blanks) and essay items are **recall tasks,** requiring students to generate the correct answers from memory. These types of items are also considered a **subjective testing** format, with the scoring more open to interpretation. Objective and subjective formats differ in three important ways:

Rubric for a Position Essay

Criteria	Points possible	Points earned
Format (typed, double-spaced)	2	
States a clear position for or against	3	
Provides appropriate level of detail describing stated position	5	
Includes arguments to support response from resources	5	
Grammar, spelling, punctuation, and clarity of writing	5	
Includes references in appropriate format for resources	5	
TOTAL	**25**	

Figure 27.1. Rubrics. Rubrics ensure consistency of grading when subjective test item formats are used.

1. *The amount of time to take the test.* While teachers may be able to ask 30 multiple-choice questions in a 50-minute class period, they may be able to ask only four essay questions in the same amount of time.

2. *The amount of time to score the test.* Scoring of objective formats is straightforward, needing only an answer key with the correct responses. If teachers use optical scanning sheets ("bubble sheets") for objective test responses, they can scan many sheets in a short amount of time. A middle school or high school teacher who uses the same 50-item test for several class periods can scan large batches of bubble sheets in minutes. Because extended short answers or essay questions involve more subjective judgments, they are more time-consuming to grade. Teachers may choose to use essays for classes with fewer students.

3. *The objectivity in grading.* Because extended short answers or essay questions are subjective, teachers can improve their objectivity in scoring these formats by using a rubric. A **rubric,** such as the example in Figure 27.1, is an assessment tool that provides preset criteria for scoring student responses, making grading simpler and more transparent. Rubrics ensure consistency of grading across students or grading sessions (when teachers grade a set of essays, stop, and return to grading).

Teachers should select the format that provides the most direct assessment of the particular skill or learning outcome being evaluated (Gronlund, 2006). As you will see next, each type of item format has its own unique characteristics. However, some general rules of item construction apply across multiple formats. All test items should:

- measure the required skill or knowledge;
- focus on important, not trivial, subject area content;
- contain accurate information, including correct spelling;
- be clear, concise, and free of bias; and
- be written at an appropriate level of difficulty and an appropriate reading level.

Alternate-Choice (True/False) Items

An **alternate-choice item** presents a proposition that a student must judge and mark as either true or false, yes or no, right or wrong. Alternate-choice items are recognition tasks because students only need to recognize whether the statement matches a fact that they have in their memory. A true/false question might state:

An equilateral triangle has three sides of equal length.	*T F*

Teachers also can design items that require multiple true/false responses. For example:

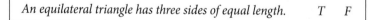

Scientists who study earthquakes have learned that:

1. *the surface of the earth is in constant motion due to forces inside the planet.*   *T   F*

2. *an earthquake is the vibrations produced by breaking rocks along a fault line.*   *T   F*

3. *the time and place of earthquakes are easy to predict.*   *T   F*

Alternate-choice questions are optimal when the subject matter lends itself to an either-or response. They allow teachers to ask a large number of questions in a short period of time (a practicality issue), making it possible to cover a wide range of topics within the domain being assessed. However, an obvious disadvantage of this format is that students have a 50% chance of getting the answer correct simply by guessing. Good alternate-choice questions are harder to write than you might expect, Teachers can use the recommendations given in Guidelines 27.1.

GUIDELINES 27.1   Developing Effective True/False Items

1. Use short statements and simple vocabulary and sentence structure. Consider the following true/false item: *"The true/false item is more subject to guessing but it should be used in place of a multiple-choice item, if well constructed, when there are insufficient plausible distractors."* Long, complex sentences such as this one are confusing and therefore more difficult to judge as true or false.

2. Include only the central idea in each statement. Consider the following true-false item: *"The true-false item, which is preferred by testing experts, is also called an alternate-response item."* This item has two ideas to evaluate: being favored by experts and being called an alternative-response item.

3. Use negative statements sparingly, and avoid double negatives. These also can be confusing.

4. Use precise wording so that the statement can unequivocally be judged true or false.

5. Write false statements that reflect common misconceptions held by students who have not achieved learning goals.

6. Avoid using statements that reproduce verbatim sentences from the textbook or reading material. Students may be able to judge the item true or false simply by memorizing and not understanding. This reduces the validity of the student's test score. Does the student *really* know the material?

7. Statements of opinion should be attributed to some source (e.g., according to the textbook; according to the research on . . .).

8. When cause-effect is being assessed, use only true propositions. For example, use *"Exposure to ultraviolet rays can cause skin cancer"* rather than *"Exposure to ultraviolet rays does not cause skin cancer."* Evaluating that the positively worded statement is true is less confusing than evaluating that the negatively worded statement is false.

9. Do not overqualify the statement in a way that gives away the answer. Avoid using specific determiners (*always, never, all, none,* and *only* tend to be false, while *usually, may,* and *sometimes* tend to be true).

10. Make true and false items of comparable length and include the same number of true and false items.

11. Randomly sort the items into a numbered sequence so that they are less likely to appear in a repetitive, predictable pattern (e.g., avoid T F T F . . . or . . . TT FF TT FF).

Sources: Ebel, 1979; Gronlund, 2006; Lindvall & Nitko, 1975.

Matching Exercises

A **matching exercise** presents students with directions for matching a list of premises and a list of responses. The student must match each premise with one of the responses. Matching is a recognition task because the answers are present in the test item. A simple matching exercise might look like this:

Directions: In the left column are events that preceded the start of the Revolutionary War. For each event, choose the date it occurred from the right column, and place the letter identifying it on the line next to the event description.

Description of events (premise list):

_____ 1. *British troops fire on demonstrators in the Boston Massacre, killing five.*

_____ 2. *British Parliament passes the Tea Act.*

_____ 3. *Parliament passes the Stamp Act, sparking protests in the American colonies.*

_____ 4. *Treaty of Paris ends French power in North America.*

Dates (response list):

a. 1763
b. 1765
c. 1768
d. 1770
e. 1773
f. 1778

Matching exercises are very useful for assessing a student's ability to make associations or see relationships between two things (e.g., words and their definitions, individuals and their accomplishments, events in history and dates). This format provides a space-saving and objective way to assess achievement of learning goals. It is versatile in that words or phrases can be matched to symbols or pictures (e.g., matching a country name to the outline of that country on a map). Well-designed matching exercises can assess students' comprehension of concepts, ideas, and principles. However, teachers often fall into the trap of using matching only for memorized lists (such as names and dates) and not developing matching exercises that assess higher-level thinking. To construct effective matching items, consider these guidelines:

- Clearly explain the intended basis for matching, as in the directions for the sample item above.
- Use short lists of responses and premises.
- Arrange the response list in a logical order. For example, in the sample item, dates are listed in chronological order.
- Identify premises with numbers and responses with letters.
- Construct items so that longer phrases appear in the premise list and shorter phrases appear in the response list.
- Create responses that are plausible items for each premise. A response that clearly does not fit any premise gives a hint to the correct answer.
- Avoid "perfect" one-to-one matching by including one or more responses that are incorrect choices or by using a response as the correct answer for more than one premise.

Multiple-choice Items

Each **multiple-choice item** contains a **stem,** or introductory statement or question, and a list of choices, called **response alternatives.** Multiple-choice items are recognition tasks because the correct answer is provided among the choices. A typical multiple-choice question looks like this:

> *What is the main topic of the reading selection Responding to Learners?*
>
> > *a. academic achievement*
> > *b. question and response techniques*
> > *c. managing student behavior*

The response alternatives include a *keyed alternative* (the correct answer) and **distractors,** or incorrect alternatives. The example includes three choices: one keyed alternative and two distractors. Other multiple-choice formats may include a four-choice option (a, b, c, d) or five-choice option (a, b, c, d, e). Guidelines 27.2 presents a set of detailed instructions for developing a multiple-choice format that addresses content and style, and offers tips for writing the stem and the choices.

Of the item formats that serve as recognition tasks, multiple-choice items are preferred by most assessment experts because this format offers many advantages. The multiple-choice format can be used to assess a great variety of learning goals, and the questions can be structured to assess factual knowledge as well as higher-order thinking. Because multiple-choice questions do not require writing, students who are poor writers have a more equal playing field for demonstrating their understanding of the content than they have when answering essay questions. All students also have less chance to guess the correct answer in a multiple-choice format than they do with true/false items or a poorly written matching exercise. Also, the distractor that a student incorrectly chooses can give the teacher insight into the student's degree of misunderstanding.

However, because multiple-choice items are recognition tasks, this format does not require the student to recall information independently. Multiple-choice questions are not the best option for assessing writing skills, self-expression, or synthesis of ideas or in situations where you want students to demonstrate their work (e.g., showing steps taken to solve a math problem). Also, poorly written multiple-choice questions can be superficial, trivial, or limited to factual knowledge.

The guidelines for writing objective items, such as those given in Guidelines 27.1 and 27.2, are especially important for ensuring the validity of classroom tests. Poorly written test items can give students a clue to the right answer. For example, **specific determiners**—extraneous clues to the answer such as *always, never, all, none, only, usually, may*—can enable students who may not know the material well to correctly answer some true/false or multiple-choice questions using testwiseness. *Testwiseness* is an ability to use test-taking strategies, clues from poorly written test items, and prior experience in test taking to improve one's score. Learned either informally or through direct instruction, it improves with grade level, experience in test taking, and motivation to do well on an assessment (Ebel & Frisbie, 1991; Sarnacki, 1979; Slakter, Koehler, & Hampton, 1970).

GUIDELINES 27.2   Developing Effective Multiple-choice Items

Content concerns:

1. Every item should reflect specific content and a single specific mental behavior, as called for in test specifications.
2. Base each item on important content to learn; avoid trivial content.
3. Use novel material to test higher-level learning. Paraphrase textbook language or language used during instruction in a test item to avoid testing for simple recall.
4. Keep the content of each item independent from content of other items on the test.
5. Avoid overly specific and overly general content when writing items.
6. Avoid opinion-based items.
7. Avoid trick items.
8. Keep vocabulary simple for the group of students being tested.

Writing the stem:

9. Ensure that the wording of the stem is very clear.
10. Include the central idea in the stem instead of in the response alternatives. Minimize the amount of reading in each item. Instead of repeating a phrase in each alternative, try to include it as part of the stem.
11. Avoid window dressing (excessive verbiage).
12. Word the stem positively; avoid negatives such as NOT or EXCEPT. If a negative word is used, use the word cautiously and always ensure that the word appears capitalized and boldface.

Writing the response alternatives:

13. Offering three response alternatives is adequate.
14. Make sure that only one of the alternatives is the right answer.
15. Make all distractors plausible. Use typical student misconceptions as your distractors.
16. Phrase choices positively; avoid negatives such as NOT.
17. Keep alternatives independent; they should not overlap.
18. Keep alternatives homogeneous in content and grammatical structure. For example, if one alternative is stated as a negative—"No running in the hall"—all alternatives should be phrased as negatives.
19. Keep all alternatives roughly the same length. If the correct answer is substantially longer or shorter than the distractors, this may serve as a clue for test-takers.
20. *None of the above* should be avoided or used sparingly.
21. Avoid *All of the above*.
22. Vary the location of the correct answer in the list of alternatives (e.g., the correct answer should not always be C).
23. Place alternatives (A, B, C, D) in logical or numerical order. For example, if a history question lists dates as the response alternatives, they should be listed in chronological order.
24. Avoid giving clues to the right answer, such as:
    a. specific determiners, including *always, never, completely,* and *absolutely*
    b. choices identical to or resembling words in the stem
    c. grammatical inconsistencies that cue the test-taker to the correct choice
    d. obvious correct choice
    e. pairs or triplets of options that clue the test-taker to the correct choice
    f. blatantly absurd, ridiculous options

Style concerns:

25. Edit and proof items.
26. Use correct grammar, punctuation, capitalization, and spelling.

Source: Adapted from Haladyna, Downing, & Rodriguez, 2002.

Short-answer/Completion Items

Short-answer/completion items come in three basic varieties. The *question variety* presents a direct question, and students are expected to supply a short answer (usually one word or phrase), as shown here:

1. What is the capital of Kentucky?	*Frankfort*
2. What does the symbol Ag represent on the periodic table?	*Silver*
3. How many feet are in one yard?	3

The *completion variety* presents an incomplete sentence and requires students to fill in the blank, as in the next examples:

1. The capital of Kentucky is _____*Frankfort*_____ .
2. $3(2 + 4) =$ __18__

The *association variety* (sometimes called the identification variety) presents a list of terms, symbols, labels, and so on for which students have to recall the corresponding answer, as shown below:

Element	Symbol
Barium	Ba
Calcium	Ca
Chlorine	Cl

Short-answer items are relatively easy to construct. Teachers can use these general guidelines to help them develop effective short-answer items:

- Use the question variety whenever possible, because it is the most straightforward short-answer design and is the preferred option of experts.
- Be sure the items are clear and concise so that a single correct answer is required.
- Put the blank toward the end of the line for easier readability.
- Limit blanks within a short-answer question to one or two.
- Specify the level of precision (a word, a phrase, a few sentences) expected in the answer so students understand how much to write in their response.

While short-answer items typically assess students' lower-level skills, such as recall of facts, they also can be used to assess more complex thinking skills if they are well designed. The short-answer format lowers a student's probability of getting an answer correct by random guessing, a more likely scenario with alternate choice and multiple choice.

Short-answer items also are relatively easy to score objectively, especially when the correct response is a one-word answer. Partial credit can be awarded if a student provides a response that is close to the correct answer but not 100% accurate. You occasionally may find that students provide unanticipated answers. For example, if you ask "Who discovered America?", student responses might include "Christopher Columbus," "Leif Erikson," "the Vikings," or "explorers who sailed across the ocean." You then would have to make a subjective judgment about whether such answers should receive full or partial credit. Because reliability decreases as scoring becomes more subjective, teachers should use a scoring key when deciding on partial credit to maintain scoring consistency from one student to the next.

Essay Tasks

Essay tasks allow assessment of many cognitive skills that cannot be assessed adequately, if at all, through more objective item formats. Essay tasks can be classified into two types. **Restricted response essay** tasks limit the content of students' answers as well as the form of their responses. A restricted response task might state: *List the three parts of the memory system and provide a short statement explaining how each part operates.* **Extended response essay** tasks require students to write essays in which they are free to express their thoughts and ideas and to organize the information as they see fit. With this format, there usually is no single correct answer; rather, the accuracy of the response becomes a matter of degree. Teachers can use these guidelines to develop effective essay questions:

- Cover the appropriate range of content and learning goals. One essay question may address one learning goal or several.

- Create essay questions that assess application of knowledge and higher-order thinking, not simply recall of facts.

- Make sure the complexity of the item is appropriate to the student's developmental level. Elementary school students might not be required to write lengthy essays in essay booklets, whereas middle school or high school students would be expected to write more detailed essays.

- Specify the purpose of the task, the length of the response, time limits, and evaluation criteria. For example, instead of an essay task that states "Discuss the advantages of single-sex classrooms," a high school teacher might phrase the task as: "You are addressing the school board. Provide three arguments in favor of single-sex classrooms." The revised essay question provides a purpose for the response and specifies the amount students need to write. Teachers also should specify how essays will be evaluated—for example, whether spelling and grammar count toward the grade and how students' opinions will be assessed.

Whether to use a restricted response format or an extended response format depends on the intended purpose of the test item as well as reliability and practicality issues. The restricted response format narrows the focus of the assessment to a specific, well-defined area. The level of specificity makes it more likely that students will interpret the question as intended. This makes scoring easier, because the range of possible responses is also restricted. Scoring is more reliable because it is easier to be very clear about what constitutes a correct answer. On the other hand, if you want to know how a student organizes and synthesizes information, the narrowly focused, restricted response format may not serve the assessment purpose well. Extended response questions are suitable for assessing students' writing skill and/or subject matter knowledge. If your learning goals involve skills such as organizing ideas, critically evaluating a certain position or argument, communicating feelings, or demonstrating creative writing skill, the extended response format provides an opportunity for students to demonstrate these skills.

Because extended responses are subjective, this format generally has poor scoring reliability. Given the same essay response to evaluate, several different teachers might award different scores, or the same teacher might award different scores to student essays at the beginning and end of a pile of tests. When the scores given are inconsistent from one response to the next, the validity of the assessment results is lessened. Also, teachers tend to evaluate the essays of different students according to different criteria, evaluating one essay in terms of its high level of creativity and another more critically in terms of grammar and spelling. A significant disadvantage is that grading extended essay responses is a very time-consuming process, especially if the teacher takes the time to provide detailed written feedback to help students improve their work.

Restricted and extended response essay items have special scoring considerations unique to the essay format. Essay responses, especially extended ones, tend to have poor scoring reliability and lower practicality. As discussed earlier, a scoring rubric can help teachers score essay answers more fairly and consistently. The following guidelines offer additional methods for ensuring consistency:

- Use a set of anchor essays—student essays that the teacher selects as examples of performance at different levels of a scoring rubric (Moskal, 2003). For example, a teacher may have a representative A essay, B essay, and so on. Anchors increase reliability because they provide a comparison set for teachers as they score student responses. A set of anchor essays without student names can be used to illustrate the different levels of the scoring rubric to both students and parents.

- If an exam has more than one essay question, score all students on the first question before moving on to the next question. This method increases the consistency and uniformity of your scoring.

- Score subject matter content separately from other factors such as spelling or neatness.

- To increase fairness and eliminate bias, score essays anonymously by having students write their names on the back of the exam.

- Take the time to provide effective feedback on essays.

- After you have designed the items for a test, do a final check of the test issues using Guidelines 27.3: Testing Checklist.

GUIDELINES 27.3   Testing Checklist

Issues	Question(s) about the test	Teacher's responsibilities
Content	What content is covered by the test?	Decide what the test results should represent and communicate to students what the test will cover.
Alignment with standards	Do the test items or tasks match the content standards (expectations for what students should know or be able to do)?	Ensure that the test is completely matched to the intended domain (all aspects of the domain are covered; no areas are covered too much or too little).
Item/task construction	Are the test questions or tasks that students are asked to perform clear? Are directions clear?	Review all test questions, prompts, directions, and other student materials for appropriate level, clarity, correct grammar, spelling, and adherence to accepted test development guidelines.
Administration conditions	Are the conditions under which students are tested conducive to them performing their best? Are time constraints appropriate?	Ensure that testing conditions are comfortable, free of distractions, and that timing does not inappropriately affect students' scores.
Scoring	How will the test be scored?	Develop scoring rubrics, answer keys, observation protocols, and so on, that are accurate, aligned with test directions, and applied objectively.
Opportunity to learn	Have all students had sufficient opportunities to learn the knowledge or skills being tested?	Ensure that the tested material has been covered in classroom instruction, activities, homework assignments, lab experiences, or other contexts, so that all students have had adequate time and opportunity to master the content.
Fairness	Are there any aspects of the test or procedures that would put some students at an unfair advantage or disadvantage?	Review items/tasks to ensure sensitivity to differences in students' gender, culture, ethnicity, language diversity, and so on, and eliminate any bias.
Accommodations	Are assessment accommodations in place for students with special needs?	Ascertain what accommodations are necessary for students to perform according to their true levels of knowledge or skill and implement these during testing. Ensure that accommodations do not provide an unfair advantage.

Adapted from Cizek, 2009.

Think about a particular unit on which your students might be tested in the grade level you intend to teach. What test item formats would you choose to use, and why? Would your choice of item formats be different for a pretest and for a test given at the end of a unit?

APPLICATION: TEST ANALYSIS AND REVISION

No test is perfect. Good teachers evaluate the tests they use and make necessary revisions to improve them. When using objective test formats such as alternate response and multiple choice, teachers can evaluate how well test items function by using **item analysis,** a process of collecting, summarizing, and using information from student responses to make decisions about each test item. When teachers use optical scanning sheets ("bubble sheets") for test responses, they can use a computer program not only to score the responses, but also to generate an item analysis. Item analysis provides two statistics that indicate how test items are functioning: an item difficulty index and an item discrimination index.

The **item difficulty index** reports the proportion of the group of test-takers who answered an item correctly, ranging from 0 to 1. Items that are functioning appropriately should have a moderate item difficulty index to distinguish students who have grasped the material from those who have not. This increases the validity of the test score. As a rule, a moderate item difficulty can range from .3 to .7. Item difficulty indexes that are very low (e.g., 0–.3) indicate that very few students answered correctly. This information can identify particular concepts that need to be retaught, provide clues about the strengths and weaknesses of instruction, or indicate test items that are poorly written and need to be revised or removed. Item difficulty indexes that are very high (e.g., .8–.9) indicate that the majority of students answered the items correctly, suggesting that the items were too easy. While we want students to perform well, items that are too easy do not discriminate between the students who know the material well and those who do not, which is one purpose of assessing student performance.

Item discrimination indexes add this crucial piece of information. An **item discrimination index** describes the extent to which a particular test item differentiates high-scoring students from low-scoring students. It is calculated as the difference between the proportion of the upper group (highest scorers) who answered a particular item correctly and the proportion of the lower group (lowest scorers) who answered that same item correctly. The resulting index ranges from –1 to +1. If a test is well constructed, we would expect all test items to be positively discriminating, meaning that those students in the highest scoring group get the items correct while those in the lowest scoring group get the items wrong. Test items with low (below .4), zero, or negative discrimination indexes reduce a test score's validity and should be rewritten or replaced. A low item discrimination index indicates that the item cannot accurately discriminate between students who know the material and those who don't. An item discrimination index of zero indicates that the item cannot discriminate *at all* between high scorers and low scorers. Items with negative discrimination indexes indicate that lower-scoring students tended to answer the items correctly while higher-scoring students tended to get them wrong. If a test contains items with negative discriminations, the total score on the exam will not provide useful information.

When item analyses suggest that particular test items did not function as expected, the source of the problem must be investigated. The item analysis may indicate that the problem stems from:

- *the item itself.* For example, multiple-choice items may have poorly functioning distractors, ambiguous alternatives, questions that invite random guessing, or items that have been keyed incorrectly.

- *student performance.* Students may have misread the item and misunderstood it. When developing a new test item, the teacher may think it is worded clearly and has one distinctly correct answer. However, item analysis might reveal that students interpreted that test item differently from the way it was intended.

- *teacher performance.* Low item difficulties, which indicate that students did not grasp the material, may suggest that the teacher's performance needs to be improved. Perhaps concepts needed further clarification or the teacher needs to consider a different approach to presenting the material.

The process of discarding certain items that did not work well, revising other items, and testing a few new items on each test eventually leads to a much higher quality of test (Nitko & Brookhart, 2007). Once "good" items have been selected, teachers can use software to store test items in a computer file so they can select a subset of test items, make revisions, assemble tests, and print out tests for use in the classroom. Certain software products even allow the teacher to sort items according to their alignment with curriculum standards. Computer applications vary in quality, cost, user-friendliness, and amount of training required for their use.

An item analysis shows that three of your test items have very low item difficulties, and you plan to revise these before you use the test next time. Because these poorly functioning items affect students' test scores, what can you do to improve the validity of your current students' test scores?

Summary

Discuss the importance of validity, reliability, fairness/equivalence, and practicality in test construction. Classroom tests should be evaluated based on their validity, reliability, fairness/equivalence, and practicality. Teachers must consider how well the test measures what it is supposed to measure (validity), how consistent the results are (reliability), the degree to which all students have an equal opportunity to learn and demonstrate their knowledge and skill (fairness/equivalence), and how economical and efficient the test is to create, administer, and score (practicality).

Explain how a test blueprint is used to develop a good test. A test blueprint is an assessment planning tool that describes the content the test will cover and the way students are expected to demonstrate their understanding of that content. A test blueprint, or table of specifications, helps teachers develop good tests because it matches the test to instructional objectives and actual instruction. Test blueprints take into consideration the importance of each learning goal, the content to be assessed, the material that was emphasized during instruction, and the amount of time available for students to complete the test.

Discuss the usefulness of each test item format. Alternate-choice items allow teachers to cover a wide range of topics by asking a large number of questions in a short period of time. Matching exercises can be useful for assessing a student's ability to make associations or see relationships between two things. Multiple-choice items are preferred by assessment experts because they focus on reading and thinking but do not require writing, give teachers insight into students' degree of misunderstanding, and can be used to assess a variety of learning goals. Short-answer questions are relatively easy to construct, can assess both lower-order and higher-order thinking skills, and minimize the chance that students will answer questions correctly by randomly guessing. Essay questions can provide an effective assessment of many cognitive skills that cannot be assessed adequately, if at all, with more objective item formats.

Compare and contrast the scoring considerations for the five test item formats. Objective formats such as alternate choice, matching, and multiple choice have one right answer and tend to be relatively quick and easy to score. Short-answer/completion questions, if well designed, also can be relatively easy to score as long as they are written clearly and require a very specific answer. Essay questions, especially extended essay formats, tend to have poor scoring reliability and lower practicality because scoring is subjective and can be time-consuming. Scoring rubrics allow teachers to score essay answers more fairly and consistently.

Describe the benefits of item analysis and revision. Item analysis determines whether a test item functions as intended, indicates areas where students need clarification of concepts, and points out where the curriculum needs to be improved in future presentations of the material. The process of discarding certain items that did not work well, revising other items, and testing a few new items on each test eventually leads to a much higher quality of test.

Key Concepts

alternate-choice item   498

content validity   493

distractors   500

equivalence   446

extended response essay   502

fairness   495

item analysis   504

item difficulty index   505

item discrimination index   505

matching exercise   499

multiple-choice item   500

objective testing   497

objectivity   494

practicality   496

recall tasks   497

recognition tasks   497

reliability   494

response alternatives   500

restricted response essay   502

rubric   498

short-answer/completion items   502

specific determiners   500

stem   500

subjective testing   497

table of specifications   496

test blueprint   496

validity   493

Case Studies
Reflect and Evaluate

EARLY CHILDHOOD: **"The Zoo"**

These questions refer to the case study on page 468.

1. Mr. Sanjay and Miss Vivian do not do any paper-and-pencil testing in this scenario. What factors should they consider when deciding whether to use traditional tests as a form of assessment?

2. If Mr. Sanjay and Miss Vivian choose to use tests or quizzes with the children, what steps should they take to ensure the validity of their results?

3. What issues could potentially interfere with the reliability of test results among preschoolers?

4. Most of the preschoolers in this classroom do not yet know how to read independently. How would this affect test construction and use for this age group?

5. Given your response to question 4, how might Mr. Sanjay and Miss Vivian assess a specific set of academic skills (e.g., letter or number recognition) with their students in a systematic way?

6. The lab school is located in a large city and has a diverse group of students. How might issues of fairness come into play when designing assessments for use with these students?   ***DIVERSITY***

ELEMENTARY SCHOOL: **"Writing Wizards"**

These questions refer to the case study on page 470.

1. Ms. Blaydes provides an answer key for the Grammar Slammer activity (quiz) and reviews it with the class. How does the use of such a key affect the level of objectivity in scoring responses?

2. Ms. Blaydes uses a matching exercise (quiz) to evaluate students' understanding of their weekly vocabulary words. What are the advantages and disadvantages of this form of assessment?

3. If Ms. Blaydes decides she wants to vary her quiz format by using multiple-choice questions instead, what factors should she keep in mind in order to write good multiple-choice questions?

4. Ms. Blaydes uses a combination of traditional tests and applied writing activities to assess her students' writing skills. Are there other subject areas in a fourth-grade classroom in which tests would be a useful assessment choice? Explain.

5. Imagine that Ms. Blaydes will be giving a social studies test and wants to incorporate writing skills as part of this assessment. What are the advantages and disadvantages of the essay format?

6. Based on what you read in the module, what advice would you give Ms. Blaydes about how to score the responses on the social studies test referred to in question 5?

MIDDLE SCHOOL: **"Assessment: Cafeteria Style"**

These questions refer to the case study on page 472.

1. From Ms. Reffert's perspective, how do the development, implementation, and grading of the multiple-choice test rate in terms of *practicality*?

2. Do 50 multiple-choice questions seem an appropriate number for a middle school exam in a 50-minute class period? Why or why not?

3. What are the advantages of using multiple-choice questions rather than one of the other question formats available (alternate choice, matching, short answer, or essay)? Would your answer vary for different subjects?

4. What are some limitations of using only multiple-choice questions to test students' understanding of course content?

5. Ms. Reffert provided a rubric to help her students better understand what was expected from them on the project option. What could she have done to clarify her expectations for those students who choose to take the exam?

6. If you were the one writing the questions for Ms. Reffert's exam, what are some guidelines you would follow to make sure the questions were well constructed?

HIGH SCHOOL: "Innovative Assessment Strategies"

These questions refer to the case study on page 474.

1. What are some advantages tests have that might explain why so many teachers at Jefferson High rely on them as a primary means of assessment?

2. In the New Hampshire humanities course described in the memo, students are asked to design their own test as part of their final project. How could these students use a test blueprint to develop a good test?

3. What criteria should the New Hampshire teacher use to evaluate the quality of the tests designed by students?

4. Imagine that a New Hampshire teacher gave a final exam using a combination of the test questions created by students. What could the teacher do to determine how the questions actually functioned?

5. The California teacher used a "dream home" project to assess his students' conceptual understanding of area relationships. Is it possible to assess this level of understanding by using multiple-choice questions on a test? Explain your answer.

6. Imagine that the Rhode Island social studies teacher wants students to pay close attention to one another's oral history presentations, so she announces that students will be given a test on the material. If she wants to test basic recall of facts and wants the test to be quick and easy to grade, which item formats would you suggest she use on her test? Explain.

28

Performance Assessment

Outline	Learning Goals
A Broader View of Assessment	
■ Performance Assessment ■ Authentic Assessment	1. Define *performance assessment* and provide examples of the formative and summative uses of performance assessment. 2. Define *authentic assessment* and identify its essential characteristics.
Application: Developing Performance Assessments	
■ Presentations ■ Projects ■ Portfolios	3. Describe the three major types of performance assessment and provide a rationale for using each type.
Application: Evaluating Performance Assessments	
■ Checklists ■ Rating Scales ■ Rubrics	4. Describe the three methods of systematically evaluating student performance.
Advantages and Disadvantages of Performance Assessment	
	5. Discuss the general advantages and disadvantages of performance assessments.
Summary **Key Concepts** **Video Applications** **Case Studies: Reflect and Evaluate**	

A BROADER VIEW OF ASSESSMENT

Since the implementation of the federal No Child Left Behind Act of 2001, educators have been required to use standardized tests for accountability purposes, but they also recognize that narrow test formats and inappropriate uses of standardized testing negatively affect the quality of instruction and student learning (Resnick & Resnick, 1992; Shepard, 2006). Dissatisfaction with the limitations of testing has led national policymakers, individuals responsible for state- and district-level assessments, and teachers interested in better uses of assessment in their own classrooms to consider assessment alternatives that give students the opportunity to show what they can "do," as well as what they know. Current trends in assessment are moving toward (McMillan, 2007a; National Research Council, 2001):

- using multiple forms of assessment,
- assessing a broader range of abilities and talents,
- assessment as an integral part of instruction, and
- assessment tasks that are relevant to real life or represent tasks common to a particular discipline.

In this module, we'll examine the ways performance assessment in the classroom can expand teachers' view of what students know and can do, while allowing them to assess students in a multidimensional way.

Performance Assessment

Performance assessment is any form of assessment that requires students to carry out an activity (*process*) or develop a *product* in order to demonstrate skill or knowledge (Airasian, 2005; Perlman, 2002). It requires students to actually demonstrate proficiency rather than simply answer questions *about* proficiency, and it asks students to perform, create, produce, or do something that involves the use of higher-level problem-solving skills (Gronlund, 2006). Performance assessments can be completed individually or as part of a group, and they may have oral and written components.

Formative versus summative uses. Like traditional forms of assessment, performance assessments can have both formative and summative uses. Consider these performance assessments:

1. A band director listens to each flute player's performance and provides suggestions for improvement.
2. A PE teacher watches a student shoot a free throw and then offers suggestions on physical stance and hand and arm movements.
3. An industrial technology teacher observes students as they use a drill press to determine whether they are operating the machinery safely.

Formative and summative assessment: See page 480.

These **formative assessments** are used to plan for instruction and to monitor progress during instruction throughout the grading period. The purpose of the assessment is to improve student performance by providing feedback *in the moment*.

Teachers also can use performance assessments as a **summative assessment** to assess achievement at the end of an instruction period. Consider these performance assessments again:

1. The band director listens to each flute player perform *in order to assign chairs in band for the next nine weeks*.
2. The PE teacher watches a student playing basketball *in order to rate the adequacy of the student's skill and participation*.
3. The industrial technology teacher observes students using the drill press *in order to grade them on the use of safety goggles*.

Process versus product. In all of these examples, the teacher is evaluating students' skills and determining how well they have met performance objectives. The examples refer to the assessment of pro-

During a formative performance assessment, the coach provides feedback in the moment to help a student improve her free throw shooting.

cesses or behaviors, yet performance assessment can also include the assessment of tangible products that students create. Most processes lead to products, so teachers might assess both as part of a single assignment. In fact, multiple processes as part of, say, a lab experiment or a research paper might lead to single or multiple products (e.g., in the lab, a finished chemical solution plus a lab report).

Matching performance assessment to instructional objectives. As a teacher, you will want to select the assessment format that provides the most direct evaluation of the particular skill or learning outcome being measured (Gronlund, 2006). As you become more familiar with different types of assessment tools through hands-on experience, you will find that you become more proficient at gauging which form of assessment best fits a situation (Struyven, Dochy, & Janssens, 2008). Before choosing to use performance assessment, you should clearly identify the purpose of the instructional activity (Moskal, 2003). If the purpose is to assess the student's ability to perform a skill, then having a student actually play a selection on the flute, for example, provides much richer, more meaningful information about the student's ability to perform that skill than simply having the student answer multiple-choice questions about flute playing.

Authentic Assessment

Authentic assessments present students with problem-solving tasks that allow them to use their knowledge and skills in a meaningful way (Nitko & Brookhart, 2007). In order to prepare students for challenges and tasks that they will face in their careers and personal lives, teachers need to give them opportunities to practice problem-solving skills related to important, real-life skills and contexts (Gulikers et al., 2008; Hambleton, 1996; Popham, 2005). Solving important problems may require locating and using resources, consulting or collaborating with other people, and integrating basic skills with higher-level thinking and creativity (Popham, 2005; Wolf, Bixby, Glenn, & Gardner, 1991). Authentic tasks share the following attributes (Powers, 2005):

Problem solving: See page 245.

- they present messy, poorly defined problems similar to the roles and challenges that students will encounter in the real world;

- they simulate ways students should use combinations of knowledge, skills, and abilities in the real world;

- they require the development of complete and well-justified responses, performances, or products; and

- they may have multiple correct solutions (although the tasks clearly specify standards and criteria for determining the possible range of correct answers).

In today's technology-rich learning environments, authentic assessments can include adaptive computer scenarios that present a student with a situation and then ask questions of or require a decision from the student. Because these presentations can be dynamic, changing depending on the student's response, each student may encounter a slightly different scenario (Nitko & Brookhart, 2007). Computer simulations can provide greater economy and consistency than real-life scenarios and also provide the advantage of computerized scoring of student responses (Epping, 2010; Jones, 1994). Research indicates that, in some cases, computer-based simulations of "hands-on" activities are just as effective as activities in which students manipulate real objects (Triona & Klahr, 2003). Skills reported to be improved on through computer simulations include reading (Willing, 1988), problem solving (Jiang & Potter, 1994; Rivers & Vockell, 1987), science process skills (e.g., measurement, data interpretation, etc.) (Geban, Askar, & Ozkan, 1992; Huppert, Lomask, & Lazarowitz, 2002), 3-D visualization

These high school students are applying skills learned in their building trades class to a Habitat for Humanity project. Why might an evaluation of their performance on the job site be considered an authentic assessment?

Technology and assessment: See page 481.

(Barnea & Dori, 1999), mineral identification (Kelly, 1997/1998), abstract thinking (Berlin & White, 1986), creativity (Michael, 2001), and algebra skills involving the ability to apply equations to real-life situations (Verzoni, 1995).

Performance assessment and authentic assessment are not necessarily synonymous (McMillan, 2003). It is possible to assign a performance task that is not authentic because, although it requires that the student perform a skill, that skill is not grounded in a meaningful, real-world context. For example, a student might be asked to go to the board and demonstrate how to solve a math problem, but if the math exercise is not tied to the solution of a complex real-world problem, it is not considered an authentic assessment.

In your own words, how would you describe the difference between performance assessment and authentic assessment? How is performance assessment used in your college courses? How might you use it in your own teaching?

APPLICATION: DEVELOPING PERFORMANCE ASSESSMENTS

After you have decided what knowledge or skills need to be assessed and have concluded that performance assessment best suits your purpose, it is time to consider which type of performance assessment is most appropriate. We'll examine the basic facets of three types of performance tasks: presentations, projects, and portfolios. Each of these performance tasks has its own unique characteristics, but first we'll consider some performance assessment guidelines that apply across multiple formats:

1. *The selected performance should reflect a valued activity.* The type of assessment you select sends a message to students about what you value and most want them to learn. For example, if you incorporate a large number of cooperative learning activities in the classroom, you are communicating the importance of interdependence and learning to work as a team.

2. *The completion of performance assessments should provide a valuable learning experience.* Performance assessments require more time to administer than other forms of assessment. The investment of this classroom time should result in a higher payoff that includes an increase both in the teacher's understanding of what students know and can do and in the students' knowledge of the intended content.

3. *The statement of goals and objectives should be clearly aligned with the measurable outcomes of the performance activity.* Figure 28.1 provides examples of performance activities and products that demonstrate the different levels of cognitive objectives in the taxonomy developed by Benjamin Bloom and his colleagues. Bloom's taxonomy presents six categories of cognitive skills (Bloom et al., 1956). Think of these six categories as a comprehensive way of considering different cognitive goals that need to be met when planning for instruction.

Bloom's taxonomy and learning objectives: See page 365.

Presentations

Several common forms of performance assessment involve a presentation of one kind or another, including demonstrations, experiments, oral presentations, and exhibitions.

Demonstrations require students to show that they can use knowledge or skills to complete a well-defined, complex task (Nitko & Brookhart, 2007). A demonstration is usually a closed-response task, meaning that there is one correct way or a best way to complete the task. Typically, a demonstration is not as long or involved as a project. Demonstrations might include preschoolers tying a shoelace, elementary school students showing the proper way to line up for a fire drill, middle school students using a microscope to view slides, and high school students driving a car.

In an **experiment,** a student plans, conducts, and interprets the results of research. Experiments allow teachers to assess whether a student can use inquiry skills and methods such as making estimates or predictions, gathering and analyzing data, drawing conclusions, stating assumptions, and presenting findings. Experiments can be used with students at all grade levels. Preschoolers might test whether certain objects sink or float, elementary school students might test different growing conditions for plants, middle school students might predict the series of steps needed to create an electrical circuit, and high school students might estimate the type of reaction that will occur when certain chemicals are mixed.

Oral presentations might include interviews, speeches, skits, debates, or other dramatizations in which students are required to verbalize their knowledge and use their oral communication skills. Written work such as a list of interview questions, the draft of a speech, note cards to be used in a debate, or the script of a skit often is submitted along with an oral presentation. As with other forms of performance assessment, oral presentations can be done individually or as a group.

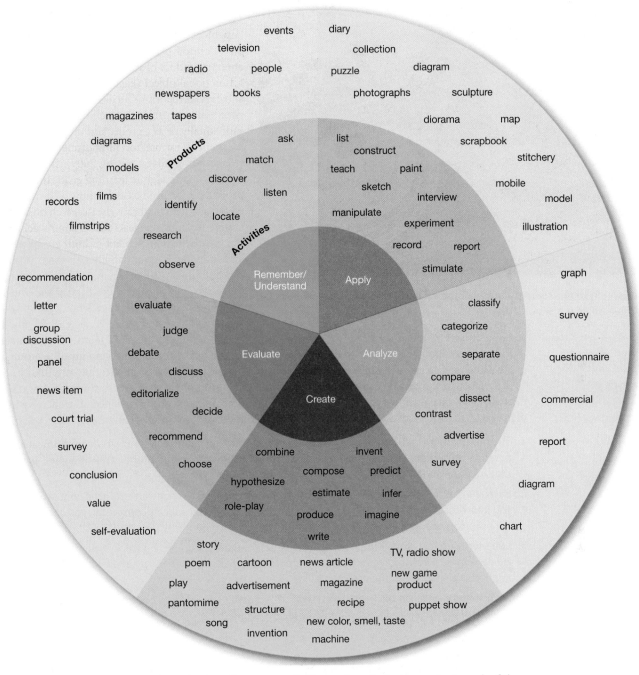

Figure 28.1. **Cognitive Categories.** Direct performance activities and products demonstrate each of the six cognitive objectives presented in Bloom's taxonomy. (Two categories, Remember and Understand, are grouped together in this diagram.)

Source: *Growing up gifted: Developing the potential of children at home and at school*, by B. Clark, 2002, Upper Saddle River, NJ: Merrill-Prentice Hall.

An **exhibition** is a public performance that serves as the culmination of a series of performances in a particular area, usually a graduation-level exercise or final class project. Exhibitions demonstrate what has been learned over the course of a unit or program of study and may require a combination of reading, writing, questioning, speaking, and listening (Davidson, 2009). Exhibitions can yield an authentic measure of students' abilities to engage in inquiry and skillful expression, and they can motivate and engage students by involving them in a public challenge. Preschoolers might exhibit their fingerpaintings or block structures, elementary school students might exhibit Young Authors stories they have written, middle school students might exhibit their Science Fair projects, and high school students might exhibit and race vehicles they have designed and built in an engineering class.

The Solar System. Creating a model of the solar system integrates many skills within a single project.

Individual and group accountability as related to learning: See page 552.

Projects

A **project** is an activity, usually completed over an extended period of time, that results in a student product of some kind, such as a model, a functional object (e.g., a map or diorama), a substantial report, or a collection of related artifacts (Banks, 2005). Projects can be completed individually or as a group, and they are an ideal assessment format for multidisciplinary tasks (MacMath, Wallace, & Chi, 2009). In addition to assessing academic learning goals, the group project can be used to assess how well students work together cooperatively. Research on cooperative learning suggests that students achieve the most when an element of both group goals and individual accountability is present (Johnson & Johnson, 2005; Slavin, 1988). The group succeeds (group goals) only when each member contributes to the project as a whole (individual accountability). For example, a teacher might assign a project in which students work in groups to visually represent the main themes in the novel *A Tale of Two Cities*. The teacher would evaluate a single product for each group and give the group a grade based on criteria such as identification of main ideas, organization, aesthetics, and originality.

The *process* of working on a project can be a worthwhile educational experience, but a project's usefulness as a form of assessment depends on how well the project task has been designed. The effective use of projects as a form of assessment requires that these four conditions be met (Nitko & Brookhart, 2007):

1. The project must focus on one or more important learning goals that are clearly communicated in advance via written instructions or a rubric that outlines grading criteria. Well-designed project tasks require students to apply a wide range of abilities and knowledge.

2. Each student must have equal access to the resources needed to create an excellent final product. If you know that students vary widely in their access to resources, such as computers, you should limit the resources they are allowed to use.

3. Long-term project work will be more successful if you keep students on track by setting intermediate deadlines, requiring regular progress reports, and helping students overcome any obstacles that might threaten to derail their work.

4. Each student must do his or her own work. If students are working on a project as a group, individual roles and responsibilities should be clearly defined.

Portfolios

How teachers can assign roles and responsibilities: See page 333.

Interest in portfolio assessment has increased dramatically in recent years (Burke, 2006; Butler & McMunn, 2006). A **portfolio** is a systematic collection of student work (Popham, 2005). Portfolios can include a wide variety of items: writing samples, artwork, graphs, diagrams, photographs, audio tapes or videotapes, teacher comments, peer comments, work in progress, revisions, and student self-analyses—anything that represents what the student has learned in the area being taught and assessed (Knotek, 2005; Wolf et al., 1991). In today's classrooms where so many students are comfortable with technoogy, teachers often use Web-based portfolios as formative assessment tools to promote student interest and learning performance (Chen & Chen, 2009). Well-designed portfolios can capture the complexity and range of a student's work. The process of selecting items for inclusion and reviewing what has been included involves critical analysis and self-reflection on the part of the student and the teacher, as both consider how best to portray what the student has learned. Older students might include written reflections about the items selected for inclusion in the portfolio. Because portfolios may include multiple samples of a student's work collected over an extended period of time, they are an excellent tool for demonstrating progress (Berryman & Russell, 2001).

Teachers can use process portfolios or best work portfolios. **Process portfolios** contain work from different stages to show a student's progress or achievement over time (Gronlund, 2006; Knotek, 2005).

They are sometimes called growth portfolios or developmental portfolios. **Best work portfolios** include a carefully selected combination of materials that showcase examples of a student's best work and serve as a final summative assessment (Johnson & Johnson, 2002). Effective use of either type of portfolio requires adherence to these guidelines:

1. *Establish the purpose of the portfolio.* Is the portfolio to be used to demonstrate progress or growth over time, or is it intended to showcase best work?

2. *Involve the student in decisions about what to include.* Many teachers allow students to have a say in what goes into their portfolios (Weasmer & Woods, 2001). If students are allowed to choose the items to be included, have them write a reflective statement telling why each piece was selected (Airasian, 2005).

3. *Review the contents of the portfolio with the student.* It is important to meet with each student on a regular basis to discuss the current state of the portfolio, review progress, and plan future work to be included (McMillan, 2007a; Weldin & Tumarkin, 1999).

4. *Set precise criteria for evaluation.* Clear and systematic criteria make the process of developing the portfolio less mysterious and make grading much more efficient (Burke, 2006; Gronlund, 2006). The criteria should allow evaluation of how well the portfolio as a whole represents the student's level of achievement (Airasian, 2005).

As a student, what is your reaction when you are assigned performance tasks? How might this influence when and how you use performance assessments as a teacher? What issues will you consider in developing performance assessments for your own students?

Student Reflection: Sample Self-assessment

Student Name: _____   Date: _____

The attached portfolio item is (e.g., first draft, poetry, concept map).

This piece of work demonstrates that I can:

_____ take risks   _____ support ideas with evidence or reasons

_____ persevere   _____ organize related ideas

_____ collaborate   _____ write using a variety of sentence structures

_____ use a writing process   _____ use effective spelling strategies

_____ participate in a discussion   _____ self-edit

_____ other: _____

Please notice:

Now I am planning to:

Student Signature: _____

Set Precise Criteria for Evaluation. Students should be involved in decisions about what to include in their portfolios. A written assessment of the contents students have chosen allows them to reflect on the quality of their work.

APPLICATION: EVALUATING PERFORMANCE ASSESSMENTS

Once the performance task has been selected, the teacher must decide how to evaluate the assessment. Whether the assessment involves a product, a performance, or both, it should be done systematically so that all students are assessed in a fair and consistent manner. Performance assessments involve a subjective evaluation of a student's performance and therefore can be subject to inconsistencies. For example, when evaluating a student presentation, one teacher might think a student "sometimes" used good eye contact while another might think the student "seldom" used good eye contact. Both teachers observed the same behavior but attached a different value to what they saw. Determining the reliability, or consistency, of the scoring of performance assessments involves **inter-rater reliability,** or the degree of consensus or similarity of ratings given by two independent raters. Like standardized achievement tests and classroom tests that use objective items (e.g., multiple choice and true/false), performance assessments must show evidence of reliability for the score or grade to be meaningful. However, reliability is more difficult to achieve with performance assessments than with more traditional forms of assessment.

Developing a scoring system—such as a checklist, rating scale, or rubric—can help teachers improve the reliability of performance assessment scores. These scoring systems provide preset criteria for evaluating student performance, making grading simpler and more transparent (Kubiszyn & Borich, 2003). They clarify what students are expected to know and do, and they make explicit how various types of knowledge and subskills in the performance are to be evaluated and weighted. The more explicit a scoring system, the more likely a teacher will be consistent in scoring across students or across class periods, increasing reliability.

The reliability of classroom tests: See page 546.

Standardized tests: See page 537.

Checklists

The use of a **checklist,** the least complex form of scoring system, is appropriate when you are looking for specific elements in a product or performance and all elements are weighted the same. Checklists provide a quick and easy way to assess based on a specified list of criteria, such as behaviors or characteristics that can be marked as Present/Absent, Complete/Incomplete, or Yes/No. Working from a prepared checklist, you mark off each item as it occurs and assign a score based on the total number of items checked. However, you give no recognition to variation in quality, and you assign no higher or lower values for how well a particular skill is executed. Checklists are especially useful for recording information during the observation of student behaviors. For example, a checklist for evaluating oral presentation skills might indicate whether the student:

_____ maintains eye contact with the audience

_____ speaks loudly enough to be heard in all parts of the room

_____ enunciates clearly

_____ uses gestures appropriately

_____ speaks for the allotted time

Rating Scales

Rating scales offer a way to attach an indication of quality to the various elements of a process or product. For example, you might rate the performance of a skill on a scale of one to ten, with ten being the best score. **Graphic rating scales** allow the rater to mark a point on a line or a continuum that reflects degrees of performance (e.g., _never, seldom, sometimes, usually, always_). **Numeric rating scales** quantify results. You might circle 1 to indicate that a certain behavior _never_ occurs, 2 to indicate that it _seldom_ occurs, 3 to indicate that it _sometimes_ occurs, 4 to indicate that it _usually_ occurs, and 5 to indicate that it _always_ occurs. This approach works best when it is set up so that the highest value is assigned to the desired response. **Descriptive rating scales** provide a description rather than simply a number or a single term for each level of performance. For example, you might rate a student's organizational skills on a project by using the following descriptors:

- _Exemplary:_ Ideas and information are very well organized.
- _Proficient:_ Some flaws in organization interfere with understanding of the project.
- _Deficient:_ The project is haphazard, with no apparent organization.

In addition to evaluating the achievement of learning objectives, rating scales can be used to evaluate student behaviors such as time on task, level of motivation, or degree of contribution to a group project.

Performance During Group Work	Unsatisfactory	Fair	Satisfactory	Good	Outstanding
Participation: Was present at all group meetings and made a significant contribution to the workload					✓
Focus: Stayed on task and encouraged others to do so			✓		
Attitude: Exhibited enthusiasm and supported the efforts of group members				✓	
Dependability: Was conscientious, thorough, reliable, accurate				✓	
Cooperation: Was willing and able to work with others to produce desired goals			✓		

Graphic Rating Scale for Evaluating a Student's Performance During Group Work. A graphic rating scale can be used to reflect degrees of performance along a continuum.

Rubrics

A **rubric** is a means of scoring a performance assessment in which multiple criteria are being assessed and the quality of the product or performance is important. Using a model to generate criteria for an assignment and using a rubric for self-assessment can help students produce better work (Andrade, Du, & Wang, 2008). Rubrics are especially appropriate for evaluating complex tasks or activities that integrate content from more than one area. Rubrics improve scoring consistency and also improve validity by clarifying the standards of achievement teachers use to evaluate students' work and communicate students' performance to parents.

A **holistic rubric,** illustrated in Example 28.1, requires the teacher to score the overall process or product as a whole, without judging the component parts separately (Nitko, 2001). Teachers using this assessment method may rely on a rubric that lists features of A work, B work, and so on, but they do not assign a specific number of points to each feature. Instead, they determine which description best fits the paper or project and grade it accordingly. Although holistic rubrics can be easier to create and score, making them faster to use, they provide less feedback to students than is possible with an analytic rubric.

With an **analytic rubric,** like the one in Example 28.2, the teacher scores separate components of the product or performance first and then sums the individual scores to obtain a total score (Moskal, 2000; Nitko, 2001). Analytic grading assigns separate scores to different criteria. For example, ideas might be worth 10 points, organization 10 points, sentence structure 10 points, and so on. This format allows the teacher to provide more detailed feedback about the strengths and weaknesses of a student's work. Sometimes, however, it may be difficult or even inappropriate to define the parts of a students' product or performance as separate and distinct. In such cases, when the overall impression or quality of the work is paramount, holistic grading may be a better choice.

Rubrics also can be classified as either generic or task-specific. A **generic rubric** provides a standard format that the teacher uses repeatedly throughout the year to evaluate a set of assignments. It contains scoring guidelines that can be applied to many different tasks (e.g., writing, science lab work, or math problem solving). Generic rubrics are useful for both teachers and students. They are an efficient tool for teachers because the same general format can be used multiple times. Repeated use of a generic rubric also encourages students to improve their performance from one task to the next because the criteria are clear and consistent. The use of a generic rubric (in an analytic format) throughout the year leads to increased student achievement (Khattri, Reeve, & Adamson, 1997). A **task-specific rubric** modifies the generic framework to match the specific learning goals of a particular task. In certain situations, an assignment is not part of a series of similar tasks, or a particular assignment has a unique set of learning objectives. In these cases, a task-specific rubric is the more appropriate choice.

Learning objectives: See page 364.

The design and scoring recommendations that follow are suitable to both analytic and holistic scoring rubrics (Arter & McTighe, 2001; Moskal, 2003). The design of effective scoring rubrics can

EXAMPLE 28.1   **Template for Holistic Rubrics**

Score	Description
5	Demonstrates complete understanding of the problem. All requirements of task are included in response.
4	Demonstrates considerable understanding of the problem. All requirements of task are included.
3	Demonstrates partial understanding of the problem. Most requirements of task are included.
2	Demonstrates little understanding of the problem. Many requirements of task are missing.
1	Demonstrates no understanding of the problem.
0	No response/task not attempted.

Source: Mertler, 2001.

EXAMPLE 28.2   **Template for Analytic Rubrics**

	Beginning 1	Developing 2	Accomplished 3	Exemplary 4	Score
Criteria #1	Description reflecting beginning level of performance	Description reflecting movement toward mastery level of performance	Description reflecting achievement of mastery level of performance	Description reflecting highest level of performance	
Criteria #2	Description reflecting beginning level of performance	Description reflecting movement toward mastery level of performance	Description reflecting achievement of mastery level of performance	Description reflecting highest level of performance	
Criteria #3	Description reflecting beginning level of performance	Description reflecting movement toward mastery level of performance	Description reflecting achievement of mastery level of performance	Description reflecting highest level of performance	
Criteria #4	Description reflecting beginning level of performance	Description reflecting movement toward mastery level of performance	Description reflecting achievement of mastery level of performance	Description reflecting highest level of performance	

Source: Mertler, 2001.

be conceptualized as a series of three basic steps, shown as the first three of seven steps in Figure 28.2 (Mertler, 2001; Montgomery, 2001; Tombari & Borich, 1999).

1. *Determine the criteria to be evaluated.* The criteria within a scoring rubric should be clearly aligned with the requirements of the task and the stated goals and objectives. These criteria should be expressed in terms of observable behaviors or product characteristics. Rubrics should be written in

specific and clear language that the students understand and should provide students with a clear description of what is expected, *before* they proceed with the assessment activity. If the language in a scoring rubric is too complex for students, the benefit of rubrics is lost.

2. *Determine the number of performance levels.* The scale used for a scoring rubric should reflect clear differences between student achievement levels. A scoring rubric that has fewer categories and clear distinctions between them is preferable to a scoring rubric that has many categories that may overlap or be difficult to interpret. The number of points assigned in each category or level should clearly reflect the value of the activity. On an analytic scoring rubric, if elements are weighted differently (e.g., weighting spelling and grammar less than content in an essay), there should be a clear reason for these differences.

3. *Define expectations clearly, beginning with the highest level of performance, and proceed with a description of each subsequent level.* This step may involve brainstorming characteristics that describe each attribute being assessed on the rubric, as well as the criteria for different levels of performance. The separation between score levels should be clear. Consider the following descriptions of a holistic five-point scale provided for a written assignment at the middle school level:

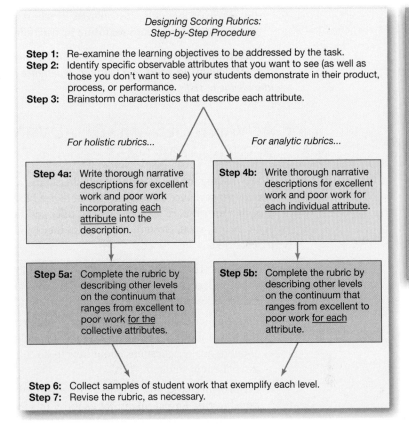

■ A score of 5 represents *outstanding* work. An essay in this category is very well-organized and coherent, clearly explains key ideas, and is free of errors in spelling, grammar, and punctuation.

■ A score of 4 represents *strong* work. An essay in this category is generally well-organized and coherent, explains key ideas, and is free of errors in spelling, grammar, and punctuation.

■ A score of 3 represents *competent* work. An essay in this category is adequately organized and developed, explains some key ideas, but may display some errors in spelling, grammar, and punctuation.

■ A score of 2 represents *insufficient* work. An essay in this category has one or more of the following weaknesses: inadequate organization or development, inadequate explanation of key ideas, little or no detail, or a pattern of errors in spelling, grammar, and punctuation.

■ A score of 1 represents *seriously flawed* work. An essay in this category contains serious or persistent problems in writing style and in mechanics, clarity, and organization of ideas.

Figure 28.2 breaks down the process into further steps that differ depending on whether the rubric is holistic or analytic.

After the rubric has been designed, teachers must consider how to use it effectively. Mathematics education professor Barbara M. Moskal (2003) offers these recommendations for scoring, interpreting, and using the results of performance assessments:

1. *The connection between the score or grade and the scoring rubric should be immediately apparent.* If an analytic rubric is used, then the report should contain the scores assigned to each analytic level. If a summary score or grade is provided, then an explanation of how the summary score or grade was determined should be included. Both students and parents should be able to understand how the final grade or score is linked to the scoring criteria.

2. *The results of the performance assessment should be used to improve instruction and the assessment process.* How can information gleaned from student responses be used to improve future classroom instruction? What did the teacher learn? How can the performance assessment and scoring rubric

Figure 28.2. Steps for Designing Rubrics. The first three steps in this flow chart form the basis for creating an effective scoring rubric. Steps 4 and 5 address differences in developing holistic and analytic rubrics.

be improved for future instruction? Teachers should use the information acquired through classroom assessment to improve future instruction and assessment.

What is the most memorable performance assessment you have completed as a student? Why was it memorable? Evaluate its value as a learning experience for you. Evaluate its value as a representation of your knowledge or skills.

ADVANTAGES AND DISADVANTAGES OF PERFORMANCE ASSESSMENT

When making the decision about whether to use a more traditional assessment (usually a test) or some type of performance assessment, teachers need to weigh the advantages and disadvantages of each approach. Performance assessments can offer several advantages over other forms of assessment (Linn & Gronlund, 2000; Oosterhoff, 1999; Rudner & Schafer, 2002) that can benefit students, teachers, and parents alike:

- Performance tasks allow students to use prior knowledge to build new knowledge structures, engage in active learning through inquiry and exploration, and construct meaning for themselves. Performance assessments can be designed to give students an opportunity to engage in self-assessment.

- Performance tasks can give teachers an opportunity to assess the processes students use, as well as their final products. These tasks assess students' ability to do things, not simply their ability to talk about or answer questions about how to do things, so in some cases they may provide a more valid assessment of students' skills.

- Performance tasks give parents an opportunity to see their children's strengths in areas that a traditional testing format might not capture. In some cases, these tasks offer parents an opportunity to share their own interests, hobbies, and experiences with their children as parent and child discuss possible options and gather necessary resources.

Despite their advantages, performance assessments are not ideal for every situation (Miller & Seraphine, 1993; Nitko & Brookhart, 2007). From a practical standpoint, completion of performance assessments may take a great deal of students' time, and the teacher must be sure that the assignment is

What Has Been Learned? Exhibitions allow students to share their work in a public format.

meaningful enough to warrant the time invested. High-quality performance assessments are difficult to design, and poorly designed performance tasks may not provide a valid assessment of what students have learned and can do (Beyreli & Ari, 2009). A student's performance on one task may tell very little about what that student can do in other areas. For example, in art class a student may be instructed to glaze a pot. The student's performance on this task provides information about how well the student can apply glazing techniques but reveals nothing about whether the student is able to successfully throw a pot on the wheel or whether the student understands the rich history of pottery as an art form. Be aware that effective scoring rubrics for performance assessments are difficult to create and that the scores may have lower reliability than other measures. Grading performance assessments can be very time-consuming, making them a less practical alternative.

Validity, a characteristic of high-quality assessment, must be carefully considered when making decisions about what form of assessment to use. Validity in the classroom context is primarily a measure of how well interpretations from assessments contribute to instructional decision making and move students toward increasing levels of competence (Brookhart, 2003; Moss, 2003). To better ensure the validity of performance assessments, the teacher should make sure the assessment (Nitko & Brookhart, 2007):

- includes content that is representative and relevant,
- represents thinking processes and skills,
- shows evidence of consistency with other assessments, and
- is part of multiple assessments across the course of a grading period.

Generally, performance assessment for summative purposes fills in the gaps left by other, more objective methods rather than being used as the sole assessment tool (Hanna & Dettmer, 2004). During the assessment process, teachers look for patterns, check for contradictory evidence, and compare the developing picture of a student's abilities to certain learning goals or standards of competence (Shepard, 2006). The inclusion of performance assessments facilitates this process by allowing the teacher to see student competencies that may not have been captured via traditional assessments. The combined use of traditional and performance assessments increases validity by presenting a more accurate and complete picture of what a student knows and is capable of doing.

How might you use performance assessments to the greatest advantage in your own teaching? In what situations might you decide not to use performance assessments?

Validity applies to classroom tests: See page 545.

Validity applies to standardized tests: See page 546.

Summary

Define *performance assessment* and provide examples of the formative and summative uses of performance assessment. Performance assessment is any assessment that requires students to carry out an activity or develop a product in order to demonstrate skill or knowledge. Formative uses of performance assessment provide feedback in the moment in order to help a student improve. Summative uses of performance assessment help the teacher evaluate students' progress, as well as the effectiveness of instructional methods, at the end of a unit or grading period.

Define *authentic assessment* and identify its essential characteristics. Authentic assessment measures important abilities using procedures that simulate the application of those abilities to real-world intellectual problems, roles, or situations. Authentic assessments present students with tasks that are complex and require students to use a combination of different types of knowledge and skills. Authentic tasks may be messy, challenging students to deal with poorly defined problems similar to the roles and issues students will encounter in the real world. The problems may have multiple correct solutions; however, standards and criteria for assessing the possible range of correct answers, performances, or products should be clearly specified.

Describe the three major types of performance assessment and provide a rationale for using each type. Projects, portfolios, and presentations are three commonly used forms of performance assessment. A project is a long-term activity that results in a student product. Well-designed project tasks allow students to apply and integrate a wide range of abilities and knowledge and, if designed as group work, can give students the opportunity to develop skill in working cooperatively. A portfolio is a systematic collection of work that can capture the complexity and range of a student's work. Because portfolios may include multiple samples of a student's work collected over an ex-

tended period of time, they are an excellent tool for demonstrating progress. Presentations can take many different forms, can be used to demonstrate what has been learned over the course of a unit or program of study, and may require a combination of reading, writing, questioning, speaking, and listening.

Describe the three methods of systematically evaluating student performance. Checklists, rating scales, and rubrics provide preset criteria for evaluating student performance, thereby making grading simpler, more transparent, and more consistent. Developing one of these scoring systems in the course of designing a performance assessment helps teachers define expectations of what students need to know and to do. If given to students at the very beginning of an assignment, these scoring systems allow students to better understand the criteria for success. Checklists are the simplest system, because the teacher simply marks whether a particular behavior or skill is present or absent. Rating scales, which can be designed in graphic, numeric, or descriptive formats, allow the teacher to indicate the level or quality of a skill performed. Rubrics provide the greatest level of detail by specifying the criteria for each level of achievement.

Discuss the general advantages and disadvantages of performance assessments. The advantages of performance assessments include their consistency with modern learning theory (building on prior knowledge, active engagement, construction of meaning); the integration of knowledge, skills, and abilities; the ability to assess the processes students use, as well as their final products; and the ability to assess what students can do, not simply what they know. Unfortunately, high-quality performance assessments can be difficult to design and time-consuming to implement and grade. Performance assessments are less objective and thus have lower reliability than other measures and, if not well designed, may also have poor validity.

Key Concepts

analytic rubric 517
authentic assessments 511
best work portfolios 515
checklist 516
demonstrations 512
descriptive rating scales 516
exhibition 513
experiment 512
formative assessments 510
generic rubric 517
graphic rating scales 516
holistic rubric 517
inter-rater reliability 516
normative rating scales 516
numeric rating scales 516
oral presentations 512
performance assessment 510
portfolio 514
process portfolios 514
project 514
rating scales 516
rubric 517
summative assessment 510
task-specific rubric 517

Video Applications

www.mhhe.com/bohlin2e

Video 1: Examples of Performance Assessment (*2 minutes*)

Clip 1 (Interview with Dr. Kunkel of the Indianapolis Key Learning Community): Process portfolios

Clip 2 (Fourth-grade gifted class): Presentations

Clip 3 (Middle school): Formative assessment

Clip 4 (Fourth- and fifth-grade gifted class): Performance of Macbeth

Case Studies
Reflect and Evaluate

EARLY CHILDHOOD: "The Zoo"

These questions refer to the case study on page 468.

1. How do Miss Vivian and Mr. Sanjay use performance assessment in their classroom?

2. Why might performance assessment be a particularly good choice for this classroom environment?

3. Would the creation of the zoo be considered an authentic task? Why or why not?

4. If Miss Vivian and Mr. Sanjay were using portfolios as a form of assessment, what possible artifacts could be included? Try to think of at least five items that would be appropriate to include.

5. How could Miss Vivian and Mr. Sanjay involve the students in the assessment process?

6. How could Mr. Sanjay have used checklists or rating scales to gather information about the students in the preschool session? What advantages would this method offer?

ELEMENTARY SCHOOL: "Writing Wizards"

These questions refer to the case study on page 470.

1. Ms. Blaydes uses many different performance tasks in her classroom to engage students in writing. What concerns about validity should she keep in mind when using performance assessments? Give specific examples.

2. What concerns about fairness should Ms. Blaydes keep in mind when using performance assessments?

3. Which elements of Ms. Blaydes's assessment of student writing could be considered authentic assessment? Why?

4. Ms. Blaydes developed an evaluation form (rubric) for invited guests to use to comment on the Young Authors submissions. What is the advantage of providing a structured rubric with preset criteria as opposed to simply asking for open-ended feedback from the evaluators?

5. If Ms. Blaydes wants to be able to provide a score when evaluating each piece of student writing, what kind of scoring system should she use? Describe how this system works.

6. Based on what you read in the module, provide at least two suggestions for how Ms. Blaydes could use computers in the assessment process.

7. If Ms. Blaydes were using portfolios as a form of assessment, what possible artifacts could be included based on what was mentioned in this case?

MIDDLE SCHOOL: "Assessment: Cafeteria Style"

These questions refer to the case study on page 472.

1. Why might Ms. Reffert's project option be classified as a type of *performance assessment*?

2. What advantages does performance assessment offer the students? The teacher?

3. What disadvantages does performance assessment present for the students? For the teacher?

4. Why is it important to use a rubric when scoring student projects?

5. What was the purpose of providing students with a copy of the rubric in advance?

6. Is the project option a form of authentic assessment? Would your answer vary depending on what each student chooses to do for his or her project? Explain.

HIGH SCHOOL: "Innovative Assessment Strategies"

These questions refer to the case study on page 474.

1. What concerns might critics of the Oregon Senior Project in English raise about reliability, validity, fairness, and practicality?

2. How might the concerns in question 1 be addressed?

3. The third phase of the Senior Project in Oregon is a formal presentation before a panel of teachers and community members. What are the advantages of having students exhibit their work publicly?

4. Is the assessment approach used by the math teacher in California a type of authentic assessment? Why or why not?

5. What kinds of information does the assessment approach referred to in question 4 provide for the teacher?

6. What are some learning objectives that could be met with the oral history project used by the teacher in Rhode Island?

7. What guidelines could Mr. Medino share with his teachers to help them decide when to use some type of performance assessment and when to continue to use traditional tests?

unit nine

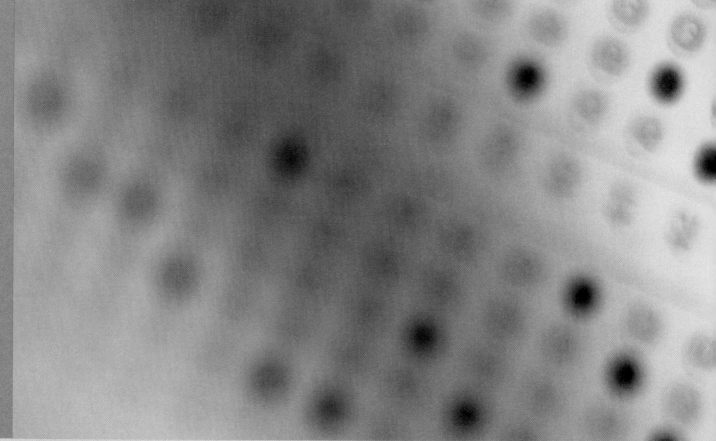

Case Studies

Early Childhood: "Kindergarten Readiness" 528

Elementary School: "Keyboard Courage" 530

Middle School: "Teachers Are Cheating?" 532

High School: "SAT Scores" 534

Module 29:
Standardized Tests and Scores

Outline and Learning Goals 536

Types of Standardized Tests 537

Basic Concepts of Measurement 541

Types of Test Scores 542

Characteristics of Good Tests 545

Summary 548

Key Concepts 548

Video Applications 549

Case Studies: Reflect and Evaluate 549

standardized testing

Module 30:
Issues in Standardized Testing

Outline and Learning Goals 551

High-stakes Testing and Accountability 552

Applications: Accommodating Students at Risk 556

Test Fairness and Test Bias 558

Teacher Certification and Licensure 560

Summary 563

Key Concepts 563

Video Applications 564

Case Studies: Reflect and Evaluate 564

Prepare:

As you read the case, make notes:

1. **WHO** are the primary participants in the case? Describe them.

2. **WHAT** is taking place?

3. **WHERE** is the case taking place? Is the environment a factor?

4. **WHEN** is the case taking place? Is the timing a factor?

Ms. Jane Walters and Ms. Sidney Theesfield are the kindergarten teachers at Bentley Elementary School in Arizona. During this week in April, the teachers are busy conducting readiness testing for the new incoming kindergarten class. The testing helps the teachers determine the strengths and weaknesses of each child so they can adapt instruction and social experiences to meet the needs of their students when the school year begins in August. Ms. Walters and Ms. Theesfield have scheduled 30-minute appointments with the parents of potential incoming kindergarten students. The teachers alternate roles, one conducting a one-on-one readiness assessment with the child while the other meets with the parent or guardian to hand out brochures about kindergarten readiness and to answer questions. Amy Shelby, a student teacher under Ms. Walters' supervision during the spring semester, will be observing some of the test administrations

Early Childhood

Kindergarten Readiness

and parent meetings. Ms. Walters and Ms. Theesfield are doing some final preparations before the appointments begin and are preparing Amy for what to expect.

Ms. Walters begins, "Now, Amy, you aren't yet qualified to give the BRIGANCE® K & 1 Screen-II that we use for testing, but you will be observing. I asked you to practice giving the test so you can ask good questions when we have finished the screening. You know we need to follow the instructions exactly as written on the testing materials, right?"

"Yes, I have been practicing at home reading the instructions to my roommate," replies Amy.

Ms. Theesfield interjects, "Well, giving the test is actually the easy part. The harder part is answering parent questions. Ms. Walters, do you remember Ms. Jackson from last November at parent-teacher conferences who wanted her daughter to skip the rest of kindergarten?" Ms. Theesfield turns to Amy and continues, "She assumed that because her daughter had a grade equivalent score of 1.2 on our district literacy assessment that she should be in first grade."

Ms. Walters replies, "Yes, it took 30 minutes to convince her that grade equivalent scores were not that meaningful and shouldn't be used to move students up or down grade levels. I am glad we decided to stop providing those scores to parents. It just causes confusion."

Amy replies, "Test scores can be hard to explain to anyone. Last night I was trying to explain the scores to my roommate. She couldn't understand why a child wouldn't be considered above average if she scored two points above the mean for the test. I tried to explain that *average* typically refers to a range of scores, not the exact mean."

"Well, we typically don't need to explain test scores to parents at this meeting. Anyway, Amy, you'll sit with me at the child screenings and parent meetings to observe," Ms. Walters replies.

As they each begin looking over the folders for their first child of the day, Ms. Theesfield says, "Amy, I forgot to ask . . . did you ever hear back about your teacher licensure test?"

Amy replies, "Yes, I passed the state licensure for Arizona, but my fiancé and I are planning to move to Utah in July, so it really doesn't do me that much good. I will have to take the state licensure exam in Utah as well. I don't understand why licensure in one state isn't good enough for every other state."

Ms. Walters announces, "Well, we could argue about state versus national licensure all day, but I see our first child has arrived."

She turns toward the doorway as she hears a family entering the classroom. "Good morning, I am Ms. Walters. You must be Maria Sanchez. I'll bet you're excited to be a kindergartener!" Ms. Walters says with a smile and a wink.

Maria doesn't say a word. She sheepishly looks toward the two ladies who have accompanied her to the screening.

The older woman turns to the younger one and says something in Spanish. The younger woman replies in Spanish and then turns to Ms. Walters. "My name is Ana. I am Maria's sister. I am the only one in our family who speaks English. I came along today to translate for my mother and sister. Is that okay?"

Ms. Walters replies, "Well, I am very glad you're here. We do have the Spanish version of the screening we use and an individual who is trained to give the screening to children who are Spanish speaking. So we won't need you to help with the screening, but you are welcome to help interpret for your mother during the parent meeting."

Ana turns to her mother, and they converse in Spanish for a minute or two. Ana asks, "Do you mean that I can't go in with Maria during her testing? My mother is concerned that she will be considered behind the other kids because of her English."

Ms. Walters assures Ana, "Please tell your mother that the entire test is given in Spanish, so the test score will be based on Maria's abilities, not her English skills. Okay?"

Again, Ana translates for her mother. The mother nods at Ms. Walters, but doesn't look convinced.

Assess

1. In your opinion, should educators conduct readiness testing for entering kindergarteners? Why or why not?

2. Why might Maria's mother be concerned about how her daughter's scores will be used by the school?

Prepare:

As you read the case, make notes:

1. **WHO** are the primary participants in the case? Describe them.

2. **WHAT** is taking place?

3. **WHERE** is the case taking place? Is the environment a factor?

4. **WHEN** is the case taking place? Is the timing a factor?

Ms. Alexandria Bowman has been the principal at Lincoln Elementary School for the past two years. The inner-city school includes a diverse group of students from various ethnic backgrounds. The school's standardized achievement test scores in reading were up two years ago from the previous year, but they have fallen this past school year below the state cutoff level in the third, fourth, and fifth grades. Before leaving for the day, Ms. Bowman sends an e-mail memo to all teachers and teacher assistants that reads:

Elementary School
Keyboard Courage

TO:	Lincoln Elementary teachers
FROM:	Ms. Bowman
Subject:	**Suggestions for Spring testing**
Date:	October 29, 2011

October 29, 2011

Good afternoon,

Our next teacher in-service training is scheduled for November 14th and will cover standardized achievement test scores. Our standardized testing scores for reading across several grades fell last year in comparison to the previous year and are below the state cutoff level. I would like each of you to send me an e-mail by next Friday with possible reasons for the decline as well as possible solutions so that we may discuss these on November 14th. Please give me specific suggestions that we can implement over the next several months in order to prepare for the spring testing session.

Sincerely,

Ms. Bowman

By morning, the principal has received a number of replies, as the teachers and staff are always more vocal online than in face-to-face interactions. The e-mails include the following:

Ms. Fernández (fourth-grade teacher): Our test scores have fallen because we have so many students who have learning disabilities and are not being provided with the appropriate accommodations. We need to do a full assessment on each child and determine the appropriate accommodations we can make to be sure our test scores are not unduly affected by this group of students in the future.

Mr. Whitney (fifth-grade teacher): The problem is that we are using a norm-referenced test and then imposing criterion-referenced test interpretations. If our scores are only slightly below average compared to the national norm, then it shouldn't matter that our scores have fallen slightly below the state cutoff for mastery. We are still within the average range. I agree we don't want this to become a slippery slope, but I also don't think we should panic just yet.

Ms. LeBlanc (reading specialist): I work with students every day who have difficulty reading a few sentences. The standardized achievement tests require a lot of reading in a short amount of time. We need to allow certain students extra time to complete the tests. I am not sure how to decide which students should get extra time or how much extra time should be allowed, but there is no way some of these children can finish the test in the time allotted.

Ms. Seifert (fifth-grade teacher assistant): Our students need more test preparation. Many students are not familiar with the test format and don't understand how to complete the computerized answer sheets. We should have practice sessions with all the students. Maybe they could take the test from last year, or we could give them similar standardized achievement tests so they can practice test-taking skills.

Ms. Rivadeneyra (special education teacher): Last year's test scores are not an accurate reflection of our students' abilities. Remember that the week before the testing session we had the shooting two blocks down and had to lock down the school until almost 5:00 P.M. that day. I would assume that many students were still shaken up about the event and didn't perform as well as expected. My guess is that the test scores would have been much better if the testing session had taken place prior to the shooting. I don't think we should get too concerned yet.

Mr. Washington (fourth-grade teacher): I don't understand the problem. Our test scores were only half a standard deviation below the national average. We have a student body made up of children from primarily lower-SES homes. Given the population we serve, why does anyone expect anything more from us?

Ms. Cong (third-grade teacher): I am very glad you are taking this so seriously. I know this is only my first year teaching, but when I saw that we had an average percentile score across the grades of 48, I was astonished. If our students didn't even get half of the questions correct on the test, we simply are not doing our jobs. I don't understand why something wasn't done the previous year when our average percentile score was even lower—46th percentile. We may need to discuss radical changes in the curriculum.

Assess

1. After reading the teachers' responses, in your opinion, how concerned should Ms. Bowman be about the fallen standardized test scores?

2. Give each person's e-mail a score based on how accurate you think the explanation is for the fallen test scores (1 = not at all accurate, 2 = somewhat accurate, 3 = very accurate). Why did you give that score?

3. Give each person's e-mail a score based on how helpful their suggestions are for improving test scores (1 = not at all helpful, 2 = somewhat helpful, 3 = very helpful). Why did you give that score?

Prepare:

As you read the case, make notes:

1. **WHO** are the primary participants in the case? Describe them.

2. **WHAT** is taking place?

3. **WHERE** is the case taking place? Is the environment a factor?

4. **WHEN** is the case taking place? Is the timing a factor?

Ms. Lisa Garrison has been at Tri-County Middle School for 12 years as a social science teacher. Currently, she is serving as the acting principal while the principal is out on medical leave for eight weeks. Ms. Garrison has asked all the teachers to stay after school today for a brief meeting on procedures regarding the two days of annual standardized testing that will take place next week. As she prepares for the meeting in her office, the teachers begin to enter the classroom adjacent to her office. She can't help but overhear some of the conversation.

She hears Ms. Haney say, "We do this every year. I don't know why we need to have this meeting."

Mr. Malcolm responds, "Well, last year there was some speculation that teachers were cheating for their students. I am sure we are going to cover that today."

Middle School

Teachers Are Cheating?

Ms. Haney replies, "I don't know what *cheating* is supposed to mean. I would never give my students the answers or extra time for the test. I have my students complete the test and write their answers in the booklet. Then, after the testing session, I take time out of my life to fill in the answer sheet with their answers. Many of them don't pay close enough attention and would get off by a line and screw up the test results. Filling in the answer sheet ensures that their answers are recorded correctly. That's not cheating."

Ms. Garrison enters the conference room. "Good afternoon, everyone. I know that you are all busy, but I just thought we should cover some of the basics of our testing procedures for next week. I'll start by asking if anyone has any questions about the procedures."

Mr. Rients asks, "Yes. This is my first year giving the tests. I have read all the instructions and time limits for the test, and I think I am set for next week. My question is about the students I have in class who typically are given extra time and assistance. What am I supposed to do with them?"

Ms. Garrison replies, "That's an excellent question. Many of you will be giving the test to students who need assistance. The various staff members involved with each of these children met a couple of weeks ago to confirm the types of accommodations the students should be given during testing sessions. I have instruction sheets here for each of those students stating exactly how they should be accommodated. I'll give you the instruction sheets for your students at the end of the meeting. So please let me know if you have any questions after you have read the instructions. Any other questions?"

"Yes, I have one," begins Ms. Haney. "I understand there was some speculation last year that the teachers didn't follow procedures correctly. Could you tell us more about that? I find it hard to believe that the teachers in this school would cheat."

Ms. Garrison replies, "I'm not sure *cheating* is the right word. The issue was that some teachers didn't follow the standard procedures laid out in the instructions for the test. For example, students must complete their own answer sheets, but some teachers filled in the sheets after the testing was completed. Also, there was some speculation that a few teachers allowed their students extra time to complete the reading comprehension section of the test. Those were the two issues raised last year, and that's exactly why we are having this meeting today. We need to be sure that we all follow the procedures exactly."

Mr. Rients asks, "Is it true that our scores last year were way above the national average? What does that mean for funding from the state? Will we receive extra funds for salary increases if the scores improve again this year?"

Ms. Garrison responds, "Our scores were only half a standard deviation above the mean. We jumped last year from the 50th percentile and a stanine score of 5 to the 63rd percentile and a stanine score of 6. If we follow the procedures *correctly* this year and our test scores go back down, we probably will be investigated more thoroughly because test scores shouldn't jump back and forth so drastically, at least not if the test is doing its job. Besides, the important information is not about how we compare to the national average. We need to be concerned about the standards set by the state after No Child Left Behind was implemented."

Assess

1. Given the information presented by Ms. Garrison, would you consider Tri-County Middle School students to be below average, average, or above average?

2. In your opinion, was Ms. Haney cheating when she completed the answer sheets for her students last year?

3. Is it fair or unfair to give students with disabilities extra time and assistance on standardized tests? Explain your answer.

Prepare:

As you read the case, make notes:

1. **WHO** are the primary participants in the case? Describe them.

2. **WHAT** is taking place?

3. **WHERE** is the case taking place? Is the environment a factor?

4. **WHEN** is the case taking place? Is the timing a factor?

Ms. Alexia Fortner arrived early this Monday morning to prepare upcoming lessons for her senior math class. Several of her students took the SAT over the weekend. She is sure much of today's discussion will surround their scores and plans for college now that they have their test scores. Over the past several weeks, Ms. Fortner tried to help prepare her students by giving them classroom tests with answer sheets, along with tips for decreasing test anxiety, and letting them use one class period to take a practice math subscale of the SAT test from the official Web site.

Ms. Fortner is particularly excited to hear from Lu Tuong, who typically is given special accommodations on the state achievement tests due to her limited English proficiency. She was particularly nervous about performing well enough on the SAT to get into a good university. Ms. Fortner spent quite some time over the past several weeks talking with Lu

High School

SAT Scores

about the possibility of attending a community college if she doesn't score well and about the importance of needing to remain calm during the test, as she tends to crumble under pressure.

Ms. Fortner greets her first student, J. T. "Well, how did you do on the SAT this weekend, J.T.?"

J. T. announces in his confident, somewhat arrogant voice, "I got a 600 on the math subscale. I'm sure I'll be able to get into the state university." He continues in a more concerned tone, "Bethany only got a 400. She cried all day yesterday and started seriously looking into community colleges. I wouldn't be surprised if she doesn't come to class today to avoid everyone asking her about it."

Lu enters the room with a shy smile and says in her choppy English, "Ms. Fortner, I got 500 on math. I think will be enough!"

Ms. Fortner replies, "Oh, that's great! You must have used some of the techniques we covered in class about relaxing, taking your time to think, and . . ."

Trevor interrupts as he enters the room, "Don't ask. Just don't anybody ask me about the SAT!"

Ms. Fortner scans the room and sees that some students are excited about their scores and ready to talk but others don't look so eager. Here comes Bethany with her head down, avoiding all eye contact. Ms. Fortner decides it's best to leave the SAT scores out of the discussion for the day. "Okay, good morning everyone, we are going to discuss the homework assignment from last week . . . ."

After school, Ms. Fortner runs into Mr. Tom Harris, one of the school counselors, in the hallway. "Hey, Ms. Fortner, did you hear the news about Lu's SAT math score? She's really excited and sure did appreciate all your help with her test anxiety problem."

"Yes, she told me first thing this morning. I'm glad I could help. Did you hear anything about Trevor?" asks Ms. Fortner. "He seemed to be very upset this morning about his score."

Mr. Harris replies, "Oh, it isn't that bad. I heard him telling somebody that he got a 600 on the math subscale. He thinks that will keep him from getting into his top pick for college. I have to admit that I was surprised his score was so low—not that 600 is low—but he is such an outstanding student and typically scores extremely high on our state achievement tests. I don't really think that score accurately represents his ability. Do you?"

"Well, I don't know his overall academic record like you do. I just know he appears to be a very bright and motivated student. I will say that he didn't seem as nervous about the test as most of the other students. It was almost like he didn't think it would be a big deal—maybe he didn't prepare well," responds Ms. Fortner.

"Well," begins Mr. Harris, "maybe his score is lower because he's Black. I know, as a Black man myself, I always got really nervous about those important tests and never seemed to score as high as I expected. I had trouble on the SAT and even later in my life on the Praxis I and Praxis II exams for teacher licensure. I think almost all standardized tests like those are biased against minority students."

Ms. Fortner replies, "That could have something to do with it. I also know he was very sick with the flu last week. It could be that his illness had something to do with it."

Assess

1. Do you think it was appropriate for Ms. Fortner to use her class time to help her students prepare for the SAT? Why or why not?

2. Based on the four students' math SAT scores provided in the case, do you think the students at this school typically are below average, average, or above average? Is there too much difference in scores to decide?

3. Do you agree with Mr. Harris that being a minority student might explain low standardized test scores? Is your answer based on opinion, experience, or other information?

"ONE THING I'LL ALWAYS BE THANKFUL FOR IS THAT I GOT HERE BEFORE THERE WERE ANY SATs."

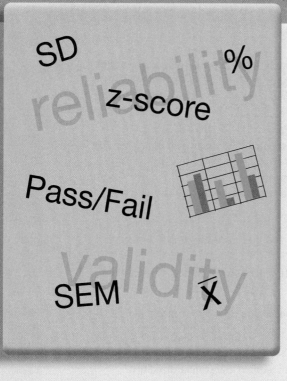

MODULE 29

Standardized Tests and Scores

Outline	Learning Goals
Types of Standardized Tests	
■ Categories of Standardized Tests ■ Criterion-referenced and Norm-referenced Tests	1. Describe the purpose of four broad categories of standardized tests and how standardized tests are used by teachers. 2. Explain the difference between criterion-referenced and norm-referenced tests.
Basic Concepts of Measurement	
■ Central Tendency and Variability ■ Normal Distribution	3. Explain the basic properties of a normal distribution.
Types of Test Scores	
■ Raw Scores ■ Percentile Scores ■ Grade-equivalent Scores ■ Standard Scores	4. Describe four types of test scores, and explain the advantages and limitations of each.
Characteristics of Good Tests	
■ Validity ■ Reliability	5. Explain why validity and reliability are two important qualities of tests and why teachers need this information about tests to interpret test scores.
Summary **Key Concepts** **Video Applications** **Case Studies: Reflect and Evaluate**	

TYPES OF STANDARDIZED TESTS

How many standardized tests have you taken in your life? Can you remember why you took them? Perhaps you took the SAT or ACT to apply for college, or the Praxis I exam to be admitted to your undergraduate education program. Before we consider why educators at all levels use standardized tests, we first need to define exactly what makes a test standardized. **Standardized tests** are distinguished by two qualities (Gregory, 2010; Haladyna, 2002):

1. They are created by testing experts at test publishing companies.
2. All students are given the test by a trained examiner under the same (hence "standardized") conditions. For example, all students are given the same directions, test items, time limits, and scoring procedures.

You're probably very familiar with tests that are *not* standardized, such as the classroom tests you have taken since elementary school. Classroom tests, often created by individual teachers, measure specific learning that occurs within a classroom and typically focus on the district's curriculum. Teachers may use classroom tests as a formative or a summative assessment of students' knowledge (Linn & Gronlund, 2000). *Assessment* includes any and all procedures used to collect information and to make inferences or judgments about an individual or a program (Reynolds, Livingston, & Willson, 2006). *Formative assessments,* such as homework assignments and quizzes, enable teachers to plan for instruction and monitor student progress throughout a grading period. To assess student achievement at the end of an instructional unit or grading period, teachers use *summative assessments* such as tests and cumulative projects.

Like some classroom tests, standardized tests typically are used for summative assessments, but they focus on broader areas of learning such as overall mathematical achievement rather than mathematical progress within a grading period. For a summary of the differences between classroom and standardized tests, see Table 29.1.

Classroom assessment: See page 477.

Classroom tests: See Module 27.

What standardized tests do you remember taking in elementary through high school? What purpose do you think they served? Think about these tests as you read about the categories of standardized tests.

TABLE 29.1	Comparison of Classroom Tests and Standardized Tests	
	Classroom test	**Standardized test**
Purpose	Formative and summative	Typically summative
Content	Specific to a content covered in the classroom over a specific time frame	Specific or general topics across many districts or states
Source of items	Created or written by the classroom teacher	Created by a panel of professional experts
Administration procedures	Can be flexible for students with disabilities and special needs	Standardized across all settings and individuals
Length	Usually short—less than an hour	Usually very long—several hours
Scoring procedures	Typically teacher-scored	Typically machine-scored
Reliability	Typically low	Typically high
Scores	Individual's number or percent correct (raw score)	Compared to predetermined criteria or norm group (converted from raw score)
Grading	Used to assign a course grade	Used to determine general ability or achievement; not used to assign course grade

Source: Haladyna, 2002.

Categories of Standardized Tests

Standardized tests have several purposes. Some standardized tests—called single-subject survey tests—contain several subtests that assess one *domain-specific* content area, such as mathematics. Other standardized tests contain a battery of several tests used in conjunction with one another to provide a broader, more *general* picture of performance that may include competencies such as vocabulary, spelling, reading comprehension, mathematics computation, and mathematics problem solving. Standardized tests fall into one of four broad categories based on their purpose (Chatterji, 2003), as described here (see Example 29.1).

1. **Standardized achievement tests** assess *current knowledge,* which can include learning outcomes and skills either in general or in a specific domain. Standardized achievement tests do not necessarily match the curriculum of any particular state or school district. Instead, they are used to identify the strengths and weaknesses of individual students as well as school districts. *Readiness tests,* like achievement tests, measure young children's current level of skill in various academic (reading, math, vocabulary) and nonacademic (motor skills, social skills) domains and are used to make placement and curricular decisions in the early elementary grades.

2. **Standardized aptitude tests** assess *future potential*—or capacity to learn—in general or in a specific domain. Aptitude tests are used for admission or selection purposes to place students in particular schools (e.g., private schools or colleges) or specific classrooms or courses (e.g., advanced mathematics). Standardized intelligence tests are considered aptitude tests because their purpose is to predict achievement in school.

   > Intelligence measured as IQ: See page 406.

3. **Career or educational interest inventories** assess individual *preferences* for certain types of activities. These inventories typically are used to assist high school and college students in planning their postsecondary education, as well as to assist companies and corporations in selecting employees. Some of these tests are also considered aptitude tests because they may predict future success.

4. **Personality tests** assess an *individual's characteristics,* such as interests, attitudes, values, and patterns of behavior. Personality tests are limited in their educational use because psychologists and

EXAMPLE 29.1   **Standardized Tests in Four Broad Areas**

	Name	Type/Purpose
Standardized achievement tests	Iowa Test of Basic Skills (ITBS)	Battery of achievement tests for grades K–8
	Tests of Achievement and Proficiency (TAP)	Battery of achievement tests for grades 9–12
	Metropolitan Achievement Test (MAT)	Battery of achievement tests for grades K–12
Standardized aptitude tests	Differential Aptitude Test (DAT)	Battery of tests to predict educational goals for students in grades 7–12
	Scholastic Assessment Test (SAT)	Single test to predict academic performance in college
	General Aptitude Test Battery (GATB)	Battery of aptitude tests used to predict job performance
	Armed Services Vocational Aptitude Battery (ASVAB)	Battery of aptitude tests used to assign armed service personnel to jobs and training programs
Career or educational interest inventories	Strong Interest Inventory (SII)	Instrument used with high school and college students to identify occupational preferences
	Kuder General Interest Survey (KGIS)	Instrument used with students in grades 6–12 to determine preferences in broad areas of interest
Personality tests	NEO Five-Factor Inventory (NEO-FFI)	Instrument to assess an individual on five theoretically derived dimensions of personality
	Minnesota Multiphasic Personality Inventory-2 (MMPI-2)	Instrument used to aid in clinical diagnosis

Source: Chatterji, 2003.

counselors with graduate-level training primarily use them for diagnosis of clinical disorders and because most personality tests are appropriate only for individuals age 18 or older.

Most standardized tests administered by teachers are given in a group format. *Group-administered tests* are relatively easy to administer and score, making them cost-effective. *Individually administered tests,* such as personality tests and IQ tests, require expert training, time to administer, and time to score and interpret, all of which lead to greater cost. Although teachers typically are not trained to administer these individual tests, they will encounter the test scores of individually administered tests in meetings to determine the eligibility of students for special education and related services.

Criterion-referenced and Norm-referenced Tests

The interpretation of test scores includes understanding not only what the test measures—general versus specific knowledge or current knowledge versus future potential—but also how test scores should be evaluated. A test score is a **measurement** that assigns a quantitative or descriptive number during the process of assessment. But a test score in itself cannot be detached from how it is evaluated. **Evaluation** is the subjective judgment or interpretation of a measurement or test score (Haladyna, 2002). For example, a student might take a test and answer 20 of 30 questions correctly (measurement), but whether that score is interpreted as a "good" score, an "improvement" from a previous score, or "substantially below" the expected score is a matter of evaluation. Standardized tests typically are designed so that any test score can be evaluated by comparing it either to a specific standard (criterion) or to data compiled from the test scores of many similar individuals (norm).

- **Criterion-referenced tests** compare an individual's score to a preset criterion, or standard of performance, for a learning objective. Many times criterion-referenced tests are used to test mastery of specific skills or educational goals in order to provide information about what an individual does and does not know. On criterion-referenced tests, test developers include test items based on their relevance to specific academic skills and curricula. The criteria are chosen because, together, they represent a level of expert knowledge. Lawyers, doctors, nurses, and teachers must take standardized tests and meet a specified criterion in order to become licensed or certified for their profession. Some tests that students take—such as state mastery tests—are also criterion-referenced tests.

- **Norm-referenced tests** compare the individual test-taker's performance to the performance of a group of similar test-takers, called the norm sample. A **norm sample** is a large group of individuals who represent the population of interest on characteristics such as gender, age, race, and socioeconomic status. For example, a norm sample for a standardized test can be all fifth-graders nationally, all fifth-graders in a state, or all fifth-graders in a district. Norm samples for nationally used standardized tests, such as the achievement tests listed in Example 29.1, need to be large (about 100,000 test-takers) and representative of the population of students in order to allow accurate interpretations. The test items on norm-referenced tests are designed to differentiate, to the greatest degree possible, between individual test-takers. For example, a norm-referenced mathematics achievement test might be used to select the top elementary school students in a school district for a gifted program with limited seats or space.

The major difference between the two types of tests is the purpose or situation for which each type of test is most useful, as summarized in Table 29.2. Many standardized group-administered achievement tests provide teachers with both a criterion-referenced and a norm-referenced interpretation of scores, as shown in Example 29.2. When dual interpretation is not available, the type of test that is used

TABLE 29.2	Comparison of Criterion-referenced and Norm-referenced Tests	
	Criterion-referenced	**Norm-referenced**
Purpose	To determine mastery at a specified level	To compare score to the performance of similar test-takers
Content	Specific to a domain or content area	Broad domain or content area
Item selection	Similar level of difficulty	Wide variability in difficulty level
Scores	Number or percent correct as compared to criteria	Standard score, percentile, or grade-equivalent score as compared to the norm group

Source: Gregory, 2010.

EXAMPLE 29.2 A Simple Standardized Test Score Report

TERRANOVA[3]

Performance on Objectives

TERRANOVA™, *Third Edition*
COMPLETE BATTERY

Individual Profile with *InView*™, Part I

PAT WASHINGTON

Grade 4

| Simulated Data |

Purpose
This report presents information about this student's performance on the *TerraNova* and *InView* assessments. Page 1 describes achievement in terms of performance on the objectives. Together with classroom assessments and classwork, this information can be used to identify potential strengths and needs in the content areas shown.

Birthdate: 02/08/98
Special Codes:
ABCDEFGHIJKLMNOPQRSTUVWXYZ
3 59 732 11 1
Form/Level: G-14

Test Date: 04/15/07 Scoring: PATTERN (IRT)
QM: 31 Norms Date: 2007

Class: JONES
School: WINFIELD
District: GREEN VALLEY

City/State: ANYTOWN, U.S.A.

Mc Graw Hill CTB McGraw-Hill

*OPI is an estimate of the number of items that a student could be expected to answer correctly if there had been 100 items for that objective.

Key

Moderate Mastery Range	
Low Mastery	O
Moderate Mastery	◒
High Mastery	●

Obj. No.	Objective Titles	Student	Nat'l OPI	Diff	Moderate Mastery Range	Objectives Performance Index (OPI)*
	Reading					
02	Basic Understanding	91	79	12	48–70	
03	Analyze Text	92	84	8	52–75	
04	Evaluate/Extend Meaning	65	66	–1	50–70	
05	Identify Rdg. Strategies	70	74	–4	45–73	
	Language					
07	Sentence Structure	63	68	–5	45–70	
08	Writing Strategies	59	74	–15	50–75	
09	Editing Skills	78	63	15	55–75	
	Mathematics					
10	Number & Num. Relations	71	69	2	47–77	
11	Computation & Estimation	83	72	11	45–75	
13	Measurement	66	86	–20	45–60	
14	Geometry & Spatial Sense	71	72	–1	50–78	
15	Data, Stats., & Prob.	61	83	–22	52–78	
16	Patterns, Funcs, Algebra	77	88	–11	44–73	
17	Prob. Solving & Reasoning	71	74	–3	52–75	
18	Communication	69	68	1	43–73	
	Science					
19	Science Inquiry	47	74	–27	50–75	
20	Physical Science	49	69	–20	52–77	
21	Life Science	46	83	–37	45–78	
22	Earth & Space Science	52	84	–32	48–73	
23	Science & Technology	48	78	–30	52–69	
24	Personal & Social Persp.	52	56	–4	50–73	
	Social Studies					
26	Geographic Perspectives	79	91	–12	48–70	
27	Historical & Cultural	84	92	–8	52–75	
28	Civics & Government	66	65	1	50–70	
29	Economic Perspectives	74	70	4	45–73	

Norm-Referenced Scores

	Scale Score	DIFF[1]	Anticipated Normal Curve Equiv.	Obtained Normal Curve Equiv.	Anticipated National Percentile	National Percentile	National Percentile Range	National Percentile Scale
Reading	664	—	35	47	23	45	32–56	
—	—	—	—	—	—	—	—	
—	—	—	—	—	—	—	—	
Language	678	Above	34	57	22	64	53–72	
—	—	—	—	—	—	—	—	
Mathematics	674	—	41	48	29	47	37–60	
—	—	—	—	—	—	—	—	
Total Score	679	Above	35	55	24	59	50–66	
Science	668	—	36	45	26	41	36–50	
Social Studies	662	—	38	43	28	37	27–48	
—	—	—	—	—	—	—	—	

National Stanine Scale

**Total Score consists of Reading, Language, and Mathematics.
[1]Above or Below appears when there is a significant difference.

will depend on the purpose. Criterion-referenced tests provide information about mastery of material but do not allow comparisons among test-takers. In contrast, norm-referenced tests do not provide information about the mastery or the strengths and weaknesses of a particular individual, but they do provide ample information for comparing test scores across individuals using several basic concepts of measurement, as discussed next.

BASIC CONCEPTS OF MEASUREMENT

In order to interpret test scores accurately, teachers must understand some basic concepts of measurement that are used in conjunction with one another to evaluate individual students as well as to evaluate groups of students, such as classrooms or school districts.

Central Tendency and Variability

One basic measure needed to form evaluations or make comparisons is **central tendency**—the score that is typical or representative of the entire group. Let's examine a set of classroom or standardized test scores. Suppose you teach a class of 11 students who receive these scores on their first exam: 63, 65, 72, 75, 76, 78, 83, 87, 87, 92, and 98. What measure will tell you the central tendency of this set of numbers? The three most common statistical descriptions of central tendency are the mean, median, and mode:

1. **Mean:** Divide the sum of all the scores by the total number of scores to find the mean, or simple average. Summing the 11 scores (sum = 876) and dividing by 11 gives mean 79.64.

2. **Median:** Find the middle score in a series of scores listed from smallest to largest. In this case, the median is 78, the middle value, because five scores are on either side. In a group with an even number of scores, the median is the midpoint, or average, of the two middle scores.

3. **Mode:** Find the most frequently occurring score in the group. In this group, the mode is 87, the only score that occurs more than once. A group of scores can be bimodal—having two modes—when two different scores occur frequently.

The mean, median, and mode all provide information about the typical score within a group but do not provide information about the **variability**—how widely the scores are distributed, or spread out, within a particular group. Compare these two groups of test scores:

Class 1 scores: 6, 7, 7, 8, 8

Class 2 scores: 4, 7, 7, 8, 10

Both classes have a mean test score of 7.2, but the scores in the second class show considerably more variation. The **range** is a simple measure of variability calculated as the difference between the highest and lowest scores. For Class 1, the range is 2 (8 minus 6), while for Class 2, the range is 6 (10 minus 4).

The most commonly used measure of variability among scores, **standard deviation (SD),** is the degree of variability in a group of scores. The standard deviation is more difficult to compute than the range: it equals the square root of each score's deviation from the mean. This sounds more complex than it is. The computation is less important than understanding the standard deviation for test score interpretation. Figure 29.1 shows the difference in variability for two groups of scores with small and large standard deviations.

- A *small* standard deviation indicates that most scores are close to the mean score of the group. For a classroom test, the teacher might hope that all students would score well and close to one another, indicating that all students are mastering the course objectives.

- A *large* standard deviation suggests that the scores are more spread out. On standardized achievement tests, a large degree of variability is not only typical but optimal, because the test items are designed to make fine discriminations in achievement among a population of students.

Figure 29.1. Normal Distributions with Large (orange) and Small (blue) Standard Deviations. In the small standard deviation, most scores are close to the mean score of the group. Scores are more spread out in a large standard deviation.

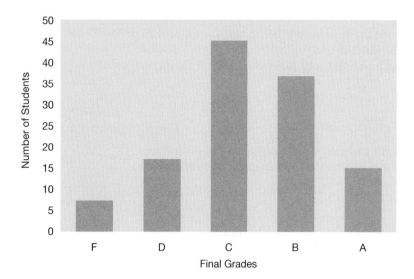

Figure 29.2. Histogram of Final Grades in an Educational Psychology Course. Final grades are indicated along the horizontal axis (x-axis), and the number of students receiving each final grade is indicated along the vertical axis (y-axis).

In the example with Class 1 and Class 2, the standard deviations are .84 (Class 1) and 2.17 (Class 2). With a small set of numbers, the variability may be obvious. However, with large groups of scores, such as the thousands of scores of students taking a standardized achievement test, the standard deviation provides a scientific measurement of the distribution of scores.

Normal Distribution

A **frequency distribution** is the simple list of all scores for a group. The scores can be depicted visually in a histogram, or bar graph. For example, Figure 29.2 depicts the final grades in an educational psychology course. Final grades are indicated along the horizontal axis (x-axis), and the number of students receiving each final grade is indicated along the vertical axis (y-axis). As Figure 29.2 shows, 7 students failed the course, 17 students received a grade of D, 45 students received a C, 37 students received a B, and 15 students received an A. In this figure more scores fall to the right (higher scores) and fewer scores fall to the left (lower scores) of the midpoint, indicating that the scores are skewed. **Skewness,** or the symmetry or asymmetry of a frequency distribution, tells how a test is working. Negatively skewed distributions (with long tails to the left), such as in Figure 29.2, indicate that the scores are piled up at the high end. Positively skewed distributions indicate that the scores are piled up at the low end (long tail to the right). Classroom tests with negative skewness are what teachers hope to achieve (i.e., mastery by most students). In standardized testing, positively skewed distributions suggest that the test had too many difficult questions, and negatively skewed distributions suggest that the test had too many easy items.

For standardized tests, we expect a frequency distribution that is symmetrical and bell-shaped, called a **normal distribution** (see Figure 29.3). Normal distributions are apparent in scores on the SAT and on IQ tests. A normal distribution has several properties:

- The mean, median, and mode are equal and appear at the midpoint of the distribution, indicating that half the scores are above the mean and half the scores are below the mean.
- Approximately 68% of scores occur within one standard deviation above and below the mean.
- Two standard deviations above and below the mean include approximately 95% of scores.
- Three standard deviations above and below the mean include approximately 99% of scores.

TYPES OF TEST SCORES

Raw Scores

Both classroom and standardized tests first yield a **raw score,** which typically is the number or percentage of correct answers. For evaluating the results of classroom tests, raw scores typically are used. For standardized criterion-referenced tests, raw scores are compared to the preset criterion for interpretation (e.g., pass/fail, mastery/nonmastery). For standardized norm-referenced tests, raw scores more commonly are converted or transformed by the test developers to help provide consistent evaluation and ease of interpretation of scores by parents and teachers. Next we consider several common norm-referenced test scores.

Percentile Scores

Percentile scores (or ranks) are derived by listing all raw scores from highest to lowest and providing information on the percentage of test-takers in the norm sample who scored below or equal to that raw score. For example, a percentile score of 80 means that the test-taker scored as well as or better than 80% of all test-takers in the norm sample. Be careful not to confuse the percentage of correct answers on a test with the percentile score, which compares individual scores among the norm sample. For example, an individual could correctly answer 65 of 100 questions (65%) on a test, but the percentile ranking of that score would depend on the performance of other test-takers. If a raw score of 65 is the mean in a normal distribution of scores (the middle value in the bell curve), then the raw score of 65 would have a percentile score of 50, meaning that 50% of the norm group scored below or equal to 65.

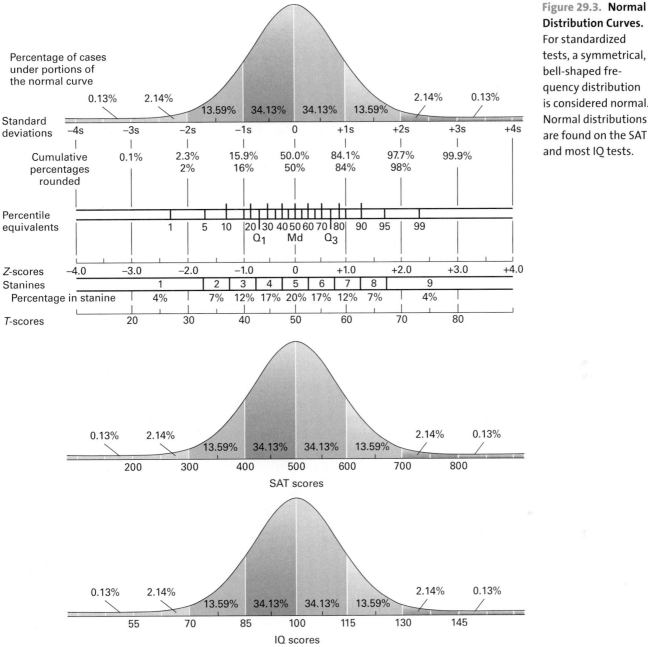

Figure 29.3. Normal Distribution Curves. For standardized tests, a symmetrical, bell-shaped frequency distribution is considered normal. Normal distributions are found on the SAT and most IQ tests.

One problem with percentile scores is that they are not equally distributed across the normal curve. A small difference in raw scores in the middle of a distribution of scores can result in a large percentile score difference, while at the extremes of the distribution (the upper and lower tails) larger raw score differences between students are needed to increase the percentile ranking. This means that percentile scores overestimate differences in the middle of the normal curve and underestimate differences at either end of the normal distribution.

As an example, take another look at Figure 29.3, the normal distribution of SAT scores for each subscale. Assume the following percentile scores:

Student A received a score of 500 → 50 percentile

Student B received a score of 600 → 84.1 percentile

Student C received a score of 700 → 97.7 percentile

Student D received a score of 800 → 99.9 percentile

Based on percentile scores, student B appears to have markedly outperformed student A (percentile score of 84.1 compared to 50), and students C and D appear to have performed very similarly (percentile scores of 97.7 and 99.9). In actuality, the difference in performance between students is exactly the same (100 points). Hence, comparisons should not be made between two students' percentile scores. The interpretation of percentile scores should only involve comparing one student's score to the performance of the entire norm group (e.g., student A performed better than or equal to 50% of all test-takers).

Grade-equivalent Scores

Grade-equivalent scores are based on the median score for a particular grade level of the norm group. For example, if the median score for all beginning sixth-graders in a norm group taking a standardized achievement test is 100, then all students scoring 100 are considered to have a grade-equivalent (GE) score of 6.0, or beginning of sixth grade. The 6 denotes grade level, and the 0 denotes the beginning of the school year. Because there are 10 months in a school year, the decimal represents the month in the school year. Suppose the median score for all sixth-graders in the seventh month of the school year is 120. Then a student earning a score of 120 would have a GE score of 6.7.

GE scores often are misused because individuals assume they are mathematical statistics for interpreting students' performance. However, GE scores function more like labels—they cannot be added, subtracted, multiplied, or divided. Because each GE score for a test (or a subtest of a test battery) is derived from the median raw score of a norm group, median raw scores will vary from year to year, from test to test, and from subtest to subtest within the same test battery. Therefore, GE scores cannot be used to compare students' improvement from year to year, students' relative strengths and weaknesses from test to test, or even students' scores on subtests of a standardized test. GE scores can be used only to describe whether a student is performing above grade level, at grade level, or below grade level.

There is a risk of misinterpreting grade-equivalent scores. A person might conclude that a student who scores above his or her actual grade level is able to be successful in an advanced curriculum or that a student who scores below grade level should be held back a grade. Suppose a second-grade student has a GE score of 5.2 on a reading achievement test. We would say that the second-grade student scored as would an average fifth-grade student in the second month of school, *if* the fifth-grade student took a reading test appropriate for second-graders. In other words, all we can say is that the second-grader is above average for his or her grade in reading achievement, not that the second-grader "reads on a fifth-grade level." The misinterpretation of GE scores stems from two problems:

1. The computation of GE scores does not use any information about the variability in scores within a distribution. The median score of all beginning sixth-graders may be 100, but there is great variability in scores among the students. Not all beginning sixth-graders will score 100. An expectation by the school district, teacher, or government that all students should reach that score is unrealistic (Anastasi & Urbina, 1997).

2. The variability in GE scores increases as grade level increases, with students at lower grade levels relatively homogeneous in performance and students at middle and high school levels showing a wide variation (Anastasi & Urbina, 1997). So a first-grade student who scores one year below grade level may be substantially below peers in achievement, while a ninth-grade student who scores one year below grade level actually may be average in achievement.

Because of the likely misinterpretation and misuse of grade-equivalent scores, most educators and psychologists do not recommend using them.

Standard Scores

Standard scores are used to simplify score differences and, in some instances, more accurately describe them than can either percentiles or grade-equivalent scores. For example, standard scores are used in interpreting IQ tests and the SAT by converting the raw scores using the mean and standard deviation. When the scores are converted, the mean for IQ tests is 100 and the standard deviation is 15, while for each subscale of the SAT the mean score is approximately 500 and the standard deviation is 100.

A common standard score is calculated by using the mean and the standard deviation (SD) to convert raw scores into **z-scores.** When raw scores are converted into z-scores using the simple formula

$$z = \frac{(\text{raw score} - \text{mean})}{\text{SD}}$$

the z-score distribution always has a mean score of 0 and a standard deviation of 1, leading to z-scores that range from -4.00 to $+4.00$, as shown in Figure 29.3. Because z-scores are based on units of standard deviations, comparisons across student scores are more precise than with percentiles or grade-equivalent scores and are less likely to be misinterpreted.

Because negative numbers can create some concern and confusion—and also have a negative connotation when interpreting students' ability or achievement—another common standardized score is the T-score. The **T-score** is also based on the number of standard deviations, but it has a mean of 50 and a standard deviation of 10 (z-scores are multiplied by 10, and then 50 is added to the product). Again, looking at Figure 29.3, we see that a T-score of 60 represents one standard deviation above the mean (+1.00 z-score) and a T-score of 40 represents one standard deviation below the mean (−1.00 z-score). T-scores typically are not used with standardized achievement or aptitude tests, but they are commonly used with personality tests and behavioral instruments, particularly those that assist in the diagnosis of disorders (Gregory, 2010).

Stanine scores are based on percentile rank but convert raw scores to a single-digit system from 1 to 9 that can be easily interpreted using the normal curve, as shown in Figure 29.3 (Gregory, 2010). The statistical mean is always 5 and comprises the middle 20 percent of scores, although scores of 4, 5, and 6 are all interpreted or evaluated as average. Stanines of 1, 2, and 3 are considered below average, and stanines of 7, 8, and 9 are considered above average. Because the scores are based on percentile rank, they do *not* provide better comparisons across scores than do z-scores and T-scores.

Teachers typically are asked to interpret standardized test scores for parents. Given a choice, which type of test score would you prefer to use in providing your interpretation and why? How comfortable would you be explaining the various other test scores?

CHARACTERISTICS OF GOOD TESTS

Several characteristics of tests and test scores are important for appropriate test-score interpretation, including:

- standardized test administration (as mentioned at the beginning of this module),
- large and representative norm samples for norm-referenced tests, and
- the use of standard scores when interpreting performance.

Teachers should evaluate two additional characteristics before selecting tests to use or interpreting test scores: validity and reliability. Without adequate evidence that test scores are reliable and valid, test-score interpretations are meaningless. Let's explore each concept in more detail.

Validity

How do we know that a test score accurately reflects what the test is intended to measure? To answer this question, we need to be able to evaluate the validity of the test score. **Validity** is the extent to which an assessment actually measures what it is intended to measure, yielding accurate and meaningful interpretations from the test score. Keep in mind that validity refers to the test *score*, not the test itself (the collection of items in a test booklet). Consider these examples:

Validity of classroom assessments: See page 494.

- Just because a test score is intended to predict intelligence, such as an IQ score of 120, does not mean that it fulfills that purpose.
- A test may have valid scores for most individuals, but the test score might be invalid for a particular individual. For example, a standardized achievement test score would not be valid for a student who takes the test without wearing his or her prescription eyeglasses. Similarly, a non–English-speaking student taking a test written in English is unlikely to receive an accurate interpretation of his or her achievement in a particular subject area based on the test score (Haladyna, 2002).

DIVERSITY

Use of standardized tests with non–English-speaking students: See page 139.

Validity is not an all-or-none characteristic (valid or invalid), and it can never be *proven*. Rather, it varies depending on the extent of the research evidence supporting a test score's validity. All validity is considered **construct validity,** or the degree to which an unobservable, intangible quality or characteristic (construct) is measured accurately. The construct validity of a test score can be supported by several types of evidence:

1. **Content validity** evidence provides information about the extent to which the test items accurately represent all possible items for assessing the variable of interest (Reynolds et al., 2006). For example, do the 50 items on a standardized eighth-grade math achievement test adequately represent the

content of eighth-grade mathematics? The issue of content validity is also relevant to classroom tests because most teachers choose a subset of questions from a pool of possible questions they could ask to represent the knowledge base for a particular learning goal.

2. **Criterion-related validity** evidence shows that the test score is related to some criterion—an outcome thought to measure the variable of interest (Reynolds et al., 2006). For example, aptitude tests used to predict college success should be related to subsequent GPA in college, an outcome measure related to a student's general aptitude (Gregory, 2010). Two types of criterion-related validity are:

   ■ **concurrent validity** evidence, based on the test score and another criterion assessed at approximately the *same time*, such as a math achievement test score and the student's current grade in math; and

   ■ **predictive validity** evidence, based on the test score and another criterion assessed in the *future*, such as an aptitude test and later college GPA.

3. **Convergent validity** evidence shows whether the test score is related to another measure of the construct. For example, a new test designed to measure intelligence should be correlated with a score on an established intelligence test.

4. **Discriminant validity** evidence demonstrates that a test score is not related to another test score that assesses a *different* construct. For example, a reading test would not be expected to correlate with a test of mental rotations or spatial abilities.

5. **Theory-based validity** evidence provides information that the test scores are consistent with a theoretical aspect of the construct (e.g., older students score higher than younger students on an achievement test).

Reliability

Reliability of classroom assessments: See page 494.

If a standardized aptitude test is given to a student on Monday and again on Friday, would you expect the test scores to be different, similar, or exactly the same? We would expect both test scores to be similar, because it would be highly improbable for the student to receive exactly the same score twice or to have two wildly divergent scores. This consistency, called the **reliability** of the test score or measurement, is measured on a continuum from high to low. A reliability index can be computed in a number of ways depending on the type of test and the test-scoring procedures. For example, administering the same aptitude test on Monday and Friday is a type of reliability procedure called *test-retest*. The computed relationship between the test and retest scores provides a reliability index. All reliability indexes, or reliability coefficients, range from 0 to 1, with higher numbers indicating higher reliability (Haladyna, 2002):

■ .90 or above is considered highly reliable,

■ between .80 and .90 is considered good, and

■ below .80 is considered questionable.

Measurement Error. All measurements, including weights on bathroom scales and scores on standardized tests, have imperfections.

To better understand reliability, let's consider another form of measurement—your bathroom scale. Have you ever stepped on the scale to weigh yourself, read the number, and then thought "That can't be right"? You step right back onto the same scale, and a slightly different weight registers (maybe one you prefer, maybe not). The difference in the weights is due to measurement error. **Measurement error** is the accumulation of imperfections that are found in all measurements. Test scores, like all other measurements, are an imperfect type of measurement. Measurement error on tests can result from a number of sources (Gregory, 2010; Reynolds et al., 2006):

■ item selection (e.g., clarity in the wording of questions),

■ test administration (e.g., a test administrator who has a harsh tone of voice and increases student anxiety),

■ individual factors (e.g., anxiety, illness, fatigue), or

■ test scoring (e.g., subjective, judgment-based assessments such as essays).

EXAMPLE 29.3   Error in Political Polls

The standard error of measurement (SEM), or margin of error, provides information used to determine a confidence interval or range in which the true score would fall. In this political poll, the President's actual approval rating is somewhere between 32% and 42%.

THE PRESIDENT'S APPROVAL RATING

APPROVE 37%

DISAPPROVE 63%

± 5% margin of error

Even though these sources of measurement error are unpredictable, developers of standardized tests estimate the amount of error expected on a given test, called the **standard error of measurement (SEM)** (also called the margin of error in public surveys such as political polls). The statistical calculation for determining the standard error of measurement is based on the reliability coefficient of the test and the standard deviation of test scores from the scores of a norm group. This calculation is not as important as how SEM can be used to interpret test scores. With an individual test score, SEM can help determine the **confidence interval,** or the range in which the individual's true score (i.e., true ability) lies. Consider this example:

A student receives a raw score of 25 on a standardized achievement test with SEM 4.

If we calculate a 68% confidence interval (the raw score plus or minus the SEM), the student's score range is 21 to 29.

We can say with 68% confidence that the student's true score is between 21 and 29 on this standardized achievement test.

We have used a 68% confidence interval with a raw score as a simple explanation of how SEM helps determine a student's true score (also see Example 29.3). However, remember that most standardized test results will report a 95% or 99% confidence interval and that the confidence intervals will use standard scores (z-scores, T-scores, stanines, etc.) rather than raw scores. Many psychologists and test developers recommend using confidence intervals to remind professionals, parents, and researchers that measurement error is present in all test scores (Gregory, 2010).

One note of caution is needed regarding the relationship between validity and reliability. Say, for example, that your bathroom scale is very reliable but you later discover that its measurement is consistently off by 10 pounds. This shows that consistent results (reliability) can be found with a measure that does not accurately assess the construct of interest (validity). In short, reliability does not lead to validity. Reliability is necessary—any test that is valid also must measure the construct of interest consistently—but it is not sufficient for achieving validity. A bathroom scale can consistently read 350 pounds for a person who actually weighs 110 pounds. In this case also, the scale is reliable but not valid. If a standardized aptitude test accurately predicts success in college (validity), the results should be consistent (reliability) across multiple testing sessions, such as early or late in twelfth grade. If the test results lack reliability, validity also is undermined.

Teachers need to evaluate the validity and reliability of a test before attempting to make test score interpretations. Most standardized tests publish the validity evidence and reliability coefficients that are used by teachers and school districts to determine which tests are "good."

Assume that your school district is using a highly reputable standardized test with a reliability coefficient above .90. One of your students performs well, as you would expect, at the beginning of the year but then performs very poorly on the same test at the end of the year. Is this student's test score valid? What might affect the reliability and validity of this student's test score?

Summary

Describe the purpose of four broad categories of standardized tests and how standardized tests are used by teachers. Standardized achievement tests are used to assess the degree of current knowledge or learning in either broad or domain-specific areas. Standardized aptitude tests assess an individual's future potential to learn in general or in domain-specific areas. Career or educational interest inventories assess preferences related to certain types of activities. Personality tests are used to assess individual characteristics. Teachers are most likely to administer group tests, which are both relatively easy to administer and cost effective. Teachers may encounter individually administered test results when determining special education eligibility.

Explain the difference between criterion-referenced and norm-referenced tests. Although some standardized tests provide both criterion-referenced and norm-referenced interpretations, the type of test or interpretation used is based on the purpose of the test. Criterion-referenced tests provide information about the mastery and the strengths and weaknesses of individual students, such as whether a particular student meets certification requirements. In contrast, norm-referenced tests allow comparisons among student scores that may be used in making decisions such as selecting the top students from a group.

Explain the basic properties of a normal distribution. The normal distribution is a special type of frequency distribution. Although some frequency distributions may be skewed, with more scores falling on the higher or lower end, the normal distribution is bell-shaped and symmetrical. The three central tendencies—mean, median, and mode—are equal to one another and appear at the midpoint of a normal distribution. The variability among scores is standard such that 68% of scores are within one standard deviation of the mean, 95% of scores are within two standard deviations of the mean, and 99% of scores are within three standard deviations of the mean.

Describe four types of test scores, and explain the advantages and limitations of each. (1) Raw scores are the number of correct answers or percentage of correct answers. They provide adequate information for classroom tests but are more difficult to interpret when comparing scores across students or groups of students. (2) Percentile scores are based on the percentage of test-takers who scored below or equal to a student's raw score. Percentile scores provide information about how well an individual performed in comparison to a group but should not be used to compare different students' scores. (3) Grade-equivalent scores represent the median score for particular grade levels indicating whether a student is scoring at grade level, below grade level, or above grade level. GE scores are commonly misinterpreted; hence, experts do not recommend their use. (4) Standard scores are derived from percentile rank scores by converting them into a single-digit system (i.e., stanines) or from raw scores by converting them into scores based on a specified mean and standard deviation (i.e., z-scores and T-scores). Standard scores typically are used for ease of interpretation, and those based on the mean and standard deviation also allow accurate comparisons among scores.

Explain why validity and reliability are two important qualities of tests and why teachers need this information about tests to interpret test scores. To determine the quality of a test, teachers should evaluate the validity evidence and reliability of test scores. Validity refers to the extent to which a test measures what it is intended to measure. Reliability of test scores refers to the consistency of the measurement, with highly reliable tests having minimal measurement error and low-quality tests having high measurement error. Teachers can use information about validity and reliability evidence to determine the quality of a test and to make decisions about whether the test should be used. The standard error of measurement also can be used to determine a confidence interval, rather than depending on a single raw or standard score. Confidence intervals remind teachers and other professionals that some measurement error is present in all tests—even high-quality tests.

Key Concepts

career or educational interest inventories   538

central tendency   541

concurrent validity   546

confidence interval   547

construct validity   545

content validity   545

convergent validity   546

criterion-referenced tests   539

criterion-related validity   546

discriminant validity   546

evaluation   539

frequency distribution   542

grade-equivalent scores   544

mean   541

measurement   539

measurement error   546

median   541

mode   541

norm-referenced tests   539

normal distribution   542

norm sample   539

percentile scores   542

personality tests   538

predictive validity   546

range   541

raw score   542

reliability   546

skewness   542

standard deviation (SD)   541

standard error of measurement (SEM)   547

standardized achievement tests   538

standardized aptitude tests   538

standardized tests   537

standard scores   544

stanine scores   545

theory-based validity   546

T-score   545

validity   545

variability   541

z-scores   544

Video Applications

www.mhhe.com/bohlin2e

Video 1: Explaining Standardized Test Scores (*8 minutes*)
This video is a mock meeting between a teacher and parent regarding a students' standardized test scores. The parent is very confused by test scores and the teacher attempts to explain percentile scores and grade equivalent scores.

Case Studies
Reflect and Evaluate

EARLY CHILDHOOD: "Kindergarten Readiness"

These questions refer to the case study on page 528.

1. The BRIGANCE® K & 1 Screen-II measures gross and fine motor skills, color recognition, knowledge of body parts, counting, oral comprehension, and many literacy and numeracy skills. In what way is this standardized readiness test like a standardized achievement test?

2. What basic concepts of measurement are used to create the range Amy refers to when explaining to her roommate that *average* typically means a range in scores?

3. Explain why grade-equivalent scores can be confusing to parents like Ms. Jackson. What types of scores could be used to better compare achievement differences among students?

4. Maria's mother is concerned about how Maria's test score will be interpreted and used. What characteristic of "good tests" is a concern for Maria's mother? Is her concern justified? Why or why not?   *DIVERSITY*

5. Suppose Maria's percentile ranking on the BRIGANCE is the 38th percentile. How would you interpret this score in relation to other students? What if another student scored at the 49th percentile? How would you compare the performance of this student to Maria's?

6. Define *validity* in your own words. Explain whether Maria's readiness test results would be valid if she took the English version of the BRIGANCE. What if she took the English version with her sister as interpreter?   *DIVERSITY*

ELEMENTARY SCHOOL: "Keyboard Courage"

These questions refer to the case study on page 530.

1. Mr. Whitney mentions the difference between norm-referenced and criterion-referenced tests. Explain whether he is accurate in his interpretation about how the test scores are used.

2. Based on the normal distribution and the information Mr. Washington provides regarding the test scores being half a standard deviation below the mean, how poorly are the students doing in comparison to students across the country?

3. If the test scores had been half a standard deviation above the national mean, would Principal Bowman have been as concerned? Why or why not?

4. Explain what is wrong with Ms. Tuong's interpretation of percentile scores.

5. Explain how the average percentile score could have increased from 46 to 48 while average scores fell below the state cutoff levels.

6. Ms. Rivadeneyra suggests that the test scores do not accurately reflect the students' abilities. What characteristic of good tests is involved here? Explain how this characteristic was influenced by the events near the school last year.

MIDDLE SCHOOL: "Teachers Are Cheating?"

These questions refer to the case study on page 532.

1. Why did Mr. Rients take so much time to prepare for the standardized testing session? What might happen if a teacher didn't prepare by reading the instructions ahead of time and noting the time limits?

2. Assume that the national test scores represent the normal distribution. Based on Acting Principal Garrison's reply that the previous year's scores were only half a standard deviation above the mean, how accurate was Mr. Rients's interpretation that the test scores were "way above the national average"? Explain your answer.

3. Ms. Garrison uses the percentile score to provide information about how the school's test scores have jumped back and forth over the past two years. Explain why this may not be the best test score to use for comparing annual progress.

4. Assume that several weeks after the testing session Ms. Garrison announces that the school's average stanine score for reading was 7. How does this compare to last year's test scores?

5. What characteristic of good tests is Ms. Garrison referring to when she says that "test scores shouldn't jump back and forth so drastically"? What characteristic of good tests is she referring to when she adds "at least not if the test is doing its job"? Why is it important for teachers to know about these characteristics?

HIGH SCHOOL: "SAT Scores"

These questions refer to the case study on page 534.

1. What type of standardized test is the SAT? Why might a student score high on an achievement test but not on the SAT?

2. Explain how a norm-referenced test, such as the SAT, can be used as a criterion-referenced test by colleges and universities for determining admissions.

3. Based on the information in the module about SAT scores, explain how much variability there was in the four students' test scores on the math subscale as presented in the case.

4. Assume that another student received a score of 700 on the math subscale. What would be the equivalent stanine score? What would be the equivalent z-score?

5. Assume that Trevor takes the SAT again next month and receives a score of 800 on the math subscale. What does the difference in his two scores indicate about the quality of the test scores? Based on the information presented in the case, what might account for the difference in Trevor's scores over such a short length of time?

No Child
LEFT BEHIND

Issues in Standardized Testing

Outline	Learning Goals
High-Stakes Testing and Accountability	
■ What Is High-Stakes Testing? ■ No Child Left Behind ■ Negative Outcomes and Test Score Pollution	1. Explain why NCLB is considered high-stakes, and describe three problems with this law. 2. Briefly explain how teachers can avoid the six negative outcomes of high-stakes testing.
Applications: Accommodating Students at Risk	
	3. Explain how accommodations improve the validity of test scores for students at risk.
Test Fairness and Test Bias	
	4. Explain the difference between test fairness and test bias and summarize the evidence for cultural test bias in standardized tests.
Teacher Certification and Licensure	
	5. Briefly summarize the two testing programs most likely to be used as the national standard in the future.
Summary **Key Concepts** **Video Applications** **Case Studies: Reflect and Evaluate**	

HIGH-STAKES TESTING AND ACCOUNTABILITY

What Is High-Stakes Testing?

While many may believe that standardized testing and the high stakes associated with test score performance are new ideas ushered in by the **No Child Left Behind Act of 2001 (NCLB),** high-stakes standardized testing has been around for more than 40 years. **High-stakes tests** refer to all tests that have significant consequences for students, teachers, administrators, or schools (Haladyna, 2002). Examples of high stakes associated with testing include:

- the publication of state and district test results in local newspapers,
- pass or fail decisions regarding grade promotion or graduation,
- pass or fail decisions about certification or licensure for entering a certain profession,
- merit pay raises or bonuses for teachers whose students have shown increased performance on standardized achievement tests,
- allocation of funding to school districts based on state test scores, and
- basing decisions about teachers' future employment on students' standardized achievement test scores.

The first wave of high-stakes testing began in response to the Soviet Union's launch of Sputnik in 1957. Politicians began to question the rigor of American education and advocated the increased use of tests to assess learning in school (Kreitzer, Madaus, & Haney, 1989). The Elementary and Secondary Education Act (ESEA) of 1965, which provided special funds and services for children from low-income families (called Title I children), was enacted in part as a response to concern that the United States was lagging behind other nations academically. Standardized testing of basic skills was used throughout the 1970s and 1980s to gauge student performance against evolving curriculum standards.

Starting in the 1990s, a second wave of testing, known as the high-stakes testing movement, became popular as a result of information from two sources:

- *A Nation at Risk,* released in 1983 by the National Commission on Education, recommended that states institute more rigorous standards to improve curricula and accountability measures and hold schools responsible for meeting those standards (U.S. Department of Education, 1983).
- Studies conducted by the International Association for the Evaluation of Educational Achievement (IEA) in the 1990s found that, compared with students in other countries, students in the United States were scoring above average in math and science in fourth grade but only at average levels by eighth grade. By 12th grade, U.S. students were scoring below average in math and science compared with students in many countries (Thomas, 2005).

The high-stakes testing movement had states, school districts, and teachers evaluate the level of student learning as a means of gathering information about possible changes needed in curriculum and teaching methods to improve student learning. States began implementing mastery tests—tests that assess students' achievement in various subjects to determine whether they have met curricular objectives. In many states, test scores were linked to high stakes such as grade promotion, graduation, and the release of test score results to the media (Thomas, 2005).

High-Stakes Testing. In some states, students who fail the standardized test but meet all other school requirements for graduation are denied a high school diploma.

A significant consequence of high-stakes testing has been the development of **accountability**—teachers and school districts are held responsible for students' performance. The U.S. Congress, concerned that states were not doing enough to promote accountability and other educational aims, enacted legislation to hold school districts responsible for student learning. In January 2002, President George W. Bush signed legislation that reauthorized ESEA and renamed it the No Child Left Behind Act of 2001 (NCLB). States do not have to abide by NCLB, but those states opting not to meet the law's requirements lose federal funding.

Do you believe teachers should be held accountable for their students' performance on high-stakes tests? Why or why not?

No Child Left Behind

GUIDING PRINCIPLES OF NCLB

When we think of NCLB, we often think of accountability. However, NCLB was built on four basic principles, of which accountability is only one. The others are expanded parental choice, expanded local control and flexibility, and reading first. Let's explore each of these.

Accountability. NCLB requires states to implement a system of accountability covering all public schools and all students. To achieve this, NCLB requires standardized testing of students in reading, math, and science every year for children in grades 3 through 8 and once for students in grades 10 through 12. Each state is allowed to create its own standardized test to match curriculum standards, or it may choose a national test that best matches its curriculum. States also are able to determine their own standards or cutoffs for four categories of success on the specified test: (1) failure, (2) basic, (3) proficient, and (4) advanced.

States must report test score results and participation rates (percentage of students taking the state test) by subgroups such as socioeconomic status, race, ethnicity, disability, and limited English proficiency to ensure that no group of students is *left behind.* One hundred percent of all subgroups are expected to achieve levels of proficiency in subject areas by 2014. NCLB requires a 95% participation rate for students in each subgroup and requires all subgroups to make **adequate yearly progress (AYP),** an annual measurable achievement goal chosen by each state to indicate movement toward proficiency. School districts that meet their state-specified AYP levels are rewarded with publicity as distinguished schools, and cash bonuses are awarded to teachers. Schools and school districts that fail to meet AYP goals can face severe consequences:

- A school is labeled "in need of improvement" if a particular subgroup fails to meet AYP goals *after two years,* or if a subgroup does not meet the 95% participation rate (Kim & Sunderman, 2005). Schools in need of improvement are required to develop a plan for improvement.

- If AYP goals are not met *after three years,* the label "in need of improvement" remains, and funding is provided to assist low-income students with educational services such as tutoring.

- If AYP goals are not met *after four years,* corrective actions are required, such as replacing staff and creating a new curriculum.

- If AYP goals are not met *after five years,* a school can be restructured, taken over by the state or a private contractor, converted to a charter school, or reconstituted with new staff (Kim & Sunderman, 2005).

Expanded parental choice. Students who attend Title I schools, which receive federal funding because of a high enrollment of students from low-income families, are able to transfer to a better public school within the district if their school fails to meet AYP goals for two consecutive years. The district must provide transportation to the new school using a portion of Title I funds.

Expanded local control and flexibility. While NCLB requires stringent accountability measures, it also provides states with greater flexibility in the use of federal funds. States can allocate up to 50% of the funds they receive to Title I schools or to any one of four state grant programs promoting (1) teacher quality, (2) educational technology, (3) safe and drug-free schools, and (4) innovative programs.

Reading first. NCLB implemented a Reading First Initiative, which makes six-year grants available to states for funding programs to ensure that every student can read by third grade. States allocate grant funds for the purpose of early K–3 reading screening to identify students at risk for reading failure and to provide research-based reading interventions in the early grades.

Although many states use standardized test scores to determine grade promotion and graduation, NCLB does not require that test results be used for those purposes. The *Standards for Educational and Psychological Testing* (AERA, 1999) provide guidelines for using test scores for promotion and graduation:

- There should be evidence that students have had an opportunity to learn the content and skills covered on a test used for decisions about grade promotion or graduation.

- There should be evidence that the test is connected to other achievement-related outcomes (e.g., other achievement tests, grades).

- Decisions about grade promotion or graduation should not be based on a single test score.

- Students should have multiple opportunities to succeed on tests used for grade promotion or graduation.

The consequences of using standardized test scores can be quite serious. Students who are required to repeat a grade due to failing the standardized test are more likely to drop out of school, and large numbers of students who fail the standardized test but meet all other school requirements for graduation are denied a high school diploma (Thomas, 2005).

PROBLEMS WITH NCLB

Although the intention of NCLB was to improve student learning and hold school districts and teachers accountable, several problems have emerged since the implementation of NCLB:

1. Because AYP levels are determined at the state level, inconsistencies exist between states such that a passing score in one state may be a failing score in another state (Thomas, 2005).

Means and variability in test scores: See page 541.

2. All schools and students are required to meet a single mean proficiency level in subjects. However, differences in average test scores among students, particularly young students, usually reflect students' cognitive skills and background characteristics before they begin school, such as preschool or early childhood education, rather than achievement as a result of later school learning (Kim & Sunderman, 2005; Waldfogel & Zhai, 2008). In addition, students who make great improvements during a school year but do not meet proficiency cut-offs are not included in measurements of AYP (Ho, 2008). Beginning in 2005, several states participated in a Growth Model Pilot Program to examine how individual student test score improvements toward proficiency might be included in accountability measures. Growth models may be most appropriate to include in accountability measures for low-achieving, high-growth schools.

DIVERSITY

3. Using mean score differences is biased against high-poverty schools and minority students. According to NCLB accountability criteria, low performance by one subgroup can result in an entire school failing to make AYP. AYP failure rates increase as schools are held accountable for additional subgroup outcomes (Kim & Sunderman, 2005; Paulson & Marchant, 2009). Many schools with high minority enrollments also have high poverty rates, so they are "doubly disadvantaged" because they need to make AYP for each minority subgroup *and* for an economically disadvantaged subgroup. A disproportionate number of minority students attend Title I schools that are required to implement federal sanctions if AYP goals are not met. In Arizona, California, Georgia, Illinois, New York, and Virginia, schools needing improvement have majority African-American and Latino enrollments, while schools meeting AYP goals have predominantly Caucasian and Asian-American enrollments (Kim & Sunderman, 2005). Recent research offers little evidence that accountability rules in California and Texas have improved the achievement level of minority students (Kane & Staiger, 2002, 2003).

4. The implementation of NCLB has done little to improve the achievement of poor-performing students in high-poverty schools or to improve the achievement gap between Black and White students (Braun, Chapman, & Vezzu, 2010; Forte, 2010). Recent research examining changes in achievement from 1992 to 2000 (pre-NCLB era) in comparison with changes from 2000 to 2007 (during the NCLB era) found only modest differences. This research suggests that accountability of NCLB to improve achievement of Black students and reduce the achievement gap between Black and White students is not substantially better than efforts deployed prior to NCLB (Braun et al., 2010).

Negative Outcomes and Test Score Pollution

Validity: See page 493.

High-stakes testing can lead to many negative outcomes for students, teachers, and schools. **Test score pollution,** one of the most severe outcomes, occurs when test scores are systematically increased or decreased due to factors unrelated to what the test is intended to measure (test score validity). In this case, the increase or decrease in test scores over time is not a true increase or decrease in student learning but rather the result of other factors, including unethical actions by teachers and administrators under pressure to meet legislated standards. The negative outcomes of high-stakes testing can show up in several ways, but each can be avoided by following the appropriate recommendations (Haladyna, 2002).

Instructional environment. The instructional environment may be negatively influenced and test score pollution may occur when teachers *"teach to the test,"* meaning that they change the curriculum or assessment procedures to closely match those of the standardized achievement tests. The district or state curriculum also may be driven by the standardized test. As the stakes increase, the curriculum typically narrows to reflect the content covered by the test (Pedulla et al., 2003; Stecher, Barron, Chun, & Ross, 2000). For these reasons, many teachers view the test preparation time and test administration time as a loss of valuable instruction time—leading to low teacher morale. This is particularly true for those teaching in high-poverty school districts or school districts with predominantly minority students, whose students are more likely to get low scores on standardized tests.   ***DIVERSITY***

❖ *Recommendations:* Although teachers tend to feel powerless to change students' scores and powerless to change public policies regarding high-stakes testing, they should teach content according to district and state curriculum standards rather than teaching to specific items on the test (Popham, 2001). When possible, teachers should be involved in making decisions about which standardized tests will be used based on how well they match the local and state curriculum standards.

Test preparation. Teachers can familiarize students with the format of a test and teach test-taking strategies. However, several test preparation practices are unethical. For example, teachers or school districts might provide students with previously used tests or expose them to the actual test prior to the standardized testing session. Concern over accountability and the sanctions associated with a test puts pressure on teachers to improve student performance (Koretz, Barron, Mitchell, & Keith, 1996). A national survey found that teachers in states implementing the high-stakes consequences of tests spent more time than teachers in low-stakes settings on test preparation, including previewing topics covered on the test, providing students with practice items, and using commercial test-preparation materials (Pedulla et al., 2003).

❖ *Recommendations:* Teachers should teach test-taking strategies to all students and familiarize their students with the format of the test by including similar formats on classroom assessments. Teachers should *not* provide students with copies of past exams or allow them to preview exams prior to the standardized testing session.

Test administration. Test administration procedures can be a source of test score pollution when certain students are given extended time limits, when students are allowed to mark their answers on their test booklets rather than on the provided computer-scored answer sheets, or when students are excluded from the testing because they are likely to have low scores (Haladyna, 2002). Although NCLB requires 95% participation, school districts have been found to systematically determine which 5% of students will be absent on the day of testing.

❖ *Recommendations:* Follow the standardized test administration procedures, such as reading only the specific directions, adhering to the standardized time limits, and accepting only the provided answer sheets. Some students may be exempted from taking the standardized achievement test when valid test scores cannot be obtained due to a severe disability or the lack of   ***DIVERSITY*** accommodations for a second language. (For more information on accommodations for students at risk, see Example 30.1 and the next section.) Teachers should follow the guidelines for removing the exemption over time and offer an alternative means of assessment.

Cheating. Cheating is an obvious way for test scores to increase without actual increases in student learning. Although we typically think of students cheating, educators also have been found to cheat on standardized tests in order to satisfy the public and legislators (Haladyna, 2002; Nichols & Berliner, 2005). Educator cheating can include reading answers to students and erasing student answers to insert the correct answer after completion of the test.

❖ *Recommendations:* Regardless of your opinion on the appropriateness of using standardized tests, do not cheat. Pay attention and report instances of student cheating. The consequences of cheating on standardized achievement tests can include having your employment terminated and/or losing your teacher certification.

Test Pollution. Student cheating is one source of test score pollution, but educators also have been found to cheat on standardized testing in order to satisfy the public and legislators.

Emotional characteristics. The emotional characteristics of test anxiety and motivation may affect students and artificially decrease or increase test scores. Young children tend to have positive views of themselves and their academic abilities and to consider standardized achievement tests as valuable and useful for teachers and school districts. As students become older and more involved in testing and grading procedures within the classroom, their positive view of themselves may diminish based on feedback about their performance. Low-achieving students in particular become less motivated and have increasing levels of test anxiety. High-achieving students, particularly older students, may have low motivation for standardized achievement tests because they understand that the task is an aid to policy decisions rather than their learning. Excessive motivational practices such as promises of parties or recognition of individual students by the school for high scores can make a difference in test scores, but the resulting test scores would reflect motivation levels rather than achievement (Haladyna, 2002).

Anxiety: See page 292.

❖ *Recommendations:* Identify and report instances in which high test anxiety may have been a factor. Prepare students by teaching ethical test preparation skills (as mentioned previously) in order to decrease test anxiety. Do not promise students excessive rewards for doing well on the test.

DIVERSITY   *Students at risk.* Students at risk—including students with disabilities or limited English proficiency and students living in poverty—are likely to decrease overall school district test performance scores.

❖ *Recommendation:* Identify students at risk and provide appropriate accommodations, as we discuss next.

DIVERSITY APPLICATIONS: ACCOMMODATING STUDENTS AT RISK

The term **students at risk** refers to a group of students considered to be at risk for not meeting standard achievement levels at school. The U.S. government uses four factors to identify children at risk: (1) a mother with less than a high school education, (2) a family using food stamps or other forms of public assistance, (3) a single-parent household, and (4) a home where the parents' primary language is not English. The first three factors are used to assess poverty, and the last factor is used to determine limited English proficiency. Students with disabilities are missing from this list of risk factors but should be included. Hence, students who are at risk for receiving low scores on high-stakes achievement tests include three groups (Haladyna, 2002):

1. *Students living in poverty.* Approximately 21% of students live in poverty. Family income levels and standardized achievement test scores are highly correlated, with students living in poverty having substantially lower test scores on a number of standardized achievement tests. Reasons for lower standardized achievement test scores among students living in poverty include poorer nutrition, less learning outside school due to lower parental education and lack of school readiness resources, a high rate of moving from one school to another, and lower-quality instruction at schools in low-income school districts. Many students living in poverty drop out of school in response to high-stakes pressure to raise their standardized achievement test scores.

Limited English Proficiency: See page 139.

2. *Students with Limited English Proficiency (LEP).* Limited English Proficiency (LEP) is the U.S. government's term for individuals whose native language is not English. Several other terms also are used within the educational context, including English-language learner (ELL) and English as a Second Language (ESL). According to the federal law regarding bilingual education, students are considered LEP if they meet one of three criteria: (1) the student was born outside the United States in a country where the native language is not English, (2) the student comes from a home environment in which English is not the spoken language, or (3) the student comes from an isolated culture such as Native Americans and Alaska natives. Approximately 14% of students in U.S. schools fall into the category of LEP. Students with LEP can be given accommodations during high-stakes testing to provide a more valid assessment of their achievement.

3. *Students with disabilities.* Approximately 11% of students in schools have some type of cognitive, behavioral, or social disability that puts them at risk for scoring lower on standardized achievement tests. Students with cognitive, emotional, or behavioral disabilities experience impairments in learning and lower academic achievement than their same-age peers. Federal laws provide guidelines for teaching and testing students with disabilities.

Students at risk need accommodations in order to have an equal opportunity to perform as well as students not at risk (Reynolds, Livingston, & Willson, 2009). **Accommodations** are changes in the way

| GUIDELINES 30.1 | **Using Standardized Tests with Students at Risk** |

- The test manual should report data indicating that test items do not show any bias—that students with disabilities and students with LEP are not disadvantaged on the test in comparison with other students.

- The test manual should identify how accommodations can be made for special populations and should offer a rationale for those recommendations so educators can interpret test scores properly.

- Accommodations should be appropriate for the individual test-taker and be based on research evidence, and all other standardized features should be maintained.

- Tests should be administered in the student's most proficient language whenever possible.

- Tests that have multiple language versions should be comparable (measuring the same thing).

- An interpreter should be fluent in both the language of the test and the individual's native language and should have expertise in providing translation.

Source: AERA, 1999.

standardized tests are administered or scored that do *not* change what is being measured. The test scores of students who are given accommodations are a more valid measure of their achievement than are the test scores of students with disabilities or limited English proficiency who are not given accommodations, and they lead to similar inferences or meaning across all students (Lissitz & Schafer, 2002). For example, students with LEP may do poorly on a math achievement test not because they have poor math skills but because they had difficulty understanding the questions and answer options given in English.

When using tests with students at risk, educators should remember the guidelines proposed in the *Standards for Educational and Psychological Testing* (AERA, 1999), as summarized in Guidelines 30.1. However, accommodations are *not* appropriate when the test being used measures skills related to the student's disability or language limitations. For example, reading the test questions out loud to a student is an acceptable accommodation in some cases, but not if the test measures reading comprehension. In this case, giving the student such an accommodation would provide an unfair advantage in the skill being measured.

Example 30.1 illustrates four broad categories of accommodations typically made for students at risk (Lissitz & Schafer, 2002; Reynolds et al., 2009):

1. *Presentation format:* The student may be presented with different directions or be given assistive devices for help in understanding the questions. For example, a student with LEP might be provided with an English-translation dictionary or an interpreter.

2. *Response format:* The format of responding to questions and providing answers may be altered. For example, a student with a motor impairment might provide oral responses to a scribe, who transfers them to the corresponding "bubbles" on a computer-scored answer sheet.

3. *Timing or scheduling:* The student might be given more time—or more sessions—to take the test, but not unlimited time. The extended time may be particularly necessary when other accommodations require more time, such as having a reader or translator.

4. *Setting:* Students may be given the test in a special setting, such as in a separate room or a special seat, rather than in the standardized group format. For example, a student with a physical disability might need to sit at a table rather than in a desk.

Accommodations vary greatly from state to state and most often are not explicitly determined by research evidence. For example, some accommodations, such as reading aloud the test questions and directions, may actually be a disadvantage to younger children (Finch, Baron, & Meyer, 2009). Further research on how well accommodations work for various items and developmental levels is needed. Typically, school officials make recommendations for how a particular student should be accommodated

EXAMPLE 30.1	Accommodations for Students at Risk
Presentation format	**Response format**
Oral exams to written exams	Oral exams to written exams
Written exams to oral exams	Written exams to oral exams
Braille format	Braillewriter to record responses
Sign language	Responding in sign language
Large print	Pointing to answer
Reader services	Having an aide mark answers
Increased spacing between items	Using a tape recorder to record responses
Reduced number of items per page	Increasing spacing on answer sheet
Rephrasing directions	Marking responses on test booklet,
Restating directions	not Scantron
Providing additional examples	
Using specialized computer programs to read text	
Timing	**Setting**
Extended time	Individual administration
More frequent breaks	Small-group administration
More sessions	Preferential seating
Sessions over more days	Study carrel to minimize distractions
Changing time of day test is given	Special lighting

Source: Reynolds, Livingston, & Willson, 2009.

Individualized Education Plan: See page 450 and page 452.

during standardized testing, as required by law. This is part of the student's *Individualized Education Plan (IEP)*—the legal contract between the parents and school officials detailing the provision of regular or special education and related services designed to meet the student's educational needs. The degree of accommodation allowed depends on the degree of risk. For example, in the area of English proficiency, most states require that students first take a basic English proficiency exam, and their score on that exam then determines the number and types of accommodations allowed. Although there are no definite criteria, some general guidelines for making accommodations include the following (Lissitz & Shafer, 2002; Reynolds et al., 2009):

- providing accommodations routinely given during classroom assessments,
- providing accommodations only when needed and promoting independence when possible, and
- continuing to evaluate the need for the accommodation and altering or ceasing the accommodation when possible.

Imagine that you are at an Individualized Education Plan meeting for an LEP student in the grade level you intend to teach. What factors should the group members consider in deciding on testing accommodations for the state mastery test?

TEST FAIRNESS AND TEST BIAS

The terms *test fairness* and *test bias* are sometimes used interchangeably, and both refer to judgments about test design and implementation. However, these two terms actually have distinct meanings and implications.

Test fairness is the broader term, addressing the ethical issue of how to use tests appropriately (Gregory, 2010). Test fairness includes aspects of test bias, equal treatment in the testing process, equal treatment of outcomes, and equal opportunities to learn the material presented on standardized achievement tests (AERA, 1999). The *Standards for Educational and Psychological Testing* (AERA, 1999) provide guidelines for fairness in testing and test uses.

The first aspect of test fairness—test bias—has received much attention in regard to standardized testing. **Test bias** is some type of systemic error in a test score (AERA, 1999) that may or may not be a function of cultural variations. The **cultural test bias hypothesis** states that standardized tests and testing procedures were designed in such a way as to have a built-in bias against groups categorized by some aspect such as gender, ethnicity, race, or socioeconomic status. The difference in group test scores is considered to be a result of the test itself and not of differences in actual group skill or ability (Reynolds et al., 2009).

The classic example used to denote cultural test bias is the difference in average IQ scores among racial groups. The average IQ score of African Americans is about one standard deviation (or 15 points) below the average score of Caucasians. When variations in socioeconomic status are controlled, African Americans' average IQ score is .5 to .7 standard deviation (or 7–10 IQ points) below that of Caucasians. Similarly, Hispanics score .5 standard deviation below Caucasians, whereas Asian Americans score equal to or better than Caucasians on standard IQ tests. These average differences in test scores across racial groups are used as evidence to support the cultural test bias hypothesis.

Two problems become evident when average group differences are used as evidence of cultural test bias. First, because the construct being measured is an unobservable characteristic (e.g., intelligence, achievement, mental ability) rather than an observable characteristic (e.g., weight, height), there is no way to substantiate that the average differences are not due to actual differences in intelligence or achievement rather than to cultural test bias (Reynolds et al., 2009). Second, test scores will vary more among individuals within the same group (within-group variability) than between two groups (between-group variability). Figure 30.1 depicts the normal distribution of scores for two groups. As you can see, the overlap between the two groups is quite large, suggesting that the between-group differences are not profound.

The generally accepted scientific method of determining cultural test bias is to examine the validity evidence. *Validity* is the extent to which an assessment actually measures what it is intended to measure, yielding accurate and meaningful interpretations from the test score. The validity of a test score can be supported by several types of evidence that might be questionable if cultural test bias actually is present (Gregory, 2010).

1. *Content validity,* or how accurately the items assess the variable of interest, may be questionable for several reasons, including these:

   ■ the information presented in an item is group-specific or offensive to one group,

   ■ the wording of the item is unfamiliar to some cultural groups and thus not understood well, or

   ■ the scoring unfairly penalizes or favors one cultural answer over equally acceptable answers in other cultures.

   Content validity analyses typically are conducted by judgmental review panels. The **judgmental review panel** comprises members of a minority group who independently rate each item for bias, sometimes following up with a group discussion. An item is deleted if a specific number of reviewers note bias in the item based on a preset criterion (Popham, 2006).

2. *Predictive validity* refers to how well the test score matches another variable to be assessed in the future. For example, SAT scores are expected to predict future college grade point averages. Predictive validity may be questionable if the test scores do not predict future performance equally well among groups, by either underpredicting or overpredicting the future performance of a particular group.

3. *Construct validity* is the degree to which an unobservable quality, such as achievement, is measured accurately. Construct validity can be assessed through particular types of item analyses. One type of item analysis, **differential item functioning (DIF),** is a statistical measure of how difficult an item is for one group versus another group. If the DIF for an item suggests that one group had more difficulty than another group, construct validity is questionable.

Research shows that American-born ethnic groups do not perform at a disadvantage on well-constructed, standardized intelligence and aptitude tests (Gregory, 2010; Reynolds et al., 2009):

DIVERSITY

Interpreting test scores: See page 545.

Validity of test scores: See page 493.

DIVERSITY

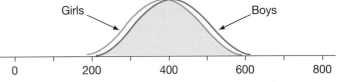

Figure 30.1. Similarities Outweigh Differences. Comparing boys' and girls' math performance historically has found mean differences, but the overlap of scores between these two groups is quite great, emphasizing the enormous variability within groups, as opposed to between groups.

- Judgmental review panels tend to be unreliable in their evaluations of culturally biased items, and thus provide little evidence of flaws in content validity.

- Tests appear to have predictive validity, because scores do *not* underpredict African Americans' future performance.

- DIF analyses of aptitude tests indicate a lack of group differences in difficulty level, providing support for construct validity.

If the cultural test bias hypothesis cannot explain the average differences found between groups on standardized tests, what else might account for the disparities? One hypothesis ascribes the differences to genetics, but little theoretical or empirical evidence supports a connection between DNA and standardized test scores. The most likely explanation is differences in environment. Minority students are more likely to be enrolled in lower-SES school districts where the quality of instruction is lower, leading to actual ability differences among groups of students. For example, more White, middle-class kindergarten students may correctly answer the question, "What is 2 plus 2?" It is hard to argue that this question is culturally biased; rather, the quality of instruction may have been poor in the lower-SES homes and school districts, leading those students to answer the question incorrectly (Popham, 2006).

Prior to reading this section, did you believe that standardized tests were biased against certain groups? On what basis did you form your opinion (personal experiences, media coverage, previous courses)? Have you changed your mind? If so, what evidence had a strong impact on your thinking?

TEACHER CERTIFICATION AND LICENSURE

Teachers, like professionals in the fields of law and medicine, must undergo high-stakes testing to satisfy the requirements of certification and licensure. **Certification** is the recognition that an individual has fulfilled certain requirements for completion of a professional training program. **Licensure,** designed to protect the public, is determined by government regulations that must be followed in order to practice a profession (e.g., law, medicine). A licensure exam is a state-mandated exam that an individual must pass before entering professional practice. Some academic programs require their students to pass a state licensure exam in order to meet the university's certification requirements. When these students graduate and receive certification, they have already passed the state licensure exam. However, not all universities require students to pass the state licensure exam in order to receive certification and graduate. Students in such programs still must pass the licensure exam before the state will allow them to practice. All states require licensure for teachers, but the licensure exam varies by state because no national examination has been established. Two testing programs have been used extensively by many states (Haladyna, 2002).

The National Board for Professional Teaching Standards (NBPTS) was developed in 1987 in response to the National Commission on Education's release of *A Nation at Risk*. The NBPTS has 63 members, primarily teachers, who are working toward the creation of national teaching standards as well as a national teacher certification testing program. Individuals seeking national certification must have three years of teaching experience and submit for review a portfolio, videotapes of their teaching, lesson plans, and samples of their students' work. The evaluation of these materials by trained professionals is very costly, leading to the imposition of an administration fee of $2,000. However, many states offer financial assistance by paying part of the fee or by increasing annual salaries when national certification is obtained. Evidence of the validity of the NBPTS testing program is accumulating, yet several issues still need to be resolved. For example, how do evaluators know whether the videotaped teaching sessions are authentic? Are the portfolio materials and samples of students' work randomly selected, or do these materials represent students' best work? Although this avenue for establishing a national teacher licensure protocol is promising, the validity of the performance assessment materials and evaluations needs further scrutiny.

Development and evaluation of performance assessments: See page 512.

The second testing program is the Praxis series, developed by the Educational Testing Service (ETS)—the nonprofit organization that develops the Advanced Placement (AP) test, the SAT, and other standardized tests. Because more than 40 states currently use all or part of the Praxis series, this testing program could become the standard for a national licensure examination. The Praxis series includes three parts:

1. *Praxis I: Academic Skills Assessment* assesses basic reading, writing, and mathematics using the Pre-Professional Skills Test (PPST). The traditional format is a paper-and-pencil test with mostly multiple-choice items and one essay. A computerized format of the test assesses the same knowledge. Many states use a passing score on the PPST as a requirement for entrance into teacher education programs.

2. *Praxis II: Subject Assessments* is intended to assess mastery of subject matter relevant to teachers. Several tests within this battery measure professional knowledge and skill and specific subject area content, and one section uses case studies from various grade levels to assess knowledge of teaching principles. The Praxis II already is used by many states as their licensure exam, and some university programs require it for certification and/or graduation.

3. *Praxis III: Classroom Performance Assessment* requires teachers in their first year of teaching to be evaluated by a trained examiner. As with the NBPTS testing program, the cost of training and scoring teaching assessments is quite high. In addition, the reliability or consistency among examiners can be problematic.

A Standard Examination for National Licensure? The Praxis series currently is used by more than 40 states and could become the standard for a national licensure examination.

Although many states still develop their own testing programs, a national licensure testing program is likely to be adopted in the near future. Individuals want more flexibility in moving from state to state and obtaining teaching positions without having to meet additional licensure requirements. Most other professions have a national organization and licensure examination to establish a level of high quality that is consistent throughout the United States. NCLB requires that all teachers be "highly qualified" as defined by the law in order for school districts to receive federal funding. NCLB specifies that a "highly qualified teacher" has:

■ earned a bachelor's or higher degree,

■ completed the state's certification and licensure requirements, and

■ demonstrated subject matter expertise in the content area he or she is teaching.

However, the term **highly qualified teacher** currently has little meaning, because certification and licensure requirements vary by state, as does the demonstration of subject matter expertise. However, differences in certification are not related to differences in teacher effectiveness. In fact, some evidence suggests that classroom performance during the first two years of teaching is a better indicator of future effectiveness than certification status (Kane, Rockoff, & Staiger, 2006).

One organization that has made great strides in bringing states together is the Interstate New Teacher Assessment and Support Consortium (INTASC), a program of the Council of Chief State School Officers. The mission of INTASC is to:

■ create educational policy on teaching that is compatible across states,

■ develop new assessment techniques for licensing and evaluating teachers,

■ develop new requirements for teacher preparation programs, and

■ create new programs for professional development.

INTASC is also developing a new licensing examination, the *Test for Teaching Knowledge.* Many teacher preparation programs already design their course content, professional experiences, and assessments around the core standards or principles developed by INTASC (see Table 30.1). The future of the teaching profession likely will be influenced by several organizations and testing programs, resulting in national standards and a licensure examination that is consistent across all states.

Review the INTASC standards in Table 30.1. Evaluate whether your teacher preparation program meets these requirements.

TABLE 30.1	Interstate New Teacher Assessment and Support Consortium (INTASC)
Standard	**Description**
1 Subject Matter	The teacher understands the central concepts, tools of inquiry, and structures of the discipline(s) he or she teaches and can create learning experiences that make these aspects of subject matter meaningful for students.
2 Student Learners	The teacher understands how children learn and develop and can provide learning opportunities that support their intellectual, social, and personal development.
3 Diverse Learners	The teacher understands how students differ in their approaches to learning and creates instructional opportunities that are adapted to diverse learners.
4 Instructional Strategies	The teacher understands and uses a variety of instructional strategies to encourage students' development of critical thinking, problem solving, and performance skills.
5 Learning Environment	The teacher uses an understanding of individual and group motivation and behavior to create a learning environment that encourages positive social interaction, active engagement in learning, and self-motivation.
6 Communication	The teacher uses knowledge of effective verbal, nonverbal, and media communication techniques to foster active inquiry, collaboration, and supportive interaction in the classroom.
7 Planning Instruction	The teacher plans instruction based upon knowledge of subject matter, students, the community, and curriculum goals.
8 Assessment	The teacher understands and uses formal and informal assessment strategies to evaluate and ensure the continuous intellectual, social, and physical development of the learner.
9 Professional Development	The teacher is a reflective practitioner who continually evaluates the effects of his/her choices and actions on others (students, parents, and other professionals in the learning community) and who actively seeks out opportunities to grow professionally.
10 Collaboration, Ethics, and Relationships	The teacher fosters relationships with school colleagues, parents, and agencies in the larger community to support students' learning and well-being.

Source: INTASC, 1992.

Summary

Explain why NCLB is considered high-stakes, and describe three problems with this law. NCLB is considered high-stakes because states, school districts, and teachers are held accountable for students' achieving a level of proficiency. Three problems that have emerged from NCLB are (1) inconsistencies among states in determining level of proficiency, (2) requirements for proficiency that do not take factors outside school into account, and (3) penalizing schools with large subgroups of students at risk such that the entire school is considered to be failing based on low scores among students in one subgroup.

Briefly explain how teachers can avoid the six negative outcomes of high-stakes testing. (1) Teachers should not teach to the test but should teach content according to district and state curriculum standards. (2) Teachers should teach test-taking strategies to all students and familiarize students with the format of the test but should not allow students to view past copies of tests or preview the current test prior to taking the examination. (3) Teachers must follow the standardized administration procedures and not allow students extended time or alternative modes of response. (4) Teachers themselves should not cheat and should pay attention to and report instances of student cheating. (5) Teachers should identify and report instances when high test anxiety may have been a factor in a student's score and should not promise students excessive rewards for doing well on the test as a way to increase motivation. (6) Teachers need to identify students at risk and provide appropriate accommodations for those students.

Explain how accommodations improve the validity of test scores for students at risk. Test scores of students at risk who are given accommodations are a more valid measure of their achievement than are test scores of students with disabilities or limited English proficiency who are not given accommodations. Accommodations include changing (1) the presentation format, such that students may be given different directions or assistive devices for help in understanding questions; (2) the response format, such that students provide answers differently from the standardized format; (3) the timing or scheduling of the test, allowing more time or more sessions to take the test; and (4) the setting, allowing students special seating. Changes in the way standardized tests are administered or scored provide students at risk an equal opportunity to succeed.

Explain the difference between test fairness and test bias, and summarize the evidence for cultural test bias in standardized tests. Test fairness is a broad concept addressing the ethical use of tests and includes aspects of test bias. Test bias is a systematic error in test scores that may or may not be based on cultural variations. Although mean differences in test scores among groups commonly is used as evidence of cultural test bias, validity evidence is more scientific. To date, research conducted on validity evidence has concluded that cultural test bias does not exist in most standardized tests.

Briefly summarize the two testing programs most likely to be used as the national standard in the future. (1) The National Board for Professional Teaching Standards (NBPTS) has created a national teacher certification testing program available for individuals with three years of teaching experience. The evaluation materials include a portfolio, videotapes of teaching, lesson plans, and samples of student work. Although this testing program is a viable contender for becoming the national teacher licensure examination, problems with the validity of the performance assessments need to be addressed. (2) The Praxis series includes three separate parts to assess academic skills, subject content, and classroom performance. The Praxis series already is used by many states to fulfill licensure requirements and is likely to be used in the future as a national examination for teacher licensure.

Key Concepts

accommodations 556

accountability 552

adequate yearly progress (AYP) 553

certification 560

cultural test bias hypothesis 559

differential item functioning (DIF) 559

highly qualified teacher 561

high-stakes tests 552

judgmental review panel 559

licensure 560

No Child Left Behind Act of 2001 (NCLB) 552

students at risk 556

test bias 559

test fairness 558

test score pollution 554

Video Applications

www.mhhe.com/bohlin2e

Video 1: Sample Standardized Test Session (*4 minutes*)
An elementary teacher gives her students a standardized test, and then she answers questions about test preparation and diversity in standardized testing.

Video 2: High-Stakes Testing (*4 minutes*)
Teachers and principals discuss issues related to high-stakes testing, including fairness in testing, teaching to the test, and accommodations for students at risk.

Video 3: No Child Left Behind (*4 minutes*)
Teachers and principals share their opinions on issues related to No Child Left Behind.

Case Studies
Reflect and Evaluate

EARLY CHILDHOOD: "Kindergarten Readiness"

These questions refer to the case study on page 528.

1. When Ms. Walters and Ms. Theesfield were children, kindergarten screenings either were not done or were not a formal process. What historical events might have led school districts to implement this type of testing?

2. Was Ms. Walters correct in offering to provide a Spanish-speaking test administrant for Maria? Why or why not?

DIVERSITY   3. According to the discussion of test fairness in the module, why wouldn't Ms. Walters allow Maria's sister, Ana, to be the interpreter for her kindergarten screening? Was it fair to eliminate her sister from the process? Why or why not?

4. Maria's mother is concerned about how Maria's test score will be interpreted by school officials and doesn't seem convinced that her daughter will receive a fair evaluation. Why might she assume there will be test bias in the screening of her daughter? How legitimate is her concern?

5. Assume that Ms. Walters and Ms. Theesfield and student teacher Amy had more time to discuss teacher licensure across states. What arguments for and against national licensure might they have presented?

6. There are high stakes associated with elementary school students' achievement scores because of NCLB's emphasis on accountability. How might kindergarten readiness tests help teachers better prepare students for meeting the requirements of NCLB? Can you think of any disadvantages of using kindergarten readiness tests?

ELEMENTARY SCHOOL: "Keyboard Courage"

These questions refer to the case study on page 530.

1. What are the ramifications for the school district if test scores fall below the AYP goals for the second year?

DIVERSITY   2. Ms. Fernández notes the large number of students at the school with learning disabilities. Based on problems associated with NCLB, explain why this may or may not be a legitimate point.

3. Ms. Seifert suggests several ways to improve students' scores by providing more test preparation. According to the description of test score pollution, which of her ideas are good and which are not? Why?

4. Why might Ms. LeBlanc's suggestion to extend the time allotted for students who have difficulty reading be an example of test score pollution? How might her suggestion be a legitimate solution?

DIVERSITY   5. Ms. Fernández suggests that the students with disabilities should have assessments and decisions should be made regarding accommodations. Who is likely to make those decisions? What are some general guidelines for providing accommodations?

MIDDLE SCHOOL: "Teachers Are Cheating?"

These questions refer to the case study on page 532.

1. Explain why meeting the state cutoff scores is more important than being above the national average of test scores.

2. The improvement in test scores over last year may be a result of test score pollution. What specific issues are raised about how test score pollution may have occurred in this school? Provide other examples of test score pollution that could occur within a school.

3. Would Ms. Haney's behavior be considered cheating? Why or why not?

4. Ms. Garrison has instruction sheets with students' accommodations to provide to teachers. She mentions that staff members involved with each of these children have confirmed the types of accommodations they should be given during testing sessions. Who are these staff members likely to be?   *DIVERSITY*

5. Based on the discussion of at-risk students in the module, what types of students would you expect to be given accommodations, and what types of accommodations might be included on the instruction sheets?   *DIVERSITY*

6. Given the information presented about Ms. Garrison, would you consider her a "highly qualified teacher" as defined by NCLB? Why or why not?

HIGH SCHOOL: "SAT Scores"

These questions refer to the case study on page 534.

1. Based on the definition presented in the module, is the SAT a high-stakes test? Why or why not?

2. Does the extra help Ms. Fortner gave the students on the SAT involve test score pollution? Why or why not?

3. What types of special accommodations is Lu likely to be given during the state achievement testing? Who would determine which accommodations she should receive?   *DIVERSITY*

4. How might Lu's test anxiety and Trevor's motivation be factors in their test scores? Does Ms. Fortner handle these issues appropriately with her students? Why or why not?

5. How likely is it that Mr. Harris's explanation of test bias accounts for Trevor's score on the SAT? Support your answer with research evidence presented in the module.   *DIVERSITY*

6. Mr. Harris took the Praxis series for teacher licensure in his state. What other types of tests are used for teacher licensure? What are some concerns with using these other tests?

HOW DOES *EdPsych* HELP YOU PREPARE FOR THE PRAXIS EXAM?

PRAXIS II™ Topics	Where to Review in *EdPsych*
I. STUDENTS AS LEARNERS **A. Student Development and the Learning Process**	
1. Theoretical foundations about how learning occurs: how students construct knowledge, acquire skills, and develop habits of mind	**Module 6:** The Brain and Development **Module 7:** Cognitive Development **Module 8:** Language Development **Module 9:** Behavioral Learning Theories **Module 10:** Social Cognitive Theory **Module 11:** Information Processing **Module 12:** Metacognition **Module 13:** Transfer of Skills and Knowledge **Module 14:** Critical Thinking and Problem Solving
Examples of important theorists:	
Jean Piaget	**Module 7**
Lev Vygotsky	**Module 7**
Howard Gardner	**Module 22**
Robert Sternberg	**Module 22**
Erik Erikson	**Module 3**
Lawrence Kohlberg	**Module 5**
Urie Bronfenbrenner	**Module 2**
David Ausubel	**Module 20**
Jerome Bruner	**Module 20**
B. F. Skinner	**Module 9**
Albert Bandura	**Module 10**
Important terms related to learning theory:	
Conservation	**Module 7**
Constructivism	**Module 7:** See "individual constructivism" and "social constructivism"
Equilibration	**Module 7**
Co-construction	**Module 7:** See "intersubjectivity"
Private speech	**Module 7:** See "egocentric speech"
Scaffolding	**Module 7**
Zone of Proximal Development	**Module 7**
Modeling	**Module 10**
Rote memorization	**Module 13**
Elaboration	**Module 11**
Organization	**Module 11**
Rehearsal	**Module 11**
Automaticity	**Module 11**
	Module 13
	Module 24

(continued)

PRAXIS II™ Topics	Where to Review in *EdPsych*
Learning (classical conditioning)	**Module 9**
Learning (operant conditioning)	**Module 9**
Learning (observational learning)	**Module 10**
Knowledge	**Module 11**
	Module 12: See "metacognitive knowledge"
Memory	**Module 11**
Schemas	**Module 11**
Transfer	**Module 13:** Transfer of Skills and Knowledge
	Module 2: Contexts of Development
	Module 3: Social Development
2. *Human development in the physical, social, emotional, moral, and cognitive domains*	**Module 4:** Emotional Development
	Module 6: The Brain and Development
	Module 7: Cognitive Development
	Module 8: Language Development
Contribution of important theorists:	
Jean Piaget	**Module 7**
Lev Vygotsky	**Module 7**
Erik Erikson	**Module 3**
Lawrence Kohlberg	**Module 5**
Carol Gilligan	**Module 5**
Major progressions in each developmental domain and the ranges of individual variation within each domain	**Module 3:** Social Development
	Module 4: Emotional Development
Impact of students' physical, social, emotional, moral, and cognitive development on their learning and how to address these factors when making decisions	**Module 5:** Moral Development
	Module 6: The Brain and Development
	Module 7: Cognitive Development
	Module 8: Language Development
How development in one domain, such as physical, may affect performance in another domain, such as social	

B. Students as Diverse Learners

	Specific coverage appears in the context of every module. Please see the diversity icon **DIVERSITY** on page margins. Also see:
	■ Module 1: Using Science to Inform Classroom Practices
	■ Module 2: Contexts of Development
	■ Module 8: See "Individual Differences in Language Acquisition"
1. *Differences in the ways students learn and perform*	■ Module 11: See "Individual Differences in Information Processing"
	■ Module 22: Intelligence
	■ Module 23: Giftedness and Creativity
	■ Module 24: Cognitive Disabilities
	■ Module 25: Emotional, Social, and Behavioral Disorders

(continued)

PRAXIS II™ Topics	Where to Review in *EdPsych*
Important terms related to diversity:	
Learning styles	**Module 22**
Multiple intelligences	**Module 6**
Performance modes, including concrete operational thinking, visual learners, and aural learners	**Module 22:** See "Teaching for Successful Intelligence"
Gender differences	Specific coverage appears in the context of every module. Please see the diversity icon **DIVERSITY** on page margins. Also see Module 1: Using Science to Inform Classroom Practices
Cultural expectations and styles	**Module 1:** Using Science to Inform Classroom Practices **Module 2:** Contexts of Development Also see: ■ Module 3 ■ Module 5 ■ Module 22
2. *Areas of exceptionality in students' learning*	**Module 23:** Giftedness and Creativity **Module 24:** Cognitive Disabilities **Module 25:** Emotional, Social, and Behavioral Disorders
Important terms related to exceptionality:	
Special physical or sensory challenges	**Module 24**
Learning disabilities	**Module 24** **Module 25**
ADHD	**Module 25**
Autism	**Module 25**
Functional and mental retardation	**Module 24**
3. *Legislation and institutional responsibilities relating to exceptional students*	**Module 24:** Cognitive Disabilities **Module 25:** Emotional, Social, and Behavioral Disorders
Important terms related to exceptionality:	
Americans with Disabilities Act (ADA); Individuals with Disabilities Education Improvement Act (IDEIA); Section 504 Protections for Students	**Module 24** **Module 25**
Inclusion	**Module 24**
Mainstreaming	**Module 24**
"Least restrictive environment"	**Module 24**
4. *Approaches for accommodating various learning styles, intelligences, or exceptionalities*	**Module 20** **Module 22** **Module 24** **Module 30:** Issues in Standardized Testing

(continued)

PRAXIS II™ Topics	Where to Review in *EdPsych*
Alternative assessment	**Module 26** **Module 28**
Testing modifications	**Module 28**
5. *Process of second language acquisition and strategies to support the learning of students*	**Module 8:** Language Development
6. *Understanding of influences of individual experiences, talents, and prior learning, as well as language, culture, family, and community values on students' learning*	Specific coverage appears in the context of every module. Please see the diversity icon **DIVERSITY** on page margins. Also see: ■ Module 1: **Using Science to Inform Classroom Practices** ■ Module 2: **Contexts of Development** ■ Module 3: **Social Development** ■ Module 8: **Language Development** ■ Module 22: **Intelligence**
Multicultural backgrounds	**Module 1:** Using Science to Inform Classroom Practices **Module 2:** Contexts of Development **Module 3:** Social Development
Age-appropriate knowledge and behavior	**Module 3:** Social Development **Module 5:** Moral Development **Module 7:** Cognitive Development
The student culture at school	**Module 2:** Contexts of Development **Module 18:** Creating a Productive Learning Environment
Family backgrounds	**Module 2:** Contexts of Development **Module 3:** Social Development
Linguistic patterns and differences	**Module 8:** Language Development
C. Student Motivation and the Learning Environment	
1. *Theoretical foundations of human motivation and behavior*	**Module 15:** Behavioral Theory **Module 16:** Cognitive Theories **Module 17:** Self Theories
2. *How knowledge of human motivation and behavior should influence strategies for organizing and supporting individual and group work in the classroom*	**Module 15** **Module 16** **Module 17** **Module 18:** Creating a Productive Learning Environment
3. *Factors and situations that are likely to promote or diminish student's motivation to learn, and how to help students to become self-motivated*	**Module 15:** Behavioral Theory **Module 17:** Self Theories
4. *Principles on effective classroom management and strategies to promote positive relationships, cooperation, and purposeful learning*	**Module 18:** Creating a Productive Learning Environment **Module 19:** Understanding and Managing Student Behavior **Module 20:** Instruction: Applying Behavioral, Cognitive, and Constructivist Approaches **Module 21:** Grouping Practices

PRAXIS

(continued)

PRAXIS II™ Topics	Where to Review in *EdPsych*
Establishing daily procedures and routines	**Module 18** **Module 20**
Establishing classroom rules	**Module 18**
Using natural and logical consequences	**Module 9:** Behavioral Learning Theories **Module 18**
Providing positive guidance	**Module 18**
Modeling conflict resolution, problem solving, and anger management	**Module 19**
Using objective behavior descriptions	**Module 19:** Understanding and Managing Student Behavior
Responding to student behavior	**Module 9:** Behavioral Learning Theories **Module 19**
Arranging classroom space	**Module 18**
II. INSTRUCTION & ASSESSMENT **A. Instructional Strategies**	
1. *Major cognitive processes*	**Module 12:** Metacognition **Module 13:** Transfer of Skills and Knowledge **Module 14:** Critical Thinking and Problem Solving
Critical thinking	**Module 14**
Creative thinking	**Module 23**
Higher-order thinking	**Module 14**
Inductive and deductive thinking	**Module 14**
Problem structuring and problem solving	**Module 14:** Critical Thinking and Problem Solving
Memorization and recall	**Module 11**
Social reasoning	**Module 5:** See "prosocial reasoning"
Representation of ideas	**Module 11:** See "schemas" and "propositional networks"
2. *Major categories, advantages, and appropriate uses of instructional strategies*	**Module 18:** Creating a Productive Learning Environment **Module 19:** Understanding and Managing Student Behavior **Module 20:** Instruction: Applying Behavioral, Cognitive, and Constructivist Approaches
	Module 21: Grouping Practices
Cooperative learning	**Module 20**
Direct instruction	**Module 20**
Discovery learning	**Module 20**
Whole-group discussion	**Module 20**
Concept mapping	**Module 11**
Questioning	**Module 14** **Module 20**
Learning centers	**Module 18**
Small-group work	**Module 20**
Project approach	**Module 28**

(continued)

PRAXIS II™ Topics	Where to Review in *EdPsych*
3. *Principles, techniques, and methods associated with major instructional strategies*	**Module 18:** Creating a Productive Learning Environment **Module 19:** Understanding and Managing Student Behavior **Module 20:** Planning for Instruction **Module 21:** Grouping Practices
Direct instruction	**Module 20:** See "Mastery Learning" Also see "Discovery Learning and Guided Discovery" and "Expository Teaching"
Student-centered methods	**Module 20**
4. *Methods for enhancing student learning through the use of a variety of resources and materials*	**Module 18:** Creating a Productive Learning Environment **Module 19:** Understanding and Managing Student Behavior **Module 20:** Instruction: Applying Behavioral, Cognitive, and Constructivist Approaches **Module 21:** Grouping Practices
Computers, internet resources, Web pages, e-mail	**Module 26**
Service learning	**Module 5**
B. Planning Instruction	
1. *Techniques for planning instruction, including addressing curriculum goals, selecting content topics, incorporating learning theory, subject matter, curriculum development, and student development and interests*	**Module 18:** Creating a Productive Learning Environment **Module 19:** Understanding and Managing Student Behavior **Module 20:** Instruction: Applying Behavioral, Cognitive, and Constructivist Approaches **Module 21:** Grouping Practices
Behavioral objectives: affective, cognitive, psychomotor, speech/language	**Module 20:** See "Bloom's taxonomy" **Module 28**
Learner objectives and outcomes	**Module 26:** Assessing Student Learning
Antibias curriculum	**Module 20**
	Module 11: Information Processing **Module 12:** Metacognition **Module 13:** Transfer of Skills and Knowledge **Module 14:** Critical Thinking and Problem Solving
2. *Techniques for creating effective bridges between curriculum goals and students' experiences*	**Module 20:** Instruction: Applying Behavioral, Cognitive, and Constructivist Approaches **Module 21:** Grouping Practices **Module 23:** Creativity and Giftedness **Module 26:** See "Assessment Planning"
Modeling	**Module 10**
Independent practice, including homework	**Module 20:** See "Direct Instruction"
Activating students' prior knowledge	**Module 11** **Module 12** **Module 13**
Encouraging exploration and problem solving	**Module 14**

(continued)

PRAXIS II™ Topics	Where to Review in *EdPsych*
C. Assessment Strategies	
1. *Types of assessments*	**Module 22:** Intelligence **Module 26:** Assessing Student Learning **Module 27:** Test Construction and Use **Module 28:** Performance Assessment **Module 29:** Standardized Tests and Scores
2. *Characteristics of assessments*	**Module 26:** Assessing Student Learning **Module 27:** Test Construction and Use **Module 28:** Performance Assessment **Module 29:** Standardized Tests and Scores **Module 30:** Issues in Standardized Testing
3. *Scoring assessments*	**Module 26:** Assessing Student Learning **Module 27:** Test Construction and Use **Module 28:** Performance Assessment
4. *Uses of assessments*	**Module 22:** Intelligence **Module 26:** Assessing Student Learning **Module 27:** Test Construction and Use **Module 28:** Performance Assessment **Module 29:** Standardized Tests and Scores **Module 30:** Issues in Standardized Testing
5. *Understanding of measurement theory and assessment–related issues*	**Module 27:** Test Construction and Use **Module 29:** Standardized Tests and Scores **Module 30:** Issues in Standardized Testing
6. *Interpreting and communicating results of assessments*	**Module 22:** Intelligence **Module 26:** Assessing Student Learning **Module 29:** Standardized Tests and Scores
III. COMMUNICATION TECHNIQUES	
A. Basic, effective verbal and nonverbal communication techniques	**Module 19:** Understanding and Managing Student Behavior **Module 22:** Intelligence
B. Effect of cultural and gender differences on communications in the classroom	**Module 8** **Module 21** **Module 22** **Module 25**
C. Types of communications and interactions that can stimulate discussion in different ways for particular purposes	**Module 12:** Metacognition **Module 8** **Module 20**
Probing for learner understanding	**Module 13** **Module 14** **Module 26**
Helping students articulate their ideas and thinking processes	**Module 11** **Module 12** **Module 21**
Promoting risk taking and problem solving	**Module 14:** Critical Thinking and Problem Solving **Module 16** **Module 23**
Facilitating factual recall	**Module 11**

(continued)

PRAXIS II™ Topics	Where to Review in *EdPsych*
Encouraging convergent and divergent thinking	**Module 23**
Stimulating curiosity	**Module 15:** See "Applications: Creating an Intrinsically Motivating Learning Environment" **Module 23:** See "Promoting Creativity"
Helping students to question	**Module 14:** Critical Thinking and Problem Solving **Module 12:** See "Reading Comprehension" **Module 20**
Promoting a caring community	**Module 18**

IV. PROFESSION & COMMUNITY
A. The Reflective Practitioner

1. *Types of resources available for professional development and learning*	**Module 1:** Using Science to Inform Classroom Practices
2. *Ability to read, understand, and apply articles and books about current research, views, ideas, and debates regarding best teaching practices*	**Module 1:** Using Science to Inform Classroom Practices
3. *Ongoing personal reflection on teaching and learning practices as a basis for making professional decisions*	**Module 1:** Using Science to Inform Classroom Practices **Module 13:** Transfer of Skills and Knowledge **Module 18:** Creating a Productive Learning Environment **Module 19:** Understanding and Managing Student Behavior Also, reflective prompts are integrated throughout the text.

B. The Larger Community

1. *Role of the school as a resource to the larger community*	**Module 2:** Contexts of Development
2. *Factors in the students' environment outside of school (family circumstances, community environments, health and economic conditions) that may influence students' life and learning*	**Module 2:** Contexts of Development **Module 19:** See "Common Causes of Misbehavior" **Module 22:** Intelligence. See "Socioeconomic and Cultural Factors"
3. *Develop and utilize active partnerships among teachers, parents/guardians and leaders in the community to support educational process*	**Module 2:** Contexts of Development **Module 18:** Creating a Productive Learning Environment
4. *Major laws related to students' rights and teacher responsibilities*	**Module 24:** Cognitive Disabilities **Module 25:** Emotional, Social and Behavioral Disorders
Appropriate education for students with special needs	**Module 24** **Module 25** **Module 30**

A

ABILITY GROUPING A method of creating groups of students who are similar in achievement or ability level. (Module 21, p. 378)

ACADEMIC INTRINSIC MOTIVATION Motivation to learn characterized by curiosity, persistence, a desire to engage in challenging and novel tasks, and a focus on mastery of knowledge and skills. (Module 15, p. 265; Module 16, p. 279)

ACADEMIC LEARNING TIME Time students spend engaged in meaningful, appropriate tasks. (Module 18, p. 332)

ACCELERATION A method recommended for gifted students in which they move quickly through grades or receive instruction above grade level in one or two subjects. (Module 23, p. 422)

ACCOMMODATION A process of adaptation in Piaget's theory that involves modifying one's existing knowledge or creating new concepts when new information cannot fit into one's existing thinking. (Module 7, p. 120)

ACCOMMODATIONS Changes in the way standardized tests are administered or scored that do not change what is being measured. (Module 30, p. 556)

ACCOUNTABILITY A significant consequence of high-stakes testing, in which teachers and school districts are held responsible or accountable for students' performance. (Module 30, p. 552)

ACHIEVEMENT GOAL A purpose for choosing to do a task and the standard that an individual constructs to evaluate performance on the task. (Module 16, p. 280)

ACRONYM A form of abbreviation in which a word is formed from the first letter of each word to be remembered. Phrases or sentences formed out of the first letter of each item in a list to be remembered. (Module 11, p. 188)

ACTION ZONE An area of the classroom in which teachers interact more frequently with students. In a classroom where desks are arranged in rows, the action zone refers to those students seated in the front and center rows. (Module 18, p. 328)

ACTIVATION LEVEL The degree to which a particular piece of information in memory is currently being attended to and mentally processed. (Module 11, p. 190)

ACTIVE LEARNING Any form of meaningful learning which involves constructing a rich knowledge base of interrelated concepts, prior knowledge, and real-life experiences. (Module 7, p. 129)

ACTIVE LISTENING Listening in a non-defensive way and responding by clarifying the message rather than criticizing. (Module 8, p. 143)

ADEQUATE YEARLY PROGRESS (AYP) An annual measurable achievement goal chosen by each state to indicate movement toward proficiency levels. (Module 30, p. 553)

ADHD See Attention-Deficit/Hyperactivity Disorder. (Module 25, p. 456)

ADOLESCENT EGOCENTRISM Difficulty differentiating between one's own thoughts and the thoughts of others. (Module 12, p. 214)

ADVANCE ORGANIZERS General information presented before instruction to provide the learner with prior knowledge and a structure in which to integrate new information. (Module 20, p. 369)

ALGORITHM A prescribed sequence of steps that, if selected and followed correctly, guarantees a correct solution. (Module 14, p. 247)

ALPHABETIC PRINCIPLE The knowledge that printed letters are represented by units of sound. (Module 24, p. 442)

ALTERNATE CHOICE Item format that presents a proposition a student must judge and mark as either true or false, right or wrong, yes or no. (Module 27, p. 498)

AMOTIVATION A lack of motivation; the least autonomous level of motivation in self-determination theory. See also self-determination. (Module 17, p. 308)

ANALOGICAL THINKING Limits the search for solutions to situations that are most similar to the one at hand. (Module 14, p. 247)

ANALYTIC RUBRIC Assessment tool used to score separate, individual parts of a product or performance first, then sum the individual scores to obtain a total score. (Module 28, p. 517)

ANALYTICAL ABILITIES One of three abilities in Sternberg's theory of successful intelligence which is characterized by skills such as analyzing, evaluating, judging, or comparing and contrasting. See also creative abilities and practical abilities. (Module 22, p. 404)

ANDROGYNOUS Having both masculine and feminine characteristics. (Module 3, p. 51)

ANXIETY Mental thoughts related to worrying and negative emotions such as nervousness or tension, which can impair academic performance. (Module 16, p. 293)

ANXIETY DISORDER A disorder which involves distressingly unpleasant and maladaptive feelings, thoughts, behaviors, and physical reactions. (Module 25, p. 453)

APPEARANCE-REALITY DISTINCTION An understanding that appearances can be deceiving or false. (Module 12, p. 212)

ARGUMENT ANALYSIS Challenging students to critically evaluate reasons in order to discriminate between those that do and do not support a particular conclusion. (Module 14, p. 244)

ARTICULATION DISORDER A speech disorder diagnosed when a familiar adult cannot understand a child's speech at age three, or when articulation errors are still evident at age eight. (Module 8, p. 142)

ASSESSMENT The process of obtaining information that is used for making decisions about curricula, students, programs, and educational policy. This term is also used to describe the actual tools (tests, papers, projects, etc.) used to gather information. (Module 26, p. 477)

ASSESSMENT PLAN Report that specifies the learning goals and types of assessment that will be used during a specific time frame. (Module 26, p. 479)

ASSIMILATION A process of adaptation in Piaget's theory that involves fitting new information or experiences into one's existing way of thinking. (Module 7, p. 120)

ATTAINMENT VALUE A component of expectancy-value theory referring to the importance of being good at a task. (Module 16, p. 280)

ATTENTION The focusing of mental processes on particular environmental stimuli. Attention is defined as a cluster of integrated events and processes that determine which stimuli receive further processing. (Module 11, p. 185)

ATTENTION-DEFICIT/HYPERACTIVITY DISORDER (ADHD) A neurological condition that impairs self-regulation, leading to problems maintaining attention, inhibiting impulsive or inappropriate responses, executive control over planning, monitoring progress, and selection of strategies in working memory. (Module 25, p. 456)

AUTHENTIC ASSESSMENT Measures important abilities using procedures that simulate the application of those abilities to real-world intellectual problems, roles, or situations. (Module 26, p. 481; Module 28, 511)

AUTHORITARIAN PARENTING High level of control in which rules are enforced, yet emotional connectedness is lacking. (Module 2, p. 32)

AUTHORITATIVE PARENTING High levels of control or enforcing rules as well as high levels of emotional connectedness. (Module 2, p. 32)

AUTISM SPECTRUM DISORDER A developmental disorder affecting social interaction, communication, and behavior. (Module 25, p. 459)

AUTOMATIC PROCESSING Skills that are applied without conscious thought. See also automaticity. (Module 11, p. 187)

AUTOMATICITY The ability to respond accurately, quickly, and using few cognitive resources such as attention and strategies while performing a mental or physical skill. (Module 11, p. 193; Module 13, 226)

AUTOMATICITY TRAINING Practice aimed at improving the accuracy and speed of reading or math skills such as word recognition or math fact retrieval. (Module 24, p. 443)

AUTONOMY A component of self-determination theory referring to a feeling of having choice and control over one's actions. (Module 17, p. 305)

B

BABBLING Repetitive consonant-vowel combinations produced by infants, such as dadadada. (Module 8, p. 134)

BACKWARD-REACHING TRANSFER Deliberately looking for knowledge learned in the past that could be useful in a current situation. (Module 13, p. 227)

BEHAVIOR SETTING A stable situation in the environment known to be correlated with specific patterns of behavior (e.g., a basketball game, a church service, a restaurant, etc). Such situations coerce children who enter them to behave in relatively homogeneous ways, regardless of the individual characteristics of the children. (Module 18, p. 333)

BELIEF PERSEVERANCE Tendency to hold onto existing ideas or beliefs even in the face of contradictory evidence. (Module 1, p. 15; Module 14, p. 246)

BEST WORK PORTFOLIO A carefully selected combination of materials that showcases examples of a student's best work and serves as final summative assessment. (Module 28, p. 515)

BETWEEN-CLASS ABILITY GROUPING A practice typical in high school that involves using test scores or past performance to place students into curriculum tracks in which all their classes are with students of similar abilities. (Module 21, p. 380)

BLOOM'S TAXONOMY A categorization of six learning objectives which includes lower-level objectives (remember, understand, apply) and higher-level objectives (analyze, evaluate, create). (Module 20, p. 365)

BROCA'S AREA Located in the left hemisphere of the brain, this area processes the understanding of language, speech, and the control of facial neurons. (Module 6, p. 112)

C

CAREER OR EDUCATIONAL INTEREST INVENTORIES Category of standardized tests that assess individual preferences toward certain types of activities. (Module 29, p. 538)

CARING ORIENTATION Moral reasoning that focuses on responding to others' needs in intimate relationships. (Module 5, p. 79)

CAUSAL ATTRIBUTIONS Explanations for why events, such as success or failure, have occurred. (Module 16, p. 282)

CELLS THAT FIRE TOGETHER, WIRE TOGETHER Phrase used to describe a pattern of increasing efficiency in the brain in which certain brain cells actually learn to fire in unison. (Module 6, p. 109)

CENTRAL EXECUTIVE The part of working memory that is responsible for monitoring and directing attention and other mental resources. (Module 11, p. 186)

CENTRAL TENDENCY A score that is typical or representative of the entire group. (Module 29, p. 541)

CENTRATION An inability to focus on two dimensions simultaneously. (Module 7, p. 122)

CEREBRAL CORTEX Extensive outer layer of gray matter of the two cerebral hemispheres, largely responsible for higher brain functions, including sensation, voluntary muscle movement, thought, reasoning, and memory. (Module 6, p. 102)

CERTIFICATION Recognition that an individual has completed certain requirements for a particular profession. (Module 30, p. 560)

CHAIN MNEMONIC A method that connects the first item to be memorized to the second, the second with the third, and so forth or an approach that incorporates items to be remembered into a catchy jingle. (Module 11, p. 188)

CHILD-DIRECTED SPEECH Language directed to infants and children characterized by high pitch, exaggerated intonations, elongated vowels, short and simple sentences, and repetition. (Module 8, p. 135)

CHRONOSYSTEM Chronological nature of development within the individual as well as the surrounding environment. (Module 2, p. 31)

CHUNKING Grouping individual groups of data into meaningful larger units. (Module 11, p. 188)

CLASS MEETINGS A format for participatory classroom management in which teachers and students make joint decisions about class rules and consequences, room arrangement, and preferred activities. (Module 18, p. 337)

CLASS-RUNNING PROCEDURES Non-academic routines that help the classroom run smoothly. (Module 18, p. 337)

CLIQUES Small peer groups of 2-8 people that are interaction-based. (Module 2, p. 37)

CODE MIXING Bilingual individuals' use of words or phrases from one language as a substitute in the other language. (Module 8, p. 140)

COGNITIVE APPRENTICESHIP An approach to learning cognitive skills within the context of authentic activities in which novices are guided, participate at a level commensurate with their ability, and gradually take over more responsibility with increasing skill. (Module 20, p. 369)

COGNITIVE-BEHAVIORAL TREATMENT (CBT) Technique that teaches students to regulate their own behavior using a series of instructions that they memorize, internalize, and apply to different school tasks. (Module 25, p. 460)

COLLECTIVE EFFICACY Belief of success about a group or social system. (Module 10, p. 180)

COGNITIVE LOAD The extent to which a task places demands on working memory. Cognitive load is dependent on factors such as complexity of the task, student's prior knowledge and skills, and supports available. (Module 11, p. 186)

COLLECTIVE SELF-EFFICACY Teachers' belief that they can positively impact student learning by working together. (Module 18, p. 343)

COMMITMENT Making decisions about areas of one's life such as educational and career goals, family obligations or goals, as well as political and religious beliefs. (Module 3, p. 49)

COMPETENCY BELIEF Belief that one has the ability to perform a task or succeed at an activity. (Module 16, p. 279)

CONCEPTUAL KNOWLEDGE A form of mental representation that reflects an understanding of declarative or procedural knowledge. (Module 11, p. 189)

CONCURRENT VALIDITY Type of criterion-validity evidence that evaluates the relationship between the test score and another criterion assessed at approximately the same time. (Module 29, p. 546)

CONDUCT DISORDER Serious behavioral disorder that involves repeatedly and purposely violating rules or laws, the rights of others, or age-appropriate societal norms. (Module 25, p. 458)

CONFIDENCE INTERVAL A range in which an individual's true score lies, based on the individual's score and the standard error of measurement for the test. (Module 29, p. 547)

CONFIRMATION BIAS Tendency to search for information that confirms our existing ideas and beliefs. (Module 1, p. 15)

CONGRUENT COMMUNICATION APPROACH An approach developed by Haim Ginott in which the teacher helps to create a supportive emotional climate for learning by using a variety of positive communication strategies. (Module 18, p. 340)

CONSENSUAL ASSESSMENT TECHNIQUE Process in which teachers collect samples of students' creative work and then rate its creativeness. (Module 23, p. 425)

CONSERVATION The understanding that quantity or amount remains the same even though appearance changes. (Module 7, p. 122)

CONSTRUCT VALIDITY The degree to which an unobservable, intangible quality or characteristic (construct) is measured accurately. (Module 29, p. 545)

CONSTRUCTIVISM A psychological paradigm that characterizes learning as a process of actively constructing knowledge. (Module 7, p. 119)

CONTENT VALIDITY Type of validity evidence that is determined by how accurately test items or questions represent all possible items and questions for assessing a content domain. In a classroom context, an assessment with high content validity accurately represents a content domain and/or reflects what teachers have actually taught. (Module 27, p. 493; Module 29, p. 545)

CONTIGUITY LEARNING Learning by simple association. (Module 9, p. 159)

CONTINGENCY CONTRACT An agreement, preferably written, between the teacher and student, that provides the following information: a) specification of appropriate student behavior; b) specification of inappropriate student behaviors; c) description of consequences for both appropriate and inappropriate behaviors. (Module 19, p. 356)

CONTINGENCY MANAGEMENT An approach to behavior modification involving the use of consequences that are tied to specific behaviors. See also contingency contract. (Module 25, p. 460)

CONTINUOUS SCHEDULE Schedule of reinforcement in which consequences are provided after every single instance of the behavior. (Module 9, p. 163)

CONTROL Behavioral aspect of parenting in which parents provide limits and discipline. (Module 2, p. 32)

CONTROLLABILITY Dimension of attributions in which the cause of an outcome is considered to be controllable by the individual or uncontrollable. (Module 16, p. 282)

CONVENTIONAL CONSEQUENCES Consequences applied in a generic fashion which are intended to serve as a form of punishment that deters future misbehavior. (Module 18, p. 336)

CONVENTIONAL LEVEL (OF MORAL REASONING) Kohlberg's second level of moral reasoning that focuses on external authorities, such as the conventions and standards of society, for determining right and wrong. (Module 5, p. 78)

CONVERGENT THINKING Reaching one conclusion or right answer. (Module 23, p. 424)

CONVERGENT VALIDITY Type of validity evidence that is determined by correlating the test score with another measure of the construct. (Module 29, p. 546)

COOPERATIVE LEARNING A method of grouping students together to work collaboratively characterized by five elements: positive interdependence, individual and group accountability, interpersonal skills, face-to-face interaction, and group processing. (Module 19, p. 370; Module 21, p. 378)

CORRELATIONAL DESIGNS Research design that attempts to make connections between two variables. (Module 1, p. 8)

COST Component of expectancy-value theory referring to the expense of engaging in the activity. (Module 16, p. 280)

CREATIVE ABILITIES One of three abilities in Sternberg's theory of successful intelligence which is characterized by the ability to generate novel ideas and take risks in pursuing implementation of ideas. See also analytical abilities and practical abilities. (Module 22, p. 405)

CREATIVE-PRODUCTIVE GIFTEDNESS Giftedness that reflects talents in generating creative ideas, problem-solving, or producing create products. (Module 23, p. 421)

CREATIVITY A variety of traits, skills, and capacities that lead an individual to think divergently and generate novel ideas or products. (Module 23, p. 424)

CRITERION-REFERENCED LETTER GRADES Grades that represent what students have accomplished relative to pre-set criteria or standards. (Module 26, p. 483)

CRITERION-REFERENCED TESTS Tests that are used to compare an individual score to a pre-set criterion for a learning objective. (Module 29, p. 539)

CRITERION-RELATED VALIDITY Type of validity evidence that is demonstrated by establishing a relationship between the test score and some criterion, usually an outcome that is thought to measure the variable of interest. (Module 29, p. 546)

CRITICAL PERIOD A prime time for learning. It was previously assumed that if a child did not acquire certain skills by a certain age, the window of opportunity would close and it would later be impossible to develop those skills. (Module 6, p. 106)

CRITICAL THINKING The process of evaluating the accuracy and worth of information and lines of reasoning. (Module 14, p. 241)

CROSS-GRADE GROUPING A procedure in which students from different grades but similar abilities are placed into homogeneous groups based on their reading or math achievement level, and each group works with different curricular materials and different methods. (Module 21, p. 381; Module 23, p. 423)

CROWDS Large, reputation-based peer groups. (Module 2, p. 37)

CUE Nonverbal event that occurs prior to a behavior. (Module 9, p. 162)

CULTURAL TEST BIAS HYPOTHESIS Tests are biased in some way for a categorical group such as gender, ethnicity, race, or socioeconomic status. (Module 30, p. 559)

CURRICULUM COMPACTING An approach to streamlining the curricular material for students who are gifted by teaching only content that has not been mastered, allowing for advanced instruction or enrichment activities in the time saved by eliminating already-learned content. (Module 23, p. 423)

CYBERBULLYING Bullying via the Internet which can take a number of forms, including misrepresenting one's identity on-line in order to trick someone, spreading lies or rumors, and posting embarrassing pictures. (Module 19, p. 358)

D

DECAY A hypothesized weakening over time of information stored in long-term memory, especially if the information is used infrequently or not at all. (Module 11, p. 192)

DECLARATIVE KNOWLEDGE Knowledge related to "what is," to the nature of how things are, were, or will be. (Module 11, p. 189)

DECODING The strategy of applying sounds to printed letters in order to identify unfamiliar words; referred to as sounding out. (Module 8, p. 137; Module 24, p. 441)

DEDUCTIVE REASONING A form of logical thinking that moves from the general to the specific. (Module 14, p. 244)

DEFICIENCY NEEDS Lower level needs in Maslow's Hierarchy of Needs: physiological, safety, love, and self-esteem. (Module 17, p. 306)

DEFICIT Performance in a domain like reading or mathematics that is poorer than both same-age peers and younger children, indicating an impairment in which students process information in a qualitatively different way than other individuals. (Module 24, p. 441)

DELIBERATE PRACTICE An intrinsic motivation to engage in extensive, long-term repetition of a skill with the desired goal of improving performance. (Module 13, p. 228)

DEMONSTRATION A type of performance task in which the student shows he can use his knowledge or skills to complete a well-defined, complex task. (Module 28, p. 512)

DESCRIPTIVE DESIGNS Research design that provides basic information about behaviors without making connections between behaviors, events, or conditions. (Module 1, p. 8)

DEVELOPMENTAL DELAY Performance in a domain such as reading or mathematics that is poorer than same-age peers but similar to younger students, indicating a slower rate of development. (Module 24, p. 441)

DEVIATION IQ A standard score derived from raw scores; it indicates a test-taker's performance relative to all other test-takers having similar characteristics. (Module 22, p. 407)

DIFFERENTIAL ITEM FUNCTIONING (DIF) A statistical measure of how difficult an item is for one group versus another group. (Module 30, p. 559)

DIRECT INSTRUCTION A teaching method based on behaviorist principles which uses teacher control, structured lessons, and extensive practice. (Module 20, p. 365)

DISABILITY The inability to perform some behavior, task, or skill. (Module 1, p. 14)

DISCIPLINE HIERARCHY List of generic consequences that increase in order of severity. (Module 18, p. 336)

DISCOVERY LEARNING An instructional method in which students discover and internalize a concept, rule, or principle by engaging in unstructured exploration of information without explicit guidance from the teacher. (Module 20, p. 368)

DISCRIMINANT VALIDITY Type of validity evidence that demonstrates a test score is not correlated to another test score that assesses a different construct. (Module 29, p. 546)

DISCRIMINATION 1) Treating students differently based on prejudice feelings or biased beliefs about a particular group; 2) learning in classical conditioning that includes differentiating between similar, but different, stimuli. (Module 1, p. 15; Module 9, p. 160)

DISEQUILIBRIUM A discrepancy between one's existing knowledge and a new experience. (Module 7, p. 120)

DISPLAY RULES Sociocultural rules governing the degree of emotional expression that is appropriate in different situations, and the coping strategies that are considered acceptable. (Module 4, p. 63)

DISTRACTORS Incorrect alternatives provided in a multiple choice question. (Module 27, p. 500)

DIVERGENT THINKING Ability to "think outside the box" by generating multiple ideas or solutions to a problem. (Module 23, p. 424)

DOCTRINE OF FORMAL DISCIPLINE Theory proposing that studying disciplines which require logical thinking could improve general mental abilities, facilitating transfer of these abilities to learning of other subjects. (Module 13, p. 226)

DUAL DISCREPANCY METHOD A method within the response-to-intervention approach to identify whether a student needs more intensive and/or more frequent intervention in which two criteria must be met: the student performs below average compared with grade-level expectations, and shows a slow rate of improvement toward benchmarks. (Module 24, p. 440)

DYSFLUENCY Articulation problems. (Module 8, p. 142)

E

EDUCATIONAL PSYCHOLOGY A discipline that links the science of psychology with educational practice. (Module 1, p. 5)

EFFICACY EXPECTATIONS Beliefs that individuals have the necessary knowledge or skills to achieve an outcome. (Module 17, p. 299)

EFFORTFUL PROCESSING Information processing which requires conscious effort and attention in order to retain and store data. (Module 11, p. 187)

EGOCENTRIC Thinking about the world primarily from one's own physical or cognitive viewpoint. (Module 7, p. 122)

EGOCENTRIC SPEECH An example of egocentrism in which children talk from the perspective of their own interests and experiences without regard for the interests and conversational contributions of the listener. (Module 7, p. 122)

EGOCENTRISM A focus on the self with little consideration for other people or their perspectives. (Module 5, p. 77)

ELABORATIVE REHEARSAL A cognitive process in which learners expand on new information based on what they already know. (Module 11, p. 187)

EMOTIONAL DISTURBANCE One of thirteen categories of disability specified by the Individuals with Disabilities Education Improvement Act. (Module 25, p. 450)

EMOTIONAL EXPRESSIVENESS The ability and degree to which one expresses positive and negative emotions appropriately. (Module 4, p. 62)

EMOTIONAL INTELLIGENCE A term originally coined by Salovey and Mayer (1990) to describe the ability to perceive, express, understand, and manage emotions. (Module 4, p. 63)

EMOTIONAL REGULATION The ability to cope with emotions such as maintaining positive emotions and avoiding the display of inappropriate emotions by monitoring and modifying emotional reactions. (Module 4, p. 66)

EMOTIONAL UNDERSTANDING The ability to differentiate and interpret one's own emotions and/or the ability to perceive and understand, and respond to the emotions of others. (Module 4, p. 64)

EMPATHY The ability to experience and understand the emotions or feelings of someone else. (Module 4, p. 66; Module 5, p. 81)

EMPATHY-BASED GUILT The feeling of pain and regret for causing distress or pain in another person. (Module 5, p. 82)

ENCODING Changing the format of new information as it is being stored in memory. (Module 11, p. 184)

ENGLISH IMMERSION A sink-or-swim approach to teaching English-language learners in which students receive all instruction in English in classes with native English-speaking peers. (Module 8, p. 140)

ENRICHMENT An approach designed to broaden and deepen the knowledge of students who are gifted while keeping them within their grade level. (Module 23, p. 423)

ENTITY VIEW OF ABILITY A pessimistic perception that one's ability is fixed (stable and uncontrollable) leading individuals to believe that their ability cannot change over time and they cannot control their level of ability. (Module 16, p. 282; Module 17, p. 302)

ENVIRONMENTAL COMPETENCE Awareness of how the physical environment impacts learning and an understanding of how to manipulate the environment to reach behavioral goals. (Module 18, p. 327)

ENVIRONMENTAL CUES Stimuli in the environment that suggest appropriate behavior. (Module 18, p. 328)

EPISODIC BUFFER A temporary storage system that integrates information from the visuospatial sketchpad, phonological loop and long-term memory into a single representation within working memory. (Module 11, p. 186)

EPISODIC KNOWLEDGE Long-term memory for information tied to a particular time and place, especially memory of the events in a person's life. (Module 11, p. 189)

EQUILIBRATION A process of maintaining a cognitive balance between our existing knowledge and new experiences. (Module 7, p. 120)

EQUIVALENCE The extent to which students are required to know and perform tasks of similar (but not identical) complexity and difficulty to earn the same grade. (Module 27, p. 496)

ETHNIC GROUP Group of people who share a similar culture or environment. (Module 1, p. 13)

ETHNIC IDENTITY Psychological attitudes and behaviors toward one's ethnic and racial group membership. (Module 3, p. 50)

EVALUATING An executive process in cognition allowing individuals to appraise the outcomes of the cognitive strategies used; the process of making subjective judgments about a student's performance or product; the subjective interpretation of a measurement or test score. (Module 12, p. 212; Module 26, p. 477; Module 29, p. 539)

EXOSYSTEM Interaction among two or more environments, one of which does not directly include the individual. (Module 2, p. 31)

EXPANSION A method of interacting with children in which adults add to—or expand—children's incomplete statements. (Module 8, p. 135)

EXPECTANCY A component of expectancy-value theory which involves a student's expectation for success; "can I do this task?" See also value. (Module 16, p. 279)

EXPERIENCE-DEPENDENT PLASTICITY The emergence of skills that are unique to particular cultures and social groups. (Module 6, p. 107)

EXPERIENCE-EXPECTANT PLASTICITY Involves windows of opportunity that may gradually close (or at least narrow) if the brain identifies the skills involved as unnecessary to the individual. (Module 6, p. 107)

EXPERIMENT A form of performance task in which a student plans, conducts, and interprets the results of research. (Module 28, p. 512)

EXPERIMENTAL DESIGNS Research design that allows cause and effect between study variables to be inferred. (Module 1, p. 8)

EXPLICIT KNOWLEDGE Long-term memories that involve deliberate or conscious recall. (Module 11, p. 189)

EXPLORATION A period of role experimentation and trying new behaviors, including contemplating morals and values. (Module 3, p. 49)

EXPLORATORY DISCUSSION The teacher raises questions in order to assess students' prior knowledge and values and to uncover their beliefs or biases. (Module 14, p. 243)

EXPOSITORY TEACHING A highly organized presentation of material from general principles to specific examples beginning with the activation of prior knowledge. (Module 20, p. 368)

EXTENDED RESPONSE ESSAY Test item that requires students to write essays in which they are free to express their thoughts and ideas, and to organize the information as they see fit. With this format, there is usually no single correct answer; rather correctness ends up being a matter of degree. (Module 27, p. 502)

EXTERNAL REGULATION The least autonomous form of extrinsic motivation in self-determination theory in which a person performs behaviors to obtain external rewards. See also self-determination. (Module 17, p. 308)

EXTINCTION Strategy used to decrease an inappropriate behavior by no longer providing reinforcement for that behavior, or ceasing to provide the pairing between stimuli and response. (Module 9, p. 160)

EXTRINSIC MOTIVATION A motivational orientation in which individuals engage in an activity or behavior to obtain an external outcome such as a reward or praise. (Module 15, p. 265; Module 16, p. 279; Module 17, p. 299)

F

FACE-TO-FACE INTERACTION A feature of cooperative learning which involves effective help and feedback to improve performance, exchanging resources effectively, challenging each other's reasoning, and motivating each other to achieve goals. (Module 21, p. 383)

FAILURE-ACCEPTING STUDENTS Students who accept failure and give up trying to demonstrate their ability because of repeated failures to perform up to their expectations. (Module 17, p. 305)

FAILURE-AVOIDING STUDENTS Students who are highly motivated to avoid failure have low motivation to approach success situations and value learning only if it makes them look competent. (Module 17, p. 304)

FAIRNESS The degree to which all students have an equal opportunity to learn and demonstrate their knowledge and skill. (Module 27, p. 495)

FALSE-BELIEFS Understanding that people can believe one thing, but be wrong. (Module 12, p. 212)

FAMILY EDUCATIONAL RIGHTS AND PRIVACY ACT (20 U.S.C. § 1232G; 34 CFR PART 99) Legislation that protects the privacy of students' academic records by specifying that parents of children under 18 years of age may review the student's school records but parents must provide written permission in order for the school to release information about a student's educational record. (Module 24, p. 433; Module 26, p. 488)

FAR TRANSFER Application of knowledge to a context that is very different from the learning context. (Module 13, p. 229)

FEMININE Stereotypical female behaviors such as being affectionate, warm, gentle, cheerful, and loyal. (Module 3, p. 51)

FETAL ALCOHOL SYNDROME If a woman drinks alcohol during her pregnancy, her baby can be born with FAS, a lifelong condition that causes physical and mental disabilities. FAS is characterized by abnormal facial features, growth deficiencies, and central nervous system (CNS) problems, as well as problems with learning, memory, attention span, communication, vision, hearing, or a combination of these. (Module 6, p. 107)

FLOW A feeling of intense engagement, enjoyment, and challenge in an activity that an individual feels is personally rewarding, causing the individual to feel at one with the task. (Module 15, p. 272)

FLYNN EFFECT A phenomenon in which IQ scores have increased over successive generations throughout the world. (Module 22, p. 409)

FORMAL ASSESSMENT A pre-planned systematic attempt to discover what students have learned. (Module 26, p. 480)

FORMATIVE ASSESSMENT Provides feedback that helps the teacher guide students' learning while it is still in progress. (Module 26, p. 480; Module 28, 510)

FORWARD-REACHING TRANSFER A principle or strategy is so well-learned or deeply understood that it becomes applicable in future learning situations. (Module 13, p. 227)

FREQUENCY DISTRIBUTION Simple list of all scores for a group. (Module 29, p. 542)

FUNCTIONAL FIXEDNESS The inability to use objects or tools in a new way. (Module 14, p. 246)

G

GENDER Social definition including behaviors learned in the environment about being either male (masculine) or female (feminine) (Module 1, p. 13; Module 3, p. 51)

GENDER IDENTITY Knowledge that one is biologically male or female. (Module 3, p. 51)

GENDER CONSTANCY Knowledge that gender will remain the same regardless of behaviors. (Module 3, p. 52)

GENDER LABELING Being able to label one's self and others as male or female. (Module 3, p. 52)

GENDER-ROLE ATTITUDE The approval or disapproval toward societal expectations for each gender. (Module 3, p. 51)

GENDER-ROLE FLEXIBILITY The ability to alter social expectations regarding gender of their own and other's behaviors. (Module 3, p. 52)

GENDER-ROLE IDENTITY Knowledge that one behaves appropriately according to societal expectations for their gender. (Module 3, p. 51)

GENDER-STABILITY Knowledge that gender will not change over time. (Module 3, p. 52)

GENERALIZATION Learning can be expanded beyond a specific stimulus to other similar stimuli. (Module 9, p. 160)

GENERIC RUBRIC A standard format that is used repeatedly throughout the year to evaluate a set of assignments. A generic rubric contains scoring guidelines that can be applied to many different tasks of similar type. (Module 28, p. 517)

GIFTEDNESS An elusive trait characterized by high achievement in one of a variety of domains. (Module 23, p. 420)

GRADE-EQUIVALENT SCORES Scores based on the median score for a particular grade-level of the norm group. (Module 29, p. 544)

GROUP FOCUS The ability to keep as many students as possible actively engaged in appropriate activities. (Module 19, p. 353)

GROUP PROCESSING A feature of cooperative learning which involves reflecting on how well the group is functioning and how to improve it. (Module 21, p. 383)

GROUP WORK A structure in which students work in groups, but do not necessarily need to work cooperatively. (Module 21, p. 382)

GROUP-ADMINISTERED IQ TESTS An approach to IQ testing in which an examiner administers an IQ test to a group of individuals in a paper-and-pencil format. (Module 22, p. 406)

GROWTH NEEDS Higher level needs in Maslow's Hierarchy of Needs: intellectual competence, aesthetic appreciation, and self-actualization. (Module 17, p. 306)

GROWTH-BASED GRADING Assigning grades by comparing a student's performance with your perceptions of his capability. (Module 26, p. 484)

GUIDED DISCOVERY A variant of discovery learning in which the teacher provides enough guidance to ensure that students discover the rule or principle to be learned. (Module 20, p. 368)

H

HETEROGENEITY Variation among individuals on an attribute, such as achievement or ability. (Module 21, p. 378)

HEURISTIC A general problem-solving strategy that relies on common sense or rule of thumb. (Module 14, p. 247)

HIGHER-ORDER THINKING Thinking that involves going well beyond information specifically learned (e.g., analyzing, applying, or evaluating it). (Module 14, p. 239)

HIGHLY QUALIFIED TEACHER Per NCLB, specifies that all teachers must have a bachelor's degree, fulfill all state certification and licensure requirements as well as demonstrate subject matter expertise. (Module 30, p. 561)

HIGH-ROAD TRANSFER Applying abstract knowledge learned in one context to a different situation. (Module 13, p. 227)

HIGH-STAKES TESTS All tests that have significant consequences for students, teachers, administrators, and schools. (Module 30, p. 552)

HOLISTIC RUBRIC Scoring criteria that require the teacher to score the overall process or product as a whole, without judging the component parts separately. (Module 28, p. 517)

HOLOPHRASTIC SPEECH Use of single words to express a larger meaning. (Module 8, p. 136)

HOME-BASED REINFORCEMENTS System in which students are given rewards (e.g., verbal, tangible, or privileges) and sanctions (e.g., loss of privileges, such as television time, snacks, or later bedtime) at home, based on their behavior at school. (Module 18, p. 341)

HOMOGENEITY Little variation among individuals on an attribute, such as achievement or ability. (Module 21, p. 378)

HOSTILE ATTRIBUTIONAL BIAS The tendency to interpret another person's intentions as hostile. (Module 5, p. 84)

HUMANISTIC THEORIES Theories which emphasize factors intrinsic to the individual, such as needs, choice, self-determination, and self-actualization as sources of motivation. (Module 17, p. 305)

HYPOTHESIS TESTING Examination of research data and results to determine what conclusions reasonably can be drawn to support or refute a stated hypotheses. (Module 14, p. 244)

I

IDENTIFIED REGULATION A slightly internalized form of regulation in self-determination theory in which individuals identify with the value of an activity and have accepted regulation of the activity as their own. See also self-determination. (Module 17, p. 308)

IDENTITY ACHIEVED Adolescents who have explored and made commitments in occupations, academic skills, friendships and values and commit to certain goals and values. (Module 3, p. 49)

IDENTITY CONSTANCY Understanding that an object remains qualitatively the same even though its appearance changes. (Module 7, p. 123)

IDENTITY DIFFUSION Adolescents who either have not yet began the process of exploration (as you might expect for younger children) or have been through the exploration process but were unable to make commitments to their goals and values. (Module 3, p. 49)

IDENTITY FORECLOSURE Adolescents who have parents that typically use an authoritarian style of parenting such as telling their adolescent who they are, what they will become, or where they will attend college are considered foreclosure. (Module 3, p. 49)

IEP TEAM A team of individuals responsible for writing and revising a student's IEP. See also Individualized Education Plan (IEP). (Module 24, p. 433)

ILL-DEFINED PROBLEM A problem in which the desired goal is unclear, the information needed to solve the problem is missing, and/or several possible solutions to the problem exist. (Module 14, p. 245)

IMAGINARY AUDIENCE Adolescent's belief that others' thoughts are focused on him or her, just as their own thoughts are focused on themselves. (Module 12, p. 214)

IMPLICIT KNOWLEDGE Knowledge that we are not conscious of recalling, but influences behavior or thought without our awareness. (Module 11, p. 189)

INCLUSION An approach to implementing the Least Restrictive Environment in which students with disabilities, even those with severe disabilities, are integrated within the regular education classroom. See also Least Restrictive Environment and Mainstreaming. (Module 24, p. 435; Module 25, p. 452)

INCREMENTAL VIEW OF ABILITY An optimistic view of ability in which one believes that ability is improvable (unstable and controllable). (Module 16, p. 000; Module 17, p. 302)

INDIVIDUAL AND GROUP ACCOUNTABILITY A feature of cooperative learning which involves group goals (group accountability) and personal responsibility for helping other members and contributing to the group goal (individual accountability). (Module 21, p. 383)

INDIVIDUAL CONSTRUCTIVISM A form of constructivism in which individuals construct meaning by themselves from their experiences. (Module 7, p. 119)

INDIVIDUAL INTEREST Interest in a particular subject or activity that is intrinsic to the individual. (Module 13, p. 234)

INDIVIDUALIZED EDUCATION PLAN (IEP) A plan for students with disabilities who are eligible for special education, which outlines curricula, educational modifications, and provision of services intended to enhance or improve the student's academic, social, or behavioral skills. (Module 24, p. 433; Module 25, p. 452)

INDIVIDUALLY-ADMINISTERED IQ TEST An approach to IQ testing in which an examiner tests an examinee one-on-one; the tester presents items orally, and sometimes uses pictures or materials such as blocks, and the examinee either responds orally or by manipulating materials. (Module 22, p. 406)

INDIVIDUALS WITH DISABILITIES EDUCATION IMPROVEMENT ACT (IDEIA) A 2004 revision of the special educational law originally passed in 1975 as the Education for All Handicapped Children Act (PL 94-142) and later revised as the Individuals with Disabilities Act (PL 101-476), which requires states to provide appropriate public education to students with disabilities aged 3 to 21. (Module 24, p. 433; Module 25, p. 450)

INDUCTIVE REASONING Logical thinking that moves from the use of specific examples to formulate a general principle. (Module 14, p. 244)

INFORMAL ASSESSMENT Ongoing, day-to-day techniques such as listening, observing students' interactions, asking questions, and reading journal entries in order to record information for the purpose of providing feedback. (Module 26, p. 480)

INFORMATION PROCESSING THEORY A theoretical perspective that focuses on the specific ways in which individuals mentally think about and "process" the information they receive. (Module 11, p. 184)

INNER SPEECH Internalized speech for regulating one's thoughts and actions. (Module 7, p. 127)

INQUIRY LEARNING An instructional activity which involves formulating research questions, collecting, analyzing and evaluating data, and communicating the results. (Module 20, p. 370)

INSTRUCTIONAL CONSEQUENCES Consequences that teach students how to correct their behavior and provide examples of how to behave properly. (Module 18, p. 336)

INSTRUCTIONAL CONVERSATIONS A method of encouraging elementary school students' interaction with and comprehension of stories during reading lessons based on Vygotsky's Zone of Proximal Development. (Module 20, p. 372)

INTEGRATED REGULATION A form of regulation in self-determination theory in which an individual has fully internalized extrinsic regulations and now takes ownership of these values. See also self-determination. (Module 17, p. 308)

INTELLECTUAL DISABILITY A disability characterized by significant limitations in intellectual functioning and adaptive behavior (formerly called mental retardation). (Module 24, p. 435)

INTERACTION PROCEDURES Rules for talking. (Module 18, p. 337)

INTERFERENCE (PROACTIVE AND RETROACTIVE) A phenomenon whereby something stored in long-term memory inhibits one's ability to remember something else correctly. (Module 11, p. 192)

INTERMITTENT SCHEDULE A schedule of reinforcement in which consequences are provided periodically for the behavior. (Module 9, p. 163)

INTERNALIZATION A developmental process; in Vygotsky's theory of cognitive development it occurs when an individual progresses from performing cognitive processes with a more capable person, socially, to performing them independently and mentally; in self-determination theory it occurs when an individual moves from less self-determined to more self-determined. (Module 7, p. 126; Module 17, p. 307)

INTERPERSONAL SKILLS A feature of cooperative learning which involves skills such as trust, communication, decision-making, leadership, and conflict resolution. (Module 21, p. 383)

INTERSUBJECTIVITY Co-construction of knowledge where two individuals who begin a task with different knowledge perspectives come to a shared understanding, each adjusting to the perspective of the other. (Module 7, p. 124)

INTERVIEWS Type of measure used in research that includes verbal questions. (Module 1, p. 10)

INTRINSIC MOTIVATION A motivational orientation in which individuals engage in an activity or behavior which is rewarding in and of itself. (Module 15, p. 265; Module 16, p. 279; Module 17, p. 299)

INTRINSIC VALUE A component of expectancy-value theory referring to interest in or enjoyment of an activity. (Module 16, p. 279)

INTROJECTED REGULATION A form of extrinsic motivation in self-determination theory in which individuals engage in an activity to comply with external pressure. See also self-determination. (Module 17, p. 308)

INTROSPECTION Awareness of thoughts. (Module 12, p. 214)

IQ-ACHIEVEMENT DISCREPANCY A method of diagnosing learning disabilities in which scores on standardized achievement tests in one or more academic subjects are significantly below what would be expected from the individual's IQ. (Module 24, p. 438)

IQ TESTS See also Group administered IQ tests and Individually administered IQ tests. (Module 22, p. 438)

ISSUE-SPECIFIC DISCUSSION Used to explore an issue or concept in depth, evaluate thoughts and perspectives, distinguish the known from the unknown, and synthesize relevant factors and knowledge. (Module 14, p. 243)

ITEM ANALYSIS The process of collecting, summarizing, and using information from student responses to make decisions about test items. (Module 27, p. 504)

ITEM DIFFICULTY INDEX A report of the proportion of the group of test-takers who answered an item correctly. (Module 27, p. 505)

ITEM DISCRIMINATION INDEX A description of the extent to which a particular test item is able to differentiate high-scoring from low-scoring students. (Module 27, p. 505)

J

JOINT ATTENTION A method of interacting with children in which adults label and talk about objects on which the child's attention is focused. (Module 8, p. 135)

JOPLIN PLAN Most famous cross-grade grouping plan, originating in 1954, in which students were assigned to cross-grade, homogeneous groups based on reading-skill level. (Module 21, p. 381)

JUDGMENTAL REVIEW PANEL Panel comprised of members of a minority group that independently rate test item for bias, sometimes followed by a group discussion. (Module 30, p. 559)

JUSTICE ORIENTATION Moral reasoning that focuses on the rights of individuals due to their focus on independence and individuality. (Module 5, p. 79)

K

KEYWORD METHOD A mnemonic technique in which an association is made between two ideas by forming a visual image of one or more concrete objects (keywords) that either sound similar to, or symbolically represent, those ideas. (Module 11, p. 188)

KWL METHOD Asks students to list their knowledge about a topic and what questions they have before instruction, and list what they learned after instruction. (Module 13, p. 232)

L

LAW OF EFFECT Behaviors that are associated with good consequences are more likely to occur, whereas behaviors that are associated with bad consequences are less likely to occur again. (Module 9, p. 161)

LEARNING Change in behavior or knowledge. (Module 9, p. 159)

LEARNING OBJECTIVE Specific descriptions of what students will know or be able to do once they have completed the lesson. (Module 20, p. 364)

LEAST RESTRICTIVE ENVIRONMENT (LRE) A legal requirement to place students with special needs in the regular classroom "to the maximum extent appropriate." (Module 24, p. 434; Module 25, p. 452)

LESSON-RUNNING PROCEDURES Specific behaviors required in order for teaching and learning to happen. (Module 18, p. 337)

LICENSURE Determined by government regulations that provide permission to practice a profession in order to protect the public. (Module 30, p. 560)

LIVE MODELS Individuals that are observed directly. (Module 10, p. 174)

LOCI METHOD A method in which you imagine a familiar place and pick out particular locations. When you need to remember a list of items, you use the locations as pegs on which to hang items to be remembered. (Module 11, p. 188)

LOCUS A dimension of attributions in which the cause of an outcome is considered to be internal or external. (Module 16, p. 282)

LOCUS OF CONTROL An individual's belief that outcomes or events are caused by either external factors outside of one's control (external locus) or internal factors (internal locus). (Module 15, p. 266)

LOGICAL CONSEQUENCES Consequences that are specific to the misbehavior itself and serve a corrective, rather than a punitive function. (Module 18, p. 336)

LONG-TERM MEMORY The component of memory that holds knowledge and skills for a relatively long period of time. (Module 11, p. 189)

LOW-ROAD TRANSFER Spontaneous, automatic transfer of highly practiced skills. (Module 13, p. 226)

M

MACROSYSTEM Broader cultural patterns such as beliefs, customs, knowledge, and morals. (Module 2, p. 31)

MAINSTREAMING An approach to implementing the Least Restrictive Environment in which students with disabilities are placed with non-disabled peers in the general education classroom when appropriate (e.g., for music, gym, art), but remain in special education classrooms for most academic subjects. See also Least Restrictive Environment and Inclusion. (Module 24, p. 435; Module 25, p. 452)

MAINTENANCE REHEARSAL Repetition of information over and over to keep it "fresh" in working memory. (Module 11, p. 187)

MAJOR DEPRESSIVE DISORDERS Mood disorders in which individuals experience at least two weeks of depressed mood or loss of interest, along with at least four additional depressive symptoms as specified in the DSM-IV-TR. (Module 25, p. 455)

MASCULINE Stereotypical male behaviors such as being athletic, aggressive, dominant, self-reliant, and independent. (Module 3, p. 51)

MASLOW'S HIERARCHY OF NEEDS A humanistic theory which emphasizes a need for self-actualization which is obtained by first satisfying lower-level deficiency needs and being needs. (Module 17, p. 305)

MASTERY GOALS Goals that focus on mastery, improving intellectually, and acquiring new skills and knowledge. (Module 13, p. 234)

MASTERY LEARNING An approach in which educational objectives are divided into small units, and students work at their own pace through each unit, progressing to the next unit only once they have achieved mastery on the current one. (Module 20, p. 367)

MASTERY-APPROACH GOALS An intrinsic motivation to focus on mastery, improving intellectually, and acquiring new skills and knowledge. (Module 16, p. 280)

MASTERY-AVOIDANCE GOALS Motivation to avoid lack of mastery or looking incompetent according to one's own criteria of performance. (Module 16, p. 280)

MATCHING EXERCISE Test format which presents students with directions for matching, a list of premises, and a list of responses. The student's job is to match each premise with one of the responses. (Module 27, p. 499)

MATTHEW EFFECT A rich-get-richer-poor-get-poorer phenomenon in which high achieving students increase their achievement at a faster rate than low-achieving students. (Module 21, p. 379)

MEAN Measure of central tendency where all scores are summed and the sum is divided by the number of scores in the group (simple average). (Module 29, p. 541)

MEANINGFUL LEARNING The process of actively constructing knowledge by selecting relevant information, organizing it, and connecting it to prior knowledge. (Module 20, p. 368)

MEANS-END ANALYSIS A heuristic in which the main problem-solving goal is divided into subgoals. (Module 14, p. 247)

MEASUREMENT A quantitative or descriptive number (score) assigned to describe the extent to which someone possesses a certain attribute or skill. (Module 26, p. 477; Module 29, p. 539)

MEASUREMENT ERROR The accumulation of imperfections which are found in all measurements. (Module 29, p. 546)

MEDIAN Measure of central tendency that is the middle score in a list of all scores. (Module 29, p. 541)

MESOSYSTEM Interaction between two or more microsystems. (Module 2, p. 31)

METACOGNITION Thinking about thinking; thinking about one's own and others' knowledge such as skills, memory capabilities, and the ability to monitor learning. (Module 12, p. 211)

METACOGNITIVE KNOWLEDGE Knowledge about our own cognitive processes, and our understanding of how to regulate those processes to maximize learning. (Module 12, p. 211)

METACOGNITIVE REGULATION The purposeful act of attempting to control one's own cognitions, beliefs, emotions, and values. (Module 12, p. 212)

METALINGUISTIC AWARENESS Knowledge about language and how it works. (Module 8, p. 137)

MICROSYSTEM Immediate environment surrounding the individual. (Module 2, p. 31)

MINDFUL ABSTRACTION A defining feature of high-road transfer in which information that is consciously and actively learned is retrieved and applied to a new situation, guided by one's metacognition. (Module 13, p. 227)

MINORITY GROUP A group of people with less power in comparison to the majority group. (Module 1, p. 13)

MISBEHAVIOR Any student behavior that disrupts the learning environment of the classroom. (Module 19, p. 347)

MNEMONIC A special memory aid or trick designed to help students learn and remember a specific piece of information. (Module 11, p. 187)

MODE Measure of central tendency that is the most frequently occurring score among the group. (Module 29, p. 541)

MODEL Individual who performs a behavior that is being observed and can be imitated. (Module 10, p. 174)

MONITORING Checking on how well your plan is working through self-testing and revising or rescheduling cognitive strategies. (Module 12, p. 212)

MORAL REALISM Piaget's first stage of moral reasoning which includes viewing right and wrong as being determined by the consequences of behavior given by adult authority figures. (Module 5, p. 77)

MORAL REASONING The thoughts or rationale for determining right and wrong. (Module 5, p. 77)

MORALITY OF COOPERATION Piaget's second stage of moral reasoning which includes understanding certain situations or under particular circumstances rules can be bent. (Module 5, p. 77)

MORATORIUM Adolescents who are actively involved in the exploration process but have not yet made decisions or commitments. (Module 3, p. 49)

MORPHEMIC INFLECTIONS Word endings. (Module 8, p. 136)

MOVEMENT MANAGEMENT Set of classroom management skills that involve the teacher's ability to keep a lesson moving at an appropriate pace to keep students engaged, to maintain smoothness (logical organization and sequencing) of instruction, and to successfully manage transitions from one activity to the next. (Module 19, p. 353)

MULTIAGE CLASSROOMS A procedure where students of varying ages are flexibly grouped within a classroom based on their current achievement, motivation, and interests. (Module 21, p. 382)

MULTIGRADE CLASSES An administrative tool in which students from different grades are put into the same class to address declining enrollments or uneven class sizes. (Module 21, p. 382)

MULTIMODAL INTERVENTIONS An approach that combines one or more of the following interventions: medication, contingency management, cognitive-behavior modification, and academic interventions. (Module 25, p. 461)

MULTIPLE-CHOICE ITEM A question format in which students must choose the correct answer from among the list of response alternatives. (Module 27, p. 500)

MYELIN A white fatty material, composed chiefly of lipids and lipoproteins, that encloses certain axons and nerve fibers. (Module 6, p. 105)

N

NARRATIVE PROGRESS REPORTS Reports prepared by teachers to provide detailed, written accounts of each student's learning and performance in class. (Module 26, p. 486)

NEAR TRANSFER The application of prior knowledge to situations that are similar but not identical to the learning context. (Module 13, p. 229)

NEGATIVE TRANSFER Occurs when previous learning hinders learning on new task. (Module 13, p. 226)

NEGLECTED YOUTH Individuals who are neither liked nor disliked by peers. (Module 2, p. 39)

NETWORK THEORY (PROPOSITIONAL NETWORKS) A theory that describes how information in memory is organized and connected within a network that is not part of conscious awareness. (Module 11, p. 190)

NEURAL PRUNING Brain cell death and/or differentiation that occurs when unnecessary neurons are eliminated during brain development. (Module 6, p. 104)

NEURON Nerve cell in the brain that sends and receives electrical signals over long distances within the body. (Module 6, p. 104)

NEUROTRANSMITTER A chemical substance that transmits nerve impulses across a synapse. (Module 6, p. 104)

NEUTRAL STIMULI All events that do not evoke an automatic response. (Module 9, p. 160)

NO CHILD LEFT BEHIND ACT OF 2001 (NCLB) Legislation that reauthorized the ESEA act to hold school districts responsible for student learning. (Module 30, p. 552)

NONGRADED PLANS Grouping students flexibly into homogeneous groups across grade or age levels. Examples are the Joplin plan and multi-age classrooms. (Module 21, p. 381)

NORM GROUP All other test-takers having characteristics similar to the individual taking a test, such as age, grade, gender, socio-economic status, ethnic or racial status, or geographic region. (Module 22, p. 407)

NORM SAMPLE A large group of individuals who represent the population of interest on numerous dimensions such as gender, age, race, and SES. (Module 29, p. 539)

NORM-REFERENCED An interpretation in which one evaluates the performance of an individual as compared to other similar test-takers. (Module 22, p. 407)

NORM-REFERENCED LETTER GRADES Grades that are based on how a student has performed in comparison with other students in the class. (Module 26, p. 484)

NORM-REFERENCED TESTS Tests that are used to compare an individual score to the scores of other students from a norm sample. (Module 29, p. 539)

O

OBJECT PERMANENCE Awareness that objects and people continue to exist even when not present. (Module 7, p. 122)

OBJECTIVE TESTING Any testing format where there is a single correct answer. (Module 27, p. 497)

OBJECTIVITY Degree to which two or more qualified evaluators would agree on what rating or score to assign to a student's performance. (Module 27, p. 494)

OBSERVATIONAL LEARNING Learning by observing and imitating others' (models) behaviors. (Module 10, p. 174; Module 19, p. 352)

OBSERVATIONS Type of measure used in research that includes watching or viewing the behavior of individuals. (Module 1, p. 10)

OPERATIONS Physical actions performed mentally. (Module 7, p. 120)

ORAL PRESENTATION Interviews, speeches, skits, debates, or other dramatizations in which students are required to verbalize their knowledge and use their oral communication skills. (Module 28, p. 512)

ORGANIZATIONAL STRATEGIES Strategies such as chunking, hierarchies, or visual imagery that help one retain new information in memory. (Module 11, p. 188)

OUTCOME EXPECTATIONS Beliefs that particular actions lead to particular outcomes in general. (Module 17, p. 299)

OVERCORRECTION Behavioral strategy used to make restitution for an inappropriate behavior by having a student perform an appropriate behavior. (Module 9, p. 168)

OVEREXTENSIONS Using a word to apply to a range of concepts. (Module 8, p. 136)

OVERLAPPING The ability to deal with misbehaviors without interrupting the flow of an ongoing lesson or activity. (Module 19, p. 353)

OVERLEARNING The process of continuing practice after students have become accurate at performing a skill. (Module 13, p. 231)

OVERREGULARIZATIONS Making an irregular word form regular by applying a rule (adding -ed to break = breaked). (Module 8, p. 137)

OVERSTRIVERS Students who are motivated by a need to perform better than others to ensure their success and prove their ability. (Module 17, p. 304)

OVERT AGGRESSION Behaviors intended to harm someone physically. (Module 2, p. 38)

P

PARALINGUISTIC CUES Language cues that are typically used to reinforce verbal content (as when a happy event is described in a joyful way). Paralinguistics may include cues such as changes in speaking rate, pitch level, or vocal quality. (Module 4, p. 65)

PERCEIVED POPULARITY Having good social skills, but may not be well-liked by peers and may display aggressive behaviors. (Module 2, p. 38)

PERCENTAGE GRADING SYSTEM A system of assigning grades based on what percentage of information a student has answered or completed correctly; all percentage grades are averaged to compute a final grade. (Module 26, p. 484)

PERCENTILE SCORES Type of test score that denotes the percentage of people in the norm sample who scored below or equal to a raw score. (Module 29, p. 542)

PERFORMANCE ASSESSMENT Any form of assessment that requires students to carry out an activity or develop a product in order to demonstrate skill or knowledge. (Module 28, p. 510)

PERFORMANCE-APPROACH GOALS An intrinsic motivation to demonstrate ability and do better than others. (Module 16, p. 280)

PERFORMANCE-AVOIDANCE GOALS Motivation to avoid lack of mastery or looking incompetent compared to the performance of peers. (Module 16, p. 281)

PERFORMANCE-CONTINGENT REWARDS Rewards that are given for mastery or for a standard of performance, which provide the individual with information about his or her ability. (Module 15, p. 268)

PERFORMANCE PRAISE Also called outcome praise; an evaluation of the end-product, such as what the student did well on an assignment. (Module 15, p. 269)

PERSON PRAISE A favorable judgment about a person's attributes or behaviors, such as being smart, or being a good speller, which implies a fixed ability that does not change. (Module 15, p. 270)

PQ4R Instructional strategy used to increase reading comprehension that includes several steps: preview, question, read, reflect, recite, and review. (Module 12, p. 217)

PRACTICAL ABILITIES One of three abilities in Sternberg's theory of successful intelligence which is characterized by the ability to apply knowledge and to effectively implement solutions in real-life contexts. See also analytical abilities and creative abilities. (Module 22, p. 405)

PRACTICALITY The extent to which the development, administration, and scoring of assessments is economical and efficient. (Module 27, p. 496)

PRAGMATICS Knowledge of the purpose of language and how language is used in social interactions. (Module 8, p. 137)

PRAISE Positive feedback on an individual's behavior or performance in verbal or written form. (Module 15, p. 269)

PRAISE-AND-IGNORE Behavioral strategy used to increase an appropriate behavior by providing reinforcement and decrease inappropriate behavior by ignoring the behavior. (Module 9, p. 167)

PRECONVENTIONAL LEVEL Kohlberg's first level of moral reasoning that includes an egocentric, self-interest view of right and wrong, not using the conventions or standards of society. (Module 5, p. 77)

PREDICTIVE VALIDITY Type of criterion-validity evidence that uses the test score and another criterion assessed in the future. (Module 29, p. 546)

PREJUDICE FEELINGS Rigid and irrational generalizations about a group or category of people. (Module 1, p. 15)

PREMACK PRINCIPLE Behavioral strategy used to increase an appropriate behavior by providing another behavior as reinforcement. (Module 9, p. 166)

PRINCIPLE OF LEAST INTERVENTION States that a teacher should react in the least intrusive way possible when dealing with misbehavior in the classroom. If the least intrusive strategy does not work, the teacher then moves along a continuum to a more intrusive approach until he/she finds a strategy that is effective. (Module 19, p. 354)

PROACTIVE CLASSROOM MANAGEMENT A preventive approach that integrates behavioral management methods with effective instruction to facilitate achievement. It focuses on the group dimensions of classroom management rather than the behavior of individual students. (Module 19, p. 350)

PROBLEM Any situation in which one is trying to reach some goal and has to find a means to do so. (Module 14, p. 245)

PROBLEM SOLVING The means we use to reach a goal in spite of an obstacle or obstacles. (Module 14, p. 245)

PROBLEM-BASED LEARNING (PBL) Experiential learning (minds-on, hands-on) organized around the investigation and resolution of messy, real-world problems. See also inquiry learning. (Module 14, p. 248)

PROCEDURAL KNOWLEDGE Knowledge concerning how to perform a certain skill or task. (Module 11, p. 189)

PROCEDURAL SUBTYPE A subtype of mathematics disability characterized by frequent use of developmentally immature procedures for solving arithmetic problems and frequent errors in executing mathematical procedures. (Module 24, p. 444)

PROCEDURES Specific descriptions of how to accomplish an activity or task in the classroom. (Module 18, p. 337)

PROCESS PORTFOLIO Collection of a student's work from different stages that shows the student's progress or achievement over time. (Module 28, p. 514)

PROCESS PRAISE An evaluation of the process taken to complete a task such as strategies, procedures, methods, approaches, and subskills for performing the task. (Module 15, p. 269)

PROJECT A long-term activity that results in a student product of some kind, such as a model, a functional object, a substantial report, or a collection. (Module 28, p. 514)

PROMPT Verbal reminder that accompanies a cue. (Module 9, p. 162)

PROSOCIAL BEHAVIOR Voluntary behavior intended to benefit others by helping or sharing. (Module 5, p. 80)

PSYCHOLOGICAL AND CULTURAL TOOLS Any symbolic system provided by culture, such as signs, language, mnemonics, concepts, activities, or social interactions. (Module 7, p. 126)

PSYCHOSOCIAL CRISIS Psychological and social challenge with two developmental outcomes, one positive and one negative. (Module 3, p. 46)

PSYCHOSOCIAL MORATORIUM A time with few responsibilities and many opportunities for exploration of different roles. (Module 3, p. 48)

PUNISHMENT A consequence of a behavior that decreases the occurrence of that behavior. (Module 9, p. 162)

Q

QUASI-EXPERIMENTAL DESIGNS Research design that attempts to demonstrate a cause-effect relationship when random assignment is not possible and manipulating the independent variable. (Module 1, p. 8)

R

RACIAL GROUP Group of people who share common biological traits. (Module 1, p. 13)

RANDOM SAMPLE Every person within the population has an equal chance of being included in the sample. (Module 1, p. 9)

RANGE Measure of variability that is the difference between the highest and the lowest score in a group of scores . (Module 29, p. 541)

RAW SCORE The number of correct answers. (Module 29, p. 542)

RECALL A memory task in which one must retrieve information in its entirety from long-term memory. (Module 11, p. 191)

RECALL TASKS Tasks that require students to generate or recall the correct answers completely from memory. Short answer and essay are item formats that involve recall of information. (Module 27, p. 497)

RECASTING A method of interacting with children in which adults reproduce children's utterances as a semantically similar expression that adds new information. (Module 8, p. 135)

RECIPROCAL QUESTIONING A method for encouraging the social negotiation of conflicting perspectives by requiring students to generate questions based on expository material and take turns asking and answering each other's questions. (Module 20, p. 372)

RECIPROCAL TEACHING A method of teaching metacognitive strategies to increase reading comprehension that includes several steps; summarizing, questioning, clarifying, and predicting. (Module 12, p. 216; Module 20, p. 372)

RECOGNITION TASKS Memory tasks that ask students to recognize correct information among irrelevant or incorrect statements. Test item formats that involve recognition include alternate choice, multiple choice, and matching. (Module 11, p. 191; Module 27, p. 497)

RECONSTRUCTION ERROR Constructing a logical but incorrect "memory" by using information retrieved from long-term memory plus one's general knowledge and beliefs about the world. (Module 11, p. 192)

REFLECTIVE PRACTICE Any technique that allows a learner to develop a conceptual understanding of content. (Module 13, p. 227)

REGION OF PROXIMAL LEARNING Proposes that individuals will study items close to being learned, but not yet mastered. (Module 12, p. 221)

REGROUPING Placing students of the same grade into homogeneous groups only for reading or mathematics based on their current skill level, and continually changing students' group placement based on re-evaluation of their skills. (Module 21, p. 381)

REHEARSAL A cognitive process in which information is repeated over and over as a possible way of learning and remembering it. When it is used to maintain information in working memory, it is called maintenance rehearsal. When it is connected with prior knowledge and expanded upon, it is called elaborative rehearsal. (Module 11, p. 187)

REINFORCEMENT A consequence that is given after display of a behavior, which will increase the likelihood that an individual will perform the behavior again. (Module 9, p. 162; Module 15, p. 265)

REINFORCING INCOMPATIBLE BEHAVIORS Behavioral strategy used to increase appropriate behavior by providing reinforcement and decrease an inappropriate behavior that cannot occur at the same time. (Module 9, p. 167)

REJECTED YOUTH Individuals who do not have good social skills, display aggressive behaviors, and tend to be less well liked by peers. (Module 2, p. 39)

RELATEDNESS A component of self-determination theory referring to the need to feel securely connected to others, which enables individuals to feel safe to explore their environment. (Module 17, p. 305)

RELATIONAL AGGRESSION Behaviors specifically intended to damage another person's relationships. (Module 2, p. 38)

RELIABILITY The consistency of the test score or results. (Module 27, p. 494; Module, 29, p. 546)

REPRIMAND Behavioral strategy used to decrease an inappropriate behavior by providing undesired verbal criticisms of behavior. (Module 9, p. 168)

RESPONSE ALTERNATIVES List of alternatives in a multiple choice item from which students must choose a correct response. (Module 27, p. 500)

RESPONSE COST Behavioral strategy used to decrease an inappropriate behavior by taking away something desired. (Module 9, p. 168)

RESPONSE SET Tendency to respond to events or situations in the way that is most familiar to us. (Module 14, p. 246)

RESPONSE-TO-INTERVENTION A method of diagnosing learning disabilities in which students identified as at risk for learning disabilities are given appropriate instructional interventions. Those who fail to respond to interventions would be considered to have a learning disability. (Module 24, p. 439)

RESPONSIVENESS Emotional component of parenting such as affection, acceptance, and caring. (Module 2, p. 32)

RESTRICTED RESPONSE ESSAY Question format that limits the content of students' answers as well as the form of their responses. (Module 27, p. 502)

RETRIEVAL CUE A hint about where to "look" for a piece of information in long-term memory. (Module 11, p. 190)

RETRIEVAL FAILURE Failure to pull up a mental record of information that has been previously learned. (Module 11, p. 192)

REVERSIBILITY Ability to manipulate one's thinking in two directions. (Module 7, p. 122)

ROTE MEMORIZATION Memorizing information without necessarily understanding it. (Module 13, p. 227)

ROUTINE A predictable schedule or course of action. (Module 18, p. 337)

RUBRIC An assessment tool that provides pre-set criteria for scoring student responses, making grading simpler and more transparent. (Module 27, p. 498; Module 28, p. 517)

RULES Statements describing a behavior that is necessary to ensure a safe and productive learning environment. (Module 18, p. 335)

S

SAMPLE Smaller set of individuals from the population of interest who are included in the research study. (Module 1, p. 9)

SATIATION Behavioral strategy used to decrease an inappropriate behavior by having a student perform the behavior until it is no longer reinforcing. (Module 9, p. 168)

SCAFFOLDING Temporary social support provided by an adult or more capable peer for a child to accomplish a task. (Module 7, p. 126)

SCHEMA THEORY Individuals use basic structures (schemas) for organizing related information and concepts within long-term memory. (Module 11, p. 190)

SCHEMES Organized patterns of physical action. (Module 7, p. 120)

SCHOOLHOUSE GIFTEDNESS Giftedness that reflects high overall cognitive ability, high achievement in particular subjects, or

efficiency in processing information and learning new things. (Module 23, p. 421)

SECTION 504 OF THE REHABILITATION ACT OF 1973 A federal anti-discrimination law protecting the rights of individuals with mental and physical disabilities. (Module 25, p. 452)

SECTION 504 PLAN A curriculum plan for students with disabilities, required by Section 504 of the Rehabilitation Act of 1973, which outlines the type of education and services needed for the student to function as adequately as non-disabled students. See also Section 504 of the Rehabilitation Act of 1973. (Module 25, p. 452)

SEDUCTIVE DETAILS Very interesting parts of a text that convey nonessential information. (Module 13, p. 235)

SEL (SOCIAL-EMOTIONAL LEARNING) A term used to describe a wide variety of programs that are designed to facilitate the development of social and emotional skills such as emotional awareness, differentiating emotions, differentiating the intensity of feelings, emotional regulation, using peer feedback, developing sensitivity to other's emotions, perspective-taking, and conflict resolution skills. (Module 4, p. 70)

SELF-ACTUALIZATION The highest level of motivation in Maslow's Hierarchy of Needs characterized by a need to satisfy one's full potential. (Module 17, p. 306)

SELF-AWARENESS The ability to recognize one's own thoughts and feelings, and to observe them in a way that allows one to understand them and make decisions about how to act on them. (Module 4, p. 64)

SELF-CONCEPT A cognitive aspect in which an individual has a perception or description about themselves. (Module 3, p. 52)

SELF-DETERMINATION Autonomy, or the feeling of having choice in one's actions rather than being controlled or pressured; also refers to a theory of motivation in which individuals are motivated intrinsically by needs for autonomy, competence, and relatedness. (Module 17, p. 305)

SELF-EFFICACY One's belief about or expectation for success on a particular task. (Module 10, p. 177; Module 17, p. 299)

SELF-ESTEEM An affective aspect in which an individual evaluates components of him or herself and feels either as good or bad. (Module 3, p. 52)

SELF-EVALUATION Determining the quality of the judgment (good or bad) and possibly providing self-imposed consequences. (Module 10, p. 179)

SELF-FULFILLING PROPHECY A groundless expectation that becomes true simply because it was expected. (Module 2, p. 36; Module 22, p. 409)

SELF-JUDGMENT Comparing one's own performance to a predetermined goal or standard. (Module 10, p. 179)

SELF-MOTIVATION The ability to generate feelings of enthusiasm, zeal, confidence, and persistence, especially during challenges and setbacks. (Module 4, p. 67)

SELF-OBSERVATION Viewing one's own behavior including possibly recording one's own behavior. (Module 10, p. 179)

SELF-REGULATION The ability to control one's emotions, cognitions, and behaviors by providing consequences to oneself. (Module 10, p. 179; Module 17, p. 301)

SELF-WORTH One's overall evaluation of worth as a person; also refers to a theory of motivation in which feelings of competence affect one's self-worth and consequently motivation to achieve in school. (Module 17, p. 303)

SEMANTIC MEMORY SUBTYPE A subtype of mathematics disability characterized by difficulty in storing arithmetic facts in long-term memory or accessing them, even after extensive drilling. (Module 24, p. 443)

SEMANTICS A component of language referring to how meaning is communicated and interpreted. (Module 8, p. 136)

SEMIOTIC FUNCTIONS An ability to use signs and symbols to represent an object. (Module 7, p. 122)

SENSITIVE PERIODS Periods in development that involve subtle changes in the brain's ability to be shaped by sensory input at a particular stage. (Module 6, p. 106)

SENSORY MEMORY A component of memory that holds incoming information in an unanalyzed form for a very brief period of time (probably less than a second for visual input and two or three seconds for auditory input). (Module 11, p. 184)

SEX The biological status of male (penis) or female (vagina). (Module 1, p. 13; Module 3, p. 51)

SEXUAL ORIENTATION Term used to denote homosexuality, heterosexuality, and bisexuality. (Module 1, p. 13)

SHAPING Behavioral strategy used to increase an appropriate behavior by reinforcing small steps toward the behavior. (Module 9, p. 167)

SHORT-ANSWER/COMPLETION TASK Test item format which requires filling in a short response, usually consisting of a word or phrase. (Module 27, p. 502)

SITUATIONAL INTEREST Immediate interest in a particular topic that a teacher creates. (Module 13, p. 234)

SKEWNESS The symmetry or asymmetry of a frequent distribution. (Module 29, p. 542)

SLEEPER EFFECT Negative effects of divorce seem dormant for many years only to arise again during adolescence. (Module 2, p. 35)

SOCIAL COMPETENCE The outcomes, skills, and processes involved in successful social interactions. (Module 3, p. 54)

SOCIAL CONSTRUCTIVISM A form of constructivism in which individuals construct meaning by interacting with others within a social and cultural context. (Module 7, p. 119)

SOCIAL ISOLATION (TIME-OUT) Behavioral strategy used to decrease an inappropriate behavior by removing an individual from a setting that includes reinforcement to a setting in which reinforcement is denied. (Module 9, p. 169)

SOCIAL REFERENCING Observation of others in an attempt to use other people's reactions to help us interpret a situation and decide how to respond. (Module 4, p. 67)

SOCIAL SKILLS The ability to reason, think through, pick up cues, and make appropriate decisions with respect to interpersonal relationships. (Module 3, p. 55)

SOCIALIZED SPEECH Speech used for communicating in a social context with adults. (Module 7, p. 127)

SOCIOECONOMIC STATUS (SES) Status of a family household that relies on the education level and occupation of family members rather than their level of income. (Module 1, p. 14)

SOCIOMETRIC POPULARITY Being well-liked by peers as well as having good social skills. (Module 2, p. 38)

SOCIOMORAL DEVELOPMENTAL DELAY Self-centered, egocentric orientation that is not replaced by the more typical advanced moral development. (Module 5, p. 82)

SPECIFIC DETERMINERS Extraneous clues to the answer of a question. (Module 27, p. 500)

SPECIFIC LANGUAGE IMPAIRMENT A disorder in which language development is significantly below age level because of difficulties in receptive and expressive language, despite normal hearing, average nonverbal intelligence, and an absence of developmental disabilities. (Module 8, p. 142)

SPECIFIC LEARNING DISABILITIES The largest special education category of disability served under the Individuals with Disabilities Education Improvement Act. (Module 24, p. 438)

SPONTANEOUS DISCUSSION Unplanned discussion that arises when students become interested in a topic, when they raise an important issue during class, or when they are on the brink of grasping an idea. (Module 14, p. 243).

SPREADING ACTIVATION Recollection of one piece of information within the network can activate recall of related or linked information. (Module 11, p. 190)

STABILITY A dimension of attributions in which the cause of an outcome is considered to be stable (unchangeable) or unstable (changeable). (Module 16, p. 282)

STANDARD DEVIATION (SD) The degree of variability in a group of scores or how much the scores deviate, or vary, around the average score. (Module 22, p. 407; Module, 29, p. 541)

STANDARD ERROR OF MEASUREMENT (SEM) Estimated amount of error expected on a given test. (Module 29, p. 547)

STANDARD SCORES Scores that are created by converting raw scores, typically using the mean and standard deviation, into scores that more easily and accurately describe score differences as compared to some other types of scores. (Module 29, p. 544)

STANDARDIZED ACHIEVEMENT TESTS Tests that assess learning outcomes and skills for broad or domain-specific learning. (Module 29, p. 538)

STANDARDIZED APTITUDE TESTS Tests that assess future potential or capacity to learn in general or in a specific domain. (Module 29, p. 538)

STANDARDIZED TESTS Tests that are created by numerous experts in the field, focus on broad areas of learning, and have standard procedures and scoring. (Module 29, p. 537)

STANDING PATTERN OF BEHAVIOR The norms and expectations associated with a particular setting. (Module 18, p. 333)

STANINE SCORES Type of standard score which converts raw scores to a single-digit system from 1 to 9. (Module 29, p. 545)

STEM An introductory statement or question that calls for a response (in a multiple-choice item). (Module 27, p. 500)

STEREOTYPE THREAT An unconscious, automatic activation of prior knowledge about a stereotype which hinders performance on cognitive tasks. (Module 22, p. 410)

STRATEGY KNOWLEDGE Knowledge about which strategies are available to aid in learning information and under what conditions or when it is best to use a particular strategy. (Module 12, p. 211)

STRUCTURED ENGLISH IMMERSION English-language learners learn subjects in English in classes separate from native-English speakers for typically one year, and teachers use materials and methods designed to accommodate students who are learning the language. Also called sheltered immersion. (Module 8, p. 140)

STUDENTS AT RISK A group of students considered to be at risk for not meeting standard achievement levels at school. (Module 30, p. 556)

STUDY-TIME ALLOCATION The amount and distribution of studying. (Module 12, p. 220)

SUBJECTIVE TESTING Any testing format where the scoring is open to interpretation. (Module 27, p. 497)

SUCCESS-ORIENTED STUDENTS Students who are intrinsically motivated, and define success in terms of becoming the best they can be, regardless of the achievements of others. (Module 17, p. 303)

SUMMATIVE ASSESSMENT A form of assessment that helps the teacher evaluate students' progress, as well as the effectiveness of instructional methods, at the end of a unit or grading period. (Module 26, p. 481; Module 28, 510)

SUSTAINING EXPECTATION EFFECT An effect whereby teachers sometimes fail to notice students' skill improvement, and therefore do not change their group placement, which inadvertently sustains students' achievement at their current level. (Module 21, p. 385)

SYMBOLIC MODELS Individuals who are observed indirectly through various forms of the media. (Module 10, p. 174)

SYNAPSE A gap between two neurons that allows transmission of messages. (Module 6, p. 104)

SYNAPTIC PRUNING Elimination of synapses. (Module 6, p. 109)

SYNAPTOGENESIS The growth of new connections in the brain, continues throughout life as individuals adapt to changing life conditions and experiences. (Module 6, p. 108)

SYNTAX The rules for combining components of language. (Module 8, p. 136)

SYSTEMATIC DESENSITIZATION A technique that combines relaxation training with gradual exposure to an anxiety-provoking stimulus to reduce anxieties and fears. (Module 25, p. 460)

SYSTEMATIC PHONICS INSTRUCTION A program that focuses on teaching children to recognize and manipulate phonemes and to then explicitly apply that knowledge to letter-sound correspondences and decoding. (Module 24, p. 442)

T

TABLE OF SPECIFICATIONS A test blueprint that is laid out in table format. (Module 27, p. 496)

TASK ANALYSIS Identification of the specific knowledge, behaviors, or cognitive processes necessary to master a particular skill. (Module 11, p. 195)

TASK KNOWLEDGE Knowledge about the difficulty or ease of a task. (Module 12, p. 211)

TASK-CONTINGENT REWARDS Rewards that are given for participating in an activity or for completing an activity without regard to performance level. (Module 15, p. 267)

TASK-SPECIFIC RUBRIC Assessment criteria that take a generic framework and modifies it to match specific learning goals of a particular task. (Module 28, p. 517)

TEACHER EFFICACY A teacher's belief that he or she has the capabilities to transmit knowledge and manage the classroom in order to teach all students effectively. (Module 10, p. 180; Module 17, p. 302)

TELEGRAPHIC SPEECH A way of ordering words according to the grammatical rules of one's language. (Module 8, p. 136)

TEMPERAMENT A pattern of responding to environmental stimuli and events that emerges early in life, is relatively enduring, and seems to have genetic origins. Temperament includes patterns of activity level, adaptability, persistence, adventurousness, shyness, inhibitedness, irritability, and distractibility. (Module 4, p. 62)

TERATOGENS Any foreign substances that can cause abnormalities in a developing fetus. (Module 6, p. 107)

TEST BIAS Systemic error in a test score that may or may not be a function of cultural variations. (Module 30, p. 559)

TEST BLUEPRINT An assessment planning tool that describes the content the test will cover and the way you expect students to demonstrate their understanding of that content. (Module 27, p. 496)

TEST FAIRNESS An ethical issue of how to use tests appropriately. (Module 30, p. 558)

TEST SCORE POLLUTION Occurs when test scores are systematically increased or decreased due to factors unrelated to what the test is intended to measure. (Module 30, p. 554)

TESTS AND SURVEYS Type of measure used in research which are typically paper-and-pencil and include a number of questions. (Module 1, p. 10)

THEORY Set of ideas used to explain a phenomenon and make prediction about behavior. (Module 1, p. 6)

THEORY OF IDENTICAL ELEMENTS A theory proposing that transfer between two learning tasks will occur if the tasks share common elements. (Module 13, p. 226)

THEORY OF MULTIPLE INTELLIGENCES A theory of intelligence proposed by Howard Gardner consisting of eight separate but interacting intelligences. (Module 22, p. 404)

THEORY OF MIND Early development of children's attempt to understand the mind and mental world. (Module 12, p. 212)

THEORY OF SUCCESSFUL INTELLIGENCE A theory proposed by Robert Sternberg in which success is defined as the ability to succeed in life and involves finding ways to effectively balance one's analytical, creative, and practical abilities. (Module 22, p. 404)

THEORY-BASED VALIDITY Type of validity evidence that demonstrates the test score is consistent with a theoretical aspect of the construct. (Module 29, p. 546)

THINKING DISPOSITION A cluster of thinking preferences, attitudes, and intentions, plus a set of capabilities that allow the preferences to become realized in a particular way. (Module 14, p. 240)

THREE-RING CONCEPTION OF GIFTEDNESS A theoretical model of giftedness which proposes that giftedness is comprised of three behaviors: above-average ability, high levels of task commitment, and high levels of creativity. (Module 23, p. 421)

TRANSFER The application of previously learned knowledge, skills, or strategies to new contexts. (Module 13, p. 226)

TRANSITIONAL BILINGUAL EDUCATION A method of bilingual instruction in which students learn subjects in their native language (as well as English-language instruction) while they are acquiring the second language. (Module 8, p. 140)

T-SCORE Type of standard score based on the units of standard deviation with a mean of 50 and standard deviation of 10. (Module 29, p. 545)

TWO-FACTOR THEORY OF INTELLIGENCE One of the first theories of intelligence which posited that performance on intelligence tests could be attributed to a general mental ability, g, and abilities in specific domains, s. See also other theories of intelligence: theory of multiple intelligences and theory of successful intelligence. (Module 22, p. 403)

TWO-WAY BILINGUAL IMMERSION A method of bilingual instruction in which students who speak English and students who speak a non-English language learn academic subjects in both languages. (Module 8, p. 140)

U

UNCONDITIONED RESPONSE The behavior that automatically occurs due to the unconditioned stimulus. (Module 9, p. 159)

UNCONDITIONED STIMULUS The behavior that evokes an automatic response. (Module 9, p. 159)

UNDEREXTENSIONS Limiting the use of a word to a subset of objects it refers to. (Module 8, p. 136)

UNINVOLVED PARENTING Lacks both control and responsiveness. (Module 2, p. 32)

USE IT OR LOSE IT PRINCIPLE The idea that practice strengthens neural connections, while infrequent use of certain skills may cause synaptic connections to weaken or degenerate. (Module 6, p. 109)

UTILITY VALUE A component of expectancy-value theory referring to the usefulness of a task for meeting short-term and long-term goals. (Module 16, p. 280)

V

VALIDITY The extent to which a test or assessment actually measures what it is intended to measure, so that meaningful interpretations can be derived from the test score. (Module 27, p. 493; Module 29, p. 545)

VALUE A component of expectancy-value theory referring to reasons for undertaking a task; "do I want to do this task?" See also expectancy. (Module 16, p. 279)

VARIABILITY Measure of how widely scores are distributed. (Module 29, p. 541)

VARIABLES The events, characteristics, or behaviors of interest in a research study. (Module 1, p. 7)

VERBAL MEDIATION A word or phrase that forms a logical connection or "bridge" between two pieces of information; used as a mnemonic. (Module 11, p. 188)

VICARIOUS PUNISHMENT Behaviors are displayed less frequently if a model has been punished for those behaviors. (Module 10, p. 177)

VICARIOUS REINFORCEMENT Behaviors are displayed more frequently if a model has been reinforced for those behaviors. (Module 10, p. 177)

VISUAL IMAGERY The process of forming mental pictures of objects or ideas. (Module 11, p. 188)

VISUAL PERSPECTIVE-TAKING Understanding that another person can see something in a different way or from a different view than themselves. (Module 12, p. 212)

VISUOSPATIAL SKETCHPAD Part of working memory. A holding system for visual and spatial information. (Module 11, p. 186)

VISUOSPATIAL SUBTYPE A subtype of mathematics disability that has not been widely investigated involving difficulties with the spatial representation of numerical information. (Module 24, p. 444)

VOLUNTEER BIAS The tendency for those who choose to participate in research studies to be different in some way from others who decline the invitation to participate. (Module 1, p. 10)

W

WAIT TIME The length of time a teacher pauses after posing a question to give students time to think before being called on to respond. (Module 11, p. 194; Module 14, p. 243)

WELL-DEFINED PROBLEM A problem in which a goal is clearly stated, all information needed to solve the problem is available, and only one correct answer exists. (Module 14, p. 245)

WERNICKE'S AREA Part of the left temporal lobe of the brain that surrounds the auditory cortex and is thought to be essential for understanding and formulating speech. Damage in Wernicke's area causes deficits in understanding spoken language. (Module 6, p. 112)

WITHIN-CLASS ABILITY GROUPING Forming groups of students in a self-contained classroom in which groups are of similar ability. (Module 21, p. 379)

WITHITNESS A teacher's ability to remain aware of and responsive to students' behaviors at all times. (Module 19, p. 353)

WORD RECOGNITION The act of identifying or recognizing individual words while reading. (Module 24, p. 441)

WORK-AVOIDANCE GOAL Motivation to avoid academic work and prefer easy tasks. (Module 16, p. 286)

WORKING-BACKWARD STRATEGY A heuristic in which you start with the final goal and think backward to identify the steps that would be needed to reach that goal. (Module 14, p. 247)

WORKING MEMORY A component of memory that holds and processes a limited amount of information; also known as short-term memory. The duration of information stored in working memory is probably about five to twenty seconds. (Module 11, p. 185)

Z

ZERO TRANSFER Occurs when previous learning has no effect on a new task. (Module 13, p. 226)

ZONE OF PROXIMAL DEVELOPMENT (ZPD) The difference between what an individual can accomplish independently and what he or she can learn with assistance from more capable individuals. (Module 7, p. 124)

Z-SCORE Standard score based on units of standard deviation ranging from −4.0 to +4.0. (Module 29, p. 544)

REFERENCES

A

Aarnoutse, C., & van Leeuwe, J. (1998). Relation between reading comprehension, vocabulary, reading pleasure, and reading frequency. *Educational Research and Evaluation, 4*(2), 143–166.

Aaron, P. G., Joshi, M., Gooden, R., & Bentum, K. (2008). Diagnosis and treatment of reading disabilities based on the component model of reading: An alternative to the discrepancy model of LD. *Journal of Learning Disabilities, 41*, 67–84.

Abbate-Vaughn, J., Frechon, O., & Wright, B. L. (2010). Accomplished urban teaching. *Theory Into Practice, 49*(3), 185–192.

Aber, J. L., Brown, J. L., & Jones, S. M. (2003). Developmental trajectories toward violence in middle childhood: Course, demographic differences, and response to school-based intervention. *Developmental Psychology, 39*, 324–348.

Abrahamsen, E., & Rigrodsky, S. (1984). Comprehension of complex sentences in children at three levels of cognitive development. *Journal of Psycholinguistic Research, 13*, 333–350.

Abrami, P. C., Bernard, R. M., Borokhovski, E., Wadem, A., Surkes, M. A., Tamim, R., & Zhang, D. (2008). Instructional interventions affecting critical thinking skills and dispositions: A stage 1 meta-analysis. *Review of Educational Research, 78*, 1102–1134.

Abramowitz, A. J., O'Leary, S. G., & Futtersak, M. W. (1988).The relative impact of long and short reprimands on children's off-task behavior in the classroom. *Behavior Therapy, 19*, 243–247.

Acee, T. W., Kim, H., Kim, H. J., Kim, J., Chu, H. R., Kim, M., Cho, Y., Wicker, F. W., & The Boredom Research Group. (2010). Academic boredom in under- and over-challenging situations. *Contemporary Educational Psychology, 35*, 17–27.

Achenbach, T. M. (1992). *Manual for the Child Behavior Checklist/2–3 and 1992 Profile*. Burlington, VT: Department of Psychiatry, University of Vermont.

Acker, M. M., & O'Leary, S. G. (1987). Effects of reprimands and praise on appropriate social behavior in the classroom. *Journal of Abnormal Child Psychology, 5*, 549–557.

Acton, H. M., & Zabartany, L. (1988). Interaction and performance within groups: Effects on handicapped and nonhandicapped students' attitudes toward their mildly mentally retarded peers. *American Journal of Mental Retardation, 93*, 16–23.

Adams, J. L. (2001). *Conceptual blockbusting* (3rd ed.). Cambridge, MA: Perseus.

Adams, L., Kasserman, J., Yearwood, A., Perfetto, G., Bransford, J., & Franks, J. (1988). The effects of facts versus problem-oriented acquisition. *Memory and Cognition, 16*, 167–175.

Adams, M. J. (1990). *Beginning to read: Thinking and learning about print*. Cambridge, MA: MIT Press.

Adams, R., & Biddle, B. (1970). *Realities of teaching*. New York: Holt, Rinehart, & Winston.

Adamson, L. B. (1996). *Communication development during infancy*. Boulder, CO: Westview Press.

Adey, P., & Shayer, M. (1993). An exploration of long-term far-transfer effects allowing an extended intervention program in the high school science curriculum. *Cognition and Instruction, 11*(1), 1–29.

Adler, P. A., & Adler, P. (1998). *Peer power: Preadolescent culture and identity*. New Brunswick, NJ: Rutgers University Press.

AERA. (1999). *Standards for educational and psychological testing*. Washington, DC: American Educational Research Association, American Psychological Association, National Council on Measurement in Education.

Aiken, E. G., Thomas, G. S., & Shennum, W. A. (1975). Memory for a lecture: Effects of notes, lecture rate and informational density. *Journal of Educational Psychology, 67*, 439–444.

Ainley, M., Hidi, S., & Berndorff, D. (2002). Interest, learning, and the psychological processes that mediate their relationship. *Journal of Educational Psychology, 94*, 545–561.

Airasian, P. (2005). *Classroom assessment* (5th ed.). New York: McGraw-Hill.

Akinbobola, A. O., & Afolabi, F. (2009). Constructivist practices through guided discovery approach: The effect on students' cognitive achievements in Nigerian senior secondary school physics. *Bulgarian Journal of Science & Education Policy, 3*(2), 233–252.

Akinsola, M. J., & Awofala, A. O. A. (2009). Effect of personalization of instruction on students' achievement and self-efficacy in mathematics word problems. *International Journal of Mathematical Education in Science & Technology, 40*(3), 389–404.

Albano, A. M., Chorpita, B. F., & Barlow, D. H. (2003). Childhood anxiety disorders. In E. J. Mash & R. A. Barkley (Eds.), *Child psychopathology* (2nd ed., pp. 279–329). New York: Guilford.

Albano, A. M., & Krain, A. (2005). Anxiety and anxiety disorders in girls. In D. J. Bell, S. L. Poster, & E. J. Mash (Eds.), *Handbook of behavioral and emotional problems in girls* (pp. 79–116). New York: Kluwer Academic/Plenum.

Alber, S. R., & Heward, W. L. (2000). Teaching students to recruit positive attention: A review and recommendations. *Journal of Behavioral Education, 10*, 177–204.

Albert, L. (1996). *Cooperative discipline*. Circle Pines, MN: American Guidance Service.

Alberto, P. A., & Troutman, A. C. (1999). *Applied behavior analysis for teachers* (5th ed.). Upper Saddle River, NJ: Prentice Hall.

Alberts, A., Elkind, D., & Ginsberg, S. (2007). The personal fable and risk-taking in early adolescence. *Journal of Youth and Adolescence, 36*(1), 71–76.

Alexander, P. A. (1996). The past, present, and future of knowledge research: A reexamination of the role of knowledge in learning and instruction. *Educational Psychologist, 31*, 89–92.

Alfassi, M., Weiss, I., & Lifshitz, H. (2009). The efficacy of reciprocal teaching in fostering the reading literacy of students with intellectual disabilities. *European Journal of Special Needs Education, 24*(3), 291–305.

Alferink, L. A., & Farmer-Dougan, V. (2010). Brain-(not) based education: Dangers of misunderstanding and misapplication of neuroscience research. *Exceptionality, 18*(1), 42–52.

Alfieri, L., Brooks, P. J., Aldrich, N. J., & Tennenbaum, H. R. (2011). Does discovery-based instruction enhance learning? *Journal of Educational Psychology, 103*(1), 1–18.

Algaze, B. (1995). Cognitive therapy, study counseling, and systematic desensitization in the treatment of test anxiety. In C. Spielberger & P. Vagg (Eds.), *Test anxiety: Theory, assessment, and treatment* (pp. 133–152). Washington, DC: Taylor & Francis.

Allen, B. A., & Boykin, A. W. (1992). African-American children and the educational process: Alleviating cultural discontinuity through prescriptive pedagogy. *School Psychology Review, 21*, 586–596.

Allington, R. L. (1980). Teacher interruption behaviors during primary-grade oral reading. *Journal of Educational Psychology, 72*, 371–374.

Allington, R. L. (1983). The reading instruction provided readers of differing reading abilities. *Elementary School Journal, 83*, 548–559.

Allington, R. L. (1984). Content coverage and contextual reading in reading groups. *Journal of Reading Behavior, 16*(2), 85–96.

Alvernini, F., Lucidi, F., & Manganelli, S. (2008). Assessment of academic motivation: A mixed methods study. *International Journal of Multiple Research Approaches, 2*(1), 71–82.

Amabile, T. M. (1983). *The social psychology of creativity.* New York: Springer-Verlag.

Amabile, T. M. (1996). *Creativity in context: Update to "The social psychology of creativity."* Boulder, CO: Westview Press.

Amabile, T. M., DeJong, W., & Lepper, M. (1976). Effects of externally imposed deadlines on intrinsic motivation. *Journal of Personality and Social Psychology, 34,* 92–98.

Amabile, T. M., & Hennessey, B. A. (1988). Story-telling: A method for assessing children's creativity. *Journal of Creative Behavior, 22,* 235–246.

Amato, P. R., & Cheadle, J. E. (2008). Parental divorce, marital conflict and children's behavior problems: A comparison of adopted and biological children. *Social Forces, 86*(3), 1139–1161.

Amato, P. R., & Keith, B. (1991). Parental divorce and the well-being of children: A meta-analysis. *Psychological Bulletin, 110*(1), 26–46.

American Association on Intellectual and Developmental Disabilities (AAIDD). (2002). *Mental retardation: Definition, classification, and systems of supports* (10th ed.). Washington, DC: American Association on Intellectual and Developmental Disabilities.

American Educational Research Association, American Psychological Association, & National Council on Measurement in Education. (1999). *Standards for educational and psychological testing.* Washington, DC: AERA.

American Philosophical Association. (1990). Critical thinking: A statement of expert consensus for purposes of educational assessment and instruction. *The Delphi Report,* Committee on Pre-College Philosophy. (ERIC Doc. No. ED 315 423).

American Psychiatric Association. (2000). *Diagnostic and statistical manual of mental disorders, text revision* (4th ed.). Washington, DC: American Psychiatric Association.

Ames, C., & Ames, R. (1990). Motivation and effective teaching. In L. Friedman (Ed.), *Good instruction: What teachers can do in the classroom.* North Central Regional Education Laboratory.

Ames, C., & Archer, J. (1988). Achievement goals in the classroom: Student learning strategies and motivation processes. *Journal of Educational Psychology, 80,* 260–267.

Ames, C. A. (1990). Motivation: What teachers need to know. *Teachers College Record, 91*(3), 409–421.

Ames, C. A. (1992). Classrooms: Goals, structures, and student motivation. *Journal of Educational Psychology, 84*(3), 261–271.

Ames, R., & Ames, C. (1984). Introduction. In R. Ames & C. Ames (Eds.), *Research on motivation in education.* New York: Academic Press.

Amspaugh, L. B. (1975). Teachers' perceptions of various characteristics of first-grade children and reading group placement (Doctoral dissertation, Ohio State University, 1974). *Dissertation Abstracts International, 35A,* 49–99.

Anastasi, A., & Urbina, S. (1997). *Psychological testing* (7th ed.). Upper Saddle River, NJ: Prentice Hall.

Anastopoulos, A. D., & Shelton, T. L. (2001). *Assessing attention-deficit/hyperactivity disorder.* New York: Kluwer Academic/Plenum.

Anderman, E. M., & Maehr, M. L. (1994). Motivation and schooling in the middle grades. *Review of Educational Research, 64*(2), 287–309.

Anderman, E. M., & Midgley, C. (1997). Changes in achievement goal orientations, perceived academic competence, and grades across the transition to middle-level schools. *Contemporary Educational Psychology, 22,* 269–298.

Anderman, E. M., & Young, A. J. (1994). Motivation and strategy use in science: Individual differences and classroom effects. *Journal of Research in Science Teaching, 31*(8), 811–831.

Anderman, L. H., & Anderman, E. M. (1999). Social predictors of changes in students' achievement goal orientations. *Contemporary Educational Psychology, 24,* 21–37.

Andersen, F. O. (2005). *International trends in primary school education: An overview based on case studies in Finland, Denmark and Japan.* Bilund, Denmark: Lego Learning Institute.

Andersen, S. M., Klatzky, R. L., & Murray, J. (1990). Traits and social stereotypes: Efficiency differences in social information processing. *Journal of Personality and Social Psychology, 59,* 192–201.

Anderson, C. W., & Smith, E. L. (1987). Teaching science. In V. Richardson-Koehler (Ed.), *Educator's handbook: A research perspective* (pp. 84–111). New York: Longman.

Anderson, J. R. (1982). Acquisition of cognitive skills. *Psychological Review, 89*(4), 369–406.

Anderson, J. R. (1990). *Cognitive psychology and its implications* (3rd ed.). New York: Freeman.

Anderson, J. R. (1995). *Learning and memory: An integrated approach.* New York: Wiley.

Anderson, J. R. (2005). *Cognitive psychology and its implications* (6th ed.). New York: Worth.

Anderson, J. R., & Bower, G. H. (1973). *Human associative memory.* Washington, DC: Winston.

Anderson, J. R., Corbett, A. T., Koedinger, K., & Pelletier, R. (1995). Cognitive tutors: Lessons learned. *Journal of the Learning Sciences, 4,* 167–207.

Anderson, J. S., Ferguson, M. A., Lopez-Larson, M., & Yurgelun-Todd, D. (2010). Topographic maps of multisensory attention. *Proceedings of the National Academy of Sciences, 2010;* DOI: 10.1073/pnas.1011616107

Anderson, L., Evertson, C., & Brophy, J. (1979). An experimental study of effective teaching in first-grade reading groups. *Elementary School Journal, 79,* 193–223.

Anderson, L., & Prawat, R. (1983). Responsibility in the classroom? A synthesis of research on teaching self-control. *Educational Leadership, 40*(7), 62–66.

Anderson, L. W., & Krathwohl, D. R. (Eds.). (2001). *A taxonomy for learning, teaching, and assessing: A revision of Bloom's Taxonomy of Educational Objectives.* New York: Longman.

Anderson, R. H., & Pavan, B. N. (1993). *Nongradedness: Helping it to happen.* Lancaster, PA: Technomic.

Andrade, H. L., Du, Y., & Wang, X. (2008). Putting rubrics to the test: The effect of a model, criteria generation, and rubric-referenced self-assessment on elementary school students' writing. *Educational Measurement: Issues & Practice, 27*(2), 3–13.

Andreano, J. M., & Cahill, L. (2009). Sex influences on the neurobiology of learning and memory. *Learning and Memory, 16,* 248–266.

Anglin, J. (1993). Vocabulary development: A morphological analysis. *Monographs of the Society for Research in Child Development, 58*(10), Serial No. 238.

Ansari, D., & Coch, D. (2006). Bridges over troubled waters: Education and cognitive neuroscience. *Trends in Cognitive Sciences, 10*(4), 146–151.

Anthony, L. G., Anthony, B. J., Glanville, D. N., Naiman, D. Q., Waanders, C., & Shaffer, S. (2005). The relationships between parenting stress, parenting behaviour, and preschoolers' social competence and behaviour problems in the classroom. *Infant and Child Development, 14*, 133–154.

Antshel, K. M., & Barkley, R. (2008). Psychosocial interventions in attention deficit hyperactivity disorder. *Child and Adolescent Psychiatric Clinics of North America, 17*(2), 421–437.

APA Zero Tolerance Task Force. (2006). *Are zero tolerance policies effective in the schools? An evidentiary review and recommendations* [Adopted by APA council of representatives]. Washington, DC: American Psychological Association.

Apple Classrooms of Tomorrow. (1995). *Changing the conversation about teaching, learning and technology: A report on 10 years of ACOT research.* Cupertino, CA: Apple Computer.

Archambault, F. X., Jr., Westberg, K. L., Brown, S. W., Hallmark, B. W., Emmons, C. L., & Zhang, W. (1993). *Regular classroom practices with gifted students: Results of a national survey of classroom teachers* (Research monograph 93102). Storrs, CT: National Research Center on the Gifted and Talented, University of Connecticut.

Argys, L. M., Rees, D. J., & Brewer, D. J. (1996). Detracking America's schools: Equity at zero cost? *Journal of Policy Analysis and Management, 15*(4), 623–645.

Armour-Thomas, E., Bruno, K., & Allen, B. A. (2006). Toward an understanding of higher-order thinking among minority students. *Psychology in the Schools, 29*(3), 273–280.

Aronson, E. (2000). *Nobody left to hate: Teaching compassion after Columbine.* New York: Worth.

Aronson, E., Blaney, N., Stephan, C., Sikes, J., & Snapp, M. (1978). *The jigsaw classroom.* Beverly Hills, CA: Sage.

Arter, J., & McTighe, J. (2001). *Scoring rubrics in the classroom.* Thousand Oaks, CA: Corwin Press.

Artiles, A. J., Trent, S. C., & Palmer, J. (2004). Culturally diverse students in special education: Legacies and prospects. In J. A. Banks & C. M. Banks (Eds.), *Handbook of research on multicultural education* (2nd ed., pp. 716–735). San Francisco: Jossey-Bass.

Ashcraft, M. H. (2006). *Cognition* (4th ed.). Upper Saddle River, NJ: Prentice Hall.

Ashman, A. (1998). Students with intellectual disabilities. In A. Ashman & J. Elkins (Eds.), *Educating children with special needs* (3rd ed.). Sydney: Prentice Hall.

Ashton, P., & Webb, R. (1986). *Making a difference: Teachers' sense of efficacy and student achievement.* New York: Longman.

Ashton, P. T. (1975). Cross-cultural Piagetian research: An experimental perspective. *Harvard Educational Review, 45*, 475–506.

Assor, A., Kaplan, H., Kanat-Maymon, Y., & Roth, G. (2005). Directly controlling teacher behaviors as predictors of poor motivation and engagement in girls and boys: The role of anger and anxiety. *Learning and Instruction, 15*, 397–413.

Assor, A., Kaplan, H., & Roth, G. (2002). Choice is good but relevance is excellent: Autonomy-enhancing and suppressing teacher behaviours in predicting students' engagement in school work. *British Journal of Educational Psychology, 72*, 261–278.

Atkeson, B. M., & Forehand, R. (1979). Home-based reinforcement programs to modify classroom behavior: A review and methodological evaluation. *Psychological Bulletin, 9*, 814–820.

Atkinson, R. C., & Shiffrin, R. M. (1968). Human memory: A proposed system and its control processes. In K. W. Spence & J. T. Spence (Eds.), *The psychology of learning and motivation: Advances in research and theory* (Vol. 2). San Diego, CA: Academic Press.

Atkinson, R. K., Derry, S. J., Renkl, A., & Wortham, D. (2000). Learning from examples: Instructional principles from the worked examples research. *Review of Educational Research, 70*, 181–214.

Attili, G., Vermigli, P., & Roazzi, A. (2010). Children's social competence, peer status, and the quality of mother-child and father-child relationships: A multidimensional scaling approach. *European Psychologist, 15*(1), 23–33.

Au, K. (1979). Using the experience-text-relationship method with minority children. *Reading Teacher, 32*(6), 677–679.

Au, T. K., Sidle, A. L., & Rollins, K. B. (1993). Developing an intuitive understanding of conservation and contamination: Invisible particles as a plausible mechanism. *Developmental Psychology, 29*, 286–299.

Ausubel, D. P. (1963). *The psychology of meaningful verbal learning.* New York: Grune & Stratton.

Ausubel, D. P. (2000). *The acquisition and retention of knowledge: A cognitive view.* Boston: Kluwer Academic.

Axtell, P. K., McCallum, R. S., & Bell, S. M. (2009). Developing math automaticity using a classwide fluency building procedure for middle school students: A preliminary study. *Psychology in the Schools, 46*(6), 526–538.

B

Backes, W., Vuurman, E., Wennekes, R., Spronk, P., Wuisman, M., Van Engelshoven, J., & Jolles, J. (2002). Atypical brain activation of reading processes in children with developmental dyslexia. *Journal of Child Neurology, 17*(12), 867–871.

Baddeley, A. (1999). *Essentials of human memory.* Philadelphia: Psychology Press.

Baddeley, A. (2000). Short-term and working memory. In E. Tulving & F. I. M. Craik (Eds.), *The Oxford handbook of memory.* New York: Oxford University Press.

Baddeley, A. D. (2001). Is working memory still working? *American Psychologist, 56*, 851–864.

Baddeley, A. D., & Hitch, G. J. (1974). Working memory. In G. A. Bower (Ed.), *The psychology of learning and motivation: Advances in research and theory, Vol. 8* (pp. 47–89). New York: Academic Press.

Baer, J., & Kaufman, J. C. (2006). Gender differences in creativity. *Journal of Creative Behavior, 42*, 75–106.

Bagwell, C. L., Coie, J. D., Terry, R. A., & Lochman, J. E. (2000). Peer clique participation and social status in preadolescence. *Merrill-Palmer Quarterly, 46*, 280–305.

Bahrick, H. P. (1984). Semantic memory content in permastore: Fifty years of memory for Spanish learned in school. *Journal of Experimental Psychology: General, 111*, 1–29.

Bahrick, H. P., Bahrick, P. O., & Wittlinger, R. P. (1975). Fifty years of memory for names and faces. *Journal of Experimental Psychology: General, 104*(1), 54–75.

Baillargeon, R. (1991). Reasoning about the height and location of a hidden object in 4.5- and 6.5-month-old infants. *Cognition, 38*, 13–42.

Baker, E. T., Wang, M. C., & Walberg, H. J. (1995). The effects of inclusion on learning. *Educational Leadership, 52*(4), 33–35.

Baker, J. A. (2006). Contributions of teacher-child relationships to positive school adjustment during elementary school. *Journal of School Psychology, 44*, 211–229.

Baker, L., & Wigfield, A. (1999). Dimensions of children's motivation for reading and their relations to reading activity and reading achievement. *Reading Research Quarterly, 34*, 452–477.

Bakker, A. B. (2005). Flow among music teachers and their students: The crossover of peak experiences. *Journal of Vocational Behavior, 66*, 26–44.

Baldie, B. (1976). The acquisition of the passive voice. *Journal of Child Language, 3,* 331–348.

Balfanz, R., Herzog, L., & MacIver, D. J. (2007). Preventing student disengagement and keeping students on the graduation path in urban middle-grades schools: Early identification and effective intervention. *Educational Psychologist, 42*(4), 223–235.

Balim, A. G. (2009). The effects of discovery learning on students' success and inquiry learning skills. *Eurasian Journal of Educational Research, 35,* 1–20.

Ball, A. F. (2002). Three decades of research on classroom life: Illuminating the classroom communicative lives of America's at-risk students. *Review of Research in Education, 26,* 71–111.

Ball, S. (1995). Anxiety and test performance. In C. Spielberger & P. Vagg (Eds.), *Test anxiety: Theory, assessment, and treatment* (pp. 107–113). Washington, DC: Taylor & Francis.

Baltes, P. (1987). Theoretical propositions of life-span developmental psychology: On the dynamics between growth and decline. *Developmental Psychology, 23,* 611–626.

Bandura, A. (1977). Self-efficacy: Toward a unifying theory of behavioral change. *Psychological Review, 84,* 191–215.

Bandura, A. (1982). Self-efficacy mechanism in human agency. *American Psychologist, 37,* 122–147.

Bandura, A. (1986). *Social foundations of thought and action: A social cognitive theory.* Englewood Cliffs, NJ: Prentice Hall.

Bandura, A. (1989). Social cognitive theory. *Annals of Child Development, 6,* 1–60.

Bandura, A. (1997). *Self-efficacy: The exercise of control.* New York: Freeman.

Bandura, A. (2000). Exercise of human agency through collective efficacy. *Current Directions in Psychological Science, 9,* 75–78.

Bandura, A. (2001). Social cognitive theory: An agentic perspective. *Annual Review of Psychology, 52,* 1–26.

Bandura, A. (2002). Social cognitive theory in cultural context. *Applied Psychology: An International Review, 51,* 269–290.

Bandura, A., & Locke, E. (2003). Negative self-efficacy and goal effects revisited. *Journal of Applied Psychology, 88,* 87–99.

Bandura, A., Ross, D., & Ross, S. (1961). Transmission of aggression through imitation of aggressive models. *Journal of Abnormal and Social Psychology, 63,* 575–582.

Bandura, A., & Schunk, D. H. (1981). Cultivating competence, self-efficacy, and intrinsic interest through proximal self-motivation. *Journal of Personality and Social Psychology, 41,* 586–598.

Banks, J. A. (2006). *Cultural diversity and education: Foundations, curriculum, and teaching* (5th ed.). Boston: Pearson Education.

Banks, J. A., & Banks, C. A. M. (1995). *Handbook of research on multicultural education.* New York: Macmillan.

Banks, S. A. (2005). *Classroom assessment: Issues and practices.* Boston: Allyn & Bacon.

Barker, G., & Graham, S. (1987). Developmental study of praise and blame as attributional cues. *Journal of Educational Psychology, 79,* 62–66.

Barker, R. (1968). *Ecological psychology: Concepts and methods for studying the environment of human behavior.* Palo Alto, CA: Stanford University Press.

Barker, R. (1971). *Midwest and its children: The psychological ecology of an American town.* Hamden, CT: Archon Books.

Barker, R. G., & Wright, H. F. (1949). Psychological ecology and the problem of psychosocial development. *Child Development, 20*(3), 131–143.

Barkley, R. A. (1990). *Attention-deficit hyperactivity disorder: A handbook for diagnosis and treatment.* New York: Guilford.

Barkley, R. A. (1997). Behavioral inhibition, sustained attention, and executive functions: Constructing a unifying theory of ADHD. *Psychological Bulletin, 121*(1), 65–94.

Barkley, R. A. (2003). Attention-deficit/hyperactivity disorder. In E. J. Mash & R. A. Barkley (Eds.), *Child psychopathology* (2nd ed., pp. 75–143). New York: Guilford.

Barkley, R. A. (2007). School interventions for attention deficit hyperactivity disorder: Where to from here? *School Psychology Review, 36*(2), 279–286.

Barkley, R. A., Shelton, T. L., Crosswait, C., et al. (2000). Multimethod psycho-educational intervention for preschool children with disruptive behavior: Preliminary results at post-treatment. *Journal of Child Psychology and Psychiatry, 41,* 319–332.

Barnea, N., & Dori, Y. J. (1999). High school chemistry students' performance and gender differences in a computerized molecular modeling environment. *Journal of Science Education and Technology, 8*(4), 257–271.

Barnes, P. (1995). *Personal, social, and emotional development of children.* Oxford: Blackwell.

Barnett, M. S., & Ceci, S. J. (2002). When and where do we apply what we learn? A taxonomy for far transfer. *Psychological Bulletin, 128*(4), 612–637.

Barnett, W. S. (2004). Does Head Start have lasting cognitive effects? The myth of fade-out. In E. Zigler & S. J. Styfco (Eds.), *The Head Start debates* (pp. 221–249). Baltimore: Paul H. Brookes.

Barnett, W. S., Yarosz, D. J., Thomas, J., Jung, K., & Blanco, D. (2007). Two-way monolingual English immersion in pre-school education: An experimental comparison. *Early Childhood Research Quarterly, 22*(3), 277–293.

Baron, J., Bazerman, M. H., & Shonk, K. (2006). Enlarging the societal pie through wise legislation: A psychological perspective. *Perspectives on Psychological Science, 1,* 23–132.

Barone, F. J. (1997). Bullying in school: It doesn't have to happen. *Phi Delta Kappan, 79,* 80–82.

Barr, R. (1995). What research says about grouping in the past and present and what it suggests about the future. In M. Radencich & L. McKay (Eds.), *Flexible grouping for literacy in the elementary grades* (pp. 1–24). Needham Heights, MA: Allyn & Bacon.

Barr, R., & Dreeben, R. (1983). *How schools work.* Chicago: University of Chicago Press.

Barrett, S., & Heubeck, B. G. (2000). Relationships between school hassles and uplifts and anxiety and conduct problems in grades 3 and 4. *Journal of Applied Developmental Psychology, 21,* 537–554.

Barron, B. J. S., Schwartz, D. L., Vye, N. J., et al. (1998). Doing with understanding: Lessons from research on problem- and project-based learning. *Journal of the Learning Sciences, 7,* 271–311.

Barron, K. E., & Harackiewicz, J. M. (2000). Achievement goals and optimal motivation: A multiple goals approach. In C. Sansone & J. M. Harackiewicz (Eds.), *Intrinsic and extrinsic motivation: The search for optimal motivation and performance* (pp. 229–254). San Diego, CA: Academic Press.

Barros, R. M., Silver, E. J., & Stein, R. E. K. (2009). School recess and group classroom behavior. *Pediatrics, 123*(2), 431–436.

Barth, A. E., Stuebing, K. K., Anthony, J. L., Denton, C. A., Mathes, P. G., Fletcher, J. M., & Francis, D. J. (2008). Agreement among response to intervention criteria for identifying responder status. *Learning and Individual Differences, 18,* 296–307.

Bascoe, S. M., Davies, P. T., Cummings, E. M., & Sturge-Apple, M. L. (2009). Children's representations of family relationships, peer information processing, and school adjustment. *Developmental Psychology, 45*(6), 1740–1751.

Basom, M. R., & Frase, L. (2004). Creating optimal work environments: Exploring teacher flow experiences. *Mentoring and Tutoring, 12,* 241–258.

Basow, S. A., & Rubin, L. R. (1999). Gender influences on adolescent development. In N. G. Johnson, M. C. Roberts, & J. Worell (Eds.), *Beyond appearance: A new look at adolescent girls* (pp. 25–52). Washington, DC: American Psychological Association.

Battistich, V., Solomon, D., Kim, D., Watson, M., & Schaps, E. (1995). Schools as communities, poverty levels of student populations, and students' attitudes, motives, and performance: A multi-level analysis. *American Educational Research Journal, 32,* 627–658.

Battistich, V., Solomon, D., Watson, M., & Schaps, E. (1997). Caring school communities. *Educational Psychologist, 32,* 137–151.

Bauer, D. J., Goldfield, B. A., & Reznick, J. S. (2002). Alternative approaches to analyzing individual differences in the rate of early vocabulary development. *Applied Psycholinguistics, 23,* 313–335.

Bauer, E. B., & Manyak, P. C. (2008). Creating language-rich instruction for English-language learners. *The Reading Teacher, 62*(2), 176–178.

Baum, S. M., Renzulli, J. S., & Hebert, T. P. (1995). Reversing underachievement: Creative productivity as a systematic intervention. *Gifted Child Quarterly, 39*(4), 224–235.

Baumann, J. F., Hoffman, J. V., Duffy-Hester, A. M., & Moon Ro, J. (2000). The first R yesterday and today: U.S. elementary reading instruction practices reported by teachers and administrators. *Reading Research Quarterly, 35,* 338–377.

Baumrind, D. (1966). Effects of authoritative parental control on child behavior. *Child Development, 37,* 887–907.

Beal, C. R., & Fleisig, W. E. (1987, April). Preschoolers' preparation for retrieval of object relocation tasks. Paper presented at the biennial meeting of the Society for Research in Child Development, Baltimore, MD.

Beaman, R., & Wheldall, K. (2000). Teachers' use of approval and disapproval in the classroom. *Educational Psychology, 20,* 431–446.

Bear, G. G. (with A. Cavalier & M. Manning). (2005). *Developing self-discipline and preventing and correcting misbehavior.* Boston: Allyn & Bacon.

Bear, G. G. (2009). The positive in positive models of discipline. In R. Gilman, E. S. Huebner, & M. Furlong (Eds.), *Handbook of positive psychology in schools* (pp. 305–321). New York: Routledge.

Beard, J. (2003). Iron deficiency alters brain development and functioning. *Journal of Nutrition, 133,* 1468–1472.

Bearison, D. J. (1982). New directions in studies of social interactions and cognitive growth. In F. C. Sarafiea (Ed.), *Social-cognitive development in context* (pp. 199–221). New York: Guilford.

Beck, I. L., & McKeown, M. G. (2001). Inviting students into the pursuit of meaning. *Educational Psychology Review, 13*(3), 225–241.

Becker, J. B., & Hu, M. (2008). Sex differences in drug abuse. *Frontiers in Neuroendocrinology, 29,* 36–47.

Becker, W. C., Madsen, C. H., Arnold, C. R., & Thomas, D. R. (1967). The contingent use of teacher attention and praise in reducing classroom behavior problems. *Journal of Special Education, 1,* 287–307.

Beery, R. G. (1975). Fear of failure in the student experience. *Personnel Guidance Journal, 54,* 190–203.

Begley, S. (2007). *Train your mind, change your brain: How a new science reveals our extraordinary potential to transform ourselves.* New York: Ballantine Books.

Beilock, S. L., Gunderson, E. A., Ramirez, G., & Levine, S. C. (2010). Female teachers' math anxiety affects girls' math achievement. *PNAS Proceedings of the National Academy of Sciences of the United States of America, 107*(5), 1860–1863.

Bell, P. A., Fisher, J. D., Baum, A., & Greene, T. C. (1990). *Environmental psychology* (3rd ed.). New York: Holt, Rinehart, & Winston.

Belsky, J., Vandell, D. L., Burchinal, M., Clarke-Stewart, K. A., McCartney, K., & Owen, M. T. (2007). Are there long-term effects of early child care? *Child Development, 78,* 681–701.

Bem, S. L. (1974). The measurement of psychological androgyny. *Journal of Consulting and Clinical Psychology, 42,* 115–162.

Bem, S. L. (1975). Sex role adaptability: One consequence of psychological androgyny. *Journal of Personality and Social Psychology, 31,* 634–643.

Bender, W. N., & Shores, C. (2007). *Response to intervention: A practical guide for every teacher.* Thousand Oaks, CA: Corwin Press.

Benedict, H. (1979). Early lexical development: Comprehension and production. *Journal of Child Language, 6,* 183–200.

Benner, S. M. (1998). *Special education issues in the context of American society.* Belmont, CA: Wadsworth.

Bereiter, C. (1995). A dispositional view of transfer. In A. McKeough, J. Lupart, & A. Marini (Eds.), *Teaching for transfer: Fostering generalization in learning* (pp. 21–34). Mahwah, NJ: Erlbaum.

Bereiter, C. (1997). Situated cognition and how I overcome it. In D. Kirshner & J. A. Whitson (Eds.), *Situated cognition: Social, semiotic, and psychological perspectives* (pp. 281–300). Mahwah, NJ: Erlbaum.

Bereiter, C., & Scardamalia, M. (1987). *The psychology of written composition.* Hillsdale, NJ: Erlbaum.

Berger, A., Kofman, O., Livneh, U., & Flenik, A. (2007). Multidisciplinary perspectives on attention and the development of self-regulation. *Progress in Neurobiology, 82*(5), 256–286.

Bergin, D. A. (1999). Influences on classroom interest. *Educational Psychologist, 34,* 87–98.

Berk, L. E. (2006). *Child development* (7th ed.). Boston, MA: Allyn & Bacon.

Berkeley, S., Bender, W. N., Peaster, L. G., & Saunders, L. (2009). Implementation of response to intervention: A snapshot of progress. *Journal of Learning Disabilities, 42*(1), 86–95.

Berko Gleason, J., Hay, D., & Cain, L. (1988). Social and affective determinants of language acquisition. In M. L. Rice & R. L. Schiefelbusch (Eds.), *The teachability of language* (pp. 171–186). Baltimore: Brookes.

Berkowitz, M. W., & Bier, M. C. (2007). What works in character education. *Journal of Research in Character Education, 5*(1), 29–48.

Berkowitz, M. W., & Grych, J. H. (1998). Fostering goodness: Teaching parents to facilitate children's moral development. *Journal of Moral Education, 27,* 371–391.

Berkowitz, M. W., & Hoppe, M. A. (2009). Character education and gifted children. *High Ability Studies, 20*(2), 131–142.

Berkowitz, M. W., Sherblom, S. A., Bier, M. C., & Battistich, V. (2006). Educating for positive youth development. In M. Killen & J. Smetana (Eds.), *Handbook of moral development.* Mahwah, NJ: Erlbaum.

Berlin, D., & White, A. (1986). Computer simulations and the transition from concrete manipulation of objects to abstract thinking in elementary school mathematics. *School Science and Mathematics, 86*(6), 468–479.

Berliner, D. C. (1988, February). *The development of expertise in pedagogy.* Paper presented at the American Association of Colleges for Teacher Education. New Orleans, LA.

Berninger, V. W., Mizokawa, D. T., & Bragg, R. (1991). Theory-based diagnosis and remediation of writing disabilities. *Journal of School Psychology, 29,* 57–79.

Bernstein, D. (1989). Language development: The school-age years. In D. Bernstein & E. Tiegerman (Eds.), *Language and communication disorders in children* (2nd ed., pp. 127–154). Upper Saddle River, NJ: Merrill/Prentice Hall.

Berry, D., & O'Connor, E. (2009). Behavioral risk, teacher–child relationships, and social skill development across middle childhood: A child-by-environment analysis of change. *Journal of Applied Developmental Psychology, 31*(1), 1–14.

Berryman, L., & Russell, D. R. (2001). Portfolios across the curriculum: Whole school assessment in Kentucky. *English Journal, 90,* 76–83.

Betancourt, H., & López, S. R. (1993). The study of culture, ethnicity, and race in American psychology. *American Psychologist, 48,* 629–637.

Betoret, F. D. (2006). Stressors, self-efficacy, coping resources, and burnout among secondary school teachers in Spain. *Educational Psychology, 26,* 519–539.

Beyreli, L., & Ari, G. (2009). The use of analytic rubric in the assessment of writing performance—inter-rater concordance study. *Educational Sciences: Theory & Practice, 9*(1), 105–125.

Bhatnagar, J. K. (1980). Linguistic behavior and adjustment of immigrant children in French and English schools in Montreal. *International Review of Applied Psychology, 2,* 141–158.

Bialystok, E. (2001). *Bilingualism in development: Language, literacy, and cognition.* Cambridge, UK: Cambridge University Press.

Biemiller, A. (1977/1978). Relationships between oral reading rates for letters, words, and simple text in the development of reading achievement. *Reading Research Quarterly, 13*(2), 223–253.

Bigge, M. L., & Shermis, S. S. (1999). *Learning theories for teachers.* New York: Longman.

Bing, N. M., Nelson, W. M., III, & Wesolowski, K. L. (2009). Comparing the effects of amount of conflict on children's adjustment following parental divorce. *Journal of Divorce and Remarriage, 50*(3), 159–171.

Birch, S. H., & Ladd, G. W. (1997). The teacher-child relationship and early school adjustment. *Journal of School Psychology, 55*(1), 61–79.

Birch, S. H., & Ladd, G. W. (1998). Children's interpersonal behaviors and the teacher-child relationship. *Developmental Psychology, 34*(5), 934–946.

Bird, S. (2010). Effects of distributed practice on the acquisition of second-language English syntax. *Applied Psycholinguistics, 31,* 635–650.

Bishop, D. (1997). *Uncommon understanding: Development and disorders of language comprehension in children.* Hove, East Sussex, UK: Psychology Press.

Bitan, T., Lifshitz, A., Breznitz, Z., & Booth, J. R. (2010). Bidirectional connectivity between hemispheres occurs at multiple levels in language processing but depends on sex. *Journal of Neuroscience, 30*(35), 11576–11585.

Bitter, G. G., & Legacy, J. M. (2006). *Using technology in the classroom* (Brief version). Boston: Allyn & Bacon.

Bjorklund, D. F. (1995). *Children's thinking: Developmental function and individual differences* (2nd ed.). Pacific Grove, CA: Brooks/Cole.

Bjorklund, D. F., & Harnishfeger, K. K. (1987). Developmental differences in the mental effort requirements for the use of an organizational strategy in free recall. *Journal of Experimental Child Psychology, 44,* 109–125.

Bjorklund, D. F., & Pellegrini, A. D. (2000). Child development and evolutionary psychology. *Child Development, 71,* 1687–1708.

Black, P., & Wiliam, D. (1998). Assessment and classroom learning. *Assessment in Education, 5,* 7–74.

Blackwell, L. S., Trzesniewski, K., & Dweck, C. S. (2007). Implicit theories of intelligence predict achievement across an adolescent transition: A longitudinal study and an intervention. *Child Development, 78,* 246–263.

Blakemore, S. J., & Firth, U. (2005). *The learning brain: Lessons for education.* Malden, MA: Blackwell.

Blanchett, W. (2006). Disproportionate representation of African American students in special education: Acknowledging the role of White privilege and racism. *Educational Researcher, 35*(6), 24–28.

Bleeker, M. M., & Jacobs, J. E. (2004). Achievement in math and science: Do mothers' beliefs matter 12 years later? *Journal of Educational Psychology, 96*(1), 97–109.

Bloom, B. S. (1971). Mastery learning. In J. H. Block (Ed.), *Mastery learning: Theory and practice.* New York: Holt, Rinehart, & Winston.

Bloom, B. S., Englehart, M. D., Frost, E. J., Hill, W. H., & Krathwohl, D. R. (1956). *Taxonomy of educational objectives.* New York: David McKay.

Blumenfeld, P., Hamilton, V., Bossert, S., Wessels, K., & Meece, J. (1983). Teacher talk and student thought: Socialization into the student role. In J. M. Levine & M. C. Wang (Eds.), *Teacher and student perceptions: Implications for learning* (pp. 143–192). Hillsdale, NJ: Erlbaum.

Blumenfeld, P., Pintrich, P., & Hamilton, V. (1986). Children's concepts of ability, effort, and conduct. *American Educational Research Journal, 23,* 95–104.

Blumenfeld, P., Pintrich, P., Meece, J., & Wessels, K. (1982). The formation and role of self-perceptions of ability in elementary classrooms. *Elementary School Journal, 82,* 401–420.

Bodrova, E., & Leong, D. (1997). *Tools of the mind: The Vygotskian approach to early childhood education.* New Jersey: Prentice-Hall.

Boekaerts, M. (1995). Self-regulated learning: Bridging the gap between metacognitive and metamotivational theories. *Educational Psychologist, 30*(4), 195–200.

Boekaerts, M. (2009). Goal-directed behavior in the classroom. In K. R. Wentzel & A. Wigfield (Eds.), *Handbook of motivation at school.* New York: Taylor & Francis.

Bohn, C. M., Roehrig, A. D., & Pressley, M. (2004). The first days of school in the classrooms of two more effective and four less effective primary-grades teachers. *Elementary School Journal, 104*(4), 269–287.

Bong, M. (2009). Age-related differences in achievement goal differentiation. *Journal of Educational Psychology, 101,* 879–896.

Bong, M., & Skaalvik, E. M. (2003). Academic self-concept and self-efficacy: How different are they really? *Educational Psychology Review, 15,* 1–40.

Bonner, F. A., II. (2000). African American giftedness. *Journal of Black Studies, 30*(5), 643–663.

Boom, J., Brugman, D., & van der Heijden, P. G. M. (2001). Hierarchical structure of moral stages assessed by a sorting task. *Child Development, 72,* 535–548.

Boon, H. J. (2007). Low- and high-achieving Australian secondary school students: Their parenting, motivations, and academic achievement. *Australian Psychologist, 42*(3), 212–225.

Boothroyd, R. A., McMorris, R. F., & Pruzek, R. (1992, April). *What do teachers know about testing and how did they find out?* Paper presented at the annual meeting of the National Council on Measurement in Education, San Francisco, CA.

Borko, H., & Shavelson, R. J. (1990). Teach decision making. In B. F. Jones & L. Idol (Eds.), *Dimensions of thinking and cognitive instruction* (pp. 311–346). Hillsdale, NJ: Erlbaum.

Borland, J. H., & Wright, L. (1994). Identifying young, potentially gifted economically disadvantaged students. *Gifted Child Quarterly, 38,* 164–171.

Borman, G. D., & Dowling, M. (2010). Schools and inequality: A multilevel analysis of Coleman's equality of educational opportunity data. *Teacher College Record, 112*(5), 1201–1246.

Bornholt, L. J. (2005). Aspects of self-knowledge about activities: An integrated model of self–concepts. *European Journal of Psychological Assessment, 21*(3), 156–164.

Bornholt, L. J., & Wilson, R. (2007). A general mediated model of aspects of self-knowledge (M-ASK): Children's participation in learning activities across social contexts. *Applied Psychology: An International Review, 56*(2), 302–318.

Botvin, G. J., Griffin, K. W., Nichols, T. R. (2006). Preventing youth violence and delinquency through a universal school-based prevention approach. *Prevention Science, 7,* 403–408.

Bouffard-Bouchard, T., Parent, S., & Larivee, S. (1991). Influence of self-efficacy on self-regulation and performance among junior and senior high-school age students. *International Journal of Behavioral Development, 14,* 153–164.

Bowlby, J. (1969). *Attachment and loss: Vol. 1. Attachment.* New York: Basic Books.

Bowlby, J. (1973). *Attachment and loss: Vol. 2. Separation.* New York: Basic Books.

Bower, G. (1969). Hierarchical retrieval schemes in recall of categorized word lists. *Journal of Verbal Learning and Verbal Behavior, 8*(3), 323–343.

Bowman, L. G., Piazza, C. C., Fisher, W. W., Hagopian, L. P., & Kogan, J. S. (1997). Assessment of preference for varied versus constant reinforcers. *Journal of Applied Behavior Analysis, 30,* 451–458.

Braaksma, M. A. H., Rijlaarsdam, G., van den Bergh, H., & van Hout-Wolters, B. H. A. M. (2004). Observational learning and its effects on the orchestration of writing processes. *Cognition and Instruction, 22,* 1–36.

Bradley, R., Danielson, L., & Doolittle, J. (2005). Response to intervention: 1997. *Journal of Learning Disabilities, 38,* 8–13.

Bradley, R. H., & Caldwell, B. M. (1984). 174 children: A study of the relationship between home environment and cognitive development during the first five years. In A. W. Gottfried (Ed.), *Home environment and early cognitive development: Longitudinal research* (pp. 5–56). San Diego, CA: Academic Press.

Bradshaw, C. P., Rodgers, C. R. R., Ghandour, L. A., & Garbarino, J. (2009). Social-cognitive mediators of the association between community violence exposure and aggressive behavior. *School Psychology Quarterly, 24*(3), 199–210.

Brainerd, C. J. (1978). Learning research and Piagetian theory. In L. S. Siegel and C. J. Brainerd (Eds.), *Alternatives to Piaget: Critical essays on the theory* (pp. 69–109). New York: Academic Press.

Brainerd, C. J. (2003). Jean Piaget, learning research, and American education. In B. J. Zimmerman & D. H. Schunk (Eds.), *Educational psychology: A century of contributions.* Mahwah, NJ: Erlbaum.

Bramen, J. E., Hranilovich, J. A., Dahl, R. E., Forbes, E. E., Chen, J., Toga, A. R., Dinov, I. D., Worthman, C. M., & Sowell, E. R. (2010). Puberty influences medial temporal lobe and cortical gray matter maturation differently in boys than girls matched for sexual maturity. *Cerebral Cortex.* doi: 10.1093/cercor/bhq137 First published online August 16, 2010.

Bransford, J., Hasselbring, T., Barron, B., Kulweicz, S., Littlefield, J., & Goin, L. (1988). Uses of macro-contexts to facilitate mathematical thinking. In R. I. Charles & E. A. Silver (Eds.), *The teaching and assessing of mathematical problem solving.* Hillsdale, NJ: Erlbaum.

Bransford, J. D., & Schwartz, D. L. (1999). Rethinking transfer: A simple proposal with multiple implications. In A. Iran-Nejad & P. D. Pearson (Eds.), *Review of research in education* (pp. 61–100). Washington, DC: American Educational Research Association.

Bransford, J. D., & Stein, B. S. (1993). *The IDEAL problem solver: A guide for improving thinking, learning, and creativity* (2nd ed.). New York: Freeman.

Bransford, J. D., Zech, L., Schwartz, D. L., Barron, B. J., Vye, N., & Cognition and Technology Group. (2000). Design environments that invite and sustain mathematical thinking. In P. Cobb (Ed.), *Symbolizing and communicating in mathematics classrooms* (pp. 275–324). Mahwah, NJ: Erlbaum.

Braun, H., Chapman, L., & Vezzu, S. (2010). The black-white achievement gap revisited. *Educational Policy Analysis archives, 18*(21), http://epaa.asu.edu/ojs/article/view/772.

Bredekamp, S., & Rosegrant, T. (1994). Learning and teaching with technology. In J. L. Wright & D. D. Shade (Eds.), *Young children: Active learners in a technological age* (pp. 53–61). Washington, DC: National Association for the Education of Young Children.

Brener, N. D., Simon, T. R., Krug, E. G., & Lowry, R. (1999). Recent trends in violence-related behaviors among high school students in the United States. *Journal of the American Medical Association, 282,* 440–446.

Bretherton, I., & Beeghly, M. (1982). Talking about internal states: The acquisition of an explicit theory of mind. *Developmental Psychology, 18,* 906–921.

Bretherton, I., Fritz, J., Zahn-Waxler, C., & Ridgeway, D. (1986). Learning to talk about emotions: A functionalist perspective. *Child Development, 57,* 529–548.

Briesch, A. M., & Chafouleas, S. M. (2009). Review and analysis of literature on self-management interventions to promote appropriate classroom behaviors (1988–2008). *School Psychology Quarterly, 24*(2), 106–118.

Brisk, M. E. (1991). Toward multilingual and multicultural mainstream education. *Journal of Education, 173*(2), 114–129.

Britner, S. L., & Pajares, F. (2006). Sources of science self-efficacy beliefs of middle school students. *Journal for Research in Science Teaching, 43,* 485–499.

Britten, J. S., & Cassidy, J. C. (2006). The technology integration assessment instrument: Understanding planned use of technology by classroom teachers. *Computers in Schools, 22*(3–4), 49–61.

Broadbent, D. E. (1958). *Perception and communication.* London: Pergamon Press.

Broadhead, M. A., Hockaday, A., Zahra, M., Francis, P. J., & Crichton, C. (2009). Scallywags—an evaluation of a service targeting conduct disorders at school and at home. *Educational Psychology in Practice, 2*(2), 167–179.

Brockner, J., & Vasta, R. (1981). Do causal attributions mediate the effects of extrinsic rewards on intrinsic interest? *Journal of Research in Personality, 15,* 201–209.

Brody, L. R. (1999). *Gender, emotion, and the family.* Cambridge, MA: Harvard University Press.

Brody, L. R., & Hall, J. A. (2008). Gender and emotion in context. In M. Lewis, J. M. Haviland-Jones, & L. F. Barrett (Eds.), *Handbook of emotions* (3rd ed., pp. 395–408). New York: Guilford Press.

Bronfenbrenner, U. (1994). Ecological models of human development. *International Encyclopedia of Education, 3*, 1643–1647.

Bronfenbrenner, U. (2005). *Making human beings human: Bioecological perspectives on human development.* Thousand Oaks, CA: Sage.

Bronstein, P., Fox, B. J., Kamon, J. L., & Knolls, M. L. (2007). Parenting and gender as predictors of moral courage in late adolescence: A longitudinal study. *Sex Roles, 56*, 661–674.

Brookhart, S. M. (2003). Developing measurement theory for classroom assessment purposes and educational uses. *Educational Measurement Issues and Practice, 22*(4), 5–12.

Brooks, L. W., & Dansereau, D. F. (1987). Transfer of information: An instructional perspective. In S. M. Cormier & J. D. Hagman (Eds.), *Transfer of learning: Contemporary research and applications* (pp. 121–150). New York: Academic Press.

Brooks-Gunn, J., Han, W. J., & Waldfogel, J. (2002). Maternal employment and child cognitive outcomes in the first three years of life: The NICHD study of early child care. *Child Development, 73*, 1052–1072.

Brophy, J. (1981). Teacher praise: A functional analysis. *Review of Educational Research, 51*(1), 5–32.

Brophy, J. (1999). Toward a model of the value aspects of motivation in education: Developing appreciation for particular learning domains and activities. *Educational Psychologist, 34*, 75–85.

Brophy, J. (2006). History of research on classroom management. In C. M. Evertson & C. S. Weinstein (Eds.), *Handbook of classroom management* (pp. 3–43). Mahwah, NJ: Erlbaum.

Brophy, J. (2008). Developing students' appreciation for what is taught in school. *Educational Psychologist, 43*(3), 132–141.

Brophy, J. E., & Evertson, C. (1976). *Learning from teaching: A developmental perspective.* Boston: Allyn & Bacon.

Brophy, J., & Evertson, C. (1978). Context variables in teaching. *Educational Psychologist, 12*, 310–316.

Brophy, J., & Good, T. (1974). *Teacher–student relationships: Causes and consequences.* New York: Holt, Rinehart, & Winston.

Brown, A. (1987). Metacognition, executive control, self-regulation and other more mysterious mechanisms. In F. E. Weinert & R. H. Kluwe (Eds.), *Metacognition, motivation, and understanding* (pp. 65–116). Hilldale, NJ: Erlbaum.

Brown, A. L., Bransford, J. D., Ferrara, R. A., & Campione, J. C. (1983). Learning, remembering, and understanding. In J. H. Flavell & E. M. Markman, *Handbook of child psychology: Vol. III, Cognitive development* (pp.77–166). New York: Wiley.

Brown, A. L., Campione, J. C., Webber, L. S., & McGilly, K. (1992). Interactive learning environments: A new look at assessment and instruction. In B. R. Gifford & M. C. O'Connor (Eds.), *Changing assessments: Alternative views of aptitude, achievement, and instruction* (pp. 37–75). Boston: Kluwer Academic.

Brown, A. L., Day, J. D., & Jones R. S. (1983). The development plans for summarizing texts. *Child Development, 54*, 968–979.

Brown, A. L., & Ferrara, R. A. (1985). Diagnosing zones of proximal development. In J. V. Wertsch (Ed.), *Culture, communication, and cognition: Vygotskian perspectives* (pp. 273–305). New York: Cambridge University Press.

Brown, A. L., & Kane, M. J. (1988). Preschool children can learn to transfer: Learning to learn and learning from example. *Cognitive Psychology, 20*, 493–523.

Brown, A. L., & Palincsar, A. S. (1987). Reciprocal teaching of comprehension strategies: A natural history of one program for enhancing learning. In J. D. Day & J. Borkowski (Eds.), *Intelligence and exceptionality: New directions for theory, assessment and instructional practice* (pp. 81–132). Norwood, NJ: Ablex.

Brown, A. L., & Palincsar, A. S. (1989). Guided, cooperative learning and individual knowledge acquisition. In L. B. Resnick (Ed.), *Knowing, learning, and instruction: Essays in honor of Robert Glaser* (pp. 393–451). Hillsdale, NJ: Erlbaum.

Brown, B. B. (1990). Peer groups and peer cultures. In S. S. Feldman & F. R. Elliot (Eds.), *At the threshold: The developing adolescent.* Cambridge, MA: Harvard University Press.

Brown, B. B. (2004). Adolescents' relationships with peers. In R. M. Lerner & L. Steinberg (Eds.), *Handbook of adolescent psychology* (2nd ed., pp. 363–394). New York: Wiley.

Brown, B. B., & Klute, C. (2006). Friendships, cliques, and crowds. In G. R. Adams & M. D. Berzonsky (Eds.), *Blackwell handbook of adolescence.* Oxford: Blackwell.

Brown, B. B., Mory, M. S., & Kinney, D. (1994). Casting adolescent crowds in a relational perspective: Caricature, channel, and context. In R. Montemayor, G. R. Adams, & T. P. Gullotta (Eds.), *Personal relationships during adolescence.* Thousand Oaks, CA: Sage.

Brown, D. F. (2002). *Becoming a successful urban teacher.* Portsmouth, NH: Heinemann.

Brown, G. D. A., Preece, T., & Hulme, C. (2000). Oscillator-based memory for serial order. *Psychological Review, 107*, 127–181.

Brown, J. S., & Burton, R. R. (1978). Diagnostic models for procedural bugs in basic mathematical skills. *Cognitive Science, 2*(2), 155–192.

Brown, J. S., Collins, A., & Duguid, P. (1989). Situated cognition and the culture of learning. *Educational Researcher, 18*(1), 32–42.

Brown, R. (1973). *A first language: The early stages.* Cambridge, MA: Harvard University Press.

Brown, R., & Bellugi, U. (1964). Three processes in children's learning of syntax. *Language and Learning* (Special issue of Harvard Educational Review), *34*, 133–151.

Brown, R., & Fraser, C. (1963). The acquisition of syntax. In C. N. Cofer & B. Musgrave (Eds.), *Verbal behavior and learning: Problems and processes* (pp. 158–201). New York: McGraw-Hill.

Brown, R., & Hanlon, C. (1970). Derivational complexity and order of acquisition. In J. R. Hayes (Ed.), *Cognition and the development of language* (pp. 11–53). New York: Wiley.

Brown, R. G. (1993). *Schools of thought.* San Francisco: Jossey-Bass.

Brown, R. P., & Day, E. A. (2006). The difference isn't black and white: Stereotype threat and the race gap on Raven's advanced progressive matrices. *Journal of Applied Psychology, 91*, 979–985.

Brown, S. W., Renzulli, J. S., Gubbins, E. J., Siegle, D., Zhang, W., & Chen, C.-H. (2005). Assumptions underlying the identification of gifted and talented students. *Gifted Child Quarterly, 49*(1), 68–79.

Brown, T. (2007). Developmental changes in human functional brain organization. Dissertation. Washington University, St. Louis, MO. Source: DAI-B 67/10, p. 5578.

Bruch, M., Juster, H., & Kaflowitz, N. (1983). Relationships of cognitive components of test anxiety to test performance: Implications for assessment and treatment. *Journal of Counseling Psychology, 30*, 527–536.

Bruel-Jungerman, E., Davis, S., Rampon, C., & Laroche, S. (2006). Long-term potentiation enhances neurogenesis in the adult dendrite gyrus. *Journal of Neuroscience, 26*(22), 5888–5893.

Bruer, J. T. (1997). Education and the brain: A bridge too far. *Educational Researcher, 26*, 4–16.

Bruer, J. T. (1999). *The myth of the first three years: A new understanding of early brain development and lifelong learning.* New York: Free Press.

Bruer, J. T., & Greenough, W. T. (2001). The subtle science of how experience affects the brain. In D. B. Bailey, Jr., J. T. Bruer, F. J. Symons, & J. W. Lichtman (Eds.), *Critical thinking about critical periods* (pp. 209–232). Baltimore: Brookes.

Bruner, J. (1961). The act of discovery. *Harvard Educational Review, 31*, 21–32.

Bruner, J. S. (1965). *The process of education.* Cambridge, MA: Harvard University Press.

Bruning, R. H., Schraw, G. J., Norby, M. M., & Ronning, R. R. (2004). *Cognitive psychology and instruction* (4th ed.). Upper Saddle River, NJ: Pearson.

Bruning, R. H., Schraw, G. J., Norby, M. M., & Ronning, R. R. (2004). *Cognitive psychology and instruction* (4th ed.). Columbus, OH: Merrill.

Bruning, R. H., Schraw, G. J., & Ronning, R. R. (1995). *Cognitive psychology and instruction* (2nd ed.). Englewood Cliffs, NJ: Prentice Hall.

Bryson, S. E. (1997). Epidemiology of autism: Overview and issues outstanding. In D. J. Cohen & F. R. Volkmar (Eds.), *Handbook of autism and pervasive developmental disorders* (2nd ed., pp. 41–46). New York: Wiley.

Büchel, C., & Sommer, M. (2004, February). Unsolved mystery: What causes stuttering? *PLoS Biology, 2*(2), 0159–0163.

Buehler, R., Griffith, D., & Ross, M. (1994). Exploring the "planning fallacy": Why people underestimate their task completion times. *Journal of Personality and Social Psychology, 67*, 366–381.

Burden, P. (2003). *Classroom management: Creating a successful learning community* (2nd ed). New York: Wiley.

Burgess, A. F., & Gutstein, S. E. (2007). Quality of life for people with autism: Raising the standard for evaluating successful outcomes. *Child and Adolescent Mental Health, 12*(2), 80–86.

Burke, K. (2003). Research on the environmental elements: Sound, light, temperature, and design. In R. Dunn & K. Griggs (Eds.), *Synthesis of the Dunn and Dunn learning style model research: Who, what, when, where, and so what?* New York: St. John's University.

Burke, K. (2006). *From standards to rubrics in six steps.* Thousand Oaks, CA: Corwin.

Burr, J. E., Ostrov, J. M., Jansen, E. A., Cullerton-Sen, C., & Crick, N. R. (2005). Relational aggression and friendship during early childhood: "I won't be your friend!" *Early Education and Development, 16*(2), 161–183.

Bursuck, W., Polloway, E. A., Plante, L., Epstein, M. H., Jayanthi, M., & McConeghy, J. (1996). Report card grading and adaptations: A national survey of classroom practices. *Exceptional Children, 62*, 301–318.

Burton, L. A., Henninger, D., & Hafetz, J. (2005). Gender differences in relations of mental rotation, verbal fluency, and SAT scores to finger length ratios as hormonal indexes. *Developmental Neuropsychology, 28*(1), 493–505.

Bussey, K., & Bandura, A. (1999). Social cognitive theory of gender development and differentiation. *Psychological Review, 106*, 676–713.

Butler, D. L. (1998). The strategic content learning approach to promoting self–regulated learning: A report of three studies. *Journal of Educational Psychology, 90*, 682–697.

Butler, R. (1998). Determinants of help seeking: Relations between perceived reasons for classroom help-avoidance and help-seeking behaviors in an experimental context. *Journal of Educational Psychology, 90*, 630–643.

Butler, R. (2000). What learners want to know: The role of achievement goals in shaping information seeking, learning, and interest.

In C. Sansone & J. M. Harackiewicz (Eds.), *Intrinsic and extrinsic motivation: The search for optimal motivation and performance* (pp. 161–194). San Diego, CA: Academic Press.

Butler, R. (2008). Ego-involving and frame of reference effects of tracking on elementary school students' motivational orientations and help seeking in math class. *Social Psychology of Education, 11*, 5–23.

Butler, S. M., & McMunn, N. D. (2006). *A teacher's guide to classroom assessment.* Thousand Oaks, CA: Corwin.

Butterworth, G. (2001). Joint visual attention in infancy. In A. Fogel (Ed.), *Blackwell handbook of infant development.* Oxford, UK: Blackwell.

Bybee, R. W. (2002). *Learning science and the science of learning.* Arlington, VA: NSTA Press.

Byrne, B. M., & Shavelson, R. J. (1986). On the structure of adolescent self-concept. *Journal of Educational Psychology, 78*, 474–481.

Byrnes, J. P. (2001). *Cognitive development and learning in instructional contexts.* Boston: Allyn & Bacon.

Byrnes, J. P. (2001). *Minds, brains, and learning: Understanding the psychological and educational relevance of neuroscientific research.* New York: Guilford Press.

Byrnes, J. P., & Fox, N. A. (1998). The educational relevance of research in cognitive neuroscience. *Educational Psychology Review, 10*, 297–342.

C

Caine, G., & Caine, R. N. (1997). *Education on the edge of possibility.* Alexandria, VA: Association for Supervision and Curriculum Development.

Cairnes, R. (1986). A contemporary perspective on social development. In P. S. Strain, M. J. Gurlanick, & H. M. Walker (Eds.), *Children's social behavior: Development, assessment and modification.* Orlando, FL: Academic Press.

Calculator, S. N. (2009). Augmentative and alternative communication (AAC) and inclusive education for students with the most severe disabilities. *International Journal of Inclusive Education, 13*(1), 93–113.

Calfee, R., & Brown, R. (1979). Grouping students for instruction. In S. L. Duke (Ed.), *Classroom management: Seventy-eighth yearbook of the National Society for the Study of Education, Part 2* (pp. 144–182). Chicago: University of Chicago Press.

Cameron, J. (2001). Negative effects of reward on intrinsic motivation—a limited phenomenon: Comment on Deci, Koestner, and Ryan (2001). *Review of Educational Research, 71*(1), 29–42.

Campbell, A., & Namy, L. (2003). The role of social-referential context in verbal and nonverbal symbol learning. *Child Development, 74*, 549–563.

Campbell, L. (1997). How teachers interpret MI theory. *Educational Leadership, 55*(1), 14–19.

Campbell, S. B., Endman, M. W., & Bernfield, G. (1977). A three-year follow-up of hyperactive preschoolers into elementary school. *Journal of Child Psychology and Psychiatry, 18*, 239–249.

Campbell, S. B., Ewing, L. J., Breaux, A. M., & Szumowski, E. K. (1986). Parent-referred problem three-year-olds: Follow-up at school entry. *Journal of Child Psychology and Psychiatry, 27*, 473–488.

Campione, J. C., & Brown, A. L. (1990). Guided learning and transfer: Implications for approaches to assessment. In N. Frederiksen, R. Glaser, A. Lesgold, & M. Shafto (Eds.), *Diagnostic monitoring of skill and knowledge acquisition* (pp. 141–172). Hillsdale, NJ: Erlbaum.

Campione, J. C., Brown, A. L., & Ferrara, R. A. (1982). Experimental and clinical interventions of retarded individuals: Intelligence, learning, and transfer. In R. Sternberg (Ed.), *Handbook of human intelligence* (pp. 392–473). New York: Cambridge University Press.

Campos, J. J., & Sternberg, C. (1981). Perception, appraisal, and emotion: The onset of social referencing. In M. E. Lamb and L. R. Sherrod (Eds.), *Infant social cognition: Empirical and theoretical considerations*. Hillsdale, NJ: Erlbaum.

Campoy, R. (2005). *Case study analysis in the classroom: Becoming a reflective practitioner*. Thousand Oaks, CA: Sage.

Canter, L., & Canter, M. (1992). *Assertive discipline: Positive behavior management for today's classroom* (2nd ed.). Santa Monica, CA: Canter & Associates.

Canter, L., & Canter, M. (1998). *First-class teacher: Success strategies for new teachers*. Santa Monica, CA: Canter & Associates.

Cardelle-Elawar, M., & Wetzel, K. (1995). Students and computers as partners in developing problem solving skills. *Journal of Research on Computing in Education, 27*(4), 378–401. Washington, DC: National Association for the Education of Young Children.

Carlo, M. S., & Royer, J. M. (1999). Cross-language transfer of reading skills. In D. A. Wagner, R. L. Venezky, & B. V. Street (Eds.), *Literacy: An international handbook* (pp. 148–154). Boulder, CO: Westview Press.

Carlson, S. M., & Moses, L. J. (2001). Individual differences in inhibitory control and children's theory of mind. *Child Development, 72,* 1032–1053.

Caro, D. H., McDonald, J. T., & Willms, J. D. (2009). Socio-economic status and academic achievement trajectories from childhood to adolescence. *Canadian Journal of Education, 32*(3), 558–590.

Carpendale, J. I. M. (2000). Kohlberg and Piaget on stages and moral reasoning. *Developmental Review, 20,* 181–205.

Carr, M., & Biddlecomb, B. (1998). Metacognition in mathematics from a constructivist perspective. In D. J. Hacker, J. Dunlosky, & A. C. Graesser (Eds.), *Metacognition in educational theory and practice* (pp. 69–91). Mahwah, NJ: Erlbaum.

Carr, M., & Davis, H. (2001). Gender differences in strategy use: A function of skill and preference. *Contemporary Educational Psychology, 26,* 330–347.

Carreker, S., & Joshi, M. (2010). Response to intervention: Are the Emperor's clothes really new? *Psicothema, 22*(4), 943–948.

Carroll, J. B. (1971). Problems of measurement related to the concept of learning for mastery. In J. H. Block (Ed.), *Mastery learning: Theory and practice* (pp. 29–46). New York: Holt, Rinehart, & Winston.

Carroll, J. B. (1992). Cognitive abilities: The state of the art. *Psychological Science, 3*(5), 266–270.

Carroll, J. B. (1993). *Human cognitive abilities: A survey of factor-analytic studies*. New York: Cambridge University Press.

Carter, K., Cushing, K., Sabers, D., Stein, P., & Berliner, D. (1988). Expert-novice differences in perceiving and processing visual classroom information. *Journal of Teacher Education, 39*(3), 25–31.

Carter, M., McGee, R., Taylor, B., & Williams, S. (2007). Health outcomes in adolescence: Associations with family, friends and school engagement. *Journal of Adolescence, 30,* 51–62.

Cartledge, G., Kea, C., & Simmons-Reed, E. (2002). Serving culturally diverse children with serious emotional disturbance and their families. *Journal of Child and Family Studies, 11*(1), 113–126.

Case, R. (1985). *Intellectual development: Birth to adulthood*. Orlando, FL: Academic Press.

Caselli, M. C., Bates, E., Casadio, P., Fenson, J., Fenson, L., Sanderl, L., & Weir, J. (1995). A cross-linguistic study of early lexical development. *Cognitive Development, 10,* 159–199.

Caspi, A. (2000). The child is father to the man: Personality continuities from childhood to adulthood. *Journal of Personality and Social Psychology, 78,* 158–172.

Caspi, A., Taylor, A., Moffitt, T. E., & Plomin, R. (2000). Neighborhood deprivation affects children's mental health: Environmental risks identified in a genetic design. *Psychological Science, 11,* 338–342.

Cassidy, J. (1999). The nature of the child's ties. In J. Cassidy & P. R. Shaver (Eds.), *Handbook of Attachment* (pp. 3–20). New York: Guilford Press.

Cassady, J. C., & Johnson, R. E. (2002). Cognitive test anxiety and academic performance. *Contemporary Educational Psychology, 27,* 270–295.

Catalano, R. F., Mazza, J. J., Harachi, T. W., Abbott, R. D., Haggerty, K. P., & Fleming, C. B. (2003). Raising healthy children through enhancing social development in elementary school: Results after 1.5 years. *Journal of School Psychology, 41*(2), 143–164.

Cates, G. L., Blum, C., & Swerdlik. M. E. (2011). *Effective RTI training and practice: Helping school and district teams improve academic performance and social behavior*. Champaign, IL: Research Press.

Catrambone, R., & Holyoak, K. J. (1989). Overcoming contextual limitations on problem-solving transfer. *Journal of Experimental Psychology: Learning, Memory, and Cognition, 15,* 1147–1156.

Catsambis, S., Mulkey, L., & Crain, R. L. (1999). To track or not to track? The social effects of gender and middle school tracking. *Research in Sociology of Education and Socialization, 12,* 135–163.

Catsambis, S., Mulkey, L., & Crain, R. L. (2001). For better or for worse? A nationwide study of the social psychological effects of gender and ability grouping in mathematics. *Social Psychology of Education, 5,* 83–115.

Cattell, R. B. (1963). Theory of fluid and crystallized intelligence: A critical experiment. *Journal of Educational Psychology, 54,* 1–22.

Cavell, T. A. (1990). Social adjustment, social performance, and social skills: A tri-component model of social competence. *Journal of Clinical Child Psychology, 19*(2), 111–112.

Cedars-Sinai Medical Center. (2010, March 28). When memory-related neurons fire in sync with certain brain waves, memories last. *ScienceDaily*. Retrieved November 4, 2010, from http://www.sciencedaily.com/releases/2010/03/100324142115.htm.

Centers for Disease Control and Prevention. (2007). Retrieved September 24, 2007, from http://www.cdc.gov/ncbddd/fas/fasask.htm.

Centers for Disease Control and Prevention. (2009). Prevalence of autism spectrum disorders—autism and developmental disabilities monitoring network, United States, 2006. In: Surveillance Summaries, December 18, 2009. 58(SS10); 1–20.

Cervantes, C. A., & Seo, M. (2005). Korean mothers' beliefs about children's emotions: An examination of parenting in a multicultural context. In J. C. Dunsmore, *Multicultural examination of parent's beliefs about children: Meanings, mechanisms, and methods*. Symposium conducted at the biennial meeting of the Society for Research in Child Development, Atlanta, GA.

Chacko, A., Pelham, W. E., Jr., Gnagy, E. M., et al. (2005). Stimulant medication effects in a summer treatment program among young children with attention-deficit/hyperactivity disorder. *Journal of the American Academy of Child and Adolescent Psychiatry, 44,* 249–257.

Chafetz, M. D. (1990). *Nutrition and neurotransmitters: The nutrient bases of behavior*. Englewood Cliffs, NJ: Prentice Hall.

Champagne, A. B., Gunstone, R. F., & Klopfer, L. E. (1985). Effecting changes in cognitive structures among physics students. In

H. T. West & A. L. Pines (Eds.), *Cognitive structure and conceptual change* (pp. 163–187). Orlando, FL: Academic Press.

Chan, D. W., Cheung, P. C., Lau, S., Wu, W. Y., Kwong, J. M., & Li, W. L. (2001). Assessing ideational fluency in primary students in Hong Kong. *Creativity Research Journal, 13*(3–4), 359–365.

Chan, L., & Dally, K. (2001). Learning disabilities: Literacy and numeracy development. *Australian Journal of Learning Disabilities, 6*(1), 12–19.

Chandler, M. A., & Chapman, M. (Eds.). (1991). *Criteria for competence.* Hillsdale, NJ: Erlbaum.

Chao, R. K., Kanatsu, A., Stanoff, N., Padmawidjaja, I., & Aque, C. (2009). Diversities in meaning and practice: The parental involvement of Asian immigrants. In N. E. Hill & R. K. Chao (Eds.), *Families, schools, and the adolescent: Connecting research, policy, and practice* (pp.110–125). New York: Teachers College Press.

Chappuis, S., & Chappuis, J. (2007–2008). The Best Value in Formative Assessment [Electronic version]. Educational Leadership, 65, 14-19. Retrieved June 24, 2008, from http://www.ascd.org.

Charles, C. M. (1999). *Building classroom discipline* (6th ed.). New York: Longman.

Charney, R. S. (2002). *Teaching children to care: Classroom management for ethical and academic growth, K–8* (Rev. ed.). Greenfield, MA: Northeast Foundation for Children.

Chart, H., Grigorenko, E. L., & Sternberg, R. J. (2008). Identification: The Aurora battery. In J. A. Plucker & C. M. Callahan (Eds.), *Critical issues and practices in gifted education* (pp. 281–301). Waco, TX: Prufrock.

Chatterji, M. (2003). *Designing and using tools for educational assessment.* Boston: Pearson.

Chen, C., & Stevenson, H. W. (1995). Motivation and mathematics achievement: A comparative study of Asian-American, Caucasian-American, and East Asian high school students. *Child Development, 66,* 1215–1234.

Chen, C. M., & Chen, M. C. (2009). Mobile formative assessment tool based on data mining techniques for supporting web-based learning. *Computers & Education, 52*(1), 256–273.

Chen, X., Li, D., Li, Z., Li, B., & Liu, M. (2000). Sociable and prosocial dimensions of social competence in Chinese children: Common and unique contributions to social, academic, and psychological adjustment. *Developmental Psychology, 36*(3), 302–314.

Chen, X., Rubin, K. H., & Bo-shu, L. (1995). Depressed mood in Chinese children: Relations with school performance and family environment. *Journal of Consulting and Clinical Psychology, 63,* 938–947.

Chen, Z., & Klahr, D. (1999). All other things being equal: Acquisition and transfer of the control of variables strategy. *Child Development, 70*(5), 1098–1120.

Cherry-Wilkinson, L., & Dollaghan, C. (1979). Peer communication in first-grade reading groups. *Theory Into Practice, 18,* 267–274.

Cheung, S. (1995). Life events, classroom environment, achievement expectation, and depression among early adolescents. *Social Behavior and Personality, 23,* 83–92.

Cheyne, J. A., & Walters, R. H. (1970). Punishment and prohibition: Some origins of self-control. *New Directions in Psychology, 4,* 281–366.

Chi, M. T. H. (1978). Knowledge structure and memory development. In R. Siegler (Ed.), *Children's thinking: What develops?* Hillsdale, NJ: Erlbaum.

Chi, M. T. H. (1987). Representing knowledge and metaknowledge: Implications for interpreting metamemory research. In F. E. Wein-

ert & R. H. Kluwe (Eds.), *Metacognition, motivation, and understanding* (pp. 239–266). Hillsdale, NJ: Erlbaum.

Chi, M. T. H. (2000). Self-explaining expository texts: The dual process of generating inferences and repairing mental models. In R. Glaser (Ed.), *Advances in instructional psychology* (Vol. 5, pp. 161–238). Mahwah, NJ: Erlbaum.

Chi, M. T. H. (2009). Active-constructive-interactive: A conceptual framework for differentiating learning activities. *Topics in Cognitive Science, 1,* 73–105.

Chi, M. T. H., Bassock, M., Lewis, M. W., Reimann, P., & Glaser, R. (1989). Self explanations: How students study and use examples in learning to solve problems. *Cognitive Science, 13,* 145–182.

Chi, M. T. H., Glaser, R., & Farr, M. (Eds.). (1988). *The nature of expertise.* Hillsdale, NJ: Erlbaum.

Chinn, C. A., & Brewer, W. F. (1998). An empirical test of a taxonomy of responses to anomalous data in science. *Journal of Research in Science Teaching, 35,* 623–654.

Chirkov, V., Ryan, R. M., & Willness, C. (2005). Cultural context and psychological needs in Canada and Brazil: Testing a self-determination approach to the internalization of cultural practices, identity, and well-being. *Journal of Cross-Cultural Psychology, 36,* 423–443.

Chong, S. L., & Siegel, L. S. (2008). Stability of computational deficits in math learning disability from second through fifth grades. *Developmental Neuropsychology, 33*(3), 300–317.

Chorzempa, B. F., & Graham, S. (2006). Primary-grade teachers' use of within-class ability grouping in reading. *Journal of Educational Psychology, 98*(3), 529–541.

Choudhury, S., Charman, T., & Blakemore, S. J. (2008). Development of the teenage brain. *Mind, Brain, & Education, 2*(3), 142–147.

Cillessen, A. H. N., & Rose, A. J. (2005). Understanding popularity in the peer system. *Current Directions in Psychological Science, 14*(2), 102–105.

Cisero, C. A., & Royer, J. M. (1995). The development and cross-language transfer of phonological awareness. *Contemporary Educational Psychology, 20,* 275–303.

Cisero, C. A., Royer, J. M., Marchant, H. G., & Jackson, S. J. (1997). Can the Computer-based Academic Assessment System (CAAS) be used to diagnose reading disability in college students? *Journal of Educational Psychology, 89*(4), 599–620.

Cizek, G. J. (2003). *Detecting and preventing classroom cheating: Promoting integrity in assessment.* Thousand Oaks, CA: Corwin.

Cizek, G. J. (2009). Reliability and validity in student achievement. *Theory Into Practice, 48,* 63–71.

Clark, B. (1990). An update on ability grouping and its importance for gifted learners. *Communicator, 20*(5), 1, 20–21.

Clark, B. (2002). *Growing up gifted: Developing the potential of children at home and at school.* Upper Saddle River, NJ: Merrill/Prentice Hall.

Clements, D. H., & Nastasi, B. K. (1993). Electronic media and early childhood education. In B. Spodek (Ed.), *Handbook of research on the education of young children* (pp. 251–275). New York: Macmillan.

Clements, D. H., & Sarama, J. (2003). Young children and technology: What does the research say? *Young Children, 58*(6), 34–40.

Clifford, M. M. (1990). Students need challenge, not easy success. *Educational Leadership, 48*(1), 22–26.

Clifford, M. M. (1991). Risk taking: Empirical and educational considerations. *Educational Psychologist, 26,* 263–298.

Cobb, P., & Bowers, J. (1999). Cognitive and situated learning perspectives in theory and practice. *Educational Researcher, 28*(2), 4–15.

Cohen, D., & Strayer, J. (1996). Empathy in conduct-disordered and comparison youth. *Developmental Psychology, 32,* 988–998.

Cohen, R. J., & Swerdlik, M. E. (2005). *Psychological testing and assessment: An introduction to tests and measurement* (6th ed.). New York: McGraw-Hill.

Cohn, M., Emrich, S. M., & Moscovitch, M. (2008). Age-related deficits in associative memory: The influence of impaired strategic retrieval. *Psychology and Aging, 23*(1), 93–103. doi:10.1037/0882-7974.23.1.93

Coie, J. D., & Dodge, K. A. (1998). Aggression and antisocial behavior. In N. Eisenberg (Ed.), *Manual of child psychology: Vol. 3. Social, emotional, and personality development* (pp. 779–862). New York: Wiley.

Colangelo, N., & Assouline, S. (2009). Acceleration: Meeting the academic and social needs of students. In L. V. Shavina (Ed.), *International Handbook on Giftedness.* Springer Science & Business Media. doi:10.1007/978-1-4020-6162-2_55

Colangelo, N., & Davis, G. A. (Eds.). (2003). *Handbook of gifted education* (3rd ed.). Boston: Allyn & Bacon.

Colby, A., & Kohlberg, L. (1987). *The measurement of moral judgment: Vol. 1. Theoretical foundations and research validation.* Cambridge, UK: Cambridge University Press.

Colby, A., Kohlberg, L., Gibbs, J., & Lieberman, M. (1983). A longitudinal study of moral judgment. *Monographs of the Society for Research in Child Development, 48* (Nos. 1/2, Serial No. 200).

Coleman, M., & Gillberg, C. (1996). *The schizophrenias: A biological approach to the schizophrenia spectrum disorders.* New York: Springer.

Coles, G. (2004). Danger in the classroom: "Brain glitch" research and learning to read. *Phi Delta Kappan, 85*(5), 344–357.

Coles, R. (1998). *The moral intelligence of children: How to raise a moral child.* New York: Plume.

Collaborative for Academic, Social, and Emotional Learning. (2003). *Safe and sound: An educator's guide to evidence-based social and emotional learning programs.* Chicago: University of Illinois at Chicago.

Collier, V. P., & Thomas, W. P. (2004). The astounding effectiveness of dual language education for all. *NABE Journal of Research and Practice, 2*(1), 1–20.

Collins, A., Brown, J. S., & Newman, S. E. (1989). Cognitive apprenticeship: Teaching the crafts of reading, writing, and mathematics. In L. B. Resnick (Ed.), *Knowing, learning, and instruction: Essays in honor of Robert Glaser* (pp. 453–494). Hillsdale, NJ: Erlbaum.

Collins, A., Hawkins, J., & Carver, S. M. (1991). A cognitive apprenticeship for disadvantaged students. In B. Means, C. Chelemer, & M. S. Knapp (Eds.), *Teaching advanced skills to at-risk students.* San Francisco: Jossey-Bass.

Colquitt, J. A., LePine, J. A., & Noe, R. A. (2000). Toward an integrative theory of training motivation: A meta-analytic path analysis of 20 years of research. *Journal of Applied Psychology, 85,* 678–707.

Compton, D. L., & Carlisle, J. F. (1994). Speed of word recognition as a distinguishing characteristic of reading disabilities. *Educational Psychology Review, 6*(2), 115–140.

Conduct Problems Prevention Research Group. (2010). The effects of a multi-year randomized clinical trial of a universal social-emotional learning program: The role of student and school characteristics. *Journal of Consulting and Clinical Psychology, 78,* 156–168. doi:10.1037/a0018607

Conner, L. N. (2007). Cueing metacognition to improve researching and essay writing in final-year high school biology class. *Research in Science Education, 37*(1), 1–16.

Conners, C. K., Epstein, J. N., March, J. S., et al. (2001). Multimodal treatment of ADHD in the MTA: An alternative outcome analysis. *Journal of the American Academy of Child and Adolescent Psychiatry, 40,* 159–167.

Connor, D. F. (2002). *Aggression and antisocial behavior in children and adolescents: Research and treatment.* New York: Guilford.

Conoley, J. C., & Goldstein, A. P. (2004). *School violence intervention: A practical handbook* (2nd ed.). New York: Guilford.

Coo, H., Ouellette-Kuntz, H., Lloyd, J. E. V., Kasmara, L., Holden, J. J. A., & Lewis, M. E. S. (2008). Trends in autism prevalence: Diagnostic substitution revisited. *Journal of Autism & Developmental Disorders, 38,* 1036–1046.

Cook, R., Tessier, A., & Armbruster, V. (1987). *Adapting early childhood curricula for children with special needs* (2nd ed.). Upper Saddle River, NJ: Merrill/Prentice Hall.

Cooper, R. (1999). Urban school reform: Student responses to detracking in a racially mixed high school. *Journal of Education for Students Placed at Risk, 4*(3), 259–275.

Cooper, R. P., & Aslin, R. N. (1990). Preference for infant-directed speech in the first month after birth. *Child Development, 61,* 1584–1595.

Copeland, W. D. (1983). *Classroom management and student teachers' cognitive abilities: A relationship.* Paper presented at the annual convention of the American Educational Research Association, Montreal.

Cordova, D. I., & Lepper, M. R. (1996). Intrinsic motivation and the process of learning: Beneficial effects of contextualization, personalization and choice. *Journal of Educational Psychology, 88,* 715–730.

Corkill, A. J. (1992). Advance organizers: Facilitators of recall. *Educational Psychology Review, 4,* 33–67.

Corno, L. (1996). Homework is a complicated thing. *Educational Researcher, 25,* 27–30.

Corpus, J. H., & Lepper, M. R. (2007). The effects of person versus performance praise on children's motivation: Gender and age as moderating factors. *Educational Psychology, 27*(4), 487–508.

Costa, A. L. (1989). Reassessing assessment. *Educational Leadership, 20*(1), 2.

Costa, A. L. (1996). Prologue. In D. Hyerle (Ed.), *Visual tools for constructing knowledge.* Alexandria, VA: Association for Supervision and Curriculum Development.

Costa, A. L., & Kallick, B. (2000). *Assessing and reporting on habits of mind.* Alexandria, VA: Association for Supervision and Curriculum Development.

Cotton, K. (1990). *Close-up no. 9: Schoolwide and classroom discipline.* Portland, OR: Northwest Regional Educational Laboratory.

Cotugno, A. J. (2009). Social competence and social skills training and intervention for children with autism spectrum disorders. *Journal of Autism & Developmental Disorders, 39,* 1268–1277.

Covington, M. (1992). *Making the grade: A self-worth perspective on motivation and school reform.* Cambridge, UK: Cambridge University Press.

Covington, M. (1998). *The will to learn: A guide for motivating young people.* New York: Cambridge University Press.

Covington, M. (2009). Self-worth theory. In K. R. Wentzel & A. Wigfield (Eds.), *Handbook of motivation at school* (pp. 142–169). New York: Routledge/Taylor & Francis Group.

Covington, M., & Beery, R. (1976). *Self-worth and school learning.* New York: Holt, Rinehart, & Winston.

Covington, M. V. (1984). The motive for self worth. In R. Ames & C. Ames (Eds.), *Research on motivation in education: Student motivation* (Vol. 1, pp. 77–113). San Diego, CA: Academic Press.

Covington, M. V. (1986). Anatomy of failure-induced anxiety: The role of cognitive mediators. In R. Schwarzer (Ed.), *Self-related cognitions in anxiety and motivation* (pp. 247–263). Hillsdale, NJ: Erlbaum.

Covington, M. V. (2000). Intrinsic versus extrinsic motivation in schools: A reconciliation. *Current Directions in Psychological Science, 9,* 22–25.

Covington, M. V., & Müeller, K. J. (2001). Intrinsic versus extrinsic motivation: An approach/avoidance reformulation. *Education Psychology Review, 13,* 157–176.

Covington, M. V., & Omelich, C. L. (1979). Effort: The double-edged sword in school achievement. *Journal of Educational Psychology, 71,* 169–182.

Covington, M. V., & Omelich, C. L. (1984a). An empirical examination of Weiner's critique of attribution research. *Journal of Educational Psychology, 76,* 1214–1225.

Covington, M. V., & Omelich, C. L. (1984b). Task-oriented versus competitive learning structures: Motivational and performance consequences. *Journal of Educational Psychology, 76,* 1038–1050.

Covington, M. V., & Omelich, C. L. (1985). Ability and effort valuation among failure-avoiding and failure-accepting students. *Journal of Educational Psychology, 77,* 446–459.

Cowan, N. (1995). *Attention and memory: An integrated framework.* New York: Oxford University Press.

Cowan, N. (2007). What infants can tell us about working memory development. In L. M. Oakes & P. J. Bauer (Eds.), *Short- and long-term memory in infancy and early childhood: Taking the first steps toward remembering* (pp. 126–150). New York: Oxford University Press.

Crago, M. (1992). Communicative interaction and second language acquisition: The Inuit example. *TESOL Quarterly, 26,* 487–505.

Craske, M. L. (1985). Improving persistence through observational learning and attribution retraining. *British Journal of Educational Psychology, 55,* 138–147.

Crawford, J. (1997). *Bilingual education: History, politics, theory, and practice* (4th ed.). Los Angeles: Bilingual Education Services.

Creel, C., & Karnes, F. A. (1988). Parental expectations and young gifted children. *Roeper Review, 11,* 48–50.

Crick, N. R., & Dodge, K. A. (1994). A review and reformulation of social information-processing mechanisms in children's social adjustment. *Psychological Bulletin, 115,* 74–101.

Crick, N. R., & Dodge, K. A. (1996). Social information-processing mechanisms in reactive and proactive aggression. *Child Development, 67,* 993–1002.

Crick, N. R., & Grotpeter, J. K. (1995). Relational aggression, gender and social-psychological adjustment. *Child Development, 66,* 710–722.

Croizet, J., Desert, M., Dutrevis, M., & Leyens, J. (2001). Stereotype threat, social class, gender, and academic underachievement: When our reputation catches up to us and takes over. *Social Psychology of Education, 4,* 295–310.

Croninger, R. G., & Lee, V. E. (2001). Social capital and dropping out of high school: Benefits to at-risk students of teachers' support and guidance. *Teacher College Record, 103*(4), 548–581.

Crosnoe, R. (2002). High school curriculum track and adolescent association with delinquent friends. *Journal of Adolescent Research, 17*(2), 143–167.

Crosnoe, R., Johnson, M., & Elder, G. (2004). Intergenerational bonding in school: The behavioral and contextual correlates of student-teacher relationships. *Sociology of Education, 77*(1), 60–81.

Crouter, A. C., Bumpus, M. F., Maguire, M. C., & McHale, S. M. (1999). Linking parents' work pressure and adolescents' well-being: Insights into dynamics in dual-earner families. *Developmental Psychology, 35*(6), 1453–1461.

Crouter, A. C., & McHale, S. (2005). The long arm of the job revisited: Parenting in dual-earner families. In T. Luster & L. Okagaki (Eds.), *Parenting: An ecological perspective.* Mahwah, NJ: Erlbaum.

Csikszentmihalyi, M. (1990). *Flow: The psychology of optimal experience.* New York: HarperCollins.

Csikszentmihalyi, M. (1990). The domain of creativity. In M. A. Runco & R. S. Albert (Eds.), *Theories of creativity* (pp. 190–212). Newbury Park, CA: Sage.

Csikszentmihalyi, M. (1996). *Creativity.* New York: HarperCollins.

Csikszentmihalyi, M. (1997). Intrinsic motivation and effective teaching: A flow analysis. In J. J. Bass (Ed.), *Teaching well and liking it: Motivating faculty to teach effectively* (pp. 72–89). Baltimore: Johns Hopkins University Press.

Csikszentmihalyi, M. (2000). *Beyond boredom and anxiety: Experiencing flow in work and play* (2nd ed.). San Francisco: Jossey-Bass.

Cullinan, D. (2007). *Students with emotional and behavioral disorders: An introduction for teachers and other helping professionals* (2nd ed.). Upper Saddle River, NJ: Merrill/Prentice Hall.

Curtis, M. (2004). Adolescents who struggle with word identification: Research and practice. In T. L. Jetton & J. A. Dole (Eds.), *Adolescent literacy research and practice* (pp. 119–134). New York: Guilford.

Curwin, R. (1992). *Rediscovering hope: Our greatest teaching strategy.* Bloomington, IN: National Education Service.

Curwin, R. L., & Mendler, A. N. (1999). *Discipline with dignity.* Alexandria, VA: Association for Supervision and Curriculum Development.

Cury, F., Elliot, A. J., Da Fonseca, D., & Moller, A. C. (2006). The social cognitive model of achievement motivation and the 2 x 2 achievement-goal framework. *Journal of Personality and Social Psychology, 90,* 666–679.

Cuttance, P., & Stokes, S. (2001). *Reporting on student and school achievement.* Sydney, Australia: University of Sydney.

D

Dalbert, C., Schneidewind, U., & Saalbach, A. (2007). Justice judgments concerning grading in school. *Contemporary Educational Psychology, 32*(3), 420–433.

Dallett, K., & Wilcox, S. G. (1968). Contextual stimuli and proactive inhibition. *Journal of Experimental Psychology, 78,* 475–480.

Damon, S., Riley-Tillman, T. C., & Fiorello, C. (2008). Comparing methods of identifying reinforcing stimuli in school consultation. *Journal of Educational & Psychological Consultation, 18*(1), 31–53.

Damon, W. (1984). Peer education: The untapped potential. *Journal of Applied Developmental Psychology, 5,* 331–343.

Damon, W. (1988). *The moral child: Nurturing children's natural moral growth.* New York: Free Press.

Daniels, L. M., Haynes, T. L., Stupnisky, R. H., Perry, R. P., Newall, N., & Pekrun, R. (2008). Individual differences in achievement goals: A longitudinal study of cognitive, emotional, and achievement outcomes. *Contemporary Educational Psychology, 33,* 584–608.

Dansereau, D. F. (1988). Cooperative learning strategies. In C. E. Weinstein, E. T. Goetz, & P. A. Alexander (Eds.), *Learning and study strategies: Issues in assessment, instruction, and evaluation* (pp. 103–120). Orlando, FL: Academic Press.

Darling-Hammond, L. (1995). Inequality and access to knowledge. In J. A. Banks & C. A. M. Banks (Eds.), *Handbook of research on multicultural education* (pp. 465–483). New York: Macmillan.

Das, J. P. (1995). Some thoughts on two aspects of Vygotsky's work. *Educational Psychologist, 30*(2), 93–97.

Das, J. P., Naglieri, J. A., & Kirby, J. R. (1994). *Assessment of cognitive processes.* Needham Heights, MA: Allyn & Bacon.

Dasen, P. R. (1977). Introduction. In P. R. Dasen (Ed.), *Piagetian psychology: Cross-cultural contributions.* New York: Gardner.

DaSilva Iddings, A. C. (2005). Linguistic access and participation: English language learners in an English-dominant community of practice. *Bilingual Research Journal, 29*(1), 165–183.

Davelaar, E. J., Goshen-Gottstein, Y., Ashkenazi, A., Haarmann, H. J., & Usher, M. (2005). The demise of short-term memory revisited: Empirical and computational investigations of recency effects. *Psychological Review, 112,* 3–42.

Davidson, J. (2009). Exhibitions: Connecting classroom assessment with culminating demonstrations of mastery. *Theory Into Practice, 48,* 36–43.

Davidson, J., & Davidson, B. (2004). *Genius denied: How to stop wasting our brightest young minds.* New York: Simon & Schuster.

Davidson, J. E., & Sternberg, R. J. (1998). Smart problem solving: How metacognition helps. In D. J. Hacker, J. Dunlosky, & A. C. Graesser (Eds.), *Metacognition in educational theory and practice* (pp. 47–68). Mahwah, NJ: Erlbaum.

Davies, P. T., & Windle, M. (2001). Interparental discord and adolescent adjustment trajectories: The potentiating and protective role of intrapersonal attributes. *Child Development, 72*(4), 1163–1178.

Davis, B. C., & Shade, D. D. (1994). *Integrate, don't isolate! Computers in the early childhood curriculum* [ERIC digest]. Urbana, IL: ERIC Clearinghouse on Elementary and Early Childhood.

Davis, G. A. (2003). Identifying creative students, teaching for creative growth. In N. Colangelo & G. A. Davis (Eds.), *Handbook of gifted education* (3rd ed., pp. 311–324). Boston: Allyn & Bacon.

Davis, G. A., & Thomas, M. A. (1989). *Effective schools and effective teachers.* Boston: Allyn & Bacon.

Davis, T. E., Ollendick, T. H., & Nebel-Schwalm, M. (2008). Intellectual ability and achievement in anxiety-disordered children: A clarification and extension of the literature. *Journal of Psychopathology & Behavioral Assessment, 30,* 43–51.

Davydov, V. V. (1972). *The types of generalization in learning.* Moscow: Pedagogika.

Davydov, V. V. (1988). The concept of theoretical generalization. *Studies in Soviet Thought, 36,* 169–202.

Day, J. D., & Cordon, L. A. (1993). Static and dynamic measures of ability: An experimental comparison. *Journal of Educational Psychology, 85,* 75–82.

Dean, Jr., D., & Kuhn, D. (2007). Direct instruction vs. discovery: The long view. *Science Education, 91*(3), 384–397.

DeAngelis, T. (2004). What's to blame for the surge in super-sized Americans? *Monitor on Psychology, 35*(1), 44–49.

Dearing, E., Kreider, H., Simpkins, S., & Weiss, H. B. (2006). Family involvement in school and low-income children's literacy: Longitudinal association between and within families. *Journal of Educational Psychology, 98,* 653–664.

DeBacker, T. K., & Nelson, R. M. (1999). Variations on an expectancy-value model of motivation in science. *Contemporary Educational Psychology, 24,* 71–94.

Debacker, T. K., & Nelson, R. M. (2000). Motivation to learn science: Differences related to gender, class type, and ability. *Journal of Educational Research, 93,* 245–254.

de Boysson-Bardies, B. (1999). *How language comes to children: From birth to two years.* Cambridge, MA: MIT Press.

de Bruyn, E. H., & Cillessen, A. H. N. (2006). Popularity in early adolescence: Prosocial and antisocial subtypes. *Journal of Adolescent Research, 21*(6), 607–627.

deCharms, R. (1968). *Personal causation: The internal affective determinants of behavior.* New York: Academic Press.

deCharms, R. (1976). *Enhancing motivation.* New York: Irvington.

Deci, E. L. (1971). Effects of externally mediated rewards on intrinsic motivation. *Journal of Personality and Social Psychology, 18,* 105–115.

Deci, E. L., Eghrari, H., Patrick, B. C., & Leone, D. R. (1994). Facilitating internalization: The self-determination theory perspective. *Journal of Personality, 62,* 119–142.

Deci, E. L., Hodges, R., Pierson, L., & Tomassone, J. (1992). Autonomy and competence as motivational factors in students with learning disabilities and emotional handicaps. *Journal of Learning Disabilities, 25,* 457–471.

Deci, E. L., Koestner, R., & Ryan, R. M. (1999a). A meta-analytic review of experiments examining the effects of extrinsic rewards on intrinsic motivation. *Psychological Bulletin, 125*(6), 627–668.

Deci, E. L., Koestner, R., & Ryan, R. M. (1999b). The undermining effect is a reality after all—extrinsic rewards, task interest, and self-determination: Reply to Eisenberger, Pierce, and Cameron (1999) and Lepper, Henderlong, and Gingras (1999). *Psychological Bulletin, 125*(6), 692–700.

Deci, E. L., Koestner, R., & Ryan. R. M. (2001). Extrinsic rewards and intrinsic motivation in education: Reconsidered once again. *Review of Educational Research, 71*(1), 1–27.

Deci, E. L., & Ryan, R. M. (1985). *Intrinsic motivation and self-determination in human behavior.* New York: Plenum Press.

Deci, E. L., & Ryan, R. M. (1992). The initiation and regulation of intrinsically motivated learning and achievement. In A. K. Boggiano & T. S. Pittman (Eds.), *Achievement and motivation: A social-developmental perspective* (pp. 9–36). New York: Cambridge University Press.

Deci, E. L., & Ryan, R. M. (2000). The "what" and the "why" of goal pursuits: Human needs and the self-determination of behavior. *Psychological Inquiry, 11,* 227–268.

Deci, E. L., & Ryan, R. M. (2002). The paradox of achievement: The harder you push, the worse it gets. In J. Aronson (Ed.), *Improving academic achievement: Contributions of social psychology* (pp. 59–85). New York: Academic Press.

Deci, E. L., Ryan, R. M., & Koestner, R. (2001). The pervasive negative effects of rewards on intrinsic motivation: Response to Cameron (2001). *Review of Educational Research, 71*(1), 43–51.

Deci, E. L., Vallerand, R. J., Pelletier, L. G., & Ryan, R. M. (1991). Motivation and education: The self-determination perspective. *Educational Psychologist, 26,* 325–346.

Dehaene, S., Spelke, E., Pinel, P., Stanescu, R., & Tsivkin, S. (1999). Sources of mathematical thinking: Behavioral and brain-imaging evidence. *Science, 284,* 970–974.

Delazer, M., Ischebeck, A., Domahs, F., et al. (2005). Learning by strategies and learning by drill—evidence from an fMRI study. *NeuroImage, 25,* 838–849.

DeLoache, J. S., Cassidy, D. J., & Brown, A. L. (1985). Precursors of mnemonic strategies in very young children's memory for the location of hidden objects. *Child Development, 56,* 125–137.

Delpit, L. (1995). *Other people's children: Cultural conflict in the classroom.* New York: New Press.

Demetriou, A., Mouyi, A., & Spanoudis, G. (2008). Modelling the structure and development of g. *Intelligence, 36*(5), 437–454.

Demo, D. H., & Acock, A. C. (1996). Family structure, family process, and adolescent well-being. *Journal of Research on Adolescence, 6,* 457–488.

DeMoss, K., Milich, R., & DeMers, S. (1993). Gender, creativity, depression, and attributional style in adolescents with high academic ability. *Journal of Abnormal Child Psychology, 21,* 455–467.

Dempster, F. N. (1991). Synthesis of research on reviews and tests. *Educational Leadership, 48*(7), 71–76.

Dempster, F. N. (1993). Resistance to interference: Developmental changes in a basic processing mechanism. In M. L. Howe & R. Pasnak (Eds.), *Emerging themes in cognitive development. Vol 1: Foundations.* New York: Springer-Verlag.

Dendato, K., & Diener, D. (1986). Effectiveness of cognitive/relaxation therapy and study-skills training in reduced self-reported anxiety and improving the academic performance of test-anxious students. *Journal of Counseling Psychology, 33,* 131–135.

Denham, C., & Lieberman, A. (1980). *Time to learn.* Washington, DC: National Institute of Education.

Denham, S. A. (1986). Social cognition, prosocial behavior, and emotion in preschoolers: Contextual validation. *Child Development, 57,* 194–201.

Denham, S. A. (1998). *Emotional development in young children.* New York: Guilford Press.

Denham, S. A., Blair, K. A., DeMulder, E., et al. (2003). Preschool emotional competence: Pathway to social competence? *Child Development, 74*(1), 238–256.

Denham, S., & Kochanoff, A. T. (2002). Parental contributions to preschoolers' understanding of emotion. *Marriage & Family Review, 34,* 311–343.

Denissen, J. J., Zarrett, N. R., & Eccles, J. S. (2007). I like to do it, I'm able, and I know I am: Longitudinal couplings between domain specific achievement, self-concept, and interest. *Child Development, 78,* 430–447.

Dennen, V. P. (2004). Cognitive apprenticeship in educational practice: Research on scaffolding, modeling, mentoring, and coaching as instructional strategies. In D. H. Jonassen (Ed.), *Handbook of research on educational communications and technology* (pp. 813–828). Mahwah, NJ: Erlbaum.

Denning, R., & Smith, P. (1997). Cooperative learning and technology. *Journal of Computers in Mathematics and Science Teaching, 16*(2–3), 177–200.

DeTemple, J. (2001). Parents and children reading books together. In D. Dickinson & P. Tabors (Eds.), *Beginning literacy with language: Young children learning at home and school* (pp. 31–51). Baltimore: Paul H. Brookes.

DeVoe, J. F., Peter, K., Kaufman, P., et al. (2003, October). *Indicators of school crime and safety: 2003 NCES2004–004/NCJ 201257.* U.S. Departments of Education and Justice, Washington, DC. Retrieved December 3, 2003, from www.ojp.usdoj. gov/bjs/.

DeVries, D., & Edwards, K. (1974). Student teams and learning games: Their effects on cross-race and cross-sex interaction. *Journal of Educational Psychology, 66*(5), 741–749.

DeVries, R. (1969). Constancy of generic identity in the years three to six. *Monographs of the Society for Research in Child Development, 34* (Serial 127).

Dewey, J. (1933). *How we think: A restatement of the relation of reflective thinking to the educational process.* Lexington, MA: Heath.

Dhopeshwarkar, G. A. (1983). *Nutrition and brain development.* New York: Plenum Press.

Diamond, M., & Hopson, J. (1998). *Magic trees of the mind: How to nurture your child's intelligence, creativity, and healthy emotions from birth through adolescence.* New York: Penguin Putman.

Dickinson, T. S. (2001). Reinventing the middle school. New York: Routledge Falmer.

Diener, C. I., & Dweck, C. S. (1978). An analysis of learned helplessness: Continuous changes in performance, strategy, and achievement cognitions after failure. *Journal of Personality and Social Psychology, 36,* 451–462.

Dion, K. K., & Dion, K. L. (2004). Gender, immigrant generation, and ethnocultural identity. *Sex Roles, 50*(5/6), 347–355.

Do, E. Y., & Gross, M. D. (2007). Environments for creativity—A lab for making things. In Proceedings of the Seventh Creativity and Cognition Conference (Washington, DC, June 13-15, 2007), ACM Press, pp. 27–36.

Dominowski, R. L. (1998). Verbalization and problem solving. In D. J. Hacker, J. Dunlosky, & A. C. Graesser (Eds.), *Metacognition in educational theory and practice* (pp. 25–45). Mahwah, NJ: Erlbaum.

Donohue, K. M., Perry, K. E., & Weinstein, R. S. (2003). Teachers' classroom practices and children's rejection by their peers. *Applied Developmental Psychology, 24,* 91–118.

Donovan, M. S., & Cross, C. T. (Eds.). (2002). *Minority students in special education.* Washington, DC: National Academy Press.

Dornbusch, S. M., Carlsmith, J. M., Bushwall, S. J., et al. (1985). Single parents, extended households, and the control of adolescents. *Child Development, 56,* 326–341.

Dotterer, A. M., McHale, S. M., & Crouter, A. C. (2009). The development and correlates of academic interests from childhood through adolescence. *Journal of Educational Psychology, 101*(2), 509–519.

Doty, G. (2001). *Fostering emotional intelligence in K–8 students.* Thousand Oaks, CA: Corwin Press.

Douglas, V. I. (2005). Cognitive deficits in children with attention deficit hyperactivity disorder: A long-term follow-up. *Canadian Psychology, 46,* 23–31.

Dowson, M., & McInerney, D. M. (2001). Psychological parameters of students' social and work avoidance goals: A qualitative investigation. *Journal of Educational Psychology, 93,* 35–42.

Doyle, A., & Aboud, F. (1995) A longitudinal study of White children's racial prejudice as a social cognitive development. *Merrill-Palmer Quarterly, 41,* 213–223.

Doyle, W. (1986). Classroom organization and management. In M. C. Wittrock (Ed.), *Handbook of research on teaching* (3rd ed., pp. 392–431). New York: Macmillan.

Doyle, W. (2006). Ecological approaches to classroom management. In C. Evertson & C. Weinstein (Eds.). *Handbook of classroom management: Research, practice, and contemporary issues* (pp. 97–125). New York: Erlbaum.

Drayer, A. M. (1979). *Problems in middle school and high school teaching: A handbook for student teachers and beginning teachers* (pp. 182–187). Boston: Allyn & Bacon.

Dreikurs, R. (1968). *Psychology in the classroom.* (2nd ed.) New York: Harper & Row.

Dreikurs, R., Grunwald, B. B., & Pepper, F. C. (1982). *Maintaining sanity in the classroom: Classroom management techniques* (2nd ed.). New York: Harper & Row.

Driscoll, M. P. (2005). *Psychology of learning for instruction.* Boston: Allyn & Bacon.

Dubois, D. L., Felner, R. D., Brand, S., Adan, A. M., & Evans, E. G. (1992). A prospective study of life stress, social support, and adaptation in early adolescence. *Child Development, 63,* 542–557.

Dudek, S. Z., Strobel, M. G., & Runco, M. A. (1993). Cumulative and proximal influences on the social environment and children's creative potential. *Journal of Genetic Psychology, 154,* 487–499.

Duffau, H., Denvil, D., Lopes, M., et al. (2002). Intraoperative mapping of the cortical areas involved in multiplication and subtraction: An electrostimulation study in a patient with a left parietal glioma. *Journal of Neurology, Neurosurgery, and Psychiatry, 73,* 733–738.

Duke, M., Forbes, H., Hunter, S., & Prosser, M. (1998). Problem-based learning: Conceptions and approaches of undergraduate students of nursing. *Advances in Health Sciences Education, 3,* 59–70.

Duncan, G. J., & Brooks-Gunn, J. (2000). Family poverty, welfare reform, and child development. *Child Development, 71,* 188–196.

Duncker, K. (1945). On problem solving (L. S. Lees, Trans.). *Psychological Monographs, 58*(5), Whole No. 270.

Dunlosky, J., & Hertzog, C. (1998). Training programs to improve learning later in adulthood: Helping older adults educate themselves. In D. J. Hacker, J. Dunlosky, & A. C. Graesser (Eds.), *Metacognition in educational theory and practice* (pp. 249–275). Mahwah, NJ: Erlbaum.

Dunn, J. (2006). Moral development in early childhood and social interaction in the family. In M. Killen & J. Smetana (Eds.), *Handbook of moral development.* Mahwah, NJ: Erlbaum.

Dunn, J., Brown, J., & Beardsall, L. (1991). Family talk about feeling states and children's later understanding of others' emotions. *Developmental Psychology, 27,* 448–455.

Dunn, R., & Griggs, S. A. (Eds.). (2003). *Synthesis of the Dunn and Dunn learning style model research: Who, what, when, where, and so what?* New York: St. John's University.

Dunsmore, J. C., Her, P., Halberstadt, A. G., & Perez-Rivera, M. B. (2009). Parents' beliefs about emotions and children's recognition of parents' emotions, *Journal of Non-Verbal Behavior, 33,* 121–140.

Dunsmore, J. C., & Karn, M. A. (2001). Mothers' beliefs about feelings and children's emotional understanding. *Early Education and Development, 12,* 117–138.

Dunsmore, J. C., & Karn, M. A. (2004). The influence of peer relationships and maternal socialization on kindergartners' developing emotion knowledge. *Early Education and Development, 15,* 39–56.

Durik, A. M., & Harackiewicz, J. M. (2007). Different strokes for different folks: How individual interest moderates the effects of situational factors on task interest. *Journal of Educational Psychology, 99*(3), 597–610.

Durik, A. M., Vida, M., & Eccles, J. S. (2006). Task values and ability beliefs as predictors of high school literacy choices: A developmental analysis. *Journal of Educational Psychology, 98*(2), 382–393.

Durlak, J. A., & Weissberg, R. P. (2005). *A major meta-analysis of positive youth development programs.* Presentation at the annual meeting of the American Psychological Association. Washington, DC.

Durlak, J., & Weissberg, R. (2010), Social and emotional learning programmes that work. *Better: Evidence-based Education* (Winter 2010), 4–5.

Durnin, J. H., Perrone, A. E., & MacKay, L. (1997). Teaching problem solving in elementary school mathematics. *Journal of Structural Learning and Intelligent Systems, 13,* 53–69.

Durston, S., Pol, H. E. H., Schnack, H. G., et al. (2004). Magnetic resonance imaging of boys with attention-deficit/hyperactivity disorder and their unaffected siblings. *Journal of the American Academy of Adolescent Psychiatry, 43*(3), 332–340.

Dusek, J. B., & McIntyre, J. G. (2006). Self-concept and self-esteem development. In G. R. Adams & M. D. Berzonsky (Eds.), *Blackwell handbook of adolescence.* Malden, MA: Blackwell.

Duthie, J. K., Nippold, M. A., Billow, J. L., & Mansfield, T. C. (2008). Mental imagery of concrete proverbs: A developmental study of children, adolescents, and adults. *Applied Psycholinguistics, 29*(1), 151–173.

Dutton, J., Dutton, M., & Perry, J. (2002). How do on-line students differ from lecture students? *Journal of Asynchronous Learning Networks Online, 6*(1).

Dweck, C. (1975). The role of expectations and attributions in the alleviation of learned helplessness. *Journal of Personality and Social Psychology, 31,* 674–685.

Dweck, C. (1985). Motivation. In R. Glaser & A. Lesgold (Eds.), *Handbook of psychology and education.* Hillsdale, NJ: Erlbaum.

Dweck, C. (2000). *Self-theories: Their role in motivation, personality, and development.* Philadelphia: Psychology Press.

Dweck, C. S. (1999). *Self-theories: Their role in motivation, personality, and development.* Philadelphia: Taylor & Francis.

Dweck, C. S. (2002). The development of ability conceptions. In A. Wigfield & J. S. Eccles (Eds.), *Development of achievement motivation* (pp. 57–88). New York: Academic Press.

Dweck, C. S. (2007). The perils and promises of praise. *Educational Leadership, 65*(2), 34–39.

Dweck, C. S., & Bush, E. S. (1976). Sex differences in learned helplessness: I. Differential debilitation with peer and adult evaluators. *Developmental Psychology, 12,* 147–156.

Dweck, C. S., Chiu, C., & Hong, Y. (1995). Implicit theories and their role in judgments and reactions: A world from two perspectives. *Psychological Inquiry, 6,* 267–285.

Dweck, C., Davidson, W., Nelson, S., & Enna, B. (1978). Sex differences in learned helplessness: II. The contingencies of evaluative feedback in the classroom, and III. An experimental analysis. *Developmental Psychology, 14,* 268–276.

Dweck, C., & Goetz, T. (1978). Attributions and learned helplessness. In W. Harvey & R. Kidd (Eds.), *New directions in attribution research. Vol. 2* (pp. 157–179). Hillsdale, NJ: Erlbaum.

Dweck, C. S., Goetz, T., & Strauss, N. L. (1980). Sex differences in learned helplessness: IV. An experimental and naturalistic study of failure generalization and its mediators. *Journal of Personality and Social Psychology, 38,* 441–452.

Dweck, C. S., & Leggett, E. L. (1988). A social-cognitive approach to motivation and personality. *Psychological Review, 95,* 256–273.

Dweck, C. S., & Master, A. (2008). Self-theories motivate self-regulated learning. In D. H. Schunk & B. J. Zimmerman (Eds.), *Motivation and self-regulated learning: Theory, research, and applications* (pp. 31–51). New York: Erlbaum.

Dweck, C. S., & Sorich, L. (1999). Mastery-oriented thinking. In C. R. Snyder (Ed.), *Coping.* New York: Oxford University Press.

Dwyer, K., Osher, D., & Warger, C. (1998). *Early warning, timely response: A guide to safe schools.* Washington, DC: U.S. Department of Education.

E

Eacott, C., & Frydenberg, E. (2009a). At-risk students in a rural context: benefits and gains from a coping skills program. *Australian Journal of Guidance and Counseling, 18*(2), 160–181.

Eacott, C., & Frydenberg, E. (2009b). Promoting positive coping skills for rural youth: Benefits for at-risk young people. *Australian Journal of Rural Health, 17,* 338–345.

Eamon, M. K. (2001). Poverty, parenting, peer and neighborhood influences on young adolescent antisocial behavior. *Journal of Social Service Research, 28*(1), 1–23.

Earl, L., & Katz, S. (2006). *Rethinking classroom assessment with purpose in mind.* Western and Northern Canadian Protocol for Collaboration in Education (WNCP). Available online at http://www.wncp.ca/.

Earl, L. M. (2003). *Assessment as learning: Using classroom assessment to maximize student learning.* Thousand Oaks, CA: Corwin Press.

Ebbinghaus, H. (1885). *Uber das Gedachtnis.* Leipzig: Duncker & Humblot. Cited in R. Klatzky (1980), *Human memory: Structures and processes.* San Francisco: Freeman.

Ebel, R. L. (1979). *Essentials of educational measurement* (3rd ed.). Upper Saddle River, NJ: Prentice Hall.

Ebel, R. L., & Frisbie, D. A. (1991). *Essentials of educational measurement* (5th ed.). Upper Saddle River, NJ: Pearson Merrill/Prentice Hall.

Ebmeier, H., & Good, T. L. (1979). The effects of instructing teachers about good teaching on mathematics achievement of fourth-grade students. *American Educational Research Journal, 16*(1), 1016.

Eccles, J., Barber, B., Jozefowicz, D., Malenchuk, O., & Vida, M. (2000). Self-evaluations of competence, task values, and self-esteem. In N. Johnson, M. Roberts, & J. Worrell (Eds.), *Girls and adolescence* (pp. 53–84). Washington, DC: APA Press.

Eccles, J., Midgley, C., & Adler, T. F. (1984). Grade-related changes in the school environment: Effects on achievement motivation. In J. G. Nicholls (Ed.), *The development of achievement motivation, Vol. 3* (pp. 283–331). Greenwich, CT: JAI Press.

Eccles, J., Roeser, R., Wigfield, A., & Freedman-Doan, C. (1999). Academic and motivational pathways through middle childhood. In L. Balter & C. Tamis-LeMonda (Eds.), *Child psychology: A handbook of contemporary issues* (pp. 287–317). Philadelphia: Psychology Press.

Eccles, J. S. (2005). Subjective task value and the Eccles et al. model of achievement-related choices. In A. J. Elliot & C. S. Dweck (Eds.), *Handbook of competence and motivation* (pp. 105–121). New York: Guilford.

Eccles, J. S., Adler, T. F., Futterman, R., Goff, S. B., Kaczala, C. M., & Meece, J. L. (1983). Expectancies, values and academic behaviors. In J. T. Spence (Ed.), *Achievement and achievement motives* (pp. 75–146). San Francisco: Freeman.

Eccles, J. S., Early, D., Frasier, K., Belansky, E., & McCarthy, K. (1996). The relation of connection, regulation, and support for autonomy to adolescents' functioning. *Journal of Adolescent Research, 12,* 263–286.

Eccles, J. S., & Midgley, C. (1989). Stage-environment fit: Developmentally appropriate classrooms for young adolescents. In C. Ames, & R. Ames (Eds.), *Research on motivation in education* (Vol. 3, pp. 139–186). San Diego, CA: Academic Press.

Eccles, J. S., Midgley, C., Wigfield, A., et al. (1993). Development during adolescence: The impact of stage-environment fit on young adolescents' experiences in schools and families. *American Psychologist, 48,* 90–101.

Eccles, J. S., Wigfield, A., & Schiefele, U. (1998). Motivation to succeed. In N. Eisenberg (Ed.), *Handbook of child psychology: Vol. 3. Social, emotional, and personality development* (5th ed., pp. 1017–1095). New York: Wiley.

Edelman, G. R. (1992). *Bright air, brilliant fire: On the matter of the mind.* New York: Basic Books.

Edelson, E. (1988). *Nutrition and the brain.* New York: Chelsea House.

Eder, D. (1983). Ability grouping and students' academic self-concepts: A case study. *Elementary School Journal, 84,* 149–161.

Egger, H. L., Costello, E. J., Erkanli, A., & Angold, A. (1999). Somatic complaints and psychopathology in children and adolescents: Stomach aches, musculoskeletal pains, and headaches. *Journal of the American Academy of Child and Adolescent Psychiatry, 38,* 852–860.

Ehlers, S., & Gillberg, C. (1993). The epidemiology of Asperger syndrome: A total population study. *Journal of Child Psychology and Psychiatry, 34,* 1327–1350.

Eibl-Eibesfeldt, I. (1971). *Love and hate: The natural history of behavior patterns.* New York: Holt, Rinehart, & Winston.

Eikeseth, S. (2009). Outcome of comprehensive psycho-educational interventions for young children with autism. *Research in Developmental Disabilities, 30*(1), 158–178.

Eisenberg, N. (1982). The development of reasoning regarding prosocial behavior. In N. Eisenberg (Ed.), *The development of prosocial behavior.* San Diego: Academic Press.

Eisenberg, N. (1986). *Altruistic emotion, cognition and behavior.* Hillsdale, NJ: Erlbaum.

Eisenberg, N., & Fabes, R. A. (1998). Prosocial development. In W. Damon (Series Ed.) & N. Eisenberg (Vol. Ed.), *Handbook of child psychology: Vol. 3. Social, emotional, and personality development.* New York: Wiley.

Eisenberg, N., Fabes, R., & Murphy, B. C. (1996). Parents' reactions to children's negative emotions: Relationship to children's social competence and comforting behavior. *Child Development, 67,* 2227–2247.

Eisenberg, N., Martin, C. L., & Fabes, R. (1996). Gender development and gender effects. In D. C. Berliner & R. C. Calfee (Eds.), *Handbook of educational psychology.* New York: Simon & Schuster Macmillan.

Eisenberg, N., Morris, A. S., McDaniel, B., & Sprinrad, T. L. (2009). Moral cognitions and prosocial responding in adolescence. In R. M. Lerner & L. Steinberg (Eds.), *Handbook of adolescent psychology* (3rd ed.). New York: Wiley.

Eisenberg, N., Shell, R., Pasternack, J., Lennon, R., Beller, R., & Mathy, R. M. (1987). Prosocial development in middle childhood: A longitudinal study. *Developmental Psychology, 23,* 712–718.

Eisenberg, N., Spinrad, T., & Sadovsky, A. (2006). Empathy-related responding in children. In M. Killen & J. Smetana (Eds.), *Handbook of moral development.* Mahwah, NJ: Erlbaum.

Eisner, E. W. (1985). *The educational imagination.* New York: Macmillan.

Ekman, P. (1994). Strong evidence for universals in facial expressions: A reply to Russell's mistaken critique. *Psychological Bulletin, 115,* 268–287.

Elfenbein, H. A. (2006). Learning in emotion judgments: Training and the cross-cultural understanding of facial expressions. *Journal of Non-Verbal Behavior, 30*(1), 21–36.

Elias, M. J. (2004). The connection between social-emotional learning and learning disabilities: Implications for intervention. *Learning Disability Quarterly, 27*(1), 53–63.

Elias, M. J., & Haynes, N. M. (2008). Social competence, social support, and academic achievement in minority, low-income, and urban elementary school children. *School Psychology Quarterly, 23*(4), 474–495.

Elias, M. J., & Schwab, Y. (2006). From compliance to responsibility: Social and emotional learning and classroom management. In C. Evertson & C. S. Weinstein (Eds.), *Handbook for classroom management: Research, practice, and contemporary issues* (pp. 309–341). Mahwah, NJ: Erlbaum.

Elias, M. J., Tobias, S. E., & Freidlander, B. S. (1999). *Emotionally intelligent parenting.* New York: Harmony/Random House.

Elias, M. J., & Weissberg, R. P. (2000). Primary prevention: Educational approaches to enhance social and emotional learning. *Journal of School Health, 70*(5), 186–190.

Elias, M. J., Zins, J. E., Weissberg, R. P., et al. (1997). *Promoting social and emotional learning: Guidelines for educators.* Alexandria, VA: Association for Supervision and Curriculum Development.

Elkind, D. (1967). Egocentrism in adolescence. *Child Development, 38,* 1025–1034.

Elliot, A. J., & Church, M. A. (1997). A hierarchical model of approach and avoidance achievement motivation. *Journal of Personality and Social Psychology, 72,* 218–232.

Elliot, A. J., & McGregor, H. A. (2001). A 2 x 2 achievement goal framework. *Journal of Personality and Social Psychology, 80*(3), 501–519.

Elliot, A. J., & McGregor, H. A., & Gable, S. (1999). Achievement goals, study strategies, and exam performance: A meditational analysis. *Journal of Educational Psychology, 91*(3), 549–563.

Elliot, A. J., & Moller, A. C. (2003). Performance-approach goals: Good or bad forms of regulation? *International Journal of Educational Research, 39,* 339–356.

Elliot, A. J., Shell, M. M., Bouas Henry, K., & Maier, M. A. (2005). Achievement goals, performance contingencies, and performance attainment: An experimental test. *Journal of Educational Psychology, 97,* 630–640.

Elliot, J. (2003). Dynamic assessment in educational settings: Realizing potential. *Educational Review, 55*(1), 15–32.

Elliott, S. N., McKevitt, B. C., & Kettler, R. J. (2002). Testing accommodations, research, and decision making. The case of "good" scores being highly valued but difficult to achieve for all students. *Measurement and Evaluation in Counseling and Development, 35,* 153–166.

Ellis, A. K. (2001). Teaching for intelligence. In A. K. Ellis (Ed.), *Research on educational innovations.* Larchmont, New York: Eye on Education.

Ellison-Wright, I., Ellison-Wright, Z., & Bullmore, E. (2008). Structural brain change in Attention Deficit Hyperactivity Disorder identified by meta-analysis. *BMC Psychiatry, 8*(51). doi:10.1186/1471-244X-8-51

Else-Quest, N. M., Hyde, J. S., & Linn, M. C. (2010). Cross-national patterns of gender differences in mathematics: A meta-analysis. *Psychological Bulletin, 136*(1), 103–127.

Emmer, E. T., Evertson, C. M., & Anderson, L. M. (1980). Effective classroom management at the beginning of the school year. *Elementary School Journal, 80*(5), 219–231.

Emmer, E. T., Evertson, C. M., & Worsham, M. E. (2006). *Classroom management for middle and high school teachers* (7th ed.). Boston: Pearson Education.

Emmer, E. T., & Stough, L. M. (2001). Classroom management: A critical part of educational psychology, with implications for teacher education. *Educational Psychologist, 36,* 103–112.

Emmer, E. T., & Worsham, M. E. (2006). *Classroom management for middle and high school teachers* (7th ed.). Boston: Allyn & Bacon.

Emond, V., Joyal, C., & Poissant, H. (2009). Structural and functional neuroanatomy of attention-deficit hyperactivity disorder (ADHD). *Encephale, 35*(2), 107–114.

Engle, R., & Kane, M. J. (2004). Executive attention, working memory capacity, and a two-factor theory of cognitive control. In B. Ross (Ed.), *The psychology of learning and motivation* (Vol. 44, pp. 145–199). New York: Elsevier.

Engle, R. W., Nations, J. K., & Cantor, J. (1990). Is "working memory capacity" just another name for word knowledge? *Journal of Educational Psychology, 82*(4), 799–804.

Enkenberg, J. (2001). Instructional design and emerging models in higher education. *Computers in Human Behavior, 17,* 495–506.

Ennis, R. (1996). Critical thinking dispositions: Their nature and assessability. *Informal Logic, 18*(2–3), 165–182.

Epping, R. J. (2010). Innovative use of Blackboard to assess laboratory skills. *Journal of Learning Design, 3*(3), 32–36.

Epstein, J. L., & MacIver, D. J. (1992). Opportunities to learn: Effects on eighth graders of curriculum offerings and instructional approaches (Report No. 34). Baltimore: Center for Research on Elementary and Middle Schools, Johns Hopkins University.

Epstein, M. H., Kinder, D., & Bursuck, D. (1989). The academic status of adolescents with behavioral disorders. *Behavioral Disorders, 14,* 157–165.

Erhardt, D., & Hinshaw, S. P. (1994). Initial sociometric impressions of attention-deficit hyperactivity disorder and comparison boys: Predictions from social behaviors and from nonbehavioral variables. *Journal of Consulting and Clinical Psychology, 62,* 833–842.

Ericsson, A. (2006). The influence of experience and deliberate practice on the development of superior expert performance. In K. A. Ericsson, N. Charness, P. J. Feltovich, & R. R. Hoffman (Eds.), *The Cambridge handbook of expertise and expert performance* (pp. 683–703). Cambridge, UK: Cambridge University Press.

Erikson, E. H. (1959/1980). *Identity and the life cycle.* New York: Norton.

Ertmer, P. A., Glazewski, K. D., Jones, D., et al. (2009). Facilitating technology-enhanced PBL in the middle school classroom: An examination of how and why teachers adapt. *Journal of Interactive Learning Research, 20*(1), 35–54.

Esposito, C. (1999). Learning in urban blight: School climate and its effects on the school performance of urban, minority, low-income children. *School Psychology Review, 28*(3), 365–377.

Esquivel, G. B. (1995). Teacher behaviors that foster creativity. *Educational Psychology Review, 7,* 185–202.

Estell, D. B., Farmer, T. W., Irvin, M. J., Crowther, A., Akos, P., & Boudah, D. J. (2009). Students with exceptionalities and the peer group context of bullying and victimization in late elementary school. *Journal of Child and Family Studies, 18,* 136–150.

Esterlee, J., & Clurman, D. (1993). *Conversations with critical thinkers.* San Francisco: The Whitman Institute.

Evans, G. W. (2004). The environment of childhood poverty. *American Psychologist, 59,* 77–92.

Evans, G. W., & English, K. (2002). The environment of poverty: Multiple stressor exposure, psychophysiological stress, and socioemotional adjustment. *Child Development, 73,* 1238–1248.

Evans, S. W., Axelrod, J. L., & Sapia, J. L. (2000). Effective school-based mental health interventions: Advancing the social skills training paradigm. *Journal of Social Health, 70,* 191–194.

Evertson., C. (1989). Improving classroom management: A school-based program for beginning the year. *Journal of Educational Research 83*(2), 82–90.

Evertson, C., & Emmer, E. (1982). Effective classroom management at the beginning of the year in junior high classes. *Journal of Educational Psychology, 74,* 485–498.

Evertson, C., & Emmer, E. (2008). *Classroom management for elementary teachers* (8th ed.). Allyn & Bacon.

Evertson, C. M., Emmer, E. T., & Worsham, M. E. (2006). *Classroom management for elementary teachers* (7th ed.) Boston: Pearson Education.

F

Fabiano, G. A., Pelham, W. E., Coles, E. K., Gnacy, E. M., Chronis-Tuscano, A., & O'Conor, B. C. (2009). A meta-analysis of behavioral treatments for attention-deficit/hyperactivity disorder. *Clinical Psychology Review, 29,* 129–140.

Fabiano, G. A., Vujnovic, R. K., Pelham, W. E., et al. (2010). Enhancing the effectiveness of special education programming for children with attention deficit hyperactivity disorder using daily report card. *School Psychology Review, 39*(2), 219–239.

Facione, F. G., Facione, N. C., & Giancarlo, C. A. (2000). The disposition toward critical thinking: Its character, measurement, and relationship to critical thinking skill. *Informal Logic, 20*(1), 61–84.

Facione, P. A. (2011). *Critical thinking: What it is and why it counts.* 2011 update. Milbrae, CA: California Academic Press.

Facione, P. A. (2011). *Think critically.* Englewood Cliffs, NJ: Pearson Education.

Falk, B., Ort, S. W., & Moirs, K. (2007). Keeping the focus on the child: Supporting and reporting on teaching and learning with a classroom-based performance assessment system. *Educational Assessment, 12*(1), 47–75.

Fanti, K. A., & Henrich, C. C. (2010). Trajectories of pure and co-occurring internalizing and externalizing problems from age 2 to age 12: Findings from the National Institute of Child Health and Human Development Study of Early Child Care. *Developmental Psychology, 46*(5), 1159–1175.

Fantuzzo, J. W., Riggio, R. E., Connelly, S., & Dimeff, L. A. (1989). Effects of reciprocal peer tutoring on academic achievement and psychological adjustment: A component analysis. *Journal of Educational Psychology, 81,* 173–177.

Farah, M. J., Betancourt, L., Shera, D. M., et al. (2008). Environmental stimulation, parental nurturance and cognitive development in humans. *Developmental Science, 11*(5), 793–801.

Farlow, L. (1995). *Cooperative learning to facilitate the inclusion of students with moderate to severe mental retardation in secondary subject-area classes.* Paper presented at the annual conference of the American Association on Mental Retardation, Boston, June 1995. Eric Document (ED 375 541).

Farmer, T. W., Estell, D. B., Bishop, J. L., O'Neal, K. K., & Cairns, B. D. (2003). Rejected bullies or popular leaders? The social relations of aggressive subtypes of rural African American early adolescents. *Developmental Psychology, 39*(6), 992–1004.

Farmer, T. W., Hall, C. M., Petrin, R., Hamm, J. V., & Dadisman, K. (2010). Evaluating the impact of a multicomponent interventional model on teachers' awareness of social networks at the beginning of middle school in rural communities. *School Psychology Quarterly, 25*(2), 94–106.

Farrington-Flint, L., Vanuxem-Cotterill, S., & Stiller, J. (2009). Patterns of problem-solving in children's literacy and arithmetic. *British Journal of Developmental Psychology, 27*(4), 815–834.

Farris, P., Fuhler, C., & Walther, M. (2004). *Teaching reading: A balanced approach for today's classrooms.* Boston: McGraw-Hill.

Fay, J., & Funk, D. (1995). *Teaching with love and logic.* Golden, CO: Love and Logic Press.

Feifer, S. G. (2008). Integrating response to intervention (RTI) with neuropsychology: A scientific approach to reading. *Psychology in the Schools, 45,* 812–825.

Feldhusen, J. F., & Moon, S. M. (1992). Grouping gifted students: Issues and concerns. *Gifted Child Quarterly, 36,* 63–67.

Feldlaufer, H., Midgley, C., & Eccles, J. S. (1988). Student, teacher, and observer perceptions of the classroom environment before and after the transition to junior high school. *Journal of Early Adolescence, 8,* 133–156.

Fenson, L., Dale, P. S., Reznick, J. S., Bates, E., Thal, D. J., & Pethick, S. J. (1994). Variability in early communicative development. *Monographs of the Society for Research in Child Development, 59*(5, Serial No. 242).

Fernald, A. (1985). Four-month-old infants prefer to listen to "motherese." *Infant Behavior and Development, 8,* 181–195.

Ferrando, M., Ferrandiz, C., Prieto, M. D., Bermejo, M. R., & Sainz, M. (2008). Creativity in gifted and talented children. *The International Journal of Creativity and Problem Solving, 18*(2), 35–47.

Fey, M., Long, S., & Finestack, L. (2003, February). Ten principles of grammar facilitation for children with specific language impairments. *American Journal of Speech–Language Pathology, 12,* 3–15.

Fichnova, K. (2002). Creative abilities of preschool-age boys and girls/Tvorive schopnosti chlapcov adievcat predskolskeho veku. *Psychologia a Patopsychologia Dietata, 37,* 306–314.

Fielder, E. D., Lange, R. E., & Winebrenner, S. (1993). In search of reality: Unraveling the myths about tracking, ability grouping and the gifted. *Roeper Review, 16,* 4–7.

Fierros, E. G., & Conroy, J. E. (2002). Double jeopardy: An exploration of restrictiveness of race in special education. In D. Losen (Ed.), *Minority issues in special education* (pp. 39–70). Cambridge, MA: The Civil Rights Project, Harvard University and Harvard Education Publishing Group.

Filby, N. N., & Barnett, B. G. (1982). Student perceptions of "better readers" in elementary classrooms. *Elementary School Journal, 82,* 435–449.

Filipek, P. A., Accardo, P. J., Baranek, G. T., et al. (1999). The screening and diagnosis of autism spectrum disorders. *Journal of Autism and Developmental Disorders, 29*(6), 439–484.

Finch, H., Baron, K., & Meyer, P. (2009). Differential item functioning analysis for accommodated versus nonaccommodated students. *Educational Assessment, 14,* 38–56.

Fine, M. A., & Harvey, J. H. (2006). Divorce and relationship dissolution in the 21st century. In M. A. Fine & J. H. Harvey (Eds.), *Handbook of divorce and remarriage.* Mahwah, NJ: Erlbaum.

Fingerhut, L. A., & Christoffel, K. K. (2002). Firearm-related death and injury among children and adolescents. *Future of Children, 12*(2), 25–37.

Finley, M. K. (1984). Teachers and tracking in a comprehensive high school. *Sociology of Education, 57,* 233–243.

Finn, J. D., & Cox, D. (1992). Participation and withdrawal among fourth-grade pupils. *American Educational Research Journal, 29*(1), 141–162.

Finn, J. D., Fish, R. M., & Scott, L.A. (2008). Educational sequelae of high school misbehavior. *Journal of Educational Research, 101*(5), 259–274.

Fischer, K. W., Bernstein, J. H., & Immordino-Yang, M. H. (Eds.). (2007). *Mind, brain and education in reading disorders.* Cambridge, UK: Cambridge University Press.

Fischer, L., Schimmel, D., & Kelly, C. (1999). *Teachers and the law.* New York: Longman.

Fischer, W. W., & Mazur, J. E. (1997). Basic and applied research on choice responding. *Journal of Applied Behavior Analysis, 30,* 387–410.

Fisher, A., & Scriven, M. (1997). *Critical thinking: Its definition and assessment.* Point Reyes, CA: Edge Press.

Fisher, C. W., Berliner, D. C., Filby, N. N., Marliave, R., Ghen, L. S., & Dishaw, M. M. (1980). Teaching behaviors, academic learning time, and student achievement: An overview. In C. Denham & A. Lieberman (Eds.), *Time to learn* (pp. 7–22). Washington, DC: National Institute of Education.

Flavell, J. H. (2000). Development of children's knowledge about the mental world. *International Journal of Behavioral Development, 24,* 15–23.

Flavell, J. H. (2004). Theory-of-mind development: Retrospect and prospect. *Merrill-Palmer Quarterly, 50,* 274–290.

Flavell, J. H., Flavell, E. R., & Green, F. L. (1983). Development of the appearance–reality distinction. *Cognitive Psychology, 15,* 95–120.

Flavell, J. H., Green, F. L., & Flavell, E. R. (1995). Young children's knowledge about thinking. *Monographs of the Society for Research in Child Development,* Serial No. 243, 60(1).

Flavell, J. H., Green, F. L., & Flavell, E. R. (2000). Development of children's awareness of their own thoughts. *Journal of Cognition and Development, 1,* 97–112.

Flavell, J. H., Miller, P. H., & Miller, S. A. (2002). *Cognitive development* (4th ed.). Upper Saddle River, NJ: Prentice Hall.

Fleischner, J. E. (1994). Diagnosis and assessment of mathematics learning disabilities. In G. R. Lyon (Ed.), *Frames of reference for the assessment of learning disabilities: New views on measurement issues* (pp. 459–472). Baltimore: Paul H. Brookes.

Fleith, D. (2000). Teacher and student perceptions of creativity in the classroom environment. *Roeper Review, 22,* 148–157.

Fletcher, J. D. (2009). From behaviorism to constructivism. In S. Tobias & T. M. Duffy (Eds.), *Constructive theory applied to instruction: Success or failure?* (pp. 242–263). New York: Taylor & Francis.

Fletcher, J. M., Barth, A. E., & Stuebing, K. K. (2011). A response to intervention (RTI) approach to SLD identification. In D. P. Flanagan & V. C. Alfonso (Eds.), *Essentials of specific learning disability and identification* (pp. 115–144). Hoboken, NJ: Wiley.

Fletcher, J. M., Lyon, G. R., Fuchs, L. S., & Barnes, M. A. (2007). *Learning disabilities: From identification to intervention.* New York: Guilford.

Fletcher, J. M., Shaywitz, S. E., Shankweiler, D. P., et al. (1994). Cognitive profiles of reading disability: Comparisons of discrepancy and low achievement definitions. *Journal of Educational Psychology, 86*(1), 6–23.

Fletcher, T., & Spielberger, C. (1995). Comparison of cognitive therapy and rational-emotive therapy in the treatment of test anxiety. In C. Spielberger & P. Vagg (Eds.), *Test anxiety: Theory, assessment, and treatment* (pp. 153–169). Washington, DC: Taylor & Francis.

Flood, W. A., Wilder, D. A., Flood, A. L., & Masuda, A. (2002). Peer-mediated reinforcement plus prompting as treatment for off-task behavior in children with Attention Deficit Hyperactivity Disorder. *Journal of Applied Behavior Analysis, 35,* 199–204.

Floyd, C. (1954). Meeting children's reading needs in the middle grades: A preliminary report. *Elementary School Journal, 55,* 99–103.

Flynn, J. R. (1984). The mean IQ of Americans: Massive gains 1932 to 1978. *Psychological Bulletin, 95,* 29–51.

Flynn, J. R. (2007). *What is intelligence?* New York: Cambridge University Press.

Folmer, A. S., Cole, D. A., Sigal, A. B., et al. (2008). Age-related changes in children's understanding of effort and ability: Implications for attribution theory and motivation. *Journal of Experimental Child Psychology, 99*(2), 114–134.

Fombonne, E. (1999). The epidemiology of autism: A review. *Psychological Medicine, 29,* 769–786.

Foorman, B. R., Francis, D. J., Winikates, P. M., Schatschneider, C., & Fletcher, J. M. (1997). Early interventions for children with reading disabilities. *Scientific Studies of Reading, 1*(3), 255–276.

Forehand, R., Thomas, A. M., Wierson, M., Brody, G., & Fauber, R. (1990). Role of maternal functioning and parenting skills in adolescent functioning following parental divorce. *Journal of Abnormal Psychology, 99*(3), 278–283.

Forte, E. (2010). Examining the assumptions underlying the NCLB federal accountability policy on school improvement. *Educational Psychologist, 45*(2), 76–88.

Foster, S. L. (2005). Aggression and antisocial behavior in girls. In D. J. Bell, S. L. Foster, & E. J. Mash (Eds.), *Handbook of behavioral and emotional problems in girls* (pp. 149–180). New York: Kluwer Academic/Plenum.

Fouad, N. A., & Smith, P. L. (1996). A test of a social cognitive model for middle school students: Math and science. *Journal of Counseling Psychology, 43,* 338–346.

Franconeri, S. L., & Simons, D. J. (2003). Moving and looming stimuli capture attention. *Perception and psychophysics, 65*(7), 999–1010.

Frankenberger, K. D. (2000). Adolescent egocentrism: A comparison among adolescents and adults. *Journal of Adolescence, 23,* 343–354.

Franklin, C., & Streeter, C. L. (1995). Assessment of middle class youth at-risk to drop out: School, psychologist and family correlates. *Children and Youth Services Review, 77,* 433–448.

Fraser, J., Goswami, U., & Conti-Ramsden, G. (2010). Dyslexia and specific language impairment: The role of phonology and auditory processing. *Scientific Studies of Reading, 14*(1), 8–29.

Frazier, T. W., Youngstrom, E. A., Glutting, J. J., & Watkins, M. W. (2007). ADHD and achievement: Meta-analysis of the child, adolescent, and adult literatures and a concomitant study with college students. *Journal of Learning Disabilities, 40*(1), 49–65.

Fredericks, J., & Eccles, J. S. (2002). Children's competence and value beliefs from childhood through adolescence: Growth trajectories in two male sex-typed domains. *Developmental Psychology, 38,* 519–533.

Fredriksen, K., & Rhodes, J. (2004). The role of teacher relationships in the lives of students. *New Directions for Youth Development, 103,* 45–54.

Freedman-Doan, C., Wigfield, A., Eccles, J., Blumenfeld, P., Arbreton, A., & Harold, R. (2000). What am I best at? Grade and gender differences in children's beliefs about ability improvement. *Journal of Applied Developmental Psychology, 21,* 379–402.

Freeland, J. T., & Noell, G. H. (1999). Maintaining accurate math responses in elementary school students: The effects of delayed intermittent reinforcement and programming common stimuli. *Journal of Applied Behavior Analysis, 32,* 211–215.

Freeman, J. (1995). Annotation: Recent studies of giftedness in children. *Journal of Child Psychology and Psychiatry, 36*(4), 531–547.

Freeman, J. B., Garcia, A. M., & Leonard, H. L. (2002). Anxiety disorders. In M. Lewis (Ed.), *Child and adolescent psychiatry: A comprehensive textbook* (3rd ed., pp. 821–834). Philadelphia: Lippincott Williams & Wilkins.

Freiburg, H. J., & Lamb, S. M. (2009). Dimensions of person-centered classroom management. *Theory Into Practice, 48,* 99–105.

Friedel, J. M., Cortina, K. S., Turner, J. C., & Midgley, C. (2010). Changes in efficacy beliefs in mathematics across the transition to middle school: Examining the effects of perceived teacher and parent goal emphases. *Journal of Educational Psychology, 102*(1), 102–114.

Fryer, J. W., & Elliot, A. J. (2008). Self-regulation of achievement goal pursuit. In D. H. Schunk & B. J. Zimmerman (Eds.), *Motivation and self-regulated learning: Theory, research, and applications* (pp. 53–75). New York: Erlbaum.

Fuchs, D., & Deshler, D. D. (2007). What we need to know about responsiveness to intervention (and shouldn't be afraid to ask). *Learning Disabilities Research and Practice, 22*(2), 129–136.

Fuchs, D., & Fuchs, L. S. (2006). Introduction to response to intervention: What, why and how valid is it? *Reading Research Quarterly, 41*, 93–99.

Fuchs, D., Mock, D., Morgan, P. L., & Young, C. L. (2003). Responsiveness-to-intervention: Definitions, evidence and implications for the LD construct. *Learning Disabilities Research & Practice, 18*, 157–171.

Fuchs, D., & Thelen, M. H. (1988). Children's expected interpersonal consequences of communicating their affective state and reported likelihood of expression. *Child Development, 59*, 1314–1322.

Fuchs, L. S., & Fuchs, D. (2007). A model for implementing responsiveness to intervention. *Teaching Exceptional Children, 39*, 14–20.

Fuchs, L. S., Fuchs, D., Kams, K., Hamlett, C. L., & Katzaroff, M. (1999). Mathematics performance assessment in the classroom: Effects on teacher planning and student problem solving. *American Educational Research Journal, 36*, 609–646.

Fuchs, L. S., Fuchs, D., Prentice, K., et al. (2003). Explicitly teaching for transfer: Effects on third-grade students' mathematical problem solving. *Journal of Educational Psychology, 95*, 293–305.

G

Gable, R. A., Hester, P. P., Hester, L. R., Hendrickson, J. M., & Sze, S. (2005). Cognitive, affective, and relational dimensions of middle school students: Implications for improving discipline and instruction. *Clearing House, 79*(1), 40.

Gage, N. L., & Berliner, D. C. (1992). *Educational psychology* (5th ed.). Boston: Houghton Mifflin.

Gajria, M., Jitendra, A. K., Sood, S., & Sacks, G. (2007). Improving comprehension of expository text in students with LD: A research synthesis. *Journal of Learning Disabilities, 40*(3), 210–225.

Galambos, N. L., Berenbaum, S. A., & McHale, S. M. (2009). Gender development in adolescence. In R. M. Lerner & L. Steinberg (Eds.), *Handbook of Adolescent Psychology* (3rd ed.). New Jersey: Wiley & Sons.

Galati, D., Scherer, K. R., & Ricci-Bitti, P. E. (1997). Voluntary facial expression of emotion: Comparing congenitally blind with normally sighted encoders. *Journal of Personality and Social Psychology, 73*, 1363–1379.

Gallagher, H., & Gallagher, S. (1994). *Teaching the gifted child*. Boston: Allyn & Bacon.

Gallagher, J. J. (1992). Gifted persons. In M. C. Alkin (Ed.), *Encyclopedia of educational research* (Vol. 2, pp. 544–549). New York: Macmillan.

Gallimore, R., & Goldenberg, C. (1992). Mapping teachers' Zone of Proximal Development: A Vygotskian perspective on teaching and teacher training. In F. Oser, A. Dick, & J.-L. Patry (Eds.), *Effective and responsible teaching: The new synthesis* (pp. 203–221). San Francisco: Jossey-Bass.

Gallimore, R., & Tharp, R. (1990). Teaching mind in society: Teaching, schooling, and literate discourse. In L. C. Moll (Ed.), *Vygotsky and education* (pp. 175–205). Cambridge, UK: Cambridge University Press.

Gamoran, A. (1990, April). *The consequences of track-related instructional differences for student achievement*. Paper presented at the annual meeting of the American Educational Research Association, Boston.

Gamoran, A. (1992). Is ability grouping equitable? *Educational Leadership, 50*(2), 11–17.

Gamoran, A. (1993). Alternative uses of ability grouping in secondary schools: Can we bring high-quality instruction to low-ability classes? *American Journal of Education, 102*(1), 1–22.

Gamoran, A., & Weinstein, M. (1998). Differentiation and opportunity in restructured schools. *American Journal of Education, 106*, 385–415.

Gao, X., & Maurer, D. (2010). A happy story: Developmental changes in children's sensitivity to facial expressions of varying intensities. *Journal of Experimental Child Psychology, 107*(2), 67–86.

Garbarino, J., & deLara, E. (2002). *And words can hurt forever: How to protect adolescents from bullying, harassment, and emotional violence*. New York: Free Press.

Garber, J., & Horowitz, J. L. (2002). Depression in children. In C. L. Hammen & I. H. Gotlib (Eds.), *Handbook of depression* (pp. 510–540). New York: Guilford.

García, E. E. (1992). "Hispanic" children: Theoretical, empirical, and related policy issues. *Educational Psychology Review, 4*(1), 69–93.

García, E. E. (1995). Educating Mexican American students: Past treatment and recent developments in theory, research, policy, and practice. In J. A. Banks & C. A. M. Banks (Eds.), *Handbook of research on multicultural education* (pp. 491–514). New York: Macmillan.

Garcia, G. E. (1991). Factors affecting the English reading test performance of Spanish-speaking Hispanic students. *Reading Research Quarterly, 26*, 371–392.

Garcia, G. E., & Pearson, P. D. (1994). Assessment and diversity. *Review of Research in Education, 20*, 337–391.

Garcia-Mila, M., & Anderson, C. (2007). Developmental change in notetaking during scientific inquiry. *International Journal of Science Education, 29*(8), 1035–1058.

Gardner, H. (1983). *Frames of mind: The theory of multiple intelligences*. New York: Basic Books.

Gardner, H. (1991). *The unschooled mind: How children think and how schools should teach*. New York: Basic Books.

Gardner, H. (1993). Introduction to the tenth-anniversary edition. *Frames of mind: The theory of multiple intelligences*. New York: Basic Books.

Gardner, H. (1995). Reflections on multiple intelligences: Myths and messages. *Phi Delta Kappan, 77*(3), 200–203.

Gardner, H. (1999). *Intelligence reframed: Multiple intelligences for the 21st century*. New York: Basic Books.

Gardner, H. (2000). *The disciplined mind: Beyond facts and standardized tests, the K–12 education that every child deserves*. New York: Penguin Books.

Gardner, H. (2006). *Multiple intelligences: New horizons*. New York: Basic Books.

Gardner, H., & Connell, M. (2000). Response to Nicholas Allix. *Australian Journal of Education, 44*, 288–293.

Gardner, H., & Moran, S. (2006). The science of multiple intelligences theory: A response to Lynn Waterhouse. *Educational Psychologist, 41*(4), 227–232.

Garlick, D. (2003). Integrating brain science research with intelligence research. *Current Directions in Psychological Science, 12*(5), 185–189.

Garner, P. W., Jones, D. C., & Miner, J. L. (1994). Social competence among low-income preschoolers: Emotion socialization practices and social cognitive correlates. *Child Development, 65,* 622–637.

Garnett, K. (1992). Developing fluency with basic number facts: Intervention for students with learning disabilities. *Learning Disabilities Research & Practice, 7,* 210–216.

Garrison, D. R., Anderson, T., & Archer, W. (2001). Critical thinking, cognitive presence, and computer conferencing in distance education. *American Journal of Distance Education, 15*(1), 7–23.

Gathercoal, F. (1993). *Judicious discipline* (3rd ed.). San Francisco: Caddo Gap Press.

Gathercoal, P., & Crowell, R. (2000). Judicious discipline. *Kappa Delta Pi, 36*(4), 173–177.

Gathercole, S. E., Pinkering, S. J., Knight, C., & Stegman, Z. (2004). Working memory skills and educational attainment: Evidence from national curriculum assessments at 7 and 14 years of age. *Applied Cognitive Psychology, 18,* 1–16.

Gavazzi, S., & Sabatelli, R. M. (1990). Family system dynamics, the individuation process, and psychosocial development. *Journal of Adolescent Research, 5,* 500–519.

Gay, G. (2000). *Culturally responsive teaching: Theory, research, and practice.* New York: Teachers College Press.

Geake, J. (2008). Neuromythologies in education. *Educational Research, 50*(2), 123–133.

Gearhart, M., & Osmundson, E. (2009). Assessment portfolios as opportunities for teacher learning. *Educational Assessment, 14*(1), 1–24.

Geary, D. (1990). A componential analysis of an early learning deficit in mathematics. *Journal of Experimental Child Psychology, 33,* 386–404.

Geary, D. C. (1993). Mathematical disabilities: Cognitive, neuropsychological, and genetic components. *Psychological Bulletin, 114,* 345–362.

Geary, D. C. (1994). *Children's mathematical development: Research and practical applications.* Washington, DC: American Psychological Association.

Geary, D. C. (1996). Sexual selection and sex differences in mathematical abilities. *Behavioral and Brain Sciences, 19,* 229–284.

Geary, D. C. (2004). Mathematics and learning disabilities. *Journal of Learning Disabilities, 37*(1), 4–15.

Geary, D. C., & Hoard, M. K. (2005). Learning disabilities in arithmetic and mathematics: Theoretical and empirical perspectives. In J. I. D. Campbell (Ed.), *Handbook of mathematical cognition* (pp. 253–267). New York: Psychology Press.

Geary, D. C., Saults, S. J., Liu, F., & Hoard, M. K. (2000). Sex differences in spatial cognition, computational fluency, and arithmetical reasoning. *Journal of Experimental Child Psychology, 77*(4), 337–353.

Geban, O., Askar, P., & Ozkan, I. (1992). Effects of computer simulations and problem solving approaches on high school students. *Journal of Educational Research, 86*(1), 5–10.

Gehlbach, H. (2004). A new perspective on perspective taking: A multidimensional approach to conceptualizing an aptitude. *Educational Psychology Review, 16,* 207–234.

Geiser, C., Lehmann, W., & Eid, M. (2008). A note on sex differences in mental rotation in different age groups. *Intelligence, 36,* 556–563.

Genesee, F., & Nicoladis, E. (1995). Language development in bilingual preschool children. In E. E. Garcia & B. McLaughlin (Eds.), *Meeting the challenge of linguistic and cultural diversity in early childhood education* (pp. 18–33). New York: Teachers College Press.

Genesee, F., Paradis, J., & Crago, M. (2004). *Dual language development and disorders: A handbook on bilingualism and second language learning.* Baltimore: Paul H. Brookes.

Genshaft, J. L., Bireley, M., & Hollinger, C. L. (1995). *Serving gifted and talented students: A resource for school personnel.* Austin, TX: Pro-Ed.

Gentile, B., Grabe, S., Dolan-Pascoe, B., Twenge, J. M., Wells, B. E., & Maitino, A. (2009). Gender differences in domain-specific self-esteem: A meta-analysis. *Review of General Psychology, 13*(1), 34–45.

Gentner, D., & Gentner, D. R. (1983). Flowing waters or teeming crowds: Mental models of electricity. In D. Gentner & A. L. Stevens (Eds.), *Mental models* (pp. 99–129). Hillsdale, NJ: Erlbaum.

Gentner, D., Loewenstein, J., & Thompson, L. (2003). Learning and transfer: A general role for analogical encoding. *Journal of Educational Psychology, 95*(2), 393–405.

Gentner, D., & Namy, L. L. (2004). The role of comparison in children's early word learning. In S. R. Waxman & D. G. Hall (Eds.), *Weaving a lexicon* (pp. 533–568). Cambridge, MA: MIT Press.

Gersten, R., Chard, D. J., Jayanthi, M., Baker, S. K., Morphy, P., & Flojo, J. (2009). Mathematics instruction for students with learning disabilities: A meta-analysis of instructional components. *Review of Educational Research, 79*(3), 1202–1242.

Gettinger, M. (1988). Methods of proactive classroom management. *School Psychology Review, 17,* 227–242.

Getzels, J. W., & Csikszentmihalyi, M. (1976). *The creative vision: A longitudinal study of problem-finding in art.* New York: Wiley.

Gibbs, J. C. (1991). Sociomoral developmental delay and cognitive distortion: Implications for the treatment of antisocial youth. In W. M. Kurtines & J. L. Gewirtz (Eds.), *Handbook of moral behavior and development: Vol. 3. Application.* Hillsdale, NJ: Erlbaum.

Gibson, S., & Dembo, M. (1984). Teacher efficacy: A construct validation. *Journal of Educational Psychology, 76,* 569–582.

Gick, M. L., & Holyoak, K. J. (1980). Analogical problem solving. *Cognitive Psychology, 12,* 306–355.

Gick, M. L., & Holyoak, K. J. (1983). Schema induction and analogical transfer. *Cognitive Psychology, 15,* 1–38.

Gick, M. L., & Holyoak, K. J. (1987). The cognitive basis for knowledge transfer. In S. M. Cormier & J. D. Hagman (Eds.), *Transfer of learning* (pp. 9–46). New York: Academic Press.

Gillies, R. (2003). The behaviors, interactions, and perceptions of junior high school students during small-group learning. *Journal of Educational Psychology, 95,* 137–147.

Gillies, R. M. (2008). The effects of cooperative learning on junior high school students' behaviours, discourse, and learning during a science-based learning activity. *School Psychology International, 29*(3), 328–347.

Gillies, R. M., & Khan, A. (2009). Promoting reasoned argumentation, problem-solving and learning during small-group work. *Cambridge Journal of Education, 39*(1), 7–27.

Gilligan, C. (1977). In a different voice: Women's conception of the self and of morality. *Harvard Educational Review, 47,* 481–517.

Gilman, B. (2008). *Challenging highly gifted learners.* Waco, TX: Prufrock Press.

Ginott, H. G. (1972). *Teacher and child.* New York: Macmillan.

Ginsburg, G. E., & Kilbourne, B. K. (1988). Emergence of vocal alternation in mother–infant interchanges. *Journal of Child Language, 15,* 221–235.

Glachan, M., & Light, P. H. (1982). Peer interaction and learning. In G. E. Butterworth & P. H. Light (Eds.), *Social cognition: Studies of the development of understanding* (pp. 238–260). Brighton, UK: Harvester Press.

Glaser, R., & Nitko, A. J. (1971). Measurement in learning and instruction. In R. L. Thorndike (Ed.), *Educational measurement* (2nd ed.). Washington, DC: American Council on Education.

Glasser, W. (1998). *Choice theory in the classroom.* New York: HarperCollins.

Glassner, A., & Schwarz, B. B. (2007). What stands and develops between creative and critical thinking? Argumentation? *Thinking Skills and Creativity, 2*(1), 10–18.

Glynn, S. M., Britton, B. K., Muth, D., & Dogan, N. (1982). Writing and revising persuasive documents: Cognitive demands. *Journal of Educational Psychology, 74,* 557–567.

Gnepp, J., & Gould, M. E. (1985). The development of personalized inferences: Understanding other people's emotional reactions in light of their prior experiences. *Child Development, 56,* 1455–1464.

Goddard, R. D., Hoy, W. K., & Woolfolk Hoy, A. (2000). Collective teacher efficacy: Its meaning, measure, and impact on student achievement. *American Educational Research Journal, 37,* 479–507.

Goddard, R. D., Hoy, W. K., & Woolfolk Hoy, A. (2004). Collective efficacy beliefs: Theoretical developments, empirical evidence, and future directions. *Educational Researcher, 33*(3), 3–13.

Godden, D. R., & Baddeley, A. D. (1975). Context-dependent memory in two natural environments: On land and underwater. *British Journal of Psychology, 66,* 325–331.

Godes, O., Hulleman, C. S., & Harackiewicz, J. M. (2007, April). *Boosting students' interest in math with utility value: Two experimental tests.* Paper presented at the annual conference of the American Educational Research Association, Chicago, IL.

Gogtay, N., Giedd, J. N., Lusk, L., et al. (2004). Dynamic mapping of human cortical development during childhood and early adulthood. *Proceedings of the National Academy of Sciences, 101*(21), 8174–8179.

Goldenberg, C. (1987). Low-income Hispanic parents' contributions to their first-grade children's word-recognition skills. *Anthropology and Education Quarterly, 18,* 149–179.

Goldenberg, C. (1992/1993). Instructional conversations: Promoting comprehension through discussion. *Reading Teacher, 46*(4), 316–326.

Goldfield, B. E., & Snow, C. E. (2005). Individual differences: Implications for the study of language acquisition. In J. B. Gleason (Ed.), *The development of language* (6th ed., p. 292–303). Boston: Pearson/Allyn & Bacon.

Goldin-Meadow, S., & Morford, M. (1985). Gesture in early child language: Studies of deaf and hearing children. *Merrill-Palmer Quarterly, 31,* 145–176.

Goldin-Meadow, S., & Mylander, C. (1983). Gestural communication in deaf children: Noneffect of parental input on language development. *Science, 221,* 372–374.

Goldstein, N. E., Arnold, D. H., Rosenberg, J. L., Stowe, R. M., & Ortiz, C. (2001). Contagion of aggression in day care classrooms as a function of peer and teacher responses. *Journal of Educational Psychology, 93,* 708–719.

Goleman, D. (1995). *Emotional intelligence.* New York: Bantam Books.

Goleman, D. (2006). Introduction. In D. Goleman, *Emotional intelligence.* New York: Bantam Books.

Goncu, A. (1993). Development of intersubjectivity in social pretend play. *Human Development, 36,* 185–198.

Gonzalez, A. R., Holbein, M. R. D., & Quilter, S. (2002). High school students' goal orientations and their relationship to perceived parenting styles. *Contemporary Educational Psychology, 27,* 450–470.

Good, C., Aronson, J., & Inzlicht, N. (2003). Improving adolescents' standardized test performance: An intervention to reduce the effects of stereotype threat. *Journal of Applied Developmental Psychology, 24,* 645–662.

Good, T. L., Biddle, B. J., & Brophy, J. E. (1975). *Teachers make a difference.* New York: Holt, Rinehart, & Winston.

Good, T. L., & Brophy, J. E. (2000). *Looking in classrooms* (8th ed.). New York: Longman.

Goodlad, J. I., & Anderson, R. H. (1987). *The non-graded elementary school.* New York: Teachers College Press.

Goodnow, J. J. (1962). A test of milieu effects with some of Piaget's tasks. *Psychological Monographs, 76* (36, Whole No. 555).

Gootman, M. E. (1998). Effective in-house suspension. *Educational Leadership, 56,* 39–41.

Gopnik, A., Meltzoff, A. N., & Kuhl, P. K. (1999). *The scientist in the crib: What early learning tells us about the mind.* New York: Perennial/HarperCollins.

Gordon, G. L. (1999). Teacher talent and urban schools. *Phi Delta Kappan, 81*(4), 304–307.

Goswami, A., & Goswami, M. (1999). *Quantum creativity: Waking up to our creative potential.* Cresskill, NJ: Hampton Press.

Goswami, U. (2004). Neuroscience and education. *British Journal of Educational Psychology, 74,* 1–14.

Goswami, U. (2008). Reading, dyslexia, and the brain. *Educational Research, 50*(2), 135–148.

Gottfredson, G., Gottfredson, D., Payne, A., & Gottfredson, N. (2005). School climate predictors of school disorder: Results from a national study of delinquency prevention in schools. *Journal of Research in Crime and Delinquency, 42,* 412–444.

Gottfried, A. E., Fleming, J. S., & Gottfried, A. W. (1994). Role of parental motivational practices in children's academic intrinsic motivation and achievement. *Journal of Educational Psychology, 86,* 104–113.

Gottfried, A. E., Fleming, J. S., & Gottfried, A. W. (1998). Role of cognitively stimulating home environment in children's academic intrinsic motivation: A longitudinal study. *Child Development, 69*(5), 1448–1460.

Gottfried, A. E., Fleming, J. S., & Gottfried, A. W. (2001). Continuity of academic intrinsic motivation from childhood through late adolescence: A longitudinal study. *Journal of Educational Psychology, 93,* 3–13.

Gottfried, A. E., & Gottfried, A. W. (1996). A longitudinal study of academic intrinsic motivation in intellectually gifted children: Childhood through early adolescence. *Gifted Child Quarterly, 40,* 179–183.

Gottwald, S., Goldbach, P., & Isack, A. (1985). Stuttering: Prevention and detection. *Young Children, 41*(1), 9–16.

Gough, D. (1991). *Thinking about thinking.* Alexandria, VA: National Association of Elementary School Principals. ED 327 980.

Graham, S. (1984). Communicating sympathy and anger to black and white students: The cognitive (attributional) consequences of affective cues. *Journal of Personality and Social Psychology, 47,* 40–54.

Graham, S. (1990). Communicating low ability in the classroom: Bad things good teachers sometimes do. In S. Graham & V. Folkes

(Eds.), *Attribution theory: Applications to achievement, mental health, and interpersonal conflict* (pp. 17–36). Hillsdale, NJ: Erlbaum.

Graham, S. (1994). Motivation in African Americans. *Review of Educational Research, 64*(1), 55–117.

Graham, S., & Barker, G. P. (1990). The down-side of help: An attributional-developmental analysis of helping behavior as a low-ability cue. *Journal of Educational Psychology, 82,* 7–14.

Graham, S., & Weiner, B. (1993). Attributional applications in the classroom. In T. M. Tomlinson (Ed.), *Motivating students to learn: Overcoming barriers to high achievement* (pp. 179–195). Berkeley, CA: McCutchan.

Graham, S., & Weiner, B. (1996). Theories and principles of motivation. In D. C. Berliner & R. C. Calfee (Eds.), *Handbook of educational psychology* (pp. 63–84). New York: Macmillan.

Graham, S., & Williams, C. (2009). An attributional approach to motivation in school. In K. R. Wentzel & A. Wigfield (Eds.), *Handbook of motivation at school* (pp. 11–33). New York: Routledge/Taylor & Francis Group.

Grant, H., & Dweck, C. S. (2003). Clarifying achievement goals and their impact. *Journal of Personality and Social Psychology, 85,* 541–553.

Gray-Little, B., & Hafdahl, A. R. (2000). Factors influencing racial comparisons of self-esteem: A quantitative review. *Psychological Bulletin, 126,* 26–54.

Green, L., Fry, A. F., & Myerson, J. (1994). Discounting of delayed rewards: A life-span comparison. *Psychological Science, 5,* 33–36.

Greenberg, M. T., Weissberg, R. P., O'Brien, M. U., et al. (2003). Enhancing school-based prevention and youth development through coordinated social, emotional, and academic learning. *American Psychologist, 58,* 466–474.

Greenfield, P. M. (1976). Cross-cultural research and Piagetian theory: Paradox and progress. In K. Riegel & J. Meacham (Eds.), *The developing individual in a changing world.* The Hague, Netherlands: Mouton.

Greenfield, P. M. (1997). You can't take it with you: Why ability assessments don't cross cultures. *American Psychologist, 52*(10), 1115–1124.

Greenlee, A., & Ogletree, E. (1993). *Teachers' attitudes toward student discipline problems and classroom management strategies.* Washington, DC: U.S. Department of Education. ERIC Clearinghouse #PSO21851.

Greenough, W. T., Black, J. E., & Wallace, C. S. (1987). Experience and brain development. *Child Development, 58,* 539–559.

Greenwood, C. (2001). Science and students with learning and behavior problems. *Behavioral Disorders, 27,* 37–52.

Gregory, A., & Cornell, D. (2009). "Tolerating" adolescent needs: Moving beyond zero tolerance policies in high school. *Theory Into Practice, 48,* 106–113.

Gregory, A., & Ripski, M. (2008). Adolescent trust in teachers: Implications for behavior in the high school classroom. *School Psychology Review, 37*(3), 337–353.

Gregory, A., Skiba, R. J., & Noguera, P. A. (2010). The achievement gap and the discipline gap: Two sides of the same coin? *Educational Researcher, 39,* 59–68.

Gregory, A., & Weinstein, R. S. (2004). Connection and regulation at home and in school: Predicting growth in achievement for adolescents. *Journal of Adolescent Research, 19,* 405–427.

Gregory, A., & Weinstein, R. S. (2008). The discipline gap and African Americans: Defiance or cooperation in the high school classroom. *Journal of School Psychology, 46,* 455–475.

Gregory, R. J. (2010). *Psychological testing: History, principles, and applications* (6th ed.). Boston: Pearson.

Gresham, F. M. (1986). Conceptual issues in the assessment of social competence. In P. S. Strain, M. J. Guralnick, & H. M. Walker (Eds.), *Children's social behavior: Development, assessment, and modification.* Orlando, FL: Academic Press.

Gresham, F. M., & Kern, L. (2004). Internalizing behavior problems in children and adolescents. In R. B. Rutherford, Jr., M. M. Quinn, & S. Mathur (Eds.), *Handbook of research in behavioral disorders* (pp. 262–281). New York: Guilford.

Gresham, F. M., Lane, K. L., & Beebe-Frankenberger, M. (2005). Predictors of hyperactive-impulsive-inattention and conduct problems: A comparative follow-back investigation. *Psychology in the Schools, 42*(7), 721–736.

Griffin, P., & Cole, M. (1999). Current activity for the future: The zoped. In P. Lloyd & C. Fernyhough (Eds.), *Lev Vygotsky: Critical assessments* (pp. 276–295). London: Routledge.

Grigorenko, E. L., Jarvin, L., & Sternberg, R. J. (2002). School-based tests of the triarchic theory of intelligence: Three settings, three samples, three syllabi. *Contemporary Educational Psychology, 27,* 167–208.

Grigorenko, E. L., & Sternberg, R. J. (1998). Dynamic testing. *Psychological Bulletin, 124,* 75–111.

Grigorova, M., Sherwin, B. B., & Tulandi, T. (2006). Effects of treatment with leuprolide acetate depot on working memory and executive functions in young premenopausal women. *Psychoneuroendocrinology, 31*(8), 935–947.

Grolnick, W. S., Deci, E. L., & Ryan, R. M. (1997). Internalization within the family: The self-determination perspective. In J. E. Grusec & L. Kuczynski (Eds.), *Parenting and children's internalization of values: A handbook of contemporary theory* (pp. 135–161). New York: Wiley.

Grolnick, W. S., Gurland, S. T., Jacob, K. F., & DeCourcey, W. (2002). The development of self-determination in middle childhood and adolescence. In A. Wigfield & J. Eccles (Eds.), *Development of achievement motivation* (pp. 147–171). New York: Academic Press.

Gronlund, N. E. (2006). *Assessment of student achievement* (8th ed.). Boston: Allyn & Bacon.

Gross, M. (1993). *Exceptionally gifted children.* London: Routledge.

Grotzer, T. A., & Perkins, D. A. (2000). Teaching of intelligence: A performance conception. In R. J. Sternberg (Ed.), *Handbook of intelligence* (pp. 492–515). New York: Cambridge University Press.

Grover, R. L., Ginsburg, G. S., & Ialongo, N. (2007). Psychosocial outcomes of anxious first graders: A seven-year follow-up. *Depression and Anxiety, 24,* 410–420.

Gruber, H. E. (1981). *Darwin on man: A psychological study of scientific creativity* (2nd ed.). Chicago: University of Chicago Press.

Guay, F., Marsh, H. W., & Boivin, M. (2003). Academic self-concept and academic achievement: Developmental perspectives on their causal ordering. *Journal of Educational Psychology, 95,* 124–136.

Guerra, N., & The Metropolitan Area Child Study Research Group. (2007). Changing the way children "think" about aggression: Social-cognitive effects of a preventive intervention. *Journal of Consulting and Clinical Psychology, 75,* 160–167.

Guilford, J. P. (1956). The structure of intellect. *Psychological Bulletin, 53,* 267–293.

Guilford, J. P. (1988). Some changes in the structure-of-intellect model. *Educational and Psychological Measurement, 48,* 1–4.

Gulikers, J. T. M., Bastiaens, T. J., Kirschner, P. A., & Kester, L. (2008). Authenticity is in the eye of the beholder: Student and teacher perceptions of assessment authenticity. *Journal of Vocational Education & Training, 60*(4), 401–412.

Gun Free Schools Act of 1994. **20 U.S.C. Chapter 70, Sec. 8921 Gun-free requirements.**

Guskey, T., & Passaro, P. (1994). Teacher efficacy: A study of construct dimensions. *American Educational Research Journal, 31,* 627–643.

Guskey, T. R., & Bailey, J. M. (2001). *Developing grading and reporting systems for student learning.* Thousand Oaks, CA: Corwin Press.

Guskey, T. R., & Jung, L. A. (2009). Grading and reporting in a standards-based environment: Implications for students with special needs. *Theory Into Practice, 48,* 53–62.

Gustafsson, J. E. (1994). Hierarchical models of intelligence and educational achievement. In A. Demetriou & A. Efklides (Eds.), *Intelligence, mind, and reasoning: Structure and development* (pp. 45–73). Amsterdam: North-Holland/Elsevier Science.

Gutiérrez, K. D., Baquedano-López, P., & Asato, J. (2001). English for the children: The new literacy of the old word order, language policy, and education reform. *Bilingual Research Journal, 24*(1 & 2), 87–112.

Gutiérrez, R., & Slavin, R. E. (1992). Achievement effects of the non-graded elementary school: A best evidence synthesis. *Review of Educational Research, 62*(4), 333–376.

Gutman, L. M., Sameroff, A., & Cole, R. (2003). Academic growth curve trajectories from first grade to twelfth grade: Effects of multiple social risks factors and preschool child factors. *Developmental Psychology, 39,* 777–790.

H

Hakim-Larson, J., Parker, A., Lee, C., Goodwin, J., & Voelker, S. (2006). Measuring parental meta-emotion: Psychometric properties of the emotion-related parenting styles self-test. *Early Education and Development, 17,* 229–251.

Haladyna, T. M. (2002). *Essentials of standardized achievement testing: validity and accountability.* Boston: Pearson.

Haladyna, T. M., Downing, S. M., & Rodriguez, M. C. (2002). A review of multiple-choice item-writing guidelines for classroom assessment. *Applied Measurement in Education, 15*(3), 309–334.

Halberstadt, A. G., & Eaton, K. L. (2002). Socialization of emotion expression, and understanding in the family. *Marriage and Family Review, 34,* 35–62.

Hale, J. B., Wycoff, K. L., & Fiorello, C. A. (2011). RTI and cognitive hypothesis testing for identification and intervention of specific learning disabilities. In D. P. Flanagan & V. C. Alfonso (Eds.), *Essentials of specific learning disability identification* (pp. 173–201). Hoboken, NJ: Wiley.

Hallahan, D. P., & Kauffman. J. (2000). *Exceptional learners* (8th ed.). Boston: Allyn & Bacon.

Hallinan, M. T., & Sorensen, A. B. (1985). Class size, ability group size, and student achievement. *American Journal of Education, 94*(1), 71–89.

Hallinan, M. T., & Sorensøn, A. B. (1987). Ability grouping and sex differences in mathematics achievement. *Sociology of Education, 60,* 63–72.

Halpern, D. F. (1997). Sex differences in intelligence: Implications for education. *American Psychologist, 52*(10), 1091–1101.

Halpern, D. F. (2000). *Sex differences in cognitive abilities* (3rd ed.). Mahwah, NJ: Erlbaum.

Halpern, D. F., & LaMay, M. L. (2000). The smarter sex: A critical review of sex differences in intelligence. *Educational Psychology Review, 12,* 229–246.

Halpern, D. F., Wai, J., & Saw, A. (2005). A psychobiosocial model: Why females are sometimes greater than and sometimes less than males in math achievement. In A. M. Gallagher & J. C. Kaufman (Eds.), *Gender differences in mathematics: An integrative approach.* Cambridge, UK: Cambridge University Press.

Hamacheck, D. (2000). Dynamics of self-understanding and self-knowledge: Acquisition, advantages, and relation to emotional intelligence. *Journal of Humanistic Counseling, Education & Development, 38*(4), 230–243.

Hambleton, R. K. (1996). Advances in assessment models, methods, and practices. In D. C. Berliner & R. C. Calfee (Eds.), *Handbook of educational psychology.* New York: Macmillan.

Hamilton, A. F., Brindley, R., & Frith, U. (2009). Visual perspective taking impairment in children with autistic spectrum disorder. *Cognition, 113*(1), 37–44.

Hamilton, R., & Ghatala, E. (1994). *Learning and instruction.* New York: McGraw-Hill.

Hamm, J. V. (2000). Do birds of a feather flock together? The variable bases for African American, Asian American and European American adolescents' selection of similar friends. *Developmental Psychology, 36*(2), 209–219.

Hammen, C., & Rudolph, K. D. (2003). Childhood mood disorders. In E. J. Mash & R. A. Barkley (Eds.), *Child psychopathology* (2nd ed., pp. 233–278). New York: Guilford.

Hammond, D. R., McBee, M. T., & Hébert, T. P. (2007). Motivational aspects of giftedness. *Roeper Review, 29*(3), 197–205.

Hampton, N. Z., & Mason, E. (2003). Learning disabilities, gender, sources of efficacy, self-efficacy beliefs, and academic achievement in high school students. *Journal of School Psychology, 41,* 101–112.

Hamre, B., & Pianta, R. (2007). Can instructional and emotional support in the first-grade classroom make a difference for children at risk of school failure? *Child Development, 76*(5), 949–967.

Han, S. S., Catron, T., Weiss, B., & Marciel, K. K. (2005). A teacher-consultation approach to social skills training for pre-kindergarten children: Treatment model and short-term outcome effects. *Journal of Abnormal Child Psychology, 33,* 681–693.

Handler, B. R. (2003, April). *Special education practices: An evaluation of educational environmental placement trends since the regular education initiative.* Paper presented at the Annual Meeting of the American Educational Research Association, Chicago, IL.

Hanich, L. B., Jordan, N. C., Kaplan, D., & Dick, J. (2001). Performance across different areas of mathematical cognition in children with learning difficulties. *Journal of Educational Psychology, 93,* 615–626.

Hanna, G. S., & Dettmer, P. A. (2004). *Assessment for effective teaching: Using context-adaptive planning.* Boston: Pearson.

Hanneke, S. (2009). *Theoretical foundations of active learning.* Doctoral dissertation. Machine Learning Department, Carnegie Mellon University.

Hara, N., Bonk, C. J., & Angeli, C. (2000). Content analysis of online discussion in an applied educational psychology course. *Instructional Science, 28*(2), 115–152.

Harackiewicz, J. M., Barron, K. E., Pintrich, P. R., Elliot, A. J., & Thrash, T. M. (2002). Revision of achievement goal theory: Necessary and illuminating. *Journal of Educational Psychology, 94,* 562–575.

Harackiewicz, J. M., Barron, K. E., Tauer, J. M., Carter, S. M., & Elliot, A. J. (2000). Short-term and long-term consequences of achievement goals in college: Predicting continued interest and performance over time. *Journal of Educational Psychology, 92,* 316–330.

Harackiewicz, J., Manderlink, G., & Sansone, C. (1984). Rewarding pinball wizardry: The effects of evaluation on intrinsic interest. *Journal of Personality and Social Psychology, 47,* 287–300.

Harari, O., & Covington, M. V. (1981). Reactions to achievement behavior from a teacher and student perspective: A developmental analysis. *American Educational Research Journal, 18,* 15–28.

Hargis, C. H. (2006). *Teaching low achieving and disadvantaged students* (3rd ed.). Springfield, IL: Charles C. Thomas.

Harkness, S. (1977). Aspects of social environment and first language acquisition in rural Africa. In C. Snow & C. Ferguson (Eds.), *Talking to children: Language input and acquisition.* Cambridge, UK: Cambridge University Press.

Harnishfeger, K. K. (1995). The development of cognitive inhibition: Theories, definitions, and research evidence. In F. Dempster & C. Brainerd (Eds.), *New perspectives in interference and inhibition in cognition.* New York: Academic Press.

Harp, S. F., & Mayer, R. E. (1997). The role of interest in learning from scientific text and illustrations: On the distinction between emotional interest and cognitive interest. *Journal of Educational Psychology, 89,* 92–102.

Harp, S. F., & Mayer, R. E. (1998). How seductive details do their damage: A theory of cognitive interest in science learning. *Journal of Educational Psychology, 90,* 414–434.

Harrington, D. M., & Anderson, S. M. (1981). Creativity, femininity and three models of psychological androgyny. *Journal of Personality and Social Psychology, 41,* 744–757.

Harrington, R. (2002). Affective disorders. In M. Rutter & E. Taylor (Eds.), *Child and adolescent psychiatry* (4th ed., pp. 463–485). Malden, MA: Blackwell Science.

Harris, B. (2008). Defining and identifying giftedness in English language learners of Mexican descent. Dissertation (publication number 3331352). Indiana University.

Harrison, A. S., & Spuler, F. B. (1983). *Hot tips for teachers.* Belmont, CA: Fearon Teacher Aids.

Harry, B., & Klingner, J. (2006). *Why are so many minority students in special education? Understanding race and disability in schools.* New York: Teachers College Press.

Hart, B., & Risley, T. (1995). *Meaningful differences in the everyday experience of young American children.* Baltimore: Paul H. Brookes.

Hart, B., & Risley, T. (1999). *The social world of children learning to talk.* Baltimore: Paul H. Brookes.

Hart, B., & Risley, T. R. (2003). The early catastrophe. The 30 million word gap. *American Educator, 27*(1), 4–9.

Harter, S. (1974). Pleasure derived from cognitive challenge and mastery. *Child Development, 45,* 661–669.

Harter, S. (1978a). Effectance motivation reconsidered: Toward a developmental model. *Human Development, 21,* 34–64.

Harter, S. (1978b). Pleasure derived from challenge and the effects of receiving grades on children's difficulty level choices. *Child Development, 49,* 788–799.

Harter, S. (1983). Developmental perspectives on the self-system. In E. M. Hetherington (Ed.), *Handbook of child psychology: Social and personality development, Vol 4* (4th ed., pp. 275–385). New York: Wiley.

Harter, S. (1990). Self and identity development. In S. S. Feldman & G. R. Elliott (Eds.), *At the threshold: The developing adolescent.* Cambridge, MA: Harvard University Press.

Harter, S. (1992). The relationship between perceived competence, affect, and motivational orientation within the classroom: Process and patterns of change. In A. Boggiano & T. Pittman (Eds.), *Achievement and motivation: A social-developmental perspective* (pp. 77–114). Cambridge, MA: Cambridge University Press.

Harter, S. (1999). *The construction of the self: A developmental perspective.* New York: Guilford.

Harter, S., & Jackson, B. K. (1992). Trait vs. nontrait conceptualizations of intrinsic/extrinsic motivational orientation. *Motivation and Emotion, 16,* 209–230.

Harter, S., Waters, P., & Whitesell, N. R. (1998). Relational self-worth: Differences in perceived worth as a person across interpersonal contexts among adolescents. *Child Development, 69,* 756–766.

Harter, S., Whitesell, N., & Junkin, L. (1998). Similarities and differences in domain-specific and global self-evaluations of learning-disabled, behaviorally disordered, and normally achieving adolescents. *American Educational Research Journal, 35,* 653–680.

Harter, S., Whitesell, N., & Kowalski, P. (1992). Individual differences in the effects of educational transitions on young adolescents' perceptions of competence and motivational orientation. *American Educational Research Journal, 29,* 777–807.

Hartup, W. W. (1996). The company they keep: Friendships and their developmental significance. *Child Development, 67,* 1–13.

Haskell, R. E. (2001). *Transfer of learning: Cognition, instruction, and reasoning.* San Diego, CA: Academic Press.

Haugland, S. W., & Wright, J. L. (1997). *Young children and technology: A world of discovery.* Boston: Allyn & Bacon.

Hawkins, J. D., Catalano, R. F., Kosterman, R., Abbott, R., & Hill, K. G. (1999). Preventing adolescent health-risk behaviors by strengthening protection during childhood. *Archives of Pediatric & Adolescent Medicine, 153,* 226–334.

Hayes, J. R. (1985). Three problems in teaching general skills. In S. F. Chipman, J. W. Segal, & R. Glaser (Eds.), *Thinking and learning skills: Vol. 1. Research and open questions* (pp. 391–406). Hillsdale, NJ: Erlbaum.

Hayes, J. R., & Simon, H. A. (1977). Psychological differences among problem isomorphs. In N. J. Castellan, P. B. Pisoni, & G. R. Potts (Eds.), *Cognitive theory* (Vol. 2, pp. 21–41). Hillsdale, NJ: Erlbaum.

Hayward, C., Wilson, K. A., Lagle, K., Kraemer, H. C., Killen, J. D., & Taylor, C. B. (2008). The developmental psychopathology of social anxiety in adolescents. *Depression and Anxiety, 25,* 200–206.

Hebb, D. O. (1949). *The organization of behavior: A neuropsychological theory.* Hoboken, NJ: Wiley.

Heine, S. J., & Hamamura, T. (2007). In search of East Asian self-enhancement. *Personality and Social Psychology Review, 11,* 1–24.

Heine, S. J., Kitayama, S., Lehman, D. R., et al. (2001). Divergent consequences of success and failure in Japan and North America: An investigation of self-improving motivations and malleable selves. *Journal of Personality and Social Psychology, 81,* 599–615.

Hemmer, P., & Steyvers, M. (2008). A Bayesian account of reconstructive memory. In V. Sloutsky, B. Love, and K. McRae (Eds.) *Proceedings of the 30th Annual Conference of the Cognitive Science Society.* Mahwah, NJ: Erlbaum.

Henderlong, J., & Lepper, M. R. (2002). The effects of praise on children's intrinsic motivation: A review and synthesis. *Psychological Bulletin, 128*(5), 774–795.

Henderson, A. T., & Berla, N. (1995). *A new generation of evidence: The family is critical to student achievement.* Washington, DC: Center for Law and Education.

Henderson, V., & Dweck, C. S. (1990). Achievement and motivation in adolescence: A new model and date. In S. Feldman and G. Elliott (Eds.), *At the threshold: The developing adolescent.* Cambridge, MA: Harvard University Press.

Hennessey, B. A. (1994). The consensual assessment technique: An examination of the relationship between ratings of product and process creativity. *Creativity Research Journal, 7,* 193–208.

Hennessey, B. A., Kim, G., Guomin, Z., & Weiwei, S. (2008). A multicultural application of the Consensual Assessment technique. *The International Journal of Creativity and Problem Solving, 18*(2), 87–100.

Henry, J., Sloane, M., & Black-Pond, C. (2007). Neurobiology and neurodevelopmental impact of childhood traumatic stress and prenatal alcohol exposure. *Language, Speech and Hearing Sciences in Schools, 38*(2), 99–108.

Hensch, T. (2004). Critical period regulation. *Annual Review of Neuroscience, 27,* 549–579.

Henson, K. T., & Eller, B. F. (1999). *Educational psychology for effective teaching.* Belmont, CA: Wadsworth.

Hershkovitz, S., Peled, I., & Littler, G. (2009). Mathematical creativity and giftedness in elementary school: Task and teacher promoting creativity for all. In R. Liekin, A. Berman, and B. Kolchu (Eds.), *Creativity in mathematics and the education of gifted students,* pp. 255–269. Rotterdam, The Netherlands: Sense Publishers.

Hertel, P. T. (1994). Depression and memory: Are impairments remediable through attentional control? *Current Directions in Psychological Science, 3,* 190–193.

Hertzog, C., & Robinson, A. E. (2005). Metacognition and intelligence. In O. Wilhelm & R. W. Engle (Eds.), *Handbook of understanding and measuring intelligence* (pp. 101–123). Thousand Oaks, CA: Sage.

Hetherington, E. M. (1991). The role of individual differences and family relationships in children's coping with divorce and remarriage. In P. A. Cowan & M. Hetherington (Eds.), *Family transitions.* Hillsdale, NJ: Erlbaum.

Hetherington, E. M. (1993). An overview of the Virginia longitudinal study of divorce and remarriage with a focus on early adolescence. *Journal of Family Psychology, 7*(1), 39–56.

Hetherington, E. M., Bridges, M., & Insabella, G. M. (1998). What matters? What does not? Five perspectives on the association between marital transitions and children's adjustment. *American Psychologist, 53*(2), 167–184.

Hetherington, E. M., Henderson, S., & Reiss, D. (1999). Adolescent siblings in stepfamilies: Family functioning and adolescent adjustment. *Monographs of the Society for Research in Child Development,* Serial No. 227.

Hidalgo, N. M., Siu, S., Bright, J. A., Swap, S. M., & Epstein, J. L. (1995). Research on families, schools, and communities: A multicultural perspective. In J. A. Banks & C. A. M. Banks (Eds.), *Handbook of research on multicultural education* (pp. 631–655). New York: Macmillan.

Hidi, S. (2000). An interest researcher's perspective: The effects of intrinsic and extrinsic factors on motivation. In C. Sansone & J. M. Harackiewicz (Eds.), *Intrinsic and extrinsic motivation: The search for optimal motivation and performance* (pp. 309–339). San Diego, CA: Academic Press.

Hidi, S., & Harackiewicz, J. (2000). Motivating the academically unmotivated: A critical issue for the 21st century. *Review of Educational Research, 70,* 151–179.

Hidi, S., Weiss, J., Berndorff, D., & Nolan, J. (1998). The role of gender, instruction and a cooperative learning technique in science education across formal and informal settings. In L. Hoffmann, A. Krapp, K. Renninger, & J. Baumert (Eds.). *Interest and learning: Proceedings of the Seeon conference on interest and gender* (pp. 215–227). Kiel, Germany: IPN.

Hiebert, E. H. (1983). An examination of ability grouping for reading instruction. *Reading Research Quarterly, 18,* 231–255.

Hill, K. T., & Wigfield, A. (1984). Test anxiety: A major educational problem and what can be done about it. *Elementary School Journal, 85,* 105–126.

Hill, N. E., & Chao, R. K. (2009). *Families, schools, and the adolescent: Connecting research, policy, and practice.* New York: Teachers College Press.

Hill, N. E., & Tyson, D. F. (2009). Parental involvement in middle school: A meta-analytic assessment of the strategies that promote achievement. *Developmental Psychology, 45*(3), 740–763.

Hilton, D. J. (2003). Psychology and the financial markets: Applications to understanding and remedying irrational decision making. In I. Brocas & J. D. Carrillo (Eds.), *The psychology of economic decisions: Vol. 1. Rationality and well-being* (pp. 273–297). Oxford, England: Oxford University Press.

Hines, M. T., & Kritsonis, W. A. (2010). The interactive effects of race and teacher self-efficacy on the achievement gap in school. *National Forum of Multicultural Issues Journal, 7*(1), 1–14.

Hinshaw, S. P., & Blackman, D. R. (2005). Attention-deficit/hyperactivity disorder in girls. In D. J. Bell, S. L. Foster, & E. J. Mash (Eds.), *Handbook of behavioral and emotional problems in girls* (pp. 117–148). New York: Kluwer Academic/Plenum.

Hinshaw, S. P., & Lee, S. S. (2003). Conduct and oppositional defiant disorders. In E. J. Mash & R. A. Barkley (Eds.), *Child psychopathology* (2nd ed., pp. 144–198). New York: Guilford.

Hittner, J. B., & Daniels, J. R. (2002). Gender-role orientation, creative accomplishments and cognitive styles. *Journal of Creative Behavior, 36,* 62–75.

Hmelo-Silver, C. E. (2004). Problem-based learning: What and how do students learn? *Educational Psychology Review, 16*(3), 235–266.

Ho, A. D. (2008). The problem with "proficiency": Limitations of statistics and policy under No Child Left Behind. *Educational Researcher, 37*(6), 351–360.

Hodge, G. K., & Nelson, N. H. (1991). Demonstrating differential reinforcement by shaping classroom participation. *Teaching of Psychology, 18,* 239–241.

Hoff, E. (2003a). The specificity of environment influence: Socioeconomic status affects early vocabulary development via maternal speech. *Child Development, 74,* 1368–1378.

Hoff, E. (2003b). Causes and consequences of SES-related differences in parent to child speech. In M. Bornstein & R. Bradley (Eds.), *Socioeconomic status, parenting, and child development* (pp. 147–160). Mahwah, NJ: Erlbaum.

Hoffman, L. W. (1974). Effects of maternal employment on the child: A review of the research. *Developmental Psychology, 10*(2), 204–228.

Hoffman, M. L. (1991). Empathy, social cognition, and moral action. In W. M. Kurtines & J. L. Gewirtz (Eds.), *Moral behavior and development: Vol. 1. Theory* (pp. 275–301). Mahwah, NJ: Erlbaum.

Hoffman, M. L. (2000). *Empathy and moral development: Implications for caring and justice.* New York: Cambridge University Press.

Hofstede, G. H. (2001). *Culture's consequences: Comparing values, behaviors, institutions and organizations across nations* (2nd ed.), Thousand Oaks, CA: Sage.

Hogan, T. P. (2007). *Psychological testing: A practical introduction.* Hoboken, NJ: Wiley.

Holmes, R. M., Pellegrini, A. D., & Schmidt, S. L. (2006). The effects of different recess timing regimens on preschoolers' classroom attention. *Early Child Development and Care, 176*(7), 735–743.

Holowka, S., & Petitto, L. A. (2002). Left hemisphere cerebral specialization for babies while babbling. *Science, 297,* 1515.

Holyoak, K. J., & Koh, K. (1987). Surface and structural similarity in analogical transfer. *Memory and Cognition, 15,* 332–340.

Homme, L. E., DeBaga, P. C., Devine, J. V., Steinhorst, R., & Rickert, E. J. (1963). Use of the Premack principle in controlling the behavior of nursery school children. *Journal of the Experimental Analysis of Behavior, 6,* 544.

Hommel, B., & Akyurek, E. G. (2009). Symbolic control of attention: Tracking its temporal dynamics. *Attention, Perception, & Psychophysics 71*(2), 385–391. doi:10.3758/APP.71.2.385

Honea, M. J. (1982). Wait time as an instructional variable: An influence on teacher and student. *Clearinghouse, 56*(4), 167–170.

Hong, E., & Milgram, R. M. (2010). Creative thinking ability: Domain generality and specificity. *Creativity Research Journal, 22*(3), 272–287.

Hong, Y. Y., Chiu, C., Dweck, C. S., Lin, D., & Wan, W. (1999). Implicit theories, attributions, and coping: A meaning system approach. *Journal of Personality and Social Psychology, 77,* 588–599.

Hooper, S. R., Wakely, M. B., de Kruif, R. E., & Swartz, C. W. (2006). Aptitude-treatment interactions revisited: Effect of metacognitive intervention on subtypes of written expression in elementary school students. *Developmental Neuropsychology, 29,* 217–241.

Hoover, J., & Oliver, R. (1996). *The bullying prevention handbook: A guide for teachers, principals, and counselors.* Bloomington, IN: National Education Service.

Hoover-Dempsey, K. V., Bassler, D. C., & Brissie, J. S. (1992). Explorations in parent–school relations. *Journal of Educational Research, 85,* 287–294.

Horgan, D. (1978). The development of the full passive. *Journal of Child Language, 5,* 65–80.

Horn, J. L. (1994). Theory of fluid and crystallized intelligence. In R. J. Sternberg (Ed.), *The encyclopedia of human intelligence* (Vol. 1, pp. 443–451). New York: Macmillan.

Horner, S. L. (2004). Observational learning during shared book reading: The effects on preschoolers' attention to print and letter knowledge. *Reading Psychology, 25,* 167–188.

Horner, S., & Gaither, S. (2006). Attribution retraining with a second-grade class. *Early Childhood Education Journal, 31,* 165–170.

Hosp, J. L., & Reschly, D. (2004). Disproportionate representation of minority students in special education: Academic, demographic, and economic predictors. *Exceptional Children, 70*(2), 185–199.

Housand, A., & Reis, S. M. (2008). Self-regulated learning in reading: Gifted pedagogy and instructional settings. *Journal of Advanced Academics, 20*(1), 108–136.

Houtz, J. C., & Krug, D. (1995). Assessment of creativity: Resolving a mid-life crisis. *Educational Psychological Review, 7,* 269–300.

Howard, E. R., Sugarman, J., & Christian, D. (2003). *Trends in two-way immersion education: A review of the research.* Washington, DC: Center for Applied Linguistics.

Howard, G. R. (1999). *We can't teach what we don't know: White teachers, multiracial schools.* New York: Teachers College Press.

Howard, V. F., Williams, B. F., Port, P. D., & Lepper, C. (2001). *Very young children with special needs* (2nd ed.). Columbus, OH: Merrill.

Howes, C., Phillipsen, L., & Peisner-Feinberg, E. (2000). The consistency of perceived teacher-child relationships between preschool and kindergarten. *Journal of School Psychology, 38,* 113–132.

Howlin, P., Mahwood, L., & Rutter, M. (2000). Autism and developmental receptive language disorder—A follow-up comparison in early adult life: II. Social, behavioral, and psychiatric outcomes. *Journal of Child Psychology and Psychiatry, 41,* 561–578.

Hubbard, J. A., & Coie, J. D. (1994). Emotional correlates of social competence in children's peer relationships. *Merrill-Palmer Quarterly, 40,* 1–20.

Hubel, D. H., & Weisel, T. N. (1962). Receptive fields, binocular transaction, and functional architecture in the cat's visual cortex. *Journal of Physiology, 160,* 106–154.

Huff, J. A. (1988). Personalized behavior modification: An in-school suspension program that teaches students how to change. *School Counselor, 35,* 210–214.

Hughes, B., Sullivan, H., & Mosley, M. (1985). External evaluation, task difficulty, and continuing motivation. *Journal of Educational Research, 78,* 210–215.

Hughes, C., Dunn, J., & White, A. (1998). Trick or Treat?: Uneven understanding of mind and emotion and executive dysfunction in hard-to-manage preschoolers. *Journal of Child Psychology and Psychiatry, 39,* 981–994.

Hughes, J., & Kwok, O. (2007). Influence of student-teacher and parent-teacher relationships on lower-achieving readers' engagement and achievement in the primary grades. *Journal of Educational Psychology, 99*(1), 39–51.

Hulit, L. M., & Howard, M. R. (2006). *Born to talk: An introduction to speech and language development.* Boston: Pearson.

Hulleman, C. S., & Harackiewicz, J. M. (2009, Dec. 4). Promoting interest and performance in high school science classes. *Science, 326,* 1410–1412.

Hulleman, C. S., Schrager, S. M., Bodmann, S. M., & Harackiewicz, J. M. (2010). A meta-analytic review of achievement goal measures: Different labels for the same constructs or different constructs with similar labels? *Psychological Bulletin, 136*(3), 422–449.

Hulleman, C. S., & Senko, C. (2010). Up and around the bend: Forecasts for achievement goal theory and research in 2020. In T. C. Urdan & S. A. Karabenick (Eds.), *The decade ahead: Theoretical perspectives on motivation and achievement* (Vol. 16A, pp. 71–104). UK: Emerald Group Publishing Limited.

Hunsaker, S. L., & Callahan, C. (1995). Creativity and giftedness: Published instrument uses and abuses. *Gifted Child Quarterly, 39,* 110–114.

Hunt, P., Farron-Davis, F., Beckstead, S., Curtis, D., & Goetz, L. (1994). Evaluating the effects of placement of students with severe disabilities in general education versus special classes. *Journal of the Association for Persons with Severe Handicaps, 19,* 200–214.

Huppert, J., Lomask, S. M., & Lazarowitz, R. (2002). Computer simulations in the high school: Students' cognitive stages, science process skills, and academic achievement in micro-biology. *International Journal of Science Education, 24*(8), 803–821.

Hussong, A. M. (2002). Differentiating peer contexts and risk for adolescent substance abuse. *Journal of Youth and Adolescence, 31*(3), 207–220.

Hyatt, K. J. (2007). Brain Gym: Building stronger brains or wishful thinking? *Remedial and Special Education, 28*(2), 117–124.

Hyde, J. S. (2005). The gender similarities hypothesis. *American Psychologist, 60*(6), 581–592.

Hyde, J. S., Fennema, E., & Lamon, S. J. (1990). Gender differences in mathematics performance: A meta-analysis. *Psychological Bulletin, 107*(2), 139–155.

Hyde, J. S., Lindberg, S. M., Linn, M. C., Ellis, A. B., & Williams, C. C. (2008, July 25). Gender similarities characterize math performance. *Science, 321,* 494–495.

Hynd, C., Holschuh, J., & Nist, S. (2000). Learning complex science information: Motivation theory and its relation to student perceptions. *Reading and Writing Quarterly, 16,* 23–58.

I

Iaria, G., Petrides, M., Dagher, A., Pike, B., & Bohbot, V. D. (2003). Cognitive strategies dependent on the hippocampus and caudate nucleus in human navigation: Variability and change with practice. *Journal of Neuroscience, 23,* 5945–5952.

Immordino-Yang, M. H. (2008). The smoke around mirror neurons: Goals as sociocultural and emotional organizers of perception and action in learning. *Mind, Brain, and Education, 2*(2), 67–73.

Immordino-Yang, M. H., & Fischer, K. W. (2009). Neuroscience bases of learning. In V. G. Aukrust (Ed.), *International Encyclopedia of Education* (3rd ed.), Section on Learning and Cognition. Oxford, England: Elsevier.

Inhelder, B., & Piaget, J. (1955). *The growth of logical thinking from childhood to adolescence.* Paris: Presses Universitaires de France.

Inhelder, B., Sinclair, H., & Bovet, M. (1974). *Learning and the development of cognition.* Cambridge, MA: Harvard University Press.

INTASC. (1992). Model standards for beginning teaching licensing, assessment, and development: A resource for state dialogue. Retrieved August 14, 2011, from http://thesciencenetwork.org/docs/BrainsRUs/Model%20Standards%20for%20Beg%20Teaching_Paliokas.pdf.

Irvine, J. J. (1990). *Black students and school failure: Policies, practices, and prescriptions.* New York: Greenwood Press.

Isbell, R. T. & Raines, S. C. (Eds.). (2007). *Creativity and the arts with young children* (2nd ed.). Clifton Park, NY: Thomson Delmar Learning.

Israel, E. (2001). *Best-ever back to school activities: Fifty winning and welcoming activities, strategies, and tips that save you time and get your school year off to a sensational start.* Jefferson City, MO: Scholastic.

Izard, C. E. (2001). Emotional intelligence or adaptive emotions? *Emotion, 1,* 249–257.

J

Jackson, P. W., Boostrom, R. E., & Hansen, D. T. (1993). *The moral life of schools.* San Francisco: Jossey-Bass.

Jacobs, G. M. (2004). A classroom investigation of the growth of metacognitive awareness in kindergarten children through the writing process. *Early Childhood Education Journal, 32,* 17–23.

Jacobs, J., Davis-Kean, P., Bleeker, M., Eccles, J., & Malanchuk, O. (2005). "I can, but I don't want to": The impact of parents, interests, and activities on gender differences in math. In A. Gallagher & J. Kaufman (Eds.), *Gender differences in mathematics: An integrative psychological approach* (pp. 73–98). New York: Cambridge University Press.

Jacobs, J. E., & Eccles, J. S. (2000). Parents, task values, and real-life achievement-related choices. In C. Sansone & J. M. Harackiewicz (Eds.), *Intrinsic and extrinsic motivation: The search for optimal motivation and performance.* San Diego, CA: Academic Press.

Jacobs, J. E., Lanza, S., Osgood, D. W., Eccles, J. S., & Wigfield, A. (2002). Changes in children's self-competence and values: Gender and domain differences across grades one through twelve. *Child Development, 73,* 509–527.

Jaffari-Bimmel, N., Juffer, F., van Ijzendoorn, M. H., Bakermans-Kranenburg, M. J., & Mooijaart, A. (2006). Social development from infancy to adolescence: Longitudinal and concurrent factors in an adoption sample. *Developmental Psychology, 42,* 1143–1153.

Jairam, D., & Kiewra, K. A. (2009). An investigation of the SOAR study method. *Journal of Advanced Academics, 20*(4), 602–629.

Jairam, D., & Kiewra, K. A. (2010). Helping students soar to success on computers: An investigation of the SOAR study method for computer-based learning. *Journal of Educational Psychology, 102*(3), 601–614.

Jalava, A. (1988). Mother tongue and identity: Nobody could see that I was a Finn. In T. Skutnabb-Kangas & J. Cummins (Eds.), *Minority education: From shame to struggle* (pp. 161–166). Bristol, PA: Multilingual Matters.

James, S. (1990). *Normal language acquisition.* Austin, TX: Pro-Ed.

Jang, H., Reeve, J., & Deci, E. L. (2010). Engaging students in learning activities: It's not autonomy support or structure, but autonomy support and structure. *Journal of Educational Psychology, 102*(3), 588–600.

Jang, H., Reeve, J., Ryan, R. M., & Kim, A. (2009). Can self-determination theory explain what underlies the productive, satisfying learning experiences of collectivistically-oriented Korean adolescents? *Journal of Educational Psychology, 101*(3), 644–661.

Jang, Y., & Huber, D. E. (2008). Context retrieval and context change in free recall: Recalling from long-term memory drives list isolation. *Journal of Experimental Psychology: Learning, Memory, and Cognition, 34*(1), 112–127.

Jarmon, L., Traphagan, T., Mayrath, M., & Trivedi, A. (2009). Virtual world teaching, experiential learning, and assessment: An interdisciplinary communication course in Second Life. *Computers and Education, 53*(1), 169–182.

Jarvin, L., & Sternberg, R. J. (2003). Alfred Binet's contributions to educational psychology. In B. J. Zimmerman & D. L. Schunk (Eds.), *Educational psychology: A century of contributions* (pp. 65–79). Mahwah, NJ: Erlbaum.

Jarvis, H. I., & Gathercole, S. E. (2003). Verbal and non-verbal working memory and achievements on national curriculum tests at 11 and 14 years. *Educational Child Psychology, 20,* 123–140.

Jennings, P. A., & Greenberg, M. (2009). The Prosocial Classroom: Teacher social and emotional competence in relation to child and classroom outcomes. *Review of Educational Research, 79,* 491–525.

Jensen, E. (1998). *Teaching with the brain in mind.* Alexandria, VA: ASCD Press.

Jensen, E. (2000). *Brain-based learning.* San Diego, CA: The Brain Store.

Jensen, M. M. (2005). *Introduction to emotional and behavioral disorders: Recognizing and managing problems in the classroom.* Upper Saddle River, NJ: Merrill/Prentice Hall.

Jensen, P. S., Hinshaw, S. P., Kraemer, H. C., Lenora, N., Newcorn, J. H., Abikoff, H. B., et al. (2001). ADHD comorbidity findings from the MTA study: Comparing comorbid subgroups. *Journal of the American Academy of Child Adolescent Psychiatry, 40*(2), 147–158.

Jeynes, W. H. (2008). Effects of parental involvement on experiences of discrimination and bullying. *Marriage and Family Review, 43*(3/4), 255–268.

Ji, P., & Weissberg, R. (2010). Implementing school-wide social and emotional learning. *Better: Evidence-based education: Social and emotional learning,* 12–13.

Jiang, Z., & Potter, W. D. (1994). A computer microworld to introduce students to probability. *Journal of Computers in Mathematics and Science Teaching, 13*(2), 197–222.

Jitendra, A. K., DuPaul, G. J., Someki, F., & Tresco, K. E. (2008). Enhancing academic achievement for children with attention-deficit hyperactivity disorder: Evidence from school-based intervention research. *Developmental Disabilities Research Reviews, 14,* 325–330.

Johnson, A. P. (2000). *Up and out: Creative and critical thinking skills to enhance learning.* Boston: Allyn & Bacon.

Johnson, C. J., & Anglin, J. M. (1995). Qualitative developments in the content and form of children's definitions. *Journal of Speech and Hearing Research, 38*(3), 612–629.

Johnson, D. W., & Johnson, R. T. (1975). *Learning together and alone: Cooperation, competition, and individualization.* Englewood Cliffs, NJ: Prentice Hall.

Johnson, D. W., & Johnson, R. T. (1978). Cooperative, competitive, and individualistic learning. *Journal of Research and Development in Education, 12,* 3–15.

Johnson, D. W., & Johnson, R. T. (1985a). Mainstreaming hearing-impaired students: The effects of effort in communicating on co-operation. *Journal of Psychology, 119,* 31–44.

Johnson, D. W., & Johnson, R. T. (1985b). Motivational processes in cooperative, competitive, and individualistic learning situations. In C. Ames & R. Ames (Eds.), *Attitudes and attitude change in special education: Its theory and practice* (pp. 118–142). New York: Academic Press.

Johnson, D. W., & Johnson, R. T. (1986). Mainstreaming and cooperative learning strategies. *Exceptional Children, 52*(6), 553–561.

Johnson, D. W., & Johnson, R. T. (1990). Cooperative learning and achievement. In S. Sharan (Ed.), *Cooperative learning: Theory and research* (pp. 23–37). New York: Praeger.

Johnson, D. W., & Johnson, R. T. (1998). Cooperative learning and social interdependence theory. In R. S. Tindale, L. Heath, J. Edwards, E. J. Posavac, F. B. Bryant, et al. (Eds.), *Theory and research on small groups* (pp. 9–35). New York: Plenum Press.

Johnson, D. W., & Johnson, R. T. (1999). *Learning together and alone: Cooperative, competitive, and individualistic learning.* Boston: Allyn & Bacon.

Johnson, D. W., & Johnson, R. T. (2000). Cooperative learning, values, and culturally plural classrooms. In M. Leicester, C. Modgill, & S. Modgill (Eds.), *Values, the classroom, and cultural diversity* (pp. 15–28). London: Cassell PLC.

Johnson, D. W., & Johnson, R. T. (2002a). Learning together and alone: Overview and meta-analysis. *Asia Pacific Journal of Education, 22,* 95–105.

Johnson, D. W., & Johnson, R. T. (2002b). *Meaningful assessment: A meaningful and cooperative process.* Boston: Allyn & Bacon.

Johnson, D. W., & Johnson, R. T. (2005). Cooperative learning. In S. W. Lee (Ed.), *Encyclopedia of school psychology.* Thousand Oaks, CA: Sage.

Johnson, D. W., & Johnson, R. T. (2009). An educational psychology success story: Social interdependence theory and cooperative learning. *Educational Researcher, 38*(5), 365–379.

Johnson, D. W., Johnson, R. T., & Smith, K. (2007). The state of cooperative learning in postsecondary and professional settings. *Educational Psychology Review, 19,* 15–29.

Johnson, D., Maruyama, G., Johnson, R., Nelson, D., & Skon, L. (1981). Effects of cooperative, competitive, and individualistic goal structures on achievement. *Psychological Bulletin, 89*(1), 47–62.

Johnson, M. H., & Munakata, Y. (2005). Processes of change in brain and cognitive development. *TRENDS in Cognitive Sciences, 9*(3), 152–158.

Johnston, M. V. (2009). Plasticity in the developing brain: Implications for rehabilitation. *Developmental Disabilities Research Reviews, 15*(2), 94–101.

Jones, E. D., & Southern, W. T. (1991). Conclusions about acceleration: Echoes of a debate. In W. Southern & E. Jones (Eds.), *The academic acceleration of gifted students* (pp. 223–228). New York: Teachers College Press.

Jones, H. (2010). National curriculum tests and the teaching of thinking skills at primary schools—Parallel or paradox? *Education 3-13, 38*(1), 69–86.

Jones, R. W. (1994). *Performance and alternative assessment techniques: Meeting the challenges of alternative evaluation strategies.* Paper presented at the Second International Conference on Educational Evaluation and Assessment, Pretoria, Republic of South Africa.

Jones, V. F., & Jones, L. S. (2007). *Comprehensive classroom management: Creating communities of support and solving problems* (8th ed.). Boston: Allyn & Bacon.

Jordan, A., Schwartz, E., & McGhie-Richmond, D. (2009). Preparing teachers for inclusive classrooms. *Teaching and Teacher Education, 25*(4), 535–542.

Jordan, N., Hanich, L. B., & Kaplan, D. (2003). A longitudinal study of mathematical competencies in children with specific mathematics difficulties versus children with comorbid mathematics and reading difficulties. *Child Development, 74,* 834–850.

Jordan, N. C. (1995). Clinical assessment of early mathematics disabilities: Adding up the research findings. *Learning Disabilities Research & Practice, 10*(1), 59–69.

Jordan, N. C., Hanich, L., & Kaplan, D. (2003). A longitudinal study of mathematical competencies in children with specific mathematics difficulties versus children with comorbid mathematics and reading difficulties. *Child Development, 74,* 834–850.

Jordan, N. C., & Montani, T. O. (1997). Cognitive arithmetic and problem solving: A comparison of children with specific and general mathematics difficulties. *Journal of Learning Disabilities, 30*(6), 624–634.

Jorgensen, G. (2006). Kohlberg and Gilligan: Duet or duel? *Journal of Moral Education, 35,* 179–196.

Joshi, M. S., & Maclean, M. (1994). Indian and English children's understanding of the distinction between real and apparent emotion. *Child Development, 65,* 1372–1384.

Josselson, R. (1988). The embedded self: I and thou revisited. In D. K. Lapsley & E. C. Power (Eds.), *Self, ego, and identity: Integrative approaches.* New York: Springer.

Joyce, B., Weil, M., & Calhoun, E. (2004). *Models of teaching* (7th ed.). Boston: Allyn & Bacon.

Juel, C. (1988). Learning to read and write: A longitudinal study of fifty-four children from first through fourth grades. *Journal of Educational Psychology, 80,* 437–447.

Jung, L. A. (2009). The challenges of grading and reporting in special education: An inclusive grading model. In T. R. Guskey (Ed.), *Practical solutions for serious problems in standards-based grading* (pp. 27–40). Thousand Oaks, CA: Corwin Press.

Jung, L. A., & Guskey, T. R. (2007). Standards-based grading and reporting: A model for special education. *Teaching Exceptional Children, 40*(2), 48–53.

Jurbergs, N., Palcic, J., & Kelley, M. L. (2007). School-home notes with and without response cost: Increasing attention and academic performance in low-income children with attention deficit/hyperactivity disorder. *School Psychology Quarterly, 22*(3), 358–379.

Juvonen, J. (2000). The social functions of attributional face-saving tactics among early adolescents. *Educational Psychology Review, 12,* 15–32.

Juvonen, J. (2007). Reforming middle schools: Focus on continuity, social connectedness, and engagement. *Educational Psychologist, 42*(4), 197–208.

K

Kagan, J., Arcus, D., Snidman, N., Wang, Y. F., Hendler, J., & Greene, S. (1994). Ease of arousal in infants: A cross-national comparison. *Developmental Psychology, 30*, 342–345.

Kagan, J., Snidman, N., & Arcus, D. (1998). Childhood derivatives of reactivity in infancy. *Child Development, 69*, 1483–1493.

Kame'enui, E. J., & Darch, C. B. (1995). *Instructional classroom management: A proactive approach to behavior management.* White Plains, New York: Longman.

Kamins, M., & Dweck, C. S. (1999). Person vs. process praise and criticism: Implications for contingent self-worth and coping. *Developmental Psychology, 35*, 835–847.

Kane, T. J., Rockoff, J. E., & Staiger, D. O. (2006). What does certification tell us about teacher effectiveness? Evidence from New York City. Retrieved May 11, 2011, from http://www.nber.org/papers/w12155.pdf?new_window=1.

Kane, T. J., & Staiger, D. O. (2002). Volatility in school test scores: Implications for test-based accountability systems. In D. Ravitch (Ed.), *Brookings papers on education policy, 2002* (pp. 235–283). Washington, DC: Brookings Institution Press.

Kane, T. J., & Staiger, D. O. (2003). Unintended consequences of racial subgroup rules. In P. E. Peterson & M. R. West (Eds.), *No child left behind? The politics and practice of school accountability* (pp. 152–176). Washington, DC: Brookings Institution Press.

Kaplan, A., & Midgley, C. (2000). The relationship between perceptions of the classroom goals structure and early adolescents' affect in school: The mediating role of coping strategies. *Learning and Individual Differences, 11*, 187–202.

Kaplan, R. M., & Saccuzzo, D. P. (2009). *Psychological testing: Principles, applications, and issues* (7th ed.). Belmont, CA: Thomson Wadsworth.

Karabenick, S. A. (2003). Seeking help in large college classes: A person-centered approach. *Contemporary Educational Psychology, 28*, 37–58.

Karpicke, J., & Roediger, H. L. (2008). The critical importance of retrieval for learning. *Science, 319*(5865), 966–968.

Karpov, Y. V. (2006). Neo-Vygotskian activity theory: Merging Vygotsky's and Piaget's theories of cognitive development. In M. A. Vanchevsky (Ed.), *Frontiers in cognitive psychology* (pp. 31–51). Hauppauge, NY: Nova Science Publishers.

Karpov, Y. V., & Bransford, J. D. (1995). L. S. Vygotsky and the doctrine of empirical and theoretical learning. *Educational Psychologist, 30*(2), 61–66.

Karrass, J., Braungart-Rieker, J., Mullins, J., & Lefever, J. (2002). Processes in language acquisition: The roles of gender, attention, and maternal encouragement of attention over time. *Journal of Child Language, 29*, 519–543.

Karweit, N. (1989). Time and learning: A review. In R. E. Slavin (Ed.), *School and classroom organization* (pp. 69–95). Hillsdale, NJ: Erlbaum.

Kasari, C., Sigman, M., Mundy, P., & Yirmiya, N. (1990). Affective sharing in the context of joint attention interactions of normal, autistic, and mentally retarded children. *Journal of Autism and Developmental Disorders, 20*(1), 87–100.

Kast, A., & Connor, K. (1988). Sex and age differences in response to informational and controlling feedback. *Personality and Social Psychology Bulletin, 14*, 514–523.

Katulak, N. A., Brackett, M. A., & Weissberg, R. P. (2009). School-based social and emotional learning (SEL) programming: Current perspectives. In A. Lieberman, M. Fullan, A. Hargreaves, & D. Hopkins (Eds.), *International handbook of educational change* (2nd ed.). New York: Springer.

Katz, I., & Assor, A. (2007). When choice motivates and when it does not. *Educational Psychology Review, 19*, 429–442.

Katz, P. A. (2003). Racists or tolerant multiculturalists? How do they begin? *American Psychologist, 58*, 897–909.

Katzir, T., & Pare-Blagoev, J. (2006). Applying cognitive neuroscience research to education: The case of literacy. *Educational Psychologist, 41*(1), 53–74.

Kaufman, A. S. (2010). "In what way are apples and oranges alike?" A critique of Flynn's interpretation of the Flynn effect. *Journal of Psychoeducational Assessment, 28*(5), 382–398.

Kaufman, J. C. (2006). Self-reported differences in creativity by ethnicity and gender. *Applied Cognitive Psychology, 20*, 1065–1082.

Kaufman, J. C., Kaufman, S. B., Beghetto, R. A., Burgess, S. A., & Persson, R. S. (2009). Creative giftedness: beginnings, developments, and future promises. In J. C. Kaufman, S. B. Kaufman, R. A. Beghetto, S. A. Burgess, & R. S. Persson (Eds.), *International handbook on giftedness.* New York: Springer.

Kaufman, J. C., Niu, W., Sexton, J. D., & Cole, J. C. (2010). In the eye of the beholder: Differences across ethnicity and gender in evaluating creative work. *Journal of Applied Social Psychology, 40*(2), 496–511.

Kauffman, J. M. (2001). *Characteristics of emotional and behavioral disorders of children and youth* (7th ed.). Columbus, OH: Merrill.

Kaufman, A., & Dodge, T. (2009). Student perceptions and motivation in the classroom: Exploring relatedness and value. *Social Psychology of Education, 12*, 101–112.

Kaufmann, D., Gesten, E., Santa Lucia, R. C., Salcedo, O., Rendina-Gobioff, G., & Gadd, R. (2000).The relationship between parenting style and children's adjustment: The parents' perspective. *Journal of Child and Family Studies, 9*(2), 231–245.

Kavale, K. (2005). Identifying specific learning disability: Is responsiveness to intervention the answer? *Journal of Learning Disabilities, 38*, 553–562.

Kavale, K. A., Kauffman, A. S., Bachmeier, R. J., & LeFevers, G. B. (2008). Response-to-intervention: Separating the rhetoric of self-congratulation from the reality of specific learning disability identification. *Learning Disabilities Quarterly, 31*, 135–150.

Kazdin, A. E. (2001). *Behavior modification in applied settings* (6th ed.). Belmont, CA: Wadsworth.

Kellough, R. D. (2005). *Your first year of teaching: Guidelines for success.* Upper Saddle River, NJ: Pearson.

Kelly, P. R. (1997/1998). Transfer of learning from a computer simulation as compared to a laboratory activity. *Journal of Educational Technology Systems, 26*(4), 345–351.

Kelsch, W., Sim, S., & Lois, C. (2010). Watching synaptogenesis in the adult brain. *Annual Review of Neuroscience, 33*, 131–149.

Kemler, D. G. (1978). Patterns of hypothesis testing in children's discriminative learning: A study of the development of problem-solving strategies. *Developmental Psychology, 14*, 653–673.

Kendziora, K., & Osher, D. (2009). *Starting to turn schools around: The academic outcomes of the Safe Schools, Successful Students initiative.* Washington, DC: American Institutes for Research.

Kent, R. D., & Miulo, G. (1995). Phonetic abilities in the first year of life. In P. Fletcher & B. MacWhinney (Eds.), *The handbook of child language* (pp.303–334). Cambridge, MA: Blackwell.

Keogh, B. K. (2003). *Temperament in the classroom.* Baltimore: Brookes.

Kernis, M. (2003). Toward a conceptualization of optimal self-esteem. *Psychological Inquiry, 14,* 1–26.

Kerr, M. M., & Nelson, C. M. (1998). *Strategies for managing problem behaviors in the classroom* (2nd ed.). Columbus, OH: Merrill.

Khattri, N., Reeve, A. L., & Adamson, R. J. (1997). *Assessment of student performance: Studies of education reform.* Washington, DC: Pelavin Research Institute.

Kierstad, J. (1985). Direct instruction and experiential approaches: Are they really mutually exclusive? *Educational Leadership, 42*(8), 25–30.

Kiewra, K. A. (1985). Investigating notetaking and review: A depth of processing alternative. *Educational Psychologist, 20,* 23–32.

Kiewra, K. A. (2002). How classroom teachers can help students learn and teach them how to learn. *Theory into Practice, 41,* 71–80.

Kiewra, K. A., DuBois, N. F., Christian, D., McShane, A., Meyerhoffer, M., & Roskelley, D. (1991). Note-taking functions and techniques. *Journal of Educational Psychology, 83,* 240–245.

Kim, A., Vaughn, S., Wanzek, J., & Wei, S. (2004). Graphic organizers and their effects on reading comprehension of students with learning disabilities: A synthesis of research. *Journal of Learning Disabilities, 37,* 105–118.

Kim, J. S., & Sunderman, G. L. (2005). Measuring academic proficiency under the No Child Left Behind Act: Implications for educational equity. *Educational Researcher, 34*(8), 3–13.

Kim, K. (2008). Underachievement and creativity: Are gifted underachievers highly creative? *Creativity Research Journal, 20*(2), 234–242.

Kimble, G. A. (2000). Behaviorism and unity in psychology. *Current Directions in Psychological Science, 9,* 208–212.

King, A. (1990). Enhancing peer interaction and learning in the classroom. *American Educational Research Journal, 27,* 664–687.

King, A. (1991). Effects of training in strategic questioning on children's problem-solving performance. *Journal of Educational Psychology, 83*(3), 307–317.

King, A. (2002). Structuring peer interaction to promote high-level cognitive processing. *Theory into Practice, 41*(1), 33–39.

King, P. M., & Kitchener, K. S. (1995). *Developing reflective judgment.* San Francisco: Jossey-Bass.

Kirk, S. A., Gallagher, J. J., Anastasiow, N. J., & Coleman, M. R. (2006). *Educating exceptional children* (11th ed.). Boston: Houghton Mifflin.

King, P. M., & Kitchener, K. S. (2002). The reflective judgment model: Twenty years of research on epistemic cognition. In B. K. Hofer & P. R. Pintrich (Eds.), *Personal epistemology: The psychology of beliefs about knowledge and knowing* (pp. 37–61). Mahwah, NJ: Erlbaum.

King, S., Waschbusch, D. A., Pelham, W. E., Frankland, B. W., Corkum, P. V., & Jacques, S. (2009). Subtypes of aggression in children with attention deficit hyperactivity disorder: Medication effects and comparison with typical children. *Journal of Clinical Child & Adolescent Psychology, 38*(5), 619–629.

Kirschner, P. A., Sweller, J., & Clark, R. E. (2006). Why minimal guidance does not work: An analysis of failure of constructivist, discovery, problem-based, experiential, and inquiry-based teaching. *Educational Psychologist, 41*(2), 75–86.

Kistner, S., Rakoczy, K., Otto, B., Dignath-van Ewijk, C., Büttner, G., & Klieme, E. (2010). Promotion of self-regulated learning in classrooms: Investigating frequency, quality, and consequences for student performance. *Metacognition and Learning, 5,* 157–171.

Kitayama, S., Park, H., Sevincer, A. T., Karasawa, M., & Uskul, A. K. (2009). A cultural task analysis of implicit independence: Comparing North America, Western Europe, and East Asia. *Journal of Personality and Social Psychology, 97*(2), 236–255.

Klahr, D., & Carver, S. M. (1988). Cognitive objectives in a LOGO debugging curriculum: Instruction, learning, and transfer. *Cognitive Psychology, 20,* 362–404.

Klahr, D., & Nigam, M. (2004). The equivalence of learning paths in early science instruction: Effects of direct instruction and discovery learning. *Psychological Science, 15*(10), 661–667.

Klassen, R. M., & Chiu, M. M. (2010). Effects on teachers' self-efficacy and job satisfaction: Teacher gender, years of experience, and job stress. *Journal of Educational Psychology, 102*(3), 741–756.

Klausmeir, H. J. (1992). Concept learning and concept teaching. *Educational Psychologist, 27,* 267–286.

Klausmeir, H. J. (2004). Conceptual learning and development. In W. E. Craighead & C. B. Nemeroff (Eds.), *The concise Corsini encyclopedia of psychology and behavioral sciences* (pp. 209–210). New York: Wiley.

Klein, M. D., Cook, R. E., & Richardson-Gibbs, A. M. (2001). *Strategies for including children with special needs in early childhood settings.* Albany, NY: Delmar.

Klein, P. S., Adi-Japha, E., & Hakak-Benizri, S. (2010). Mathematical thinking of kindergarten boys and girls: Similar achievement, different contributing processes. *Educational Studies in Math, 73,* 233–246.

Kling, K. C., Hyde, J. S., Showers, C. J., & Buswell, B. N. (1999). Gender differences in self-esteem: A meta-analysis. *Psychological Bulletin, 125,* 470–500.

Klingner, J. K., Vaughn, S., & Boardman, A. (2007). *Teaching reading comprehension to students with learning difficulties: What works for special-needs learners.* New York: Guilford.

Knotek, S. (2005). Portfolio assessment. In S. W. Lee (Ed.), *Encyclopedia of school psychology.* Thousand Oaks, CA: Sage.

Knudsen, E. I. (1999). Early experience and critical periods. In M. J. Zigmond (Ed.), *Fundamental neuroscience* (pp. 637–654). San Diego, CA: Academic Press.

Knudsen, E. I. (2004). Sensitive periods in the development of brain and behavior. *Journal of Cognitive Neuroscience, 16*(8), 1412–1425.

Kochanska, G., Gross, J. N., Lin, M.-H., & Nichols, K. E. (2002). Guilt in young children: Development, determinants, and relations with a broader system of standards. *Child Development, 73,* 461–482.

Koegel, L. K., Koegel, R. L., & Dunlap, G. (1996). *Positive behavior support: Including people with difficult behavior in the community.* Baltimore: Paul H. Brookes.

Koegel, L. K., Koegel, R. L., Harrower, J. K., & Carter, C. M. (1999). Pivotal response I: Overview of approach. *Journal of the Association for Persons with Severe Handicaps, 24,* 174–185.

Koestner, R., Ryan, R. M., Bernieri, F., & Holt, K. (1984). Setting limits on children's behavior: The differential effects of controlling versus informational styles on intrinsic motivation and creativity. *Journal of Personality, 52,* 233–248.

Koestner, R., Zuckerman, M., & Koestner, J. (1987). Praise, involvement, and intrinsic motivation. *Journal of Personality and Social Psychology, 53,* 383–390.

Koestner, R., Zuckerman, M., & Koestner, J. (1989). Attributional focus of praise and children's intrinsic motivation: The moderating role of gender. *Personality and Social Psychology Bulletin, 15,* 61–72.

Kogan, E. (2001). *Gifted bilingual students.* New York: Peter Lang.

Kogan, N. (1974). Creativity and sex differences. *Journal of Creative Behavior, 8*, 1–14.

Kohlberg, L. (1963). The development of children's orientations toward moral order: Sequence in the development of moral thought. *Vita Humana, 6*, 11–33.

Kohlberg, L. (1975). The cognitive-developmental approach to moral education. *Phi Delta Kappan, 57*, 670–677.

Kohlberg, L. (1981). *The philosophy of moral development* (*Essays on moral development*, Vol. 1). San Francisco: Harper & Row.

Kohlberg, L. (1984). *The psychology of moral development: The nature and validity of moral stages* (*Essays on moral development*, Vol. 2). San Francisco: Harper & Row.

Kohlberg, L., Yaeger, J., & Hjertholm, E. (1968). Private speech: Four studies and a review of theories. *Child Development, 39*, 691–736.

Kohler, F. W., Anthony, L. J., Steighner, S. A., & Hoyson, M. (2001). Teaching social interaction skills in the integrated preschool: An examination of naturalistic tactics. *Topics in Early Childhood Special Education, 21*(2), 93–113.

Kohn, A. (1996). *Beyond discipline: From compliance to community.* Alexandria, VA: Association for Supervision and Curriculum Development.

Koong, C. S., & Wu, C. Y. (2011). The applicability of interactive item templates in varied knowledge types. *Computers and Education, 56*(3), 781–801.

Korenman, S., Miller, J., & Sjaastad, J. (1995). Long-term poverty and child development in the United States: Results from the NLSY. *Children and Youth Services Review, 17*, 127–155.

Koretz, D., Barron, S., Mitchell, K., & Keith, S. (1996). *Perceived effects of the Maryland school performance assessment program* (CSE Technical Report 409). Los Angeles: National Center for Research on Evaluation, Standards, and Student Testing.

Kornell, N., & Metcalfe, J. (2006). Study efficacy and the region of proximal learning framework. *Journal of Experimental Psychology: Learning, Memory, and Cognition, 32*, 609–622.

Kornhaber, M., Fierros, E., & Veenema, S. (2004). *Multiple intelligences: Best ideas from research and practice.* Boston: Allyn & Bacon.

Kosslyn, S. M., & Koening, O. (1992). *Wet mind: The new cognitive neuroscience.* New York: Free Press.

Kostelnik, M., Soderman, A., & Whiren, A. (2004). *Developmentally appropriate curriculum: Best practices in early childhood education.* Upper Saddle River, NJ: Merrill/Prentice Hall.

Kounin, J. S. (1970). *Discipline and group management in classrooms.* New York: Holt, Rinehart, & Winston.

Kourilsky, M. L., & Wittrock, M. C. (1992). Generative teaching: An enhancement strategy for the learning of economics in cooperative groups. *American Educational Research Journal, 29*(4), 861–876.

Kousoulas, F. (2010). The interplay of creative behavior, divergent thinking, and knowledge base in students' creative expression during learning activity. *Creativity Research Journal, 22*(4), 387–396.

Kousoulas, F., & Mega, G. (2009). Students' divergent thinking and teachers' ratings of creativity: Does gender play a role? *Journal of Creative Behavior, 43*(3), 209–222.

Koustaal, W., & Cavendish, M. (2006). Using what we know: Consequences of intentionally retrieving gist versus item-specific information. *Journal of Experimental Psychology: Learning, Memory, and Cognition, 32*(4), 778–791.

Kramarski, B., & Mevarech, Z. R. (2003). Enhancing mathematical reasoning in the classroom: The effects of cooperative learning and metacognitive training. *American Educational Research Journal, 40*, 281–310.

Krapp, A. (1999). Interest, motivation and learning: An educational–psychological perspective. *European Journal of Psychology of Education, 14*, 23–40.

Krebs, S. S., & Roebers, C. M. (2010). Children's strategic regulation, metacognitive monitoring, and control processes during test-taking. *British Journal of Educational Psychology, 80*(3), 325–340.

Kreitzer, A. E., Madaus, G. F., & Haney, W. (1989). Competency testing and dropouts. In L. Weis, E. Farrar, & H. G. Petrie (Eds.) *Dropouts from school: Issues, dilemmas, and solutions* (pp. 129–152). Albany, NY: State University of New York Press.

Krezmien, M. P., Leone, P. E., & Achilles, G. M. (2006). Suspension, race, and disability: Analysis of statewide practices and reporting. *Journal of Emotional and Behavioral Disorders, 14*(4), 217–226.

Kroesbergen, E. H., & Van Luit, J. E. H. (2005). Constructivist mathematics education for students with mild mental retardation. *European Journal of Special Needs Education, 27*(1), 107–116.

Krohne, H. (1992). Developmental conditions of anxiety and coping: A two-process model of child-rearing effects. In K. Hagtvet & T. Johnson (Eds.), *Advances in test anxiety and research*, Vol. 7 (pp. 143–155). Amsterdam: Swets & Zeitlinger.

Krumboltz, J. D., & Krumboltz, H. B. (1972). *Changing children's behaviors.* Englewood Cliffs, NJ: Prentice Hall.

Krumboltz, J. D., & Yeh, C. J. (1996). Competitive grading sabotages good teaching. *Phi Delta Kappan, 78*, 324–326.

Kryspin, W. J., & Feldhusen, J. F. (1974). *Developing classroom tests.* Edina, MN: Burgess.

Kubiszyn, T., & Borich, G. (2003). *Educational testing and measurement: Classroom application and practice* (7th ed.). New York: Wiley.

Kucan, L., Palincsar, A. S., Khasnabis, D., & Chang, C. (2009). The Video Viewing Task: A source of information for assessing and addressing teacher understanding of text-based discussion. *Teaching and Teacher Education, 25*, 415–423.

Kuhl, P. K. (2004). Early language acquisition: Cracking the speech code. *Neuroscience, 5*, 831–843.

Kuhura-Kojima, K., & Hatano, G. (1989). Strategies of recognizing sentences among high and low critical thinkers. *Japanese Psychological Research 3*(1), 1–9.

Kuhura-Kojima, K., & Hatano, G. (1991). Contribution of content knowledge and learning ability to the learning of facts. *Journal of Educational Psychology, 83*(2), 253–263.

Kulhavy, R. W., Lee, J. B., & Caterino, L. C. (1985). Conjoint retention of maps and related discourse. *Contemporary Educational Psychology, 10*, 28–37.

Kulieke, M., Bakker, J., Collins, C., et al. (1990). *Why should assessment be based on a vision of learning?* Oak Brook, IL: North Central Regional Educational Laboratory.

Kulik, C. C., Kulik, J. A., & Bangert-Drowns, R. L. (1990). Effectiveness of mastery learning programs: A meta-analysis. *Review of Educational Research, 60*, 265–299.

Kulik, J. A. (1992). *An analysis of the research on ability grouping: Historical and contemporary perspectives.* Storrs, CT: National Research Center on the Gifted and Talented, University of Connecticut.

Kulik, J., & Kulik, C. (1987). Effects of ability grouping on student achievement. *Equity and Excellence, 23*(1–2), 22–30.

Kulik, J. A., & Kulik, C. C. (1988). Timing of feedback and verbal learning. *Review of Educational Research, 58*, 79–97.

Kulik, J. A., & Kulik, C. C. (1990). Ability grouping and gifted students. In N. Colangelo & G. A. Davis (Eds.), *Handbook of gifted education* (pp. 178–196). Boston: Allyn & Bacon.

Kulik, J. A., & Kulik, C. C. (1992). Meta-analytic findings on grouping programs. *Gifted Child Quarterly, 36*(2), 73–77.

Kulik, J. A., & Kulik, C. C. (2004). Meta-analytic findings on grouping programs. In L. E. Brody (Ed.), *Grouping and acceleration practices in gifted education* (pp. 105–114). Thousand Oaks, CA: Corwin Press.

Kurdek, L. A., & Sinclair, R. J. (1988). Relation of eighth graders' family structure, gender, and family environment with academic performance and school behavior. *Journal of Educational Psychology, 80*(1), 90–94.

Kusche, C. A., & Greenberg, M. T. (2001). PATHS in your classroom: Promoting emotional literacy and alleviating emotional distress. In J. Cohen (Ed.), *Social emotional learning and the elementary school child: A guide for educators* (pp. 140–161). New York: Teachers College Press.

L

Laakso, A., Vilkman, H., Bergman, J., et al. (2002). Sex differences in striatal presynaptic dopamine synthesis capacity in healthy subjects. *Biological Psychiatry, 52,* 759–763.

LaFontana, K. M., & Cillessen, A. H. N. (2002). Children's perceptions of popular and unpopular peers: A multi-method assessment. *Developmental Psychology, 38,* 635–647.

La Freniere, P., & Sroufe, L. A. (1985). Profiles of peer competence in the preschool interrelations between measures, influence of social ecology, and relation to attachment history. *Developmental Psychology, 21,* 56–69.

Lai, A. F., Chen, D. J., & Chen, S. L. (2008). Item attributes analysis of computerized test based on IRT-A comparison study on static text/graphic presentation and interactive multimedia presentation. *Journal of Educational Multimedia & Hypermedia, 17*(4), 531–559.

Lalley, J. P., & Gentile, J. P. (2009). Classroom assessment and grading to assure mastery. *Theory Into Practice, 48,* 28–35.

Lam, L. T., & Kirby, S. L. (2002). Is emotional intelligence an advantage? An exploration of the impact of emotional and general intelligence on individual performance. *Journal of Social Psychology, 142*(1), 133–143.

Landrum, T. J., & Kaufman, J. M. (2006). Behavioral approaches to classroom management. In C. M. Evertson & C. S. Weinstein (Eds.), *Handbook of classroom management: Research, practice and contemporary issues* (pp. 47–71). Mahwah, NJ: Erlbaum.

Lane, K. L., Gresham, F. M., & O'Shaughnessy, T. E. (2002). *Interventions for children with or at risk for emotional and behavioral disorders.* Boston: Allyn & Bacon.

Langer, E. J. (1993). A mindful education. *Educational Psychologist, 28*(1), 43–50.

Langer, J. A. (2000). Excellence in English in middle and high school: How teachers' professional lives support student achievement. *American Educational Research Journal, 37,* 397–439.

Langley, A. K., Bergman, R. L., McCracken, J., & Piacentini, J. C. (2004). Impairment in childhood anxiety disorders: Preliminary examination of the Child Anxiety Impact Scale–Parent Version. *Journal of Child and Adolescent Psychopharmacology, 14,* 105–114.

Lapsley, D. K. (1993). Toward an integrated theory of adolescent ego development: The "new look" at adolescent egocentrism. *American Journal of Orthopsychiatry, 63,* 562–571.

Lapsley, D. K. (2006). Moral stage theory. In M. Killen & J. Smetana (Eds.), *Handbook of moral development.* Mahwah, NJ: Erlbaum.

Larkin, J. H. (1989). What kind of knowledge transfers? In L. B. Resnick (Ed.), *Knowing, learning, and instruction* (pp. 283–305). Hillsdale, NJ: Erlbaum.

Lassig, C. J. (2009) Promoting creativity in education—from policy to practice: An Australian perspective. In *Proceedings of the 7th ACM Conference on Creativity and Cognition: Everyday Creativity,* October 27–30, 2009, University of California, Berkeley, CA.

Laurendeau-Bendavid, M. (1977). Culture, schooling, and cognitive development: A comparative study of children in French Canada and Rwanda. In P. R. Dasen (Ed.), *Piagetian psychology: Cross-cultural contributions* (pp. 123–168). New York: Gardner Press.

Lave, J. (1988). *Cognition in practice.* Cambridge, UK: Cambridge University Press.

Lave, J., & Wenger, E. (1991). *Situated teaming: Legitimate peripheral participation.* Cambridge, UK: Cambridge University Press.

Lawton, J. T., & Hooper, F. H. (1978). Piagetian theory and early childhood education: A critical analysis. In L. S. Siegel and C. J. Brainerd (Eds.), *Alternatives to Piaget: Critical essays on the theory* (pp. 169–199). New York: Academic Press.

Lay, R., & Wakstein, J. (1985). Race, academic achievement, and self-concept of ability. *Research in Higher Education, 22,* 43–64.

Lazar, I., & Darlington, R. (1982). Lasting effects of early education: A report from the consortium for longitudinal studies. *Monographs of the Society for Research in Child Development, 47*(2–3) (Serial No. 195).

Leach, D. J., and Byrne, M. K. (1986). Some "spill-over" effects of a home-based reinforcement programme in a secondary school. *Educational Psychology, 6*(3), 265–276.

Leap, W. L. (1981). American Indian language maintenance. *Annual Review of Anthropology, 10,* 209–236.

LeBlanc, R. S., Muise, J. G., & Blanchard, L. (1992). Backward masking in children and adolescents: Sensory transmission, accrual rate, and asymptotic performance. *Journal of Experimental Child Psychology, 53,* 105–114.

Lederer, J. M. (2000). Reciprocal teaching of social studies in inclusive elementary classrooms. *Journal of Learning Disabilities, 33*(1), 91–106.

LeDoux, J. E. (2000). Emotional circuits in the brain. *Annual Review of Neuroscience, 23,* 155–184.

Lee, S.-H., Simpson, R. L., & Shogren, K. A. (2007). Effects and implications of self-management for students with autism: A meta-analysis. *Focus on Autism and Other Developmental Disabilities, 22*(1), 2–13.

Lefebvre, L. (2006). Social intelligence and forebrain size in birds. In J. Kaas (Ed.), *The evolution of nervous systems* (Vol. 2, pp 229–236). Oxford: Elsevier.

LeFever, G. B., Arcona, A. P., & Antonuccio, D. O. (2003). ADHD among American school children: Evidence of overdiagnosis and overuse of medication. *The Scientific Review of Mental Health Practice, 2*(1), 49–60.

Leflot, G., Lier, P. A. C., Onghena, P., & Colpin, H. (2010). The role of teacher behavior management in the development of disruptive behaviors: An intervention study with the Good Behavior game. *Journal of Abnormal Child Psychology, 38*(6), 869–882.

Legault, L., Green-Demers, I., & Pelletier, L. (2006). Why do high school students lack motivation in the classroom? Toward an understanding of academic amotivation and the role of social support. *Journal of Educational Psychology, 98*(3), 567–582.

of instructional methods, at the end of a unit or grading period. (Module 26, p. 481; Module 28, 510)

SUSTAINING EXPECTATION EFFECT An effect whereby teachers sometimes fail to notice students' skill improvement, and therefore do not change their group placement, which inadvertently sustains students' achievement at their current level. (Module 21, p. 385)

SYMBOLIC MODELS Individuals who are observed indirectly through various forms of the media. (Module 10, p. 174)

SYNAPSE A gap between two neurons that allows transmission of messages. (Module 6, p. 104)

SYNAPTIC PRUNING Elimination of synapses. (Module 6, p. 109)

SYNAPTOGENESIS The growth of new connections in the brain, continues throughout life as individuals adapt to changing life conditions and experiences. (Module 6, p. 108)

SYNTAX The rules for combining components of language. (Module 8, p. 136)

SYSTEMATIC DESENSITIZATION A technique that combines relaxation training with gradual exposure to an anxiety-provoking stimulus to reduce anxieties and fears. (Module 25, p. 460)

SYSTEMATIC PHONICS INSTRUCTION A program that focuses on teaching children to recognize and manipulate phonemes and to then explicitly apply that knowledge to letter-sound correspondences and decoding. (Module 24, p. 442)

T

TABLE OF SPECIFICATIONS A test blueprint that is laid out in table format. (Module 27, p. 496)

TASK ANALYSIS Identification of the specific knowledge, behaviors, or cognitive processes necessary to master a particular skill. (Module 11, p. 195)

TASK KNOWLEDGE Knowledge about the difficulty or ease of a task. (Module 12, p. 211)

TASK-CONTINGENT REWARDS Rewards that are given for participating in an activity or for completing an activity without regard to performance level. (Module 15, p. 267)

TASK-SPECIFIC RUBRIC Assessment criteria that take a generic framework and modifies it to match specific learning goals of a particular task. (Module 28, p. 517)

TEACHER EFFICACY A teacher's belief that he or she has the capabilities to transmit knowledge and manage the classroom in order to teach all students effectively. (Module 10, p. 180; Module 17, p. 302)

TELEGRAPHIC SPEECH A way of ordering words according to the grammatical rules of one's language. (Module 8, p. 136)

TEMPERAMENT A pattern of responding to environmental stimuli and events that emerges early in life, is relatively enduring, and seems to have genetic origins. Temperament includes patterns of activity level, adaptability, persistence, adventurousness, shyness, inhibitedness, irritability, and distractibility. (Module 4, p. 62)

TERATOGENS Any foreign substances that can cause abnormalities in a developing fetus. (Module 6, p. 107)

TEST BIAS Systemic error in a test score that may or may not be a function of cultural variations. (Module 30, p. 559)

TEST BLUEPRINT An assessment planning tool that describes the content the test will cover and the way you expect students to demonstrate their understanding of that content. (Module 27, p. 496)

TEST FAIRNESS An ethical issue of how to use tests appropriately. (Module 30, p. 558)

TEST SCORE POLLUTION Occurs when test scores are systematically increased or decreased due to factors unrelated to what the test is intended to measure. (Module 30, p. 554)

TESTS AND SURVEYS Type of measure used in research which are typically paper-and-pencil and include a number of questions. (Module 1, p. 10)

THEORY Set of ideas used to explain a phenomenon and make prediction about behavior. (Module 1, p. 6)

THEORY OF IDENTICAL ELEMENTS A theory proposing that transfer between two learning tasks will occur if the tasks share common elements. (Module 13, p. 226)

THEORY OF MULTIPLE INTELLIGENCES A theory of intelligence proposed by Howard Gardner consisting of eight separate but interacting intelligences. (Module 22, p. 404)

THEORY OF MIND Early development of children's attempt to understand the mind and mental world. (Module 12, p. 212)

THEORY OF SUCCESSFUL INTELLIGENCE A theory proposed by Robert Sternberg in which success is defined as the ability to succeed in life and involves finding ways to effectively balance one's analytical, creative, and practical abilities. (Module 22, p. 404)

THEORY-BASED VALIDITY Type of validity evidence that demonstrates the test score is consistent with a theoretical aspect of the construct. (Module 29, p. 546)

THINKING DISPOSITION A cluster of thinking preferences, attitudes, and intentions, plus a set of capabilities that allow the preferences to become realized in a particular way. (Module 14, p. 240)

THREE-RING CONCEPTION OF GIFTEDNESS A theoretical model of giftedness which proposes that giftedness is comprised of three behaviors: above-average ability, high levels of task commitment, and high levels of creativity. (Module 23, p. 421)

TRANSFER The application of previously learned knowledge, skills, or strategies to new contexts. (Module 13, p. 226)

TRANSITIONAL BILINGUAL EDUCATION A method of bilingual instruction in which students learn subjects in their native language (as well as English-language instruction) while they are acquiring the second language. (Module 8, p. 140)

T-SCORE Type of standard score based on the units of standard deviation with a mean of 50 and standard deviation of 10. (Module 29, p. 545)

TWO-FACTOR THEORY OF INTELLIGENCE One of the first theories of intelligence which posited that performance on intelligence tests could be attributed to a general mental ability, g, and abilities in specific domains, s. See also other theories of intelligence: theory of multiple intelligences and theory of successful intelligence. (Module 22, p. 403)

TWO-WAY BILINGUAL IMMERSION A method of bilingual instruction in which students who speak English and students who speak a non-English language learn academic subjects in both languages. (Module 8, p. 140)

U

UNCONDITIONED RESPONSE The behavior that automatically occurs due to the unconditioned stimulus. (Module 9, p. 159)

UNCONDITIONED STIMULUS The behavior that evokes an automatic response. (Module 9, p. 159)

UNDEREXTENSIONS Limiting the use of a word to a subset of objects it refers to. (Module 8, p. 136)

UNINVOLVED PARENTING Lacks both control and responsiveness. (Module 2, p. 32)

USE IT OR LOSE IT PRINCIPLE The idea that practice strengthens neural connections, while infrequent use of certain skills may cause synaptic connections to weaken or degenerate. (Module 6, p. 109)

UTILITY VALUE A component of expectancy-value theory referring to the usefulness of a task for meeting short-term and long-term goals. (Module 16, p. 280)

V

VALIDITY The extent to which a test or assessment actually measures what it is intended to measure, so that meaningful interpretations can be derived from the test score. (Module 27, p. 493; Module 29, p. 545)

VALUE A component of expectancy-value theory referring to reasons for undertaking a task; "do I want to do this task?" See also expectancy. (Module 16, p. 279)

VARIABILITY Measure of how widely scores are distributed. (Module 29, p. 541)

VARIABLES The events, characteristics, or behaviors of interest in a research study. (Module 1, p. 7)

VERBAL MEDIATION A word or phrase that forms a logical connection or "bridge" between two pieces of information; used as a mnemonic. (Module 11, p. 188)

VICARIOUS PUNISHMENT Behaviors are displayed less frequently if a model has been punished for those behaviors. (Module 10, p. 177)

VICARIOUS REINFORCEMENT Behaviors are displayed more frequently if a model has been reinforced for those behaviors. (Module 10, p. 177)

VISUAL IMAGERY The process of forming mental pictures of objects or ideas. (Module 11, p. 188)

VISUAL PERSPECTIVE-TAKING Understanding that another person can see something in a different way or from a different view than themselves. (Module 12, p. 212)

VISUOSPATIAL SKETCHPAD Part of working memory. A holding system for visual and spatial information. (Module 11, p. 186)

VISUOSPATIAL SUBTYPE A subtype of mathematics disability that has not been widely investigated involving difficulties with the spatial representation of numerical information. (Module 24, p. 444)

VOLUNTEER BIAS The tendency for those who choose to participate in research studies to be different in some way from others who decline the invitation to participate. (Module 1, p. 10)

W

WAIT TIME The length of time a teacher pauses after posing a question to give students time to think before being called on to respond. (Module 11, p. 194; Module 14, p. 243)

WELL-DEFINED PROBLEM A problem in which a goal is clearly stated, all information needed to solve the problem is available, and only one correct answer exists. (Module 14, p. 245)

WERNICKE'S AREA Part of the left temporal lobe of the brain that surrounds the auditory cortex and is thought to be essential for understanding and formulating speech. Damage in Wernicke's area causes deficits in understanding spoken language. (Module 6, p. 112)

WITHIN-CLASS ABILITY GROUPING Forming groups of students in a self-contained classroom in which groups are of similar ability. (Module 21, p. 379)

WITHITNESS A teacher's ability to remain aware of and responsive to students' behaviors at all times. (Module 19, p. 353)

WORD RECOGNITION The act of identifying or recognizing individual words while reading. (Module 24, p. 441)

WORK-AVOIDANCE GOAL Motivation to avoid academic work and prefer easy tasks. (Module 16, p. 286)

WORKING-BACKWARD STRATEGY A heuristic in which you start with the final goal and think backward to identify the steps that would be needed to reach that goal. (Module 14, p. 247)

WORKING MEMORY A component of memory that holds and processes a limited amount of information; also known as short-term memory. The duration of information stored in working memory is probably about five to twenty seconds. (Module 11, p. 185)

Z

ZERO TRANSFER Occurs when previous learning has no effect on a new task. (Module 13, p. 226)

ZONE OF PROXIMAL DEVELOPMENT (ZPD) The difference between what an individual can accomplish independently and what he or she can learn with assistance from more capable individuals. (Module 7, p. 124)

Z-SCORE Standard score based on units of standard deviation ranging from −4.0 to +4.0. (Module 29, p. 544)

Lehman, S., Schraw, G., McCrudden, M., & Hartley, K. (2007). Processing and recall of seductive details in scientific text. *Contemporary Educational Psychology, 32,* 569–587.

Lehmann, M., & Hasselhorn, M. (2010). The dynamics of free recall and their relation to rehearsal between 8 and 10 years of age. *Child Development, 81*(3), 1006–1020.

Leinhardt, G., Weidman, C., & Hammond, K. M. (1987). Introduction and integration of classroom routines by expert teachers. *Curriculum Inquiry, 17*(2), 135–175.

Lemerise, E. A., & Arsenio, W. F. (2004). An integrated model of emotion processes and cognition in social information processing. *Child Development, 71*(1), 107–118.

Lent, R. W., Lopez, F. G., Brown, S. D., & Gore, P. A. (1996). Latent structure of the sources of mathematics self-efficacy. *Journal of Vocational Behavior, 49,* 292–308.

Lentz, F. E. (1988). Reductive procedures. In J. C. Witt, S. N. Elliott, & F. M. Gresham (Eds.), *Handbook of Behavior Therapy in Education.* New York: Plenum Press.

Leondari, A., & Gonida, E. (2007). Predicting academic self-handicapping in different age groups: The role of personal achievement goals and social goals. *British Journal of Educational Psychology, 77,* 595–611.

Leontiev, A. N. (1961). Learning as a problem in psychology. In N. O'Connor (Ed.), *Recent Soviet psychology* (pp. 227–246). Nw York: Liveright.

Leontiev, A. N., & Luria, A. R. (1972). Some notes concerning Dr. Fodor's "Reflections on L. S. Vygotsky's thought and language." *Cognition, 1,* 311–316.

Lepper, M. R., Corpus, J. H., & Iyengar, S. S. (2005). Intrinsic and extrinsic motivational orientations in the classroom: Age differences and academic correlates. *Journal of Educational Psychology, 97*(2), 184–196.

Lepper, M. R., & Greene, D. (1978). *The hidden costs of reward.* Hillsdale, NJ: Erlbaum.

Lepper, M. R., & Henderlong, J. (2000). Turning "play" into "work" and "work" into "play": Twenty-five years of research on intrinsic versus extrinsic motivation. In C. Sansone & J. M. Harackiewicz (Eds.), *Intrinsic and extrinsic motivation: The search for optimal motivation and performance* (pp. 257–307). New York: Academic Press.

Lepper, M. R., & Malone, T. W. (1987). Intrinsic motivation and instructional effectiveness in computer-based education. In R. E. Snow & M. J. Fair (Eds.), *Cognitive and affective process analyses* (Vol. 3, pp. 255–286). Mahwah, NJ: Erlbaum.

Lepper, M. R., Sethi, S., Dialdin, D., & Drake, M. (1997). Intrinsic and extrinsic motivation: A developmental perspective. In S. S. Luthar, J. A. Burack, D. Cicchetti, & J. R. Weisz (Eds.), *Developmental psychopathology: Perspectives on adjustment, risk, and disorder* (pp. 23–50). New York: Cambridge University Press.

Lerman, D. C., & Iwata, B. A. (1995). Prevalence of the extinction burst and its attenuation during treatment. *Journal of Applied Behavior Analysis, 28,* 93–94.

Lesgold, A. M. (1988). Problem solving. In R. J. Sternberg & E. E. Smith (Eds.), *The psychology of human thoughts.* New York: Cambridge University Press.

Lessow-Hurley, J. (2000). *The foundations of dual language instruction* (3rd ed.). White Plains, NY: Longman.

Leu, D., & Kinzer, C. (1995). *Effective reading instruction.* Englewood Cliffs, NJ: Merrill/Prentice Hall.

Levesque, C., Zuehike, A. N., Stanek, L. R., & Ryan, R. M. (2004). Autonomy and competence in German and American university students: A comparative study based on self-determination theory. *Journal of Educational Psychology, 96,* 68–84.

Levin, J., & Nolan, J. F. (2000). *Principles of classroom management* (3rd ed). Boston: Allyn & Bacon.

Levy, L. J., Astur, R. S., & Frick, K. M. (2005). Men and women differ in object memory but not performance of a virtual radial maze. *Behavioral Neuroscience, 119,* 853–862.

Lewinsohn, P. M., & Essau, C. A. (2002). Depression in adolescents. In C. L. Hammen & I. H. Gotlib (Eds.), *Handbook of depression* (pp. 541–559). New York: Guilford.

Lewis, A., & Smith, D. (1993). Defining higher order thinking. *Theory Into Practice, 32*(3), 131–137.

Liberman, I. Y., Shankweiler, D., & Liberman, A. M. (1989). The alphabetic principle and learning to read. In D. Shankweiler, & I. Y. Liberman, (Eds.), *Phonology and reading disability: Solving the reading puzzle* (pp. 1–33). Ann Arbor, MI: University of Michigan Press.

Lichtenstein, E. H., & Brewer, W. F. (1980). Memory for goal-directed events. *Cognitive Psychology, 12,* 415–445.

Lichtenstein, S., & Slovic, P. (Eds.). (2006). *The construction of preference.* Cambridge, UK: Cambridge University Press.

Lindberg, S. M., Hyde, J. S., & Hirsch, L. M. (2008). Gender and mother-child interactions during mathematics homework. *Merrill-Palmer Quarterly, 54,* 232–255.

Lindberg, S. M., Hyde, J. S., Peterson, J. L., & Linn, M. C. (2010). New trends in gender and mathematics performance: A meta-analysis. *Psychological Bulletin, 136*(6), 1123–1135.

Lindholm-Leary, K. J. (2001). *Dual language education.* Avon, UK: Multilingual Matters.

Lindholm-Leary, K. J. (2004–2005). The rich promise of two-way immersion. *Educational Leadership, 62*(4), 56–59.

Lindner, E. G. (2006). Emotion and conflict: Why it is important to understand how emotions affect conflict and how conflict affects emotions. In M. Deutsch, P. T. Coleman, & E. C. Markus (Eds.), *The handbook of conflict resolution: Theory and practice* (pp. 268–293). San Francisco: Jossey-Bass.

Lindsay, G., Dockrell, J., Letchford, B., & Mackie, C. (2002). Self-esteem of children with specific speech and language difficulties. *Child Language Teaching and Therapy, 18,* 125–143.

Lindvall, C. M., & Nitko, A. J. (1975). *Measuring pupil achievement and aptitude* (2nd ed.). New York: Harcourt Brace Jovanovich.

Linn, R. L., & Gronlund, N. E. (2000). *Measurement and assessment in teaching* (8th ed.). Upper Saddle River, NJ: Prentice Hall.

Linnenbrink, E. A., & Pintrich P. R. (2003). The role of self-efficacy beliefs in student engagement and learning in the classroom. *Reading and Writing Quarterly, 19,* 119–137.

Linnenbrink, E. A. (2005). The dilemma of performance-approach goals: The use of multiple goal contexts to promote students' motivation and learning. *Journal of Educational Psychology, 97,* 197–213.

Linnenbrink, E. A., & Fredericks, J. A. (2007). Developmental perspectives on achievement motivation: Personal and contextual influences. In J. Y. Shah & W. L. Gardner (Eds.), *Handbook of motivation science: The social psychological perspective* (pp. 448–517). New York: Guilford.

Lisonbee, J., Mize, J., Payne, A. L., & Granger, D. (2008). Children's cortisol and the quality of teacher-child relationships in child care. *Child Development, 79*(6), 1818–1832.

Lissitz, R. W., & Schafer, W. D. (2002). *Assessment in educational reform: Both means and ends.* Boston: Allyn & Bacon.

Little, M., & Hopkins, C. (2010). Will PATHS lead to the fourth "R"? *Better: Evidence-based Education: Social and Emotional Learning* (Winter 2010), 8–9.

Little, S. G., & Akin-Little, A. (2008). Psychology's contributions to classroom management. *Psychology in the Schools, 45*(3), 227–234.

Ljungdahl, L., & Prescott, A. (2009). Teachers' use of diagnostic testing to enhance students' literacy and numeracy learning. *International Journal of Learning,16*(2), 461–475.

Lloyd, L. (1999). Multi-age classes and high ability students. *Review of Educational Research, 69*(2), 187–212.

LoCicero, K. A., & Ashbly, J. S. (2000). Multidimensional perfectionism in middle school age gifted students: A comparison to peers from the general cohort. *Roeper Review, 22*(3), 182–185.

Locke, J. (1892). Some thoughts concerning education. In R. H. Quick (Ed.), *Locke on education* (pp. 1–236). Cambridge, UK: Cambridge University Press. (Original work published in 1690.)

Locke, J. L. (1983). *Phonological acquisition and change.* New York: Academic Press.

Locke, J. L. (1995). Development of the capacity for spoken language. In P. Fletcher & B. MacWhinney (Eds.), *The handbook of child language* (pp. 278–302). Cambridge, MA: Blackwell.

Lockl, K., & Schneider, W. (2007). Knowledge about the mind: Links between theory of mind and later metamemory. *Child Development, 78*(1), 148–167.

Lomawaima, K. T. (2003). Educating Native Americans. In J. A. Banks & C. A. M. Banks (Eds.), *Handbook of research on multi-cultural education* (2nd ed., pp. 441–461). New York: Wiley.

Longo, C. (2010). Fostering creativity or teaching to the test: Implications of state testing on the delivery of science instruction. *The Clearing House, 83,* 54–57.

Lopes, P., & Salovey, P. (2004). Toward a broader education: Social, emotional, and practical skills. In J. E. Zins, R. P. Weissberg, M. C. Wang, & H. J. Walberg (Eds.), *Building school success on social and emotional learning.* New York: Teachers College Press.

Lou, Y., Abrami, P. C., Spence, J. C., Poulsen, C., Chambers, B., & d'Apollonia, S. (1996). Within-class grouping: A meta-analysis. *Review of Educational Research, 66*(4), 423–458.

Lourenço, O., & Machado, A. (1996). In defense of Piaget's theory: A reply to 10 common criticisms. *Psychological Review, 103*(1), 143–164.

Loveless, T. (1999). Will tracking reform promote social equity? *Educational Leadership, 56*(7), 28–32.

Loyens, S., Kirschner, P. A., & Paas, F. (2009). *Problem-based learning.* APA Educational Psychology Handbook.

Loyens, S. M. M., Magda, J., & Rikers, R. M. J. P. (2008). Self-directed learning in problem-based learning and its relationships with self-regulated learning. *Educational Psychology Review, 20,* 411–427.

Lu, Z.-L., Williamson, S. J., & Kaufman, L. (1992). Behavioral lifetime of human auditory sensory memory predicted by physiological measures. *Science, 258,* 1668–1670.

Lubart, T., & Zenasni, F. (2010). A new look at creative giftedness. *Gifted and Talented International, 25*(1), 53–57.

Luckasson, R., Borthwick-Duffy, S., Buntinx, W. H. E., et al. (2002). *Mental retardation: Definition, classification, and systems of supports* (10th ed.). Washington, DC: American Association on Intellectual and Developmental Disabilities.

Luekens, M. T., Lyter, D. M., & Fox, E. E. (2004). *Teacher attrition and mobility: Results from the teacher follow-up survey 2000–2001.* (NCES 2004-301). U.S. Department of Education. Washington, DC: National Center for Education Statistics.

Luiten, J., Ames, W., & Ackerson, G. (1980). A meta-analysis of the effects of advance organizers on learning and retention. *American Educational Research Journal, 17*(2), 211–218.

Lund, N., & Duchan, J. (1988). *Assessing children's language in naturalistic contexts.* Upper Saddle River, NJ: Prentice Hall.

Lynch, J. P. (2002, October). Trends in juvenile violent offending: An analysis of victim survey data. *Juvenile Justice Bulletin.* Retrieved December 3, 2003, from www.ojjdp.ncjrs.org/pubs/delinq .html#191052.

Lynch, S., & Mills, C. (1990). The skills reinforcement program (SRP): An academic program for high-potential minority youth. *Journal for the Education of the Gifted, 21,* 95–102.

Lynn, R. (1998). In support of the nutrition theory. In U. Neisser (Ed.), *The rising curve* (pp. 207–215). Washington, DC: American Psychological Association.

Lyon, G. R. (1995). Toward a definition of dyslexia. *Annals of Dyslexia, 45,* 3–27.

Lyon, G. R., Fletcher, J. M., Shaywitz, S. E., et al. (2001). Rethinking learning disabilities. In C. E. Finn, Jr., A. J. Rotherham, & C. R. Hokanson, Jr. (Eds.), *Rethinking special education for a new century* (pp. 259–287). Washington, DC: Thomas B. Fordham Foundation and Progressive Policy Institute.

M

Ma, H. J., Wan, G., & Lu, E. Y. (2008). Digital cheating and plagiarism in schools. *Theory Into Practice, 47,* 197–203.

Ma, X. (1999). A meta-analysis of the relationship between anxiety toward mathematics and achievement in mathematics. *Journal for Research in Mathematics Education, 30,* 520–540.

Maag, J. W. (2001). Rewarded by punishment: Reflections on the disuse of positive reinforcement in schools. *Exceptional Children, 67,* 173–186.

Maatta, S., & Nurmi, J. (2007). Achievement orientations, school adjustment, and well-being: A longitudinal study. *Journal of Research on Adolescence, 17,* 789–812.

Maccoby, E. E. (1990). The role of gender identity and gender constancy in sex-differentiated development. In K. Shrader (Ed.), *New directions for child development.* San Francisco: Jossey-Bass.

MacIver, D., Stipek, D., & Daniels, D. (1991). Explaining within-semester changes in student effort in junior high school and senior high school courses. *Journal of Educational Psychology, 83,* 201–211.

Mackenzie, A. A., & White, R. T. (1982). Fieldwork in geography and long-term memory structures. *American Educational Research Journal, 19*(4), 623–632.

MacKinnon, D. W. (1965). Personality and the realization of creative potential. *American Psychologist, 20,* 365.

Mackintosh, N. J. (1996). Sex differences in IQ. *Journal of Biosocial Science, 28*(4), 559–571.

Maclean, M., Bryant, P. E., & Bradley, L. (1987). Rhymes, nursery rhymes, and reading in early childhood. *Merrill-Palmer Quarterly, 33,* 255–281.

MacLeod, M. D., & Saunders, J. (2008). Retrieval inhibition and memory distortion: Negative consequences of an adaptive process. *Current Directions in Psychological Science, 17*(1), 26–30.

MacMath, S., Wallace, J., & Chi, X. (2009). Curriculum integration: Opportunities to maximize assessment as, of, and for learning. *McGill Journal of Education, 44*(3), 451–466.

MacMillan, D. L., & Siperstein, G. N. (2002). Learning disabilities as operationally defined in schools. In R. Bradley, L. Danielson, & D. P.

Hallahan (Eds.), *Identification of learning disabilities: Research to practice* (pp. 287–333). Mahwah, NJ: Erlbaum.

Madaus, J. W., & Shaw, S. F. (2006). The impact of the IDEA 2004 on transition to college for students with learning disabilities. *Learning Disabilities Research and Practice, 21*(4), 273–281.

Madsen, C. H., Becker, W. C., & Thomas, D. R. (1968). Rules, praise, and ignoring: Elements of elementary classroom control. *Journal of Applied Behavior Analysis, 1,* 139–150.

Maehr, M. L., & Midgley, C. (1991). Enhancing student motivation: A schoolwide approach. *Educational Psychologist, 26,* 399–427.

Maehr, M. L., & Nicholls, J. G. (1980). Culture and achievement motivation: A second look. In N. Warren (Ed.), *Studies in cross-cultural psychology, Vol. 2* (pp. 221–267). New York: Academic Press.

Maehr, M. L., & Zusho, A. (2009). Achievement goal theory: The past, present, and future. In K. R. Wentzel & A. Wigfield (Eds.), *Handbook of motivation in school* (pp. 77–104). New York: Routledge/Taylor & Francis Group.

Magee, M., & Perkins, D. (2010). Implementing a SEL programme. *Better: Evidence-based Education: Social and Emotional Learning* (Winter 2010), 10–11.

Mager, R. (1975). *Preparing instructional objectives* (2nd ed.). Belmont, CA: Lake.

Maier, N. R. F. (1933). An aspect of human reasoning. *British Journal of Psychology, 24,* 144–155.

Maier, N. R. F. (1937). Reasoning in rats and human beings. *Psychological Review, 44,* 365–378.

Maite, G. (2009). A comparative analysis of empathy in childhood and adolescence: Gender differences and associated socioemotional variables. *International Journal of Psychology & Psychological Therapy, 9*(2), 217–235.

Maker, C. J. (1996). Identification of gifted minority students: A national problem, needed changes and a promising solution. *Gifted Child Quarterly, 40,* 41–50.

Malone, M. R., & Lepper, M. R. (1983). Making learning fun. In R. E. Snow & J. F. Marshall (Eds.), *Aptitude, learning , and instruction: Cognitive and affective process analyses, Vol. 3* (pp. 223–253). Hillsdale, NJ: Erlbaum.

Malti, T., Gasser, L., & Buchmann, M. (2009). Aggressive and prosocial children's emotion attributions and moral reasoning. *Aggressive Behavior, 35,* 95–102.

Mandara, J. (2006). The impact of family functioning on African American males' academic achievement: A review and clarification of the empirical literature. *Teachers College Record, 108*(2), 206–223.

Manderlink, G., & Harackiewicz, J. (1984). Proximal vs. distal goal setting and intrinsic motivation. *Journal of Personality and Social Psychology, 47,* 918–928.

Mangels, J. A., Piction, T. W., & Craik, F. I. (2001). Attention and successful episodic encoding: An event-related potential study. *Brain Research, 11,* 77–95.

Manning, B. H. (1991). *Cognitive self-instruction for classroom processes.* Albany, NY: New York Press.

Mansell, W., & Morris, K. (2004). A survey of parents' reactions to the diagnosis of autistic spectrum disorder by a local service. *Autism, 8,* 387–407.

March, J. G., & Olson, J. P. (1989). *Rediscovering institutions: The organizational basis of politics.* New York: Free Press.

Marcia, J. E. (1966). Development and validation of ego-identity status. *Journal of Personality and Social Psychology, 3,* 551–558.

Marcia, J. E. (1987). The identity status approach to the study of ego identity development. In T. Honess & K. Yardley (Eds.), *Self and identity: Perspectives across the lifespan.* New York: Routledge & Kegan Paul.

Marcia, J. E. (1994). The empirical study of ego identity. In H. A. Bosma, T. L. G. Graafsma, J. D. Grotevant, & D. J. de Levita (Eds.), *Identity and development: An interdisciplinary approach.* Thousand Oaks, CA: Sage.

Marcotte, D., Lévesque, N., & Fortin, L. (2006). Variations of cognitive distortions and school performance in depressed and nondepressed high school adolescents: A two-year longitudinal study. *Cognitive Therapy Research, 30,* 211–225.

Marinak, B. A., & Gambrell, L. B. (2008). Intrinsic motivation and rewards: What sustains young children's engagement with text? *Literacy Research and Instruction, 47,* 9–26.

Marini, A., & Genereux, R. (1995). The challenge of teaching for transfer. In A. McKeough, J. Lupart, & A. Marini (Eds.), *Teaching for transfer: Fostering generalization in learning* (pp. 1–20). Mahwah, NJ: Erlbaum.

Markus, H. R. (2008). Pride, prejudice, and ambivalence: Toward a unified theory of race and ethnicity. *American Psychologist, 63*(8), 651–670.

Marschark, M., West, S. H., Nall, L., & Everhart, V. (1986). Development of creative language devices in signed and oral production. *Journal of Experimental Child Psychology, 41,* 534–550.

Marsh, H. W., Hau, K. T., & Kong, C. K. (2002). Multilevel causal ordering of academic self-concept and achievement: Influence of language of instruction (English compared with Chinese) for Hong Kong students. *American Educational Research Journal, 39,* 727–763.

Marsh, H. W., Trautwein, U., Ludtke, O., Koller, O., & Baumert, J. (2005). Academic self-concept, interest, grades, and standardized test scores: Reciprocal effects models of causal ordering. *Child Development, 76,* 397–416.

Marshall, H. H., & Weinstein, R. S. (1984). Classroom factors affecting students' self-evaluations: An interactional model. *Review of Educational Research, 54,* 301–325.

Marshall, I. H. (2002). *A study of the factors contributing to the attrition rate of public school teachers in Texas* (Doctoral dissertation, Texas A & M University, Kingsville Corpus Christi).

Marshall, S. P. (1994). Our gifted children: Are they asking too much? *Gifted Child Quarterly, 38,* 187–192.

Martin, A. J., Marsh, H. W., McInerney, D. M., Green, J., & Dowson, M. (2007). Getting along with teachers and parents: The yields of good relationships for students' achievement motivation and self-esteem. *Australian Journal of Guidance & Counseling, 17,* 109–125.

Martin, N. (Ed.). (1987). *Writing across the curriculum.* Upper Montclair, NJ: Boynton/Cook.

Martinez-Roldan, C. M., & Lopez-Robertson, J. M. (2000). Initiating literature circles in a first-grade bilingual classroom. *The Reading Teacher, 53*(4), 270–281.

Martinussen, R., Hayden, J., Hogg-Johnson, S., & Tannock, R. (2005). A meta-analysis of working memory impairments in children with attention-deficit/hyperactivity disorder. *Journal of the American Academy of Child and Adolescent Psychiatry, 44*(4), 377–384.

Marzano, R. J. (1993). How classroom teachers approach the teaching of thinking. *Theory into Practice, 32*(3), 154–160.

Marzano, R. J. (1995). Critical thinking. In J. H. Block, S. T. Everson, & T. R. Guskey (Eds.), *School improvement programs* (pp. 57–76). New York: Scholastic.

Marzano, R. J. (2000). *Transforming classroom grading*. Alexandria, VA: Association for Supervision and Curriculum Development.

Marzano, R. J., Brandt, R. S., Hughes, C. S., et al. (1988). *Dimensions of thinking: A framework for curriculum and instruction*. Alexandria, VA: Association for Supervision and Curriculum Development.

Marzano, R. J., & Marzano, J. S. (2009). In K. Ryan & J. M. Cooper (Eds.), *Kaleidoscope: Classic and contemporary readings in education* (pp. 160–167).

Marzano, R. J., Pickering, D. J., & Pollack, J. E. (2005). *Classroom instruction that works: Research-based strategies for increasing student achievement*. Upper Saddle River, NJ: Merrill/Prentice Hall.

Masataka, N. (1992). Pitch characteristics of Japanese maternal speech to infants. *Journal of Child Language, 19*, 213–224.

Maslow, A. H. (1943). A theory of human motivation. *Psychological Review, 50*, 370–396.

Maslow, A. H. (1954). *Motivation and personality*. New York: Harper.

Maslow, A. H. (1987). *Motivation and personality* (3rd ed.). Delhi, India: Pearson Education.

Mason, D. A., & Good, T. L. (1993). Effects of two-group and whole-class teaching on regrouped elementary students' mathematics achievement. *American Educational Research Journal, 30*, 328–360.

Masters, M. S., & Sanders, B. (1993). Is the gender difference in mental rotation disappearing? *Behavior Genetics, 23*, 337–341.

Mastropieri, M. A., & Scruggs, T. E. (1984). Generalization: Five effective strategies. *Academic Therapy, 19*(4), 427–431.

Mastropieri, M. A., & Scruggs, T. E. (2005). Feasibility and consequences of response to intervention: Examination of the issues and scientific evidence as a model for the identification of individuals with learning disabilities. *Journal of Learning Disabilities, 38*, 525–531.

Mastropieri, M. A., Scruggs, T. E., & Butcher, K. (1997). How effective is inquiry learning for students with mild disabilities? *Journal of Special Education, 31*(2), 199–211.

Mastropieri, M. A., Scruggs, T. E., Hamilton, S. L., Wolfe, S., Whedon, C., & Canevaro, A. (1996). Promoting thinking skills of students with learning disabilities: Effects on recall and comprehension of expository prose. *Exceptionality, 6*, 1–11.

Mather, M., & Sutherland, M. R. (2011). Arousal-biased competition in perception and memory. *Perspectives on Psychological Science, 6*, 114–133.

Mathieson, L. C., & Crick, N. R. (2010). Reactive and proactive subtypes of relational and physical aggression in middle childhood: Links to concurrent and longitudinal adjustment. *School Psychology Review, 39*(4), 601–611.

Matson, J. L., & Nebel-Schwalm, M. (2007). Assessing challenging behaviors in children with autism spectrum disorders: A review. *Research in Developmental Disabilities, 28*(6), 567–579.

Matsumoto, D., & Ekman, P. (1989). American–Japanese cultural differences in intensity ratings of facial expressions of emotion. *Motivation and Emotion, 13*, 143–157.

Matsumura, L. C., Slater, S. C., & Crosson, A. (2008). Classroom climate, rigorous instruction and curriculum, and students' interactions in urban middle schools. *Elementary School Journal, 108*(4), 293–312.

Mau, W. C., & Bikos, L. H. (2000). Educational and vocational aspirations of minority and female students: A longitudinal study. *Journal of Counseling and Development, 78*, 186–194.

Maudsley, G., Williams, E. M. I., & Taylor, D. C. M. (2008). Problem-based learning at the receiving end: A 'mixed methods' study of junior medical students' perspectives. *Advances in Health Sciences Education, 13*, 435–451.

Mayer, D. P. (1998). Do new teaching standards undermine performance on old tests? *Educational Evaluation and Policy Analysis, 15*, 1–16.

Mayer, J., Salovey, P., & Caruso, D. (2004). Emotional intelligence: Theory, findings, and implications. *Psychological Inquiry, 15*(3), 197–215. doi: 10.1207/s15327965pli1503_02

Mayer, J. D., DiPaolo, M. T., & Salovey, P. (1990). Perceiving affective content in ambiguous visual stimuli: A component of emotional intelligence. *Journal of Personality Assessment, 54*, 772–781.

Mayer, R. (2000). Intelligence and education. In R. J. Sternberg (Ed.), *Handbook of intelligence* (pp. 519–533). New York: Cambridge University Press.

Mayer, R. E. (1992). Guiding students' cognitive processing of scientific information. In M. Pressley, K. Harris, & J. Guthrie (Eds.), *Promoting academic competence and literacy: Cognitive research and instructional innovation* (pp. 243–258). Orlando, FL: Academic Press.

Mayer, R. E. (1996). Learning strategies for making sense out of expository text: The SOI model for guiding three cognitive processes in knowledge construction. *Educational Psychology Review, 8*, 357–371.

Mayer, R. E. (2001). *Multimedia learning*. New York: Cambridge University Press.

Mayer, R. E. (2003). *Learning and instruction*. Upper Saddle River, NJ: Merrill/Prentice Hall.

Mayer, R. E. (2004). Should there be a three-strikes rule against pure discovery learning? The case for guided methods of instruction. *American Psychologist, 59*(1), 14–19.

Mayer, R. E., Quilici, J. L., & Moreno, R. (1999). What is learned in an after-school computer club? *Journal of Educational Computing Research, 20*, 223–235.

Mayer, R. E., & Wittrock, M. C. (1996). Problem-solving transfer. In D. C. Berliner & R. C. Calfee (Eds.), *Handbook of educational psychology* (pp. 47–62). New York: Simon & Schuster/Macmillan.

Mayes, S. D., Calhoun, S. L., & Crowell, E. W. (2000). Learning disabilities and ADHD: Overlapping spectrum disorder. *Journal of Learning Disabilities, 33*, 417–424.

Mayo, M. W., & Christenfeld, N. (1999). Gender, race, and performance expectations of college students. *Journal of Multicultural Counseling and Development, 27*, 93–104.

McBride, R. E., Xiang, P., Wittenburg, D., & Shen, J. (2002). An analysis of preservice teachers' dispositions toward critical thinking: A cross-cultural perspective. *Asia-Pacific Journal of Teacher Education, 30*, 131–140.

McCabe, D. P. (2008). The role of covert retrieval in working memory span tasks: Evidence from delayed recall tests. *Journal of Memory and Language, 58*, 480–494.

McCabe, D. P., & Castel, A. D. (2008). Seeing is believing: The effect of brain images on judgments of scientific reasoning. *Cognition, 107*, 343–352.

McCartney, K., et al. (2010). Testing a series of causal propositions relating time in child care to children's externalizing behavior. *Developmental Psychology, 46*(1), 1–17.

McCaslin, M., & Good, T. (1996). The informal curriculum. In D. Berliner & R. Calfee (Eds.), *Handbook of educational psychology* (pp. 47–62). New York: Macmillan.

McCoach, D. B., Kehle, T. J., Bray, M. A., & Siegle, D. (2001). Best practices in the identification of gifted students with learning disabilities. *Psychology in the Schools, 38*(5), 403–411.

McComas, J. J., Thompson, A., & Johnson, L. (2003). The effects of presession attention on problem behavior maintained by different reinforcers. *Journal of Applied Behavior Analysis, 36,* 297–307.

McCombs, B. L. (2001). Self-regulated learning and academic achievement: A phenomenological view. In B. J. Zimmerman & D. H. Schunk (Eds.), *Self-regulated learning and academic achievement: Theory, research, and practice* (pp. 67–123) (2nd. ed.). Mahwah, NJ: Erlbaum.

McCrudden, M. T., & Corkill, A. J. (2010). Verbal ability and the processing of scientific text with seductive detail sentences. *Reading Psychology, 31,* 282–300.

McDaniel, M. A. (2005). Big-brained people are smarter: A meta-analysis of the relationship between in vivo brain volume and intelligence. *Intelligence, 33,* 337–346.

McDonough, G. P. (2005). Moral maturity and autonomy: Appreciating the significance of Lawrence Kolhberg's Just Community. *Journal of Moral Education, 34,* 199–213.

McEwen, B. S. (1995). Stressful experience, brain, and emotions: Developmental, genetic, and hormonal influences. In M. S. Gazzaniga (Ed.), *The cognitive neurosciences* (pp. 1117–1135). Cambridge, MA: MIT Press.

McFaul, S. A. (1983). An examination of direct instruction. *Educational Leadership, 40*(7), 67–69.

McGee, C. L., Bjorkquist, O. A., Price, J. M., Mattson, S. N., & Riley, E. P. (2009). Social information processing skills in children with histories of heavy prenatal alcohol exposure. *Journal of Abnormal Child Psychology, 37*(6), 817–830.

McGhee, P. (1979). *Humor: Its origin and development.* San Francisco: W. H. Freeman & Company.

McGoey, K. E., & DuPaul, G. J. (2000). Token reinforcement and response cost procedures: Reducing the disruptive behavior of preschool children with attention-deficit/hyperactivity disorder. *School Psychology Quarterly, 15,* 330–343.

McGoey, K. E., Schneider, D. L., Rezzetano, K. M., Prodan, T., & Tankersley, M. (2010). Classwide intervention to manage disruptive behavior in the kindergarten classroom. *Journal of Applied School Psychology, 26,* 247–261.

McGregor, H. A., & Elliot, A. J. (2002). Achievement goals as predictors of achievement-relevant processes prior to task engagement. *Journal of Educational Psychology, 94*(2), 381–395.

McIntyre, T. (1990). The teacher's role in cases of suspected child abuse. *Education and Urban Society, 22*(3), 300–306.

McIntyre, T. (2011). New UH study links job stress in teachers to student achievement. PRNewswire/USNewswire. Retrieved August 15, 2011, from http://www.uh.edu/news-events/stories/2011articles/May2011/teacherstress.php.

McKenzie, J. A. (1986). The influence of identification practices, race, and SES on the identification of gifted students. *Gifted Child Quarterly, 30*(2), 93–95.

McLean, J., & Snyder-McLean, L. (1999). *How children learn language.* San Diego, CA: Singular Publishing Group.

McLennan, J. D., Lord, C., & Schopler, E. (1993). Sex differences in higher-functioning people with autism. *Journal of Autism and Developmental Disorders, 23,* 217–227.

McLoyd, V. C. (1998). Socioeconomic disadvantage and child development. *American Psychologist, 53,* 185–204.

McMaster, K., & Fuchs, D. (2002). Effects of cooperative learning on the academic achievement of students with learning disabilities: An update of Tateyama-Sniezek's review. *Learning Disabilities Research and Practice, 17,* 107–117.

McMillan, J. H. (2003). Understanding and improving teachers' classroom assessment decision-making: Implications for theory and practice. *Educational Measurement: Issues and Practice, 22*(4), 34–43.

McMillan, J. H. (2007a). *Classroom assessment* (4th ed.). Boston: Allyn & Bacon.

McMillan, J. H. (2007b). Formative classroom assessment: The key to improving student achievement. In J. H. McMillan (Ed.), *Formative classroom assessment: Theory into practice* (pp. 1–7). New York: Teachers College Press.

McMullin, D., & Steffen, J. (1982). Intrinsic motivation and performance standards. *Social Behavior and Personality, 10,* 47–56.

McNeill, J., & Fowler, S. (1996, Summer). Using story reading to encourage children's conversations. *Teaching Exceptional Children, 28*(4), 43–47.

McWilliam, E. (2005). Unlearning pedagogy. *Journal of Learning Design, 1*(1), 1–11.

Means, M. B., & Knapp, M. S. (1991). Cognitive approaches to teaching advanced skills to educationally disadvantaged students. *Phi Delta Kappan, 73*(4), 282–289.

Means, M. B., & Knapp, M. S. (1994). Cognitive approaches to teaching advanced skills to educationally disadvantaged students. In H. F. Clarizio, W. A. Mehrens, & W. G. Hapkiewicz (Eds.), *Contemporary issues in educational psychology* (6th ed., pp. 180–190). New York: McGraw-Hill.

Medley, D., Soar, R., & Coker, H. (1984). *Measurement-based evaluation of teacher performance.* New York: Longman.

Meece, J. (1981). *Individual differences in the affective reactions of middle and high school students to mathematics: A social cognitive perspective.* Unpublished doctoral dissertation, University of Michigan.

Meece, J. L., Glienke, B. B., & Askew, K. (2009). Gender and motivation. In K. R. Wentzel & A. Wigfield (Eds.), *Handbook of motivation at school* (pp. 412–431). New York: Routledge/Taylor & Francis Group.

Meece, J. L., Glienke, B. B., & Burg, S. (2006). Gender and motivation. *Journal of School Psychology, 44,* 351–373.

Meece, J. L., Herman, P., & McCombs, B. L. (2003). Relations of learner-centered teaching practices to adolescents' achievement goals. *International Journal of Educational Research, 39*(4–5), 457–475.

Meece, J. L., & Miller, S. D. (2001). A longitudinal analysis of elementary school students' achievement goals in literacy activities. *Contemporary Educational Psychology, 26,* 454–480.

Meece, J. L., & Painter, J. (2008). Gender, self-regulation, and motivation. In D. H. Schunk & B. J. Zimmerman (Eds.), *Motivation and self-regulated learning: Theory, research, and applications* (pp. 339–367). New York: Erlbaum.

Meehan, S. K., Randhawa, B., Wessel, B., & Boyd, L. A. (2010) Implicit sequence-specific motor learning after subcortical stroke is associated with increased prefrontal brain activations: An fMRI Study. *Human Brain Mapping 32*(2), 290–303.

Meese, R. L. (2001). *Teaching learners with mild disabilities: Integrating research and practice* (2nd ed.). Belmont, CA: Thomson/Wadsworth.

Mehan, H. (1974). Accomplishing classroom lessons. In A. Cicourel, K. Jennings, S. Jennings, et al. (Eds.), *Language use and school performance.* New York: Academic Press.

Melnick, S. M., & Hinshaw, S. P. (1996). What they want and what they get: The social goals of boys with ADHD and comparison boys. *Journal of Abnormal Child Psychology, 24,* 169–185.

Mendez, L. M. R., & Knoff, H. M. (2003). Who gets suspended from school and why: A demographic analysis of schools and disciplinary infractions in a large school district. *Education and Treatment of Children, 26*(1), 30–51.

Menendez, A. L., Payne, L. D., & Mayton, M. R. (2008). The implementation of positive behavioral support in an elementary school: Processes, procedures and outcomes. *Alberta Journal of Educational Research, 54*(4), 448–462.

Menyuk, P. (1988). *Language development: Knowledge and use.* Glenview, IL: Scott, Foresman/Little, Brown.

Mercer, C. D., Jordan, L., Allsopp, D. H., & Mercer, A. R. (1996). Learning disabilities definitions and criteria used by state education departments. *Learning Disability Quarterly, 19*, 217–232.

Merikangas, K. R. (2005). Anxiety disorders: Epidemiology. In B. J. Sadock & V. A. Sadock (Eds.), *Kaplan and Sadock's comprehensive textbook of psychiatry* (Vol. I, pp. 1720–1727). Philadelphia: Lippincott Williams & Wilkins.

Mertler, C. A. (2001). *Designing scoring rubrics for your classroom.* Retrieved August 15, 2011, from http://www.learner.org/workshops/tfl/resources/s7_rubrics.pdf.

Merton, R. K. (1948). The self-fulfilling prophecy. *Antioch Review, 8*, 193–210.

Merzenich, M. M. (2001). Cortical plasticity contributing to child development. In J. L. McClelland & R. S. Siegler (Eds.), *Mechanisms of cognitive development: Behavioral and neural perspectives* (pp. 67–95). Mahwah, NJ: Erlbaum.

Mesquita, B., & Frijda, N. H. (1992). Cultural variations in emotion: A review. *Psychological Bulletin, 112*, 179–204.

Mestre, J. P. (1984). The problem with problems: Hispanic students and math. *Bilingual Journal, 32*, 15–19.

Mestre, J. P., & Cocking, R. R. (2000). The science of learning. Special Issue of *Journal of Applied Developmental Psychology, 21*(1), 1–135.

Metcalfe, J. (2000). Metamemory: Theory and data. In E. Tulving & F. I. M. Craik (Eds.), *The Oxford handbook of memory* (pp. 197–211). Oxford, UK: Oxford University Press.

Metcalfe, J. (2002). Is study time allocated selectively to a region of proximal learning? *Journal of Experimental Psychology: General, 131*, 349–363.

Metcalfe, J., & Finn, B. (2008). Evidence that judgments of learning are causally related to study choice. *Psychonomic Bulletin and Review, 15*(1), 174–179.

Metcalfe, J., & Kornell, N. (2005). A region of proximal learning model of study time allocation. *Journal of Memory and Language, 52*, 463–477.

Metcalfe, J., & Mischel, W. (1999). A hot/cool system analysis of delay of gratification: Dynamics of willpower. *Psychological Review, 106*, 3–19.

Meyer, K. A. (2003). Face-to-face versus threaded discussions: The role of time and higher-order thinking. *Journal of Asynchronous Learning Networks, 7*(3), 55–65.

Meyer, P. J., & Setzer, J. C. (2009). A comparison of bridging methods in the analysis of NAEP trends with the new race subgroup definitions. *Journal of Educational Measurement, 46*, 104–128.

Meyer, W. U., Bachmann, M., Biermann, U., Hempelmann, M., Plöger, F. O., & Spiller, H. (1979). The informational value of evaluative behavior: Influences of praise and blame on perceptions of ability. *Journal of Educational Psychology, 71*, 259–268.

Michael, K. Y. (2001). The effect of a computer simulation activity versus hands-on activity in product creativity in technology education. *Journal of Technology Education, 13*(1), 31–43.

Mickelson, R. (1990). The attitude–achievement paradox among black adolescents. *Sociology of Education, 63*, 44–61.

Micklo, S. (1993). Perceived problems of public school pre-kindergarten teachers. *Journal of Research in Childhood Education, 8*(1), 57–68.

Middleton, M., & Midgley, C. (1997). Avoiding the demonstration of lack of ability: An under explored aspect of goal theory. *Journal of Educational Psychology, 89*, 710–718.

Midgley, C. (2002). *Goals, goal structures, and adaptive learning.* Mahwah, NJ: Erlbaum.

Midgley, C., Anderman, E., & Hicks, L. (1995). Differences between elementary and middle school teachers and students: A goal theory approach. *Journal of Early Adolescence, 15*, 90–113.

Midgley, C., & Feldlaufer, H. (1987). Students' and teachers' decision-making fit before and after the transition to junior high school. *Journal of Early Adolescence, 7*, 225–241.

Miller, D., & Hom, H. (1997). Conceptions of ability and the interpretation of praise, blame, and material rewards. *Journal of Experimental Education, 65*, 163–177.

Miller, G. A. (1956). The magical number seven, plus or minus two: Some limits on our capacity for processing information. *Psychological Review, 63*, 81–97.

Miller, K., & Baillargeon, R. (1990). Length and distance: Do preschoolers think that occlusion brings things together? *Developmental Psychology, 26*, 103–114.

Miller, R., & Gentry, M. (2010). Developing talents among high-potential students from low-income families in an out-of-school enrichment program. *Journal of Advanced Academics, 21*(4), 594–627.

Miller-Washington, C. D. (2010). Unraveling the gift: A study of classroom teachers' perceptions of African Americans' giftedness. Dissertation (publication number 3411958).

Mills, C. J., & Durden, W. G. (1992). Cooperative learning and ability grouping: An issue of choice. *Gifted Child Quarterly, 36*(1), 11–16.

Milton, J., Solodkin, A., Hlusik, P., & Small, S. (2007). The mind of expert motor performance is cool and focused. *Neuroimage, 35*(2), 804–813.

Miranda, A., & Presentación, M. J. (2000). Efficacy of cognitive-behavioral therapy in the treatment of children with ADHD, with and without aggressiveness. *Psychology in the Schools, 37*, 169–182.

Miranda, A., Presentación, M. J., & Soriano, M. (2002). Effectiveness of a school-based multicomponent program for the treatment of children with ADHD. *Journal of Learning Disabilities, 35*, 546–562.

Miri, B., David, B. C., & Uri, Z. (2007). Purposely teaching for the promotion of higher-order thinking skills: A case of critical thinking. *Research in Science Education, 37*(4), 353–369.

Mischel, W., Shoda, Y., & Rodriguez, M. L. (1989). Delay of gratification in children: *Science, 244*, 933–938.

Moeller, J., & Koeller, O. (1999). Spontaneous cognitions following academic test results. *Journal of Experimental Education, 67*, 150–164.

Moffitt, T. E., Caspi, A., Harkness, A. R., & Silva, P. A. (1993). The natural history of change in intellectual performance: Who changes? How much? Is it meaningful? *Journal of Child Psychology and Psychiatry, 34*, 455–506.

Molden, D., & Dweck, C. (2000). Meaning and motivation. In C. Sansone & J. Harackiewicz (Eds.), *Intrinsic and extrinsic motivation: The search for optimal motivation and performance* (pp. 131–159). San Diego, CA: Academic Press.

Molfese, D. L., Molfese, V. J., Key, A. F., & Kelly, S. D. (2003). Influence of environment on speech-sound discrimination: Findings from a longitudinal study. *Developmental Neuropsychology, 24*(2 & 3), 541–558.

Moll, L. C. (2001). Through the mediation of others: Vygotskian research on teaching. In V. Richardson (Ed.), *Handbook of research on teaching* (pp. 111–129). Washington, DC: American Educational Research Association.

Moller, A. C., & Elliot, A. J. (2006). The 2 x 2 achievement goal framework: An overview of empirical research. In A. Mittel (Ed.), *Focus on educational psychology* (pp. 307–326). New York: Nova Science Publishers.

Monteiro, M. B., de Franca, D. X., & Rodrigues, R. (2009). The development of intergroup bias in childhood: How social norms can shape children's racial behaviours. *International Journal of Psychology, 44*(1), 29–39.

Montessori, M. (1964). *Advanced Montessori method.* Cambridge, MA: Bentley.

Montgomery, J. (2002, February). Understanding the language difficulties of children with specific language impairments: Does verbal working memory matter? *American Journal of Speech Language Pathology, 11,* 77–91.

Montgomery, K. (2001). *Authentic assessment: A guide for elementary teachers.* New York: Longman.

Moody, S. W., Vaughn, S., & Schumm, J. S. (1997). Instructional grouping for reading. *Remedial and Special Education, 18,* 347–356.

Moore, D., & Davenport, S. (1988). *The new improved sorting machine.* Madison, WI: National Center on Effective Secondary Schools.

Moore, L. M. (1989). Ethnic group differences in the Armed Services Vocational Aptitude Battery (ASVAB) performance of American youth: Implications for career prospects. In B. Gifford (Ed.), *Test policy and test performance: Education, language, and culture* (pp. 183–229). Boston: Kluwer Academic.

Morin, V. A., & Miller, S. P. (1998). Teaching multiplication to middle school students with mental retardation. *Education and Treatment of Children, 21,* 22–36.

Morris, R. J., & Kratochwill, T. R. (1983). *Treating children's fears and phobias. A behavioral approach.* New York: Pergamon.

Morris, R. J., & Kratochwill, T. R. (1998). Fears and phobias. In R. J. Morris & T. R. Kratochwill (Eds.), *The practice of child therapy* (3rd ed.). Needham Heights, MA: Allyn & Bacon.

Morrisette, P., Ricard, M., & Gouin-Decarie, T. (1995). Joint visual attention and pointing in infancy: A longitudinal study of comprehension. *British Journal of Developmental Psychology, 13,* 163–177.

Morrison, M., & Dungan, R. (1992). *The identification of creative thinking ability: A multifactored approach.* Columbus, OH: Ohio Department of Education.

Morrow, L. (1989). *Literacy development in the early years.* Upper Saddle River, NJ: Prentice Hall.

Morton, J. B., & Trehub, S. E. (2001). Children's understanding of emotion in speech. *Child Development, 72,* 834–843.

Moshman, D. (1997). Pluralist rational constructivism. *Issues in Education: Contributions from Educational Psychology, 3,* 229–234.

Moskal, B. M. (2000). Scoring rubrics: What, when, and how? *Practical Assessment, Research, & Evaluation, 7*(3). Retrieved August 15, 2011, from http://PAREonline.net/getvn.asp?v=7&n=3.

Moskal, B. M. (2003). Recommendations for developing classroom performance assessments and scoring rubrics. *Practical Assessment, Research, & Evaluation, 8*(14). Retrieved July 13, 2008, from http://PAREonline.net/getvn.asp?v=8&n=14.

Moss, P. A. (2003). Reconceptualizing validity for classroom assessment. *Educational Measurement: Issues and Practice, 22*(4), 13–25.

Moyer, P. S. (2002). Are we having fun yet? How teachers use manipulatives to teach mathematics. *Educational Studies in Mathematics, 47,* 175–197.

MTA Cooperative Group. (1999a). Effects of comorbid anxiety, poverty, session attendance, and community medication on treatment outcome in children with attention deficit/hyperactivity disorder. *Archives of General Psychiatry, 56,* 1088–1096.

MTA Cooperative Group. (1999b). Fourteen-month randomized clinical trial of treatment strategies for attention-deficit hyperactivity disorder. *Archives of General Psychiatry, 56,* 1073–1086.

Mucherah, W., & Yoder, A. (2008). Motivation for reading and middle school students' performance on standardized testing in reading. *Reading Psychology, 29*(3), 214–235.

Mueller, C. M., & Dweck, C. S. (1998). Praise for intelligence can undermine children's motivation and performance. *Journal of Personality and Social Psychology, 75,* 33–52.

Mulkey, L. M., Catsambis, S., Steelman, L. C., & Crain, R. L. (2005). The long-term effects of ability grouping in mathematics: A national investigation. *Social Psychology of Education, 8,* 137–177.

Murayama, K., & Elliot, A. J. (2009). The joint influence of personal achievement goals and classroom goal structures on achievement-related outcomes. *Journal of Educational Psychology, 101,* 432–447.

Murdock, T. B. (1999). The social context of risk: Status and motivational predictors of alienation in middle school. *Journal of Educational Psychology, 91,* 62–75.

Murphy, P. K., Wilkinson, I. A. G., Soter, A. O., Hennessey, M. N., & Alexander, J. F. (2009). Examining the effects of classroom discussion on students' comprehension of text: A meta-analysis. *Journal of Educational Psychology, 101*(3), 740–764.

Murphy, P. K., & Woods, B. S. (1996). Situating knowledge in learning and instruction. *Educational Psychologist, 31,* 141–145.

Muzzatti, B., & Agnoli, F. (2007). Gender and mathematics: Attitudes and stereotype threat susceptibility in Italian children. *Developmental Psychology, 43,* 747–759.

Murray, J. (2006, May). Pedagogical implications of cognitive science research. *Independent Teacher* (e–journal).

Murray-Close, D., Crick, N. R., & Calotti, K. (2006). Children's moral reasoning regarding physical and relational aggression. *Social Development, 15,* 345–372.

Myers, D. G. (2002). *Intuition: Its powers and perils.* New Haven, CT: Yale University Press.

Myers, D. G. (2005). *Exploring psychology* (6th ed. in modules). New York: Worth.

N

Nagy, W., & Anderson, R. C. (1984). How many words are there in printed school English? *Reading Research Quarterly, 19,* 304–330.

Nair, H., & Murray, A. D. (2005). Predictors of attachment security in preschool children from intact and divorced families. *The Journal of Genetic Psychology, 166*(3), 245–263.

Nairne, J. S. (2002) The myth of the encoding-retrieval match. *Memory, 10,* 389–395.

Naoi, N., Yokoyama, K., & Yamamoto, J. (2007). Intervention for tact as reporting in children with autism. *Research in Autism Spectrum Disorders, 1,* 174–184.

National Association of Secondary School Principals. (2006). *Breaking ranks in the middle: Strategies for leading middle level reform.* Reston, VA: Author.

National Center for Education Statistics. (2000, January). *America's kindergarteners.* Washington, DC: U.S. Department of Education. Office of Educational Research and Improvement (Report No. NCES–2000–070).

National Center for Innovation and Education. (1999). Lessons for life: How smart schools boost academic, social, and emotional intelligence. Bloomington, IN: HOPE foundation (www.communitiesofhope.org).

National Commission on Teaching and America's Future. (2003, January). *No dream denied: A pledge to America's children.* Washington, DC.

National Reading Panel. (2000). *Teaching children to read: An evidence-based assessment of the scientific research literature on reading and its implications for reading instruction* (NIH Pub. No. 00–4769). Washington, DC: National Institutes of Health.

National Research Center on Learning Disabilities. (2007). *Responsiveness to intervention in the SLD determination process* [Brochure]. Lawrence, KS: Author.

National Research Council. (2000a). *How people learn: Brain, mind, experience and school.* Washington, DC: National Academy Press.

National Research Council. (2000b). *Improving intergroup relations among youth.* Washington, DC: National Research Council.

National Research Council. (2001). *Adding it up: Helping children learn mathematics.* J. Kilpatrick, J. Swafford, & B. Find-ell (Eds.), Mathematics Learning Study Committee, Center for Education, Division of Behavioral and Social Sciences and Education. Washington, DC: National Academy Press.

National Research Council. (2001). *Knowing what students know.* Washington, DC: National Academic Press.

National Science Foundation. (2008). *Science and engineering indicators 2008.* Retrieved August 15, 2011, from http://www.nsf.gov/statistics/seind08.

Naveh-Benjamin, M. (1991). A comparison of training programs intended for different types of test-anxious students: Further support for an information processing model. *Journal of Educational Psychology, 83*(1), 134–139.

Naveh-Benjamin, M., McKeachie, W. J., & Lin, Y. G. (1987). Two types of test-anxious students: Support for an information processing model. *Journal of Educational Psychology, 79*(2), 131–136.

Neisser, U. (1967). *Cognitive psychology.* New York: Appleton-Century-Crofts.

Neisser, U., Boodoo, G., Bouchard, T. J., Jr., et al. (1996). Intelligence: Knowns and unknowns. *American Psychologist, 51*(2), 77–101.

Nel, P. W., Keville, S., Ford, D., et al. (2008). Close encounters of the uncertain kind: Reflections on doing problem-based learning (PBL) for the first time. *Reflective Practice, 9,* 197–206.

Nelsen, J. (1997). No more logical consequences—at least hardly ever! Focus on solutions. *Empowering People Catalog,* Winter/Spring, 8.

Nelsen, J. L., Lott, L., & Glenn, H. (2000). *Positive discipline in the classroom* (3rd ed.). Roseville, CA: Prima.

Nelson, C. A., Thomas, K. M., & de Haan, M. (2006). Neural bases of cognitive development. In W. Damon & R. Lerner (Eds.), *Handbook of child psychology* (6th ed.). New York: Wiley.

Nesbit, J. C., & Adesope, O. (2006). Learning with concept and knowledge maps: A meta-analysis. *Review of Educational Research, 76,* 413–448.

Nesdale, D., & Pickering, K. (2006). Teachers' reactions to children's aggression. *Social Development, 15*(1), 109–127.

Neufang, S., Specht, K., Hausmann, M., et al. (2009). Sex differences and the impact of steroid hormones on the developing human brain. *Cerebral Cortex, 19*(2): 464–473. doi: 10.1093/cercor/bhn100

Newell, A., & Simon, H. A. (1972). *Human problem solving.* Englewood Cliffs, NJ: Prentice Hall.

Newman, B. M., & Newman, P. R. (2001). Group identity and alienation: Giving the we its due. *Journal of Youth and Adolescence, 30,* 515–538.

Newman, F. M. (1990). Higher-order thinking in teaching social studies: A rationale for the assessment of classroom thoughtfulness. *Journal of Curriculum Studies, 22,* 41–56.

Newson, J., & Newson, E. (1975). Intersubjectivity and the transmission of culture: On the social origins of symbolic functioning. *Bulletin of the British Psychological Society, 28,* 437–446.

Ng, F. F.–Y., Pomerantz, E. M., & Lam, S.–F. (2007). European American and Chinese parents' responses to children's success and failure: Implications for children's responses. *Developmental Psychology, 43*(5), 1239–1255.

Nicholls, J. (1979). Development of perception of own attainment and causal attributions for success and failure in reading. *Journal of Educational Psychology, 71,* 94–99.

Nicholls, J., Cobb, P., Wood, T., Yackel, E., & Patashnick, M. (1990). Assessing students' theories of success in mathematics: Individual and classroom differences. *Journal for Research in Mathematics Education, 21,* 109–122.

Nichols, S. L., & Berliner, D. C. (2005). The inevitable corruption of indicators and educators through high-stakes testing. Retrieved May 11, 2011, from http://www.peecworks.org/PEEC/PEEC_Gen/00490D09-007EA7AB.0/Nichols%20Berliner%20high%20stakes%20testing.pdf.

Nickerson, R. S. (1984). Kinds of thinking taught in current programs. *Educational Leadership, 42*(1), 26–37.

Nickerson, R. S., Perkins, D. N., & Smith, E. E. (1985). *The teaching of thinking.* Hillsdale, NJ: Erlbaum.

Nicoladis, E., & Genesee, F. (1996). Word awareness in second language learners and bilingual children. *Language Awareness, 5,* 80–90.

Nicoladis, E., & Genesee, F. (1997). Language development in preschool bilingual children. *Journal of Speech–Language Pathology and Audiology, 21*(4), 258–270.

Niebuhr, K., & Niebuhr, R. (1999). An empirical study of student relationships and academic achievement. *Education, 119*(4), 679–681.

Niiya, Y., Crocker, J., & Bartmess, E. N. (2004). From vulnerability to resilience: Learning orientations buffer contingent self-esteem from failure. *Psychological Science, 15,* 801–805.

Nilson, L. B. (2003). *Teaching at its best: A research-based resource for college instructors* (2nd ed.). Boston: Jossey-Bass.

Nippold, M., & Duthie, J. (2003). Mental imagery and idiom comprehension: A comparison of school-age children and adults. *Journal of Speech, Language, and Hearing Research, 46,* 788–799.

Nirmalakhandan, N. (2007). Computerized dynamic assessment. Paper presented at International Conference on Engineering Education, Coimbra, Portugal, September 3–7, 2007.

Nisbett, R. (1995). Race, IQ, and scientism. In S. Fraser (Ed.), *The bell curve wars: Race, intelligence, and the future of America* (pp. 36–57). New York: Basic Books.

Nishina, A., Juvonen, J., & Witkow, M. R. (2005). Sticks and stones may break my bones, but names will make me feel sick: The psychosocial, somatic, and scholastic consequences of peer harassment. *Journal of Clinical Child and Adolescent Psychology, 34,* 37–48.

Nitko, A. J. (2001). *Educational assessment of students* (3rd ed.). Upper Saddle River, NJ: Merrill.

Nitko, A. J., & Brookhart, S. M. (2007). *Educational assessment of students* (5th ed.). Upper Saddle River, NJ: Pearson Merrill/Prentice Hall.

Noam, G. G., Warner, L. A., & Van Dyken, L. (2001). Beyond the rhetoric of zero tolerance: Long-term solutions for at-risk youth. *New Directions for Youth Development, 92,* 155–182.

Norlander, T., Erixon, A., & Archer, T. (2000). Psychological androgyny and creativity: Dynamics of gender-role and personality traits. *Social Behavior and Personality, 28,* 423–436.

Nottlemann, E. D., & Hill, K. T. (1977). Test anxiety and off-task behavior in evaluative situations. *Child Development, 48,* 225–231.

Nucci, L. (2006). Education for moral development. In M. Killen & J. Smetana (Eds.), *Handbook of moral development.* Mahwah, NJ: Erlbaum.

O

O'Connor, K. (2007). *A repair kit for grading: Fifteen fixes for broken grades.* Portland, OR: Educational Testing Service.

O'Leary, K., & O'Leary, S. (Eds.). (1977). *Classroom management: The successful use of behavior modification* (2nd ed.). New York: Pergamon.

O'Leary, K. D., Kaufman, K. F., Kass, R. E., & Drabman, R. S. (1970). The effects of loud and soft reprimands on the behavior of disruptive students. *Exceptional Children, 37,* 145–155.

O'Mara, A. J., Marsh, H. W., Craven, R. G., & Debus, R. L. (2006). Do self-concept interventions make a difference? A synergistic blend of construct validation and meta-analysis. *Educational Psychologist, 41,* 181–206.

Oakes, J. (1985). *Keeping track: How schools structure inequality.* New Haven. CT: Yale University Press.

Oakes, J. (1990a). *Multiplying inequalities: The effects of race, social class, and tracking on opportunities to learn mathematics and science.* Santa Monica, CA: The RAND Corporation.

Oakes, J. (1990b). Opportunities, achievement, and choice: Women and minority students in science and math. *Review of Research in Education, 16,* 153–222.

Oakes, J. (1992). Can tracking research inform practice? Technical, normative, and political considerations. *Educational Researcher, 27*(4), 12–21.

Oakes, J., & Guiton, G. (1995). Matchmaking: The dynamics of high school tracking decisions. *American Educational Research Journal, 32,* 3–33.

Oakes, J., & Wells, A. S. (2002). Detracking for high student achievement. In L. Abbeduto (Ed.), *Taking sides: Clashing views and controversial issues in educational psychology* (2nd ed., pp. 26–30). Guilford, CT: McGraw-Hill/Duskin.

Oberauer, K. (2002). Access to information in working memory: Exploring the focus of attention. *Journal of Experimental Psychology: Learning, Memory, and Cognition, 28,* 411–421.

Oberauer, K. (2005). Control of the contents of working memory—a comparison of two paradigms and two age groups. *Journal of Experimental Psychology: Learning, Memory, and Cognition, 31,* 714–728.

Obler, L., & Gjerlow, K. (1999). *Language and the brain.* New York: Cambridge University Press.

Ochs, E., & Schieffelin, B. B. (1984). Language acquisition and socialization: Three developmental stories and their implications. In R. Shweder and R. LeVine (Eds.), *Developmental pragmatics* (pp. 276–320). New York: Academic Press.

Ogbu, J. U. (1994). Racial stratification and education in the United States: Why inequality persists. *Teachers College Record, 96*(2), 264–298.

Ogbu, J. U. (2003). *Black American students in an affluent suburb: A study of academic disengagement.* Mahwah, NJ: Erlbaum.

Ogden, M. H. (1968). The fulfillment of promise: Forty-year follow-up of the Terman gifted group. *Genetic Psychology Monographs, 77,* 3–93.

Ogle, D. S. (1986). K-W-L group instructional strategy. In A. S. Palincsar, D. S. Ogle, B. F. Jones, & E. G. Carr (Eds.), *Teaching reading as thinking* (Teleconference Resource Guide, pp. 11–17). Alexandria, VA: Association of Supervision and Curriculum Development.

Okagaki, L., & Sternberg, R. J. (1993). Parental beliefs and children's school performance. *Child Development, 64,* 36–56.

Ollendick, T., King, N., & Muris, P. (2002). Fears and phobias in children: Phenomenology, epidemiology, and aetiology. *Child and Adolescent Mental Health, 7,* 98–106.

Olson, R. K., Wise, B., Ring, J., & Johnson, M. (1997). Computer-based remedial training in phoneme awareness and phonological decoding: Effects on the posttraining development of word recognition. *Scientific Studies of Reading, 1*(3), 235–253.

Oosterhoff, A. (1999). *Developing and using classroom assessments* (2nd ed.). Upper Saddle River, NJ: Prentice Hall.

Orlofsky, J. L., Marcia, J. E., & Lesser, R. M. (1973). Ego identity status and the intimacy versus isolation crisis of young adulthood. *Journal of Personality and Social Psychology, 27,* 211–219.

Ornstein, P. A., Naus, M. J., & Liberty, C. (1975). Rehearsal and organizational processes in children's memory. *Child Development, 46,* 818–830.

Ornstein, R. (1997). *The right mind: Making sense of the hemispheres.* San Diego: Harcourt Brace.

Osborn, A. (2006). Public school teacher attrition and organizational health: A comparative study. Doctoral dissertation, University of Texas at Austin.

Osborne, R. J., & Wittrock, M. C. (1983). Learning science: A generative process. *Science Education, 67,* 489–504.

Osburn, H. K., & Mumford, M. D. (2006). Creativity and planning: Training interventions to develop creative problem-solving skills. *Creativity Research Journal, 18*(2), 173–190.

Osgood, C. E. (1949). The similarity paradox in human learning. *Psychological Review, 56,* 132–143.

Osher, D., Bear, G. G., Sprague, J. R., & Doyle, W. (2010). How can we improve school discipline? *Educational Researcher, 39*(1), 48–58.

Osher, D., Cartledge, G., Oswald, D., Sutherland, K. S., Artiles, A. J., & Coutinho, M. (2004). Cultural and linguistic competency and disproportionate representation. In R. B. Rutherford, M. M. Quinn, & S. B. Mathur (Eds.), *Handbook of research in emotional and behavioral disorders* (pp. 54–77). New York: Guilford Press.

Osher, D., Morrison, G., & Bailey, W. (2003). Exploring the relationship between student mobility and dropout among students with emotional and behavioral disorders. *Journal of Negro Education, 72,* 79–96.

Osher, D., Sprague, R., Weissberg, R. P., Axelrod, J., Keenan, S., & Kendziora, K. (2008). A comprehensive approach to promoting social, emotional, and academic growth in contemporary schools. In A. Thomas & J. Grimes (Eds.), *Best practices in school psychology* (Vol. 4, pp. 1263–1278). Bethesda, MD: National Association of School Psychologists.

Ostad, S. A. (1998). Developmental differences in solving arithmetic word problems and simple number-fact problems: A comparison of mathematically normal and mathematically disabled children. *Mathematical Cognition, 4,* 1–19.

Osterman, K. (2010). Teacher practice and students' sense of belonging. In T. Lovat, R. Toomey, & N. Clement (Eds.), *International Research Handbook on Values Education and Student Wellbeing, Part 1* (pp. 239–260).

Ostrov, J. M., & Crick, N. R. (2007). Forms and functions of aggression during early childhood: A short-term longitudinal study. *School Psychology Review, 36*(1), 22–43.

Otting, H., & Zwaal, W. (2006). Critical task characteristics in problem-based learning. *Industry and Higher Education, 20*(5), 347–357.

Otto, B. (2006). *Language development in early childhood* (2nd ed.). Upper Saddle River, NJ: Merrill/Prentice Hall.

Owens, R. (1988). *Language development.* Upper Saddle River, NJ: Merrill/Prentice Hall.

Owens, R. (2005). *Language development: An introduction* (6th ed.). Boston: Allyn & Bacon.

P

Paivio, A. (1971). *Imagery and verbal processes.* Fort Worth, TX: Harcourt Brace.

Pajares, F., & Johnson, M. J. (1996). Self-efficacy beliefs in the writing of high school students: A path analysis. *Psychology in the Schools, 33,* 163–175.

Pajares, F., Johnson, M. J., & Usher, E. L. (2007). Sources of writing self-efficacy beliefs of elementary, middle, and high school students. *Research in the Teaching of English, 42,* 104–120.

Pajares, F., & Kranzler, J. (1995). Self-efficacy beliefs and general mental ability in mathematical problem solving. *Contemporary Educational Psychology, 20,* 426–443.

Pajares, F., & Valiante, G. (2001). Influence of self-efficacy on elementary students' writing. *Journal of Educational Research, 90*(6), 353–360.

Palincsar, A. S. (1998). Social constructivist perspectives on teaching and learning. In J. T. Spence, J. M. Darley, & D. J. Foss (Eds.), *Annual review of psychology* (pp. 345–375). Palo Alto, CA: Annual Reviews.

Palincsar, A. S. (2003). Ann L. Brown: Advancing a theoretical model of learning and instruction. In B. J. Zimmerman & D. H. Schunk (Eds.), *Educational psychology: A century of contributions* (pp. 459–476). Mahwah, NJ: Erlbaum.

Palincsar, A. S., & Brown, A. L. (1984). Reciprocal teaching of comprehension-fostering and comprehension-monitoring activities. *Cognition & Instruction, 1,* 117–175.

Palincsar, A. S., Brown, A. L., & Martin, S. M. (1987). Peer interaction in reading comprehension instruction. *Educational Psychologist, 22,* 231–253.

Paller, K. A., Ranganath, C., Gonsalves, B., et al. (2003). Neural correlates of person recognition. *Learning and Memory, 10,* 253–260.

Palmer, E. J. (2005). The relationship between moral reasoning and aggression, and the implications for practice. *Psychology, Crime and Law, 11,* 353–361.

Panferov, S. (2010). Increasing ELL parent involvement in our schools; Learning from the parents. *Theory Into Practice, 49,* 106–112.

Paris, S. G., Byrnes, J. P., & Paris, A. H. (2001). Constructing theories, identities, and actions of self-regulated learners. In B. J. Zimmerman & D. H. Schunk (Eds.), *Self-regulated learning and academic achievement: Theoretical perspectives* (2nd ed., pp. 253–287). Mahwah, NJ: Erlbaum.

Park, K. A., & Walters, E. (1989). Security of attachment and preschool friendships. *Child Development, 60,* 1076–1081.

Park, S. H., & Ertmer, P. A. (2008). Impact of problem-based learning (PBL) on teachers' beliefs regarding technology use. *Journal of Research on Technology in Education, 40*(2), 247–267.

Parker, W. D. (1997). An empirical typology of perfectionism in academically talented children. *American Educational Research Journal, 34,* 545–562.

Parrish, T. (2002). Racial disparities in the identification, funding, and provision of special education. In D. Losen (Ed.), *Minority issues in special education* (pp. 15–38). Cambridge, MA: Civil Rights Project, Harvard University and Harvard Education Publishing Group.

Parsley, K., & Corcoran, C. A. (2003). The classroom teacher's role in preventing school failure. *Kappa Delta Pi Record, 39*(2), 84–87.

Pastor, P. N., & Reuben, C. A. (2008). Diagnosed attention deficit hyperactive disorder and learning disability: United States, 2004-2006. National Center for Health Statistics. *Vital Health Statistics, 10,* 237.

Pastorelli, C., Caprara, G. V., Barbaranelli, C., Rola, J., Rozsa, S., & Bandura, A. (2001). The structure of children's perceived self-efficacy: A cross-national study. *European Journal of Psychological Assessment, 17,* 87–97.

Patall, E. A., Cooper, H., & Wynn, S. R. (2010). The effectiveness and relative importance of choice in the classroom. *Journal of Educational Psychology, 102*(4), 896–915.

Patrick, H., Anderman, L. H., Ryan, A. M., Edelin, K. C., & Midgley, C. (2001). Teachers' communication of goal orientations in four fifth grade classrooms. *Elementary School Journal, 102,* 35–58.

Patrick, H., Neighbours, C., & Knee, C. R. (2004). Appearance-related social comparisons: The role of contingent self-esteem and self-perceptions of attractiveness. *Personality and Social Psychology Bulletin, 30,* 501–514.

Patrick, H., Turner, J. C., Meyer, D. K., & Midgley, C. (2003). How teachers establish psychological environments during the first days of school: Associations with avoidance in mathematics. *Teachers College Record, 105,* 1521–1558.

Patterson, K., & Wright, A. (1990). The speech, language of hearing-impaired child: At-risk academically. *Childhood Education, 67*(2), 91–95.

Patterson, P. O. (1989). Employment testing and Title VII of the Civil Rights Act of 1964. In B. Gifford (Ed), *Test policy and the politics of opportunity allocation: The workplace and the law* (pp. 83–120). Boston: Kluwer Academic.

Paul, R., Binker, A. J. A., Martin, D., & Adamson, K. (1989). *Critical thinking handbook: High school.* Rohnert Park, CA: Center for Critical Thinking and Moral Critique.

Paul, R., & Elder, L. (2006). *The miniature guide to critical thinking: Concepts and tools.* Dillon Beach, CA: Foundation for Critical Thinking.

Paulesu, E., Démonet, J.-F., Fazio, F., et al. (2001). Dyslexia: Cultural diversity and biological unity. *Science, 291,* 2165–2167.

Paulson, S. E., & Marchant, G. J. (2009). Background variables, levels of aggregation, and standardized test scores. *Education Policy Analysis Archives, 17*(22), http://epaa.asu.edu/epaa/v17n22/.

Pavlov, I. (1927/1960). *Conditioned reflexes: An investigation of the physiological activity of the cerebral cortex.* Oxford: Oxford University Press.

Payne, A., Whitehurst, G., & Angell, A. (1994). The role of home literacy environment in the development of language ability in preschool children from low-income families. *Early Childhood Research Quarterly, 9*(3–4), 427–440.

Payne, S. C., Youngcourt, S. S., & Beaubien, J. M. (2007). A meta-analytic examination of the goal orientation nomological net. *Journal of Applied Psychology, 92,* 128–150.

Payton, J., Weissberg, R. P., Durlak, J. A., et al. (2008). *The positive impact of social and emotional learning for kindergarten to eighth-grade students.* Chicago: Collaborative for Academic, Social, and Emotional Learning (CASEL), www.casel.org.

Pea, R. D. (1987). Socializing the knowledge transfer problem. *International Journal of Educational Research, 11,* 639–663.

Pearson, B. (1998). Assessing lexical development in bilingual babies and toddlers. *International Journal of Bilingualism, 2*(3), 347–372.

Pedulla, J., Abrams, L., Madaus, G., Russell, M., Ramos, M., & Miao, J. (2003). *Perceived effects of state-mandated testing programs on teaching and learning: Findings from a national survey of teachers.* Chestnut Hill, MA: National Board on Educational Testing and Public Policy, Boston College.

Peled, Z., & Wittrock, M. C. (1990). Generative meanings in the comprehension of word problems in mathematics. *Instructional Science, 19,* 171–205.

Pelham, W. E., & Molina, B. S. G. (2003). Childhood predictors of adolescent substance use in a longitudinal study of children with ADHD. *Journal of Abnormal Psychology, 112,* 497–507.

Pellegrini, A., & Smith, P. K. (1993). School recess. *Review of Educational Research, 63,* 51–67.

Pellegrini, A. D. (2002). Bullying, victimization, and sexual harassment during the transition to middle school. *Educational Psychologist, 37,* 151–163.

Pellegrini, A. D., & Bohn, C. M. (2005, January/February). The role of recess in children's cognitive performance and school adjustment. *Educational Researcher, 34*(1), 13–19.

Pellegrini, A. D., Huberty, P. D., & Jones, I. (1995). The effects of recess timing on children's playground and classroom behaviors. *American Educational Research Journal, 32,* 845–864.

Pellegrino, J. W., Chudowsky, N., & Glaser, R. (2001). Knowing what students know. Washington, DC: National Academy Press.

Pepicello, W., & Weisberg, R. (1983). Linguistics and humor. In P. McGhee & J. Goldstein (Eds.), *Handbook of humor research: Vol. 1. Basic issues* (pp. 59–83). New York: Springer-Verlag.

Perez, B. (2004). *Becoming biliterate: A study of two-way bilingual immersion education.* Mahwah, NJ: Erlbaum.

Perfetti, C., & Bolger, D. (2004). The brain might read that way. *Scientific Studies of Reading, 8,* 293–304.

Perfetti, C. A. (1985). *Reading ability.* New York: Oxford University Press.

Perfetti, C. A. (1992). The representation problem in reading acquisition. In P. B. Gough, L. Ehri, & R. Treiman (Eds.), *Reading acquisition* (pp. 145–174). Hillsdale, NJ: Erlbaum.

Perfetti, C. A., & Lesgold, A. M. (1977). Discourse comprehension and sources of individual differences. In M. Just & P. Carpenter (Eds.), *Cognitive processes in comprehension* (pp. 141–183). Hillsdale, NJ: Erlbaum.

Perkins, D., Jay, E., & Tishman, S. (1993). Beyond abilities: A dispositional theory of thinking. *Merrill-Palmer Quarterly, 39*(1), 1–21.

Perkins, D., Jay, E., & Tishman, S. (1993). New conceptions of thinking: From ontology to education. *Educational Psychologist, 28*(1), 67–85.

Perkins, D. F., & Borden, L. M. (2003). Positive behaviors, problem behaviors, and resiliency in adolescence. In R. M. Lerner, M. A. Easterbrooks, & J. Mistry (Eds.), *Handbook of psychology: Vol. 6. Developmental psychology* (pp. 373–394). Hoboken, NJ: Wiley.

Perkins, D. N. (1995). *Outsmarting IQ: The emerging science of learnable intelligence.* New York: Free Press.

Perlman, C. (2002). An introduction to performance assessment scoring rubrics. In C. Boston (Ed.), *Understanding scoring rubrics* (pp. 5–13). University of Maryland: ERIC Clearinghouse on Assessment and Evaluation.

Perrin, J. S., Herve, P. Y., Leonard, G., et al. (2008). Growth of white matter in the adolescent brain: Role of testosterone and androgen receptor. *The Journal of Neuroscience, 28*(38), 9519–9524.

Perry, M. (1991). Learning and transfer: Instructional conditions and conceptual change. *Cognitive Development, 6,* 449–468.

Peterfalvi, B. (2001). Obstacles et situations didactiques en sciences: Processus intellectuels et confrontations. L'exemple des transformations de la matière. Ph.D. dissertation, Université de Rouen.

Peterson, L. R., & Peterson, M. J. (1959). Short-term retention of individual items. *Journal of Experimental Psychology, 58,* 193–198.

Peterson, P. L. (1988). Teachers' and students' cognitional knowledge for classroom teaching and learning. *Educational Researcher, 17*(5), 5–14.

Peterson, P. L., Fennema, E., Carpenter, T. P., & Loef, M. (1989). Teachers' pedagogical content beliefs in mathematics. *Cognition and Instruction, 6,* 1–40.

Petitto, L. A., & Dunbar, K. (In press). New findings from educational neuroscience on bilingual brains, scientific brains, and the educated mind. In K. Fischer & T. Katzir (Eds.), *Building usable knowledge in mind, brain, and education.* Cambridge, UK: Cambridge University Press.

Petitto, L. A., Holowka, S., Sergio, L. E., & Ostry, D. (2001a). Language rhythms in baby hand movements. *Nature, 413,* 35–36.

Petitto, L. A., Katerelos, M., Levy, B. G., Gauna, K., Tetreault, K., & Ferraro, V. (2001b). Bilingual signed and spoken language acquisition from birth: Implications for the mechanisms underlying early bilingual language acquisition. *Journal of Child Language, 28*(2), 453–496.

Peverly, S. T., Brobst, K. E., Graham, M., & Shaw, R. (2003). College adults are not good at self-regulation: A study on the relationship of self-regulation, note taking, and test taking. *Journal of Educational Psychology, 95,* 335–346.

Peverly, S. T., Brobst, K. E., & Morris, K. S. (2002). The contribution of reading comprehension ability and metacognitive control to the development of studying in adolescence. *Journal of Research in Reading, 25,* 203–216.

Pew Internet and American Life Project. (2007). Cyberbullying and online teens. Retrieved August 15, 2011, from http://www.pewinternet.org/PPF/r/216/report_display.asp.

Pfeifer, M., Goldsmith, H. H., Davidson, R. J., & Rickman, M. (2002). Continuity and change in inhibited and uninhibited children. *Child Development, 73,* 1474–1485.

Pfeiffer, S. I., & Blei, S. (2008). Gifted identification beyond the IQ test: Rating scales and other assessment procedures (pp. 177–198). In S. Pfeiffer (Ed.), *Handbook of giftedness in children: Psychoeducational theory, research, and best practices.* New York: Springer.

Pfiffner, L. J., & Barkely, R. A. (1998). Treatment of ADHD in school settings. In R. A. Barkley (Ed.), *Attention-deficit hyperactivity disorder: A handbook for diagnosis and treatment* (2nd ed., pp. 458–490). New York: Guilford Press.

Pfiffner, L. J., & O'Leary, S. G. (1987). The efficacy of all-positive management as a function of the prior use of negative consequences. *Journal of Applied Behavior Analysis, 20,* 265–271.

Phi Delta Kappa/Gallup. (2010). Highlights of the 2010 Phi Delta Kappa/Gallup Poll. *Phi Delta Kappan,* September 2010, pp. 8–26.

Phinney, J. S. (1989). Stages of ethnic identity in minority group adolescents. *Journal of Early Adolescence, 9,* 163–173.

Phinney, J. S. (1990). Ethnic identity in adolescents and adults: Review of research. *Psychological Bulletin, 108*(3), 499–514.

Piaget, J. (1924). *Judgment and reasoning in the child.* Neuchatel, Switzerland: Delachaux et Niestle.

Piaget. J. (1926). *The child's conception of the world.* Paris: Alcan.

Piaget, J. (1932). *The moral judgment of the child.* Glencoe, IL: Free Press.

Piaget, J. (1945/1962). *Play, dreams, and imitation in childhood.* New York: Norton.

Piaget, J. (1950). *The psychology of intelligence.* London: Routledge & Kegan Paul.

Piaget, J. (1954). *The construction of reality in the child.* New York: Basic Books.

Piaget, J. (1962). *Comments on Vygostky's critical remarks concerning "The Language and Thought of the Child," and "Judgment and Reasoning in the Child."* Boston: MIT Press.

Piaget, J. (1963). *Origins of intelligence in children.* New York: Norton.

Piaget, J. (1970). Piaget's theory. In P. H. Mussen (Ed.), *Carmichael's manual of child psychology* (pp. 703–732). New York: Wiley.

Piaget, J. (1972). *The psychology of intelligence.* Totowa, NJ: Littlefield Adams.

Piaget, J. (1972a). Intellectual evolution from adolescence to adulthood. *Human Development, 15,* 1–12.

Piaget, J. (1972b). *Problems of genetic psychology.* Paris: Gonthier.

Piaget, J. (1976a). Postscript. *Archives de Psychologie, 44,* 223–228.

Piaget, J. (1976b). *The grasp of consciousness: Action and concept in the young child.* Cambridge, MA. Harvard University Press.

Piaget, J. (1985). *The equilibration of cognitive structures: The central problem of intellectual development* (T. Brown & K. L. Thampy, Trans.). Chicago: University of Chicago Press.

Pickar, D. B., & Tori, C. D. (1986). The learning disabled adolescent: Eriksonian psychosocial development, self-concept, and delinquent behavior. *Journal of Youth and Adolescence, 15*(5), 429–440.

Pierce, W., Lemke, E., & Smith, R. (1988). Critical thinking and moral development in secondary students. *High School Journal, 71*(3), 120–126.

Piirto, J. (2007). *Talented children and adults: Their development and education* (3rd ed.). Waco, TX: Prufrock Press.

Pillow, B. H. (2002). Children's and adults' evaluation of the certainty of deductive inferences, inductive inferences, and guesses. *Child Development, 73,* 779–792.

Pinker, S. (1997). *How the mind works.* New York: Norton.

Pintrich, P. R. (2000). An achievement goal theory perspective on issues in motivation terminology, theory, and research. *Contemporary Educational Psychology, 25,* 92–104.

Pintrich, P. R. (2003). A motivational science perspective on the role of student motivation in learning and teaching. *Journal of Educational Psychology, 95,* 667–686.

Pintrich, P. R., & DeGroot, E. V. (1990). Motivational and self-regulated learning components of classroom academic performance. *Journal of Educational Psychology, 82,* 33–40.

Pintrich, P. R., & Garcia, T. (1991). Student goal orientation and self-regulation in the college classroom. In M. L. Maehr & P. R. Pintrich (Eds.), *Advances in motivation and achievement: Goals and self-regulatory processes, Vol. 7* (pp. 371–402). Greenwich, CT: JAI Press.

Pintrich, P. R., & Schunk, D. H. (2002). *Motivation in education: Theory, research, and applications* (2nd ed.). Upper Saddle River, NJ: Merrill/Prentice Hall.

Pittman, T. S., Cooper, E. E., & Smith, T. W. (1977). Attribution of causality and the overjustification effect. *Personality and Social Psychology Bulletin, 3,* 280–283.

Plake, B. S., Impara, J. C., & Fager, J. J. (1993). Assessment competencies of teachers: A national survey. *Educational Measurement: Issues and Practice, 10*(4), 12–15.

Plaks, J., Stroessner, S., Dweck, C., & Sherman, J. (2001). Person theories and attention allocation: Preferences for stereotypic versus counterstereotypic information. *Journal of Personality and Social Psychology, 80,* 876–893.

Plant, R., & Ryan, R. M. (1985). Intrinsic motivation and the effects of self-consciousness, self-awareness, and ego-involvement: An investigation of internally controlling styles. *Journal of Personality, 53,* 435–449.

Plass, J. A., & Hill, K. T. (1986). Children's achievement strategies and test performance: The role of time pressure, evaluation, anxiety, and sex. *Developmental Psychology, 22,* 31–36.

Pluess, M., & Belsky, J. (2010). Differential susceptibility to parenting and quality of child care. *Developmental Psychology, 46*(2), 379–390.

Pogrow, S. (2005). HOTS revisited: A thinking development approach to reducing the learning gap after grade 3. *Phi Delta Kappan, 87,* 64–75.

Polloway, E. A., Epstein, M. H., Bursuck, W. D., Roderique, T. W., McConeghy, J. L., & Jayanthi, M. (1994). Classroom grading: A national survey of policies. *Remedial and Special Education, 15,* 162–170.

Poncy, B. C., Skinner, C. H., & O'Mara, T. (2006). Detect, practice, and repair: The effects of a classwide intervention on elementary students' math-fact fluency. *Journal of Evidence-Based Practices for Schools, 7*(1), 47–68.

Pong, S. (1997). Family structure, school context, and eighth-grade math and reading achievement. *Journal of Marriage and the Family, 59*(3), 734–746.

Pong, S. (1998). The school compositional effect of single parenthood on 10th-grade achievement. *Sociology of Education, 71*(1), 23–43.

Pong, S., Hao, L., & Gardner, E. (2005). The roles of parenting styles and social capital in the school performance of immigrant Asian and Hispanic adolescents. *Social Science Quarterly, 86*(4), 928–950.

Popham, W. J. (1978). *Criterion referenced measurement.* Englewood Cliffs, NJ: Prentice-Hall.

Popham, W. J. (2001). Teaching to the test. *Educational Leadership, 58*(6), 16–20.

Popham, W. J. (2005). *Classroom assessment* (4th ed.). Boston: Allyn & Bacon.

Popham, W. J. (2006). *Assessment for educational leaders.* Boston: Pearson.

Popham, W. J. (2008). *Transformative assessment.* Alexandria, VA: Association for Supervision and Curriculum Development.

Popham, W. J. (2009). Assessment literacy for teachers: Faddish or fundamental? *Theory Into Practice, 48,* 4–11.

Pornari, C., & Wood, J. (2010). Peer and cyber aggression in secondary school students: The role of moral disengagement, hostile attribution bias, and outcome expectancies. *Aggressive Behavior, 36*(2), 81–94.

Portrat, S., Camos, V., & Barrouillet, P. (2009). Working memory in children: A time-constrained functioning similar to adults. *Journal of Experimental Child Psychology, 102*(3), 368–374.

Posner, M. I. (1995). Attention in cognitive neuroscience: An overview. In M. S. Gazzaniga (Ed.), *The cognitive neurosciences* (pp. 615–624). Cambridge, MA: MIT Press.

Posner, M. I., & Raichle, M. E. (1994). *Images of mind.* New York: Scientific American Library.

Posner, M. I., & Rothbart, M. K. (2007). *Educating the human brain.* Washington, DC: American Psychological Association.

Postma, A., Jager, G., Kessels, R. P. C., Koppeschaar, H. P. F., & van Honk, J. (2004). Sex differences for selective forms of spatial memory. *Brain Cognition, 54,* 24–34.

Potter, D. (2010). Psychosocial well-being and the relationship between divorce and children's academic achievement. *Journal of Marriage and Family, 72*(4), 933–946.

Powers, K. (2005). Authentic assessment. In S. W. Lee (Ed.), *Encyclopedia of school psychology.* Thousand Oaks, CA: Sage.

Prawat, R. S. (1989). Promoting access to knowledge, strategy, and disposition in students: A research synthesis. *Review of Educational Research, 59,* 1–41.

Preckel, F., Götz, T., & Frenzel, A. (2010). Ability grouping of gifted students: Effects on academic self-concept and boredom. *British Journal of Educational Psychology, 80*(3), 451–472.

Preckel, F., Goetz, T., Pekrun, R., & Kleine, M. (2008). Gender differences in gifted and average-ability students: Comparing girls' and boys' achievement, self-concept, interest, and motivation in mathematics. *Gifted Child Quarterly, 52*(2), 146–159.

Premack, D. (1959). Toward empirical behavior laws: I. Positive reinforcement. *Psychological Review, 66,* 219–233.

Premack, D. (1963). Rate differential reinforcement in monkey manipulation. *Journal of Experimental Analysis of Behavior, 6,* 81–89.

Premack, D. (1965). Reinforcement theory. In D. Levine (Ed.), *Nebraska Symposium on Motivation.* Lincoln, NE: University of Nebraska Press.

Pressley, M., & Woloshyn, V. (1995). *Cognitive strategy instruction that really improves children's academic performance.* Cambridge, MA: Brookline Books.

Prinstein, M. J., & La Greca, A. M. (2002). Peer crowd affiliation and internalizing distress in childhood and adolescence: A longitudinal follow-back study. *Journal of Research on Adolescence, 12*(3), 325–351.

Proctor, C. P., August, D., Carlo, M. S., & Snow, C. E. (2006). The intriguing role of Spanish language vocabulary knowledge in predicting English reading comprehension. *Journal of Educational Psychology, 98*(1), 159–169.

Proshansky, E., & Wolfe, M. (1974). The physical setting and open education. *School Review, 82,* 557–574.

The Psychological Corporation. (2001). *The Wechsler Individual Achievement Test-II.* San Antonio, TX: Author.

Puckett, M. B., Aikins, J. W., & Cillessen, A. H. N. (2008). Moderators of the association between relational aggression and perceived popularity. *Aggressive Behavior, 34*(6), 563–576.

Pugh, K. J., & Bergin, D. A. (2006). Motivational influences on transfer. *Educational Psychologist, 41*(3), 147–160.

Puma, M. J., Jones, C. C., Rock, D., & Fernandez, R. (1993). *Prospects: The Congressionally mandated study of educational growth and opportunity.* Interim Report. Bethesda, MD: Abt Associates.

Purdie, N., & Hattie, J. (1996). Cultural differences in the use of strategies for self-regulated learning. *American Educational Research Journal, 33,* 845–871.

Pylyshyn, Z. W. (1984). *Computation and cognition.* Cambridge, MA: MIT Press.

Q

Quadrel, M. J., Fischhoff, B., & Davis, W. (1993). Adolescent (in)vulnerability. *American Psychologist, 48,* 102–116.

R

Rafferty, Y. (2005). Benefits and risks of reverse inclusion for preschoolers with and without disabilities: Perspectives of parents and providers. *Journal of Early Intervention, 27*(3), 173–192.

Ramey, C. T. (1994). Abecedarian project. In R. J. Sternberg (Ed.), *Encyclopedia of human intelligence* (Vol. 1, pp. 1–3). New York: Macmillan.

Randhawa, B. (1994). Self-efficacy in mathematics, attitudes, and achievement of boys and girls from restricted samples in two countries. *Perceptual and Motor Skills, 79,* 1011–1018.

Raphael, T., & Hiebert, E. (1996). *Creating an integrated approach to literacy instruction.* Fort Worth, TX: Harcourt Brace.

Rapport, M. D., Murphy, H. A., & Bailey, J. S. (1982). Ritalin vs. response cost in the control of hyperactive children: A within-subject comparison. *Journal of Applied Behavior Analysis, 15,* 205–216.

Rathunde, K., & Csikszentmihalyi, M. (2005). Middle school students' motivation and quality of experience: A comparison of Montessori and traditional school environments. *American Journal of Education, 111,* 341–371.

Ratner, N. (2004, January). Caregiver–child interactions and their impact on children's fluency: Implications for treatment. *Language, Speech and Hearing Services in Schools, 35,* 46–56.

Rayner, K., Foorman, B. R., Perfetti, C. A., Pesetsky, D., & Seidenberg, M. S. (2001). How psychological science informs the teaching of reading. *Psychological Science in the Public Interest, 2,* 31–74.

Read, C. R. (1991). Achievement and career choices: Comparisons of males and females. *Roeper Review, 13,* 188–193.

Reddy, G. L., Ramar, R., & Kusama, A. (2000). *Education of children with special needs.* New Delhi: Discovery.

Reed, S. K. (1987). A structure-mapping model for word problems. *Journal of Experimental Psychology: Learning, Memory, and Cognition, 13*(1), 124–139.

Reed, S. K., Ernst, G. W., & Banerji, R. (1974). The role of analogy in transfer between similar problem states. *Cognitive Psychology, 6,* 436–450.

Reese, E., Bird, A., & Tripp, G. (2007). Children's self-esteem and moral self: Links to parent-child conversations regarding emotion. *Social Development, 16*(3), 460–478.

Reeve, J. (2009). Why teachers adopt a controlling motivating style toward students and how they can become more autonomy supportive. *Educational Psychologist, 44*(3), 159–175.

Reeve, J., & Deci, E. L. (1996). Elements of the competitive situation that affect intrinsic motivation. *Personality and Social Psychology Bulletin, 22,* 24–33.

Reeve, J., & Jang, H. (2006). What teachers say and do to support students' autonomy during a learning activity. *Journal of Educational Psychology, 98,* 209–218.

Reeve, J., Jang, H., Carrell, D., Barch, J., & Jeon, S. (2004). Enhancing high school students' engagement by increasing their teachers' autonomy support. *Motivation and Emotion, 28,* 147–169.

Reid, D. K., & Knight, M. G. (2006). Disability justifies exclusion of minority students: A critical history grounded in disability studies. *Educational Researcher, 35*(6), 18–23.

Reis, S. M., & Boeve, H. (2009). How academically gifted elementary, urban students respond to challenge in an enriched, differentiated reading program. *Journal for the Education of the Gifted, 33*(2), 203–240.

Reis, S. M., & Purcell, J. H. (1993). An analysis of content elimination and strategies used by elementary classroom teachers in the curriculum compacting process. *Journal for the Education of the Gifted, 16*(2), 147–170.

Reis, S. M., & Renzulli, J. S. (2004). Current research on the social and emotional development of gifted and talented students: Good news and future possibilities. *Psychology in the Schools, 41*(1).

Rejskind, G. (2000). TAG teachers: Only the creative need apply. *Roeper Review, 22*, 153–157.

Renkl, A., Mandl, H., & Gruber, H. (1996). Inert knowledge: Analyses and remedies. *Educational Psychologist, 31*, 115–121.

Renne, C. H. (1997). *Excellent classroom management.* Belmont, CA: Wadsworth.

Renzulli, J. S. (1978a). *The compactor.* Mansfield Center, CT: Creative Learning Press.

Renzulli, J. S. (1978b). What makes giftedness? Reexamining a definition. *Phi Delta Kappan, 60*, 180–184, 261.

Renzulli, J. S. (1988). *Technical report of research studies related to the enrichment triad/revolving door model* (3rd ed.). Teaching The Talented (TTT) program, University of Connecticut.

Renzulli, J. S. (1990). A practical system for identifying gifted and talented students. *Early Child Development and Care, 63*, 9–18.

Renzulli, J. S. (1999). What is this thing called giftedness, and how do we develop it? A twenty-five-year perspective. *Journal for the Education of the Gifted, 23*(1), 3–54.

Renzulli, J. S. (2002). Emerging conceptions of giftedness: Building a bridge to the new century. *Exceptionality, 10*(2), 67–75.

Renzulli, J. S. (2011). Kappan Classic: What makes giftedness?: Reexamining a definition. *Phi Delta Kappan, 92*(8), 81–88.

Renzulli, J. S., & Reis, S. M. (1991). The reform movement and the quiet crisis in gifted education. *Gifted Child Quarterly, 35*, 26–35.

Renzulli, J. S., & Reis, S. M. (2004). Curriculum compacting: A research-based differentiation strategy for culturally diverse talented students. In D. Boothe & J. C. Stanley (Eds.), *In the eyes of the beholder: Critical issues for diversity in gifted education* (pp. 87–100). Waco, TX: Prufrock Press.

Renzulli, J. S., Smith, L., & Reis, S. (1982). Curriculum compacting: An essential strategy for working with gifted students. *Elementary School Teacher, 82*(3), 185–194.

Reschly, D. J., & Hosp, J. L. (2004). State SLD policies and practices. *Learning Disability Quarterly, 27*, 197–213.

Rescorla, R. A. (1988). Pavlovian conditioning: It's not what you think. *American Psychologist, 43*, 151–160.

Resing, W. C. M., & Tunteler, E. (2007). Children becoming more intelligent: Can the Flynn effect be generalized to other child intelligence tests? *International Journal of Testing, 7*(2), 191–208.

Resnick, L. B. (1987). *Education and learning to think.* Washington, DC: National Academy Press.

Resnick, L. B. (1988). Treating mathematics as an ill-structured discipline. In R. I. Charles & A. E. Silver (Eds.), *The teaching and assessing of mathematical problem solving* (pp. 32–60). Mahwah, NJ: Erlbaum.

Resnick, L. B., & Omanson, S. F. (1987). Learning to understand arithmetic. In R. Glaser (Ed.), *Advances in instructional psychology* (Vol. 3, pp. 41–95). Hillsdale, NJ: Erlbaum.

Resnick, L. B., & Resnick, D. P. (1992). Assessing the thinking curriculum: New tools for education reform. In B. R. Gifford & M. C. O'Connor (Eds.), *Changing assessments: Alternative views of ap-*

titude, achievement, and instruction (pp. 37–75). Boston: Kluwer Academic.

Rest, J. R., Thomas, S. J., & Edwards, L. (1997). Designing and validating a measure of moral judgment: Stage preference and stage consistency approaches. *Journal of Educational Psychology, 89*, 5–28.

Retelsdorf, J., Butler, R., Streblow, L., & Schiefele, U. (2010). Teachers' goal orientations for teaching: Associations with instructional practices, interest in teaching, and burnout. *Learning and Instruction, 20*, 30–46.

Reyna, C. (2000). Lazy, dumb, or industrious: When stereotypes convey attribution information in the classroom. *Educational Psychology Review, 12*, 85–110.

Reyna, C., & Weiner, B. (2001). Justice and utility in the classroom: An attributional analysis of the goals of teachers' punishment and intervention strategies. *Journal of Educational Psychology, 93*, 309–319.

Reyna, V. F., & Farley, F. (2006). Risk and rationality in adolescent decision-making. *Psychological Science in the Public Interest, 7*, 1–44.

Reyna, V. F., & Lloyd, F. J. (2006). Physician decision-making and cardiac risk: Effects of knowledge, risk perception, risk tolerance, and fuzzy processing. *Journal of Experimental Psychology: Applied, 12*, 179–195.

Reynolds, C. R., Chastain, R. L., Kaufman, A. S., & McLean, J. E. (1987). Demographic characteristics and IQ among adults: Analysis of the WAIS-R standardization sample as a function of the stratification variables. *Journal of School Psychology, 25*, 323–342.

Reynolds, C. R., Livingston, R. B., & Willson, V. (2009). *Measurement and assessment in education* (2nd ed.). Boston: Pearson.

Rhode, G., Jensen, W. R., & Reavis, H. K. (1992). *The tough kid book: Practical classroom management strategies.* Longmont, CO: Sopris West.

Rholes, W., Blackwell, J., Jordan, C., & Walters, C. (1980). A developmental study of learned helplessness. *Developmental Psychology, 16*, 616–624.

Rich, L. E. (2004). Bringing more effective tools to the weight-loss table. *Monitor on Psychology, 4*(1), 52–55.

Richards, J. (2006). Setting the stage for student engagement. *Kappa Delta Pi Record, 42*, 92–94.

Richardson, T. M., & Benbow, C. P. (1990). Long-term effects of acceleration on the social-emotional adjustment of mathematically precocious youths. *Journal of Educational Psychology, 82*(3), 464–470.

Richardson, R. C., Tolson, H., Huang, T., & Lee, Y. (2009). Character education: Lessons for teaching social and emotional competence. *Children and Schools, 31*(2), 71–78.

Ridgway, A., Northup, J., Pellegrini, A., LaRue, R., & Hightshoe, A. (2003). Effects of recess on the classroom behavior of children with and without attention-deficit hyperactivity disorder. *School Psychology Quarterly, 18*, 253–268.

Rimm-Kaufman, S. E., Curby, T. W., Grimm, K. J., Nathanson, L., & Brock, L. L. (2009). The contribution of children's self-regulation and classroom quality to children's adaptive behaviors in the kindergarten classroom. *Developmental Psychology, 45*(4), 958–972.

Rimm-Kaufman, S. E., Early, D., Cox, M., et al. (2002). Early behavioral attributes and teachers' sensitivity as predictors of competent behavior in the kindergarten classroom. *Journal of Applied Developmental Psychology, 23*, 451–470.

Rincon, E. (1980). Test speededness, test anxiety, and test performance: A comparison of Mexican American and Anglo American high school juniors. Doctoral dissertation, University of Texas at Austin. *Dissertation Abstracts International, 40,* 5772A.

Risch, N. L., & Kiewra, K. A. (1990). Content and form variations in note taking: Effects among junior high students. *Journal of Educational Research, 83,* 355–357.

Rist, R. (1970). Student social class and teacher expectations: The self-fulfilling prophecy in ghetto education. *Harvard Educational Review, 40,* 411–451.

Ritchie, W. C., & Bhatia, T. K. (Eds.). (1999). *Handbook of child language acquisition.* Orlando, FL: Academic Press.

Ritter, K. (1978). The development of knowledge of an external retrieval cue strategy. *Child Development, 49,* 1227–1230.

Rivera, S. M., Reiss, A. L., Eckert, M. A., & Menon, V. (2005). Developmental changes in mental arithmetic: Evidence for increased specialization in the left inferior parietal cortex. *Cerebral Cortex, 15,* 1779–1790.

Rivers, R. H., & Vockell, E. (1987). Computer simulations to stimulate scientific problem solving. *Journal of Research in Science Teaching, 25*(4), 403–415.

Roberts, G., Torgesen, J. K., Boardman, A., & Scammacca, N. (2007). Evidence-based strategies for reading instruction of older students with learning disabilities. *Learning Disabilities Research and Practice, 23*(2), 63–69.

Robinson, A. (1990). Point–counterpoint: Cooperation or exploitation? The argument against cooperative learning for talented students. *Journal for the Education of the Gifted, 14,* 9–27.

Robinson, A., & Clinkenbeard, P. R. (1998). Giftedness: An exceptionality examined. In J. T. Spence, J. M. Darley, & D. J. Foss (Eds.), *Annual review of psychology* (pp. 117–139). Palo Alto, CA: Annual Reviews.

Robinson, C., Menchetti, B., & Torgesen, J. (2002). Toward a two-factor theory of one type of mathematics disabilities. *Learning Disabilities Research and Practice, 17,* 81–89.

Robinson, D. H. (1998). Graphic organizers as aids to test learning. *Reading Research and Instruction, 37,* 85–105.

Robinson, D. H., Funk, D. C., Beth, A., & Bush, A. M. (2005). Changing beliefs about corporal punishment: Increasing knowledge about ineffectiveness to build more consistent moral and informational beliefs. *Journal of Behavioral Education, 14,* 117–139.

Robinson, R. P. (1961). *Effective study.* New York: Harper & Row.

Roe, A. (1952). *The making of a scientist.* New York: Dodd, Mead.

Roediger, H. L., & Guynn, M. J. (1996) Retrieval processes. In E. L. Bjork and R. A. Bjork (Eds.), *Memory* (pp. 197–236). San Diego: Academic Press.

Roediger, H. (1997). Memory: Explicit and implicit. Paper presented at the Symposium, Recent Advances in Research on Human Memory, National Academy of Sciences, Washington, DC.

Roeser, R., Eccles, J., & Sameroff, A. (1998). Academic and emotional functioning in early adolescence: Longitudinal relations, patterns, and predictions by experience in middle school. *Development and Psychopathology, 10,* 321–352.

Roeser, R., Eccles, J., & Sameroff, A. (2000). School as a context of early adolescents' academic and social-emotional development: A summary of research findings. *Elementary School Journal, 100,* 443–471.

Rogers, K. B. (1991). *The relationship of grouping practices to the education of the gifted and talented learner.* Storrs, CT: National Research Center on the Gifted and Talented.

Rogers, K. B. (1993). Grouping the gifted and talented: Questions and answers. *Roeper Review, 16,* 8–12.

Rogers, K. B. (2002). Grouping the gifted and talented. *Roeper Review, 24,* 103–108.

Rogers, S. J. (1996). Brief report: Early intervention in autism. *Journal of Autism and Developmental Disorders, 26*(2), 243–246.

Rogoff, B. (1990). *Apprenticeship in thinking.* New York: Oxford University Press.

Rogoff, B. (2001). *Everyday cognition: Its development in social context.* New York: Replica Books.

Rogoff, B. (2003). *The cultural nature of human development.* New York: Oxford University Press.

Rogoff, B., & Chavajay, P. (1995). What's become of research on the cultural basis of cognitive development? *American Psychologist, 50,* 859–877.

Rohrbeck, C. A., Ginsburg-Block, M. D., Fantuzzo, J. W., & Miller, T. R. (2003). Peer-assisted learning interventions with elementary school students: A meta-analytic review. *Journal of Educational Psychology, 94*(2), 240–257.

Roid, G. (2003). *Stanford-Binet intelligence scales* (5th ed.). Itasca, IL: Riverside.

Rollins, P. (2003). Caregivers' contingent comments to 9-month-old infants: Relationship with later language. *Applied Psycholinguistics, 24,* 221–234.

Root-Bernstein, M. (2009) Imaginary wordplay as an indicator of creative giftedness. In L. V. Shavinina (Ed.), *International handbook on giftedness* (pp. 599–616). New York: Springer.

Rose, A. J., Swenson, L. P., & Carlson, W. (2004). Friendships of aggressive youth: Considering the influences of being disliked and of being perceived as popular. *Journal of Experimental Child Psychology, 88,* 25–45.

Rose, L. C., & Gallup, A. M. (1999). The 31st annual Phi Delta Kappa/Gallup Poll of the public's attitude toward public schools. *Phi Delta Kappan, 81*(1), 41–58.

Rose, M. (1989). *Lives on the boundary: The struggles and achievements of America's underprepared.* New York: Free Press.

Rosenbaum, J. E. (1980). Social implications of educational grouping. *Review of Research in Education, 8,* 361–401.

Rosenberg, M., Schooler, C., Schoenbach, C., & Rosenberg, F. (1995). Global self-esteem and specific self-esteem: Different concepts, different outcomes. *American Sociological Review, 60,* 141–156.

Rosenfield, P., Lambert, N., & Black, A. (1985). Desk arrangement effects on pupil classroom behavior. *Journal of Educational Research, 77*(1), 101–108.

Rosenholtz, S. J., & Simpson, C. (1984). The formation of ability conceptions: Developmental trend or social construction? *Review of Educational Research, 54*(1), 31–63.

Rosenshine, B. (1971). *Teaching behaviours and student achievement.* London: National Foundation for Educational Research.

Rosenshine, B. (1979). Content, time, and direct instruction. In P. Peterson & H. Wahlberg (Eds.), *Research on teaching: Concepts, findings, and implications* (pp. 28–56). Berkeley, CA: McCutchan.

Rosenshine, B. (1985). Direct instruction. In T. Husen & T. N. Postlethwaite (Eds.), *International Encyclopedia of Education* (Vol. 3, pp. 1395–1400). Oxford, UK: Pergamon Press.

Rosenshine, B. (1988). Explicit teaching. In D. Berliner & B. Rosenshine (Eds.), *Talks to teachers* (pp. 75–92). New York: Random House.

Rosenshine, B., & Meister, C. (1994). Reciprocal teaching: A review of the research. *Review of Educational Research, 64*(4), 479–530.

Rosenshine, B., & Stevens, R. (1986). Teaching functions. In M. Wittrock (Ed.), *Handbook of research on teaching* (3rd ed., pp. 376–391). New York: Macmillan.

REFERENCES

Rosenthal, R. (1995). Critiquing Pygmalion: A 25-year perspective. *Current Directions in Psychological Science, 4*, 171–172.

Rosenweig, M. R. (1969). Effects of heredity and environment on brain chemistry, brain anatomy, and learning ability in the rat. In M. Monosevitz, G. Lindzey, & D. D. Thiessen (Eds.), *Behavioral genetics*. New York: Appleton-Century-Crofts.

Ross, B. H. (1987). This is like that: The use of earlier problems and the separation of similarity effects. *Journal of Experimental Psychology: Learning, Memory, and Cognition, 13*, 629–639.

Ross, B. H. (1989). Distinguishing types of superficial similarities: Different effects on the access and use of earlier problems. *Journal of Experimental Psychology: Learning, Memory, and Cognition, 15*, 456–468.

Ross, D. M., & Ross, S. A. (1982). *Hyperactivity: Current issues, research, and theory*. New York: Wiley.

Ross, J., & Bruce, C. (2007). Professional development effects on teacher efficacy: Results of randomized field trial. *Journal of Educational Research, 101*(1), 50–60.

Ross, J. A. (1998). The antecedents and consequences of teacher efficacy. In J. Brophy (Ed.), *Research on teaching* (Vol. 7, pp. 49–74). Greenwich, CT: JAI Press.

Rotenberg, K. J., & Mayer, E. V. (1990). Delay of gratification in Native and White children: A cross-cultural comparison. *International Journal of Behavioral Development, 13*, 23–30.

Roth, G., Assor, A., Kanat-Maymon, Y., & Kaplan, H. (2007). Autonomous motivation for teaching: How self-determined teaching may lead to self-determined learning. *Journal of Educational Psychology, 99*(4), 761–774.

Rothbart, M. K., Ellis, L. K., & Posner, M. I. (2004). Temperament and self-regulation. In R. F. Baumeister & K. D. Vohs (Eds.), *Handbook of self-regulation*. New York: Guilford Press.

Rothbaum, F., Weisz, J., Pott, M., Miyake, K., & Morelli, G. (2000). Attachment and culture: Security in the United States and Japan. *American Psychologist, 55*, 1093–1104.

Rotter, J. (1966). Generalized expectancies for internal versus external control of reinforcement. *Psychological Monographs, 1* (Whole No. 609).

Rotter, J. (1990). Internal versus external control of reinforcement: A case history of a variable. *American Psychologist, 45*, 489–493.

Rowan, B., & Miracle, A. W., Jr. (1983). Systems of ability grouping and the stratification of achievement in elementary schools. *Sociology of Education, 56*, 133–144.

Rowe, M. B. (1987). Wait time: Slowing down may be a way of speeding up. *American Educator, 11*(1), 38–44, 47.

Rowe, S. M., & Wertsch, J. V. (2002). Vygotsky's model of cognitive development. In U. Goswami (Ed.), *Blackwell handbook of childhood cognitive development* (pp. 538–554). Malden, MA: Blackwell.

Royer, J. M. (1997). A cognitive perspective on the assessment, diagnosis, and remediation of reading skills. In G. Phye (Ed.), *Handbook of academic learning* (pp. 199–234). New York: Academic Press.

Royer, J. M., & Sinatra, G. M. (1994). A cognitive theoretical approach to reading diagnostics. *Educational Psychology Review, 6*(2), 81–113.

Royer, J. M., & Tronsky, L. N. (1998). Addition practice with math disabled students improves subtraction and multiplication performance. *Advances in Learning and Behavioral Disabilities, 12*, 185–217.

Royer, J. M., Tronsky, L. N., Chan, Y., Jackson, S. J., & Marchant, H. (1999). Math-fact retrieval as the cognitive mechanism underlying gender differences in math test performance. *Contemporary Educational Psychology, 24*, 181–266.

Rudasill, K. M., Gallagher, K. C., & White, J. M. (2010). Temperamental attention and activity, classroom emotional support, and academic achievement in third grade. *Journal of School Psychology, 48*(2), 113–134.

Rudasill, K. M., Rimm-Kaufman, S. E., Justice, L. M., & Pence, K. (2006). Temperament and language skills as predictors of teacher-child relationship quality in preschool. *Early Education and Development, 17*(2), 271–291.

Rugg, M. D., Johnson, J. D., Park, H., & Uncapher, M. R. (2008). Encoding-retrieval overlap in human episodic memory: A functional neuroimaging perspective. In W. S. Sossin, J. C. Lacaille, V. F. Castellucci, & S. Belleville (Eds.), *Progress in brain research* (Vol. 169), 339–352.

Runco, M. A. (Ed.). (1996). *Creativity from childhood through adulthood: The developmental issues*. San Francisco: Jossey-Bass.

Runco, M. A., & Nemiro, J. (1994). Problem finding, creativity, and giftedness. *Roeper Review, 16*, 235–241.

Russell, R. L., & Ginsburg, H. P. (1984). Cognitive analysis of children's mathematical difficulties. *Cognition and Instruction, 1*, 217–244.

Rutter, M. (1978). Diagnosis and definition. In M. Rutter & E. Schloper (Eds.), *Autism: A reappraisal of concepts and treatment* (pp. 1–26). New York: Plenum.

Ryan, A. M., & Patrick, H. (2001). The classroom social environment and changes in adolescents' motivation and engagement during middle school. *American Educational Research Journal, 38*, 437–460.

Ryan, R. M. (1995). Psychological needs and the facilitation of integrative processes. *Journal of Personality, 63*, 397–427.

Ryan, R. M., Connell, J. P., & Deci, E. L. (1985). A motivational analysis of self-determination and self-regulation in education. In C. Ames & R. Ames (Eds.), *Research on motivation in education* (Vol. 2, pp. 13–51). San Diego: Academic Press.

Ryan, R. M., & Deci, E. L. (2000a). Self-determination theory and the facilitation of intrinsic motivation, social development and well-being. *American Psychologist, 55*, 68–78.

Ryan, R. M., & Deci, E. L. (2000b). Intrinsic and extrinsic motivation: Classic definitions and new directions. *Contemporary Educational Psychology, 25*, 54–67.

Ryan, R. M., Deci, E. L., & Grolnick, W. S. (1995). Autonomy, relatedness, and the self: Their relation to development and psychopathology. In D. Cicchetti & D. J. Cohen (Eds.), *Developmental psychopathology, Vol. I: Theory and methods* (pp. 618–655). New York: Wiley.

Ryan, R. M., & Grolnick, W. S. (1986). Origins and pawns in the classroom: Self-report and projective assessments of individual differences in children's perceptions. *Journal of Personality and Social Psychology, 50*, 550–558.

Ryan, R. M., Mims, V., & Koestner, R. (1983). Relation of reward contingency and interpersonal context to intrinsic motivation: A review and test using cognitive evaluation theory. *Journal of Personality and Social Psychology, 45*, 736–750.

Ryan, R. M., & Stiller, J. (1991). The social contexts of internalization: Parent and teacher influences on autonomy, motivation, and learning. In M. L. Maehr & P. L. Pintrich (Eds.), *Advances in motivation and achievement* (Vol. 7, pp. 115–149). Greenwich, CT: JAI Press.

S

Saavedra, L. M., Silverman, W. K., Morgan-Lopez, A. A., & Kurtines, W. M. (2010). Cognitive behavioral treatment for childhood anxiety disorders: Long-term effects on anxiety and secondary disorders in young adulthood. *The Journal of Child Psychology and Psychiatry, 51*(8), 924–934.

Sabatelli, R. M., & Mazor, A. (1985). Differentiation, individuation, and identity formation: The integration of family system and individual developmental perspectives. *Adolescence, 20*, 619–633.

Sabers, D. S., Cushing, K. S., & Berliner, D. C. (1991). Differences among teachers in a task characterized by simultaneity, multidimensionality, and immediacy. *American Educational Research Journal, 28*(1), 63–88.

Sachs, J. (1989). Communication development in infancy. In J. Berko Gleason (Ed.), *The development of language* (pp. 39–61). Upper Saddle River, NJ: Merrill/Prentice Hall.

Sadker, M., Sadker, D., & Klein, S. (1991). The issue of gender in elementary and secondary education. In G. Grant (Ed.), *Review of research in education* (pp. 269–334). Washington, DC: American Educational Research Association.

Sadoski, M., & Paivio, A. (2001). *Imagery and text: A dual coding theory of reading and writing.* Mahwah, NJ: Erlbaum.

Safdar, S., Freidlmeier, W., Matsumoto, D., et al. (2009). Variations of emotional display rules within and across cultures: A comparison between Canada, USA, and Japan. *Canadian Journal of Behavioural Science, 41*(1), 1–10.

Saffran, E. M., & Schwartz, M. F. (2003). Language. In M. Gallagher & R. J. Nelson (Eds.), *Handbook of psychology: Vol. 3. Biological psychology* (pp. 595–627). Hoboken, NJ: Wiley.

Saleh, M., Lazonder, A. W., & Jong, T. D. (2005). Effects of within-class ability grouping on social interaction, achievement, and motivation. *Instructional Science, 33*, 105–119.

Salend, D., & Sonnenschein, P. (1989). Validating the effectiveness of a cooperative learning strategy through direct observation. *Journal of School Psychology, 27*(1), 47–58.

Salomon, G., & Globerson, T. (1987). Skill may not be enough: The role of mindfulness in learning and transfer. *International Journal of Educational Research, 11*, 623–637.

Salomon, G., & Perkins, D. (1989). Rocky roads to transfer: Re-thinking mechanisms of a neglected phenomenon. *Educational Psychologist, 18*, 42–50.

Salovey, P., & Mayer, J. D. (1990). Emotional intelligence. *Imagination, Cognition, and Personality, 9*, 185–211.

Sanders, J. R., Hills, J. R., Nitko, A. J., et al. (1990). Standards for teacher competence in educational assessment of students. *Educational Measurement: Issues and Practices, 9*, 30–31.

Santiago, R. (1994). The interdependence between linguistic and cognitive performance among bilingual preschoolers with differing home language environments. In D. MacLaughlin & S. McEwen (Eds.), *Proceedings of Boston University Conference on Language Development, 19*, 511–520. Somerville, MA: Cascadilla Press.

Sapp, M. (1999). *Test anxiety: Applied research, assessment, and treatment interventions* (2nd ed.). New York: University Press of America.

Sarnacki, R. E. (1979). An examination of test-wiseness in the cognitive test domain. *Review of Educational Research, 49*, 252–279.

Saucier, D. M., Green, S. M., Leason, J., MacFadden, A., Bell, S., & Elias, L. J. (2002). Are sex differences in navigation caused by sexually dimorphic strategies or by differences in the ability to use the strategies? *Behavioral Neuroscience, 116*, 403–410.

Saunders, W., & Goldenberg, C. (1992, April). Instructional conversations on transition students' concepts of "friendship": An experimental study. Paper presented at the Annual Meeting of the American Educational Research Association, San Francisco.

Saunders, W., & Goldenberg, C. (1999). The effects of instructional conversations and literature logs on limited- and fluent-English-proficient students' story comprehension and thematic understanding. *Elementary School Journal, 99*(4), 277–301.

Savion, L. (2009). Clinging to discredited theories: Understanding obstacles to learning. *International Journal of Learning, 16*(2), 85–93.

Saxe, G. B. (2002). Candy selling and math learning. In C. Desforges & R. Fox (Eds.), *Teaching and learning: The essential readings* (pp. 86–106). Malden, MA: Blackwell.

Scardamalia, M., & Bereiter, C. (1985). Fostering the development of self-regulation in children's knowledge processing. In S. F. Chipman, J. W. Segal, & R. Glaser (Eds.), *Thinking and learning skills: Research and open questions* (pp. 563–577). Hillsdale, NJ: Erlbaum.

Scardamalia, M., & Bereiter, C. (1986). Research on written composition. In M. C. Wittrock (Ed.), *Handbook of research on teaching* (3rd ed., pp. 778–803). New York: Macmillan.

Scardamalia, M., Bereiter, C., & Goelman, H. (1982). The role of production factors in writing ability. In M. Nystrand (Ed.), *What writers know* (pp. 173–210). New York: Academic Press.

Scardamalia, M., Bereiter, C., & Steinbach, R. (1984). Teachability of reflective processes in written composition. *Cognitive Science, 8*, 173–190.

Scarr, S. (1998). American child care today. *American Psychologist, 53*, 95–108.

Schachar, H. (2003). Who gains what from cooperative learning: An overview of eight studies. In R. Gillies & A. Ashman (Eds.), *Cooperative learning: The social and intellectual outcomes of learning in groups* (pp. 103–118). London: Routledge/Falmer.

Schachar, R., & Tannock, R. (2002). Syndromes of hyperactivity and attention deficit. In M. Rutter & E. Taylor (Eds.), *Child and adolescent psychiatry* (4th ed., pp. 399–418). Malden, MA: Blackwell Science.

Schacter, D. L., Gilbert, D. T., & Wenger, D. M. (2009). *Psychology.* New York: Worth.

Schalock, R. L., Borthwick-Duffy, S. A., Bradley, V. J., et al. (2009). *Intellectual disability: Definition, classification, and systems of supports* (11th ed.). Washington, DC: American Association on Intellectual and Developmental Disabilities.

Schaps, E. (2007). Community in school: The heart of the matter. In P. Honston, A. Blankstein, & R. Cole (Eds), *Spirituality in educational leadership.* Thousand Oaks, CA: Cormin Press, 73–87.

Schaps, E. (2010). How a changing society changes SEL. *Better: Evidence-based Education: Social and Emotional Learning* (Winter 2010), 20–21.

Schell, L. M., & Burden, P. R. (1992). *Countdown to the first days of school.* West Haven, CT: NEA Professional Library.

Scherer, N., & Olswang, L. (1984). Role of mothers' expansions in stimulating children's language production. *Journal of Speech and Hearing Research, 27*, 387–396.

Schewel, R. H., & Waddell, J. G. (1986). Metacognitive skills: Practical strategies. *Academic Therapy, 22*, 19–25.

Schickedanz, J., York, M., Stewart, I., & White, D. (1990). *Strategies for teaching young children.* Upper Saddle River, NJ: Prentice Hall.

Schiefele, U. (1991). Interest, learning, and motivation. *Educational Psychologist, 26*, 299–323.

Schieffelin, F., & Ochs, E. (1986). Language socialization. *Annual Review of Anthropology, 15*, 163–246.

Schirrmacher, R. (2006). *Art and creative development for young children* (5th ed.). Clifton Park, NY: Thomson.

Schliemann, A. D., & Acioly, N. M. (1989). Mathematical knowledge developed at work: The contribution of practice versus the contribution of schooling. *Cognition and Instruction, 6*, 185–221.

Schloss, P. J., & Smith, M. A. (1994). *Applied behavior analysis in the classroom.* Boston: Allyn & Bacon.

Schlotz, W., Jones, A., Phillips, D., Gale, C. R., Robinson, S. M., & Godfrey, K. M. (2010). Lower maternal folate status in early pregnancy is associated with childhood hyperactivity and peer problems in offspring. *Journal of Child Psychology and Psychiatry, 51*(5), 594–602.

Schmader, T. (2002). Gender identification moderates stereotype threat effects on women's math performance. *Journal of Experimental Social Psychology, 38*, 194–201.

Schmader, T., & Johns, M. (2003). Converging evidence that stereotype threat reduces working memory capacity. *Journal of Personality and Social Psychology, 85*, 440–452.

Schmidt, W. H., McKnight, C. C., & Raizen, S. A. (1996). *Executive summary: A splintered vision: An investigation of U.S. science and mathematics education.* Retrieved August 15, 2011, from http://ustimss.msu.edu/splintrd.pdf.

Schneider, B. A., Trehub, S. E., & Bull, D. (1979). The development of basic auditory processes in infants. *Canadian Journal of Psychology, 33*, 306–319.

Schneider, W. (1985). Training high-performance skills: Fallacies and guidelines. *Human Factors, 27*(3), 285–300.

Schneider, W., & Shiffrin, R. M. (1985). Categorization (restructuring) and automatization: Two separable factors. *Psychological Review, 92*(3), 424–428.

Scholz, U., Dona, B. G., Sud, S., & Schwarzer, R. (2002). Is general self-efficacy a universal construct? Psychometric findings from 25 countries. *European Journal of Psychological Assessment, 18*(3), 242–251.

Schunk, D. (1989). Self-efficacy and cognitive skill learning. In C. Ames & R. Ames (Eds.), *Research on motivation in education: Goals and cognitions, Vol. 3* (pp. 13–44). San Diego, CA: Academic Press.

Schunk, D. (2001). Social cognitive theory and self-regulated learning. In B. J. Zimmerman & D. H. Schunk (Eds.), *Self-regulated learning and academic achievement: Theoretical perspectives* (2nd ed., pp. 125–152). Mahwah, NJ: Erlbaum.

Schunk, D. (2003). Self-efficacy for reading and writing: Influence of modeling, goal setting, and self-evaluation. *Reading and Writing Quarterly, 19*, 159–172.

Schunk, D., & Hanson, A. (1985). Peer models: Influence on children's self-efficacy and achievement. *Journal of Educational Psychology, 77*, 313–322.

Schunk, D., & Hanson, A. R. (1989). Self-modeling and children's cognitive skill learning. *Journal of Educational Psychology, 81*, 155–163.

Schunk, D., & Zimmerman, B. (1997). Social origins of self-regulatory competence. *Educational Psychologist, 32*, 195–208.

Schunk, D., & Zimmerman, B. (2007). Influencing children's self-efficacy and self-regulation of reading and writing through modeling. *Reading and Writing Quarterly, 23*, 7–25.

Schunk, D. H. (1981). Modeling and attributional feedback effects on children's achievement: A self-efficacy analysis. *Journal of Educational Psychology, 74*, 93–105.

Schunk, D. H. (1987). Peer models and children's behavioral change. *Review of Educational Research, 57*, 149–174.

Schunk, D. H. (2000). *Learning theories* (3rd ed.). Upper Saddle River, NJ: Merrill/Prentice Hall.

Schunk, D. H. (2004). *Learning theories: An educational perspective* (4th ed.), Upper Saddle River, NJ: Pearson.

Schunk, D. H. (2008). Attributions as motivators of self-regulated learning. In D. H. Schunk & B. J. Zimmerman (Eds.), *Motivation and self-regulated learning: Theory, research, and applications* (pp. 245–266). New York: Erlbaum.

Schunk, D. H., & Meece, J. L. (2006). Self-efficacy development in adolescence. In F. Pajares & T. Urdan (Eds.), *Self-efficacy beliefs of adolescents* (pp. 71–96). Greenwich, CT: Information Age.

Schunk, D. H., & Miller, S. D. (2002). Self-efficacy and adolescents' motivation. In F. Pajares & T. Urdan (Eds.), *Academic motivation of adolescents* (pp. 29–52). Greenwich, CT: Information Age.

Schunk, D. H., & Pajares, F. (2002). The development of academic self-efficacy. In A. Wigfield & J. Eccles (Eds.), *Development of achievement motivation* (pp. 15–31). San Diego: Academic Press.

Schunk, D. H., & Pajares, F. (2009). Self-efficacy theory. In K. R. Wentzel, & A. Wigfield (Eds.), *Handbook of motivation at school* (pp. 35–53). New York: Routledge/Taylor & Francis Group.

Schussler, D. L. (2009). Beyond content: How teachers manage classrooms to facilitate intellectual engagement for disengaged students. *Theory Into Practice, 48*, 114–121.

Schwalbe, M. L., & Staples, C. L. (1991). Gender differences in sources of self-esteem. *Social Psychology Quarterly, 54*, 158–168.

Schweinle, A., Turner, J. C., & Meyer, D. K. (2008). Understanding young adolescents' optimal experiences in academic settings. *The Journal of Experimental Education, 77*(2), 125–143.

Sciutto, M. J., & Eisenberg, M. (2007). Evaluating the evidence for and against the overdiagnosis of ADHD. *Journal of Attention Disorders, 11*(2), 106–113.

Scott, L. (2007). The child who stutters at school: Notes to the teacher. Retrieved September 21, 2007, from http://www.stutteringhelp.org/Portals/english/0042NT.pdf.

Scruggs, T. E., & Mastropieri, M. A. (1994). Successful mainstreaming in elementary science classes: A qualitative study of three reputational cases. *American Educational Research Journal, 31*, 785–811.

Sedek, G., & McIntosh, D. (1998). Intellectual helplessness: Domain specificity, teaching styles, and school achievement. In M. Kofta, G. Weary, & G. Sedek (Eds.), *Personal control in action: Cognitive and motivational mechanisms* (pp. 419–443). New York: Plenum Press.

Seginer, R. (2006). Parents' educational involvement: A developmental ecological perspective. *Parenting: Science and Practice, 6*, 1–48.

Seijts, G. H., & Latham, G. P. (2001). The effect of learning, outcome, and proximal goals on a moderately complex task. *Journal of Organizational Behavior, 22*, 291–302.

Sejnowski, T. J., & Churchland, P. S. (1989). Brain and cognition. In M. I. Posner (Ed.), *Foundations of cognitive science* (pp. 301–358). Cambridge, MA: MIT Press.

Seligman, M., & Maier, S. (1967). Failure to escape traumatic shock. *Journal of Experimental Psychology, 74*, 1–9.

Seligman, M. E. P. (1994). *What you can change and what you can't.* New York: Alfred A. Knopf.

Selman, R. L. (1971a). Conceptual role-taking development in early childhood. *Proceedings of the Annual Convention of the American Psychological Association*, Vol. 6, pp. 155–156.

Selman, R. L. (1971b). The relation of role taking to the development of moral judgment in children. *Child Development, 42*, 79–91.

Semrud-Clikeman, M. (2005). Neuropsychological aspects for evaluating learning disabilities. *Journal of Learning Disabilities, 38*, 563–568.

Serna, L., Lambros, K. M., Nielsen, E., & Forness, S. R. (2002). Head Start children at risk for emotional or behavioral disorders: Behavioral profiles and clinical implications of a primary prevention program. *Behavioral Disorders, 27,* 137–141.

Serna, L., Nielsen, E., Mattern, N., & Forness, S. R. (2003). Primary mental health prevention in Head Start classrooms: Partial replication with teachers as intervenors. *Behavioral Disorders, 23,* 124–129.

Serrano, R., & Howard, E. R. (2003). Maintaining Spanish proficiency in the United States. In L. Sayahi (Ed.), *Selected proceedings of the first workshop on Spanish sociolinguistics* (pp. 77–88). Somerville, MA: Cascadilla Proceedings Project.

Shabani, D. B., Katz, R. C., Wilder, D. A., Beauchamp, K., Taylor, C. R., & Fischer, K. J. (2002). Increasing social initiations in children with autism: Effects of a tactile prompt. *Journal of Applied Behavior Analysis, 35,* 79–83.

Shaffer, D. R. (2000). *Social and personality development* (4th ed.). Belmont, CA: Wadsworth.

Shatz, M. (1994). *A toddler's life: Becoming a person.* New York: Oxford University Press.

Shavelson, R. J., & Baxter, G. P. (1991). Performance assessment in science. *Applied Measurement in Education, 4,* 347–362.

Shavelson, R. J., Berliner, D. C., Ravitch, M. M., & Loeding, D. (1974). Effects of position and type of question on learning from prose material: Interaction of treatments with individual differences. *Journal of Educational Psychology, 66,* 40–48.

Shaw, T. J. (1983). The effect of a process-oriented science curriculum upon problem-solving ability. *Science Education, 67,* 615–623.

Shaywitz, B. A., Shaywitz, S. E., Blachman, B. A., et al. (2004). Development of left occipitotemporal systems for skilled reading in children after a phonologically-based intervention. *Biological Psychiatry, 55*(9), 926–933.

Shaywitz, B. A., Shaywitz, S. E., Pugh, K. R., et al. (2002). Disruption of posterior brain systems for reading in children with developmental dyslexia. *Biological Psychiatry, 52*(2), 101–110.

Shek, D. T. L. (2005). Paternal and maternal influences on the psychological well-being, substance abuse, and delinquency of Chinese adolescents experiencing economic disadvantage. *Journal of Clinical Psychology, 61*(3), 219–234.

Shen, J., Zhang, N., Zhang, C., Calderella, P., Richardson, M. J., & Shatzer, R. H. (2009). Chinese elementary school teachers' perceptions of students' classroom behaviour problems. *Educational Psychology, 29*(2), 187–201.

Shepard, L. A. (2000). The role of assessment in a learning culture. *Educational Researcher, 29*(7), 4–14.

Shepard, L. A. (2006). Classroom assessment. In R. L. Brennan (Ed.), *Educational measurement* (4th ed.). Westport, CT: American Council on Education and Praeger Publishers.

Sheridan, S. M., Hungelmann, A., & Maughan, D. P. (1999). A contextualized framework for social skills assessment, intervention, and generalization. *School Psychology Review, 28,* 84–103.

Shernoff, D. J., & Csikszentmihalyi, M. (2009). Flow in schools. Cultivating engaged learners and optimal learning environments. In R. Gilman, E. S. Huebner, & M. J. Furlong (Eds.), *Handbook of positive psychology in schools* (pp. 131–146). New York: Routledge/Taylor & Francis.

Sherwin, B. B., & Tulandi, T. (1996). Add-back estrogen reverses cognitive deficits induced by a gonadotropin-releasing-hormone agonist in women with leiomyomata uteri. *Journal of Clinical Endocrinology and Metabolism, 81,* 2545–2549.

Shields, C. (1995). A comparison study of student attitudes and perceptions in homogeneous and heterogeneous classrooms. *Roeper Review, 17,* 234–238.

Shimamura, A. P. (1994). The neuropsychology of metacognition. In J. Metcalfe & A. P. Shimamura (Eds.), *Metacognition: Knowing about knowing* (pp. 253–276). Cambridge, MA: MIT Press.

Shimamura, A. P. (1995). Memory and frontal lobe function. In M. S. Gazzaniga (Ed.), *The cognitive neurosciences* (pp. 803–813). Cambridge, MA: MIT Press.

Shochet, L. M., Dadds, M. R., Ham, D., & Montague, R. (2006). School connectedness is an underemphasized parameter in adolescent mental health: Results of a community prediction study. *Journal of Clinical Child and Adolescent Psychology, 35*(2), 170–179.

Shore, R. (1997). *Rethinking the brain: New insights into early development.* New York: Families and Work Institute.

Sieber, J., O'Neil, H., & Tobias, S. (1977). *Anxiety, learning, and instruction.* Hillsdale, NJ: Erlbaum.

Sieber, R. T. (1979). Classmates as workmates: Informal peer activity in the elementary school. *Anthropology and Education Quarterly, 10,* 207–235.

Siegler, R. S., & Alibali, M. W. (2005). *Children's thinking* (4th ed.). Upper Saddle River, NJ: Pearson/Prentice Hall.

Sierens, E., Vansteenkiste, M., Goossens, L., Soenens, B., & Dochy, F. (2009). The synergistic relationship of perceived autonomy support and structure in the prediction of self-regulated learning. *British Journal of Educational Psychology, 79,* 57–68.

Silk, J. A., Steinberg, L., & Morris, A. S. (2003). Adolescents' emotion regulation in daily life: Links to depressive symptoms and problem behavior. *Child Development, 74,* 1869–1880.

Silver, E. A., Ghousseini, H., Gosen, D., Charalambous, C., & Strawhun, B. (2005). Moving from rhetoric to praxis: Issues faced by teachers in having students consider multiple solutions for problems in the mathematics classroom. *Journal of Mathematical Behavior, 24,* 287–301.

Silverman, I., Choi, J., & Peters, M. (2007). The hunter-gatherer theory of sex differences in spatial abilities: Data from 40 countries. *Archives of Sexual Behavior, 36,* 261–268.

Silvia, P. J. (2005). What is interesting? Exploring the appraisal structure of interest. *Emotion, 5,* 89–102.

Silvia, P. J. (2006). *Exploring the psychology of interest.* New York: Oxford University Press.

Simmon, R. G. (1987). Self-esteem in adolescence. In T. Honess & K. Yardley (Eds.), *Self and identity: Perspectives across the lifespan.* New York: Routledge & Kegan Paul.

Simons-Morton, B., & Chen, R. (2009). Peer and parent influences on school engagement among early adolescents. *Youth and Society, 41*(1), 3–25.

Simonton, D. K. (2000). Creativity: Cognitive, personal, developmental, and social aspects. *American Psychologist, 55,* 151–158.

Simos, P. G., Fletcher, J. M., Sarkari, S., Billingsley, R. L., Denton, C., & Papanicolaou, A. C. (2007). Altering the brain circuits for reading through intervention: A magnetic source imaging study. *Neuropsychology, 21*(4), 485–496.

Simos, P. G., Pugh, K., Menci, E., et al. (2009). Temporal course of word recognition in skilled readers: A magnetoencephalography study. *Behavioural Brain Research, 197*(1), 45–54.

Simpkins, S. D., Davis-Kean, P. E., & Eccles, J. S. (2006). Math and science motivation: A longitudinal examination of the links between choice and beliefs. *Developmental Psychology, 42,* 70–83.

Singer, F. M. (2007). Beyond conceptual change: Using representations to integrate domain-specific structural models in learning mathematics. *Mind, Brain, and Education, 1*(2), 84–97.

Singh, K., Bickley, P., Trivette, P., Keith, T. Z., Keith, P. B., & Anderson, E. (1995). The effects of four components of parental involvement on eighth-grade student achievement: Structural analysis of NELS-88 data. *School Psychology Review, 24*, 299–317.

Singley, M. K., & Anderson, J. R. (1989). *The transfer of cognitive skill.* Cambridge, MA: Harvard University Press.

Siok, W. T., Perfetti, C. A., Jin, Z., & Tan, L. H. (2004). Biological abnormality of impaired reading is constrained by culture. *Nature, 431*, 71–76.

Skiba, R., & Peterson, R. (1999). The dark side of zero tolerance: Can punishment lead to safe schools? *Phi Delta Kappan, 80*, 372–379.

Skinner, B. F. (1953). *Science and human behavior.* New York: Macmillan.

Skinner, B. F. (1954). The science of learning and the art of teaching. *Harvard Education Review, 14*, 86–97.

Skinner, B. F. (1957). *Verbal behavior.* Upper Saddle River, NJ: Prentice–Hall.

Skinner, E. A., & Belmont, M. J. (1993). Motivation in the classroom: Reciprocal effects of teacher behavior and student engagement across the school year. *Journal of Educational Psychology, 85*(4), 571–581.

Skoumios, M., & Hatzinikita, V. (2008). Development of pupils' competences to identify obstacles during research-based science teaching. *International Journal of Learning, 14*(9), 237–247.

Slakter, M. J., Koehler, R. A., & Hampton, S. H. (1970). Grade level, sex, and selected aspects of test-wiseness. *Journal of Educational Measurement, 7*, 119–122.

Slavin, R. E. (1978). Student teams and achievement divisions. *Journal of Research and Development in Education, 12*, 39–49.

Slavin, R. E. (1980). Cooperative learning. *Review of Educational Research, 50*(2), 315–342.

Slavin, R. E. (1986). *Using student team learning* (3rd ed.). Baltimore: Johns Hopkins University Center for Research on Elementary and Middle Schools.

Slavin, R. E. (1987a). Ability grouping and student achievement in elementary schools: A best-evidence synthesis. *Review of Educational Research, 57*(3), 293–336.

Slavin, R. E. (1987b). Grouping for instruction in elementary school. *Educational Psychologist, 22*(2), 109–127.

Slavin, R. E. (1988). Cooperative learning and student achievement. *Educational Leadership, 46*(2), 31–33.

Slavin, R. E. (1990). Achievement effects of ability grouping in secondary schools: A best-evidence synthesis. *Review of Educational Research, 60*, 471–499.

Slavin, R. E. (1990). Mastery learning re-reconsidered. *Review of Educational Research, 60*(2), 300–302.

Slavin, R. E. (1991). Synthesis of research on cooperative learning. *Educational Leadership, 48*(5), 71–82.

Slavin, R. E., Lake, C., Chambers, B., Cheung, A., & Davis, S. (2009). Effective reading programs for the elementary grades: A best-evidence synthesis. *Review of Educational Research, 79*(4), 1391–1466.

Slavin, R. E., Leavey, M., & Madden, N. A. (1984). Combining cooperative learning and individualized instruction: Effects on student mathematics achievement, attitudes and behaviors. *Elementary School Journal, 84*, 409–422.

Slavin, R. E., & Madden, N. (1989). What works for students at risk: A research synthesis. *Educational Leadership, 46*(5), 4–13.

Slavin, R. E., Madden, N. A., & Stevens, R. J. (1990). Cooperative learning models for the three R's. *Educational Leadership, 47*(4), 22–28.

Smith, D. D. (2006). *Introduction to special education: Teaching in an age of opportunity* (5th ed.). Boston: Allyn & Bacon.

Smith, K., Johnson, D. W., & Johnson, R. (1982). Effects of cooperative and individualistic instruction on the achievement of handicapped, regular, and gifted students. *Journal of Social Psychology, 116*, 277–283.

Smith, L. (1993). *Necessary knowledge: Piagetian perspectives on constructivism.* Hillsdale, NJ: Erlbaum.

Smith, L. (2002). Piaget's model. In U. Goswami (Ed.), *Blackwell handbook of childhood cognitive development* (pp. 515–537). Malden, MA: Blackwell.

Smith, N. B., & Robinson, H. A. (1980). *Reading instruction for today's children.* New York: Prentice Hall.

Smolucha, L., & Smolucha, F. (1998). The social origins of mind: Post-Piagetian perspectives on pretend play. In O. N. S. B. Saracho (Ed.), *Multiple perspectives on play in early childhood education* (pp. 34–58). SUNY series *Early childhood education: Inquiries and insights.* Albany, NY: State University of New York Press.

Snow, C. E. (1986). Conversations with children. In P. Fletcher & M. Garman (Eds.), *Language acquisition: Studies in first language development* (pp. 69–89). Cambridge, UK: Cambridge University Press.

Snow, C. E., & Goldfield, B. A. (1983). Turn the page please: Situation-specific language learning. *Journal of Child Language, 10*, 551–569.

Snow, C. E., Tabors, P. O., & Dickinson, D. K. (2001). Language development in the preschool years. In D. K. Dickinson & P. O. Tabors (Eds.), *Beginning literacy with language* (pp. 1–25). Baltimore: Brookes.

Snyder, J., Brooker, M., Patrick, M., Snyder, A., Schrepferman, L., & Stoolmiller, M. (2003). Observed peer victimization during early elementary school: Continuity, growth, and relation to risk for child antisocial and depressive behavior *Child Development, 74*(6), 1881–1898. doi:10.1046/j.1467-8624.2003.00644.x

Soenens, B., & Vansteenkiste, M. (2005). Antecedents and outcomes of self-determination in three life domains: The role of parents' and teachers' autonomy support. *Journal of Youth and Adolescence, 34*, 589–604.

Solomon, D., & Kendall, A. J. (1976). Individual characteristics and children's performance in "open" and "traditional" classroom settings. *Journal of Educational Psychology, 65*, 613–625.

Solomon, D., Watson, M. S., & Battistich, V. A. (2001). Teaching and schooling effects on moral/prosocial development. In V. Richardson (Ed.), *Handbook of research on teaching* (4th ed., pp. 566–603). Washington, DC: American Educational Research Association.

Solso, R. L. (2001). Brain activities in a skilled versus a novice artist: An fMRI study. *Leonardo, 34*(1), 31–34. doi:10.1162/00240940130052479

Songer, N. B., Kelcey, B., & Gotwals, A. W. (2009). How and when does complex reasoning occur? Empirically driven development of a learning progression focused on complex reasoning about biodiversity. *Journal of Research in Science Teaching, 46*(6), 610–613.

Soodak, L. C. (2003). Classroom management in inclusive settings. *Theory Into Practice, 42*(4), 327–333.

Sowell, E. R., Leow, A. D., Bookheimer, S. Y., et al. (2010). Differentiating prenatal exposure to methamphetamine and alcohol versus alcohol and not methamphetamine using tensor-based brain morphometry and discriminant analysis. *The Journal of Neuroscience, 30*(11), 3876–3885.

Sparrow, S. S., Balla, D. A., & Cicchetti, D. V. (1984). *Vineland Adaptive Behavior Scales*. Circle Pines, MN: American Guidance Service.

Spearman, C. E. (1904). General intelligence objectively determined and measured. *American Journal of Psychology, 15*, 201–293.

Spearman, C. E. (1927). *The nature of "intelligence" and the principles of cognition* (2nd ed.). London: Macmillan.

Speicher, B. (1994). Family patterns of moral judgment during adolescence and early adulthood. *Developmental Psychology, 30*, 624–632.

Spelke, E. S., & Newport, E. L. (1998). Nativism, empiricism, and the development of knowledge. In W. Damon (Series Ed.) & D. Kuhn & R. S. Siegler (Vol. Eds.), *Handbook of child psychology; Vol. 2. Cognition, perception, and language* (5th ed., pp. 275–340). New York: Wiley.

Spencer, S. J., Steele, C. M., & Quinn, D. M. (1999). Stereotype threat and women's math performance. *Journal of Experimental Social Psychology, 35*, 4–28.

Sperling, G. (1960). The information available in brief visual presentations. *Psychological Monographs, 74* (11, Whole No. 498).

Spinath, B., & Spinath, F. M. (2005). Longitudinal analysis of the link between learning motivation and competence beliefs among elementary school children. *Learning and Instruction, 15*, 87–102.

Spiro, R., Feltovich, P. J., Jacobsen, M. J., & Coulson, R. L. (1991). Cognitive flexibility, constructivism, and hypertext: Random access instruction for advanced knowledge acquisition in ill-structured domains. *Educational Technology, 31*(5), 24–33.

Spoth, R. L., Clair, S., Shin, C., & Redmond, C. (2006). Long-term effects of universal preventative interventions on methamphetamine use among adolescents. *Archives of Pediatric and Adolescent Medicine, 160*, 876–882.

Spronken-Smith, R. A., & Harland, A. (2009). Learning to teach with problem-based learning. *Active Learning in Higher Education, 10*, 138–153.

Squibb, B., & Dietz, S. (2000). *Learning activities for infants and toddlers: An easy guide for everyday use*. Washington, DC: Children's Resources International.

Squire, L. R., & Alvarez, P. (1998). Retrograde amnesia and memory consolidation: A neurobiological perspective. In L. R. Squire & S. M. Kosslyn (Eds.), *Findings and current opinion in cognitive neuroscience* (pp. 75–84). Cambridge, MA: MIT Press.

Stahl, S. (1998). Teaching children with reading problems to decode: Phonics and "not-phonics" instruction. *Reading and Writing Quarterly: Overcoming Learning Difficulties, 14*(2), 165–188.

Stainback, S., & Stainback, W. (1996). *Inclusion: A guide for educators*. Baltimore: Paul H. Brookes.

Staley, J. K., Krishnan-Sarin, S., Zoghbi, S., et al. (2001). Sex differences in [123I]b-CIT SPECT measures of dopamine and serotonin transporter availability in healthy smokers and nonsmokers. *Synapse, 41*, 275–284.

Stanovich, K. (2003). Understanding the styles of science in the study of reading. *Scientific Studies of Reading, 7*, 105–126.

Stanovich, K. E. (1986). Matthew effects in reading: Some consequences of individual differences in the acquisition of literacy. *Reading Research Quarterly, 21*(4), 360–406.

Stanovich, K. E. (1988). Explaining the differences between the dyslexic and the garden-variety poor reader: The phonological-core variable-difference model. *Journal of Learning Disabilities, 21*(10), 590–604, 612.

Stanovich, K. E. (1990). Concepts in developmental theories of reading skill: Cognitive resources, automaticity, and modularity. *Developmental Review, 10*, 72–100.

Stanovich, K. E. (1991a). Conceptual and empirical problems with discrepancy definitions of reading disability. *Learning Disability Quarterly, 14*, 269–280.

Stanovich, K. E. (1991b). Discrepancy definitions of reading disability: Has intelligence led us astray? *Reading Research Quarterly, 26*(1), 7–29.

Stanovich, K. E. (1993). A model for studies of reading disability. *Developmental Review, 13*, 225–245.

Stanovich, K. E., & Siegel, L. S. (1994). Phenotypic performance profile of children with reading disabilities: A regression-based test of the phonological-core variable-difference model. *Journal of Educational Psychology, 86*(1), 24–53.

Stanovich, K. E., & West, R. E. (2000). Individual differences in reasoning: Implications for the rationality debate? *Behavior and Brain Sciences, 23*, 646–665.

Star, J., & Rittle-Johnson, B. (2007). Developing flexible knowledge. The case of equation solving. *Learning and Instruction*. doi:10.1016/j.learninstruc.2007.09.018

Star, J. R., & Seifert, C. (2006). The development of flexibility in equation solving. *Contemporary Educational Psychology, 31*, 280–300.

Stecher, B., Barron, S., Chun, T., & Ross, K. (2000). *The effects of the Washington state education reform on schools and classrooms* (CSE Technical Report 525). Los Angeles: National Center for Research on Evaluation, Standards, and Student Testing.

Steele, C. M. (1997). A threat is in the air: How stereotypes shape intellectual identity and performance. *American Psychologist, 52*, 613–629.

Steele, C. M., & Aronson, J. (1998). Stereotype threat and the intellectual test performance of African Americans. *Journal of Personality and Social Psychology, 69*, 797–811.

Steele, F. I. (1973). *Physical settings and organization development*. Reading, MA: Addison-Wesley.

Steffens, M. C., Jelenec, P., & Noack, P. (2010). On the leaking math pipeline: Comparing implicit math-gender stereotypes and math withdrawal in female and male children and adolescents. *Journal of Educational Psychology*. doi:10.037/a0019920

Steffy, B. E., Wolfe, M. P., Pasch, S. H., & Enz, B. J. (2000). *Life cycle of the career teacher*. Thousand Oaks, CA: Corwin Press.

Stein, M. A., Szumowski, E., Blondis, T. A., & Roizen, N. J. (1995). Adaptive skills dysfunction in ADD and ADHD children. *Journal of Child Psychology and Psychiatry, 36*, 663–670.

Steinberg, L. S. (1996). *Beyond the classroom: Why school reform has failed and what parents need to do*. New York: Simon & Schuster.

Steinberg, L., & Morris, A. S. (2001). Adolescent development. *Annual Review of Psychology, 52*, 83–110.

Steiner, H. H., & Carr, M. (2003). Cognitive development in gifted children: Toward a more precise understanding of emerging differences in intelligence. *Educational Psychology Review, 15*(3), 215–246.

Steinmetz, H., Herzog, A., Schlaug, G., Huang, Y., & Lanke, R. (1995). Brain (a)symmetry in monozygotic twins. *Cerebral Cortex, 5*, 296–300.

Stemler, S. E., Grigorenko, E. L., Jarvin, L., & Sternberg, R. J. (2006). Using the theory of successful intelligence as a basis for augmenting AP exams in psychology and statistics. *Contemporary Educational Psychology, 31*, 344–376.

Stemler, S. E., Sternberg, R. J., Grigorenko, E. L., Jarvin, L., & Sharpes, K. (2009). Using the theory of successful intelligence as a framework for developing assessments in AP physics. *Contemporary Educational Psychology, 34*, 195–209.

Stephanou, G. (2008). Students' value beliefs, performance expectations, and school performance: The effect of school subject and gender. *Hellenic Journal of Psychology, 5*(3), 231–257.

Sternberg, R. J. (Ed.). (1990). *Wisdom: Its nature, origins, and development.* Cambridge, UK: Cambridge University Press.

Sternberg, R. J. (1996a). Myths, countermyths, and truths about intelligence. *Educational Researcher, 25*(2), 11–16.

Sternberg, R. J. (1996b). *Successful intelligence: How practical and creative intelligence determine success in life.* New York: Simon & Schuster.

Sternberg, R. J. (1997). What does it mean to be smart? *Educational Leadership, 54*(6), 20–24.

Sternberg, R. J. (1998). Principles of teaching for successful intelligence. *Educational Psychologist, 33*(2–3), 65–72.

Sternberg, R. J. (Ed.). (1999a). *Handbook of creativity.* Cambridge, UK: Cambridge University Press.

Sternberg, R. J. (1999b). The theory of successful intelligence. *Review of General Psychology, 3*(4), 292–316.

Sternberg, R. J. (2000). Identifying and developing creative giftedness. *Roeper Review, 23,* 60–64.

Sternberg, R. J. (2002). Individual differences in cognitive development. In U. Goswami (Ed.), *Blackwell handbook of childhood cognitive development* (pp. 600–619). Malden, MA: Blackwell.

Sternberg, R. J. (2003a). Contemporary theories of intelligence. In W. M. Reynolds & G. E. Miller (Eds.), *Handbook of psychology: Educational psychology* (Vol. 7, pp. 23–45). Hoboken, NJ: Wiley.

Sternberg, R. J. (2003b). Giftedness according to the theory of successful intelligence. In N. Colangelo & G. A. Davis (Eds.), *Handbook of gifted education* (pp. 55–60). Boston: Allyn & Bacon.

Sternberg, R. J. (2004). Culture and intelligence. *American Psychologist, 59*(5), 325–338.

Sternberg, R. J. (2005). Intelligence, race, and genetics. *American Psychologist, 60*(1), 46–59.

Sternberg, R. J. (2006a). Creating a vision of creativity: The first 25 years. *Psychology of Aesthetics, Creativity, and the Arts, S*(1), 2–12.

Sternberg, R. J. (2006b). How can we simultaneously enhance both academic excellence and diversity? *College and University, 81*(1), 17–23.

Sternberg, R. J. (2006c). The nature of creativity. *Creativity Research Journal, 18*(1), 87–98.

Sternberg, R. J. (2007). Who are the bright children? The cultural context of being and acting intelligent. *Educational Researcher, 36*(3), 148–155.

Sternberg, R. J. (2008). Wisdom, intelligence and creativity synthesized: A model of giftedness. In T. Balchin, B. J. Hymer, and D. J. Matthews (Eds.), *The Routledge-Falmer international companion to gifted education.* London: Routledge-Falmer.

Sternberg, R. J. (2010a). WICS: A new model for cognitive education. *Journal of Cognitive Education and Psychology, 9*(1), 36–47.

Sternberg, R. J. (2010b). Assessment of gifted students for identification purposes: New techniques for a new millennium. *Learning and Individual Differences, 20,* 327–336.

Sternberg, R. J., & Coffin, L. A. (2010). Kaleidoscope: Admitting and developing new leaders for a changing world. *New England Journal of Higher Education, 24*(3), 12–13.

Sternberg, R. J., Conway, B. E., Ketron, J. L., & Bernstein, M. (1981). People's conceptions of intelligence. *Journal of Personality and Social Psychology, 41,* 37–55.

Sternberg, R. J., Ferrari, M., Clinkenbeard, P., & Grigorenko, E. L. (1996). Identification, instruction, and assessment of gifted children: A construct validation of a triarchic model. *Gifted Child Quarterly, 40,* 129–137.

Sternberg, R. J., Forsythe, G. B., Hedlund, J., et al. (2000). *Practical intelligence in everyday life.* Cambridge, UK: Cambridge University Press.

Sternberg, R. J., & Grigorenko, E. L. (2003). Teaching for successful intelligence: Principles, procedures, and practices. *Journal for the Education of the Gifted, 27*(2–3), 207–228.

Sternberg, R. J., & Grigorenko, E. L. (2004). Successful intelligence in the classroom. *Theory Into Practice, 43,* 274–280.

Sternberg, R. J., Grigorenko, E. L., Ferrari, M., & Clinkenbeard, P. (1999). A triarchic analysis of an aptitude-treatment interaction. *European Journal of Psychological Assessment, 15*(1), 1–11.

Sternberg, R. J., Grigorenko, E. L., & Zhang, L. (2008). Styles of learning and thinking matter in instruction and assessment. *Perspectives on Psychological Science, 3*(6), 486–506.

Sternberg, R. J., & Kaufman, J. C. (1998). Human abilities. *Annual Review of Psychology, 49,* 479–502.

Sternberg, R. J., & Lubart, T. I. (1995). *Defying the crowd: Cultivating creativity in a culture of conformity.* New York: Free Press.

Sternberg, R. J., & Lubart, T. I. (1999). Investing in creativity. *American Psychologist, 51*(7), 677–688.

Sternberg, R. J., & O'Hara, L. A. (1999). Creativity and intelligence. In R. J. Sternberg (Ed.), *Handbook of creativity* (pp. 251–272). Cambridge, UK: Cambridge University Press.

Sternberg, R. J., Torff, B., & Grigorenko, E. L. (1998a). Teaching for successful intelligence raises school achievement. *Phi Delta Kappan, 79,* 667–669.

Sternberg, R. J., Torff, B., & Grigorenko, E. L. (1998b). Teaching triarchically improves school achievement. *Journal of Educational Psychology, 90,* 1–11.

Sternberg, R. J., & Williams, W. M. (1996). *How to develop student creativity.* Alexandria, VA: Association for Supervision and Curriculum Development.

Stetsenko, A., Little, T. D., Gordeeva, T., Granshof, M., & Oettingen, G. (2000). Gender effects in children's beliefs about school performance: A cross-cultural study. *Child Development, 71,* 517–527.

Stevens, R. J., Madden, N. A., Slavin, R. E., & Farnish, A. M. (1987). Cooperative integrated reading and composition: Two field experiments. *Reading Research Quarterly, 22,* 433–454.

Stevens, T., Olivárez, A., Jr., & Hamman, D. (2006). The role of cognition, motivation, and emotion in explaining the mathematics achievement gap between Hispanic and White students. *Hispanic Journal of Behavior Sciences, 28,* 161–186.

Stevens, T., Olivárez, A., Lan, W. Y., Tallent-Runnels, M. K. (2004). Role of mathematics self-efficacy and motivation in mathematics performance across ethnicity. *Journal of Educational Research, 97*(4), 208–221.

Stevenson, D. L., & Baker, D. P. (1987). The family–school relation and the child's school performance. *Child Development, 58,* 1348–1357.

Stevenson, H. W., Chen, C., & Uttal, D. H. (1990). Beliefs and achievement: A study of black, white, and Hispanic children. *Child Development, 61,* 508–523.

Stewart, S. C., Evans, W. H., & Kaczynski, D. J. (1997). Setting the stage for success: Assessing the instructional environment. *Preventing School Failure, 41,* 53–56.

Stiggins, R., & Chappuis, J. (2008). Enhancing student learning [Electronic version]. *District Administration, 44*(1). Retrieved June 24, 2008, from http://www.districtadministration.com/ViewArticle.aspx?articleid=1362

Stiggins, R., Rubel, E., & Quellmalz, E. (1986). *Measuring thinking skills in the classroom.* Washington, DC: National Education Association.

Stiles, J., Bates, E. A., Thal, D., Trauner, D. A., & Reilly, J. (2002). Linguistic and spatial cognitive development in children with pre- and perinatal focal brain injury: A ten-year overview from the San Diego Longitudinal Project. In M. H. Johnson, Y. Munakata, & R. O. Gilmore (Eds.), *Brain development and cognition: A reader* (2nd ed., pp. 272–291). Oxford, UK: Blackwell.

Stiles, J., & Thal, D. (1993). Linguistic and spatial cognitive development following early focal brain injury: Patterns of deficit and recovery. In M. H. Johnson (Ed.), *Brain development and cognition: A reader* (pp. 643–664). Oxford, UK: Blackwell.

Stipek, D. (1984). The development of achievement motivation. In R. Ames & C. Ames (Eds.), *Research on motivation in education, Vol. 1* (pp. 145–174). Orlando: Academic Press.

Stipek, D. (2002). *Motivation to learn: Integrating theory and practice* (4th ed.). Boston: Allyn & Bacon.

Stipek, D., de la Sota, A., & Weishaupt, L. (1999). Life lessons: An embedded classroom approach to preventing high-risk behaviors among preadolescents. *Elementary School Journal, 99*(5), 433–452.

Stipek, D., & Tannatt, L. (1984). Children's judgments of their own and their peers' academic competence. *Journal of Educational Psychology, 76,* 75–84.

Stipek, D. J. (1996). Motivation and instruction. In D. C. Berliner & R. C. Calfee (Eds.), *Handbook of educational psychology* (pp. 85–113). New York: Simon & Schuster Macmillan.

Stipek, D. J., & Daniels, D. H. (1990). Children's use of dispositional attributions in predicting the performance and behavior of classmates. *Journal of Applied Developmental Psychology, 11,* 13–28.

Stone, L. B., Uhrlass, D. J., & Gibb, B. E. (2010). Co-rumination and lifetime history of depressive disorders in children. *Journal of Clinical Child and Adolescent Psychology, 39*(4), 597–602.

Stormont, M., Stebbins, M. S., & Holliday, G. (2001). Characteristics and educational support needs of underrepresented gifted adolescents. *Psychology in the Schools, 38,* 413–423.

Strain, P. S., & Danko, C. D. (1995). Caregivers' encouragement of positive interaction between preschoolers with autism and their siblings. *Journal of Emotional and Behavioral Disorders, 3*(1), 2–12.

Streitmatter, J. L. (1989). Identity development and academic achievement in early adolescence. *Journal of Early Adolescence, 9,* 99–111.

Struyven, K., Dochy, F., & Janssens, S. (2008). The effects of hands-on experience on students' preferences for assessment methods. *Journal of Teacher Education, 59*(1), 69–88.

Sullivan, M. A., & O'Leary, S. G. (1990). Maintenance following reward and cost token programs. *Behavior Therapy, 21,* 139–149.

Sullivan, T. N., Farrell, A. D., & Kliewer, W. (2006). Peer victimization in early adolescence: Association between physical and relational victimization and drug use, aggression, and delinquent behaviors among urban middle school students. *Development and Psychopathology, 18,* 119–137.

Sun, Y., & Li, Y. (2002). Children's well-being during parents' marital disruption process: A pooled time-series analysis. *Journal of Marriage and Family, 64*(2), 472–488.

Sun, Y., & Li, Y. (2009). Postdivorce family stability and changes in adolescents' academic performance. *Journal of Family Issues, 30*(11), 1527–1555.

Sunstein, C. R. (2005). Moral heuristics. *Behavioral and Brain Sciences, 28,* 531–573.

Supovitz, J. A., & Turner, H. M. (2000). The effects of professional development on science teaching practices and classroom culture. *Journal of Research in Science Teaching, 37*(9), 963–980.

Sutton, R. E., Mudrey-Camino, R., & Knight, C. C. (2009). Teachers' emotion regulation and classroom management. *Theory Into Practice, 48,* 130–137.

Suzuki, L. A., & Valencia, R. R. (1997). Race-ethnicity and measured intelligence. *American Psychologist, 52*(10), 1103–1114.

Swan, A. (1993). Helping children who stutter: What teachers need to know. *Childhood Education, 69*(3), 138–141.

Swanson, J. M., Kraemer, H. C., Hinshaw, S. P., et al. (2001). Clinical relevance of the primary findings of the MTA: Success rates based on severity of ADHD and ODD symptoms at the end of treatment. *Journal of the American Academy of Child and Adolescent Psychiatry, 40,* 1–12.

Swanson, T. C. (2005). Twenty ways to provide structure for children with learning and behavior problems. *Intervention in School and Clinic, 40* (3), 182–187.

Swift, J. N., & Gooding, C. T. (1983). Interaction of wait time feedback and questioning instruction on middle school science teaching. *Journal of Research in Science Teaching, 20,* 721–730.

Swinkels, S. H. N., Dietz, C., Van Daalen, E., Kershof, I. H. G. M., Van Engeland, H., & Buitelaar, J. K. (2006). Screening for autism spectrum disorders in children aged 14 to 15 months. I: The development of the Early Screening of Autistic Traits Questionnaire (ESAT). *Journal of Autism and Developmental Disorders, 36,* 723–732.

Sykes, G. (1996). Reform of and as professional development. *Phi Delta Kappan, 77*(7), 464–467.

Sylvan, L. J., & Christodoulou, J. A. (2010). Understanding the role of neuroscience in brain-based products: A guide for educators and consumers. *Mind, Brain and Education, 4*(1), 1–7.

Sze, K. M., & Wood, J. J. (2008). Enhancing CBT for the treatment of autism spectrum disorders and concurrent anxiety. *Behavioural and Cognitive Psychotherapy, 36,* 403–409.

T

Tach, L. M., & Farkas, G. (2006). Learning-related behaviors, cognitive skills, and ability grouping when schooling begins. *Social Science Research, 35*(4), 1048–1079.

Tackett, J. L. (2010). Toward an externalizing spectrum in *DSM-V*: Incorporating developmental concerns. *Child Development Perspectives, 4*(3), 161–167.

Tafa, E. M. (2002). Corporal punishment: The brutal face of Botswana's authoritarian schools. *Educational Review, 54,* 17–26.

Tager-Flusberg, H. (1997). Putting words together: Morphology and syntax in the preschool years. In J. Berko Gleason (Ed.), *The development of language* (4th ed.). Boston: Allyn & Bacon.

Tajika, H., & Nakatsu, N. (2005). Using a metacognitive stragtegy to solve mathematical problems. *Bulletin of the Aichi University of Education, 54,* 1–9.

Tajika, H., Nakatsu, N., Nozaki, H., Neumann, E., & Maruno, S. (2007). Effects of self-explanation as a metacognitive strategy for solving mathematical word problems. *Japanese Psychological Research, 49*(3), 222–233.

Tam, H., Jarrold, C., Baddeley, A. D., & Sabatos-DeVito. M. (2010). The development of memory maintenance: Children's use of phonological rehearsal and attentional refreshment in working memory tasks. *Journal of Experimental Child Psychology, 107*(3), 306–324.

Tam, V. C. W., & Lam, R. S. Y. (2003). Parenting style of Chinese fathers in Hong Kong: Correlates with children's school-related performance. *International Journal of Adolescent Medicine and Health, 15*(1), 51–62.

Tamis-LeMonda, C. S., Bornstein, M. H., & Baumwell, L. (2001). Maternal responsiveness and children's achievement of language milestones. *Child Development, 72*(3), 748–767.

Tang, Y., Zhang, W., Chen, K., et al. (2006). Arithmetic processing in the brain shaped by cultures. *Proceedings of the National Academy of Science USA, 103*, 10775–10780.

Tangney, J. P. (2001). Constructive and destructive aspects of shame and guilt. In A. C. Bohart & D. J. Stipek (Eds.), *Constructive and destructive behavior: Implications for family, school, and society* (pp. 127–145). Washington, DC: American Psychological Association.

Tarim, K. (2009). The effects of cooperative learning on preschoolers' mathematics problem-solving ability. *Educational Studies in Mathematics, 72*, 325–340.

Tashiro, A., Makino, H., & Gage, F. H. (2007). Experience-specific functional modification of the dentate gyrus through adult neurogenesis: A critical period during an immature stage. *Journal of Neuroscience, 27*(13), 3252–3259.

Taylor, A. Z., & Graham, S. (2007). An examination of the relationship between achievement values and perceptions of barriers among low-SES African American and Latino students. *Journal of Educational Psychology, 99*(1), 52–64.

Taylor, B. A., & Levin, L. (1998). Teaching a student with autism to make verbal initiations: Effects of a tactile prompt. *Journal of Applied Behavior Analysis, 31*, 651–654.

Taylor, O. (1977). Sociolinguistic dimension in standardized testing. In M. Saville-Troike (Ed.), *Georgetown University Roundtable on Language and Linguistics* (pp. 257–266). Washington, DC: Georgetown University Press.

Taylor, R. L., Sternberg, L., & Richards, S. B. (1995). *Exceptional children: Integrating research and teaching* (2nd ed.). San Diego, CA: Singular.

Tebo, M. G. (2000, April). Zero tolerance, zero sense. *American Bar Association Journal.* Retrieved January 19, 2007, from www.abanet.org/journal/apr00/04FZERO.html.

Tella, A., Tella, A., & Adeniyi, O. (2009). Locus of control, interest in schooling, self-efficacy, and academic achievement. *Cypriot Journal of Educational Sciences, 4*(3), 168–182.

Temple, E., et al. (2003). Neural deficits in children with dyslexia ameliorated by behavioral remediation: Evidence from functional MRI. *Proceedings of the National Academy of Sciences USA, 100*, 2860–2865.

Terman, L. M. (1959). *Genetic studies of genius: The gifted group at mid-life.* Stanford, CA: Stanford University Press.

Terwel, J., van Oers, B., van Dijk, I., & van den Eeden, P. (2009). Are representations to be provided or generated in primary mathematics education? Effects on transfer. *Educational Research and Evaluation, 15*(1), 25–44.

Tharp, R. G. (1989). Psychocultural variables and constants: Effects on teaching and learning in schools. *American Psychologist, 44*, 349–359.

Tharp, R. G., & Gallimore, R. (1988). *Rousing minds to life: Teaching, learning, and schooling in social context.* Cambridge, UK: Cambridge University Press.

Thatcher, R. W., North, D. M., & Biver, C. J. (2009), Self-organized criticality and the development of EEG phase reset. *Human Brain Mapping, 30*, 553–574.

Thelen, E., & Smith, L. B. (1998). Dynamic systems theories. In W. Damon (Editor-in-chief) and R. M. Lerner (Vol. Ed.), *Handbook of child psychology: Vol. 1. Theoretical models of human development.* New York: Wiley.

Theriot, M. T., & Dupper, D. R. (2010). Student discipline problems and the transition from elementary to middle school. *Education and Urban Society, 42*(2), 205–222.

Thomas, A., & Chess, S. (1977). *Temperament and development.* New York: Bruner/Mazel.

Thomas, E. L., & Robinson, H. A. (1972). *Improving reading in every class: A sourcebook for teachers.* Boston: Allyn & Bacon.

Thomas, R. M. (2005). *High stakes testing: Coping with collateral damage.* Mahwah, NJ: Erlbaum.

Thomas, R. M., Hotsenpiller, G., & Peterson, D. A. (2006). Acute psychosocial stress reduces cell survival in adult hippocampal neurogenesis without altering proliferation. *Journal of Neuroscience, 27*(11), 2734–2743.

Thompson, J. G. (2002). *First-year teacher's survival kit: Ready-to-use strategies, tools, and activities for meeting the challenges of each school day.* San Francisco: Jossey-Bass.

Thompson, P. M., Giedd, J. N., Woods, R. P., MacDonald, D., Evans, A. C., & Toga, A. W. (2000). Growth patterns in the developing brain detected by using continuum mechanical tensor maps. *Nature, 404*, 190–193.

Thompson, R. A. (1998). Early sociopersonality development. In W. Damon (Series Ed.) & N. Eisenberg (Vol. Ed.), *Handbook of child psychology: Vol. 3. Social, emotional, and personality development* (5th ed.). New York: Wiley.

Thorkildsen, T. A., & Nicholls, J. G. (1998). Fifth-graders' achievement orientations and beliefs: Individual and classroom differences. *Journal of Educational Psychology, 90*, 179–201.

Thorndike, E. L. (1898). Animal intelligence: An experimental study of the associate processes in animals. *Psychological Review Monograph Supplement, 2*, 1–8.

Thorndike, E. L. (1923). The influence of first-year Latin upon the ability to read English. *School and Society, 17*, 165–168.

Thorndike, E. L. (1924). Mental discipline in high school studies. *Journal of Educational Psychology, 15*, 1–22, 83–98.

Thornton, C. A., & Toohey, M. A. (1985). Basic math facts: Guidelines for teaching and learning. *Learning Disabilities Focus, 1*(1), 44–57.

Thurstone, L. L. (1938). *Primary mental abilities.* Chicago: University of Chicago Press.

Thurstone, L. L. (1947). *Multiple-factor analysis.* Chicago: University of Chicago Press.

Tisak, M. S., Tisak, J., & Goldstein, S. E. (2006). Aggression, delinquency, and morality: A social-cognitive perspective. In M. Killen & J. Smetana (Eds.), *Handbook of moral development.* Mahwah, NJ: Erlbaum.

Tishman, S., Jay, E., & Perkins, D. N. (1993). Teaching thinking dispositions: From transmission to enculturation. *Theory Into Practice, 33*(3), 147–153. Retrieved August 15, 2011, from http://learnweb.harvard.edu/alps/thinking/docs/article2.html.

Tishman, S., Perkins, D. N., & Jay, E. (1995). *The thinking classroom: Learning and teaching in culture of thinking.* Boston: Allyn & Bacon.

Titze, C., Jansen, P., & Heil, M. (2010). Mental rotation performance in fourth graders: No effects of gender beliefs (yet?). *Learning and Individual Differences, 20*, 459–463.

Tobias, S. (1992). The impact of test anxiety cognition in school learning. In K. A. Hagtvet & T. B. Johnsen (Eds.), *Advances in test anxiety research, Vol. 7* (pp. 18–31). Amsterdam: Swets & Zeitlinger.

Tobin, K. (1987). The role of wait time in higher cognitive level learning. *Review of Educational Research, 57*(1), 69–95.

Tokuhama-Espinosa, T. (2008). The scientifically substantiated art of teaching: A study in the development of standards in the new academic field of neuroeducation (mind, brain, and education science). Dissertation.

Tollefson, N. (2000). Classroom applications of cognitive theories of motivation. *Educational Psychology Review, 12*(1), 63–83.

Tombari, M., & Borich, G. (1999). *Authentic assessment in the classroom: Applications and practice.* Upper Saddle River, NJ: Merrill.

Tomlinson, C. (2005). Quality curriculum and instruction for highly able students. *Theory into Practice, 44*(2), 160–166.

Tomlinson, C. A., & McTighe, J. (2006). *Integrating differentiated instruction and understanding by design.* Alexandria, VA: ASCD.

Topman, R., Kleijn, W., van der Ploeg, H., & Masset, E. (1992). Test anxiety, cognitions, study habits and academic performance: A prospective study. In K. Hagtvet & T. Johnsen (Eds.), *Advances in test anxiety research. Vol. 7* (pp. 239–259). Amsterdam: Swets & Zeitlinger.

Toppino, T. C., Kasserman, J. E., & Mracek, W. A. (1991). The effect of spacing repetitions on the recognition memory of young children and adults. *Journal of Experimental Child Psychology, 51,* 123–138.

Torff, B. (2005). Developmental changes in teachers' beliefs about critical thinking activities. *Journal of Educational Psychology, 97*(1), 13–22.

Torgesen, J. K. (2000). Individual differences in response to early interventions in reading: The lingering problem of treatment resisters. *Learning Disabilities Research and Practice, 15*(1), 55–64.

Torgesen, J. K., Alexander, A. W., Wagner, R. K., Rashotte, C. A., Voeller, K. K. S., & Conway, T. (2001). Intensive remedial instruction for children with severe reading disabilities: Immediate and long-term outcomes from two instructional approaches. *Journal of Learning Disabilities, 34*(1), 33–58, 78.

Torgesen, J. K., & Mathes, P. G. (2000). *A basic guide to understanding and teaching phonological awareness.* Austin, TX: Pro-Ed.

Torgesen, J. K., Wagner, R. K., & Rashotte, C. A. (1997). Prevention and remediation of severe reading disabilities: Keeping the end in mind. *Scientific Studies of Reading, 1*(3), 217–234.

Torgesen, J. K., Wagner, R. K., & Rashotte, C. A. (1999). *Test of word reading efficiency.* Austin, TX: Pro-Ed.

Torgesen, J. K., Wagner, R. K., Rashotte, C. A., Herron, J., & Lindamood, P. (2010). Computer-assisted instruction to prevent early reading difficulties in students at risk for dyslexia: Outcomes from two instructional programs. *Annals of Dyslexia, 60,* 40–56.

Torp, L., & Sage, S. (2002). *Problems as possibilities: Problem-based learning for K–16 education* (2nd ed., pp. 15–16). Alexandria, VA: Association of Supervision and Curriculum Development.

Torrance, E. P. (1960). Creativity: Second Minnesota Conference on Gifted Children. Minneapolis: Center for Continuation Study, University of Minnesota.

Torrance, E. P. (1962). *Guiding creative talent.* Englewood Cliffs, NJ: Prentice-Hall.

Torrance, E. P. (1966). *The Torrance tests of creative thinking: Norms-technical manual.* Lexington, MA: Personal Press.

Torrance, E. P. (1974). *Torrance tests of creative thinking.* Lexington, MA: Personal Press. Treatment for Adolescents with Depression Study Team. (2004). Fluoxetine, cognitive-behavioral therapy, and their combination for adolescents with depression: Treatment for Adolescents with Depressions Study (TADS) randomized controlled trial. *Journal of the American Medical Association, 292,* 807–820.

Towle, P. O., Visintainer, P. F., O'Sullivan, C., Bryan, N. E., & Busby, S. (2009) Detecting autism spectrum disorder from early intervention charts: Methodology and preliminary findings. *Journal of Autism Disorder, 39,* 444–452.

Treatment for Adolescents with Depression Study Team. (2004). Fluoxetine, cognitive-behavioral therapy, and their combination for adolescents with depression: Treatment for Adolescents with Depressions Study (TADS) randomized controlled trial. *Journal of the American Medical Association, 292,* 807–820.

Triona. L. M., & Klahr, D. (2003). Point and click or grab and heft: Comparing the influence of physical and virtual instructional materials on elementary students' ability to design experiments. *Cognition and Instruction, 21,* 149–173.

Trumbull, E., & Farr, B. (2000). *Grading and reporting student progress in an age of standards.* Norwood, MA: Christopher-Gordon.

Tsang, C. L. (1989). Informal assessment of Asian Americans: A cultural and linguistic mismatch? In B. Gifford (Ed.), *Test policy and test performance: Education, language, and culture* (pp. 231–254). Boston: Kluwer Academic.

Tsay, M., & Brady, M. (2010). A case study of cooperative learning and communication pedagogy: Does working in teams make a difference? *Journal of the Scholarship of Teaching and Learning, 10*(2), 78–89.

Tschannen-Moran, M., Woolfolk Hoy, A., & Hoy, W. K. (1998). Teacher efficacy: Its meaning and measure. *Review of Educational Research, 68,* 202–248.

Tschannen-Moran, M., & Woolfolk Hoy, A. (2001). Teacher efficacy: Capturing an elusive construct. *Teaching and Teacher Education, 17,* 783–805.

Tudge, J., & Scrimsher, S. (2003). Lev S. Vygotsky on education: A cultural-historical, interpersonal, and individual approach to development. In B. J. Zimmerman & D. H. Schunk (Eds.), *Educational psychology: A century of contributions* (pp. 207–228). Mahwah, NJ: Erlbaum.

Turiel, E. (1983). *The development of social knowledge: Morality and convention.* San Francisco: Jossey-Bass.

Turnbull, A. P., & Turnbull, H. R. (2001). *Families, professionals, and exceptionality: Collaborating for empowerment* (4th ed.). Upper Saddle River, NJ: Merrill/Prentice Hall.

Turnbull, R., Turnbull, A., Shank, M., Smith, S., & Leal, D. (2002). *Exceptional lives: Special education in today's schools* (3rd ed.). Upper Saddle River, NJ: Merrill/Prentice Hall.

Turner, J., & Paris, S. G. (1995). How literacy tasks influence children's motivation for literacy. *Reading Teacher, 48*(8), 662–673.

Turner, J. C., & Meyer, D. K. (2004). A classroom perspective on the principle of moderate challenge in mathematics. *Journal of Educational Research, 97,* 311–318.

Turner, J. C., Meyer, D. K., Midgley, C., & Patrick, H. (2003). Teacher discourse and sixth graders' reported affect and achievement behaviors in two high-mastery/high performance mathematics classrooms. *The Elementary School Journal, 103,* 357–378.

Turner, L. A., & Johnson, B. (2003). A model of mastery motivation for at-risk preschoolers. *Journal of Educational Psychology, 95*(3), 495–505.

Turner, M. A. (1999). Annotation: Repetitive behaviour in autism: A review of psychological research. *Journal of Child Psychology and Psychiatry and Allied Disciplines, 40,* 839–849.

Twenge, J. M., & Campbell, W. K. (2002). Self-esteem and socioeconomic status: A meta-analytic review. *Personality and Social Psychology Review, 6,* 59–71.

Twenge, J. M., & Campbell, W. K. (2008). Increases in positive self-views among high school students: Birth-cohort changes in anticipated performance, self-satisfaction, self-liking, and self-competence. *Psychological Science, 19*(11), 1082–1086.

U

U.S. Department of Education. (1983). *A nation at risk: The imperative for educational reform.* Retrieved August 15, 2011, from http://www2.ed.gov/pubs/NatAtRisk/index.html.

U.S. Department of Education. (2009). *Twenty-eighth annual report to Congress on the implementation of the Individuals with Disabilities Education Act, 2006, Vol. 1.* Office of Special Education and Rehabilitative Services, Washington DC: U.S. Government Printing Office.

U.S. Department of Health and Human Services, Administration on Children, Youth, and Families. (2006). Child maltreatment 2004: Reports from the states to the National Child Abuse and Neglect Data System. Washington, DC: Government Printing Office.

Umana-Taylor, A. J., Gonzales-Backen, M. A., & Guimond, A. B. (2009). Latino adolescents' ethnic identity: Is there a developmental progression and does growth in ethnic identity predict growth in self-esteem? *Child Development, 80*(2), 391–405.

Unsworth, N., & Engle, R. W. (2007). The nature of individual differences in working memory capacity: Active maintenance in primary memory and controlled search from secondary memory. *Psychological Review, 114*(1), 104–132.

Urdan, T. (2004). Predictors of academic self-handicapping and achievement: Examining achievement goals, classroom goal structures, and culture. *Journal of Educational Psychology, 96,* 251–264.

Urdan, T., & Mestas, M. (2006). The goals behind performance goals. *Journal of Educational Psychology, 98*(2), 354–365.

Urdan, T., Midgley, C., & Anderman, E. M. (1998). The role of classroom goal structure in students' use of self-handicapping strategies. *American Educational Research Journal, 35*(1), 101–122.

Usher, E. L., & Pajares, F. (2006a). Inviting confidence in school: Invitations as a critical source of the academic self-efficacy beliefs of entering middle school students. *Journal of Invitational Theory and Practice, 12,* 7–16.

Usher, E. L., & Pajares, F. (2006b). Sources of academic and self-regulatory efficacy beliefs of entering middle school students. *Contemporary Educational Psychology, 31,* 125–141.

Usher, E. L., & Pajares, F. (2008). Sources of self-efficacy in school: Critical review of the literature and future directions. *Review of Educational Research, 78*(4), 751–796.

V

Vagg, P., & Spielberger, C. (1995). Treatment of test anxiety: Application of the transactional process model. In C. Spielberger & P. Vagg (Eds.), *Test anxiety: Theory, assessment, and treatment* (pp. 197–215). Washington, DC: Taylor & Francis.

Vaillancourt, T., & Hymel, S. (2006). Aggression and social status: The moderating roles of sex and peer-valued characteristics. *Aggressive Behavior, 32,* 396–408.

Valentine, J. C., DuBois, D. L., & Cooper, H. (2004). The relation between self-beliefs and academic achievement: A meta-analytic review. *Educational Psychologist, 39,* 111–133.

Valeski, T., & Stipek, D. (2001). Young children's feelings about school. *Child Development, 72*(4), 1198–1213.

Vallerand, R. J., Pelletier, L. G., Blais, M. R., Brière, N. M., Senécal, C., & Vallières, E. F. (1993). On the assessment of intrinsic, extrinsic, and amotivation in education: Evidence on the concurrent and construct validity of the academic motivation scale. *Educational and Psychological Measurement, 53,* 159–172.

Vandell, D. L., Belsky, J., Burchinal, M., Steinberg, L., & Vandergrift, N. (2010). Do effects of early child care extend to age 15 years? Results from the NICHD study of Early Child Care and Youth Development. *Child Development, 81*(3), 737–756.

VanDerHeyden, A. M., & Burns, M. (2010). *Essentials of response to intervention.* Hoboken, NJ: Wiley.

Van Houten, R., Nau, P. A., MacKenzie-Keating, S. E., Sameoto, D., & Colavecchia, B. (1982). An analysis of some variables influencing the effectiveness of reprimands. *Journal of Applied Behavior Analysis, 15,* 65–83.

van Laar, C. (2000). The paradox of low academic achievement but high self-esteem in African American students: An attributional account. *Educational Psychology Review, 12*(1), 33–61.

van Merrienboer, J. J. G., & Sweller, J. (2005). Cognitive load theory and complex learning: Recent developments and future directions. *Educational Psychology Review, 17*(2). doi:10.1007/s10648-005-3951-0

Van Meter, P., Yokoi, L., & Pressley, M. (1994). College students' theory of note-taking derived from their perceptions of note-taking. *Journal of Educational Psychology, 86,* 323–338.

Van Overwalle, F., & De Metsenaere, M. (1990). The effects of attribution-based intervention and study strategy training on academic achievement in college freshmen. *British Journal of Educational Psychology, 60,* 299–311.

Vansteenkiste, M., & Deci, E. L. (2003). Competitively contingent rewards and intrinsic motivation: Can losers remain motivated? *Motivation and Emotion, 27*(4), 273–299.

Vansteenkiste, M., Lens, W., & Deci, E. L. (2006). Intrinsic versus extrinsic goal contents in self-determination theory: Another look at the quality of academic motivation. *Educational Psychologist, 41*(1), 19–31.

Vansteenkiste, M., Lens, W., De Witte, S., De Witte, H., & Deci, E. L. (2004). The "why" and "why not" of job search behavior: Their relation to searching, unemployment experience and well-being. *European Journal of Social Psychology, 34,* 345–363.

Vansteenkiste, M., Matos, L., Lens, W., & Soenens, B. (2007). Understanding the impact of intrinsic versus extrinsic goal framing on exercise performance: The conflicting role of task and ego involvement. *Psychology of Sport and Exercise, 8*(5), 771–794.

Vansteenkiste, M., Niemiec, C. P., & Soenens, B. (2010). The development of the five mini-theories of self-determination theory: An historical overview, emerging trends, and future directions. In T. C. Urdan, & S. A. Karabenick (Eds.), *The decade ahead: Theoretical perspectives on motivation and achievement, Volume 16A* (pp. 105–165). Bingley, UK: Emerald Group Publishing.

Vansteenkiste, M., Simons, J., Lens, W., Sheldon, K.M., & Deci, E. L. (2004). Motivating learning, performance, and persistence: The synergistic effects of intrinsic goal contents and autonomy-supportive contexts. *Journal of Personality and Social Psychology, 87,* 246–260.

Vansteenkiste, M., Zhou, M., Lens, W., & Soenens, B. (2005). Experiences of autonomy and control among Chinese learners. Vitalizing or immobilizing? *Journal of Educational Psychology, 97,* 468–483.

VanTassel-Baska, J. (1998). *Excellence in educating gifted and talented learners* (3rd ed.). Denver, CO: Love Publishing.

VanTassel-Baska, J., Feng, A. X., Swanson, J. D., Quek, C., & Chandler, K. (2009). Academic and affective profiles of low-income, minority, twice-exceptional gifted learners: The role of gifted program membership in enhancing self. *Journal of Advanced Academics, 20*(4), 702–739.

Vardi, I., & Ciccarelli, M. (2008).Overcoming problems in problem-based learning: A trial of strategies in an undergraduate unit. *Innovations in Education and Teaching International, 45*(4), 345–354.

Varma, S., McCandliss, B., & Schwartz, D. L. (2008). Scientific and pragmatic challenges for bridging education and neuroscience. *Educational Researcher, 37*(3), 140–152.

Varma, S., & Schwartz, D. L. (2008). How should educational neuroscience conceptualize the relation between cognition and brain function? Mathematical reasoning as a network process. *Educational Research, 50*(2), 149–161.

Varnum, M. E., Grossman, I., Kitayama, S., & Nisbett, R. E. (2010). The origin of cultural differences in cognition: Evidence for the social orientation hypothesis. *Current Directions in Psychological Science, 19*(1), 9–13.

Vaughn, S., Linan-Thompson, S., & Hickman, P. (2003). Response to instruction as a means of identifying students with reading/learning disabilities. *Exceptional Children, 69*, 391–409.

Veenman, S. (1995). Cognitive and noncognitive effects of multigrade and multiage classes: A best–evidence synthesis. *Review of Educational Research, 65*(4), 319–381.

Veenman, S. (1997). Combination classrooms revisited. *Educational Research and Evaluation, 3*(3), 262–276.

Verhoeven, L., van Leeuwe, J., & Vermeer, A. (2011). Vocabulary growth and reading development across the elementary school years. *Scientific Studies of Reading, 15*(1), 8–25.

Verhulst, F. C. (2001). Community and epidemiological aspects of anxiety disorders in children. In W. K. Silverman & P. D. A. Treffers (Eds.), *Anxiety disorders in children and adolescents: Research, assessment, and intervention* (pp. 293–312). New York: Cambridge University Press.

Verzoni, K. A. (1995). *Creating simulations: Expressing life-situated relationships in terms of algebraic equations.* Paper presented at the Annual Meeting of the Northeastern Educational Research Association, Ellenville, NY.

Victor, A., Wozniak, J. R., & Chang, P. (2008). Environmental correlates of cognition and behavior in children with fetal alcohol spectrum disorders. *Journal of Human Behavior in the Social Environment, 18*(3), 288–300.

Viel-Ruma, K., Houchins, D., Jolivette, K., & Benson, G. (2010). Efficacy beliefs of special educators: The relationships among collective efficacy, teacher self-efficacy, and job satisfaction. *Teacher Education & Special Education, 33*(3), 225–233.

Villa, R. A., & Thousand, J. (2000). *Restructuring for caring and effective education.* Baltimore: Paul H. Brookes.

Volkmar, F. R., Szatmari, P., & Sparrow, S. S. (1993). Sex differences in pervasive developmental disorders. *Journal of Autism and Developmental Disorders, 23*, 579–591.

Voyer, D., Voyer, S., & Bryden, M. P. (1995). Magnitude of sex differences in spatial abilities: A meta-analysis and consideration of critical variables. *Psychological Bulletin, 117*, 250–270.

Vygotsky, L. S. (1962). *Thought and language.* Cambridge, MA: MIT Press.

Vygotsky, L. S. (1978). *Mind in society: The development of higher psychological processes.* Cambridge, MA: Harvard University Press.

Vygotsky, L. S. (1987). *The collected works of L. S. Vygotsky: Vol. 1. Problems of general psychology* (R. W. Rieber & A. S. Carton, Vol. Eds.; N. Minick, Trans.). New York: Plenum.

Vygotsky, L. S. (1993). *The collected works of L. S. Vygotsky: Vol. 2. The fundamentals of defectology (abnormal psychology and learning disabilities).* (R. W. Rieber & A. S. Carton, Vol. Eds.; N. Minick, Trans.). New York: Plenum. (Chapters originally written between 1924 and 1935.)

Vygotsky, L. S. (1994). The problem of the environment. In R. van der Veer & J. Valsiner (Eds.), *The Vygostsky reader* (pp. 338–354). Oxford, UK: Blackwell. (Originally published in 1935.)

Vygotsky, L. S. (1998). In R. W. Rieber (Vol. Ed.) and M. J. Hall (Trans.), *The collected works of L. S. Vygotsky: Vol. 5. Child psychology.* New York: Plenum. (Chapters originally written between 1930 and 1934.)

W

Wagner, R. K., Torgesen, J. K., & Rashotte, C. A. (1994). The development of reading-related phonological processing abilities: New evidence of bi-directional causality from a latent variable longitudinal study. *Developmental Psychology, 30*, 73–87.

Wagner, T., Kegan, R., Lahey, L., et al. (2006). *Change leadership: A practical guide to transforming our schools.* San Francisco: Jossey-Bass.

Waldfogel, J., & Zhai, F. (2008). Effects of public preschool expenditures on the test scores of fourth graders: Evidence from TIMSS. *Educational Research and Evaluation, 14*(1), 9–28.

Waldron, N. L. (1998). The effects of an inclusive school program on students with mild and severe learning disabilities. *Exceptional Children, 64*, 395–405.

Walker, H. M., Colvin, G., & Ramsey, E. (1995). *Antisocial behavior in schools: Strategies and best practices.* Pacific Grove, CA: Brooks/Cole.

Walker, H. M., Seeley, J. R., Small, J., et al. (2009). A randomized controlled trial of the First Step to Success Early Intervention: Demonstration of program efficacy outcomes in a diverse, urban school district. *Journal of Emotional and Behavioral Disorders, 17*(4), 197–212.

Walker, J., & Shea, T. (1995). *Behavior management: A practical approach for educators* (6th ed.). Englewood Cliffs, NJ: Merrill.

Walker, J. E., Shea, T. M., & Bauer, A. M. (2004). *Behavior management: A practical approach for educators* (8th ed.). New Jersey: Pearson.

Walker, J. M. T., & Hoover-Dempsey, K. V. (2006). Research on parental involvement important to classroom management. In C. M. Evertson & C. S. Weinstein (Eds.), *Handbook of classroom management: Research, practice, and contemporary issues.* Mahwah, NJ: Erlbaum.

Walker, L., de Vries, B., & Trevethan, S. D. (1987). Moral stages and moral orientations in real-life and hypothetical dilemmas. *Child Development, 58*(3), 842–858.

Walker, L. J. (2006). Gender and morality. In M. Killen & J. Smetana (Eds.), *Handbook of moral development* (pp. 93–115). Mahwah, NJ: Erlbaum.

Wallas, G. (1926). *The art of thought.* New York: Harcourt Brace.

Wallis, C., & Steptoe, S. (2006). How to bring our schools out of the 20th century. *Time.* Retrieved August 15, 2011, from http://www.time.com/time/magazine/article/0,9171,1568480,00.html.

Waltman, K. K., & Frisbie, D. A. (1994). Parents' understanding of their children's report cards. *Applied Measurement in Education, 2*, 223–240.

Wambugu, P. W., & Changeiywo, J. M. (2008). Effects of mastery learning approach on secondary school students' physics achievement. *Eurasia Journal of Mathematics, 4*(3), 293–302.

Ward, N. S., & Frackowiak, R. S. (2006). The functional anatomy of cerebral reorganisation after focal brain injury. *Journal of Physiology–Paris, 99*(4–6), 425–436.

Warner, C. M., Fisher, P. H., Shrout, P. E., Rathor, S., & Klein, R. G. (2007). Treating adolescents with social anxiety disorder in school: An attention control trial. *Journal of Child Psychology and Psychiatry, 48*(7), 676–686.

Warren, H. K., & Stifter, C. A. (2008). Maternal emotion-related socialization and preschoolers' developing emotion self-awareness. *Social Development, 17*(2), 239–258.

Warren-Leubecker, A., & Bohannon, J. N. (1983). The effects of verbal feedback and listener type on the speech of pre-school children. *Journal of Experimental Child Psychology, 35,* 540–548.

Wartenburger, I., Heekeren, H. R., Abutalebi, J., Cappa, S. F., Villringer, A., & Perani, D. (2003). Early setting of grammatical processing in the bilingual brain. *Neuron, 37,* 159–170.

Waschbusch, D. A. (2002). A meta-analytic examination of comorbid hyperactive-impulsive-attention problems and conduct problems. *Psychological Bulletin, 128,* 118–150.

Waterhouse, L. (2006). Multiple intelligences, the Mozart effect, and emotional intelligence: A critical review. *Educational Psychologist, 41*(4), 207–225.

Waters, S., Cross, D., & Shaw, T. (2010). Does the nature of schools matter? An exploration of selected school ecology factors on adolescent perceptions of school connectedness. *British Journal of Educational Psychology, 80,* 381–402.

Waters, J., & Sroufe, L. A. (1983). Social competence as a developmental construct. *Developmental Review, 3,* 79–97.

Watkins, M. J. (1979). Engrams as cuegrams and forgetting as cue overload: A cueing approach to the structure of memory. In C. R. Puff (Ed.), *Memory and organization structure* (pp. 173–195). New York: Academic Press.

Watson, J. B. (1913). Psychology as the behaviorist views it. *Psychological Review, 20,* 158–177.

Watson, J. B., & Rayner, R. (1920). Conditioned emotional reactions. *Journal of Experimental Psychology, 3,* 1–14.

Watson, M., & Ecken, L. (2003). *Learning to trust: Transforming difficult elementary classrooms through developmental discipline.* San Francisco: Jossey-Bass.

Watt, H. (2004). Development of adolescents' self-perceptions, values, and task perceptions. *Child Development, 75,* 1556–1574.

Watts, G. H., & Anderson, R. C. (1971). Effects of three types of inserted questions on learning from prose. *Journal of Educational Psychology, 62,* 387–394.

Weasmer, J., & Woods, A. (2001). Encouraging student decision making. *Kappa Delta Pi Record, 38,* 40–42.

Webb, N. M. (1984). Sex differences in interaction and achievement in cooperative small groups. *Journal of Educational Psychology, 74,* 475–484.

Webb, N. M. (1985). Gender differences in small group interaction and achievement in high- and low-achieving classes. In L. C. Wilkinson & C. B. Marrett (Eds.), *Gender differences in classroom interaction* (pp. 209–236). New York: Academic Press.

Webb, N. M. (1989). Peer interaction and learning in small groups. *International Journal of Educational Research, 13,* 21–39.

Webb, N. M. (1991). Task-related verbal interaction and mathematics learning in small groups. *Journal of Research in Mathematics Education, 22,* 366–369.

Webb, N. M. (2008). Learning in small groups. In T. L. Good (Ed.), *21st century education: A reference handbook* (pp. 203–211). Thousand Oaks, CA: Sage.

Webb, N. M., & Palincsar, A. S. (1996). Group processes in the classroom. In D. C. Berliner & R. C. Calfee (Eds.), *Handbook of educational psychology* (pp. 841–873). New York: Prentice Hall.

Weber, W. A., & Roff, L. A. (1983). A review of teacher education literature on classroom management. In W. A. Weber, L. A. Roff, J. Crawford, & C. Robinson (Eds.). *Classroom management: Reviews of the teacher education and research literature* (pp. 7–42). Princeton, NJ: Educational Testing Service.

Webster-Stratton, C., Reid, M. J., & Stoolmiller, M. (2008). Preventing conduct problems and improving school readiness: Evaluation of the Incredible Years Teacher and Child Training Programs in high-risk schools. *Journal of Child Psychology and Psychiatry, 49*(5), 471–488.

Wechsler, D. (2003). *WISC–IV administration and scoring manual.* San Antonio, TX: Psychological Corporation.

Wehmeier, P. M., Schacht, A., & Barkley, R. A. (2010). Social and emotional impairment in children and adolescents with ADHD and the impact on quality of life. *Journal of Adolescent Health, 46,* 209–217.

Weiner, B. (1982). An attributionally based theory of motivation and emotion: Focus, range, and issues. In N. T. Feather (Ed.), *Expectations and actions.* Hillsdale, NJ: Erlbaum.

Weiner, B. (1990). History of motivational research in education. *Journal of Educational Psychology, 82*(4), 616–622.

Weiner, B. (1992). *Human motivation: Metaphors, theories and research.* Newbury Park, CA: Sage.

Weiner, B. (1994). Integrating social and personal theories of achievement striving. *Review of Educational Research, 64,* 557–573.

Weiner, B. (2000). Intrapersonal and interpersonal theories of motivation from an attributional perspective. *Educational Psychology Review, 12,* 1–14.

Weiner, B. (2010). The development of an attribution-based theory of motivation: A history of ideas. *Educational Psychologist, 45*(1), 28–36.

Weinstein, C. E., & Mayer, R. E. (1986). The teaching of learning strategies. In M. C. Wittrock (Ed.), *Handbook of research on teaching* (3rd ed.). New York: Macmillan.

Weinstein, C. S. (2003). *Secondary classroom management: Lessons from research and practice* (2nd ed.). New York: McGraw-Hill.

Weinstein, C. S., & Mignano, A. J. (2003). *Elementary classroom management: Lessons from research and practice* (3rd ed.). New York: McGraw-Hill.

Weinstein, C. S., & Mignano, A. J. (2007). *Elementary classroom management: Lessons from research and practice* (4th ed.). New York: McGraw-Hill.

Weinstein, C. S., & Mignano, A. J. (2011). *Elementary classroom management: Lessons from research and practice* (5th ed.). New York: McGraw-Hill.

Weinstein, C. S., Tomlinson-Clarke, S., & Curran, M. (2004). Toward a conception of culturally responsive classroom management. *Journal of Teacher Education, 55*(1), 25–38.

Weinstein, R. (1993). Children's knowledge of differential treatment in school: Implications for motivation. In T. Tomlinson (Ed.), *Motivating students to learn: Overcoming barriers to high achievement* (pp. 197–224). Berkeley, CA: McCutchan.

Weinstein, R., Madison, S., & Kuklinski, M. (1995). Raising expectations in schooling: Obstacles and opportunities for change. *American Educational Research Journal, 32,* 121–159.

Weinstein, R. S. (1993). Children's knowledge of differential treatment in school: Implications for motivation. In T. M. Tomlinson

(Ed.), *Motivating students to learn: Overcoming barriers to high achievement* (pp. 197–224). Berkeley, CA: McCutchan.

Weir, E., & Bianchet, S. (2004). Developmental dysfluency: Early intervention is key. *Canadian Medical Association Journal, 170*(12), 1790–1791.

Weisberg, D. S., Keil, F. C., Goodstein, J., Rawson, E., & Gray, J. R. (2008). The seductive allure of neuroscience explanations. *Journal of Cognitive Neuroscience, 20,* 470–477.

Weiser, D. A., & Riggio, H. R. (2010). Family background and academic achievement: Does self-efficacy mediate outcomes? *Social Psychology of Education, 13*(3), 367–383.

Weiss, M., & Weiss, G. (2002). Attention deficit hyperactivity disorder. In M. Lewis (Ed.), *Child and adolescent psychiatry: A comprehensive textbook* (3rd ed., pp. 645–670). Philadelphia: Lippincott Williams & Wilkins.

Weiss, S. J., St. John Seed, M., & Harris-Muchell, C. (2007). The contribution of fetal drug exposure to temperament: Potential teratogenic effects on neuropsychiatric risk. *Journal of Child Psychology and Psychiatry, 48*(8), 773–784.

Weissberg, R. P., & Greenberg, M. T. (1998). School and community competence-enhancement and prevention programs. In W. Damon (Series Ed.) & I. E. Sigel & K. A. Renninger (Vol. Eds.), *Handbook of child psychology: Vol. 4. Child psychology in practice* (5th ed., pp. 877–954). New York: Wiley.

Weisz, V. I., & Argibav, P. F. (2009). A putative role for neurogenesis in neurocomputational terms: Inferences from a hippocampal model. *Cognition, 112*(2), 229–240.

Weldin, D. J., & Tumarkin, S. R. (1999). Parent involvement: More power in the portfolio process. *Childhood Education, 75,* 90–96.

Weller, E. B., Weller, R. A., Rowan, A. B., & Svadjian, H. (2002). Depressive disorders in children and adolescents. In M. Lewis (Ed.), *Child and adolescent psychiatry: A comprehensive textbook* (3rd ed., pp. 767–781). Philadelphia: Lippincott Williams & Wilkins.

Weller, L. D. (2001). Building validity and reliability into classroom tests. *NASSP Bulletin, 85,* 32–37.

Wentzel, K. R. (1997). Student motivation in middle school: The role of perceived pedagogical caring. *Journal of Educational Psychology, 89*(3), 411–419.

Wentzel, K. R. (2002). Are effective teachers like good parents? Interpersonal predictors of school adjustment in early adolescence. *Child Development, 73,* 287–301.

Wentzel, K. R. (2003a). Motivating students to behave in socially competent ways. *Theory Into Practice, 42*(4), 319–326.

Wentzel, K. R. (2003b). School adjustment. In W. M. Reynolds & G. E. Miller (Eds.), *Handbook of psychology, Vol. 7. Educational psychology* (pp. 235–258). Hoboken, NJ: Wiley.

Wentzel, K. R., Battle, A., Russell, S. L., & Looney, L. B. (2010). Social supports from teachers and peers as predictors of academic and social motivation. *Contemporary Educational Psychology, 35,* 193–202.

Werner, N. E., & Crick, N. R. (2004). Maladaptive peer relationships and the development of relational and physical aggression during middle childhood. *Social Development, 13*(4), 495–514.

West, R. F., Toplak, M. E., & Stanovich, K. E. (2008). Heuristics and biases as measures of critical thinking: Associations with cognitive ability and thinking dispositions. *Journal of Educational Psychology, 100*(4), 930–941.

Westberg, K. L., Archambault, F. X. Jr., Dobyns, S. M., & Salvin, T. J. (1993). *An observational study of instructional and curricular practices used with gifted and talented students in regular classrooms* (research monograph 93104). Storrs, CT: National Research Center on the Gifted and Talented, University of Connecticut.

Western and Northern Canadian Protocol for Collaboration in Education. (2006). *Rethinking classroom assessment with purpose in mind: Assessment for learning, assessment as learning, assessment of learning.* Crown in Right of the Governments of Alberta, British Columbia, Manitoba, Northwest Territories, Nunavut, Saskatchewan, and Yukon Territory as represented by their Ministers of Education. Retrieved August 16, 2011, from http://www.wncp.ca/media/40539/rethink.pdf.

Westwood, P. (2003). *Commonsense methods for children with special educational needs: Strategies for the regular classroom* (4th ed.). New York: Routledge Falmer.

Wexler, J., Edmonds, M. S., & Vaughn, S. (2007). Teaching older readers with reading difficulties. In N. Mather (Ed.), *Evidence based interventions for students with learning and behavioral challenges* (pp. 193–214). Mahwah, NJ: Erlbaum.

Whalon, K., & Hanline, M. F. (2008). Effects of a reciprocal questioning intervention on the question generation and responding of children with Autism Spectrum Disorder. *Education and Training in Developmental Disabilities, 43*(3), 367–387.

Wheelcock, A. (1992). The case for untracking. *Educational Leadership, 50*(2), 6–10.

White, K. R. (1982). The relation between socioeconomic status and academic achievement. *Psychological Bulletin, 91,* 461–481.

White, L., & Genesee, F. (1996). How native is near-native? The issue of ultimate attainment in adult second language acquisition. *Second Language Research, 12,* 233–265.

White, R. W. (1959). Motivation reconsidered: The concept of competence. *Psychological Review, 66,* 297–333.

White, T., Schmidt, M., Kim, D., & Calhoun, V. D. (2010). Disrupted functional brain connectivity during verbal working memory in children and adolescents with schizophrenia. *Cerebral Cortex, 21*(3), 510–518.

Whitington, V., & Floyd, I. (2009). Creating intersubjectivity during socio-dramatic play at an Australian kindergarten. *Early Child Development and Care, 179*(2), 143–156.

Wigfield, A., & Cambria, J. (2010a). Expectancy-value theory: Retrospective and prospective. In T. C. Urdan & S. A. Karabenick (Eds.), *The decade ahead: Theoretical perspectives on motivation and achievement* (pp. 35–70). UK: Emerald Publishing.

Wigfield, A., & Cambria, J. (2010b). Students' achievement values, goal orientations and interest: Definitions, development, and relations to achievement outcomes. *Developmental Review, 30,* 1–35.

Wigfield, A., & Eccles, J. S. (1989). Test anxiety in elementary and secondary students. *Educational Psychologist, 24,* 159–183.

Wigfield, A., & Eccles, J. (1994). Children's competence beliefs, achievement values, and general self-esteem: Change across elementary and middle school. *Journal of Early Adolescence, 14,* 107–137.

Wigfield, A., Eccles, J., Yoon, K., et al. (1997). Changes in children's competence beliefs and subjective task values across the elementary school years: A three-year study. *Journal of Educational Psychology, 89*(3), 451–469.

Wigfield, A., & Eccles, J. S. (2000). Expectancy-value theory of achievement motivation. *Contemporary Educational Psychology, 25,* 68–81.

Wigfield, A., & Eccles, J. S. (2002). The development of competence beliefs, expectancies for success, and achievement values from childhood through adolescence. In A. Wigfield & J. S.

Eccles (Eds.), *Development of achievement motivation* (pp. 91–120). San Diego, CA: Academic Press.

Wigfield, A., Eccles, J. S., Schiefele, U., Roeser, R. W., & Davis-Kean, P. (2006). Development of achievement motivation. In W. Damon & R. M. Lerner (Eds.), *Handbook of child psychology* (pp. 933–1002). Hoboken, NJ: Wiley.

Wigfield, A., Tonks, S., & Klauda, S. L. (2009). Expectancy-value theory. In K. R. Wentzel & A. Wigfield (Eds.), *Handbook of motivation at school* (pp. 55–75). New York: Routledge/Taylor & Francis Group.

Wigfield, A., & Wagner, A. L. (2005). Competence, motivation, and identity development during adolescence. In A. J. Elliot & C. S. Dweck (Eds.), *Handbook of competence and motivation* (pp. 222–239). New York: Guilford.

Wiggins, G. (1998). *Educative assessment: Designing assessment to inform and improve student performance.* San Francisco: Jossey-Bass.

Wiggins, G., & McTighe, J. (1998). *Understanding by design.* Alexandria, VA: Association for Supervision and Curriculum Development.

Wilkins, J. L. M. (2004). Mathematics and science self-concept: An internal investigation. *Journal of Experimental Education, 72*(4), 331–346.

Williams, L. R., Lejuez, C. W., Reynolds, E. K., et al. (2010). Early temperament, propensity for risk-taking, and adolescent substance-related problems: A prospective multi-method investigation. *Addictive Behaviors, 35*(12), 1148–1151.

Willing, R. (1988). Computer simulations: Activating content reading. *Journal of Reading, 31*(5), 400–409.

Willingham, D. T. (2004). *Cognition: The thinking animal* (2nd ed.). Upper Saddle River, NJ: Prentice Hall.

Willingham, D. T., & Lloyd, J. W. (2007). How educational theories can use scientific data. *Mind, Brain, and Education, 1*(3), 140–149.

Willingham, W. W., & Cole, N. S. (1997). *Gender and fair assessment.* Hillsdale, NJ: Erlbaum.

Wilson, J. H. (2006). Predicting student attitudes and grades from perceptions of instructors' attitudes. *Teaching of Psychology, 33,* 91–95.

Wilson, J. H., & Wilson, S. B. (2007). The first day of class affects student motivation: An experimental study. *Teaching of Psychology, 34*(4), 226–231.

Wilson, R. A. (2003). *Special educational needs in the early years.* New York: Routledge Falmer.

Windschitl, M. (2002). Framing constructivism in practice as the negotiation of dilemmas: An analysis of the conceptual, pedagogical, cultural, and political challenges facing teachers. *Review of Educational Research, 72,* 131–175.

Wing, C., & Scholnick, E. (1981). Children's comprehension of pragmatic concepts expressed in "because," "although," "if" and "unless." *Journal of Child Language, 8,* 347–365.

Wininger, S. R., & Norman, A. D. (2010). Assessing coverage of Maslow's theory in Educational Psychology textbooks: A content analysis. *Teaching Educational Psychology, 6*(1), 33–48.

Wink, J., & Putney, L. (2002). *A vision of Vygotsky.* Boston: Allyn & Bacon.

Winn, W. (1991). Learning from maps and diagrams. *Educational Psychology Review, 3,* 211–247.

Winner, E. (1996). *Gifted children: Myths and realities.* New York: Basic Books.

Winner, E. (2000). The origins and ends of giftedness. *American Psychologist, 55*(1), 159–169.

Winston, J. S., Strange, B. A., O'Doherty, & Dolan, R. J. (2002). Automatic and intentional brain responses during evaluation of trustworthiness of faces. *Nature Neuroscience, 5,* 277–283.

Winzer, M., & Grigg, N. (1992). *Educational psychology in the Canadian classroom.* Scarborough, ON: Prentice Hall Canada.

Wixted, J. T., & Ebbesen, E. B. (1991). On the form of forgetting. *Psychological Science, 2,* 409–415.

Wolf, D., Bixby, J., Glenn, J., III, & Gardner, H. (1991). To use their minds well: New forms of student assessment. *Review of Research in Education, 17,* 31–74.

Wolfe, P. (2001). *Brain matters: Translating research into classroom practice.* Alexandria, VA: ASCD.

Wolters, C. (2004). Advancing achievement goal theory: Using goal structures and goal orientations to predict students' motivation, cognition, and achievement. *Journal of Educational Psychology, 96,* 236–250.

Wolters, C. A., & Daugherty, S. G. (2007). Goal structures and teachers' sense of efficacy: Their relation and association to teaching experience and academic level. *Journal of Educational Psychology, 99*(1), 181–193.

Woltz, D. J., & Was, C. A. (2007). Available but unattended conceptual information in working memory: Temporarily active semantic content or persistent memory for prior operations? *Journal of Experimental Psychology: Learning, Memory, and Cognition, 33*(1), 155–168.

Wolvin, A., & Coakley, C. (1985). *Listening.* Dubuque, IA: William C. Brown.

Wong, H. K., & Wong, R. T. (1998). *How to be an effective teacher: The first days of school.* Mountain View, CA: Harry K. Wong.

Wood, D., Kaplan, R., & McLloyd, V. C. (2007). Gender differences in the educational expectations of urban, low-income African American youth: The role of parents and the school. *Journal of Youth Adolescence, 36,* 417–427.

Wood, D. J. (1989). Social interaction as tutoring. In M. H. Bornstein & J. S. Bruner (Eds.), *Interaction in human development.* Hillsdale, NJ: Erlbaum.

Wood, D. J., Bruner, J. S., & Ross, G. (1976). The role of tutoring in problem solving. *Journal of Child Psychology and Psychiatry, 17,* 89–100.

Wood, J. (2006). Effect of anxiety reduction on children's school performance and social adjustment. *Developmental Psychology, 42*(2), 345–349.

Wood, J. J., Chiu, A. W., Hwang, W., Jacobs, J., & Ifekwunigwe, M. (2008). Adapting cognitive-behavioral therapy for Mexican-American students with anxiety disorders: Recommendations for school psychologists. *School Psychology Quarterly, 23*(4), 515–532.

Wood, J. J., Drahota, A., Sze, K., Har, K., Chiu, A., & Langer, D. A. (2009). Cognitive behavioral therapy for anxiety in children with autism spectrum disorders: A randomized, controlled trial. *Journal of Child Psychology and Psychiatry, 50*(3), 224–234.

Woodward, J., & Baxter, J. (1997). The effects of an innovative approach to mathematics on academically low-achieving students in inclusive settings. *Exceptional Children, 63,* 373–388.

Woolfolk, A. E., & Brooks, D. M. (1985). The influence of teachers' nonverbal behaviors on students' perceptions and performance. *Elementary School Journal, 85,* 513–528.

Woolfolk, A. E., & Hoy, W. K. (1990). Prospective teachers' sense of efficacy and beliefs about control. *Journal of Educational Psychology, 82,* 81–91.

Woolfolk, A. E., Rosoff, B., & Hoy, W. K. (1990). Teachers' sense of efficacy and their beliefs about managing students. *Teaching and Teacher Education, 6*(2), 137–148.

X

Xie, H., Cairns, B. D., & Cairns, R. B. (2005). The development of aggressive behaviors among girls: Measurement issues, social functions, and differential trajectories. In D. J. Pepler, K. C. Madsen, C. Webster, & K. S. Levene (Eds.), *The development and treatment of girlhood aggression.* New Jersey: Erlbaum.

Xie, H., & Shi, B. (2009). Gender similarities and differences in preadolescent peer groups. *Merrill-Palmer Quarterly, 55*(2), 157–183.

Y

Yairi, E., & Ambrose, N. (2005). *Early childhood stuttering: For clinicians by clinicians.* Austin, TX: Pro-Ed.

Yamasue, H., Abe, O., Suga, M., et al. (2008). Sex-linked neuroanatomical basis of human altruistic cooperativeness. *Cerebral Cortex, 18*(10), 2331–2340.

Yang, J., Hou, C., Ma, N., et al. (2007). Enriched environment treatment restores impaired hippocampal synaptic plasticity and cognitive deficits induced by prenatal chronic stress. *Neurobiology of Learning and Memory, 87*(2), 257–263.

Yang, Y. C., & Ahn, S. H. (2007). The effects of synchronous online discussion on the improvement of critical thinking skills. *Korean Journal of Thinking and Problem Solving, 17*(1), 41–50.

Yang, Y. T. C., & Chou, H. A. (2008). Beyond critical thinking skills: Investigating the relationship between critical thinking skills and dispositions through different online instructional strategies. *British Journal of Educational Technology, 39*(4), 666–684.

Youniss, J., McLellan, J. A., & Strouse, D. (1994). "We're popular, but we're not snobs": Adolescents describe their crowds. In R. Montemayor, G. R. Adams, & T. P. Gullotta (Eds.), *Personal relationships during adolescence.* Thousand Oaks, CA: Sage.

Yoon, U., Fahim, C., Perusse, D., & Evans, A. C. (2010). Lateralized genetic and environmental influences on human brain morphology of 8-year-old twins. *NeuroImage, 53*(3), 1117–1125.

Yu, L., & Suen, H. K. (2005). Historical and contemporary exam-driven education fever in China. *KEDI Journal of Educational Policy, 2,* 1, 17–33.

Yung, B. H. W. (2001). Three views of fairness in a school-based assessment scheme of practical work in biology. *International Journal of Science Education, 23,* 985–1005.

Z

Zatz, S., & Chassin, L. (1985). Cognitions of test-anxious children under naturalistic test-taking conditions. *Journal of Consulting and Clinical Psychology, 53,* 393–401.

Zeidner, M. (1998). *Text anxiety: The state of the art.* New York: Plenum.

Zeidner, M., & Nevo, B. (1992). Test anxiety in examinees in a college admissions testing situation: Incidence, dimensionality, and cognitive correlates. In K. Hagtvet & T. Johnsen (Eds.), *Advances in test anxiety research, Vol. 7* (pp. 288–303). Amsterdam: Swets & Zeitlinger.

Zentall, S. R., & Morris, B. J. (2010). "Good job, you're so smart": The effects of inconsistency of praise type on young children's motivation. *Journal of Experimental Child Psychology, 107,* 155–163.

Zentall, S. S. (1993). Research on the educational implications of attention deficit hyperactivity disorder. *Exceptional Children, 60,* 143–153.

Zhang, D. (2006). *Theoretical and empirical studies on mathematics teaching for "two basics" in China* [in Chinese]. Shanghai, China: Shanghai Educational Press.

Zhu, X., & Simon, H. A. (1987). Learning mathematics from examples and by doing. *Cognition and Instruction, 4,* 137–166.

Zigler, E., & Berman, W. (1983). Discerning the future of early childhood intervention. *American Psychologist, 38,* 894–906.

Zigler, E., & Gilman, E. (1998). The legacy of Jean Piaget. In G. A. Kimble & M. Wertheimer (Eds.), *Portraits of pioneers in psychology* (pp. 145–160). Washington, DC: American Psychological Association.

Zigler, E., Hodapp, R. M., & Edison, M. R. (1990). From theory to practice in the care and education of mentally retarded individuals. *American Journal on Mental Retardation, 95,* 1–12.

Zimmerman, B. J. (1998). Academic studying and the development of personal skill: A self-regulatory perspective. *Educational Psychologist, 33*(3), 73–86.

Zimmerman, B. J. (2000). Self-efficacy: An essential motive to learn. *Contemporary Educational Psychology, 25,* 82–91.

Zimmerman, B. J. (2001). Theories of self-regulated learning and academic achievement: An overview and analysis. In B. J. Zimmerman & D. H. Schunk (Eds.), *Self-regulated learning and academic achievement: Theoretical perspectives* (2nd ed., pp. 1–38). Mahwah, NJ: Erlbaum.

Zimmerman, B. J., Bandura, A., & Martinez-Pons, M. (1992). Self-motivation for academic attainment: The role of self-efficacy beliefs and personal goal setting. *American Educational Research Journal, 29,* 663–676.

Zimmerman, B. J., & Kitsantas, A. (1997). Developmental phases in self-regulation: Shifting from progress to outcome goals. *Journal of Educational Psychology, 89,* 29–36.

Zimmerman, B. J., & Martinez-Pons, M. (1990). Student differences in self-regulated learning: Relating grade, sex, and giftedness to self-efficacy and strategy use. *Journal of Educational Psychology, 82,* 51–59.

Zimmerman, B. J., & Schunk, D. J. (2001). *Self-regulated learning and academic achievement: Theoretical perspectives* (2nd ed.). Mahwah, NJ: Erlbaum.

Zins, J. E., Bloodworth, M. R., Weissberg, R. P., & Wahlberg, H. J. (2004). The scientific base linking social and emotional learning to school success. In J. Zins, M. Bloodworth, R. Weissberg, & H. Wahlberg (Eds.), *Building academic success on social and emotional learning: What does the research say?* (pp. 3–22). New York: Teachers College Press.

Zins, J. E., Payton, J. W., Weissberg R. P., & O'Brien, M. U. (2007). Social and emotional learning and successful school performance. In G. Matthews, M. Zeidner, & R. D. Roberts (Eds.), *Emotional intelligence: Knowns and unknowns* (pp. 376–395). New York: Oxford University Press.

Zohar, A., & Dori, Y. J. (2003). Higher-order thinking skills and low-achieving students: Are they mutually exclusive? *Journal of the Learning Sciences, 12*(2), 145–181.

Zusho, A., & Pintrich, P. R. (2003). A process-oriented approach to culture: Theoretical and methodological issues in the study of culture and student motivation in a multicultural context. In F. Salili & R. Hoosain (Eds.), *Teaching, learning, and motivation in a multicultural context* (pp. 33–65). Greenwich, CT: Information Age.

Module 1

[**page 12 Table 1.2:** "INTASC Standards"] From www.ccsso.org/projects/Interstate_New_Teacher_Assessment_and_Support_Consortium/#resource. Reprinted with the permission of the Council of Chief State School Officers.

Module 4

[**page 71 Table 4.2:** "Planning Lessons that Integrate Emotional Intelligence"] From G. Doty, *Fostering Emotional Intelligence in K-8 Students* (Thousand Oaks, Calif.: Corwin Press, 2001), p. 14. Copyright © 2001 by Sage Publications, Inc. Reprinted with permission.

Module 6

[**page 103, Figure 6.1:** "Review of Brain Structures and Functions"] Adapted and reprinted with the permission of Massoud Bina, MD. Copyright © 1997. Reprinted with permission.

[**page 106 Figure 6.5:** "Brain Development"] Copyright © 2009 by Dwayne Godwin and Jorge Cham, all rights reserved.

[**page 109 Figure 6.7:** "Areas of the Brain Involved in Reading"] From www.brainconnection.com. Reprinted with the permission of PositScience Corporation.

Module 7

[**page 123 Figure 7.1:** "Piaget's Conservation Tasks"] From R. S. Siegler and M. W. Allball, *Children's Thinking, Fourth Edition*. Copyright © 2005. Reprinted the with permission of Pearson Education, Upper Saddle River, NJ.

Module 8

[**page 138 Table 8.2:** "Benchmarks of Normal Development in Phonological Awareness"] From J. K. Torgesen and P. G. Mathes, *A Basic Guide to Understanding, Assessing, and Teaching Phonological Awareness* (Austin, Tex.: Pro-Ed, 2000), p. 7. Copyright © 2000 by Pro-Ed, Inc. Reprinted with permission.

Module 11

[**page 186 Figure 11.2:** "Baddeley's Model of Working Memory"] Redrawn from Figure 1 from http://www.smithsrisca.demon.co.uk/PSYbaddeley2000.html. Copyright © 2004 by Derek J. Smith. Reprinted with the permission of Derek J. Smith.

[**page 196:** Harley Schwadron cartoon, "Refresh my memory, Ms. Hamish.] Reprinted with the permission of CartoonStock Ltd., www.cartoonstock.com.

Module 12

[**page 217 Example 12.3:** "Reciprocal Dialogue Example"] From A. S. Palincsar and A. L. Brown, "Reciprocal teaching of comprehension-fostering and comprehension-monitoring activities" from Cognition & Instruction 1 (1984): 117–175. Copyright © 1984 Routledge. Reprinted by permission of Taylor & Francis Book Group.

[**page 219 Example 12.4:** "Sample Procedural Facilitations"] Adapted from M. Scardamalia, C. Bereiter, and R. Steinbach, "Teachability of reflective processes in written composition" from Cognitive Science 8 (1984): 173–190. Copyright © 1984 Routledge. Reprinted by permission of Taylor & Francis Book Group.

[**page 220, Figure 12.2a:** "Note-Taking Techniques"] From K. A. Kiewra, "How classroom teachers can help students learn and teach them how to learn" from Theory into Practice 41 (2002): 71–80. Copyright © 2002 College of Education, The Ohio State University. Reprinted by permission of Routledge/Taylor & Francis Group.

Module 13

[**page 232 Example 13.2:** "Mathematical Problem Solving with Lower Achievers"] Adapted from M. B. Means and M. S. Knapp, "Cognitive approaches to teaching advanced skills to educationally disadvantaged students" in H. F. Clarizio, W. A. Mehrens, and W. G. Hapkiewicz (Eds.), *Contemporary issues in educational psychology, Sixth Edition.* Copyright © 1994. Reprinted by permission of McGraw-Hill, Inc.

Module 14

[**page 242 Table 14.2:** "Qualitative Dimensions of Critical Thought"] From R. Paul and L. Elder, *The Miniature Guide to Critical Thinking: Concepts and Tools.* Copyright © 2006. Reprinted with the permission of the Foundation for Critical Thinking, www.criticalthinking.org.

[**page 243 Example 14.1:** "Question Sets That Can Be Used Effectively in Class Discussions"] Adapted from R. Paul, A. J. A. Binker, D. Martin, and K. Adamson, *Critical Thinking Handbook: High School.* Copyright © 1989. Adapted with the permission of the Foundation for Critical Thinking, www.criticalthinking.org.

[**page 247 Table 14.3:** "IDEAL Problem-solving Steps] From J. D. Bransford and B. S. Stein, *The IDEAL Problem Solver: A guide for improving thinking, learning, and creativity, Second Edition.* Copyright © 1983, 1993 W.H. Freeman & Company, Inc. Used with permission.

Module 15

[**page 271 Table 15.1:** "Guidelines for Effective Praise"] From J. Brophy, "Teacher praise: A functional analysis" from Review of Educational Research 51.1 (1981): 5–32. Copyright © 1981 by the American Educational Research Association. Reprinted by permission of Sage Publications, Inc.

Module 16

[**page 290 Example 16.1:** "Sample Questions to Assess Student Attributions"] From D. Stipek, *Motivation to Learn: Integrating Theory and Practice.* Copyright © 2002. Reprinted with permission of Pearson Education, Inc.

[**page 292 Example 16.2:** "Behaviors Indicating Learned Helplessness"] From D. Stipek, *Motivation to Learn: Integrating Theory and Practice.* Copyright © 2002. Reprinted by permission from Pearson Education, Inc.

Module 17

[**page 304 Figure 17.1:** "Four Types of Students"] From M. V. Covington and K. J. Mueller, "Intrinsic versus Extrinsic Motivation: An approach/avoidance reformulation" from Education Psychology

Review 13, no. 2 (2001): 157–176. Copyright © 2001. Reprinted by permission of Springer.

[**page 307 Figure 17.3:** "A Taxonomy of Human Motivation"] Adapted from R. M. Ryan, and E. L. Deci, "Self-determination theory and the facilitation of intrinsic motivation, social development, and well-being" from American Psychologist 55.1 (January 2000): 72. Copyright © 2000 American Psychological Association. Used with permission.

Module 18

[**page 331 Example 18.4:** "Basic Components of a Lesson Plan"] Adapted from J. G. Thompson, *First-Year Teacher's Survival Kit: Ready to use strategies, tools, and activities for meeting the challenge of each school day, Second Edition.* Copyright © 2007 by John Wiley & Sons, Inc. Adapted with permission of John Wiley & Sons, Inc.

[**page 334 Guideline 18.1:** "Establishing Norms and Expectations"] Adapted from S. C. Stewart, W. H. Evans, and D. J. Kaczynski, "Setting the stage for success: Assessing the instructional environment" from Preventing School Failure 41, no 2 (1997): 53–56. Copyright © 1997 by Routledge. Adapted by permission of Routledge/Taylor & Francis.

[**page 339 Guideline 18.3:** "Dos and Don'ts in Developing Strong Teacher-Student Relationships"] From American Psychological Association, "Improving Students' Relationships with Teachers to Provide Essential Supports for Learning," www.apa.org/education/k12/relationships.aspx. Reprinted with the permission of the American Psychological Association.

Module 19

[**page 349 cartoon**] CALVIN AND HOBBES © 1995 Watterson Dist. by Universal Press Syndicate. Reprinted with permission. All rights reserved.

[**page 351 Example 19.2:** "Models of Classroom Management and Discipline"] Adapted from C. M. Charles, *Building Classroom Discipline, Sixth Edition.* Copyright © 1999. Adapted with the permission of Pearson Education, Inc.

Module 20

[**page 373 Table 20.2:** "Components of Instructional Conversations"] Adapted from C. Goldenberg, "Instructional Conversations: Promoting comprehension through discussion" from The Reading Teacher 46.4 (1992/1993): 316–326. Copyright © 1992. Adapted with the permission of the International Reading Association.

[**page 374 Example 20.2:** "Question Stems for Reciprocal Questioning"] Adapted from A. King, "Structuring peer interaction to promote high-level cognitive processing" from Theory into Practice 41.1 (2002): 33–39. Copyright © 2002 College of Education, The Ohio State University. Adapted with the permission of Routledge/Taylor & Francis Group.

Module 22

[**page 407 Table 22.2:** "Description of selected WISC-IV Subtests"] Simulated items similar to those in the Wechsler Intelligence Scale for Children–Fourth Edition. Copyright © 2003 by NCS Pearson, Inc. Reproduced with permission. All rights reserved. "Wechsler Intel-

ligence Scale for Children" and "WISC" are trademarks, in the U.S. and/or other countries, of Pearson Education, Inc. or its affiliate(s).

[**page 412 Table 22.3:** "Multiple Intelligences Theory: Guidelines and Misapplications"] From H. Gardner, "Reflections on multiple intelligences: Myths and messages" from Phi Delta Kappan 77.3 (1995): 200–203. Copyright © 1995. Reprinted with the permission of Phi Delta Kappa International.

[**page 414 Table 22.4:** "Teaching to Analytical, Creative, and Practical Abilities"] From R. J. Sternberg, "What does it mean to be smart?" from Educational Leadership 54.6 (1997): 20–24. Copyright © 1997. Reprinted with the permission of ACSD.

Module 23

[**page 424 cartoon**] Copyright © 2005 by Randy Glasbergen. Used with permission.

Module 26

[**page 477, logo**] Used with permission of the National Association of Secondary School Principals, parent organization of the National Honor Society.

[**page 482 Table 26.1:** "Assessment Tool Kit"] From Lorna M. Earl, Steven Katz, and Western and Northern Canadian Protocol for Collaboration in Education, *Rethinking Classroom Assessment with Purpose in Mind: Assessment for Learning, Assessment as Learning, Assessment of Learning.* Winnipeg, MB: Manitoba Education, Leadership and Youth, 2006. Available online at www.wncp.ca. Adapted with permission.

[**page 485 Figure 26.1:** "Five-step inclusive grading model"] From Thomas R. Guskey and Lee Ann Jung, "Grading and Reporting in a Standards-Based Environment: Implications for Students with Special Needs" from Theory into Practice 48 (2009): 57. Copyright © 2009 College of Education and Human Ecology, The Ohio State University. Reprinted by permission of Routledge/Taylor & Francis Group.

[**page 488 Guideline 26.3:** "Parent-Teacher Conferences"] Adapted from J. G. Thompson, *First-Year Teacher's Survival Kit: Ready to use strategies, tools, and activities for meeting the challenge of each school day, Second Edition.* Copyright © 2007 by John Wiley & Sons, Inc. Adapted with permission of John Wiley & Sons, Inc.

Module 27

[**page 495 Example 27.1:** "Time Requirements for Certain Assessment Tasks"] From A. J. Nitko and S. M. Brookhart, *Educational Assessment of Students, Fifth Edition.* Copyright © 2007. Reprinted by permission of Pearson Education, Inc., Upper Saddle River, NJ.

[**page 497 Example 27.2:** "Test Blueprint for a High School Science Unit"] Adapted from W. J. Kryspin and J. F. Feldhusen, *Developing Classroom Tests.* Copyright © 1974. Reprinted by permission of Pearson Education, Inc., Upper Saddle River, NJ.

[**page 501 Guideline 27.2:** "Writing Multiple-choice Items"] Adapted from T. M. Haladyna, S. M. Downing, and M. C. Rodriquez, "A review of multiple-choice item-writing guidelines for classroom assessment" from Applied Measurement in Education 15.3 (2002): 309–334. Copyright © 2002 by Routledge. Adapted by permission of Routledge/Taylor & Francis Group.

[**page 504 Guideline 27.3:** "Testing Checklist"] Adapted from G. J. Cizek, "Reliability and validity in student achievement" from *Theory into Practice* 48 (2009): 63–71. Copyright © 2009 College of Education, The Ohio State University. Reprinted by permission of Routledge/Taylor & Francis Group.

Module 28

[**page 513 Figure 28.1:** "Cognitive Categories"] From B. Clark, *Growing Up Gifted: Developing the potential of children at home and at school.* Copyright © 2002. Reprinted by permission of Pearson Education, Inc., Upper Saddle River, NJ.

[**page 518 Example 28.1:** "Template for Holistic Rubrics"] From C. A. Mertler, "Designing scoring rubrics for your classroom" from *Practical Assessment, Research, and Evaluation* 7.25 (2001). Reprinted with permission.

[**page 518 Example 28.2:** "Template for Analytic Rubrics"] From C. A. Mertler, "Designing scoring rubrics for your classroom" from *Practical Assessment, Research, and Evaluation* 7.25 (2001). Reprinted with permission.

Unit 9

[**page 535 cartoon**] © Sidney Harris. www.ScienceCartoonsPlus.com. Used with permission.

Module 29

[**page 537 Table 29.1:** "Comparison of Classroom Tests and Standardized Tests"] From T. M. Haladyna, *Essentials of Standardized Achievement Testing: Validity and Accountability.* Copyright © 2002. Reprinted by permission of Pearson Education, Inc.

[**page 538 Example 29.1:** "Examples of Standardized Tests in Four Broad Areas"] From M. Chatterji, *Designing and Using Tools for Educational Assessment.* Copyright © 2003. Reprinted by permission of Pearson Education, Inc.

[**page 539 Table 29.2:** "Comparison of Criterion-referenced and Norm-referenced Tests"] From R. J. Gregory, *Psychological Testing: History, Principles, and Applications, Sixth Edition* (Boston: Pearson, 2010). Copyright © 2010. Reprinted by permission of Pearson Education, Inc.

[**page 540 Example 29.2:** "A Simple Standardized Test Score Report"] From *TerraNova, Third Edition* Individual Profile. Copyright © 2003 CTB/McGraw-Hill. Reprinted by permission.

Module 30

[**page 557 Guidelines 30.1:** "Using Standardized Tests with Students at Risk"] From American Educational Research Association, *Standards for educational and psychological testing.* Copyright © 1999. Reprinted with the permission of the American Educational Research Association.

[**page 558 Example 30.1:** "Accommodations for Students at Risk"] From C. R. Reynolds, R. B. Livingston, and V. Willson, *Measurement and Assessment in Education.* Copyright © 2006. Reprinted by permission of Pearson Education, Inc.

[**page 562 Table 30.1:** "Interstate New Teacher Assessment and Support Consortium (INTASC) Principles"] From INTASC (1992). Reprinted with the permission of the Council of Chief State School Officers.

PHOTO CREDITS

Module 1

Opener: © Kevin Dodge/Corbis; **p. 6:** © Pixland/PunchStock; **p. 10:** © David Buffington/Getty Images; **p. 11:** © Lambert/Hulton Archive/Getty Images; **p. 14:** © Alamy Images

Unit 1

Opener: © Marcy Maloy/Photodisc/Getty Images; **p. 23:** © Myrleen Ferguson Cate/PhotoEdit; **p. 25:** © PhotoAlto/Laurence Mouton/Getty Images; **p. 27:** © David Young-Wolff/PhotoEdit; **p. 29:** © Ron Chapple/Thinkstock Images/Punchstock

Module 2

Opener: © Amy Etra/PhotoEdit; **p. 36:** © MM Productions/Corbis; **p. 37:** © Sean Justice/Corbis; **p. 38 (left):** © SW Productions/Photodisc/Getty Images; **p. 38 (right):** © BananaStock/PunchStock; **p. 40:** © Siri Stafford/Digital Vision/PunchStock

Module 3

Opener: © Blend Images/Getty Images; **p. 47:** © DAJ/Getty Images; **p. 48:** © Digital Vision; **p. 49:** © Corbis Super RF/Alamy; **p. 56:** © Laurence Mouton/PhotoAlto Agency/Getty Images

Module 4

Opener: © RubberBall; **p. 63 (left):** © Reuters/Corbis; **p. 63 (middle):** © Jose Luis Pelaez Inc/Blend Images/Corbis; **p. 63 (right):** © BananaStock; **p. 66 (top left):** © Dale Durfee/Stone/Getty Images; **p. 66 (top middle):** © SuperStock; **p. 66 (top right):** © Dkal Inc./Getty Images; **p. 66 (bottom left & middle):** © SuperStock; **p. 66 (bottom right):** © Index Stock/Photolibrary/Getty Images; **p. 68:** © David Lassman/Syracuse Newspapers/The Image Works; **p. 70:** © Spencer Platt/Getty Images; **p. 72:** © Michael Newman/PhotoEdit

Module 5

Opener: © Emely/zefa/Corbis; **pp. 80, 83, 84:** © Michael Newman/PhotoEdit; **p. 87:** © Michael Buckner/Getty Images

Unit 2

Opener: © Ingram Publishing/SuperStock; **p. 93:** © Radius Images/Alamy; **p. 95:** © Cindy Charles/PhotoEdit; **p. 97:** © Geoff Brightling/Getty Images; **p. 99:** © Getty Images

Module 6

Opener: © Royalty-Free/Corbis; **p. 102:** © Eric Van Den Brulle/Getty Images; **p. 107 (left):** © VCL/Antonio Mo/Getty Images; **p. 107 (right):** © Creatas; **p. 108:** Streissguth, A. P., & Little, R. E. (1994). "Unit 5: Alcohol, Pregnancy, and the Fetal Alcohol Syndrome: Second Edition" of the Project Cork Institute Medical School Curriculum (slide lecture series) on Biomedical Education: Alcohol Use and Its Medical Consequences, produced by Dartmouth Medical School; **p. 110:** © Stockbyte/Getty Images; **p. 113:** © Arthur Tilley/Getty Images

Module 7

Opener: © David Young-Wolff/PhotoEdit, **p. 121 (top left):** © Doug Goodman/Photo Researchers; **p. 121 (top right):** © BananaStock/PunchStock; **p. 121 (bottom left):** © Michael Scott for McGraw-Hill Companies; **p. 121 (bottom right):** © Jon Feingersh/Getty Images; **p. 127:** © Digital Vision/PunchStock

Module 8

Opener: © Image Source/Alamy, **p. 135:** © BananaStock/Picture-Quest; **p. 136:** © James Woodson/Getty Images; **p. 137:** © Brand X Pictures/PunchStock; **p. 141:** © Image Source/Getty Images; **p. 143:** © Jose Luis Pelaez Inc./Blend Images/Jupiterimages

Unit 3

Opener: © Jeff Cadge/Photographer's Choice/Getty Images; **p. 150:** © Tom Grill/Corbis; **p. 152:** © Getty Images; **p. 155:** © Comstock Select/Corbis; **p. 157:** © David Young-Wolff/PhotoEdit

Module 9

Opener: © Suzie Ross/McGraw-Hill; **p. 159:** © Robert W. Ginn/PhotoEdit; **p. 160:** © Mike Kemp/Rubberball Productions/Getty Images; **p. 163:** © Royalty-Free/Corbis; **p. 166:** © Mary Kate Denny/PhotoEdit; **p. 167:** © Kevin Dodge/Corbis

Module 10

Opener: © Stockbyte/Getty Images; **p. 174:** Bandura, A., Ross, D., & Ross, S. A. (1961). Transmission of aggressions through imitation of aggressive models. Journal of Abnormal and Social Psychology, 63(3), 575–582. Reprinted with permission.; **p. 175 (both):** © Getty Images; **p. 176:** © Michael Newman/PhotoEdit; **p. 178 (top):** © Jon Feingersh/Blend Images/Getty Images; **p. 178 (bottom):** Courtesy of the White House

Module 11

Opener: © Jack Hollingsworth/Corbis; **p. 185:** © John Berry/Syracuse Newspapers/The Image Works; **p. 187 (top):** © Royalty-Free/Corbis; **p. 187 (bottom):** © Image Source/PunchStock; **p. 191:** © D. Hurst/Alamy; **p. 194:** © Ableimages/Riser/Getty Images

Unit 4

Opener: © ColorBlind Images/Iconica/Getty Images; **p. 203:** © Ariel Skelley/Blend Images/Getty Images; **p. 204:** © PhotoLink/Photodisc/Getty Images; **p. 207:** © Tim O'Leary/zefa/Corbis; **p. 209:** © Justin Guariglia/National Geographic/Getty Images

Module 12

Opener: © Thinkstock/Corbis, **p. 213:** © Michael Newman/PhotoEdit; **p. 214:** © Pixland/Corbis

Module 13

Opener: © Tobi Corney/Getty Images; **p. 226:** © Karl Weatherly/Getty Images; **p. 227:** © Corbis Premium RF/Alamy; **p. 228:** © Goodshoot/PunchStock

Module 14

Opener: © Radius Images/Alamy; **p. 239:** © Harald Sund/Photographer's Choice/Getty Images; **p. 240 (left):** Library of Congress; **p. 240 (right):** © Getty Images; **p. 244:** © Photodisc/SuperStock; **p. 249:** © 2005 Jim West/The Image Works

Unit 5

Opener: © Brand X/Jupiter Images; **p. 257:** © Image Source/AGE fotostock; **p. 259:** © Blend Images/Alamy; **p. 261, 263:** © image100 Ltd.

Module 15

Opener: © Image Source/Getty Images; **p. 266:** © i love images/Jupiter Images; **p. 267:** Courtesy of the Authors; **p. 272:** © David Deas/Getty Images; **p. 273:** © Jim Cummins/Corbis

Module 16

Opener: © Stockbyte/PunchStock; **p. 280:** © Stockdisc/PunchStock; **p. 286:** © John Birdsall/The Image Works; **p. 288 (both):** © Royalty-Free/Corbis; **p. 289:** © GoGo Images/Jupiter Images

Module 17

Opener: © The McGraw-Hill Companies/Andrew Resek, photographer; **p. 299:** From The Little Engine that Could by Watty Piper, illustrated by George and Doris Hauman, © & TM Penguin Group (USA) Inc. The Little Engine That Could, "I Think I Can" and all related titles, logos, and characters are trademarks of Penguin Group (USA) Inc. Used by permission. All rights reserved; **p. 300:** © Daniel Pangbourne/Digital Vision/Getty Images; **p. 303:** © Stockbyte/Getty Images; **p. 305:** © Randy Faris/Corbis

Unit 6

Opener: © Blend Images/Getty Images; **p. 318:** © Jose Luis Pelaez/Iconica/Getty Images; **p. 321:** © AAGAMIA/Iconica/Getty Images; **p. 323:** © Jeff Greenberg/PhotoEdit; **p. 325:** © Royalty-Free/Corbis

Module 18

Opener: © Blend Images/Getty Images; **p. 330 (both):** Courtesy of the Authors; **p. 333:** © Andersen Ross/Blend Images /Jupiter Images; **p. 337:** © Purestock/Getty Images; **p. 338:** © altrendo images/Getty Images

Module 19

Opener: © Digital Vision/Getty Images ; **p. 347:** © Pixland/PunchStock; **p. 350:** © Royalty Free/Corbis; **p. 352:** © Peter Hvizdak/The Image Works; **p. 335:** © Brand X Pictures/PunchStock; **p. 358:** © Image Source Black/Alamy

Module 20

Opener: © dynamicgraphics/Jupiterimages; **p. 367:** © Photodisc/Getty Images; **p. 369:** © Phillip Spears/Getty Images

Module 21

Opener: © Bill Aron/Photo Edit; **p. 378:** © McGraw-Hill Companies Inc./Ken Karp, photographer; **p. 379:** © Ableimages/Digital Vision/Getty Images

Unit 7

Opener: © Corbis; **p. 395:** © Jutta Klee/ableimages/Corbis; **p. 396:** © Michael Newman/PhotoEdit; **p. 399:** © Erik Isakson/Tetra Images/Corbis; **p. 401:** © Ocean/Corbis

Module 22

Opener: © Ingram Publishing; **p. 406:** © Joel Gordon

Module 23

Opener: © Getty Images; **p. 419:** © Royalty-Free/Corbis; **p. 423:** © Dimitri Vervitsiotis/Getty Images; **p. 425:** © Image Club; **p. 427:** © David Young-Wolff/PhotoEdit

Module 24

Opener: © JGI/Jamie Grill/Getty Images; **p. 437:** © Jupiterimages/Getty Images

Module 25

Opener: © PhotoConcepts/Getty Images; **p. 547:** © Mike Kemp/Rubberball Productions/Getty Images; **p. 459:** © MGM-UA/Photofest

Unit 8

Opener: © SW Productions/Photodisc/Getty Images; **p. 469:** © Ellen B. Senisi/The Image Works; **p. 471:** © Ellen Senisi/The Image Works; **p. 475:** © David Lassman/Syracuse Newspapers/The Image Works

Module 26

Opener: © Scott Speakes/Corbis; **p. 477:** Used with permission of the National Association of Secondary School Principals, parent organization of the National Honor Society; **p. 481:** © BananaStock/PictureQuest; **p. 488:** © SW Productions/Photodisc/Getty Images

Module 27

Opener: © Liquidlibrary/Jupiterimages; **p. 495:** © Image Source/Alamy

Module 28

Opener: © Corbis/age fotostock; **p. 510, 511:** © Corbis; **p. 514:** © Michael Newman/PhotoEdit; **p. 520:** © Creatas/PunchStock

Unit 9

Opener: © Comstock/PictureQuest; **p. 529:** © Robin Sachs/PhotoEdit; **p. 533:** © Bob Daemmrich/The Image Works

Module 29

p. 546: © Royalty-Free/Corbis

Module 30

p. 552: © BananaStock/PunchStock; **p. 555:** © PhotoAlto/Eric Audras/Getty Images; **p. 561:** © McGraw-Hill

A

ability, 282–283
ability attributions, 286, 286t
ability grouping, 301, 378
abstraction, 229
abuse
  emotional, 34t
  physical, 34t
  sexual, 34t
academic achievement
  self-efficacy, and, 179
  socioeconomic status, and, 14
academic intrinsic motivation
  cognitive theory, 279
  defined, 265
academic learning time, 332
academic performance
  ADHD, and, 457
  anxiety, and, 454
  autism spectrum disorders, and, 460
  conduct disorder, and, 458
  depression, and, 455
academic socialization, 341
acceleration, 422, 423
accommodation
  cognitive adaptation, 120
  students with disabilities, 556
accountability, 552, 553
achievement. See academic
  achievement
"Achievement Gap" case study, 2–3
achievement goal, 280
acronym, 188, 216
action zone, 328
activation level, 191
active exploration of the physical
  environment, 120
active learning, 129
active listening, 143
active long-term memory (ALTM), 186
adaptive behavior, 436
adequate yearly progress (AYP), 553, 554
ADHD. See attention-deficit
  hyperactivity disorder (ADHD)
admissions, assessment for, 477
adolescence, 46t
  emotional development milestones,
    65t
  identity vs. identity diffusion, 46t, 48
  social competence characteristics, 57
adolescent egocentrism, 214
advance organizer, 369
Advanced Placement (AP) test, 560
African Americans, 13
  cultural beliefs, 42
  intellectual disabilities, 436
  intelligence testing, 410
  IQ score average, 559

motivation, 289
parents' expectations, 42
self-efficacy, 301
self-esteem, 54
aggression
  gender, and, 38
  overt, 38, 82
  relational, 38, 39, 82
"Air" case study, 202–203
Alaska Natives, 13
Albert, Linda, 336
algorithm, 247
alphabetic principle, 442
alternate-choice item, 498
ALTM. See active long-term memory
  (ALTM)
ambience, classroom, 327
American Indians, 13
amygdala, 113
analogical thinking, 247
analogical transfer, 227
analytic rubric, 517, 518
analytical abilities, 404, 419
analytical thinking, 240
androgynous gender-role identity, 51,
  52
anxiety, 292–294, 348
anxiety disorder, 453–455
AP test. See Advanced Placement (AP)
  test
appearance-reality distinctions, 212
appropriate education, IDEIA/Section
  504, 452
argument analysis, 244
Armed Services Vocational Aptitude
  Battery (ASVAB), 538
articulation, 370
articulation disorder, 142
articulation problems, 142
Asian Americans, 13
  cultural beliefs, 42
  motivation, 289
  parents' expectations, 42
assessment. See also tests
  advantages/disadvantages, 520–521
  authentic, 481, 511–512
  data using, 482
  defined, 477
  evaluation of, 516–520
  formal, 480
  formative, 480–481, 510
  grading procedures, 483–485
  informal, 480
  method selection, 480–482
  parent-teacher communication,
    486–488
  performance, 510–511
  planning, 479–483

portfolio, 514–515
presentation, 512–513
project, 514
purposes of, 477
report cards/narrative reports,
  485–486
summative, 480–481, 510
teacher competence standards,
  478–479
tool kit, 482t
"Assessment: Cafeteria Style" case
  study, 472–473
assessment plan, 479
assimilation, 120
ASVAB. See Armed Services Vocational
  Aptitude Battery (ASVAB)
attachment theory, 46
attainment value, 280
attention, 110
  information processing theory, 185
  social cognitive theory, 176
attentional limits, 194, 194
attention-deficit hyperactivity disorder
  (ADHD), 456–458
  characteristics, 457
  combined subtype, 456
  comorbidity, 456
  developmental differences, 456–457
  diagnosis, 456
  interventions, 461–462
  memory research, 110
  predominantly hyperactive-
    impulsive subtype, 456
  predominantly inattentive subtype,
    456
  school performance/relationships,
    457
attribution theory, 282–284, 284t
Ausubel, David, 368
authentic activities, 273, 310
authentic assessments, 481, 511
authentic tasks, 404
authoritarian parenting, 32
authoritative parenting, 32, 300
autism spectrum disorders, 459–460
automatic processing, 187, 187
automaticity
  external memory aids, compared,
    195
  information processing theory, 193
  intelligence, and, 414
  transfer, of skills/knowledge, 226, 231
  word recognition training, 443
autonomy, 305
autonomy vs. shame/doubt,
  toddlerhood, 46–47, 46t
autonomy-supportive learning,
  308–309, 309t

avoidance goals, 280
AYP. *See* adequate yearly progress (AYP)

B

babbling, 134, 136
Back to School Night, 342
backward-reaching transfer, 227
Baddeley's model of working memory, 186*f*
Bandura, Albert, 174, 177
"Basketball Star" case study, 26–27
Baumrind, Diana, 32
Baumrind's parenting practices, 32*t*
behavior management. *See* misbehavior
behavior setting, 333
behavioral disorders. *See* emotional/social/behavioral disorders
behavioral learning theories
   assumptions, 159
   classical conditioning, 159–161
   classroom applications, 166–169
   operant conditioning, 161–166. *See also* operant conditioning
behavioral theory
   classroom applications, 273–274
   flow theory, 272
   motivation, defined, 265–266
   praising students for learning, 269–272
   rewarding students for learning, 266–269
belief perseverance, 15, 246
belongingness, 50
"Bending the Rules" case study, 156–157
best practices, *11*
best work portfolios, 515
between-class ability grouping, 380–381
bilingual language acquisition, 139–141
biological maturation, 119
biological theories, 51
bisexuality, 13
Bloom, Benjamin, 239, 512
Bloom's taxonomy
   instruction planning, 365, 365*t*
   performance assessments, 512, 513*f*
   thinking skills, 239
bodily-kinesthetic intelligence, 404, 405*t*, 419, *419*
brain development
   activity during learning, 108–109
   brain activity during learning, 108–109
   brain structure/function, 102–104, 103*f*
   "brain-based learning" recommendations, 113–114

critical periods, 106
developmental processes, 104–105
emotion, 112–113
environment stimulation, 106
factors affecting, 105–108
gender differences, 108
genetics, 106
language, and, 134
math, 112
memory, 110–111
nutrition, and, 107
old *vs.* new thinking, 101*t*
plasticity, 107
reading, 111
research, and teaching, 109–114
research, classroom applications, 110–114
research, relevance of, 101–102
sensitive periods, 106–107
synoptic density, 105*f*
teratogens, 107
tools for studying the brain, 102*t*
Brain Gym, 113–114
brain hemispheres, 101
brain stem, 103, 103*f*
"brain-based learning" recommendations, 113–114
Broca's area, 103, 103*f*, 112
Bronfenbrenner, Urie, 348
Bronfenbrenner's biological model, 31*f*, 348
Brophy, Jere, 270, 271, 271t
Bruner, Jerome, 126
bullying, 39, 358
   conventional reasoning, 79
   cyberbullying, 358
   misbehavior, 348
Bush, George W., 552

C

Caine, Geoffrey, 113
Caine, Renata, 113
Canter, Lee, 351
Canter, Marlene, 351
CAPTA. *See* Child Abuse Prevention and Treatment Act (CAPTA)
career/educational interest inventories, 538
caring orientation, 79
case study research, 7
CASEL. *See* Collaborative for Academic, Social, and Emotional Learning (CASEL)
CAT scans, 102*t*
"Caterpillar Circle" case study, 318–319
causal attributions, 282
CBT. *See* cognitive-behavioral treatment (CBT)

cell body, 104
central executive, 186
central tendency, 541
centration, 122
cerebellum, 103, 103*f*
cerebrum (cerebral cortex), 102, 103, 134
certification
   assessment for, 477
   teachers, 560
chain mnemonic, 188, 216
cheating, 79, 356–357, 555
checklist, 516
"Cheetahs, Lions, and Leopards" case study, 396–397
child abuse. *See* abuse
Child Abuse Prevention and Treatment Act (CAPTA), 33
child-directed speech, 135*t*
chronic tardiness, 356
chronosystem, 31
chunking, 188
CIRC. *See* Cooperative Integrated Reading and Composition model (CIRC)
City University of New York (CUNY) Graduate Center, 15
class meeting, 337, *337*
classical conditioning, 159–161
classroom. *See also* schools
   emotional displays by students, *63*
   environmental cues, 328–330
   floor plan, examples, *328, 329*
   motivation techniques, 290–291
   positive relationships, 311
   procedures/routines, 337
   room arrangement, 327
   rules/consequences, 335–337
   safety, 322–323
   seating patterns, 327–328
classroom management/discipline models, 351
classroom practices, 10–16
"Classroom Safety" case study, 322–323
classroom stimuli, *185*
class-running procedures, 337
cliques, 37
coaching, 369
code mixing, 140
cognitive apprenticeship, 369, *369*
cognitive development
   constructivist theories, 119–126. *See also* constructivist theories
   issues, 126–128
   language, and, 127–128
   Piaget's theory, 119–124
   Vygotsky's theory, 124–126
cognitive disabilities
   classroom guidelines/applications, 436–438

IDEIA 2004, 433
intellectual disabilities, identifying, 435–436
mathematics disability, 443–445
planning/placement, 434–435
reading disability, 441–443
special education referral/eligibility, 433–434
specific learning disabilities (LD), 438–441
cognitive learning theory, teaching methods, 368–369
cognitive load, 186
cognitive-behavioral treatment (CBT), 460–461
Collaborative for Academic, Social, and Emotional Learning (CASEL), 72
collaborative group activities, 273
collective efficacy, 180
collective self-efficacy, 343
Coloroso, Barbara, 351
combination classes, 382
combined ADHD subtype, 456
commitment, 49
common sense, *vs.* scientific approaches, 6
competence
    emotional, 54
    environmental, 327–330
    social. *See* social competence
    teacher competence standards, 478–479
competency belief, 279
complaining, 355
comprehension, 371–374
computer simulations, 511
computerized axial tomography (CAT scans), 102*t*
concepts, 122
conceptual knowledge, 189, 365
conceptual skills, 436
concrete operational stage, *121, 123*
concurrent validity, 546
conditional knowledge, 211
conditioned response, 160
conditioned stimulus (CS), 160
conduct disorder, 458
confidence, 240
confidence interval, 547
confirmation bias, 15
congruent communication approach, 340
consensual assessment technique, 425
consequences
    classroom rules, and, 335–337
    conventional, 336
    effective use by teachers, 163–166
    instructional, 336
    logical, 336, 355, 358

conservation, 122
construct validity, 545, 559
constructivism, 119, 369–374
constructivist theories, 108
    effective teaching, and, 128–129
    Piaget, 119–124. *See also* Piaget's theory of cognitive development
    Vygotsky, 124–126. *See also* Vygotsky's theory of cognitive development
content validity
    classroom tests, 493
    standardized tests, 545–546, 559
context, 191
contiguity learning, 159, *159*
contingency contract, 356, *357*
contingency management, 460
continuous schedule, 163
continuum of research designs, *9*
control, 32
controllability, 282, 283*f*
controlled practice, 366
controlling praise, 270
conventional consequences, 336
conventional domain, 83
conventional level, 77*t*, 78
convergent thinking, 229, 424
convergent validity, 546
Cooper, Robert, 386
Cooperative Discipline (Albert), 336
Cooperative Integrated Reading and Composition model (CIRC), 384*t*
cooperative learning, 370–371, 382–385
    characteristics, 382–383
    cognitive disabilities, 437
    defined, 378
    effectiveness, 383–385
    skill-based cooperative methods, 384*t*
    teacher efficacy, 302
correlation coefficient, 7
correlational research designs, 7, 8*t*
cost, 280
counseling, assessment for, 477
CRCM. *See* Culturally Responsive Classroom Management (CRCM)
creative abilities, 405, 419
creative-productive giftedness, 421
creativity, 424–428, 426–427
    assessment methods, 425
    characteristics, 424–425
    checklist, *426*
    classroom applications, 427–428
    ethnicity/gender, and, 426–427
    identifying, 425–427
Crick, Nicki, 67
criterion-referenced letter grades, 483
criterion-referenced tests, 539, 539*t*

criterion-related validity, 546
critical period, brain development, 106
critical thinking, 241–245
    argument analysis, 244–245
    classroom application, 242–244
    defined, 241–242
    hypothesis testing, 244
    inductive/deductive reasoning, 244
    writing techniques, 244
critical thought, qualitative dimensions, 242*t*
cross-grade grouping, 381, 423
cross-sectional studies, 9
crowds, 37
"Cry Baby" case study, 22–23
CS. *See* conditioned stimulus (CS)
Csikzentmihalyi, Mihalyi, 272
cues, 162
cultural differences
    information processing theory, 193
    math processing, 112
    reading, and, 111
    self-efficacy, 178
    student-teacher relationships, 339
cultural factors, 41–42
cultural test bias hypothesis, 559
cultural tools, 126
Culturally Responsive Classroom Management (CRCM), 339
curriculum, and moral development, 86–87
curriculum compacting, 423, 424
Curwin, Richard, 351
cyberbullying, 358

D

daily lesson plans, 331
Damon, William, 85
dangerous behaviors, 358–360
DAT. *See* Differential Aptitude Test (DAT)
declarative knowledge, 189, 211, 364
decoding, 111, 137, 441
decontextualized learning, 266
deductive reasoning, 244, *244*
deficiency needs, 306
deficit, 441
deliberate practice, 228, *228*
demandingness, 85
democratic processes, 85
demonstrations, 512
dendrites, 104, 104*f*
depression, 455
descriptive rating scales, 516
descriptive research designs, 7, 8*t*
despair *vs.* integrity, late adulthood, 46*t*, 49
Detect-Practice-Repair (DPR), 445

development contexts
cultural factors, 41–42
family, 31–36. *See also* family
parental employment, 40–41
peers, 36–40. *See also* peer relations
developmental delay, 441, 442
developmental discipline, 86
developmental disorders, 453, 462
developmental factors
misbehavior, 348–349
motivational change, 287
deviation IQ, 407
Dewey, John, 369
diagnosis, assessment for, 477
DIF. *See* differential item functioning
(DIF)
Differential Aptitude Test (DAT), *538*
differential item functioning (DIF),
559
direct instruction, 365–367, 437
disability, 14. *See also* cognitive
disabilities
intellectual, 435–438
overview, 433*f*
disability referral form, *451*
discipline, 86
discovery learning, 368
discrepancy reduction model, 221
discriminant validity, 546
discrimination, 15, 160
disequilibrium, 120, 273
display rules, 63
distractors, 500
distributed practice, 191, 366
divergent thinking, 424, *424*
diversity
addressing, 13–16
student-teacher relationships, 339
divorce/remarriage, 34–36
doctrine of formal discipline, 226
Dodge, Kenneth, 67, 83
domain-general strategies, 112
domain-specific strategies, 112
DPR. *See* Detect-Practice-Repair (DPR)
Dreikurs, Rudolf, 351
dual discrepancy method, 440
dynamic testing, 128
dysfluency, 142, 144*t*

E

early childhood. *See also* infancy;
preschool; toddlerhood
"Air" case study, 202–203
articulation problems, 142
"Caterpillar Circle" case study,
318–319
"Cry Baby" case study, 22–23

emotional development milestones,
65*t*
emotional understanding, 64
"Fire Safety" case study, 92–93
"Kindergarten Readiness" case study,
528–529
"Letter *P* Day" case study, 394–395
"Pinch" case study, 150–151
"Worksheets, The" case study,
256–257
"Zoo, The" case study, 468–469
"Ecosystem" case study, 320–321
Edison, Thomas, 240
educational psychology, 6–16
classroom practices, 10–16
defined, 5–6
diversity, 13–15
INTASC Core Teaching Standards
2011, 12
philosophies of teaching, 10–13
research, 7–10. *See also* research
studies
science of, 6–10
Educational Testing Service (ETS), 560
EEG. *See* electroencephalography (EEG)
efficacy expectations, 299
effort, 178
effortful processing, 187, *187*
egocentric speech, 122
egocentrism, 77, 122
adolescent, 214
EI. *See* emotional intelligence (EI)
Eisenberg, Nancy, 80, 85*t*
Eisenberg's theory of prosocial moral
reasoning, 80
elaborative rehearsal, 187
electroencephalography (EEG), 102*t*
elementary school
"Cheetahs, Lions, and Leopards" case
study, 396–397
"Ecosystem" case study, 320–321
"Keyboard Courage" case study,
530–531
"Project Night" case study, 94–95
"Reading About Pirates" case study,
204–205
"Silly Students" case study, 152–153
"Team" case study, 24–25
within-class ability grouping, 385
"Writer's Block" case study, 258–259
"Writing Wizards" case study,
470–471
elicited imitation, 134
ELL. *See* English-language learner (ELL)
emotional abuse, 34*t*
emotional arousal, 300
emotional competence, 54
emotional context, 191

emotional development
emotion, defined, 62–63
emotional intelligence dimensions,
63–68. *See also* emotional
intelligence (EI)
emotionally intelligent teaching,
68–72
milestones, 65*t*
social-emotional learning (SEL),
70–72
emotional disturbance, 450
emotional expressiveness, 54–55, 62
emotional intelligence (EI), 63–68
classroom emotions, 68
emotional regulation, 66–67
emotional understanding, 64–65
emotionally-intelligent teaching,
68–72
relationships, 67–68
responding to others' emotions,
65–66
self-motivation, 67
*Emotional Intelligence: Why It Can
Matter More than IQ* (Goleman), 63
emotional regulation, 55, 66–67, 340
emotional triggers, *70*
emotional understanding, 55, 64–65
emotional/social/behavioral disorders,
450–453
ADHD, 456–458
anxiety, 453–455
autism spectrum disorders, 459–460
characteristics, 453–460
conduct disorder, 458
depression, 455
IDEIA, 450–453
interventions, 460–462
special education referral/eligibility,
450–453
emotions, 62, , 112–113
empathy, 66, 81–82
empathy-based guilt, 82
empirical learning, 127
encoding
information processing theory, 184
metacognition, 218
English Acquisition Act, 141
English as a Second Language (ESL), 556
English immersion, 140–141, 140*t*
English-language learner (ELL), 556
enrichment, 423
entity view of ability, 282, 302
environmental competence, 327–330
environmental cues, 328–330
environmental factors, and
misbehavior, 348–350
episodic buffer, 186
episodic knowledge, 189

epistemology, 119
equilibrium, 120
equivalence, 496
Erikson, Erik, 46
Erikson's psychosocial theory, 46–49
erogenous grouping, 387
ESL, English as a Second Language (ESL)
ethnic differences
    cooperative learning, and, 385
    creativity, and, 426–427
    intelligence, and, 410
    motivation, and, 289, *289*
    self-efficacy, 300–301
    student-teacher relationships, 339
ethnic group, 13
ethnic identity, 50–51, *51*
ethnic involvement, 50
ETS. *See* Educational Testing Service (ETS)
evaluating, 212
evaluation, 477, 539
evidence-based practice, 11
"Exam Grades" case study, 262–263
excessive talking, 355
exclusionary policies, 360
executive control functions, 212
exhibition, 513, 520
exosystem, 31
expansion, 135*t*
expectancies, 279
expectancy-value theory, 279, 284*t*
expectations
    behavior management, 352
    behavior setting, 333–337
    efficacy, 299
    outcome, 299
experience-dependent plasticity, 107
experience-expectant plasticity, 107
experiment, 512
experimental research designs, 8, 8*t*
explaining, 369
explicit knowledge, 189
exploration, 49, 370
exploratory discussion, 243
expository teaching, 368–369
expulsion policies, 360
extended response essay, 502
external locus, 282, 283*f*
external storage, 219
externalizing disorders, 453, 461
extinction, 160, 168
extinction burst, 168
extrinsic motivation, 265–266, 279, 299

F

face-to-face interaction, 371, 383
facial expressions, 66, 66*f*
fading, 126, 370

failure-accepting students, 305
failure-avoiding students, 304–305
fairness, 495
false-beliefs, 212
family, 31–36
    Baumrind's parenting practices, 32*t*
    child abuse/neglect, 33–34*t*
    divorce/remarriage, 34–36
    emotional expressiveness, 62
    family transitions, *36*
    moral development, 84–85
    parenting practices, 32–34
family conflict, 35
Family Educational Rights and Privacy
    Act (FERPA), 433, 488
family transitions, *36*
family-school relations, 341
far transfer, 229
FAS. *See* fetal alcohol syndrome (FAS)
fear, 113
feedback, 311
feminine gender-role identity, 51, 52
FERPA. *See* Family Educational Rights
    and Privacy Act (FERPA)
fetal alcohol syndrome (FAS), 107, 107*f*
fighting, 358, 360
"Fire Safety" case study, 92–93
fixed schedules, 163
flexibility, classroom, 327
floor plan, examples, *328, 329*
flow theory, 272
Flynn effect, 409
fMRI. *See* functional magnetic
    resonance imaging (fMRI)
fMRS. *See* functional magnetic
    resonance spectroscopy (fMRS)
forgetting, 191–192
formal assessment, 480
formal operational stage, *121, 123*–124
formative assessment, 367, 480–481,
    510, *510*
forward-reaching transfer, 227
frequency distribution, 542
friendships, 36
    peer context, 36–38
    preschool-age, *37*
"Frogs" case study, 96–97
frontal lobe, 103, 103*f*
functional fixedness, 246
functional magnetic resonance
    imaging (fMRI), 102*t*, 105
functional magnetic resonance
    spectroscopy (fMRS), 102*t*

G

Gamoran, Adam, 386
Gardner, Howard, 113

Gardner's multiple intelligences. *See*
    theory of multiple intelligences
GATB. *See* General Aptitude Test
    Battery (GATB)
Gates, Bill, 240
Gathercoal, Forrest, 335
GE scores. *See* grade-equivalent (GE)
    scores
gender, 13, 51
gender constancy, 52–53
gender differences
    aggression, and, *38*
    creativity, and, 426–427
    emotional expression, and, 63
    human brain development, 108
    intelligence, 410–412
    motivation, and, 287–288
    self-efficacy theory, 300
gender identity, 51
gender labeling, 52
gender schemas, 52
gender stability, 52
gender-role flexibility, 52
gender-role identity, 51
General Aptitude Test Battery (GATB),
    538
general crystallized intelligence (Gc),
    403
general fluid intelligence (Gf), 403
generalization, 160, 437
generativity *vs.* stagnation, middle
    adulthood, 46*t*, 48–49
generic rubric, 517
genetic epistemology, 119
genetics, and brain development, 106
Gibbs, John C., 82
giftedness, 420–424
    characteristics, 420–421
    identifying, 421–422
    multidimensional assessment, 422
    standardized IQ scores, 421–422
    teaching gifted students, 422–424
Gilligan, Carol, 78–79
Ginott, Haim, 338, 340, 351
Glasser, William, 351
Glenn, Stephen, 336
goal orientations, 285–286
    changes in, 285–286
    mastery-approach goals, 280, 281*t*,
      301
    performance-approach goals, 280,
      280, 281*t*, 301
    performance-avoidance goals, 281
    work-avoidance, 286
goal theory, 280–282, 284*t*
goals, 311
Goleman, Daniel, 63, 64
Gordon, Thomas, 351

grade-equivalent (GE) scores, 544
grading model, 483
grading on the curve, 484
grading practices, 311
grading procedures, 483–485
graphic rating scales, 516
group focus, 353
group processing, 371, 383, 388, 388*f*
group work, 382
group-administered IQ tests, 406
group-administered tests, 539
grouping practices
    ability grouping, 378–382
    between-class ability grouping,
        380–381
    classroom applications, 385–388
    cooperative learning, 382–385
    flexible grouping methods, 381–382
    within-class ability grouping, *378*, 379
growth need, 306
guidance/counseling, assessment for,
    477
guided discovery, 368
guided practice, 366
guilt *vs.* initiative, preschoolers, 46*t*,
    47, *47*

H

hands-on learning, 437, *437*
harassment, 79
Harrison, Ann, 352
hazing, 79
Head Start, 409
heredity, 408–409
heterogeneity, 378
heterosexuality, 13
heuristic, 247
hierarchical grouping, 188, 188*f*
high school
    "Bending the Rules" case study,
        156–157
    "Exam Grades" case study, 262–263
    "I Don't Understand" case study,
        208–209
    "Innovative Assessment Strategies"
        case study, 474–475
    "Noon Supervised Study" case study,
        400–401
    "Refusal to Dress" case study,
        324–325
    "SAT Scores" case study, 534–535
    "Steal, Cheat, and Fight" case study,
        28–29
    "Substitute, The" case study, 98–99
    tracking, 386
higher-order thinking, 239, 239*t*
highly qualified teacher, 561

high-road transfer, 227, 229
high-stakes testing, 552–556
hippocampus, 110
Hoffman, Martin, 81, 85*t*
holistic rubric, 517, *518*
holophrastic speech, 136, *136*
home-based reinforcements, 341
home-school connections, 341–342
homework
    failure to do, 356
    as punishment, 166
homogeneity, 378
homosexuality, 13
"honor system," 311
hostile attributional bias, 84
humanistic theories, 306
hypothalamus, 103
hypothesis testing, 244

I

"I Don't Understand" case study,
    208–209
IDEAL problem-solving steps, 246–247,
    247*t*
IDEIA 2004. *See* Individuals with
    Disabilities Education Improvement
    Act (IDEIA 2004)
identity
    ethnic, 50–51
    gender, 51–52
    Marcia's categories of identity
        achievement commitment, 49, 50*t*
        statuses, 49–50
identity achieved, 49, 50*t*
identity constancy, 123
identity development, 48
identity diffusion, 49–50, 50*t*
identity foreclosure, 49, 50*t*
identity statuses, 49
identity *vs.* identity diffusion, 46*t*, 48
IEP. *See* Individualized Education Plan
    (IEP)
ill-defined problems, 245
illumination, 424
imaginary audience, 214, *214*
imitation, language development,
    134–135
immoral behaviors, 356–358
implicit knowledge, 189
inclusion, 435, 452
incremental view of ability, 282, 302
incubation, 424
independent practice, 366
individual constructivism, 119
individual interest, 234
individual/group accountability, 370,
    383

Individualized Education Plan (IEP)
    grading considerations, 485
    special education referral/eligibility,
        433, 452, 453
    standardized tests, 558
individually administered IQ tests, 406,
    406
individually administered tests, 539
Individuals with Disabilities Education
    Improvement Act (IDEIA 2004), 433,
    450–453
induction, 85
inductive reasoning, 244
industry *vs.* inferiority, school age, 46*t*,
    47–48
infancy, 46, 46*t*
    emotional development milestones,
        65*t*
    trust *vs.* mistrust, 46, 46*t*
inferiority *vs.* industry, school age, 46*t*,
    47–48
informal assessment, 480
information processing theory
    assumptions, 184
    classroom applications, 193–196
    individual differences, 192–193
    long-term memory, 189–192
    sensory memory, 184–185
    three stage model, 184–193
    working memory, 182–189. *See also*
        working memory
informational praise, 270
initiative *vs.* guilt, preschoolers, 46*t*,
    47, *47*
inner speech, 127
"Innovative Assessment Strategies"
    case study, 474–475
inquiry learning, 370, 370*f*
instruction
    advanced, gifted students, 422–424
    direct, 365–367, 437
instructional consequences, 336
instructional conversations, 144, 372,
    373*t*
instructional environment, 554–555
instructional planning, 330–332
INTASC. *See* Interstate New Teacher
    Assessment and Support Consortium
    (INTASC)
integrity *vs.* despair, late adulthood,
    46*t*, 49
intellectual curiosity, 240
intellectual disability, 435–438
intelligence
    biological issues, 408
    classic views, 403
    classroom applications, multiple
        intelligences theory, 412–413

classroom applications, successful intelligence theory, 413–414
contemporary views, 403–406
ethnicity, and, 410
Gardner's theory of multiple intelligences, 404
gender, and, 410–412
IQ measurement, 406–408
SES, and, 409
Sternberg's theory of successful intelligence, 404–406
interaction procedures, 337
interference, 192
intermittent schedule, 163, *163*
internal locus, 282, 283*f*
internalization, 126, 307
internalizing disorders, 453, 461
interpersonal authority stage, 77*t*
interpersonal intelligence, 404, 405*t*, 419
interpersonal objectives, 387
interpersonal skills, 371, 383
inter-rater reliability, 516
Interstate New Teacher Assessment and Support Consortium (INTASC), 12*t*, 561, 562*t*
intersubjectivity, 124
interval schedules, 163
interviews, 10
intimacy *vs.* isolation, young adulthood, 46*t*, 48
intolerable behaviors, 347, 348
intrapersonal intelligence, 404, 405*t*, 419
intrinsic motivation
cognitive theory, 279
cooperative learning, 371
defined, 265–266
self theories, 299
self-determination, 307, 308
intrinsic value, 279
introspection, 213
Iowa Test of Basic Skills (ITBS), *538*
IQ tests, 406–408
cognitive disabilities, 436
giftedness, identifying, 421
group administered, 406
individually administered, 406
IQ-achievement discrepancy, 438
KTEA-II, 438
Stanford-Binet Intelligence Scales-V, 406, 436
Wechsler Intelligence Scale for Children, Fourth Edition (WISC-IV), 406, 436
IQ-achievement discrepancy, 438
isolation *vs.* intimacy, young adulthood, 46*t*, 48

issue-specific discussion, 243
ITBS. *See* Iowa Test of Basic Skills (ITBS)
item analysis, 504
item difficulty index, 505
item discrimination index, 505

J

jigsaw method, 383, *383*
Johnson methods, 383
joint attention, 135*t*
Joplin plan, 381
judgmental review panel, 559
"Judicious Discipline" program, 335
justice orientation, 79

K

Kansas State University, 15
Kaufman Test of Educational Achievement II (KTEA-II), 438
"Keyboard Courage" case study, 530–531
keyed alternative, 500
keyword method, 188, 216
KGIS. *See* Kuder General Interest Survey (KGIS)
"Kindergarten Readiness" case study, 528–529
"King Washington" case study, 206–207
knowledge
conceptual, 189, 365
conditional (strategy), 211
declarative, 189, 211, 364
episodic, 189
explicit, 189
implicit, 189
metacognitive, 211
procedural, 189, 211, 365
Kohlberg, Lawrence, 77–78, 85, 85*t*
Kohlberg's theory of moral reasoning, 77–78, 77*t*
Kounin, Jacon, 351
KTEA-II. *See* Kaufman Test of Educational Achievement II (KTEA-II)
Kuder General Interest Survey (KGIS), *538*
KWL method, 232, 233*f*

L

language development. *See also* speech
bilingual language acquisition, 139–141
biological basis, 134
classroom applications, 143–144
cognitive development, and, 127
early childhood language acquisition, 136–139

English Acquisition Act, 141
English immersion, 140–141, 140*t*
imitation/reinforcement, 134–135
individual differences, 141–143
language acquisition, 134–136
social interactions, 135–136
two-way bilingual immersion (TWBI), 140*t*, 141
late adulthood, 46*t*, 49
law of effect, 161
learned behavior, 239
learned helplessness, 292, 305
learning
cooperative, 370–371
decontextualized, 266
defined, 159
discovery, 368
guided discovery, 368
inquiry, 370, 370*f*
mastery, *367*, 367–368
meaningful, 368
objectives, 364
learning objectives, 364–365
least restrictive environment (LRE), 434–435, 452
LEP. *See* Limited English Proficiency (LEP)
lesson-running procedures, 337
"Letter *P* Day" case study, 394–395
licensure, 560
Limited English Proficiency (LEP), 556
linguistic intelligence, 404, 405*t*, 419
live models, 174, *176*
Loci method, 188, 216
locus, 282, 283*f*
external, 282, 283*f*
internal, 282, 283*f*
locus of control, 266
logical consequences, 336, 355, 358
logical-mathematical intelligence, 404, 405*t*, 419
longitudinal designs, 9
long-range plans, 331
long-term memory, 189–192
Lott, Lynn, 336
lower-order thinking, 239, 239*t*
low-road transfer, 226, *226*, 227–230
LRE. *See* least restrictive environment (LRE)

M

macrosystem, 31
magnetic resonance imaging (MRI), 102*t*
magnetoencephalography (MEG), 102*t*
Maier, Norman R., 239
mainstreaming, 435, 452

maintenance rehearsal, 187
major depressive disorders, 455
malingering, 355
manipulatives, 444
mapping, 229
Marcia, James, 49
Marcia's categories of identity
  achievement commitment, 50*t*
Marsh, Herbert W., 53
masculine gender-role identity, 51, 52
Maslow, Abraham, 306
Maslow's hierarchy of needs, 306, 306*f*
massed practice, 191
mastery goals, 234, 311
mastery learning, *367*, 367–368
mastery-approach goals
  goal theory, 280, 281*t*
  self-efficacy, 301
MAT. *See* Metropolitan Achievement
  Test (MAT)
matching exercise, 499
math, 112
"Math Review, The" case study,
  260–261
"Math Troubles" case study, 398–399
mathematics disability (MD), 443–445
Matthew effect, 379, *379*
MD. *See* mathematics disability (MD)
mean, 541
meaningful learning, 368
meaningful verbal learning, 368
means-end analysis, 247
measurement, 477
measurement error, 546, *546*
measures, research studies, 10
median, 541
MEG. *See* magnetoencephalography
  (MEG)
memory
  See active long-term memory
    (ALTM), 186
  echoic, 185
  iconic, 185
  long-term, 189–192
  sensory, 184–185, 192
  working. *See* working memory
Mendler, Allen, 351
mental retardation, 435
mesosystem, 31
metacognition, 240
  defined, 211
  factor affecting development/use,
    215
  importance of, 211–212
  note taking, 218–220
  reading comprehension, 215–218
  special cases, 212–214
  studying, 220–221

writing skills, 218
metacognitive knowledge, 211
metacognitive regulation, 212
metalinguistic awareness, *137*, 137–138,
  139
Metropolitan Achievement Test (MAT),
  538
MI theory. *See* theory of multiple
  intelligences
microsystem, 31
middle adulthood, 46*t*, 48–49
middle school
  "Achievement Gap" case study, 2–3
  "Assessment: Cafeteria Style" case
    study, 472–473
  "Basketball Star" case study, 26–27
  "Classroom Safety" case study,
    322–323
  "Frogs" case study, 96–97
  "King Washington" case study,
    206–207
  "Math Review, The" case study,
    260–261
  "Math Troubles" case study, 398–399
  "Study Hall" case study, 154–155
  "Teachers Are Cheating?" case study,
    532–533
  tracking, 386
mild misbehaviors, 347, 348
mindful abstraction, 227
Minnesota Multiphasic Personality
  Inventory-2 (MMPI-2), *538*
minority group, 13
misbehavior
  anticipation/prevention of potential
    problems, 353
  common causes, 348–350
  dangerous behaviors, 358–360
  defined, 347–348
  degrees/types, 347–348
  expectations, establishing, 352
  immoral behaviors, 356–358
  intermediate concerns, 356
  modeling/reinforcing desired
    behaviors, 352
  models of classroom management/
    discipline, 351
  principle of least intervention,
    354–355
  proactive classroom management,
    350
  routine disruptions, 355
  self-regulation skills, 353–354
mistrust *vs.* trust, infancy, 46, 46*t*
MMPI-2. *See* Minnesota Multiphasic
  Personality Inventory-2 (MMPI-2)
mnemonics, 187, 188, 216
mode, 541

model, observational learning, 174–176
modeling, 85, 369
moderate misbehaviors, 347, 348
monitoring, 212, 221
moral development
  aggressive behavior, 82–84
  cognitive developmental moral
    reasoning, 77–79
  family context, 84–85
  peer context, 85–86
  prosocial behavior, 79–82
  school context, 86–87
moral domain, 83
moral realism, 77
moral reasoning, 77
morality of cooperation, 77
morality of individual principles stage,
  77*t*
morality of social contract stage, 77*t*
moratorium, 49, 50*t*
morphemic inflections, 136
Moskal, Barbara M., 519
motivation
  amotivation, 308
  anxiety, 292–294
  attribution theory, 282–284
  behavioral definition, 265
  classroom-level techniques,
    290–291
  cognitive theories, 279–285
  developmental changes, 285–297
  ethnic differences, 289, *289*
  expectancy-value theory, 279–280
  external regulation, 308
  extrinsic, 265–266, 299
  gender differences, 287–288
  giftedness, 420
  goal theory, 280–282
  grades, and, 484–485
  identified regulation, 308
  integrated regulation, 308
  intrinsic, 265–266, 299, 308
  introjected regulation, 308
  learned helplessness, 292
  self-determination, and, 307
  self-efficacy, and, 299–302
  self-worth, and, 303
  social cognitive theory, 176
  student-level techniques, 289–290
  taxonomy, 307*f*
motor cortex, 103, 103*f*
movement management, 353
MRI. *See* magnetic resonance imaging
  (MRI)
multiage classrooms, 382
multigrade classes, 382
multimodal intervention, 461
multiple-choice item, 500

musical intelligence, 404, 405t, 419
myelin, 104, 105

N

naive hedonistic stage, 77, 77t
narrative reports, 485–486
National Board for Professional
    Teaching Standards (NBPTS), 560
National Research Center on Rural
    Education Support (NRCRES), 15
naturalistic intelligence, 404, 405t, 419
NBPTS. See National Board for
    Professional Teaching Standards
    (NBPTS)
NCLB Act. See No Child Left Behind
    (NCLB) Act
near transfer, 229
negative attitudes, ethnicity and, 50
negative punishment, 163
negative reinforcement, 163
negative transfer, 226, 368
neglect, 34t
neglected youth, 39–40
Nelsen, Jane, 336
NEO Five-Factor Inventory (NEO-FFI),
    538
network theory, 190
neural pruning, 104
neurons, 104, 104f
neuroscience research, 101
neurotransmitters, 104, 104f
neutral stimuli, 160
Nickerson, Raymond, 244
No Child Left Behind (NCLB) Act, 6, 303
    guiding principles, 553–554
    high-stakes testing, 552
    problems with, 554
nongraded plans, 381
"Noon Supervised Study" case study,
    400–401
norm group, 407
norm sample, 539
normal distribution, 542
norm-referenced interpretation, 407
norm-referenced letter grades, 484
norm-referenced tests, 539, 539t
norms, 333–337
note taking, 218–219
NRCRES. See National Research Center
    on Rural Education Support (NRCRES)
numeric rating scales, 516
nurturance, 85
nutrition, brain development, 107

O

Oakes, Jeannie, 386
Obama, Barack, 179

object permanence, 122
objective testing, 497
objectivity, 494
observational learning, 174–177, 352
observations, 10
occipital lobe, 103, 103f
one-on-one time, 72
Open House, 342
open-mindedness, 240
operant conditioning, 161–166, 365
operations, 120
oral presentations, 512
organization, 194
organizational strategies, 188
outcome expectations, 299
out-of-school suspensions, 166
output stage, anxiety, 293
overcorrection, 168
overextensions, 136
overlapping, 353
overlearning, 231, 437
overregularizations, 137
overstrivers, 303
overt aggression, 38

P

PALS. See Peer-Assisted Learning
    Strategies (PALS)
paralinguistic cues, 65
parents/parenting
    authoritarian, 32
    authoritative, 32
    autonomy-supportive, 308
    Baumrind's parenting practices, 32t
    child abuse/neglect, 33–34t
    home-school connections, 341–342
    parent-teacher conferences, 342
    parental employment, and, 40–41
    permissive, 32
    practices, 32–33
    uninvolved, 32
parent-teacher communication,
    486–488
parent-teacher conferences, 342, 487
parietal lobe, 103, 103f
passing notes, 355
past performance, 300
PATHS curriculum, 71
Pavlov, Ivan Petrovich, 160
PBL. See problem-based learning (PBL)
peer groups, 36–38
peer relations, 36–40, 340
    friendships/peer groups, 36–38
    moral development, 85–86
    neglected youth, 39–40
    popularity, 38–39
    rejected growth, 39

peer selection process, 37
peer social status, 38
peer socialization process, 37
Peer-Assisted Learning Strategies
    (PALS), 384t
perceived popularity, 38–39
percentage grading system, 484
percentile scores, 542–544
performance assessment, 510–511. See
    also assessment
performance praise, 269
performance-approach goals
    goal theory, 280, 280, 281t
    self-efficacy, 301
performance-avoidance goals, 281
performance-contingent rewards, 268,
    269
permissive parenting, 32
persistence, 178
person knowledge, 211
person praise, 270
personal domain, 83
personal fable, 214
personal reward stage, 77
personality tests, 538
perspective taking, 80, 81
PET scan, 102t
philosophies of teaching, 10–13
Phinney, Jean S., 50
phonological awareness, 137
phonological loop, 186
physical abuse, 34t
physical context, 191
physical factors, misbehavior, 348
physical punishment, 165–166
**Piaget, Jean, 77, 85, 85t, 119–124, 127,
    128, 129, 273, 369**
Piaget's conservation tasks, 123f
Piaget's theory of cognitive
    development, 119–124
    basic tenets, 119–120
    concrete operational stage, 121, 123
    formal operational stage, 123–124
    pre-operational stage, 121, 122–123
    sensorimotor stage, 121, 121–122
    stage model, 120–124
    Vygotsky's criticism, 125
"Pinch" case study, 150–151
pituitary gland, 103
planning, 212, 221
plasticity, 106–107
point grading system, 484
popularity, 38–39
portfolio, 514
positive attitudes, and ethnicity, 50
positive interdependence, 370, 382
positive justice, 80
positive practice, 167–168

positive punishment, 163
positive reinforcement
  behavioral learning theories, 163
  emotional/social/behavioral
    disorders, 460
  language development, 134–135
positive transfer, 226
positron emission tomography (PET
  scan), 102t
postconventional level, 77t, 78
poverty, 556
PQ4R, 216
practical abilities, 405, 419
practical skills, 436
practicality, 496
practice, 110
practicing, 370
pragmatics, 137, 139
praise, 269–272, 284
  effective use, 270–272
  informational, 270
  performance praise, 269–270
  person praise, 270
  process praise, 269–270
praise-and-ignore, 167
Praxis I: Academic Skills Assessment, 561
Praxis II: Subject Assessments, 561
Praxis III: Classroom Performance
  Assessment, 561
Praxis series, 560, 561
preconventional level, 77
predictive validity, 546, 559
predominantly hyperactive-impulsive
  ADHD subtype, 456
predominantly inattentive ADHD
  subtype, 456
prejudice feelings, 15
Premack principle, 166–167, 167
pre-operational stage, 121, 122–123
preparation, 424
preprocessing stage, anxiety, 293
preschool, 46t
  emotional development milestones,
    65t
  initiative vs. guilt, 46t, 47, 47
  social competence characteristics, 57
presentations, 512–513
pretend play, 127, 128
principle of least intervention, 354–355
proactive classroom management, 350
proactive interference, 192
problem, 245
problem solving, 245–249
  algorithms, 247
  defined, 245–246
  general/specific strategies, 246–247
  heuristics, 247–248
  obstacles, 246

problem-based learning, 248–249
problem-based learning (PBL),
  248–249, 249
problem-solving transfer, 227, 227
procedural facilitations, 218
procedural knowledge, 189, 211, 365
procedural subtype, 444
procedures, 337
process portfolios, 514
process praise, 269
processing stage, anxiety, 293
production, social cognitive theory, 176
productive behavior, 239
project, 514
"Project Night" case study, 94–95
prompts, 162
propositional network, 190
prosocial behavior, 79–82
prosociality, 55
psychological punishment, 166
psychological tools, 126
psychology. See educational
  psychology
Psychology of Intelligence, The (Piaget),
  120
psychosocial crisis, 46
psychosocial factors, misbehavior, 348
psychosocial moratorium, 48
pull-out program, 452
punishment
  behavioral learning theories, 162, 162,
    163, 164–165
  extra homework, 166
  out-of-school suspensions, 166
  physical, 165–166
  psychological, 166
  recess withdrawal, 166, 166
  vicarious, 177
punishment/obedience stage, 77t

Q

quasi-experimental research, 8–9, 8t
question variety, 502
questioning, 242–244

R

racial group, 13
random sample, 9
range, 541
rating scales, 516, 517
ratio schedule, 163
raw score, 542
RD. See reading disability (RD)
reading, 109f
  brain development, 111
  comprehension, 215–217

language development, 143, 143
"Reading About Pirates" case study,
  204–205
reading disability (RD), 441–443
Reading First Initiative, 553
reasoning, 239
  deductive, 244
  inductive, 244
  moral, 77
recall, 191, 191
recall tasks, 497
recasting, 135t
recess, 166, 166
reciprocal teaching, 215, 231, 372–374
recognition, 228
recognition tasks, 191, 191, 497
reconstruction error, 192
Redl, Fritz, 351
reflection, 370
reflective practice, 227
"Refusal to Dress" case study, 324–325
region of proximal learning, 221
regrouping, 381
Rehabilitation Act of 1973, Section 504,
  452
rehearsal, 187
reinforcement
  behavior management, 352
  behavioral learning theories, 162–165
  home-based, 341
  incompatible behaviors, 167
  motivation, and, 265
  negative. See negative reinforcement
  positive. See positive reinforcement
  vicarious, 177
rejected youth, 39
relatedness, 305
relational aggression, 38, 39
relationships
  ADHD, and, 457
  anxiety, and, 454
  autism spectrum disorders, and, 460
  conduct disorder, and, 458
  depression, and, 455
  positive, 311
  student-student, 340
  teacher-student, 307, 338, 338–340
relevance, 195
reliability
  classroom tests, 494
  inter-rater, 516
  standardized tests, 546–547
remarriage, 34–36
Renzulli, Joseph, 420, 421
report cards, 485–486
reprimand, 168
reproductive thinking, 239
research design, 7–9

research studies
  correlational designs, 7, 8*t*
  descriptive designs, 7, 8*t*
  experimental designs, 8, 8*t*
  measures, 10
  neuroscience, 101
  quasi-experimental designs, 8–9, 8*t*
  research material, 6
  samples, 9–10
response alternatives, 500
response cost, 168–169, 460
response distribution effect, 177
response facilitation effect, 176–177
response inhibition effect, 177
response set, 246
response-to-intervention (RTI),
  439–441
responsiveness, 32
restricted response essay, 502
retention, social cognitive theory, 176
retrieval cues, 191
retrieval failure, 192
retroactive interference, 192
reversibility, 122
rewards, 266–269
  effective use of, 268–269
  performance-contingent, 267, 269
  task-contingent, 267
room arrangement, 327
Ross, Gail, 126
rote memorization, 227
routine, 337
RTI. *See* response-to-intervention (RTI)
rubric, 498, 517–520
rules, 335–337

S

sample, 9–10
"SAT Scores" case study, 534–535
satiation, 168
scaffolding, 370
  automaticity, 231
  reciprocal teaching, 372
schema theory, 190
schemes, 120
school performance. *See* academic
  performance
school-age, 46*t*
school-age children. *See also*
  elementary school; high school;
  middle school
  emotional development milestones,
    65*t*
  industry *vs.* inferiority, 46*t*, 47–48
  social competence characteristics, 57
school-based interventions, 87
schoolhouse giftedness, 421

schools. *See also* classroom
  home-school connections, 341–342
  moral development, 86–87
scientific approach. *See* educational
  psychology
scientific concepts, 127
scientific method, 370
SD. *See* standard deviation (SD)
seating arrangements, 327–328, *328*
Section 504 of the Rehabilitation Act of
  1973, 452
Section 504 plan, 452
seductive details, 235
SEL. *See* social-emotional learning (SEL)
self-actualization, 306
self-awareness, 64
self-concept, 52, 53
self-determination, 273, 309–310, 310*t*
self-determination theory, 305–309
self-efficacy
  creativity, and, 425
  expectancies, 279
  motivation, and, 299–302
  self theories compared, 309–310,
    310*t*
  social cognitive theory, 177–179
  teacher efficacy, 302–303
  theory, 299–303
self-esteem, 52, 54
self-evaluation, 179
self-fulfilling prophecy, 36, 409
self-handicapping strategies, 281, 281*t*,
  304–305
self-identification, 50
self-judgment, 179
self-motivation, 67
self-observation, 179
self-regulation
  social cognitive theory, 179–180, 180*f*,
    301
  teaching, 353
self-worth, 309–310, 310*t*
self-worth theory, 303–305
Selman, Robert L., 81, 85*t*
SEM. *See* standard error of
  measurement (SEM)
semantic memory subtype of MD, 443
semantics, 136, 138
semiotic functions, 122
sensitive periods, brain development,
  106
sensorimotor stage, *121*, 121–122
sensory cortex, 103, 103*f*
sensory memory, 184–185, 192
service learning, 86
SES. *See* socioeconomic status (SES)
sex, 13, 51
sexual abuse, 34*t*

sexual orientation, 13
shame/doubt *vs.* autonomy,
  toddlerhood, 46–47, 46*t*
shaping, 167
short-answer/completion items, 502
SII. *See* Strong Interest Inventory (SII)
"Silly Students" case study, 152–153
situated cognition, 369
situational interest, 234
skewness, 542
skills-based cooperative methods, 384*t*
skills-focused methods, 383
Skinner, B. F., 161, 351
sleeper effect, 35
SLI. *See* specific language impairment
  (SLI)
SOAR method, 221
sociability, 55
social adjustment, 54–55
social authority stage, 77*t*
"social brain," *113*
social cognitive theory, 174
  assumptions, 174
  collective efficacy, 180
  observational learning, 174–177
  self-efficacy, 177–179
  self-regulation, 179–180
  teacher efficacy, 180
social competence, 54–57
  characteristics of, 57
  social adjustment, 54–55
  social performance, 55
  social skills, 55–57
social constructivism, 119
social development
  Erikson's psychosocial theory, 46–49
  ethnic identity, 50–51
  gender identity, 51–52
  identity statuses, 49–50
  self-concept, 52–53
  self-esteem, 54
  social competence, 54–57. *See also*
    social competence
social disorders. *See* emotional/social/
  behavioral disorders
social domain model, 83
social experiences, 120
social interactions, 135
social isolation (time-out), 169
social learning theory, 51–52, 174
social performance, 55
social referencing, 67
social skills, 55–56, 436
social-emotional learning (SEL), 70–72
social-information processing, 83–84,
  84
socialized speech, 127
sociodramatic play, 128

socioeconomic status (SES)
  cognitive disabilities, and, 436
  cooperative learning, and, 385
  diversity, 14
  intelligence, and, 409
  self-esteem, 54
sociometric popularity, 38
sociomoral developmental delay, 82
Socrates, 239
spatial intelligence, 404, 405t, 419
Spearman, Charlie, 403
Spearman's Two-factor Theory of
  intelligence, 403, 403f
special education referral/eligibility,
  433–434, 438–441, 450–452
specific determiners, 500
specific language impairment (SLI),
  142–143
specific learning disabilities (LD),
  438–441
speech. *See also* language
  articulation disorder, 142
  child-directed, 135t
  dysfluency, 142, 144t
  egocentric, 122
  holophrastic, 136, *136*
  inner, 127
  socialized, 127
  specific language impairment (SLI),
    142–143
  stuttering, 142
  telegraphic, 136–139
Sperling, George, 185
split-grade classes, 382
spontaneous concepts, 127
spontaneous discussions, 243
spreading activation, 190
Spuler, Frances, 352
stability, 282, 283f
STAD. *See* Student Teams–Achievement
  Division (STAD)
stagnation *vs.* generativity, middle
  adulthood, 46t, 48–49
standard deviation (SD), 407, 541
standard error of measurement (SEM),
  547
standard scores, 544–545
standardized achievement tests, 538
standardized aptitude tests, 538
standardized tests
  categories, 538–539
  central tendency, 541
  classroom tests, compared, 537t
  criterion-referenced, 539
  grade-equivalent scores, 544
  high-stakes testing, 552–556
  normal distribution, 542
  norm-referenced, 539

percentile scores, 542–544
raw scores, 542
reliability, 546–547
simple test score report, example,
  540
standard scores, 544–545
students at risk, accommodating,
  556–558
teacher certification/licensure,
  560–562
test bias, 559
test fairness, 558–560
types, 537–541
validity, 545–546
variability, 541–542
*Standards for Educational and
  Psychological Testing*, 557
standing pattern of behavior, 333
Stanford-Binet Intelligence Scales-V,
  406, 436
stanine scores, 545
status quo, challenging, 87
"Steal, Cheat, and Fight" case study,
  28–29
stealing, 357–358
stem, 500
stereotype threat, 410
Sternberg, Robert, 68
Sternberg's theory of successful
  intelligence. *See* theory of successful
  intelligence
storage decay, 192
story grammar, 190
strategy knowledge, 211
stress, 113
Strong Interest Inventory (SII), *538*
structured English immersion, 140t, 141
student behavior. *See* misbehavior
Student Teams–Achievement Division
  (STAD), 384t
students
  failure-accepting, 305
  failure-avoiding, 304–305
  overstrivers, 303
  success-oriented, 303
  teacher-student relationships, 307
  types, 304f
students at risk, 556–558
students with disabilities. *See also*
  cognitive disabilities
  classroom management, 327
  cooperative learning, 371
  grading considerations, 485
  grouping practices, 387
  standardized tests, 556
student-student relationships, 340
student-teacher relationships, 307, *338*,
  338–340

"Study Hall" case study, 154–155
studying, 220–221
study-test overlap, 191
study-time allocation, 220
stuttering, 142
subjective testing format, 497
"Substitute, The" case study, 98–99
success-oriented students, 303
summative assessment, 367, 480–481,
  510
surveys, 10
sustaining expectation effect, 385
symbolic models, 174, *175*
sympathy, 81
synapse, 104, 104f
synaptic density, *105*
synaptic pruning, 109
synaptogenesis, 108
syntax, 136–139
systematic desensitization, 460
systematic phonics instruction, 442
systematic planning, 240

T

table of specifications, 496
TAI. *See* Team-Assisted
  Individualization (TAI)
talking back, 356
TAP. *See* Tests of Achievement and
  Proficiency (TAP)
tardiness, 356
task analysis, 195
task knowledge, 211
task-contingent rewards, 267
task-specific rubric, 517
Taxonomy of Educational Objectives
  (Bloom et al.), 239
teacher efficacy, 180, 302–303
teacher-parent communication,
  486–488
"Teachers Are Cheating?" case study,
  532–533
teachers/teaching
  autonomy-supportive, 308
  behavior setting, 333–337
  certification/licensure, 560
  challenges, 5
  competence standards, 478–479
  educational psychology, 6–16. *See
    also* educational psychology
  emotionally-intelligent teaching,
    68–72
  environmental competence, 327–330
  gifted students, 422–424
  instructional planning, 330–332
  opportunities, 5
  parent-teacher conferences, 342

reactions/evaluations, 283–284
strategies, 427
teacher attitudes, 427
teaching as decision-making, 5–6
time management, 332–333
teacher-student relationships, 307, *338*, 338–340
teaching methods
cognitive apprenticeships, 369, *369*
cooperative learning, 370–371
direct instruction, 365–367
discovery learning, 368
expository teaching, 368–369
guided discovery, 368
inquiry learning, 370, *370f*
instructional conversations, 372, *373t*
mastery learning, *367*, 367–368
meaningful learning, 368
reciprocal questioning, 372–374
reciprocal teaching, 372
"Team" case study, 24–25
Team-Assisted Individualization (TAI), *384t*
Teams-Games-Tournament (TGT), *384t*
teasing, 356
telegraphic speech, 136
temperament, 62
temporal lobe, 103, *103f*
teratogens, 107
Terman, Lewis, 421
test administration, 555
test bias, 559
test blueprint, 496, 497
test fairness, 558
Test for Teaching Knowledge, 561
test preparation, 555
test score pollution, 554–556
tests. *See also* standardized tests
alternate-choice item, 498–499
analysis/revision, 504–505
blueprint development, 496–497
characteristics, 493–496
equivalence, 496
essay tasks, 502–504
fairness, 495–496
matching exercise, 499–500
multiple-choice item, 500–502
objectivity, 494
practicality, 496
reliability, 494
research measures, 10
test items, 497–504
validity, 493
Tests of Achievement and Proficiency (TAP), *538*
testwiseness, 500
TGT. *See* Teams-Games-Tournament (TGT)

theft, 357–358
theoretical learning, 127
theories, 6
theory of identical elements, 226
theory of mind, 212
theory of multiple intelligences, 404, 405
classroom applications, 412–413
creativity, 420
giftedness, 419
theory of successful intelligence, 404–406
classroom applications, 413–414
giftedness, 419
theory-based validity, 546
thinking dispositions, 240
thinking skills, *239*
Thorndike, Edward, 161, 226
three-ring conception of giftedness, 421
time management, 332–333
time-out, 169
toddlerhood, 46–47, *46t*
autonomy *vs.* shame/doubt, 46, *46t*
emotional development milestones, *65t*
token economy, 460
Torrance Tests of Creative Thinking (TTCT), 425
tracking, 380–381
transfer (of skills/knowledge)
classroom application, 230–235
defined, 226
high-road, 227, 229
low-road, 226, *226*, 227–230
negative, 226, 368
positive, 226
specific *vs.* general, 226
zero, 226
zero transfer, 368
transitional bilingual education, 140, *140t*
triadic reciprocal determination model of causality, 177, *177*
trust, 86
trust *vs.* mistrust, infancy, 46, *46t*
truth-seeking, 240
T-score, 545
TTCT. *See* Torrance Tests of Creative Thinking (TTCT)
two-factor theory of intelligence, 403, *403f*
two-way bilingual immersion (TWBI), *140t*, 141

U

unconditioned response (UCR), 159, 160
unconditioned stimulus (UCS), 159, 160

underextensions, 136
uninvolved parenting, 32
unit plans, 331
University of Chicago Urban Education Institute, 15
use-it-or-lose-it principle, 109
utility value, 280

V

validity
classroom tests, 493
concurrent, 546
construct, 559
convergent, 546
criterion-related, 546
discriminant, 546
performance assessment, 521
predictive, 546, 559
standardized tests, 545–546, 559
theory-based, 546
values, 279–280
vandalism, 358
variability, 541–542
variable schedules, 163
variables, 7
verbal mediation, 188
verbal persuasion, 300
verbal reprimand, 460
verification, 424
vicarious experiences, 300, *300*
vicarious punishment, 177
vicarious reinforcement, 177
Vineland Adaptive Behavior Scales, 436
violence, 358–360
visibility, classroom, 327
visual imagery, 188
visual perspective-taking, 212–213, *213*
visuospatial sketchpad, 186
visuospatial subtype, 444
volunteer bias, 10
Vygotsky, Lev Semenovich, 119, 124–126, 128, 129, 369
Vygotsky's theory of cognitive development, 124–126
criticism of Piaget's theory, 125
Zone of Proximal Development (ZPD), 124

W

wait time, 194, 243
Waiting for Superman, 14
Washington State University, 15
Wattenberg, William, 351
Wechsler Intelligence Scale for Children, Fourth Edition (WISC-IV), 406, 436

well-defined problems, 245
Wernicke's area, 103, 103f, 112
WISC-IV. *See* Wechsler Intelligence
    Scale for Children, Fourth Edition
    (WISC-IV)
within-class ability grouping, *378*, 379,
    385
withitness, 353
Wood, David, 126
word recognition, 441
work-avoidance goal orientation, 286
working memory, 185–189
    capacity/duration, 186–187
    chunking, 188

elaborative rehearsal, 187
encoding processes, 187–189
hierarchies, 188
individual differences in information
    processing, 192–193
maintenance rehearsal, 187
visual imagery, 188
working-backward strategy, 247
"Worksheets, The" case study,
    256–257
"Writer's Block" case study, 258–259
writing skills, 218
writing techniques, 244
"Writing Wizards" case study, 470–471

Y

young adulthood, 46t
    intimacy *vs.* isolation, 46t, 48

Z

Zero Tolerance policy, 360
zero transfer, 226, 368
Zone of Proximal Development (ZPD),
    124, 126, 127, 372
"Zoo, The" case study, 468–469
ZPD. *See* Zone of Proximal
    Development (ZPD)
z-scores, 544